HANDBOOK OF PSYCHOLOGICAL ASSESSMENT

HANDBOOK OF PSYCHOLOGICAL ASSESSMENT

Fifth Edition

Gary Groth-Marnat

WILEY

John Wiley & Sons, Inc.

This book is printed on acid-free paper. ∞

Copyright © 2009 by John Wiley & Sons, Inc. All rights reserved.

Published by John Wiley & Sons, Inc., Hoboken, New Jersey.
Published simultaneously in Canada.

For general information on our other products and services please contact our Customer Care Department within the U.S. at (800) 762-2974, outside the United States at (317) 572-3993 or fax (317) 572-4002.

Wiley also publishes its books in a variety of electronic formats. Some content that appears in print may not be available in electronic books. For more information about Wiley products, visit our website at www.wiley.com.

Library of Congress Cataloging-in-Publication Data:

Groth-Marnat, Gary.
    Handbook of psychological assessment / Gary Groth-Marnat. —5th ed.
      p. cm.
   Includes bibliographical references and index.
    ISBN 978-0-470-08358-1 (cloth)
      1. Psychological tests. 2. Personality assessment. I. Title.
  BF176.G76 2009
  150.28'7—dc22

                                   2008032243

Printed in the United States of America

10 9 8 7 6 5 4 3 2 1

To My Students

Contents

Preface

My dear readers. Thank you so much for your support in buying and reading this book. My intention has been to create a resource that will cover the A to Z of assessment. In other words, my aim has been to provide guidance that extends from larger issues on assessment, to clarifying the referral question, and through to writing up the report and consulting with your referral sources and clients. I hope it brings clarity, practical guidelines, insights, and useful strategies to your work. Feedback on the previous editions assures me that this is often the case. This fact makes it worth all those long hours hidden away inside a small room incubating ideas and reading, writing, revising, and editing.

As with the previous editions, I have tried to integrate the best of science with the best of practice. Necessarily, psychological assessment involves technical knowledge. But in presenting this technical knowledge, I have tried to isolate, extract, and summarize in as clear a manner as possible the core information that is required for practitioners to function competently. At the same time, assessment is also about the very human side of understanding, helping, and making decisions about people. I hope I have been able to comfortably blend this technical (science) side with the human. An assessment that does not have at least some heart to it is cold and lacking. To keep in touch with the practitioner/human side of assessment, I have continually maintained an active practice in which I have tried to stay close to and interact with the ongoing personal and professional challenges of practitioners. I hope that within and between the sentences in the book, my active involvement with the world of practice is apparent.

It has been seven years since the previous (fourth) edition. During that time, much has changed and much has remained the same. The big tests that professional psychologists use most frequently are unchanged. This is reflected in that the numbers and titles of the chapters are the same as they were in the fourth edition. However, there are important changes within these chapters. Two of the most important are revised chapters incorporating the Wechsler Adult Intelligence Scale, Fourth Edition (WAIS-IV) and the Wechsler Memory Scale, Fourth Edition (WMS-IV). Another revision has been a somewhat more narrow focus for the chapter on screening for neuropsychological impairment, which has involved a focus on the Bender Visual Motor Gestalt Test, Second Edition (Bender-II) in combination with the relatively recently developed (1998) Repeatable Battery for the Assessment of Neuropsychological Status (RBANS). These are two fairly brief screening tests for neuropsychological impairment. The RBANS involves assessing a fairly wide number of domains (memory, visuospatial, attention, language) using revisions of assessment tools that have been frequently used in clinical neuropsychology. A final noteworthy addition has been the inclusion of greater information on diversity as reflected by separate test-related chapter subheadings entitled "Use with Diverse Groups." This section reflects the more extensive use of assessment for a wide variety of populations and the importance of competently and sensitively working with diverse populations.

There are also many smaller changes throughout this fifth edition. It has been fully updated with new research in the field. There has also been greater emphasis on making assessment more user friendly and consumer oriented. This is reflected in suggestions for using everyday language in reports, connecting interpretations to actual client behavior, strategies for wording interpretations in a manner likely to enhance client growth, and the importance of collaborating with clients. Some chapters have organized interpretations by using bulleted phrases. Information on the Minnesota Multiphasic Personality Inventory-2 Restructured Form (MMPI-2 RF), MMPI-2 Personality Psychopathology Five (PSY-5), and the latest norms for the Rorschach have also been included. The psychological report writing chapter has been completely updated, including a new sample of psychological reports. I trust that these changes will provide readers with the best and the most practical of what can be available in assessment.

The development of *Handbook of Psychological Assessment* has been a group effort. It started many years ago with ideas and cowriting with my colleague Dorothy Morena. We both wanted to develop a resource that would assist students with all phases of psychological assessment. My sincere thanks to her. A series of editors at John Wiley & Sons have been invaluable, including Herb Reich, Jennifer Simon, Tracey Belmont, Lisa Gebo, and Peggy Alexander. In addition, Sweta Gupta at Wiley has been of great assistance. I have very much enjoyed and appreciated my relationship with Wiley; not only have I been treated as a respected author, but they have also welcomed me into the Wiley "family." Valuable input from colleagues have included Steve Smith, Larry Beutler, Steve Finn, Alan Kaufman, Dawn Flanagan, Greg Meyer, Joni Mihura, and the invaluable and nonstop list of articles from the Kenneth Pope Listerv. Much-appreciated reviews of the fourth edition were provided by Deborah Hammels and Kayreen Burns. James Holdnack and his colleagues at Pearson Assessment were extremely helpful and generous in getting me advance information on the WAIS-IV and WMS-IV. Pacifica Graduate Institute has been a supportive and much-appreciated environment for developing this fifth edition. Particular thanks are due to my colleagues in the clinical psychology program, support staff, as well as the organizational leadership of Allen Bishop, Jim Broderick, Cindy Carter, and Steve Aizenstat. Finally, much of my professional work is devoted toward helping students to achieve the best of what they are capable of. In return, they have helped me refine this fifth edition. As a result, special thanks go to particularly helpful students, including Lisa Nowinski, Dori Pelz-Sherman, Paulsen Veliyannoor, Julie Robarts, and Ari Davis. Accordingly, this fifth edition is dedicated to past, current, and future students.

Gary Groth-Marnat
Hollister Ranch
June 15, 2008

Chapter 1

INTRODUCTION

The *Handbook of Psychological Assessment* is designed to develop a high level of practitioner competence by providing relevant practical, research, and theoretical information. It can serve as both a reference and instructional guide. As a reference book, it aids in test selection and the development of a large number and variety of interpretive hypotheses. As an instructional text, it provides students with the basic tools for conducting an integrated psychological assessment. The significant and overriding emphasis in this book is on assessing areas that are of practical use in evaluating individuals in a clinical context. It is applied in its orientation, and for the most part, I have kept theoretical discussions to a minimum. Many books written on psychological testing and the courses organized around these books focus primarily on test theory, with a brief overview of a large number of tests. In contrast, my intent is to focus on the actual processes that practitioners go through during assessment. I begin with such issues as role clarification and evaluation of the referral question and end with treatment planning and the actual preparation of the report itself.

One of the crucial skills that I hope readers of this text will develop, or at least have enhanced, is a realistic appreciation of the assets and limitations of assessment. This includes an appraisal of psychological assessment as a general strategy as well as an awareness of the assets and limitations of specific instruments and procedures. A primary limitation of assessment lies in the incorrect handling of the data, which is not integrated in the context of other sources of information (behavioral observations, history, other test scores). Also, the results are not presented in a way that helps solve the unique problems clients or referral sources are confronting. To counter these limitations, the text continually provides practitioners with guidelines for integrating and presenting the data in as useful a manner as possible. The text is thus not so much a book on test interpretation (although this is an important component) but on test integration within the wider context of assessment. As a result, psychologists should be able to create reports that are accurate, effective, concise, and highly valued by the persons who receive them.

ORGANIZATION OF THE HANDBOOK

My central organizational plan for the *Handbook of Psychological Assessment* replicates the sequence practitioners follow when performing an evaluation. They are initially concerned with clarifying their roles, ensuring that they understand all the implications of the referral question, deciding which procedures would be most appropriate for the assessment, and reminding themselves of the potential problems associated with clinical judgment (Chapter 1). They also need to understand the context in which they will conduct the assessment. This understanding includes appreciating the issues, concerns, terminology, and likely roles of the persons from these contexts. Practitioners also must have clear ethical guidelines, know how to work with persons from diverse backgrounds, and recognize issues related to computer-assisted assessment and the ways that the preceding factors might influence their selection of procedures (see Chapter 2).

Once practitioners have fully understood the preliminary issues discussed in Chapters 1 and 2, they must select different strategies of assessment. The three major strategies are interviewing, observing behavior, and psychological testing. An interview is likely to occur during the initial phases of assessment and is also essential in interpreting test scores and understanding behavioral observations (see Chapter 3). The assessment of actual behaviors might also be undertaken (see Chapter 4). Behavioral assessment might be either an end in itself or an adjunct to testing. It might involve a variety of strategies, such as the measurement of overt behaviors, cognitions, alterations in physiology, or relevant measures from self-report inventories.

The middle part of the book (Chapters 5 through 13) provides a general overview of the most frequently used tests. Each chapter begins with an introduction to the test in the form of a discussion of its history and development, current evaluation, and procedures for administration. The main portions of these chapters provide a guide for interpretation, which includes such areas as the meaning of different scales, significant relations between scales, frequent trends, and the meaning of unusually high or low scores. When appropriate, there are additional subsections. For example, Chapter 5, "Wechsler Intelligence Scales," includes additional sections on the meaning of IQ scores, estimating premorbid IQ, and assessing special populations. Likewise, Chapter 11, "Thematic Apperception Test," includes a summary of Murray's theory of personality because knowledge of his concepts is a prerequisite for understanding and interpreting the test. Chapter 12, "Screening and Assessing for Neuropsychological Impairment," varies somewhat from the preceding format in that it is more a compendium and interpretive guide to some of the most frequently used short neuropsychological tests, along with a section on special considerations in conducting a neuropsychological interview. This organization reflects the current emphasis on and strategies for assessing patients with possible neuropsychological dysfunction.

Several of the chapters on psychological tests are quite long, particularly those for the Wechsler intelligence scales, Minnesota Multiphasic Personality Inventory, and the Rorschach. These chapters include extensive summaries of a wide variety of interpretive hypotheses intended for reference purposes when practitioners must generate interpretive hypotheses based on specific test scores. To gain initial familiarity with the tests, I recommend that practitioners or students carefully read the initial sections (history and development, psychometric properties, etc.) and then skim through the interpretation sections more quickly. This provides the reader with a basic familiarity with the procedures and types of data obtainable from the tests. As practical test work progresses, clinicians can then study the interpretive hypotheses in greater depth and gradually develop more extensive knowledge of the scales and their interpretation.

Based primarily on current frequency of use, these tests are covered in this text: the Wechsler intelligence scales (WAIS-IV/WISC-IV), Wechsler Memory Scales (WMS-IV), Minnesota Multiphasic Personality Inventory (MMPI-2), Millon Clinical Multiaxial Inventory (MCMI-III), Bender Visual Motor Gestalt Test-II, Repeatable Battery for the Assessment of Neuropsychological Status (RBANS), Rorschach, and the Thematic Apperception Test (TAT; Camara, Nathan, & Puente, 2000; C. Piotrowski & Zalewski, 1993; Robin, Barr, & Burton, 2005; Watkins, 1991; Watkins, Campbell, Nieberding, & Hallmark, 1995). The California Personality Inventory (CPI) was selected because of the importance of including a broad-based inventory of normal functioning along with its excellent technical development and relatively large research base (Anastasi & Urbina, 1997; Baucom, 1985; Gough, 2000; Wetzler, 1990). I also included a chapter on the most frequently used brief, symptom-focused inventories because of the increasing importance of monitoring treatment progress and outcome in a cost- and time-efficient managed care environment (Eisman, 2000; C. Piotrowski, 1999). The preceding instruments represent the core assessment devices used by most practitioners.

Finally, the clinician must generate relevant treatment recommendations and integrate the assessment results into a psychological report. Chapter 14 provides a systematic approach for working with assessment results to develop practical, evidence-based treatment recommendations. Chapter 15 presents guidelines for report writing, a report format, and four sample reports representative of the four most common types of referral settings (medical setting, legal context, educational context, psychological clinic). Thus, the chapters follow a logical sequence and provide useful, concise, and practical knowledge.

ROLE OF THE CLINICIAN

The central role of clinicians conducting assessments should be to answer specific questions and aid in making relevant decisions. To fulfill this role, clinicians must integrate a wide range of data and bring into focus diverse areas of knowledge. Thus, they are not merely administering and scoring tests. A useful distinction to highlight this point is the contrast between a psychometrist and a clinician conducting psychological assessment (Maloney & Ward, 1976; Matarazzo, 1990). Psychometrists tend to use tests merely to obtain data, and their task is often perceived as emphasizing the clerical and technical aspects of testing. Their approach is primarily data oriented, and the end product is often a series of traits or ability descriptions. These descriptions are typically unrelated to the person's overall context and do not address unique problems the person may be facing. In contrast, psychological assessment attempts to evaluate an individual in a problem situation so that the information derived from the assessment can somehow help with the problem. Tests are only one method of gathering data, and the test scores are not end products but merely means of generating hypotheses. Psychological assessment, then, places data in a wide perspective, with its focus being problem solving and decision making.

The distinction between psychometric testing and psychological assessment can be better understood and the ideal role of the clinician more clearly defined by briefly elaborating on the historical and methodological reasons for the development of the psychometric approach. When psychological tests were originally developed, group measurements of intelligence met with early and noteworthy success, especially in military and industrial settings where individual interviewing and case histories were too expensive and time consuming. An advantage of the data-oriented intelligence tests was that they appeared to be objective, which would reduce possible interviewer bias. More important, they were quite successful in producing a relatively high number of true positives when used for classification purposes. Their predictions were generally accurate and usable. However, these facts created the early expectation that all assessments could be performed using the same method and would provide a similar level of accuracy and usefulness. Later assessment strategies often tried to imitate the methods of earlier intelligence tests for variables such as personality and psychiatric diagnosis.

A further development consistent with the psychometric approach was the strategy of using a "test battery." It was reasoned that if a single test could produce accurate descriptions of an ability or trait, administering a series of tests could create a total picture of the person. The goal, then, was to develop a global yet definitive description for the person using purely objective methods. This goal encouraged the idea that the tool (psychological test) was the best process for achieving the goal, rather than being merely one technique in the overall assessment procedure. Behind this approach were the concepts of *individual differences* and *trait psychology*. These assume that one of the best ways to describe the differences among individuals is to measure their strengths and weaknesses with respect to various traits. Thus, the clearest approach to the study of personality involved developing a relevant taxonomy of traits and then creating tests to measure these traits. Again, there was an emphasis on the tools as primary, with a deemphasis on the input of the clinician. These trends created a bias toward administration and clerical skills. In this context, the psychometrist requires little, if any, clinical expertise other than administering, scoring, and interpreting tests. According to such a view, the most preferred tests would be machine-scored true-false or multiple-choice constructed so that the normed scores, rather than the psychometrist, provide the interpretation.

The objective psychometric approach is most appropriately applicable to ability tests such as those measuring intelligence or mechanical skills. Its usefulness decreases, however, when users attempt to assess personality traits such as dependence, authoritarianism, or anxiety. Personality variables are far more complex and, therefore, need to be validated in the context of history, behavioral observations, and interpersonal relationships. For example, a moderately elevated score on a scale measuring high energy level takes on an entirely different meaning for a high-functioning physician than for an individual with a history of mood disorders and associated work and interpersonal difficulties. When the purely objective psychometric approach is used for the evaluation of problems in living (coping more effectively, resolving interpersonal relationship, etc.), its usefulness is questionable.

Psychological assessment is most useful in the understanding and evaluation of personality and especially of problems in living. These issues involve a particular problem situation having to do with a specific individual. The central role of the clinician performing psychological assessment is that of an expert in human behavior who must deal with complex processes and understand test scores in the context of a person's life. The clinician must have knowledge concerning problem areas and, on the basis of this knowledge, form a general idea regarding behaviors to observe and areas in which to collect relevant data. Doing this involves an awareness and appreciation of multiple causation, interactional influences, and multiple relationships. As Woody (1980) has stated, "Clinical assessment is individually oriented, but it always considers social existence; the objective is usually to help the person solve problems."

In addition to an awareness of the role suggested by psychological assessment, clinicians should be familiar with core knowledge related to measurement and clinical practice. This includes descriptive statistics, reliability (and measurement error), validity (and the meaning of test scores), normative interpretation, selection of appropriate tests, administration procedures, variables related to diversity (ethnicity, race, age, gender), testing individuals with disabilities, and an appropriate amount of supervised experience (Turner, DeMers, Fox, & Reed, 2001). Persons performing psychological assessment should also have basic knowledge related to the demands, types of referral questions, and expectations of various contexts—particularly employment, education, vocational/career, health care (psychological, psychiatric, medical), and forensic. Furthermore, clinicians should know the main interpretive hypotheses in psychological testing and be able to identify, sift through, and evaluate a series of hypotheses to determine which are most relevant and accurate. For each assessment device, clinicians must understand conceptually what they are trying to test. Thus, rather than merely knowing the labels and definitions for various types of anxiety or thought disorders, clinicians should also have in-depth operational criteria for them. For example, the concept of intelligence, as represented by the IQ score, can sometimes appear misleadingly straightforward. Intelligence test scores can be complex, however, involving a variety of cognitive abilities, the influence of cultural factors, varying performance under different conditions, and issues related to the nature of intelligence. Unless clinicians are familiar with these areas, they are not adequately prepared to handle IQ data.

The above knowledge should be integrated with relevant general coursework, including abnormal psychology, the psychology of adjustment, clinical neuropsychology, psychotherapy, and basic case management. A problem in many training programs is that, although students frequently have a knowledge of abnormal psychology, personality theory, and test construction, they usually have insufficient training to integrate their knowledge into the interpretation of test results. Their training focuses on developing competency in administration and scoring rather than on knowledge relating to what they are testing.

The approach in this book is consistent with that of psychological assessment: Clinicians should be not only knowledgeable about traditional content areas in psychology and the various contexts of assessment but also able to integrate the test data into a relevant description of the person. This description, although focusing on the individual, should take into account the complexity of his or her social environment, personal history, and behavioral observations. Yet the goal is not merely to describe the person but rather to develop relevant answers to specific questions, aid in problem solving, and facilitate decision making.

PATTERNS OF TEST USAGE IN CLINICAL ASSESSMENT

Psychological assessment is crucial to the definition, training, and practice of professional psychology. Fully 91% of all practicing psychologists engage in assessment (Watkins et al., 1995), and 64% of all nonacademic advertisements listed assessment as an important prerequisite (Kinder, 1994). Assessment skills are also strong prerequisites for internships and postdoctoral training. The theory and instruments of assessment can be considered the very foundation of clinical investigation, applied research, and program evaluation. In many ways, psychological assessment is professional psychology's unique contribution to the wider arena of clinical practice. The early professional psychologists even defined themselves largely in the context of their role as psychological testers. Practicing psychologists spend 10% to 25% of their time conducting psychological assessment (Camara et al., 2000; Watkins, 1991; Watkins et al., 1995).

Although assessment has always been a core, defining feature of professional psychology, the patterns of use and relative importance of assessment have changed with time. During the 1940s and 1950s, psychological testing was frequently the single most important activity of professional psychologists. In contrast, the past 60 years have seen psychologists become involved in a far wider diversity of activities. Lubin and his colleagues (Lubin, Larsen, & Matarazzo, 1984; Lubin, Larsen, Matarazzo, & Seever, 1985, 1986) found that the average time spent performing assessment across five treatment settings was 44% in 1959, 29% in 1969, and only 22% in 1982. The average time spent in 1982 performing assessments in the five different settings ranged from 14% in counseling centers to 31% in psychiatric hospitals (Lubin et al., 1984, 1985, 1986). Camara et al. (2000) found that the vast majority of professional psychologists (81%) spend 0 to 4 hours a week conducting formal assessment, 15% spend 5 to 20 hours a week, and 4% spend more than 20 hours. The gradual decrease in the total time spent in assessment is due in part to the widening role of psychologists. Whereas in the 1940s and 1950s a practicing psychologist was almost synonymous with a tester, professional psychologists currently are increasingly involved in administration, consultation, organizational development, and many areas of direct treatment (Bamgbose, Smith, Jesse, & Groth-Marnat, 1980; Groth-Marnat, 1988; Groth-Marnat & Edkins, 1996). Decline in testing has also been attributed to disillusionment with the testing process based on criticisms about the reliability and validity of many assessment devices (Garb, Wood, Nezworski, Grove, & Stejskal, 2001; Wood, Lilienfeld, Garb, & Nezworski, 2000; Ziskin & Faust, 1995) and reductions in reimbursement (Cashel, 2002). In addition, psychological assessment has come to include a wide variety of activities beyond merely the administration and interpretation of traditional tests. These include conducting structured and unstructured interviews, behavioral observations in natural settings, observations of interpersonal interactions, neuropsychological assessment, behavioral assessment, and using assessment findings as part of the overall therapeutic process (Finn, 2007; Garb, 2007).

The relative popularity of different traditional psychological tests has been surveyed since 1935 in many settings, such as academic institutions, psychiatric hospitals, counseling centers, veterans administration centers, institutions for the developmentally disabled, private practice, and various memberships and professional organizations. Surveys of test usage have usually found that the 10 most frequently used tests are the Wechsler intelligence scales, Minnesota Multiphasic Personality Inventory, Rorschach, Bender Visual Motor Gestalt Test, Thematic Apperception Test, projective drawings (Human Figure Drawing, House-Tree-Person), Wechsler Memory Scale, Beck Depression Inventory, Millon Clinical Multiaxial Inventories, and California Psychological Inventory (Camara et al., 2000; Kamphaus, Petoskey, & Rowe, 2000; Lubin et al., 1985; C. Piotrowski & Zalewski, 1993; Watkins, 1991; Watkins et al., 1995). The pattern for the 10 most popular tests has remained quite stable since 1969 except that the Millon Clinical Multiaxial Inventory is now ranked number 10 and Human Figure Drawings have decreased to 13 (Camara et al., 2000). The pattern of test usage varies somewhat across different studies and varies considerably from setting to setting. Schools and centers for the intellectually disabled emphasize tests of intellectual abilities, such as the WISC-IV and behavior rating scales; counseling centers are more likely to use vocational interest inventories; and psychiatric settings emphasize tests assessing level of pathology, such as the MMPI-2 or MCMI-III.

One clear change in testing practices has been a relative decrease in the use and status of projective techniques (Groth-Marnat, 2000b; C. Piotrowski, 1999). Criticisms have been wide ranging but have centered on overly complex scoring systems, questionable norms, subjectivity of scoring, poor predictive utility, and inadequate or even nonexistent validity (Garb, 2005a; Garb et al., 2001; Miller, 2007; Pruitt, Smith, Thelen, & Lubin, 1985; D. Smith & Dumont, 1995). Further criticisms include the extensive time required to effectively learn the techniques, heavy reliance of projective techniques on psychoanalytic theory, and the greater time and cost efficiency of alternative objective tests. These criticisms have usually occurred from within the academic community where they are used less and less for research purposes (C. Piotrowski, 1999; C. Piotrowski & Zalewski, 1993; Watkins, 1991). As a result of these criticisms, there has been a slight but still noteworthy reduction in the use of the standard projective tests in professional practice (Archer, Buffington-Vollum, Stredny, & Handel, 2006; Camara et al., 2000; Kamphaus et al., 2000; C. Piotrowski, 1999). Although there has been a reduction, the Rorschach and TAT are still among the ten most frequently used instruments in adult clinical settings. This can be attributed to lack of time available for practitioners to learn new techniques, expectations that students in internships know how to use them, unavailability of other practical alternatives, and the fact that clinical experience is usually given more weight by practitioners than empirical evidence. This suggests distance between the quantitative, theoretical world of the academic and the practical, problem-oriented world of the practitioner. In fact, assessment practices in many professional settings seem to have little relationship to the number of research studies done on assessment tools, attitudes by academic faculty, or the psychometric quality of the test (Garb, Wood, Lilienfeld, & Nezworski, 2002). In contrast to the continued use of projective instruments in adult clinical settings, psychologists in child settings are likely to rely more on behavior rating scales (i.e., Child Behavior Checklist) than projective tests (Cashel, 2002; Kamphaus et al., 2000; Miller, 2007).

The earliest form of assessment was through clinical interview. Clinicians such as Freud, Jung, and Adler used unstructured interaction to obtain information regarding history, diagnosis, or underlying structure of personality. Later clinicians taught interviewing by providing outlines of the areas that should be discussed. During the 1960s and 1970s, much criticism was directed toward the interview, leading many psychologists to perceive interviews as unreliable and lacking empirical validation. Tests, in many ways, were designed to counter the subjectivity and bias of interview techniques. During the 1980s and 1990s, a wide variety of structured interview techniques gained popularity and have often been found to be reliable and valid indicators of a client's level of functioning. Structured interviews such as the Diagnostic Interview Schedule (DIS; Robins, Helzer, Cottler, & Goldring, 1989), Structured Clinical Interview for the DSM (SCID; Spitzer, Williams, & Gibbon, 1987), and Renard Diagnostic Interview (Helzer, Robins, Croughan, & Welner, 1981) are often given preference over psychological tests. These interviews, however, are very different from the traditional unstructured approaches. They have the advantage of being psychometrically sound even though they might lack important elements of rapport, idiographic richness, and flexibility that characterize less structured interactions (Garb, 2007; Rogers, 2001).

A further trend has been the development of neuropsychological assessment (see Groth-Marnat, 2000a; Lezak, 2004). The discipline is a synthesis between behavioral neurology and psychometrics and was created from a need to answer questions such as the nature of a person's organic deficits, severity of deficits, localization, and differentiating between functional versus organic impairment. The pathognomonic sign approach and the psychometric approaches are two clear traditions that have developed in the discipline. Clinicians relying primarily on a pathognomonic sign approach are more likely to interpret specific behaviors such as perseverations or weaknesses on one side of the body, which are highly indicative of the presence and nature of organic impairments. These clinicians tend to rely on the tradition of assessment associated with Luria (Bauer, 1995; Luria, 1973) and base their interview design and tests on a flexible method of testing possible hypotheses for different types of impairment. In contrast, the more quantitative tradition represented by Reitan and his colleagues (Reitan & Wolfson, 1993; Russell, 2000) is more likely to rely on critical cutoff scores, which distinguish between normal and brain-damaged persons. Reitan and Wolfson (1985, 1993) have recommended using an impairment index, which is the proportion of brain-sensitive tests that fall into the brain-damaged range. In actual practice, most clinical neuropsychologists are more likely to combine the psychometric and pathognomonic sign approaches (Rabin, Barr, & Burton, 2005). The two major neuropsychological test batteries are the Luria-Nebraska Neuropsychological Battery (Golden, Purisch, & Hammeke, 1985) and the Halstead Reitan Neuropsychological Test Battery (Reitan & Wolfson, 1993). A typical neuropsychological battery might include tests specifically designed to assess organic impairment along with tests such as the MMPI, Wechsler intelligence scales, and the Wide Range Achievement Test (WRAT-III). As a result, extensive research over the past 15 to 20 years has been directed toward developing a greater understanding of how the older and more traditional tests relate to different types and levels of cerebral dysfunction.

During the 1960s and 1970s, behavior therapy was increasingly used and accepted. Initially, behavior therapists were concerned with an idiographic approach to the functional analysis of behavior. As their techniques became more sophisticated, formalized methods of behavioral assessment began to arise. These techniques arose in part from dissatisfaction with the *Diagnostic and Statistical Manual of Mental Disorders,* 2nd Edition (*DSM-II*; American Psychiatric Association, 1968) methods of diagnosis as well as from a need to have assessment relate more directly to treatment and its outcomes. There was also a desire to be more accountable for documenting behavior change over time. For example, if behaviors related to anxiety decreased after therapy, the therapist should be able to demonstrate that the treatment had been successful. Behavioral assessment could involve measurements of movements (behavioral checklists, behavioral analysis), physiological responses (galvanic skin response [GSR], electromyograph [EMG]) or self-reports (self-monitoring, Beck Depression Inventory, assertiveness scales). Whereas the early behavioral assessment techniques showed little concern with the psychometric properties of their instruments, there has been an increasing push to have them meet adequate levels of reliability and validity (First, Frances, Widiger, Pincus, & Davis, 1992; Follette & Hayes, 1992). Despite the many formalized techniques of behavioral assessment, many behavior therapists feel that an unstructured idiographic approach is most appropriate.

Traditional means of assessment, then, have decreased because of an overall increase in other activities of psychologists and an expansion in the definition of assessment. Currently, a psychologist doing assessment might include such techniques as interviewing, administering, and interpreting traditional psychological tests (MMPI-2/MMPI-A, WAIS-III, etc.), naturalistic observations, neuropsychological assessment, and behavioral assessment. In addition, professional psychologists might be required to assess areas that were not given much emphasis before the 1980s: personality disorders (borderline personality, narcissism), stress and coping (life changes, burnout, existing coping resources), hypnotic responsiveness, psychological health, adaptation to new cultures, and the changes associated with increasing modernization. Additional areas might include family systems interactions, relation between a person and his or her environment (social climate, social supports), cognitive processes related to behavior disorders, and level of personal control (self-efficacy). All these require clinicians to be continually aware of new and more specific assessment devices and to maintain flexibility in the approaches they take.

The future of psychological assessment will probably be most influenced by the trends toward computerized assessment, adaptation to managed health care, and distance health care delivery (Groth-Marnat, 2000b; Groth-Marnat, 2008; Kay, 2007). Computerized assessment is likely to enhance efficiency through rapid scoring, complex decision rules, reduction in client-practitioner contact, novel presentation of stimuli (i.e., virtual reality), and generation of interpretive hypothesis (Lichtenberger, 2006). Future assessments are also likely to tailor the presentation of items based on the client's previous responses (Forbey & Ben-Porath, 2007). Unnecessary items will not be given with one result being that a larger amount of information will be obtained through the presentation of relatively fewer items. This time efficiency is in part stimulated by the cost-savings policies of managed care, which require psychologists to demonstrate the cost-effectiveness of their services (Groth-Marnat, 1999; Groth-Marnat & Edkins, 1996). In assessment, this means linking assessment with treatment planning. Thus, psychological reports of the future are likely to spend relatively less time on client dynamics and more time on details related to specific intervention strategies. Whereas considerable evidence supports the cost-effectiveness of using psychological tests in organizational contexts, health care similarly needs to demonstrate that assessment can increase the speed of treatment as well as optimize treatment outcome (Blount et al., 2007; Groth-Marnat, 1999; Groth-Marnat, Roberts, & Beutler, 2001; Lambert & Hawkins, 2004; Yates & Taub, 2003).

A further challenge and area for development is the role assessment will play in distance health (Leigh & Zaylor, 2000; Murphy, Levant, Hall, & Glueckauf, 2007). It might be particularly important for users of these facilities to be screened (or screen themselves) in order to optimally tailor interventions. In addition, distance assessment as a means in and of itself is likely to become important as well. This might require professional psychologists to change their traditional face-to-face role to one of developing and monitoring new applications as well as consulting/collaborating with clients regarding the results of assessments derived from the computer.

EVALUATING PSYCHOLOGICAL TESTS

Before using a psychological test, clinicians should investigate and understand the theoretical orientation of the test, practical considerations, the appropriateness of the standardization sample, and the adequacy of its reliability and validity. Often, helpful descriptions and reviews that relate to these issues can be found in the test manuals as well as past and future editions of the *Mental Measurements Yearbook* (Plake, Impara, & Spies, 2003), *Tests in Print* (L. L. Murphy, Impara, & Plake, 2006), *Tests: A Comprehensive Reference for Assessment in Psychology, Education, and Business* (Maddox, 2003), and *Measures for Clinical Practice: A Sourcebook* (Fischer & Corcoran, 2007). Reviews can also be found in assessment-related journals such as the *Journal of Personality Assessment, Journal of Psychoeducational Assessment*, and *Educational and Psychological Measurement*. Table 1.1 outlines the more important questions that should be answered. The issues outlined in this table are discussed further. The discussion reflects the practical orientation of this text by focusing on problems that clinicians using psychological tests are likely to confront. It is not intended to provide a comprehensive coverage of test theory and construction; if a more detailed treatment is required, the reader is referred to one of the

Table 1.1.   Evaluating a Psychological Test

Theoretical Orientation

1. Do you adequately understand the theoretical construct the test is supposed to be measuring?
2. Do the test items correspond to the theoretical description of the construct?

Practical Considerations

1. If reading is required by the examinee, does his or her ability match the level required by the test?
2. How appropriate is the length of the test?

Standardization

1. Is the population to be tested similar to the population the test was standardized on?
2. Was the size of the standardization sample adequate?
3. Have specialized subgroup norms been established?
4. How adequately do the instructions permit standardized administration?

Reliability

1. Are reliability estimates sufficiently high (generally around .90 for clinical decision making and around .70 for research purposes)?
2. What implications do the relative stability of the trait, the method of estimating reliability, and the test format have on reliability?

Validity

1. What criteria and procedures were used to validate the test?
2. Will the test produce accurate measurements in the context and for the purpose for which you would like to use it?

many texts on psychological testing (e.g., Aiken & Groth-Marnat, 2006; R. Kaplan & Saccuzzo, 2005).

Theoretical Orientation

Before clinicians can effectively evaluate whether a test is appropriate, they must understand its theoretical orientation. Clinicians should research the construct that the test is supposed to measure and then examine how the test approaches this construct. This information can usually be found in the test manual. If for any reason the information in the manual is insufficient, clinicians should seek it elsewhere. Clinicians can frequently obtain useful information regarding the construct being measured by carefully studying the individual test items. Usually the manual provides an individual analysis of the items, which can help the potential test user evaluate whether they are relevant to the trait being measured.

Practical Considerations

A number of practical issues relate more to the context and manner in which the test is used than to its construction. First, tests vary in terms of the level of education (especially reading skills) that examinees must have to understand them adequately. The examinee must be able to read, comprehend, and respond appropriately to the test. Second, some tests are too long, which can lead to a loss of rapport with or extensive frustration on the part of the examinee. Administering short forms of the test may reduce these problems, provided these forms have been properly developed and are treated with appropriate caution. Finally, clinicians have to assess the extent to which they need training to administer and interpret the instrument. If further training is necessary, a plan must be developed for acquiring this training.

Standardization

Another central issue relates to the adequacy of norms (see Cicchetti, 1994). Each test has norms that reflect the distribution of scores by a standardization sample. The basis on which individual test scores have meaning relates directly to the similarity between the individual being tested and the sample. If a similarity exists between the group or individual being tested and the standardization sample, adequate comparisons can be made. For example, if the test was standardized on European American college students between the ages of 18 and 22, useful comparisons can be made for college students in that ethnic and age bracket (if we assume that the test is otherwise sufficiently reliable and valid). The more dissimilar the person is from this standardization group (e.g., different national group, over 70 years of age), the less useful the test is for evaluation. The examiner may need to consult the literature to determine whether research that followed the publication of the test manual has developed norms for different groups. This is particularly important for tests such as the MMPI and the Rorschach in which norms for various cross-national populations have been published.

Three major questions that relate to the adequacy of norms must be answered. The first is whether the standardization group is representative of the population on which the examiner would like to use the test. The test manual should include sufficient information to determine the representativeness of the standardization sample. If this information is insufficient or in any way incomplete, it greatly reduces the degree of confidence with which clinicians can use the test. The ideal and current practice is to use stratified random sampling. However, because this can be an extremely costly and time-consuming procedure, many tests are quite deficient in this respect. The second question is whether the standardization group is large enough. If the group is too small, the results may not give stable estimates because of too much random fluctuation. Finally, a good test has specialized subgroup norms as well as broad national norms. Knowledge relating to subgroup norms gives examiners greater flexibility and confidence if they are using the test with similar subgroup populations (see Dana, 2005). This is particularly important when subgroups produce sets of scores that are significantly different from the normal standardization group. These subgroups can be based on factors such as ethnicity, sex, geographic location, age, level of education, socioeconomic status, or urban versus rural environment. Knowledge of each of these subgroup norms allows for a more appropriate and meaningful interpretation of scores.

Standardization can also refer to administration procedures. A well-constructed test should have instructions that permit the examiner to give the test in a structured manner similar to that of other examiners and also to maintain this standardized administration between one testing session and the next. Research has demonstrated that varying the instructions between one administration and the next can alter the types and quality of responses the examinee makes, thereby compromising the test's reliability. Standardization of administration should refer not only to the instructions but also to ensuring adequate lighting, quiet, no interruptions, and good rapport.

Reliability

The reliability of a test refers to its degree of stability, consistency, predictability, and accuracy. It addresses the extent to which scores obtained by a person are the same if the person is reexamined by the same test on different occasions. Underlying the concept of reliability is the possible range of error, or error of measurement, of a single score. This is an estimate of the range of possible random fluctuation that can be expected in an individual's score. It should be stressed, however, that a certain degree of error or noise is always present in the system, from such factors as a misreading of the items, poor administration procedures, or the changing mood of the client. If there is a large degree of random fluctuation, the examiner cannot place a great deal of confidence in an individual's scores. The goal of a test constructor is to reduce, as much as possible, the degree of measurement error, or random fluctuation. If this is achieved, the difference between one score and another for a measured characteristic is more likely to result from some true difference than from some chance fluctuation.

Two main issues relate to the degree of error in a test. The first is the inevitable, natural variation in human performance. Usually the variability is less for measurements of ability than for those of personality. Whereas ability variables (intelligence, mechanical aptitude, etc.) show gradual changes resulting from growth and development, many personality traits are much more highly dependent on factors such as mood. This is particularly true in the case of a characteristic such as anxiety. The practical significance of this in evaluating a test is that certain factors outside the test itself can serve to reduce the reliability that the test can realistically be expected to achieve. Thus, an examiner should generally expect higher reliabilities for an intelligence test than for a test measuring a personality variable such as anxiety. It is the examiner's responsibility to know what is being measured, especially the degree of variability to be expected in the measured trait.

The second important issue relating to reliability is that psychological testing methods are necessarily imprecise. For the hard sciences, researchers can make direct measurements, such as the concentration of a chemical solution, the relative weight of one organism compared with another, or the strength of radiation. In contrast, many constructs in psychology are often measured indirectly. For example, intelligence cannot be perceived directly; it must be inferred by measuring behavior that has been defined as being intelligent. Variability relating to these inferences is likely to produce a certain degree of error resulting from the lack of precision in defining and observing inner psychological constructs. Variability in measurement also occurs simply because people have true (not because of test error) fluctuations in performance between one testing session and the next. Whereas it is impossible to control for the natural variability in human performance, adequate test construction can attempt to reduce the imprecision that is a function of the test itself. Natural human variability and test imprecision make the task of measurement extremely difficult. Although some error in testing is inevitable, the goal of test construction is to keep testing errors within reasonably accepted limits. A high correlation is generally .80 or more, but the variable being measured also changes the expected strength of the correlation. Likewise, the method of determining reliability alters the relative strength of the correlation. Ideally, clinicians should hope for correlations of .90 or higher in tests that are used to make decisions about individuals, whereas a correlation of .70 or more is generally adequate for research purposes.

The purpose of reliability is to estimate the degree of test variance caused by error. The four primary methods of obtaining reliability involve determining (a) the extent to which the test produces consistent results on retesting (test-retest), (b) the relative accuracy of a test at a given time (alternate forms), (c) the internal consistency of the items (split-half and coefficient alpha), and (d) the degree of agreement between two examiners (interscorer). Another way to summarize this is that reliability can be time to time (test-retest), form to form (alternate forms), item to item (split-half/coefficient alpha), or scorer to scorer (interscorer). Although these are the main types of reliability, there is a fifth type, the Kuder-Richardson; like the split-half, it is a measurement of the internal consistency of the test items. However, because this method is considered appropriate only for tests that are relatively pure measures of a single variable, it is not covered in this book.

Test-Retest Reliability

Test-retest reliability is determined by administering the test and then repeating it on a second occasion. The reliability coefficient is calculated by correlating the scores obtained by the same person on the two different administrations. The degree of correlation between the two scores indicates the extent to which the test scores can be generalized from one situation to the next. If the correlations are high, the results are less likely to be caused by random fluctuations in the condition of the examinee or the testing environment. Thus, when the test is being used in actual practice, the examiner can be relatively confident that differences in scores are the result of an actual change in the trait being measured rather than random fluctuation.

A number of factors must be considered in assessing the appropriateness of test-retest reliability. One is that the interval between administrations can affect reliability. Thus, a test manual should specify the interval as well as any significant life changes that the examinees may have experienced, such as counseling, career changes, or psychotherapy. For example, tests of preschool intelligence often give reasonably high correlations if the second administration is within several months of the first one. However, correlations with later childhood or adult IQ are generally low because of innumerable intervening life changes. One of the major difficulties with test-retest reliability is the effect that practice and memory may have on performance, which can produce improvement between one administration and the next. This is a particular problem for speeded and memory tests such as those found on the Digit Symbol and Arithmetic subtests of the WAIS-IV. Additional sources of variation may be the result of random, short-term fluctuations in the examinee or of variations in the testing conditions. In general, test-retest reliability is the preferred method only if the variable being measured is relatively stable. If the variable is highly changeable (e.g., anxiety), this method is usually not adequate.

Alternate Forms

The alternate forms method avoids many of the problems encountered with test-retest reliability. The logic behind alternate forms is that, if the trait is measured several times on the same individual by using parallel forms of the test, the different measurements should produce similar results. The degree of similarity between the scores represents the reliability coefficient of the test. As in the test-retest method, the interval between administrations should always be included in the manual as well as a description of any significant intervening life experiences. If the second administration is given immediately after the first, the resulting reliability is more a measure of the correlation between forms and not across occasions. Correlations determined by tests given with a wide interval, such as two months or more, provide a measure of both the relation between forms and the degree of temporal stability.

The alternate forms method eliminates many carryover effects, such as the recall of previous responses the examinee has made to specific items. However, there is still likely to be some carryover effect in that the examinee can learn to adapt to the overall style of the test even when the specific item content between one test and another is unfamiliar. This is most likely when the test involves some sort of problem-solving strategy in which the same principle in solving one problem can be used to solve the next one. An examinee, for example, may learn to use mnemonic aids to increase his or her performance on an alternate form of the WAIS-III Digit Symbol subtest.

Perhaps the primary difficulty with alternate forms lies in determining whether the two forms are actually equivalent. For example, if one test is more difficult than its alternate form, the difference in scores may represent actual differences in the two tests rather than differences resulting from the unreliability of the measure. Because the test constructor is attempting to measure the reliability of the test itself and not the differences between the tests, the difference between test scores could confound and lower the reliability coefficient. Alternate forms should be independently constructed tests that use the same specifications, including the same number of items, type of content, format, and manner of administration.

A final difficulty is encountered primarily when there is a delay between one administration and the next. With such a delay, the examinee may perform differently because of short-term fluctuations such as mood, stress level, or the relative quality of the previous night's sleep. Thus, an examinee's abilities may vary somewhat from one examination to another, thereby affecting test results. Despite these problems, alternate forms reliability has the advantage of at least reducing, if not eliminating, many carryover effects of the test-retest method. A further advantage is that the alternate test forms can be useful for other purposes, such as assessing the effects of a treatment program or monitoring a patient's changes over time by administering the different forms on separate occasions.

Internal Consistency: Split-half Reliability and Coefficient Alpha

The split-half method and coefficient alpha are the best techniques for determining reliability for a trait with a high degree of fluctuation. Because the test is given only once and the items are correlated with each other, there is only one administration, and it is not possible for the effects of time to intervene as they might with the test-retest method. Thus, the split-half method and coefficient alpha give measures of the internal consistency of the test items rather than the temporal stability of different administrations of the same test. To determine split-half reliability, the test is often split on the basis of odd and even items. This method is usually adequate for most tests. Dividing the test into a first half and second half can be effective in some cases but is often inappropriate because of the cumulative effects of warming up, fatigue, and boredom, all of which can result in different levels of performance on the first half of the test compared with the second. In contrast, coefficient alpha correlates the items with each other to determine their consistency.

As is true with the other methods of obtaining reliability, the split-half method and coefficient alpha have limitations. When a test is split in half, there are fewer items on each half, which results in wider variability because the individual responses cannot stabilize as easily around a mean. As a general principle, the longer a test is, the more reliable it is because the larger the number of items, the easier it is for the majority of items to compensate for minor alterations in responding to a few of the other items. As with the alternate forms method, differences in content may exist between one half and another.

Interscorer Reliability

In some tests, scoring is based partially on the judgment of the examiner. Because judgment may vary between one scorer and the next, it may be important to assess the extent to which reliability might be affected. This is especially true for projectives and even for some ability tests where hard scorers may produce results somewhat different from easy scorers. This variance in interscorer reliability may apply for global judgments based on test scores, such as brain-damaged versus normal, or for small details of scoring, such as whether a person has given a shading versus a texture response on the Rorschach. The basic strategy for determining interscorer reliability is to obtain a series of responses from a single client and to have these responses scored by two different individuals. A variation is to have two different examiners test the same client using the same test and then to determine how close their scores or ratings of the person are. The two sets of scores can then be correlated to determine a reliability coefficient. Any test that requires even partial subjectivity in scoring should provide information on interscorer reliability.

The best form of reliability is dependent on both the nature of the variable being measured and the purposes for which the test is used. If the trait or ability being measured is highly stable, the test-retest method is preferable, whereas split-half is more appropriate for characteristics that are highly subject to fluctuations. When using a test to make predictions, the test-retest method is preferable because it gives an estimate of the dependability of the test from one administration to the next. This is particularly true if, when determining reliability, an increased time interval existed between the two administrations. If, on the other hand, the examiner is concerned with the internal consistency and accuracy of a test for a single, one-time measure, either the split-half or the alternate forms would be best.

Another consideration in evaluating the acceptable range of reliability is the format of the test. Longer tests usually have higher reliabilities than shorter ones. Also, the format of the responses affects reliability. For example, a true-false format is likely to have a lower reliability than multiple choice because each true-false item has a 50% possibility of the answer being correct by chance. In contrast, each question in a multiple-choice format having five possible choices has only a 20% possibility of being correct by chance. A final consideration is that tests with various subtests or subscales should report the reliability for the overall test as well as for each of the subtests. In general, the overall test score has a significantly higher reliability than its subtests. For example, the overall IQ on the WAIS-IV has a higher reliability than any of the more specific and shorter subtests used to calculate the IQ. In estimating the confidence with which test scores can be interpreted, the examiner should take into account the lower reliabilities of the subtests. For example, a Full Scale IQ on the WAIS-III can be interpreted with more confidence than the specific subscale scores.

Most test manuals include a statistical index of the amount of error that can be expected for test scores, which is referred to as the *standard error of measurement* (SEM). The logic behind the SEM is that test scores consist of both truth and error. Thus, there is always noise or error in the system, and the SEM provides a range to indicate how extensive that error is likely to be. The range depends on the test's reliability so that the higher the reliability, the narrower the range of error. The SEM is a standard deviation score so that, for example, a SEM of 3 on an intelligence test would indicate that an individual's score has a 68% chance of being ±3 IQ points from the estimated true score. This is because the SEM of 3 represents a band extending from −1 to +1 standard deviations above and below the mean. Likewise, there would be a 95% chance that the individual's score would fall within a range of ±6 points from the estimated true score. From a theoretical perspective, the SEM is a statistical index of how a person's repeated scores on a specific test would fall around a normal distribution. Thus, it is a statement of the relationship among a person's obtained score, his or her theoretically true score, and the test reliability. Because it is an empirical statement of the probable range of scores, the SEM has more practical usefulness than a knowledge of the test reliability. This band of error is also referred to as a *confidence interval*.

The acceptable range of reliability is difficult to identify and depends partially on the variable being measured. In general, unstable aspects (states) of the person produce lower reliabilities than stable ones (traits). Thus, in evaluating a test, the examiner should expect higher reliabilities on stable traits or abilities than on changeable states. For example, a person's general fund of vocabulary words is highly stable and therefore produces high reliabilities. In contrast, a person's level of anxiety is often highly changeable. This means examiners should not expect nearly as high reliabilities for anxiety as for an ability measure such as vocabulary. A further consideration, also related to the stability of the trait or ability, is the method of reliability that is used. Alternate forms are considered to give the lowest estimate of the actual reliability of a test, while split-half provides the highest estimate. Another important way to estimate the adequacy of reliability is by comparing the reliability derived on other similar tests. The examiner can then develop a sense of the expected levels of reliability, which provides a baseline for comparisons. In the example of anxiety, a clinician may not know what is an acceptable level of reliability. A general estimate can be made by comparing the reliability of the test under consideration with other tests measuring the same or a similar variable. The most important thing to keep in mind is that lower levels of reliability usually suggest that less confidence can be placed in the interpretations and predictions based on the test data. However, clinical practitioners are less likely to be concerned with low statistical reliability if they have some basis for believing the test is a valid measure of the client's state at the time of testing. The main consideration is that the sign or test score does not mean one thing at one time and something different at another.

Validity

The most crucial issue in test construction is validity. Whereas reliability addresses issues of consistency, validity assesses what the test is to be accurate about. A test that is valid for clinical assessment should measure what it is intended to measure and should also produce information useful to clinicians. A psychological test cannot be said to be valid in any abstract or absolute sense, but more practically, it must be valid in a particular context and for a specific group of people (Messick, 1995). Although a test can be reliable without being valid, the opposite is not true; a necessary prerequisite for validity is that the test must have achieved an adequate level of reliability. Thus, a valid test is one that accurately measures the variable it is intended to measure. For example, a test comprising questions about a person's musical preference might erroneously state that it is a test of creativity. The test might be reliable in the sense that if it is given to the same person on different occasions, it produces similar results each time. However, it would not be reliable in that an investigation might indicate it does not correlate with other more valid measurements of creativity.

Establishing the validity of a test can be extremely difficult, primarily because psychological variables are usually abstract concepts, such as intelligence, anxiety, and personality. These concepts have no tangible reality, so their existence must be inferred through indirect means. In addition, conceptualization and research on constructs undergo change over time requiring that test validation go through continual refinement (G. Smith & McCarthy, 1995). In constructing a test, a test designer must follow two necessary, initial steps. First, the construct must be theoretically evaluated and described; second, specific operations (test questions) must be developed to measure it. Even when the designer has followed these steps closely and conscientiously, it is sometimes difficult to determine what the test really measures. For example, IQ tests are good predictors of academic success, but many researchers question whether they adequately measure the concept of intelligence as it is theoretically described. Another hypothetical test that, based on its item content, might seem to measure what is described as musical aptitude may in reality be highly correlated with verbal abilities. Thus, it may be more a measure of verbal abilities than of musical aptitude.

Any estimate of validity is concerned with relationships between the test and some external independently observed event. The *Standards for Educational and Psychological Testing* (American Educational Research Association [AERA], American Psychological Association [APA], & National Council for Measurement in Education [NCME], 1999; G. Morgan, Gliner, & Harmon, 2001) list the three main methods of establishing validity as content-related, criterion-related, and construct-related.

Content Validity

During the initial construction phase of any test, the developers must first be concerned with its content validity. *Content validity* refers to the representativeness and relevance of the assessment instrument to the construct being measured. During the initial item selection, the constructors must carefully consider the skills or knowledge area of the variable they would like to measure. The items are then generated based on this conceptualization of the variable. At some point, it might be decided that the item content overrepresents, underrepresents, or excludes specific areas, and alterations in the items might be made accordingly. If experts on subject matter are used to determine the items, the number of these experts and their qualifications should be included in the test manual. The instructions they received and the extent of agreement between judges should also be provided. A good test covers not only the subject matter being measured but also additional variables. For example, factual knowledge may be one criterion, but the application of that knowledge and the ability to analyze data are also important. Thus, a test with high content validity must cover all major aspects of the content area and must do so in the correct proportion.

A concept somewhat related to content validity is face validity. These terms are not synonymous, however, because *content validity* pertains to judgments made by experts, whereas *face validity* concerns judgments made by the test users. The central issue in face validity is test rapport. Thus, a group of potential mechanics who are being tested for basic skills in arithmetic should have word problems that relate to machines rather than to business transactions. Face validity, then, is present if the test looks good to the persons taking it, to policymakers who decide to include it in their programs, and to other untrained personnel. Despite the potential importance of face validity in regard to test-taking attitudes, disappointingly few formal studies on face validity are performed and/or reported in test manuals.

In the past, content validity has been conceptualized and operationalized as being based on the subjective judgment of the test developers. As a result, it has been regarded as the least preferred form of test validation, albeit necessary in the initial stages of test development. In addition, its usefulness has been focused primarily at achievement tests (how well has this student learned the content of the course?) and personnel selection (does this applicant know the information relevant to the potential job?). More recently, it has become used more extensively in personality and clinical assessment (Ben-Porath & Tellegen, 2008; Butcher, Graham, Williams, & Ben-Porath, 1990; Harkness, McNulty, Ben-Porath, & Graham, 2002; Millon, 1994). More recent use of content validity has paralleled more rigorous and empirically based approaches to content validity along with a closer integration to criterion and construct validation.

Criterion Validity

A second major approach to determining validity is criterion validity, which has also been called *empirical* or *predictive validity*. Criterion validity is determined by comparing test scores with some sort of performance on an outside measure. The outside measure should have a theoretical relation to the variable that the test is supposed to measure. For example, an intelligence test might be correlated with grade point average; an aptitude test, with independent job ratings or general maladjustment scores on other tests measuring similar dimensions. The relation between the two measurements is usually expressed as a correlation coefficient.

Criterion-related validity is most frequently divided into either concurrent or predictive validity. *Concurrent validity* refers to measurements taken at the same, or approximately the same, time as the test. For example, an intelligence test might be administered at the same time as assessments of a group's level of academic achievement. *Predictive validity* refers to outside measurements that were taken some time after the test scores were derived. Thus, predictive validity might be evaluated by correlating the intelligence test scores with measures of academic achievement a year after the initial testing. Concurrent validation is often used as a substitute for predictive validation because it is simpler, less expensive, and not as time consuming. However, the main consideration in deciding whether concurrent or predictive validation is preferable depends on the test's purpose. Predictive validity is most appropriate for tests used for selection and classification of personnel. This may include hiring job applicants, placing military personnel in specific occupational training programs, screening out individuals who are likely to develop emotional disorders, or identifying which category of psychiatric populations would be most likely to benefit from specific treatment approaches. These situations all require that the measurement device provide a prediction of some future outcome. In contrast, concurrent validation is preferable if an assessment of the client's current status is required rather than a prediction of what might occur to the client at some future time. The distinction can be summarized by asking "Is Mr. Jones maladjusted?" (concurrent validity) rather than "Is Mr. Jones likely to become maladjusted at some future time?" (predictive validity).

An important consideration is the degree to which a specific test can be applied to a unique work-related environment (see Hogan, Hogan, & Roberts, 1996). This consideration relates more to the social value and consequences of the assessment than the formal validity as reported in the test manual (Messick, 1995). In other words, can the test under consideration provide accurate assessments and predictions for the environment in which the examinee is working? To answer this question adequately, the examiner must refer to the manual and assess the similarity between the criteria used to establish the test's validity and the situation to which he or she would like to apply the test. For example, can an aptitude test that has adequate criterion validity in the prediction of high school grade point average also be used to predict academic achievement for a population of college students? If the examiner has questions regarding the relative applicability of the test, he or she may need to undertake a series of specific tasks. The first is to identify the required skills for adequate performance in the situation involved. For example, the criteria for a successful teacher may include such attributes as verbal fluency, flexibility, and good public speaking skills. The examiner then must determine the degree to which each skill contributes to the quality of a teacher's performance. Next, the examiner has to assess the extent to which the test under consideration measures each of these skills. The final step is to evaluate the extent to which the attribute that the test measures is relevant to the skills the examiner needs to predict. Based on these evaluations, the examiner can estimate the confidence that he or she places in the predictions developed from the test. This approach is sometimes referred to as *synthetic validity* because examiners must integrate or synthesize the criteria reported in the test manual with the variables they encounter in their clinical or organizational settings.

The strength of criterion validity depends in part on the type of variable being measured. Usually, intellectual or aptitude tests give relatively higher validity coefficients than personality tests because there are generally a greater number of variables influencing personality than intelligence. As the number of variables that influences the trait being measured increases, it becomes progressively more difficult to account for them. When a large number of variables are not accounted for, the trait can be affected in unpredictable ways. This situation can create a much wider degree of fluctuation in the test scores, thereby lowering the validity coefficient. Thus, when evaluating a personality test, the examiner should not expect as high a validity coefficient as for intellectual or aptitude tests. A helpful guide is to look at the validities found in similar tests and compare them with the test being considered. For example, if an examiner wants to estimate the range of validity to be expected for the extraversion scale on the Myers Briggs Type Indicator, he or she might compare it with the validities for similar scales found in the NEO-PIR and Eysenck Personality Questionnaire. The relative level of validity, then, depends both on the quality of the construction of the test and on the variable being studied.

An important consideration is the extent to which the test accounts for the trait being measured or the behavior being predicted. For example, the typical correlation between intelligence tests and academic performance is about .50 (Neisser et al., 1996). Because no one would say that grade point average is entirely the result of intelligence, the relative extent to which intelligence determines grade point average has to be estimated. It can be calculated by squaring the correlation coefficient and changing it into a percentage. Thus, if the correlation of .50 is squared, it comes out to 25%, indicating that 25% of academic achievement can be accounted for by IQ as measured by the intelligence test. The remaining 75% may include factors such as motivation, quality of instruction, and past educational experience. The problem facing the examiner is to determine whether 25% of the variance is sufficiently useful for the intended purposes of the test. This determination ultimately depends on the personal judgment of the examiner.

The main problem confronting criterion validity is finding an agreed-on, definable, acceptable, and feasible outside criterion. Whereas for an intelligence test the grade point average might be an acceptable criterion, it is far more difficult to identify adequate criteria for most personality tests. Even with so-called intelligence tests, many research-ers argue that it is more appropriate to consider them tests of scholastic aptitude rather than of intelligence. Yet another difficulty with criterion validity is the possibility that the criterion measure will be inadvertently biased. Referred to as *criterion contamination,* this occurs when knowledge of the test results influences an individual's later perform-ance. For example, a supervisor in an organization who receives such information about subordinates may act differently toward a worker placed in a certain category after being tested. This situation may set up negative or positive expectations for the worker, which could influence his or her level of performance. The result is likely to artificially alter the level of the validity coefficients. To work around these difficulties, especially in regard to personality tests, a third major method must be used to determine validity.

Construct Validity

The method of construct validity was developed in part to correct the inadequacies and difficulties encountered with content and criterion approaches. Early forms of con-tent validity relied too much on subjective judgment, while criterion validity was too restrictive in working with the domains or structure of the constructs being measured. Criterion validity had the further difficulty in that there was often a lack of agreement in deciding on adequate outside criteria. The basic approach of construct validity is to assess the extent to which the test measures a theoretical construct or trait. This assessment involves three general steps. Initially, the test constructor must make a careful analysis of the trait. This is followed by a consideration of the ways in which the trait should relate to other variables. Finally, the test designer needs to test whether these hypothesized rela-tionships actually exist (Foster & Cone, 1995). For example, a test measuring dominance should have a high correlation with the individual accepting leadership roles and a low or negative correlation with measures of submissiveness. Likewise, a test measuring anxi-ety should have a high positive correlation with individuals who are measured during an anxiety-provoking situation, such as an experiment involving some sort of physical pain. As these hypothesized relationships are verified by research studies, the degree of confi-dence that can be placed in a test increases.

There is no single, best approach for determining construct validity; rather, a variety of different possibilities exist. For example, if some abilities are expected to increase with age, correlations can be made between a population's test scores and age. This may be appropriate for variables such as intelligence or motor coordination, but it would not be applicable for most personality measurements. Even in the measurement of intelligence or motor coordination, this approach may not be appropriate beyond the age of maturity. Another method for determining construct validity is to measure the effects of experimen-tal or treatment interventions. Thus, a posttest measurement may be taken following a period of instruction to see if the intervention affected the test scores in relation to a pre-vious pretest measure. For example, after an examinee completes a course in arithmetic, it would be predicted that scores on a test of arithmetical ability would increase. Often correlations can be made with other tests that supposedly measure a similar variable. However, a new test that correlates too highly with existing tests may represent needless duplication unless it incorporates some additional advantage, such as a shortened format, ease of administration, or superior predictive validity. Factor analysis is of particular rel-evance to construct validation because it can be used to identify and assess the relative strength of different psychological traits. Factor analysis can also be used in the design of a test to identify the primary factor or factors measured by a series of different tests. Thus, it can be used to simplify one or more tests by reducing the number of categories to a few common factors or traits. The factorial validity of a test is the relative weight or loading that a factor has on the test. For example, if a factor analysis of a measure of psychopathology determined that the test was composed of two clear factors that seemed to be measuring anxiety and depression, the test could be considered to have factorial validity. This would be especially true if the two factors seemed to be accounting for a clear and large portion of what the test was measuring.

Another method used in construct validity is to estimate the degree of internal consistency by correlating specific subtests with the test's total score. For example, if a subtest on an intelligence test does not correlate adequately with the overall or Full Scale IQ, it should be either eliminated or altered in a way that increases the correlation. A final method for obtaining construct validity is for a test to converge or correlate highly with variables that are theoretically similar to it. The test should not only show this convergent validity but also have discriminate validity, in which it would demonstrate low or negative correlations with variables that are dissimilar to it. Thus, scores on reading comprehension should show high positive correlations with performance in a literature class and low correlations with performance in a class involving mathematical computation.

Related to discriminant and convergent validity is the degree of sensitivity and specificity an assessment device demonstrates in identifying different categories. *Sensitivity* refers to the percentage of true positives that the instrument has identified, whereas *specificity* is the relative percentage of true negatives. A structured clinical interview might be quite sensitive in that it would accurately identify 90% of schizophrenics in an admitting ward of a hospital. However, it may not be sufficiently specific in that 30% of schizophrenics would be incorrectly classified as either normal or having some other diagnosis. The difficulty in determining sensitivity and specificity lies in developing agreed-on, objectively accurate outside criteria for categories such as psychiatric diagnosis, intelligence, or personality traits.

As indicated by the variety of approaches discussed, no single, quick, efficient method exists for determining construct validity. It is similar to testing a series of hypotheses in which the results of the studies determine the meanings that can be attached to later test scores (Foster & Cone, 1995; Messick, 1995). Almost any data can be used, including material from the content and criterion approaches. The greater the amount of supporting data, the greater is the level of confidence with which the test can be used. As a result, construct validity represents the strongest and most sophisticated approach to test construction. In many ways, all types of validity can be considered as subcategories of construct validity. Construct validation involves theoretical knowledge of the trait or ability being measured, knowledge of other related variables, hypothesis testing, and statements regarding the relationship of the test variable to a network of other variables that have been investigated (G. T. Smith, 2005). Thus, construct validation is a never-ending process in which new relationships always can be verified and investigated.

VALIDITY IN CLINICAL PRACTICE

Although a test may have been found to have a high level of validity during its construction, it does not necessarily follow that the test is also valid in a specific situation with a particular client. A test can never be valid in any absolute sense because, in practice, numerous variables might affect the test results. A serious issue, then, is the degree of validity generalization that is made. In part, this generalization depends on the similarity between the population used during various stages of test construction and the population and situation that it is being used for in practice. Validity in clinical practice also depends on the extent to which tests can work together to improve each other's accuracy. Some tests thus show incremental validity in that they improve accuracy in increments as increasing numbers of data sources are used. *Incremental validity*, then, refers to the ability of tests to produce information above what is already known. Another important consideration is the ability of the clinician to generate hypotheses, test these hypotheses, and blend the data derived from hypothesis testing into a coherent, integrated picture of the person. Maloney and Ward (1976) refer to this latter approach to validity as *conceptual validity* because it involves creating a conceptually coherent description of the person.

Incremental Validity

For a test to be considered useful and efficient, it must be able to produce accurate results above and beyond the results that could be obtained with greater ease and less expense (Hunsley & Meyer, 2003). If equally accurate clinical descriptions could be obtained through such basic information as biographical data and knowing the referral question, there would be no need for psychological tests. Incremental validity also needs to be evaluated in relation to cost-effectiveness. A psychological test might indeed demonstrate incremental validity by increasing the relative proportions of accurate diagnoses, or hit rates, by 2%. However, practitioners need to question whether this small increase in accuracy is worth the extra time involved in administering and interpreting the test. Clinicians might direct their time more productively toward direct treatment.

In the 1950s, one of the theoretical defenses for tests having low reliabilities and validities was that, when used in combination, their accuracy could be improved. In other words, results from a series of different tests could provide checks and balances to correct for inaccurate interpretations. A typical strategy used to empirically test for this was to first obtain biographical data, make interpretations and decisions based on this data, and then test its accuracy based on some outside criterion. Next, a test such as the MMPI could be given; then the interpretations and decisions based on it could likewise be assessed for accuracy. Finally, clinicians could be given both sets of data to assess any improvements in the accuracies of interpretation/decisions between either of the first two conditions and the combined information.

It would seem logical that the greater the number of tests used, the greater would be the overall validity of the assessment battery. However, research on psychological tests used in clinical practice has often demonstrated that they have poor incremental validity. An older but representative study by Kostlan (1954) on male psychiatric out-patients compared the utility of a case history, Rorschach, MMPI, and a sentence completion test. Twenty experienced clinicians interpreted different combinations of these sources of test data. Their conclusions were combined against criterion judges who used a lengthy checklist of personality descriptions. The conclusions were that, for most of the data, the clinicians were no more accurate than if they had used only age, occupation, education, marital status, and a basic description of the referral question. The exception was that the most accurate descriptions were based on a combination of social history and the MMPI. In contrast, psychological tests have sometimes clearly demonstrated their incremental validity. S. Schwartz and Wiedel (1981) demonstrated that neurological residents gave more accurate diagnoses when an MMPI was used in combination with history, electroencephalogram (EEG), and physical exam. This was probably not so much because of a specific MMPI neurological profile but rather that the MMPI increased diagnostic accuracy by enabling the residents to rule out other possible diagnoses.

Often clinical psychologists attempt to make a series of behavioral predictions based on complex psychological tests. Although these predictions may show varying levels of accuracy, a simpler and more effective means of achieving this information might be to simply ask the clients to predict their own behaviors. In some circumstances, self-prediction has been found to be more accurate than psychological tests, whereas in others, tests have been found to be more accurate (Shrauger & Osberg, 1981). Advantages of self-assessment are that it can be time-efficient, cost-effective, and facilitate a collegial relationship between assessor and client. In contrast, difficulties are that, compared with formal testing, self-assessment may be significantly more susceptible to social desirability, attributional errors, distortions caused by poor adjustment, and the relative self-awareness of the client. These factors need to be carefully considered before deciding to use self-assessment versus formal psychological tests. Although the incremental validity of using self-assessment in combination with formal testing has not been adequately researched, it would seem that this is conceptually a potentially useful strategy for future research.

Reviews of studies on incremental validity (Garb, 1998b, 2003, 2005b) have provided a number of general conclusions. The addition of an MMPI to background data has consistently led to increases in validity although the increases were quite small when the MMPI was added to extensive data. The addition of projective tests to a test battery did not generally increase incremental validity. Lanyon and Goodstein (1982) have argued that case histories are generally preferable to psychological test data. Furthermore, a single test in combination with case history data is generally as effective as a large number of tests with case history data. Some studies have found that the MMPI alone was generally found to be preferable to a battery containing the MMPI, Rorschach, and sentence completion (Garb, 1984, 1994a, 1998b, 2005b). In contrast, other studies have found that the Rorschach can add incremental validity to a test battery (G. Meyer, 1997; Weiner, 1999).

In defense of the poor incremental validity of many of the traditional clinical tests are weaknesses and unanswered questions relating to the preceding research. First, few studies have looked at statistically derived predictions and interpretations based on optimal multiple cutoff scores or multiple regression equations. However, more recent research, particularly on tests such as the MMPI-2 and CPI, has emphasized this approach. For example, combined weightings on such variables as specific CPI scores, Scholastic Aptitude Test (SAT) scores, grade point average (GPA), and IQ can be combined to predict success in specific programs (see Chapter 9). Further research using this approach may yield greater incremental validity for a wide number of assessment techniques. Second, few studies on incremental validity have investigated the ways in which different tests might show greater incremental validity in specific situations for specific populations. Instead, most research has focused on the validity of global personality descriptions, without tying these descriptions to the unique circumstances or contexts persons might be involved in. Finally, as most previous studies have focused on global personality descriptions, certain tests demonstrate greater incremental validity when predicting highly specific traits and behaviors.

Conceptual Validity

A further method for determining validity that is highly relevant to clinical practice is conceptual validity (Maloney & Ward, 1976). In contrast to the traditional methods (content validity, etc.), which are primarily concerned with evaluating the theoretical constructs in the test itself, conceptual validity focuses on individuals with their unique histories and behaviors. It is a means of evaluating and integrating test data so that the clinician's conclusions make accurate statements about the examinee. There are similarities with construct validity in that construct validity also tries to test specific hypothesized relationships between constructs. Conceptual validity is likewise concerned with testing constructs, but in this case the constructs relate to the individual rather than to the test itself.

In determining conceptual validity, the examiner generally begins with individuals for whom no constructs have been developed. The next phase is to observe, collect data, and form a large number of hypotheses. If these hypotheses are confirmed through consistent trends in the test data, behavioral observations, history, and additional data sources, the hypotheses can be considered to represent valid constructs regarding the person. The focus is on an individual in his or her specific situation, and the data are derived from a variety of sources. The conceptual validity of the constructs is based on the logicalness and internal consistency of the data. Unlike construct validity, which begins with previously developed constructs, conceptual validity produces constructs as its end product. Its aim is for these constructs to provide valid sources of information that can be used to help solve the unique problems that an individual may be facing.

CLINICAL JUDGMENT

Any human interaction involves mutual and continually changing perceptions. *Clinical judgment* is a special instance of perception in which the clinician attempts to use whatever sources are available to create accurate descriptions of the client. These sources may include test data, case history, medical records, personal journals, and verbal and nonverbal observations of behavior. Relevant issues and processes involved in clinical judgment include data gathering, data synthesis, the relative accuracy of clinical versus statistical/actuarial descriptions, and judgment in determining what to include in a psychological report. This sequence also parallels the process clinicians go through when assessing a client.

Data Gathering and Synthesis

Most of the research related to the strengths and weaknesses of data gathering and synthesis has focused on the assessment interview (see Chapter 3). However, many of the issues and problems related to clinical judgment during interviewing also have implications for the gathering and synthesis of test data. One of the most essential elements in gathering data from any source is the development of an optimum level of rapport. Rapport increases the likelihood that clients will give their optimum level of performance. If rapport is not sufficiently developed, it is increasingly likely that the data obtained from the person will be inaccurate.

Another important issue is that the interview itself is typically guided by the client's responses and the clinician's reaction to these responses. A client's responses might be nonrepresentative because of factors such as a transient condition (stressful day, poor night's sleep, etc.) or conscious/unconscious faking. The client's responses also need to be interpreted by the clinician. These interpretations can be influenced by a combination of personality theory, research data, and the clinician's professional and personal experience. The clinician typically develops hypotheses based on a client's responses and combines his or her observations with his or her theoretical understanding of the issue. These hypotheses can be further investigated and tested by interview questions and test data, which can result in confirmation, alteration, or elimination of the hypotheses. Thus, bias can potentially enter into this process from a number of different directions, including the types of questions asked, initial impressions, level of rapport, or theoretical perspective.

The clinician typically collects much of the initial data regarding a client through unstructured or semistructured interviews. Unstructured approaches in gathering and interpreting data provide flexibility, focus on the uniqueness of the person, and are ideographically rich. In contrast, an important disadvantage of unstructured approaches is that a clinician, like most other persons, can be influenced by a number of personal and cultural biases. For example, clinicians might develop incorrect hypotheses based on first impressions (primacy effect). They might end up seeking erroneous confirmation of incorrect hypotheses by soliciting expected responses rather than objectively probing for possible disconfirmation. Thus, clinicians might be unduly influenced by their preferred theory of personality, halo effects, self-fulfilling prophecies, expectations, and cultural stereotypes. These areas of potential sources of error have led to numerous questions regarding the dependability of clinical judgment.

Accuracy of Clinical Judgments

After collecting and organizing their data, clinicians then need to make final judgments regarding the client. Determining the relative accuracy of these judgments is crucial. In some cases, clinical judgment is clearly in error, whereas in others it can be quite accurate. To increase accuracy, clinicians need to know how errors might occur, how to correct these errors, and the relative advantages of specialized training.

A possible source of inaccuracy is that clinicians frequently do not take into account the base rate, or the rate at which a particular behavior, trait, or diagnosis occurs in the general population (Faust, 1991; S. Hawkins & Hastie, 1990; Wedding & Faust, 1989). For example, an intake section of a psychiatric hospital might evaluate a population of whom 50% could be considered to be schizophrenic. A clinician who would randomly diagnose patients as either schizophrenic or nonschizophrenic would be correct 50% of the time. Thus, even a 60% correct diagnosis of schizophrenia would exceed the base rate (or chance occurrence) by only 10%. It is also rare for clinicians to receive feedback regarding either the accuracy of their diagnoses or other frequently used judgments, such as behavioral predictions, personality traits, or the relative success of their recommendations (Garb, 1989, 1994a, 1998b, 2005b). Thus, it is possible that inaccurate strategies for arriving at conclusions will be continued with little likelihood of correction.

A further source of error is that information obtained earlier in the data collection process is frequently given more importance than information received later (primacy effect). This means that different starting points in the decision-making process may result in different conclusions. This can be further reinforced if clinicians make early judgments and then work to confirm these judgments through seeking supporting information. The resulting *confirmatory bias* can be especially likely to occur in a hypothesis-testing situation in which clinicians do not adequately seek information that could disconfirm as well as confirm their hypothesis (Haverkamp, 1993). The most problematic examples occur when clinicians interpret a client's behavior and then work to persuade the client that their interpretation is correct (Loftus, 1993).

Research on person perception accuracy indicates that, even though no two persons are uniformly accurate, some persons are much better at accurately perceiving others. Taft (1955) and P. E. Vernon (1964) summarize the early research on person perception accuracy by pointing out that accuracy is not associated with age (in adults); there is little difference in accuracy between males and females (although females are slightly better); and accurate perceptions of others are positively associated with intelligence, artistic/ dramatic interests, social detachment, and good emotional adjustment. Authoritarian personalities tend to be poor judges. In most instances, accuracy is related to similarity in race and cultural backgrounds (P. Shapiro & Penrod, 1986). In some cases, accuracy by psychologists may be only slightly related to their amount of clinical experience (Garb, 1989, 1992, 1994a, 1998b, 2005b); and, for some judgments, psychologists may be no better than certain groups of nonprofessionals, such as physical scientists and personnel workers (Garb, 1992, 1994a, 1998b, 2005b). Relatively higher rates of accuracy were achieved when clinical judgments based on interviews were combined with formal assessments and when statistical interpretive rules were used. When subjective test interpretation was combined with clinical judgment, it was questionable whether any increase in accuracy was obtained (Garb, 1984, 1989).

It would be logical to assume that the more confidence clinicians feel regarding the accuracy of their judgments, the more likely it would be that their judgments would be accurate. In several studies, however, confidence was often not related to accuracy (E. Kelly & Fiske, 1951; Kleinmuntz, 1990). Kelly and Fiske even found that degree of confidence was inversely related to predicting the success of trainees in a Veterans Administration training program. Several studies (Kareken & Williams, 1994; Lichtenstein & Fischoff, 1977) concluded that persons were generally overconfident regarding judgments; and when outcome knowledge was made available, clinicians typically overestimated what they thought they knew before receiving outcome knowledge (Hawkins & Hastie, 1990). This is usually referred to as *hindsight bias* ("I would have known it all along") and is usually accompanied by a denial that the outcome knowledge has influenced judgment. Paradoxically, as knowledge and experience in an area increase, there is generally a decrease in confidence regarding judgments. This observation was found to be true unless the clinicians were very knowledgeable, in which case they were likely to have a moderate level of confidence (Garb, 1989). Confidence was also more accurate if participants were made socially accountable for their judgments (Ruscio, 2000). Thus, the more experienced clinicians and persons who were more socially accountable were able to more accurately rate their level of confidence.

Crucial to clinical judgment is whether clinicians can make judgments better than laypersons and whether amount of clinical training can increase accuracy. This is a particularly important issue if psychologists are offering their services as expert witnesses to the legal justice system. Research reviews generally support the value of clinical training, but this is dependent on the domain being assessed. For example, Garb (1992) has concluded, "Clinicians are able to make reliable and valid judgments for many tasks, and their judgments are frequently more valid than judgments by laypersons" (p. 451). In particular, clinicians have been found to make more accurate judgments relating to relatively complex technical areas such as clinical diagnosis, ratings of mental status, many domains related to interview information, short-term (and possibly long-term) predictions of violence, psychological test interpretation (WAIS, MMPI), forensic knowledge, competency evaluations, neuropsychological test results, psychotherapy data, and biographical data (see primarily Garb, 1998b, but also 1984, 1989, 1992, 1994a). In contrast, trained clinicians were no better than less experienced persons (laypersons, novice trainees) in making judgments based on projective test results and in making personality descriptions based on face-to-face interaction (Garb, 2005b; Witteman & van den Bercken, 2007).

The preceding material indicates that errors in clinical judgment can and do occur. It is thus crucial, especially when appearing as an expert witness, that clinicians be familiar with the relevant literature on clinical judgment and, based on this information, take steps to improve their accuracy. Accordingly, Garb (1994a, 1998b, 2005b) and Wedding and Faust (1989) have made the following recommendations:

1. To avoid missing crucial information, clinicians should use comprehensive, structured, or at least semistructured approaches to interviewing. This is especially

important in cases where urgent clinical decisions (danger to self or others) may need to occur.

2. Clinicians should not only consider the data that supports their hypotheses, but also carefully consider or even list evidence that does not support their hypotheses. This will likely reduce the possibility of hindsight and confirmatory bias.

3. Diagnoses should be based on careful attention to the specific criteria contained in the *DSM-IV-TR* (2000; or *International Classification of Disorders* [*ICD-10*]). In particular, this means not making errors caused by inferences biased by gender and ethnicity.

4. Because memory can be a reconstructive process subject to possible errors, clinicians should avoid relying on memory and, rather, refer to careful notes as much as possible.

5. In making predictions, clinicians should attend to base rates as much as possible. Such a consideration potentially provides a rough estimate of how frequently the behavior will occur in a given population or context. Any clinical predictions, then, are guided by this base rate occurrence and are likely to be improvements on the base rate.

6. Clinicians should seek feedback when possible regarding the accuracy and usefulness of their judgments. For example, psychological reports should ideally be followed up with rating forms (that can be completed by the referral sources) relating to the clarity, precision, accuracy, and usefulness of the information and recommendations contained in the reports.

7. Clinicians should learn as much as possible regarding the theoretical and empirical material relevant to the person or group they are assessing. This would potentially help to develop strategies for obtaining comprehensive information, allow clinicians to make correct estimates regarding the accuracy of their judgments, and provide them with appropriate base rate information.

8. Familiarity with the literature on clinical judgment should be used to continually update practitioners on past and emerging trends.

Sometimes in court proceedings, psychologists are challenged regarding the difficulties associated with clinical judgment. If the preceding steps are taken, psychologists can justifiably reply that they are familiar with the literature and have taken appropriate steps to guard against inaccuracies in clinical judgment. More important, the quality of service related to clients and referral sources is also likely to be enhanced.

Clinical versus Actuarial Prediction

Over 50 years ago, Meehl (1954) published a review of research comparing the relative accuracy of clinical judgment to statistical formulas when used on identical sets of data (life history, demographic data, test profiles). The clinical approach used clinicians' judgment, whereas the actuarial approach used empirically derived formulas, such as single/multiple cutoffs and regression equations, to come to decisions regarding a client. His review covered a large number of settings including military placement, college success, criminal recidivism, and benefit from psychotherapy. He concluded that statistical decisions consistently outperformed clinical judgments (Meehl, 1954, 1965). This resulted in some lively debate in the journals, with Meehl's conclusions generally being supported (Aegisdottir et al., 2006; Garb, 1994b; Grove, Zald, Lebow, Snitz, & Nelson, 2000; Kleinmuntz, 1990). The magnitude of this difference has been estimated to be a 13% greater accuracy using actuarial methods when compared with clinical judgment.

Despite the empirical support for an actuarial approach, several practical and theoretical issues need to be considered. A clinical approach to integrating data and arriving at conclusions allows a clinician to explore, probe, and deepen his or her understanding in many areas. These frequently involve areas that tests or statistical formulas cannot measure. Often an interview is the only means of obtaining observations of behavior and unique aspects of history. Idiosyncratic events with a low frequency of occurrence may significantly alter a clinician's conclusions although no formulas take these events into account. It is quite common for unique, rare events to have occurred at some time in a client's life; and, during the process of assessment, they are frequently relevant and can often alter the conclusions of many, if not most, clinical assessments. Not only do unique aspects of a person change interpretations, but typically an assessment for a person needs to be focused for a specific context and specific situation that he or she is involved in. When the focus changes from institutional to individual decision making, the relevance of statistical rules becomes less practical (McGrath, 2001; Vane & Guarnaccia, 1989). Not only are individuals too multifaceted for simple actuarial formulas, but also their unique situations, contexts, and the decisions facing them are even more multifaceted.

A further difficulty with a purely actuarial approach is that development of both test reliability and validity, as well as actuarial formulas, requires conceiving the world as stable and static. For such approaches to be useful, the implicit assumption is that neither people nor criteria change. In contrast, the practitioner must deal with a natural world that is imperfect, constantly changing, does not necessarily follow rules, is filled with constantly changing perceptions, and is subject to chance or at least impossible-to-predict events. Thus, even when statistical formulas are available, they may not apply. This distinction between the statistical orientation of the psychometrician and the natural environment of the practitioner underlies the discrepancy between their two worlds (Beutler, 2000). Practitioners must somehow try to combine these two modes of analysis, but often find the task difficult. It may be true that controlled studies generally favor a statistical approach over a clinical one but, at the same time, that truth is seldom useful to the practitioner involved in the changing and unique world of practice (Bonarius, 1984).

Bonarius (1984) presents a conceptual alternative to this dilemma. The first step is to alter mechanistic views of prediction. Instead, clinicians might avoid the term *prediction* altogether and use *anticipation*. Anticipating future possibilities implies a cognitive constructional process rather than a mechanical process. It admits that the world can never be perfect in any mechanistic sense and that there is no such thing as an average person in an average situation engaged in an average interaction. Furthermore, the creation of future events is shared by coparticipants. Clients take an active part in formulating and evaluating their goals. The success of future goals depends on the degree of effort they are willing to put into them. The coparticipants share responsibility for the future. Thus, the likelihood that future events will occur is related to both cognitive constructions of an idiosyncratic world and interaction between participants.

Ideally, clinicians need to be aware of and to use, whenever available, actuarial approaches, such as multiple cutoffs and regression equations. Doing so would be particularly important for situations where there are clearly defined outcomes, errors are costly, and clinicians need to have maximum accountability. Such situations might include suicide, violence, sexual offending, recidivism, relapse, postparole adjustment, malingering, response to psychotherapy, academic performance, vocational success, psychiatric prognosis, or success in training programs. Despite over 50 years of research and debates, actuarial strategies are still not widely available except within forensic contexts. In addition, many of the formulas are not yet ready for "prime time" (Aegisdottir et al., 2006). It is hoped that at some time in the near future, a set of optimal, well-validated actuarial formulas will be widely available along with user-friendly programs on using them (Groth-Marnat, 2000b, in press). The results from such formulas will still need to be integrated with data and inferences obtainable only through clinical means. Although it is unlikely that actuarial prediction rules will replace clinical judgment, formal prediction rules can and should be used more extensively as a resource to improve the accuracy of clinical decision making.

Psychological Report

An accurate and effective psychological report requires that clinicians clarify their thinking and crystallize their interpretations. The report ties together all sources of information, often combining complex interprofessional and interpersonal issues. All the advantages and limitations involved with clinical judgment either directly or indirectly affect the report. The focus should be a clear communication of the clinician's interpretations, conclusions, and recommendations. Chapter 15 provides in-depth information on the psychological report as it relates to relevant research, guidelines, format, and sample reports.

PHASES IN CLINICAL ASSESSMENT

An outline of the phases of clinical assessment can provide both a conceptual framework for approaching an evaluation and a summary of some of the points already discussed. Although the steps in assessment are isolated for conceptual convenience, in actuality, they often occur simultaneously and interact with one another. Throughout these phases, the clinician should integrate data and serve as an expert on human behavior rather than merely an interpreter of test scores. Doing so is consistent with the belief that a psychological assessment can be most useful when it addresses specific individual problems and provides guidelines for decision making regarding these problems.

Evaluating the Referral Question

Many of the practical limitations of psychological evaluations result from an inadequate clarification of the problem. Because clinicians are aware of the assets and limitations of psychological tests, and because clinicians are responsible for providing useful information, it is their duty to clarify the requests they receive. Furthermore, they cannot assume that initial requests for an evaluation are adequately stated. Clinicians may need to uncover hidden agendas, unspoken expectations, and complex interpersonal relationships as well as explain the specific limitations of psychological tests. One of the most important general requirements is that clinicians understand the vocabulary, conceptual model, dynamics, and expectations of the referral setting in which they will be working (Turner et al., 2001).

Clinicians rarely are asked to give a general or global assessment but instead are asked to answer specific questions. To address these questions, it is sometimes helpful to contact the referral source at different stages in the assessment process. For example, it is often important in an educational evaluation to observe the student in the classroom environment. The information derived from such an observation might be relayed back to the referral source for further clarification or modification of the referral question. Likewise, an attorney may wish to somewhat alter his or her referral question based on preliminary information derived from the clinician's initial interview with the client.

Acquiring Knowledge Relating to the Content of the Problem

Before beginning the actual testing procedure, examiners should carefully consider the problem, the adequacy of the tests they will use, and the specific applicability of that test to an individual's unique situation. This preparation may require referring both to the test manual and to additional outside sources. Clinicians should be familiar with operational definitions for problems such as anxiety disorders, psychoses, personality disorders, and organic impairment so that they can be alert to their possible expression during the assessment procedure. Competence in merely administering and scoring tests is insufficient to conduct effective assessment. For example, the development of an IQ score does not necessarily indicate that an examiner is aware of differing cultural expressions of intelligence or of the limitations of the assessment device. It is essential that clinicians have in-depth knowledge about the variables they are measuring or their evaluations are likely to be extremely limited.

Related to knowledge regarding relevant variables is the relative adequacy of the test in measuring the variable being considered. Evaluating the relative adequacy of the test includes learning about certain practical considerations, the standardization sample, and reliability and validity (see Table 1.1). It is important that the examiner also consider the problem in relation to the adequacy of the test and decide whether a specific test or tests can be appropriately used on an individual or group. Doing this demands knowledge in such areas as the client's age, sex, ethnicity, race, educational background, motivation for testing, anticipated level of resistance, social environment, and interpersonal relationships. Finally, clinicians need to assess the effectiveness or utility of the test in aiding the treatment process.

Data Collection

After clarifying the referral question and obtaining knowledge relating to the problem, clinicians can then proceed with the actual collection of information. This may come from a wide variety of sources, the most frequent of which are test scores, personal history, behavioral observations, and interview data. Clinicians may also find it useful to obtain school records, previous psychological observations, medical records, police reports, or discuss the client with parents or teachers. It is important to realize that the tests themselves are merely a single tool, or source, for obtaining data. The case history is of equal importance because it provides a context for understanding the client's current problems and, through this understanding, renders the test scores meaningful. In many cases, a client's history is of even more significance in making predictions and in assessing the seriousness of his or her condition than his or her test scores. For example, a high score on depression on the MMPI-2 is not as helpful in assessing suicide risk as are historical factors, such as the number of previous attempts, age, sex, details regarding any previous attempts, and length of time the client has been depressed. Of equal importance is that the test scores themselves are usually not sufficient to answer the referral question. For specific problem solving and decision making, clinicians must rely on multiple sources and, using these sources, check to assess the consistency of the observations they make.

Interpreting the Data

The end product of assessment should be a description of the client's present level of functioning and considerations relating to etiology, prognosis, and treatment recommendations. Etiologic descriptions should avoid simplistic formulas and should instead focus on the influence exerted by several interacting factors. These factors can be divided into primary, predisposing, precipitating, and reinforcing causes, and a complete description of etiology should take all of these into account. Further elaborations may also attempt to assess the person from a systems perspective in which the clinician evaluates patterns of interaction, mutual two-way influences, and the specifics of circular information feedback. An additional crucial area is to use the data to develop an effective plan for intervention (see Beutler, Clarkin, & Bongar, 2000; Beutler & Groth-Marnat, 2003; Hersen, 2008; Jongsma, Peterson, & Bruce, 2006; Maruish, 2004). Clinicians should also pay careful attention to research on, and the implications of, incremental validity and continually be aware of the limitations and possible inaccuracies involved in clinical judgment. If actuarial formulas are available, they should be used when possible. These considerations indicate that the description of a client should not be a mere labeling or classification but should rather provide a deeper and more accurate understanding of the person. This understanding should allow the examiner to perceive new facets of the person in terms of both his or her internal experience and his or her relationships with others.

To develop these descriptions, clinicians must make inferences from their test data. Although such data is objective and empirical, the process of developing hypotheses, obtaining support for these hypotheses, and integrating the conclusions is dependent on the experience and training of the clinician. This process generally follows a sequence of developing impressions, identifying relevant facts, making inferences, and supporting these inferences with relevant and consistent data. Maloney and Ward (1976) have conceptualized a seven-phase approach (Figure 1.1) to evaluating data. They note that, in actual practice, these phases are not as clearly defined as indicated in Figure 1.1 but often occur simultaneously. For example, when a clinician reads a referral question or initially observes a client, he or she is already developing hypotheses about that person and checking to assess the validity of these observations.

Phase 1

The first phase involves collecting data about the client. It begins with the referral question and is followed by a review of the client's previous history and records. At this point, the clinician is already beginning to develop tentative hypotheses and to clarify questions for investigation in more detail. The next step is actual client contact, in which the clinician conducts an interview and administers a variety of psychological tests. The client's behavior during the interview, as well as the content or factual data, is noted. Out of this data, the clinician begins to make his or her inferences.

Phase 2

Phase 2 focuses on the development of a wide variety of inferences about the client. These inferences serve both a summary and explanatory function. For example, an examiner may infer that a client is depressed, which also may explain his or her slow performance, distractibility, flattened affect, and withdrawn behavior. The examiner may then wish to evaluate whether this depression is a deeply ingrained trait or more a reaction to a current situational difficulty. This may be determined by referring to test scores, interview data, or any additional sources of available information. The emphasis in the second phase is on developing multiple inferences that should initially be tentative. They serve the purpose of guiding future investigation to obtain additional information that is then used to confirm, modify, or negate later hypotheses.

Phase 3

Because the third phase is concerned with either accepting or rejecting the inferences developed in Phase 2, there is constant and active interaction between these phases.

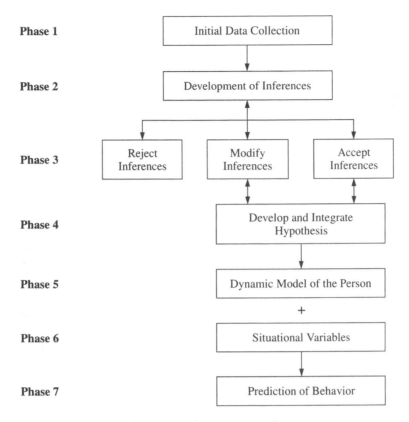

Figure 1.1.   Conceptual model for interpreting assessment data
Adapted from Maloney and Ward, 1976, p. 161. Reprinted with permission from *Psychological Assessment: A Conceptual Approach*, by M. P. Maloney and M. P. Wark, New York: Oxford University Press, 1976.

Often, in investigating the validity of an inference, a clinician alters either the meaning or the emphasis of an inference or develops entirely new ones. Rarely is an inference entirely substantiated, but rather the validity of that inference is progressively strengthened as the clinician evaluates the degree of consistency and the strength of data that support a particular inference. For example, the inference that a client is anxious may be supported by WAIS-III subscale performance, MMPI-2 scores, and behavioral observations, or it may only be suggested by one of these sources. The amount of evidence to support an inference directly affects the amount of confidence a clinician can place in this inference.

Phase 4

As a result of inferences developed in the previous three phases, the clinician can move in Phase 4 from specific inferences to general statements about the client. Doing this involves elaborating each inference to describe trends or patterns of the client. For example, the inference that a client is depressed may result from self-verbalizations in which the client continually criticizes and judges his or her behavior. This may also be expanded to give information regarding the ease or frequency with which a person might enter into the depressive state. The central task in Phase 4 is to develop and begin to elaborate on statements relating to the client.

Phases 5, 6, 7

The fifth phase involves a further elaboration of a wide variety of the personality traits of the individual. It represents an integration and correlation of the client's characteristics. It may include describing and discussing general factors, such as cognitive functioning, affect and mood, and interpersonal-intrapersonal level of functioning. Although Phases 4 and 5 are similar, Phase 5 provides a more comprehensive and integrated description of the client than Phase 4. Finally, Phase 6 places this comprehensive description of the person into a situational context, and Phase 7 makes specific predictions regarding his or her behavior. Phase 7 is the most crucial element involved in decision making and requires that the clinician take into account the interaction between personal and situational variables.

Establishing the validity of these inferences presents a difficult challenge for clinicians because, unlike many medical diagnoses, psychological inferences usually cannot be physically documented. Furthermore, clinicians are rarely confronted with feedback about the validity of these inferences. Despite these difficulties, psychological descriptions should strive to be reliable, have adequate descriptive breadth, and possess both descriptive and predictive validity. *Reliability of descriptions* refers to whether the description or classification can be replicated by other clinicians (interdiagnostician agreement) as well as by the same clinician on different occasions (intradiagnostician agreement). The next criterion is the breadth of coverage encompassed in the classification. Any classification should be broad enough to encompass a wide range of individuals yet specific enough to provide useful information regarding the individual being evaluated. *Descriptive validity* involves the degree to which individuals who are classified are similar on variables external to the classification system. For example, are individuals with similar MMPI-2 profiles also similar on other relevant attributes, such as family history, demographic variables, legal difficulties, or alcohol abuse? Finally, *predictive validity* refers to the confidence with which test inferences can be used to evaluate future outcomes. These may include academic achievement, job performance, or the outcome of treatment. Making accurate predictions is one of the most crucial functions of testing. Unless inferences can be made that effectively enhance decision making, the scope and relevance of testing are significantly reduced. Although these criteria are difficult to achieve and to evaluate, they represent the ideal standard for which assessments should strive.

RECOMMENDED READING

Aiken, L. R., & Groth-Marnat, G. (2006). *Psychological testing and assessment* (12th ed.). Boston, MA: Pearson Education.

Garb, H. N. (2005a). Clinical judgment and decision making. *Annual Review of Psychology, 1,* 67–89.

Groth-Marnat, G. (2000). Visions of clinical assessment: Then, now, and a brief history of the future. *Journal of Clinical Psychology, 56,* 349–365.

Kubiszyn, T. W., Meyer, G. J., Finn, S. E., Eyde, L. D., Kay, G. G., Moreland, K. L., et al. (2000). *Empirical support for psychological assessment in clinical care settings. Professional Psychology, 31,* 119–130.

Matarazzo, J. D. (1990). Psychological assessment versus psychological testing: Validation from Binet to the school, clinic, and courtroom. *American Psychologist, 45,* 999–1017.

Meyer, G. J., Finn, S. E., Eyde, L., Kay, G. G., Moreland, K. L., Dies, R. R., et al. (2001). Psychological testing and psychological assessment. *American Psychologist, 56,* 128–165.

Chapter 2

CONTEXT OF CLINICAL ASSESSMENT

Although general knowledge regarding tests and test construction is essential, practitioners must consider a wide range of additional issues to place testing procedures and test scores in an appropriate context. These considerations include clarifying the referral question, understanding the referral context, following ethical guidelines, identifying and working with test bias, selecting the most appropriate instrument for the variable or problem being studied, and making appropriate use of computer-assisted interpretation.

TYPES OF REFERRAL SETTINGS

Throughout the assessment process, practitioners should try to understand the unique problems and demands encountered in different referral settings. Otherwise, examiners—despite being skilled in administering and interpreting tests—may provide much useless information to their referral source and perhaps even administer a needless series of tests. That is, a thorough investigation of the underlying motive for a referral can sometimes lead to the discovery that evaluation through testing is not warranted.

Errors in test interpretation frequently occur because clinicians do not respond to the referral question in its broadest context. In turn, requests for psychological testing are often worded vaguely: "I would like a psychological evaluation on Mr. Smith," or "Could you evaluate Jimmy because he is having difficulties in school?" The request seldom states a specific question that must be answered or a decision that must be made, when in fact this is usually the position that the referral source is in. For example, a school administrator may need testing to support a placement decision, a teacher may want to prove to parents that their child has a serious problem, or a psychiatric resident may not be comfortable with the management of a patient. An organization's surface motive for testing may be as vague as a statement that the procedure is a matter of policy. Greater clarification is necessary before clinicians can provide useful problem-solving information. Furthermore, many of these situations have hidden agendas that may not be adequately handled through psychological testing alone. One of the most useful questions in addressing these issues is to ask what decisions need to be made regarding the patient.

It must be stressed that the responsibility for exploring and clarifying the referral question lies with the clinician, who should actively work with the referral source to place the client's difficulty in a practicable context. Clinicians must understand the decisions that the referral source is facing as well as the available alternatives and the relative usefulness of each of these alternatives. Clinicians also need to specify the relevance of the psychological evaluation in determining different alternatives and their possible outcomes. They should make clear the advantages and usefulness of psychological testing but should also explain the limitations inherent in test data.

To help clarify the referral question, as well as develop a relevant psychological evaluation, clinicians should become familiar with the types of environments in which they will be working. The most frequent environments are the psychiatric setting, the general medical setting, the legal context, the educational context, and the psychological clinic.

Psychiatric Setting

Levine (1981) has summarized the important factors for a psychologist to be aware of in a psychiatric setting. These referrals typically come from a psychiatrist, who may be asking the referral question in the role of administrator, psychotherapist, or physician. Each role presents unique issues for the psychiatrist, and clinicians have a primary responsibility to develop evaluations that directly address the problems at hand.

One of the main roles a psychiatrist fills is administrator in a ward. Ward administrators frequently must make decisions about problems such as suicide risk, admission/discharge, and the suitability of a wide variety of medical procedures. While retaining primary responsibility, a psychiatrist often uses information from other persons to help with decisions. This represents a change from the typical role of psychiatrists 30 years ago when they were mainly concerned with diagnosis and treatment. Currently, issues about custody, freedom of the patient, and the safety of society have taken over as the primary focus. From the perspective of psychologists performing assessments, this means that making a formal *DSM-IV-TR* (American Psychiatric Association, 2000) psychiatric diagnosis is usually not sufficient in and of itself. For example, a patient may be diagnosed bipolar, but this label does not indicate the level of dangerousness that the patient poses to himself or herself or to others. After patients have been admitted to a psychiatric setting, many practical questions have to be answered, such as the type of ward in which to place them, the activities in which they should be involved, and the method of therapy that would be most likely to benefit them.

Initially, the psychologist must determine exactly what information the ward administrator is looking for, particularly concerning any decisions that must be made about the patient. Psychologists in psychiatric settings who receive vague requests for "a psychological" sometimes develop a standard evaluation based on their preconception of what this term implies. They may evaluate the patient's defense mechanisms, diagnosis, cognitive style, and psychosocial history without addressing the specific decisions that have to be made or perhaps covering only two or three relevant issues and omitting others. To maximize the usefulness of an evaluation, examiners must be especially aware of, and sensitive to, psychiatric administrators' legal and custodial responsibilities.

In contrast to the concerns of ward administrators, the standard referral questions from psychiatrists evaluating a patient for possible psychotherapy involve the appropriateness of the client for such therapy, the strategies that are most likely to be effective, and the likely outcome of therapy. These assessments are usually clear-cut and typically do not present any difficulties. Such an evaluation can elaborate on likely problems that may occur during the course of therapy, capacity for insight, diagnosis, coping style, level of resistance, degree of functional impairment, and problem complexity (see Chapter 14).

If a referral is made during therapy, however, a number of problem areas may exist that are not readily apparent from the referral question. The assessor must investigate these complicating factors along with potential decisions derived from the assessment information. An area of potential conflict arises when psychiatrists are attempting to fulfill roles of both administrator (caretaker) and psychotherapist and yet have not clearly defined these roles either for themselves or for their patients. The resulting ambiguity may cause the patient to feel defensive and resistant and the psychiatrist to feel that the patient is not living up to the therapist's expectations. Elaboration of a specific trait or need in the patient cannot resolve this conflict, but must occur in the context of interactions between the therapist and the patient. A standard psychological evaluation investigating the internal structure of the patient does not address this issue.

A second possible problem area for clients referred in the midst of therapy can be the result of personal anxiety and discomfort on the therapist's part. Thus, issues such as countertransference and possibly the therapist's unreasonable expectations may be equally or even more important than looking at a patient's characteristics. If role ambiguity, countertransference, or unreasonable expectations are discovered, they must be elaborated and communicated in a sensitive manner.

When psychiatrists are acting in the role of physician, they and the psychologist may have different conceptual models for describing a patient's disorder. Whereas psychiatrists function primarily from a disease or medical model, psychologists may speak in terms of difficulties in living with people and society. In effectively communicating the results of psychological evaluations, examiners must bridge this conceptual difference. For example, a psychiatrist may ask whether a patient has a dissociative disorder, whereas a psychologist may not believe that the label *dissociative disorder* is useful or even a scientifically valid concept. The larger issue, however, is that the psychiatrist is still faced with some practical decisions. In fact, the psychiatrist may share some of the same concerns regarding dissociative disorders, but this conceptual issue may not be particularly relevant in dealing with the patient. Legal requirements or hospital policies might require that the patient be given a traditional diagnosis. The psychiatrist may also have to decide whether to give antipsychotic medication, electroconvulsive therapy, or psychotherapy. For a patient who is diagnosed as schizophrenic rather than brain-damaged or personality-disordered, then (given a hospital's current and economic policy considerations), the psychiatrist may decide on antipsychotic medication. An effective examiner should be able to see beyond possible conceptual differences and instead address practical considerations. A psychiatrist may refer a defensive patient who cannot or will not verbalize his or her concerns and ask whether this person is schizophrenic. Beyond this are factors such as the quality of the patient's thought processes and whether the person poses a danger to himself or herself or to others. Thus, the effective examiner must translate his or her findings into a conceptual model that is both understandable by a psychiatrist and useful from a task-oriented point of view.

General Medical Setting

It has been estimated that as many as two-thirds of patients seen by physicians have primarily psychosocial difficulties, and of those with clearly established medical diagnoses, between 25% to 50% have specifically psychological disorders in addition to medical ones (Asaad, 2000; Katon & Walker, 1998; McLeod, Budd, & McClelland, 1997; Mostofsky & Barlow, 2000). Most of these psychological difficulties are neither diagnosed nor referred for treatment (American Journal of Managed Care, 1999; Blount et al., 2007; Borus, Howes, Devins, & Rosenberg, 1988; Mostofsky & Barlow, 2000). In addition, many traditionally "medical" disorders such as coronary heart disease, asthma, allergies, rheumatoid arthritis, ulcers, and headaches have been found to possess a significant psychosocial component (Blount et al., 2007; Groth-Marnat & Edkins, 1996). Not only are psychological factors related to disease, of equal importance, they are related to the development and maintenance of health. In addition, the treatment and prevention of psychosocial aspects of "medical" complaints have been demonstrated to be cost-effective for areas such as preparation for surgery, smoking cessation, rehabilitation of chronic pain patients, obesity, interventions for coronary heart disease, and patients who are somatizing psychosocial difficulties (Blount et al., 2007; Chiles, Lambert, & Hatch,

1999; Groth-Marnat & Edkins, 1996; Groth-Marnat, Edkins, & Schumaker, 1995; Sobel, 2000). A complete approach to the patient, then, involves an awareness of the interaction between physical, psychological, and social variables (Kaslow et al., 2007; G. Schwartz, 1982). Thus, psychologists have the potential to make an extremely important contribution. To adequately work in general medical settings, psychologists must become familiar with medical descriptions, which often means learning a complex and extensive vocabulary (see Robinson & Baker, 2006). Another issue is that, even though physicians often draw information from several sources to aid in decision making, they must take ultimate responsibility for their decisions.

The most frequent situations in which physicians might use the services of a psychologist involve the presence of an underlying psychological disorder, possible emotional factors associated with medical complaints, assessment for neuropsychological deficit, psychological treatment for chronic pain, the treatment of chemical dependency, patient management, and case consultation (Bamgbose et al., 1980; Groth-Marnat, 1988; Pincus, Pechura, Keyser, Bachman, & Houtsinger, 2006). Although a medical exam may not suggest any physical basis for the patient's complaints, the physician still has to devise some form of treatment or at least an appropriate referral. This is crucial in that a significant portion of patients referred to physicians do not have any detectable physical difficulties and their central complaint is likely to be psychological (Asaad, 2000; Blount et al., 2007; Maruish, 2002; Mostofsky & Barlow, 2000). The psychologist can then elaborate and specify how a patient can be treated for possible psychosocial difficulties (Kaslow et al., 2007; Wickramasekera, 1995a, 1995b). Doing this may require using not only the standard assessment instruments but also more specialized ones, such as the Millon Behavioral Health Inventory or the Millon Behavioral Medicine Diagnostic (Bockian, Meagher, & Millon, 2000; Maruish, 2000; Millon, 1997).

Another area that has greatly increased in importance is the psychological assessment of a patient's neuropsychological status (see Chapter 12). Whereas physicians attempt to detect physical lesions in the nervous system, the neuropsychologist has traditionally been more concerned with the status of higher cortical functions. Another way of stating this: Physicians evaluate how the *brain* is functioning, whereas the neuropsychologist evaluates how the *person* is functioning as a result of possible brain abnormalities. The typical areas of assessment focus primarily on the presence of possible intellectual deterioration in areas such as memory, sequencing, abstract reasoning, spatial organization, and executive abilities (Groth-Marnat, 2000b). Such referrals, or at least screening for neuropsychological deficit, typically account for approximately a third of all psychological referrals in psychiatric and medical settings. In the past, neuropsychologists have been asked to help determine whether a patient's complaints were "functional" or "organic." The focus now is more on whether the person has neuropsychological deficits that may contribute to or account for observed behavioral difficulties than on either/or distinctions (Loenberger, 1989). Physicians often want to know whether a test profile suggests a specific diagnosis, particularly malingering, conversion disorder, hypochondriasis, organic brain syndrome, or depression with pseudoneurological features. Further issues that neuropsychologists often address include the nature and extent of identified lesions, localization of lesions, emotional status of neurologically impaired patients, extent of disability, and suggestions for treatment planning such as recommendations for cognitive rehabilitation, vocational training, and readjustment to family and friends (Lemsky, 2000; Lezak, 2004; Snyder, Nussbaum, & Robins, 2006).

A physician might also request a psychologist to conduct a presurgical evaluation to assess the likelihood of a serious stress reaction to surgery. Finally, physicians—particularly pediatricians—are often concerned with detecting early signs of serious psychological disorder, which may have been brought to their attention by parents, other family members, or teachers. In such situations, the psychologist's evaluation should assess not only the patient's present psychological condition but also the contributing factors in his or her environment, and should provide a prediction of the patient's status during the next few months or years. When the patient's current condition, current environment, and future prospects have been evaluated, the examiner can then recommend the next phase in the intervention process. A psychologist may also consult with physicians to assist them in effectively discussing the results of an examination with the patient or the patient's family.

Legal Context

During the past 30 years, the use of psychologists in legal settings has become more prevalent, important, and accepted (see Goldstein, 2007; Otto & Heilburn, 2002). Psychologists might be called in at any stage of legal decision making. During the investigation stage, they might be consulted to assess the reliability of a witness or to help evaluate the quality of information by a witness. The prosecuting attorney might also need to have a psychologist evaluate the quality of another mental health professional's report, evaluate the accused person's competency, or help determine the specifics of a crime. A defense attorney might use a psychologist to help in supporting an insanity plea, to help in jury selection, or to document that brain damage has occurred. A judge might use a psychologist's report as one of a number of factors to help determine a sentence, a penal officer might wish consultation to help determine the type of confinement or level of dangerousness, or a parole officer might need assistance to help plan a rehabilitation program. Even though a psychologist might write a legal report, he or she is likely to actually appear in court in only about 1 in every 10 cases.

The increasing use and acceptance of psychologists in legal contexts have resulted in a gradual clarification of their roles (Goldstein, 2007; Otto & Heilburn, 2002) as well as a proliferation of forensic specific assessment instruments (Archer, 2006; Archer et al., 2006; Heilbrun, Marczyk, & Dematteo, 2002). However, acclimatizing to the courtroom environment is often difficult because of the quite different roles between courtroom and clinic as well as the need to become familiar with specialized legal terms such as *diminished capacity* and *insanity*. In addition, many attorneys are familiar with the same professional literature that psychologists read and may use this information to discredit a psychologist's qualifications, methods of assessment, or conclusions (Ziskin & Faust, 2008). Psychologists are also required to become increasingly sophisticated in their evaluation of possible malingering and deception (see review on kspope.com/assess/malinger.php).

Each psychologist appearing in court must have his or her qualifications approved. Important areas of consideration are the presence of clinical expertise in treating specialty disorders and relevant publication credits. Evaluation of legal work by psychologists indicates they are generally viewed favorably by the courts and may have reached parity with psychiatrists (Sales & Miller, 1994).

As outlined by the American Board of Forensic Psychology, the practice of forensic psychology includes training/consultation with legal practitioners, evaluation of populations likely to encounter the legal system, and the translation of relevant technical psychological knowledge into usable information. Psychologists are used most frequently in child custody cases, competency of a person to dispose of property, juvenile commitment, comprehension of Miranda rights, potential for having given a false confession, and personal injury suits in which the psychologist documents the nature and extent of the litigant's suffering or disability (stress, anxiety, cognitive deficit).

An essential requirement when working in the legal context is for psychologists to modify their language. Many legal terms have exact and specific meanings that, if misunderstood, could lead to extremely negative consequences. Words such as *incompetent, insane,* or *reasonable certainty* may vary in different judicial systems or from state to state. Psychologists must familiarize themselves with this terminology and the different nuances involved in its use. Psychologists may also be requested to explain in detail the meaning of their conclusions and how these conclusions were reached. Whereas attorneys rarely question the actual data that psychologists generate, the inferences and generalizability of these inferences are frequently placed under scrutiny or even attacked. Often this questioning can seem rude or downright hostile, but in most cases, attorneys are merely doing their best to defend their client. Proper legal protocol also requires that the psychologist answer questions directly rather than respond to the implications or underlying direction suggested by the questions. Furthermore, attorneys (or members of the jury) may not be trained in or appreciate the scientific method, which is the mainstay of a psychologist's background. In contrast, attorneys are trained in legal analysis and reasoning, which subjectively focus on the uniqueness of each case rather than on a comparison of the person to a statistically relevant normative group (see Hilsenroth & Stricker, 2004).

Two potentially problematic areas lie in evaluating insanity and evaluating competency. Although the insanity plea has received considerable publicity, very few people make the appeal; and, of those who do, few have it granted. It is usually difficult for an expert witness to evaluate such cases because of the problem of possible malingering to receive a lighter sentence and the possible ambiguity of the term *insanity*. Usually a person is considered insane in accordance with the McNaughton Rule, which states that persons are not responsible if they did not know the nature and extent of their actions and if they cannot distinguish that what they did was wrong according to social norms. In some states, the ambiguity of the term is increased because defendants can be granted the insanity plea if it can be shown they were insane at the time of the incident. Other states include the clause of an "irresistible impulse" to the definition of insanity. Related to insanity is whether the defendant is competent to stand trial. *Competence* is usually defined as the person's ability to cooperate in a meaningful way with the attorney, understand the purpose of the proceedings, and understand the implications of the possible penalties. To increase the reliability and validity of competency and insanity evaluations, specialized assessment techniques have been developed; for example, the MacArthur Competence Assessment Tool (Poythres et al., 1999) and the Evaluation of Competency to Stand Trial-Revised (Rogers, Tillbrook, & Sewell, 2004) and the Rogers Criminal Responsibility Scales (R. Rogers, 1984).

The prediction of dangerousness has also been a problematic area. Because actual violent or self-destructive behavior is a relatively unusual behavior (low base rate), any cutoff criteria typically are going to produce a high number of false positives (Mulvey & Cauffman, 2001). Thus, people incorrectly identified may potentially be detained and understandably be upset. However, the negative result of failure to identify and take action against people who are potentially violent makes erring on the side of caution more acceptable. Attempts to use special scales on the MMPI (Overcontrolled Hostility Scale; Megargee & Mendelsohn, 1962) or a 4-3 code type (see Chapter 7) have not been found to be sufficiently accurate for individual decision making. However, significant improvements have been made in predicting dangerousness and reoffending by using actuarial strategies, assessing for the presence of antisocial features, collateral sources, formal ratings, and summed ratings, which include relevant information on developmental influences, possible events that lower thresholds, arrest record, life situation, and situational triggers such as interpersonal stress and substance intoxication

(Monahan & Steadman, 2001; Monahan et al., 2000; Steadman et al., 2000; Tolman & Rotzien, 2007). The legal/justice system is most likely to give weight to those individual assessment strategies that combine recidivism statistics, tests specifically designed to predict dangerousness, summed ratings, and double administrations of psychological tests to assess change over time. Representative and frequently used tests are the Historical Clinical Risk-20 (for violence risk assessment; Webster, Douglas, Eaves, & Hart, 1997) and the Static 99 (for sexual reoffending risk; Hanson & Thornton, 1999). In contrast, informal clinical interviews are clearly considered to be insufficient (Tolman & Rotzien, 2007).

Psychologists are sometimes asked to help with child custody decisions. Guidelines for developing child custody evaluations and child protection evaluations have been developed by the American Psychological Association (APA) (Guidelines for Child Custody Evaluations in Divorce Proceedings, APA, 1994 and Guidelines for Psychological Evaluations in Child Protection Matters, APA, 1998; www.apa.org/practice/childcustody). The central consideration is to determine which arrangement is in the child's best interest. Areas to be considered include the mental health of the parent, the quality of love and affection between the parent and child, the nature of the parent-child relationship, and the long-term effect of the different decisions on the child (Ackerman, 2006a, 2006b). Often psychological evaluations are conducted on each member of the family using traditional testing instruments. Specific tests, such as the Bricklin Perceptual Scales (Bricklin, 1984), have also been developed.

A final, frequently requested service is to aid in the classification of inmates in correctional settings. One basic distinction is between merely managing the person versus attempting a program of rehabilitation. Important management considerations are levels of suicide risk, appropriateness of dormitory versus a shared room, possible harassment from other inmates, or degree of dangerousness to others. Rehabilitation recommendations may need to consider the person's educational level, interests, skills, abilities, and personality characteristics related to employment.

Academic/Educational Context

Psychologists are frequently called on to assess children who are having difficulty in, or may need special placement in, the school system. The most important areas are evaluating the nature and extent of a child's learning difficulties, measuring intellectual strengths and weaknesses, assessing behavioral difficulties, creating an educational plan, estimating a child's responsiveness to intervention, and recommending changes in a child's program or placement (Sattler & Hoge, 2006; Sattler, 2008). Any educational plan should be sensitive to the interactions among a child's abilities, diversity considerations, the child's personality, the characteristics of the teacher, and the needs and expectations of the parents.

A typical educational placement begins with a visit to the classroom for observation of a child's behavior under natural conditions. A valuable aspect of this is to observe the interaction between the teacher and child. Typically, any behavioral difficulty is closely linked with the child-teacher interaction. Sometimes the teacher's style of responding to a student can be as much a part of the problem as the student. Consequently, classroom observations can cause discomfort to teachers and should be handled sensitively.

Observing the child in a wider context is, in many ways, contrary to the tradition of individual testing. However, individual testing all too frequently provides a relatively limited and narrow range of information. If it is combined with a family or classroom assessment, additional crucial data may be collected, but there is also likely to be significant resistance. This resistance may result from legal or ethical restrictions regarding the scope of the services the school can provide or the demands that a psychologist can make on the student's parents. Often there is an initial focus on, and need to perceive, the student as a "problem child" or "identified patient." This may obscure larger, more complex, and yet more significant issues, such as marital conflict, a disturbed teacher, misunderstandings between teacher and parents, or a conflict between the school principal and the parents. All or some of these individuals may have an investment in perceiving the student as the person with the problem rather than acknowledging that a disordered school system or significant marital turmoil may be responsible. An individually oriented assessment may be made with excellent interpretations, but unless wider contexts are considered, understood, and addressed, the assessment may very well be ineffective in solving both the individual difficulties and the larger organizational or interpersonal problems.

Most assessments of children in a school context include behavioral observations, a test of intellectual abilities such as the WISC-IV, Stanford Binet-V, Woodcock-Johnson Psychoeducational Battery-III (Woodcock, McGrew, & Mather, 2001), or Kaufman Assessment Battery for Children-II (K-ABC-II; A. Kaufman & Kaufman, 2004), and tests of personality functioning. In the past, assessment of children's personality generally relied on projective techniques. However, many projective tests have been found to have inadequate psychometric properties and are time consuming to administer, score, and interpret. As a result, a wide variety of behavioral ratings instruments have begun to replace the use of projective instruments (Kamphaus et al., 2000). These include the Achenbach Child Behavior Checklist (Achenbach & Rescorla, 2001), Conners' Parent Rating Scale-Revised (Conners, 1997), Conners' Teacher Rating Scale-Revised (Conners, Sitarenios, Parker, & Epstein, 1998), and the Behavior Assessment System for Children-2 (BASC-2; Reynolds & Kamphaus, 2004). A number of sound objective instruments, such as the Personality Inventory for Children-2 (PIC-2; Lachar & Gruber, 2001), have also been developed. The inventory was designed along similar lines as the MMPI but is completed by a child's parent. It produces 4 validity scales to detect faking and 12 clinical scales, such as Depression, Family Relations, Delinquency, Anxiety, and Hyperactivity. Assessment of adolescent personality can be done effectively with the MMPI-A or the Millon Adolescent Clinical Inventory (MACI; Millon, 1993). Additional well-designed scales that have become increasingly used are the Vineland Adaptive Behavior Scales (Sparrow, Balla, & Cicchetti, 1984), the Wechsler Individual Achievement Test-2 (WIAT-2; Psychological Corporation, 2001), and the Wide Range Achievement Test-IV (WRAT-IV; Wilkinson & Robertson, 2007).

Any report written for an educational setting should focus not only on a child's weaknesses but also on his or her strengths. Understanding a child's strengths can potentially be used to increase a child's self-esteem as well as to create change in a wide context. Recommendations should be realistic and practical. Recommendations can be developed most effectively when the clinician has a thorough understanding of relevant resources in the community, the school system, and the classroom environment. This understanding is particularly important because the quality and resources available between one school or school system and the next can vary tremendously. Recommendations typically specify which skills need to be learned, how these can be learned, a hierarchy of objectives, and possible techniques for reducing behaviors that make learning difficult.

Recommendations for special education should be made only when a regular class would clearly not be equally beneficial. However, the recommendations are not the end product. They are beginning points that should be elaborated and modified depending on the initial results. Ideally, a psychological report should be followed up with continuous monitoring.

The assessment of children should be carried out in two phases. The first phase should assess the nature and quality of the child's learning environment. If the child is not exposed to adequate quality instruction, he or she cannot be expected to perform well. Thus, it must first be demonstrated that a child has not been learning even with appropriate instruction. The second phase involves a comprehensive assessment battery, which includes measures of intellectual abilities, academic skills, adaptive behavior, and screening out any biomedical disorders that might disrupt learning. Intellectual abilities might involve memory, spatial organization, abstract reasoning, and sequencing. Regardless of students' academic and intellectual abilities, they will not perform well unless they have relevant adaptive abilities, such as social skills, adequate motivation, and ability to control impulses. Assessing a child's values and attitudes toward education may be particularly important because they determine whether the student is willing to use whatever resources he or she may have. Likewise, the person's level of personal efficacy helps to determine whether the person is able to perform behaviors leading toward attaining the goals he or she values. Physical difficulties that might interfere with learning include poor vision, poor hearing, hunger, malnutrition, or endocrine dysfunction.

The preceding considerations clearly place the assessment of children in educational settings into a far wider context than merely the interpretation of test scores. Relationships among the teacher, family, and student need to be assessed, along with the relative quality of the learning environment. Furthermore, the child's values, motivation, and sense of personal efficacy need to be taken into consideration, along with possible biomedical difficulties. Examiners need to become knowledgeable regarding the school and community resources as well as learn new instruments that have demonstrated relatively high levels of reliability and validity.

Psychological Clinic

In contrast to the medical, legal, and educational institutions where the psychologist typically serves as a consultant to the decision maker, the psychologist working in a psychological clinic is often the decision maker. A number of frequent types of referrals come into the psychological clinic. Perhaps the most common ones are individuals who are self-referred and are seeking relief from psychological turmoil. For most of these individuals, extensive psychological testing is not relevant and, in fact, may be contraindicated because the time spent in testing is usually time that could best be applied toward treatment. However, brief instruments targeted toward assessing client characteristics most relevant toward treatment planning can help to develop treatments that will speed the rate of treatment as well as optimize outcome (see Chapters 13 and 14). Brief instruments can also be used to monitor response to therapy, make relevant alterations, and thus increase the likelihood of successful intervention (Lambert & Hawkins, 2004). There may also be certain groups of self-referred clients about whom the psychologist may question whether the treatment available in a psychological clinic is appropriate. These clients can include persons with extensive medical problems, individuals with legal complications that need additional clarification, and persons who may require inpatient treatment. With these cases, it might be necessary to obtain additional information through psychological testing. However, the main purpose of the testing would be to aid in decision making rather than to serve as a direct source of help for the client.

Two other situations in which psychological assessment may be warranted involve children who are referred by their parents for school or behavioral problems and referrals from other decision makers. When referrals are made for poor school performance or behavioral problems involving legal complications, special precautions must be taken before testing. Primarily, the clinician must develop a complete understanding of the client's social network and the basis for the referral. This complete understanding may include a history of previous attempts at treatment and a summary of the relationship among the parents, school, courts, and child. Usually a referral comes at the end of a long sequence of events, and it is important to obtain information regarding these events. After the basis of the referral has been clarified, the clinician may decide to have a meeting with different individuals who have become involved in the case, such as the school principal, previous therapists, probation officer, attorney, or teacher. This meeting may uncover myriad issues that require decisions, such as referral for family therapy, placement in a special education program, a change in custody agreements between divorced parents, individual therapy of other members of the family, and a change in school. All of these may affect the relevance of, and approach to, testing, but these issues may not be apparent if the initial referral question is taken at face value. Sometimes psychologists are also confronted with referrals from other decision makers. For example, an attorney may want to know if an individual is competent to stand trial. Other referrals may involve a physician who wants to know whether a head-injured patient can readjust to his or her work environment or drive a car, or the physician may need to document changes in a patient's recovery.

So far, this discussion on the different settings in which psychological testing is used has focused on when to test and how to clarify the manner in which tests can be most helpful in making decisions. Several additional summary points must be stressed. As has been discussed previously, a referral source sometimes is unable to adequately formulate the referral question. In fact, the referral question is usually neither clear nor concise. It is the clinician's responsibility to look beyond the referral question and determine the basis for the referral in its widest scope. Thus, an understanding must be developed of the complexity of the client's social setting including interpersonal factors, family dynamics, and the sequence of events leading to the referral. In addition to clarifying the referral question, a second major point is that psychologists are responsible for developing knowledge about the setting for which they are writing their reports. This knowledge includes learning the proper language, the roles of the individuals working in the setting, the choices facing decision makers, and the philosophical and theoretical beliefs they adhere to. It is also important that clinicians understand the values underlying the setting and assess whether these values coincide with their own. For example, psychologists who do not believe in aversion therapy, capital punishment, or electroconvulsive therapy may come into conflict while working in certain settings. Psychologists, thus, should clearly understand how the information they give their referral source will be used. It is essential for them to appreciate that they have a significant responsibility, because decisions made regarding their clients, which are often based on assessment results, can frequently be major changing points in a client's life. If the possibility exists for the information to be used in a manner that conflicts with the clinician's value system, he or she should reconsider, clarify, or possibly change his or her relationship to the referral setting.

A final point is that clinicians should not allow themselves to be placed into the role of a "testing technician" or psychometrist. This role ultimately does a disservice to the client, the practitioner, and the profession. Clinicians should not merely administer, score, and interpret tests but should also understand the total referral context in its broadest sense. This means they also take on the role of an expert who can integrate data from a variety of sources. Tests, by themselves, are limited in that they are not flexible or sophisticated enough to address themselves to complex referral questions. Levine (1981) writes:

> [The formal research on test validity is] not immediately relevant to the practical use of psychological tests. The question of the value of tests becomes not "Does this test correlate with a criterion?" or "Does the test accord with a nomological net?" but rather "Does the use

of the test improve the success of the decision making process?" by making it either more efficient, less costly, more accurate, more rational, or more relevant. (p. 292)

All of these concerns are consistent with the emphasis on an examiner fulfilling the role of an expert clinician performing psychological assessment rather than a psychometrist acting as a technician.

ETHICAL PRACTICE OF ASSESSMENT

Ethical guidelines reflect values that professional psychology endorses. These include client safety, confidentiality, the reduction of suffering, fairness, and advancing science. These guidelines have largely evolved through careful considerations of how these values are expressed in ideal practice. Unfortunately, many of the ethical codes have been refined due to conflicts and criticisms related to assessment procedures. Criticism has been directed at the use of tests in inappropriate contexts, confidentiality, cultural bias, invasion of privacy, release of test data, and the continued use of tests that are inadequately validated. These criticisms have resulted in restrictions on the use of certain tests, greater clarification within the profession regarding ethical standards, and increased skepticism from the public. To deal with these potential difficulties as well as conduct useful and accurate assessments, clinicians need to be aware of the ethical use of assessment tools. The American Educational Research Association (AERA) and other professional groups have published guidelines for examiners in their Standards for Educational and Psychological Tests (1999) and the Ethical Principles of Psychologists and Code of Conduct (American Psychological Association, 2002). A special series in the *Journal of Personality Assessment* (Russ, 2001) also elaborates on ethical dilemmas found in training, medical, school, and forensic settings. The next section outlines the most important of these guidelines along with additional related issues. It is roughly organized in the chronological sequence psychologists are likely to encounter as they work their way through the beginning and on to the final stages of assessment.

Developing a Professional Relationship

Assessment should be conducted only in the context of a clearly defined professional relationship. This means that the nature, purpose, and conditions of the relationship are discussed and agreed on. Usually the clinician provides relevant information, followed by the client's signed consent. Information conveyed to the client usually relates to the type and length of assessment, alternative procedures, details relating to appointments, the nature and limits of confidentiality, financial requirements, and additional general information that might be relevant to the unique context of an assessment (see Pope, 2007a,b and Zuckerman's [2003] *Paper Office* for specific guidelines, formats, and forms for informed consent).

An important area to be aware of is the impact the quality of the relationship can have on both assessment results and the overall working relationship. It is the examiner's responsibility to recognize the possible influences he or she may exert on the client and to optimize the level of rapport. For example, enhanced rapport with older children (but not younger ones) involving verbal reinforcement and friendly conversation has been shown to increase WISC-R scores by an average of 13 IQ points compared with an administration involving more neutral interactions (Feldman & Sullivan, 1971). This is a difference of nearly 1 full standard deviation. It has also been found that mildly disapproving comments such as "I thought you could do better than that" resulted in significantly lowered performance when compared with either neutral or approving ones (Witmer, Bornstein, & Dunham, 1971). In a review of 22 studies, Fuchs and Fuchs (1986) concluded that, on the average, IQ scores were 4 points higher when the examiner was familiar with the child being examined than when he or she was unfamiliar with the child. This trend was particularly pronounced for lower socioeconomic status children. Whereas there is little evidence (Lefkowitz & Fraser, 1980; Sattler, 1973a, 1973b; Sattler & Gwynne, 1982) to support the belief that African American students have lower performance when tested by European American examiners, it has been suggested that African American students are more responsive to tangible reinforcers (money, candy) than are European American students, who generally respond better to verbal reinforcement (Schultz & Sherman, 1976). However, in a later study, Terrell, Taylor, and Terrell (1978) demonstrated that the main factor was the cultural relevance of the response. They found a remarkable 17.6-point increase in IQ scores when African American students were encouraged by African American examiners with culturally relevant comments such as "nice job, blood" or "good work, little brother." Thus, the rapport and feedback, especially if that feedback is culturally relevant, can significantly improve test performance. As a result, the feedback, and level of rapport should, as much as possible, be held constant from one test administration to the next.

A variable extensively investigated by Rosenthal and his colleagues is that a researcher/examiner's expectations can influence another person's level of performance (R. Rosenthal, 1966). This has been demonstrated with humans as well as laboratory rats. For example, when an experimenter was told to expect better performances from rats that were randomly selected from the same litter as "maze bright" (compared with "maze dull"), the descriptions of the rats' performance given by the experimenter conformed to the experimenter's expectations (R. Rosenthal & Fode, 1963). Despite criticisms that have been leveled at his studies and the finding that the magnitude of the effect was not as large as originally believed (Barber & Silver, 1968; Elashoff & Snow, 1971), Rosenthal maintains that an expectancy effect exists in some situations and suggests that the mechanisms are through minute nonverbal behaviors (H. Cooper & Rosenthal, 1980). He maintains that the typical effects on an individual's performance are usually small and subtle, and occur in some situations but not in others. The obvious implication for clinicians is that they should continually question themselves regarding their expectations of clients and check to see whether they may in some way be communicating these expectations to their clients in a manner that confounds the results.

An additional factor that may affect the nature of the relationship between the client and the examiner is the client's relative emotional state. It is particularly important to assess the degree of the client's motivation and his or her overall level of anxiety. There may be times in which it would be advisable to discontinue testing because situational emotional states may significantly influence the results of the tests. At the very least, examiners should consider the possible effects of emotional factors and incorporate these into their interpretations. For example, it might be necessary to increase the estimate of a client's optimal intellectual functioning if the client was extremely anxious during administration of an intelligence test.

A final consideration, which can potentially confound both the administration and, more commonly, the scoring of responses, is the degree to which the examiner likes the client and perceives him or her as warm and friendly. Several studies (Sattler, Hillix, & Neher, 1970; Sattler & Winget, 1970) have indicated that the more the examiner likes the client, the more likely he or she will be to score an ambiguous response in a direction favorable to the client. Higher scores can occur even on items in which the responses are not ambiguous (Egeland, 1969; Simon, 1969). Thus, "hard" scoring, as opposed to more lenient scoring, can occur at least in part because of the degree of subjective liking the examiner feels toward the client. Again, examiners should continually check themselves to assess whether their relationship with the client is interfering with the objectivity of the test administration and scoring.

Issues Related to Informed Consent

Psychologists should obtain informed consent for assessment procedures. Any consent involves a clear explanation of what procedures will occur, the relevance of the testing, and how the results will be used (see Pope, 2007a; kspope.com/consent/index/php?). This means that examiners should always have a clear conception of the specific reasons for giving a test. It should be stressed that the information is usually considered to be confidential. However, exceptions to confidentiality may occur in situations involving child/elder abuse, danger to self or others, and information that has been requested based on a subpoena. The information should be provided in clear, straightforward language that can be understood by the client. Unfortunately, many formal consent forms are written at a level far above the reading comprehension level of a large proportion of clients.

Informed consent involves communicating not only the rationale for testing but also the kinds of data obtained and the possible uses of the data. This fact does not mean the client should be shown the specific test subscales beforehand but rather that the nature and intent of the test should be described in a general way. For example, if a client is told that a scale measures "sociability," this foreknowledge might alter the test's validity in that the client may answer questions based on popular, but quite possibly erroneous, stereotypes. Introducing the test format and intent in a simple, respectful, and forthright manner significantly reduces the chance that the client will perceive the testing situation as an invasion of privacy.

Sometimes clinicians will have provided clear information and the client has agreed to the procedures, but unforeseen events not covered in the information may occur. This might occur when the examiner discovers aspects of the client that he or she would rather keep secret. Thus assessment may entail an invasion of privacy. The Office of Science and Technology (1967), in a report entitled "Privacy and Behavioral Research," has defined privacy as "the right of the individual to decide for him/herself how much he will share with others his thoughts, feelings, and facts of his personal life" (p. 2). This right is considered to be "essential to insure dignity and freedom of self determination" (p. 2). The invasion of privacy issue usually becomes most controversial with personality tests because items relating to motivational, emotional, and attitudinal traits are sometimes disguised. Thus, persons may unknowingly reveal characteristics about themselves that they would rather keep private. Similarly, many persons consider their IQ scores to be highly personal. Public concern over this issue culminated in an investigation by the Senate Subcommittee on Constitutional Rights and the House Subcommittee on Invasion of Privacy. Neither of these investigations found evidence of deliberate or widespread misuse of psychological tests (Brayfield, 1965).

Dahlstrom (1969) has argued that public concern over the invasion of privacy is based on two basic issues. The first is that tests have been oversold to the public, with a resulting exaggeration of their scope and accuracy. The public is usually not aware of the limitations of test data and may often feel that tests are more capable of discovering hidden information than they actually are. The second misconception is that it is not necessarily wrong to obtain information about persons that they either are unaware of themselves or would rather keep private. The more important issue is how the information is used. Furthermore, the person who controls where or how this information is used is generally the client. The ethical code of the American Psychological Association (2002) specifically states that information derived by a psychologist from any source can be released only with the permission of the client. Although there may be exceptions regarding the rights of minors, or when clients are a danger to themselves or others, the ability to control the information is usually clearly defined as being held by the client. Thus, the public is often uneducated regarding its rights and typically underestimates the power the public has in determining how the test data will be used.

Whereas concerns about invasion of privacy relate to the discovery and misuse of information that clients would rather keep secret, *inviolacy* involves the actual negative feelings created when clients are confronted with the test or test situation. Inviolacy is particularly relevant when clients are asked to discuss information they would rather not think about. For example, the MMPI contains questions about many ordinarily taboo topics relating to sexual practices, toilet behavior, bodily functions, and personal beliefs about human nature. Such questions may produce anxiety by making the examinees more aware of deviant thoughts or repressed unpleasant memories. Many individuals obtain a certain degree of security and comfort by staying within familiar realms of thought. Even to be asked questions that may indicate the existence of unusual alternatives can serve as an anxiety-provoking challenge to personal rules and norms. This problem is somewhat related to the issue of invasion of privacy and it, too, requires one-to-one sensitivity as well as clear and accurate information about the assessment procedure.

Another issue is that during personnel evaluations, participants might feel pressured to reveal personal information on tests because they aspire to a certain position. Also, applicants may unknowingly reveal information because of subtle, nonobvious test questions, and, perhaps more important, they have no control over the inferences that examiners make about the test data. However, if a position requires careful screening and if serious negative consequences may result from poor selection, it is necessary to evaluate an individual as closely as possible. Thus, the use of testing for personnel in the police, delicate military positions, or important public duty overseas may warrant careful testing.

In a clinical setting, obtaining personal information regarding clients usually does not present problems. The agreement that the information be used to help clients develop new insights and change their behavior is generally clear and straightforward. However, should legal difficulties arise relating to areas such as child abuse, involuntary confinement, or situations in which clients may be a danger to themselves or others, ethical questions often arise. Usually there are general guidelines regarding the manner and extent to which information should be disclosed. These are included in the American Psychological Association's *Ethical Principles of Psychologists and Code of Conduct* (2002), and test users are encouraged to familiarize themselves with these guidelines. Professional psychologists can also consult with colleagues, their insurance companies, or the APA ethics office (apa.org/ethics).

Labeling and Restriction of Freedom

When individuals are given a medical diagnosis for physical ailments, the social stigmata are usually relatively mild. In contrast are the potentially damaging consequences of many psychiatric diagnoses. A major danger is the possibility of creating a self-fulfilling prophecy based on the expected roles associated with a specific label. Many of these expectations are communicated nonverbally and are typically beyond a person's immediate awareness (H. Cooper & Rosenthal, 1980; R. Rosenthal, 1966). Other self-fulfilling prophecies may be less subtle; for example, a juvenile with minor but poor sexual boundaries might be labeled as a "sex offender," which would then result in quite restrictive treatment along with quite public distribution of the label.

Just as labels imposed by others can have negative consequences, self-acceptance of labels can likewise be detrimental. Clients may use their labels to excuse or deny responsibility for their behavior. This is congruent with the medical model, which usually assumes that a "sick" person is the victim of an "invading disorder." Thus, in our society, "sick" persons are not considered to be responsible for their disorders. However, the acceptance of this model for behavioral problems may perpetuate behavioral disorders because persons see themselves as helpless, passive victims under the power of mental health "helpers" (Szasz, 1987). This sense of helplessness may serve to lower their ability to deal effectively with new stress. In contrast to this sense of helplessness is the belief that clients require an increased sense of responsibility for their lives and actions to effectively change their behavior.

A final difficulty associated with labeling is that it may unnecessarily impose limitations on either an individual or a system by restricting progress and creativity. For example, an organization may conduct a study to determine the type of person who has been successful at a particular type of job and may then develop future selection criteria based on this study. This can result in the future selection of relatively homogeneous employees, which in turn could prevent the organization from changing and progressing. There may be a narrowing of the "talent pool," in which people with new and different ideas are never given a chance. In other words, what has been labeled as adaptive in the past may not be adaptive in the future. One alternative to this predicament is to look at future trends and develop selection criteria based on these trends. Furthermore, diversity might be incorporated into an organization so that different but compatible types can be selected to work on similar projects. Thus, clinicians should be sensitive to the potential negative impact resulting from labeling by outside sources or by self-labeling, as well as to the possible limiting effects that labeling might have.

Competent Use of Assessment Instruments

To correctly administer and interpret psychological tests, an examiner must have proper training, which generally includes adequate graduate course work combined with lengthy supervised experience (Turner et al., 2001). Clinicians should have a knowledge of tests and test limitations, and should be willing to accept responsibility for competent test use. Intensive training is particularly important for individually administered intelligence tests and for the majority of personality tests. Students who are taking or administering tests as part of a class requirement are not adequately trained to administer and interpret tests professionally. Thus, test results obtained by students have questionable validity, and they should clearly inform their subjects that the purpose of their testing is for training purposes only.

In addition to the preceding general guidelines for training, examiners should also acquire a number of specific skills (Moreland, Eyde, Robertson, Primoff, & Most, 1995; Turner et al., 2001). These include the ability to evaluate the technical strengths and limitations of a test, the selection of appropriate tests, knowledge of issues relating to the test's reliability and validity, and interpretation with diverse populations. Examiners need to be aware of the material in the test manual as well as relevant research both on the variable the test is measuring and the status of the test since its publication. This is particularly important with regard to newly developed subgroup norms and possible changes in the meaning of scales resulting from further research. After examiners evaluate the test itself, they must also be able to evaluate whether the purpose and context for which they would like to use it are appropriate. Sometimes an otherwise valid test can be used for purposes it was not intended for, resulting in either invalid or useless inferences based on the test data. Examiners must also be continually aware of, and sensitive to, conditions affecting the examinee's performance. These conditions may include expectations on the part of the examiner, minor variations from the standardized instructions, degree of rapport, mood of the examinee, or timing of the test administration in relation to an examinee's life changes. To help develop accurate conclusions, examiners should have a general knowledge of the diversity of human behavior. Different considerations and interpretive strategies may be necessary for various ethnic groups, sex, sexual orientation, or persons from different countries (see Dana 2005; Nguyen, Huang, Arganza, & Liao, 2007). A final consideration is that, if interns or technicians are administering the tests, an adequately trained psychologist should be available as a consultant or supervisor.

Specific data-based guidelines for test user qualifications have been developed by relevant professional organizations (APA, 1988; Turner et al., 2001) and these guidelines have been incorporated by most organizations selling psychological tests. Qualification forms request information regarding the purpose for using tests (counseling, research, personnel selection), area of professional expertise (marriage and family, social work, school), level of training (degrees, licenses), specific courses taken (descriptive statistics, career assessment), and quality control over test use (test security, appropriate tailoring of interpretations). Persons completing the forms certify that they possess appropriate training and competencies and agree to adhere to ethical guidelines and legal regulations regarding test use.

In addition to being appropriately trained to use tests themselves, psychologists should not promote the use of psychological techniques by persons who are not qualified. This does not mean that all psychological tests should be used exclusively by psychologists because many tests are available to other professionals. However, psychologists should be generally aware of which tests require a high level of training (i.e., individually administered IQ tests) and those that are more generally available.

One of the important aspects of competent test use is that the tests should be used only for the purposes they were designed for. Typically, tests being extended beyond what they were designed for have been done in good faith and with good intentions. For example, an examiner might use a TAT or Rorschach as the primary means of inferring an individual's IQ. Similarly, the MMPI-2 or MCMI-III, which was designed to assess the extent of psychopathology in an individual, might be inappropriately used to assess a normal person's level of functioning. Although some conclusions can be drawn from the MMPI-2 relating to certain aspects of a normal person's functioning, or although IQ estimates based on projectives can be made, they should be considered extremely tentative. These tests were not designed for these purposes, and, as a result, such inferences do not represent the strengths of the tests. A somewhat more serious misuse can occur when a test such as the MMPI-2 is used to screen applicants for some types of personnel selection. Results from MMPI-2-type tests are likely to be irrelevant for assessing most job-related skills. Of equal importance is that the information derived from the MMPI-2 is typically of a highly personal nature and, if used in many types of personnel selection, is likely to represent an invasion of privacy.

Interpretation and Use of Test Results

Interpreting test results should never be considered a simple, mechanical procedure. Accurate interpretation means not simply using norms and cutoff scores but also taking into consideration unique characteristics of the person combined with relevant aspects of the test itself. Whereas tests themselves can be validated, the integration of information from a test battery is far more difficult to validate. It is not infrequent, for example, to have contradictions among different sources of data. It is up to the clinician to evaluate these contradictions to develop the most appropriate, accurate, and useful interpretations. If there are significant reservations regarding the test interpretation, these should be communicated, usually in the psychological report itself.

A further issue is that test norms and stimulus materials eventually become outdated. As a result, interpretations based on these tests may become inaccurate. For this reason, clinicians need to stay current on emerging research and new versions of tests. A rule of thumb is that if a clinician has not updated his or her test knowledge in the past 10 years, he or she is probably not practicing competently.

Part of remaining current means that psychologists should select their testing instruments, as well as any scoring and interpretation services, based on evidence related to the validity of the programs or tests. Part of this requires knowledge of the context of the situation (Turner et al., 2001). A well-validated test might have been found to be quite valid in one context or population but not for another. Another issue that might have ethical considerations is conversion to or use of computerized or Internet-assisted technology (McMinn, Buchanan, Ellens, & Ryan, 1999; McMinn, Ellens, & Soref, 1999). Ultimately, any interpretations and recommendations regarding a client are the responsibility of the clinician. Placing a signature on a report means that the clinician is taking responsibility for the contents of the report. Indeed, an important difference between an actuarial formula or automated report and a practitioner is that the practitioner ultimately will be held accountable.

Communicating Test Results

Psychologists should ordinarily give feedback to the client and referral source regarding the results of assessment (Lewak & Hogan, 2003; see Pope, 1992, 2007b, and on http://kspope.com/assess/feedabs1.php for forms and guidelines). This should be done using clear, everyday language. If the psychologist is not the person giving the feedback, this should be agreed on in advance and the psychologist should ensure that the person providing the feedback presents the information in a clear, competent manner. Unless the results are communicated effectively, the purpose of the assessment is not likely to be achieved. This effective feedback involves understanding the needs and vocabulary of the referral source, client, and other persons, such as parents or teachers, who may be affected by the test results. Initially, there should be a clear explanation of the rationale for testing and the nature of the tests being administered. This explanation may include the general type of conclusions that are drawn, the limitations of the test, and common misconceptions surrounding the test or test variable. If a child is being tested in an educational setting, a meeting should be arranged with the school psychologist, parents, teacher, and other relevant persons. Such an approach is crucial for IQ tests, which are more likely to be misinterpreted, than for achievement tests. Feedback of test results should be given in terms that are clear and understandable to the receiver. Descriptions are generally most meaningful when performance levels are clearly indicated along with behavioral references. For example, in giving IQ results to parents, it is only minimally relevant to say that their child has an IQ of 130 with relative strengths in spatial organization, even though this may be appropriate language for a formal psychological evaluation. A more effective description might be that their child is "currently functioning in the top 2% when compared with his or her peers and is particularly good at organizing nonverbal material such as piecing together puzzles, putting together a bicycle, or building a playhouse."

In providing effective feedback, the clinician should also consider the personal characteristics of the receiver, such as his or her general educational level, relative knowledge regarding psychological testing, and possible emotional response to the information

(Finn, 2007). The emotional reaction is especially important when a client is learning about his or her personal strengths or shortcomings. Facilities should be available for additional counseling, if needed. If properly given, feedback is not merely informative but can actually serve to reduce symptomatic distress and enhance self-esteem (Armengol, Moes, Penney, & Sapienza, 2001; Finn & Tonsager, 1992; Lewak & Hogan, 2003). Thus, providing feedback can actually be part of the intervention process itself. Because psychological assessment is often requested as an aid in making important life decisions, the potential impact of the information should not be underestimated. Clinicians are usually in positions of power, and with that power comes responsibility in that the information clients receive and the decisions they make based on this information is often with them for many years.

Maintenance of Test Security and Release of Test Data

If test materials were widely available, it would be easy for persons to review the tests, learn the answers, and respond according to the impression they would like to make. Thus, the materials would lose their validity. Not only is maintaining test security an ethical obligation, but it is a legal requirement related to trade secrets and agreements made with the test publisher when materials are purchased. Psychologists should make all reasonable efforts to ensure that test materials are secure. Specifically, all tests should be kept locked in a secure place and no untrained persons should be allowed to review them. Any copyrighted material should not be duplicated (see Zuckerman [2003] for forms and guidelines).

The security of assessment results should also be maintained. This usually means that only persons designated by the client (usually the referral source and client) should see the results. In reality, however, this ethical principal may sometimes be difficult to achieve. For example, many medical contexts expect most relevant treatment information (including psychological assessment results) to be kept in clients' charts. Typically, all members of the treatment team have access to the charts (Claassen & Lovitt, 2001). On one level, this access represents a conflict between psychological and medical guidelines. On another level, it represents a conflict between benefit to the patient (that may be enhanced by the treatment team having access to his or her records) and patient autonomy (patient control over who and where information should go). Security of assessment results can also be compromised when a large number of organizations (insurance company, interacting rehabilitation provider, referral source) all want access to patient records. This issue arises frequently in the managed health care environment. The security of client records also becomes more tenuous when large interconnected databases potentially have access to patient data (McMinn, Buchanan, et al., 1999; McMinn, Ellens, et al., 1999).

In some clinical and legal contexts, the court or the opposing counsel may wish to see actual client data. This data can be released if the client authorizes it or if the material has been subpoenaed. Ideally, however, the examiner should recommend that a qualified person be present to explain the results. This recommendation is consistent with the principle that the examiner protect the client from potential harm. If the examiner feels that releasing the test data may result in "substantial harm" to the client or "misuse or misrepresentation of the data," (APA, 2002, p. 14), he or she may have the option of refraining from releasing the data. This situation has the potential of resulting in a conflict between legal and ethical requirements.

One important distinction is between "test data" and "test materials." *Test data* refers to raw and scaled scores, such as subscale scores and test profiles. In contrast, *test materials* refers to "manuals, instruments, protocols, and test questions and stimuli" (APA, 2002, p. 14).

Interestingly, test material turns into test data when a psychologist places the client's name on it. Since actual items should not be released, it would thus be important for clinicians to make sure they do not place client-identifying information on what might be copyrighted or restricted material. This is crucial since psychologists can release test data, but they cannot release test materials, such as actual test items. As stated, the release of test materials would constitute a breach of trade secrets, copyright, and the conditions of purchase (Behnke, 2004). One exception to this point is that the material may be released to persons who are properly qualified (Tranel, 1994). Another exception is when a subpoena specifically squashes these terms of purchase, copyright, and trade secrets.

ASSESSING DIVERSE GROUPS

Competence in assessing diverse groups is an essential part of professional practice. This fact is highlighted by increased globalization, extensive immigration, controversies over potential test bias when used with diverse groups, cross-national adaptation of common instruments, and the American Psychological Association's requirement that professional psychologists be trained to work with diverse groups. In the United States, the minority population now comprises a third of the population (100 million people; United States Census Bureau, 2007). Hispanics make up the largest minority (44.3 million), and there are an estimated 40 million African Americans, and approximately 15 million Asian Americans. Additional data indicate that nearly 21 million minorities live in California with the result that 57% of California is comprised of "minorities" (and 75% of Hawaii). Many minority populations in the United States are underrepresented and underserved (Levine, 2007). Thus, developing guidelines for competent assessment is crucial. The guidelines are centered on language skills, cultural competency, assessing cultural/racial identity, appropriate use of instruments, diagnostic issues, and interpretation guidelines (see Dana, 2005).

Language Skills

Evaluating a client's language proficiency is a first step in assessing diverse clients. Based on this evaluation, it may be necessary, or at least advisable, to conduct the assessment in the client's native language. The sufficiently knowledgeable clinician can conduct the assessment him- or herself. Sometimes a translator or referral to another clinician who speaks the language may be required. If the client is reasonably proficient in English, then it may be possible to conduct the assessment in English. However, clinicians should be aware of how this might alter the interaction. For example, a client who is struggling with English may appear to be uncooperative or to have flat affect when in reality this impression is created primarily due to language difficulties. It may also be advisable to use assessment instruments that have been translated into the client's native language.

Cultural Competency

Cultural competency on the part of clinicians begins with self-exploration of personal histories, attitudes, and knowledge. This involves understanding their exposure to various cultures as well as the degree of comfort with these cultures. It is natural to feel more resonant with some cultures as opposed to others. Often attitudes can be subtle and unconscious; for example, clinicians might have a sense of white privilege yet may have difficulty acknowledging these feelings. These attitudes are typically transmitted through nonverbal rather than verbal means.

Based on personal exploration and knowledge of a culture, clinicians need to develop optimal strategies of service etiquette. One strategy may involve level of formality. For example, Native Americans are likely to be more comfortable with minimal formality whereas Asian Americans usually expect more formal interactions characterized by a logical, structured approach. Other factors are the extent of eye contact, physical proximity, volume of voice, and the extent to which emotions are conveyed. For example, some cultures defer to persons perceived as being of higher status by decreasing the volume of their voice and minimizing eye contact. Clinicians who are knowledgeable about these differences should be both accepting of them and not misinterpret these behaviors as indicating depression or evasiveness. At the same time, these behaviors may make it more difficult to detect depression when it is actually present. A further variable is the time involved prior to the client becoming self-disclosing. Some cultures expect extensive preliminaries, perhaps to the point of having mutual acquaintances approve of the clinician prior to more formal clinical work. In contrast, other cultures are quite comfortable with becoming more self-disclosing and "task oriented" with minimal preliminaries. Taking into account each of these factors may make the difference between developing good rapport with accurate assessment results versus poor rapport resulting in inaccurate assessment data.

Cultural/Racial Identity

Cultural identity is a crucial aspect of explaining thoughts, feelings, and behaviors. It is thus important to understand this fact when conducting individual assessment. However, cultural identity varies according to the extent that a person identifies with his or her culture. Some individuals have quite strong identifications with their cultures. As a result, careful consideration of whether standard tests are appropriate to use with them is required. It may be necessary to use test translations, different norms, translators, or instruments specific to their culture. In contrast, other clients might have early experience with a culture but have later become quite acculturated into the dominant culture. As a result, standard tests might be used with more confidence.

Level of identity can be informally assessed through interview. There are also a variety of more formal instruments that ask questions related to variables such as language proficiency/preference, religious beliefs, foods, family structure, value orientation, socioeconomic status, collectivism/individualism, and culture-specific traditions, customs, and identifications. A sample of frequently used measures follows (see review by Dana, 2005):

African Americans: African American Acculturation Scale (Landrine & Klonoff, 1994)

Asian Americans: Asian Values Scale (Kim, Atkinson, & Yang, 1999)

Hispanic/Latinos: Acculturation Rating Scale for Mexican Americans (Cuellar, Arnold, & Maldonado, 1995)

Native Americans and Alaska Natives: Northern Plains Bicultural Immersion Scale (Allen, 1998)

One caution with these instruments is that sometimes individuals have quite different origins within the general group the instrument is trying to measure. This is particularly true for Hispanics and Asian Americans. For example, there are significant differences between Hispanics from Mexico and those from Argentina. Similarly, Japanese, Chinese, Koreans, and Hmong have many differences between their cultures. Despite this fact, a scale such as the Asian Values Scale tries to look at the commonalities among these groups.

Test Equivalence and Appropriate Use of Instruments

Whether an instrument is appropriate is based on a number of considerations, including the client's level of acculturation, language preference, language proficiency, availability of translations of the instrument, whether the construct is the same for the client's culture, availability of norms, and availability of possibly more appropriate alternatives specific to the client's culture. At the core of whether of not the test is appropriate is evaluating the equivalence of the test. Equivalence can be organized according to linguistic, conceptual, and metric equivalence. (See Table 2.1.)

If a test is not equivalent, it may result in bias against the group or individual it is evaluating. *Bias in testing* refers to the presence of systematic error in the measurement of certain factors (e.g., academic potential, intelligence, psychopathology) among certain individuals or groups (Suzuki, Meller, & Ponterotto, 1996). The possible presence of bias toward minority groups has resulted in one of the most controversial issues in psychological testing. More specifically, critics believe that psychological tests are heavily biased in favor of, and reflect the values of, European American, middle-class society. They argue that such tests cannot adequately assess intelligence or personality when applied to minority groups. Whereas the greatest controversy has arisen from the use of intelligence tests, the presence of cultural bias is also relevant in the use of personality testing. Over the past 20 years, discussion over bias has shifted from controversy over the nature and extent of bias to a more productive working through of how to make the most valid and equitable assessment based on current knowledge (see Dana, 2005; Geisinger, 2003; Handel & Ben-Porath, 2000).

The original controversies over test bias centered on determining whether tests are as valid for minority groups as for nonminorities. Undoubtedly, differences exist in mean test scores; however, the meaning that can be attributed to these differences has been strongly debated. A further question lies in identifying the cause of these differences. Some theorists have argued that the differences are primarily the result of environmental factors (Kamin, 1974; R. Rosenthal & Jacobson, 1968), whereas others stressed hereditary determination (A. R. Jensen, 1969, 1972; Rushton, 1994). Although the debate is not resolved, guidelines have been established by the Equal Employment Opportunity Commission (EEOC) for the use of psychological tests with minority groups in educational and industrial settings. The basic premise is that a screening device (psychological test) can have an adverse impact if it screens out a proportionally larger number of minorities than nonminorities. Furthermore, it is the responsibility of

Table 2.1. **Summary of test equivalence**

Type	Definition	Issues/strategies
Linguistic	Wording and content	Translate into new language and then retranslate again ("backtranslate"), consider idioms and pictures, *adapt* not merely literal translation
Conceptual	Construct has same meaning	Same as construct validity, makes similar predictions, correlation, and factor analysis
Metric	Same psychometric features	Distributions, ranges, stability, comparable reliability, and validity, do scores mean the same things

the employer to demonstrate that the procedure produces valid inferences for the specific purposes for which the employer would like to use it. If an industrial or educational organization does not follow the guidelines as defined by the EEOC (1970), the Office of Federal Contract Compliance has the direct power to cancel any government contract that the institution might have.

Linguistic Equivalence

As summarized in Table 2.1, the first area of concern is *linguistic equivalence*, which is whether the test has been translated accurately. On the surface, this may mean simply translating the administration instructions and test items into the language of interest. One strategy to assist with this is to use "back-translation." In back-translation, once the test is translated, it is then translated back into the original language. If the meanings of the items are still the same, then the back-translation helps to ensure that the translation has been made correctly. A further issue is that sometimes idioms need to be comparable. Similar to this issue is that not only verbal materials but also pictures should be made comparable. For example, a picture of a stereotypically appearing person depicted in one culture should be similarly made to look stereotypical in the culture the test has been translated into. This goes beyond merely translating the test and into an "adaptation" of the test (sometimes referred to as "functional equivalence").

Conceptual Equivalence

A further concern is *conceptual equivalence,* which requires the constructs to have the same meaning in various cultures. Sometimes the equivalence of the constructs is clear whereas at others it is more difficult to determine. For example, "dominance" as a personality trait may seem to be something that would be conceptually equivalent in all cultures. This fact is partially true, but nuances may make the concept somewhat different in various cultures. More collectivist cultures may emphasize the obligation to the group or family as being a more important aspect of dominance than individualistic cultures. It should be noted that various aspects of conceptual equivalence may emerge during translations of the test. For this reason, linguistic and conceptual equivalence are somewhat overlapping strategies.

More formal procedures for establishing conceptual equivalence might include investigating patterns of correlation through convergent and discriminant validity. A favored means of determining equivalence is factor analysis. It would be predicted that if indeed the concepts are comparable, then the same factors would emerge on the test when evaluated using samples from different cultures.

Metric Equivalence

The final means of establishing equivalence is through *metric equivalence*. This term refers to whether the instrument has similar psychometric properties across different groups/cultures. The extent the psychometric properties are different or not can include evaluating such areas as content, criterion, and construct validity. Note that a prerequisite for metric equivalence is that conceptual equivalence needs to be demonstrated first.

One of the initial things that persons reviewing tests will notice is that there are items on tests that appear irrelevant and possibly unfair for various groups. For example, a person from different ethnic or cross-national groups could not reasonably be expected to know prominent political leaders in the country where the test was developed. On the surface, it would appear that the test was culturally biased. Within the United States, early intuitive observations seemed to suggest that many African American children and other minorities usually do not have the opportunity to learn the types of material contained in many of the test items. Thus, their lower scores may represent not a lack of "intelligence" but merely a lack of familiarity with European American, middle-class culture. Critics of the tests point out that it would clearly be unfair to assess a European American's "intelligence" based on whether he or she knows idioms or facts specific to a certain ethnic minority or national group. Low scores would simply measure an individual's relative familiarity with the knowledge contained within the group rather than his or her specific "mental strengths."

If this reasoning is used, many IQ and aptitude tests may appear on the surface to be culturally biased. However, studies in which researchers, to the best of their ability, eliminated biased test items or items that statistically discriminated between minorities and nonminorities did not alter total test scores (Reynolds, 2000). In a representative study, 27 items were removed from the SAT that consistently differentiated minorities from nonminorities. This did little to change either the test takers' individual scores or the differences between the two groups (Flaugher & Schrader, 1978). Thus, the popular belief, based on a superficial appraisal of many psychological tests, that biased items are responsible for test differences does not appear to be supported by research.

Although test differences between minority and nonminority groups have frequently been found, the meaning and causes of these differences are open to debate. For example, it has been demonstrated that African Americans consistently scored 12 to 15 IQ points lower than European Americans on the WISC-III and WAIS-III (Heaton, Taylor, & Manly, 2003; Prifitera, Weiss, & Saklofske, 1998). When African Americans and European Americans of equal socioeconomic status were compared, the differences in IQ scores were reduced to 11 to 13 IQ points (Heaton et al., 2003). Performance by Hispanics is about 7 IQ points lower than European Americans, and Asian Americans have been found to have IQ scores roughly equal to European Americans. Personality tests have also been found to have differences among various ethnic groups within the United States. For example, some studies (Dahlstrom, Lachar, & Dahlstrom, 1986b; Timbrook & Graham, 1994) have found that African Americans have five T-score higher mean scores for MMPI scales F, 8, and 9. However, these differences were either decreased or found to be insignificant when groups were matched for age and education. This point suggests that socioeconomic factors may be an important reasons for score differences. Socioeconomic status still accounts for only part of the reason for differences in test performance on cognitive tests, however (Sackett, Borneman, & Connelly, 2008). Other possible reasons are lack of belief in the impact of effort, level of acculturation, the effects of discrimination, gaps in general skills, or possible genetic differences. The reasons for these differences have been hotly debated. At this point the relative extent of these factors is unclear (see Neisser et al., 1996, and W. M. Williams, 2000, Special Series in *Psychology, Public Policy, and Law*).

Another consideration related to metric equivalence is the adequacy of the predictive validity of various tests when used with minority groups. Because one of the main purposes of these tests is to predict later performance, it is essential to evaluate the extent to which the scores in fact adequately predict areas such as a minority's performance in college. A representative group of studies indicates that the SAT scores actually overpredict how well some minorities will perform in college (Hunter & Schmidt, 1996, 2000; A. R. Jensen, 1984; Sackett et al., 2008). Intelligence test scores have also been found to consistently predict African American work performance as accurately as European American performance (Hunter & Schmidt, 1998). Furthermore, both the WISC and the WISC-R are equally as effective in predicting the academic achievement of both African Americans and European Americans in primary and secondary schools (Neisser et al., 1996; Reynolds & Hartlage, 1979).

A number of tests have been developed with the partial intent of using them in the assessment of ethnic minorities and cross-national groups. These tend to emphasize nonverbal tasks and include the Leiter International Performance Scale, Peabody Picture Vocabulary Test-III, Raven's Progressive Matrices, the Universal Nonverbal Intelligence Test, and the Test of Nonverbal Abilities (Bracken & McCallum, 1998; McCallum, Bracken, & Wasserman, 2001). Some of these tests have been found to have minimal cultural bias (see Kaufman & Lichtenberger, 2006). In addition, the Kaufman Assessment Battery for Children-II (K-ABC-II; Kaufman, Lichtenberger, & Fletcher-Janzen) demonstrates minimal cultural bias. Mean IQ scores for European Americans, African Americans, and Hispanics are relatively close; and there is some evidence that reliability and concurrent validity is comparable for different ethnic populations (Kaufman et al., 2005).

As is true for ability tests and tests of scholastic aptitude, personality tests have the potential to be biased. The main research in this area has been performed on the MMPI/MMPI-2 and has consistently indicated that minority groups do score differently than do nonminorities (see section on "Use with Diverse Groups" in Chapter 7). However, these differences have not been found to be consistent across all populations (Greene, 1987, 1991, 2000). For example, African Americans from forensic, psychiatric, and vocational populations have been found to have varying patterns of mean scale elevations when compared to the mean scale elevations for European Americans. Even if consistent score differences were found, this does not mean these differences will be of sufficient magnitude to alter a clinician's interpretations, nor does it mean that predictions based on empirical criteria will be different. Studies using empirical criteria for prediction indicate that the MMPI does not result in greater descriptive accuracy for European Americans than for African Americans (Elion & Megargee, 1975; Green, 1991, 2000; Green & Kelly, 1988).

Reviews of MMPI/MMPI-2 performance for Asian Americans, African Americans, Hispanics, and Native Americans have concluded that since no consistent patterns have emerged between various ethnic groups, it is premature to use different ethnically based norms (J. R. Graham, 2006; Greene, 1987, 1991; G. C. N. Hall, Bansal, & Lopez, 1999; Schinka, LaLone, & Greene, 1998). What seems to affect MMPI profiles more than ethnicity are moderator variables such as socioeconomic status, intelligence, and education. Furthermore, the existing differences may result from true differences in behavior and personality caused by the greater stresses often encountered by minorities. J. Graham (1987) suggests that, when MMPI scores are deviant, the clinician should tentatively accept these scores but make special efforts to explore the person's life situation and level of adjustment, and integrate this information with the test scores.

From this discussion, it should be obvious that developing test equivalence is complicated and the meanings of various patterns of scores are far from being resolved. Several general solutions have been suggested (see Suzuki et al., 1996). These include improving selection devices, developing different evaluation criteria, improving general skills, and changing social environments. Improving the use of selection devices involves paying continual attention to, and obtaining greater knowledge of, the meaning of different scores for different subgroups. Doing this may include tailoring specific test scores to the types of decisions individuals may make in their lives.

Another approach to solving the problem of potential test equivalence and bias is to develop different and more adequate criterion measures. For example, objective measures of work performance may be more accurate predictors than formal tests. These predictions of work performance may be higher if made by persons who share similar ethnic backgrounds. Related to this point, it may be crucial to consider the impact of various settings. For example, if a European American and a Hispanic attorney are placed in settings in which they work with Hispanics, it is probable that the Hispanic attorney would be more effective because he or she will have increased rapport and greater familiarity with the language and values of his or her clientele.

Another solution involves changing the social environment. Part of the rationale for emphasizing this approach is the belief that the differences in test scores between minorities and nonminorities are not because of test bias but rather because tests accurately reflect the effects of an unequal environment and unequal opportunities (Reynolds, 2000). Even though, in some situations, different minority norms and additional predictive studies on minority populations are necessary, the literature suggests that tests are not as biased as they have been accused of being (see Sackett et al., 2008). Removing seemingly biased or discriminating items still results in the same mean test scores, ability tests often still provide accurate predictions of grade point average for both minorities and nonminorities, and the MMPI-2 often makes behavioral predictions that are equally accurate for various ethnic groups. These facts suggest that tests themselves are often not the problem but merely the means of establishing that, often, inequalities exist between ethnic groups. The goal should be to change unequal environments that can ideally increase a population's skills as measured by current tests of aptitude, IQ, and achievement. Whereas improving selection devices and developing different criterion measures are still important, future efforts should also stress more equal access to educational and career opportunities.

Probably the most important strategy is to maintain a flexible attitude combined with the use of alternative assessment strategies. Doing this changes the focus from merely establishing test equivalence to using a wide array of alternate assessment strategies. Thus, nonverbal techniques might be used, such as the Universal Nonverbal Intelligence Test (Bracken & McCallum, 1998), Raven's Progressive Matrices Test, or emphasis on the perceptual/nonverbal subtests of the WAIS-IV/WISC-IV. In addition, "dynamic testing," in which actual observations of the benefit a person receives from learning situations, also shows promise in assessing the extent to which a client can benefit from educational interventions (learning potential; Grigorenko & Sternberg, 1998). Material beyond tests, such as teacher reports, discussions with parents, history, and behavioral observations, should also have a greater significance.

Diagnostic Issues

DSM-IV-TR diagnosis needs to be considered within the context of cultural considerations. In addition to noting the cultural identity of the client, it is also crucial to carefully listen to cultural explanations of the client's difficulty. One category of presentation is the so-called culture-bound syndrome that is outlined in the *DSM-IV-TR*. For example, *latah* (mainly Southeast Asia) is a reaction to sudden fear that results in a dissociative state along with associated behaviors of command obedience and repetitive behaviors. Less dramatic are how the presence of oppression and discrimination among ethnic groups might contribute to misdiagnosing a person as being paranoid. A further example is how a disorder such as depression might be presented in primarily physiological terms within some cultures. In such cases, the external presentation would need to be decoded in order to identify the underlying depression. Research has clearly demonstrated varying rates of diagnoses in various cultures (Nguyen et al., 2007). What is less clear is whether these varying diagnoses represent underdiagnosis, overdiagnosis, or misdiagnosis. The practical implication is that when errors in diagnosis do occur, they have the potential to result in poor decisions and incorrect treatment. It might also be necessary to consider combining standard psychological treatments along with culture-specific interventions.

Interpretation Guidelines

The preceding discussion clearly indicates that ensuring accurate interpretations for diverse groups is challenging but also essential. Acculturation, equivalence, cultural competence, and the client's self-description within the context of his or her culture all need to be taken into account. Clinicians also need to incorporate what is known about how the instruments function within various cultures, including translations, idioms, norms, and various types of validity. However, it is nearly impossible to definitively demonstrate equivalence due to the many steps and issues involved. Due to this fact, clinicians need to be both flexible and sensitive. For example, the pathological aspects of a high score on MMPI-2 scale 6 (Paranoia) may need to be moderated if elevated for a client who has experienced racial discrimination. Similarly, indicators of low emotional expressiveness on the Rorschach may need to be modified if the person's emotional responses seemed to be "blunted" due to struggles with English as a second language. Often a phrase needs to be included in a report such as ". . . results need to be treated with caution since the instruments have not been adequately adapted for use within the client's culture." Inserting a phrase such as this means that there are no clear specific strategies, but instead there are general guidelines to work with. Information and guidelines relevant to specific tests are included in each of the test-related chapters (see "Use with Diverse Groups").

SELECTING PSYCHOLOGICAL TESTS

The most important factor in test selection is the extent to which the test is useful in answering the referral question. An assessment of neurological patients might use tests sensitive to cerebral deficit; depressed patients might be given the Beck Depression Inventory-II (A. T. Beck, Steer, & Brown, 1996); and pain patients might be given the McGill Pain Questionnaire (Melzack, 1975), Millon Behavioral Health Inventory (Millon, Green, & Meagher, 2000), or Illness Behavior Questionnaire (Pilowski, Spence, Cobb, & Katsikitis, 1984).

Another important factor in test selection is a particular practitioner's training, experience, personal preferences, and familiarity with relevant literature. For example, a clinician who has received training in the MMPI-2 might be concerned about its ability to assess personality disorders and may rather choose to use an instrument such as the MCMI (Millon, 1994). Clinicians might also select an instrument because it has practical efficiency in terms of time and economy (Groth-Marnat, 1999). Thus, they may wish to use simple behavioral predictions made by the client rather than use more expensive, time-consuming, and, quite possibly, less accurate tests (Shrauger & Osberg, 1981). Computer-assisted instruments may also help to lower the costs of assessment primarily by reducing direct practitioner time and achieving greater speed for scoring and hypothesis generation. A final crucial factor is that the assessment instrument should have good psychometric properties (see Hunsley & Mash, 2008).

The most frequently used assessment techniques are included in the following chapters 3–13. Contact details for the major psychological distributors, along with a partial listing of tests they carry, are listed in Appendix A on page 605. Additional information on tests and assessment can be found by contacting various organizations that focus on assessment and are listed in Appendix B on page 609. Various combinations of tests typically constitute a core battery used by clinicians. However, it is often necessary to expand such a core battery depending on the specifics of the referral question. Table 2.2 provides a listing of the domains for assessment along with relevant tests.

Table 2.2.   Assessment instruments relevant for specific response domains

Cognitive functioning
  General functioning
    Mental Status Examination
    Mini-Mental Status Examination (MMSE)
  Intellectual functioning
    Wechsler Adult Intelligence Scale-IV
    Wechsler Intelligence Scale for Children-IV
    Stanford-Binet (5th ed.)
    Kaufman Assessment Battery for Children-II
    Woodcock-Johnson Psychoeducational Battery-IV
  Memory functions
    Wechsler Memory Scale-IV
    Rey Auditory Verbal Learning Test
    California Verbal Learning Test
    Benton Visual Retention Test
  Visuoconstructive abilities
    Bender Visual Motor Gestalt Test
    Drawing tests
  Content of thought processes
    Thematic Apperception Test
    Children's Apperception Test

Emotional functioning and level of psychopathology
  General patterns and severity
    Minnesota Multiphasic Personality Inventory-2
    Millon Clinical Multiaxial Inventory-III
    Millon Adolescent Clinical Inventory
    Rorschach
    Symptom Checklist 90-Revised
    Brief Symptom Inventory
    Personality Inventory for Children-2
  Depression
    Beck Depression Inventory-II
    Hamilton Rating Scale for Depression
    Children's Depression Inventory
  Anxiety
    State-Trait Anxiety Inventory
    Fear Survey Schedule
    Anxiety Disorders Interview Schedule
  Sexual disturbance
    Derogatis Sexual Functioning Inventory
  Marital/family disturbance
    Dyadic Adjustment Scale
    Family Environment Scale
    Marital Satisfaction Inventory

Interpersonal patterns
    California Psychological Inventory
    Rathus Assertiveness Schedule
    Therapeutic Reactance Scale
    Taylor Johnson Temperament Analysis

Continued

Table 2.2.   Continued

General personality measures
  Sixteen Personality Factors
  NEO-PI-R
  Myers Briggs Type Indicator
  Adjective Checklist
  Sentence completion tests
Academic/school adjustment
  Achenbach Child Behavior Checklist
  Vineland Social Maturity Scale
  Connors Behavior Rating Scales
  Kinetic School Drawing
  Behavior Assessment System for Children-2
Academic achievement
  Woodcock Johnson Tests of Achievement-III
  Wide Range Achievement Test-III
  Wechsler Individual Achievement Test
Adaptive Level
  AAMD Adaptive Behavior Scale
  Vineland Adaptive Behavior Scale
Vocational interests
  Career Assessment Inventory
  Kuder Occupational Interest Survey
  Self-Directed Search
  Strong Interest Inventory
Alcohol abuse
  Michigan Alcoholism Screening Test
  Alcohol Use Inventory
Diagnosis
  Diagnostic Interview Schedule
  Schedule for Affective Disorders and Schizophrenia
  Structured Clinical Interview for DSM
  Structured Interview for DSM Personality Disorders
  Diagnostic Interview for Children and Adolescents
Prognosis and risk
  Suicide potential
      Scale of Suicide Ideation
      Beck Hopelessness Scale
  Schizophrenia prognosis
      Camberwell Family Interview

Although some of the tests described in Table 2.2 are thoroughly described in specific chapters dedicated to them, others may be relatively unfamiliar, and practitioners should obtain additional information on them. Various sources are available for information about these and other tests. Such sources can provide important information for deciding whether to obtain the tests and incorporate them into a battery. Probably the most useful is the *Mental Measurements Yearbook*, which contains a collection of critical test reviews that include evaluations of the tests and an overview on the tests. The 17th *Mental Measurements Yearbook* was published in 2007 (Geisinger, Spies, Carlson, & Plake, 2007) but it may be necessary to consult previous editions as not all tests are reviewed again in each new edition. The reviews are available in book form as well as online

(*Mental Measurement Database*; see www.unl.edu/buros/). *Tests in Print VII* (Murphy, Spies, & Plake, 2006) is associated with the *Mental Measurements Yearbook* but, rather than focusing on evaluating tests, lists information on each test, such as title, population it was designed for, available subtests, updating, author(s), and publisher. A further listing, description, and evaluation of tests can be found in Maddox (2003), *Tests: A Comprehensive Reference for Assessment in Psychology, Education, and Business* (5th ed.), which provides descriptive information on more than 3,500 tests. Practitioners interested in obtaining information on rating scales and other measures used in clinical practice might consult *Measures for Clinical Practice and Research: A Sourcebook* (Fischer & Corcoran, 2007). In *Assessments That Work,* Hunsley and Mash (2008) present tests according to types of disorders and provide descriptions of these tests along with ratings of their psychometric properties. Neuropsychological tests are reviewed in the preceding resources as well as in Lezak's (2004) *Neuropsychological Assessment*, Strauss, Sherman, and Spreen (2006) *A Compendium of Neuropsychological Tests,* and specialty journals in neuropsychology, particularly *Neuropsychology Review*. A careful review of the information included in these references often will answer questions clinicians might have related to a test's psychometric properties, usefulness, appropriateness for different populations, details for purchasing, and strengths and limitations. Most of the questions listed in Table 1.1 (see Chapter 1) can be answered by consulting the preceding resources.

An important and current trend in research and practice on psychological assessment is the use of tests to generate a treatment plan (Beutler & Groth-Marnat, 2003: Jongsma, Peterson, & Bruce, 2006; Maruish, 2004). Indeed, a basic objective of psychological assessment is to provide useful information regarding the planning, implementation, and evaluation of treatment. With the increased specificity of both treatment and assessment, this goal is becoming possible. For example, oppositional, resistant clients have been found to have optimal treatment outcomes when either self-directed or paradoxical interventions have been used (Beutler, Clarkin, & Bongar, 2000; Beutler, Sandowicz, Fisher, & Albanese, 1996). In addition, a problem's severity has clear implications for the restrictiveness of treatment (inpatient, outpatient) as well as treatment duration and intensity. Thus, clinicians should not select tests based simply on their diagnostic accuracy or psychometric properties; they should also be concerned with the functional utility of the tests in treatment planning. Accordingly, Chapter 14 presents a systematic, integrated approach to transforming assessment results into a series of clear treatment recommendations.

Two special concerns in selecting tests are faking and the use of short forms. In many situations, clinicians might be concerned that persons will either consciously or unconsciously provide inaccurate responses (see kspope.com/assess/). Malingering ("inconsistent effort") is becoming an increasingly important issue, especially in forensic settings, where personal gain may result in presenting "fake bad" results. Thus, clinicians may want to pay particular attention to validity scales built in to tests (i.e., MMPI-2, MCMI-III, CPI) as well as use specialty instruments designed to detect faking. Although controversial, many projective techniques may be resistant to attempts at faking. Concerns regarding the time required for assessment may cause examiners to consider selecting short forms of instruments such as the WAIS-IV or WISC-IV. Although many short forms for cognitive tests seem sufficiently valid for screening purposes, their use as substitutes for the longer forms is not acceptable (A. Kaufman, Kaufman, Balgopal, & McLean, 1996; A. Kaufman & Lichtenberger, 2002). Most past attempts to develop short forms for the longer objective personality tests such as the MMPI-2 have not been successful (Butcher, 2006a). However, future computerized applications that tailor items based on a client's previous responses (adaptive testing) may result in the development of shortened administrations with acceptable psychometric properties (Forbey & Ben-Porath, 2007). In addition, the recent 338-item MMPI-2 Restructured form has been found to be an acceptable short form (Ben-Porath & Tellegen, 2008).

During the evaluation of single cases, such as in clinical diagnoses and counseling, clinicians do not usually use formal combinations of test scores. Rather, they rely on their past judgment, clinical experience, and theoretical background to interpret and integrate test scores. However, for personnel decisions, academic predictions, and some clinical decisions (recidivism rate, suicide risk), clinicians may be advised to use statistical formulas (Aegisdottir et al., 2006). The two basic approaches for combining test results are multiple regression equations and multiple cutoff scores. Multiple regression equations are developed by correlating each test or subtest with a criterion. The higher the correlation, the greater is the weight in the equation. The correlation of the entire battery with the criterion measure gives an indication of the battery's highest predictive validity. For example, high school achievement can be predicted with this regression equation, which combines IQ and CPI subtests:

$$\text{Achievement} = .786 + .195 \text{ Responsibility} + .44 \text{ Socialization}$$
$$- .130 \text{ Good Impression} + .19 \text{ Achievement via Conformance}$$
$$+ .179 \text{ Achievement via Independence} + .279 \text{ IQ}$$

This equation raises the correlation with GPA to .68 as compared with .60 when using IQ alone (Megargee, 1972). This correlation indicates that academic achievement is dependent not only on intellectual factors but also on psychosocial ones, such as responsibility, socialization, achievement via independence, and achievement via conformance, all of which are measured by the CPI. The second strategy, multiple cutoff scores, involves developing an optimum cutoff for each test or subtest. If the person is above a certain specified score (i.e., above the brain-damaged or schizophrenic range), the score can be used to indicate the presence of a certain characteristic. Although not all tests have equations or cutoffs developed for them, the decision to include a test in a battery may depend in part on the presence of such formal extensions of the tests. In addition, many of the computer-assisted interpretive packages use various actuarial formulas (usually in combination with expert interpretations) to develop their interpretations.

COMPUTER-ASSISTED ASSESSMENT

During the past 30 years, computer-assisted assessment has grown exponentially. By 1990, 17% of practicing psychologists frequently used computer-generated narratives, with an additional 36% using them on an occasional basis (Spielberger & Piotrowski, 1990). By 1999, the number of psychologists stating that they used some form of computer-assisted testing had increased to 40% (McMinn, Buchanan, et al., 1999). More than 400 software packages are available, many of which are listed in various catalogs published and distributed by test suppliers. At present, computers are used mainly for their clerical efficiency in scoring and data storage and to generate interpretive reports. Future uses of computers are likely to include features such as innovative presentation of items (i.e., adaptive testing), networked norms, novel presentation of stimuli (i.e., virtual reality), psychophysiological monitoring, and artificial intelligence (Garb, 2000; Groth-Marnat, 2000a, in press). Computing in mental health has included not only computer-assisted assessment but also computer interviews, computerized diagnosis, computer-aided instruction, direct treatment intervention, clinical consultation, and simulated psychiatric interviews (Lichtenberger, 2006; McMinn, Buchanan, et al., 1999).

Computer-assisted administration and interpretation in neuropsychology have seen a number of particular advances (see special series review by Kane, 2007). Batteries have been developed mainly in large organizational contexts (military, Federal Aviation Authority) and focused on specialized types of problems. For example, the Neuro-behavioral Evaluation System is particularly sensitive to the impact of environmental toxins (Groth-Marnat, 1993), COGSCREEN has been used in the selection of airline pilots, and the military's UTCPAB was originally developed to assess the impact of drugs in the workplace. The Cambridge Neuropsychological Test Automated Batteries (CANTAB) have been found to detect and locate brain damage including early signs of Alzheimer's, Parkinson's, and Huntington's disease (Fray, Robbins, & Sahakian, 1996; Luciana, 2003). Although the computer-assisted programs show considerable promise, they are currently used less than the more familiar individually administered neuropsychological tests or test batteries (Camara et al., 2000; Luciana, 2003).

Computer-assisted assessment has a number of advantages. Computers can save valuable professional time, potentially improve test-retest reliability, reduce possible tester bias, and reduce the cost to the consumer by improving efficiency (Butcher, Perry, & Hahn, 2004; Groth-Marnat, 1999: Kane, 2007; Luciana, 2003). Even greater benefits may someday be realized by incorporating more complicated decision rules in interpretation, collecting data on response latency and key pressure, incorporating computer-based models of personality, tailoring future questions to a client based on past responses, and estimating the degree of certainty of various interpretations (Groth-Marnat, 2000a, 2000b; Lichtenberger, 2006).

In the past, computer-assisted assessment has resulted in considerable controversy within mental health publications (Faust & Ziskin, 1989; Groth-Marnat & Schumaker, 1989), the popular media (C. Hall, 1983), and professional publications outside the mental health area (Groth-Marnat, 1985). A primary issue has been untested reliability and validity. Research on reliability, however, has typically indicated that computerized administrations have generally excellent reliability that is at least equivalent to the paper-and-pencil versions (Campbell et al., 1999; Kane, 2007; Luciana, 2003). In addition, computer-administered versus paper-and-pencil results for traditional tests have generally been found to result in negligible differences in scores (Butcher et al., 2004; Finger & Ones, 1999). This finding supports the view that if a paper-and-pencil version of the test is valid, a computerized version will also have equal validity resulting from the comparability in scores.

A further issue is the validity of computer-based test interpretation. Butcher et al. (2004) concluded that in the vast majority of computer-based interpretations, 60% of the interpretations were appropriate. Shorter to midlength narratives were generally considered to have a higher proportion of valid interpretations when compared with longer ones. In addition, the narrative statements contained in the computer-based reports were comparable to the types of statements made by clinicians. While this finding generally supports the use of computer-based interpretations, the fact that 40% or more of interpretations were not considered accurate means that the computer-based reports should be carefully evaluated. Thus, cutting and pasting computerized narratives into reports results in unacceptably high error rates. Indeed, 42% of psychologists surveyed felt this procedure raised ethical concerns (McMinn, Ellens, et al., 1999). The previous summary clearly emphasizes that computer-based reports should not be used to replace clinical judgment but should instead be used as an adjunct to provide possible interpretations that the clinician needs to verify.

The Association of Test Publishers (2000) has attempted to clarify standards in their *Guidelines for Computer-Based Testing* (along with the 2001 APA ethics code). They stress that only persons who meet the requirements for using psychological tests in general should use computer-based assessments (Turner, DeMers, Fox, & Reed, 2001). Specifically, users should have an understanding of psychological measurement, validation procedures, and test research. They should also limit their use of computerized techniques to those areas they are competent to use. They should be knowledgeable regarding how computer-based scores were generated and how interpretations have been made. Finally, they should be able to evaluate whether the computer-based procedures are applicable to how they will be used.

The preceding difficulties associated with computer-assisted assessment suggest a number of guidelines for users (Butcher et al., 2004; Groth-Marnat & Schumaker, 1989). First, practitioners should not blindly accept computer-based narrative statements but rather should ensure, to the best of their ability, that the statements are both linked to empirically based research and placed in the context of the unique history and unique situation of the client. Computers have, among other benefits, the strong advantage of offering a wide variety of possible interpretations to the clinician, but these interpretations still need to be critically evaluated. Far greater research needs to be performed on both the meaning of computer-administered test scores and on the narrative interpretations based on these scores. The developers of software should also be encouraged to provide enough information in the manual to allow proper evaluation of the programs and should develop mechanisms to ensure the updating of obsolete programs.

RECOMMENDED READING

Butcher, J. N., Perry, J. N., & Hahn, J. (2004). Computers in clinical assessment: Historical developments, present status, and future challenges. *Journal of Clinical Psychology, 60*, 331–345.

Dana, R. H. (2005). *Multicultural assessment: Principles, applications, and examples*. Mahwah, NJ: Erlbaum.

Heilbrun, K., Marczyk, G. G., & Dematteo, D. (2002). *Forensic mental health assessment: A casebook*. New York: Oxford University Press.

Hunsley, J., & Mash, E. J. (Eds.). (2008). *Assessments that work*. New York: Oxford University Press.

Pope, K. (2007a). Informed consent in psychotherapy and counseling: Forms, standards, guidelines, and references. Retrieved November 2, 2007, from http://kspope.com/consent/index.php.

Pope, K. (2007b). Responsibilities in providing psychological test feedback to clients. Retrieved November 2, 2007 from http://kspope.com/assess/feedabs1.php.

Yaloff, J., & Brabender, V. (2001). Ethical dilemmas in personality assessment courses: Using the classroom for in vivo training. *Journal of Personality Assessment, 77*, 203–213.

Zuckerman, E. L. (2003). *The paper office: Forms, guidelines, and resources to make your practice work ethically, legally, and profitably*. New York: Guilford Press.

Chapter 3

THE ASSESSMENT INTERVIEW

Probably the single most important means of data collection during psychological evaluation is the assessment interview. Without interview data, most psychological test results are meaningless. The interview also provides potentially valuable information that may be otherwise unobtainable, such as behavioral observations, idiosyncratic features of the client, and the person's reaction to his or her current life situation. In addition, interviews are the primary means for developing rapport.

Sometimes an interview is mistakenly thought to be simply a conversation. In fact, the interview and conversation differ in many ways. An interview typically has a clear sequence and is organized around specific, relevant themes because it is meant to achieve defined goals. Unlike a normal conversation, the assessment interview may even require the interviewer and interviewee to discuss unpleasant facts and feelings. Its general objectives are to gather information that cannot easily be obtained through other means, establish a relationship that is conducive to obtaining the information, develop greater understanding in both the interviewer and interviewee regarding problem behavior, and provide direction and support in helping the interviewee deal with problem behaviors. The interviewer must not only direct and control the interaction to achieve specific goals but also have knowledge about the areas to be covered in the interview.

A basic dimension of an interview is its degree of structure. Some interviews allow the participants to freely drift from one area to the next, whereas others are highly directive and goal oriented, often using structured ratings and checklists. The more unstructured formats offer flexibility, possibly high rapport, the ability to assess how clients organize their responses, and the potential to explore unique details of a client's history. Unstructured interviews, however, have received frequent criticism, resulting in widespread distrust of their reliability and validity. As a result, highly structured and semistructured interviews have been developed that provide sound psychometric qualities, the potential for use in research and the capacity to be administered by less trained personnel.

Regardless of the degree of structure, any interview needs to accomplish specific goals, such as assessing the client's strengths, level of adjustment, the nature and history of the problem, diagnosis, and relevant personal and family history. Techniques for accomplishing these goals vary from one interviewer to the next. Most practitioners use at least some structured aids, such as intake forms that provide identifying data and basic elements of history. Obtaining information through direct questions on intake forms frees the clinician to investigate other aspects of the client in a more flexible, open-ended manner. Clinicians might also use a checklist to help ensure that they have covered all relevant areas. Other clinicians continue the structured format throughout most of the interview by using one of the formally developed structured interviews, such as the Schedule for Affective Disorders and Schizophrenia (SADS) or Structured Clinical Interview for the *DSM-IV* (SCID).

HISTORY AND DEVELOPMENT

Early Developments

The earliest form of obtaining information from clients was through clinical interviewing. At first, these interviews were modeled after question-and-answer medical formats, but later, the influence of psychoanalytic theories resulted in a more open-ended, free-flowing style. Parallel to the appearance of the psychoanalytically oriented interview was the development of the more structured and goal-oriented mental status examination originally formulated by Adolf Meyer in 1902. The mental status examination assessed relevant areas of a client's current functioning, such as general appearance, behavior, thought processes, thought content, memory, attention, speech, insight, and judgment. Professionals also expressed early interest in the relationship between biographical data and the prediction of occupational success or prognosis for specific disorders.

Regardless of the style used, the interviews all had these common objectives: to obtain a psychological portrait of the person, to conceptualize what is causing the person's current difficulties, to make a diagnosis, and to formulate a treatment plan. The difficulty with unstructured interviews is that they were (and still are) considered to have questionable reliability, validity, and cost-effectiveness. The first standardized psychological tests were developed to overcome these limitations. Tests could be subjected to rigorous psychometric evaluation and were more economical because they required less face-to-face contact with the person(s) being evaluated.

Developments during the 1940s and 1950s

During the 1940s and 1950s, researchers and clinicians began conceptualizing and investigating these critical dimensions of interviews:

1. Content versus process
2. Goal orientation (problem solving) versus expressive elements
3. Degree of directiveness
4. Amount of structure
5. The relative amount of activity expressed by the participants

These issues have been the focus of numerous research studies. A representative and frequently cited study on interviewer style was reported by W. Snyder (1945), who found that a nondirective approach was most likely to create favorable changes and self-exploration in clients. In contrast, a directive style using persuasion, interpretation, and interviewer judgments typically resulted in clients being defensive and resistant to expressing difficulties. Strupp (1958) investigated the experience-inexperience dimension and found, among other things, that experienced interviewers expressed more warmth, a greater level of activity, and a greater number of interpretations. Level of empathy did not alter, regardless of the interviewer's degree of experience. Further, representative studies include Porter's (1950) in-depth evaluation of the effects of different types of responses (evaluative, probing, reassuring) and R. Wagner's (1949) early review, which questioned the reliability and validity of employment interviews.

Developments during the 1960s

A considerable amount of research in the 1960s was stimulated by C. Rogers (1961), who emphasized understanding the proper interpersonal ingredients necessary for an optimal therapeutic relationship (warmth, positive regard, genuineness). Elaborating on Roger's ideas, Truax and Carkhuff (1967) developed a five-point scale to measure interviewer understanding of the client. This scale was used for research on interviewing and therapist training, and as support for a client-centered theoretical orientation. Additional research efforts were also directed toward listing and elaborating on different categories of interactions, such as clarification, summarizing, and confrontation.

Other investigators conceptualized interviewing as an interactive system in which the participants simultaneously influenced each other (Matarazzo, 1965; Watzlawick, Beavin, & Jackson, 1966). This emphasis on an interactive, self-maintaining system became the core for most early and later formulations of family therapy. The 1960s also saw the development and formalization of behavioral assessment, primarily in the form of goal-directed interviews that focused on understanding current and past reinforcers as well as on establishing workable target behaviors. Proponents of behavioral assessment also developed formal rating instruments and self-reports for areas such as depression, assertiveness, and fear.

Some attempts were made at integrating different schools of thought into a coherent picture, such as Beier's (1966) conceptualization of unconscious processes being expressed through nonverbal behaviors that could then be subject to covert social reinforcement. However, the 1960s (and part of the 1970s) were mostly characterized by a splintering into different schools of conflicting and competing ideologies. For example, client-centered approaches emphasized the importance of staying with the client's self-exploration; behavioral interviews emphasized antecedents and consequences of behavior; and family therapy focused on interactive group processes. Parallel progress was made within each of these different schools and within different disciplines, but little effort was devoted to cross-fertilization and/or integration.

Throughout the 1950s and 1960s, child assessment was conducted primarily through interviews with parents. Direct interviews with the child were considered to be for therapeutic purposes rather than for assessment. Differential diagnosis was unusual; almost all children referred to psychiatric clinics were either undiagnosed or diagnosed as "adjustment reactions" (Rosen, Bahn, & Kramer, 1964). Early research by Lapouse and Monk (1958, 1964) using structured interviews indicated that mothers were more likely to report overt behaviors that are bothersome to adults (thumb-sucking, temper tantrums), but children were more likely to reveal covert difficulties (fears, nightmares). Somewhat later, P. Graham and Rutter (1968), using structured interviews of children (rather than a parent), found interrater agreement was high for global psychiatric impairment (.84); moderate for attentional deficit, motor behavior, and social relations (.61 to .64); and low for more covert difficulties, such as depression, fears, and anxiety (.30).

Developments during the 1970s

Assessment with adults and children during the 1970s saw a further elaboration and development of the trends of the 1960s as well as increased emphasis on structured interviews. The interest in structured interviews was fueled largely by criticisms about the poor reliability of psychiatric diagnosis. A typical structured interview would be completed by the interviewer either during or directly after the interview, and the data would be transformed into such scales as organicity, disorganization, or depression-anxiety.

Initial success with adult structured interviews (e.g., Present State Examination, Renard Diagnostic Interview) encouraged thinking regarding the further development of child-structured interviews both for global ratings and specific content areas. Child assessment became concerned not only with information derived from parents but also with the child's own experience. There was a trend toward direct questioning of the child, greater emphasis on differential diagnosis, and the development of parallel versions of structured interviews for both the parent(s) and child.

Behavioral strategies of interviewing for both children and adults not only emphasized the interviewee's unique situation but also provided a general listing of relevant areas for consideration. Kanfer and Grimm (1977) outlined the areas an interviewer should assess as:

1. Behavioral deficiencies
2. Behavioral excesses
3. Inappropriate environmental stimulus control
4. Inappropriate self-generated stimulus
5. Problem reinforcement contingencies

In a similar categorization, Lazarus (1973, 2005) developed his BASIC-ID model, which described a complete assessment as involving behaviors (B), affect (A), sensation (S), imagery (I), cognition (C), interpersonal relations (I), and need for pharmacological intervention/drugs (D).

Additional themes in the 1970s included interest in biographical data, online computer technology, and the training of interviewer skills. Specifically, efforts were made to integrate biographical data for predicting future behavior (suicide, dangerousness, prognosis for schizophrenia) and for inferring current traits. J. W. Johnson and Williams (1977) were instrumental in developing some of the earliest online computer technology to collect biographical data and to integrate it with test results. Although training programs were devised for interviewers, a central debate was whether interview skills could actually be significantly learned or improved (Wiens, 1976).

Whereas most reviews of the literature in the 1970s emphasized the advantages of a comprehensive structured format, family therapists were dealing with group processes in which formal interview structure was typically deemphasized. Because most family therapists were observing fluid interactional processes, they needed to develop a vocabulary different from that used in traditional psychiatric diagnosis. In fact, *DSM* categories were usually considered irrelevant because they described static characteristics of individuals rather than ongoing group processes. Few, if any, structured formats were available to assess family relationships.

Developments during the 1980s

Many of the trends, concepts, and instruments developed in the 1960s and 1970s were further refined and adapted for the 1980s. One important effort was the adaptation of many instruments to the *DSM-III* (1980) and *DSM-III-R* (1987). In addition, the increased delineation of childhood disorders required greater knowledge related to differential diagnosis and greater demand for structured interviews as adjuncts to assessment. Many of the efforts were consistent with the use of specific diagnostic criteria along with a demand for efficiency, cost-effectiveness, and accountability. Despite concerns regarding computer-based interpretations (Groth-Marnat & Schumaker, 1989), some of these functions were beginning to be performed by specific computer programs. Because interviews were becoming increasingly structured, with the inclusion of scales and specific diagnostic strategies, the distinction between tests and interviews was becoming less clear. In some contexts, aspects of interviewing were even replaced with computer-requested and computer-integrated information and combined with simple programs to aid in diagnosis, such as DIANO III (Spitzer, Endicott, & Cohen, 1974) and CATEGO (Wing, Cooper, & Sartorius, 1974). During the mid- and late 1980s, most clinicians, particularly those working in large institutions, used a combination of structured interviews and open-ended unstructured approaches. Some research focused on the importance of the initial interview regarding clinical decision making and later therapeutic outcome (Hoge, Andrews, Robinson, & Hollett, 1988; Turk & Salovey, 1985). There was also a greater appreciation and integration of the work from different disciplines and from differing theoretical persuasions (Hersen, 1988). Finally, greater emphasis was placed on the impact and implications of culture and gender on the assessment process (L. Brown, 1990).

The 1990s and into the Millennium

Two of the defining features of psychology in the 1990s were managed health care and the controversy over the validity of repressed memories. Both of these issues had significant implications for interviewing. Managed health care emphasized the cost-effectiveness of providing health services; and for interviewing, this means developing the required information in the least amount of time. Doing this may mean streamlining interviews by maximizing computer-derived information or paper-and-pencil forms. The use of computer-assisted interviewing brings up the larger issue of the extent to which practitioners need to spend face-to-face time with the client versus deriving information through other means. The development of single-session therapy (Hoyt, 1994) illustrates the potential brevity of information that might be required before making therapeutic interventions. There was also recognition that precise patient-treatment matching can optimize the treatment and potentially the cost-effectiveness of psychosocial interventions (Antony & Barlow, 2002; Beutler & Clarkin, 1990; Beutler, Clarkin, & Bongar, 2000).

The controversy over repressed memories has forced interviewers to clarify the extent to which the information they derive from clients represents literal as opposed to narrative truth. Research has consistently indicated that client self-reports are reconstructions of events (Henry, Moffitt, Caspi, Langley, & Silva, 1994; Loftus, 1993) and are likely to be particularly questionable for retrospective reports of psychosocial variables (Garb, 2007; Henry et al., 1994; Piasecki, Hufford, Solhan, & Trull, 2007). The even greater challenge to interviewers is to ensure that their interviewing style and method of questioning are not distorting the information derived from clients. This issue becomes intensely highlighted during interviews to investigate the possibility of childhood sexual abuse (see guidelines in S. White & Edelstein, 1991).

Further, continuing themes in the 1990s and into the millennium were the importance of interview strategies for special populations and the development of new technologies. It is clear that many diverse populations are more likely to be misdiagnosed. At least in part, this misdiagnosis results in worse outcomes compared with majority groups (Neighbors et al., 2007; Nguyen et al., 2007). The potential for misdiagnoses for minority groups demands that clinicians be aware of their biases, become knowledgeable regarding these subgroups, and make appropriate modifications to their interviews. Several new technologies are currently both available and becoming progressively more utilized. These include computer-administered interviews (Garb, 2007) as well as data derived from electronic diaries (Piasecki et al., 2007), and ambulatory sensors (Haynes & Yoshioka, 2007) that become a part of clinical interviews. The themes and issues related to cost-effectiveness, patient-treatment matching, recovered memories, use of new interview technologies, and strategies for interviewing special populations will continue to be important themes throughout the first one or two decades of the millennium.

ISSUES RELATED TO RELIABILITY AND VALIDITY

Although the interview is not a standardized test, it is a means of collecting data and, as such, can and should be subjected to some of the same types of psychometric considerations as a formal test. Evaluating the psychometric properties of interviews is important because interviews might introduce numerous sources of bias, particularly if the interviews are relatively unstructured. Reliability of interviewers is usually discussed in relation to interrater (interviewer) agreement. R. Wagner's (1949) early review of the literature found tremendous variation, ranging from .23 to .97 ($Mdn = .57$) for ratings of personal traits and $-.20$ to .85 ($Mdn. = .53$) for ratings of overall ability. Later reviews have generally found similar variations in interrater agreement (Arvey & Campion, 1982; L. Ulrich & Trumbo, 1965). The problem then becomes how to determine which ratings to trust and which to view with skepticism. Of particular relevance is why some interviewers focus on different areas and have different biases. A consistent finding is that, when interviewers were given narrow areas to assess and were trained in interviewer strategies, interrater reliability increased (Dougherty, Ebert, & Callender, 1986; Zedeck, Tziner, & Middlestadt, 1983). The consensus was that highly structured interviews were more reliable (Garb, 2007; Huffcutt & Arthur, 1994). However, increased structure undermines one of the greatest strengths of interviews—their flexibility. In many situations, a free-form, open-ended approach may be the only way to obtain some types of information.

Research on interview validity has typically focused on various sources of interviewer bias. Halo effects result from the tendency of an interviewer to develop a general impression of a person and then infer other seemingly related characteristics. For example, clients who are considered to express warmth may be seen as more competent or mentally healthy than they actually are. This clustering of characteristics may be incorrect, thereby producing distortions and exaggerations. Similarly, first impressions have been found to bias later judgments (W. Cooper, 1981). Confirmatory bias might occur when an interviewer makes an inference about a client and then directs the interview to elicit information that confirms the original inference. This bias typically occurs when clinicians develop initial diagnostic impressions from historical information and then ignore later relevant information since they are too busy confirming their initial impressions. In addition, a psychoanalytically oriented interviewer might direct questions related to early childhood traumas, possibly incorrectly confirming traditional psychoanalytic explanations of current adult behaviors. Similar to halo effects is the finding that one specific outstanding characteristic (educational level, physical appearance, etc.) can lead an interviewer to judge other characteristics that he or she incorrectly believes are related to the outstanding one. For example, physical attractiveness has been found to create interviewer bias in job applicants (Gilmore, Beehr, & Love, 1986). In a clinical context, physical attractiveness may result in practitioners' either deemphasizing pathology or, on occasion, exaggerating pathology because of discomfort the interviewer may feel over his or her feelings of attraction (L. Brown, 1990). Interviewers also may focus incorrectly on explanations of behavior that emphasize traits rather than situational determinants (Ross, 1977). This error is particularly likely when the interpretation of interview data relies heavily on psychological tests, because tests, by their nature, conceptualize and emphasize static characteristics of the person rather than ongoing interactional processes.

In addition to the interviewer's perceptual and interactional biases, interviewees themselves may distort their responses. For example, they may present an overly favorable view of themselves, particularly if they are relatively naive regarding their motivations. Distortions are most likely found in sensitive areas, such as sexual behavior. Some specific areas of distortions are represented by the finding that victims of automobile accidents typically exaggerated the amount of time they lost from work, 40% of respondents provided overestimates of their contributions to charity, and 17% of respondents reported their ages incorrectly (R. Kahn & Cannell, 1961). More extreme cases of falsification occur with outright (conscious) lies, delusions, confabulations, and lies by pathological (compulsive) liars that they partially believe themselves (Kerns, 1986). Inaccuracies based on retrospective accounts have been found to most likely occur related to psychosocial information (e.g., family conflict, onset of psychiatric symptoms) compared with variables such as change of residence, reading skill, height, and weight (B. Henry et al., 1994).

Reviews of interview validity, in which interviewer ratings were compared with outside criterion measures, have, like reliability measures, shown tremendous variability ranging from −.05 to +.75 (Arvey & Campion, 1982; Henry et al., 1994; Huffcutt & Arthur, 1994; J. Hunter & Hunter, 1984; L. Ulrich & Trumbo, 1965). One clear finding is that validity increases as the structure of the interview format increases (Huffcutt & Arthur, 1994; Marchese & Muchinsky, 1993). For example, a meta-analysis by Wiesner and Cronshaw (1988) found that unstructured interviews had validity coefficients of .20, structuring the interview increased the validity to .63, and structured interviews by a panel using consensus ratings increased validity coefficients to a quite respectable .64. However, the validity seems to vary according to the type of variable that is being assessed. Situational employment interviews (asking the interviewee what he or she would do in a particular situation) had higher validities (.50) than interviews used to assess past job-related behavior (.39) or rate psychological qualities such as dependability (.29; McDaniel et al., 1994). It has also been found that interview accuracy increases more when interviewees are held accountable for the process they went through when coming to their decisions, compared to being held accountable for the accuracy of their predictions (procedural versus outcome accountability; Brtek & Motowidlo, 2002).

The previous brief review indicates that adding structure to interviews and paying close attention to the procedure by which decisions are made typically results in higher levels of validity. It also means that information derived from unstructured interviews should be treated cautiously and treated as tentative hypotheses that need to be supported by other means. Interviewers should also continually question the extent to which their particular style, attitudes, and expectations might be compromising interview validity. Given the difficulties related to unstructured formats, a variety of formal structured clinical interviews has been developed. Additional information on the reliability and validity of the most frequently used structured clinical interviews is provided in the last section of this chapter.

ASSETS AND LIMITATIONS

Both structured and unstructured interviews allow clinicians to place test results in a wider, more meaningful context. In addition, biographical information from interviews can be used to help predict future behaviors; what a person has done in the past is an excellent guide to what he or she is likely to continue doing in the future. Factors for predicting suicide risk, success in certain occupations, and prognosis for certain disorders can usually be most effectively accomplished by attending to biographical data rather than test scores.

Because tests are almost always structured or "closed" situations, the unstructured or semistructured interview is typically the only time during the assessment process when the clinician can observe the client in an open, ambiguous situation. Observations can be made regarding how persons organize their responses, and inferences can be derived from subtle, nonverbal cues. These inferences can be followed up with further, more detailed questioning. This flexibility inherent in unstructured and semistructured interviews is frequently their strongest advantage over standardized tests. The focus during unstructured interviews is almost exclusively on the individual rather than on how that individual does or does not compare with a larger normative comparison group. Some types of information can be obtained only through this flexible, person-centered approach, which allows the interviewer to pay attention to idiosyncratic factors. In crisis situations when relatively rapid decisions need to be made, it can be impractical to take the time required to administer and interpret tests, leaving interviews and rapid screening devices as the only means of assessment. Finally, interviews allow clinicians to establish rapport and encourage client self-exploration. Rarely do clients reveal themselves or perform optimally on tests unless they first sense trust, openness, and a feeling of being understood.

The greatest difficulty with unstructured interviews is interviewer bias from perceptual and interactional processes such as the halo effect, confirmatory bias, and the primacy effect. This bias typically results in considerable variability for both reliability and validity as well as in difficulty comparing one subject with the next. One of the main reasons for diagnostic disagreement is variations in the information obtained (information variance) and variations in the criteria (criterion variance) used to conclude the presence or absence of a condition. Varation in interviewing strategies means that different practitioners develop and ask a wide variety of questions and apply standards for the presence of a condition, such as depression, in an inconsistent fashion. A further difficulty is the high cost of using trained interviewers for large-scale epidemiological studies.

Structured interviews have many distinct advantages over unstructured approaches. Because structured interviews have more psychometric precision, the results enable comparability between one case or population and the next. The standardized presentation allows for the development of reliable ratings, reduces information variance, and uses consistent diagnostic criteria (Garb, 2007; Summerfeldt & Antony, 2002). In addition, the comprehensiveness of many structured interviews reduces the likelihood of missing a diagnosis or set of relevant symptomology. Partially because of these advantages, structured clinical interviews have progressed from being used primarily for research to use in a number of clinical settings. At issue, however, is the time required for structured interviews. The more recently developed computer-assisted programs offer a potential method of countering this difficulty (Epstein & Klinkenberg, 2001; Garb, 2007). In addition, computer-administered interviews are comprehensive, and clients are more likely to disclose highly sensitive information when compared with clinician-administered interviews (Garb, 2007). Instruments such as the Diagnostic Interview Schedule and Diagnostic Interview for Children and Adolescents have been designed for administration by lay interviewers, thereby reducing the time required by professionals.

Although structured interviews generally have higher psychometric properties than unstructured formats, they tend to overlook the idiosyncrasies and richness of the person. In many cases, these unique aspects may go undetected and yet may make a significant difference in interpreting test scores or making treatment recommendations. Although still somewhat controversial (Helzer & Robins, 1988), another criticism of many clinicians and researchers is that a highly structured approach may not create enough rapport for the client to feel sufficiently comfortable about revealing highly personal information. This is truer for the highly structured interviews, such as the Diagnostic Interview Schedule, than for a semistructured instrument, such as the Schedule for Affective Disorders and Schizophrenia, which includes an initial, relatively unstructured component. However, M. Rosenthal (1989) has noted that rapport with structured instruments can be enhanced through carefully educating the client as to the importance and procedures of these more structured approaches.

Although many of the structured interviews have demonstrated adequate reliability, studies relating to validity have primarily focused on the general level of impairment or simple discriminations between psychiatric and nonpsychiatric populations. There has been considerable controversy over what exactly is an acceptable outside criterion measure regarding the "true" diagnosis. In-depth studies of construct validity or incremental validity have yet to be performed. Furthermore, far more work needs to be done on the treatment utility of structured interviews in areas such as prognosis, selection of treatment, and likely response to specific forms of pharmacological or psychotherapeutic interventions.

THE ASSESSMENT INTERVIEW AND CASE HISTORY

General Considerations

The previously mentioned historical and psychometric considerations indicate that no single correct way exists to conduct an unstructured or semistructured interview. Interviewer style is strongly influenced by theoretical orientation and by practical considerations. Persons strongly influenced by client-centered theories tend to be nondirective and avoid highly structured questions. This is consistent with the underlying belief that persons have the inner ability to change and organize their own behaviors. The goal of a client-centered interview, then, is to create the type of interpersonal relationship most likely to enhance this self-change. In contrast, a behavioral interview is more likely to be based on the assumption that change occurs because of specific external consequences. As a result, behavioral interviews are relatively structured because they are directed toward obtaining specific information that would help to design strategies based on altering external conditions. In addition, different interviewing styles and strategies work well with some clients but may be relatively ineffective with others.

A useful distinction is between a diagnostic interview and one that is more informal and exploratory. The goal of a diagnostic interview is to develop a specific diagnosis, usually based on the multiaxial *DSM-IV* model (see Othmer & Othmer, 1994; R. Rogers, 1995; Sommers-Flanagan & Sommers-Flanagan, 2003). Developing a diagnosis might follow a five-step process in which the clinician develops diagnostic clues, considers these in relation to diagnostic criteria, takes a psychiatric history, and, based on this information, develops a multiaxial diagnosis with corresponding estimates of prognosis (Othmer & Othmer, 1994). Such an interview is likely to be directive with a careful consideration of inclusion and exclusion criteria for different disorders. It is most likely to occur in a psychiatric or general medical setting. In contrast, many practitioners do not believe in the value of formal diagnosis and, accordingly, do not pursue a formal *DSM-IV* (1994) diagnosis. They might be more concerned with areas such as a client's coping style, social supports, family dynamics, or the nature of the disability. As such, their interviews might be less directive and more flexible. Again, neither style is right or wrong, but instead one style may be appropriate and effective in one context (or client) whereas it is ineffective or inappropriate in another context.

Often interviewers might wish to construct a semistructured interview format by listing in sequence the types of questions they would like to ask the person. To construct such a list, interviewers might consult Table 3.1 to note possibly relevant areas. Each of these areas might then be converted into specific questions. For example, the first few areas might be converted into this series of questions:

- "What are some important concerns that you have?"
- "Could you describe the most important of these concerns?"

- "When did the difficulty first begin?"
- "How often does it occur?"
- "Have there been any changes in how often it has occurred?"
- "What happens after the behavior(s) occurs?"

Table 3.1.   Checklist for an assessment interview and case history

History of the Problem

Description of the problem	Intensity and duration
Initial onset	Previous treatment
Changes in frequency	Attempts to solve
Antecedents/consequences	Formal treatment

Family Background

Socioeconomic level	Cultural background
Parent's occupations(s)	Parent's current health
Emotional/medical/history	Family relationships
Married/separated/divorced	Urban/rural upbringing
Family constellation	

Personal History

Infancy

Developmental milestones	Early medical history
Family atmosphere	Toilet training
Amount of contact with parents	

Early and Middle Childhood

Adjustment to school	Peer relationships
Academic achievement	Relationship with parents
Hobbies/activities/interests	Important life changes

Adolescence

All areas listed for early and middle childhood	Early dating
	Reaction to puberty
Presence of acting out (legal, drugs, sexual)	Childhood abuse

Early and Middle Adulthood

Career/occupational	Domestic violence
Interpersonal relationships	Medical/emotional history
Satisfaction with life goals	Relationship with parents
Hobbies/interests/activities	Economic stability
Marriage	Substance abuse

Late Adulthood

Medical history	Reaction to declining abilities
Ego integrity	Economic stability

Miscellaneous

Self-concept (like/dislike)	Somatic concerns (headaches, stomach-aches, etc.)
Happiest/saddest memory	
Earliest memory	Events that create happiness/sadness
Fears	Recurring/noteworthy dreams

Because clients vary regarding their personal characteristics (age, educational level, degree of cooperation) and type of presenting problem (childhood difficulties, legal problems, psychosis), the questions necessarily need to vary from person to person. Furthermore, any series of questions should not be followed rigidly but with a certain degree of flexibility, to allow exploring unique but relevant areas that arise during the interview.

Good interviewing is difficult to define, partly because different theoretical perspectives exist regarding clinician-client interaction. Furthermore, clinicians achieve successful interviews not so much by what they do or say but by making sure they express the proper attitude. Whereas clinicians from alternative theoretical persuasions might differ regarding areas such as their degree of directiveness or the type of information they should obtain, they would all agree that certain aspects of the relationship are essential (Patterson, 1989). These aspects include the interviewer's expression of sincerity, acceptance, understanding, genuine interest, warmth, and a positive regard for the worth of the person. If clinicians do not demonstrate these qualities, they are unlikely to achieve the goals of the interview, no matter how these are defined.

Patient ratings of the quality of interviews have been found to be dependent on the extent to which interviewers can understand the patient's emotions and detect emotional messages that are only partially expressed, particularly as these emotions are likely to be indirect and conveyed through nonverbal behaviors. Understanding a client's emotional responses is especially relevant in clinical interviews that focus on a client's personal difficulties. Typically, words are inadequate to accurately describe problem emotions, so interviewers must infer them from paraverbal or nonverbal expression. Reliance on nonverbal cues is highlighted by the assumption that nonverbal aspects of communication are likely to be a more powerful method of conveying information. For example, eye contact is most likely to convey involvement; rigidity of posture might suggest client defensiveness; and hand movements often occur beyond the person's conscious intent, suggesting nervousness, intensity, or relaxation. Mehrabian (1972) has supported this perspective with his estimates that the message received is 55% dependent on facial expression, 38% by tone, and only 7% by the content of what is said.

Interviewers vary in the extent to which they take notes during the interview. Some argue that note taking during an interview might increase a client's anxiety, raise questions regarding anonymity, increase the likelihood that he or she will feel like an object under investigation, and create an unnatural atmosphere. In contrast, many interviewers counter these arguments by pointing out that a loss of rapport rarely results solely from note taking during the interview, assuming, of course, that the interviewer can still spend a sufficient amount of time attending to the client. Ongoing note taking is also likely to capture more details and result in less memory distortion than recording material after the interview has been completed. Thus, an intermediate amount of note taking during the interview is recommended. If the interview is audiotaped or videotaped, the reasons for this procedure need to be fully explained, along with the assurance of confidentiality and the procuring of a signed agreement. Although audiotape or videotape recording is often awkward at first, usually the interviewer and client quickly forget that it is occurring.

Interview Tactics

Numerous tactics or types of statements have been proposed and studied. These include the clarification statement, verbatim playback, probing, confrontation, understanding, active listening, reflection, feedback, summary statement, random probing, self-disclosure, perception checking, use of concrete examples, and therapeutic double binds. Additional relevant topics are the importance of eye contact, self-disclosure, active listening, and touch. These areas are beyond the scope of this chapter, but the interested reader is referred to excellent discussions by Cormier and Cormier (1998), Sommers-Flanagan and Sommers-Flanagan (2003), Sattler and Hoge (2005), and Zuckerman (2005). The most relevant skills for interviewing do not come so much from memorizing interviewing tactics but develop from reviewing actual live or taped interview sessions. However, several important tactics of interviewing are described because they provide a general interviewing strategy.

Preliminaries

During the initial phase of the interview, practitioners need to ensure that they deal adequately with the following issues:

1. Organize the physical characteristics of the interview situation so that the room looks used but not untidy; lighting is optimal; seating is arranged so that the interviewer and client are neither too close nor too far and so that eye level is approximately equal.
2. Introduce yourself and indicate how you prefer to be addressed (Doctor, first name, etc.) and clarify how the client prefers to be addressed.
3. State the purpose of the interview, check the client's understanding of the interview, and clarify any discrepancies between these two understandings.
4. Explain how the information derived from the interview will be used.
5. Describe the confidential nature of the information, the limits of confidentiality, and special issues related to confidentiality (e.g., how the information might be obtained and used by the legal justice system). Further, explain that the client has the right not to discuss any information he or she does not wish to disclose. If the information will be sent to other persons, obtain a signed release of information.
6. Explain the role and activities you would like the client to engage in, the instruments that are likely to be used in the assessment, and the total length of time required. In some circumstances, this may be formalized into a written contract (Handelsman & Galvin, 1988).
7. Make sure that any fee arrangements have been clarified, including the hourly rate, total estimated cost, the amount the client versus a third party is likely to need to pay, and the interval between billing and the expected payment.

With the possible exception of fee arrangement (item 7), the preceding issues should be handled by a mental health practitioner rather than a secretary or receptionist. Covering these areas during the preliminary stages of the interview is likely to reduce the likelihood of miscommunications and later difficulties.

Directive versus Nondirective Interviews

The degree to which clinicians choose to be structured and directive during an interview depends on both theoretical and practical considerations. If time is limited, the interviewer needs to be direct and to the point. The interviewer will use a different approach for assessing a person who has been referred and will be returning to the referring person than for a person before conducting therapy with him or her. An ambiguous, unstructured approach probably makes an extremely anxious person even more anxious, while a direct approach may prove more effective. A passive, withdrawn client also is likely to initially require a more direct question-and-answer style. As stated previously, a less structured style often encourages deeper client self-exploration, enables clinicians to observe the client's organizational abilities, and may result in greater rapport, flexibility, and sensitivity to the client's uniqueness.

Frequently, behavioral interviews are characterized as being structured and directed toward obtaining a comprehensive description of actual behaviors and relevant cognitions, attitudes, and beliefs (see Chapter 4). Behavioral interviewing is often contrasted with the more unstructured psychodynamic approach, which investigates underlying motivations and hidden dynamics and assesses information that may not be within the person's ordinary awareness. Typically, these approaches are perceived as competing and mutually exclusive. Haas, Hendin, and Singer (1987) point out that this either/or position is not only unnecessary but unproductive, because each style of interviewing provides different types of information that could potentially compensate for the other's weaknesses. Using both approaches might increase interview breadth and validity. Exploring multiple facets of the person may include direct behavioral data (public communication), self-description, and private symbolization (Leary, 1957). Each of these levels may be useful for different purposes, and the findings from each level might be quite different from one another.

Sequence of Interview Tactics

Most authors recommend that interviewers begin with open-ended questions and, after observing the client's responses, use more direct questions to fill in gaps in their understanding (Beutler & Groth-Marnat, 2003; Othmer & Othmer, 2002; Sommers-Flanagan & Sommers-Flanagan, 2003). Although this sequence might begin with open-ended questions, it should typically lead to interviewer responses that are intermediate in their level of directiveness, such as facilitating comments, requesting clarification, and possibly confronting the client with inconsistencies.

An important advantage of open-ended questions is that they require clients to comprehend, organize, and express themselves with little outside structure. This is perhaps the only occasion in the assessment process that makes this requirement of clients, because most tests or structured interviews provide guidance in the form of specific, clear stimuli. When clients are asked open-ended questions, they will be most likely to express significant but unusual features about themselves. Verbal fluency, level of assertiveness, tone of voice, energy level, hesitations, and areas of anxiety can be noted. Hypotheses can be generated from these observations and further open-ended or more direct questions used to test these hypotheses. In contrast to these advantages, open-ended questions can potentially provide an overabundance of detailed, vague, and tangential information.

Interviewer responses that show an intermediate level of directiveness are facilitation, clarification, empathy, and confrontation. Facilitation of comments maintains or encourages the flow of conversation. This might be accomplished verbally ("Tell me more . . ." "Please continue...") or nonverbally (eye contact, nodding). These requests for clarification might be used when clients indicate, perhaps through subtle cues, that they have not fully expressed something regarding the topic of discussion. Requests for clarification can bring into the open material that was only implied. In particular, greater clarification might be achieved by requesting the client to be highly specific, such as asking him or her to provide concrete examples (a typical day or a day that best illustrates the problem behavior). Empathic statements ("It must have been difficult for you") can also facilitate client self-disclosure.

Sometimes interviewers might wish to confront, or at least comment on, inconsistencies in a client's information or behavior. Carkhuff (1969) has categorized the potential types of inconsistencies as being between what a person is versus what he or she wants to be, what he or she is saying versus what he or she is doing, and between the person's self-perception versus the interviewer's experience of the person. A confrontation might also challenge the improbable content of what he or she is reporting ("tall" stories).

The purpose of confrontations during assessment is to obtain more in-depth information about the client. In contrast, therapeutic confrontations are used to encourage client self-exploration and behavior change. If a practitioner is using the initial interview and assessment as a prelude to therapy, this distinction is less important. However, a confrontational style can produce considerable anxiety, which should be created only if sufficient opportunity exists to work through the anxiety. Usually a client is most receptive to confrontations when they are posed hypothetically as possibilities to consider rather than as direct challenges. Confrontations also require a sufficient degree of rapport to be sustained; unless this rapport is present, confrontations probably result in client defensiveness and a deterioration of the relationship.

Finally, direct, close-ended questions can be used to fill in gaps in what the client has stated. Thus, a continual flow can be formed between client-directed or client-organized responses and clinician-directed responses. This sequence, beginning with open-ended questions, then moving to intermediately structured responses (facilitation, clarification, confrontation), and finally ending in directive questions, should not be rigid but should vary throughout the interview.

Comprehensiveness

The basic focus of an assessment interview should be to define the problem behavior (nature of the problem, severity, related affected areas) and its causes (conditions that worsen or alleviate it, origins, antecedents, consequences). Interviewers might wish to use a checklist, such as the one in Table 3.1, to ensure they are covering most relevant areas. In using such a checklist, the interviewer might begin with a general question, such as "How were you referred here?" or "What are some areas that concern you?" Observations and notes can then be made about the way the client organizes his or her responses, what he or she says, and the way he or she says it. The interviewer could use facilitating, clarifying, and confronting responses to obtain more information. Finally, the interviewer could review the checklist on family background to see if all relevant areas were covered sufficiently. If some areas or aspects of areas were not covered, the interviewer might ask direct questions, such as "What was your father's occupation?" or "When did your mother and father divorce?" The interviewer could then begin the same sequence for personal history related to infancy, middle childhood, and so on. Table 3.1 is not comprehensive but is intended as a general guide for most interview situations. If practitioners generally evaluate specific client types (child abuse, suicide, brain-impaired), this checklist may need additional guidelines and/or be used as an adjunct to commercially available structured interviews, such as the Personality Disorder Examination (Loranger, 1988), Neuropsychological Status Examination (Schinka, 1983), or Lawrence Psychological-Forensic Examination (Lawrence, 1984).

Avoidance of "Why" Questions

It is best to avoid "why" questions because they are likely to increase client defensiveness. A "why" question typically sounds accusatory or critical and thus forces the client to account for his or her behavior. In addition, clients are likely to become intellectual in this situation, thereby separating themselves from their emotions. An alternative approach is to preface the question with either "What is your understanding of ..." or "How did it occur that ..." rather than "why?" These options are more likely to result in a description rather than a justification and to keep clients more centered on their emotions.

Nonverbal Behaviors

Interviewers should also be aware of their own as well as their clients' nonverbal behaviors. In particular, interviewers might express their interest by maintaining eye contact, being facially responsive, and attending verbally and nonverbally, such as through occasionally leaning forward.

Concluding the Interview

Any interview is bound by time constraints. An interviewer might help to ensure observance of these constraints by alerting the client when only 5 or 10 minutes remain until the arranged completion of the interview. This allows the client or interviewer to obtain final relevant information. There should also be an opportunity for the client to ask any questions or provide comments. At the end of an interview or assessment session, the interviewer should summarize the main themes of the interview and, if appropriate, make any recommendations.

MENTAL STATUS EXAMINATION

The mental status exam was originally modeled after the physical medical exam; just as the physical medical exam is designed to review the major organ systems, the mental status exam reviews the major systems of psychiatric functioning (appearance, cognitive function, insight, etc.). Since its introduction into American psychiatry by Adolf Meyer in 1902, it has become the mainstay of patient evaluation in most psychiatric settings. Most psychiatrists consider it as essential to their practice as the physical examination is in general medicine (Rodenhauser & Fornal, 1991).

A mental status examination can be used as part of a formal psychological assessment for a variety of reasons. A brief mental status examination might be appropriate before assessment to determine the appropriateness of more formal psychological testing. If, for example, a patient was unable to determine where he or she was and had significant memory impairments, testing with most instruments might be too difficult and could thereby result in needless distress. Such a screening might also be used to determine basic case management issues such as hospitalization or placing the patient under close observation. A mental status examination can also be used as part of an assessment using formal psychological tests. The "raw" data from the exam can be selectively integrated with general background information to present a coherent portrait of the person and assist in diagnosis.

Despite its popularity among psychiatrists, this form of interviewing is not typically used by psychologists, partly because many areas reviewed by the mental status exam are already covered during the assessment interview and through the interpretation of psychological test results. Many psychological tests cover these areas in a more precise, in-depth, objective, and validated manner with scores being compared to appropriate norms. A client's appearance, affect, and mood are usually noted by attending to behavioral observations. A review of the history and nature of the problem is likely to pick up areas such as delusions, misinterpretations, and perceptual disorders (hallucinations). Likewise, interview data and psychological test results typically assess a client's fund of knowledge, attention, insight, memory, abstract reasoning, and level of social judgment. However, the mental status examination reviews all of the preceding areas in a relatively brief, systematic manner. Furthermore, there are situations, such as intakes in an acute medical or psychiatric hospital, where insufficient time is available to evaluate the client with psychological tests.

Numerous sources in the psychiatric literature provide thorough guidelines for conducting a mental status exam (Crary & Johnson, 1981; H. Kaplan & Sadock, 2001; Othmer & Othmer, 2002; Robinson, 2001; Sommers-Flanagan & Sommers-Flanagan, 2003), and R. Rogers (2001) has provided a review of the more structured mental status exams. This literature indicates that practitioners vary widely in how they conduct the mental status examination. The most unstructured versions involve merely the clinician's use of the mental status examination as a set of general guidelines. The more structured versions range from comprehensive instruments that assess both general psychopathology and cognitive impairment to those that focus primarily on cognitive impairment. For example, the comprehensive North Carolina Mental Status Examination (Ruegg, Ekstrom, Evans, & Golden, 1990) includes 36 items that are rated on a 3-point scale (not present, slight or occasional, marked or repeated) to cover the important clinical dimensions of physical appearance, behavior, speech, thought processes, thought content, mood, affect, cognitive functioning, orientation, recent memory, immediate recall, and remote memory. Another similar comprehensive instrument is the Missouri Automated Mental Status Examination Checklist (Hedlund, Sletten, Evenson, Altman, & Cho, 1977), which requires the examiner to make ratings on nine areas of functioning: general appearance, motor behavior, speech and thought, mood and affect, other emotional reactions, thought content, sensorium, intellect, and insight and judgment. The checklist includes 119 possible ratings, but the examiner makes ratings in only those areas he or she judges to be relevant.

Despite extensive development, the more comprehensive mental status examinations have not gained wide acceptance. In contrast, the narrower structured mental status examinations that focus more exclusively on cognitive impairment are used quite extensively. One of the most popular has been the Mini Mental Status Examination (Folstein, Folstein, & McHugh, 1975). It comprises 11 items designed to assess orientation, registration, attention, calculation, and language. It has excellent interrater and test-retest reliabilities (usually well above .80), correlates with WAIS IQs (.78 for verbal IQ), and is sensitive to global and left-hemisphere deficits (but not right-hemisphere impairment; R. Rogers, 1995; Tombaugh, McDowell, Kristjansson, & Hubley, 1996). Clinicians who wish to develop knowledge and skills in conducting mental status examinations are encouraged to consult the preceding sources.

The following descriptions of the typical areas covered serve as a brief introduction to this form of interviewing. The outline is organized around the categories recommended by Crary and Johnson (1981), and a checklist of relevant areas is included in Figure 3.1. Interviewers can answer the different areas on the checklist either during or after a mental status examination. The tabled information can then be used to answer relevant questions relating to the referral question, to help in diagnosis, or to add to other test data. Such a checklist is important because clinicians not using similar checklists have been found to frequently omit crucial information (Ruegg et al., 1990).

General Appearance and Behavior

This area assesses material similar to that requested in the "behavioral observations" section of a psychological report (see Chapter 15). A client's clothing, posture, gestures, speech, personal care/hygiene, and any unusual physical features, such as physical handicaps, tics, or grimaces, are noted. Attention is given to the degree to which his or her behavior conforms to social expectations, but this is placed in the context of his or her culture and social position. Additional important areas are facial expressions, eye contact, activity level, degree of cooperation, physical attractiveness, and attentiveness. Is the

Name _____   Observer's Name _____

			No Data	Present	Absent
APPEARANCE		1. unkempt, unclean, disheveled.............			
		2. clothing and/or grooming atypical........			
		3. unusual physical characteristics.........			
COMMENTS RE APPEARANCE:					
BEHAVIOR	Posture	4. slumped....................................			
		5. rigid, tense..............................			
	Facial Expression Suggests	6. anxiety, fear, apprehension..............			
		7. depression, sadness......................			
		8. anger, hostility.........................			
		9. absence of feeling, blandness...........			
		10. atypical, unusualness....................			
	General Body Movements	11. accelerated, increased speed............			
		12. decreased, slowed.......................			
		13. atypical, unusual.......................			
		14. restlessness, fidgetiness...............			
	Speech	15. rapid speech............................			
		16. slowed speech...........................			
		17. loud speech.............................			
		18. soft speech.............................			
		19. mute....................................			
		20. atypical quality, slurring, stammer......			
BEHAVIOR	Therapist-Patient Relationship	21. domineering, controlling................			
		22. submissive, overly compliant, dependent..			
		23. provocative, hostile, challenging.......			
		24. suspicious, guarded, evasive............			
		25. uncooperative, non-compliant............			
COMMENTS RE BEHAVIOR:					
FEELING (AFFECT AND MOOD)		26. inappropriate to thought content........			
		27. increased lability of affect............			
		predominant mood is:			
		28. blunted, dull, bland....................			
		29. euphoria, elation.......................			
		30. anger, hostility........................			
		31. anxiety, fear, apprehension.............			
		32. depression, sadness.....................			
COMMENTS RE FEELING:					
PERCEPTION		33. illusions...............................			
		34. auditory hallucinations.................			
		35. visual hallucinations...................			
		36. other types of hallucinations...........			
COMMENTS RE PERCEPTION:					
THINKING	Intellectual Functioning	37. impaired level of consciousness..........			
		38. impaired attention span, distractible....			
		39. impaired abstract thinking..............			
		40. impaired calculation ability............			
		41. impaired intelligence...................			
	Orientation	42. disoriented to person...................			
		43. disoriented to place....................			
		44. disoriented to time.....................			
	Memory	45. impaired recent memory..................			
		46. impaired remote memory..................			
	Insight	47. denies presence of psychological problems.........................			
		48. blames others or circumstances for problems.........................			
	Judgment	49. impaired ability to make routine decisions.........................			
		50. impaired impulse control................			
THINKING	Thought Content	51. obsessions..............................			
		52. compulsions.............................			
		53. phobias.................................			
		54. depersonalization.......................			
		55. suicidal ideation.......................			
		56. homicidal ideation......................			
		57. delusions...............................			
	Stream of Thought	58. associational disturbance...............			
COMMENTS RE THINKING:					

DIAGNOSIS: _____

as manifested by the following M.S.E. items

____ ____ ____ ____ ____ ____

____ ____ ____ ____ ____ ____

Figure 3.1   Format for mental status and history

From "Mental Status Examination" by W. G. Crary and C. W. Johnson, 1981. In, Johnson, C. W., Snibbe, J. R., and Evans, L. A. (Eds.), *Basic Psychopathology: A Programmed Text, 2nd ed.* Lancaster: MIP Press, pp. 55-56. With kind permission of Springer Science and Business Media.

client friendly, hostile, seductive, or indifferent? Do any bizarre behaviors or significant events occur during the interview? In particular, speech might be fast or slow, loud or soft, or include a number of additional unusual features. Figure 3.1 includes a systematic checklist of relevant areas of behavior and appearance.

Feeling (Affect and Mood)

A client's *mood* refers to the dominant emotion expressed during the interview, whereas *affect* refers to the client's range of emotions. Information related to affect and mood is inferred from the content of the client's speech, facial expressions, and body movements. The type of affect can be judged according to variables such as its depth, intensity, duration, and appropriateness. The client might be cold or warm, distant or close, labile, and, as is characteristic of schizophrenia, his or her affect might be blunted or flattened. The client's mood might also be euphoric, hostile, anxious, or depressed.

Perception

Different clients perceive themselves and their world in a wide variety of ways. It is especially important to note whether there are any illusions or hallucinations. The presence of auditory hallucinations are most characteristic of schizophrenics, whereas vivid visual hallucinations are more characteristic of persons with organic brain syndromes.

Thinking

Intellectual Functioning

Any assessment of higher intellectual functioning needs to be made in the context of a client's educational level, socioeconomic status, and familiarity and identification with a particular culture. If a low level of intellectual functioning is consistent with a general pattern of poor academic and occupational achievement, a diagnosis of intellectual disability might be supported. However, if a person performs poorly on tests of intellectual functioning and yet has a good history of achievement, organicity might be suspected.

Intellectual functioning typically involves reading and writing comprehension, general fund of knowledge, ability to do arithmetic, and the degree to which the client can interpret the meaning of proverbs. Throughout the assessment, clinicians typically note the degree to which the client's thoughts and expressions are articulate versus incoherent. Sometimes clinicians might combine assessments of intellectual functioning with some short, formal tests such as the Bender, with an aphasia screening test, or even with portions of the WAIS-III or WISC-III.

Orientation

The ability of clients to be oriented can vary in the degree to which they know who they are (person), where they are (place), and when current and past events have occurred or are occurring (time). Clinical observation indicates the most frequent type of disorientation is for time; disorientation for place and person occurs less frequently. When disorientation does occur for place, and especially for person, the condition is relatively severe. Disorientation is most consistent with organic conditions. If a person is oriented in all three spheres, this is frequently abbreviated as "oriented X3."

Related to the orientation of clients is their *sensorium,* which refers to how intact their physiological processes are to receiving and integrating information. *Sensorium* might refer to hearing, smell, vision, and touch and might range from being clouded to clear. Can the client attend to and concentrate on the outside world, or are these processes interrupted? The client might experience unusual smells, hear voices, or have the sense that his or her skin is tingling. *Sensorium* can also refer to the client's level of consciousness, which may vary from hyperarousal and excitement to drowsiness and confusion. Disorders of a client's sensorium often reflect organic conditions but may also be consistent with psychosis.

Memory, Attention, and Concentration

Because memory retrieval or acquisition requires attention and concentration, these three functions are frequently considered together. Long-term memory is often assessed by requesting information regarding the client's general fund of information (e.g., important dates, major cities in a country, three major heads of state since 1900). Some clinicians include the Information or Digit Span subtests from the WAIS-IV/WISC-IV or other formal tests of a similar nature. Recall of a sentence or paragraph might be used to assess short-term memory for longer, more verbally meaningful information. In addition, clients' long-term memory might be evaluated by measuring recall of their major life events, and the accuracy of their recall can be compared with objective records of these events (e.g., year graduated from high school, date of marriage). It is often useful to record any significant distortions of selective recall in relation to life events as well as to note the client's attitudes toward his or her memory.

Short-term memory might be assessed by either requesting that clients recall recent events (most recent meal, how they got to the appointment) or by having them repeat digits forward and backward. Again, the WAIS-IV/WISC-IV Digit Span subtest, or at least a similar version of it, might be used. Serial sevens (counting forward by adding seven each time) can be used to assess how distractible or focused they are. Persons who are anxious and preoccupied have a difficult time with serial sevens as well as with repeating digits forward and, especially, backward.

Insight and Judgment

Clients vary in their ability to interpret the meaning and impact of their behavior on others. They also vary widely in their ability to provide for themselves, evaluate risks, and make plans. Adequate insight and judgment involves developing and testing hypotheses regarding their own behavior and the behavior of others. Clients also need to be assessed to determine why they believe they were referred for evaluation and, in a wider context, their attitudes toward their difficulties. How do they relate their past history to current difficulties, and how do they explain these difficulties? Where do they place the blame for their difficulties? Based on their insights, how effectively can they solve problems and make decisions?

Thought Content

A client's speech can often be considered a reflection of his or her thoughts. The client's speech may be coherent, spontaneous, and comprehensible or may contain unusual features. It may be slow or fast, be characterized by sudden silences, or be loud or unusually soft. Is the client frank or evasive, open or defensive, assertive or passive, irritable, abusive, or sarcastic? Consideration of a person's thoughts is often divided into thought content and thought processes. Thought contents such as delusions might suggest a psychotic condition, but delusions may also be consistent with certain organic disorders, such as dementia or chronic amphetamine use. The presence of compulsions or obsessions should be followed up with an assessment of the client's degree of insight into the appropriateness of these thoughts and behaviors. Thought processes such as the presence of rapid changes in topics might reflect flighty ideas. The client might also have difficulty producing a sufficient number of ideas, include an excessive number of irrelevant associations, or ramble aimlessly.

INTERPRETING INTERVIEW DATA

Interpreting and integrating interview data into the psychological report inevitably involves clinical judgment. Even with the use of structured interviews, the clinician still must determine which information to include or exclude. Thus, all the potential cautions associated with clinical judgment need to be considered (see Chapter 1). Caution is particularly important because life decisions and the success of later treatment may be based on conclusions and recommendations described in the report.

Several general principles can be used to interpret interview data. The interview is the primary instrument that clinicians use to develop tentative hypotheses regarding their clients. Thus, interview data can be evaluated by determining whether these hypotheses are supported by information outside the interview. Interview data that is supported by test scores can be given greater emphasis in the final report if it is relevant to the referral question. Even material that is highly supported throughout different phases of the interview process should not be included unless it relates directly to the purpose of the referral.

There is a continuum in handling interview information that varies according to the extent the information will be interpreted. On one hand, the information might be merely reorganized into a chronological history of the person's life. This would emphasize repeating the information in as objective and accurate a manner as possible. Typically this is done in the history section of a psychological report. On the other hand, interview data can be considered raw data to be interpreted. It is thus similar to the data from formal psychological tests. It might, therefore, be used to make inferences related to a client's personality, coping style, or mood and affect.

One method of organizing interview information is to use the information to develop a coherent narrative of the person's life. For example, describing how early family patterns resulted in emotionally sensitive areas ("scar" tissue) can be used to help explain current symptom patterns and difficulties in interpersonal relationships. A different sort of history might trace how interest in a vocation was first begun (early childhood daydreams regarding occupations) and how this progressed and developed as the person matured. Another person might present difficulties related to authority figures. Specific details relating to these difficulties might emerge, such as the client's feeling like a martyr and eventually inappropriately expressing extreme anger toward the authority figure(s). A careful review of the client's history might reveal how he or she becomes involved in these recurring relationships and how he or she typically attempts to resolve them. Persons who are frequently depressed might distance themselves from others by their behavior and then be confused about why relationships seem to be difficult. Often these themes emerge during a carefully conducted interview, yet aspects of the themes (or the entire themes themselves) are not apparent to the interviewee.

Interview data might also be organized around various domains (see further discussion in Chapter 15). A grid can be used to organize these domains. The various domains might be listed on the left side of the grid with the top of the grid listing the sources of data (of which the interview might be one of a variety of sources of information; see Figure 15.1 in Chapter 15). Domains might include mood and affect, cognitions, level of resistance, symptom patterns, or coping style. This approach treats interview data in much the same manner as data from psychological tests.

There is no one strategy for sensitizing interviewers to the types and patterns of recurring themes they may encounter during interviews. Inevitably, clinical judgment is a significant factor. The accuracy and types of judgments depend on the theoretical perspective of the interviewer, knowledge regarding the particular difficulty the interviewer is investigating, past experience, types of questions asked, and purpose of the interview.

STRUCTURED INTERVIEWS

Standardized psychological tests and structured interviews were developed to reduce the problems associated with open-ended interviews. They both serve to structure the stimuli presented to the person and reduce the role of clinical judgment. Because structured interviews generate objective ratings on the same areas, they have the advantage of making possible comparisons between one case or population and the next. Typically, these interviews vary in their degree of structure, the relative expertise required to administer them, and the extent to which they serve as screening procedures designed for global measurement or as tools used to obtain specific diagnoses.

Before structured interviews could be developed, clear, specific criteria needed to be created relating to symptom patterns and diagnoses. Developing these clear, specific criteria ideally helped to reduce the amount of error caused by vague guidelines for exclusion or inclusion in different categories (*criterion variance*). These criteria then needed to be incorporated into the interview format and interview questions. *Information variance* refers to the variability in amount and type of information derived from interviews with patients. In most unstructured interviews, information variance is caused by the wide differences in content and phrasing because of factors such as the theoretical orientation of the interviewer. Structured interviews correct for this by requesting the same or similar questions from each client.

The first popular system of specific criterion-based diagnosis was developed by Feighner et al. (1972) and provided clear, behaviorally oriented descriptions of 16 psychiatric disorders based on the *DSM-II* (1968). Clinicians using the Feighner criteria were found to have an immediate and marked increase in interrater diagnostic reliability. The descriptions of and relevant research on the Feighner criteria were published in Woodruff, Goodwin, and Guze's (1974) book, *Psychiatric Diagnosis.* Several interviews, such as the Renard Diagnostic Interview (Helzer et al., 1981), incorporated the Feighner criteria. Spitzer, Endicott, and Robins (1978) further altered and elaborated the Feighner criteria to develop the Research Diagnostic Criteria. Simultaneous with the development of the Research Diagnostic Criteria, Endicott and Spitzer (1978) developed the Schedule for Affective Disorders and Schizophrenia (SADS), which was based on the new Research and Diagnostic Criteria. When new versions of the *DSM* were published (1980, 1987, 1994, 2000), revisions of previous interviews typically incorporated the most recent *DSM* criteria along with elements of the Feighner criteria and/or the Research Diagnostic Criteria.

As noted earlier, the reliability of structured interviews has been found to vary depending on the specificity or precision of the rating or diagnosis. Whereas the highest reliabilities have been found for global assessment (presence/absence of psychopathology), much lower reliabilities have generally been found for the assessment of specific types of behaviors or syndromes. Likewise, high reliabilities have been found for overt behaviors, but reliability has been less satisfactory for more covert aspects of the person, such as obsessions, fears, and worries. Reliability also tends to be lower when clinicians are asked to attempt exact estimates regarding behavioral frequencies and for inferences of multifaceted aspects of the person derived from complex clinical judgments.

Most early studies on validity were based on item content (content validity) or degree of accuracy in distinguishing between broad areas of psychopathology (psychiatric/ nonpsychiatric). More recent trends have attempted to assess the accuracy of far more specific areas. However, most validity studies have suffered from an absence of clear, commonly agreed-on criteria. Although structured interviews were attempts to improve on previous, imperfect instruments (unstructured interviews, standardized tests), the structured interviews themselves could not be compared with anything better. For example, the "procedural validity" strategy is based on comparing lay interviewers' diagnoses with diagnoses derived from trained psychiatrists. Although the psychiatrist's diagnosis may be better than the layperson's, diagnoses by trained psychiatrists still cannot be said to be an ultimate, objective, and completely accurate standard. Furthermore, there is confusion about whether actual validity is being measured (which would assume psychiatrists' diagnoses are the true, accurate ones) or merely a version of interrater reliability. At the core of this issue is the very nature of how diagnosis is defined and the degree to which it is actually helpful in treatment (see Beutler & Malik, 2002; Widiger & Clark, 2000).

Future studies need to involve aspects of what has previously been discussed as construct validity. The focus on construct validity means looking more carefully at structured interviews in relationship to etiology, course, prognosis, and treatment utility relating to areas such as the appropriate selection of types of treatments and the likelihood of favorable responses to these treatments. Validity studies also need to look at the interaction between and implications of multiple criterion measures, including behavioral assessment, checklists, rating scales, self-report inventories, biochemical indices, and neuropathological alterations.

Since the mid-1970s, there has been a proliferation of structured interviews for a wide range of areas. Clinicians working in specific areas often select structured interviews directed toward diagnosing the disorders they are most likely to encounter. For example, some situations might benefit from using the Anxiety Disorders Interview Schedule (T. Brown, DiNardo, & Barlow, 1994) to make clear distinctions between anxiety disorders and substance abuse and between psychosis and major affective disorders. Other contexts might be best served by the Eating Disorder Examination (EDE; Z. Cooper & Fairburn, 1987) or the Structured Interview for *DSM-IV* Dissociative Disorders (SCID-D; Steinberg, 1993). Three categories of structured interviews with representative frequently used instruments are included in Table 3.2 and have been extensively reviewed in R. Roger's (1995) *Diagnostic and Structured Interviewing: A Handbook for Psychologists.* One consideration in selecting these instruments is that, because most structured interviews are undergoing continuous revisions, the most up-to-date research should be consulted to ensure that practitioners obtain the most recently revised versions. The following pages provide an overview of the most frequently used and most extensively researched structured interviews.

Structured Clinical Interview for the *DSM-IV*

The SCID (First, Spitzer, Gibbon, & Williams, 1996, 1997; Spitzer et al., 1987) is the most frequently used structured interview (see description and updates at www.scid4.org). It is a clinician-administered, comprehensive broad-spectrum instrument that adheres closely to the *DSM-IV*-TR decision trees for psychiatric diagnosis. A certain degree

Table 3.2.   Frequently used structured interviews by categories

I. *Assessment of Axis I disorders*
   Schedule of Affective Disorders and Schizophrenia (SADS) and Schedule of
   Affective Disorders and Schizophrenia for School-Age Children (K-SADS)
   Diagnostic Interview Schedule (DIS) and Diagnostic Interview for Children (DISC)
   Structured Clinical Interview for *DSM-IV* (SCID)
   Diagnostic Interview for Children and Adolescents (DICA)

II. *Assessment of Axis II disorders*
   Structured Interview for *DSM-IV* Personality Disorders (SIDP)
   Personality Disorder Examination (PDE)
   Structured Clinical Interview for *DSM-III-R* Personality Disorders (SCID-II)

III. *Focused structured interviews*
   Anxiety Disorders Interview Schedule (ADIS)
   Diagnostic Interview for Borderlines (DIB)
   Psychopathy Checklist (PCL)
   Structured Interview for *DSM-IV*-Dissociative Disorders (SCID-D)
   Structured Interview of Reported Symptoms (SIRS)
   Psychosocial Pain Inventory (PSPI)
   Comprehensive Drinker Profile (CDP)
   Eating Disorder Examination (EDE)
   Structured Interview of Sleep Disorders (SIS-D)
   Substance Use Disorders Diagnostic Schedule (SUDDS)

of flexibility is built in so that administration can be tailored to different populations and contexts. Thus, slightly different forms are used for psychiatric patients (SCID-In/Patient), outpatients (SCID-Out/Patients), and nonpatients (SCID-Non/Patients). Criticisms that the early version of the SCID had sacrificed clinical information so that it would be more user-friendly for clinicians resulted in a revision that emphasized a clear, easy-to-use version for clinical contexts (the SCID-Clinical Version or SCID-CV; First et al., 1997) and a longer, more in-depth version for research (SCID-I or SCID-Research Version; First, Spitzer, et al., 1996). Whereas these versions of the SCID are directed toward Axis I diagnoses, a separate version has been developed for the diagnosis of Axis II disorders (SCID-II; Spitzer, Williams, Gibbon, & First, 1990). A further variation, the SCID-D-Revised (Steinberg, 1993), has been developed using *DSM-IV* criteria for the assessment of dissociative disorders. The SCID and its variations include several open-ended questions as well as a skip structure, which enables the interviewer to branch into new areas dependent on the client's previous responses. Because clinical judgment is essential throughout the interview, the SCID should be administered only by trained professionals. To increase incremental validity, the authors encourage the inclusion of relevant additional data in making final diagnostic decisions.

The SCID, along with its variations, is the most comprehensive structured interview available. As a result, administration time can be considerable even with the in-built screening questions and skip structure. Many individual clinicians and treatment sites deal with this by primarily administering the modules they are most concerned with. For example, a treatment center specializing in substance abuse might administer the module for Psychoactive Substance Use Disorders along with the SCID-II when the comorbidity of personality disorders is suspected. Administration time might also be reduced by administering the computerized mini-SCID (First, Gibbon, Williams, & Spitzer, 1996), which has been designed to screen for possible Axis I disorders. In addition, a computerized SCID-II (AutoSCID-II; First, Gibbon, et al., 1996) that can also potentially reduce clinician time is available (www.mhs.com). Although it can be administered by telephone, this procedure is discouraged, given the poor agreement between telephone and face-to-face diagnoses (Cacciola, Alterman, Rutherford, McKay, & May, 1999).

The reliability studies have resulted in overall moderate, but quite variable, test-retest and interrater reliabilities (First & Gibbon, 2004). For example, interrater agreement using the SCID-II for common diagnostic categories ranges between .40 and .86 with a mean of .59 (First, Spitzer, Gibbon, & Williams, 1995). Riskind, Beck, Berchick, Brown, and Steer (1987) found that several difficult-to-distinguish diagnostic categories had relatively good levels of interrater agreement. These included generalized anxiety disorders (.79, 86% agreement), depressive disorders (.72, 82% agreement; Riskind et al., 1987), panic disorders (k=.86), and major depression (k = .81; J. Reich & Noyes, 1987). Test-retest reliabilities over a two-week interval for psychiatric patients was fair to good (overall weighted kappas = .61) but poor for nonpatients (overall weighted kappas = .37; J. B. Williams et al., 1992).

For the most part, validity studies of the SCID have assumed that *DSM-IV* diagnoses are the benchmark for making comparisons of diagnostic accuracy. Thus, "procedural validity" has often been assumed since the SCID has closely paralleled the diagnostic criteria derived from the *DSM-IV* (R. Rogers, 2001). A representative validity study found good agreement (k = .83) between interviewer ratings and cross ratings of interviewer videotapes by two senior psychiatrists (Maziade et al., 1992). Other studies have found considerable diagnostic overlap within Axis I disorders and between Axis I and Axis II disorders (Alnacs & Torgerson, 1989; Brawman-Mintzer et al., 1993). However, evaluating the meaning of this overlap is difficult because the extent to which it is caused by instrument error versus true comorbidity (i.e., the frequent occurrence of anxiety and depression) is difficult to determine. In contrast to these mostly favorable studies, a number of studies have found generally poor agreement between SCID and clinician-based diagnosis (Shear et al., 2000; Steiner, Tebes, Sledge, & Walker, 1995). In summary, the strength of the SCID is its impressive breadth of coverage, use of modules targeted toward specific areas, and close parallel with the *DSM-IV*. Its weaknesses are its wide variation in reliability and its need for further validity studies, particularly relating it to other diagnostic measures.

Schedule for Affective Disorders and Schizophrenia

The SADS (Endicott & Spitzer, 1978) is a clinician-administered, extensive, semistructured interview that has been the most widely used structured interview for clinical research purposes. Although it was originally designed for differential diagnosis between affective disorders and schizophrenia, it has evolved to include a much wider range of symptoms and allows the interviewer to consider many different diagnostic categories. A wide range of disorders is considered within the SADS, but its primary strength lies in obtaining fine detail regarding different subtypes of affective disorders and schizophrenia (Rogers, Jackson, & Cashiel, 2004). The interview rates clients on six gradations of impairment from which diagnoses are reached using the clear, objective categories derived from Spitzer et al.'s (1978) Research Diagnostic Criteria (RDC). The SADS is divided into adult versions for current symptoms, occurrence of lifetime symptoms, and degree of change. There is a further version for the assessment of children's difficulties (K-SADS). Two modifications for the SADS have been the inclusion of anxiety disorders (SADS-LA; Fyer, Endicott, Manuzza, & Klein, 1985, 1995) and eating disorders (EAT-SADS-L; Herzog, Keller, Sacks, Yeh, & Lavori, 1992).

Adult Version

The adult version of the SADS (Endicott & Spitzer, 1978) is designed to be administered in two different parts, the first focusing on the client's current illness and the second on past episodes. This division roughly corresponds with the three different versions of the SADS. The first is the regular version (SADS), the second is the lifetime version (SADS-L, which is actually the second half of the SADS), and the third is the SADS-C, which measures changes in the client. The SADS-L is directed toward diagnosing the possible presence of psychiatric disturbance throughout the person's life. The SADS and SADS-L are the most extensively used. Because the questions in the SADS are directed toward current symptoms and those symptoms experienced one week before the illness, it is most appropriate for administration when the client is having current difficulties. In contrast, the SADS-L is most appropriate when there is no current illness. To make accurate ratings, interviewers are allowed to use a wide range of sources (client's family, medical records) and ask a number of different questions. Final ratings are made on a 6-point Likert-type scale. Administration involves more than 200 items and takes from 1.5 to 2 hours and should be conducted only by a psychiatrist, psychologist, or psychiatric social worker. The end product is eight summary scales:

1. Mood and ideation
2. Endogenous features
3. Depressive-associated features
4. Suicidal ideation and behavior
5. Anxiety
6. Manic syndrome
7. Delusions-hallucinations
8. Formal thought disorder

Interrater reliabilities for the specific diagnostic categories have been found to be quite high, with the exception of the Formal Thought Disorder Scale (Endicott & Spitzer, 1978). The low reliability of this scale may have been because few of the patients in the Endicott and Spitzer sample showed clear patterns of disordered thoughts, which resulted in high variability for the ratings. Test-retest reliabilities were likewise good, ranging from .88 for Manic Disorders to .52 for Chronic and Intermittent Depressive Disorder (Spiker & Ehler, 1984). The exception was a low reliability for schizoaffective, depressed (.24), but this was probably because of the small number of patients included in this category, which resulted in limited variance. Using a different and possibly more appropriate statistical method, reliability increased to .84. Overall, the SADS has demonstrated excellent reliability, particularly for interrater and test-retest reliabilities related to current episodes of psychiatric disturbance.

Validity studies have been encouraging because expected relationships have been found between SADS scores and external measures of depression, anxiety, and psychosis. For example, M. H. Johnson, Margo, and Stern (1986) found that relevant SADS measures could effectively discriminate between patients with depression and paranoid and nonparanoid schizophrenia. In addition, the SADS depression measures effectively rated the relative severity of a patient's depression. For example, Coryell et al. (1994) found clear consistency between different levels of depression. The authors suggest that incremental validity might be increased by having clients referred for a medical examination to screen out physical difficulties that might be resulting in central nervous system dysfunction. The authors also recommend that interviewers try to increase validity by always including the best available information (family history, structured tests, other rating schedules) before making final ratings. The SADS has been used to predict the clinical features, course, and outcome of various disorders, including major depression (Coryell et al., 1994), schizophrenia (Stompe, Ortwein-Swoboda, Strobl, & Friedman, 2000), and bipolar disorder (Vieta et al., 2000). A number of studies has also successfully used the SADS to detect family patterns of schizophrenia (Stompe et al., 2000) and obsessive-compulsive disorders (Bienvenu et al., 2000).

Child Version

The SADS for School-Age Children (Kiddie-SADS-P, K-SADS-P; Ambrosini, 2000; Puig-Antich & Chambers, 1978) is a semistructured interview developed for children between ages 6 and 18. The K-SADS has come out in versions to be used in epidemiological research (K-SADS-E), to assess present and lifetime psychopathology (K-SADS-P/L), and present levels of symptomology (K-SADS-P). Although much of the K-SADS is based on research with major depressive disorders of prepubertal children, it also covers a wide range of disorders, such as phobias, conduct disorders, obsessive-compulsive disorders, and separation anxiety.

The interview should be administered by a professional clinician who has been trained in the use of the K-SADS and is familiar with *DSM-IV*-TR criteria. All versions are administered to both the parent and the child. Any discrepancies between the two sources of information are clarified before final ratings are made. Total administration time is approximately 1.5 hours per informant (3 hours total). The first phase is a 15- to 20-minute unstructured interview in which rapport is developed as well as an overview of relevant aspects of history, including the frequency and duration of presenting symptoms, their onset, and whether the parents have sought previous treatment. This is followed by structured questions regarding symptoms, which are rated on a Likert scale, with 1 representing "not at all" and 7 indicating that they are "extreme." A skip structure is built into the format so that interviewers can omit irrelevant questions. Interviewers are allowed to use their judgment regarding the wording and the type and number of questions. Finally, ratings are made regarding behavioral observations (appearance, attention, affect). Interviewers are also asked to rate the completeness and reliability of the interview and to make a global assessment of pathology (degree of symptomatology and level of impairment).

Test-retest and interrater reliability for the K-SADS has been good with a general trend for each version to have improved reliabilities. Ambrosini (2000), for example, reported that the K-SADS-P/L had test-retest reliabilities ranging from 1.00 (lifetime occurrence of major depression) to .55 (for lifetime occurrence for attention deficit disorder). However, overall reliabilities have been lower for the K-SADS (and K-SADS-III-R) than for the adult SADS, but this is to be expected given the relative changeableness and less well-developed language skills found with children (Ambrosini, Metz, Prabucki, & Lee, 1989; Chambers et al., 1985). Validity studies indicate that relevant K-SADS measures correlated highly with diagnoses for conduct disorders, schizophrenia, and depression (Apter, Bleich, Plutchik, Mendelsohn, & Tyrano, 1988). Additional expected correlations have been found between SADS measures and ratings of adolescent mood (E. Costello, Benjamin, Angold, & Silver, 1991) and the Child Behavior Checklist (Achenbach & Edelbrock, 1983; Ambrosini, 2000). Finally, follow-up studies on adolescents diagnosed with disorders (i.e., depression) have found a continued risk for later affective difficulties (i.e., Lewinsohn, Rohde, Klein, & Seeley, 1999).

Collectively, the different versions of the SADS provide a thorough, well-organized interview with unparalleled coverage of the subtypes and gradations of the severity of mood disorders. The SADS has also been well accepted in research and clinical settings. It has strong interrater reliability and provides good ratings of symptom severity, measures associated symptoms, includes guidelines for possible malingering, and has strong evidence of convergent validity (see R. Rogers, 2001; Rogers et al., 2004). In contrast, its weaknesses include a relatively narrow band of diagnosis compared with some of the other available instruments, such as the SCID or DIS. In addition, the diagnoses are based on RDC rather than the more recent *DSM-III-R* or *DSM-IV*-TR criteria. This criticism is somewhat moderated, however, by many of the RDC and *DSM-III/DSM-IV*-TR criteria being nearly the same, especially for childhood disorders. Finally, administration and interpretation of the SADS require extensive training (usually a week) as well as a good working knowledge of differences between the SADS/RDC and *DSM-III-R/DSM-IV*-TR criteria.

Diagnostic Interview Schedule

In contrast to the SADS, which is semistructured and requires administration by trained professionals, the DIS (Robins, Helzer, Croughan, & Ratcliff, 1981) is highly structured and was designed specifically by the National Institute of Mental Health (Division of Biometry and Epidemiology) to be administered by nonprofessional interviewers for epidemiological studies (see Helzer & Robins, 1988). It has been updated for the *DSM-III-R* (DIS-III-R; Robins et al., 1989) and the *DSM-IV* (DIS-IV; Robins, Cottler, Bucholz, & Compton, 1996). The latest version (DIS-IV) includes 19 modules with more than 30 Axis I diagnoses and one Axis II diagnosis (antisocial personality). This modular format allows for tailoring various portions of the DIS-IV to the interests of the researcher or clinician. However, clinical judgment is reduced to a minimum by using verbatim wording, specific guidelines, a clear flow from one question to the next, and simple yes-no answers. Thus, the DIS is far more economical to administer than the SADS. Total administration time is 60 to 90 minutes. Studies have generally indicated that results are comparable between trained clinicians and nonprofessional interviewers (Helzer, Spitznagel, & McEvoy, 1987).

Adult Version

The original version of the DIS was derived from the format of the earlier Renard Diagnostic Interview. However, diagnosis for the DIS-IV is based exclusively on *DSM-IV* criteria. Initially, questions are directed toward obtaining information regarding the client's life, and information is also requested regarding more current symptoms based on the past two weeks, past month, past six months, and past year. Specific probe questions distinguish whether a symptom is clinically significant. A total of 470 potential clinical ratings are made and organized around 24 major categories. Administration time is approximately 60 to 90 minutes.

Computerized administration and scoring programs are available that can generate *DSM-IV*-based diagnoses. However, computer-based diagnoses on early versions of the DIS were found to generate an average of 5.5 possible diagnoses compared with an average of 2.6 for nonstructured interviews (Wyndowe, 1987). Patient acceptance for the computer administration has been found to be high, although the average administration time is somewhat longer than the clinician-interviewed version.

Studies of the reliability and validity of the DIS have been both variable and controversial. Although much of this research was done on pre–DIS-IV versions, the similarity of format and content between the DIS and DIS-IV suggests that much of this earlier research is pertinent. The comparability of diagnosis by professionals and nonprofessionals using the DIS has generally been supported. This finding suggests that nonprofessionals can effectively use it to help gather data for large epidemiological studies. For example, Robins et al. (1981) found diagnostic agreement between psychiatrists and nonprofessional interviewers to be .69. The sensitivity (percent interviewees correctly identified) of the DIS varied according to type of diagnosis but had a mean of 75% with a mean specificity (percent noncases correctly identified) of 94%. More recent studies have similarly concluded that the specificity is stronger than its sensitivity (Eaton, Neufeld, Chen, & Cai, 2000; J. Murphy, Monson, Laird, Sobol, & Leighton, 2000). However, data on sensitivity and specificity were based on using psychiatrists' diagnoses as the true index of diagnostic accuracy. The difficulties in considering psychiatrists' ratings as the truly accurate or "gold standard" criterion for validity have already been noted; therefore, it is probably best to consider the preceding data on sensitivity and specificity as forms of interrater reliability rather than concurrent validity. In contrast to this study, Vandiver and Sheer (1991) found somewhat modest median test-retest reliabilities ranging between .37 and .46.

Although many of the DIS ratings between professional and lay interviewers were equivalent, Helzer et al. (1985) found that, when compared with psychiatrists, nonprofessional interviewers tended to overdiagnose major depression. In contrast to Helzer et al. (1987), Folstein et al. (1985) did not find a sufficiently high rate of agreement between diagnoses by a panel of psychiatrists and diagnoses by the DIS to warrant its use in epidemiological studies. Specifically, it was found that the DIS generated more cases of depression and schizophrenia and fewer cases of alcoholism and antisocial personality (Cooney, Kadden, & Litt, 1990; Folstein et al., 1985). Eaton et al. (2000) has noted that false-negative diagnoses for many cases could be attributed mainly to failure by patients to report symptoms based on life crises or medical conditions. In contrast, the DIS has been found to be comparable with other commonly used psychiatric rating devices, such as the Psychiatric Diagnostic Interview (Folstein et al., 1985; R. Weller et al., 1985). However, both diagnostic strategies may contain inaccuracies, and it is difficult to tell in which areas these inaccuracies occurred (R. Weller et al., 1985). The DIS has had the greatest difficulty accurately diagnosing borderline conditions and patients in remission, but this is to be expected because these are the most problematic diagnoses for many other assessment strategies (Robins & Helzer, 1994). In contrast, Swartz et al. (1989) were able to find quite respectable sensitivities (85.7%) and specificities (86.2%) for borderline conditions using a DIS borderline index.

Child Version

The Diagnostic Interview Schedule for Children (DISC; Costello, Edelbrock, Duncan, & Kalas, 1984; Shaffer, Fisher, Lucas, Dulcan, & Schwab-Stone, 2000) is similar to the adult version in that it is highly structured and designed for nonprofessional interviewers. It differs in that it is designed to be given as both a child interview (DISC-C) and parent interview (DISC-P). There have also been versions designed for teachers (Teacher DISC), screening (DISC Predictive Scales), young adults (Young Adult DISC), and administrations that can be given by computer or audiotape (Lucas et al., 2001; Shaffer et al., 2000). Ratings are coded as 0 (not true), 1 (somewhat true), or 2 (very often true). *DSM-IV* diagnoses are generated based on the combined ratings for the child and parent interviews. Some of the more problematic diagnoses (autism, pervasive developmental disorder, pica) are based on an interview with the parent only. The entire interview takes an average of 70 minutes per informant and 90 to 120 minutes per patient, but an explicit skip structure can enable some interviews to be somewhat shorter. The most recent modification of the DISC (DISC-IV; Robins et al., 1996; Shaffer et al., 2000) was designed to be compatible with *DSM-IV* and *ICD-10* criteria. The DISC-IV comprises six modules, each of which comprises the major diagnostic clusters (Anxiety, Mood, Disruptive, Substance Use, Schizophrenia, Miscellaneous).

DISC test-retest reliability (one-year interval) for *DSM-IV* diagnoses in a clinical sample was good to adequate with parent ratings having higher reliabilities (.54 to .79) than child interviews (.25 to .92; Shaffer et al., 2000). However, test-retest reliabilities for a community sample were generally quite poor for child interviews (.27 to .64) but adequate for parent interviews (.45 to .68; Shaffer et al., 2000). Children's reliability increased with age, which is expected considering their increase in intellectual abilities, greater memory, and improved language comprehension and expression. In contrast, reliabilities based on ratings from interviews with the parents decreased with the child's age, probably because the parents have progressively less contact with their child.

Research on the validity of the DISC has found that discriminations between psychiatric and pediatric groups were good for children with severe diagnoses and severe symptoms but not for children with mild-to-moderate difficulties (Shaffer et al., 2000). Discriminations based on interviews with parents were generally more accurate than those based on children (E. Costello, Edelbrock, & Costello, 1985). Accuracy was also higher for externalizing than internalizing disorders (Friman et al., 2000). In addition, comparisons between psychiatric and pediatric referrals indicated that psychiatric referrals had more symptom scores and more psychiatric diagnoses than pediatric referrals (E. Costello et al., 1985). The DISC has also been found to identify risk factors for substance abuse (Greenbaum, Prange, Friedman, & Silver, 1991) and to predict behaviors related to conduct and oppositional disorders (Friman et al., 2000). Ratings between DISC and clinician-based diagnosis were moderate to good (.29 to .74 for parent and .27 to .79 for child; Shaffer et al., 2000) in research settings and followed strict diagnostic guidelines. However, there was very poor agreement between DISC and clinician-based diagnosis when the clinicians performed diagnosis in everyday clinical settings (A. L. Jensen & Weisz, 2002). This may reflect not so much a weakness of the DISC itself but more that there are considerable differences between how diagnosis is achieved in research as opposed to practice contexts. In summary, the DISC has strengths in that it has good reliability and validity among clinical samples involving parent interviews, especially when the problems are related to externalizing disorders. However, the DISC is more problematic when ratings are based on child interviews, particularly among community samples and for internalizing disorders.

Diagnostic Interview for Children and Adolescents

The Renard Diagnostic Interview (Helzer et al., 1981) inspired both the DIS and the Diagnostic Interview for Children and Adolescents (DICA; Herjanic & Campbell, 1977; Herjanic & Reich, 1982). It has been through several revisions, which have incorporated the different editions of the *DSM* and elements of the DIS (W. Reich, 2000). Similar to the DIS, the DICA has been designed for administration by lay interviewers. The most recent version was published in 1997 and is available in child, adolescent, and parent versions (W. Reich, 2000). The DICA can be administered to children between ages 6 and 17 years. The format is semistructured and primarily organized around different themes, such as behavior at home, behavior at school, and interpersonal relationships with peers. Additional content areas are substance abuse and the presence of syndromes such as anxiety disorders, mania, and affective disorders. Elaborate instructions are given for skipping irrelevant items, and total administration time is between one and two hours. The administration begins with an interview of both the parent and child, which is designed to establish baseline behaviors and to obtain relevant chronological information. The parent is then questioned about the child to determine the possible appropriateness of common *DSM-IV* diagnostic categories. The final step is to administer a "Parent Questionnaire," which requests additional medical and developmental history and addresses possible diagnoses that have not been covered by previous questioning.

Reliability of the DICA has been quite variable. Test-retest reliability has been quite good, mostly ranging between .76 and .90 (Bartlett, Schleifer, Johnson, & Keller, 1991; Earls, Reich, Jung, & Cloninger, 1988). However, test-retest reliability for child (6 to 12) ADHD was low (.32) and oppositional disorder was low to adequate (.46; W. Reich, 2000). Reliability has been found to be lowest for questions that were complex, related to time, and for children with the highest level of functional impairment. In contrast, questions with the highest reliability were related to frequency and to externalizing symptoms (Perez, Ascaso, Massons, & Chaparro, 1998). Most cross-informant (parent-child) agreement related to specific symptoms has been disappointingly low (.19 to .54; Herjanic & Reich, 1982). The highest level of agreement was for the oldest children and the lowest for younger groups (W. Reich, 2000). Whereas mothers reported more behavioral symptoms, children were more likely to report subjective complaints.

Validity studies on the DICA indicate that it can accurately make the somewhat gross distinction between middle- to older-aged children who were referred to a general psychiatric clinic from those referred to a pediatric clinic (Herjanic & Campbell, 1977). However, there was considerable overlap for children between ages six and eight, thus suggesting that a greater possibility of misdiagnosis exists for children in this age range. The DICA was found to be most effective for assessing relationship problems, less effective for academic difficulties, and least effective for assessing school problems, somatic complaints, and neurotic symptoms (Herjanic & Campbell, 1977). In addition, adolescents diagnosed with depression on the DICA also had corresponding elevations on the Beck Depression Inventory (Martin, Churchard, Kutcher, & Korenblum, 1991). W. Reich (2000) reported that as the genetic similarity of persons diagnosed with bipolar disorder decreased, their level of psychopathology on the DISC correspondingly decreased. In summary, the psychometric properties of the DICA have been variable; more studies are needed to substantiate its validity, particularly concurrent validity (R. Rogers, 2001).

RECOMMENDED READING

Garb, H. N. (2007). Computer-administered interviews and rating scales. *Psychological Assessment*, *19*, 4–13.

Othmer, E., & Othmer, S. C. (2002). *The clinical interview using DSM-IV-TR. Vol. 1: Fundamentals.* Washington, DC: American Psychiatric Press.

Rogers, R. (2001). *Handbook of diagnostic and structured interviewing.* New York: Guilford Press.

Sommers-Flanagan, R., & Sommers-Flanagan, J. (2003). *Clinical interviewing* (3rd ed.). Hoboken, NJ: John Wiley & Sons.

Summerfeldt, L. J., & Antony, M. (2002). *Structured and semistructured diagnostic interviews.* In M. Antony & D. H. Barlow (Eds.), *Handbook of assessment and treatment planning for psychological disorders.* New York: Guilford Press.

Chapter 4

BEHAVIORAL ASSESSMENT

Behavioral assessment is one of a variety of assessment traditions, such as projective testing, neuropsychological assessment, and objective testing. Behavioral assessment distinguishes itself by being a set of specific techniques as well as a way of thinking about behavior disorders and how these disorders can be changed. One of its core assumptions is that behavior can be most effectively understood by focusing on preceding events and resulting consequences. Out of this core assumption has come a surprisingly diverse number of assessment methods, including behavioral interviewing, several strategies of behavioral observation, measurement of relevant cognitions, psychophysiological assessment, and a variety of self-report inventories.

Behavioral assessment can be most clearly defined by contrasting it with traditional assessment. One of the most important comparisons is the emphasis that behavioral assessment places on situational determinants of behavior. This emphasis means that behavioral assessment is concerned with a full understanding of the relevant antecedents and consequences of behavior. In contrast, traditional assessment is often perceived as more likely to view behavior as the result of enduring, underlying traits. It is this underlying difference in conceptions of causation that explains most of the other contrasts between the two traditions. An extension of this conceptual difference is that behavioral assessment goes beyond the attempt to understand the contextual or situational features of behavior and, more important, concerns itself with ways to change these behaviors. There is a close connection between assessment itself and its implications for treatment. Thus, behavioral assessment is more direct, utilitarian, and functional.

The perceived limitations of traditional assessment were a major factor in stimulating the development of behavioral assessment. Specifically, traditional assessment was considered to focus too extensively on abstract, unobservable phenomena that were distant from the actual world of the client. In addition, behaviorists felt that traditional clinical psychology had stagnated because its interventions were not sufficiently powerful and too much emphasis was placed on verbal therapy. The concepts of traditional assessment seemed to exist in an abstract world divorced from the immediate realities and requirements of behavior change. The result of many traditional procedures seemed to be a large quantity of information that had little direct relevance to treatment intervention and outcome. However, this is a stereotyped, somewhat polarized view of traditional (and behavioral) assessment in that there has been considerable and increasing emphasis on the treatment implications and situational context of information derived from traditional methods of assessment. This stereotyped view is meant to highlight differences between the two strategies rather than to capture the complexities and similarities between them.

A further contrast between behavioral and traditional assessment is that behavioral assessment is concerned with clearly observable aspects in the way a person interacts with his or her environment. A typical behavioral assessment might include specific *measures of behavior* (overt and covert), *antecedents* (internal and external), *conditions surrounding behaviors*, and *consequences*. This knowledge can then be used to specify methods for changing relevant behaviors. Although some behavioral assessors might take selected personality traits into account, these traits would be considered relevant only if they had direct implications for therapy. For example, certain personality styles interact with the extent and type of depressive cognitions (Alloy et al., 1999), and the existence of a personality disorder typically predicts therapeutic outcome (see Nelson-Gray & Farmer, 1999). This focus on the person and his or her unique situation is quite different from psychodynamic, biochemical, genetic, or normative trait models.

The behavioral approach stresses that different behavior disorders are typically expressed in a variety of modes. These might include overt behaviors, cognitions, changes in physiological states, and patterns of verbal expressions. This approach implies that different assessment strategies should be used for each of these modes (S. Haynes & O'Brien, 2000). An inference based on one mode does not necessarily generalize to another. For example, anxiety for one person may be caused and maintained primarily by the person's cognitions and only minimally by poor social skills. Another person might have few cognitions relating to anxiety but be anxious largely because of inadequate social skills. The person with inadequate social skills might be most effectively treated through social skills training and only minimally helped through approaches that alter irrational thoughts (see Breitholtz, Johansson, & Ost, 1999). It should also be noted that altering a person's behavior in one mode is likely to affect other modes, and these effects might have to be considered.

Whereas the preceding information presents a relatively rigid and stereotyped distinction between traditional and behavioral assessment, most practicing clinicians, including those who identify themselves as behavior therapists, typically combine and adopt techniques from both traditions (Haynes & Heiby, 2004; Hersen, 2006). Combining both traditions is consistent with the finding that between 50% and 80% of clinicians who described themselves as being behaviorally oriented reported using structured personality tests such as the MMPI (Guevremont & Spiegler, 1990; Watkins, Campbell, & McGregor, 1990). Watkins et al. even found that about 50% used projective tests and the Rorschach was used by a full 32%. Thus, behavioral assessment has become increasingly eclectic and now is usually perceived as part of mainstream assessment rather than as a new and contrasting alternative. Traditional and behavioral approaches have now come to resemble each other in many areas. In particular, behavioral assessment has gone through both a turning inward and a turning outward toward traditional psychometric approaches. The turning inward is most apparent in that internal behavioral repertoires and aspects of cognition are seen as essential for a complete understanding of the person (Glass & Merluzzi, 2000; Lodge, Tripp, & Harte, 2000; Nezu, Nezu, Peacock, & Girdwood, 2004). Specific cognitive techniques include having the person think aloud as he or she is involved in a specific situation, sampling thoughts when a beeper goes off, and using a wide variety of self-statement inventories. Behavioral assessment has turned outward in that it has become increasingly concerned with traditional psychometric considerations. This concern with psychometric evaluation has included assessing the reliability and validity of behavioral observations, self-report inventories, and diagnoses (S.N. Haynes, 2006; Hersen, 2006).

The assumptions and perspectives of behavioral assessment have resulted in an extremely diverse number of approaches and an even wider variety of specific techniques. These approaches and their corresponding techniques can be organized into the areas of behavioral interviewing, behavioral observation, cognitive behavioral assessment, psychophysiological assessment, and self-report inventories. Each of these areas was developed within a wider historical context extending over several decades.

HISTORY AND DEVELOPMENT

Treatment based on behavioral principles has a long history, dating back to the days of Little Albert and his fear of white, furry objects (M. Jones, 1924). However, extensive, well-defined behavioral assessment strategies that were consistent with behavioral therapy were relatively slow to develop. The earliest formal use of behavioral assessment occurred in industrial and organizational settings (Hartshorne & May, 1928; Office of Strategic Services Staff, 1948), but behavioral assessment did not become popular in the clinical context until the mid- to late 1960s. This was probably because of the powerful influence of psychodynamic approaches among clinicians who were taught to "look beneath the surface" to understand the "true" causes of behavior. Perhaps in part as a reaction to this indirect and inferential approach to understanding the person, the earliest forms of behavioral assessment focused almost exclusively on observable behaviors. Although organismic variables such as cognitions, feelings, and psychophysiological responses were acknowledged, they were not considered important influences on behavior and, as a result, were not stressed in assessment and treatment. Instead, behavioral assessment was consistent with the then-dominant operant conditioning paradigm in that it focused on identifying discrete behavioral responses, target behaviors, and reinforcers that could change specific behaviors. Measurement of these areas typically quantified the frequency, rate, and duration of relevant behaviors (Ullman & Krasner, 1965). The result was numerous, highly innovative assessments of overt behaviors. Typically, interventions involved single cases, which was consistent with their idiographic approach.

Early definitions of behavioral assessment were created partially by making contrasts with traditional psychodynamic approaches. Each had different aims (identification of problem behaviors versus classification), assumptions (behavior is caused by situations versus enduring traits), and applications (direct observation versus indirect inferences). In particular, Mischel (1968) attacked the very nature of traits by arguing that they were fictions based on distortions of language (a preponderance of static descriptions), the result of consistency of roles and situations (not inner traits), perceptual bias based on needs for predictability, and the rarity of disconfirmation when traits are (incorrectly) inferred. This attack fueled a lengthy controversy, which was relevant to behavioral assessment in that Mischel's perspective was used to argue for a focus on situational determinants of behavior. Proponents of behavioral assessment (along with psychiatry itself) were also dissatisfied with traditional *DSM-II* diagnosis, which had poor reliability and validity and did not seem to relate to the real world of the client or have direct treatment utility.

During the 1970s, there was a much greater emphasis on a wider approach. The typical single case study format gave way to assessment within a much larger context, such as schools, businesses, families, and differing sociocultural frameworks. This assessment approach was based partially on the observation that these larger contexts could have considerable influence on the person, so that effective individual change often required change in these wider contexts. A refocusing on larger contexts was also motivated by challenges to the strict operant paradigm in that, while effective in controlled situations (hospital ward, Skinner box, prison), had questionable social validity and doubtful long-term clinical impact (Goldfried, 1983; Milne, 1984). Assessment was also widened by arguments to focus on the wider aspects of the person, which meant not only behavior but also feelings, sensations, internal imagery, cognitions, interpersonal relations, and psychophysiological functioning (Lazarus, 1973, 2005). This emphasis on a multimodal or multifaceted approach forced the mainstream of behavioral assessment to accept a number of indirect measures, such as self-reports, ratings by significant others, and cognitions (Cone, 1977,

1978). Relevant publications were the first editions of *Behavioral Assessment: A Practical Handbook* (Hersen & Bellack, 1976), *Handbook of Behavioral Assessment* (Ciminero, Calhoun, & Adams, 1977), and the journals *Behavioral Assessment* and the *Journal of Behavioral Assessment*, both of which began in 1979.

The 1980s and 1990s saw a proliferation of publications in the field of behavioral assessment, a dramatic reevaluation of some of its most basic assumptions, and the incorporation of influences from other traditions and disciplines. In particular, psychiatry had similar difficulties with the *DSM-II* as behavioral assessment and began to develop strategies quite similar to those of behavioral assessment. The Problem Oriented Record (Weed, 1968) was introduced into many general hospital and psychiatric settings to improve diagnostic and treatment practices by providing behavior-specific databases, problem lists, treatment plans, and follow-up data. It thereby more effectively tied in the relationship between assessment and treatment, and more clearly delineated diagnostic issues. Perhaps of greater importance, *DSM-III-R* and *DSM-IV* were similar to the efforts of behavioral assessment in that each diagnostic category was developed using behavior-specific descriptions. Numerous publications have worked to integrate behavioral assessment with traditional psychiatric diagnosis (First et al., 1992; Follette & Hayes, 1992; Hersen, 2005, 2006; Nelson-Gray & Paulson, 2004) in areas such as depression (R. Nelson & Maser, 1988), the diagnosis of childhood disorders (Hersen, 2005), and personality disorders (Nelson-Gray & Farmer, 1999). The perspectives of psychiatry and behavioral assessment have been further linked by the *Journal of Behavior Therapy and Experimental Psychiatry*.

The development and expansion of behavioral medicine and neuropsychology has also drawn extensively on behavioral assessment strategies in the evaluation of headaches, coronary heart disease, Reynaud's disease, asthma, chronic pain, sleep disturbances, and brain-behavior relationships (Franzen, 2004; Williamson, Veron-Guidry, & Kiper, 1998). Behavioral assessment strategies have also focused on complex causal models as well as unstable, transitional behaviors (S. N. Haynes, 1995; O'Brien, Kaplar, & McGrath, 2004). Thus, not only has behavioral assessment increasingly accepted the contributions of other disciplines and alternative models of conceptualizing behavior, but many of the most honored behavioral techniques have been challenged (Goldfried, 1983). For example, clinical judgment in the context of structured interviews has been accepted, diagnostic classification is now considered potentially useful, reliance solely on behavioral observations is perceived in some contexts as inappropriate, and indirect measurement is often seen as essential. In addition, more inferential techniques, such as measuring underlying cognitive structures (schemas) that organize more specific thoughts and behaviors, have now become a frequent part of behavioral assessment (Linscott & DiGiuseppe, 1998). This focus on internal aspects of behavior is contrasted by a dramatic decrease in the early, time-honored focus on measuring observable frequencies of target behaviors (Glass & Merluzzi, 2000; Guevremont & Spiegler, 1990).

In essence, the 1980s and 1990s witnessed a significant reappraisal and expansion of what is involved in behavioral assessment. In 1989, Birchler summarized his review of behavioral assessment by noting "Behavioral assessment as we may have known it in the recent past is in a rapidly changing process of (choose one): disarray, revision, broad expansion, advancement, confusion, and/or extinction" (p. 385). There has certainly been a significant blurring and cross-fertilization between behavioral assessment and other forms of assessment (S. Haynes & O'Brien, 2000). This blurring and cross-fertilization is in part reflected in the fact that the *Behavioral Assessment* journal and the *Journal of Behavioral Assessment* have changed their names and content to include wider aspects of psychopathology and more traditional assessment tools (i.e., MMPI-2, MCMI-III).

Current directions include analog and virtual reality assessment, advances in psycho-physiological assessment, utilization of innovative technology, use of ambulatory sensors, assessment of clients in their natural environments, and greater applications for special populations (Haynes & Yoshioka, 2007; Hersen, 2005, 2006; Piasecki et al., 2007). Future directions that have been highlighted by Ollendick, Alvarez, and Greene (2004) are the need to focus more on developmental factors, incremental validity when using multiple assessment methods, and the inclusion of culturally sensitive approaches.

ISSUES RELATED TO RELIABILITY AND VALIDITY

Traditional psychometric considerations for behavioral assessment are difficult to summarize because of the wide diversity of techniques and the differences in assumptions regarding the focus, nature, and causes of behavior. Whereas traditional assessment stresses the relative stability of various characteristics, behavioral assessment assumes variability based largely on environmental factors. A finding such as low test-retest reliability is more likely to be interpreted in the behavioral context because of true variance resulting from environmental conditions rather than error in the data collection procedure. Furthermore, behavioral assessment stresses the importance of individually tailored approaches emphasizing the client's idiosyncrasies. In this context, normative comparisons are frequently seen as both irrelevant and inappropriate. Despite these issues, many from within the area of behavioral assessment have successfully argued for evaluating behavioral assessment techniques with traditional psychometric approaches (Cone, 1998; S. N. Haynes, 2006). For example, interobserver agreement for behavioral observations is essential before the data gathered from this approach can be trusted. Evaluating interobserver agreement is typically determined by calculating the percentage of interrater agreement. Likewise, data derived from self-reports in areas such as assertiveness and fear need to demonstrate that the findings can be generalized to other situations, such as role plays, simulations, and, especially, daily life.

The earliest forms of behavioral assessment relied primarily on behavioral observation and assumed that the direct observation of specific behaviors was sufficiently clear, reliable, and accurate. The emphasis was primarily on determining a functional analysis between behavior and its antecedents and consequences. In an activity such as pressing a bar for reinforcement, the behavior could be easily recorded by an electronic detector, and, therefore, the reliability of the measure could be considered to be quite high. However, with behaviors that are more difficult to define, the reliability of measurement, especially when based on behavioral observation, cannot be assumed. For example, fingernail-biting might be defined merely by the person touching his or her face, or it may involve touching the mouth, actually chewing the nail, or removing part of the nail or perhaps the entire nail. The issue of precise definition and accurate measurement of the behavior becomes even more problematic when dealing with internal cognitions, in which the clinician is completely dependent on self-reports rather than on direct observation.

The level of reliability across different observational strategies has varied. In general, material derived from behavioral observation during behavioral assessment can be influenced by observer expectations in similar ways, as has been found by experimental research (H. Cooper & Rosenthal, 1980; Orne, 1962; R. Rosenthal, 1966). Consistent with this fact is the finding that interrater agreement has been quite variable for areas such as overt difficulties and underlying mechanisms (Persons, Mooney, & Padesky, 1995). In situations such as natural observation in which observer bias, outside factors (such as interference from nontarget persons), and a lack of clear definitions are likely to create variability in observer ratings, reliability can be expected to be relatively low. Further sources of observer error include halo effects, primacy effects, failure to score a behavior that has occurred, rating toward the center of the scale, and leniency or generosity of scoring. When bias is reduced by using highly structured procedures, reliability increases. Thus, a procedure such as systematic sampling, in which clear strategies are used to determine when and how the behavior will be measured, has generally been more reliable and accurate than naturalistic observation (Cunningham & Thorp, 1981). Although reliability has been found to increase in controlled situations where the observers know that they themselves are being evaluated for accuracy (Romanczyk, Kent, Diament, & O'Leary, 1973), this outside monitoring of observers rarely occurs in clinical situations. Thus, it cannot be assumed that the reliability found in clinical situations is as high as for controlled studies in which evaluators are themselves being evaluated. General guidelines for increasing reliability in clinical situations include having two observers compare their results, providing careful instructions when a client is asked to monitor his or her own behavior, specifying target behaviors, clearly wording items on self-reports, taking care in the construction of instruments, and thoroughly training observers such as parents or teachers. Reliability of ratings is also likely to be increased by paying closer attention to contextual variables (J. G. Beck, 1994; S. N. Haynes, 2006; S. N. Haynes & O'Brien, 2000).

During the 1960s and 1970s, the validity of various assessment procedures depended primarily on informal content validity. Questionnaires and observational strategies were based on rational considerations regarding what was to be studied and how these measurements were to be made. Few efforts were made to develop empirically derived categories. For example, the assessment of depression might have been based on knowledge about the typical thoughts depressed people seem to have as well as additional variables that seem important regarding social supports and typical antecedent events. The various areas of observation were selected mostly based on what rationally seemed to be the most critical considerations. Since the early 1980s, increased work has gone into assessing the validity of various methods of behavioral assessment. In general, few validity studies have been performed on behavioral interviews and naturalistic observations, whereas much more has been done on behavioral questionnaires. Most validity studies have been conducted by using relevant outside criteria. Many of the same issues have come up with criterion validity for behavioral assessment as for traditional assessment, including difficulty generalizing to different populations, settings, and methods of administration.

The early behavioral self-report questionnaires relied on content and face validity. Because these questionnaires represented new techniques with a different underlying philosophy, it was believed that they did not have to be judged using the same criteria as the older and more traditional psychometric tests. They were considered to be direct reports of client behaviors, and thus little psychometric validity was reported. R. Kaplan and Saccuzzo (1993) criticize this initial focus on content and face validity by stating that behavioral self-reports may be "repeating history and reinventing the wheel" (p. 493). They further point out that the "early paper-and-pencil structured personality tests which were finally abandoned in the 1930s are indeed difficult to distinguish from many present-day (behavioral) self-report procedures" (p. 494). Many early behavioral self-report questionnaires could have been best described as "idiosyncratic clinical tools" rather than psychometrically sound tests. The problems of response bias, questionable reliability and validity, no norms, and assumed client truthfulness need to be addressed for any standardized instrument, including behavioral procedures.

As a result of these criticisms, much greater attention was focused on behavioral techniques, especially self-report inventories. However, the success of these efforts has been quite variable. For example, the Rathus Assertiveness Schedule (RAS; Rathus, 1973) has been subjected to traditional psychometric procedures and illustrates the difficulties encountered in this and other similar behavioral inventories. Whereas Heimberg, Harrison, Goldberg, Desmarais, and Blue (1979) did not find a very high correspondence between scores on the RAS and observational reports of role plays in an inmate population, the RAS did relate to nonassertiveness in a group of dental students (Rathus, 1972). However, a difficulty with relating assertiveness in role-play situations, which most of the preceding studies used, is that assertiveness in role plays may not relate to assertiveness in naturalistic situations (Bellack, Hersen, & Turner, 1979). Perhaps when subjects are asked to role-play, they can alter their daily level of assertiveness to "act the part" correctly (Higgins, Alonso, & Pendleton, 1979). The RAS similarly has poor criterion validity based on instructor evaluations of observed assertive behavior and grades in a communication course (Tucker, Weaver, Duran, & Redden, 1983). Thus, even though the RAS is a frequently used device in both research and clinical settings, the meaning of the scores might be difficult to evaluate. Other behavioral self-report questionnaires have experienced similar problems.

ASSETS AND LIMITATIONS

Probably the greatest advantage of behavioral assessment is that its practitioners have continually paid attention to its relevance toward treatment. Any measurement of problem behaviors is usually directly tied to how these behaviors can be changed. Furthermore, relevant behaviors are given an empirical functional analysis, which enables clinicians to make baseline measurements of behavior and to assess the antecedents and consequences of these behaviors. An initial functional analysis can then allow clinicians to evaluate whether change has actually occurred during or after treatment. Although many techniques have not been through rigorous traditional validity studies, the emphasis on treatment validity has proven to be attractive to many practitioners. Thus, behavioral assessment is particularly useful for persons using a hypothesis-testing approach and for those who wish to have clear accountability that change has actually taken place. In some situations, however, behavioral assessment can be tied too closely to treatment, particularly in legal assessments or other situations in which assessment and therapy are separate.

A further asset is that behavioral assessment offers a wide range of possible techniques for use in extremely varied contexts. These strategies include self-reports, naturalistic observation, physiological monitoring, ambulatory sensors, structured observation, and self-monitoring. Variations in techniques are consistent with the view that a complete understanding of the person requires multiple modes of assessment. The different assessment modes might involve relevant aspects of person-situation interaction, physiological changes, cognitions, interpersonal relationships, overt behaviors, feelings, imagery, and aspects of the person's larger social system. Many behavioral assessment models organize their approach around stimulus, organism, response, and contingencies (Goldfried, 1982b). Other approaches rely on Lazarus BASIC-ID (Lazarus, 2005) or on Kanfer and Saslow's (1969) functional analysis of behavioral excesses and deficits. These approaches place the person in a much wider context than traditional assessment procedures.

Behavioral assessment is particularly appropriate when a presenting problem is determined primarily by environmental factors. In most cases, a clear, functional relationship (environmental interaction) can be established for disorders such as phobias, marital difficulties, acting out, temper tantrums, and inappropriate classroom behavior. If these behaviors are frequent in occurrence (i.e., smoking, classroom acting out), it is fairly easy to develop a baseline and monitor change. However, quite unique behavior that occurs infrequently (i.e., relapse into substance abuse, or bringing firearms to school) may be much more difficult to measure and monitor (J. Nelson, Roberts, Rutherford, Mathur, & Aaroe, 1999). In addition, behavioral assessment is somewhat less relevant when environmental factors account for a smaller portion of the variance. This may be the case when organic factors may be more important than environmental ones, such as in chronic schizophrenia, certain types of headaches, and head injuries. Although behavioral assessment and intervention can still be effective for such problems, greater difficulties are involved because the environment is relatively less important.

A previously described but extremely important drawback of many behavioral assessment strategies is that they have poor or, at least, untested psychometric properties. Often the attempts to establish reliability and validity have been disappointing. In addition, the accuracy of behavioral observation and interviewing can be distorted because of observer bias, halo effects, primacy effects, low interobserver agreement, confirmatory bias, and so forth.

Although cognitive behavioral assessment has been given increased importance over the past 20 years, in many ways it is contrary to the original spirit of behavioral assessment's emphasis on direct observation. Cognitive assessment is necessarily unobservable and relies on client self-reports. Difficulties might include differences in meaning between the client and the clinician, response biases, assumed honesty of reporting, and assumptions about the equivalence of internal dialogues and their verbal descriptions.

A final limitation of behavioral assessment is that it often requires extensive resources in terms of time, personnel, and equipment. This is particularly true for psychophysiological and observational methods. Surveys indicate that while clinicians do use direct observation, they do so only on an occasional basis (Elliot, Miltenberger, Kaster-Bundgaard, & Lumley, 1996; Guevremont & Spiegler, 1990). In contrast, they are much more likely to use interviews with the client, interviews with significant others, self-monitoring, and behavioral rating scales. As a result, behavioral assessment is frequently limited to interviews and questionnaires (Guevremont & Spiegler, 1990; Sayers & Tomcho, 2006). An additional drawback is that many behavioral instruments have not been designed to deal with problems frequently encountered in clinical practice, such as dissociative disorders, paranoia, and hypochondriasis.

STRATEGIES OF BEHAVIORAL ASSESSMENT

Behavioral assessment has given rise to numerous and highly varied techniques, many of which are described in *Comprehensive Handbook of Psychological Assessment (Volume 3): Behavioral Assessment* (S. N. Haynes & Heiby, 2004); *Clinician's Handbook of Adult Behavioral Assessment* (Hersen, 2006) *Clinician's Handbook of Child Behavioral Assessment* (Hersen, 2005); and *Dictionary of Behavioral Assessment Techniques* (Hersen & Bellack, 2002). For example, there are an estimated 300 questionaires that can be conceptualized as behaviorally oriented self-report instruments (Hersen & Bellack, 2002). Despite this diversity, behavioral assessment strategies can be organized into the general categories of behavioral interviewing, behavioral observation, cognitive behavioral assessment, psychophysiological assessment, and self-report inventories. Each of these approaches varies in the degree to which it emphasizes direct versus indirect measures of the person as well as in the extent to which it relies on inference. For example, cognitive assessment is more indirect than behavioral observation and relies much more on inferences regarding the degree to which cognitions affect and interact with overt behavior. However, all of these techniques stress developing a functional analysis of behavior through understanding person-environment interaction. They also emphasize that each aspect of assessment is directly relevant to treatment planning and evaluation.

Behavioral Interviewing

Behaviorally oriented interviews generally focus on describing and understanding the relationships between antecedents, behaviors, and consequences (ABC). In addition, a baseline or pretreatment measure of behavior is developed through a systematic consideration of the frequency, intensity, and duration of relevant behaviors. Behaviors might also be provided with a description of specific behavioral excesses and deficits (Kanfer & Saslow, 1969). Any goal must be capable of being measured and tested in an objective and reliable way, and the client should agree on its relevance (Gresham, 1984). Although the behavioral approach might seem long and involved, the process is simplified by considering only areas that are relevant for treatment.

Despite this emphasis on treatment utility, it is essential to place each aspect of the information derived from a behavioral interview into a wide context. A basic description of a target behavior is simplistic because it does not take into account an interactionist model. For example, a phobia is likely to create difficulties in the client's relationships, which could undermine the person's sense of competence. The person might then react by becoming highly dependent on a primary relationship, reinforcing the sense of helplessness. The helplessness might then reinforce a fear of not being able to cope, which can then interact with and quite possibly exacerbate the phobia. Thus, a complete interview would evaluate not only the existence of and nature of the phobia but also the effect of the phobia on relationships, work effectiveness, and self-statements. Whereas the earlier behavioral interviews of the 1960s and 1970s often had a narrow focus, current models of behavioral assessment emphasize taking this wider context into consideration (Nezu et al., 2004).

The general purpose of the behavioral interview is multifaceted. It might help identify relevant target behaviors or select additional behavioral assessment procedures. It also provides an opportunity to obtain informed consent, obtain a history of the problem, identify causal factors related to the presenting problem, develop a functional analysis of the problem behavior, increase client motivation, design intervention programs, and evaluate the effectiveness of previously attempted interventions.

The initial phase of a behavioral interview needs to include many of the elements relevant for traditional interviews. A sufficient degree of rapport needs to be established, a statement needs to be developed of the general and specific purposes of the interview, and a review should be made of the client's relevant history. However, history tends to be deemphasized in favor of current behaviors because the main cause of client behavior is considered situational rather than historical. Common clinician approaches involve reflective comments, probing, understanding, and expressed empathy. Open-ended questions can be followed up with more direct questioning. However, the extensive use of nondirective techniques is inappropriate in that the clinician must set a clear direction and have the client answer direct questions relevant to a behaviorally oriented approach.

Sometimes clients provide excellent descriptions of their problems and can specify relevant antecedent and consequent conditions. Other clients experience difficulty describing the events surrounding the decision to seek treatment, elaborating on their feelings, stating who referred them, or providing information about how other people might be perceiving their problem. Because a careful behavioral analysis requires a complete description of problem behaviors, the client and therapist must work to establish the extent of the difficulty, where it occurs, when it occurs, and its effects on relationships. Sometimes it is helpful to have the client keep a diary of relevant events and observations. New technologies using electronic devices are now available to assist with ongoing self-monitoring (Piasecki et al., 2007). Often clients describe and define their difficulties by relying extensively on general trait descriptions rather than on more behaviorally oriented ones. A behavioral interviewer, then, needs to work with the client to develop specific and easily observable descriptions. For example, if a client says he or she is a "depressed type of person," this might translate into specific types of behaviors (slow movement, spending too much time in bed, avoiding people, being nonassertive), cognitions (that he or she is no good, a failure), and feelings (hopelessness, apathy). The belief in an underlying permanent trait (illness) needs to be reframed as a group of specific behaviors that are potentially changeable. This reframing process, in itself, is likely to be beneficial to clients because they will be better able to see specific things they can do to change how they feel. Speaking in concrete behavioral terms rather than abstractions is also likely to increase mutual understanding between client and therapist.

A wide-based behavioral assessment should describe not only the specific presenting problem but also the manner in which the problem has generalized into other areas. In particular, this assessment might involve information about the larger social system. Often the client's school, work, or family situation can be incorporated into the assessment and treatment program to ensure both immediate and long-term success. In contrast, if a narrow approach to change is taken, the client may attempt to express his or her newly acquired behavior in contexts that are not supportive of it. As a result, previous problem behavior might once again develop to the exclusion of newer, more adaptive behavior. This might be true if the client developed new, effective behaviors that were learned only in the narrow context of the practitioner's office.

An interview should end by providing the client with a summary of the information obtained, an explanation of additional information that is required, and an estimate of the likely success of treatment (Sayers & Tomcho, 2006). If further information is required, the clinician and client should agree on what is needed and how to obtain it. This need for additional information might involve instructions for keeping an effective diary, requests for observations from other people, or techniques for self-monitoring of different behaviors. If the interview is a prelude to therapy, additional information should be given about possible strategies for intervention, the length of treatment, possible financial and emotional costs, and assurances that the client will have input into all decisions.

Because most interviews tend to be somewhat informal and haphazard, they frequently provide information with low reliability and validity. For example, T. Wilson and Evans (1983) found a low level of reliability among clinicians trying to specify appropriate target behaviors. Some authors urge that behavioral interviews be structured and standardized. Kratochwill (1985) has suggested that interviews be planned around a four-stage problem-solving process. The first stage is *problem identification* in which the problem is specified and explored, and procedures are established to measure current performance and desired target behaviors. The vague and generalized descriptions that clients typically come in with are developed into specific behavioral descriptions. Next, a *problem analysis* is performed by assessing the client's resources and by noting the relevant environmental conditions influencing behavior and the context in which the behavior excesses or deficits occur. An interview also needs to establish how a *plan might be implemented*, which would include ongoing procedures for collecting data relevant to the progress of the treatment. Finally, strategies for *treatment evaluation* should be specified by considering the pre- and posttreatment measures to determine whether the intervention was successful.

Witt and Elliott (1983) provide this somewhat similar outline of expected accomplishments for any behavioral interview:

1. Initially, provide the client with an overview of what needs to be accomplished and why a clear and detailed specification of the problem behavior is important.
2. Identify the target behavior(s) and articulate them in precise behavioral terms.
3. Identify the problem frequency, duration, and intensity ("How many times has it occurred today," "How long has it been going on," etc.).
4. Identify conditions in which the problem occurs in terms of its antecedents, behaviors, and consequences.
5. Identify the desired level of performance and consider an estimate of how realistic this is and possible deadlines.
6. Identify the client's strengths.
7. Identify the procedures for measuring relevant behaviors: What will be recorded, who will record it, how will it be recorded, when and where will it be recorded?
8. Identify how the effectiveness of the program will be evaluated.
9. After completing discussion of the preceding areas, summarize it to ensure that the client understands and agrees.

This outline should not be followed rigidly but should be used as a general guideline. However, each behavioral assessment should have accomplished all nine areas before completion.

Behavioral Observation

In some cases, the behavioral interview is itself sufficient to obtain an adequate assessment. However, some form of actual behavioral observation is often required before, during, and/or after treatment. The particular method for observing behavior is usually decided on during the initial interview. Whereas the interview is directed primarily toward obtaining verbal information from the client, behavioral observation is used to decide on and actually carry out specific strategies and techniques of measuring the relevant areas of behavior discussed during the interview (see Suen & Rzasa, 2004). In some cases, such as assessing the developmentally disabled, resistant clients, or very young children, behavioral observation may become one of the most important means of assessment. These observations might be made by the professional who is actually conducting the treatment or by someone else who is more involved in the client's life, such as a teacher, parent, spouse, or self-monitoring by the client. The most frequent approaches are narrative recording, interval recording, event recording, and ratings recording.

The first behavioral observation task is to select relevant target behaviors, which can vary from a single response set to a larger interactive unit. The target behavior should either involve the problem behavior itself or relate to it in a meaningful way. Decisions must be made regarding the number of behaviors to record and the relative complexity of the recording method. Both the recording method and the target behavior need to be manageable and should avoid being overly complex. The target behavior can best be clarified by beginning with a narrative description of the client's difficulty and then further specified by considering the antecedents and consequences related to the problem behavior.

All behaviors to be measured must have objective, complete definitions that allow clear observations of the measures of the behavior. In particular, the definition should avoid abstract and highly inferential terms, such as apathy or sadness, and instead translate such terms into specific behaviors. Any description of the target behavior should involve an easy-to-read dictionary-type definition, an elaboration of the behavior, and specifications regarding precisely when the behavior occurs, as well as descriptions of borderline examples and clear nonexamples. In measuring behavioral frequencies, the practitioner must clearly define when the behavior begins and ends. This might be easy for measuring the number of cigarettes a person smokes or the number of times a child bangs his or her head but is more difficult when measuring less clearly defined behaviors, such as the number of aggressive acts a person makes or frequency of nonassertive behaviors. Recordings should also measure the duration of behaviors and their intensity. For example, how hard a child bangs his or her head and the total time engaged in the activity have implications for the urgency and strength of the treatment approach.

The different devices used to make recordings might include various combinations of golf counters, stopwatches, pencil-and-paper forms, or electromechanical devices such as an event recorder with buttons that can be pressed when various categories of behaviors occur. Handheld computers are becoming more common as well as video and audio recordings.

The settings of behavioral observation can range from those that are natural to those that are highly structured. Natural, or in vivo, settings might include the home, classroom, business, or playground. Observations made from these types of settings are likely to be directly relevant to and reflective of the client's life. Natural settings are most effective when assessing high-frequency behaviors and/or more global behaviors, such as attentional deficits, social withdrawal, or depressive behaviors. They are also useful when measuring the amount of change the client has made following intervention. However, natural settings present difficulties because of the extensive time required to make observations. Furthermore, natural settings are problematic when trying to measure infrequently occurring behaviors (aggression, nonassertiveness) or behaviors that typically occur in the absence of others (fire-setting, suicide). To counter the difficulties inherent in naturalistic observation, practitioners may wish to create analog situations such as role plays or work simulations that elicit specific types of behaviors. Such environments are especially important for infrequent behaviors. However, inferences need to be derived cautiously from observations in these structured or analog situations, as they may not generalize into the client's actual life.

When clinicians are concerned that observations made by a person outside the client's environment might contaminate the results, they may wish to train persons who are already a part of the client's natural setting, such as parents, teachers, or spouses. This might help prevent subjects from changing their behaviors simply because they are aware that they are being observed ("reactivity"). These more natural observers can be much less obtrusive than an outside professional. The training of observers needs to include a clear rationale for measuring the behavior with emphasis on making accurate and objective recordings. Observers should memorize the recording code, practice making the recordings, and receive feedback about the relative accuracy of their recordings. Precautions should be taken to avoid observer error, such as through observer bias, leniency, lapses in concentration, and discussion of data with other observers. Sometimes reliability might be checked by comparing the degree of agreement between different observers rating the same behaviors. Trained observers should be used cautiously because widely varying levels of inter-observer agreement have been noted (G. Margolin, Hattem, John, & Yost, 1985).

A system of coding behaviors usually needs to be developed so that recordings are abbreviated and simplified. If too many codes are used, it is difficult for recorders to recall them, especially if behaviors occur in rapid succession. Both the type of recording method (narrative recording, event recording, etc.) and the coding system depend largely on the goals of assessment. A coding system that is clear, simple, and closely connected to the presenting problem is likely to be both useful and reliable. Important considerations in selecting a recording and coding system are the number of times the behavior needs to be observed, the length of observation periods, when to make the recording, the type of recording to be made, and the target behaviors to be recorded. The following sections describe the most frequently used recording systems, along with examples of different methods of coding.

Narrative Recording

Narrative recording requires that the observer simply make note of behaviors of interest. There is little quantification, and the observations can vary in the degree of inferences made. For example, an observer may stick closely to direct descriptions of behavior, such as noting that someone frequently laughs and smiles at his or her friends, or may infer from these behaviors that the client has good peer relations. The primary value of narrative recordings is that they may help define future, more specific areas that can then be measured in a quantitative manner. Thus, narrative recording is usually a precursor to alternative forms of measurement. It has the advantages of potentially discovering relevant behaviors; it can elaborate on these behaviors; it requires little, if any, equipment; and numerous hypotheses can be generated from the narrative descriptions. Limitations are that it does not enable the observer to quantify the observations, it may have questionable validity, and the usefulness of the observations depends largely on the individual skill of the observer.

Interval Recording

A clinician may choose to record whether selected aspects of behavior occur within predetermined intervals. As a result, this technique is also referred to as *time sampling*, *interval sampling*, or *interval time sampling*. Usually the intervals vary from 5 to 30 seconds and may be based either on set schedules for each observation period (e.g., every 5 minutes) or may be selected randomly. Interval recording is most appropriately used for measurements of overt behaviors with moderate frequencies (e.g., once every 5 to 20 seconds) are required and when these behaviors do not have any clear beginning or end. Examples might include behaviors such as walking, listening, playing, reading, or looking up and down.

When developing a strategy for interval recording, clinicians must decide on the length of time between each observation, the method of recording, and the length of the observation period. Deciding on which strategy to use depends largely on the type of behavior. For example, different types of verbal interaction may vary in length and, for that reason, the observation periods must be adjusted. Some strategies might require the observer to alternate between recording (e.g., for 10 seconds), then observing (e.g., for 20 seconds), and then going back to recording the observation just made. Cues regarding the beginning and end of each behavior must be specified. The target behaviors for observation are derived from information based on such sources as the initial interview, self-report inventories, narrative observations, and especially descriptions of the presenting problem. The focus of observation may also vary between different people, such as husband, wife, teacher, child, or client. Sometimes clinicians or researchers arrange to have an outside person observe the same client behaviors. The interrater reliability of the observations can then be established by calculating the percentage of agreement between the two raters (see Suen & Rzasa, 2004). A representative interval recording chart, with instructions on how to develop such a chart, are provided in Figure 4.1.

Interval recording is time efficient and highly focused on specific behaviors, and has the potential to measure almost any behavior. Interval recording is not designed to assess

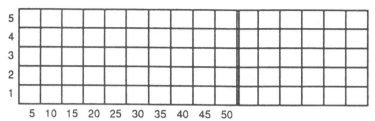

a. Graph paper with series of columns, each five blocks high. Double heavy line marks off 10 columns, for a 50-minute period.

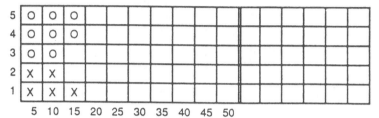

b. Chart after 13 minutes of monitoring pupil's behavior. First two columns are completed and the third is partially completed. If the pupil behaves appropriately during the next (14th) minute, the observer will mark an "X" in the third column just above the other "X." If the pupil misbehaves, the observer will mark an "O" in that column just under the other two "Os."

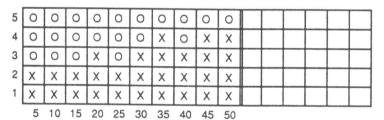

c. Chart after observer has completed the 50-minute period.

Figure 4.1.   Example of interval recording

the quality of the target behaviors, however, and can be artificial or may overlook other important behaviors.

Event Recording

Whereas interval recording depends on measurements defined by units of time that are imposed on target behaviors, event recording depends on the occurrence of the behavior itself. The observer must wait for the target behavior to occur and then record relevant details of the behavior. Examples of behaviors most appropriate for event recording are aggressive actions, greetings, or use of verbal expressions such as assertion or profanity.

The basic design of event recording systems is to note the behavior's frequency, duration, and intensity and to record the behavior on such devices as a checklist, golf counter, or personal digital assistant (PDA). Although the main emphasis is on quantifying the frequency of responding, its duration also can be measured with a stopwatch. The intensity of the behavior can be noted by simply specifying whether it was slight, moderate, or strong. A representative example of an event-recording chart is included in Figure 4.2.

Intervals in minutes

Behavior	Totals	Person Observed	5	10	15	20	25	30
Getting out of seat	⟨27⟩	Subject	▢	L'	▢	ː	·	··
	8	Comparison	··	⁄	ː ⁄	·		·
Request-ing help	5	Subject		·		ː·		⁄
	11	Comparison	··	ː·	ː·	⁄	⁄	·

Figure 4.2.   Example of event recording within 5-minute intervals

Event recording is especially good for recording behaviors having low frequencies and measuring changes in behaviors over time, and for use in studying many different types of behavior. However, event recording is relatively poor at measuring behaviors that do not have clear beginnings and endings, and presents difficulties in keeping the attention of observers for behaviors of long durations. Because event recording does not provide information regarding sequences of behaviors, it is difficult to make inferences about how and why behaviors occur.

Ratings Recording

Rather than recording direct observations of behaviors, clinicians may wish to obtain general impressions of relevant dimensions of behaviors and have these impressions rated on a checklist or scale. Such measures tend to be more global and may involve more abstract terms, such as the client's level of cooperativeness or ability to maintain self-care. Typically, ratings recordings are made after a period of observation. A typical format might request the evaluator to rate, on a scale from 1 to 5 or 1 to 7, the client's frequency of temper tantrums, quality of peer relations, or conscientiousness. For example, the Motivation Assessment Scale (MAS; Durand & Crimmins,1992) is a 16-item questionnaire that evaluates the functional significance of behavior related to the dimensions of sensory, escape/avoidance, social attention, and tangible rewards. Although the MAS is a frequently used instrument, the level of interrater agreement has been found to be quite variable, as has its internal consistency and factor structure (see Kearney, Cook, Chapman, & Bensaheb, 2006). An example of a completed MAS is illustrated in Figure 4.3.

Ratings recordings can potentially be used for a wide variety of behaviors. Other advantages are that the data can be subjected to statistical analysis; the ratings can be made for either individuals or groups; and because of the time efficiency of ratings recordings, they are likely to be cost-effective. Disadvantages include possibly low inter-rater agreement because of the subjectivity of the ratings; little information regarding antecedent and consequent events; and possibly inaccurate ratings, especially if much time elapses between making the observations and making the ratings.

Cognitive Behavioral Assessment

Over the past 30 years, considerable research has been conducted on understanding the cognitive processes underlying behavior disorders. Relevant areas include the self-statements associated with different disorders, the underlying structure or cognitive organization related to these disorders, differences between cognitive distortions in pathological versus normal behavior, and cognitive alterations that occur during therapy. This research has considerably influenced and altered the nature of behavioral assessment. In particular,

Name Bill   Rater Mark   Date 7/16/88

Behavior Description Hitting objects (e.g., tops of tables) with his hand.

Setting Description One-to-one instructional settings in school

Instructions: The **Motivation Assessment Scale** is a questionnaire designed to identify those situations in which an individual is likely to behave in certain ways. From this information, more informed decisions can be made concerning the selection of appropriate reinforcers and treatments. To complete the **Motivation Assessment Scale**, select one behavior that is of particular interest. It is important that you identify the behavior *very specifically*. *Aggressive*, for example, is not as good a description as *hits his sister*. Once you have specified the behavior to be rated, read each question carefully and circle the *one* number that best describes your observations of this behavior.

QUESTIONS

ANSWERS

		Never	Almost Never	Seldom	Half the Time	Usually	Almost Always	Always
1.	Would the behavior occur continuously, over and over, if this person was left alone for long periods of time? (For example, several hours.)	(0)	1	2	3	4	5	6
2.	Does the behavior occur following a request to perform a difficult task?	0	1	2	3	4	(5)	6
3.	Does the behavior seem to occur in response to your talking to other persons in the room?	0	(1)	2	3	4	5	6
4.	Does the behavior ever occur to get a toy, food, or activity that this person has been told that he or she can't have?	0	1	2	(3)	4	5	6
5.	Would the behavior occur repeatedly, in the same way, for very long periods of time, if no one was around? (For example, rocking back and forth for over an hour.)	(0)	1	2	3	4	5	6
6.	Does the behavior occur when *any* request is made of this person?	0	1	2	3	(4)	5	6
7.	Does the behavior occur whenever you stop attending to this person?	0	(1)	2	3	4	5	6
8.	Does the behavior occur when you take away a favorite toy, food, or activity?	0	1	2	3	(4)	5	6
9.	Does it appear to you that this person enjoys performing the behavior? (It feels, tastes, looks, smells, and/or sounds pleasing.)	0	(1)	2	3	4	5	6
10.	Does this person seem to do the behavior to upset or annoy you when you are trying to get him or her to do what you ask?	0	1	2	3	4	(5)	6
11.	Does this person seem to do the behavior to upset or annoy you when you are not paying attention to him or her? (For example, if you are sitting in a separate room, interacting with another person.)	0	1	(2)	3	4	5	6
12.	Does the behavior **stop** occurring shortly after you give this person the toy, food or activity he or she has requested?	0	1	2	3	(4)	5	6
13.	When the behavior is occurring, does this person seem calm and unaware of anything else going on around him or her?	(0)	1	2	3	4	5	6

Figure 4.3.   A completed Motivation Assessment Scale for Bill's object hitting in one-to-one instructional settings

QUESTIONS   ANSWERS

	Never	Almost Never	Seldom	Half the Time	Usually	Almost Always	Always
14. Does the behavior stop occurring shortly after (one to five minutes) you stop working or making demands of this person?	0	1	2	3	4	5	(6)
15. Does this person seem to do the behavior to get you to spend some time with him or her?	0	(1)	2	3	4	5	6
16. Does the behavior seem to occur when this person has been told that he or she can't do something he or she had wanted to do?	0	1	2	(3)	4	5	6

	Sensory		Escape		Attention		Tangible
	1. O	2.	5	3.	1	4.	3
	5. O	6.	4	7.	1	8.	4
	9. 1	10.	5	11.	2	12.	4
	13. O	14.	6	15.	1	16.	3
Total score =	1		20		5		14
Mean score =	0.25		5.0		1.25		3.5
Relative ranking =	4		1		3		2

Figure 4.3.   Continued.

Source: From *Severe Behavior Problems: A Functional Communication Training Approach,* pp. 80–82, by V. M. Durand, 1990, New York: Guilford: © 1990 by Guilford Press. Reprinted by permission.

researchers have developed specific techniques for assessing cognitive processes, such as having the person think aloud, listing different thoughts, thought sampling at various intervals, and a wide variety of self-statement inventories.

This internal perspective is quite different from the early emphasis of behavioral assessment, which focused almost exclusively on observable overt behavior. This transition has come about because of persuasive evidence for the relationship between behavior and cognitions (Alloy et al., 1999; Bandura, 1986; Garratt, Ingram, Rand, & Sawalani, 2007; Haaga, Dyck, & Ernst, 1991; Kendall & Treadwell, 2007). Cognitive processes not only change during the course of effective therapy but may be causally related to both the development as well as the maintenance of different types of disorders (Alloy et al., 1999; Breitholtz et al., 1999; Brewin, 1996; Garratt et al., 2007). Some approaches assume that altering cognitions can be sufficiently powerful to change behaviors. However, there are also a number of significant limitations with cognitive behavioral assessment. All material is necessarily derived from the client's self-reports of his or her internal processes and, as such, may be subject to a number of distortions. Clients can usually recall and describe the results of their cognitive processes, but they have much greater difficulty describing how they arrived at these conclusions. The actual processes may need to be inferred based on complicated analyses of the results derived from intricate assessment strategies. In addition, remembering events seems to be a reconstructive process in which each successive recall can be altered based on the person's needs, biases, and expectations (Henry et al., 1994; Lindsay & Read, 1995; Loftus, 1993). These inherent difficulties have led some traditional behaviorists to question the theoretical and practical appropriateness of cognitive assessment.

A relevant finding is that the popular belief in the "power of positive thinking" is simplistic because it is not a very good predictor of adjustment. What seems more important is the absence of negative statements or what Kendall and Hollon (1981) have referred to as "the power of nonnegative thinking." Furthermore, the effect of negative self-talk is greater than the ability of positive thinking to counter negative internal dialogue. As might be expected, gains in therapy have been associated with reductions in negative self-statements (Garratt et al., 2007; Kendall & Treadwell, 2007). Another issue is that relevant cognitions such as self-efficacy vary across cultures. For example, many nonwestern cultures have been found to have lower levels of self-efficacy; this is particularly true among persons from more collectivist cultures (Klassen, 2004). Despite this finding, levels of self-efficacy were actually more predictive of relevant behaviors among these cultures. Clinicians conducting cognitive and other forms of assessments need to take these contextual variables into consideration.

The two major strategies of cognitive assessment are through various self-report inventories and techniques of recording cognitions. Each of these general strategies has strengths and weaknesses and is appropriate in different situations for different types of clients.

Cognitive Self-Report Inventories

There has been a tremendous expansion in the number and frequency of use of cognitive self-report inventories. Guevremont and Spiegler (1990) noted that they were used nearly as frequently as behavioral interviewing and twice as often as direct observation (Guevremont & Spiegler, 1990). They have the general advantages of having strong face validity and are both easy and inexpensive to administer. However, their psychometric properties vary greatly, and many instruments in frequent use are quite poor in this regard. Typically, they involve between 20 and 100 items, with respondents asked to indicate their degree of endorsement of each item on a Likert-type scale. Many instruments have been tailored toward specific domains such as depression, fears and anxieties, self-efficacy, imagery, social skills (especially assertiveness), eating disorders, and marital problems. The main domains for cognitive self-report inventories and the most frequently used instruments in these domains are summarized in Table 4.1. It is beyond the scope of this chapter to review them, but useful information can be obtained in Bellack and Hersen (1998) and Hersen and Bellack (2002).

Table 4.1.   Cognitive self-report measures

Domain	Instruments
Depression	Dysfunctional Attitudes Scale
	Cognitive Bias Questionnaire (child and adult versions)
	Automatic Thoughts Questionnaire
	Beck Depression Inventory-II
	Attributional Styles Questionnaire
Fears and Anxieties	Social Avoidance and Distress Scale
	Fear of Negative Evaluation Scale
	Social Interaction Self-statement Test
	Irrational Beliefs Test
	Rational Behavior Inventory
	Fear Survey Schedule
Eating Disorders	Eating Attitudes Test
	Bulimia Test-Revised
	Cognitive Error Questionnaire (modified for eating disorders)

Table 4.1.   Continued

Domain	Instruments
Social Skills	Rathus Assertiveness Inventory
	Wolpe-Lazarus Assertion Inventory
	Gambrill Assertion Inventory
	Bakker-Assertiveness Schedule
	Conflict Resolution Inventory
	Survey of Heterosexual Interactions
	Stanford Shyness Scale
Marital Relationships	Relationship Attribution Measure
	Relationship Belief Inventory
	Dyadic Attribution Inventory
	Marital Attitude Survey
	Specific Relationship Standards

Theories of the cognitive processes of *depression* suggest that it is maintained by characteristic and repetitive thoughts that are self-perpetuating (Alloy et al., 1999; Garratt et al., 2007). A. T. Beck (1967) originally listed the cognitions associated with depression as involving *arbitrary inference* (making inferences without substantiating evidence), *selective abstraction* (making a broad judgment based on a minor aspect of an event), *overgeneralization* (extrapolating in an unjustified fashion from a minor event), and *magnification/minimization* (overemphasizing negative events; minimizing positive ones). Although these processes seem to be related to depression, a simple cause-effect model between depression and specific cognitions does not appear to be warranted, and further clarification is required (Greenberg, 2007). The most frequently used inventories to assess depressogenic cognitions are the Dysfunctional Attitudes Scale (A. Weissman & Beck, 1978), the Cognitive Bias Questionnaire (Hammen, 1978; Hammen & Krantz, 1976), Automatic Thoughts Questionnaire (Hollon & Kendall, 1980; Ingram et al., 1995), and Beck Depression Inventory (BDI-II; A. T. Beck et al., 1996). More extensive coverage of the BDI/BDI-II can be found in Chapter 13. In addition, the Attributional Styles Questionnaire (Seligman, Abramson, Semmel, & von Baeyer, 1979) is sometimes used to better understand the manner in which a client construes the causes for various behaviors, particularly those related to depression (i.e., learned helplessness).

A wide number of measures have been developed related to a person's *fears and anxieties* (see McGlyn & Rose, 1998). The main cognitions that seem to characterize social phobias are interpersonal threat along with beliefs that positive interpersonal feedback is incorrect (Kendall & Treadwell, 2007; Sewitch & Kirsch, 1984). The importance of a cognitive assessment of social phobias is underscored by research suggesting that cognitive deficits and distortions are more important in causing and maintaining the difficulty than deficits in social skills (Heimberg, 1994). Social phobics are more likely to recall negative information, fear social embarrassment, interpret ambiguous feedback negatively, underestimate their own performance, expect more negative evaluations from others, and have more negative self-statements before interactions (Breitholtz et al., 1999; Cacioppo, Glass, & Merluzzi, 1979; Hope & Heimberg, 1993). Assessment of the relative rate of occurrence of each of these areas can provide specific treatment suggestions regarding which processes need to be modified. The most frequently used instruments in the cognitive assessment of social phobias are the Social Avoidance and Distress Scale (Watson & Friend, 1969), Fear of Negative Evaluation Scale (FNE; Watson & Friend, 1969), and the Social Interaction Self-Statement Test (Glass, Merluzzi, Biever, & Larsen, 1982). Many of the self-statements described by research on social phobias and measured by tests such as the Social Interaction Self-Statement Test are quite similar to the ones described by A. T. Beck (1967) as characteristic of depression. These similarities raise the still-unresolved issue of whether specific irrational beliefs are related to specific disorders or whether there is a nonspecific (yet generally negative) effect of irrational beliefs (see Heimberg, 1994). Although less work has been done on generalized anxiety, two frequently used tests are the Irrational Beliefs Test (R. Jones, 1969) and the somewhat similar 70-item Rational Behavior Inventory (Shorkey, Reyes, & Whiteman, 1977). The many versions of the Fear Survey Schedule (Wolpe & Lang, 1964, 1969, 1977) and the Fear Survey Schedule for Children (Ollendick, 1978, 1983) do not measure specific cognitions related to fear, but they are both frequently used and quite useful in detailing the various categories of fear a client might have.

Several strategies have been used in the assessment of *eating disorders* based on the observations that this class of disorders involves considerable cognitive distortions (Mizes & Christiano, 1994). Some authors have taken a previously developed scale, such as the Cognitive Error Questionnaire (Lefebvre, 1981), and modified it to evaluate the cognitive distortions specific to eating disorders (Dritschel, Williams, & Cooper, 1991). The Eating Attitudes Test (Garner & Garfinkel, 1979) and the Bulimia Test-Revised (Thelan, Farmer, Wonderlich, & Smith, 1991) both have strong psychometric properties and focus primarily on cognitions related to eating and weight control. A further strategy is to have eating-disordered persons monitor their self-statements in their natural environments (Zotter & Crowther, 1991). The value of such strategies is the indication that cognitive behavioral instruments can be tailored toward specific disorders and the information derived from these strategies has direct relevance for treatment as it provides clinicians with specific cognitions to work with.

The area that has dominated the assessment of *social skills* has been assertiveness. Such assessment typically rates not only cognitions related to assertive behavior but also specific behaviors and skills. A wide variety of self-report inventories has been developed, including the Wolpe-Lazarus Assertion Inventory (Wolpe & Lazarus, 1966), Gambrill Assertion Inventory (Gambrill & Richey, 1975), Bakker Assertiveness Inventory (Bakker, Bakker-Rabdau, & Breit, 1978), and the Conflict Resolution Inventory (McFall & Lillesand, 1971). However, the RAS (Rathus, 1973) has been the most extensively used, and relevant normative data are available for normal college students (Quillan, Besing, & Dinning, 1977) as well as for psychiatric populations (Rathus & Nevid, 1977). Respondents are requested to rate, on a 6-point scale, how descriptive each statement is. A +3 indicates that the statement is "very uncharacteristic of me" and a –3 indicates that it is "very characteristic." In addition to the original 30-item schedule, two other versions have been developed for special populations. The modified RAS (MRAS; Del Greco, Breitbach, & McCarthy, 1981) was developed for young adolescents. A simplified version is available that requires a minimum 6th-grade reading level in contrast to the 10th-grade reading level required for the regular version (SRAS; McCormick, 1984). Additional, nonassertiveness social skills inventories include the Survey of Heterosexual Interactions (Twentyman & McFall, 1975) and the Stanford Shyness Survey (Zimbardo, 1977).

Assessing *marital relationships* involves gathering information about a wide range of behaviors with a particular focus on the strengths and weaknesses of the relationship, goals for change, and attempts the couple has made to change in the past (see Birchler & Fals-Stewart, 2006). Much of this information can and should be obtained through a careful interview. Areas related to cognitive assessment are the differing perceptions of each spouse, the perceived causes (attributions) for why the persons act in certain ways, expectations for future behavior, assumptions about relationships (roles, scripts), and standards by which the relationship is judged. Many of these areas can be evaluated through the use of cognitive self-report inventories. Some of the more frequent and well-researched instruments are the Relationship Attribution Measure (Fincham & Bradbury, 1992), Relationships Beliefs Inventory (Eidelstein & Epstein, 1982), Dyadic Attribution Inventory (Baucom, Sayers, & Duhe, 1989), Marital Attitude Survey (Pretzer, Epstein, & Fleming, 1992), and Specific Relationship Standards (Baucom, Epstein, Rankin, & Burnett, 1996).

Self-efficacy has received considerable interest, particularly because it has been related to a variety of different predictions relevant to treatment (Bandura, 1986). Assessment is usually accomplished by simply having clients rate the degree to which they believe they are able to accomplish a certain skill or goal (i.e., stop smoking). Useful distinctions should be made between the level of strength of self-efficacy and its generalizability from one situation to the next. Because some question exists regarding the degree to which self-efficacy can be related from one situation to the next, specific measurements are often used for different areas (depression, assertion, smoking, etc.). A person having a high level of self-efficacy is likely to have positive expectations about his or her effectiveness to judge and deal effectively with situations. Self-efficacy is developed as a result of the attainments someone has achieved in the past, vicarious (observational) experiences, verbal persuasion, and physiological states. An assessment of self-efficacy is especially important in understanding the antecedent and retrospective accounts of the effect and quality of the behavior. The relative level of self-efficacy has been found to predict a wide number of variables, including general therapy outcome, in the treatment of smoking and relapse rate from self-regulatory training (see Bandura, 1997).

Imagery has frequently been observed to relate to a person's presenting problem in the form of fantasies, daydreams, and different dreaming states. A depressed person may continually repeat images of being criticized, the anxious person might replay scenes of danger, and the paranoid person might frequently review images of persecution. Knowing a person's relative ability to produce and control images may be important in predicting response to treatment that requires the formation of images, such as systematic desensitization, covert desensitization, covert aversive conditioning, and certain types of relaxation procedures (Sheikh, 2003). Extensive experimental work has been conducted on imagery in areas such as the different dimensions of imagery (C. Parks, 1982), differences between waking and nonwaking imagery (Cartwright, 1986), and the effects of conscious and unconscious images on behavior (Horowitz, 1985). Persons wishing to assess both clinical imagery and other aspects of cognitions might use one or several of the strategies described below that have been developed to assess cognitions.

Recording Cognitions

In addition to the many self-report inventories available, a number of strategies have been developed for recording cognitions in a less-structured manner. C. Parks and Hollon (1988) have listed and summarized these methods used by previous researchers:

Thinking Aloud. Clients are requested to verbalize their ongoing thoughts, with these verbalizations usually extending for 5 to 10 minutes (Lodge et al., 2000). A similar technique is free association, in which the client is asked to simply say whatever comes to mind rather than report on his or her ongoing inner thoughts. A potential problem is that the procedure may feel unnatural and, therefore, provide a sample different from normally occurring internal thoughts. Also, the client may have no opportunity to verbalize competing thoughts with the result that the reported thoughts will most likely be a limited portion of the total cognitions. In addition, clients may not report everything honestly. A factor that is likely to make the verbally reported thoughts different from actual ongoing processes is that, typically, people change the topic of ongoing internal dialogues every 5 to 6 seconds, whereas verbal reports of these dialogues may have topic changes only on the average of every 30 seconds.

Private Speech. Sometimes children's cognitions can be assessed by paying close attention to barely audible speech they make while engaged in various activities. It is believed that these private verbalizations are closely aligned to inner thoughts.

Articulated Thoughts. Clinicians may wish to create structured situations or simulations that parallel the problems the client reports. For example, an analog situation may be created that demands the client to be assertive or be exposed to criticism or phobic stimuli (Rosqvist et al., 2006). The person can then be asked to articulate the thoughts he or she is experiencing during these situations. Typical thoughts can be noted and inferences made regarding how they relate to the problem behaviors.

Production Methods. Instead of asking clients to articulate their thoughts during a simulation, an actual naturalistic situation (criticism, phobic stimuli, etc.) can occur, with clients then noting and recording the typical thoughts they have related to these situations. As such, these methods might also be referred to as in vivo self-reports.

Endorsement Method. The client might be presented with either a standardized (e.g., Irrational Beliefs Test, Cognitive Bias Questionnaire) or an informally developed list of items and then be requested to rate frequency of occurrence, strength of belief, and how the item might be uniquely represented in the person's cognitions. These items might include ratings of the frequency of such thoughts as "What's the use" or "I can't do anything right." Potential difficulties with this technique are the effects of the demand characteristics of the situation and social desirability. An underlying and questionable assumption behind the technique is that the relevant cognitions are in the client's conscious awareness.

Thought Listing. Instead of developing a continuous description of ongoing thoughts, clients might be asked simply to summarize their relevant thoughts. These thoughts might be elicited by a specific stimulus, problem area, or merely attending to or anticipating a stimulus.

Thought Sampling. A sample of a person's thoughts might be obtained by setting a prompt (e.g., a beep on a PDA), then having the client describe the thoughts he or she was having just before the interruption by the prompt.

Event Recording. The client might be asked to wait until a relevant event occurs (e.g., hand washing for an obsessive-compulsive), at which point the thoughts related to these events are written down. Instead of merely waiting for a problem or spontaneously occurring behavior, a client might also be asked to describe the thoughts related to the expression of new and desired behaviors, such as assertion. The relevant thoughts about these behaviors might then be used to increase the likelihood of their continued occurrence.

Psychophysiological Assessment

A complete understanding of the person involves an assessment of not only behavioral, affective, and cognitive modes but also of the ways these interact with and are dependent on physiological functioning. Such psychophysiological assessments have recently become easier to make because of increased interest and knowledge regarding instrumen-tation (magnetic resonance imaging [MRI], electronics, computers), operant conditioning of behaviors that at one time were considered involuntary, physiological and neurochemi-cal aspects of behavior, and behavioral medicine (Larkin, 2006). The most frequently assessed physiological responses are heart rate, blood pressure, skin temperature, muscle tension, vasodilation, galvanic skin response (GSR), and brain activity as measured by electroencephalograms (EEGs). By quantifying data gathered through these areas, psy-chological problems can be translated into more precise physiological indices.

One of the first relevant studies to relate psychological and physiological modes indicated that fear and anger had different physiological responses in blood pressure and skin conductance (Ax, 1953). This result suggested that these and other psychologi-cal variables might be measured in ways other than through self-report inventories. More recently, it has been found that patients with obsessive-compulsive disorder had greater activation of the orbitofrontal region of the cortex (Anderson & Savage, 2004). A further representative area of research has involved the relationship between different personality variables and psychophysiological measurement. Clients with antisocial personalities have been found to have lower skin conductance than those with anxiety disorders (Lorber, 2004). Polygraph testing to detect lying, while still in extensive use, has not been found to be particularly effective at detecting those who lie from those who are telling the truth (Iacano & Patrick, 2006). In contrast, greater promise has been demonstrated differenti-ating true from faked memory loss using event-related potentials (ERPs). Physiological baseline measures for an area such as anxiety can and have been used to monitor the effectiveness of treatment for social phobias, generalized anxiety disorders, and obses-sive-compulsive disorders (Larkin, 2006). Although most of the previously mentioned studies represent very general correlations among such variables as emotions, personality, behavioral disorders, and outcome assessment, they show considerable potential for future assessment, should these measures become more refined.

In addition to the usual knowledge relating to psychological assessment, clinicians who obtain and interpret psychophysiological data must have knowledge in anatomy, electronics, and the physiology of cardiovascular, musculoskeletal, neurological, respira-tory, electrodermal, ocular, and gastrointestinal response systems. This extensive back-ground is particularly important because instrumentation presents a number of special problems. A variety of confounding factors may be present, such as the effect of slowing respiratory rate to alter cardiac output or the effect of eye roll on measured brain activity. Filters might be necessary to exclude noise in the system. The techniques are also intru-sive, thereby making the situation artificial. As a result, it may not be correct to generalize to outside aspects of the client's life or between different response modes. A wide vari-ety of difficulties may arise regarding meaningful psychological interpretations based on the physiological data. In the future, the development of better instruments and improved methods of computer analysis are likely to increase the utility of psychophysiological assessment and overcome many of these difficulties.

RECOMMENDED READING

Haynes, S. N., & Heiby, E. M. (Eds.). (2004). *Comprehensive handbook of psychological assessment. Behavioral assessment* (Vol. *3*). Hoboken, NJ: John Wiley & Sons.

Hersen, M. (Ed.). (2006). *Clinician's handbook of adult behavioral assessment.* New York: Elsevier.

Hersen, M., & Bellack, A. S. (Eds.). (2002). *Dictionary of behavioral assessment techniques* (2nd ed). New York: Pergamon Press.

Chapter 5

WECHSLER INTELLIGENCE SCALES

The Wechsler intelligence scales are individually administered, composite intelligence tests in a battery format. They assess different areas of intellectual abilities and create a situation in which aspects of personality can be observed. The most recent versions (WAIS-IV and WISC-IV) provide an overall, or "Full Scale IQ," as well as specific index scores that can be calculated using various combinations of subtests. The Wechsler intelligence scales are considered to be among the best of all psychological tests because they have sound psychometric properties and produce information relevant to practitioners. As a result, they have become the most frequently used tests in clinical practice (Archer, Buffington-Vollum, Stredny, & Handel, 2006; Camara, Nathan, & Puente, 2000; Watkins, Campbell, Nieberding, & Hallmark, 1995).

TESTING OF INTELLIGENCE: PRO AND CON

The testing of intelligence has had a consistent history of misunderstanding, controversy, and occasional misuse (Bartholomew, 2006: D. Flanagan & Harrison, 2005; Weinberg, 1989). Criticisms have ranged from moral indictments against labeling individuals, to cultural bias, and even to accusations of flagrant abuse of test scores. Although valid criticisms can be made against testing intelligence, such procedures also have a number of advantages.

One of the main assets of intelligence tests is their accuracy in predicting future behavior. Initially, Alfred Binet was able to achieve a certain degree of predictive success with his scales, and, since that time, test procedures have become progressively more refined and accurate. More recent studies provide ample support that intelligence tests can predict an extremely wide number of variables. In particular, IQ tests are excellent predictors of academic achievement (A. Kaufman & Lichtenberger, 2006; Neisser et al., 1996) and occupational performance (J. Hunter & Schmidt, 1996; F. Schmidt & Hunter, 1998, 2004; Wagner, 1997), and are sensitive to the presence of neuropsychological deficit (Groth-Marnat, Gallagher, Hale, & E. Kaplan, 2000; Lezak, Howieson, & Loring, 2004). However, certain liabilities are also associated with these successes. First, intelligence tests can be used to classify children into stereotyped categories, which limit their freedom to choose fields of study. Furthermore, IQ tests are quite limited in predicting nontest or nonacademic activity, yet they are sometimes incorrectly used to make these inferences (Snyderman & Rothman, 1987; Sternberg, 2003). It should also be stressed that intelligence tests are measures of a person's current level of functioning and, as such, are best used for making short-term predictions. Long-term predictions, although attempted frequently, are less accurate because there can be many uncontrolled, influencing variables. Similarly, even short-term academic placements made solely on the basis of an IQ score have a high chance of failure because all the variables that may be crucial for success are not and cannot be measured by an intelligence test. It can sometimes be tempting for test users to extend the meaning of test scores beyond their intended scope, especially in relation to the predictions they can realistically be expected to make.

In addition to predicting academic achievement, IQ scores have also been correlated with occupation, ranging from highly trained professionals with mean IQs of 125, to unskilled workers with mean IQs of 87 (Reynolds, Chastain, Kaufman, & McLean, 1987). Correlations between job proficiency and general intelligence have been highest in predicting relatively more complex jobs (.58) than less demanding occupations (.23; F. Schmidt & Hunter, 2004). They have also reported moderately high correlations between general intelligence and success for managers (.53), salespersons (.61), and clerks (.54). For intellectually demanding tasks, nearly half the variance related to performance criteria can be accounted for by general intelligence (F. Schmidt & Hunter, 2004; F. Schmidt, Ones, & Hunter, 1992). The use of intelligence tests for personnel selection has demonstrated financial efficacy for organizations (F. Schmidt & Hunter, 1998). In addition, the accuracy of using IQ tests can be incrementally increased by combining the results with integrity tests, work samples, and structured interviews (F. Schmidt & Hunter, 1998, 2004).

Another important asset of intelligence tests, particularly the WAIS-IV and WISC-IV, is that they provide valuable information about a person's cognitive strengths and weaknesses. They are standardized procedures whereby a person's performance in various areas can be compared with that of age-related peers. In addition, useful comparisons can be made regarding a person's pattern of strengths and weaknesses. The WAIS-IV, WISC-IV, and other individually administered tests provide the examiner with a structured context in which a variety of tasks can be used to observe the unique and personal ways the examinee approaches cognitive tasks. Through a client's interactions with both the examiner and the test materials, an initial impression can be made of the individual's self-esteem, behavioral idiosyncrasies, anxiety, social skills, and motivation, while also obtaining a specific picture of intellectual functioning.

Intelligence tests often provide clinicians, educators, and researchers with baseline measures for use in determining either the degree of change that has occurred in an individual over time or how an individual compares with other persons in a particular area or ability. These distinctions may have important implications for evaluating the effectiveness of an educational program or for assessing the changing abilities of a specific student. In cases involving recovery from a head injury or readjustment following neurosurgery, it may be extremely helpful for clinicians to measure and follow the cognitive changes that occur in a patient. Furthermore, IQ assessments may be important in researching and understanding more adequately the effect on cognitive functioning of environmental variables, such as educational programs, family background, and nutrition. Thus, these assessments can provide useful information about cultural, biological, maturational, or treatment-related differences among individuals.

A criticism leveled at intelligence tests is that almost all have an inherent bias toward emphasizing convergent, analytical, and scientific modes of thought. Thus, a person who emphasizes divergent, artistic, and imaginative modes of thought may be at a distinct disadvantage. Some critics have even stressed that the current approach to intelligence testing has become a social mechanism used by people with similar values to pass on educational advantages to children who resemble themselves. Not only might IQ tests tend to place creative individuals at a disadvantage, but also they are limited in assessing nonacademically oriented intellectual abilities (Gardner, 2006; Snyderman & Rothman, 1987; Sternberg, 2003). Thus, social acumen, success in dealing with people, the ability to handle the concrete realities of the individual's daily world, social fluency, and specific tasks, such as purchasing merchandise, are not measured by standard intelligence tests (Sternberg, 2003). More succinctly, people are capable of many more cognitive abilities than can possibly be measured on an intelligence test.

Misunderstanding and potential misuse of intelligence tests frequently occur when scores are treated as measures of innate capacity. The IQ is not a measure of an innate fixed ability, nor is it representative of all problem-solving situations. It is a specific and limited sample, made at a certain point in time, of abilities that are susceptible to change because of a variety of circumstances. It reflects, to a large extent, the richness of an individual's past experiences. Although interpretation guidelines are quite clear in pointing out the limited nature of a test score, there is a tendency to look at test results as absolute facts reflecting permanent characteristics in an individual. People often want a quick, easy, and reductionist method to quantify, understand, and assess innate cognitive abilities, and the IQ score has become the most widely misused test score to fill this need.

An important limitation of intelligence tests is that, for the most part, they are not concerned with the underlying processes involved in problem solving. They focus on the final product or outcome rather than on the steps involved in reaching the outcome. They look at the "what" rather than the "how" (Embretson, Schneider, & Roth, 1986; E. Kaplan et al., 1999; Milberg, Hebbgen, & Kaplan, 1996). Thus, a low score on Arithmetic might result from poor attention, difficulty understanding the examiner because of disturbances in comprehension, or low educational attainment. The extreme example of this "end product" emphasis is the global IQ score. When the examiner looks at the myriad assortment of intellectual abilities as a global ability, the complexity of cognitive functioning may be simplified to the point of being almost useless. The practitioner can apply labels quickly and easily, without attempting to examine the specific strengths and weaknesses that might make precise therapeutic interventions or knowledgeable recommendations possible. Such thinking detracts significantly from the search for a wider, more precise, and more process-oriented understanding of mental abilities.

A further concern about intelligence tests involves their limited usefulness in assessing minority groups with divergent cultural backgrounds. It has been stated that intelligence-test content is biased in favor of European American, middle-class values. Critics stress that minorities tend to be at a disadvantage when taking the tests because of deficiencies in motivation, lack of practice, lack of familiarity with culturally loaded items, and difficulties in establishing rapport. Numerous arguments against using intelligence tests for the assessment and placement of minorities have culminated in legal restrictions on the use of IQ scores. However, traditional defenses of IQ scores suggest that they are less biased than has been accused (see the "Use with Diverse Groups" section later in this chapter). The issue certainly has not been resolved, but clinicians should continue to be aware of this dilemma, pay attention to subgroup norms, and interpret minority group IQ scores cautiously.

Finally, many people feel that their IQs are deeply personal pieces of information. They would prefer that others, even a psychologist who is expected to observe confidentiality, not be allowed access to this information. This problem is further compounded when IQ scores might be given to several different persons, such as during legal proceedings or personnel selection.

Intelligence tests provide a number of useful and well-respected functions. They can adequately predict short-term scholastic performance; assess an individual's relative strengths and weaknesses; predict occupational achievement; reveal important personality variables; and permit the researcher, educator, or clinician to trace possible changes in an individual or population. However, these assets are helpful only if the limitations of intelligence tests are adequately understood and appropriately taken into consideration. They are limited in predicting certain aspects of occupational success and nonacademic skills, such as creativity, motivational level, social acumen, and success in dealing with people. Furthermore, IQ scores are not measures of an innate, fixed ability, and their use in classifying minority groups has been questioned. Finally, there has been an overemphasis on understanding the end product of cognitive functioning and a relative neglect in appreciating underlying cognitive processes.

HISTORY AND DEVELOPMENT

During the 1930s, Wechsler began studying a number of standardized tests and selected 11 different subtests to form his initial battery. His search for subtests was in part guided by his conception that intelligence is global in nature and represents a part of the greater whole of personality. Several of his subtests were derived from portions of the 1937 revision of the Stanford-Binet (Comprehension, Arithmetic, Digit Span, Similarities, and Vocabulary). The remaining subtests came from the Army Group Examinations (Picture Arrangement), Koh's Block Design (Block Design), Army Alpha (Information, Comprehension), Army Beta (Digit Symbol-Coding), Healy Picture Completion (Picture Completion), and Pinther-Paterson Test (Object Assembly). These subtests were combined and published in 1939 as the Wechsler-Bellevue Intelligence Scale. The Wechsler-Bellevue had a number of technical deficiencies primarily related to both the reliability of the subtests and the size and representativeness of the normative sample. Thus, it was revised to form the Wechsler Adult Intelligence Scale (WAIS) in 1955; another revised edition (WAIS-R) was published in 1981. The 1981 revision was based on 1,880 individuals who were generally representative of the 1970 census and categorized into nine different age groups.

The Wechsler Adult Intelligence Scale-III (WAIS-III) replaced the earlier (1981) WAIS-R. The primary reason for the revision was to update the norms. Additional reasons included extending the age range, modifying items, developing a higher IQ "ceiling" and "floor," decreased reliance on timed performance, developing index/factor scores, creating linkages to other measures of cognitive functioning/achievement, and extensive testing of reliability and validity. Despite these changes, many of the traditional features of the WAIS-R were maintained, including the six Verbal subtests and the five Performance subtests. Maintaining these clusters of subtests still enabled practitioners to calculate the Full Scale, Verbal, and Performance IQs. An added feature of the WAIS-III was the inclusion of three new subtests, which enabled the calculation of four index scores. Thus, the WAIS-III was not merely a renormed "face-lift"; it also enabled the clinician to do more with the different test scores, such as being able to assess persons with either greater age or IQ ranges as well as linking scores with the Wechsler Memory Scales or calculating both IQ and index/factor scores.

The Wechsler Adult Intelligence Scale—Fourth Edition (WAIS-IV) is the most recent revision of the evolving Wechsler intelligence scales (Wechsler, 2008a,b). The general purpose of the revision was to update norms, improve floors and ceilings, improve psychometric properties, reduce testing time, and conorm it with the Wechsler Memory Scale-Fourth Edition (WMS-IV; see Table 5.1) and the Wechsler Individual Achievement Test-II (WIAT). One of the most obvious changes has been the elimination of the time-honored verbal versus performance IQ. Instead, the WAIS-IV uses the traditional Full Scale IQ along with four index scores (Verbal Comprehension, Working Memory, Perceptual Reasoning, and Processing Speed). The major rationale for the elimination of the Verbal-Performance IQs is that they are not pure measures but typically combine a number of different abilities. For example, the Verbal IQ included measures of verbal abilities as well as working memory. Thus, it was not a unitary measure of an ability. In contrast, relying on the four index scores ensures that relatively pure, theoretically sound measures

Table 5.1.   Major changes on the WAIS-IV

Elimination of Verbal and Performance IQs

Updated norms

15 subtests (versus 14 on the WAIS-III)

Computation of Full Scale IQ and Indexes based on 10 core subtests

General Ability Index (optional index that combines Verbal Comprehension and Perceptual Reasoning)

3 newly developed subtests (Visual Puzzles, Figure Weights, Cancellation)

Deletion of 2 subtests (Object Assembly, Picture Arrangement)

Organization of subtests into core and supplemental

Renaming of the Perceptual Organization Index to the Perceptual Reasoning Index

Inclusion of process scoring options for Block Design, Digit Span, Letter-Number Sequencing

Potential for shortened administration using only the 10 core subtests (for FSIQ + Indexes)

Greater attention to floor and ceilings

Normed linkages with the Wechsler Memory Scale-IV

Upgrade kit for specialist neuropsychologists and geropsychologists

of abilities have been made. This reliance on a Full Scale IQ plus the four indexes parallels a similar development for the WISC-IV (Wechsler, 2003). In addition, the WAIS-IV includes an optional General Ability Index that combines the Verbal Comprehension and Perceptual Reasoning index scores. An upgrade of the WAIS-IV for neuropsychologists and geropsychologists became available in 2009 (*WAIS-IV/WMS-IV Advanced Clinical Solutions,* Pearson, 2009c).

A further feature of the WAIS-IV has been the deletion, addition, and revision of subtests. In addition, subtests have been organized according to core and supplemental subtests. The core subtests are used to develop the index scores (see Table 5.2). However, if a core subtest is "spoiled" (i.e., made invalid) or if practitioners are unable to administer a core subtest, they can use one of the supplemental subtests instead. Supplemental subtests can also be administered to find additional information regarding a client's level of functioning. For example, the new Cancellation subtest might be added to Symbol Search and Coding to add further information related to a client's ability to process information rapidly. Many of the subtests have undergone revisions to enhance clarity of instructions, refine scoring rules, change stimuli, and include different items.

New norms have been developed for the WAIS-IV derived from 2,200 persons between the ages of 16 and 90 stratified according to sex, education, ethnicity, and geographical region. These norms closely correspond to the 2005 U.S. census data. Whereas 200 examinees were included for the age bands between 16 and 60, only 100 examinees have been included for the age bands between 70 and 90. The WAIS-IV has been conormed with the WMS-IV and Wechsler Individual Achievement Test-II. Norms and patterns of responses have been developed for special groups, including mild cognitive impairment, borderline intellectual functioning, traumatic brain injury, Alzheimer's disease, attention deficit hyperactivity disorder (ADHD), reading disorder, math disorder, autism, Asperger's syndrome, and depression.

The original Wechsler-Bellevue Scale was developed for adults, but in 1949, Wechsler developed the Wechsler Intelligence Scale for Children (WISC) so that children from the age of 5 years 0 months could be assessed in a similar manner. Easier items, designed

Table 5.2.   Organization of WAIS-IV subtests

Index	Core subtests	Supplemental subtests
Verbal Comprehension	Similarities	Comprehension
	Vocabulary	
	Information	
Perceptual Reasoning	Block Design	Figure Weights
	Matrix Reasoning	Picture Completion
	Visual Puzzles	
Working Memory	Digit Span	Letter-Number Sequencing
	Arithmetic	
Processing Speed	Symbol Search	Cancellation
	Coding	

for children, were added to the original scales and standardized on 2,200 European American boys and girls selected to be representative of the 1940 census. However, some evidence shows that Wechsler's sample may have been overrepresentative of children in the middle and upper socioeconomic levels. Thus, ethnic minorities and children from lower socioeconomic levels may have been penalized when compared with the normative group. The WISC was revised in 1974 and standardized on a new sample that was more accurately representative of children in the United States. The WISC-III (Wechsler, 1991) was released in 1991; its major change was the inclusion of four factor/index scores (Verbal Comprehension, Perceptual Organization, Freedom from Distractibility, and Processing Speed). The new Processing Speed factor involved the inclusion of a new Symbol Search subtest along with the older Coding subtest. As with the earlier WISC-R, the standardization and reliability were excellent. The scales were standardized on 2,200 children between the ages of 6 and 16 who closely matched the 1988 census. The sample consisted of 100 boys and 100 girls for each of the different age groups.

The WISC-IV (2003) was noteworthy in that it contained more changes than any other previous edition (see Table 5.3). The most obvious change was the elimination of the time-honored Verbal and Performance IQ. There was instead a greater reliance on interpretation using a combination of the four index scores along with the global Full Scale IQ (see Table 5.4). The indexes have also been refined by the inclusion of a five new subtests (and the deletion of Picture Arrangement, Object Assembly, and Mazes). Completely new norms for the WISC-IV were developed that closely represented the U.S. census. A further potentially useful feature was the publication of the WISC-IV Integrated (Wechsler et al., 2004), which allows for 12 additional procedures that enable specialty practitioners the option of analyzing the underlying processes clients go through when making their responses (see McCloskey & Maerlander, 2005).

One of the motivations for the WAIS-IV and WISC-IV revisions was to update the instruments' theoretical foundations. To a certain extent, this has been done. The importance of fluid intelligence has been reflected in the introduction of a new subtest that assesses this area of intellectual functioning (Matrix Reasoning, Picture Concepts, Word Reasoning, Visual Puzzles, and Figure Weights). In addition, the concepts of working memory and processing speed have been incorporated and refined. The result has been changes and refinements in the subtests and psychometric properties included in the Working Memory and Processing Speed indexes. It should also be noted that the factor

Table 5.3. **Major changes on the WISC-IV**

Elimination of Verbal and Performance IQs

Updated norms

Fifteen subtests (versus 13 on the WISC-III)

Computation of IQ and Indexes based on 10 core subtests

Introduction of five new WISC-IV subtests:

Three newly developed subtests (Word Reasoning, Cancellation, and Picture Concepts) plus downward extensions of two WAIS-III subtests (Matrix Reasoning, and Letter-Number Sequencing)

Three deleted subtests (Picture Arrangement, Object Assembly, and Mazes)

New organization of subtests into core and supplemental

Introduction of seven Process scores

Longer administration time with all 15 subtests (65–80 minutes versus 50–70 minutes for the WISC-III)

Potential for shortened administration using only the 10 core subtests (for FSIQ + Indexes)

Greater attention to floor and ceilings

Normed linkages with the Wechsler Individual Intelligence Test-II

IQs below 70 now called "Extremely Low" versus the "Intellectually Deficient" title on the WISC-III

Table 5.4. **Organization of WISC-IV indexes and subtests**

Index	Core subtests	Supplemental subtests
Verbal Comprehension	Similarities	Information
	Vocabulary	Word Reasoning
	Comprehension	
Perceptual Reasoning	Block Design	Picture Completion
	Picture Concepts	
	Matrix Reasoning	
Working Memory	Digit Span	Arithmetic
	Letter-Number Sequencing	
Processing Speed	Coding	Cancellation
	Symbol Search	

structure of the more recent revisions of the Wechsler intelligence scales has resulted in a de facto theory of intelligence defined by the Full Scale IQ in combination with the functions measured by the four indexes. However, neither the WAIS-IV nor the WISC-IV has been organized around a specific theory of intelligence. In contrast, revisions of the K-ABC, Stanford Binet-5, and the Woodcock Johnson-III, each of which took place in the first few years of the 21st century, were closely aligned to the Cattell-Horn-Carrol (CHC) theory of intelligence. Some have stated that the Wechsler intelligence scales have been overburdened by their traditions, resulting in a failure to make major adaptations to evolving knowledge related to intelligence (Flanagan & Kaufman, 2004).

In 1967, the Wechsler Preschool and Primary Scale of Intelligence (WPPSI) was first published for the assessment of children between the ages of 4 and 6 years 6 months. Just as the WISC is a downward extension of the WAIS, so the WPPSI is generally a downward extension of the WISC in which easier but similar items are used. Although most of the scales are similar in form and content to the WISC, a number are unique to the WPPSI. The WPPSI was revised in 1989 (WPPSI-R; Wechsler, 1989) and again in 2002 (WPPSI-III; Wechsler, 2002c).

RELIABILITY AND VALIDITY

WAIS-IV Reliability and Validity

The reliabilities for the WAIS-IV are generally quite high (Wechsler, 2008b). Areas of note are that average split-half reliability for the Full Scale IQ (FSIQ) is an extremely high .98 (Wechsler, 2008b). Average split-half reliabilities for the other combined or "composite" scores are only slightly lower and range from a high of .96 for the Verbal Comprehension index to a low of .90 for Processing Speed. Average split-half reliability for the subtests ranged from excellent (i.e., Vocabulary r = .94, Digit Span r = .93) to an acceptable .78 for Cancellation. All subtests except Cancellation were above .81. These good to excellent reliabilities were found not only for the standardization sample but also among various clinical populations (i.e., brain injured, ADHD, Alzheimer's disease). The average standard error of measurement for various WAIS-IV scores indicates a small band of error (i.e., Full Scale IQ = 2.16, Verbal Comprehension Index = 2.12, Processing Speed Index = 4.24). Calculating the Standard Error of Measure for each of the composite scores is a standard procedure on the WAIS-IV Record Form so that it is reported for all examinees. The Average test-retest reliabilities (8–82 days, M = 22 days) for the Full Scale IQ was quite high (r = .96) and the composite scores were similarly high, ranging from .96 for Verbal Comprehension to a low of .87 for Processing Speed. These reliabilities are among the best for any test available and, in almost all cases, represent a slight improvement over the WAIS-III.

While these test-retest reliabilities indicate a high degree of temporal stability, there is still some degree of improvement on retesting because of practice effects. Improved performance due to retesting is important to understand; clinicians need to know when to attribute an increase in scores to practice effects and when this might indicate actual clinical improvement. Over the retesting interval (8–82 days, M = 22 days), the Full Scale IQ was found to increase by 4.7 points. The lowest increase was for Verbal Comprehension (2.5 points) followed by Working Memory (3.1), Perceptual Reasoning (3.9), and Processing Speed (4.4). These increases are not only statistically significant but may have clinical significance when making inferences about the extent to which real improvement/deterioration has occurred for a particular client. Thus, a client who has a Perceptual Reasoning increase of 4 points on retesting may not really be improving in everyday functions but merely demonstrating practice effects. A difference of 15 points on the earlier WAIS-III Full Scale IQ (for ages 16 to 54) was found to be necessary to infer that there had been an actual improvement in abilities (A. Kaufman & Lichtenberger, 2002). Research with the WAIS-R indicated that these practice effects can occur up to 9 months later even among head-injured patients. However, retest gains have also been found to diminish with advancing age (J. Ryan, Paolo, & Brungardt, 1990; Wechsler, 2008a, 2008b).

Because extensive validity studies exist for the WAIS-III, one of the most important steps in WAIS-IV validation was to determine the comparability between the two tests. As expected, correlations were found to be quite high. The WAIS-IV and WAIS-III Full Scale IQ correlation was .94 (Wechsler, 2008b). The four indexes were similarly high, ranging from .91 for Verbal Comprehension to .84 for Perceptual Reasoning/Perceptual Organization. This finding suggests that the WAIS-IV measures essentially the same constructs as the WAIS-III. Noteworthy high correlations between WAIS-IV and WAIS-III

[handwritten margin note: could this indicate that verbal comp. is a static aspect of intelligence when compared to others?]

subtests were .90 for Information, .87 for Vocabulary, and .85 for Coding. In contrast, a relatively low correlation was found for Picture Completion (.65). Correlations between the WAIS-IV and WISC-IV for a group of 16-year-olds were quite high (Full Scale IQ = .91, Verbal Comprehension = .88, Perceptual Reasoning = .77, Working Memory = .78, Processing Speed = .77). The correlations between the WAIS-IV and Wechsler Memory Scale-III were .61 for the Working Memory Index. A similar .59 correlation was found between the Full Scale IQ and the WMS-III General Memory Index. These moderate correlations are expected, given that the WAIS-IV and WMS-III measure somewhat different but still overlapping constructs. Correlations between achievement were, as expected, in the moderate to high range (WAIS-IV Full Scale IQ and Wechsler Individual Achievement Test-II Total Achievement = .88).

The WAIS-IV has also been found to produce expected patterns of correlation with a number of additional standard ability measures (Wechsler, 2008b). The Delis-Kaplan Executive Functioning System (Delis, Kaplan, & Kramer, 2001) is a series of subtests that measure various aspects of a client's ability to initiate, plan, and flexibly monitor their behavior. Representative correlations were a .22 between Perceptual Reasoning and the ability to fluidly produce the names of classes of objects (Category Fluency) and a correlation of .77 with Full Scale IQ and the ability to flexibly and rapidly connect combinations of letters and numbers (Trail Making). The California Verbal Learning Test-II (Delis, Kramer, Kaplan, & Ober, 2000) measures how well a person can recall lists of words that are read to them. Correlations between the WAIS-IV Full Scale IQ and a series of trials on learning word lists ranged from .48 to .32 (Wechsler, 2008b). A final representative test is the Repeatable Battery for the Assessment of Neuropsychological Status (RBANS; Randolph, 1998), which measures various domains of cognitive functioning (see Chapter 12). Correlations between the WAIS-IV Full Scale IQ and the RBANS Total Score was .75. The WAIS-IV Index scores and RBANS Total Score correlations were slightly lower, ranging from a high of .72 for Perceptual Reasoning to a low of .54 for Processing Speed. This overview of WAIS-IV correlations with various standardized measures provides strong support for WAIS-IV validity.

Factor analysis of the WAIS-IV has supported the presence of g in that most subtests correlate with each other as well as with the FSIQ at least to a moderate extent (Wechsler, 2008b). Dividing subtests into four indexes is supported by current theories of intelligence as well as factor-analytic procedures (Wechsler, 2008b). However, Arithmetic was found to load on both the Verbal Comprehension as well as the Working Memory factors. This is consistent with conceptualizations of Arithmetic in that it involves both verbal abilities as well as working memory. In addition, the new Figure Weights subtest was found to load highly on both Perceptual Reasoning and Working Memory. Again, these high loadings are expected, given that Figure Weights involve visual reasoning, but this reasoning is related to quantitative manipulations. Future research likely will further refine these findings and present alternative factor alternatives.

Various clinical populations have patterns of deficits in learning, cognition, and memory (see Wechsler, 2008b). It thus is to be expected that the WAIS-IV would be sensitive to these patterns. This finding was somewhat supported in that the mean WAIS-IV Full Scale IQ (M = 81.2) and index scores for Alzheimer's disease patients were low compared with their age-related peers. Comparisons among the index scores indicated differential cognitive abilities in that the mean Verbal Comprehension Index was relatively higher (86.2) than Processing Speed (76.6). However, it would have been expected that the Working Memory Index would have been somewhat lower than the mean of 84.3, given the considerable memory complaints among this population. Traumatic brain-injured patients had a somewhat similar pattern in that verbal abilities were relatively spared (relatively higher Verbal Comprehension mean of 92.1) when compared with a relatively lower Processing Speed (80.5). This finding indicates that the WAIS-III is sensitive to the difficulties these patient populations have with rapidly processing and consolidating information.

The mean WAIS-IV Full Scale IQ (96.9) for clients diagnosed with attention deficit hyperactivity disorder (ADHD) did not differ substantially from the standardization sample. In addition, their mean Working Memory Index score (94.7) was only slightly lower than their Verbal Comprehension mean scores (100.9). This finding suggests that the WAIS-IV is not particularly sensitive to the attentional problems of this group, perhaps because the WAIS-IV is administered in a structured testing situation with few distractions. In contrast, real-world environments are likely to have multiple concurrent attentional demands that would be much more difficult for these clients to ignore. Subjects diagnosed with reading-related learning disabilities were found to have mean Working Memory scores (88.9) that were significantly below the WAIS-IV standardization sample (101.1). Learning-disabled persons with mathematical difficulties similarly had the greatest difficulty with Working Memory (84.1) when compared with matched controls derived from the standardization sample (98.7). This finding reflects the common difficulties related to tasks requiring short-term memory and attention. These examples of research described in the *WAIS-IV Technical and Interpretive Manual* suggest that the WAIS-IV is sensitive to the types of cognitive difficulties found among various patient groups.

WISC-IV Reliability and Validity

Reliability on the WISC-IV is generally excellent. Internal consistency reported in the Technical Manual for the Full Scale IQ ranges from .96 to .97 (M = .97). The mean internal consistencies for the individual index scores range from .91 to .92. The mean internal consistencies for 12 of the 15 subtests ranged from a low of .79 for Symbol Search and Cancellation to a high of .90 for Letter-Number Sequencing. Test-retest reliability (average 32-day interval) for the Full Scale IQ was .89. The four index test-retest reliabilities range from a high of .79 for Processing Speed to a relative low of .89 for Verbal Comprehension. Average test-retest stability for the subtests ranged from a high of .85 for Vocabulary to a low of .68 for Symbol Search. It should be noted, however, that this data represents reliabilities that were averaged across the 11 age groups. Reliabilities for certain age groups can vary substantially. For example, 12 of the 15 subtest coefficients for the 6- to 7-year age group were found to be below .80.

An important issue related to test-retest reliability is how to interpret changes in scores. The Technical Manual indicates that, over a 9-week interval, there was an average increase of 5.6 points on the Full Scale IQ. The index scores had increases of 2.1 points for Verbal Comprehension, 5.2 points for Perceptual Reasoning, 2.6 points for Working Memory, and 7.1 points for Processing Speed. This finding means that increases over a time interval of 9 weeks or less will need to be substantially greater than the listed scores to indicate actual increases in ability. If the increases are within the magnitude indicated here, they are more likely to be due to practice effects. It should be particularly noted that Processing Speed and Perceptual Reasoning have quite large practice effects (7.1 and 5.2, respectively). More research is needed to determine the impact of practice effects over a longer interval and with different groups (i.e., brain injured, learning disabled).

The WISC-III had well-substantiated validity, and it can be cautiously assumed that much of this research can be transferred to the WISC-IV. This idea is partially supported in that 56% of the items are shared. In addition, there are moderate to high correlations between the WISC-III and WISC-IV Full Scale IQs, index scores, and subtests (i.e., Full Scale IQ = .87, Verbal Comprehension = .85, Perceptual Reasoning/Perceptual Organization Index = .70, Working Memory/Freedom from Distractibility = .74, Processing Speed = .81). Criterion validity has been performed on several Pearson Assessment (previously Psychological Corporation) tests with generally favorable results. For example, the WISC-IV Full Scale IQ and General Memory and Attention/Concentration scores on the Children's Memory Scale correlated .61 and .72 respectively. Correlations with the BarOn Emotional Quotients were low to nonsignificant, which is what would be expected, given that they are theoretically assessing different variables. Finally, correlations with the WISC-IV Full Scale IQ and the Adaptive Behavior Assessment Scale-Teacher were also supportive (i.e., General Adaptive = .58 and Conceptual = .63). The Technical Manual also provides studies of 16 different groups. For example, a closed head injury group had a mean Processing Speed score of 85 compared to a mean Full Scale IQ of 90. In contrast, children who were considered to be intellectually gifted had Full Scale IQ scores of 123.5 with Verbal Comprehension scores of 124.7.

Factor analyses generally has supported the four-factor model that was originally reported in the Technical Manual and is reflected in the four index scores (Sattler & Dumont, 2004; Watkins, Wilson, Kotz, Carbone, & Babula, 2006). However, even though Sattler and Dumont (2004) found support for the factor structure, it can also vary according to the age of the sample. For example, Information was found to have a factor loading of only .25 with the Verbal Comprehension Index at age 8. A similar low factor loading was a .22 for Symbol Search on Processing Speed. In addition, nearly all the subtests are good to fair measures of g (Sattler & Dumont, 2004) and have good to fair specificity. The exception is Cancellation, which is a poor measure of g and has poor subtest specificity.

A contrast to these factor-analytic findings is that the factor structure of the WISC-IV does not optimally reflect the four indexes but instead is best reflected in various dimensions of the Cattell-Horn-Carrol (CHC) theory of intelligence (Flanagan & Kaufman, 2004; Keith, Fine, Taub, Reynolds, & Kanzler, 2006). Specifically, Keith et al. (2006) found that their factor structure best fit measures of crystallized ability (Gc), visual processing (Gv), fluid reasoning (Gf), short-term memory (Gsm), and processing speed (Gs). The practical implications of this finding are that interpretations are likely to be most accurate and most consistent with theory when clusters of subtests are arranged according to these constructs (Flanagan & Kaufman, 2004; Keith, Fine, Taub, Reynolds, & Kranzler, 2006). Thus the Verbal Processing Speed Index still can be organized according to the traditional index cluster (Digit Symbol-Coding and Symbol Search). Verbal Processing Speed similarly measures the speed by which the client processes information (or general speed/Gs, in CHC terminology). In contrast, Block Design and Picture Completion measure the CHC dimension of visual processing (Gv), which represents a different cluster than the indexes presented in the WISC-IV Technical Manual.

ASSETS AND LIMITATIONS

Since their initial publication, the Wechsler intelligence scales have been used in numerous research studies and have become widely used throughout the world. Thus, they are familiar to both researchers and practitioners and also have a long and extensive history of continued evaluation. This enormous research base allows practitioners to make relatively accurate predictions regarding clients. Inconsistencies between an individual's performance and relevant research can also be noted, alerting the practitioner that he or she needs to develop and pursue further hypotheses. Furthermore, the subtests are relatively easy to administer, and the accompanying manuals provide clear instructions, concise tables, and excellent norms.

Norms for both the WAIS-IV and WISC-IV represent a further clear strength. The size is adequate and, for the most part, has corresponded to the demographics of the U.S. census. Cross-national use has been developed through research on how residents in other countries perform. Sampling on the WAIS-IV and WISC-IV for African American and Hispanics closely approximated U.S. Census data. A further important feature is that the WAIS-IV was conormed with the Wechsler Memory Scale-IV (WMS-IV) and the Wechsler Individual Achievement Test. Thus, a high degree of confidence can be placed in comparing scores between these tests. Finally, the WAIS-IV has extended its age range to include the performance for persons in the 70- to 90-year range. This is an important feature, given the increases in knowledge related to this age group along with the expanding number of persons over 65.

Of perhaps even more practical importance to the clinician is the clear, precise data obtained regarding the person's cognitive functioning from the IQ, index, and subtest scores. For example, high scores on the Verbal Comprehension Index indicate good verbal abilities and that the person has benefited from formal education. In contrast, a low score on Processing Speed suggests the person would have difficulty processing information quickly. Clinicians can become extremely sensitive to the different nuances and implications of various patterns of scores. Thus, many of these interpretive guidelines, particularly for the IQ and index scores, have substantial theoretical and empirical support.

A final, but extremely important, asset of the Wechsler scales is their ability to aid in assessing personality variables. This assessment can be done by directly observing the individual as he or she interacts with the examiner, studying the content of test item responses, or evaluating information inferred from the individual's pattern of subtest scores. For example, a person who scored low on Digit Span, Arithmetic, and Coding is likely to be experiencing anxiety, to have an attentional deficit, or a combination of both. On the other hand, it might be hypothesized that a person who scored high on Comprehension is likely to have good social judgment. Despite attempts to establish patterns of subtest scores for different psychiatric groups, few clear findings have emerged (Piedmont, Sokolov, & Fleming, 1989a, 1989b). Thus, the Wechsler scales should not be seen as similar to "personality scales" or "clinical scales." Rather, the subject's subtest patterns, behavior surrounding the test, and qualitative responses to the items should be considered as a means of generating hypotheses related to personality. In this context, the Wechsler intelligence scales are noteworthy in the degree to which they can provide personality variables and clinical information.

One significant criticism leveled at the Wechsler scales has been their lack of data supporting their ecological (or everyday) validity (Groth-Marnat & Teal, 2000; Reinecke, Beebe, & Stein, 1999; Sbordone & Long, 1996). Knowing a test's ecological validity is particularly important as referral questions are increasingly related to a client's everyday levels of functioning (i.e., extent of disability, ability to function independently, everyday aspects of memory). Although the Wechsler scales have been correlated with other measures, including the Stanford-Binet and academic achievement, for the most part, there has been a notable lack of comparisons with behavior external to the scales themselves, despite the belief that many significant areas of a person, such as adaptive behavior, personal competence, and need for achievement, are separate (but related) constructs (Greenspan & Driscoll, 1997; Sternberg, 2003). In particular, the meanings associated with subtest scores should be investigated in more depth. For example, Picture Completion has traditionally been considered a measure of a person's ability to distinguish relevant from irrelevant details in his or her environment, yet this assumption has not been adequately tested. Likewise, no studies have been made to determine if high or low Digit Span scores relate to actual day-by-day behaviors, such as recalling telephone numbers, facility with computer programming sequences, or following directions.

An extension of this concern is that a number of authors have criticized what they believe is an overinterpretation of subtest and index scores (Glutting, Watkins, Konold, & McDermott, 2006; Konold, Glutting, McDermott, Kush, & Watkins, 1999). Specifically, they believe that individual subtest reliabilities are too low and not sufficiently specific for interpreting individual profiles. For example, they note that, compared with g (as represented by the Full Scale IQ), WISC-IV index scores do not account for a sufficient proportion of the variance in predicting achievement (Glutting et al., 2006). As a result, index interpretation does not demonstrate sufficient incremental increases in prediction. In addition, the ipsative patterns of subtest strengths and weaknesses are not sufficiently stable over time (Macmann & Barnett, 1997). Clinicians might therefore be advised to rely on the Full Scale IQ rather than index scores when making academic (and possibly other) predictions. Various authors counter this belief by emphasizing the importance of hypothesis testing, combining interpretations with external criteria, and noting the conceptual importance of the complexity of intelligence (A. Kaufman, 1994, 1999; A. Kaufman & Lichtenberger, 2000, 2002, 2006; Lezak, 1988, 2004; Milberg et al., 1996).

There are several additional limitations to the Wechsler scales. Some critics believe that norms may not be applicable for ethnic minorities or persons from lower socioeconomic backgrounds (see next section, "Use with Diverse Groups"). In addition, the complexity of scoring, particularly the numerous calculations required for the Wechsler intelligence scales, is likely to increase the probability of clerical errors by examiners (Linger, Ray, Zachar, Underhill, & LoBello, 2007; Loe, Kadlubek, & Marks, 2007; Slate & Hunnicutt, 1988; Slate, Jones, & Murray, 1991). A further potential difficulty is that when supplementary subtests are substituted for core subtests, it is unclear how these supplementary subtests will affect the Full Scale IQ or index scores. As a result, supplementary subtests should be given only under unusual circumstances, such as when one of the core subtests has been "spoiled."

A further issue is that there is a certain degree of subjectivity when scoring many of the items on Comprehension, Similarities, and Vocabulary. Thus, a "hard" scorer may develop a somewhat lower score than an "easy" scorer. This is particularly true for Similarities, Comprehension, and Vocabulary, where scoring criteria are less clear than for other subtests. The Wechsler scales, like other tests of intelligence, are also limited in the scope of what they can measure. They do not assess some important factors, such as need for achievement, motivation, creativity, or success in dealing with people (Gardner, 2006; Sternberg, 2003).

It should finally be noted that the WAIS-IV and WISC-IV have continued the traditional measurement of intelligence as represented by the Stanford-Binet scales and the earlier versions of the Wechsler scales. Although their revisions have provided features such as updated norms and index scores (especially the inclusion of Working Memory and Processing Speed), the underlying theories and essential construction of these scales have remained relatively unchanged for well over 50 years, despite numerous developments in both theory and measurement. These developments include the Cattell-Horn-Carroll (CHC) theory (see Flanagan & Kaufman, 2004), Luria's PASS (Planning-Attention-Successive-Sequencing: Luria, 1980) model, Gardner's independent competencies (Gardner, 2006), various theories on emotional intelligence (Bar-On, 1998; Ciarochi, Chan, & Caputi, 2000), and commonsense problem solving (Sternberg et al., 1995). Thus, one criticism of the Wechsler intelligence scales is that they have not responded to more current views on intelligence (A. Kaufman & Lichtenberger, 2002, 2006; Sternberg, 2003; Sternberg & Kaufman, 1998). It remains to be seen whether newer models and assessment tools will have much of an impact on assessing either intelligence or, especially, the frequency to which the Wechsler scales will be used in this process.

USE WITH DIVERSE GROUPS

Each of the considerations discussed in Chapter 2 (see "Assessing Diverse Groups") should be taken into account when evaluating a person from a diverse background. Doing this involves evaluating the client's level of acculturation and language proficiency as well as the cultural competency of the examinee. In addition, a high degree of flexibility should occur both when conducting the assessment and when making interpretations. Different accommodations and strategies need to be made based on the outcome of these considerations.

One of the key issues when assessing diverse clients is determining the extent that the instruments used might be biased. Evaluating for test bias can be partially informed by the considerable research devoted to evaluating the extent that intelligence tests such as the Wechsler intelligence scales are biased when used to assess various minority groups in the United States. The majority of these studies have been done with groups that are reasonably well acculturated and with moderate to good English skills. Reviews of this research have generally concluded (i.e., Kaplan & Sacuzzo, 2005; Sattler, 2008) that intelligence tests are not as biased as has been assumed. For example, deletion of items that appear to have biased content seems to make little difference in overall scores (i.e., Sandoval, 1979). Numerous validity studies have also found that intelligence tests make academic predictions as accurately for minority groups as for majority groups (i.e., Weiss, Prifitera, & Roid, 1993; Sattler, 2008). Factor-analytic research indicates that the same construct is being measured across various minority groups (i.e., Gutkin & Reynolds, 1981). Finally, Japanese populations, who come from a quite different culture than that of the United States, had mean scores that were actually higher than the U.S. standardization group (Lynn, 1977).

[handwritten margin note: This is because the education system is not designed to be supportive or inclusive of minority groups]

Thus, research supports the use of the Wechsler intelligence scales for use with minority groups in the United States. The central problem does not seem to be the tests themselves. Although these tests are far from perfect, they provide the sort of information they were intended to provide. The main problem seems to be unequal opportunities that are accurately reflected in how various disadvantaged groups perform on intelligence tests. Despite the conclusion that cognitive tests generally measure what they intend to measure, clinicians still need to take extra care to insure that accurate data and conclusions are developed. These general and specific guidelines seem appropriate:

- Make extra efforts to insure that clients feel comfortable and welcomed.
- *[handwritten margin note: How?]* Make extra efforts to increase motivation; encourage clients to do their best.
- Make sure that communication is as clear as possible, especially if there are differences in accents between the clinician and the client.
- *[handwritten margin note: ✱]* Resources beyond merely tests should have a greater significance with diverse clients (teacher reports, discussions with parents, history, behavioral observations) than for majority clients.
- If language and culture appear to have been a factor in lowering the client's performance, subtests that seem to be less influenced by culture and language should be the focus of interpretation. (Deemphasize language-based subtests such as Vocabulary and instead emphasize nonverbal tests such as Block Design, Matrix Reasoning, and Visual Puzzles.)
- When assessing persons from cultures that deemphasize performing tasks rapidly (i.e., South Pacific islands), deemphasize speeded subtests (Processing Speed Index, Coding, Symbol Search, Cancellation).

- Be cautious interpreting PRI<VCI differences for right-hemisphere-damaged African Americans and Native Americans; the differences have been found to be less when compared with European Americans (based on PIQ<VIQ for the WAIS-R and WAIS-III; see A. Kaufman & Lichtenberger, 2006).
- Be cautious interpreting VCI<PRI differences for left-hemisphere-damaged African Americans; the expected verbal-nonverbal difference found among European Americans has not been found in this population (based on VIQ<PRI for the WAIS-R and WAIS-III; see A. Kaufman & Lichtenberger, 2006).

When clinicians determine that clients are highly identified with their culture and have minimal proficiency with English, many of the same considerations still apply. Specifically, clinicians should make extra efforts to assure that clients are comfortable, made to feel welcome, and encouraged to do their best and that communication is clear. Nontest information should also be carefully considered. If it is decided to administer the Wechsler intelligence scales, nonverbal subtests should be given greater emphasis. Verbal-oriented tests should never be used for interpretations for clients who do not have at least adequate English language proficiency. In some cases it might be advisable to use an interpreter. If an interpreter is used, it would be important to locate one who is familiar not only with the client's language but with the person's values, culture, and ideology. However, using an interpreter also means that the test administration will not be standard; as a result, there may be a reduction in test validity. In particular, it may be more difficult to translate some of the directions and responses. The meaning and level of difficulty of some of the items might change. For example, vocabulary items might be either more or less difficult in the client's native language. It may be advisable to use one of the 20 language translations of the Wechsler intelligence scales. Clinicians also need to carefully evaluate when there are significant language differences when working with clients from cross cultural backgrounds.

One strategy for assessing clients who are highly identified with their own culture and do not have proficiency with English may be to use alternative nonverbal tests. These might be used in conjunction with the Wechsler intelligence scales or be the sole means of assessing intelligence. Examples are the Comprehensive Test of Nonverbal Intelligence (Hammill, Pearson, & Wiederholt, 1997), Universal Nonverbal Intelligence Test (Bracken & McCallum, 1998), and the Wechsler Nonverbal Intelligence Test (Wechsler & Naglieri, 2006). One of the main motivations for developing these tests was for use with quite diverse populations who do not have English proficiency. However, even some groups with good English proficiency might benefit from more nonverbally oriented procedures. For example, Native Americans have been found to score up to 25 or 30 points higher on nonverbal tests when compared with verbal tests (McShane & Plas, 1984). Thus, using nonverbal tests will illustrate their strengths. In addition, measures of a client's ongoing learning abilities (so-called dynamic testing) shows promise in assessing the extent to which a client can benefit from various learning environments (learning potential; Sternberg & Grigorenko, 2002).

Persons with visual, hearing, or motor disabilities present different challenges for clinicians. If clients have visual impairments, subtests with visual components cannot be administered (i.e., Coding, Symbol Search, Block Design, Matrix Reasoning). Instead, greater reliance will need to be placed on auditory/verbal subtests. Different considerations will need to be made for persons with hearing impairments. For these clients, more reliance will need to be given to nonverbal tests. Specialty nonverbally oriented tests might be considered. Sometimes clinicians may decide to use an interpreter (i.e., American Sign Language). While this means that a greater variety of tests can be administered, it also means the administration is nonstandardized, with the resulting potential for reduced validity. Clinicians will need to evaluate whether the greater variety of tests that can be administered will compensate for the potential loss of validity. The *WAIS-IV Administration and Scoring Manual* provides recommendations on which subtests to use with different types of interpreters (i.e., American Sign Language versus Cured Speech). For example, the Arithmetic subtest does not seem to be significantly altered with American Sign Language but, due to sign language supplying unintended cures, the Vocabulary subtest does seem to be significantly modified and therefore may not produce valid scores.

MEANING OF IQ SCORES

Because only a weak and vague relation exists between theories of intelligence and the Wechsler intelligence scales, it is important for all persons involved with testing to understand the meaning of IQ scores. Untrained persons are particularly likely to misinterpret IQ scores, which may result in poor decisions or negative attitudes toward either the client or the testing procedure itself. The meaning of IQ scores can be partially clarified by elaborating on some of the more common misinterpretations. IQ is often incorrectly believed to be fixed, unchangeable, and innate. Although there does tend to be considerable stability of IQ scores throughout adulthood ($r=.85$; Schuerger & Witt, 1989), it is possible for changes in IQ to occur, particularly among children (Perkins & Grotzer, 1997). For example, the greatest longitudinal increases in IQs occurred among children who were from homes that provided strong encouragement and avoided severe forms of punishment (McCall, Appelbaum, & Hogarty, 1973). Similarly, Sameroff, Seifer, Baldwin, and Baldwin (1993) found that multiple environmental risk factors (e.g., number of major stressful events, mother's mental health) were able to predict one-third to one-half of IQ variance between the ages of 4 and 13. In addition, education can increase aspects of IQ primarily related to crystallized intelligence even among adults. Thus, IQ can be related to a number of environmental influences.

In addition, IQ scores are not exact, precise measurements; rather, they are estimates in which there is an expected range of fluctuation between one performance and the next. Finally, tests such as the Wechsler scales measure only a limited range of abilities, and a large number of variables usually considered "intelligent" are beyond the scope of most intelligence tests. No test or battery of tests can ever give a complete picture; tests can only assess various areas of functioning. In summary, an IQ is an estimate of a person's current level of functioning as measured by the various tasks required in a test.

An assumption of any global IQ score is that it derives from a wide array of interacting abilities. A subtest such as Information assesses specific areas of a person's range of knowledge and is related to general intelligence. However, optimal performance on the Information subtest is influenced by achievement orientation, curiosity, culture, and the person's interests. More general prerequisites are that the client must comprehend what has been requested, be motivated to do well, follow directions, provide a response, and understand English. Factors such as persistence and drive are also likely to influence any type of task presented to the person. The tasks included in IQ tests are those, based on judgments by psychometrists, most valued by Western society. In other words, they relate to and are predictive of relevant skills outside the testing situation. It is certainly possible to test a much wider range of areas (as in Guilford's Structure of Intelligence), but these are not routinely done since they are often of little relevance in predicting academic achievement or vocational performance.

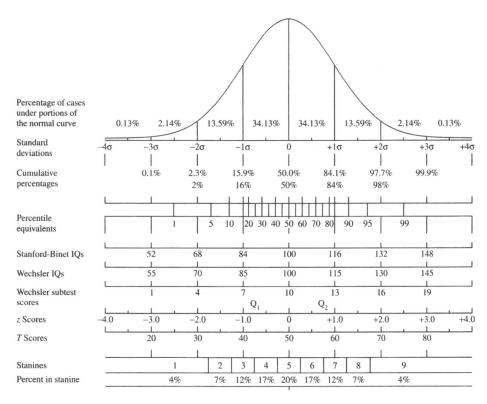

Figure 5.1.   Relationship of Wechsler scores to various types of standard measures

Despite the many relevant areas measured by IQ tests, practitioners need to observe some humility when making predictions based on them. Many persons with quite high IQs achieve little or nothing. Having a high IQ is in no way a guarantee of success but merely means that one important prerequisite has been met. In contrast, persons with relatively low IQs have more severe limitations placed on them. As a result of their relatively narrower range of options, predictions regarding their behavior tend to be more accurate. However, it is possible that persons with average or below-average WAIS-IV/WISC-IV IQs may have high levels of interpersonal, practical, or emotional "intelligence," which may help them compensate for lower levels of formal intelligence.

Regardless of the person's IQ range, clinicians should be clear regarding the likely band of error (standard error of measurement). It is often useful to include the standard error of measurement in a report. For example, the WAIS-IV Full Scale IQ has an average standard error of measurement of (2.16; Wechsler, 2008b). Thus, a particular IQ has a 95% chance of being within 2.16 IQ points of a person's obtained IQ. The WISC-IV has a slightly (higher) average standard error of measurement of 2.68 for the Full Scale IQ (Wechsler, 2003). Error can also be the result of unforeseen events beyond the context of IQ tests. Although 50% to 75% of the variance of children's academic success is dependent on nonintellectual factors (persistence, personal adjustment, family support), most of a typical assessment is spent evaluating IQ. Some of these nonintellectual areas might be quite difficult to assess, and others might even be impossible to account for. For example, a student might unexpectedly develop an excellent relationship with a new teacher, which significantly changes his or her attitude toward school, thereby stimulating his or her interest to passionately pursue a specific area. Thus, any meaning attached to an IQ score should acknowledge the possible effects of uncertainty both in the measurement itself and from the wider context of the person's life.

Another important aspect of IQ is the statistical meaning of the different scores. Binet originally conceptualized intelligence as the difference between a person's mental age and his or her chronological age. Binet's formulation was found to be inadequate and has been replaced by the use of the deviation IQ. The assumption behind the deviation IQ is that intelligence falls around a normal distribution (see Figure 5.1). The interpretation of an IQ score, then, is straightforward because it gives the relative position of a person compared with his or her age-related peers. The IQ can thus be expressed in deviation units away from the norm. The Wechsler Full Scale IQ and the four indexes have a mean of 100 and a standard deviation of 15. Scores also can be easily translated into percentile equivalents. For example, an IQ of 120 is 1.33 standard deviations above the mean and places an individual in the 91st percentile (see *WAIS-IV Administration and Scoring Manual* Tables A.3 to A.7 and the *WISC-IV Administration and Scoring Manual* Table A.6 for conversions). Thus, this person's performance is better than 91% of his or her age-related peers. The IQ cutoff for mental retardation is 70, which indicates that such individuals are functioning in the lowest 2% when compared with their age-related peers.

A final consideration is the different classifications of intelligence. Table 5.5 lists commonly used diagnostic labels and compares them with IQ ranges and percentages. These terms are taken from the 2008 WAIS-IV Record forms. Thus, an IQ can be expressed conceptually as an estimate of a person's current level of ability, statistically as a deviation score that can be transformed into percentile equivalents, and diagnostically using common terms for classification.

CAUTIONS AND GUIDELINES IN ADMINISTRATION

The Wechsler manuals generally provide quite clear guidelines for administration and scoring. Despite this clarity, the number of administration and scoring errors on the part of both trainee and experienced clinicians is far higher than they should be (Alfonso, Johnson, Patinella, & Radar, 1998; Linger et al., 2007; Loe et al., 2007; Moon, Blakey, Gorsuch, & Fantuzzo, 1991; Moon, Fantuzzo, & Gorsuch, 1986; Slate & Hunnicutt, 1988; Slate et al., 1991). One way of reducing clerical errors is to use the computer scoring software developed by Pearson Assessment (i.e., WAIS-IV Scoring Assistant, WAIS-IV

Table 5.5.   WAIS-IV/WISC-IV intelligence classifications

Classifications	More value-neutral terms	Corresponding IQ range
Very superior	Upper extreme	130+
Superior	Well above average	120–129
High average	High average	110–119
Average	Average	90–109
Low average	Low average	80–89
Borderline	Well below average	70–79
Extremely low	Lower extreme	69 and below

Source: Intelligence classifications adapted from WAIS-IV and WISC-IV Record forms.

Writer, WISC-IV Scoring Assistant, WISC-IV Writer). Even with repeated administration of the Wechsler scales, examiners often end up "practicing their mistakes" rather than correcting them (Slate et al., 1991). The causes of these errors include lack of proper instruction, lack of clarity between academic versus clinical site regarding where training is supposed to occur, carelessness, variations in the quality of the examiner-examinee relationship, and work overload for clinicians (Slate & Hunnicutt, 1988). One approach to reducing errors is awareness regarding the most frequent general categories of errors. The most common errors have been found to be (Loe et al., 2007; Slate & Hunnicutt, 1988):

1. Failing to query verbal responses.
2. Assigning too many points to an answer (leniency by examiner).
3. Failing to record examinee responses, circle scores, or record times (errors of administration).
4. Failing to question responses when required by test manual (poor reading and recalling of information in the manual).
5. Questioning examinee inappropriately (poor reading and/or incorrect integration of the manual).
6. Assigning too few points when required by test manual (examiner scores too hard).
7. Incorrectly converting raw score to standard score (clerical error).
8. Failing to assign correct points for nonverbal items (clerical and timing errors).
9. Incorrectly calculating raw score for subtest totals (clerical error).
10. Incorrectly calculating chronological age (clerical error).

Whereas this list covers quite general categories, Moon et al. (1991) have developed a list of the most frequently occurring specific errors along with concrete, specific recommendations to correct for these errors. However, it should be cautioned that these errors may not necessarily be the ones that occur most frequently for the latest versions of the Wechsler intelligence scales (WAIS-IV/WISC-IV):

1. Recite digits (on Digit Span) and digits and letters (on Letter-Number Sequencing) at the rate of one per second with the pitch of the voice dropping on the last digit/letter of each trial.
2. State during the introduction that each task begins with easy questions and ends with difficult ones. Examiners may also note that not everyone is expected to succeed on all problems.
3. Record responses verbatim on Vocabulary. At times, the examinee provides so much detail that this is not possible, but the essential components should be written down verbatim. This can be facilitated by the use of abbreviations.
4. Properly orient blocks (on Block Design) at the examinee's midline.
5. The first time the examinee points out a nonessential part on Picture Completion, the examiner should say, "Yes, but what is the most important thing missing?"
6. Attempt to elicit the examinee's perception of the testing situation and correct any misconceptions.
7. Check to see if the examinee is comfortable.

Despite clear guidelines in the manual as well as awareness of frequent errors, examiners are still likely to make mistakes. Thus, optimal training guidelines should be incorporated into graduate programs and continuing education. A recommended format is the Mastery

Model, which involves these steps: (a) 1 to 2 hours studying the manual, (b) viewing a videotape of a flawless WAIS-IV/WISC-IV administration, (c) viewing a videotaped lecture of major pitfalls of administration, (d) successfully detecting errors in a videotaped flawed WAIS-IV/WISC-IV administration, and (e) actually administering the WAIS-IV/WISC-IVs to be evaluated by a rating device such as Sattler's (2008) "Administrative Checklist for the WISC-IV" (pp. 40–49). Such procedures are likely to significantly shorten the length of training time and number of training administrations and yet significantly increase the level of competence related to Wechsler scale administration and scoring (Moon, Fantuzzo, & Gorsuch, 1986; Slate et al., 1991).

The *WAIS-IV Administration and Scoring Manual* indicates that the average time to administer the 10 core subtests used to determine the Full Scale IQ and 4 index scores for the normative sample ranged between 67 and 100 minutes. Including all the supplemental subtests took an additional 20 to 24 minutes. However, research with the WAIS-III, found that, for a heterogeneous clinical population, the average time was somewhat longer than that reported in the manual (Ryan, Lopez, & Werth, 1998). It may be that future research with the WAIS-IV will find that administration time among clinical populations is longer than the time estimated in the manual. Time estimates given in the WISC-IV manual to administer the 10 core subtests used to calculate the Full Scale IQ and 4 index scores ranged from 65 to 80 minutes. Research with a school population found that the range was a bit wider (42–100+ minutes) with an average length of 72 minutes (Ryan, Glass, & Brown, 2007). These times were for administration only and did not include time required for scoring, breaks, or interpretation, which usually takes an additional 50 to 60 minutes. One practical implication is that clinicians may need to take extra time for some clients, especially those who are slow, fatigue easily, or provide overly detailed responses. In some cases it might be necessary to assess such clients over two separate sessions. Finally, clinicians should make realistic appraisals of required times and use these estimates to make sure that they are appropriately compensated.

WAIS-IV/WISC-IV SUCCESSIVE-LEVEL INTERPRETATION PROCEDURE

The successive-level approach to interpreting Wechsler scores represents an integration and synthesis of the approaches outlined by major resources in the field (Flanagan & Kaufman, 2004; Kaufman & Lichtenberger, 2006; Kaufman & Flanagan, in press; Sattler, 2008). This approach provides clinicians with a sequential, five-level format for working with and discussing a person's performance. The underlying purpose for each of these steps should be based on confirming, disconfirming, or altering hypotheses based on patterns of scores combined with relevant background information. The next section of this chapter ("Wechsler Subtests") covers descriptions of the Wechsler subtests, including the more frequently encountered abilities associated with these subtests. This section can serve as a summary and quick reference for clinicians, especially in analyzing test profiles (Levels II and III).

Examiners who are relatively unfamiliar with the Wechsler scales are likely to find the level of detail in these interpretation procedures and Wechsler subtest sections somewhat daunting because of their complexity. It is recommended that they read the interpretation procedures first to gain familiarity with the material. It might be particularly helpful to review the summary of these procedures in Table 5.6, both before and after reading this section. Table 5.6 can also serve as a useful future quick reference guide when actually

Table 5.6.   Summary of successive five-level WAIS-IV/WISC-IV interpretive procedures

Level I. Interpret the Full Scale IQ

Determine percentile rankings and IQ classifications

Level II. Interpret index scores and CHC groupings

Interpret *personal* strengths and weaknesses (*ipsatively*) for the examinee if significant discrepancies occur between clusters of index scores; *normative* interpretations can still be made whether significant differences occur or not

  a. *Index scores:* Verbal Comprehension, Perceptual Reasoning, Working Memory, Processing Speed
  b. *CHC groupings:* Fluid Reasoning, Verbal Fluid Reasoning, Nonverbal Fluid Reasoning, Lexical Knowledge, General Information, Visual Processing, Mental Manipulation, Visual Motor Speed, Problem Solving without Visual Motor Speed, Long Term Memory, Short Term Memory (note that all core and supplemental subtests must be given to calculate CHC groupings)

Level III. Interpret Subtest Variability

Level IV. Qualitative/process Analysis

Level V. Analyze Intrasubtest Variability

working with Wechsler protocols. After perusing the "Interpretation Procedures" section, student examiners should next obtain a completed WAIS-IV/WISC-IV profile, preferably one they themselves have administered, and then work through the levels of interpretation in a sequential manner. Doing this should add the required level of clarity and integration of the material to enable examiners to work more confidently with future protocols.

An ideal set of interpretive statements is one that is not only accurate but also gives the sense of what the cognitive ability measures and connects it with the client's everyday functioning. It should ideally use everyday language with a minimum of technical terms. However, often this is a difficult interpretive skill to develop. The following five general strategies might be used to expand on cognitive interpretations:

1. Make an initial general statement ("excellent verbal abilities [VCI = 125, top 5% of age-related peers])," etc.).
2. Elaborate by listing subcomponents of ability ("good fund of general information, word knowledge.").
3. Give qualitative description of test responses ("could easily define quite difficult words" or "accurately described the similarities between two related objects or ideas") or test items ("was able to recall the accomplishments of famous people and accurately describe a variety of scientific facts").
4. Give qualitative description of history/behavioral observations ("She quickly, concisely, and accurately answered questions.").
5. Provide implications for everyday life ("She would be able to easily understand complex conversations" or "would do well in verbally oriented occupations").

It would rarely be necessary to use all of these strategies. In some cases it might be necessary to use only the first one. In other situations, especially when the interpretation is crucial to the referral question, it might be important to use three or four of them. One caution related to the third strategy is that the actual items should not be described since this would be a breach of test security. Instead, a general description or alternative examples illustrating the types of items that were administered and answered might be provided.

These are principles to keep in mind when working through the interpretation procedures:

- The successive steps begin with the most general aspects of the WAIS-IV/WISC-IV (Full Scale IQ) and gradually work their way to more specific aspects of the person's performance (indexes, CHC groupings, qualitative responses to individual items, etc.).
- Examiners can interpret the more global measures (Full Scale IQ, Global Ability Index) with greater meaning, usefulness, and certainty if there is not a high degree of difference among the index scores (23 points for both the WAIS-IV and WISC-IV between the highest and lowest index scores) or other groupings. With increasing differences, the purity of the global measures becomes contaminated so that interpretations of these global measures become less meaningful. For example, if there is a pattern in which the Verbal Comprehension and Working Memory Indexes are significantly different from each other, it makes more sense to focus on these two indexes rather than the more global Full Scale IQ (or Global Ability Index).
- The recommended level set to establish significant difference is the .05 level. This is true for differences through all levels of interpretation including indexes and additional groupings. It is felt that this level of significance is sufficiently rigorous for clinical purposes. If either less stringent ($p=.15$) or more stringent ($p=.01$) levels are desired, relevant tables can be found in the WAIS-IV and WISC-IV Administration and Scoring Manuals (Wechsler, 2003a, 2008a). When possible, Bonferroni corrections have been included to correct for the possible statistical error resulting from inflation of significant results because of the number of comparisons.
- To determine whether index scores are significantly (.05 level) discrepant from each other, tables can be consulted in the manuals (Table B.1, p. 230 in the *WAIS-IV Administration and Scoring Manual* and Table B.1, p. 256 in the *WISC-IV Administration and Scoring Manual*). Thus, comparisons are made between the different pairs of indexes.
- In contrast to the previous procedure for discrepancies between indexes, subtest fluctuations are based on *comparisons with mean scores*. One strategy is to compare the scaled score of each individual subtest with the mean for all the subtests administered (and then calculate the difference that the subtests fluctuate from this mean to see if the difference is significant). An alternative strategy is to find the mean of the subtests within the index scores (rather than for the mean for the 10 core subtests) to see if the subtest scores are significantly different.
- Any interpretations, especially those related to the more specific levels (Levels III, IV, and V), should be considered as tentative hypotheses requiring support from additional sources of information (behavioral observations, school records, etc.). Preferably, each hypothesis should be supported by at least two additional sources. This process of hypothesis generation, confirmation/disconfirmation, and integration with other sources is not merely a statistical procedure but also involves considerable clinical wisdom and judgment.

Level I. Full Scale IQ (and Global Ability Index)

An examinee's Full Scale IQ should be considered first because it provides the basis and context for evaluating other cognitive abilities. It is generally the single most reliable and valid score. The Full Scale IQ gives the person's relative standing in comparison with his or her age-related peers and provides a global estimate of his or her overall mental abilities. It is often useful to transform the Full Scale IQ into a percentile rank (see

WAIS-IV Administration and Scoring Manual, Tables A.3–A.7, pp. 220–225 or *WISC-IV Administration and Scoring Manual*, Appendix A.6, pp. 239–240) or intelligence classification (see Table 5.5 or WAIS-IV/WISC-IV Record forms). This is especially important when relating test results to untrained persons because both percentile rank and intelligence classifications are usually less subject to misinterpretation than IQ scores. Many examiners also prefer to include the standard error of measurement (SEM) as an estimate of the confidence ("confidence intervals") that can be placed in the obtained score. For example, a Full Scale IQ of 110 has a 95% probability of falling between 105 and 115 IQ points. This clarifies that the IQ score is not a precise number but is rather a range with an expected margin of error. However, including the confidence intervals in actual reports is likely to be more technical detail than most referral sources need. One classification, "Borderline," might potentially be misinterpreted, because it might be confused with the *DSM-IV* psychiatric diagnosis of *Borderline Personality*. Examiners might counter this by clarifying in parentheses that the "Borderline" range can also be described as "Well below Average."

Although the Full Scale IQ is the most stable and well-validated part of the Wechsler scales, its significance becomes progressively less important as the fluctuations increase between index scores and other groupings. When such fluctuations occur, it is incumbent on the examiner to work in more detail to extract the significance of these relative strengths and weaknesses. The next four successive levels of interpretation provide a sequential method of accomplishing this goal.

The Global Ability Index (GAI; WAIS-IV only) is an alternative global measure of intelligence. It is calculated by using only the three subtests used for the Verbal Comprehension Index and the three subtests used for the Perceptual Reasoning Indexes. Therefore, it eliminates using the Working Memory and Processing Speed subtests. This is important since Working Memory and Processing Speed are the indexes that are most sensitive to deterioration. This finding is consistent with the finding that 65% of examinees with a wide variety of cognitive difficulties had GAI index scores that were significantly higher than their Full Scale IQs (Wechsler, 2008b). Thus, calculating the difference between Full Scale IQ and GAI provides an index of the degree to which brain- and age-sensitive subtests are lowering a person's overall level of functioning (see WAIS-IV Technical and Interpretive Manual for guidelines). The general descriptions noted for describing the Full Scale IQ also apply to the GAI.

Level II. Indexes and Additional Groupings

The second level of interpretation is to consider index scores and additional groupings. The .05 level of significance is consistently used to determine if fluctuations are significant. In some cases, procedures and formulas are provided to determine the significance of various fluctuations and to convert scores into the familiar IQ-related standard scores having a mean of 100 and standard deviation of 15. (See summary of formulas in Appendix C on pages 611–619)

Step IIa. Index Scores

The core level of interpretation is the index scores. These represent an optimal level of specificity. In contrast, the Full Scale IQ is so general that it does not provide much information related to a client's strengths and weaknesses. The subtests, however, are quite narrow measures of and their reliability and validity are sufficiently low that relying on them for interpretation has been seriously questioned (Glutting et al., 2006; Konold et al., 1999). Thus the indexes provide a sound, empirically and conceptually based means of understanding more detailed aspects of the person's intellectual functioning. Examples are provided to illustrate how high or low scores might translate into everyday functioning.

Indexes should be interpreted only if they represent unitary abilities. A unitary ability is one in which there is less than a 5-point subscale difference among the subtests within the index. If the difference between the highest and the lowest subtest score is 5 or more subscale points, then that index should not be interpreted. Instead, proceed to Level IIa to investigate whether there are additional meaningful groupings or not.

One important consideration is whether relative index weaknesses are cause for concern. Cause for concern depends on how low the person performed relative to the rest of the population. For example, a person may have a Verbal Comprehension Index of 125 but a Processing Speed Index of 100. This finding represents considerable variation such that it is safe to conclude that the speed with which the person processes information is a relative weakness. This can be considered a *personal* (or "ipsative") weakness since it is a weakness relative to the examinee's other score. However, since Processing Speed is still in the average range, it is not likely to create problems in adapting to most everyday situations. The situation is quite different if there is a similar 25-point Verbal Comprehension-Processing Speed difference but with Verbal Comprehension being 100 and Processing Speed being 75. The Processing Speed score of 75 strongly suggests difficulties in the person's ability to function adequately if given even minimally demanding tasks, such as clerical procedures. It can thus be considered not only a *personal* weakness but also a *normative* weakness since it is quite low compared with the person's age-related peers. In the examples given later of everyday functioning listed under each of the indexes, it is essential to understand that these examples refer to normative strengths/weaknesses rather than merely relative/ipsative strengths/weaknesses.

A further strategy for interpreting index scores is to note whether there are significant differences among various pairs. Discrepancy comparisons are part of the standard scoring procedure for the WAIS-IV and WISC-IV. Calculations include whether the differences are significant and the frequency with which the difference occurs in the standardization sample (base rate; see *WAIS IV Administration and Scoring Manual* Tables B.1 and B.2, pp. 230–231). For example, if a person's WAIS-IV Perceptual Reasoning Index was 15 points higher than his or her Processing Speed Index (PRI>PSI), this difference would clearly exceed the .05 level for all age groups (as per Table B.1) and, according to Table B.2, a PRI-PSI difference of 15 points occurred in only 15% of the standardization sample.

The next and more challenging step is to determine what the significance is for this difference. On one hand it might simply represent natural variations in the person's abilities. Indeed, it is quite natural for variations in abilities to occur for many people, especially for persons in the high IQ range. In the last example of the relatively higher Perceptual Reasoning versus Processing Speed, this difference might reflect a person who worked in a nonverbal area (i.e., skilled craftsperson) and had a corresponding slow, deliberate work style. Thus it may not be clinically significant. In contrast, another person may have the previous pattern but may have sustained a recent head injury. The slow Processing Speed might reflect the impact of this injury, especially if the person had been employed in an occupation that required rapid processing of information. The much slower speed would then have practical significance in that the person may have a particularly difficult time readjusting to work.

Step IIb. Cattell-Horn-Carroll (CHC) Groupings

Interpreting additional clusters of subtests can be based on CHC concepts (Kaufman & Lichtenberger, in press; Flanagan & Ortiz, 2001; Flanagan & Kaufman, 2004). This can only be done if all 15 subtests have been administered. As with the Full Scale IQ and Index scores, it is first necessary to decide whether the clusters represent unitary abilities. A unitary cluster is defined by there being less than 5 scaled score points among the subtests comprising the Index. If there are 5 or more points, it suggests the cluster score is not unitary. Accordingly, they should not be interpreted. It is then incumbent on the clinician to determine whether or not there are other combinations of subtests that help explain the client's cognitive abilities.

The following list of CHC-based WAIS-IV groupings developed by Kaufman and Lichtenberger (in press) provides the name of the CHC grouping, the WAIS-IV subtests that comprise the grouping, and a brief description of the abilities that are measured by the grouping. The definitions were derived from Flanagan and Ortiz (2001), Flanagan and Kaufman (2004), and Kaufman and Lichtenberger (in press). Unfortunately tables to calculate the WAIS-IV significance of differences along with conversion tables are not yet available. However, relevant tables will be available when Kaufman and Lichternberger's (in press) *Essentials of WAIS-IV assessment* becomes available.

1. *Fluid Reasoning (Matrix Reasoning + Figure Weights).* Mental operations required for a novel task, the operations cannot be done automatically; examples include accurately perceiving relationships among patterns, drawing inferences, recognizing and forming concepts, solving problems, making inferences, understanding implications, reorganizing and transforming information, extrapolating.

2. *Verbal Fluid Reasoning (Similarities + Comprehension).* Involves fluid reasoning (see above) specific to verbal material, includes depth and breadth of acquired knowledge through interacting with culture and then ability to apply this knowledge.

3. *Lexical Knowledge (Vocabulary + Similarities).* Breadth and depth of accumulated knowledge of a culture and how to apply this knowledge, application of word knowledge.

4. *General Information (Comprehension + Information).* Range of general information.

5. *Visual Processing (Block Design + Visual Puzzles).* Perception, generation, synthesis, manipulation, transformation, storage, and retrieval of visual information; examples include perceiving and manipulating spatial patterns, maintaining spatial orientation, interpreting how objects change as they move through space, mentally reversing and rotating objects.

6. Mental Manipulation (Letter-Number Sequencing + Digit Span).

7. *Visual Motor Speed (Block Design + Coding + Symbol Search).* Each of these subtests requires that participants process visual information as rapidly as possible. This grouping, and the interpretations dependent on it, is almost identical to the Processing Speed Index. However, Block Design has been added to the grouping since it also has a timed component.

8. Problem-Solving without Visual Motor Speed (Matrix Reasoning + Visual Puzzles or Matrix Reasoning + Visual Puzzles + Picture Completion + Figure Weights). This grouping assesses how effectively a person can solve visual information without needing to make a motor response. It therefore provides an alternative measure of visual fluid reasoning that is somewhat different from the WAIS-IV Perceptual Reasoning Index. Developing this grouping might be particularly useful for clients who have physical impairments from arthritis or neurological complications.

9. *Long-Term Memory (Vocabulary + Information).* Range of general information combined with word knowledge both of which are stored in long term memory.

10. *Short-Term Memory (Letter-Number Sequencing + Digit Span).* Holding and using information in immediate awareness; this involves divided attention and managing a limited amount of information in short-term memory; limited to seven "chunks" of information (plus or minus two); examples are remembering telephone numbers, ability to hold directions in memory long enough to complete a task.

A similar listing of CHC groupings has been developed for the WISC-IV by Flanagan and Kaufman (2004).

1. Fluid Reasoning (Gf Matrix Reasoning + Picture Concepts + Arithmetic)
2. *Verbal Fluid Reasoning* (Similarities + Word Reasoning)
3. Nonverbal Fluid Reasoning (Gf; Matrix Reasoning + Picture Concepts)
4. Lexical Knowledge (Word Reasoning + Vocabulary)
5. General Information (Comprehension + Information)
6. Visual Processing (Gv; Block Design + Picture Completion)
7. Long Term Memory (Information + Vocabulary)
8. Short Term Memory (Letter-Number Sequencing + Digit Span)

In contrast to the WAIS-IV, difference and conversion tables are currently available for the WISC-IV. These enable scaled scores for each of the above WISC-IV clusters to be calculated by first summing the subtest scaled scores. Score conversions can then be made by referring to Appendix C (on pages 611–619). The resulting scaled scores are equivalent to the Index Scores in that they will have a mean of 100 and a standard deviation of 15.

The cluster scaled scores can be used to make *normative* comparisons. Thus a Visual Processing score of 85 would indicate the client is one standard deviation below their age-related peers in this ability. They would most likely have a difficult time making sense of and solving problems related to what they see. Interventions might include breaking visual information into basic, step-by-step instructions or highlighting the most crucial visual information for them to notice.

In addition to these normative comparisons, interpretation can also involve understanding the client's personal strengths and weaknesses compared with their own performance (*ipsative* comparisons). Ipsative comparisons that portray an examinees *personal* strengths and weaknesses can be made by comparing relevant pairs of clusters. The most useful comparisons are listed in Table 5.7. In order for the differences to be interpretable (significantly different) they must vary at or greater than the magnitude indicated in the "Amount of Difference" column. For example, if a child's Verbal Fluid Reasoning is 24 or more scaled score points higher than their Visual Processing, it would suggest that a relative strength would be in their ability to understand, reason through, and solve verbal problems. In contrast, they would have much more difficulty performing similar procedures with nonverbal information.

Level III. Interpreting Subtest Variability

The next step is to consider the degree to which the individual subtests deviate from the Full Scale IQ or the index scores. This information can then be used to develop interpretations that have been made based on the Full Scale IQ and index scores. The outcome should be a description of a person's relative cognitive strengths and weaknesses.

Table 5.7.   Size of difference between pairs of clinical clusters needed to be considered unusually large or uncommon

Cluster comparison	Amount of difference
Fluid Reasoning *(Gf)*—Visual Processing *(Gv)*	21
Nonverbal Fluid Reasoning (*Gf*-nonverbal)—Visual Processing *(Gv)*	24
Verbal Fluid Reasoning (*Gf*-verbal)—Nonverbal Fluid Reasoning (*Gf*-nonverbal)	24
Lexical Knowledge (*Gc*-VE)—General Information (*Gc*-K0)	17
Long-Term Memory (*Gc*-LTM)—Short-Term Memory (*Gsm*-WM)[a]	24
Long-Term Memory (*Gc*-LTM)—Verbal Fluid Reasoning (*Gf*-verbal)	17

Note: "Unusually large or uncommon" denotes differences occurring less than 10% of the time in the WISC-IV Standardization Sample.

[a]The Short-Term Memory (*Gsm*-WM) Cluster is identical to the WISC-IV Working Memory Index (WMI).

Source: Wechsler Intelligence Scale for Children–Fourth Edition. Copyright © 2003 by Harcourt Assessment, Inc. Reproduced by permission of the publisher. All rights reserved. *Wechsler Intelligence Scale for Children* and *WISC* are trademarks of Harcourt Assessment, Inc., registered in the United States of America and/or other jurisdictions.

A listing and discussion of the meaning of each subtest and the abilities it measures is provided in the next major section of this chapter ("Wechsler Indexes and Subtests"). Clinicians can refer to this section as well as to information on how to assess diverse populations in developing their own hypotheses about important dimensions of high and low scores. Readers may also wish to refer to Flanagan and A. Kaufman (2004), A. Kaufman and Lichtenberger (2006), and Sattler (2008), who have provided detailed lists of hypotheses and useful tables for various combinations of high and low subtest scores. However, Level III interpretation is necessary only if there is sufficient subtest scatter. If all the subtests are fairly even, it is not necessary to attempt subtest profile interpretation.

As was noted previously, subtest interpretation has been the source of controversy in that some authors have pointed out that the subtests are not sufficiently reliable, do not have enough subtest specificity, and do not provide sufficient incremental validity beyond what might be accounted for by the Full Scale IQ (Konold et al., 1999; Watkins, Glutting, & Lei, 2007; McDermott, Fantuzzo, Glutting, Watkins, & Baggaley, 1992; Watkins, Glutting, & Lei, 2007). Criticism of subtest interpretation has mainly been based on empirical concerns, but there are also underlying conceptual differences centered around whether intelligence is mainly accounted for by *g* ("lumpers") as opposed to its being composed of a number of different components ("splitters"). This debate seems to have been present almost as long as conceptions of intelligence have been in existence. One common response to this issue is that subtest interpretation is not merely an empirical activity but also involves a clinical process of hypothesis testing and integrating a variety of sources of data (A. Kaufman & Lichtenberger, 2006; Lezak et al., 2004).

As a result of the difficulties with subtest interpretation, the major focus should be on the index and CHC groupings. These provide a much stronger basis for making interpretations. In some cases, however, investigating subtests can be useful. These steps are recommended to interpret subtest variability: (a) Determine whether subtest fluctuations are significant (see "Determining Strengths and Weaknesses" sections of the Record Form); (b) develop hypotheses related to the meaning of the relative high/low scores; and (c) integrate these hypotheses with additional relevant information regarding the examinee. Clinicians should *never* interpret subtests merely by noting what seems to be high/low subtests and then listing the abilities provided in the subtest descriptions. Interpreters who merely list the subtest's abilities as they are listed in a book will make incorrect and even potentially damaging conclusions about the examinee. Clinicians need to be aware that interpreting subtest variability involves clinical judgment guided by theory, observation, and an integration of the specifics of each case. Because there is little research base to support this process, interpreting subtest variability should be approached with caution. Again, the preferable method of working with subtest variability is to note various clusters (see interpretive level II). Inferences based on one or two subtests should be considered quite tentative.

The challenge with interpreting high/low subtests is that any subtest will involve a series of different abilities. Just because a subtest or group of subtests has been designated as a relative strength or weakness does not mean that it is clear which of the various functions involved with the subtest is a strength or weakness. It is the examiner's responsibility to become actively engaged with the pattern of subtests, behavioral observations, and any other relevant sources of information necessary to determine which ability or abilities are high and low for the person. For example, Coding requires rapidly processing the digit-symbols, planning, sequencing, learning the digit-symbol pairs, making the actual response, and a high level of motivation. For one person, scoring low in Coding might reflect poor speed, for another it might reflect difficulties with short-term memory, and for a third it might reflect poor motivation. If a clinician noted a relatively low score on Coding, he or she might make sure that other sequencing-oriented tasks (i.e., Digit Span, Arithmetic, Letter-Number Sequencing) were also low. If this was the case, it would support the interpretation that sequencing was a problem. If this was not the case, then an alternative explanation needs to be determined. Thus a clinician might suspect that slow speed was the problem. If the examinee has done poorly due to slow speed, then it would be expected that other speeded tests would also be low (check Symbol Search and Cancellation). Sometimes behavioral observations might be useful. Thus, a person scoring low in Coding due to visual acuity might be struggling with seeing the images or have corrective lenses that are only partially effective.

Another example might be a clinician who is trying to decide whether the examinee prefers a simultaneous or sequential style of processing information. A relevant behavior for careful observation would be the way the examinee worked on Block Design. Did he or she proceed in a step-by-step sequence, trying to match each block with a segment of the picture, or, rather, did he or she try to understand the design as a whole while attempting to complete the task? A final relevant example might be low scores on Arithmetic, Digit Span, Coding, Letter-Number Sequencing, and Symbol Search. Each of these subtests requires a high level of motivation. Indeed, sometimes they have been referred to as validity indicators because they are likely to be lowered as a result of poor motivation. Rather than work to decipher the examinee's low abilities as reflected in these subtests, the clinician might decide that behavioral observations more accurately suggest the person was not expending a sufficient amount of effort.

This procedure should follow statistical principles for calculating subtest strengths and weaknesses, but at the same time it should not be a rigid, mechanical process. For example, a client who presents with subjective complaints related to poor sequencing (e.g., difficulty following directions, placing things in the wrong order) may not necessarily have all the expected WAIS-IV/WISC-IV subtests quite within the statistically interpretable range (indicated as subtest "strengths" and "weaknesses" on the Record Form). However, given the quite clear symptom reports (and possibly behavioral observations), practitioners may still choose to interpret the sequencing-related subtests. In contrast, another client might have most sequencing subtests in the statistically significant range but poor sequencing was neither a symptom complaint nor were behavioral observations noted that would have been consistent with poor sequencing. As a result, the hypothesis of poor sequencing might be rejected as not applying to the person. The outlined procedure, then, should be used for hypothesis generation in which other factors beyond the mechanical interpretation procedure can confirm or disconfirm these hypotheses.

Level IV. Qualitative/Process Analysis

In addition to interpreting subtest variability, a qualitative/process approach tries to understand the underlying reasons why a score was high/low. A general strategy is to look at the content of responses, especially on Information, Vocabulary, Comprehension, and Similarities. Frequently the presence of unique, highly personal, or unusual responses can suggest some important dimensions of an individual's intellectual or personality functioning (see Groth-Marnat et al., 2000; E. Kaplan et al., 1991, 1999). For example, some responses may reflect aggressive tendencies, concrete thinking, or unusual associations. A highly aggressive person might provide unusual responses on some of the Vocabulary items, or a person with paranoid personality characteristics might provide rigid, cautious, and legalistic responses. Similarly, impulsivity might be suggested by persons who quickly place incorrect blocks together on Block Design and then do not reflect on whether their designs were correct.

A more formal approach is to work with the process scores. For example, providing a timed versus an untimed (No Time Bonus) administration and scoring for Block Design enables clinicians to understand the relative extent that fast or slow responses determined a client's score. These procedures are not used to help compute the Full Scale IQ, Index, or additional cluster scores. In addition, they are optional procedures; they are quite time consuming and should not be routinely calculated unless there is some reason to suspect they might yield additional information. Another reason for not routinely calculating these procedures is that more research needs to be performed to better understand the meaning of norms, cutoff scores, and the degree to which they increase interpretive accuracy. However, they can be used to help generate hypotheses related to the client's functioning. The various process scores can be divided into four clusters based on which subtests they refer to:

1. *Process score related to Block Design*

    Block Design No Time Bonus (BDN). The usual Block Design subtest score does not provide information on the extent to which speed versus difficulty with visuoconstructive abilities have impacted the score. Some children may have intact visuoconstrucitve abilities but, due to a cautious problem-solving style, slow cognitive processing, or physical difficulties, may have low scores on the usual Block Design index score. The Block Design No Time Bonus (BDN) scoring reduces but does not completely eliminate the importance of speed. The reason that it does not completely eliminate the importance of speed is that, in order to obtain points, clients must still perform the task correctly within the maximum time limit. A client who does much better on BDN compared with the normal scoring is likely to have good visuoconstructive abilities but, for some reason, does not work quickly (check also the Processing Speed Index and subscale scores on Coding, Symbol Search, and Cancellation)

2. *Process scores related to Digit Span*

    Digit Span Forward (DSF), Digit Span Backward (DSB), and Digit Span Sequencing (DSS; WAIS-IV only). It is sometimes useful to compare a client's performance for Digit Span Forward versus Digits Span Backward. Digit Span Forward is a fairly, simple, straightforward procedure. As a result, it is fairly stable in that it resists cognitive deterioration. In contrast, DSB and Digit Span Sequencing (WAIS-IV only) require more attention, concentration, and ability to manipulate numbers. It is thus useful to compare scores on DSF with scores on DSB. If DSB is much lower than DSF, it suggests cognitive deterioration related to poor attention, sequencing, chunking, and visualizing the numbers. It is also useful (WAIS-IV) to compare DSF with DSS since, as with DSB, the sequencing task is more difficult. A significantly lower score on DSS similarly reflects deterioration in attention, sequencing, chunking, and visualizing numbers.

Longest Digit Span Forward (LDSF) versus *Longest Digit Span Backward* (LDSB). This score represents a variation on DSF versus DSB and is derived by simply noting the longest number of digits recalled forward versus the longest recalled backward. As such, it is a raw rather than a scaled score. The reason for this is that sometimes it is useful to double check DSF versus DSB. The interpretation is essentially the same as for DSF versus DSB.

Longest Digit Span Sequence (LDSS) versus *Longest Letter-Number Sequence* (LLNS; WAIS-IV only). This score represents a variation on LDSF versus LDSB. It is similarly based on raw scores derived from noting the longest number of digits recalled forward versus the longest recalled backward. The interpretation is essentially the same as for LDSF versus LDSB.

3. *Letter-Number Sequencing (LLNS; WAIS-IV only)*

The LLNS score is a raw score based on the total number of letters and numbers that were recalled on the last correct trial. This score may provide additional information on how a client performed on Letter-Number Sequencing, especially if performance on the previous items was quite variable.

4. *Process scores related to Cancellation Random (CAR) versus Cancellation Structured (CAS; WISC-IV only)*

Item 1 of Cancellation has objects arranged in a random order. In contrast, Item 2 includes the added feature that the objects are lined up in even rows. This means that the task for Item 2 is somewhat easier than that for Item 1. It is expected that the greater structure of Item 2 would result in better performance. (See Tables A.8 and B.9 in the *WISC-IV Administration and Scoring Manual* for conversion and comparisons.) The improved performance assumes, of course, that the child actually benefits from the greater structure. Thus, the extent to which the child benefits from the structure can be determined by comparing Cancellation Random (CAR) with Cancellation Structured (CS).

These process scores allow clinicians to elaborate on the meanings of individual subtests in more detail. An expanded series of subtest stimuli, alternative administrations, and scorings can be found in the *WISC-IV Integrated* upgrade and the *WAIS-IV/WMS-IV Advanced Clinical Solutions*.

Level V. Intrasubtest Variability

A further, potentially important area of analysis involves looking at the patterns of performance within the items of each subtest. These items are arranged in sequences that become progressively more difficult. Thus, a normal and expected pattern would have the examinee pass the initial items and slowly but evenly begin to fail more difficult ones. A more sporadic pattern, in which the examinee misses initial easier items but passes later more difficult ones, may suggest an attentional deficit or specific memory losses, particularly related to retrieval difficulties (E. Kaplan et al., 1991; E. Kaplan et al., 1999). If performance is highly sporadic, the reason should be explored further. For example, clients might be consciously faking if they miss every other item, miss extremely easy items, and/or appear much more alert than their obtained IQ. Sporadic performance might also be characteristic of patients with brain damage with diffuse cortical (Mittenberg, Hammeke, & Rao, 1989) or subcortical involvement (Godber, Anderson, & Bell, 2000). An analysis of the intrasubtest scatter can provide a type of information different from that obtained merely by looking at the quantitative-scaled scores. It should be noted, however, that research on this is equivocal given that J. Ryan, Paul, and Arb (1999) were unable to find high subtest scatter on the Information subtest among patients who had documented retrieval difficulties.

WECHSLER INDEXES AND SUBTESTS

To understand the Wechsler intelligence scales, it is useful to understand the various abilities that the indexes and subtests measure. This section describes the indexes and subtests and presents the different abilities involved in each of the 15 WAIS-IV and WISC-IV subtests, followed by a discussion of their relevant features, including the possible meanings associated with high or low scores. Subtest abilities and factor loadings for the WAIS-IV are based on research reviewed in the *WAIS-IV Technical and Interpretive Manual* (Wechsler, 2008). Descriptions of the subtest abilities and data on factor loadings presented for the WISC-IV subtests are derived from A. Kaufman and Lichtenberger (2006), Flanagan and Kaufman (2004), and Sattler (2008).

In keeping with the overall approach of this book, any interpretations suggested in the discussion of the subtests should be considered tentative. They are merely beginning possibilities that must be explored further and placed in a proper context. In addition, no subtest is a pure measurement of any single intellectual ability; rather, each represents a combination of skills. It is important to emphasize that a low or high score on a specific subtest can occur for a variety of reasons, which the examiner must consider in interpreting the overall profile. This section is most helpful only after practitioners are familiar with the subtest stimuli and administration procedures outlined in the WAIS-IV and WISC-IV manuals.

Verbal Comprehension Index/Subtests

The Verbal Comprehension Index (WAIS-IV: Vocabulary, Similarities, and Information; WISC-IV: Similarities and Vocabulary) is a relatively pure, refined measure of verbal abilities. The material presented to examinees is in the form of oral questions that they need to answer. An examinee's score on Verbal Comprehension reflects the extent to which he or she understands the meanings of words, can conceptualize verbal information, the extent of factual knowledge related to verbal material, and ability to adequately express the material in words. Thus they measure an individual's proficiency in these areas:

- The ability to work with abstract semantic information.
- The amount and degree of benefit a person has received from his or her educational background.
- Verbal memory abilities.
- Verbal fluency.

Everyday examples of persons scoring high suggest that they will be able to easily understand spoken communication, easily construct sentences, be verbally fluent, will likely do well in verbally oriented occupations, and have interests in educational activities. In contrast, persons scoring low may have difficulties with spoken language, struggle over fluidly coming up with the correct words, and have little interest in educational or intellectual pursuits.

These considerations should be tempered by the fact that the subtests on the Verbal Comprehension Index are more influenced by cultural factors than other subtests. In contrast, many of the more nonverbally oriented subtests comprising most of the Perceptual Reasoning and Processing Speed indexes are considered to be somewhat more culture free. If an individual does significantly better (9 points or more for the WAIS-IV or 11 points or more for the WISC-IV) on the Verbal Comprehension Index compared with the Perceptual Reasoning Index, this difference may indicate a number of interpretative possibilities, including a relatively high level of education; a tendency toward overachieving; psychomotor slowing because of depression; difficulty working with practical tasks; deficits in nonverbal abilities; poor visual-motor integration; a quick, impulsive work style resulting in relatively more errors on Perceptual Reasoning subtests (A. Kaufman & Lichtenberger, 2006; Lezak et al., 2004; Sattler, 2008). In addition, persons from professional occupations, with high educational attainment, and with high IQs in general are likely to have quite high Verbal Comprehension Index scores.

Similarities (WAIS-IV/WISC-IV Core Subtest)

- Logical abstract reasoning*
- Verbal concept formation or conceptual thinking.
- Distinguishing essential from nonessential details.
- Associative ability combined with language facility.

The Similarities subtest requires verbal concept formation and abstract reasoning ability. These functions mediate an awareness of the belonging-togetherness of objects and events of the day-to-day world. An essential aspect of adjusting to one's environment is the use of these abilities to clarify, reduce, and classify the style and manner to which a response is made. Inductive reasoning is required, as the examinee must move from particular facts to a general rule or principle. Implicit in the test is the ability of individuals to use long-term memory and to apply elegant expressions in their responses. The more precise and abstract the expression, the higher the score, which indicates that verbal fluency is an important determinant. Correct responses to the last few items indicate a particularly high level of abstraction. Individuals with a good ability for insight and introspection tend to perform highly on this subtest; thus, it may be used as an indicator of favorable prognosis for psychotherapy. Scores decrease significantly in schizophrenics, rigid or inflexible thinkers, and patients with senile conditions. Examiners can, therefore, use this subtest to gain further information regarding the nature of an examinee's idiosyncratic or pathological form of concept formation.

---

*Abilities followed by an asterisk indicate specific abilities and traits strongly associated with the subtest under discussion here through page 165.

High scorers show good verbal concept formation, which, if unusually high, may reflect intellectualizing tendencies. Low scorers show poor abstraction abilities, literalness, and inflexible thinking. The Similarities subtest in adult protocols is the most sensitive subtest to left-hemisphere lesions, particularly lesions to the left temporal and/or left frontal regions (Dobbins & Russell, 1990).

Vocabulary (WAIS-IV/WISC-IV Core Subtest)

The Vocabulary subtest includes these abilities or traits:

- Language development.*
- Word knowledge.*
- General verbal intelligence.
- Language usage and accumulated verbal learning ability.
- Rough measure of the subject's optimal intellectual efficiency.
- Educational background.
- Range of ideas, experiences, or interests that a subject has acquired.

The Vocabulary subtest is a test of accumulated verbal learning and represents an individual's ability to express a wide range of ideas with ease and flexibility. It may also involve the person's richness of ideas, long-term memory, concept formation, and language development. Vocabulary is noteworthy in that it is one of the most reliable Verbal Comprehension subtests (WAIS-IV test-retest reliability = .89; WISC- test-retest reliability = .92) and, like Information, it is highly resistant to neurological deficit and psychological disturbance (Lezak et al., 2004; Reitan & Wolfson, 1993). Although the Vocabulary subtest holds up with age, it tends to fall off with those people for whom visual-spatial skills are far more important than verbal abilities. Vocabulary generally reflects the nature and level of sophistication of the person's schooling and cultural learning. Vocabulary is primarily dependent on the wealth of early educational environment, but it is susceptible to improvement by later experience or schooling. Vocabulary, along with Information, is the least variable of all the subtests, and subtest scores below the Vocabulary level sometimes imply a drop of efficiency in that function. Vocabulary is the best single indicator of general intelligence (WAIS-IV/WISC-IV .72 correlation with the Full Scale IQ). Because of its high degree of stability, Vocabulary is often used as an indicator of a person's intellectual potential and to make an estimate of the premorbid level of functioning (see subsection on estimating premorbid IQ in the "Assessing Brain Damage" section).

The Vocabulary responses are similar to Comprehension and Similarities in that a qualitative analysis often provides useful information relating to the examinee's thought processes, background, life experiences, and response to frustration. It is often important to explore incorrect responses to determine whether they were guesses, clang associations (e.g., "ponder" meaning "to pound" or "assemble" meaning to "resemble"), concrete thinking, bizarre associations, or overinclusive reasoning. Even when a response is correct, a consideration of the style used to approach the word and specific content can be helpful.

High scores suggest high general intelligence and indicate that the examinee can adequately recall past ideas and form concepts relating to these ideas. Persons with high scores have a wide range of interests and a good fund of general information, and may have high needs for achievement. Clinical populations who score high on Vocabulary may use compulsive or intellectualizing defense mechanisms. Low scores suggest a limited educational background, low general intelligence, poor language development, lack of familiarity with English, and/or poor motivation.

Information (WAIS-IV Core Subtest, WISC-IV Supplemental Subtest)

- Range of general factual knowledge.*
- Old learning or schooling.
- Intellectual curiosity or urge to collect knowledge.
- Alertness to day-to-day world.
- Long-term memory.

The Information subtest samples the type of knowledge that average persons with average opportunities should be able to acquire. This knowledge is usually based on habitual, overlearned material, particularly in the case of older children and adults. Both Information and Vocabulary are highly resistant to neurological deficit and psychological disturbance (Lezak et al., 2004; Reitan & Wolfson, 1993) and are two of the most stable subtests. Because of this stability, Wechsler referred to them as "hold" tests as opposed to "no-hold" tests, which he theorized are more sensitive to deterioration and such situational variables as anxiety and fatigue (i.e., Arithmetic, Coding, Block Design). Furthermore, both these subtests are good measures of general intelligence and are highly correlated with educational level (A. Kaufman & Lichtenberger, 2006) and WAIS-IV and WISC-IV Full Scale IQs. Research has shown that the earlier WAIS-R Information and Vocabulary subtests have predicted college grade-point average as accurately as well-established college aptitude tests (Feingold, 1983). It is for these reasons that Information (along with Vocabulary and Arithmetic) is included in Bannatyne's Acquired Knowledge category. It also loads most strongly (.84) on the Verbal Comprehension factor.

Although performance on the Information subtest involves remote memory and alertness to the environment, it is influenced only to a small extent by conscious effort and is believed to be only minimally affected by factors such as anxiety. To score well, the individual must have been exposed to a highly varied past environment, have an intact long-term memory, and possess a wide range of interests.

A high score on this subtest suggests that the examinee has good long-term memory, cultural interests, strong educational background, positive attitude toward school, good verbal ability, and possibly intellectualization as his or her most frequently used defense mechanism. Low scorers may show superficiality of interests, lack of intellectual curiosity, cultural deprivation, or lack of familiarity with Western (primarily American) culture. (However, note the availability of numerous foreign-country adaptations.) Failing initial easy items combined with success on more difficult ones (high intrasubtest variability; see Level IV procedure) may suggest difficulties with retrieval, although research substantiating this hypothesis has been equivocal (E. Kaplan et al., 1991; Mittenberg et al., 1989; J. Ryan & Paul, 1999). High intrasubtest scatter may also suggest the possibility of malingering or poor motivation.

Comprehension (WAIS-IV Supplemental Subtest, WISC-IV Core Subtest)

- Demonstration of practical knowledge.*
- Knowledge of conventional standards of behavior.*
- Ability to evaluate past experience; that is, proper selection, organization, and emphasis of facts and relationships.*
- Abstract thinking and generalization (later items only).*
- Social maturity, social judgment, common sense, or judgment in practical social situations.

- Grasp of social milieu; for example, information and knowledge of moral codes, social rules, and regulations
- Reality awareness, understanding, and alertness to the day-to-day world.

Comprehension has often been considered to reflect the extent to which an examinee adheres to conventional standards, has benefited from past cultural opportunities, and has a well-developed conscience. However, formal studies have generally not supported a relationship between Comprehension and various measures of social intelligence (see Beebe, Pfiffner, & McBurnett, 2000). Comprehension is also, at least in part, a test of information, which is supported by its high correlation (low- to mid-70s, depending on age) with the Information and Vocabulary subtests. Comprehension involves an adaptive response by the individual to a situation that requires him or her to select the most efficient way of dealing with a specific problem. The examinee not only must possess relevant information but also must appropriately use this information for decision making. In this sense, the Comprehension subtest goes one step beyond the degree of complexity and synthesis required for the Information subtest. Like Vocabulary and Information, it measures general verbal ability (.79 correlation with WAIS-IV VCI, .86 correlation with WISC-IV VCI). Not only must the examinee have the necessary information, but he or she also must apply it in a coherent, problem-oriented manner. Thus, a Comprehension score significantly below the Information score suggests that an examinee is not effectively using his or her knowledge.

In assessing an examinee's responses, it can be important to distinguish between actually dealing with the material to develop an original response and merely repeating over-learned concepts. For example, parroting answers to "forest," "parole system," or the proverbs does not indicate full comprehension and may simply be based on past experience rather than on accurate problem solving, good judgment, or abstract reasoning. Thus, basic rule-of-thumb answers can significantly increase the total number of correct responses. However, in the later items, a correct response requires higher-level problem solving, and these items, therefore, can still be a good measure of general intelligence instead of merely rote memorization.

Personality variables, especially those relating to judgment, are important areas to consider in this subtest. In particular, poor levels of adjustment can lower scores on Comprehension. Clinicians should note the pattern of responses, clichés, literalness, and any circumscribed responses. In contrast, good judgment involves the ability to engage in discriminative activity. Failure on the easy items even though later, more difficult items are passed indicates impaired judgment. It is important to note emotional implications on this subtest because emotional responsiveness influences the way a person evaluates environmental events. For example, individuals who are highly analytical and use these analytical abilities to avoid emotions may have difficulty understanding the social components of situations as presented in Comprehension.

High scorers show reality awareness, capacity for social compliance, good judgment, and emotionally relevant use of information. Low scorers, especially if they have 4 or more subscale points below Vocabulary, might have poor judgment, impulsiveness, and hostility against their environment. Mentally disturbed persons often do poorly on Comprehension, which may be the result of disturbed perceptions, idiosyncratic thinking, impulsiveness, or antisocial tendencies.

Word Reasoning (Not Available on the WAIS-IV, WISC-IV Supplemental Subtest)

- Verbal reasoning.*
- Verbal abstraction.*
- Deductive reasoning.*

- Ability to develop alternative concepts.
- Synthesizing ability.
- Verbal comprehension.

The child is asked to identify the common concept after a series of one to three clues. Each clue becomes progressively more specific. The child must first comprehend the purpose of the subtest, understand the clues, test out various hypotheses, and decide on what he or she feels is the best concept to solve the problem. The subtest thus requires children to generate different concepts, understand the relationships between them, and test to make sure they have developed the best option.

One of the main features of Word Reasoning is that it loads strongly on the Verbal Comprehension Index (average loading = .66). It is also a good measure of g (54% of its variance can be accounted for by g) and has a moderate correlation with the Full Scale IQ ($r = .65$). It also has a moderate correlation with the Perceptual Reasoning Index ($r = .52$). Its highest subtest correlation is with Vocabulary ($r = .66$). It has a relatively high reliability ($r = .80$).

High scores suggest good deductive reasoning, good ability to generate alternative concepts, good analogical reasoning, good ability to understand relationships, good vocabulary, and a high motivation to achieve. In contrast, low scores indicate poor deductive reasoning, difficulty generating alternative concepts, poor word knowledge, and possibly low motivation.

Perceptual Reasoning Index/Subtests

The Perceptual Reasoning Index (PRI) is a relatively pure measure of perceptual abilities (WAIS-IV: Block Design, Matrix Reasoning, Visual Puzzles; WISC-IV: Block Design, Picture Concepts, Matrix Reasoning). An examinee's score reflects the extent to which he or she has good nonverbal, fluid reasoning; can integrate nonverbal material; pays close attention to detail; and accurately responds to the visuospatial material presented to him or her. Many of these abilities involves using the kind of visuospatial and visuomotor skills to solve problems that are not taught in formal academic schooling. The Perceptual Reasoning Index reflects proficiency in these areas:

- The individual's degree and quality of nonverbal contact with the environment.
- The ability to integrate perceptual stimuli with relevant motor responses.
- The capacity to work in concrete situations.
- The ability to evaluate visuospatial information.

Everyday examples of persons who score high in Perceptual Reasoning include good ability to follow maps, accurately driving from one place to the next, correctly assembling objects, finding objects in a house/office, drawing a design, or the ability to work with nonverbal material. In contrast, low scores suggest that the person may have a difficult time following spatial directions, finding objects placed in a house/office, accurately drawing designs, repairing broken objects, or estimating distance.

Perceptual Reasoning subtests are generally less affected by educational background than are the Verbal Comprehension subtests. If an individual does significantly (.05 level) better (9 points or more on the WAIS-IV, 11 or more points on the WISC-IV) on the Perceptual Reasoning Index compared with the Verbal Comprehension Index, this may indicate a number of interpretive possibilities, including superior perceptual organizational abilities, a tendency toward low academic achievement, possible acting out (juvenile delinquency), an individual who could be described as a doer rather than a thinker, a person from a relatively low socioeconomic background, presence of a language deficit, poorly developed auditory conceptual/processing skills, or that immediate problem solving is better developed than problem solving based on accumulated knowledge.

Block Design (WAIS-IV/WISC-IV Core Subtest)

- Analysis of whole into component parts.*
- Spatial visualization.*
- Nonverbal concept formation.
- Visuomotor coordination and perceptual organization.
- Capacity for sustained effort; concentration.
- Visual-motor-spatial coordination; manipulative and perceptual speed.

The Block Design subtest involves nonverbal problem-solving skills because it emphasizes analyzing a problem into its component parts and then reintegrating these parts into a cohesive whole. The examinee must apply logic and reasoning in a manner that will solve spatial relationship problems. As a test of nonverbal concept formation, Block Design demands skills in perceptual organization, spatial visualization, and abstract conceptualization. The Block Design subtest is sturdy and reliable, correlating highly with general intelligence, and is not likely to be lowered except by the effects of depression or organic impairment. It also has been found to relate to everyday measures of spatial abilities (Groth-Marnat & Teal, 2000). To perform well, examinees must be able to demonstrate a degree of abstraction that is free from literal concreteness. They must also make a distinction between part and whole by demonstrating both analytic and synthetic skills. This test involves an ability to shift the frame of reference while maintaining a high degree of flexibility. The examinee must also be able to inhibit impulsive tendencies and to persist in a designated task.

An important feature of Block Design is that it enables an examiner actually to observe the examinee's response. Some subjects are easily discouraged and give up, while others insist on completing the task even if they have to work beyond the time limit. In approaching the task, one subject might impulsively place the blocks together in a nonrandom sequence, whereas another subject might demonstrate a meticulous sequential style, thereby revealing preferences for either a holistic simultaneous or a more sequential problem-solving style. Additional observations can reveal factors such as hand preference, motor coordination, speed of information processing, frustration tolerance, and ability to benefit from feedback. A highly reflective or compulsive style can lower scores because of the resulting extended time for completing the task. Placing blocks outside the 2×2 or 3×3 configuration is a further behavioral observation that reflects poor visuospatial skills (Kramer, Kaplan, & Huckeba, 1999). Thus, potentially valuable information can be obtained by observing and recording differences in solving the Block Design tasks.

Block Design is also a nonverbal, relatively culture-free test of intelligence. It is reliable in that it correlates highly with general intelligence (.66 correlation with the WAIS-IV Full Scale IQ, .61 correlation with the WISC-IV Full Scale IQ), but it has a relatively low correlation with education. Thus, the Block Design subtest is only minimally biased by an examinee's cultural or educational background. Block Design scores can therefore be important tools in assessing the intellectual potential of persons from diverse cultural and intellectual backgrounds.

Block Design is an excellent indicator of right-hemisphere brain damage and is especially sensitive to right parietal lesions (Lezak et al., 2004; Reitan & Wolfson, 1992, 1993).

Right-lesion patients tend to make errors because they might distort the designs, misperceive aspects of them, or become disoriented when attempting to complete them. In contrast, left-lesion patients, particularly if the lesion is in the parietal lobe, are not nearly as likely to have a poor Block Design score. However, when they do, it is likely to be expressed in design simplification, confusion, and a concrete approach to reproducing the design (Lezak et al., 2004). Inattention (neglect) can be reflected by the examinee's failing to complete the right or left portion of the design. For example, only 6 or 7 of the blocks might be used when attempting to complete a 9-block design (Lezak et al., 2004). Block Design is typically one of the lowest subtests in Alzheimer's patients. It is sensitive to the early phases of the disease and thus can be useful in differentiating between Alzheimer's and pseudodementing conditions such as depression (Fuld, 1984; La Rue & Jarvik, 1987).

High scorers show a good capacity for visuospatial perception, visuomotor speed, a good ability to concentrate, and excellent nonverbal concept formation. Low scores suggest poor perceptual abilities, difficulties with visual integration, and problems in maintaining a sustained effort.

Matrix Reasoning (WAIS-III/WISC-IV Core Subtest)

- Visual-spatial reasoning.*
- Abstract reasoning.*
- Visual organization.*
- Simultaneous processing of visuospatial information.
- Analysis of wholes into component parts.

High scores on Matrix Reasoning suggest good visual information processing and nonverbal abstract reasoning skills. On the WAIS-IV, Matrix Reasoning is combined with Block Design and Visual Puzzles to form the Perceptual Reasoning Index. In contrast, the WISC-IV uses Block Design but then adds Picture Completion to form the Perceptual Reasoning Index. Matrix Reasoning is untimed (except for the 30 seconds maximum on the WAIS-IV) and is therefore useful for persons from older age groups who might do poorly on some of the other timed tests. It also does not penalize those who have a reflective, cautious problem-solving style. Matrix Reasoning is relatively culture free and requires only a minimal amount of visuomotor coordination because the subject merely points to the correct response. Conceptually, Matrix Reasoning is similar to the Halstead Reitan Category Test and Raven's Progressive Matrices. However, future studies will need to determine the nature and degree of correspondence between these measures.

One of the rationales for Matrix Reasoning was to develop a visuospatial subtest with good psychometric properties that could replace the psychometrically poor Object Assembly subtest. Matrix Reasoning has been found to have test-retest stabilities ranging from .74 to .92, SEM of .95 to .99, and factor loadings of .73 to .69 on the Perceptual Reasoning Index. It is an excellent measure of general intelligence (.67 correlation with WAIS-IV Full Scale IQ and .64 with the WISC-IV Full Scale IQ).

High scores might indicate good nonverbal abstract reasoning abilities, a preference for simultaneous processing of information, and excellent visual information processing. Low scores might suggest low visual concept formation, poor or at least rigid visual reasoning, or poor concentration. Negativism might be indicated if the examinee seems unmotivated and replies with wording such as "none of them match."

Visual Puzzles (WAIS-IV Core Subtest, Not Available on the WISC-IV)

- Visual recognition and identification.*
- Perception of the parts in relation to the whole.*

- Visual spatial reasoning.*
- Analysis of wholes into component parts.
- Capacity for sustained visual effort; concentration.
- Fluid reasoning.

Visual Puzzles is a new subtest developed for the WAIS-IV. It requires examinees to first view a completed design at the top of a page. They must then look at six possible design fragments at the bottom of the page and select the three that, when combined, would re-create the original design at the top of the page. It is thus similar to solving a puzzle. However, examinees do not actually manipulate any objects. The task is performed completely based on visual reasoning. Examinees must analyze the original shape and then synthesize which of the alternative shapes are correct. It is thus a measure of visual and analogical reasoning (Wechsler, 2008a). The *WAIS-IV Technical and Interpretive Manual* (Wechsler, 2008a) reported that similar measures have been found to involve "visual perception, broad visual intelligence, fluid intelligence, simultaneous processing, spatial visualization and manipulation, and the ability to anticipate relationships among parts" (p. 14).

High scores indicate good nonverbal reasoning, ability to concentrate, and a good ability to integrate visuospatial integration. In contrast, low scores suggest problems with integrating nonverbal material, possible problems with concentration, and possible visual neglect.

Figure Weights (WAIS-IV Supplementary Subtest, Not Available on the WISC-IV)

- Nonverbal mathematical reasoning.*
- Quantitative and analogical reasoning.*
- Visual concentration combined with an ability to visually organize material.
- Capacity for sustained effort.

Figure Weights is a new subtest developed for the WAIS-IV and appropriate for examinees between the ages of 16 and 69. Examinees are first shown a picture at the top of the stimulus card depicting two measuring scales with various shapes on the trays. The scales on the left are balanced as indicated by the two trays being at the same level. The scales on the right are also balanced in that they are similarly at the same level. There are objects in the left tray but the right tray is empty, with a question mark appearing above the empty tray. The examinee is then requested to select which of five sets of objects at the bottom of the stimulus card would be necessary to balance the scale depicted at the top right side of the stimulus card (and with the question mark on top of the tray). Figure Weights is a nonverbal test of mathematical reasoning. It involves quantitative and analogical reasoning and inductive or deductive logic. To a certain extent, the task is similar to Arithmetic in that it involves sustained effort and concentration. However, the Arithmetic subtest requires examinees to hold details of the problem in their memory and work with this information (working memory). In contrast, Figure Weights has the problem depicted visually. As a result, the importance of remembering the various components of the problem is minimized. In addition, the Arithmetic subtest is verbal (except for the early extremely easy items) whereas Figure Weights is nonverbal.

High scores suggest good nonverbal quantitative reasoning, excellent concentration, and a good ability to organize nonverbal information. In contrast, low scores might indicate poor nonverbal quantitative reasoning and difficulties with concentration. A potentially useful contrast is to compare scores on Arithmetic with those on Figure Weights (see WAIS-IV Table B.3). If scores are the same, it suggests a person's quantitative abilities are equal for both verbal and nonverbal information. However, a significantly higher Arithmetic score (3 or more subscale points) suggests that verbal quantitative abilities are better developed. In contrast, a relatively higher Figure Weights score (3 or more subscales scores) would indicate that the examinee's nonverbal quantitative abilities are better.

Picture Completion (WAIS-IV/WISC-IV Supplementary Subtest)

- Visual alertness.*
- Visual recognition and identification (long-term visual memory).*
- Awareness of environmental detail; reality contact.
- Perception of the whole in relation to its parts; visual conceptual ability.
- Ability to differentiate essential details from nonessential details.
- Visual concentration combined with an ability to visually organize material.

The Picture Completion subtest is a measure of visual concentration and is a nonverbal test of general information. It involves discovering consistency and inconsistency by paying close attention to the environment and accessing remote memory. It is dependent on, and also draws on, an individual's experience with his or her culture. Thus, persons who are unfamiliar with common features of American/Western society may make errors because of a lack of experience rather than a lack of intelligence. Persons will also make errors if they are unable to detach themselves emotionally from the material, thereby making accurate discriminations difficult. For example, passive, dependent personalities might make errors because they notice the absence of people controlling the actions in the pictures. Typical responses might be that "there's nobody holding the pitcher," "there are no people rowing the boat," or "there's no flagpole." Sometimes negative, inflexible, oppositional individuals state that there is nothing missing in the pictures.

High scorers are able to recognize essential visual information, are alert, and demonstrate good visual acuity. Low scores indicate poor concentration and inadequate visual organization. Impulsiveness can often produce lowered performance because the examinee may make a quick response without carefully analyzing the whole picture.

Picture Concepts (Not Available on WAIS-IV, WISC-IV Supplemental Subtest)

- Nonverbal concept formation.*
- Perceptual recognition.
- Abstract, categorical reasoning.

Clients are initially requested to look at two rows of pictures. They are then asked to determine which picture in the first row goes together with one of the pictures from the second row (i.e., they might both be animals or means of transport). Later items use three instead of two rows. Clients must first scan the pictures and determine which categories the pictures belong to. They must then decide which is the most important characteristic that the picture on the first row shares with the picture on the second row. Picture Concepts is thus a measure of nonverbal concept formation. It functions as a nonverbal parallel to the verbally oriented Similarities subtest.

Picture Concepts is a moderate measure of g (37% of its variance is accounted for by g) and has a low to moderate correlation with the WISC-IV Full Scale IQ ($r = .6$). It is a moderate contributor to the Perceptual Reasoning Index (loading = .40) and has ample specificity. It is moderately reliable ($r = .82$) and has its highest correlation with Matrix Reasoning ($r = .47$).

In order to interpret Picture Concepts, it is often useful to note if there are any visual difficulties or signs of negativism. It is also important to notice whether clients respond in a rapid, impulsive manner or one that is more reflective. Once the subtest is completed, it is sometimes useful to develop a better understanding of the reasoning behind clients' problem solving. This can be done by asking why they made the response they did. It might also be useful to check whether clients have performed much higher or lower on the Similarities subtest. Scores that are relatively higher on Picture Concepts suggest that abstract reasoning is better for nonverbal than for verbal material. In contrast, lower scores on Picture Concepts indicate that nonverbal abstract reasoning is superior.

High scores suggest good nonverbal concept formation, good flexibility of thinking, and good logical and abstract thinking. Low scores indicate poor nonverbal concept formation, rigid thought processes, and poor abstract reasoning. However, sometimes low scores might reflect good abstract reasoning but the responses are based on more unconventional, innovative means of perceiving relationships between pictures. Questioning clients about their responses might help determine whether their answers were wrong due to their not understanding the problem or simply due to them understanding it correctly but developing unconventional responses.

Working Memory Index/Subtests

Working Memory (WAIS-IV/WISC-IV: Digit Span, Arithmetic, Letter-Number Sequencing) is a more complex and controversial construct than the constructs measured in the other indexes. It has been related primarily to concentration, attention, and short-term memory. Because the term *memory* is in the title, clinicians sometimes are tempted to think of it as a measure of memory. Instead, it is a narrow measure of the ability to hold and manipulate information for a short period of time. Whereas this ability is certainly related to and a prerequisite for many aspects of memory, it is not the same as memory. As such, interpreting high (or low) scores as indicating that the client has good (or poor) "memory" should never be done. In addition, the subtests focus on auditory/verbal aspects of working memory rather than on visual components (see Leffard et al., 2006). Sequencing is also crucial for Working Memory subtests because each of the subtests requires that the respondent place numbers and symbols in their proper order. Wielkiewicz (1990) has suggested that the low scores on Working Memory can reflect not only poor concentration, memory, and sequencing but also difficulties with executive functioning. Specifically, the person experiences difficulty attending to stimuli and simultaneously performing other mental tasks (e.g., listening to spoken digits and storing them while simultaneously reversing them and then repeating them backward). Good performance also requires a high level of motivation. As a result of these diverse functions, a low Working Memory Index is also likely to lower performances in other areas, and this should be considered when estimating the person's overall potential. Thus, Working Memory represents a proficiency in these areas:

- Concentration and attention.*
- The ability to hold and manipulate information in short-term memory.*
- Short-term memory.
- Sequencing.
- Facility with numbers.
- Mental flexibility (especially for Digit Span backward, Digit Span Sequencing, and Letter-Number Sequencing).

Persons scoring high would be expected to be good at recalling phone numbers, evaluating checks in a restaurant, following a sequence of (verbal) instructions, concentrate on a task without being distracted, and can easily do two things at the same time. In contrast, low scores might indicate that the person would have a difficult time paying attention to a lecture, recalling phone numbers, following a sequence of instructions, and doing two things at the same time, or they might be quite anxious.

It is crucial to consider a variety of interpretive possibilities to interpret the Working Memory Index. Often behavioral observations can be crucial. A client who frequently asks to have the questions repeated might have a high level of distractibility. Alternatively, a high degree of motor activity or excessive talking might highlight a client's high level of anxiety. If number skills have not been developed, the client might ask to write out the numbers related to the arithmetic problems or count out the numbers with his or her fingers.

The association between Working Memory and ADHD has been equivocal. It would seem that conceptually Working Memory would be the lowest index score (Mayes & Calhoun, 2007). However, often this has not been found (Reinecke et al., 1999; Wechsler, 2003b, 2008b). As mentioned previously, this may be due partially to the structured nature of the testing situation, which eliminates most distractions. In contrast, a real-world environment typically has many competing distractions that a person with ADHD may have a difficult time screening out. As a result, clinicians need to look at additional sources of information including corroborating sources and rating scales (i.e., Connors's Rating Scales, Child Behavior Checklist, Behavior Assessment System for Children).

Digit Span (WAIS-IV/WISC-IV Core Subtest)

- Immediate rote recall.*
- Reversibility; ability to shift thought patterns (from digits forward to digits backward).*
- Concentration and attention.
- Auditory sequencing.
- Rote learning.

Digit Span is considered to be a test of short-term memory and attention. The subject must recall and repeat auditory information in the proper sequence. Bannatyne (1974) has further described this as "auditory vocal sequencing memory." Correct responses require a two-step process. First, the information must be accurately received, which requires attention and encoding. Persons who are easily distractible have difficulty in this phase. Second, the examinee must accurately recall, sequence, and vocalize the information. Persons who can perhaps receive the information correctly may still have a problem at this phase if they have short-term memory difficulties because they cannot hold the memory trace long enough. Sometimes the previous digit is forgotten as they are attempting to vocalize a present one. Digits Forward is a simpler, more straightforward task requiring rote memory than Digits Backward. The examinee usually must hold the memory longer and also transform it before making a restatement. Thus, a good performance on Digits Backward is likely to reflect a person who is flexible, can concentrate, and is tolerant of stress. High Digits Backward scores may also involve the ability to form, maintain, and scan visual mental images formed from the auditory stimulus (Lezak et al., 2004; Sattler, 2008; Wielkiewicz, 1990). Similarly, Digit Span Sequencing is a more difficult task than Digit Span Forward in that it requires the client not only to recall the digits but to also make an internal manipulation of them and rearrange them in the correct sequence. As a result, DSS has been found to be particularly sensitive to the impact of Alzheimer's disease and traumatic brain injury (Wechsler, 2008). A Digit Forward score that is 4 or more points higher than DSS is significant and should be investigated further (see WAIS-IV Administrative Scoring Tables C.2, C.3, C.4, pp. 247–249).

Passive, anxiety-free individuals seem to do best on Digit Span test. It requires an effortless and relatively unhampered contact with reality, which is characterized by open receptivity to incoming information. Performance is greatly hampered by increased anxiety or tension, and the Digit Span subtest is considered the most susceptible to the effects of anxiety. Other subtests that also are sensitive to the effects of anxiety are Arithmetic, Coding, and Letter-Number Sequencing. On the WAIS-IV, Digit Span and Arithmetic form the Working Memory Index and are generally (along with the Processing Speed subtests) the most sensitive subtests to brain damage, mental retardation, and learning disabilities (Lezak et al., 2004; Wechsler, 2003b). Similarly, the Digit Span subtest (and Letter-Number Sequencing) is included in the WISC-IV Working Memory Index.

Persons who score high have good auditory short-term memory and excellent attention and may be relatively unaffected by stress and anxiety. However, just because a person has good short-term auditory memory for digits does not necessarily mean that his or her memory for more complicated information, such as music or verbally relevant information, is also good. These more complex features of memory may have to be assessed by other means. The rare event of Digits Backward being longer than Digits Forward (.9% of adult WAIS-III profiles, .2% of children's protocols; Wechsler, 2003b) suggests that the individual has excellent numerical abilities. Low scores on Digit Span indicate difficulty concentrating, which may be the result of anxiety or unusual thought processes. A large discrepancy (5 digits) in favor of Digits Forward versus Digits Backward can suggest the presence of an organic deficit, particularly if the overall backward Digit Span score is below scores for tests such as Information and Vocabulary. Whereas Digits Forward is fairly stable and resistant to deterioration, Digits Backward and Digit Span Sequencing are far more difficult than Digits Forward and are quite sensitive to deterioration (see subsection on estimating premorbid IQ in the "Assessing Brain Damage" section). Whereas Digits Forward is more likely to be lowered by left-hemisphere lesions, lowered Digits Backward is more consistent with either diffuse or right-frontal involvement (Lezak et al., 2004; Rapport, Webster, & Dutra, 1994). Lowered performance for both Digit Span Backward and Coding (previously Digit Symbol) occur with the diffuse damage associated with exposure to solvents (Groth-Marnat, 1993; Morrow, Furman, Ryan, & Hodgson, 1988).

Arithmetic (WAIS-IV Core Subtest, WISC-IV Supplemental Subtest)

- Computational skill.*
- Auditory short-term memory.
- Sequencing ability.
- Numerical reasoning and speed of numerical manipulation.
- Concentration and attention/low distractibility.
- Reality contact and mental alertness (i.e., active relationship to the outside world).
- School learning (earlier items)/acquired knowledge.
- Logical reasoning, abstraction, and analysis of numerical problems (later items).

The Arithmetic subtest requires focused concentration as well as basic mathematical skills and an ability to apply these skills. The skills required to complete this test are usually acquired by the time a person reaches junior high school; therefore, low scores are more likely to be the result of poor concentration. Arithmetic is likely to be more challenging and stressful than tests such as Information and Vocabulary, both because the task itself is more demanding and because the test is timed. Thus, persons who are susceptible to the disruptive effects of anxiety are likely to be adversely affected. However, examiners may want to establish whether the person simply lacks the necessary skills or had difficulty concentrating. This can be assessed by readministering items that the examinee had previously missed, but allowing the person to use paper and pencil without a time limit. Under these circumstances, persons with adequate mathematical knowledge who are distractible should be able to complete the items correctly.

Individuals from higher socioeconomic backgrounds, obedient teacher-oriented students, and persons with intellectualizing tendencies usually do well on this subtest. A helpful formula is that Information plus Arithmetic equals school achievement. Because numbers come from the outside environment and create rule and direction, some individuals react rebelliously. This is particularly true for antisocial personalities. Histrionic personalities, who do not readily accept outside direction and generally refuse to take responsibility for their behaviors, may likewise do poorly. This is not to suggest that lowered Arithmetic scores are diagnostic of these clinical groups, but rather that this lowering may at times be consistent with the way these individuals interact with their environment.

High scorers show alertness, capacity for concentration, freedom from distractibility, and good short-term auditory memory, and may use intellectualizing defenses. Low scorers show poor mathematical reasoning, lack of capacity to concentrate, distractibility, and poor auditory short-term memory. A poor educational background in which adequate mathematical skills have not been developed can also account for lowered performance.

Letter-Number Sequencing (WAIS-IV Supplemental Subtest, WISC-IV Core Subtest)

- Auditory short-term memory.*
- Sequencing ability.*
- Concentration and attention.*

A good performance on Letter-Number Sequencing suggests that the person has good sequencing, attention, and concentration. The subtest requires the person to attend to a series of letters and numbers that have been read to him or her, hold them in memory, manipulate them into a new order, and repeat the new sequence. When combined with Arithmetic on the WISC-IV, it forms the Working Memory Index. (On the WAIS-IV, it is a supplemental subtest.)

Psychometrically, Letter-Number Sequencing is good to adequate. WAIS-IV test-retest reliability has been found to be .80, the SEM is 1.03, and it has a factor loading of .69 with the Working Memory Index. On the WISC-IV it has been found to have a test-retest reliability of .83 (for all ages), SEM of .97, and a factor loading of .62 with the Working Memory Index.

High scores suggest that the examinee has good short-term auditory memory, is able to effectively sequence auditory information, is persistent, and has good working memory. In contrast, a low score indicates the person has difficulties with auditory sequencing, has poor short-term auditory memory, is inattentive, and may also be impulsive, anxious, or poorly motivated.

Processing Speed Index/Subtests

The Processing Speed Index (PSI; WAIS-IV/WISC-IV: Symbol Search, Coding) reflects the mental and motor speed with which a person can solve nonverbal problems. Further subtest support for this index can be found if the person also has correspondingly high (or low) performances on the timed nonverbal Block Design subtest. In addition to mental and motor speed, the Processing Speed factor is a measure of a person's ability to plan, organize, and develop relevant strategies. Because speed and concentration require good test-taking attitudes, Processing Speed (as well as Working Memory) can also be lowered by poor motivation to perform well. For this reason, these two indexes are sometimes referred to as *validity* factors. Whether a lowered performance is the result of poor motivation often is best assessed by behavioral observations in combination with clarification and consideration of the presenting problem. An overly reflective problem-solving style could also lower the Processing Speed factor because the person would take too much time cautiously considering his or her response to each item. Thus, Processing Speed represents proficiency in these areas:

- Speed of processing information.
- Planning and organization.
- Motor control.
- Motivation.

People who score high generally can solve problems quickly, are likely to be fast readers, dial a telephone number rapidly, can quickly find a telephone number in a phone book, may do well in occupations that require rapid responding, and would be able to quickly locate food items on a shelf. In contrast, persons who score low may require extra time to learn material, be slow picking up objects, be slow readers, be hesitant, carefully reflect on their answers before giving them, or take a relatively long time to find food items on a shelf.

Processing Speed is noteworthy in that it is the index that is most sensitive to cognitive problems caused by a wide variety of disorders including dementia, traumatic brain injury, ADHD, and learning disabilities (Wechsler, 2008a). It is also the index that begins to decrease the earliest (during the 20s), with a more precipitous drop in the mid-30s (A. Kaufman & Lichtenberger, 2006). The other indexes, particularly Verbal Comprehension, are more resistant to the effects of aging. Low scores on Processing Speed can also reflect poor motor control and be associated with problems with sensory acuity. Among persons with high IQs and those labeled as gifted, Processing Speed is often the lowest index (with Verbal Comprehension being the highest; Wechsler, 2008a).

Coding (Previously Called Digit Symbol; WAIS-IV/WISC-IV Core Subtest)

- Psychomotor speed.*
- Ability to follow directions.*
- Clerical speed and accuracy.*
- Visual short-term memory.*
- Paper-pencil skills.*
- Ability to learn an unfamiliar task; capacity for learning and responding to new visual material.
- Some degree of flexibility; ability to shift mental set.
- Capacity for sustained effort, attention, concentration, and mental efficiency.
- Associative learning and ability to imitate newly learned visual material.
- Sequencing ability.

Visuomotor integration is implied by good performance on Coding. However, the most important functions necessary for a high score are psychomotor speed combined with good recall for the symbol-digit pairs. This test involves appropriately combining the newly learned memory of the digit with the symbol, as well as adequate spatial-motor orientation, followed by executing the half-habituated activity of drawing the symbol. The subtest also requires the ability to learn an unfamiliar task, accuracy of eye-hand coordination, attentional skills, short-term memory, and the ability to work under pressure. This is a delicate and complex interaction, which can be disturbed because of difficulties with any of the preceding skills. In contrast to Vocabulary, which is a highly stable subtest, Coding is extremely sensitive to the effects of either organic or functional impairment. In particular, depressed patients and patients with brain damage have a difficult time with this subtest. It is also the subtest that is most influenced by age. For example, a WAIS-IV raw score required to achieve a subscale score of 10 for the 70- to 74-year-old group would obtain a subscale score of only 6 when compared with the 20- to 34-year-old reference group.

Coding pairs with Symbol Search to form the Processing Speed Index. Coding is a fair measure of general intelligence (.59 correlation with the WAIS-IV Full Scale IQ, .63 correlation with the Full Scale IQ on the WISC-IV).

Because visuomotor coordination (particularly visual acuity and motor activity) is implied, it is not surprising to find that those individuals with high reading and writing experience are among the high scorers. Functions that are implicit in the task are rapid visual, spatial, and motor coordination as well as the executive action of drawing the symbol. Because this task requires sustained attention and quick decision making, anxious hesitancy, obsessiveness, deliberation, and perfectionism significantly lower scores. This difficulty might be somewhat counteracted by informing persons who appear perfectionistic and reflective that they need only make their responses legibly but it does not need to be perfect. Persons who are extremely competitive but also become highly anxious in competitive situations may also be adversely affected. Coding scores can be lowered by anxiety; the psychomotor slowing found in depressive states or the confused orientation of schizophrenics likewise produces a decrease in performance. Thus, a rough index of the severity of a person's depression can be assessed by comparing the relative lowering of Coding with other more stable subtests. Of particular significance is that Coding is one of the most sensitive subtests to the effects of any type of organic impairment (Lezak et al., 2004; Wechsler, 2008a; Reitan & Wolfson, 1993), and it tends to be one of the lower scores found in learning-disabled individuals (Bannatyne, 1974; Groth-Marnat, 2001; A. Kaufman & Lichtenberger, 2006). Even in persons with minimal brain damage, Coding is still likely to be the lowest subtest overall (Lezak et al., 2004, Reitan & Wolfson, 1993). In addition, patients with rapidly growing tumors are more likely to have lower scores than those with slow-growing tumors (Reitan & Wolfson, 1993).

Because Coding requires such a diverse range of abilities, high or low scores can potentially indicate a wide number of possibilities. Therefore, clinicians need to work particularly hard to extract the significance of scores by integrating them with other relevant measures, behavioral observations, and medical/personal history. To illustrate how this has been done, the WAIS-III included two optional procedures to help determine whether an examinee's score was attributable primarily to visual memory, graphomotor speed, or a combination of both. The first procedure ("Incidental Learning") assessed how intact visual memory was by first requesting patients to recall as many of the digit-symbol pairs as possible and then simply to recall as many symbols as possible (without the associated numbers). These two related tasks were untimed. In contrast, "Digit Symbol-Copy" assessed graphomotor speed by presenting the examinee with a series of symbols and then requesting that he or she write down as many of the symbols as possible in boxes directly under the symbol. Examinees were given 90 seconds to write down as many of the symbols as possible. Various combinations of high and low scores could help to understand the underlying processes involved with Coding. For example, if a client did poorly on

Digit Symbol-Coding and Incidental Learning was high (e.g., good visual memory) but Digit Symbol-Copy was low (e.g., slowed graphomotor speed), it suggested the reason for the poor performance was slow graphomotor speed. However, this procedure was not continued on the WAIS-IV.

High scorers potentially have excellent visuomotor ability, mental efficiency, capacity for rote learning of new material, and quick psychomotor reactions. Lower scorers may have reduced capacity for visual associative learning, impaired visuomotor functioning, and poor mental alertness.

Symbol Search (WAIS-IV/WISC-IV Core Subtest)

- Speed of visual search.*
- Speed of processing information.
- Planning.
- Encoding information in preparation for further processing.
- Visuomotor coordination.
- Learning ability.

Symbol Search was designed to be as pure a test as possible of information-processing speed. It pairs nicely with Coding because, conceptually, they assess similar areas, as is more formally indicated by relatively high correlations (WAIS-IV, .65; WISC-IV, .53) between the two subtests. Together, they form the Processing Speed factor. Symbol Search is psychometrically a relatively good subtest. Test-retest over a 8- to 82-day ($M = 22$) interval was .81 for the WAIS-IV and .80 for the WISC-IV. It correlated relatively highly with the Full Scale (WAIS-IV, .64; WISC-IV, .66) and Processing Speed (WAIS-III, .91; WISC-III, .87) composites.

High scores suggest that the individual can rapidly absorb information as well as integrate and respond to this information. In addition, it suggests good levels of visuomotor coordination, short-term visual memory, planning, general learning, and a high level of attention and concentration. Low scores suggest slow mental processes; visual-perceptual difficulties; possibly poor motivation and/or anxiety; difficulties with short-term visual memory; or a reflective, perfectionistic, or obsessive problem-solving style.

Cancellation (WAIS-IV/WISC-IV Supplemental Subtest)

- Perceptual recognition.*
- Perceptual discrimination.*
- Perceptual scanning ability.*
- Speed and accuracy.*
- Attention and concentration.*
- Visuomotor coordination.

The examinee is shown a page with a few selected shapes or pictures in one area. There are a larger number of shapes/pictures that include both the original shapes as well as a large variety of other shapes/pictures. Examinees are requested to scan the area with the wide variety of shapes/pictures and then draw a line through only those shapes/pictures from the selected few shapes/picture. Thus, examinees must scan the shapes/pictures, recognize the correct ones, make the motor task of crossing them out, remember what they are supposed to be looking for, and maintain a constant level of attention. It is important that examinees make the discriminations as quickly as possible. The WAIS-IV has increased the difficulty of this task by requiring examinees to identify both shape and color. On the WISC-IV this subtest consists of two items that are in the form of two sets of pictures. One item consists of a haphazard arrangement of pictures ("random arrangement"), and the second item consists of pictures in neat rows ("structured arrangement"). Most of the time it is sufficient to calculate the combined scores on these two items. However, sometimes it can be useful to obtain separate scores for the random versus the structured arrangement (see Cancellation Random/CAR versus Cancellation Structured/ CS process scorings in the *WAIS-IV Administration and Scoring Manual*).

The WAIS-IV Technical and Interpretive Manual reported that the Cancellation subtest is similar to other subtests that measure "processing speed, visual selective attention, vigilance, perceptual speed, and visual motor ability" (Wechsler, 2008a). Within neuropsychological contexts, low scores on cancellation-type subtests have been found among patients with visual neglect, motor perseveration, and difficulties inhibiting their responses (Lezak et al., 2004).

The main advantage of the Cancellation subtest is that it has a fairly high loading on the Processing Speed Index (.56 with the WAIS-IV, .65 with the WISC-IV). As would be expected, the correlation between Cancellation and the Processing Speed Index is moderate (.49 for the WAIS-IV, .41 for the WISC-IV). In contrast, it has quite low correlations with the other indexes as well as with the Full Scale IQ (.26 for the WAIS-IV/WISC-IV). Thus, it is a poor measure of *g*. It is a fairly reliable (.79 test-retest on the WISC-IV, .71 test-retest on the WISC-IV) and has high specificity for all ages.

Cancellation is a particularly useful subtest for identifying the poor distractibility that typically occurs with attention deficit disorder or traumatic brain injury. Often it is quite useful to determine whether low scores on Cancellation are due to distractibility, slow speed, or disturbances with visual recognition.

High scores indicate excellent processing speed, good attention and concentration, good perceptual recognition, good scanning abilities, and high motivation. Conversely, low scores suggest slow processing speed, distractibility, poor perceptual recognition, poor scanning abilities, and poor motivation.

ASSESSING BRAIN DAMAGE

General Principles

The Wechsler intelligence scales measure many abilities that are likely to be lowered by brain damage. These include memory, learning, perceptual organization, problem solving, and abstract reasoning. As a result, the Wechsler intelligence scales are typically a core feature of any neuropsychological battery (Groth-Marnat, 2000b; Lezak et al., 2004). At one time, it was hoped that the Wechsler intelligence scales, along with other more specialized psychological tests, could be used in the actual diagnosis of brain damage. Despite some noteworthy success in this area, it is currently more typical for psychological tests to be used in the assessment of the effects a known lesion is likely to have on a person's cognitive and adaptive functioning. Thus, the Wechsler intelligence scales, along with other specific tests of neurocognitive ability, are not tests specifically sensitive to brain damage. Rather, they are tests that can reflect the effects of brain damage as well as a variety of other conditions.

During the earlier development of the WAIS and WISC, Wechsler (1958) hoped that brain damage could be discriminated based on relative lowerings in subtests that were most sensitive to neurological impairment. He referred to these brain-sensitive tests as *no-hold* tests (Digit Span, Digit Symbol, Similarities, Block Design) and contrasted them with *hold* tests, which were believed to be far more resistant to impairment (Information, Object Assembly, Picture Completion, Vocabulary). Although the distinction between hold and no-hold tests has some truth, the use of such a distinction in diagnosing brain damage has been found to result in too many misclassifications. Vogt and Heaton (1977) summarized the reasons for this lack of success by pointing out:

- There is no single pattern of brain damage, so highly variable test responses can be expected.
- The hold/no-hold distinction does not account for other significant factors, such as the age when the brain damage occurred, environmental variables, education, location of the lesion, and whether the lesion is recent versus chronic.
- The Wechsler intelligence scales do not measure many important abilities related to brain damage.

More recent work supports the theory that there is no specific brain damage profile (Groth-Marnat et al., 2000; Lezak et al. 2004). Some persons with brain damage produce low IQs, whereas for others, IQs are still high. Sometimes there is a high level of subtest scatter; at other times, scores on the subtests and indexes are quite even. Thus, brain damage may cause a general lowering on all or most subtests; at other times, there may be a lowering of only specific subtests. The most general indicator for the detection of brain damage is whether a person's scores (either general or specific) are lower than expected given his or her socioeconomic status, age, education, occupation, and other relevant areas of his or her history.

One of the older conventional wisdoms about brain damage is that left-hemisphere involvement is more likely to lower the verbal abilities, whereas right-hemisphere involvement results in relatively lower scores on nonverbal abilities. This finding would be reflected on the WAIS-IV in that patients with left-hemisphere damage would be expected to have relatively lower scores on the Verbal Comprehension Index than scores on the Perceptual Reasoning Index (VCI<PRI). In contrast, patients with right-hemisphere damage would be expected to have lower scores on Perceptual Reasoning than Verbal Comprehension (PRI<VCI; see previous discussion under "Index Score Interpretation"). Research using earlier versions of the Wechsler intelligence scales using Verbal versus Performance IQs has found that sometimes this laterality effect occurred; at other times, it has not (Aram & Ekelman, 1986; R. A. Bornstein, 1983; A. Kaufman & Lichtenberger, 2002, 2006; Larrabee, 1986; Lezak et al., 2004). In general, right-hemisphere lesions are likely to produce greater verbal-nonverbal discrepancies than left-hemisphere lesions (see review by A. Kaufman & Lichtenberger, 2006). Probably the safest approach is that a VCI-PRI difference is not diagnostic either of brain damage in general or, more specifically, of damage to one or hemisphere or the other. However, a significant VCI-PRI difference can at times be consistent with this hypothesis. Specifically, a lowered Verbal Comprehension score suggests the possibility of language impairment whereas a relatively lower Perceptual Reasoning Index suggests right-hemisphere impairment. Clinicians should use avoid overinterpreting a person's results and should consider other means of investigation, including knowledge of health status, medical history, and additional specialized psychological tests.

A finding noted in the *WAIS-IV Technical and Interpretive Manual* (Wechsler, 2008a) is that brain damage is most likely to impact a person's processing speed (see also Fisher, Ledbetter, Cohen, Marmor, & Tulsky, 2000; K. Hawkins, 1998). Patients with both traumatic brain injury and Alzheimer's disease all had Processing Speed as their lowest score. In contrast, verbal abilities were better preserved. This finding reflects the fact that persons with brain impairment tire easily and have difficulties with concentration and attention. In addition, Perceptual Reasoning and Working Memory were lower among brain-injured patients. Perceptual Reasoning as well as Working Memory and Processing Speed involves fluid intelligence. From a theoretical perspective, fluid intelligence is tied more to an intact brain structure and also is assessed more clearly by the ongoing problem-solving tasks presented in the Perceptual Reasoning subtests. Thus, a destruction of brain tissue would be more likely to lower fluid intelligence, which would be reflected in lowered Perceptual Reasoning subtest scores. This hypothesis can be further assessed by calculating the Cattell-Horn-Carroll subtest groupings for fluid intelligence (see "WAIS-IV/WISC-IV Successive Level Interpretation Procedure" section, Level IIb).

Many of the inferences related to brain damage depend on profile analysis. Useful material relevant to brain damage can be found in the discussion of Levels II through V under the "Interpretation Procedure" section in this chapter and in the relevant discussions for each subtest in the "Wechsler Subtests" section. Much of this interpretation depends on hypothesis testing in which the practitioner integrates knowledge about the person, brain function, Wechsler subtests, and past clinical experience. Often no clear, empirically based guidelines exist. Accuracy of any inferences is based partially on whether they make neuropsychological sense. However, one generally accepted principle is that inter-subtest scatter is most likely to occur with focal lesions of recent origin (see A. Kaufman & Lichtenberger, 2006). In contrast, a general lowering of all abilities (low subtest scatter) is more likely with either chronic lesions or diffuse degenerating diseases (e.g., exposure to neurotoxins; Groth-Marnat, 1993; L. Miller, 1993).

One useful strategy developed by E. Kaplan and her colleagues is to work toward parceling out the underlying processes responsible for scores on the Wechsler intelligence scales (Milberg et al., 1996). Alternative administration guidelines, error categories, useful tables, and interpretive procedures have been developed for the *WAIS-IV/WMS-IV (Advanced Clinical Solutions,* Pearson, 2009c) and the WISC-IV (*WISC-IV Integrated*; Wechsler et al., 2004). For example, a clinician might be interested to know if a client's poor performance on Information or Vocabulary resulted from lack of knowledge or problems with retrieval. This might be determined by presenting him or her with multiple-choice formats that assist with the retrieval process (recognition of correct answers rather than the much more difficult task of having to recall them). If a client does significantly better on the multiple-choice format than the standard format, it suggests that the lowering was caused by retrieval difficulties. The WAIS-IV has incorporated some of these strategies into the process scores. For example, the Digit Span subtest has separate scores for Digit Span Forward, Digit Span Backward, and Digit Span Sequencing. DSB and DSS are more difficult than simply repeating the digits forward. As a result, the backward and especially the sequencing tasks are more sensitive to brain-injured patients in that they obtain fairly low scores on these versions when compared to the overall score on the Digit Span subtest (Wechsler, 2008a). Another strategy built in to the process approach is to carefully investigate various error categories (Groth-Marnat et al., 2000; E. Kaplan et al., 1991, 1999). For example, visual neglect might be indicated by not noticing details on the left (usually) side of pictures on Picture Completion or making errors on the left side of the designs for Block Design.

When the preceding strategies, principles, and cautions are taken into account, clinicians can generate and test useful hypotheses developed from different patterns of subtest scores. The next list summarizes some of the most frequently supported hypotheses about specific subtests or patterns of subtests:

- The Processing Speed Index and its related subtests (Symbol Search and Coding) is the most brain-sensitive Wechsler index and can be lowered by lesions in any location. A lowering implies difficulties with speed of information processing and/ or learning, sequencing, rote learning, concentration (especially with lowerings in Digit Span and Arithmetic), and visuomotor abilities (K. Hawkins, 1998; Lezak et al., 2004; Reitan & Wolfson, 1992; Wechsler, 1997b, 2008a).

- Block Design is also brain sensitive, especially to either left or right parietal lesions (Golden, 1976; Lezak et al., 2004; McFie, 1960, 1969). A lowering implies visuospatial problems and possible difficulty in constructing objects (constructional apraxia: note quality of drawings; Kramer et al., 1999; Zilmer, Bell, Fowler, Newman, & Stutts, 1991). The Block Design No Time Bonus process score removes the timed variable. If the score is still low, hypotheses that visuospatial problems are present are strengthened (Wechsler, 2008a).

- Both Digit Span and Arithmetic are frequently lowered in brain-damaged populations, particularly with left-hemisphere lesions (A. Kaufman & Lichtenberger, 2006; Lezak et al., 2004; McFie, 1960, 1969). Lowering suggests poor concentration and attention and, if Digits Backward is significantly lower than Digits Forward (generally 5 or more digits), a significantly reduced level of mental flexibility and/or difficulty forming and maintaining a visual image of the digits. It may also suggest difficulties in a person's executive functions related to selecting a key stimulus, attending to it, and maintaining the information in short-term storage while simultaneously performing other mental tasks (Wielkiewicz, 1990).

- Vocabulary, Information, and Picture Completion have often been used as a rough estimate of a person's premorbid level of functioning because they are relatively unaffected by lesions. An important exception is that children who are brain damaged often score lowest on the Vocabulary subtest (Boll, 1974; Reitan, 1974b; Reitan & Wolfson, 1992). In addition, Information and Vocabulary are generally lowered (especially relative to Similarities) in patients with left-temporal damage, suggesting difficulties with word comprehension, retrieval, and language expression (Dobbins & Russell, 1990). Picture Completion, while usually resistant to brain damage, might be lowered because of difficulties involving vision, especially visual agnosia (difficulty recognizing objects; E. Kaplan et al., 1991, 1999). Thus, always considering Vocabulary, Information, and Picture Completion as indicators of premorbid functioning can potentially result in incorrect inferences. As a result, scores on these three subtests should be interpreted in relation to what is known about brain-behavior relationships.

- The Similarities subtest, especially in relation to Information and Vocabulary, is most likely to be lowered with left-frontal lesions and suggests difficulty with verbal reasoning and verbal concept formation (Dobbins & Russell, 1990).

- Qualitative responses, particularly related to error categories (even when the subtests are not lowered), can provide useful information related to brain damage. Some responses might suggest poor judgment and impulsivity, whereas others might indicate concrete thinking in which the person is bound by the stimulus value of the item (e.g., a season of the year might be described as "hot, dry" rather than the more abstract reference to a season; or the clang response to a word such as "empathy" being defined as "empty"). Other persons might report they once knew the answer but have forgotten, which can be assessed through multiple-choice options. Diffuse brain damage (but not focal) might also be consistent with a high degree of intratest scatter in which the client misses easy items but correctly answers later, more difficult ones (Mittenberg et al., 1989). This finding suggests retrieval failure and/or the random loss of previously stored information. This intrasubtest scatter is most likely to occur on Vocabulary, Comprehension, Information, Similarities, and Picture Completion.

Estimating Premorbid IQ

Professional psychologists are frequently confronted with the need to estimate a client's premorbid level of functioning. In an ideal situation, previous IQ results derived before the injury could be obtained and compared with the current level of functioning. Even in this situation, clinicians should be aware that a decline in *overall* performance should not be inferred unless there is a significantly lower current IQ than had been obtained from a premorbid IQ assessment. A discrepancy of 12 or more Full Scale IQ points on the WAIS-R when compared with a Full Scale IQ on the WAIS-III would result in an 80% accurate detection of adults who had actually suffered a cognitive decline (Graves, Carswell, & Snow, 1999). It should also be stressed that there still might be quite specific areas of decline that are not sensitive to the global measure of IQ scores.

In most cases, premorbid IQ results are not available; therefore, clinicians must rely on other strategies to infer premorbid ability. These strategies include historical achievement-based records, current measures of ability that are not sensitive to decline ("hold" measures), demographic-based regression equations, or a combination of these. Useful historical records might include grade-point average, Scholastic Achievement Test scores, work achievement records, achievement tests, or peer ratings (see Baade & Schoenberg, 2004). The age of the person, as well as relevant aspects of the injury (i.e., size and location of the lesion, recency of injury), might also be important to consider.

A further strategy for estimating premorbid ability is to note performances on Wechsler subtests that are considered most resistant to neurological impairment (Information, Picture Completion, and especially Vocabulary). As discussed previously, these subtests have often been considered to reflect the person's past level of functioning and have therefore been referred to as *hold* subtests. Administering an achievement test such as the Wide Range Achievement Test (WRAT-III) or Wechsler Individual Achievement Test (WIAT-II) might accomplish a similar purpose. One difficulty is that for many clients, especially those who are well educated, this method is likely to overestimate premorbid IQ. In contrast, it would be likely to underestimate premorbid IQ for subgroups whose premorbid Performance Scales are typically greater than Verbal Scales (i.e., Native Americans, Hispanics, bilinguals, persons with low educational attainment, blue-collar workers). It would also underestimate premorbid ability among patients who have had impairment to their verbal abilities.

A related technique is to consider the person's two or three highest subtests (regardless of whether the subtests are brain sensitive or non–brain sensitive) and then use these to estimate the person's premorbid level of functioning. Despite its occasional usefulness, this procedure is likely to result in a high number of misclassifications because it does not consider crucial factors such as the person's age, educational level, or location of the lesion (Matarazzo & Prifitera, 1989). In addition, it is quite common for normal persons to have significant variability in their performance, especially those with high IQs. As a result, clients with high IQs are likely to have significantly inflated estimates of their premorbid level of functioning.

A variation of this hold procedure is to use a reading test, such as the National Adult Reading Test (NART; H. Nelson & Williams, 1991) or Wechsler Test of Adult Reading

(WTAR; Wechsler, 2001). The NART and WTAR were designed by selecting 50 irregularly spelled words (i.e., yacht, naive) that are unlikely to be pronounced correctly unless the client has previous knowledge of the words. This relatively pure recognition task places minimal demands on memory and problem-solving abilities. A NART-estimated WAIS-R Full Scale IQ 20 points higher than a person's obtained IQ suggests intellectual decline (80% accuracy for those with actual decline; Graves et al., 1999). The WTAR has been found to correlate highly with other measures of premorbid functioning and to be quite stable despite cognitive changes measured by other tests (Green et al., 2008). However, this stability assumes that the injury would not have affected the person's reading ability. Despite the usefulness of the NART/NART-R and WTAR, the previous caveats related to demographics (ethnicity, education) would also be relevant for these reading tests.

Other efforts to determine premorbid IQ have used regression equations based on demographic variables (education, occupation, etc.). One of the most extensively researched is the Barona Index (Barona, Reynolds, & Chastain, 1984). To correctly classify (80% accuracy) clients with true cognitive decline, a discrepancy of 25 IQ points would be required (Graves et al., 1999). Unfortunately, this discrepancy is sufficiently large such that other more straightforward procedures (i.e., previous work performance, grade-point average, medical records) would be likely to be more accurate. In addition, the index is likely to be inaccurate for persons with either extremely high (above 120) or extremely low (below 69) IQs (Barona et al., 1984; Graves et al., 1999; Veiel & Kooperman, 2001), and the formulas are likely to overestimate most premorbid IQ levels (Eppinger, Craig, Adams, & Parsons, 1987).

Research with the WAIS-III found a series of algorithms that were useful in estimating premorbid IQ. An example that can be used for general clinical purposes is listed next (Oklahoma Premorbid Intelligence Estimate [OPIE-3]; Schoenberg, Duff, Scott, & Adams, 2003):

OPIE-3 (2 subtests) using Vocabulary and Matrix Reasoning; SEE = 6.63

$$FSIQ=45.997+.652 \text{ (Vocabulary)}+1.287 \text{ (Matrix Reasoning)}+1.57 \text{(Age in years)}$$
$$+1.034 \text{ (Education)}+0.652 \text{ (Ethnicity)}-1.015 \text{ (Gender)}$$

Education: 1 = 0–8 years, 2 = 9–11 years, 3 = 12 years, 4 = 13–15 years, 5 = 16+ years

Ethnicity: 1 = African American, 2 = Hispanic, 3 = Other, 4 = Caucasian

Gender: 1 = male, 2 = female

Note: Only raw scores should be used for the subtest scores.

Schoenberg et al. (2003) clarify that alternate equations should be used if the Vocabulary and Matrix Reasoning scaled scores are discrepant (see worksheet in Strauss et al., 2006). However, there have been sufficient changes on the WAIS-IV that the Schoenberg et al. (2003) formulas are likely to be obsolete. It is expected that algorithms based on the WAIS-IV will be forthcoming.

Research with children has found that a series of algorithms based on the WISC-IV standardization sample have been able to predict premorbid IQ (Schoenberg, Lange, Brickell, & Saklofske, 2007). This algorithm was found to be the most accurate and used a combination of demographics and raw scores on Vocabulary, Matrix Reasoning, Information and Picture Completion:

$$IQ=81.64+(\text{Vocabulary } 0.682)+(\text{Matrix Reasoning } 1.088)+(\text{Information } 0.719)+$$
$$(\text{Picture Completion } 0.317)+(\text{Age in years } -4.729)+(\text{Parental education}$$
$$0.413)+\text{Ethnicity}+\text{Gender}$$

Parental education: Number of years of parental education (if two parents, use the average of both parents)

Ethnicity: Caucasian (nil), African American (–1.646) Hispanic (0.126), Asian (3.475)

Gender: Male (nil), Female (3.127)

Note: Only raw scores should be used for the subtest scores.

The total mean IQ using this formula was 99.73 with a standard deviation of 13.53, and the correlation between the estimated Full Scale IQ and the actual WISC-IV Full Scale IQ was .86 (Schoenberg et al., 2007). Fifty percent of estimated IQ scores were ±5 points from the actual Full Scale IQs and 82% were within ±10 IQ points. Predictions were less accurate for children in the Superior range of intelligence (= 130) or at the Borderline or below range (= 79). One caution is that the preceding data was developed from healthy persons without any known neuropsychological impairment. Whether these predictions will be as accurate for clinical populations has not yet been determined. However, research using similar procedures on patients with known neuropsychological impairment for the WAIS-R, WAIS-III, and WISC-III found that the algorithms made accurate estimates (Axelrod, Vanderploeg, & Schinka, 1999; Schoenberg et al., 2003; Vanderploeg, Schinka, Baum, Tremont, & Mittenberg, 1998). Thus, it is likely that future research with clinical populations using the WISC-IV and the preceding algorithms will provide accurate predictions.

Due to the considerable legal implications combined with the error rate, estimating premorbid IQ has been a controversial procedure (see Veiel & Koopman, 2001). These review points seem crucial:

- The equations should be used to supplement but not replace a careful evaluation of crucial information, such as work history and medical records.
- Formal cutoffs should be used. Rarely, for example, would an obtained IQ 5 to 10 points below the estimated "premorbid IQ" suggest actual cognitive decline in a person's *overall* ability. However, this still does not preclude the possible presence of quite specific deficits (i.e., facial recognition, short-term visual memory).
- The likelihood of errors increases when equations based on demographics or subtests are used with persons with IQs suspected of being extremely high or extremely low (below 80 or above 120).

Alzheimer's Disease

The initial symptoms of Alzheimer's disease are apathy, a decline in short-term memory, and difficulties with problem solving. Underlying these changes are reductions in cholinergic activity. Currently, neuropsychological assessment, particularly with the Wechsler intelligence scales, is one of a variety of diagnostic procedures to increase the accuracy of diagnosis as well as to understand the nature and extent of a patient's difficulties. Cognitive assessment is often used in conjunction with medically based diagnostic procedures, such as identifying the presence of an Alzheimer's dementia autosomal mutation among direct relatives, biomarkers in the cerebrospinal fluid, medial temporal lobe atrophy based on magnetic resonance imaging (MRI), and patterns of brain activity noted on positron emission tomography (PET) functional neuroimaging (Dubois et al., 2007).

Ideally, a unique cognitive pattern would identify the presence of Alzheimer's disease. While a clear, distinct pattern has not been identified, research has found that nonverbal abilities seem to be more sensitive to impairment than verbal abilities. Earlier research with the WAIS-R found that a full 52% of Alzheimer's disease patients had Verbal greater than Performance IQ scores of 15 points or more (Fuld, 1984). Similarly, the WAIS-IV Verbal Comprehension Index ($M = 86.2$) has been found to be 10 points higher than Processing Speed ($M = 76.6$) among a sample of patients with probable mild Alzheimer's (Wechsler, 2008a). Thus, Processing Speed is the subtest that is most sensitive to the early presence of Alzheimer's disease. However, Processing Speed is also the subtest that is most sensitive to many if not most types of cognitive impairment. Additional lowerings in index scores were found in Working Memory ($M = 84.3$) and Perceptual Reasoning ($M = 85.8$). The subtests that were most sensitive to being lowered by mild Alzheimer's disease were Symbol Search, Information, Coding, and Arithmetic.

The WAIS-IV and its predecessors are useful in the assessment of Alzheimer's disease in that they assess a wide range of general as well as specific cognitive functions. Many of these functions will be lowered as a result of Alzheimer's disease and other forms of dementia. However, crucial functions are not measured by the Wechsler intelligence scales. Memory is one of the most important features of Alzheimer's disease yet the Wechsler intelligence scales do not measure this function in much depth or breadth. As a result, specialized memory scales, such as the Wechsler Memory Scales-IV, are crucial. Other functions that might need to be assessed through additional instruments include word naming (i.e., Boston Naming Test; Goodglass & Kaplan, 1983), verbal fluency (i.e., Controlled Oral Word Association Test; Benton & Hamsher, 1989), and executive functions (i.e., Delis-Kaplan Executive Function System; Delis, Kaplan, & Kramer, 2001). In addition, specialized dementia batteries, such as the CERAD battery (Morris et al., 1989), have been assembled based on tests that have been found to be the most sensitive to Alzheimer's disease.

ASSESSING ADDITIONAL SPECIAL POPULATIONS

Learning Disabilities

Learning disabilities make up a complex, heterogeneous, loosely defined disorder with a wide variety of manifestations and many different theories regarding causation (A. Kaufman & Lichtenberger, 2006; Sattler, 2008). A central component of all definitions is that learning disabilities involve difficulties in developing skills in reading (most commonly), writing, listening, speaking, reasoning, spelling, or math. This cluster of difficulties is sometimes summarized as poor information processing. Further essential features are these: Learning-disabled persons have adequate intelligence, show a significant discrepancy between achievement and intellectual ability, and have a disorder that is considered primarily intrinsic to the person, presumably because of central nervous system dysfunction. The underachievement cannot be primarily the result of an intellectual disability (mental retardation), brain damage, behavior problems, sensory handicaps, or environmental disadvantage.

The major purpose of learning disability assessment is to identify a client's strengths and weaknesses to be able to decide on an appropriate placement and to design an optimal program. Relevant areas to assess include developmental-cognitive processes, achievement, environmental demands, reactions of others to the client's difficulties, and the possible interaction of additional factors, such as fear of failure, overall level of interpersonal adjustment, and family history of similar difficulties. The Wechsler scales are typically considered essential as a means of identifying the client's overall level of functioning and specific cognitive strengths and weaknesses and to eliminate the possibility of intellectual disability (mental retardation). Other tests are usually required: achievement tests, measures of adaptive behavior, visuomotor tests, assessments of auditory and visual processing, and measures of emotional and behavioral problems, for example (see Sattler, 2008).

Researchers have expended considerable effort in searching for a specific Wechsler scale profile that is unique to learning-disabled populations (see Level IIIb in "Interpretation Procedure" section). WAIS-III revealed evidence for an ACID profile (comprised of Arithmetic, Coding/Digit Symbol, Information, and Digit Span); 24% of those diagnosed with learning disabilities had a partial (three out of the four subtests as the lowest scores) ACID profile, and 6.5% had a full (all four of the subtests as the lowest) ACID profile (Wechsler, 1997a). This is higher than the standardization sample. The WAIS-III index scores of Working Memory and Processing Speed (compared to Perceptual Organization and Verbal Comprehension) were also found to be particularly low among a sample of adults diagnosed with reading disabilities (Wechsler, 1997a). This finding has led A. Kaufman and Lichtenberger (1999, 2006) to suggest the possible utility of combining the five subtests in these lowest indexes into a SCALD profile (Symbol Search, Digit Symbol-Coding, Arithmetic, Letter-Number Sequencing, Digit Span).

The recent WAIS-IV has been considerably revised compared to the WAIS-III, and these profiles are not likely to be as relevant. For example, Letter-Number Sequencing on the WAIS-IV is categorized as a supplementary subtest. However, the *WAIS-IV Technical and Interpretive Manual* reported that the lowest index score for persons with a reading disorder was for Working Memory ($M = 88.9$). Subtest scores were lowest for Letter-Number Sequencing, Arithmetic, and Vocabulary. Students with reading disorder were similarly found to have Working Memory as their lowest index score ($M = 84.1$); as would be expected, Arithmetic was their lowest subtest (along with Figure Weights and Letter-Number Sequencing). This information is consistent with the finding that persons with learning disabilities have problems with sequencing and attention.

The ACID profile has also received some support with the WISC-III; most studies have found that approximately 20% of persons with learning disabilities had either a partial or full ACID profile (A. Kaufman, 1994; A. Kaufman & Lichtenberger, 2002; Mayes, Calhoun, & Crowell, 1998; Stanton & Reynolds, 1998). A somewhat similar WISC-III profile substitutes the Symbol Search subtest for Information, resulting in the SCAD (Symbol Search, Coding, Arithmetic, Digit Span) profile. These four subtests emphasize the functions of speed of information processing, visual short-term memory, and visuomotor coordination (Symbol Search and Coding), as well as number ability and sequencing (Arithmetic and Digit Span). These are specifically the types of functions that many learning-disabled individuals (as well as many other types of persons with brain dysfunctions) have difficulty with. Accordingly, children with learning disabilities and attention deficit disorder have been found to score particularly low on the SCAD profile (A. Kaufman, 1994; Mayes et al., 1998; Stanton & Reynolds, 1998). Similarly, children diagnosed with ADHD have performed relatively poorly on the WISC-III Freedom from Distractibility factor (Anastopoulos, Spisto, & Maher, 1994). This finding should be used with caution, however, because a relatively large proportion of children with ADHD still do not have this profile. In addition, S. Ward, Ward, Hatt, Young, and Mollner (1995) did not find support for the SCAD profile among learning-disabled children.

Research with the WISC-IV has not yet evaluated the ACID and SCALD profiles. However, the lowest index score among learning-disabled persons has been reported to be for Working Memory ($M = 87.0$; Mayes & Calhoun, 2007; Wechsler, 2003b;). The lowest subtest scores for reading-disordered persons were for Vocabulary, Letter-Number Sequencing, Information, and Arithmetic. WISC-IV index scores for math-disordered persons were low for all composite scores except for Processing Speed. As would be expected, the lowest subtest score was Arithmetic with Digit Span Backward also being low.

Another way to understand learning disabilities and related disorders is to use Bannatyne's categories, which conceptualize learning-disabled performances as highest on subtests requiring spatial abilities (Object Assembly, Block Design, Picture Completion) in which little or no sequencing is required (Bannatyne, 1974). Conceptual skills are intermediate (Comprehension, Similarities, Vocabulary), and subtests requiring sequencing abilities (Digit Span, Digit Symbol-Coding, Picture Arrangement) are lowest. Thus, spatial abilities among many learning disabled persons are believed to be greater than their conceptual abilities, which, in turn, are greater than their sequential abilities. A fourth category, Acquired Knowledge (Information, Arithmetic, Vocabulary), is also sometimes used as a rough index of the extent to which the person has accumulated school-related facts and skills (see Level III, Interpreting Subtest Variability, in "Interpretation Procedures" section). Even though these findings might suggest a greater degree of subtest scatter among learning-disabled persons, research has not provided clear support for this finding (Greenway & Milne, 1999).

Collectively, the preceding profiles suggest that many learning-disabled individuals perform best on tasks requiring holistic, right-brain, simultaneous processing (Picture Completion, Block Design) and worst on those requiring sequential processing (Digit Span, Digit Symbol/Coding, Picture Arrangement), which is expressed in difficulties with planning, reading, and numerical ability. Wielkiewicz (1990) has further suggested that these subtests indicate a poorly functioning executive ability in which the individual experiences difficulty attending to stimuli while simultaneously performing other mental tasks.

Reviews and cross-validation of Bannatyne's and ACID/SCAD profiles have produced inconsistent results (see Groth-Marnat, 2001). Only some groups of learning-disabled students in some studies showed the Bannatyne Spatial > Conceptual > Sequential pattern (Katz et al., 1993; A. Kaufman, 1994; A. Kaufman & Lichtenberger, 2006). This is not surprising given the many different modes of expression found under the umbrella term *learning disabilities* (A. Kaufman & Kaufman, 2006). In addition, Bannatyne's pattern has not been found to be unique to learning disabilities; it frequently occurs in a diverse number of groups, including juvenile delinquents and emotionally handicapped children (see Groth-Marnat, 2001). Although only minimal support exists for Bannatyne's categories as a diagnosis for learning disabilities, they are far from useless. The four categories (Spatial, Conceptual, Sequential, Acquired Knowledge) can be invaluable for interpreting relative strengths and weaknesses for learning-disabled persons as well as for other groups. While research has not been able to produce a unique "learning-disabled profile," the research invested in this effort has resulted in a useful means of analyzing Wechsler scale profiles.

Given the previous research, these conclusions are warranted (adapted from Groth-Marnat, 2001):

- The Full Scale IQ can be used most appropriately in the assessment of persons with learning disabilities to estimate their overall potential and assist in excluding possible explanations for poor academic performance, other than learning disabilities (i.e., intellectual disabilities/mental retardation).

- There is moderate to equivocal evidence that some profiles (relatively low Processing Speed and Working Memory/Freedom from Distractibility, Spatial > Conceptual > Sequential, ACID, SCAD, SCALD) occur more frequently in learning-disabled populations compared to the general population. However, these patterns need to be updated and validated for the WAIS-IV and WISC-IV.

- These profiles are not unique to learning disabilities but often occur in other groups as well (juvenile delinquents, ADHD, emotionally handicapped).

- If a person does have a "learning-disabled" Wechsler profile (ACID, etc.), it is *consistent with, although not necessarily diagnostic of*, learning disabilities.
- The majority of learning-disabled persons *do not* have Wechsler "learning disabled" profiles. Thus, the absence of one of the profiles *does not exclude* a diagnosis of learning disabilities.
- The various patterns of Wechsler subtests can, at times, be used to further understand individual cases of persons experiencing learning difficulties.

Intellectual Disability (Mental Retardation)

Intellectual disability (mental retardation) is a nonspecific, heterogeneous disorder that occurs during a person's early developmental stages (birth to 18 years; Schalock, Luckasson, Shogren, Borthwick-Duffy, Bradley, et al., 2007). It is defined in part as involving subaverage general intellectual performance, which in turn is defined as less than 2 standard deviations below average. Of equal importance are difficulties in adaptive behavior, and any assessment of intellectual disability must demonstrate both a low intelligence level (2 standard deviations below the mean) and evidence that the person cannot function independently or deal effectively with day-to-day life problems (American Psychiatric Association, 2000). Poor independent functioning must include at least two adaptive skill areas including communication, self-care, home living, social skills, community use, self-direction, health and safety, functional academics, leisure, and work. Classification of intellectual disabilities should identify the person's psychological and emotional strengths and weaknesses, overall physical health, and current environmental placement. The AIDD guidelines stress that this assessment should lead to a profile that places less emphasis on describing the level of disability (mild, moderate, severe) and more on identifying the types and intensities of supports required by the person. These supports might be intermittent, limited, extensive, or pervasive. Thus, recently there has been a move away from describing the disability in favor of using information about the person to identify how the person's functioning could best be optimized by the best support available for him or her. With appropriate supports, the person's functioning should be able to improve over time. In addition, assessment should take into consideration cultural and linguistic diversity, the context of the community environment, and balance out the individual's adaptive limitations with his or her adaptive skills and personal capabilities.

The AAID guidelines emphasize the interaction of the person with the environment. In particular, they encourage any assessment to focus on the level and intensity of required support with a philosophy of empowering the person. As such, there has been a relative deemphasis on the global IQ score along with the elimination of person-oriented levels of disability. This does not mean that IQ scores are not important, but there is more of a focus on treatment and community-oriented descriptions. In somewhat of a contrast to this trend are the guidelines in the *DSM-IV-TR* (2000), which continue to classify the degree of severity (and corresponding diagnostic code) based on these IQ ranges: 50–55 to 70 (mild); 35–40 to 50–55 (moderate); 20–25 to 35–40 (severe); below 20–25 (profound); and severity unspecified (mental retardation is presumed to exist but intelligence is untestable by standard tests). The implications are that, for most contexts, clinicians should follow the AAID guidelines because they are more useful, more clearly tied to recommendations, represent the most current thinking in the field, and are in accordance with national recommendations. However, there may be certain situations in some contexts where *DSM-IV-TR* guidelines might be required.

Although intellectual disability (mental retardation) is a heterogeneous disorder, there is consensus that it consists of two general categories. Nonorganic (or familial) retardation is caused by low genetic inheritance, poor environment, and possibly some organic factors. Persons with familial retardation constitute the upper realms of intelligence (50 to 69) and adaptive functioning among persons with intellectual disabilities and can be educated. Organic retardation is frequently severe (IQ less than 50) and is more closely associated with neurological dysfunction and genetic impairment. Persons with this disorder typically require more supervision and care but usually can be taught to manage some routine day-to-day activities.

A typical assessment battery for the diagnosis and assessment of mental intellectual disability includes the WISC-IV or other individually administered intelligence tests (K-ABC-II, Stanford-Binet-IV), an achievement test (Wide Range Achievement Test-IV, Wechsler Individual Achievement Test-II, Kaufman Test of Educational Achievement), and measures of adaptive functioning (Adaptive Behavior Assessment System, AAMD Adaptive Behavior Scale, or Vineland Adaptive Behavior Scales). Further information from interviews, behavioral observations, and medical records is also essential. An important purpose of a test such as the WISC-IV is to establish the client's general intelligence level so that it can be placed into the context of other relevant information. When determining the cutoff IQ for diagnosis, the test's range of error should be taken into account. This means that the IQ cutoff criteria are somewhere between 70 and 75. The most difficult subtests for intellectually disabled persons are Information, Arithmetic, and Vocabulary (primarily the Verbal Comprehension factor), while the easiest subtests are Picture Completion and Object Assembly (primarily the Perceptual Organization factor; Mueller, Dash, Matheson, & Short, 1984).

Gifted Children

Gifted children are frequently defined as having IQs of 130 or higher. Children who have a single outstanding ability, such as art, music, or math, are also frequently classified as gifted even though their IQs may not necessarily be above 130. One caution is that portions of the WISC-IV and WAIS-IV place considerable emphasis on speeded performance. Thus, a person who was generally gifted, but did not express this giftedness in a rapid manner, would not be expected to do well on the Processing Speed Index. This fact may need to be taken into account when making interpretations. However, formal IQ tests may not be particularly good if a single outstanding ability is used to determine whether a particular child is gifted. Additional assessment strategies for children should include samples of their work, achievement tests, rating forms, or designation by a highly qualified person.

An essential goal of assessing for giftedness is to optimize (rather than "normalize") the child's abilities so that a greater likelihood exists that the child will eventually make a significant contribution to society. Assessment of gifted persons will typically recommend an appropriate educational placement and provide general guidelines for program planning. IQ, in itself, is in many ways a limited definition of giftedness. Many persons with extremely high IQs do not accomplish anything of significance. A high IQ (or outstanding talent in a specific area) is merely one of a variety of prerequisites. The interactions of internal motivation, discipline, and environmental opportunities, such as appropriate instruction, are of equal importance.

Caution should also be used when using tests such as the WISC-IV to assess gifted persons who demonstrate high creativity. Often highly intelligent people are not particularly creative, a fact that is supported by the low correlation between intelligence tests and creativity (Amabile, 1983). For abilities such as artistic or musical creativity, measures outside

IQ testing may prove to be of greater importance. These measures might include a list of creative achievements, nomination by a qualified person, and specific tests of creativity.

SHORT FORMS

Dozens of short forms for the Wechsler intelligence scales have been developed to provide a more time-efficient means of estimating IQ. These short forms reduce administration time by either giving selected subtests or deleting specific items (early easy ones, odd or even items). Although time-efficient, these short forms tend to provide less information about a person's cognitive abilities, produce a wider band of error than a full administration, result in less clinical information, and are often of questionable accuracy when used for intelligence classifications (J. Kaufman & A. Kaufman, 2001; Silverstein, 1990). Indeed, J. Kaufman and A. Kaufman (2001) have recommended not using short forms, especially when well-developed alternative brief intelligence tests are available. However, short forms can serve as screening devices, which are best used when the purpose of evaluation is other than for intellectual assessment. The results can be used either as a rough indicator of intelligence or as a basis for determining whether a more complete cognitive assessment is necessary. None of the short forms should be confused with a full intellectual assessment or even with a valid indicator of IQ. For this reason, it is important to clearly specify on the report that the indicated IQ is an estimate (indicate as *Est* next to the IQ score) and that a "brief WAIS-IV/WISC-IV" was given. If this is not specified, the IQ derived from the short form may be confused with a full administration, and later decisions may be incorrectly based on the misleadingly described results.

The basic requirement for any short form is a minimum correlation of .90 with the full administration. Even at the .90 level, the band of error is considerably wider than for an IQ derived from a full administration. Calculations indicate that at a .90 correlation, two-thirds of the IQs fall within 9 points of a person's actual IQ and a full one-third are 10 or more points away from the actual IQ (L. Schwartz & Levitt, 1960). In addition to these psychometric considerations, short forms might be selected based on the type of clinical information needed or special client characteristics (i.e., handicapped, non-English-speaking background).

Many clinicians calculate short-form IQs by prorating the subtest scores—that is, by calculating the mean subtest score for the subtests that were given. This mean can then be multiplied by the total number of core subtests (10) to derive an estimated Full Scale sum of scaled scores. Once this estimate of sum of scaled scores has been determined, relevant tables in the manual(s) can be consulted to determine the estimated IQs. The *WAIS-IV Administration and Scoring Manual* provides some prorating for calculating the Full Scale IQ when nine subtests have been given (see Table A.9, p. 227) or for calculating the Verbal Comprehension Index and Perceptual Reasoning Index when two subtests have been given (see Table A.8, p. 226). Unfortunately, prorating may produce error by failing to consider the relative reliabilities of the different subtests that were used. To counter this problem for the WISC-IV, Sattler (2008) has provided conversion tables for combinations of two, three, and five subtest short forms (see Tables A-9 through A-12, pp. 32–37). Sattler (2008) has also provided a formula (see Table D-11, pp. 185) for obtaining deviation IQs from short forms. Similar resources for the WAIS-IV are not yet available.

Wechsler Abbreviated Measure of Intelligence (WASI)

The Psychological Corporation developed the Wechsler Abbreviated Scale of Intelligence (WASI; Wechsler, 1997a) as a means of providing clinicians and researchers with a short, reliable measure of intelligence linked to the WAIS-III (and WISC-III). The WASI includes four subtests (Vocabulary, Similarities, Block Design, and Matrix Reasoning), which have a similar format and similar content as the WAIS-III subtests with the same names. The selection of these subtests was based in part on high loadings on g, along with evidence suggesting bilateral hemispheric activation on most complex cognitive tasks (Springer & Deutsch, 1998). The WASI yields both Verbal and Performance IQs, as well as a Full Scale IQ. The WASI was nationally standardized using a population ranging between ages 6 and 89. Because the subtests were linked to the longer Wechsler intelligence scales, the WASI provides reliable estimates of full WAIS-III and WISC-III IQs. The *WISC-IV Administration and Scoring Manual* has provided tables for predicting WISC-IV scores based on the WASI (see Appendix C, p. 246). Resources for making WAIS-IV predictions are not currently available. Administration time can be reduced even further by using a two-subtest form (Vocabulary and Matrix Reasoning), which takes approximately 15 minutes but yields only a Full Scale IQ estimate. If a brief, Wechsler-based version of intelligence is desired, it is strongly recommended that the WASI be used in preference to the short forms described next.

Best Two- and Three-Subtest Short Forms

One of the most popular two-subtest short forms uses Vocabulary and Block Design. Administration time is approximately 20 minutes, and correlations with the full-administration Full Scale IQ are generally in the .90 range (Sattler, 2001, 2008). In two-thirds of the cases, IQs fall within 7 points of a person's actual IQ, and one-third of the scores have an error of eight points or greater. Conceptually, Vocabulary and Block Design are good tests to use because they are both good measures of g, are quite stable, and represent a sample subtest from both the Verbal Comprehension and the Perceptual Reasoning indexes. However, research with the WAIS-R suggests it might potentially underestimate the IQs of African Americans because these two subtests are typically their lowest scores (A. Kaufman et al., 1988). Furthermore, persons with high IQs are likely to have a greater margin of error when short forms are used to estimate their IQs because of the greater degree of subtest scatter among this subgroup (Matarazzo, Daniel, Prifitera, & Herman, 1988). If examiners wish to add a third subtest, the inclusion of Similarities, Information, Comprehension, Picture Arrangement, and Picture Completion have each been found to increase correlations into the low .90s (Sattler, 2001, 2008).

Best Four-Subtest Short Forms

Short forms using any four combinations of Vocabulary, Similarities, Symbol Search, Arithmetic, Coding, Block Design, Arithmetic, Matrix Reasoning, Digit Span, and Information are likely to produce correlations with the Full Scale IQ in the mid-.90s (Sattler, 2008). Decisions on which subtests to include may depend on the type of information that is required. For example, including Vocabulary provides an indication of a person's verbal abilities and is the best predictor of Full Scale IQ. However, for ethnic minorities who might have English as their second language, a focus on nonverbal subtests may provide better estimate of their abilities (i.e., Block Design, Matrix Reasoning) than verbal subtests such as Vocabulary. In order to screen for impaired cognitive functioning, "brain-sensitive" tests such as Coding and Symbol Search might be important to include. If more verbally oriented subtests are given (Vocabulary, Information), it may overestimate their level of functioning.

Seven-Subtest Short Forms

One strategy is to delete the most time-consuming subtests and give as many of the shorter subtests as possible. For example, J. Ryan and Ward (1999) developed a WAIS-III seven-subtest short form (Information, Digit Span, Arithmetic, Similarities, Picture Completion, Block Design, Coding), which takes 35 minutes to administer. A slight variation from this short form is to substitute Matrix Reasoning for Block Design. This combination is likely to also be time efficient for the WAIS-IV, but the administration time and reliability and validity data have not been calculated. However, data on the WAIS-III indicated that estimated Full Scale IQ scores were nearly as reliable as for full-administration IQs with the average Full Scale standard error of measurement being 2.80 (and 2.72 for the version with Matrix Reasoning) versus 2.58 for the full WAIS-III Full Scale IQ (J. Ryan & Ward, 1999). Correlations between the J. Ryan and Ward (1999) seven-subtest short form and a full administration were .98 for the Full Scale IQ, .97 for the Verbal IQ, and .95 for the Performance IQ (.96 using Matrix Reasoning). Thus, the psychometric properties of the seven-subtest short form are excellent.

Additional Short Forms (Satz-Mogel/Yudin and Modified Formats)

An alternative to administering various combinations of subtests is to use every subtest but limit the number of items from each one. The most frequently used variation is the Satz and Mogel (1962) approach, which was originally developed for the WAIS but can also be used for the WAIS-IV. The procedure is to administer every third item for Information and Vocabulary and multiply the scores by 3 to obtain the raw scores. Only odd items would be administered for Similarities, Arithmetic, Block Design, Visual Puzzles, and each score is multiplied by 2 to obtain the respective scaled scores. Full administrations would be given for Digit Span, Coding, Matrix Reasoning, and Symbol Search. The entire procedure for the WAIS-III took approximately 40 minutes, and the derived IQs had correlations similar to the best four-subtest variations. A distinct advantage over four-subtest variations is that the Satz-Mogel approach samples a wider range of areas. This is likely to increase the stability of scores over a wider variety of populations and allows clinicians to develop inferences over a larger number of behaviors. Research with the WAIS-III has indicated that IQs derived from the Satz-Mogel usually did not vary more than 6 points when compared with the full administration (J. Ryan, Lopez, & Werth, 1999). In addition, a full 86% of the clients had the same IQ classifications. A caution is that, although a score is provided for each subtest, it is inappropriate to attempt a profile analysis because the individual subtests are not sufficiently reliable (J. Ryan et al., 1999). Given that it would take only an additional 20 minutes to administer the entire battery, the entire administration seems a worthwhile time investment.

A WISC-IV equivalent of the Satz-Mogel approach would have the same advantages and disadvantages and follow a nearly identical procedure. However, Arithmetic and Information would not be given because they are optional subtests; Coding would be given in its entirety. In addition, every other item would be given for the core WISC-IV Picture Concepts subtest.

A final approach is the elimination of early, easy items on each of the subtests. This is most appropriate for relatively bright subjects but should be used cautiously with persons of below-average intelligence. Cella (1984) provided WAIS-R guidelines for the number of items to be omitted based on a subject's performance on the Information subtest. Research on the WAIS-IV using this format has not been conducted. However, research with the WAIS-R has been found to have an almost exact correlation (.99) with a full administration and yet can reduce the total administration time by 25%. Despite this high correlation, some caution should be exercised regarding Cella's Modified Format and the Satz-Mogel approaches. First, lowered internal consistency is likely to reduce subtest reliabilities sufficiently to render profile analysis questionable. Second, examinees are disadvantaged because they are not able to have as many previous subtest items to practice on (as items are skipped) before more difficult items are administered. The result may be that the norms for the full administration may not necessarily apply to the shortened versions. Again, the slight reduction in time is probably not worth the loss of psychometric quality.

RECOMMENDED READING

Flanagan, D. P., & Kaufman, A. S. (2004). *Essentials of WISC-IV assessment*. Hoboken, NJ: John Wiley & Sons.

Kaufman, A. S., & Lichtenberger, E. O. (2006). *Assessing adolescent and adult intelligence* (3rd ed.). Boston: Allyn & Bacon.

Kaufman, A. S., & Lichtenberger, E. O. (in press). *Essentials of WAIS-III assessment*. Hoboken, NJ: John Wiley & Sons, Inc.

Sattler, J. M. (200). *Assessment of children: Cognitive functions* (5th ed.). San Diego, CA: Author.

Chapter 6

WECHSLER MEMORY SCALES

The Wechsler memory scales are individually administered, composite batteries designed to enable the user to better understand various components of a patient's memory. Now in its fourth edition (WMS-IV), it has been conormed with the WAIS-IV. Another major feature is that it provides a full range of memory functioning and has been carefully designed according to current theories of memory. As a result of these features, it typically is considered to be a core component of any thorough cognitive assessment (Rabin et al., 2005), which is reflected in its being ranked as the ninth most frequently used test by clinical psychologists (and third by neuropsychologists; Camara et al., 2000).

Memory complaints are extremely prevalent among client populations. These complaints are associated with anxiety, schizophrenia, depression, head injuries, stroke, learning disabilities, and neurotoxic exposure. For example, the impact of alcohol and other drugs on memory might need to be evaluated carefully. In occupational contexts, one similarly might need to evaluate the impact of exposure to industrial agents (lead, mercury, organic solvents) that can potentially result in impaired memory function. The increasingly aging population means that distinguishing normal memory loss from the early expression of dementia will become progressively more important. One crucial differential diagnosis is to distinguish between pseudodementia resulting from depression and Alzheimer's disease. As various drugs are developed for treating cognitive difficulties, it also will become increasingly important to monitor client improvement with a particular emphasis on memory functions. This array of symptoms suggests a developmental perspective; children are most likely to experience memory complaints related to learning disabilities, adults typically experience difficulties because of neurotoxic exposure or head injuries, and older populations have memory problems related to dementing conditions.

Many of the early conceptualizations of memory considered it a unitary process. From a practical assessment perspective, it was not necessary to have a composite battery that assessed various components of memory. In contrast, more recent conceptualizations consider memory to have various components (see Lezak et al., 2004). One major distinction is between short-term and long-term memory (sometimes described as primary and secondary memory storage, respectively). For memory to be stored effectively, there also needs to be some active engagement on the part of the person. Thus, "working memory" was conceptualized as containing an executive component that initiated, monitored, and evaluated information. It also included an attentional component that had a limited capacity. A further well-supported distinction is between memory that is conscious and reflected in verbal reports of facts, events, and experiences (*declarative, explicit,* or *episodic* memory) versus memory that is more unconscious and measured implicitly by changes in performance (*procedural* or *implicit* memory). Finally, memory can involve various sensory components, particularly visual and auditory modes of processing.

HISTORY AND DEVELOPMENT

In some ways, the development of the Wechsler memory scales have paralleled the development of knowledge on memory. Each of the four editions has increasingly incorporated advances in the theoretical understanding of memory. The original Wechsler Memory Scale (WMS; Wechsler, 1945) reflected the earlier nonspecific conceptualizations of memory. It was composed of brief procedures on memory for number sequences, recalling a story, simple visual designs, and paired words. The advantage of using a variety of procedures was that a client might have intact memory for visual information but not auditory information or vice versa. Despite the fact that the early WMS procedures could be *logically* divided into visuospatial versus auditory tasks, the overall scoring was a composite Memory Quotient that, similar to the Wechsler intelligence scale Intelligence Quotients (IQs), had a mean of 100 and a standard deviation of 15. This was extremely valuable information for clinicians because they could easily compare a client's IQ with his or her Memory Quotient. Any large discrepancy could be investigated further. The WMS was also quite popular as it was a relatively brief procedure, typically taking about 15 minutes to complete. Because retesting a client would be likely to result in practice effects, it had the further advantage of having a parallel form. As a result of these advantages, it became a ubiquitous procedure among clinicians.

The WMS had surprising longevity, considering that a formal new version did not become available until 1987 (a 42-year interval). The WMS was limited, however, because it included unsophisticated methods of scoring the various procedures. In addition, the algorithms to determine the Memory Quotient were overly simple because they did not consider a sufficient number of client variables. The norms were derived from a small sample of 200 patients between the ages of 25 and 50 at the Bellevue Hospital in New York. Scores for either older or younger persons were extrapolated from this sample but were not based on actual participants. In addition, the alternate form was rarely used, and the research supporting it was quite limited. Finally, it did not reflect advances in knowledge related to memory processes.

One early attempt to correct for the deficiencies of the WMS was Russell's (1975, 1988) adaptation in which he administered two of the subtests (Logical Memory and Visual Reproduction) in an immediate format combined with a delay of 30 minutes. This allowed comparisons to be made between short-term and long-term memory. Research on Russell's WMS supported the predicted difference between left-hemisphere (relatively lowered auditory recall based on Logical Memory) and right-hemisphere (relatively lowered visual reproduction based on Visual Reproduction) lesions. Despite these advantages, the psychometrics were weak, and the test was poorly standardized. Unfortunately, it was titled the Wechsler Memory Scale-Revised (WMS-R). This could create confusion because The Psychological Corporation developed a full revision of the WMS that was also titled the *Wechsler Memory Scale-Revised*. Subsequent publications have attempted to clarify the two versions by referring to them as either Russell's WMS-R *or the* WMS-R.

The 1987 revision (Wechsler Memory Scales-Revised or WMS-R) was a significant improvement over the WMS. It had age-related norms for nine different age groups ranging between 16 and 17 years for the youngest group and 70 to 74 years for the oldest group. The standardization sample was composed of 316 persons, who had characteristics that closely approximated 1980 census data. There were approximately 50 subjects in each of the age groups. Whereas the WMS had only 1 composite Memory Quotient, the WMS-R had 12 subtests from which these five composite scores could be derived: General Memory, Attention-Concentration, Verbal Memory, Visual Memory, and Delayed Recall. Each of the index scores had a mean of 100 and a standard deviation of 15. This division into index scores is consistent with theories that have divided memory into short term versus long term (note the Delayed Recall used to assess long-term memory) and verbal/auditory versus visual (note the Verbal Memory and Visual Memory indexes).

Reliability of the WMS-R was generally low to adequate (internal consistency ranged from .44 to .88 and test-retest ranged from .51 to .60) The index standard error of measure ranged from a high of 8.47 for the Visual Memory Index to a low of 4.86 for the Attention-Concentration Index (Wechsler, 1987). Similar to studies on reliability, the validity of the WMS-R was good to adequate. Factor-analytic studies supported either a two- (Bornstein & Chelune, 1988; Roid, Prifitera, & Ledbetter, 1988; Wechsler, 1987) or three-factor solution (Bornstein & Chelune, 1988). A wide range of studies supported the ability of the WMS-R to distinguish between normal and clinical groups (A. Hawkins, Sullivan, & Choi, 1997; Reid & Kelly, 1993; Wechsler, 1987), distinguish the relative severity of deficits based on subjective complaints (Gass & Apple, 1997), provide an index that related to client ratings of level of everyday memory (Reid & Kelly, 1993), and predict the degree of brain atrophy (Gale, Johnson, Bigler, & Blatter, 1995). In addition, the Attention-Concentration Index was found to be one of the most sensitive measures in identifying cognitive impairment (M. Schmidt, Trueblood, Merwin, & Durham, 1994). Despite a conceptual basis for believing that visual and verbal memory would relate to brain laterality of deficits, research on this has produced inconsistent results (Chelune & Bornstein, 1988; Loring, Lee, Martin, & Meador, 1989).

The WMS-R had clear advantages over the WMS because it had a far better normative base, was validated on diverse populations, had quite extensive studies performed on it, and divided memory into various indexes, thereby allowing the possibility for measuring various aspects of memory. Nevertheless, its weaknesses resulted in a revision within a relatively short period. One of the most serious limitations of the WMS-R has been the relatively low reliabilities of the subtests and indexes (Elwood, 1991), which likely significantly reduced the accuracy of measurements. In addition, the different indexes are probably not very good measures of specific components of memory. This is not to say they are not sensitive to both *general* cognitive impairment and the *degree* of that impairment. However, the specific nature of the impairment cannot be determined accurately by referring to the specific indexes despite the fact that the index names suggest that this differentiation can be made. Finally, current theories of memory were not used in the design of the WMS-R (Lichtenberger, Kaufman, & Lai, 2002).

The Memory Scale-III was published just 10 years after the release of the WMS-R (Wechsler, 1997a, 2002a). The new revision was designed not merely as a face-lift of the WMS-R but rather a "state of the art assessment instrument that comprehensively addresse[d] the complexity of brain/behavior relationships involved in learning and memory" (Edith Kaplan in the foreword to the WMS-III manual, p. iii). To accomplish this goal, new subtests were added, scoring procedures were made more sophisticated, stimulus materials were changed, and new index configurations were developed. This resulted in 6 primary and 5 optional subtests that were organized into index scores. Whereas the manual stated that it is possible to administer the 6 primary subtests in 30 to 35 minutes, research with a clinical population indicated that it took 42 minutes to administer the 11 primary subtests (see Axelrod, 2001). An abbreviated version was published in 2002 that reduced the administration time to 15 to 20 minutes (Wechsler Memory Scale-III Abbreviated; Wechsler 2002b).

One of the most important aspects of the WMS-III is that it was developed simultaneously with the WAIS-III. This enabled the two tests not only to share two subtests but also to be conormed. The normative sample consisted of 1,250 adults ranging between 16 and 89 years. Instead of 9 groups, as in the WMS-R, the WMS-III had 13 different groups. These groups not only had more subjects (50 in each group for the WMS-R versus 100 for the first 11 groups of the WMS-III) but also extended to a far higher age range (74 for the WMS-R versus 89 for the WMS-III). This is appropriate because one of the more important functions of memory assessment is to evaluate older clients.

The WMS-III had better reliability than its predecessor. The *WAIS-III/WMS-III Technical Manual* indicated that internal consistency for the primary subtest scores ranges between .74 and .93 for all age groups. As would be expected, the primary indexes had better internal consistencies of .82 or higher. Test-retest reliabilities for all age groups over a 2- to 12-week interval mostly ranged between .62 and .82 for the individual subtests and between .75 and .88 for the indexes. The *Technical Manual* stated that even those subtests requiring the most judgment (Logical Memory I and II, Family Pictures I and II, Visual Reproduction I and II) had interscorer reliabilities above .90.

Factor analyses reported in the 1997 *WMS-III Technical Manual* concluded that a three-factor model composed of Working Memory, Visual Memory, and Auditory Memory most closely fit the data. In contrast, the 2002 *Technical Manual* found that a five-factor model composed of Working Memory, Auditory Immediate Memory, Visual Immediate Memory, Auditory Delayed Memory, and Visual Delayed Memory fit the age groups from 30 to 64 and 65 to 89. For ages 30 to 89, this closely corresponded to five of the eight index scores. The change in factor structure between the younger and older age groups is also consistent with findings that the components of memory become more clearly distinguishable ("dissociated") with age (Dolman, Roy, Dimeck, & Hall, 2000). Thus, the index scores might become more meaningful with older populations. However, it should be noted that for most populations, there was a correlation of .98 between Immediate Memory and General Memory (K. Hawkins, 1998; Weiss & Price, 2002). This finding suggests that much of the time, these indexes were redundant. Other research has found a four-factor model (Auditory, Visual, Working Memory, Learning; Price, Tulsky, Millis, & Weiss, 2002) and a two-factor model (Wilde et al. 2003).

There was ample evidence that the WMS-III effectively differentiated between clinical and normal populations. Various clinical groups (Alzheimer's, Huntington's, and Parkinson's disease; multiple sclerosis; chronic alcohol abuse; temporal lobe epilepsy; schizophrenia) consistently scored lower than the standardization sample (D. Fisher et al., 2000; K. A. Hawkins, 1998; Psychological Corporation, 1997). For example, Korsakoff's patients typically have severe difficulties with encoding and storing new information, but their attention and working memory are normal. This finding was reflected on the WMS-III index performances wherein Working Memory was in the normal range but all other index scores were in the impaired range (Psychological Corporation, 1997). In addition, patients with mild Alzheimer's disease scored in the 60 to 71 range for most of the primary indexes except for a mean score of 80 for Working Memory (Psychological Corporation, 1997). Fisher et al. found that patients with moderate to severe traumatic brain injury scored low on all indexes. This finding is also consistent with the finding that clinician ratings of the severity of brain injury were accurately reflected on scores on the WMS-III (Makatura, Lam, Leahy, Castillo, & Kalpakjian, 1999). The previous sampling of studies indicates that many of the predicted theoretical and clinical patterns of performance were supported.

Despite the relative success of the WMS-III, there were still a number of limitations. Some of the most important of these limitations were the equivocal factor structure, long testing time for older adults, subtest overlap with the WAIS-III, and problems with some of the subtests (Faces, Family Pictures, Verbal Paired Associates). In order to correct for these limitation in the WMS-III and refine memory assessment further, the Wechsler Memory Scale-IV was developed and published in 2009 (Pearson, 2009a, 2009b). To counteract the WMS-III limitations, the WMS-IV organized the indexes according to a clear factor structure, tried to reduce the administration time (especially for older adults), eliminated the subtest overlap with the WAIS-IV (deleted Digit Span and Letter-Number Sequencing), and eliminated some of the subtests specific to the WMS-III (Faces, Family Pictures, Spatial Span, Word Lists). Additional innovations were increasing the score ranges (ceiling and floor), focusing on *visual* working memory tasks (versus the WAIS-IV *auditory* working memory tasks), an additional new subtest (Spatial Addition), clarifying/simplifying some of the scoring procedures (Visual Reproduction), and modifying some of the WMS-III subtests (Logical Memory, Verbal Paired Associates, Symbol Span, Designs).

These efforts resulted in six subtests plus an additional optional Brief Cognitive Screen (see Table 6.1). Most of the subtests are administered a first time, then readministered following a 20- to 30-minute delay. Theoretical and factor analyses clustered the subtests according to five indexes (see Table 6.2). This is in contrast to the seven indexes for the WMS-III. Another major change was the development of one battery for adults (*WMS-IV: Adult Battery*; ages 16 to 69) and a slightly modified battery for older adults (*WMS-IV: Older Adult Battery*; ages 65 to 90, see Table 6.3). The advantage of the Older Adult Battery is that administration time is shorter but only four indexes can be calculated. In order to assist with interpretation, a series of "contrast scores" were included that determine whether differences between subtests were large enough to be interpretable. For example, a Visual Memory Index that was significantly higher than a client's Auditory Memory Index suggests that visual ability is a relative strength. Interpretation of these differences could assist with diagnosis and guide the development of treatment recommendations.

Table 6.1. WMS-IV subtest names, descriptions, and abilities measured

Subtest title	Description
Brief Cognitive Status (Optional)	Basic tasks include orientation (year, date, etc.), mental control (i.e. counting backwards), drawing a clock, recall of objects that had been named previously, inhibition of responses, and verbal production. A total score is derived to provide an estimate of any major cognitive impairment (*gross cognitive impairment***).
Logical Memory (Ages 16–90)	I*: Two short stories are read and examinees are requested to repeat as many details as possible. Older adults (65–90) are presented with only one story presented twice (*short-term auditory–verbal memory*). II: Examinees are again asked to recall as many of the details as possible. (*long term auditory-verbal recall*) They are then asked yes/no questions about details in the stories (*long-term auditory–verbal recognition*).
Verbal Paired Associates (Ages 16–90)	I: A list of pairs of words are read (i.e. "dark . . . light"). The first word of the pair is read again and the examinee is asked to remember what the second word of the pair is (i.e. (dark . . .?") (*short-term auditory learning*). II: The examinee is again read the first word in the list and requested to recall the correct paired word (i.e. "light . . .?"). (*long-term auditory memory*) They are then read a list of paired words and asked which pairs were/were not read to them in condition I. (*long-term auditory recognition*). They are then asked (optional task) to say as many of the word pairs as they can recall (*long-term auditory recall information*).
Designs (Ages 16–69)	I: The examinee is shown a series of designs placed on a grid (10 seconds). The grid is removed and a new grid is presented along with a set of designs. Examinees must then identify where on the grid the original designs belong. (*short-term spatial memory*).

Table 6.1. Continued

Subtest title	Description
	II: Examinees are shown designs and grids and asked to reproduce the original placement of the designs on the grid (long-term visuospatial memory). They are then shown grids with designs on them and asked to recognize which designs are the same as in the immediate (I) condition (*long-term visual recognition*).
Visual Reproduction (Ages 16–90)	I: Five designs are shown to the examinee for 10 seconds. He or she must then draw the designs from memory (*short-term visual memory*). II: Examinees are requested to draw the original designs from memory (free recall task) (*long-term visual memory*). Next the examinee is asked to identify which of six designs on a page is the same as the design shown in condition I (*long-term visual recall*). Finally (optional task), examinees are shown the original designs and requested to draw them (copy phase; *visuospatial construction*).
Spatial Addition (Ages 16–90)	Examinees are show two grids with blue and red circles. They are then asked to add or subtract the location of the circles but are guided by a set of rules (*visual-spatial working memory*).
Symbol Span (Ages 16–90)	Examinees are first shown a page with a series of abstract symbols. They are then shown a different array of symbols and are asked to identify the correct order that they were presented on the original page (*visual-sequencing working memory*).

*I indicates that the procedure was administered and then their memory for the activity was assessed immediately afterward ("immediate" condition). In contrast, II indicates that a variation on the original procedure (I) occurred 20–30 minutes later ("delayed" condition).

**The phrases in italics indicate the type of memory function that is measured by the subtest.

Source: Adapted from Table 1.1 from the *WMS-IV Administration and Scoring Manual* by Pearson, 2009, Pearson, Inc.

Table 6.2. WMS-IV: Adult Battery (ages 16–69) indexes, primary subtests

Indexes	Subtests used to calculate indexes
Auditory Memory	Logical Memory I, Verbal Paired Associates I, Logical Memory II, Verbal Paired Associates II
Immediate Memory	Logical Memory I, Verbal Paired Associates I, Designs I, Visual Reproduction I
Delayed Memory	Logical Memory II, Verbal Paired Associates II, Designs II, Visual Reproduction II
Visual Memory	Designs I, Visual Reproduction I, Designs II, Visual Reproduction II
Visual Working Memory	Spatial Addition, Symbol Span

Table 6.3. WMS-IV: Older Adult Battery (ages 65–90) indexes and primary subtests

Indexes	Subtests used to calculate indexes
Auditory Memory	Logical Memory I, Verbal Paired Associates I, Logical Memory II, Verbal Paired Associates II
Immediate Memory	Logical Memory I, Verbal Paired Associates I, Visual Reproduction I
Delayed Memory	Logical Memory II, Verbal Paired Associates II, Visual Reproduction II
Visual Memory	Visual Reproduction I, Visual Reproduction II

The standardization sample for the WMS-IV was representative of the 2005 U.S. census of persons between the ages of 16 and 90. As such, the sample reflects the U.S. population based on age, sex, race/ethnicity, education level, and geographic region. A total of 1,400 examinees were included with 100 in each of 14 age bands. A wide variety of exclusion criteria were used to make sure that inappropriate persons were not included (i.e., persons with dementia, psychosis, medication that might impair their performance). The WMS-IV was conormed with the WAIS-IV, thereby making comparisons between the two instruments more appropriate.

RELIABILITY AND VALIDITY

The WMS-IV has good to excellent reliability. Subtest internal consistency among the normative groups was highest for Visual Reproduction II (.97) and Verbal Paired Associates (.94) and lowest for Visual Reproduction (.74) and Verbal Paired Associates (.76; Pearson, 2009a). Internal consistency among a wide variety of clinical groups (i.e., Alzheimer's disease, traumatic brain injury) was even higher. As would be expected, the index score internal consistencies were all excellent, ranging from a high of .98 for Visual Memory (SEM = 3.04) to a low of .93 for Visual Working Memory (SEM = 3.71; Pearson, 2009a). Subtest test-retest reliabilities over a 14- to 84-day interval ($M = 23$ days) ranged between .77 for Spatial Addition and a low of .59 for Designs I (Spatial scoring category). Since the index scores have a larger number of items/subtests, it would be expected that their test-retest reliabilities would be higher than for the individual subtests. This finding was supported in that the index test-retest reliabilities ranged from a high of .83 (Auditory Memory and Visual Working Memory) to a low of .81 (Visual Memory and Immediate Memory).

Extensive and quite supportive evidence for the validity of the WMS-IV is presented in the *WMS-IV Technical and Interpretive Manual* (Pearson, 2009a), which can be organized according to content validity, correlations among the WMS-IV subtests/indexes themselves, factor analyses, correlations with other measures, and relationships with special groups (i.e., traumatic brain injury, intellectual disabilities, Alzheimer's disease). Content validity was based on a combination of research on previous versions of the Wechsler memory scales, expert review, client feedback, and research on the cognitive processes clients underwent when responding to the test items. Based on this information, the test items were modified and eventually evolved into the current WMS-IV. As a result, considerable efforts have been made to develop and refine their content validity.

The WMS-IV technical manual presents additional information related to correlations among the various subtest/index scores. Ideally, subtests/indexes on a test such as the WMS-IV would be expected to have positive correlations with similar tests (convergent validity) and low or nonexistent correlations with tests that do not seem similar (discriminant validity). Among the WMS-IV subtests/indexes themselves, they would all be expected to have at least some correlation with each other since each of the subtests measure, to some extent, the common variable of memory. This was indeed the case. In addition, similar abilities would be expected to have somewhat higher correlations than those with dissimilar abilities. Thus, a verbal subtest such as Logical Memory I was found to have a moderate correlation with Verbal Paired Associates (.44). In contrast, a lower correlation was found between Verbal Paired Associates (a verbal subtest) and the more visual subtest of Spatial Addition (.31). However, the correlation between the Delayed Memory and the Immediate Memory indexes was quite high, .87. This finding is high enough to suggests that the subtests may be measuring quite similar constructs.

In contrast, the Auditory Memory and Visual Memory indexes were only moderately correlated (.64), suggesting that the auditory and visual memory components of the WMS-IV are adequately differentiated.

Previous factor analysis of earlier editions of the Wechsler Memory Scales resulted in inconsistent findings, which created considerable debate regarding the true structure of the instruments and called into question the accuracy of some WMS-R/WMS-III index groupings. As a result, the WMS-IV closely adhered to a factor-analytically supported three-factor model comprised of Auditory Memory, Visual Memory, and Working Memory. Immediate Memory and Delayed Memory indexes were also included even though they were highly correlated. The rationale for including these last two indexes was that they have been found to be clinically useful constructs among some clinical groups where short-term acquisition of memory occurs but then decays over time (Millis, Malina, Bowers, & Ricker, 1999).

A wide number of correlations with other similar measures support the concurrent validity of the WMS-IV. For example, the correlation between the California Verbal Learning Test-II (learning trials 1–5) and the WMS-IV Auditory Memory Index was .63 (Pearson, 2009b). Similarly, correlations between the Children's Memory Scales (CMS; for 16-year-olds) and the WMS-IV ranged between a high of .74 (for Immediate Memory-CMS General Memory) to a low of .25 (for Auditory Memory-CMS Visual Immediate). In addition to correlations with specific measures of memory, the WMS-IV technical manual provides numerous correlations with more general ability measures. For example, index correlations with the WAIS-IV ranged from .71 (between Full Scale IQ and Visual Working Memory) to a low of .40 (between Auditory Memory and Processing Speed). As would be expected, the highest subtest correlations were between WMS-IV and WAIS-IV spatial measures (i.e., Spatial Addition-Block Design $r = .51$). One of the most important functions of a psychological test is to make accurate predictions related to everyday behavior. In support of this, the WMS-IV demonstrated positive correlations with a measure of independent living (the Independent Living Scales; i.e., Immediate Memory Index and Independent Living Scale Full Scale score $r = .51$). Finally, measures of achievement were moderately correlated with various scores on the Wechsler Individual Achievement Test-II (i.e., Visual Working Memory Index and Mathematics score $r = .77$).

The WMS-IV technical manual provides results for a wide variety of special groups. A sampling of some of these results is provided here for persons with mild intellectual disabilities, Alzheimer's disease, traumatic brain injury, and schizophrenia. Again, data has been highly supportive of the validity of the WMS-IV. As would be expected, scores for moderately intellectually disabled persons ranged between a low of 49 on Immediate Memory to a high of 54 for Auditory Memory. Patients in the early stages of Alzheimer's disease typically report memory as being their primary complaint. As a result, it would be expected that their WMS-IV scores would be lower than their WAIS-IV scores. This expectation was supported; mean WMS-IV scores for mild Alzheimer's patients ranged between 64 for Delayed Memory and 72 for Immediate Memory. In contrast, their mean WAIS-IV General Ability Index was a significantly higher 87. The subtests that were the most difficult for patients with mild Alzheimer's were Logical Memory (Scaled score $M = 2.20$) and Verbal Paired Associates (Scaled score $M = 2.05$). It was found that patients with mild to severe traumatic brain injury had WMS-IV scores that were significantly lower than the standardization group, ranging from a high of 86 for Visual Working Memory to a low of 78 for Delayed Memory. Schizophrenics also had lower WMS-IV scores, ranging between a high of 82 for Visual Memory to a low of 77 for Immediate Memory.

Research reported in the *WMS-IV Technical and Interpretive Manual* amply support differentiating between normal and clinical groups. However, what is particularly crucial for the practicing clinician is to determine whether the individual indexes can accurately measure subcomponents of memory. Factor-analytic studies and determining whether patterns of scores match theories of memory are particularly important. As noted previously, the WMS-IV indexes were carefully organized according to the results of factor analysis. A further area of investigation is to see whether expected index patterns occur among specific types of clinical populations. For example, it would be hoped that the WMS-IV visual and auditory index scores would reliably differentiate patients with right-hemisphere brain damage (lower visual memory scores) from those with left-hemisphere brain damage (lower verbal/auditory scores). Some support for this was found among right temporal lobe epilepsy patients, who had lower Visual Memory scores ($M = 86$) compared to scores on Auditory Memory ($M = 95$). In contrast, left temporal lobe epilepsy patients had, as expected, lower Auditory Memory scores ($M = 78$) than Visual Memory scores ($M = 98$). Additional future research will no doubt investigate the extent to which the WMS-IV can differentiate discrete components of memory.

ASSETS AND LIMITATIONS

The WMS-IV is generally an excellent instrument capable of measuring a wide range of memory functioning. It has been based on theoretical research into the processes of memory, it has excellent standardization, and most research indicates solid empirical support. Subtests found to be problematic on the WMS-III were eliminated or modified, and a new subtest was added. There are only five indexes (four for the Older Adult Battery), and these are consistent with theories of memory, have generally good empirical support, and should make interpretation easier than the seven indexes developed for the WMS-III. The WMS-IV has been conormed with the WAIS-IV, which allows practitioners to make realistic comparisons between performance on the two instruments. In addition, the shorter format for older adults (ages 65–90) has advantage of making the Older Adult Battery more user friendly for this population. The WMS-IV is clearly an improvement over previous editions.

The scoring and administration of the WMS-IV is, for the most part, clearly described in the manual. The artwork is also clear, as is the Record Form. However, Logical Memory does not present guidelines regarding the speed at which the stories should be read. It also does not have guidelines for intonations, pauses, or inflections. Examiner variation in each of these areas may, therefore, result in the potential for error. For the WMS-III, Lichtenberger et al. (2002) recommended that the test developers introduce an audiotaped administration. This might be considered for the WMS-IV as well. A further issue with both Logical Memory I and II is its high degree of cultural loading; therefore, persons whose first language is not English may be disadvantaged on this subtest.

The original WMS had the advantage of taking only 15 minutes to administer. The WMS-III increased the administration time to an average of 42 minutes, but it may have actually taken up to 100 minutes for some clinical populations (Lichtenberger et al., 2002). Since the WMS-IV reduced the number of subtests and resulting indexes, it would seem reasonable that administration times would be shorter than for the WMS-III. However, administration times reported in the *WMS-IV Administration and Scoring Manual* (p. 14) indicated that for most participants, the total time for administering the WMS-IV Adult Battery was 75 to 77 minutes. The WMS-IV Older Adult Battery administration times were shorter, between 35 to 41 minutes for most participants. Currently these administration times should be considered quite tentative since the data was derived from inexperienced examiners (James Holdnack, personal communication, January 1, 2008).

It is fair to assume that administration times would become faster with greater experience. Future studies will more precisely determine administration times among experienced examiners and for various clinical populations.

In the past, practitioners concerned with time efficiency used short forms of the WMS-III/WMS-R. For example, a three-subtest WMS-III short form consisted of Logical Memory, Verbal Paired Associates, and either Faces or Family Pictures and correlated at a .97 level with General Memory (and Immediate Memory; Axelrod, Ryan, & Woodward, 2001). A two-subtest short form composed of Logical Memory and Verbal Paired Associates had a quite similar correlation of .96 with General Memory (and Immediate Memory). These two short forms accounted for 95% and 87% of the variance in General Memory and Immediate Memory, respectively (Axelrod & Woodward, 2000). Concerns with developing a formal short form resulted in the *WMS-III Abbreviated* (Wechsler, 2002b), which used four WMS-III subtests that could be used to calculate visual and auditory memory indexes. Clearly clinicians are concerned with time efficiency and probably will use various short forms of WMS-IV. One feature that would have been good to include in the WMS-IV resources would have been guidance on how this could be best accomplished. Future research probably will establish these guidelines.

The WMS-IV was designed to be a fairly comprehensive measure of memory as reflected in the five indexes (four for older adults). There are also numerous methods for displaying and analyzing various combinations of scores, including index scores, scaled scores, percentiles, confidence intervals, graphical displays, subtest variability within indexes, contrast scores between subtests, contrast scores between indexes, and comparisons between the WAIS-IV and WMS-IV. The numerous options for displaying and organizing scores is clearly an advantage in that it allows clinicians to extend the possible meanings of test scores. For example, clinicians can determine whether an examinee's long-term (delayed) memory is significantly higher/lower than his or her short-term (immediate) memory. The *WAIS-IV/WMS-IV Advanced Clinical Solutions* (Pearson, 2009c) will provide additional strategies for analysis, including forensic applications, considerations for older populations, demographically corrected norms, and information on whether changes in scores on repeat testing represent reliable change. Difficulties with the sheer number of options are the extensive time required for training and an increased possibility that clerical errors will occur for scoring (Hopwood & Richard, 2005; Ryan & Schnakenberg-Ott, 2003). In addition, the large number of comparisons increases the likelihood that seemingly meaningful differences will occur simply due to chance ("random" significance). Both scoring errors and random significance may result in incorrect interpretations, leading to poor patient care. Clinicians must take particular care to make sure their interpretations are accurate.

An important unanswered question with the WMS-IV is the extent to which it actually measures the various components of memory. Its divisions (and corresponding indexes) into visual, auditory, and working memories are well supported. However, the distinction between immediate and delayed memory is not as well supported. This difficulty was also noted on the WMS-III. As a result, clinicians who note differences between the Immediate and Delayed Indexes should seek further support based on other measures and relevant history. A related and important issue is that the various components of memory (and corresponding indexes) are likely to perform differently across various clinical populations and age groups. A final unanswered question in need of further exploration is the extent to which the WMS-IV indexes relate to aspects of everyday memory. This question is often crucial for clinicians; many referral questions ask such things how much supervision the patient might need or whether the client can return to work. Given the considerable research that resulted from the WMS-III, these and many additional questions will no doubt be answered over the next few years.

USE WITH DIVERSE GROUPS

Since the WMS-IV is a measure of cognitive abilities, many of the considerations that apply to the Wechsler intelligence scales also apply to the WMS-IV, including level of acculturation, language proficiency, ensuring rapport, encouraging optimal effort, paying particular attention to nontest information, and caution interpreting the meanings of verbal (auditory) versus nonverbal (visual) comparisons. However, an important contrast between the Wechsler intelligence scales and the WMS-IV is that general ability measures, such as the Wechsler intelligence scales, typically are used to determine functional level compared to the general population. This is often the goal for psychoeducational assessments, assessing intellectual deficiency, and vocational assessments. In these situations, demographically adjusted norms are not recommended (see "Use with Diverse Groups" in Chapter 5) and the norms provided in the WMS-IV manuals should be adequate. In contrast, the WMS-IV is much more frequently used to determine neuropsychological diagnosis and level of impairment. In these cases, using demographically corrected norms are recommended (Heaton et al., 2003; Strauss et al., 2006; Wechsler, 2002a). The main rationale here is that, rather than normative comparisons being made, comparisons are typically made between a client's current status and a presumed premorbid level of functioning. Demographically corrected norms are more likely to give a more accurate estimate of premorbid level.

Research on the WMS-III found that the highest scores occurred among European Americans followed by Hispanics; the lowest scores were found among African Americans (Heaton, Taylor, & Manly, 2003; Heaton, Miller, Taylor, & Grant, 2004). Thus, using the norms provided in the *WMS-III Administration and Scoring Manual* may result in overestimating the number of African Americans and other minorities who are "impaired." Normative adjustment for age, education, gender, and ethnicity were prepared for the WMS-III (Heaton et al., 2003; Heaton et al., 2004), and these authors are likely to develop demographically corrected norms for the WMS-IV. Demographic corrections will also be available in the upcoming *WAIS-IV/WMS-IV Advanced Clinical Solutions* (Pearson, 2009c). Until these norms are available, clinicians should proceed with caution when assessing persons from various ethnic groups. Clinicians should also take a careful history to make sure that ethnicity is indeed the actual variable that needs to be corrected. Other possibilities that might lower performance include quality of education, quality of the home environment, socioeconomic status, level/persistence of poverty, and health/nutritional status.

Some clients with physical, sensory, or language limitations might need special consideration with test administration and interpretation (see guidelines in Sattler, 2008, and Strauss et al., 2006). For example, it might be advisable to administer only the Auditory Memory and Symbol Span subtests to persons with physical difficulties (Pearson, 2009b). In contrast, it might be appropriate to give only the visual subtests and not the auditory (verbal) subtests to persons with language difficulties. If a client is not fluent in English, it might be advisable to administer the WMS-IV in a client's native language. However, the advantages of greater comprehension should be balanced with the reduction in test validity resulting from nonstandardized administration. Any modification of test administration should be noted on the Record Form and in the psychological report.

INTERPRETATION PROCEDURE

The WMS-IV measures a wide range of different functions. As a result, interpretation can be complex. The strategies to be described focus on index scores and comparisons between various combinations of index scores. Since referral questions frequently ask how a patient's memory compares with his or her overall ability, a section has been included on various relationships between scores on the WAIS-IV and various WMS-IV scores. This interpretive approach is designed to focus on the most important dimensions of the WMS-IV. More detailed information on a wider range of interpretive strategies can be found in the *WMS-IV Technical and Interpretive Manual* and will be available when a new edition of *Essentials of WMS-III Assessment* (Lichtenberger et al., 2002) becomes available with WMS-IV updates.

Often psychological reports include quite technical interpretative phrases. For example, a clinician might write something like "Ms. Memory's auditory immediate memory was statistically higher than her visual immediate memory." This may be an accurate interpretation, but, at the same time, it is likely to be understood by a relatively narrow group of readers. Typically a much wider audience will read the reports. As a result, clinicians may wish to use an interpretive phrase, such as "Ms. Memory's ability to recall information that has been spoken to her was much better (top 50% of the population) than her ability to remember information she has seen (lower 2% of the population)." This statement might be linked to actual test behavior, such as "She had a difficult time recalling details of designs she had been shown and then requested to draw." Another option would be to link test scores to examples of everyday behavior, such as "This suggests she would have problems remembering whom she had met previously or how she had gotten from one place to the next."

Prior to administering the WMS-IV primary indexes, clinicians may choose to give the optional Brief Cognitive Screening Exam (see Table 6.1). This example presents clients with a series of fairly basic tasks, such as recalling the date/day/month, counting backward, drawing a clock, or naming objects they had been previously shown. A total score can be used to obtain a general sense of any major cognitive difficulties. Thus this exam serves a similar function as a mental status examination (see Chapter 3). Scores are converted into classification labels for Average (25–100%), Low Average (10–24%), Borderline (5–9%), Low (2–4%), and Very Low (<2%). As can be seen, scores are not so much geared toward high and superior levels of functioning but more toward distinguishing various levels of poor functioning. If a patient obtains a low or very low score, the clinician may even decide not to proceed with the more demanding tasks of the primary WMS-IV subtests.

Prior to interpreting the WMS-IV, clinicians should thoroughly understand these essential principles:

- The WMS-IV index and subtest scores are arranged in the same format as the WAIS-IV. The indexes have a mean of 100 with a standard deviation of 15. The range (floor and ceiling) extends from 4 standard deviations above the mean (160) to 4 standard deviations below the mean (40). Percentile ranks are calculated as part of the standard scoring procedure. Subtest scores have a mean of 10 and a standard deviation of 3 (range is 1–19).

- Whereas the index and subtest scores provide information on how the patient performs in relation to their age-related peers, "contrast scores" measure the differences between two scores. One ability score is referred to as the "control," since it becomes the basis of comparison; the second one is referred to as the "dependent" measure. For example, a clinician might wish to note whether patients' memory for information they have seen (based on their Visual Memory Index) is significantly lower than for information they have heard (based on their Auditory Memory Index). In this case, the Auditory Memory Index is the control measure; Visual Memory is being contrasted with it and thus is the dependent measure.

- Memory is a complex function that can be influenced by factors other than memory itself. These factors include poor hearing, language impairment, visual difficulties, poor attention, general intellectual impairment, and impaired executive functioning. The possibility of comorbid conditions should always be considered when trying to determine the reasons for difficulties in memory (i.e., traumatic brain injury being comorbid with a learning disability or the side effects of medication). It is incumbent on clinicians to identify whether low scores on the WMS-IV are due to specific problems with memory or are secondary to one or more of the factors just listed.

- Patterns of WMS-IV scores cannot be used to diagnose specific clinical conditions or to make diagnoses. In other words, there is no WMS-IV score "fingerprint" that is specific to a given condition. However, when combined with other information, WMS-IV can be a potentially crucial source of information to help with diagnosis.

- When the WMS-IV is used with diverse groups, clinicians should carefully consider clients' acculturation and language facility. Proficiency with American English often allows examinees to understand the directions more easily and to encode, consolidate, and retrieve the information. This is likely to be more important for auditory information when compared to more visually oriented tasks.

- Clinicians should be careful not to overinterpret WMS-IV scores. Sometimes overinterpretation can occur from relying on a single low subtest score. In contrast, it is not unusual for average healthy persons to have one low score (Brooks, Iverson, Holdnack, & Feldman, 2008). Another potential source of overinterpretation is to confuse statistical significance with clinical significance. In other words, just because a formal calculation has found that a low score is statistically significant does not mean that this indicates an "impairment," "deficit," or "pathology." A closer inspection of cumulative percentages may reveal that many differences occur relatively frequently in the normal population. Thus normal patterns of individual differences in memory abilities should not be confused with cognitive impairments. Finally, overinterpretation potentially can occur when a large number of scores are analyzed such that some of the comparisons might be mistaken as being clinically significant when in reality they might merely be a random event ("random spurious significance").

- Different clinicians may vary in their determinations of whether a score is "impaired." As a general rule of thumb, WMS-IV index scores of 70 (2 standard deviations below the norm or lower second percentile) occurred in the most impaired clinical groups used in the validation studies (Alzheimer's disease, mild/moderate intellectual disability). In contrast, borderline to low average scores (70–85) occurred among clinical groups that were less impaired (schizophrenics, patients who had had their temporal lobes removed, moderate to severe traumatic brain-injured patients). However, this impairment should also be considered within the context of a client's overall abilities and occupation. For example, attorneys who rely heavily on auditory/verbal skills may have considerable difficulty functioning in the profession if their auditory/verbal memory performance has been lowered into the average to low-average range.

- The main focus of interpretation should be on the index scores, which represent robust, psychometrically sound measures. In contrast, subtest scores are not as psychometrically sound. As a result, there is a minimal emphasis on subtest interpretation in the next section. Instead, subtests should be used to develop tentative hypotheses in need of further support (see Table 6.1). Subtests can also be used to make qualitative descriptions that can assist report readers to understand the types of behaviors on which the interpretations have been based (i.e., "For example, Mr. Memory did poorly at recalling details of a brief short story that was read to him").

- When minimal variability among the subtests compromises an index, the index itself can be interpreted with a high level of confidence. In contrast, high subtest variability suggests that the unity of the index might be compromised due to the disparate abilities that may be present. This does not invalidate the index, but it does challenge clinicians to determine why there was less consistency in performance.

INTERPRETING PATTERNS OF INDEX SCORES

The purpose of interpreting patterns of index scores is to better understand a person's memory-related strengths and weaknesses. Initially, clinicians might do this by noting the absolute values of the index scores. These values will provide comparisons with the standardization group. For example, a relatively low score on Visual Memory might indicate a relative weakness in this modality compared to the examinee's age-related peers. In contrast, a low score on Auditory Memory might suggest difficulties with recalling verbally meaningful information. However, clinicians should also be aware that fluctuations can occur for a number of different reasons. It is up to each clinician to evaluate these various possibilities by carefully integrating additional relevant information. Therefore, the index "interpretations" listed in this section should be considered tentative.

Another strategy is to compare various combinations of index scores. Instead of making normative comparisons, this level of interpretation compares clients with their own relative strengths and weaknesses (so-called ipsative analysis). The comparisons included here are based on those distinctions that are both most clinically useful and have received empirical and theoretical support. Thus a clinician may wish to know if visual or auditory modalities are relatively stronger or weaker. A second issue relates to whether a low score on visual working memory is really due to poor *working* memory or is rather the result of poor visual memory in general. A final assessment issue relates to differences between immediate (short-term) and long-term (delayed) memory. Thus, a delayed memory that is significantly lower than immediate memory suggests that there is a decay (forgetting) of memory over time. These three comparisons are described in the next section and can be formally determined by calculating and referring to the "Index-level contrast scaled scores" on the WMS-IV Record Form (and calculated by using conversion tables in Appendix G, Table G.12, of the *WMS-IV Administration and Scoring Manual*). Knowledge related to each of these components of memory has relevance for diagnosis and treatment planning as well as for understanding normal levels of strengths and weaknesses.

The next section briefly describes the index or contrast scores, then summarizes what a high or low score means along with some examples of how the abilities measured by the indexes might occur in everyday life. Finally, consideration is given to understanding more in-depth aspects of the index, especially when there is wide variability or scores among the subtests.

Auditory Memory Index

The Auditory Memory Index (AMI) requires people to attend to information that has been presented to them orally. They then must comprehend the information and repeat it immediately after it has been presented. They must later recall the information again after a 20- to 30-minute delay. One subtest of the Auditory Memory Index (Logical Memory) requires examinees to repeat a brief story that has been read to them. The second subtest (Verbal Paired Associates) requests examinees to learn pairs of words that belong together (i.e., "dark . . . *light*"; see Table 6.1).

High scores on the Auditory Verbal Index indicate that the person has excellent abilities attending to and recalling information that he or she has heard. In contrast, low scores suggest the person will have difficulties attending to and recalling information that he or she has heard. Everyday examples might include recalling material presented in lectures, oral directions, remembering conversations a few days later, recalling shopping items without the help of a list, or phone numbers that the person has been told. Persons with low scores might need to write down oral information. Assuming their visual memory is intact, they might also learn to translate the information into visual cues (visual reminders or "mind maps" of more complex information).

Although the WMS-IV norms provided in the administration/scoring and technical/ interpretive manuals do not take into account sex differences, females typically perform better than males on Verbal Paired Associates. Analysis of the 1997 WMS-III found that females had a mean of 10.58 versus a mean of 8.46 for males on total recall scaled scores (Basso, Harrington, Matson, & Lowery, 2000). This effect was moderately strong (approximately 3 subscale points) and should therefore be considered when making interpretations. Although formal analysis has not yet been done on the WMS-IV, this same sex difference is likely to occur and will be included as part of the demographically corrected norms in the upcoming *WAIS-IV/WMS-IV Advanced Clinical Solutions.*

One potentially useful behavioral observation is that excessive embellishment of stories on Logical Memory I and II may be a maneuver to compensate for or cover up difficulty remembering accurate information. Such embellishment may result in coherent elaboration or more illogical confabulations. A further behavioral observation is to note whether a client remembers primarily the global gist of the story as opposed to quite specific linear details. This result may suggest a global, holistic mode of processing as opposed to a more linear approach.

If all the scores for the subtests comprising Auditory Memory are relatively close together, interpretation of the Auditory Memory Index is fairly straightforward. In some situations, there might be fluctuations among the different scores (see Table F.1 in the *WMS-V Administration and Scoring Manual* and Record Form for "Subtest-level differences within indexes"), which would then require careful consideration of why these scores were discrepant. This can best be done by considering the differences and similarities of the subtests. The Logical Memory tasks require examinees to recall information that has been read in a short story format. In contrast, Verbal Associates requires examinees to learn pairs of words (i.e., "high . . . *low"*) over four consecutive learning trials. These two subtests are similar in that the information is not only for auditory recall but for auditory *verbal* information (rather than musical or other types of sounds). However, they are different in that Logical Memory requires examinees to learn more complex, verbally relevant information whereas Verbal Paired Associates is for simple pairs of words and involves a prompt (one word is used as a prompt for the person to repeat the second/ paired word). A discrepancy between these subtests might be explained by understanding the differences between them. For example, a relatively higher Logical Memory suggests that the person is better able to attend to and consolidate more complex, verbally meaningful information.

Another consideration when parsing discrepancies might be to note whether the delayed portions of the subtests (Logical Memory II, Verbal Paired Associates II) are significantly higher or lower than the immediate versions (Logical Memory I, Verbal Paired Associates I). In other words, are examinees' short-term memory better or worse than their long-term memory? For example, if the delayed versions were significantly lower, it suggests that examinees forget over time information what they have heard and initially learned. In order to help understand this distinction further, clinicians should note the Immediate and Delayed Memory indexes. In addition, they should obtain information from the client and informants to see if there are noteworthy examples of material that initially has been learned but seems to have been forgotten a short time later.

Visual Memory Index

The tasks on the Visual Memory Index require examinees to recall designs from memory and either to draw them or to place them in the correct spatial location (see Tables 6.1, 6.2, and 6.3). As a result, it measures their memory for both visual details and where visual information should be located. Since examinees must respond to information both immediately after it has been presented and after a 20- to 30-minute delay, the Visual Memory Index is a measure of both short-term and long-term visual memory.

High scores on the Visual Memory Index suggest that examinees have good abilities in recalling the details and location of information they have seen. In contrast, low scores indicate problems with remembering the details and location of information they have seen. Everyday examples might include remembering whom they had seen earlier in the day, where something has been left in the house, how they had gotten from one place to the next, or finding where their car was parked in a parking lot. Patients with low scores might compensate by writing events that have occurred in a diary or writing down directions in a verbal form.

If all the subtest scores in the Visual Memory Index are similar, index interpretation can be fairly straightforward because the abilities that have been measured are more likely to be unitary. Interpretation is more complicated in cases where there is wide variability among the subtest scores, suggesting that there may be quite specific visual memory difficulties (see Table F.1 in the *WMS-V Administration and Scoring Manual* and Record Form for "Subtest-level differences within indexes"). Visual Reproduction (I and II) requires examinees to look at a design and then draw it. Not only must they recall the design itself, but they also must go through the perceptual process of internally reconstructing it along with the external motor task of actually drawing the design. In contrast, Designs (I and II) requires examinees to look at the location of objects on a grid and later recall where the designs belonged on the grid. Thus the Designs subtest has more of a spatial component than Visual Reproduction. In contrast, Visual Reproduction has more of a psychomotor reconstructive component. Discrepancies between scores on these subtests might be explained by understanding the differences in the tasks. For example, a significantly lower Visual Reproduction score compared with Designs might be due to examinees having difficulties with the task of having to draw the design. It should be noted that the Older Adult Battery does not include Designs I and II.

A further comparison might be made between the immediate and delayed portions of the subtests on Visual Memory. If scores for delayed visual memory tasks were significantly lower than those for immediate tasks, it suggests that the visual information that has been learned has been forgotten over time. Support for this, and other related inferences, should be obtained by noting performance on the Immediate and Delayed Indexes as well as obtaining information on the client's everyday behavior. For example, do other people in the client's life describe noteworthy instances in which the client seems to have rapidly forgotten information that has been seen (i.e., recalling who was at a meeting)?

Auditory Memory Index versus Visual Memory Contrast Scaled Score

One of the basic distinctions supported by WMS-IV factor analysis is between auditory and visual memory. The difference between these modalities (and the indexes that measure them) thus can be used to hypothesize relative auditory versus visual strengths and weaknesses. Thus it answers the question "Is this client stronger, weaker, or the same when auditory and visual memory abilities are compared?" A significant difference can indicate either lifelong patterns related to differences in abilities or acquired deficits in these modalities. The WMS-IV converts differences between index scores into scaled scores with means of 10 and standard deviations of 3 (see *WMS-IV Administration and Scoring Manual* Appendix G, Table G.12, and Record Form for "Index-level contrast scaled scores"). A score of 7 (16th percentile) indicates that the examinee's visual memory is in the low-average range compared with his or her auditory memory. Lower scores exaggerate this difference and suggest visual memory impairment. In contrast, a score of 13 or greater (84th percentile) suggests that the examinee's auditory memory is a relative strength compared with his or her visual memory.

Some research has found hemispheric laterality differences in patients with visual versus auditory memory impairments. Specifically laterality differences have been noted previously; patients with unilateral left-hemisphere damage have been found to do more poorly for verbal-auditory information than for visual information (K. Hawkins, 1998; Pearson, 2009a). For example, they would be expected to have particular difficulty when given verbal directions. In contrast, they might perform far better when shown a visual map of how to get from one place to the next. In contrast, patients with unilateral right-hemisphere damage would be expected to do more poorly on visual memory tasks. Thus, they would be expected to benefit more from auditory-verbal directions than from directions that were visually presented. However, visual memory performance was found to be the most sensitive to any type of brain damage, and patients with both unilateral right- and left-hemisphere damage performed poorly on visual memory types of tasks (Pearson, 2009a). If one modality was found to be relatively stronger than another, this stronger modality might be used to maximize learning. For example, if a person achieved a low score on auditory memory tasks, he or she might use learning strategies that capitalized on visual modes (or vice versa).

Visual Working Memory

The Visual Working Memory Index assesses a person's ability to temporarily attend to, organize, and manipulate visuospatial information (see Table 6.1). Note that it is not included on the Older Adult Battery. Visual Working Memory is similar to the WAIS-IV Working Memory Index in that both indexes evaluate the degree to which a person can hold and manipulate information for a short period of time. However, the WAIS-IV is specific to auditory-verbal material. It includes tests that require examinees to repeat a series of numbers, perform arithmetic problems that have been orally presented, and reorganize numbers and letters. In contrast, the WMS-IV has developed a quite different measure of working memory that is specific to visual information. The WMS-IV Visual Working Memory subtests require examinees to add/subtract visual information (Spatial Addition) and to arrange visual information into the correct sequence.

High scores on Visual Working Memory suggest that the person has excellent abilities holding and manipulating visual information. In contrast, low scores indicate the person has difficulties with visual information. Everyday examples might include being able to concentrate on a visual task without being distracted, staying focused on reorganizing furniture in a house, reorganizing the sequences of images on a computer screen, or tracking cards that have been seen in a card game.

Interpretation of the Visual Working Memory Index is made easier when the subtest scores are all within the same range, which indicates that the ability is more unitary. In contrast, subtest scores that are quite variable suggest that the ability may be due to more specific aspects of visual working memory (see Table F.1 in the *WMS-IV Administration and Scoring Manual* and Record Form for "Subtest-level differences within indexes"). As with previous indexes, it is incumbent on the clinician to parse these abilities in order to better understand the meaning of the index score. The Spatial Addition subtest requires examinees to look at two grids with different color circles. They must then add or subtract the location of the circles by following a set of rules. It is thus a spatial equivalent to the WAIS-IV Arithmetic subtest. Symbol Span shows examinees a series of abstract symbols on a page. They are then shown a different page with an array of symbols, including some from the previous page. They must identify which symbols had been shown to them previously and then indicate the order in which they were presented on the original page. The task is thus a visual analog to the WAIS-IV Digit Span subtest. Whereas Spatial Addition seems to be more of a visual "arithmetic" subtest (addition of the symbols is involved), Symbol Span involves more visual sequencing (items must be placed in the correct order). Clinicians should take these differences into account when understanding discrepant scores between the subtests. For example, a much lower Symbol Span subtest suggests that visual sequencing may be a particular difficulty for the examinee.

Visual Working Memory Index versus Visual Memory Index Contrast Scaled Score

An important consideration in understanding an examinee's performance on Visual Working Memory is whether it is due to poor working memory itself or rather to poor visual memory in general. In other words, is the problem a visual memory impairment beyond merely difficulties with working memory? Clinicians can determine the answer by checking to see if there is a significant difference between Visual Working Memory and Visual Memory. The WMS-IV converts differences between index scores into scaled scores with means of 10 and standard deviations of 3 (see *WMS-IV Administration and Scoring Manual* Appendix G, Table G.12, and Record Form for "Index-level contrast scaled scores"). A score of 7 (16th percentile) indicates that examinees' visual memory is in the low-average range compared to their relatively higher visual *working* memory. This finding suggests that their visual memory is probably the reason why their visual *working* abilities are low. For example, patients who have had their right temporal lobes removed were found to have contrast scores of 7.7 (Pearson, 2009a), which reflects poor visual memories. This somewhat low score is what would be expected, given that the right temporal lobe processes information related to visual memory. In contrast, a scaled score of 13 (84th percentile) suggests that clients have higher visual memory relative to their visual *working* memory. Thus it can be concluded that visual memory was not the reason why their visual *working* memory was low. In such cases, more faith can be placed in the interpretation that it was visual *working* memory itself that caused the low performance.

Sometimes scores on both the Visual Working Memory and Visual Memory indexes are low. In these cases, the contrast score is also likely to be low. This situation likely is caused by poor visual memory processes in general. It may also reflect interference on the tasks due to impaired visual perception.

Immediate Memory Index

Short-term (immediate) and long-term (delayed) memory are two of the crucial distinctions related to understanding memory. The WMS-IV Immediate Memory Index assesses how well examinees can recall both verbal and visual information immediately after the information has been presented. It includes tasks that require examinees to recall a story that has been read to them, learn words that are paired, draw designs from memory, and recall the correct location where designs should be placed on a grid (see Tables 6.1, 6.2, and 6.3).

High scores suggest that a client has good short-term memory for recalling information that they have heard (auditory-verbal) and information that they have seen (visual). In contrast, low scores indicate that a client has difficulty with these abilities. Everyday examples might include being able to recall a license plate they have seen, a phone number they have been told to remember, or where items belong in a cupboard. However, the above examples all relate to information that they can recall on a short-term (immediate) basis. It does not necessarily imply that they will be able to recall it over a longer duration.

Interpretation of the Immediate Memory Index is relatively clear when all the subtests scores are fairly even. This means that the ability being measured is unitary. In contrast, variation among the subtests means that the score might have occurred due to more specific factors (see Table F.1 in the *WMS-IV Administration and Scoring Manual* and Record Form for "Subtest-level differences within indexes"). The most obvious factor might have been due to differences in auditory as opposed to visual abilities. Thus clinicians might note scores on the Auditory and Visual Memory Indexes as well as the Auditory Memory Index versus Visual Memory Contrast Scaled Score. For example, if the Immediate Memory Index score was low but the Visual score was much lower than the score for the Auditory Index, it suggests that the relatively poor performance on visual material was mainly responsible for the poor performance on the Immediate Memory Index.

Delayed Memory Index

In addition to measuring short-term (immediate) memory, the WMS-IV also measures the extent to which examinees retain the information. This is measured by requesting examinees to recall details of the information that has been presented to them in each of the primary subtests following a 20- to 30-minute delay. Clients must first attend to the information and then encode, consolidate, retrieve, and provide the correct answer after the delay.

Persons with high scores on Delayed Memory can be expected to be good at retaining and retrieving information they have learned. In contrast, persons with low scores can be expected to have difficulty retaining and retrieving information. Everyday examples might include long-term recall of instructions, times of meetings, where things should be placed in cupboards, and repeating jokes or stories they have heard.

The Delayed Memory Index is comprised of many memory components since it requires that clients first accurately encode and consolidate short-term ("immediate") information and then must recall it at a later time. It involves both visual and auditory information. As a result, it can be conceptualized as a measure of global memory (similar to the General Memory Index on the 1997 WMS-III; James Holdnack, personal communication, January 6, 2009).

As with the previous indexes, subtest scores on the Delayed Memory Index that are similar mean that the ability is a unitary construct. As a result, the index can be interpreted with confidence. In contrast, a high level of variability challenges the clinician to determine if there are more specific abilities that resulted in the subtest variability (see Table F.1 in the *WMS-IV Administration and Scoring Manual* and Record Form for "Subtest-level differences within indexes"). Doing this can be particularly challenging since the Delayed Memory score represents the end product of a potentially wide number of processes (attending to the test material, good visual/auditory perception, encoding, consolidation, retrieval, expressing the response). As a result, a wide variety of reasons can disrupt performance on Delayed Memory. One potentially important distinction is between visual and auditory-verbal modalities. Clinicians might inspect possible differences in subtest scores to determine if the visual subtest scores are higher/lower than the auditory-verbal scores. They might also check the Visual and Auditory Index scores and note especially the Auditory Memory Index versus Visual Memory contrast scaled score. If, for example, the auditory scores were significantly lower than the visual scores, it suggests that the client's auditory memory might be the reason for the low score on the Delayed Memory Index.

One possible explanation for a low Delayed Memory score might be that people had a difficult time retrieving the information even though they had learned it successfully. Thus they might not have been able to "recall" the correct answers, but, if given a chance, they might be able to "recognize" the correct answers. This finding can be parsed by having administered the recognition procedures (see WMS-IV Record Form "Process Score Conversion" section). They might have scored poorly in the standard scores on the primary subtests, but their recognition scores might have been quite good. Everyday examples might be persons who have extensive tip-of-the-tongue struggles or who say "I know I know the answer but I just can't remember it," or can get the correct answer with minor prompting.

Immediate Memory Index versus Delayed Memory Index Contrast Scaled Score

The distinction between short-term (immediate) and long-term (delayed) memory is often important for practicing clinicians. Thus a referral question might be "Does this patient have impairments in forgetting material she has previously learned?" In contrast, the memory of some examinees actually might improve over time since they need the extra time to consolidate the information. A question relating to this issue might be: "Does the examinee have an improvement in memory over time?" If delayed memory is considerably lower than immediate memory (see *WMS-IV Administration and Scoring Manual* Appendix G, Table G.12, and Record Form for "Index-level contrast scaled scores"), it suggests that the person can learn material initially but that the information decays over a period of time. It should be stressed in this regard that performance on immediate memory becomes the benchmark for how much information has been lost. In other words, unless a person has learned something initially, there is nothing to lose. The exception might be that a person has acquired information but then may not be able to recall it due to poor retrieval. However, recognizing the information is generally a much easier task; the person might be able to recognize information accurately even though he or she may not be able to recall/retrieve that information. A number of procedures are available on the WMS-IV to contrast a person's recall with recognition (see Record Form for relevant "Process Score Conversions" and "Subtest-Level Contrast Scaled Scores" scores).

One issue is that factor analysis of the immediate/delayed distinction on the WMS-IV may not be as strong as would be optimal (Pearson, 2009). This issue is consistent with the finding that there was a quite high (.87) correlation between the Immediate Memory and Delayed Memory Indexes, as was also the case for the WMS-III (K. A. Hawkins, 1998; Millis et al., 1999; Weiss & Price, 2002). Clinically this means that most of the time, the index scores will not reveal a significant difference between the two abilities. Despite these findings, it was decided to include Immediate and Delayed Memory Indexes on the WMS-IV, since they can still provide potentially useful clinical information (Millis et al., 1999). In other words, there may be some populations (i.e., Korsakoff's disease, older populations) who can repeat information they have just seen or heard but forget it a short time later. This situation can be suspected in cases where informants state that clients seem to understand and can repeat information but cannot say what they saw or heard the next day.

COMPARING SCORES ON THE WAIS-IV AND THE WMS-IV

One of the most important referral questions is whether a client's memory is low compared to his or her other, more general abilities. The question may be phrased in this way: "Is this client's memory consistent with his general level of cognitive functioning?" A comparison between performance on the WMS-IV and performance on the WAIS-IV allows a clinician to answer this question. It thus places memory performance within a larger context. Thus general ability (WAIS-IV) provides a baseline or comparison point for evaluating the extent that memory (on the WMS-IV) has declined. This assumes, of course, that the more general abilities measured on the WAIS-IV are relatively stable. In contrast, memory is usually considered to be more sensitive to decline, a finding consistent with the fact that memory often is patients' main concern. For example, memory is usually the main complaint reported by patients with traumatic head injury or Alzheimer's disease. In contrast, their other more general abilities tend to be more stable.

Previous versions of the Wechsler memory scales used a total or general score that could be compared with a person's Full Scale IQ. The original WMS allowed practitioners to calculate a "Memory Quotient," and the 1997 WMS-III had a General Memory Index. Differences between the general ability and the memory scores were fairly easy to explain to referral sources or family members. Clinicians could use a phrase such as "Joe's overall mental abilities were in the average range (50th percentile) but, in contrast, his memory was much lower since he was in the bottom 5% of the population." Instead, the WMS-IV makes comparisons between each of its index scores and the WAIS-IV General Ability Index. The General Ability Index was used since it is comprised of verbal (Verbal Comprehension Index) and performance/nonverbal (Perceptual Reasoning Index) abilities. Both these abilities/indexes tend to be fairly resistant to the impact of most clinical disorders. As such, they are quite stable. In contrast, speed (Processing Speed Index) and attention/manipulation (Working Memory Index) are quite sensitive to a variety of clinical conditions. Thus many of the conditions that would be likely to lower memory also would be likely to lower speed and attention (Processing Speed and Working Memory indexes). The General Ability Index is likely to be a more stable benchmark for comparison than the Full Scale IQ, which includes all four WAIS-IV indexes (including measures of speed and attention). In other words, the General Ability Index–WMS-IV index comparisons are likely to be more sensitive to difficulties with memory when compared to using Full Scale IQ–WMS-IV index comparisons.

The Record Form allows for completion of a wide number of ability-memory comparisons (see the Record Form "Ability-Memory Analysis" section that uses Tables B.1–B.16 on pp. 200–218 of the *WMS-IV Technical and Interpretive Manual*). Most clinicians focus primarily on comparisons between the General Ability Index and the WMS-IV index scores. For that reason, we describe only those scores in this chapter. Some examiners may want to make more detailed comparisons between additional combinations of the WMS-IV index and WAIS-IV index scores. All differences are converted to contrast scaled scores with a mean of 10 and a standard deviation of 3. A score of 7 (16th percentile) indicates that the memory index is unexpectedly low (a relative weakness) compared with the General Ability Index. Lower scores exaggerate this difference and suggest the possibility of memory impairment specific to the index. In contrast, a score of 13 or greater (84th percentile) suggests that the examinee's memory index is unexpectedly high (a relative strength) compared with his or her General Ability Index. One caution is that, with so many potential comparisons, the possibility of random spurious significant differences increases. In other words, some of the "significant" differences may not actually be clinically accurate descriptions of the client. As a result, clinicians should be careful not to overinterpret the difference scores.

The next descriptions are quite brief. Clinicians who want more detailed interpretations can read information under each of the WMS-IV indexes; that material includes a description of the index, a listing of the types of tasks involved, a brief interpretation of the meaning of high/low scores, and everyday examples (see "Interpret Patterns of Index Scores" earlier in this chapter).

General Ability Index versus Auditory Memory Index

A low score (below 7) indicates that the information that clients have recalled based on having heard it is a weakness compared with their overall ability. High scores (above 13) indicate that their memory for information they have heard is a relative strength.

General Ability Index versus Visual Memory Index

A low score (below 7) indicates that the information that clients have recalled based on having seen it is a weakness compared with their overall ability. This index has been found to be one of the most sensitive measures of impairment (Pearson, 2009a). High scores (above 13) indicate that their memory for information they have seen is a relative strength.

General Ability Index versus Visual Working Memory Index

A low score (below 7) indicates that clients' ability to concentrate on, hold, organize, and manipulate complex visual information is a relative weakness compared with their overall ability. They are likely to have difficulty working with both where the information was located ("visual space") and the details of what was seen ("visual details"). High scores (above 13) indicate that holding and manipulating visual information (both spatially and for details) is a relative strength.

General Ability Index versus Immediate Memory Index

A low score (below 7) indicates that clients' short-term ("immediate") memory for information they have seen or heard is a relative weakness compared with their overall ability. High scores (above 13) indicate that their short-term ("immediate") memory is a relative strength.

General Ability Index versus Delayed Memory Index

A low score (below 7) indicates that clients' long-term ("delayed") memory for information they have seen or heard is a relative weakness compared with their overall ability. This measure is one of the more clinically sensitive measures (Pearson, 2009a). High scores (above 13) indicate that their long-term ("delayed") memory for information they have seen or heard is a relative strength. "Long"-term assessment on this index was based on a 20- to 30-minute delay. Since the Delayed Memory Index is comprised of many memory components, it can be conceptualized as a measure of global memory (similar to the General Memory Index on the 1997 WMS-III). Given its sensitivity combined and the fact that it is a global measure of memory, it should be one of the most important comparisons.

ADDITIONAL CONSIDERATIONS: MALINGERING AND EVALUATING CHANGE

Secondary gain is frequently an issue for assessments related to personal injury litigation, workers' compensation, long-term disability, or defendants in criminal injury proceedings. Due to the potential for gain, malingering is a distinct possibility. Surveys of neuropsychologists found that estimates for feigning deficits were as high as 30% among personal injury and workers' compensation cases (Mittenberg et al., 2002) and up to 40% for litigants involved with traumatic brain injury (Larrabee, 2005). Memory problems are particularly likely to be exaggerated since they are often the most frequently reported problems among these populations. As a result, clinicians need to be particularly careful to evaluate the validity of a client's complaints. Terms that are similar to malingering but somewhat more neutral include "suboptimal performance," "inconsistent effort," or "feigning."

A number of specialty instruments are available to detect suboptimal cognitive effort and are recommended to help make a more definitive assessment (see Boone, 2007; Larrabee, 2005; Strauss et al. 2006). Best practice even requires multiple measures to be used. Possible strategies to detect malingering on the WMS-IV might be to focus on the Logical Memory Delayed Recognition task that requests clients to state whether (yes or no) an item was included in one of the previously read stories. Because random guessing would produce a score of 50%, scores of less than this suggest that the client is malingering (see Killgore & Dellapietra, 2000). Malingering may also be suggested if recognition does not improve in comparison to recall because recognition tasks are easier than free recall tasks. A final quite general indicator is dramatic differences between a person's day-to-day functioning (based on corroborating sources) and performance on WMS-III measures. The *WAIS-IV/WMS-IV Advanced Clinical Solutions* (Pearson, 2009c) will provide additional strategies to detect malingering, including analyses of guessing for Logical Memory Recognition, Verbal Paired Associates, Designs Spatial, and Designs Content (James Holdnack, personal communication, January 7, 2008). If an examinee performs lower than guessing on the listed subtests, malingering is a possibility.

Sometimes Wechsler memory scale scores are used to document deterioration or to monitor improvement. It is tempting to peruse pretest and posttest scores and quickly infer that some sort of actual change has occurred in the patient's level of functioning. For example, a client might have had a WMS-IV Delayed Memory Index score of 80 directly after a head injury and, 3 months later, achieved a score of 85. It might be inferred that the patient's memory has improved. However, this finding does not take into consideration factors such as practice effects, regression to the mean, or the relative reliability of the measure. The improvement between the pretest of 80 and the posttest of 85 might simply be the result of the patient's practicing the tasks 3 months previously, or the difference might simply be measurement error (reflected in its test-retest reliability). The *WAIS-IV/WMS-IV Advanced Clinical Solutions* (Pearson, 2009c) will provide strategies for calculating whether actual change has occurred ("reliable change index"). However, these calculations will account for the unreliability of the instrument, which does not necessarily mean that the personal or social significance of the change in scores has been demonstrated (see Beutler & Moleiro, 2001). Determining the personal and clinical meaning of changed scores requires clinicians to integrate information from a wider variety of sources to support any inferences related to actual change in the client's functioning.

RECOMMENDED READING

Heaton, R. K., Taylor, M. J., & Manly, J. (2003). *Demographic effects and use of demographically corrected norms with the WAIS-III and WMS-III.* In D. S. Tulsky, D. H. Saklofske,G. J. Chelune, R. K. Heaton, & R. J. Ivnik (Eds.), *Clinical interpretation of the WAIS-III and WMS-III* (pp. 181–210). San Diego: Academic Press.

Strauss, E., Sherman, E. M. S., & Spreen, O. (2006). *Memory.* In O. Spreen & E. Strauss (Eds.), *A compendium of neuropsychological tests: Administration, norms, and commentary* (3rd ed.) (pp. 679–686). New York: Oxford University Press.

Chapter 7

MINNESOTA MULTIPHASIC PERSONALITY INVENTORY[†]

The Minnesota Multiphasic Personality Inventory (MMPI)* is a standardized questionnaire that elicits a wide range of self-descriptions scored to give a quantitative measurement of an individual's level of emotional adjustment and attitude toward test taking. Since its original development by Hathaway and McKinley in 1940, the MMPI has become the most widely used clinical personality inventory, with more than 10,000 published research references (Archer et al., 2006; Boccaccini & Brodsky, 1999; Camara et al., 2000; C. Piotrowski, 1999). Thus, in addition to its clinical usefulness, the MMPI has stimulated a vast amount of literature.

The 1943 MMPI test format consisted of 504 affirmative statements that could be answered "True" or "False." The number of items was later increased to 566 through the inclusion of repeat items and Scales 5 (Masculinity-Femininity) and 0 (Social Introversion). The 1989 restandardization retained the same basic format but altered, deleted, and/or added a number of items, which resulted in a total of 567. The different categories of responses can be either hand or computer scored and summarized on a profile sheet. An individual's score as represented on the profile form can then be compared with the scores derived from different normative samples.

The original MMPI had 13 standard scales, of which 3 related to validity and 10 related to clinical or personality indices. The more recent MMPI-2 and MMPI-A have maintained the original 10 clinical/personality scales as well as the original 3 validity scales, but the total number of validity scales has been increased (see Table 7.1). The clinical and personality scales are known both by their scale numbers and by scale abbreviations. Additional options are available to refine the meaning of the clinical scales as well as provide additional information. These options include scales based on item content (content scales), refinement of the clinical scales (restructured clinical scales), subscales for the clinical and personality scales based on clusters of content-related items (Harris-Lingoes subscales), assessment of items and item clusters that relate to relevant dimensions (critical items), and empirically derived new scales (supplementary scales). New scales are still being researched and reported in the literature. The result of these developments is an extremely diverse and potentially useful test that can be interpreted, refined, and expanded from a variety of different perspectives.

The contents for the majority of MMPI questions are relatively obvious and deal largely with psychiatric, psychological, neurological, or physical symptoms. However, some of the questions are psychologically obscure because the underlying psychological process they are assessing is not intuitively obvious. For example, item 68, "I sometimes

Table 7.1   Validity, Basic (Clinical), and Content Minnesota Multiphasic Personality Inventory Scales

Name	Abbreviation	Scale No.	No. of Items
Validity scales			
Cannot say	?		
Variable response inconsistency	VRIN		98
True response inconsistency	TRIN		40
Infrequency	F		60
Back F	Fb		40
Infrequency-Psychopathology	Fp		27
Fake Bad Scale	FBS		
Lie	L		15
Correction	K		30
Superlative Self Presentation	S		50
Basic (clinical) scales			
Hypochondriasis	Hs	1	32
Depression	D	2	57
Hysteria	Hy	3	60
Psychopathic deviant	Pd	4	50
Masculinity-femininity	Mf	5	56
Paranoia	Pa	6	40
Psychasthenia	Pt	7	48
Schizophrenia	Sc	8	78
Hypomania	Ma	9	46
Social introversion	Si	0	69
Content scales			
Anxiety	ANX		23
Fears	FRS		23
Obsessiveness	OBS		16
Depression	DPS		33
Health concerns	HEA		36
Bizarre mentation	BIZ		23
Anger	ANG		16
Cynicism	CYN		23
Antisocial practices	ASP		22
Type A	TPA		19
Low self-esteem	LSE		24
Social discomfort	SOD		24
Family problems	FAM		25
Work interference	WRK		33
Negative treatment indicators	TRT		26

tease animals," is empirically answered "False" more frequently by depressed subjects than normals. Thus, it was included under Scale 2 (Depression) even though it does not, on the surface, appear to directly assess an individual's degree of depression. For the most part, however, the statements are more direct and self-evident, such as item 56, "I wish I could be as happy as others seem to be" (True) or 146, "I cry easily" (True), both of which also reflect an examinee's level of depression. The overall item content is extremely varied and relates to areas such as general health, occupational interests, preoccupations, morale, phobias, and educational problems.

After a test profile has been developed, the scores are frequently arranged or coded in a way that summarizes and highlights significant peaks and valleys. However, to accurately interpret the test, both the overall configuration of the different scales and the relevant demographic characteristics of the client must be taken into consideration. In many instances, the same scaled score on one test profile can mean something quite different on another person's profile when the elevations or lowerings of other scales are also considered. For example, an elevated Scale 3 (Hysteria) may indicate an individual who denies conflict, demands support from others, expresses optimism, and is somewhat interpersonally naive. However, if this elevation is also accompanied by a high 4 (Psychopathic Deviate), there is likely to be a strong undercurrent of repressed anger. This anger is usually expressed indirectly, and any negative effects on others are likely to be strongly denied. Thus, it is important for the clinician to avoid the use of purely quantitative or mechanical formulas for interpreting the profile and instead examine the scores in the overall context of the other scale elevations and lowerings. A particular scale should be examined not only in the context of the overall test configuration, but also using additional sources, such as demographic characteristics (age, education, socioeconomic status, ethnicity), behavioral observations, other psychometric devices, and relevant history can often increase the accuracy, richness, and sensitivity of personality descriptions.

A further important, general interpretive consideration is that the scales represent measures of personality traits rather than simply diagnostic categories. Although the scales were originally designed to differentiate normal from abnormal behavior, it is generally regarded as far more useful to consider that the scales indicate clusters of personality variables. For example, Scale 2 (Depression) may suggest characteristics such as mental apathy, self-deprecation, and a tendency to worry over even relatively small matters. This approach characterizes the extensive research performed on the meanings of the two highest scales (2-point code types), which are summarized later in this chapter. Rather than merely labeling a person, this descriptive approach creates a richer, more in-depth, and wider assessment of the individual who is being tested.

HISTORY AND DEVELOPMENT

The original development of the MMPI was begun in 1939 at the University of Minnesota by Starke R. Hathaway and J. Charnley McKinley. They wanted an instrument that could serve as an aid in assessing adult patients during routine psychiatric case workups and that could accurately determine the severity of their disturbances. Furthermore, Hathaway and McKinley were interested in developing an objective estimate of the change produced by psychotherapy or other variables in a patient's life.

The most important approach taken during construction of the MMPI was empirical criterion keying. This refers to the development, selection, and scoring of items within the scales based on some external criterion of reference. Thus, if a clinical population was given a series of questions to answer, the individuals developing the test would select questions for inclusion or exclusion based on whether this clinical population answered differently from a comparison group. Even though a theoretical approach might be used initially to develop test questions, the final inclusion of questions would not be based on this theoretical criterion. Instead, test questions would be selected based on whether they were answered in a direction different from a contrasted group. For example, a test constructor may believe that an item such as "Sometimes I find it almost impossible to get out of bed in the morning" is a theoretically sound statement to use in assessing depression. However, if a sample population of depressed patients did not respond to that question differently from a normative group, the item would not be included. Thus, if a person with hysterical traits answers "True" to the statement "I have stomach pains," whether he or she actually does have stomach pains is less important, from an empirical point of view, than the fact that the individual says he or she does. In other words, the final criterion for inclusion of items in an inventory is based on whether these items are responded to in a significantly different manner by a specified population sample.

Using this method, Hathaway and McKinley began with an original item pool of more than 1,000 statements derived from a variety of different sources, including previously developed scales of personal and social attitudes, clinical reports, case histories, psychiatric interviewing manuals, and personal clinical experience. Of the original 1,000 statements, many were eliminated or modified. The result was 504 statements that were considered to be clear, readable, not duplicated, and balanced between positive and negative wording. The statements themselves were extremely varied and were purposely designed to tap as wide a number of areas in an individual's life as possible. The next step was to select different groups of normal and psychiatric patients to whom the 504 questions could be administered. The normals were primarily friends and relatives of patients at the University of Minnesota hospitals who were willing to complete the inventory. They consisted of 226 males and 315 females, who were screened with several background questions about age, education, marital status, occupation, residence, and current medical status. Individuals who were under the care of a physician at the time of the screening were excluded from the study. This group was further augmented by the inclusion of other normal subjects, such as recent high school graduates, Work Progress Administration workers, and medical patients at the University of Minnesota hospitals. This composite sample of 724 individuals was closely representative in terms of age, sex, and marital status of a typical group of individuals from the Minnesota population, as reflected in the 1930 census. The clinical group comprised patients who represented the major psychiatric categories being treated at the University of Minnesota hospitals. These patients were divided into clear subgroups of approximately 50 in each category of diagnosis. If a patient's diagnosis was at all in question, or if a person had a multiple diagnosis, he or she was excluded from the study. The resulting subgroups were hypochondriasis, depression, hysteria, psychopathic deviate, paranoia, psychasthenia, schizophrenia, and hypomania.

After the normals and psychiatric patients had been administered the 504-item scale, Hathaway and McKinley could then compare their responses. Each item that correctly differentiated between these two groups was included in the resulting clinical scale. For example, an item such as "I feel vague aches and pains in my stomach" might be answered "True" by 20% of a sample of hypochondriacs and by only 2% of the normals. It could thus be included in the clinical scale for hypochondriasis. The comparisons, then, were between each clinical group and the group of normals rather than among the different clinical groups themselves. This was the selection procedure used to develop tentative clinical scales.

Still another step was included in the scale constructions. The fact that an item was endorsed differently by the group of 724 Minnesota normals than by the patients from various clinical populations did not necessarily indicate that it could be used successfully for clinical screening purposes. Thus, an attempt was made to cross-validate the scales by selecting a new group of normals and comparing their responses with a different group of clinical patients. The items that still provided significant differences between these groups were selected for the final version of the scales. It was reasoned, then, that these items and the scales comprising these items would be valid for differential diagnosis in actual clinical settings.

Whereas this procedure describes how the original clinical scales were developed, two additional scales that used slightly different approaches were also included. Scale 5 (Masculinity-Femininity) was originally intended to differentiate male homosexuals from males with a more exclusively heterosexual orientation. However, few items were found that could effectively perform this function. The scale was then expanded to distinguish items that were characteristically endorsed in a certain direction by the majority of males from those that were characteristically endorsed in a certain direction by females. This was accomplished in part by the inclusion of items from the Terman and Miles I Scale (1936). The second additional scale, Social Introversion (Si), was developed by Drake in 1946. It was initially developed by using empirical criterion keying in an attempt to differentiate female college students who participated extensively in social and extracurricular activities from those who rarely participated. It was later generalized to reflect the relative degree of introversion for both males and females.

It soon became apparent to the test constructors that persons could alter the impression they made on the test because of various test-taking attitudes. Hathaway and McKinley thus began to develop several scales that could detect the types and magnitude of the different test-taking attitudes most likely to invalidate the other clinical scales. Four scales were developed: the Cannot say (?), the Lie (L), the Infrequency (F), and the Correction (K). The Cannot say (?) scale is simply the total number of unanswered questions. If a high number of these are present, it would obviously serve to reduce the validity of the overall profile. High scores on the Lie scale indicate a naive and unsophisticated effort on the part of the examinee to create an overly favorable impression. The items selected for this scale were those that indicated a reluctance to admit to even minor personal shortcomings. The Infrequency (F) scale is composed of those items endorsed by fewer than 10% of normals. A high number of scorable items on the F scale, then, reflects that the examinee is endorsing a high number of unusually deviant responses.

Correction (K), which reflects an examinee's degree of psychological defensiveness, is perhaps the most sophisticated of the validity scales. The items for this scale were selected by comparing the responses of known psychiatric patients who still produced normal MMPIs (clinically defensive) with "true" normals who also produced normal MMPIs. Those items that differentiated between these two groups were used for the K scale. Somewhat later, the relative number of items endorsed on the K scale was used as a "correction" factor. The reasoning behind this was that, if some of the scales were lowered because of a defensive test-taking attitude, a measure of the degree of defensiveness could be added into the scale to compensate for this. The result would theoretically be a more accurate appraisal of the person's clinical behavior. The scales that are not given a K correction are those whose raw scores still produced an accurate description of the person's actual behavior. However, there have been some questions regarding the effectiveness of the K correction in some settings. As a result, clinicians have the choice of whether they wish to use MMPI-2 profile sheets with or without the K correction, and the MMPI-A has omitted the use of the K correction altogether.

Since the publication of the original MMPI, special scales and numerous adjunctive approaches to interpretation have been developed. A primary strategy has been content interpretation. The most frequently have been the Harris and Lingoes subscales, Wiggins Content Scales, and several different listings of critical items. These scales can potentially provide important qualitative information regarding an examinee. In addition, many supplementary scales have been developed, such as the Anxiety Scale, the MacAndrew Scale to assess the potential for substance abuse, and the Ego Strength Scale to estimate the extent to which a person will benefit from insight-oriented therapy. Each of these approaches can be used as an adjunct in interpreting the traditional clinical scales and/ or experimental scales for assessing or researching specific populations (Butcher, 2006a, 2006b; Graham, 2006; Butcher, Graham, Williams, & Ben-Porath, 1990; C. Williams, Butcher, Ben-Porath, & Graham, 1992).

In addition to innovations in scales and interpretations, the MMPI has been used in a wide number of settings for extremely diverse areas. Most studies have focused on the identification of medical and psychiatric disorders as well as on uses in forensic contexts (Deardorff, 2000; Greene, 2000; K. Pope, Butcher, & Seelen, 2000), and on expanding or further understanding the psychometric properties of the MMPI. Other frequent topics include alcoholism, aging, locus of control, computer-based interpretation, chronic pain, and the assessment of different occupational groups. The MMPI has been translated into a number of different languages and has been used in a wide range of different cross-cultural contexts (see Butcher, 1996, 2004; Cheung & Ho, 1997; Greene, 1991; G. Hall, Bansal, & Lopez, 1999; Handel & Ben-Porath, 2000).

Criticisms of the original MMPI have primarily centered on its growing obsolescence, difficulties with the original scale construction, inadequacy of its standardization sample, and difficulties with many of the items (Helmes & Reddon, 1993). Problems with the items included sexist wording, possible racial bias, archaic phrases, and objectionable content. In addition, the original norms had poor representation of minorities and were inappropriate in making comparisons with current test takers. Further problems have related to inconsistent meanings associated with *T* score transformations.

These criticisms led to an extensive restandardization of the MMPI, which began in 1982. Despite the need to make major changes, the restandardization committee wanted to keep the basic format and intent of the MMPI as intact as possible so that the extensive research base collected over the past 50 years would still be applicable to the restandardized version. As a result, the following six goals were established:

1. The deletion of obsolete or objectionable items.
2. Continuation of the original validity and clinical scales.
3. The development of a wide, representative normative sample.
4. Norms that would most accurately reflect clinical problems and would result in a uniform percentile classification.
5. The collection of new clinical data that could be used in evaluating the items and scales.
6. The development of new scales.

The restandardization used a special research form consisting of the original 550 items (of which 82 were modified) and additional 154 provisional items used for the development of new scales. Even though 82 of the original items were reworded, their psychometric properties apparently were not altered (Ben-Porath & Butcher, 1989). The resulting 704-item form (Form AX) was administered to 1,138 males and 1,462 females from seven different states, several military bases, and a Native American reservation. The subjects were between the ages of 18 and 90 and were contacted by requests through direct mail, advertisements in the media, and special appeals. The resulting restandardization sample was highly similar to the 1980 U.S. census in almost all areas with the exception that they were somewhat better educated than the overall population.

The MMPI-2 (Butcher, Dahlstrom, Graham, Tellegen, & Kaemmer, 1989; Butcher, Graham, Ben-Porath, Tellegen, Dahlstrom, & Kaemmer, 2001) differs from the older test in a number of ways. The T scores that subjects obtain are generally not as deviant as those from the earlier version. In addition, the T scores were designed to produce the same range and distribution throughout the traditional clinical scales (except for Scales 5 and 0). The practical result is that T scores of 65 or greater are considered to be in the clinical range (versus a cutoff score of 70 for the MMPI). Also, the percentile distributions are uniform throughout the different clinical scales (whereas they were unequal for the MMPI). The test booklet itself contains 567 items, but the order has been changed so that the traditional scales (3 validity and 10 clinical) can be derived from the first 370 items. The remaining 197 items (371 to 567) provide different supplementary, content, and research measures. A number of new scales were included along with new, subtle, adjunctive measures of test validity, separate measures of masculinity and femininity, and 15 additional content scales measuring specific personality factors (Anxiety, Health concerns, Cynicism, etc.). An extensive research base has accumulated related to areas such as the validity of MMPI/MMPI-2 code types, use with special populations, the ability to distinguish over- or underreporting of symptoms, and comparability between the original MMPI, MMPI-2, and MMPI-A.

Two ongoing criticisms of the MMPI-2 are that the scales are too heterogeneous and the test is simply too long. As a result, work has progressed to refine the basic clinical scales by extracting the common or shared variable of demoralization. The result has been the shorter and more homogeneous Restructured Clinical (RC) scales (Tellegen et al., 2003). Further, five core personality scales related to psychopathology have been developed (Personality Psychopathology Five [PSY-5]; Harkness et al., 2002). These and other developments have, to a certain extent, provided alternatives to the heterogeneous and more-difficult-to-interpret original clinical scales. By combining these scale groupings with the validity and additional scales, a 388-item restructured short form has become available (MMPI-2 Restructured Form [MMPI-2-RF]; Ben-Porath & Tellegen, 2008). A final short form is through computer-adapted assessment (MMPI-2-CA; Forbey & Ben-Porath, 2007) in which future items are selected based on responses to past items. It is still uncertain the extent to which these short forms will be embraced by the clinical and research community.

Early on, it was noticed that the original MMPI produced different scale elevations for adolescents than for adults. This recognition resulted in the development of different sets of recommended norms for use with adolescent populations (Archer, 1987; Colligan & Offord, 1989; Klinefelter, Pancoast, Archer, & Pruitt, 1990; Marks, Seeman, & Haller, 1974). However, many practitioners and researchers felt that, even with the use of adolescent norms, there were still considerable difficulties. Specifically, the test was too long, the reading level was too high, there was a need for contemporary norms, more of the content needed to assess problems specifically related to adolescents, and some of the language was outmoded and/or inappropriate (Archer, Maruish, Imhof, & Piotrowski, 1991). In response to these issues, the restandardization committee for the MMPI-2 decided in 1989 to develop the MMPI-Adolescent (MMPI-A), which was first made available in 1992 (Butcher et al., 1992). It was normed against a generally representative group of 805 males and 815 females between the ages of 14 and 18. The main discrepancy between the normative group and comparison with U.S. census data was that the parents of the normative group were better educated. Despite the similarity with the MMPI and MMPI-2, there are several important differences. Fifty-eight items were deleted from the original standard scales, some of the wording of items was changed, and new items relevant to adolescent concerns were included. The result has been the inclusion of four new validity scales (VRIN, TRIN, *F*1, *F*2) in addition to the earlier validity scales (*L*, *F*, *K*). There are also six supplementary scales (e.g., Immaturity Scale, Anxiety, Repression) and additional newly developed content scales (e.g., A-dep/Adolescent Depression). To counter claims that the MMPI is too long, especially for adolescents, the MMPI-A contains 478 items, thereby shortening the administration time. This can be shortened even further by administering only the first 350 items, still sufficient to obtain the validity and standard clinical scales. Thus, the MMPI-A is strongly related to the MMPI and MMPI-2 (and their respective databases) but also has a number of important distinctive features of its own.

RELIABILITY AND VALIDITY

Reliability studies on the original MMPI indicate that it had moderate levels of temporal stability and internal consistency. For example, Hunsley, Hanson, and Parker (1988) completed a meta-analysis of studies performed on the MMPI between 1970 and 1981 and concluded, "All MMPI scales are quite reliable, with values that range from a low of .71 (Scale *Ma*) to a high of .84 (Scale *Pt*)" (p. 45). Their analysis was derived from studies that included a wide range of populations, intervals that ranged from one day to two years, and a combined sample size exceeding 5,000. In contrast to Hunsley et al., some authors have reported that the fluctuations in some of the scales are sufficiently wide to question their reliabilities (Hathaway & Monachesi, 1963; Mauger, 1972). Proponents of the MMPI counter that some fluctuation in test scores is to be expected. This is especially true for psychiatric populations because the effects of treatment or stabilization in a temporary crisis are likely to be reflected in a patient's test performance (J. Graham, Smith, & Schwartz, 1986). Bergin (1971) has demonstrated that Scale 2 (Depression) is particularly likely to be lowered after successful treatment. Similarly, Scale 7 (Psychasthenia) would be likely to alter according to a person's external situation. Thus, test-retest reliability may actually be an inappropriate method of evaluating these scales for certain populations. This defense of the test's reliability is somewhat undermined by the observation that test-retest reliability is actually slightly more stable for psychiatric populations than for normals. Whereas the median range for psychiatric patients is about .80, median reliabilities for normals are about .70. Split-half reliabilities are likewise moderate, having an extremely wide range from .05 to .96, with median correlations in the .70s (Hunsley et al., 1988).

Reliability reported in the MMPI-2 manual indicates moderate test-retest reliabilities. However, test-retest reliabilities were calculated for a narrow population over short-term retesting intervals. Reliabilities for normal males over an average interval of 8.58 days (*Mdn* = 57 days) ranged from a low of .67 for Scale 6 to a high of .92 for Scale 0 (Butcher et al., 1989). A parallel sample of females over the same retesting interval produced similar reliabilities ranging from .58 (Scale 6) to .91 (Scale 0). Standard error of measurements for the different scales ranged from 2 to 3 raw score points (Butcher et al., 1989, 2001; Munley, 1991).

One difficulty with the MMPI/MMPI-2 lies in the construction of the scales themselves. The intercorrelations between many of the scales are quite high, which results primarily from the extensive degree of item overlap. Sometimes the same item will be used simultaneously for the scoring of several different scales, and most of the scales have a relatively high proportion of items common to other scales. For example, Scales 7

(Psychasthenia) and 8 (Schizophrenia) have high overlap, which is reflected in correlations ranging from .64 to .87, depending on the population sampled (Butcher et al., 1989; Dahlstrom & Welsh, 1960). Scale 8, which has the highest number of items (78), has only 16 items that are unique to it (Dahlstrom, Welsh, & Dahlstrom, 1972). Similarly, Scale *F* (Infrequency) is highly correlated with Scales 7 (*Pt*), 8 (*Sc*), and the Bizarre Mentation content scale. The practical implication is that interpreters need to be quite cautious about inferring a "fake bad" profile if profile *F* is elevated along with 7 (*Pt*), 8 (*Sc*), and Bizarre Mentation. Several factor-analytic studies have been conducted that were motivated in part by a need to further understand the high intercorrelations among scales. These studies have not found any consistent numbers and types of factors. The numbers of factors range between 2 (Dahlstrom, Welsh, & Dahlstrom, 1975; Dahlstrom et al., 1972; D. Jackson, Fraboni, & Helms, 1997) and 9 (Archer & Krishnamurthy, 1997a; Costa, Zonderman, Williams, & McCrae, 1985) and even up to 21 (J. H. Johnson, Null, Butcher, & Johnson, 1984). This suggests that these factors are not highly differentiated.

The different scales correlate so highly, in part, because the original selection of the items for inclusion in each scale was based on a comparison of normals with different clinical groups. The items, then, were selected based on their differentiation of normals from various psychiatric populations rather than on their differentiation of one psychiatric population from another. Although the psychiatric groups varied from the normals on several traits, this manner of scale construction did not develop accurate measurements of these different traits. Rather, the scales are filled with many heterogeneous items and measure multidimensional, often poorly defined attributes. This approach has also led to many items being shared with other scales. In contrast, an approach in which specific psychiatric groups had been compared with one another would have been more likely to have resulted in scales with less item overlap and with the ability to measure more unidimensional traits.

A partial defense of item overlap is that for complex, multidimensional variables such as pathological syndromes, important relationships would be expected with other similar constructs. If these other constructs were being measured on the same test, it would further be expected that there would be scale overlap on these theoretically and clinically related syndromes (Dahlstrom et al., 1972). For example, depression is a common feature among several categories of psychopathology. Thus, it would be theoretically related to conditions such as hypochondriasis, schizophrenia, and anxiety. This means that it would be expected that the common occurrence of depression would result in intercorrelations between scales and would produce scales that, while intercorrelated, would still have subtle and clinically different meanings (Broughton, 1984). Thus, the multidimensionality of the scales combined with their item overlap would be not so much a weakness of the MMPI/MMPI-2/MMPI-A but would be expected, given the nature of the constructs. Accurate interpretation, however, would need to include an awareness of the subtle differences and similarities between scales.

An issue related to MMPI/MMPI-2/MMPI-A scale multidimensionality is that elevations can often occur for a variety of reasons. For example, an elevation on 4 (Psychopathic Deviance) might result from family discord, poor peer relations, alienation from self and society, and/or acting out associated with legal difficulties. A person interpreting an elevated Scale 4 (Psychopathic Deviance) might potentially infer antisocial acting out when family discord is the major reason for the scale elevation. To enhance the likelihood of accurate interpretations, practitioners need to carefully evaluate the meanings of scale elevations. This might include looking at the content of selected items (critical items), scoring the Harris-Lingoes subscales, considering the meanings of content or supplementary scales, reviewing scores on the restructured clinical scales, referring to published MMPI research, and integrating the results from the client's history and relevant behavioral observations. Differentiating which of these scale dimensions is most relevant can be quite challenging for the practitioner.

A further difficulty relating to scale construction is the imbalance in the number of true and false items. In the L scale, all the items are scorable if answered "False"; on the K scale, 29 of 30 items are scored if answered "False"; and Scales 7, 8, and 9 have a ratio of approximately 3 to 1 of true compared with false items. The danger of this imbalance is that persons having response styles of either acquiescing ("yea-saying") or disagreeing ("naysaying") may answer according to their response style rather than to the content of the items. A more theoretically sound approach to item construction would have been to include an even balance between the number of true and false answers. Some authors (A. Edwards, 1957, 1964; D. Jackson et al., 1997) have even suggested that test results do not reflect psychological traits as much as generalized test-taking attitudes. Thus, a controversy has arisen over "content variance," in which an examinee is responding to the content of the items in a manner that will reflect psychological traits rather than "response-style variance," in which responses reflect more the examinee's tendency to respond in a certain biased direction. In a review of the literature, Koss (1979) concluded that, although response sets can and do exist, the examinee's tendency to respond accurately to the item content is far stronger. The MMPI-2 restandardization committee has also developed the Variable Response Inconsistency (VRIN) and True Response Inconsistency (TRIN) scales to help detect invalid profiles caused by inconsistent or contradictory responding. These scales have been specifically designed to detect either response acquiescence or response nonacquiescence and thus should help counter the potential complications resulting from imbalanced keying.

The difficulties associated with reliability and scale construction have led to challenges to the MMPI's validity. Rodgers (1972) has even referred to the MMPI as a "psychometric nightmare." However, although the psychometric difficulties have presented problems, this has been somewhat compensated by extensive validity studies. More specifically, the meanings of 2- and 3-point profile code types have been extensively researched, as have the contributions that the MMPI can make toward assessing and predicting specific problem areas. There are at least 8,000 studies investigating profile patterns, and this number is continually increasing (see, e.g., Butcher 2006a; DuAlba & Scott, 1993; Gallucci, 1994; J. Graham, Ben-Porath, & McNulty, 1999; McNulty, Ben-Porath, & Graham, 1998). These studies provide extensive evidence of the MMPI's construct validity. For example, elevations on Scales 4 (*Pd*) and 9 (*Ma*) have been associated with measures of impulsivity, aggression, substance abuse, and sensation seeking among adolescent inpatients (Gallucci, 1994). In addition, the degree to which individuals improve from psychotherapy was predicted based on elevations on the content scales of Anxiety (*ANX*) and Depression (*DEP*; Chisholm, Crowther, & Ben-Porath, 1997). Finally, high scores on Scale 0 (*Si*) have been associated with persons who have low self-esteem, social anxiety, and low sociability (Sieber & Meyers, 1992). Individual clinicians can consult research on code types to obtain specific personality descriptions and learn of potential problems to which a client may be susceptible. The extensiveness and strength of these validity studies have usually been regarded as major assets of the MMPI and are important reasons for its continued popularity.

In addition to studying the correlates of code type, another approach to establishing validity is to assess the accuracy of inferences based on the MMPI. Early studies by Kostlan (1954) and Little and Shneidman (1959) indicated that the MMPI is relatively more accurate than other standard assessment instruments, especially when the MMPI was combined with social case history data. This incremental validity of the MMPI has been supported in later reviews by Garb (1998b) and J. Graham and Lilly (1984). For example, the accuracy of neurologists' diagnoses was found to increase when they added an MMPI to their patient data (S. Schwartz & Wiedel, 1981). Garb (1998b) concluded that the MMPI was more accurate than social history alone, was superior to projectives, and that the highest incremental validity was obtained when the MMPI was combined with social history. In addition, incremental validity of the new MMPI-2 content scales has been found in that they both expanded on and increased the validity of the standard clinical scales (Barthlow, Graham, Ben-Porath, & McNulty, 1999; Ben-Porath, McCully, & Almagor, 1993). The restructured clinical scales have also been found to have better discriminant validity than the basic clinical scales (Sellbom, Ben-Porath, & Graham, 2006).

ASSETS AND LIMITATIONS

The previous discussion on reliability and validity highlights several issues associated with the MMPI. These include moderate levels of reliability, extensive length, and problems related to the construction of the scales, such as item overlap, high intercorrelations among scales, and multidimensional poorly defined variables. Some of the older criticisms of the original MMPI relating to obsolete norms, offensive items, and poorly worded items have been largely corrected with the publication of the MMPI-2 and MMPI-A. The MMPI also has a number of strengths along with other weaknesses.

One caution stemming from the construction of the original MMPI is that it generally does not provide much information related to normal populations. The items were selected on the basis of their ability to differentiate a bimodal population of normals from psychiatric patients. Thus, extreme scores can be interpreted with a high degree of confidence, but moderate elevations must be interpreted with appropriate caution. An elevation in the range of 1 standard deviation above the mean is more likely to represent an insignificant fluctuation of a normal population than would be the case if a normally distributed group had been used for the scale construction. This is in contrast to a test such as the California Personality Inventory (CPI), which used a more evenly distributed sample (as opposed to a bimodal one) and, as a result, can make meaningful interpretations based on moderate elevations. The MMPI-2 partially addresses this difficulty as it has used broad contemporary norms for its comparisons, combined with uniform T scores (Tellegen & Ben-Porath, 1992). However, evaluation of normals can be complicated by the observation that normal persons sometimes achieve high scores. Despite these difficulties, the use and understanding of nonclinical populations have been increasing (Keiller & Graham, 1993). In particular, uses have included screening personnel for sensitive jobs, such as air traffic controllers, police officers, and nuclear plant operators.

Although there have been a number of notable improvements with the MMPI-2, issues have been raised regarding comparability between the two versions. In defense of their comparability are the many similarities in format, scale descriptions, and items. In particular, Ben-Porath and Butcher (1989) found that the effects of rewriting 82 of the MMPI items for inclusion in the MMPI-2 were minimal. The rewritten items had no effect on any of the validity, clinical, or special scales when comparisons were made between administrations of the original and restandardized versions using college students. This finding provided some support for Butcher and Pope's (1989) contention that the MMPI-2 validity and clinical scales measure "exactly what they have always measured" (p. 11). Further studies have generally found that there are few differences based on individual scale comparisons (Ben-Porath & Butcher, 1989; Chojnacki & Walsh, 1992; Harrell, Honaker, & Parnell, 1992; L. Ward, 1991). Similarly, number of elevated scales between the two forms does not seem to be significantly different, and there has been 75%

agreement regarding whether a subject's profile was considered to be within normal limits (Ben-Porath & Butcher, 1989).

Despite these similarities, the use of the restandardization norms and the use of uniform T scores have created differences in 2-point codes among different population samples, including differences among 31% of the code types derived from general psychiatric patients (Butcher et al., 1989), 22% of peace officers (Hargrave, Hiatt, Ogard, & Karr, 1994), 39% to 42% of psychiatric inpatients (D. Edwards, Morrison, & Weissman, 1993; H. Weissman, 1992), and a full 50% of both university students (H. Weissman, 1992) and forensic populations (Humphrey & Dahlstrom, 1995). The greatest level of disagreements was for poorly defined code types (mild to moderate elevations combined with more than two "competing" scales). In contrast, well-defined code types (highly elevated and without "competing" third- or fourth-most elevated scales) had considerably higher concordance (Tellegen & Ben-Porath, 1993). This fact suggests that special care should be taken regarding poorly defined code types, and, if more than two scales are elevated, the meanings of the relatively high scales not included in the code should be given particular interpretive attention.

These discrepancies in code types seem to question the exact transferability of past code type research on the MMPI onto the more recent MMPI-2 (and MMPI-A). However, the most important question is the extent to which the MMPI-2 accurately describes an individual's relevant behaviors. The research that has been done on the MMPI-2 does support the conclusion that scores on the MMPI-2 predict the same sorts of behaviors that were found with the earlier MMPI. (Archer, Griffin, & Aiduk, 1995; Butcher et al., 2001; J. Graham et al., 1999; Timbrook & Graham, 1994). As research continues to explore the MMPI-2 (and MMPI-A) validity, it will progressively mean that interpretations based on these newer versions can rely on their own research base rather than having to depend on the earlier work done with the MMPI.

As highlighted in the previous section, a traditional asset of the MMPI/MMPI-2/MMPI-A has been extensive and ongoing code type studies. However, difficulties with these studies have been noted. First, some studies have tried to be extremely inclusive in deciding which codes to evaluate. In contrast, others have been quite restrictive (i.e., including only clearly defined code types). Inclusion/exclusion among the different studies has ranged from 24% to 99% (McGrath & Ingersoll, 1999a). The practical implication for clinicians is considering the degree to which their code type classifications parallel those of research. If specific clinicians are highly inclusive about what they consider to be interpretable code types, they may place unwarranted faith in their interpretations if the body of research they are drawing from has used quite restrictive criteria (i.e., J. Graham et al., 1999 used only well-defined code types). A further concern is that the mean effect size across studies was quite variable, with a high of .74 and low of .02 (McGrath & Ingersoll, 1999b; G. Meyer & Archer, 2001). In addition, effect sizes were found to vary among different scales and code types. Therefore, practitioners may not only be placing unwarranted faith in some of their interpretations, but also the validity of the interpretations they do make is likely to vary according to which scale/code type they are interpreting.

In all versions of the MMPI, the scale labels can be misleading because they use traditional diagnostic categories. A person might read a scale such as Schizophrenia and infer that a person with a peak on that scale, therefore, fits the diagnosis of schizophrenia. Although it was originally hoped that the MMPI could be used to make differential psychiatric diagnoses, it was soon found that it could not adequately perform this function. Thus, even though schizophrenics score high on Scale 8, so do other psychotic and nonpsychotic groups. Also, moderate elevations can occur for some normal persons. With each progressive edition of the *Diagnostic and Statistical Manual of Mental Disorders* (*DSM*; American Psychiatric Association [APA] 1968, 1980, 1994, 2000), the labels given to the scale names have become progressively more outdated. This potentially causes confusion related to diagnosis because the scales reflect these outdated categories. For example, Scales 1, 2, and 3 are called the *neurotic triad*, and Scale 7 is labeled *Psychasthenia*; yet clinicians are often faced with the need to translate these outdated designations into *DSM-IV-TR* (APA, 2000) terminology. This difficulty has been somewhat alleviated through research detailing the frequencies which various diagnoses derived from recent editions of the *DSM* occur on the different code types (Bagby, Marshall, Basso, Nicholson, Bacchiochi, & Miller, 2005; Morey, Blashfield, Webb, & Jewell, 1988; Vincent et al., 1983). *DSM-III/DSM-IV* translations have been further aided through the use of different content, supplementary, and restructured scales that allow for broader descriptions of symptom patterns (Barthlow et al., 1999; Butcher 2006a, 2006b; Butcher et al., 1990; Graham, 2006; C. Williams et al., 1992).

To compensate for the difficulties related to scale labels, clinicians should become aware of the current meanings of the scales based on research rather than the meanings implied by the often misleading scale titles. This approach can be aided in part by using scale numbers rather than titles. For example, Scale 8 suggests attributes such as apathy, feelings of alienation, philosophical interests, poor family relations, and unusual thought processes rather than schizophrenia. It is the clinician's responsibility to determine which of these attributes are most characteristic of the person being evaluated. Clinicians should also be aware of the relationships among scales as represented by the extensive research performed on 2- and 3-point code types. Usually the patterns or profiles of the scales are far more useful and valid than merely considering individual scale elevations. The extensive research in this area represents what is probably the strongest asset of the MMPI. This volume of work has prevented the MMPI from becoming obsolete and has been instrumental in transforming it from a test of psychiatric classification into a far more wide-band personality inventory.

A further significant asset is the MMPI's immense popularity and familiarity within the field. Extensive research has been performed in a variety of areas, and new developments have included abbreviated forms, new scales, the use of critical items, an adolescent version, and computerized interpretation systems. The MMPI has been translated into more than 50 languages and is available in numerous countries. Normative and validity studies have been conducted on several different cultural groups (see Butcher, 1996, 2004; Handel & Ben-Porath, 2000), which makes possible the comparison of data collected from varying cultures. In contexts where no norms have been developed, at least the test format lends itself to the development of more appropriate norms that can then be used in these contexts.

A complicating aspect of the MMPI is that interpretations often need to take into account many demographic variables (Schinka, LaLone, & Greene, 1998). It has been demonstrated that age, sex, race, place of residence, intelligence, education, and socioeconomic status are all related to the MMPI scales. Often the same relative elevation of profiles can have quite different meanings when corrections are made for demographic variables. Some of the more important and well researched of these are discussed later in the chapter (see the section titled "Use with Diverse Groups").

The advantages and cautions for using the MMPI, MMPI-2, and MMPI-A indicate that a considerable degree of psychological sophistication by clinicians is necessary. Both their assets and limitations need to be understood and taken into account. The limitations for the original MMPI are numerous and include moderately adequate reliability, heterogeneity of the clinical scales, offensive items, limited usefulness for normal populations, misleading labels for the scales, and excessive length. However, the limitations of the MMPI-2 are balanced by a number of significant assets. For example, the excessive length can be countered either by administering only the first 370 items (or the first 350 items for the MMPI-A) or by using the MMPI-2 Restructured Form (388 items). An additional important strength is the extensive research relating to the meanings of the different scales and the relationships among scales. Extensive strategies are also in place to help refine and expand the meanings of scale elevations by using alternative scales (content, Harris-Lingoes, supplementary). Further assets are the MMPI-2's familiarity in the field, the development of subgroup norms, and extensive research in specific problem areas. Of central importance is that the MMPI has repeatedly proven itself to have practical value for clinicians, especially because the variables that the scales attempt to measure are meaningful and even essential areas of clinical information. The over 10,000 studies on or using it, combined with its extensive clinical use, provide ample evidence of its popularity.

USE WITH DIVERSE GROUPS

Age

A significant feature of adolescent populations is a general elevation on many of the original MMPI scales. This was particularly true for scales related to level of energy (9) and rebellious acting out (4). These generally higher elevations have led to considerable controversy over whether adolescents have more actual pathology (based on external behavioral correlates) or whether they merely have higher scores without correspondingly higher pathology (Archer, 1984, 1987, 1992a; Janus, Tolbert, Calestro, & Toepfer, 1996).The controversy has encouraged efforts to more clearly understand behavioral correlates of adolescent profiles (Archer, 2005; Archer & Jacobson, 1993; Basham, 1992; Janus et al., 1996). The controversy has also led to the development of the MMPI-A. The general consensus seems to be that using the MMPI-A (and norms based on it) results in behavioral descriptions that are at least as accurate as descriptors based on the MMPI/MMPI-2 (Archer, 1992a, 1992b; Butcher et al., 1992; Janus et al., 1996; Weed, Butcher, & Williams, 1994).

Sometimes clinicians are faced with deciding whether to use the MMPI-2 or MMPI-A with 18-year-olds. If they are living independently and are relative mature, the MMPI-2 should be used (Graham, 2006). In contrast, if they are still living at home and are relatively immature, the MMPI-A is recommended.

As people age, they generally have reduced energy and greater focus on health concerns. Whereas this trend is reflected in scores on the MMPI-2 of older adults, these changes tend to be fairly small (less than 5 T scores) and clinically nonsignificant (Graham, 2006). As a result, using separate norms for older adults has not been recommended.

Ethnicity

The MMPI/MMPI-2 has been extensively studied to determine how appropriate it is to use with culturally divergent groups. This research has centered around both ethnically different (minority) groups within the United States as well as its use in different countries. There are a wide variety of possible reasons why persons from different cultural groups might score in a certain direction. Although scores may be due to the accurate measurement of different personality traits, they may also be the result of cultural tendencies to acquiesce by giving socially desirable responses, differing beliefs about modesty, role conflicts, or varying interpretations of the meaning of items. Profiles may also reflect the results of racial discrimination in that scales associated with anger, impulsiveness, and frustration may be elevated.

MMPI/MMPI-2 research on ethnic groups within the United States has centered on differences between African versus European Americans. Research on African American versus European Americans' MMPI performance has frequently indicated that African Americans are more likely to score higher on Scales *F*, 8, and 9 (Green & Kelley, 1988; Gynther & Green, 1980; Smith & Graham, 1981). This finding has resulted in considerable controversy over whether these differences indicate higher levels of actual pathology or merely reflect differences in perceptions and values without implying greater maladjustment. If the differences did not reflect greater actual pathology, then specialized subgroup norms would be required to correct for this source of error. However, reviews of over 30 years of research have concluded that, although African versus European American differences could be found for some populations, there was no consistent pattern to these differences across all populations (Greene, 1987, 1991; G. Hall, Bansal, & Lopez, 1999). What seemed of greater significance was the role of moderator variables, such as education, income, age, and type of pathology. When African American and European American psychiatric patients were compared according to level of education and type of pathology, their MMPI/MMPI-2 performances were the same (McNulty, Graham, Ben-Porath, & Stein, 1997; Timbrook & Graham, 1994). In other words, behavioral correlates between African American and European American MMPI performance have generally not found differences between the two groups. For example, ratings by clinicians (McNulty, Graham, Ben Porath, & Stein, 1997) and partners (Timbrook & Graham, 1994) were equally as accurate for both groups. In addition, the main behavioral features of 68/86 code types between African Americans and European Americans were the same (Clark & Miller, 1971). Furthermore, predictions based on African American and European American juvenile delinquents' MMPI scores were equally accurate for African Americans and European Americans (Green & Kelley, 1988; Timbrook & Graham, 1994). A final crucial finding has been that, even when mean differences have been found, they have been less than 5 *T* score points difference (G. Hall et al., 1999; Stukenberg, Brady, & Klinetob, 2000). The magnitude of this difference is not clinically meaningful. Based on the preceding findings, it would be premature to develop and use separate norms for African Americans. However, it still is important for clinicians to continually be aware of any possible culturally relevant factors (i.e., effects of discrimination) that may cause unique elevations in an individual African American's profile.

Native Americans scored higher on a number of MMPI-2 scales (*L*, *F*, *K*, 4, 8, 9, *HEA*, *BIZ*, *CYN*, *ASP*, *TRT*), a finding likely to reflect cultural differences rather than actual psychopathology (Robin, Greene, Albaugh, Caldwell, & Goldman, 2003). As a result, low elevations should be interpreted with caution. In contrast, once scores become higher than $T = 65$, the elevations are likely to reflect actual psychopathology.

Similar to African American versus European American comparisons, no consistent patterns have been found across different populations for Hispanics and Asian Americans. Differences between Latino Americans and European Americans have generally been found to be less than African American or European American differences (Greene, 1991). The largest difference was that male Latinos scored higher on Scale 5 than male European Americans (G. Hall et al., 1999). However, all differences were still less than 5 *T* score points (G. Hall et al., 1999). Given the reviews of ethnicity and the

MMPI/MMPI-2 (Graham, 2006; Greene, 1987, 1991; G. Hall et al., 1999; Schinka et al., 1998), these conclusions seem warranted:

- Even when ethnic differences have been found between various groups, overall these differences are less than 5 T score points (less than 10% of the variance) and are therefore not clinically meaningful.
- It would be premature to develop new norms for ethnic groups, particularly since moderator variables (socioeconomic standing [SES], age) seem to explain most of the variance in performance.
- It may at times be useful to consider the meanings of ethnic score differences for specific ethnic subgroups. For example, Latino workers' compensation cases may be more likely to somatize psychological distress as reflected by greater elevations on 1 (*Hs*), 2 (*D*), and 3 (*Hy*) than European Americans (DuAlba & Scott, 1993). In addition, higher *CYN* (Cynicism) and *ASP* (Antisocial Practices) found among African American as opposed to European American forensic populations are likely to represent clinically meaningful differences (Ben-Porath, Shondrick, & Stafford, 1995).
- Low scores for Native Americans are likely to reflect cultural factors rather than psychopathology, but higher elevations (above $T = 65$) are likely to reflect actual psychopathology.
- Future research should consider within-group ethnic differences including degree of identification with his or her ethnic group, acculturation, language fluency, perceived minority status, and degree to which they feel discriminated.
- More research needs to investigate the relationship between ethnicity and the many supplementary and content scales.

The MMPI/MMPI-2 has not only been used with ethnic groups within the United States; it has also been used in a wide variety of different countries. An important rationale for this use is that it is more efficient to adapt and validate the MMPI/MMPI-2 for a different country than go to the far more extensive effort of developing a whole new test for the culture. Examples of countries where adaptations have occurred include such diverse areas as China, Israel, Pakistan, South Africa, Chili, Mexico, and Japan (see Butcher, 1996). Whenever clinicians work with different cross-national groups, they should consult the specific norms that have been developed for use with these groups as well as become familiar with any research that may have been carried out with the MMPI on these groups. Useful sources are Butcher's (1996) *International Adaptations of the MMPI-2* and reviews of cross-cultural research by Greene (1987, 1991, pp. 338–354) and G. Hall et al. (1999).

ADMINISTRATION

The MMPI-2 can be administered to persons who are 16 years of age or older with an eighth-grade reading level. As noted, it is possible to administer the MMPI-2 to persons between the ages of 16 and 18, but adolescent norms need to be used. However, the preferred option for individuals between ages 14 and 18 is to have them take the MMPI-A. It is often helpful to augment the standard instructions on the MMPI-2 and MMPI-A booklets. In particular, examiners should explain to clients the reason for testing and how the results will be used. It might also be pointed out that the test was designed to determine whether someone has presented himself or herself in an either unrealistically positive or exaggeratedly disturbed manner. Thus, the best strategy is to request that examinees be as honest and as clear as possible. Finally, it might be clarified that some, or even many, of the questions might seem a bit unusual. They have been developed to assess individuals with a wide range of personality styles and problem presentations. If they do not apply to the person taking the test, this should be indicated with either a true or false response. Including this additional information is likely to result in less anxiety, more accurate responses, and greater rapport. Completion times for all persons taking the test should be noted.

The MMPI-2 and MMPI-A have only one booklet form, although these are available in either softcover or hardcover. Completion of the first 370 items on the MMPI-2 and first 350 items on the MMPI-A allows for the scoring of the basic validity and standard clinical scales. The final 197 MMPI-2 and 128 MMPI-A items are used for scoring different supplementary and content scales. An online computer administration is available through National Computer Systems. For persons who have special difficulties, an individual (Box) form and a tape-recorded form have been developed. The Box form is most appropriate for persons who have difficulties concentrating and/or reading. Each item is presented on a card, which the person is requested to place into one of three different sections to indicate a "true," "false," or "cannot say" response. The tape-recorded form is used for persons who have reading difficulties because of factors such as illiteracy, blindness, or aphasia.

The sometimes-prohibitive length of the MMPI has encouraged the development of numerous short forms. However, most of these have not been found to be sufficiently reliable or valid (Butcher & Hostetler, 1990; Butcher & Williams, 2000; J. Graham, 2000). One acceptable abbreviated form is to administer all the items necessary for scoring only the basic validity and standard clinical scales (e.g., the first 370 MMPI-2 items or the first 350 MMPI-A items). Two other options are to use either the 388-item MMPI-2 Restructured Form or a computer-adapted administration (Forbey & Ben-Porath, 2007).

Some clinicians allow the client to take the MMPI under unsupervised conditions (such as at home). Butcher and Pope (1989) stress that this is not recommended, for the following reasons:

- The conditions are too dissimilar from those used for the normative samples and any significant change in proceedings might alter the results.
- Clients might consult others to determine which answers to make.
- The clinician cannot be aware of possible conditions that might compromise reliability and validity.
- There is no assurance that the client will actually complete the protocol himself or herself.

Thus, any administration should closely follow the administration procedures used for the normative samples. This means providing clear, consistent instructions, ensuring that the directions are understood, providing adequate supervision, and making sure the setting will enhance concentration by limiting noise and potential interruptions.

INTERPRETATION PROCEDURE

The following eight steps are recommended for interpreting MMPI-2/MMPI-A profiles. These steps should be followed with a knowledge and awareness of the implications of age, culture, intellectual level, education, level of functioning as well as the reason, motivation, and context of assessment. While looking at the overall configuration of the test (Steps 4, 5, and 6), clinicians can elaborate on the meanings of the different scales and the relationships among scales by consulting the interpretive hypotheses associated with them. These can be found in later sections of this chapter on validity scales, clinical scales, and 2-point codes as well as in sections on the content, supplementary, and restructured scales. The discussion of the various scales and codes represents an integration and summary of both primary sources and the following MMPI-2/MMPI-A resources: Archer (2005); Butcher (2000, 2006b); Butcher et al. (2001); Friedman, Lewak, Nichols, and Marks (2000); J. Graham (2006); Greene (2000); and Greene and Clopton (1994). In particular, the subsections on treatment implications have drawn on the work of Butcher (1990), Freidman et al. (2000), and Greene and Clopton (1994). Occasionally, additional quite recent material and/or relevant reviews/meta-analyses have been cited either to update material related to scale descriptions or to highlight important areas of research.

Step 1. Completion Time

The examiner should note the length of time required to complete the test. For a mildly disturbed person who is 16 years or older with an average IQ and eighth-grade education, the total completion time for the MMPI-2 should be approximately 90 minutes. Computer administrations are usually 15 to 30 minutes shorter (60 to 75 minutes in total). The MMPI-A usually takes 60 minutes to complete with computer administrations taking 15 minutes less time (45 minutes in total). If 2 or more hours are required for the MMPI-2 or 1.5 or more for the MMPI-A, the next interpretive possibilities must be considered:

- Major psychological disturbance, particularly a severe depression or functional psychosis.
- Obsessive indecision.
- Below-average IQ or poor reading ability resulting from an inadequate educational background.
- Cerebral impairment.

If, however, an examinee finishes in less than 60 minutes, the examiner should suspect an invalid profile, an impulsive personality, or both.

Note any erasures or pencil points on the answer sheet. The presence of a few of these signs may indicate that the person took the test seriously and reduces the likelihood of random marking; a great number of erasures may reflect obsessive-compulsive tendencies.

Step 2. Score and Plot the Profile

Complete the scoring and plot the profile. Specific directions for tabulating the MMPI-2 raw scores and converting them into profiles are provided in Appendix D on page 621. If examiners would like to score and profile the content scales, Harris-Lingoes and *Si* content subscales, the most frequently used supplementary scales, restructured clinical scales, or the personality psychopathology five scales, additional keys and profile forms may be obtained through National Computer Systems. In addition to the possibility of scoring alternative scales, clinicians should compile further information, including IQ scores, relevant history, demographic variables, and observations derived from Steps 1 and 2.

Score the critical items and note which ones indicate important trends. It is often helpful at some point to review these items with the client and obtain elaborations. In particular, it is essential to determine whether the person understood what the item was asking. Similarly, it can sometimes be helpful to examine the answer sheet and note which, if any, questions were omitted. A discussion with the client about why he or she chose not to respond might shed additional light on how he or she is functioning psychologically and what areas are creating conflict for him or her.

Step 3. Organize the Scales and Identify the Code Type

The scores can be summarized by simply listing the scores according to the order in which they appear on the profile sheet (VRIN, TRIN, *L*, *Fb*, *Fp*, *L*, *K*, *S*, 1, 2, 3, etc.) with their *T* scores to the right of these scales. For the purposes of communicating scale scores, *T* scores rather than raw scores should be used.

Developing summary codes ("code types") provides a shorthand method of recording MMPI-2/MMPI-A results. Code types can be determined simply by looking at the two highest scale elevations. For example, the two highest scores in a profile might be 8 and 7 resulting in an 87/78 code type. The 87/78 code type can then be looked up in the Two-Point Codes section to obtain various descriptions relating to that code type. Note that Scales 5 (Masculinity-Femininity) and 0 (Social Introversion) are not strictly clinical scales, so they are not used in determining code type. Examiners should keep in mind that only well-defined code types can be safely interpreted (Butcher, 1999; D. Edwards et al., 1993; Greene, 2000; McNulty et al., 1998; Tellegen & Ben-Porath, 1993). A well-defined code type is considered one in which the elevated scales are above 65 and the scales used to determine the code type are 5 or more *T* score points above the next highest scales. Less well-defined profiles should be interpreted by noting each scale that is elevated and then integrating the meanings derived from the different descriptors.

Step 4. Determine Profile Validity

Assess the validity of the profile by noting the pattern of the validity scales. There are a number of indicators suggesting invalid profiles, which are described in the next section. However, the basic patterns include a defensive style in which pathology is minimized (elevated *L*, *K*, and *S* on the MMPI-2 and *L* and *K* on the MMPI-A), an exaggeration of pathology (elevated *F*, *Fb*, *Fp*, FBS on the MMPI-2 or *F*, *F1*, or *F2* on the MMPI-A), or an inconsistent response pattern (elevated VRIN or TRIN). In addition, clinicians should consider the context of the assessment to determine whether a defensive, fake bad, or inconsistent response style supports what is known about the client. In particular, the examiner should determine the likelihood that the examinee would potentially gain by over- or underreporting psychopathology.

Step 5. Determine Overall Level of Adjustment

Note the number of scales over 65 and the relative elevation of these scales. The degree to which *F* is elevated can also be an excellent indicator of the extent of pathology (assuming that it is not so high as to indicate an invalid profile). The greater the number and relative elevation of these scales, the more the individual is likely to have difficulties carrying out basic responsibilities and experience social and personal discomfort.

Step 6. Describe Symptoms, Behaviors, and Personality Characteristics

This step represents the core process in interpretation. Mild elevations on individual scales (*T* = 60–65) represent tendencies or trends in the individual's personality. Interpretations should be treated cautiously with the more extreme descriptors being deleted or rephrased to represent milder characteristics. Scores in this range on the MMPI-A are highlighted by shading, thereby designating a marginal or transitional zone between normality and pathology. Elevations above 65 on the MMPI-2 and MMPI-A are more strongly characteristic of the individual and, with progressively greater increases, are more likely to represent core features of personality functioning. However, basing interpretations solely on specific T score elevations may be misleading because a client's demographic characteristics or level of functioning might alter the interpretations. For example, a high-functioning professional with a mild to moderate score on 2 (depression) probably indicates a level of introspection and mild dysphoria that he or she is able to effectively control. In contrast, a similar elevation on a low-functioning psychiatric patient is more likely to reflect aspects of psychopathology. Furthermore, different authors use different criteria for determining high and low scores. Some authors have used T score ranges (e.g., $T = 70$–80); others have defined elevated scores as the upper quartile; and still others have defined a high score as the highest in a profile regardless of other T score elevations. As a result, the descriptors in the following sections on interpretation do not designate specific T score elevations. Instead, more general descriptions associated with high and low scores have been provided. Clinicians will need to interpret the accuracy of these potential meanings by taking into consideration not merely the elevations but other relevant variables as well. In addition, each of the descriptions is modal. They should be considered as possible interpretations that will not necessarily apply to all persons having a particular score. They are merely hypotheses in need of further verification. This point is highlighted by the finding that somewhere in the range of 40% of computer-generated descriptors do not apply to the person being assessed (Butcher et al., 2000).

Whereas T scores are not provided for most scale interpretations, they have been included in the subsection on validity scales. Validity T and sometimes raw scores are included because there is extensive research on optimal cutoff scores.

During the interpretive process, do not merely note the meanings of the individual scales but also examine the overall pattern or configuration of the test and note the relative peaks and valleys. Typical configurations, for example, might include the "conversion V," reflecting a possible conversion disorder or elevated Scales 4 and 9, which reflect a high likelihood of acting-out behavior. Note especially any scales greater than 65 or less than 40 as being particularly important for the overall interpretation. The meaning of 2-point code configurations can be determined by consulting the corresponding section in this chapter ("Two-Point Codes"). When working to understand the meaning of a profile with two or more elevated clinical scales, it is recommended that clinicians read the descriptors for the individual scales as well as relevant 2-point code descriptions. It is also recommended that, when reading about elevations on single scales, clinicians should read the meanings of high and low elevations as well as the more general information on the relevant scale. Further elaboration on the meaning of the scale elevations and code types can be obtained by scoring and interpreting the content scales, Harris-Lingoes, and *Si* subscales, supplementary scales, restructured clinical scales, and/or the critical items; these scales are discussed later in this chapter. When interpretive information is available, clinicians can examine an individual's profile in combination with the requirements of the referral questions to determine relevant descriptions for each of these areas.

Many of the client descriptions focus on client deficits. As a result, clinicians often struggle to translate these interpretations into everyday, client-friendly language. To assist with this, client feedback statements derived from Lewak et al. (1990) are included in the individual clinical scale descriptions. The language has been selected to be empathic, enhance rapport, and increase the possibility of client growth. These statements can also be edited to develop more client-focused interpretations for use in actual reports. For example, the statement "Your body is a source of constant worry and fear for you..." becomes "The client's body is a source of constant worry and fear for them..." (see description under "Scale 1/Hypochnodriasis"). Note that Scales 5 and 0 are not considered clinical scales; as a result, no client feedback statements have been included.

Clearly Defined Profiles

As noted previously, a clearly defined code type is indicated by both a high elevation and either single scales, which are elevated with no other "competing" scale elevations (so-called spike profiles), or clear code types in which the elevated scales in the code types similarly do not have competing scales that are close to the degree of elevations of the scales in the code. Well-defined elevations indicate greater validity of the relevant descriptors (McNulty et al., 1998). In addition, they are more likely to be stable over time (high test-retest reliability).

Poorly Defined Profiles

If the elevation is not particularly high (generally $T = 60–65$), the interpretations need to be modified by either toning down the descriptors to a more normal level or deleting the more extreme descriptors. Often the content, Harris-Lingoes, restructured clinical, and supplementary scales can be useful in understanding the meaning of elevations in the $T = 60–64$ range. If the profile is poorly defined because there are additional scales that "compete" with the scales in the code type (e.g., 27/72 code type but with Scales 1 and 8 also elevated nearly as high as Scales 2 and 7), several strategies need to be used. The safest and most conservative strategy is to consider descriptors that occur in common among all the different elevated scales as the most valid (e.g., anxiety is likely to be a common descriptor for elevations on Scales 1, 2, 7, and 8; this is strengthened if 7 is the most highly elevated scale). In addition, examiners need to make an effort to understand and integrate the interpretations given under each of the individual scale descriptions. Furthermore, the meanings of alternative code type combinations need to be considered and integrated (e.g., if Scales 2, 7, 1, and 8 are all elevated, these code type descriptors need to be considered: 27/72, 18/81, 87/78, 12/21, 17/71, and 28/82). Finally, with poorly defined elevations, it becomes increasingly important to use the content, Harris-Lingoes, supplementary, and restructured clinical scales to more fully understand and refine the meanings of the clinical scale elevations.

Use of Content Scales

The content scales can be used to supplement, extend, confirm, and refine interpretations derived from the basic validity and standard clinical scales. Furthermore, some of the content scales (e.g., TPA/Type A, WRK/Work Interference) provide additional information not included in the clinical scales. The adult content scales are divided into the clusters of internal symptoms, external aggressive tendencies, negative self-view, and general problem areas. Similarly, the adolescent content scales are divided into scales reflecting interpersonal functioning, treatment recommendations, and academic difficulties (see "Content Scales" section).

Harris-Lingoes and Si Subscales

To understand which personality and clinical variables of a person might have been responsible for elevating the clinical scales, clinicians might wish to selectively use the rationally devised Harris-Lingoes and Social Introversion subscales. These scales (or subscales) organize clusters of content-related items so that the different dimensions of the scales can be more clearly differentiated. For example, it might be found that an elevation on Scale 4 (Psychopathic Deviate) resulted primarily from family discord. In contrast, criminal acting out might be suggested by subscale elevations on authority conflict and social imperturbability. This would then have implications for both interpretations and case management (see "Harris-Lingoes Scales" section).

Critical Items

Clinicians may also wish to evaluate the meanings of content related to specific items the client has endorsed by investigating critical items (see scoring of "Critical Items" section).

Supplementary (Including Psychopathology Personality Five/PSY-5) Scales

The empirically derived supplementary scales can also be used to both refine the meanings of the clinical scales and add information not included in the clinical scales (see "Supplementary and PSY-5 Scales" sections).

Restructured Clinical Scales

The restructured clinical scales represent purer measures of the clinical scales. These purer measures were developed by extracting the common factor of demoralization. As such, elevations on these scales represent clearer measures of the types of variables the basic clinical scales are trying to measure. (see section, MMPI-2-Restricted Clinical Scales)

Low Scale Scores

Low scale scores (below T score of 35 or 40) on the clinical scales may represent strengths, and these strengths might correspond in an opposite direction to the interpretations for the high scores. For example, a low score on Scale 1 (Hypochondriasis) might suggest an absence of physical complaints and health-related concerns. However, research in this area is both minimal and equivocal. As a result, this area of interpretation has not been included in the interpretive statements. However, sufficient research is available for low scores on some of the validity scales and scales 5 (Masculinity/Femininity) and 0 (Social Introversion) such that interpretations have been included.

Specific Interpretive Guidelines Organized around Symptom Domains

The following topic areas and interpretive strategies are intended to be basic, rule-of-thumb approaches to help guide hypothesis generation around specific areas. There are certainly other relevant areas, but the ones listed can generally be considered the most important. These guidelines will serve to alert clinicians to specific areas, clinicians will still need to investigate these areas in far more depth by consulting relevant scale descriptors and patterns between scales. Clinicians may also wish to consult one of the MMPI-2/MMPI-A resources listed in the Recommended Readings to further extend and expand on the meanings of different profiles.

Suppression (Constriction). Scales 5 (*Mf*) and 0 (*Si*) are sometimes referred to as suppressor scales because, if either or both are elevated, they tend to suppress, or "soften," the expression of characteristics suggested by other elevated scores.

Acting Out (Impulsivity). In contrast to Scales 5 (*Mf*) and 0 (*Si*), Scales 4 (*Pd*) and 9 (*Ma*) are sometimes referred to as "releaser" or "excitatory scales." If one or both are elevated, the person is likely to act out difficulties. This hypothesis is further strengthened if 0 (*Si*) is also quite low.

Internalizing Coping Style. Similar to the preceding two guidelines are indicators of internalizing versus externalizing coping styles. If the combined scores for Scales 4 (*Pd*),

6 (*Pa*), and 9 (*Ma*) are lower than the combined scores for 2 (*D*), 7 (*Pt*), and 0 (*Si*), the individual can be considered to have an internalizing coping style.

Externalizing Coping Style. In contrast to the preceding, an individual who has combined scores on 4 (*Pd*), 6 (*Pa*), and 9 (*Ma*) that are greater than his or her combined scores on 2 (*D*), 7 (*Pt*), and 0 (*Si*) can be considered to have an externalizing coping style.

Overcontrol (Repression). Rigid overcontrol of impulses, particularly hostility, is suggested by elevations on 3 (*Hy*) and the *O-H* (Overcontrolled Hostility) supplementary scale.

Anger (Loss of Control). Angry loss of control is suggested by elevations on the ANG (Anger) content scale.

Subjective Distress. A general check on the degree of subjective stress a person is encountering can be determined by noting the degree to which scales 2 (*D*) and 7 (*Pt*) are elevated.

Anxiety. Elevations on Scale 7 (*Pt*), especially if 7 (*Pt*) is greater than 8 (*Sc*), suggest anxiety.

Depression. A high score on 2 (*D*) combined with a low score on 9 (*Ma*) is particularly indicative of depression.

Mania. A high score on 9 (*Ma*) combined with a low score on 2 (*D*) suggests mania.

Psychosis. A high score on 8 (*Sc*) and BIZ (Bizarre Mentation), especially if 8 (*Sc*) is 10 points or more higher than 7 (*Pt*), suggests psychosis.

Confusion and Disorientation. Elevations above $T = 80$ on F, 8 (*Sc*), and 7 (*Pt*) suggest a confused, disoriented state. Confusion can also be suggested if the mean for all eight clinical scales (this excludes Scales 5 and 0, as these are not strictly clinical scales) is greater than $T = 70$.

Suspicion and Mistrust. If 6 (*Pa*) is moderate to highly elevated and, especially if 6 is the highest scale, suspicion and mistrust is strongly indicated.

Introversion. Introversion is indicated by elevations on the 0 (*Si*) scale.

Obsessiveness. Obsessiveness is indicated by elevations on 7 (*Pt*; especially when this is the highest point) and elevations on the OBS (Obsessiveness) content scale.

Cynicism. Cynicism is indicated by elevations on the CYN (Cynicism) content scale.

Drug or Alcohol Problems. Elevations on Scales 4 (*Pd*), 2 (*D*), and 7 (*Pt*) are consistent with (although not diagnostic of) drug- and alcohol-related problems. Lifestyle and personality patterns consistent with, and suggesting proneness to drug and alcohol patterns, are indicated by elevations on MAC-R and the Alcohol Potential Scale (APS). Clear awareness of and open discussion of alcohol and/or drug problems are indicated by elevations on the Alcohol Acknowledgment Scale (AAS).

Quality and Style of Interpersonal Relations. Scales that are most useful for understanding the patterns of interpersonal relations include:

- 0 (*Si*; level of sociability, shyness, social avoidance, alienation).
- Social Discomfort Scale (SOD; social discomfort).
- 1 (*Hs*; complaining, critical, demanding, indirect expression of hostility, passive, preoccupied with self).
- 4 (*Pd*; good first impressions but use others for their own needs, outgoing, talkative, energetic but also shallow and superficial, and impulsive).
- 6 (*Pa*; moralistic, suspicious, hypersensitive, resentful, guarded).
- 8 (*Sc*; isolated from social environment, seclusive, withdrawn, inaccessible, feels misunderstood).
- Marital Distress Scale (MDS; presence of marital conflict).
- Dominance (*Do*; assertive, dominant, takes the initiative, confident).

Step 7. Provide Diagnostic Impressions

Although the original MMPI and the MMPI-2/MMPI-A have not been successful in leading directly to diagnosis, they can often contribute considerable information relevant to diagnostic formulations. In the section on code types, possible *DSM-IV-TR* diagnoses consistent with each code type have been included. Clinicians should consider these, along with additional available information, to help make an accurate diagnosis. In some contexts and for some types of referral questions, formal diagnosis will be relevant; but for other contexts and referral questions, formal diagnosis will be neither required nor appropriate (e.g., employment screening). A further review of the considerations and guidelines described in Step 6 might be useful in extracting relevant information for diagnosis.

Step 8. Elaborate on Treatment Implications and Recommendations

Often, one of the most valuable services a practitioner can provide is to predict the client's likelihood of benefiting from interventions. This typically means elaborating on the person's strengths and weaknesses, level of defensiveness, ability to form a treatment relationship, predicted response to psychotherapy (note especially *Es* [Ego Strength] and TRT scales), antisocial tendencies, and level of insight. Much of this information is summarized at the ends of the subsections on scale elevations and code types. If doing extensive work with specific types of clients, clinicians might need to expand on the knowledge relating to types and outcome of treatments by referring to the extensive research base that is available (e.g., chronic pain, substance abuse, outcomes related to specific code types). Butcher and Perry's (2008) *Psychological Assessment in Treatment Planning: Use of the MMPI-2 and BTPI* can be particularly helpful in this regard. Treatment responsiveness might be further extended into providing suggestions for tailoring specific interventions for client profiles and types of problems. Reviewing the areas, considerations, and guidelines described in Step 6 might be useful in extracting information relevant to treatment planning. A further useful resource in this process is Maruish's (1999) *Use of Psychological Testing for Treatment Planning and Outcome Assessment*. Lewak et al. (1990) not only provide suggestions for treatment but also outline a step-by-step procedure for translating MMPI-2 results into clear, relevant feedback for the client. These steps include specific issues for the client background and early life experiences and self-help suggestions. A listing of feedback statements derived from Lewak et al. (1990) is included in the individual scale descriptions (see "Step 6" section). These statements can be used to provide feedback in a user-friendly manner, which will be likely to increase rapport and optimize client growth. In addition, a manual by Finn (1996) for using the MMPI-2 as a therapeutic intervention is available (see also Finn, 2007).

COMPUTERIZED INTERPRETATION

Computerized interpretation systems are an important and frequently used adjunct to MMPI interpretation. The number of such services has grown considerably since 1965, when the first system was developed by the Mayo Clinic. Major providers are Pearson Assessments (previously National Computer Systems), Psychological Assessment Resources, Caldwell Report, Western Psychological Services, Psychometric Software, Psych Screen, Automated Assessment Associates, and BehaviorData. A description and evaluation of many of these services are included in past and current editions of the *Mental Measurements Yearbook* (the most recent/17th edition was edited by Geisinger et al., 2007) and a review by Williams and Weed (2004). The best sources will be the most recent listings found in test publisher catalogs (see Appendix A on p. 605) or on service provider Web sites.

Caution in the use of different computer-based interpretive systems is important because the interpretive services and software packages are highly variable in terms of quality, and most have untested or only partially tested validity. Many do not specify the extent to which they were developed using empirical guidelines versus clinical intuition. Each computerized system has a somewhat different approach. Some provide screening, descriptive summaries, and cautions related to treatment, whereas others provide extensive elaborations on interpretations or may provide optional interpretive printouts for the clients themselves. Even the best programs will produce a combination of accurate as well as inaccurate interpretations (Butcher et al., 2000).

The rationale behind computerized systems is that they are efficient and can accumulate and integrate large amounts of information derived from the vast literature on the MMPI, which even experienced clinicians cannot be expected to recall. However, questions have been raised regarding misuse (Groth-Marnat, 1985; Groth-Marnat & Schumaker, 1989). In particular, computerized services are limited to standard interpretations and are not capable of integrating the unique variables usually encountered in dealing with clinical cases. This is a significant factor, which untrained personnel may be more likely to either overlook or inadequately evaluate. In response to these issues, the American Psychological Association developed a set of guidelines to ensure the proper use of computerized interpretations (American Psychological Association, 1986, 1994). It should be stressed that although computerized systems can offer information from a wide variety of accumulated data, their interpretations are still not end products. Like all test data, they need to be placed in the context of the client's overall background and current situation and integrated within the framework of additional test data (see Lichtenberger, 2006; McMinn, Ellens, et al., 1999).

VALIDITY SCALES

The MMPI was one of the first tests to develop scales to detect whether respondents were answering in such a manner as to invalidate the overall results. This tradition has continued and been expanded in the MMPI-2 and MMPI-A. Meta-analyses of studies on the various validity scales generally indicate that they are able to detect faking effectively. Probably the most effective strategy is the F scale's ability to detect overreporting of pathology (R. Baer, Kroll, Rinaldo, & Ballenger, 1999; Bagby, Buis, & Nicholson, 1995; Iverson, Franzen, & Hammond, 1995; G. Meyer & Archer, 2001). The K scale, while still useful, is somewhat less effective in detecting underreporting (R. Baer, Wetter, & Berry, 1992; Putzke, Williams, Daniel, & Boll, 1999). However, adding supplementary validity scales (Social Desirability scale, Superlative scale) to L and K can serve to increase the detection of underreporting (Bagby, Rogers, Nicholson, et al., 1997). Despite the consensus related to the accuracy of detection, a concern is that a wide range of cutoff scores are recommended depending on the group being assessed (Bagby et al., 1994, 1995; L. Stein, Graham, & Williams, 1995). For example, optimal cutoff scores for normals faking bad are lower than psychiatric patients faking bad (Berry, Baer, & Harris, 1991; J. Graham et al., 1991). An unresolved issue is whether normals who are motivated to fake bad as well as given information on how to fake (e.g., symptom patterns of individuals with posttraumatic stress disorder, paranoid schizophrenia, schizophrenia) can avoid detection. Some research indicates that, even with motivation and a clear strategy, they still cannot avoid detection (Wetter, Baer, Berry, Robinson, & Sumpter, 1993), whereas other research suggests that strategic (informed) fakers can consistently produce profiles that are indistinguishable from true patients (R. Rogers, Bagby, & Chakraborty, 1993; Wetter & Deitsch, 1996). Attempts to fake bad might be particularly likely to succeed if subjects are given information on the design and intent of the validity scales (Lamb, Berry, Wetter, & Baer, 1994) and are familiar with the type of disorder they are faking (Bagby, Rogers, Buis, et al., 1997).

It should be noted that the MMPI-2 provides the option of profile sheets that can include either *K* corrections or sheets that omit this procedure. The MMPI-A does not include the *K* correction on its profile sheets because, in some contexts, particularly those for adolescents, the *K* correction is not appropriate (Colby, 1989).

? "Scale" (Cannot Say; *Cs*)

The ? scale (abbreviated by either ? or *Cs*) is not actually a formal scale but merely represents the number of items left unanswered on the profile sheet. The MMPI-2 does not even include a column for profiling a ? (*Cs*) scale but merely provides a section to include the total number of unanswered questions. The usefulness of noting the total number of unanswered questions is to provide one of several indices of a protocol's validity. If 30 or more items are left unanswered, the protocol is most likely invalid and no further interpretations should be attempted. This is simply because an insufficient number of items have been responded to, which means less information is available for scoring the scales. Thus, less confidence can be placed in the results. To minimize the number of "cannot say" responses, the client should be encouraged to answer all questions.

High number of ? (30+)

* Difficulties with reading, psychomotor retardation, indecision, confusion, or extreme defensiveness (consistent with severe depression, obsessional states, extreme intellectualization, or unusual interpretations of the items).
* Legalistic overcautiousness or a paranoid condition.
* Perception that the unanswered items are irrelevant.

VRIN (Variable Response Inconsistency Scale)

The VRIN comprises pairs of selected questions that would be expected to be answered in a consistent manner if the person is approaching the testing in a valid manner. Each pair of items is either similar or opposite in content. It would be expected that similar items would be answered in the same direction. If a person answers in the opposite direction, then it indicates an inconsistent response and is, therefore, scored as 1 raw score on the VRIN scale. Pairs of items with opposite contents would be expected to be answered in opposite directions. If, instead, these pairs are answered in the same direction, this would represent inconsistent responding, which would also be scored as 1 raw score point on the VRIN scale.

High VRIN (MMPI-2 *T* = 80; MMPI-A *T* = 80) or Moderate (MMPI-2 70–79; MMPI-A 70–74)

* Indiscriminate responding; profile should be considered invalid and should not be interpreted (especially if *F* is also high).

TRIN (True Response Inconsistency Scale)

The MMPI-2 and MMPI-A TRIN scales are like the VRIN scale in comprising pairs of items. However, only pairs with opposite contents are included. This means there would be two ways for a person to obtain a response that would be scored on the VRIN scale. A "True" response to both items would indicate inconsistency and would, therefore, be scored as plus 1 raw score point. A "False" response to both pairs would also indicate inconsistency but would be scored as minus 1 point (negative scores are avoided by adding a constant).

Very High (MMPI-2 $T = 80$; MMPI-A $T = 80$) or Moderate (MMPI-2 70–79; MMPI-A 70–74)

- Person is indiscriminately answering "True" to the items (acquiescence or yea-saying).

F Scale (Infrequency)

The F (Infrequency) scale measures the extent to which a person answers in an atypical and deviant manner. The MMPI and MMPI-2 F scale items were selected based on their endorsement by less than 10% of the population. Thus, from a statistical definition, they reflect nonconventional thinking. This nonconventional thinking may include endorsing items that all rules should be thrown away or that the examinee would like to visit novel places. These items do not cohere around any particular trait or syndrome. High scores indicate the examinee is answering in a scorable direction to a wide variety of unusual characteristics. As might be expected, high scores on F are typically accompanied by high scores on many of the clinical scales. High scores can often be used as a general indicator of pathology. In particular, high scores can reflect unusual feelings caused by some specific life circumstance to which the person is reacting. This might include grieving, job loss, or divorce. A person scoring high may also be "faking bad," which could serve to invalidate the protocol. No exact cutoff score is available to determine whether a profile is invalid or is accurately reflecting pathology. Even T scores from 70 to 90 do not necessarily reflect an invalid profile, particularly among prison or inpatient populations. In general, moderate elevations represent an openness to unusual experiences and possible psychopathology, but it is not until more extreme elevations that an invalid profile is suspected. Further information can be obtained by consulting the F back scale (see section entitled "*Fb* (*F* back) Scale").

The 66-item MMPI-A F scale was constructed similar to the MMPI-2 F scale. However, because adolescents are more likely to endorse unusual experiences, a more liberal criterion of 20% endorsement was used for inclusion. The MMPI-A F scale was further divided into $F1$ scales to assess validity for the first portion of the booklet (clinical scales) and $F2$ to assess the last portion of the book (supplementary and content scales; $F1$ and $F2$).

High Scores on F (approximating $T = 100$; fake bad cutoff for inpatients = 100, cutoff for outpatients $T = 90$, cutoff for nonclinical settings $T = 80$; cutoff for MMPI-A = 79)

- Invalid profile, possibly caused by clerical errors in scoring, random responding, false claims by the client regarding symptoms, resistance to testing, malingering.
- Extremely high F (100+); may possibly accurately reflect psychopathology, but this will correspond with possible hallucinations, delusions of reference, poor judgment, disorientation, restlessness, dissatisfaction, and/or extreme withdrawal (check for consistency with history).

Moderate Scores ($T = 70$–90)

- Attempt to draw attention to distress as a "cry for help" (and are in need of assistance).

- Unconventional and unusual thoughts, may be rebellious, antisocial, and/or having difficulties in establishing a clear identity.
- Slightly elevated ($T = 65$ to 75) and person does not seem to be pathological, he or she might be curious, complex, psychologically sophisticated, opinionated, unstable, and/or moody.

Low Scores on F

- Clients perceive the world as most other people do.
- Possible denial of difficulties if their history indicates psychopathology ("faking good"; note the relative elevation on K and L).

Fb (F back) Scale (MMPI-2); F1 and F2 (MMPI-A)

The 40-item MMPI-2 Fb was designed to identify a "fake bad" mode of responding for the last 197 items. This might be important because the traditional F scale was derived only from items taken from what are now the first 370 questions on the MMPI-2. Without the Fb scale, no check on the validity of the later questions would be available. It might be possible for a person to answer the earlier items accurately and later change to an invalid mode of responding. This is important for the supplementary and content scales because many of them are derived either partially or fully from the last 197 questions. The Fb scale was developed in the same manner as the earlier F scale in that items with low endorsement frequency (less than 10% of nonpatient adults) were included. Thus, a high score suggests the person was answering the items in an unusual mode. As with the F scale, this could indicate either generalized pathology or that the person was attempting to exaggerate his or her level of symptomatology.

Somewhat similar to the MMPI-2, the MMPI-A includes a 66-item F scale that is divided into $F1$ and $F2$ subscales. The $F1$ scale is composed of 33 items, all of which appear on the first half (initial 236 items) of the MMPI-A booklet, and relates to the standard clinical scales. In contrast, the 33-item $F2$ scale is composed of items on the last half of the booklet (final 114 items) and relates to the supplementary and clinical scales. The $F1$ and $F2$ scales can be interpreted in much the same way as for F and Fb on the MMPI-2. However, the Fb scale has not been found to be as effective a predictor of malingering as the F scale (Iverson et al., 1995).

High Fb (and $F1$ and $F2$; $T = 90$ for nonclinical settings and 110 for clinical settings)

- Possible exaggeration of psychopathology (see considerations under "F Scale").

Fp (Infrequency-Psychopathology) Scale

Because the F scale is typically elevated among psychiatric patients, it is often difficult to differentiate between persons with true psychopathology and those who have some psychopathology but are nonetheless faking bad. This is particularly true if the psychopathology is quite severe. The history of the person (e.g., degree of preexisting psychopathology) and context of the referral (e.g., possible gain for faking bad) can often be quite useful in making this distinction. To further assist with this differentiation, Arbisi and Ben-Porath (1995) developed a set of 27 items that were infrequently answered even by psychiatric inpatients. (In contrast, the F scale was developed from infrequently answered questions by the normative sample.)

High Fp ($T = 94$ for men and $T = 97$ for women)

- Faking psychopathology among psychiatric patients.

Fake Bad Scale (*FBS*)

The fake bad scale (*FBS*) was developed in the hopes that it could detect personal injury claimants who were exaggerating their difficulties (Lees-Haley, English, & Glenn, 1991). Research has been equivocal with concerns related to false positives (Rogers, Sewell, Martin, & Vitacco, 2003). In contrast, other studies have provided more supportive research (Greiffenstein, Fox, & Lees-Haley, 2007) and indicate it is one of the best MMPI-2 scales for detecting faking (Nelson, Sweet, & Demakis, 2006).

High *FBS* (moderately indicative if raw score = 22, more strongly indicated by a raw score = 28)

- Fake bad/malingering. Raw scores of 28 or higher reduce the possibility of false positives.

L (Lie) Scale

The *L* or lie scale consists of 15 items that indicate the extent to which a client is attempting to describe himself or herself in an unrealistically positive manner. Thus, high scorers describe themselves in an overly perfectionistic and idealized manner. The items consist of descriptions of relatively minor flaws to which most people are willing to admit. Thus, persons scoring high on the *L* scale might state that they never get angry or that they like everyone they meet.

High Scores on *L* (*T* = 65)

- Person is describing self in an overly favorable light due to conscious deception.
- Person is describing self an overly favorable light due to an unrealistic view of himself or herself; may be inflexible, unoriginal, and unaware of the impressions he or she makes on others; perceives world in a rigid, self-centered manner.
- Poor insight due to denial of flaws.
- Low tolerance to stress.
- Poor candidates for psychotherapy.
- Extremely high scores would suggest that such persons are ruminative, extremely rigid, and will experience difficulties in relationships (i.e., paranoids who place considerable emphasis on denying their personal flaws and instead project them onto others).
- Extremely high scores might be due to conscious deception by antisocial personalities.

Low Scores on *L* (*T* = 35–45)

- Frank and open regarding responses to items.
- Able to admit minor faults in themselves, may also be articulate, relaxed, socially ascendant, and self-reliant.
- Possibly somewhat sarcastic and cynical.

K (Correction) Scale

The *K* scale was designed to detect clients who are describing themselves in overly positive terms. It, therefore, has a similarity with the *L* scale. The *K* scale, however, is more subtle and effective. Whereas only naive, moralistic, and unsophisticated individuals would score high on *L*, more intelligent and psychologically sophisticated persons might have somewhat high *K* scores and yet be unlikely to have any significant elevation on *L*.

Moderate scorers often have good ego strength, effective emotional defenses, good contact with reality, and excellent coping skills. Typically, they are concerned with, and often skilled in, making socially acceptable responses. As might be expected, K scores are inversely related to scores on Scales 8, 7, and 0. Elevations on K can also represent ego defensiveness and guardedness. This might occur with persons who avoid revealing themselves because of their personality style or because something might be gained by conveying a highly favorable impression (e.g., employment, child custody evaluations). There is no clear cutoff for differentiating among positive ego strength (adjustment), ego defensiveness, and faking good. A general guideline is that the more ego-defensive the person is, the more likely it is that some of the clinical scales might also be elevated. Helpful information can also be obtained through relevant history and the context of the testing (legal proceedings, employment evaluation, etc.).

Because a defensive test-taking approach is likely to suppress the clinical scales, a K correction is added to five of the MMPI-2 clinical scales (1/*Hs*, 4/*Pd*, 7/*Pt*, 8/*Sc*, 9/*Ma*) to compensate for this defensiveness. This correction is obtained by taking a designated fraction of K and adding it to the relevant scale (see directions in Appendix C on pp. 611–619). However, the basis of the K correction has been called into question. It has been omitted from the MMPI-A, and the MMPI-2 contains separate scoring sheets with and without the K correction so that examiners can decide whether they wish to use it.

High Scores on K ($T = 65$ or 70)

- Person is attempting to describe self in an overly favorable light, denying difficulties.
- May have aswered false to all items (naysaying; check TRIN and VRIN).
- If profile is considered valid, persons are presenting an image of being in control and functioning effectively, but they will overlook any faults they might have.
- Likely to have poor insight and resist psychological evaluation, limited benefit from psychotherapy.
- Intolerant of nonconformity in others, may perceive nonconformists as weak.
- Use of denial, poor insight, unaware of the impression he or she makes on others.
- Shy, inhibited, low level of social interaction (check *Si*).

Moderate Scores on K ($T = 56$–64)

- Moderate levels of defensiveness.
- Potential positive qualities: independent, self-reliant, express an appropriate level of self-disclosure, have good ego strength, good verbal ability and social skills.
- Might admit to some "socially acceptable" difficulties but minimize other important conflicts.
- Unlikely to seek help.
- Moderate scores in adolescents contraindicate acting out.

Low Scores on K

- Fake bad profile, exaggeration of pathology (check F, Fb, $F1$, and $F2$).
- In an otherwise valid profile, client might be disoriented and confused, extremely self-critical, cynical, skeptical, dissatisfied, and have inadequate defenses.
- Poor self-concept, low level of insight.
- Low scores among adolescents are not uncommon and may reflect a greater level of openness and sensitivity to their problems, consistent with their undergoing a critical self-assessment related to establishing a clear sense of identity.

S (Superlative) Scale

Because the *K* and *L* scales have been found to be only moderately effective in differentiating persons who fake good, the S scale was developed in the hopes that it might more accurately identify those persons attempting to appear overly virtuous (Butcher & Han, 1995). The 50 items of the scale were developed by noting the differences in item endorsement between persons in an employment situation who were likely to be presenting themselves in an extremely favorable light (i.e., airline pilots applying for a job) and the responses of the normative sample. The resulting 50 items relate to contentment with life, serenity, affirming human goodness, denial of irritability/anger, patience, and denial of moral flaws. Thus, persons endorsing a high number of these items are presenting themselves as getting along very easily with others, being free from psychological problems, and having a strong belief in human goodness.

The scale does seem to be effective in discriminating nonpatients who were requested to present themselves in an extremely favorable light (pretending they were applying for a highly desired job) from those who were requested to respond in an honest manner (R. Baer, Wetter, Nichols, et al., 1995). However, the *L* and *K* scales are equally as good in detecting clinical populations who are underreporting psychopathology (R. Baer & Miller, 2002; R. Baer, Wetter, & Berry, 1995).

CLINICAL SCALES

Scale 1. Hypochondriasis (*Hs*)

Scale 1 was originally designed to distinguish hypochondriacs from other types of psychiatric patients. Although it can suggest a diagnosis of hypochondriasis, it is most useful as a scale to indicate a variety of personality characteristics that are often consistent with, but not necessarily diagnostic of, hypochondriasis.

High Scores on Scale 1

- High concern with illness and disease.
- Rarely act out directly but express hostility indirectly, likely to be critical of others.
- Complaints usually related to a wide variety of physical difficulties; complaints are vague and diffuse and will often shift to various locations on their bodies.
- Complaints typically include epigastric complaints, pain, fatigue, and headaches.
- Complaints are used to manipulate and control others, thereby creating interpersonal distress.
- Symptoms are usually not reactions to situational stress but more of long-standing duration.
- Moderate scores may have a true organic basis for their difficulties, but they are still likely to exaggerate their physical difficulties.
- Typically experience little overt anxiety.
- Stubborn, pessimistic, narcissistic, and egocentric.
- Egocentric, immature, pessimistic, sour, whiny, and passive-aggressive.
- Perceived by others as dull, unenthusiastic, ineffective, and unambitious.
- Level of efficiency is reduced, but they are rarely completely incapacitated.
- Overuse the medical system. Histories usually reveal numerous visits to a wide variety of practitioners. They will recite a long series of symptom complaints (sometimes referred to as an "organ recital").

- Refuse to believe assurances that their difficulties have no organic basis.
- Investigate for possible prescription medication abuse.
- Extremely high scores suggest person has a wide variety of symptom-related complaints, extremely constricted (possibly consistent with psychotic-like features [schizoid, schizoaffective, schizophrenic, psychotic depression] who is having bodily delusions; check elevations on Scales 6, 7, 8, and 9).

Related Scale Elevations
- Often elevated along with Scales 2, 3, and 7; reflects corresponding levels of depression, denial, conversions, or anxiety states.
- If Scale 7 is elevated, indicates better prognosis for psychotherapy, clients' level of anxiety is high enough to motivate them to change.
- "Conversion V" (elevations on Scales 1 and 3 with a significant lowering of 10 or more points on 2); person converts psychological conflicts into bodily complaints (see 13/31 code type).

Treatment Implications
- Have often rejected and criticized the "help" that has been offered to them.
- Resist any suggestion that their difficulties are even partly psychologically based.
- Psychotherapy is usually difficult due to their poor insight.
- Pessimistic about being helped, argumentative with professional staff (confirm/disconfirm this by checking the TRT/Negative Treatment Indicators content scale).
- Require repeated assurance that they have been well understood and that their symptoms will not be ignored.
- Framing interventions with biomedical terminology may make interventions more acceptable (e.g., biofeedback procedures might be described as "neurological retraining").

Client Feedback Statements[†]   Your body is a constant source of anxiety and fear for you, so right now your worries about health take up most of your time and energy. So much of your time is spent worrying about your physical well-being that it is hard for you to accomplish anything, to find outside interests or things you can do that will not incur additional pain. You also may consult a number of physicians for your symptoms without any benefit or relief. Your apprehension and concern about your physical health may leave you feeling somewhat defeated, pessimistic, and bitter. When people try to force you not to focus on your physical problems, you tend to resist them. You feel they do not understand what you are going through. Financial worries, family problems, confrontations, or heavy responsibilities tend to aggravate your physical problems. You may have developed a number of ways to get people to help you. At the same time, however, you resent not being able to do things for yourself. People with your profiles often had periods during childhood when they were seriously ill or extremely frightened by the possibility of being physically harmed. Perhaps an explosive or abusive parent or perhaps a serious accident or illness in the family predisposed you to this fear for your physical well-being. When your physical problems and fears seem to get worse, see if, in fact, you are not angry or even afraid of something else. Try to enjoy the times you do feel physically well. Give yourself permission to let go of your fears about your body whenever you feel well.

MMPI-A Considerations   The preceding descriptors are relevant for adolescent profiles. They also suggest school-related difficulties. Girls are likely to experience family problems (marital disagreements, financial concerns) and eating disorders. However, elevations on this scale are relatively rare among adolescents.

Scale 2. Depression (*D*)

The 57 items of Scale 2 relate to brooding, physical slowness, subjective feelings of depression, mental apathy, and physical malfunctioning. High scores may indicate difficulties in one or more of these areas. Patients seeking inpatient psychiatric treatment are most likely to have Scale 2 as the highest point on their profiles. As would be expected, elevations on 2 typically decrease after successful psychotherapy. The relative elevation on Scale 2 is the single best predictor of a person's level of satisfaction, sense of security, and degree of comfort. Persons who score high on 2 are usually described as self-critical, withdrawn, aloof, silent, and retiring. Adolescents typically score slightly lower than nonpatient adults whereas older adults score 5 to 10 points higher.

High Scores on Scale 2
- Suggests reactive depression (particularly if 2 is the only high point).
- Confronting difficulties with pessimism, helplessness, and hopelessness; this may be part of characteristic personality features exaggerated due to current problems.
- Sense of inadequacy, poor morale, difficulty concentrating; may be severe enough to create difficulties in working effectively.
- Depression can be seen as both a symptom as well as a means of coping by numbing self to future painful feelings or situations.
- Retiring, shy, aloof, timid, inhibited but also irritable, high-strung, and impatient.
- Highly sensitive to criticism.
- Avoid confrontations at all costs, possibly avoiding interpersonal relationships in general.
- Conventional, cautious, passive, and unassertive; higher scores indicate an exaggeration of these trends.
- Excessive worry over even minor problems.
- Possibly impaired ability to deal effectively with interpersonal problems.
- Possible psychomotor retardation, lethargy, and withdrawal.
- Possible preoccupation with death and suicide; check to determine possible inpatient treatment based on whether client is danger to self.

Related Score Elevations
- Elevated Scales 1, 2, and 3 are referred to as the neurotic triad: wide variety of complaints, including not only depression but also somatic complaints, irritability, difficulties with interpersonal relationships, work-related problems, and general dissatisfaction (see code types 12/21, 13/31, 23/32).
- Associated elevation on 7 (2 and 7 referred to as the distress scales): index of personal pain, anxiety, and discomfort, tense, nervous, intropunitive, self-critical; favorable sign for psychotherapy since person is motivated to change and is introspective and self-aware (see code types 27/72).
- Elevations on Scales 2 and 8: depression is characterized by unusual thoughts, disaffiliation, isolation, and alienation (see code type 28/82).
- Corresponding elevations on 1 (also HEA, and Harris-Lingoes *D*3/Physical Malfunctioning): variety of somatic complaints including feeling sluggish, tense, low energy.

Treatment Implications

- Check for whether external (reactive) or internal (endogenous) factors are responsible for depression.
- Check for relative contribution of cognitions, social support, and the prevalence of vegetative symptoms; focus treatment accordingly.
- Check for suicide potential, particularly if the elevations are high to extremely high with corresponding elevations on 4, 7, 8, and/or 9 (note that no clear "suicidal profile" accurately predicts suicide). Any suggestion of suicidal behavior on the profile should be investigated further through a careful assessment of additional relevant variables (demographics, presence, clarity, lethality of plan, etc.).
- Moderate depression possible positive sign for psychotherapy since clients are likely to be highly motivated (but check possible negative indicators with elevations on TRT/Negative Treatment Indicators, *L*, *K*, and 1), but extremely high score may indicate they are too depressed to experience sufficient motivation to change.

Client Feedback Statements[†]   You are generally a thoughtful, circumspect, and analytical person who takes life and responsibilities very seriously. However, right now some of your strengths may be working against you, for you are feeling very dejected, gloomy, and depressed. You are probably spending most of your time thinking about things you have done or said and feeling hopeless about things ever changing. While you may be able to do some basic chores, you may find little motivation to pursue enjoyable activities. In fact, low energy is probably a cause of concern to you. Unfortunately, you probably blame yourself for your loss of energy and lack of interest. This compounds your sense of hopelessness, helplessness, and despair. At the same time, your sadness and despair helps to make you feel numb as a means of protecting you from future painful feelings and situations. By not allowing yourself to experience hope, you can protect yourself from future losses. Your sleep may be constantly interrupted so you awaken feeling tired and without energy. Your appetite may be markedly diminished, or you may take comfort in eating. Your interest in sex may be low. You may find it difficult to concentrate, make decisions, and plan for the future. Try to find small rewards and pleasures that you can give yourself on a daily basis and keep a record of these. When you feel pessimistic about the future, force yourself (if necessary) to write down some of the things that have gone well for you recently, so you can keep things in perspective. Try to stop constantly blaming yourself for things you think have gone wrong. Begin a regular exercise program. Keep a record of your accomplishments and things that you have done well.

MMPI-A Considerations   The preceding MMPI-2 descriptors and use of the Harris-Lingoes scales are also relevant for adolescents, particularly for girls. In addition, high adolescent scores on 2 suggest school-related difficulties (check A-sch/School Problems content scale) and a worsening of arguments between their parents (check_A-fam/Family Problems content scale). They are less likely to act out but more likely to report eating problems (especially females), somatic complaints, and low self-esteem. Interpersonally, they will be introverted with a few friends.

Scale 3. Hysteria (*Hy*)

Scale 3 was originally designed to identify patients who had developed a psychogenically based sensory or motor disorder. The 60 items primarily involve specific physical complaints and a defensive denial of emotional or interpersonal difficulties. The types of physical complaints are generally quite specific and include areas such as fitful sleep, nausea, vomiting, headaches, and heart or chest pains (check HEA/Health Concerns scale). The important feature of persons who score high on this scale is that they simultaneously report specific physical complaints but also use a style of denial in which they may even express an exaggerated degree of optimism. One of the important and primary ways in which they deal with anxiety and conflict is to channel or convert these difficulties onto the body. Thus, their physical complaints serve as an indirect expression of these conflicts. Their traits might be consistent with a histrionic personality in that they will demand affection and social support but do so in an indirect and manipulative manner. They are also likely to be socially uninhibited and highly visible. They can easily initiate relationships, yet their relationships are likely to be superficial. They will approach others in a self-centered and naive manner. They might act out sexually or aggressively but have a convenient lack of insight into either their underlying motives or their impact on others. However, Scale 3 is quite heterogeneous in its item composition. The Harris-Lingoes item analysis has divided these into denial of social anxiety, need for affection, lassitude-malaise, somatic complaints, and inhibition of aggression. If Scale 3 is clearly elevated and a clinician is unclear regarding the meaning of the elevation, it can often be useful to formally score the Harris-Lingoes subscales (see section on Harris-Lingoes subscales).

High Scores on Scale 3

- Extraverted, dramatic, attention seeking.
- Highly conforming, immature, naive, childishly self-centered, impulsive.
- Strong needs for approval, support, and affection; will attempt to obtain these through indirect and manipulative means, interpersonally indirect.
- Difficulty expressing hostility and resentment.
- Will communicate with others to create an impact rather than to convey specific information.
- Will perceive events globally rather than attend to specific and often relevant details of a situation.
- Low levels of anxiety, tension, depression; rarely report serious psychopathology such as hallucinations, delusions, and suspiciousness.
- Presence of functionally related somatic complaints.
- Physical difficulties typically worsen in response to increases in stress levels, typically disappear when stress is reduced (especially with $T = 80$).
- Complaints can be either quite vague or quite specific and are of unknown origin.
- Clients will explain symptoms in purely medical terms, will seek medical rather than psychological treatment.
- Use of denial combined with dissociation.
- Low insight; deny difficulties and have a strong need to see themselves in a favorable light.
- Increasingly higher scores reflect exaggeration of denial, somatization, dissociation, immaturity, suggestibility, and low levels of insight.
- Persons with moderate scores may have good levels of adjustment, especially if educated and from higher socioeconomic groups.
- Persons with moderate scores may be presenting a favorable impression for employment (reflects endorsement of items denying any abnormality).

Related Scale Elevations

- Note "Conversion V" (in 1 descriptions; see also code types 12/21, 13/31, and 23/32).
- High 2 with K: person is likely to be inhibited, affiliative, overconventional, have an exaggerated need to be liked and approved of by others (especially if scales F and 8 are also low).
- High 3 reduces the likelihood the person will be psychotic, even though Scales 6 and 8 might be relatively high.

Treatment Implications

- Enthusiastic, optimistic initial response to therapy, partially based on strong needs to be liked.
- Slow to gain insight into underlying motives for behavior due to extensive denial and repression, will deny presence of psychological problems.
- Often look for simplistic, medical, concrete, naive solutions.
- Will try to manipulate therapist into supportive, nonconfrontational role; if defenses are challenged, they might become more manipulative, perhaps resorting to complaints of mistreatment and not being understood, possibly even becoming verbally aggressive.
- Core conflicts centered on issues of dependence versus independence.
- Direct suggestion focusing on short-term goals is often effective in creating change.

Client Feedback Statements[†]   You tend to be an agreeable, even sentimental and romantic person who yearns for a life where people are kind and loving to each other. Very likely you work hard avoiding interpersonal difficulties or holding controversial views. You probably seek out situations where you can please others, make them happy, and relieve them of suffering. Your discomfort with anger probably makes it difficult for you to confront people. People with your profile are often seen as playful and childlike because of their extreme discomfort with the adult world of competition, greed, and cruelty. Serious and painful responsibilities are something you avoid. You are easily influenced by other people's philosophies and think that you should think, want, and do what they do. Holding your feelings in and trying to stay positive, however, is putting stress on your body and you may be having all or any of the following symptoms: headaches, backaches, neckaches, stomachaches, nausea, or dizziness. These symptoms probably get worse as your stress increases and may change depending on what kind of stress you are under. Rejection and anger from others are extremely painful for people with your profile. Perhaps as a child one of your parents was explosive or abusive and frightened you. Your reaction very likely was to try to be brave and to look for a positive outcome. You may have learned to be totally unaware of your anger. Headaches, stomachaches, low back pain, or other physical symptoms are often caused by unfelt and unexpressed angry and negative feelings. When you experience physical symptoms, such as headaches, stomachaches, and the like, look to see if you are struggling with some angry feelings that are difficult to express. Whenever you find yourself even mildly resentful or angry toward someone, try to express your feelings to them immediately even in small matters. Try to see what is negative, as well as positive, in any given situation and try to balance the two extremes.

MMPI-A Considerations   While the interpretations for adults with elevated Scale 3 can also be made with adolescents, they should be done with caution because of questions related to questionable validity with this population. In particular, the Harris-Lingoes subscales can help to clarify the meanings of scale elevations. Females (but not males) are still likely to have somatic complaints in response to stress. Males are more likely to have both school problems (check A-sch/School Problems content scale) and a history of suicidal ideation and gestures. However, Scale 3 is rarely a high point among adolescent males.

Scale 4. Psychopathic Deviate (*Pd*)

The purpose of Scale 4 is to assess the person's general level of social adjustment. The questions deal with areas such as degree of alienation from family, social imperviousness, difficulties with school and authority figures, and alienation from self and society (see ANG/Anger and FAM/Family Problems content scales). The original purpose of the scale was to distinguish those persons who had continuing legal difficulties yet were of normal intelligence and did not report having experienced cultural deprivation. They were people who seemed unconcerned about the social consequences of their behavior and yet did not appear to suffer from neurotic or psychotic difficulties. An important rationale for developing the scale is that high scorers might not be engaged in acting out at the time of testing. In fact, they may often make an initial good impression, which could sometimes be described as charming. Recent friends and acquaintances may not believe that they could even be capable of antisocial behavior. However, under stress or when confronted with a situation that demands consistent, responsible behavior, they would be expected to act out in antisocial ways. Even though they might get caught, these persons would have a difficult time learning from their mistakes.

Different relatively normal groups will often have somewhat elevated Scale 4 profiles. This might include counterculture groups, which reflect their relative disregard for the values and beliefs of mainstream culture. Similarly, African Americans often score higher, which might reflect their feelings that many of the rules and laws of the dominant culture are unfair and serve to disadvantage them. Normal persons who are graduate students in the humanities and social sciences often have somewhat elevated scores. More positive characteristics to be found with moderate elevations include frankness, deliberateness, assertion, sociability, and individualism. In addition, normal persons who are extraverted, risk takers, and have unconventional lifestyles (skydivers, police officers, actors) are also likely to have somewhat elevated Scale 4 profiles.

High Scores on Scale 4

- Problems with persons in authority.
- Frequent marital and work difficulties.
- Poor tolerance for boredom.
- Angry disidentification with family, society, or both.
- Relationships shallow and characterized by recurrent turmoil, difficulty forming long-term loyalties.
- May make an initial good impression; eventually they will have an outbreak of irresponsible, untrustworthy, and antisocial behavior.
- Slow to learn from the consequences of their behavior despite having been caught.
- When confronted with the consequences of their actions, may experience genuine remorse, but this is usually short-lived.
- Difficulty in learning from experience makes benefiting from psychotherapy difficult.
- Will blame others, particularly their families, when things go wrong.

- High scorers on 4 are often perceived as angry, alienated, impulsive, and rebellious (see ASP/Antisocial Practices content scale) but also outgoing, extraverted, talkative, active, and self-centered.
- Frequent history of involvement with the legal system; extensive alcohol or drug abuse.
- Extremely high scores: aggressive or even assaultive, unstable, irresponsible, self-centered, legal difficulties.
- Moderate scores: adventurous, pleasure-seeking, sociable, self-confident, assertive, unreliable, resentful, and imaginative.

Related Scale Elevations

- Elevated 4 and 9 (see 49/94 code type and ASP/Antisocial Practices and ANG/Anger content scales): presence of energy to act on underlying feelings of anger and impulsiveness, history of extensive impulsive behavior, behaviors have resulted in damage to family's reputation, possible involvement with criminal activity. Moderate elevations on Scales 4 and 9 suggest behaviors with possibly a good level of adjustment.
- High 4 and 8 (see 48/84 code type): psychotic expression of antisocial behavior.
- High 4 accompanied by a high 3 (see 34/43 code type): antisocial behavior might be expressed in covert or disguised methods, person might manipulate others to act out for him or her.
- High 4 and 2 (see 24/42 code type); person has been caught performing antisocial acts, feels temporary guilt and remorse for his or her behaviors.

Treatment Implications

- May be initially perceived as good candidates for psychotherapy (they are usually verbally fluent, energetic) but underlying hostility, impulsiveness, and feelings of alienation eventually surface; likely to blame others for the problems they have encountered.
- Initial agreement to psychotherapy may be to avoid negative consequences. When these are removed (end of parole, spouse moves back in), they usually terminate treatment (see TRT/Negative Treatment Indicators content scale).
- Difficulty committing themselves to any, including the therapeutic, relationship.
- If low subjective distress (low Scales 2 and 7), their motivation for change is likely to be particularly low.
- Short-term goals that focus on documenting clear behavior change (rather than merely verbalizing it) would be indicated.
- External motivation for therapy (e.g., condition of parole or continued employment) might will increase the likelihood that they will follow through on treatment.

Client Feedback Statements[†]   You are very independent and rather uncomfortable working for others. Right now it is difficult for you to care about others and you do not want to get involved with them for fear they will disappoint you or let you down. You want to protect yourself, you do not want to count on anyone again, so you will keep your distance and stay uninvolved and emotionally numb. That way, you hope to avoid a repetition of previous pain. You are probably a survivor. You learned to take care of yourself at an early age. This may have left you with a cynical view of the world in which real love and caring does not exist. You may also feel angry, bitter, and defeated in your relationships. You have a low tolerance for frustration, and you may find yourself restless and impulsive, especially when stressed. You like immediate gratification. You want what you want, and want it right now.

In some cases this can lead to problems with the law and to problems with authority as well. You are likely to have had numerous relationships with the opposite sex, but there was little real intimacy or satisfaction. In fact, letting yourself really care about someone is difficult because you do not expect people to care about you. You often view the world as a cruel and heartless place. As a result, you fear that if you are not vigilant and should become vulnerable, others will use you and take advantage of you. People with your profile often grew up in environments where they had to care for themselves because the authority figures in their lives could not be trusted to meet their needs. You may remember specific occasions in your childhood when you were particularly disappointed.

When you get bored and look for excitement, find things to do that are not dangerous, illegal, or destructive. When you set a goal, try to give yourself small rewards along the way so that you do not think about quitting before you have given it a real try. Find ways to express your anger before it starts to build instead of letting it accumulate and explode.

MMPI-A Considerations   Adolescents frequently have elevations on Scale 4, and it will be their highest overall scale. A full one-third of the clinical sample used in the development of the MMPI-A had elevations of 65 or more. These generally high scores most likely reflect their often turbulent attempts to form a sense of identity and achieve independence from their parents. Thus, the elevation might be part of a temporary phase of development rather than a permanent enduring trait. However, high or extremely high scores will still reflect significant levels of pathology. Such scores are associated with delinquents who commit antisocial acts (see A-ang/Anger and A-con/Conduct Problems scales), are in conflict with their families (see A-fam/Family Problems), school-related difficulties (see A-Sch/School Problems), and are involved with drugs and/or alcohol (see MAC-R, ACK/ Alcohol Drug Acknowledgment, and PRO/Alcohol Proneness supplementary scales). Often they report little guilt for this acting out and appear impervious to punishment. Additional difficulties might include externalizing behavior problems (lying, cheating, stealing, temper outbursts, jealousy) and school dropout. Boys frequently report physical abuse and having run away; girls similarly report physical abuse but also having been sexually abused. They are also likely to be sexually active. Often they are not particularly motivated to become involved in therapy. Because Scale 4 is quite heterogeneous with a correspondingly high number of descriptors, a formal scoring and inspection of the Harris-Lingoes scales often can be extremely useful in determining which of the scale descriptors is most appropriate.

Scale 5. Masculinity-Femininity (*Mf*)

This scale was originally designed to identify males who were having difficulty with homosexual feelings and gender-identity confusion. However, it has been largely unsuccessful because a high score does not seem to clearly and necessarily relate to a person's sexual preference. Instead, it relates to the degree to which a person endorses items related to traditional masculine or feminine roles or interests. Males who have completed university degrees will usually score 5 *T* scores higher (*T* = 60–65) than the standardization sample; and those with less than a high school education will score, on average, 5 *T* scores lower. Interpretations, therefore, should consider the influence of education. In contrast, the correlation between females and education is quite small (–.15 correlation). The item content seems to be organized around these five dimensions: personal and emotional stability, sexual identification, altruism, feminine occupational identification, and denial of masculine occupations. The items are scored in the opposite direction for females. Thus, high scores for males have traditionally been used to suggest a nonidentification with stereotyped masculine interests, whereas a high score for females has traditionally been used to suggest an identification with these masculine interests.

An important consideration regarding Scale 5 is that it is not an actual clinical scale in the same sense as most of the other scales. It does not actually assess any pathological syndromes and thus does not provide clinical information. As a result, a "treatment implications" section has not been included. However, it can be useful in providing color or tone to the other scales. Interpretations should first be made of the other scales, and then the meaning of the relative score on Scale 5 should be taken into consideration. For example, an elevation on Scale 4 (*Pd*) would indicate that the person is impulsive, might act out under stress, and feels alienated from him- or herself or society. If the person scoring a high 4 is a male and also scores low on Scale 5, he would be likely to express his dissatisfaction through action, have low insight into his behavior, and place emphasis on physical strength. In contrast, a male with a high scale on 4 accompanied by a high score on 5 suggests that he will be more introspective, sensitive, articulate, and may channel his or her antisocial feelings toward creating social change. As noted previously, the person's level of education and socioeconomic status should be taken into account when deciding whether the score is "high" or "low."

High Scores on Scale 5 (Males)

- Aesthetic and artistic interests.
- Little interest in stereotypically masculine interests.
- More likely than most men to be involved in child rearing and housekeeping.
- Insightful, sensitive, and introspective (qualities conducive to benefiting from psychotherapy).
- Reduced likelihood that any existing pathology will be acted out.
- Low scores on Scale 5 (males).
- Stereotypically male interests, occupations, hobbies, and other activities.
- Presenting themselves as extremely "masculine."

High Scores on Scale 5 (Females)

- Interest in traditionally masculine interests and activities.
- Involved in occupations that are more frequently occupied by males.
- Possible difficulty engaging in traditional psychotherapy because they usually do not value introspection and insight, might have difficulty articulating their problems and expressing emotions.

Low Scores on Scale 5 (Females)

- Endorsement of many traditionally feminine roles, behaviors, and interests.
- Considerable satisfaction is likely to be derived from involvement as mothers and spouses.

MMPI-A Considerations   Scale 5 elevations for males were rare on both the MMPI-A clinical and normative samples. Males who do score high will seem interested in stereotypically feminine interests, deny stereotypically masculine interests, and are less likely to act out. If there are correspondingly high elevations on other scales suggesting acting out (Scales 4, 9, *F*), these should be given more consideration than the suppression value of an elevated Scale 5. Further research needs to be conducted on the behavioral correlates of both high- and low-scoring adolescent females. However, tentative interpretations would indicate that high-scoring females have stereotypically masculine interests.

Scale 6. Paranoia (*Pa*)

Scale 6 was designed to identify persons with paranoid conditions or paranoid states. It measures a person's degree of interpersonal sensitivity, self-righteousness, and suspiciousness. Many of the 40 items center on areas such as ideas of reference, delusional beliefs, pervasive suspiciousness, feelings of persecution, grandiose self-beliefs, and interpersonal rigidity. Whereas some of the items deal with overt psychotic content, other less extreme questions ask information related to the perceived ulterior motives of others. The Harris-Lingoes subscales divide the items in Scale 6 into ideas of external influence, poignancy (feelings of being high strung, sensitive, having stronger feelings than others, and a sense of interpersonal distance), and naiveté (overly optimistic, high morality, denial of hostility, overly trusting, and vulnerability to being hurt).

Mild elevations on Scale 6 suggest that the person is emotional, softhearted, and experiences interpersonal sensitivity. As the elevation increases, a person's suspicion and sensitivity become progressively more extreme and consistent with psychotic processes. He or she may have delusions, ideas of self-reference, a grandiose self-concept, and disordered thought processes. In contrast, low-scoring persons are seen as being quite balanced. However, there are some differences between the descriptions given for low-scoring males as opposed to low-scoring females. Low-scoring males are described as cheerful, decisive, self-centered, lacking in a strong sense of conscience, and having a narrow range of interests. Females are somewhat differently described as mature and reasonable.

In some ways, Scale 6 is quite accurate in that high-scoring persons will usually have significant levels of paranoia. However, the contents of most of the 40 items are fairly obvious. Thus, a person wanting to conceal his or her paranoia, because of fear over the imagined consequences of detection, could do so quite easily. Because of this fact, it might be possible for low or moderate scores to still be consistent with paranoia. This is especially true for bright and psychologically sophisticated persons. They might mask their paranoia not only on the test but also in real life. Thus, they might be a member of some extreme political group or religious cult that provides some degree of social support for their underlying paranoid processes. However, if the scale is clearly elevated, it is an excellent indication of paranoia.

High Scores on Scale 6

- Highly suspicious, vengeful, brooding, resentful, and angry.
- Will feel mistreated and typically misinterpret the motives of others, feeling that they have not received a fair deal in life.
- May have a thought disorder with accompanying ideas of reference, delusional thinking, fixed obsessions, compulsions, and phobias.
- Extremely rigid thinking, argumentative.
- May easily misinterpret the benign statements of others as personal criticisms.
- Will enlarge on and brood over partially or wholly invented criticisms.
- Underlying feelings of anger expressed in a rigidly moralistic and intellectual manner.
- Will reduce anxiety through intellectualization.
- Use projection to deny underlying feelings of hostility.
- Personal hostility might be expressed through indirect means (yet appear outwardly self-punishing).
- Will feel as if they have gotten an unfair deal from life, will resent family members.
- Moderate elevations: much less likely to reflect overtly psychotic trends but will still be suspicious, argumentative, potentially hostile, and quite sensitive in interpersonal relationships.

- Mild elevations (for nonpatient groups) are usually described in relatively favorable terms: hardworking, industrious, moralistic, sentimental, softhearted, peaceable, generous, trusting unless betrayed, intelligent, poised, rational, fair-minded, and with a broad range of interests.
- Mild elevations (for nonpatient groups) may also be: submissive, prone to worry, high strung, dependent, and lacking in self-confidence.
- Mild elevations (for psychiatric patients): oversensitive, slightly paranoid, suspicious, feel as if their environment is not sufficiently supportive.

Related Scale Elevations

- High 6 and 8 (see 68/86 code type): highly suggestive of paranoid schizophrenia.
- Corresponding elevation on Scale 3 (see 36/63 code type): will repress their hostile and aggressive feelings and appear naive, positive, and accepting; may easily enter into superficial relationships but after these relationships deepen, their underlying suspiciousness, hostility, ruthlessness, and egocentricity would become more openly expressed.

Treatment Implications

- Provides an index of the degree to which clients can develop a trusting relationship, their attitudes toward authority figures, and their degree of flexibility.
- Psychotherapy may be extremely difficult because of their rigidity, poor level of insight, and suspiciousness (check TRT/Negative Treatment Indicators Content scale).
- Are often argumentative, cynical, and resentful, thereby making it difficult to establish a relationship of mutual trust, empathy, and respect.
- Do not like to discuss emotional issues, overvalue rationality, and are likely to blame others for their difficulties.
- Frequently will not return following the initial session, will leave feeling that they have not been understood. Major challenge with an intake is to make sure that they feel understood (see "Client Feedback Statements").
- Might attempt to manipulate the therapist by implicitly suggesting they will terminate.
- Very high scores (check *BIZ*/Bizarre Mentation and critical item clusters related to mental confusion and persecutory ideas subscales) may require medication.
- Evaluate potential for dangerousness toward others if brooding and resentment are particularly pronounced.

Client Feedback Statements[†]   Currently you are feeling extremely sensitive to criticism, attack, or judgment. You are also very cautious about revealing to others your deepest thoughts and feelings. This is probably because you fear you may reveal too much and your self-revelations will be used against you. You are wary of being a victim of someone else's power. This makes you very cautious and concerned about the motives of others. If you care about someone deeply, it frightens you because you feel vulnerable to them. You feel that this gives them control over you and then they may hurt you. Being rational and fair is also extremely important to you, and you expect others to be this way as well. There are times when you become so angry that it is hard for you to forgive the person who you see as the source of your anger and who has frustrated you. People with your profile often were reared in households where their parents were controlling and judgmental. As a child you may have felt unfairly or unjustly criticized and attacked. At present you may experience some fears of being criticized, which makes you feel very tense and cautious. It reawakens your vulnerability to being dominated and controlled. At times when you feel you are being criticized unfairly, remember that not all criticism is intended as a personal attack on you. If you find yourself feeling mildly criticized by someone, observe to see if your feelings get hurt and you withdraw rather than standing up to argue your case.

MMPI-A Considerations Elevations are consistent with academic problems including poor grades and suspension (check A-sch/School Problems content scale). Clinical girls report significant disagreements with their parents (check A-fam/Family Problems content scale). Clinical boys are described as hostile, withdrawn, immature, and argumentative; they feel persecuted and are not well liked by their peers. In addition, they are perceived as being overly dependent on adults, attention-seeking, resentful, anxious, and obsessed; they feel as if they are bad and deserving of punishment. Because the items on the MMPI, MMPI-2, and MMPI-A are the same, the Harris-Lingoes scales can be used to understand possible patterns of item endorsement.

Scale 7. Psychasthenia (*Pt*)

The 48 items on Scale 7 were originally designed to measure the syndrome of psychasthenia. Although psychasthenia is no longer used as a diagnosis, it was current when the MMPI was originally developed. It consisted of compulsions, obsessions, unreasonable fears, and excessive doubts. Thus, it is quite similar to what today would be an anxiety disorder with obsessive-compulsive features. However, there are important differences between Scale 7 and obsessive-compulsive disorder. Scale 7 measures more overt fears and anxieties that the person might be experiencing (check also ANX/Anxiety). In contrast, persons having an obsessive-compulsive disorder could potentially score quite low on 7 because their behaviors and obsessions are effective in reducing their levels of anxiety (check the OBS/Obsessiveness content scale). Although an elevation on Scale 7 may suggest the possibility of an obsessive-compulsive disorder, other anxiety-related disorders or situational states could also produce an elevation.

Scale 7 is the clinical scale that most clearly measures anxiety and ruminative self-doubt. Thus, along with elevations on Scale 2, it is a good general indicator of the degree of distress the person is undergoing. High scorers are likely to be tense, indecisive, obsessionally worried, and have difficulty concentrating. In a medical context, they are prone to overreact to even minor medical complaints. They are usually rigid, agitated, fearful, and anxious. The most frequent complaints will be related to cardiac problems as well as difficulties related to their gastrointestinal or genitourinary systems. In nonmedical and more normal populations, high scorers are likely to be high strung, articulate, individualistic, and perfectionistic, with extremely high standards of morality.

High Scores on Scale 7
- Apprehensive, worrying, perfectionistic, tense, difficulty concentrating.
- Highly introspective, self-critical, self-conscious, and feel a generalized sense of guilt.
- Wide variety of superstitious fears.
- Orderly, conscientious, reliable, persistent, organized.
- Often moralistic with high standards for themselves and others.
- Lack in originality.
- Even minor problems might become sources of considerable concern.
- Will overreact and exaggerate the importance of events.
- Will use rationalization and intellectualization (usually without success) to reduce anxiety; these defenses are rarely successful.

- Defenses against their anxiety could be expressed in a variety of rituals.
- Experience self-doubt, rigid, meticulous, apprehensive, uncertain, indecisive.
- Social difficulties, frequently worrying about their degree of acceptance and popularity.
- Extremely high scores: disruption in a person's ability to perform daily activities.

Related Scale Elevations
- Moderate elevation on 7 and 2 (see 27/72 code type): good prognosis for therapy because clients are sufficiently uncomfortable to be motivated to change.
- Scale 7 relatively higher (10 *T* score points or more) than 8 (see 78/87 code type): person is still anxious about and struggling with an underlying psychotic process; better prognosis.
- Scale 7 relatively lower than 8 (10 *T* score points or more): person is likely to have given up attempting to fight the disorder, psychotic processes are either of a chronic nature or likely to become more chronic; poor prognosis.

Treatment Implications
- Usually highly motivated to change, will usually stay in therapy, progress tends to be slow although steady.
- Immediate task is to work directly with their anxiety (cognitive restructuring, hypnosis, relaxation, or systematic desensitization).
- Anxiety may be sufficiently high that a short-term regimen of antianxiety medication. This should be considered to help clients work more constructively in a therapeutic context and function in their daily activities.
- Insight-oriented therapy should be used with caution; they will have a tendency to intellectualize and ruminate indefinitely without making any concrete changes, may be overly perfectionistic and rigid, thereby making it difficult for them either to accept insights or to integrate them in a flexible, problem-solving manner.

Client Feedback Statements[†]   Right now you are feeling constantly on the alert as if danger lurked around every corner. It is hard for you to think clearly, remember things, or concentrate, because you are constantly distracted and fretful about details. You may find yourself making "mental lists" of all the things you have to worry about to avoid some unpredictable catastrophe. You might have developed a number of habits or superstitions that serve to reduce their anxiety. You tend to be a careful, thorough, and persevering person who attends to every detail. Confrontations with others that might lead to anger are frightening, and you tend to avoid them. Being angry with others causes you to feel guilty, tense, and uncomfortable. Consequently, being assertive is generally difficult for you, and you may allow others to push you around or take advantage of you. People with your profile often were reared in homes where they were subjected to unreasonable or unexpected and frightening events. They tried to protect themselves from the unexpected by analyzing and predicting the future and thereby avoiding any future painful event. Whenever you find yourself tense and highly alert, take some time to think of a peaceful and relaxing scene. Once you make a decision, do not go back over it and reanalyze it. When something does go wrong, try not to punish and blame yourself as a bad person.

MMPI-A Considerations   Few descriptors have been found for adolescents with high scores on *Pt* in part because, it is speculated, an early (adolescent) rigid personality style may not become problematic until later in adult life. Girls from clinical populations are likely to be depressed, may make suicidal threats, are more likely to steal, and report significant disagreements with their parents. Boys from clinical populations are likely to have low self-confidence and may have been sexually abused. However, more research needs to be performed to more clearly understand the behavioral correlates of high–Scale 7–scoring adolescents.

Scale 8. Schizophrenia (*Sc*)

Scale 8 was originally designed to identify persons who were experiencing schizophrenic or schizophrenic-like conditions. This goal has been partially successful in that a diagnosis of schizophrenia is raised as a possibility in the case of persons who score extremely high. However, even persons scoring quite high would not necessarily fulfill the criteria for schizophrenia, in part because the items in the scale cover a highly diverse number of areas. Thus, elevations can occur for a variety of reasons, which means that the descriptions of high scorers would also be quite varied. The items assess areas such as social alienation, apathy, poor family relations, unusual thought processes, and peculiarities in perception. Other questions are intended to measure reduced efficiency, difficulties in concentration, general fears and worries, difficulty coping, and problems delaying impulses. Because of the many scale items, heterogeneity of their content, and the resulting numerous potential descriptors for individuals scoring high on Scale 8, it can be useful to consult the Harris-Lingoes subscales to more fully understand the meanings of elevations. The following six different content areas have been described by Harris and Lingoes (1968):

1. Social alienation.
2. Emotional alienation.
3. Lack of ego mastery-cognitive (strange thought processes, fear of losing his or her mind, difficulty concentrating, feelings of unreality).
4. Lack of ego mastery-cognative (difficulty coping with everyday life, low interest in life, hopelessness, depression).
5. Lack of ego mastery-defective inhibition (impulsive, hyperactive, sense of being out of control, impulsive, laughing or crying spells).
6. Bizarre sensory experiences.

In general, an elevated score on Scale 8 suggests the person feels alienated, distant from social situations, and misunderstood. He or she might have a highly varied fantasy life and, when under stress, will withdraw further into fantasy. Others will most likely perceive the person as eccentric, seclusive, secretive, and inaccessible. He or she will often have a difficult time maintaining a clear and coherent line of thought. Communication skills will be poor; other people often will feel they are missing some important component of what this individual is trying to say. The person will typically not make clear and direct statements and often will have difficulty focusing on one idea for very long.

Adolescents score higher on Scale 8, which might be consistent with their greater openness to unusual experiences, turmoil in establishing a solid sense of identity, and greater feelings of alienation. Some groups of relatively normal persons might have mild elevations on 8. These might include individuals developing sensory impairments, persons with organic brain disorders, or unconventional persons who identify with the counterculture. Persons who have had a variety of drug experiences may score somewhat higher on 8. This may reflect the direct effects of the drugs themselves rather than suggest greater levels of pathology.

High Scores on Scale 8

- Unusual beliefs, unconventional.
- Possible difficulty concentrating and focusing attention.
- Moderately elevated: merely aloof, different, approach tasks from an innovative perspective; may have philosophical, religious, or abstract interests; little concern with concrete matters.
- Moderately elevated: described by others as shy, aloof, and reserved.
- Higher elevations: greater difficulties organizing and directing thoughts, aggressive, resentful, and/or hostile feelings yet cannot express these feelings.
- Positive qualities might include being peaceable, generous, sentimental, sharp-witted, interesting, creative, and imaginative.
- Very high elevations: bizarre mentation, delusions, highly eccentric behaviors, poor contact with reality, and possibly hallucinations (see BIZ/Bizarre Mentation content scale), feel incompetent, inadequate, and be plagued by a wide variety of sexual preoccupations, self-doubts, and unusual religious beliefs.
- Very high scores: reflect unusual experiences reported by extremely anxious patients, adolescent adjustment reactions, prepsychotics, borderline personalities, or relatively well-adjusted persons who are malingering.

Related Scale Elevations

- Elevations on 4 and 8 (see 48/84 code type): extremely distrustful, alienated from their world, environment perceived as dangerous, likely to react to others in a hostile and aggressive fashion.
- High 8 and 9 (see 89/98 code type): likely to constantly deflect the direction of conversation, frequently diverting it to unusual tangents, distorted view of their world, and they have the energy to act on these distorted perceptions.
- Elevated 8 and F, 2, 4, and 0: schizoid profile.

Treatment Implications

- Very high scores: difficulty trusting others and developing relationships resulting in difficulty with psychotherapy, especially during its initial stages.
- After initial therapy, individuals often stay in therapy longer than many other types of clients, may eventually develop a relatively close and trusting client/therapist relationship.
- Treatment should be focused around working on specific current problems the client is dealing with.
- Often prognosis is poor due to the often-chronic nature of clients' difficulties.
- With extremely disorganized thought processes, referral for medication might be indicated.

Client Feedback Statements[†]   You are probably feeling very separate from others, and it is hard for you to know how others feel toward you. You are probably confused about your thoughts and moods and wonder if there is something really wrong with you. Perhaps you feel that if people get too close to you and come to know you, they will somehow discover that something is wrong with you and reject you. Very likely you spend a good deal of time daydreaming, and it is hard for you to organize your thoughts or make decisions and get things accomplished. Often odd and unpredictable things that are uncomfortable and even terrifying will intrude into your thinking. You may feel very lonely, but at the same time you desperately avoid getting close to people and allowing them to get close to you. If anyone is hostile or angry toward you, it completely disorganizes you, making it hard for you to think clearly and respond. There are times when you may say something you think is appropriate, funny, or sympathetic to someone, and they will respond in an angry or indifferent way. People with your profile often grew up in homes where they were subjected to a great deal of anger and hostility from the important adults in their lives. You may have protected yourself by daydreaming and trying to escape into fantasies. If you find yourself in a sad or bad mood and feel alienated from others, rather than withdrawing into the mood, force yourself to find something to do that could make you feel better. Talk yourself out of withdrawing as a solution. When you feel a bad mood coming on, avoid scolding yourself and feeling that you are a terrible person. Although it may seem difficult, focus on thoughts that make you feel good, even if you must force yourself to do so.

MMPI-A Considerations Both boys and girls report a higher rate of having several school-related problems, with boys frequently being suspended and girls being unlikely to report having had any significant achievements (check A-sch/School Problems content scale). In addition, the possibility of sexual abuse should be investigated. Girls are likely to report increased disagreements with their parents (check A-fam/Family Problems content scale) and, among clinical populations, may be aggressive, threaten suicide, act out, and have outbursts of temper. In contrast, clinical boys are described as having behaviors such as being guilt-prone, shy, withdrawn, fearful, and perfectionistic; showing low self-esteem; being "clingy"; and having somatic complaints (nausea, headaches, dizziness, stomach pains). Clinical boys with quite high elevations might also have psychotic features, including delusions, hallucinations, ideas of reference, grandiose beliefs, or peculiar speech and mannerisms (check A-biz/Bizarre Mentation content scale).

Scale 9. Hypomania (*Ma*)

The 46 items on Scale 9 were originally developed to identify persons experiencing hypomanic symptoms. These symptoms might include cyclical periods of euphoria, increased irritability, and excessive unproductive activity that might be used as a distraction to stave off an impending depression. Thus, the items are centered on topics such as energy level, irritability, egotism, and expansiveness. The Harris-Lingoes subscales classify the content of the items under amorality, psychomotor acceleration, imperturbability, and ego inflation. However, hypomania occurs in cycles. Thus, persons in the acute phase were unable to be tested because of the seriousness of their condition. Further, some persons might score quite low on Scale 9, which might reflect the depressive side of their cycle. These low scorers, then, might still develop a hypomanic state and may have actually been hypomanic in the past.

The scale is effective not only in identifying persons with moderate manic conditions (extreme manic patients would be untestable) but also in identifying characteristics of nonpatient groups. A full 10% to 15% of normals have elevations on this scale, suggesting characteristics such as an unusually high drive level. Males with moderate to mild elevations and with no history of psychiatric disturbance might be described as warm, enthusiastic, outgoing, and uninhibited. They would most likely be able to expend a considerable amount of energy over a sustained period of time. They might also be easily offended, hyperactive, tense, and prone to periods of worry, anxiety, and depression. Others might describe them as expressive, individualistic, generous, and affectionate. Nonpatient females are likely to be frank, courageous, talkative, enthusiastic, idealistic, and versatile. Their husbands are likely to describe them as making big plans, wearing strange or unusual clothes, stirring up excitement, becoming very excited for no reason, being risk takers, and telling people off. High-scoring males were described by their wives as demanding excessive attention, being bossy, talking back to others without thinking, whining, and taking nonprescription drugs.

Age and race are important when evaluating what should be considered a high or low score. Some studies have indicated that certain populations of African Americans score higher than European Americans. Also, younger populations (adolescents and college-age students) score somewhat higher than nonpatient adults. In contrast, elderly persons often score quite low on Scale 9.

High Scores on Scale 9

- Extremely high scores: moderate manic episode, will be maladaptively hyperactive, poorly focused, flighty ideas, inflated sense of self-importance, and low impulse control.
- Possibly perceived as creative, enterprising, and ingenious, but what they can actually accomplish is unrealistic.
- Unwarranted sense of optimism.
- Become irritable at relatively minor interruptions and delays.
- Expend a considerable amount of energy, but their activity is usually unproductive because it is unfocused.
- Increased energy may serve to distract them from painful feelings or situations.
- Possible good initial impression because they are enthusiastic, friendly, and pleasant, but also deceptive, manipulative, and unreliable, ultimately causing interpersonal difficulties.
- Quickly develop relationships with others, but these relationships will be superficial.
- Will be perceived as restless and agitated.
- Moderate elevations: often more able to focus and direct their energy in productive directions.
- Moderate elevations among nonpatients: direct, energetic, enthusiastic, sociable, independent, optimistic, have a wide range of interests, might also be somewhat guileful, overactive, impulsive, persuasive, and prefer action to thought.
- Might sometimes show mood difficulties and experience elation without cause.
- Self-centered and impulsive.
- Scores alone not sufficient to distinguish a person who is energetic, optimistic, and focused from a person who is scattered, ineffective, and hyperactive (note critical items, Harris-Lingoes subscales, integrate relevant historical information).

Related Scale Elevations

- High 9 and 2 (note: these are usually negatively correlated): reflects an agitated state, person is attempting to defend self from underlying hostile and aggressive impulses, might be highly introspective and narcissistically self-absorbed. 9 and 2 can also be elevated for certain types of organically impaired patients.
- High 9 with low 2 and 7: suggests a minimum of psychological distress. Males are likely to have a compulsive need to seek power and place themselves in narcissistically competitive situations. With elevated K, these males are likely to be managerial, autocratic, and power hungry, and expend a considerable degree of effort organizing others. Self-esteem would often be dependent on eliciting submission and weakness from others (what they usually receive is a grudging deference rather than admiration).

Females having this profile are likely to be prone to exhibitionistic self-display and to be extremely concerned with their physical attractiveness.

- Low scores (T = 40): likely to be apathetic, depressed, fatigued, pessimistic, feel inadequate.

Treatment Implications

- Distractibility and overactivity often make psychotherapy difficult. Clients resist focusing on problems by diverging onto irrelevant tangents and object to psychological interpretations of their behavior.
- May develop grandiose plans for change, but these are seldom followed through.
- Tend to use denial and avoid self-examination.
- Low frustration for tolerance and frequent irritability might result in dramatic therapy sessions.
- Frequent disregard for prearranged appointment times, cancel because they are too busy.
- High resistance indicates they might optimally benefit from non- or self-directive interventions or paradoxical strategies.
- Evaluate for the possibility of a bipolar disorder with follow-up for appropriate medication.
- Check for alcohol or drug abuse (check MAC-R, AAS/Addiction Acknowledgment scale, and APS/Addiction Potential scale).
- Low score on 9: difficulty becoming motivated, require a concrete action program with a high degree of structure.

Client Feedback Statements[†]   You are a person with a very high level of energy and you are unusually optimistic, even in situations where other people might feel defeated or disgruntled. You may find yourself so optimistic that you make promises that are hard to keep. Working on one task is difficult for you. You get very excited by the prospect of something new, and then it is hard for you to rest or to focus on the task at hand. You need novelty, excitement, and challenge. You may find yourself impatient with others. The world appears to be moving too slowly for you. This high level of activity may be a means by which you cope with underlying painful feelings. Make a list of things you wish to do in the immediate future and start to do them, one by one, without being distracted. Try to finish one thing before beginning another. Reward yourself frequently and regularly for completing tasks. Try not to commit yourself to too many task and activities. Do not make any changes in your career or life goals until you have discussed these and thought them through with someone else.

MMPI-A Considerations   Moderate elevations suggest that the individual is enthusiastic, animated, and takes an interest in things. However, higher elevations suggest underachievement in school and problems at home (check A-sch/School Problems and A-fam/Family Problems content scales). Scale 9 elevations might also reflect irrational, manic behaviors and antisocial acts (check A-con/Conduct Problems content scale). Among boys, amphetamine use is relatively common. They are typically insensitive to criticism, do not like to reflect on their behavior, and are, therefore, unmotivated to become involved in therapy. They may also believe that they know more than authority figures and feel that such persons punish people unjustly. They might be self-confident, oppositional, take advantage of others, and deny any social discomfort.

Scale 0. Social Introversion (*Si*)

This scale was developed from the responses of college students on questions relating to an introversion-extraversion continuum. It was validated based on the degree to which the students participated in social activities. High scores suggest that the respondent is shy, has limited social skills, feels uncomfortable in social interactions, and withdraws from many interpersonal situations. In particular, these individuals may feel uncomfortable around members of the opposite sex. They would prefer to be alone or with a few close friends than with a large group. One cluster of items deals with self-depreciation and neurotic maladjustment, whereas the other group deals with the degree to which the person participates in interpersonal interactions. The different item contents have been further organized around the areas of shyness/self-consciousness, social avoidance, and the extent that a person feels alienated from self and others (Ben-Porath, Hostetler, Butcher, & Graham, 1989). These contents form subscales that can be used in conjunction with the Harris-Lingoes subscales to help determine the different variables related to why a person had an elevation on Scale 0 (see section on Harris-Lingoes and *Si* subscales).

Scale 0 is similar to 5 in that it is used to "color" or provide a different emphasis to the other clinical scales. Thus, interpretations should first be made without considering 5 and 0; later, the implications of these scales should be included. As a result, code types involving 0 have not been included in the section on 2-point codes. Elevations on 0 help provide information on the other scales by indicating how comfortable persons are with interactions, their degree of overt involvement with others, the effectiveness of their social skills (check SOD/Social Discomfort content scale), and the likelihood that they will have a well-developed social support system. A low score on 0 will often reduce the degree of pathology that might otherwise be suggested by elevations on the other scales. A low 0 also suggests that, even if persons have a certain level of pathology, they are able to find socially acceptable outlets for these difficulties. In contrast, a high 0 suggests an exaggeration of difficulties indicated by the other scales. This is particularly true if 0, 2, and 8 are all elevated. This finding suggests that the person feels socially alienated, withdrawn, is self-critical, and has unusual thoughts. However, he or she is not likely to have an adequate social support group to help in overcoming these difficulties. Although an elevated 0 can suggest an increase in personal difficulties, it often reflects a decreased likelihood of acting out. This finding is further supported by corresponding elevations on 2 and 5 (for males or a lowering for females). As a result, 0, 2, and 5 are often referred to as *inhibitory scales*.

High Scores on Scale 0

- Feel uncomfortable in group interactions, may have poorly developed social skills.
- Self-effacing, lacking in self-confidence, submissive, shy, timid.
- Others might experience them as cold, distant, rigid, difficult to get to know.
- Extremely high scorers: withdrawn, ruminative, indecisive, insecure, retiring, uncomfortable regarding their lack of interaction with others, sensitive to the judgments others make of them.
- Will not have a well-developed social support group to help them overcome difficulties.
- Moderate scores: dependable, conservative, cautious, unoriginal, serious, overcontrolled.
- Normal males who score high on 0: modest, inhibited, lacking in self-confidence, generally deficient in poise and social presence.
- Normal females who score moderately high: similarly described as modest, shy, self-effacing, sensitive, and prone to worry.

Treatment Implications

- High scorers (extremely introverted): difficulty engaging in therapy because they are shy, withdrawn, and anxious; would take time to develop a therapeutic relationship; may expect the therapist to be directive and dominate. A withdrawn and nondirective therapist might increase such a client's anxiety, resulting in premature termination.
- Might appear unmotivated and passive but internally they are likely to feel high strung and anxious (check LSE/Low Self-Esteem, A-lse/Low Self-Esteem, SOD/Social Discomfort, and A-sod/Social Discomfort content scales).
- Likely to be overcontrolled and experience considerable difficulties in making changes.
- Group treatment and social skills training are often appropriate interventions. It is essential that the group should be supportive and accepting, thereby increasing the likelihood that clients would experiment with new behaviors.
- Low scorers (extremely extraverted): possible difficulty due to superficial orientation, disinclination to reflect inwardly.

MMPI-A Considerations   Among adolescents, high scores on 0 are a clear indication of difficulties in social relationships, particularly related to low self-esteem and social withdrawal. The behavioral correlates for girls suggest that they are withdrawn, shy, fearful, depressed, may have had suicidal ideation and/or gestures, have eating problems, are socially withdrawn, and have only a few friends. Elevations also suggest an inhibitory effect in that they are unlikely actually to act out on their pathology. Thus, they rarely report difficulties with drugs or alcohol, delinquency, sexual acting out, and have little interest in heterosexual relationships. There are less behavioral correlates for boys, but high scores do suggest that they are unlikely to participate in school activities.

Low Scores on Scale 0

- Warm, outgoing, assertive, self-confident, verbally fluent, gregarious.
- Strong need to be around other people.
- Concerned with power, recognition, status.
- May be opportunistic, exhibitionistic, manipulative, and self-indulgent; in extreme cases they might also be immature, self-indulgent, superficial.
- Normal males: sociable, expressive, socially competitive, verbally fluent.
- Normal females: sociable, talkative, assertive, enthusiastic, adventurous.
- Extremely low scores: may have highly developed social techniques but behind their external image, they may have feelings of insecurity with a strong need for social approval, hypersensitive, difficulties dealing with feelings of dependency, large number of superficial friends but probably do not feel close to anyone.

2-POINT CODES

Code-type interpretation often produces more accurate and clinically useful interpretations than merely interpreting individual scales. The basis of code-type interpretation depends on empirical correlations among various classes of nontest behavior. The 2-point codes included in the following section have been selected based on their frequency of occurrence, the thoroughness of the research performed on them, and their relative clinical importance. Thus, some combinations of code types will not be discussed.

   Code-type interpretation is most appropriate for disturbed populations in which *T* score elevations are at least 65 on the MMPI-2 or MMPI-A. The descriptions are clearly oriented around the pathological dimensions of an individual. The 2-point code descriptions, then, do not have the same divisions into low, moderate, and high elevations as the individual scores but are directed primarily toward discussions of high elevations. When considering 2-point codes that are in the moderate range (MMPI-2 $T = 60–70$), interpretations should be made with caution and the more extreme descriptions should be considerably modified or excluded.

Usually, the elevation of one scale in relation to the other does not make much difference as long as the elevations are still somewhat similar in magnitude. A general approach is that, if one scale is 10 points or more higher than the other, the higher one gives more color to, or provides more emphasis for, the interpretation. Specific elaborations are made for scales in which a significant difference between their relative elevations is especially important. If the scales have an equal magnitude, they should be given equal emphasis.

In some cases, more than two scales will be equally elevated, thereby making it difficult to clearly establish which scales represent the 2-point code. In these cases, clinicians should look at the descriptions provided for other possible combinations. For example, if Scales 2, 7, and 8 are elevated for a particular profile, the clinician should look up the 27/72 code as well as codes 78/87 and 28/82. The descriptions for the code type with the highest elevations and those descriptors that are common between the different code descriptions are most likely to be valid. However, multiple elevations also raise the issue of the generalizability of the MMPI descriptors (which the majority of research has been derived from) and the MMPI-2 (Butcher et al., 1990; Butcher & Williams, 2000; D. Edwards et al., 1993; Humphrey & Dahlstrom, 1995; Tellegen & Ben-Porath, 1993). Up to 50% of the code types have been found to differ, which is particularly true for poorly defined code types. This fact potentially compromises the validity of the code-type descriptions. A more cautious approach would be to rely more on the single-scale descriptors.

In developing meaningful interpretations, it is important to continually consider the underlying significance of elevated scales. Doing this requires considering factors such as the manner in which the scales interact, the particular category of psychopathology they suggest, and their recurring patterns or themes. When possible, *DSM-IV-TR* classifications have been used, but the term *neurosis* is used occasionally because of its ability to summarize a wide variety of disorders and/or its ability to refer to a cluster of related scales (e.g., "neurotic triad"). Some characteristics described in the code types will be highly accurate for a specific person, whereas others will not be particularly relevant or accurate. Clinicians, then, will need to continually reflect on their data to develop descriptions and diagnoses that are both accurate and relevant.

The code types from the MMPI-A should be used with considerable caution because there is currently insufficient research on the behavioral correlates of these code types. In contrast, there is considerable research on the correlates of individual MMPI-A scale elevations. With this caution in mind, it is recommended that clinicians tentatively use the code types described in the following pages to help generate hypotheses concerning adolescent functioning. Doing this is partially justified in that many of the MMPI code type correlates are common for both adults and adolescents (Archer, 1992a). In addition, the majority of the code types derived from the MMPI will be the same for the MMPI-A, especially if the code types are well defined. If there are differences between adult and adolescent descriptors, or if no adolescent descriptors are available, this will be noted in the code-type descriptions.

12/21

Symptoms and Behaviors

- Complaints revolve around physical symptoms; can be either organic or functional (check the HEA/Health Concerns content scale).

- Common complaints: pain, irritability, anxiety, physical tension, fatigue, overconcern with physical functions.
- Significant level of depression is present.
- Characteristically handle psychological conflict through repression and by attending to real, exaggerated, or imagined physical difficulties.
- Even if physical difficulties are organically based, symptoms will be exaggerated and used to manipulate others. They elaborate their complaints beyond what can be physically confirmed, often doing so by misinterpreting normal bodily functions.
- Have learned to live with their complaints and use them to achieve their own needs.
- More frequently encountered in males and older persons.
- Pattern 1 (generalized hypochondriac): significant depressive features, self-critical, indirect, manipulative; if difficulties are solely functional, they are more likely to be shy and withdrawn. Persons with a significant organic component are likely to be loud complainers. Complaints are usually focused around the trunk of the body and involve the viscera (in contrast to the 13/31 code in which complaints are more likely to involve the central nervous system and peripheral limbs; see 13/31 code type).
- Pattern 2 (chronic pain patient): have given in to their pain and learned to live with it. Expression of pain is likely to be exaggerated, used to manipulate others. Check for history of drug or alcohol abuse as means of self-medication.
- Pattern 3 (patients with recent, severe accident): Their elevations on Scales 1 and 2 reflect an acute, reactive depression that occurs in response to the limiting effects of their condition.
- Some heavy drinkers have elevations on 1, 2, 3, and 4; they experience considerable physical discomfort, digestive difficulties, tension, depression, hostility, poor work and relationship histories.

Personality and Interpersonal Characteristics
- Introverted, shy, self-conscious, passive dependent.
- May harbor resentment against persons for not providing them with sufficient attention and emotional support.
- Interpersonally sensitive and manipulate others through references to their symptoms.

Treatment Implications
- Lack insight, not psychologically sophisticated, resent any implications that their difficulties may be even partially psychological (check the TRT/Negative Treatment Indicators scale).
- Difficult to take responsibility for their behavior.
- Typically seek medical explanations and solutions for their difficulties.
- Somatize stress, thus they are able to tolerate high levels of discomfort before being motivated to change.
- Generally not good candidates for psychotherapy, especially if the therapy is insight oriented.

13/31

Symptoms and Behaviors
- Classic conversion V (Scale 2 is 10 points or more lower than 1 or 3: as 2 becomes lower in relation to 1 and 3, the likelihood of a conversion disorder increases,

strengthened in males who have correspondingly high Scales 4 and 5 and in females with a correspondingly high 4 but lowered 5).

- 13/31 is more frequent in females and the elderly than in males and younger persons.
- Very little anxiety due to conversion into physical complaints (check corresponding elevations of Scales 2 and 7 since sometimes anxiety is present).
- If anxiety/depression are present: conversions are currently unable to eliminate their conflicts effectively.
- Extensive complaining about physical difficulties.
- Complaints typically involve problems related to eating, such as obesity, nausea, anorexia nervosa, or bulimia; also psychogenic seizures or psychogenic paralysis.
- Possible presence of vague "neurological" difficulties, such as dizziness, numbness, weakness, and fatigue.
- Occasional sense of indifference (marked lack of concern) regarding symptoms.
- Strong need to appear rational and socially acceptable, yet nonetheless control others through histrionic and symptom-related means.
- Often try and appear psychologically hypernormal (check K and L).
- Even if complaints were originally caused by an organic impairment, there will be both exaggeration and a strong functional basis to symptoms.
- Scale 3 higher than 1: certain degree of optimism; complaints will most likely be to the trunk of the body (i.e., gastrointestinal disorders, or diseases of the lungs or heart); strong use of denial and repression, passive, sociable, and dependent; manipulate others through complaints about their "medical" problems.
- Scale 3 is lower than 1: significantly more negative; any conversion is likely to be to the body extremities, such as the hands or legs.
- High 13/31 and very high 8 and 2: somatic delusions.
- Symptom-related complaints will usually increase with stress. When stress decreases, symptoms will often disappear.
- Frequent diagnoses: major affective disorders (major depression, dysthymic disorder), hypochondriasis, conversion disorder, passive-aggressive personality, histrionic personality.
- High 13/31 occurs among pain patients with organic injuries whose symptoms typically worsen under stress.
- Malingering of somatic complaints might be indicated if potential gain is a factor and 13/31 is quite high (especially if 3 is above $T = 80$) even if F is not elevated (because patients want to emphasize their psychological normality but exaggerate the specifically physical nature of their difficulties).

Personality and Interpersonal Characteristics
- Superficial relationships, with extensive repression of hostility.
- Often interactions will have an exhibitionistic flavor.
- Others describe them as selfish, immature, and egocentric but also as being outgoing, extraverted, and with strong needs for affection.
- Lack insight into their problems, use denial, and will often blame others for their difficulties (check the Repression/R scale).
- Usually extremely threatened by any hint that they are unconventional. Will organize themselves around ideals of service to others. Relationships and actual degree of involvement tend to be superficial.

- May feel resentment and hostility toward persons whom they feel have not provided them with sufficient attention and emotional support.
- Conversion V in normal range (1 and 3 at or slightly below 65 on the MMPI-2): optimistic but somewhat immature and tangential, responsible, helpful, normal, sympathetic.

Treatment Implications
- Difficulties in psychotherapy: lack insight; avoid introspection; need to appear hypernormal; prefer simple, concrete answers to their difficulties.
- Might respond to either direct suggestions or placebos, especially if the placebos are given in a medical context.
- Stress inoculation to reduce stress might be helpful.
- Describe any psychosocial interventions using medical terminology (i.e., biofeedback or other stress reduction techniques might be referred to as *neurological retraining*).
- Treatment is often terminated prematurely, especially if their defenses are challenged.
- Psychotherapeutic challenges are further increased with presence of personality disorder (check for comorbid narcissistic, dependent, antisocial, or borderline personality).

14/41 (Rare Code)

Symptoms and Behaviors
- Severely hypochondriacal; egocentric, demand attention, express continuous concern with physical complaints.
- May have history of alcohol abuse, drug addiction, and poor work and personal relationships. (Check WRK/Work Interference, MAC-R/MacAndrew Alcoholism scale, APS/Addiction Potential scale, and AAS/Addiction Acknowledgment scale to refine interpretations.)
- Indecisive, rebellious.
- Frequent diagnoses: hypochondriasis, personality disorder (especially antisocial personality); relatively higher 4 suggests antisocial personality; relatively higher 1 suggests hypochondriasis. Profiles involving "neurotic" features (anxiety, somatoform, dissociative, and dysthymic disorders) will have relatively higher Scale 1 with 2 and/or 3.

Personality and Interpersonal Characteristics
- Ongoing personality difficulties: acting out, poor judgment, extremely manipulative (but rarely extremely antisocial).
- Resentful of any rules and limits that are imposed on them.
- Rebellious toward their homes and parents, but these feelings are not likely to be expressed openly.
- Able to maintain control of impulses but will do so in a bitter, pessimistic, self-pitying manner.
- Described by others as demanding, grouchy, and dissatisfied (check the CYN/Cynicism, ASP/Antisocial Practices, and FAM/Family Problems scales).

Treatment Implications
- Resistant to therapy but may have satisfactory response to short-term, symptom-oriented treatment.
- Long-term therapy will be difficult, characterized by sporadic participation.

- Sessions may become somewhat tense because of their level of resentment and hostility, which is sometimes expressed toward the therapist (check the TRT/Negative Treatment Indicators and ANG/Anger scales).

18/81

Symptoms and Behaviors

- Variety of vague, unusual complaints (check the HEA/Health Concerns scale).
- Confused, disoriented, distracted, difficulty concentrating.
- Their focus on physical symptoms serves as a way to organize their thoughts, although the beliefs related to these symptoms may represent delusions.
- Ability to deal with stress and anxiety is extremely limited.
- Interpersonal relationships will be experienced with considerable distance and alienation.
- They will often feel hostile and aggressive but will usually keep these feelings inside. When they do express their feelings, it will be made in an extremely inappropriate, abrasive, belligerent manner.
- Perceived by others as eccentric or even bizarre.
- Will distrust others and may disrupt relationships because of their difficulty controlling hostility.
- Possible paranoid ideation (possibly, although not necessarily, reflected in an elevated Scale 6).
- Elevated 18/81 along with 2: emphasize self-critical, pessimistic dimensions.
- Elevated 18/81 along with 7: emphasize the presence of fears and anxiety (check the ANX/Anxiety, A/Anxiety, FRS/Fears, and OBS/Obsessions scales).
- Elevated 18/81 along with 3: conversions and/or somatic delusions.
- Frequent diagnoses: schizophrenia (especially with elevated F) hypochondriasis (with lower F), anxiety disorder (with elevated 7).

Personality and Interpersonal Characteristics

- Personality difficulties of a long-standing nature.
- Low trust, feelings of social inadequacy.
- Feel socially isolated and alienated.
- Histories often reveal a nomadic lifestyle, poor work histories (check the WRK/Work Interference scale).

Treatment Implications

- Difficulty engaging them in therapy due to poor insight.
- Distrustful, pessimistic, alienated, and even hostile (check the TRT/Negative Treatment Indicators scale).

19/91 (Rare Code)

Symptoms and Behaviors

- Possible organic difficulties relating to endocrine dysfunction or the central nervous system; gastrointestinal difficulties, exhaustion, headaches.
- Extensive complaining, overconcern with physical difficulties.

- May paradoxically attempt to deny and conceal complaints; may invest significant energy in avoiding confrontations relating to their complaints yet will make a display of these techniques of avoidance.
- Extraverted, talkative, and outgoing but also tense and restless.
- Possibly in a state of turmoil and experiencing anxiety and distress.
- Extremely high expectations yet goals will be poorly defined and often unobtainable.
- If complaints have no organic basis, their behavior may be an attempt to stave off an impending depression. Depression will be related to strong but unacceptable dependency needs.
- Frequent diagnoses: hypochondriasis, manic states (may occur simultaneously). May be in response to, and exacerbated by, an underlying organic condition, an impending depression, or both; passive-aggressive personality (especially if 4 and 6 are elevated).

Personality and Interpersonal Characteristics
- Superficial appearance of being outgoing, assertive, and ambitious.
- Underlying passive-dependent core.

Treatment Implications
- Reluctant to accept psychological explanation for complaints (check the TRT/Negative Treatment Indicators scale).

23/32

Symptoms and Behaviors
- Lacking in energy, weak, apathetic, listless, depressed, anxious.
- Frequently report gastrointestinal complaints.
- Feel inadequate, difficulty accomplishing daily activities.
- Much of their energy is invested in excessively controlling their feelings and behavior.
- Although situational stress may serve to increase their depression, usually this depression is long-standing; they have learned to live with their unhappiness and general lack of satisfaction.
- Not very involved or interested in life and have difficulty initiating activities.
- Males: ambitious, industrious, serious, competitive, immature dependent; strive for increased responsibilities yet also fear them; want to appear normal and receive recognition for their accomplishments yet they often feel ignored; their level of work adjustment is often inadequate.
- Females: more apathetic and weak, and experience significant levels of depression, resigned to long-term unhappiness and a lack of satisfaction, probably significant marital strife (check the FAM/Family Problems scale) but they rarely seek divorce.
- Frequent diagnoses: somatoform disorder, frequently among chronic pain patients, affective disorders, high Scale 4 (angry, brooding component to depression, underlying antisocial thoughts, yet their external behavior is usually overcontrolled) with high Scale 6 (depression relates to extreme interpersonal sensitivity, distrust), with high 0 (socially withdrawn, introspective), with high F and/or 8 (major depression with psychotic features).

Personality and Interpersonal Characteristics

- Passive, docile, dependent; typically obtain nurturance from others.
- Obtain security by keeping relationships superficial.
- Uncomfortable around members of the opposite sex, may experience sexual maladjustment, including impotence or frigidity.
- Perceived as immature, childish, socially inadequate.
- Feel the need to achieve and be successful but are afraid of the added pressure this might produce.
- Superficially appear as if they are driven to succeed but are anxious regarding competitive situations.

Treatment Implications

- Rarely volunteer for psychotherapy.
- Poor insight.
- Usually do not show significant improvement during treatment; therapy represents a threat to their use of denial and avoidance.
- Highly invested in medical explanations for their complaints.
- Seek medical "solutions" to interpersonal conflicts through methods such as tranquilizers and pain medications.
- Difficulty tolerating any discomfort but seem resigned to live with their unhappiness.
- Conflicts are likely to be somatized.
- Since distress is usually quite high, some method of symptom relief is indicated, possibly antidepressant medication.
- Supportive (rather than insight-oriented) psychotherapy is often beneficial.

24/42

Symptoms and Behaviors

- Difficulty maintaining control over antisocial impulses.
- Experience guilt and anxiety regarding the consequences of their actions; anxiety usually occurs too late to serve as an effective deterrent; difficulty planning ahead.
- When guilt and anxiety are reduced, there is usually further acting out. (24/42 code often represents an antisocial personality who has been caught.)
- Depression is probably situational; distress probably reflects fear of external consequences rather than an actual internalized moral code.
- Check for heavy drinking and/or drug abuse, which serves as a form of self-medication for depression (check the MAC-R, ACK/Alcohol Acknowledgment, and APS/Alcohol Potential scales).
- Poor interpersonal relationships, numerous family difficulties (check the FAM/Family Problems scale).
- Sporadic employment; prospects for long-term employment are rarely favorable (check the WRK/Work Interference scale).
- Check for numerous legal complications (check the ASP/Antisocial Practices scale).
- With high 6: may feel justified in externalizing their anger because of real or imagined wrongs committed against them.
- With low 6: Suppression or unconscious denial of hostility.

- With high 9: extremely dangerous and volatile, may have committed violent behaviors.
- Frequent diagnoses: passive-aggressive or antisocial personalities (especially with high 6), adjustment disorder with a depressed mood; if depression is chronic then anxiety, conversions, and depression (neurotic features) will be predominant (especially if Scales 1 and 3 are also high). If depression is reactive, this more likely represents an antisocial personality who has been apprehended; substance abuse may be either the primary difficulty or may occur in addition to the other disorders suggested earlier, extremely elevated 4 (above 90) a psychotic or prepsychotic process may be present especially if F and 8 are also high.

Personality and Interpersonal Characteristics

- Initial impression of friendliness or even charm; at their best, they can appear sociable, competent, enthusiastic, outgoing.
- In a hospital setting, these patients may attempt to manipulate staff.
- Produce resentment in interpersonal relationships over the long term.
- Superficially competent and confident but feel self-conscious and an underlying sense of dissatisfaction.
- Respond to failures with pessimism, self-criticism, self-doubt.
- Will often develop passive-dependent relationships to deal with feelings of self-doubt.

Treatment Implications

- Frequent pattern found in alcohol and drug treatment programs.
- Regardless of setting or reason for referral, check for substance abuse (also check the AAS/Addiction Acknowledgment scale).
- Long-standing personality difficulties that often make therapy difficult; promise to change due to guilt, guilt is generally authentic, but their acting out is usually resistant to change.
- Effective therapy: Clear limits, change in environment, warm supports, continual contact.
- External monitoring of their treatment is essential (i.e., legal or work-related); perhaps conduct treatment in a controlled environment.
- Long-term success in therapy is poor, likely to terminate when confronted with situational stress or when external motivators (e.g., legal) have been eliminated.
- Group interventions are likely to be more effective than individual treatment since they are highly influenced by peers.

26/62

Symptoms and Behaviors

- Extreme sensitivity to real or imagined criticism.
- Even minor criticism is brooded over and elaborated on.
- Will sometimes interpret the statements of others in a way that creates rejection, but conclusions will be based on insufficient data.
- Described by others as resentful, aggressive, hostile.
- Self-fulfilling and self-perpetuating dynamic: will often reject others first as a means of protection from perceived impending rejection by others. This results in other people avoiding them; the avoidance provides evidence that they are being rejected,

which gives them a justification for feeling and expressing anger. They blame others for their difficulties, yet others have difficulty understanding the part they play in creating the interpersonal responses directed toward them.

- Long histories of difficulties with interpersonal relationships.
- Frequent diagnoses: dysthymic disorder; passive-aggressive personality (with elevated 4); likelihood of a psychotic or prepsychotic condition, especially paranoid schizophrenia (especially if 7, 8, and 9 are also high); well controlled, well-defined paranoid system with a generally adequate level of adjustment if 2, 6, and *F* are only moderately elevated.

Personality and Interpersonal Characteristics

- Likely to have poor interpersonal relationships due to their hostility and hypersensitivity (check the FAM/Family Problems and CYN/Cynicism scales).
- Blaming, resentful, hostile, possibly passive-aggressive qualities, usually of a long-standing nature and difficult to alter.

Treatment Implications

- Challenge to develop and maintain rapport and trust; must continually disengage from hostility and suspiciousness (check the ANG/Anger scale).
- Assess for possible underlying psychotic processes.

27/72

Symptoms and Behaviors

- Code is extremely common in psychiatric populations; reflects persons who are depressed, agitated, restless, and nervous.
- Scales 2 and 7 reflect the relative degree of subjective turmoil the person is experiencing, referred to as the *distress scales* (also check ANX/Anxiety, A/Anxiety, FRS/Fears, OBS/Obsessiveness scales).
- Excessive worry, often overreact to real or imagined events.
- Obsessive, experience a wide variety of phobias and fears (check the FRS/Fears scale).
- Strong and inflexible consciences, will often be extremely religious in a rigidly fundamental manner.
- Possibly slowed speech and movements.
- Insomnia.
- Feelings of social and sexual inadequacy.
- Spend a good deal of time anticipating problems before they actually occur.
- Feel vulnerable to actual or imagined threats.
- Physical complaints may include weakness, fatigue, chest pain, constipation, and dizziness (check the HEA/Health Concerns scale).
- Occurs more frequently with males 27 years or older from higher educational backgrounds.
- Frequent diagnoses: affective disorders (particularly major affective disorder), adjustment disorder with depressed mood, anxiety disorders (particularly obsessive-compulsive disorder), personality disorders (avoidant, compulsive, passive-aggressive); may be normals who are fatigued and exhausted but who also have a high degree of rigidity and excessive worry only (with moderate elevations).

- With accompanying high 4: anxious and depressed because of poor judgment related to self-indulgence, particularly related to problem alcohol or drug use (check MAC-R, AAS/Addiction Acknowledgment, APS/Addiction Potential scales).

Personality Characteristics

- Perfectionistic, meticulous.
- High need for recognition.
- Difficulty asserting themselves, self-blaming, self-punishing, passive-dependent (check the SOD/Social Discomfort scale).
- Will rarely be argumentative or provocative.
- Most are married, courtships were fairly brief, many marrying within one month of their initial dating.
- Described by others as docile and dependent, typically elicit nurturance, excessive reliance on friends and family.
- They feel inadequate, insecure, deal with feelings of hostility in an intropunitive manner.

Treatment Implications

- Good prognosis for therapy with moderate elevations; person is introspective and is experiencing a sufficient amount of distress to be motivated to change.
- Clients typically express a great deal of pessimism regarding treatment and the future in general.
- Their psychological distress is ordinarily reactive; in time, they can be expected to improve.
- The disorder usually takes between one month and one year to develop.
- Will typically be their first need for intervention.
- Extremely high scores: Person may be too agitated to focus and concentrate; medication may be necessary for person to function in a psychotherapeutic context.
- Suicidal thoughts are a definite possibility (especially with high 6 and 8); carefully evaluate for dangerousness.
- Are often extremely self-critical during therapeutic sessions, require considerable emotional support.
- Prone to being perfectionistic, guilty, with frequent unproductive periods of rumination.
- Although obsessive about change, they often have a difficult time actually attempting new behaviors.
- Generally establish new relationships relatively easily; these are frequently deep and of long duration.
- With high 4: drinking patterns might be of a long-standing nature, therefore complicating any interventions (assess early in treatment). Do not do well in individual insight-oriented therapy. Likely to terminate prematurely. May be an initial "honeymoon" effect in which changes have apparently been made. During times of stress they are likely to act out and undermine any progress. Will most likely benefit from group interventions with a focus on clear, specific goals that would include, among other things, environmental changes.

28/82

Symptoms and Behaviors

- Depression, anxiety, insomnia, fatigue, weakness.
- Mental confusion, memory impairments, difficulty concentrating.

- Agitated, tense, "jumpy."
- Motivation to achieve is characteristically low, poor level of efficiency.
- Unoriginal, stereotyped, apathetic, indifferent.
- Excessive guilt, self-punitive.
- Fears relating to difficulty controlling emotions and impulses, including suicide.
- May cope by denying unacceptable impulses, sometimes results in dissociative periods of acting out.
- Possible delusions and hallucinations (especially if Scale 8 is greater than 85).
- Note highly diverse description of attributes only some of which may be present in any specific case (see descriptions under Scales 8 and 2). It is crucial to examine data other than mere Scale 8 elevation (critical items, clinical interview data; personal history; Harris-Lingoes scales; content scales particularly BIZ/Bizarre Mentation, FRS/Fears, OBS/Obsessions, LSE/Low Self-Esteem, SOD/Social Discomfort).
- Possible diagnoses: major affective disorder (bipolar-depressed or major depression), schizophrenia or schizoaffective disorder, personality disorders (borderline, avoidant, obsessive-compulsive, schizoid; features likely to include liability, emotional instability, acting out).

Personality and Interpersonal Characteristics
- Resentful, unassertive, dependent, irritable.
- Suspicious, extremely sensitive to criticism.
- Interpersonal ambivalence.
- May feel withdrawn, alienated.

Treatment Implications
- Multiple problems related to expressing anger, relationship difficulties, and social withdrawal.
- Might lose control over feelings of anger, which may be directed toward therapist during times of stress.
- Likely to feel ambivalence toward relationships in general resulting in resistance to therapy; ambivalence may make it difficult to experiment with new strategies learned in therapy.
- Therapy tends to be long term.
- Therapist can provide potential point of stability in an otherwise chaotic and unpredictable life.
- Assess for suicide potential both during the initial session(s) and throughout treatment.
- May require medication during times of crises to control thoughts and feelings.

29/92

Symptoms and Behaviors
- High level of energy.
- Energy may be associated with a loss of control, or it may serve to defend against experiencing underlying depressive feelings; speeding up activity can distract themselves from unpleasant depressive experiences.
- May use alcohol either to relax or to decrease depression; sporadic alcohol abuse is common.

- Anxiety and depression are likely to be present; will ruminate on feelings of worthlessness.
- Tension, restlessness.
- Somatic complaints (especially upper gastrointestinal).
- Among younger persons, 29/92 might reflect vocational crisis with a resulting loss of identity.
- Sometimes brain-injured persons have this profile; reflects their feeling of loss of control over thoughts and feelings, attempts to compensate by speeding up their level of activity.
- Frequent diagnoses: mixed bipolar depression—both scales can change according to the particular phase the patient is in (state-dependent scales), cyclothymic disorder, brain injured.

Personality and Interpersonal Characteristics
- Inadequacy, worthlessness.
- Person may deny these feelings and defend against them with excessive activity.
- Typically perceived as self-absorbed and self-centered.
- High needs for achievement but may paradoxically set self up for failure.

Treatment Implications
- Alternating periods of intense activity followed by exhaustion and depression.
- Major challenge of treatment is to stabilize mood and activity swings.
- Treatment may be complicated by a long-standing history of alcohol or drug abuse.
- Carefully monitor suicide potential.
- Depression may not be immediately apparent, but careful consideration of the client's background will usually reveal long-term but sporadic phases of depression.

34/43

Symptoms and Behaviors
- Immature, self-centered.
- High level of anger that they have difficulty expressing; anger will often be expressed in an indirect, passive-aggressive style.
- Continually trying to conform and please other people but still experience a considerable degree of anger, they struggle to find ways of controlling or discharging it.
- Anger stems from a sense of alienation and rejection by family members.
- Poor insight regarding their own behavior. Lack of insight even more pronounced with high 6; anger will be projected onto others.
- Females: more likely than males to have vague physical complaints such as headaches, blackouts, and upper-gastrointestinal complaints; still relatively free from extensive levels of anxiety; relationships will be superficial and characterized by naive expectations and a perfectionistic view of the world; gloss over and deny conflicts.
- Frequent diagnoses: passive-aggressive interactional style, histrionic or borderline personalities, adjustment disorder with depressed mood (or mixed emotional features), fugue states in which aggressive and/or sexual impulses will be acted out (if both 3 and 4 are extremely elevated; T greater than 85).

Personality and Interpersonal Characteristics

- Significant conflicts relating to dependence versus independence.
- Demand approval and affection but also have underlying feelings of anger that can easily become activated by criticism.
- Superficially conforming, but underneath they have strong feelings of rebelliousness.
- Past interpersonal relationships have been difficult; history of acting out, marital discord, alcohol abuse (check the MAC-R, AAS/Addiction Acknowledgment Scale, APS/Addiction Potential Scale, and MDS/Marital Distress scales).
- Will project blame onto others; low insight regarding this coping style.
- Might at times vicariously act out their aggression by developing a relationship with an individual who directly and spontaneously expresses his or her hostility. Such a relationship might be characterized by the 34/43 individual's covertly encouraging and fueling the other person's angry expressions yet, on a more superficial social level, disapproving of the other person.

Treatment Implications

- Stormy treatment sessions because the therapeutic relationship will be treated in a similar way as other relationships.
- Central issues will be self-control and difficulty taking responsibility for behaviors.
- Will terminate therapy out of anger and frustration.
- Internal motivation to seek therapy is often lacking, have been forced into treatment through external pressures (spouses, work, legal justice system).
- Arrange for some external monitoring and external motivation to keep them in treatment.
- Group therapy can be quite effective since they are relatively more responsive to peer (versus authority) pressures.

36/63

Symptoms and Behaviors

- Extremely sensitive to criticism.
- Will repress hostile and aggressive feelings.
- Fearful, tense, anxious.
- May complain of physical difficulties (headaches or stomach problems).
- Overtly deny suspiciousness and competitiveness, see the world in naively accepting, positive, perfectionistic terms.
- When 6 is higher than 3 (more than 5 points): will attempt to develop some sense of security in their lives by seeking power and prestige.
- When 3 is higher than 6 (more than 5 points): will deny any conflicts or problems, will idealize both themselves and their world, will be more likely to develop somatic complaints rather than paranoid ideation, chance of a psychotic process is significantly reduced.

Personality and Interpersonal Characteristics

- Will harbor feelings of resentment and hostility, especially toward family members, but unlikely to express these feelings directly.
- Naive and gullible.
- Can quickly and easily develop comfortable, superficial relationships.
- As relationship's depth and closeness increases, underlying hostility, egocentricity, and even ruthlessness become more apparent.

Treatment Implications

- Limited ability to acquire personal insight, psychologically unsophisticated, resent suggestions that their difficulties may be even partially psychological (check the TRT/Negative Treatment Indicators scale).
- Will blame their personal problems on others, thereby creating difficulties in therapeutic relationship.
- Will typically terminate abruptly and unexpectedly.
- Can be ruthless, defensive, uncooperative.
- Core issue will be having them take responsibility for their feelings and behaviors.

38/83 (Rare Code)

Symptoms and Behaviors

- Anxiety, depression.
- Complaints include headaches, gastrointestinal disturbances, numbness.
- May have a series of obscure, intractable somatic complaints.
- Thought disturbances including mental confusion, disorientation, difficulties with memory and, at times, delusional thinking (especially when 8 is significantly higher than Scale 3; check BIZ/Bizarre Mentation).
- Experience turmoil, feel tense, fearful, worried.
- Outwardly apathetic and withdrawn.
- Will describe their difficulties in a vague, guarded, and nonspecific manner.
- With elevated *K* and low *F*: affiliative, inhibited, overconventional, exaggerated need to be liked and approved of by others; unrealistic yet unassailable optimism; emphasize harmony, perhaps even at the cost of sacrificing their own needs, attitudes, and beliefs; extremely uncomfortable with anger and will avoid it at all costs; will avoid independent decision making and many other situations in which they must exert their power. Due to exaggerated optimism and denial of personal conflicts, they rarely appear in mental health clinics; almost as if any feelings of anger, tension, or defeat are intolerable; these feelings seem to represent both a personal failure and, perhaps more important, a failure in their attempts at controlling their world by developing an overconventional, exaggeratedly optimistic, inhibited stance.
- Frequent diagnoses: somatoform or dissociative disorders (when 3 is relatively higher than 8, and 8 and/or *F* is less than 70), possible schizophrenia (when 8 and *F* both highly elevated).

Personality and Interpersonal Characteristics

- Immature, dependent, strong needs for attention and affection.
- Superficially conventional, stereotyped, unoriginal.
- Despite unusual internal experiences, they are uncomfortable with these processes and will limit them by being intropunitive.
- Their unusual experiences and thoughts will make them feel socially alienated, but they have strong needs to appear normal and strong needs for affection.
- If others knew how unusual their experiences were, they feel they would be rejected; thus they develop extremely dependent relationships.
- To protect themselves, they use extensive denial, which makes their capacity for insight poor.

Treatment Implications

- Difficult to engage in therapy since they are typically apathetic and uninvolved in life activities.
- Treatment further complicated by low level of insight.
- They place considerable effort into appearing normal despite considerable unusual underlying processes.
- Individual insight-oriented therapy is contraindicated.
- May be responsive to a highly supportive, directive approach.

45/54

Symptoms and Behaviors

- Difficulty incorporating societal values.
- Can usually control antisocial feelings but may have brief episodes of acting out associated with low frustration tolerance and underlying anger and resentment.
- Usual coping style is through passive-aggressive means.
- The 45/54 code should in no way be considered diagnostic of homosexuality (see Scale 5 descriptor).
- Note: Scale 5 is not considered as a "clinical" scale but more provides the "tone" for the clinical scales. For example, a profile in which 4, 5, and 6 are all high might be interpreted as if it were a 46/64 code type, but the high 5 for a male would decrease the likelihood of acting out.
- Males: this code type occurs much more frequently among men, openly nonconformist, psychologically sophisticated; if they are from higher educational levels, they will be more likely to direct their dissatisfaction into social causes and express organized dissent toward the mainstream culture; with high 9, they will be dissatisfied with their culture, sensitive, and aware but will also have the energy to attempt to create change.
- Males with high 4, 9 and low 5: high probability of sexual acting out ("Don Juan" personality), self-centered, difficulty delaying gratification, behind overt display of affection is an underlying current of hostility.
- Females: openly rebelling against traditional feminine role; often rebellion is motivated by intense fear related to developing dependent relationships. Alternatively they may merely be involved in a subculture or occupation that emphasizes traditionally male-oriented activities.

Personality and Interpersonal Characteristics

- Immature, self-centered, inner-directed.
- Nonconformist, likely to openly express this nonconformity in a challenging, confrontational manner.
- May have significant problems with sexual identity, possibly experience sexual dysfunction.
- Possible ambivalence relating to strong but unrecognized dependency needs.

Treatment Implications

- Guarded and defensive about revealing themselves.
- Capable of thinking clearly, good insight.
- Rarely report for treatment because they typically are satisfied with themselves and their behavior.

- Do not usually report being emotionally distressed.
- Typical issues relate to dominance and dependence.
- Significant change is unlikely because of the chronic, ingrained nature of their personality.

46/64

Symptoms and Behaviors
- Hostile, brooding, distrustful, irritable, immature, self-centered.
- Continually blame others for their personal faults; this prevents them from developing insight into their own feelings and behavior because they are constantly focusing on the behavior of others rather than their own.
- Note history of drug addiction or alcohol abuse (check the MAC-R, AAS/Addiction Acknowledgment, and APS/Addiction Potential scales).
- Males with high 8s: psychotic, especially paranoid schizophrenic or prepsychotic; with 2 and/or 3 also elevated, the chances of a borderline condition are significantly increased. Will be angry and have significant conflicts relating to their own denied but strong needs for dependency, will rebel against authority figures, may use suicidal threats to manipulate others.
- Females: may be psychotic or prepsychotic but are more often passive-aggressive personalities; with high 3 they will have intense needs for affection and will be egocentric, demanding, but resentful of the demands placed on them by others.

Personality and Interpersonal Characteristics
- Passive dependency.
- Adjustment difficulties associated with hostility, anger, mistrust, and blame of others.
- Avoid deep involvement.
- Are perceived as sullen, argumentative, obnoxious, resentful of authority (check the ANG/Anger scale).
- Usually unable to form close relationships; significant levels of social maladjustment.
- Minimal self-criticism, highly defensive, argumentative (especially with high L and K).
- Highly sensitive to real or imagined criticism from others, often inferring hostility or rejection when this was not intended.
- To avoid rejection and maintain a certain level of security, they become extremely adept at manipulating others.

Treatment Implications
- Suspicious and even antagonistic toward treatment.
- Treatment typically occurs at the insistence of someone else.
- Project the blame for any difficulties onto someone else.
- Treatment plans should be concrete, clear, realistic, and described in a way that does not arouse suspicion or antagonism.
- Therapeutic relationship is difficult to establish; once established, is likely to be somewhat turbulent.
- Carefully monitor angry acting out.

47/74

Symptoms and Behaviors

- Brooding and resentful.
- Experience guilt over behavior.
- Insensitive to the feelings of others but intensely concerned with their own responses and feelings; justify insensitivity because they feel rejected or restricted by others.
- Predictable interpersonal cycle: express anger with little control over their behavior, resulting in impulsive acting out (check the ASP/Antisocial Practices and ANG/ Anger scales), will feel guilty over behavior, followed by a phase of excessive overcontrol accompanied by guilt, brooding, and self-pity (check the O-H/Over-Controlled Hostility scale). Frustrated by these feelings, they may then attempt to selfishly meet their needs through alcohol abuse, promiscuity, or further aggressive acting out. Cycle is usually resistant to change.
- Frequently leads to legal, work-, and home-related difficulties.
- Even though guilt and remorse are genuine (even excessive), their self-control is still inadequate and acting out continues.
- Frequent diagnoses: antisocial personality, anxiety disorder, alcohol/drug abuse (check the MAC-R, AAS/Alcohol Acknowledgment, APS/Alcohol Potential scales), miscellaneous conditions with impulsive-compulsive styles (e.g., eating disorder programs for persons with bulimia).

Personality and Interpersonal Characteristics

- Insecurity and ambivalence regarding dependency.
- Need frequent reassurances that they are worthy.

Treatment Implications

- Early treatment characterized by sincere remorse and need to change; as guilt diminishes, acting out again occurs. (Be suspicious of early "easy" gains.)
- Limit-setting will be met with anxiety and resentfulness; often they either test the limits or completely ignore them.
- Acting out followed by guilt is a chronic pattern.
- Therapeutic attempts to decrease anxiety may actually result in increased acting out because the control created by guilt and remorse might be diminished.
- May respond well to reassurance and support.
- Long-term, fundamental change will be difficult to achieve.

48/84

Symptoms and Behaviors

- Strange, eccentric, emotionally distant, severe problems with adjustment.
- Behavior is unpredictable, erratic; may involve strange sexual obsessions and responses.
- Antisocial behavior has resulted in legal complications (check the ASP/Antisocial Practices).
- Very little empathy, nonconforming, impulsive.
- Possibly members of strange religious cults or unusual political organizations.

- Early family histories: learned that relationships were dangerous; constant confrontation with intense family conflicts; felt alienated, hostile, rejected; attempted to compensate with counter rejection and other forms of retaliation.
- Erratic academic performance, characterized by underachievement.
- With high F and low 2: aggressive, cold, punitive, inspire guilt and anxiety in others. Often they take on roles in which such behavior is socially sanctioned (i.e., rigid law enforcement officer, overzealous member of the clergy, strict school disciplinarian). Behavior may range all the way from merely stern, punitive, and disapproving, to actual clinical sadism. Underneath these overt behaviors they usually have a deep sense of alienation, vulnerability, and loneliness, which may give rise to feelings of anxiety and discomfort.
- Males: frequent criminal behavior (especially with high 9). Crimes are often bizarre, impulsive, poorly planned, self-defeating, eventually result in self-punishment, occur without apparent reason, are extremely violent, involve homicide and/or sexual assault.
- Females: less likely to act criminally. Relationships will usually be primarily sexual, rarely become emotionally close; relationships will be with men who are significantly inferior to themselves (often described as losers).
- Frequent diagnoses: schizoid or paranoid personality, psychotic reaction, paranoid schizophrenia (especially with high 6).

Personality and Interpersonal Characteristics
- Deep needs for attention and affection.
- Frequently set themselves up for rejection and failure.
- Deep feelings of insecurity, poor self-concept.
- Poor interpersonal judgment, inadequate communication; others feel as if they are missing important elements or significant connotations of what the 48/84 individual is saying, but they cannot figure out exactly what or why.

Treatment Implications
- Difficult to establish therapeutic relationship since clients are aloof and unconventional.
- Sessions are likely to be chaotic with difficulty focusing on relevant areas. There will be so many different problems to work on it will be difficult to know where to begin. It is easy to get sidetracked, as a result sessions may seem relatively unproductive.
- Long-standing drug- and alcohol-related problems may complicate treatment.
- Acting out may further complicate treatment.
- Since they are mistrustful, they are likely to terminate prematurely.

49/94

Symptoms and Behaviors
- Feel alienated.
- Antisocial tendencies with the energy to act on these tendencies.
- Self-indulgent, sensation seeking, impulsive, oriented toward pleasure, irritable, extraverted, violent, manipulative, energetic.
- Poorly developed conscience, marked lack of concern for rules and conventions.
- Free from anxiety, talkative, articulate, charming; can often make a good initial impression.
- Relationships are usually shallow; any sort of deeper contact with them brings out the more problematic sides of their personality.

- History typically reveals extensive legal, family, and work-related difficulties (check ASP/Antisocial Practices and WRK/Work Interference).
- Pattern is highly resistant to change when found in persons over age 30.
- Adolescent males: associated with delinquency.
- With low 0: highly developed social techniques, will use these skills to manipulate others; may be involved in elaborate, antisocial con games.
- With high 3: decreases the chance of acting out; expression of hostility is likely to be similar to that of the 34/43 code in that it will be indirect and often passive-aggressive.
- With high 6: therapists should use extreme caution, very dangerous, poor judgment, acting out will often be violent and bizarre, will appear justified to themselves because of strong feelings of resentment.
- Frequent diagnoses: antisocial personality (but use caution when categorizing adolescents, as these scales are commonly elevated for both normal and abnormal adolescents), manic state, or schizophrenia (with high 8).

Personality and Interpersonal Characteristics
- External facade of confidence and security but underlying immaturity, dependence, and insecurity.
- Narcissistic, great difficulty establishing deep emotional closeness.
- Difficulty delaying gratification, will often exercise poor judgment.
- Perceived by others as extraverted, talkative, uninhibited, restless, needing emotional stimulation and excitement.
- Initial good impression, but their antisocial style will soon become apparent.
- Will rationalize their shortcomings and blame their problems on others.

Treatment Implications
- Numerous difficulties encountered in therapy: problem focusing, constantly embarking on irrelevant tangents, difficulty delaying gratification, do not learn from experience, primarily concerned with self-gratification (often at the expense of others), frequently irritable, if confronted by a therapist will express their fairly extensive hostility, typically cope through conning other people.
- May use charm laced with occasional belligerence. When this behavior occurs, it is advisable to confront it as soon as possible.
- Treatment is likely to be slow, frustrating, often unproductive.
- Rarely volunteer for therapy, typically referred by the court system or at the insistence of someone else (e.g., employer, spouse).
- External monitoring is usually required to keep them in treatment.
- Because their anxiety level is quite low, they will not be motivated to change.
- Group treatment has been reported to be relatively helpful; behavioral modification can often help them develop better coping styles.
- Termination is usually premature and associated with clients feeling bored with the sessions, acting out, or a combination of the two.

68/86

Symptoms and Behaviors
- Suspicious, distrustful; perceive the intentions of others as suspect and questionable.
- Interpersonally distant, few or no friends.

- Inhibited, shy, resentful, anxious, difficulty accepting or appropriately responding to the demands made of them.
- Highly involved in fantasy world.
- Uncooperative, apathetic, poor judgment.
- Experience difficulty concentrating.
- Sense of reality is poor.
- Often experience guilt, inferiority, mental confusion.
- Flat affect.
- Unusual, even bizarre thoughts, delusions of grandeur and/or self-reference.
- Internally quite anxious.
- Past work history is often (surprisingly) adequate (provided the elevations on 6 and 8 are not extremely high).
- Intensification of their symptoms brought on by stress will usually disrupt their ability to work.
- Typically single and younger than 26 years of age.
- If they are married, their spouses are frequently also emotionally disturbed.
- Highly elevated *F* with Scales 6 and 8 above 80 does not necessarily indicate an invalid profile.
- Frequent diagnoses: paranoid schizophrenia (especially with high 4 and if 8 is relatively higher than 7) with depression (elevated 2), inappropriate affect, phobias, and paranoid delusions; note "paranoid valley" (when 7 is 10 points or more lower than Scales 6 and 8), which emphasizes the presence of paranoid ideation; possibly organic brain disorders.

Personality and Interpersonal Characteristics
- Insecure, low self-confidence, poor self-esteem (check LSE/Low Self-Esteem).
- Others perceive them as being unfriendly, negativistic, moody, and irritable.
- High social discomfort; will feel most relaxed when alone, will generally avoid deep emotional ties (check SOD/Social Discomfort).
- Poorly developed defenses.
- Usually regress under stress.

Treatment Implications
- Numerous issues related to further assessment and case management due to significant level of psychopathology: inpatient or outpatient treatment, danger to self or others, possible psychopharmacological intervention and maintenance, basic daily living skills.
- Training in basic social skills, assertiveness, job interviewing, and knowledge of resources to resort to when their symptoms increase.
- Insight-oriented therapy is often contraindicated as self-reflection might result in further regression.
- Concrete, behaviorally oriented method of intervention is likely to be more successful.
- Patient may have unusual or even bizarre belief systems with quite different sets of logic from the therapist (check the BIZ/Bizarre Mentation scale), which is likely to make cognitively based interventions difficult.
- Level of suspicion and projection of blame will present further challenges.

- Mistrust, poor social skills, and social discomfort may make it likely for them to have difficulty forming a therapeutic relationship.
- Sessions will often seem slow, unproductive, and characterized by long periods of silence.
- Impulsivity and regression likely to provide further treatment challenges.

69/96

Symptoms and Behaviors
- Excited, oversensitive, mistrustful, energetic, irritable.
- Difficulty thinking.
- Obsessional, ruminative, overideational.
- May have clear or subtle signs of a thought disorder including delusions, difficulty concentrating, hallucinations, tangential associations, incoherent speech.
- May appear perplexed and disoriented.
- Feel extremely vulnerable to real or imagined threats, experience anxiety much of the time.
- Reactions to stress can result in their becoming either overly excited or apathetic and withdrawn.
- Typical response to stress is to withdraw into fantasy.
- Difficulty modulating their expression of emotions.
- Exercise poor judgment.
- Frequent diagnoses: schizophrenia (paranoid type), mood disorder.

Personality and Interpersonal Characteristics
- Mistrustful and suspicious.
- High needs for affection; relationships will often be passive-dependent.
- Clear discrepancy between how they describe themselves and how others perceive them; they describe themselves as calm, easygoing, happy, in good health; others describe them as hostile, angry, and overreactive to even minor stress.

Treatment Implications
- 69/96 is characteristic of inpatient populations.
- Psychopharmacological interventions to help control disorganized thinking or regulate mood can often be extremely effective.
- Due to disorganized, regressive, and ruminative thought processes, insight-oriented therapy is usually not effective.
- Lack of trust and suspiciousness often makes it difficult to form a therapeutic relationship.
- If a trusting relationship can be developed, concrete, problem-focused approaches are most effective.

78/87

Symptoms and Behaviors
- Agitation is often sufficiently intense to disrupt their daily activities.
- Profile represents a reaction to a specific crisis; may have been previously functioning at an adequate level until some event or series of events triggered a collapse in their defenses ("nervous breakdown").

- Low level of self-confidence, common feelings include guilt, inferiority, confusion, worry, fear.
- Insomnia, hallucinations, delusions.
- Note extent and relation between elevations on 7 and 8 since this is important diagnostically and prognostically; if 7 is higher (at least 5 to 10 points) than 8, then condition is more susceptible to improvement and tends to be more benign (regardless of the elevation of 8, as long as 7 maintains its relatively higher position). When 7 is higher, this suggests that the person is still actively fighting the problem and has some defenses still working; this suggests an anxiety disorder rather than psychosis since ingrained bizarre thought patterns and withdrawn behavior have not yet become established. A relatively higher Scale 8 (at least 5 to 10 points) reflects a more fixed pattern, which is more difficult to treat (particularly if Scale 8 is over 75). If 7 and 8 are both greater than 75 (with Scale 8 relatively higher), this suggests an established schizophrenic pattern (especially if the neurotic triad is low; check BIZ/Bizarre Mentation). Even if schizophrenia can be ruled out, the condition tends to be extremely resistant to change (i.e. severe, alienated personality disorder).
- With elevated 2: dysthymic or obsessive-compulsive disorder.

Personality and Interpersonal Characteristics
- Feel inferior, inadequate, indecisive, insecure.
- Often passive-dependent relationships, difficulties asserting themselves in heterosexual relationships.
- Difficulty developing and sustaining relationships, may have difficulties related to sexual performance.
- Preoccupied with excessive and unusual sexual fantasies.
- Often feel extremely uncomfortable in most social relationships (check SOD/Social Discomfort scale).
- Likely to defend themselves with excessive withdrawal.

Treatment Implications
- 78/87 often occurs among psychiatric patients.
- Possible significant suicidal risk; check elevation on 2, relevant critical items, take a careful history, ask relevant questions related to the client's thought processes.

89/98

Symptoms and Behaviors
- Highly energetic, perhaps to the point of hyperactivity.
- Emotionally labile, tense, disorganized.
- Possible delusions of grandeur, sometimes with a religious flavor (especially with a high 6).
- Tangential, bizarre speech, possibly characterized by neologisms, clang associations, and echolalia (check BIZ/Bizarre Mentation).
- Unrealistic goals and expectations lead them often to make extensive plans that are far beyond their ability to accomplish; aspirations will be significantly higher than their actual achievements.
- Severe symptoms related to insomnia.
- High likelihood of serious psychopathology.

- Frequent diagnoses: schizophrenia, schizoaffective disorder with manic states, severe personality disorder; the relative elevation of F can be used as an index of severity.

Personality and Interpersonal Characteristics

- Childish, immature interpersonal relationships.
- Fearful, distrustful, irritable, distractible.
- Highly talkative and energetic but will also prefer to withdraw from interpersonal relationships, resist any deep involvement.
- Grandiose and boastful but with underlying feelings of inferiority and inadequacy.
- Demand considerable attention, will become hostile and resentful when needs are not met (check ANG/Anger).

Treatment Implications

- Because they are highly distractible and tangential, psychotherapeutic approaches with them are extremely difficult.
- Poor insight, will resist psychological interpretations, cannot focus on any one area for any length of time.
- Defend themselves using denial, grandiose thoughts, and an inflated sense of self-worth; challenging these defenses is likely to provoke irritability, anger, or even aggression.
- If extensive delusions and hallucinations are present, antipsychotic medication may be indicated, or mood stabilizers if a mood disorder is predominant.

MMPI-2 CONTENT SCALES

One of the earliest efforts to develop a series of MMPI content scales was by Wiggins (1966, 1971), who organized scales based on an overall analysis of the contents of the MMPI items. He began with item clusters that were based on areas such as authority conflicts and social maladjustment. These clusters were revised and refined using factor analysis and evaluations of internal consistency. During the 1989 restandardization of the MMPI, many of the items relating to the Wiggins scales were altered or deleted. As a result, Butcher et al. (1990) developed a new set of 15 different content scales. At first, provisional content scales were developed by rationally sorting the items into different content categories. These categories were then refined statistically by making item-scale correlations with psychiatric inpatients and correlations between the scales. Further validity studies have confirmed that they are at least as valid as the MMPI/MMPI-2/MMPI-A empirically derived clinical scales (Barthlow et al., 1999; Ben-Porath, Butcher, & Graham, 1991; Ben-Porath et al., 1993; Butcher & Williams, 2000). A further advantage over the clinical scales is that they measure single dimensions. The practical significance is that they can be relatively easily interpreted using rational, intuitive strategies. In contrast, the MMPI clinical and validity scales are multidimensional. Thus, they require clinicians to work with them to extract the most useful and valid interpretations, often from a wide variety of possible descriptors.

An important function of the content scales is the ability to use them to refine the meanings of the clinical scales. For example, if an individual obtains an elevation on 4 (Psychopathic Deviance), clinicians can note possible corresponding elevations on FAM (Family Problems) and ASP (Antisocial Practices). If FAM is elevated but not ASP, the elevated 4 has more to do with family alienation and conflict than criminal and other forms of antisocial behavior. Thus, the content scales can incrementally increase the validity of the clinical scales (Barthlow et al., 1999; Ben-Porath et al., 1993).

In addition to clarifying the meanings of the scales, their interpretations and implications can also be extended. For example, elevations on 1, 2, and 3 are consistent with pain patients. However, in considering their prognosis for rehabilitation programs, it would also be important to assess their attitudes toward returning to work by noting the scores on WRK (Work Interference) and responsiveness to treatment by noting scores on TRT (Negative Treatment Indicators; M. Clark, 1996; Deardorff, 2000). Elevations above 65 on the content scales indicate that many of the descriptors for the scale apply to the person. Scales that are mildly elevated (60 to 64 inclusive) suggest that several of the behaviors apply to the person. Thus, the inclusion of the new MMPI-2 and MMPI-A content scales represents potentially important and easily interpreted dimensions of assessment. The content scales can be divided into the clusters described next relating to internal symptoms, external aggression, negative self-views, and general problem areas.

Internal Symptomatic Behaviors

ANX/Anxiety. Generalized anxiety, somatic difficulties, worries, insomnia, ambivalence, tension, a feeling that life is a strain, fear of losing his or her mind, pounding heart and shortness of breath, concentration problems, difficulties making decisions; symptoms clearly perceived and admitted to by the client.

FRS/Fears. Multiple specific fears (nuisance animals, blood, dirt, leaving home, natural disasters, mice, snakes, etc.).

OBS/Obsessiveness. Ruminates, difficulty with decision making, resistant to change, needless repetitive counting, may have compulsive behaviors such as counting or alphabetizing his or her experience; worried, sometimes overwhelmed by his or her own thoughts; others become easily impatient with the person. Persons with low scores are likely to be relaxed, secure, and unlikely to be depressed.

DEP/Depression. High number of depressive thoughts, uninterested in life; feeling of emptiness; feeling of having committed unpardonable sins; cries easily; unhappy; possible suicidal ideation; sense that other people are not sufficiently supportive; sensitive to rejection, tense, passive feeling of hopelessness; helplessness about the future.

HEA/Health Concerns. Numerous physical complaints regarding gastrointestinal, neurological, sensory, skin, cardiovascular, and/or respiratory difficulties; problems of adjustment; worried and nervous; lacking in energy.

BIZ/Bizarre Mentation. Psychotic thought processes, hallucinations (auditory, visual, olfactory), paranoid beliefs, strange thoughts, delusions.

External Aggressive Tendencies

ANG/Anger. Difficulties in controlling anger, irritable, impatient, annoyed, stubborn, may swear; episodes of loss of control, possibly breaking objects or actually being physically abusive. Persons scoring low are unlikely to be depressed or have significant family problems.

CYN/Cynicism. Distrust of other people; fear of being used or that others will lie and cheat them; belief that the only reason for others not lying or cheating is fear of being caught; negativity toward friends and associates, belief that people are friendly only for selfish reasons. Persons with low scores might be highly achievement oriented.

ASP/Antisocial Practices. Past legal and/or academic problem behaviors; expectation that others will lie; support of illegal behavior; enjoyment of criminal behavior of others; thought patterns that characterize criminal behavior, whether such behavior actually occurs or not. ASP has been found to be a better predictor (greater sensitivity and specificity) of antisocial personality disorder than *Pd* (Psychopathic deviance; S. Smith, Hilsenroth, Castlebury, & Durham, 1999) with a recommended cutoff of 55 or 60 (rather than the suggested cutoff of 65 implied by the MMPI-2).

TPA/Type A. Driven, hardworking, competitive, hostile, irritable with time constraints, overbearing, annoyed with interruptions, tries to do more and more in less and less time, blunt and direct, petty regarding minor details. (This scale is a better construct for use with males than females.)

Negative Self-View

LSE/Low Self-Esteem. Low self-confidence, feeling of insignificance, negative beliefs regarding self (clumsy, inept, unattractive), acutely aware of faults, feeling of being disliked by others, sometimes overwhelmed by his or her own faults, difficulty accepting compliments from others. Conversely, low scores suggest the person is secure, relaxed, and unlikely to be depressed.

General Problem Areas Cluster

SOD/Social Discomfort. Shy, withdrawn, uneasy with others, introverted, dislikes social events, prefers to be alone. Persons with low scores are likely to be secure, relaxed, achievement oriented, assertive, and unlikely to be depressed or experience somatic symptoms.

FAM/Family Problems. Family discord, unhappy childhood, difficult and unhappy marriages, families that do not express much love but are rather quarrelsome and unpleasant, possibly an abusive childhood.

WRK/Work Interference. Personal difficulties that interfere with work; tension, worry, obsessiveness, difficulty concentrating, career indecision and/or dissatisfaction, poor concentration, dislike of coworkers; difficulty initiating work-related activities; little family support for career choice; easily defeated by difficulties.

TRT/Negative Treatment Indicators. Dislike or distrust of helping professionals, discomfort in discussing difficulties, low level of disclosure, resistance to change, disbelief in the possibility of change, belief that no one can really understand or help them, preference for giving up rather than facing a crisis.

MMPI-A CONTENT SCALES

The MMPI-A content scales were developed and refined in much the same way as the MMPI-2 content scales. Some of the items were changed to be more relevant for adolescent populations. In addition, some new scales, such as the Adolescent-School Problems scale (instead of the adult WRK/Work Interference scale), were added, and others, such as the TPA (Type A) scale, were dropped because they were not considered relevant for adolescents. Elevations above 65 indicate that there has been extensive endorsement of the problems indicated in the scales whereas a mild elevation (60 to 64 inclusive) suggests that several of the descriptors apply to the person.

A-anx/Adolescent-Anxiety. High scores suggest tension, nervousness, worry, sleep-related difficulties (nightmares, difficulty with sleep onset, early-morning awakening); life feels like a strain; problems seem as if they are insurmountable; there are feelings of impending doom, fears of losing his or her mind, confusion and difficulty concentrating, increase in family discord; girls in clinical settings report feeling depressed and have somatic complaints.

A-obs/Adolescent-Obsessiveness. High scores suggest excessive worry, ruminations, obsessive counting of objects, extreme fear regarding making changes, difficulty making decisions, obsessing over past events or behaviors; others lose patience with them; boys in clinical settings are described as anxious, overly concerned with the future, dependent, worried, preoccupied, resentful, feel as if they deserve punishment; girls in clinical settings may have suicidal ideation and/or have actually made suicidal gestures.

A-dep/Adolescent-Depression. High scores suggest fatigue, crying spells, self-criticism, feelings of being condemned and unworthy, feelings of hopelessness; life is uninteresting, suicidal ideation is present; there is difficulty initiating activities, dissatisfaction; boys in clinical settings might be further assessed for a history of abuse; girls in clinical settings have depression and low self-esteem; girls in school settings are likely to have poor grades, are unlikely to have noteworthy personal achievements, and are likely to be concerned about being overweight.

A-hea/Adolescent-Health. Elevations indicate the presence of health problems that result in school absence and limit their physical activities; complaints cover several different physical areas including gastrointestinal (nausea, vomiting, constipation, stomach trouble), sensory problems (poor eyesight, hearing difficulty), neurological complaints (convulsions, paralysis, numbness, dizzy spells, fainting), cardiovascular problems (heart or chest pains), skin disorders, respiratory problems, excessive worry over health and belief that all related problems would be fine if their health difficulties could be solved; in clinical settings, they are likely to report being afraid of school; in school settings, they are likely to have academic and behavioral difficulties (school suspensions, course failures, low grades); girls in clinical settings are likely to report an increase in disagreements with parents; boys in clinical settings are described as anxious, worried, guilt prone, accident prone, perfectionistic (but less bright), clinging, fearful, and more likely to have lost weight.

A-aln/Adolescent-Alienation. High scores indicate a high level of emotional distance, a feeling that no one really understands or cares for them, a sense that they are getting a raw deal from life, difficulty getting along with others, not liked, others are unkind and even out to get them; there is a belief that others have more fun than they do, low self-disclosure is likely; others interfere with their attempts to succeed; they feel anxious when talking to a group and are likely to have poor grades in school; girls may have a problem with weight gain; girls in clinical settings have few or no friends, increase in disagreements with parents; boys in clinical populations have low self-esteem and poor social skills.

A-biz/Adolescent-Bizarre Mentation. High scores indicate very strange thoughts and experiences; possibly auditory, olfactory, and visual hallucinations; paranoid thoughts (plotted against, someone is trying to kill them); possible beliefs that evil spirits or ghosts are trying to control them; girls in clinical settings probably come from dysfunctional families, parents and/or siblings might have arrest records; boys in clinical settings are likely to have been under the supervision of a child protective worker, likely to exhibit bizarre and possibly psychotic behavior; individuals from school settings are likely to have numerous difficulties including poor grades, suspensions, and course failures.

A-ang/Adolescent-Anger. High scores indicate that the person finds it difficult controlling anger, feels like breaking or smashing things, sometimes yelling to make a point and throwing tantrums to get his or her way; feels like getting into fistfights; shows irritability when others try to hurry him or her, impatient, especially likely to get into fights when drinking, likely to act out in school and/or home; adolescents in clinical settings are extremely interested in violence and aggression, histories of assault; described as angry, resentful, impulsive, moody, externalize behaviors; boys in clinical settings are described as attention seeking, resentful, anxious, self-condemning but also dependent and clinging, may have a history of sexual abuse; girls in clinical settings are likely to be aggressive, delinquent, have been arrested, act out sexually (promiscuity), are flirtatious, wear provocative clothes, need to be supervised around boys.

A-con/Adolescent-Conduct Problems. Elevations suggest that the client is oppositional, has legal problems, peer group is often in trouble; behavior problems including lying, stealing, shoplifting, swearing, vandalism; likely to enjoy other people's criminal behavior, might also enjoy making other people afraid of them; uses drugs and alcohol, has record of poor academic performance and school-related behavior problems (course failures, suspensions, lying and cheating), disobedient, impulsive; clinical girls are described as impulsive, angry, unpredictable, sexually active, provocative, resentful, impatient, require supervision around boys, unlikely to be depressed.

A-cyn/Adolescent Cynicism. Persons scoring high are endorsing statements that they distrust other people. They believe that if other people are nice, it is only because they are trying to take unfair advantage of the people they are being nice to. Accordingly, high scorers feel guarded and misunderstood. Because they feel that others are out to get them and mainly concerned with self-interest, persons scoring high feel justified in having misanthropic attitudes. They may also believe that others are jealous of them.

A-lse/Adolescent-Low Self-Esteem. High scores indicate that the individual feels unattractive, useless, has little ability, many faults, low self-confidence, unable to do anything particularly well including planning own future, confused and forgetful, difficulty accepting compliments, susceptible to social pressure, passive; high-scoring boys should be further assessed for the possibility of sexual abuse; girls are likely to report weight gain, poor grades, and no noteworthy personal achievements; boys in clinical settings are described as having poor social skills; girls in clinical settings will be depressed, are likely to have learning disabilities, have increasing numbers of conflicts with their parents, suicidal thoughts, and possibly suicidal gestures.

A-las/Adolescent-Low Aspirations. High scores indicate a low level of interest, especially academically; the person dislikes studying, reading, listening to lectures (especially science); has problems initiating activities, gives up easily, dislikes facing difficult situations; has low expectations for achievement and little interest in continuing on to college; described by others as lazy, has poor grades, little interest in school activities; clinical girls are likely to report sexual acting out, very unlikely to report having won a prize or award; clinical boys are likely to have been truant in school and run away from home.

A-sod/Adolescent-Social Discomfort. High scores indicate that the person is shy, prefers to be alone, difficulty making friends, extremely uncomfortable when addressing a group, dislikes parties and crowds, difficult to get to know, uncomfortable meeting new people, dislikes initiating conversations, might actively avoid others, unlikely to report using drugs or alcohol; boys are likely to avoid school activities; girls in clinical settings are unlikely to be involved in acting out, are uninterested in boys, have few friends, may be depressed, have eating difficulties; may be fearful, withdrawn, physically weak; and are not likely to be involved with drugs, alcohol, or irresponsible behavior.

A-fam/Adolescent-Family Problems. High scorers are likely to have extensive difficulties with parents and other family members including fault-finding, jealousy, little love, serious arguments, poor communication; they long for the day when they can finally leave home, feel that parents punish them unfairly, show little acceptance of responsibility around home, feel that they cannot depend on their family in times of need; beatings and runaways are possible, however, problems usually do not extend into the legal justice system; there may be some school-related difficulties (low grades, suspensions); may reflect marital difficulties of parents; girls in school settings report possible exam failure and/or weight gain; in clinical settings, there may be more externalizing behaviors including lying, cheating, stealing as well as somatic complaints, crying, guilt, timidity, and withdrawal; boys in clinical settings are described as sad, secretive, uncommunicative, disliked, self-conscious, unloved, dependent, resentful, attention seeking, and self-blaming; girls in clinical settings are typically described as immature, likely to fight, cruel, destructive, secretive, self-conscious, hyperactive, provocative, sexually acting out (promiscuity), and preoccupied with sex; further assessment should include possible sexual abuse for girls and possible physical abuse for boys.

A-sch/Adolescent-School. High scores indicate a wide number of school-related difficulties including low grades, truancy, easily upset by school events, learning disabilities, low level of social competence, boredom, suspensions, dislike of school, disciplinary actions, difficulty concentrating, probations, and negative attitudes toward teachers; feels that school is a waste of time; often school-related difficulties are specific to school itself and do not spill over into other areas; boys from clinical populations are likely to have run away, been irresponsible, and have a history of drug use, particularly amphetamines; they should be further evaluated for the possibility of sexual abuse; girls from clinical populations may have learning disabilities and/or academic underachievement.

A-trt/Adolescent-Negative Treatment Indicators. High scores indicate negative attitudes and feelings toward health care professionals; they do not like to share personal information with others; they feel that they can never really be understood and others do not really care what happens to them; they will have anxiety related to people asking them personal questions; they have difficulty planning for the future and are unwilling to take responsibility for the negative things in their lives; they feel that they have many secrets they need to keep to themselves.

HARRIS-LINGOES AND *Si* SUBSCALES

One of the more popular developments has been the reorganization by Harris and Lingoes (1955/1968) of the standard scales into more homogeneous content categories. These subscales were constructed by intuitively grouping together items that seemed to reflect single traits or attitudes contained in the already existing MMPI Scales 2, 3, 4, 6, 8, and 9. Ben-Porath et al. (1989) further developed subscales similar to the Harris-Lingoes subscales for Scale 0. No subscales were developed for 1 and 7 because these were considered to be relatively homogeneous in their item content. These same subscales have been carried over for use with the MMPI-A. The subscales and a brief summary of the meanings associated with high scores are provided in this section. These summaries are derived from material by Harris and Lingoes (1968), and extensions of these materials as summarized by Butcher et al. (1990), Butcher and Williams (2000), J. Graham (2006), Greene (2000), and Levitt and Gotts (1995). Scoring templates and profile sheets for the MMPI-2 and MMPI-A Harris-Lingoes subscales are available from Pearson Assessments.

Although the Harris and Lingoes subscales show high intercorrelations with the parent scales (Harris & Lingoes, 1968) and relevant code types (McGrath, Powis, & Pogge, 1998), the internal consistency of the subscales is somewhat low (.04 to .85; Gocka, 1965). Several initial validity studies are available (Boerger, 1975; Calvin, 1975;

N. Gordon & Swart, 1973) that demonstrate the potential clinical usefulness of these subscales. The Social Introversion subscales have been found to account for 90% of the variance of the *Si* scale, and convergent and discriminant validity was demonstrated based on an analysis of spouses' ratings of each other (Ben-Porath et al., 1989). The practical importance of both sets of subscales is that they provide a useful supplement for interpreting the original scales. For example, a clinician can assess whether a person scoring high on Scale 4 (Psychopathic Deviate) achieved that elevation primarily because of family discord (*Pd* 1), authority problems (*Pd* 2), or social imperturbability (*Pd* 3). This breakdown is likely to be quite helpful in interpreting why a client received a high score that was unexpected based on the person's history. It might also be quite useful in interpreting the significance associated with moderate elevations ($T = 60$–65). A further situation to score and interpret the Harris-Lingoes scales is to understand the possible reasons for contradictory descriptions such as might emerge if both Scales 2 and 9 were elevated. However, if the clinical scales are either in the normal range, or quite high, the Harris-Lingoes scales are not particularly useful. Only Harris-Lingoes and *Si* subscale elevations of $T = 65$ or greater should be interpreted.

The Harris-Lingoes and *Si* subscales should not be used for routine interpretations because they are quite time consuming to hand-score. Rather than scoring all the Harris-Lingoes and *Si* subscales, clinicians can select and score only those that are relevant for refining and clarifying the meanings of clinical scales that are in question. Despite some validity efforts, the amount of research available is still inadequate, and, in many cases, the internal consistency of the subscales is insufficient. Thus, any interpretations should be made cautiously and be considered as hypotheses in need of further support. This is particularly true for the MMPI-A, in which there has been even less investigation using the Harris-Lingoes and *Si* subscales than for the MMPI/MMPI-2. Furthermore, item deletions and alterations between the MMPI/MMPI-2 and MMPI-A, primarily for the *Si* scale, bring into question the transferability of the Harris-Lingoes and *Si* scales with the adolescent version of the MMPI.

Scale 2. Depression

D*1*/*Subjective Depression.* Unhappy, low energy, sense of inferiority, low self-confidence, socially uneasy, few interests.

D*2*/*Psychomotor Retardation.* Low energy, immobilized, socially withdrawn, listless.

D*3*/*Physical Malfunctioning.* Reports wide variety of physical symptoms, preoccupied with health, denial of good health.

D*4*/*Mental Dullness.* Low energy, pessimistic, little enjoyment of life; difficulties with concentration, attention, and memory; apathetic.

D*5*/*Brooding.* May feel as if he or she is losing control of his or her thoughts; broods, cries, ruminates, feels inferior, and is hypersensitive.

Scale 3. Hysteria

Hy*1*/*Denial of Social Anxiety.* Extraverted, comfortable with social interaction, minimally influenced by social standards.

Hy*2*/*Need for Affection.* Strong needs for affection with fears that these needs will not be met, denies negative feelings toward others.

Hy*3*/*Lassitude-Malaise.* Subjective, discomfort, poor health, fatigued, poor concentration, insomnia, unhappiness.

Hy4/*Somatic Complaints.* Wide variety of physical complaints, denial of hostility toward others.

Hy5/*Inhibition of Aggression.* Denial of hostility and anger, interpersonally hypersensitive.

Scale 4. Psychopathic Deviate

Pd1/*Familial Discord.* Family that was critical, unsupportive, and interfered with independence.

Pd2/*Authority Conflict.* Rebellion against societal rules, beliefs of right/wrong that disregard societal norms, legal/academic difficulties.

Pd3/*Social Imperturbability.* Opinionated, socially confident, outspoken.

Pd4/*Social Alienation.* Isolated from others, feels poorly understood.

Pd5/*Self-Alienation.* Unhappy with self, guilt and regret regarding past behavior.

Scale 6. Paranoia

Pa1/*Persecutory Ideas.* Perceives world as dangerous, feels poorly understood, distrustful.

Pa2/*Poignancy.* Feels lonely, tense, hypersensitive, possibly high sensation seeking.

Pa3/*Naiveté.* Overly optimistic, extremely high moral standards, denial of hostility.

Scale 8. Schizophrenia

Sc1/*Social Alienation.* Feels unloved, mistreated, and possibly persecuted.

Sc2/*Emotional Alienation.* Depression, fear, possible suicidal wishes.

Sc3/*Lack of Ego Mastery, Cognitive.* Strange thoughts, sense of unreality, poor concentration and memory, loss of mental control.

Sc4/*Lack of Ego Mastery, Conative.* Depressed, worried, fantasy withdrawal, life is too difficult, possible suicidal wishes.

Sc5/*Lack of Ego Mastery, Defective Inhibition.* Sense of losing control of impulses and feelings, labile, hyperactive, cannot control or recall certain behaviors.

Sc6/*Bizarre Sensory Experiences.* Hallucinations, peculiar sensory and motor experiences, strange thoughts, delusions.

Scale 9. Hypomania

Ma1/*Amorality.* Selfish, poor conscience, manipulative; justifies amoral behavior by believing others are selfish and opportunistic.

Ma2/*Psychomotor. Acceleration* Restless, hyperactive, accelerated thoughts and behaviors, seeks excitement to reduce boredom.

Ma3/*Imperturbability.* Unaffected by concerns and opinions of others, denies feeling socially anxious.

Ma4/*Ego Inflation.* Unrealistic perception of abilities, resentful of demands placed on himself or herself.

Scale 0. Social Introversion

Si1/*Shyness.* Easily embarrassed, reluctant to initiate relationships, socially uncomfortable, shy.

Si2/*Social Avoidance.* Dislike and avoidance of group activities, parties, social activities.

Si3/*Self/Other Alienation.* Poor self-esteem, self-critical, low self-confidence, sense of ineffectiveness.

CRITICAL ITEMS

An alternative to content analysis, other then scoring and interpreting actual scales, is to interpret the meanings of single items or clusters of items that seem, based on their content, to relate to different areas of psychopathology (depressed suicidal ideation, mental confusion, etc.) or direction on these items could represent serious pathology, regardless of how the person responded on the remainder of the inventory. These items have been referred to as *pathognomonic items*, *stop items*, or, more frequently, *critical items*. It has been assumed that the direction in which a person responds represents a sample of the person's behavior and acts like a short scale that indicates his or her general level of functioning. The critical items are most useful when clinicians look at the individual item content in relation to the specific types of information that the item reveals. This information might be used to guide further interviewing. However, some caution should be taken in their interpretation, as they are both subject to an acquiescing response set (most items are keyed in the "True" direction) and faking bad. They should not be considered to be scales but rather direct communications to the clinician about areas specific to the item content. A listing of critical items can be found in the MMPI-2 manual (Butcher et al., 2001); these items typically are scored by most computer-assisted programs.

While lists of critical items have been included in the MMPI-2 manual (Butcher et al., 2001), clinicians should use these lists with caution in reference to adolescents. First, normal adolescents as well as clinical populations of adolescents endorse, on average, twice the number of critical items as normal adults (Archer & Jacobson, 1993). In addition, normal adolescents and clinical populations endorse item frequencies about equally, thereby suggesting that the items themselves should not be used to differentiate between these two groups. This means that empirical attempts to develop critical item lists for adolescents might be quite difficult. As for the MMPI/MMPI-2, clinicians should not treat the different clusters of critical items as rough scales to be interpreted. Rather, the individual item content should be used to develop specific interview questions, and the relative deviancy of these items should be handled with appropriate tolerance.

MMPI-2 AND MMPI-A SUPPLEMENTARY SCALES

Since the initial publication of the MMPI, more than 450 new scales have been developed. Some of these have been developed for normals and are unrelated to pathology, such as dominance (*Do*) and social status (*St*). Other scales relate more directly to pathological dimensions, and often use the data from Hathaway and McKinley's original standardization sample or the more recent restandardization group. Scoring is possible only if the entire 567 MMPI-2 or 478 MMPI-A items are given. Although exact cutoffs for determining high scores have not been specified, they are generally $T = 65$. Scoring templates and profile sheets are available through Pearson Assessments. The scales selected for inclusion on this profile sheet are considered most useful, have been most extensively researched, or show promise in terms of future usefulness and/or are likely to be researched more extensively in the future. The following lists provide the names and interpretations surrounding scale elevations.

MMPI-2 Supplementary Scales

A/Anxiety. High scores indicate that the person is upset, shy, retiring, insecure, has low self-confidence, is inhibited, uncertain, hesitant, conforming, under stress, and has extreme difficulty making decisions. Low scores indicate that the individual is extraverted, secure, relaxed, energetic, competitive, and generally has an absence of emotional difficulties.

R/Repression. High scorers tend to be submissive, overcontrolled, slow, clear thinking, conventional, formal, cautious, use denial and rationalization, and go to great lengths to avoid unpleasant interpersonal situations. Low scorers are likely to be dominant, enthusiastic, excitable, impulsive, self-indulgent, outspoken, and achievement oriented.

Es/Ego Strength. This scale assesses the degree to which a client is likely to benefit from psychotherapy, but it is probably specific to predicting the response of neurotic patients to insight-oriented therapy; it is probably not useful for other types of patients or other kinds of treatments. High scores suggest these persons can benefit from psychotherapy because they are likely to be adaptable and possess personal resources; have good reality contact; are tolerant, balanced, alert; have a secure sense of reality; will seek help in situational difficulties; possess strongly developed interests; are persistent; can deal effectively with others; have a sense of personal adequacy; can easily gain social acceptance; and have good physical health. Low scores reflect general maladjustment. These people are likely to have low self-esteem, a poor self-concept; lack personal resources; feel insecure; are rigid and moralistic; have chronic physical problems; possess fears and phobias; are confused and helpless, have chronic fatigue; may be withdrawn and seclusive, inhibited; have personality rather than situational problems and poor work histories; and will, therefore, have difficulty benefiting from psychotherapy.

Do/Dominance. Elevations indicate that the individual is self-confident, realistic, task oriented; feels a sense of duty toward others; is competent to solve problems, socially dominant, poised, and self-assured in working with groups; takes the initiative in relationships; possesses strong opinions; perseveres at tasks; and has a good ability to concentrate. The scale is useful and frequently used in personnel selection (e.g., police officer selection).

Re/Responsibility. High scores suggest that the individual possesses high standards, a strong sense of justice and fairness, strong (even rigid) adherence to values; is self-confident, dependable, trustworthy. The scale is a general index of positive personality characteristics; often useful in personnel screening.

Mt/College Maladjustment. High scores indicate general maladjustment among college students; they are likely to be worried, anxious, and procrastinate; they are pessimistic, ineffectual, somatize stress, and feel that, much of the time, life is a strain.

PK/Posttraumatic Stress Disorder Scale. High scores indicate emotional distress, depression, anxiety, sleep disturbances, guilt, loss of control over thinking, a feeling of being misunderstood and mistreated by others. The scale does not determine that trauma has actually occurred but indicates that the symptoms reported are consistent with persons exposed to traumatic events; the existence of a trauma still needs to be determined through other means.

MDS/Marital Distress Scale. High scores indicate the person is experiencing marital distress; this scale is more specifically related to marital difficulties than either the FAM content scale or Scale 4 (both of which assess relationship difficulties not necessarily specific to marriage). MDS should be interpreted only for persons who are married, separated, or divorced.

Ho/Hostility Scale. Highs scores are characterized by being cynical, mistrusting, suspicious, unfriendly, and angry. However, they may not express their hostility in overt ways. They are likely to perceive others as being hostile and to blame others for their problems. As a result, they typically have low levels of social support. They have poor self-concepts and may be depressed. anxious, and experience somatic difficulties. They may have serious health problems.

O-H/Overcontrolled Hostility Scale. High scores suggest that the person is emotionally constricted, bottles up anger, and may overreact, possibly becoming physically or verbally aggressive; the aggressiveness usually occurs as rare incidents in a person who is otherwise extremely well controlled. The scale is most useful in understanding past behavior rather than predicting the likelihood of future hostility. Some persons who score high are not actively struggling to control dangerous hostility but are very well controlled and highly socialized. Thus, the scale is more directly a measure of persons who deny aggressive actions and are somewhat constricted; therapy, at least initially, might seem superficial and lacking in affect.

MAC-R/MacAndrew Alcoholism Scale-Revised. The MAC-R scale is best considered a measure of the potential for substance abuse. It differentiates between outpatient alcoholics and nonalcoholic psychiatric outpatients and identifies persons who are at risk of later developing alcohol-related problems. The potential to become involved in alcohol use is assessed rather than current alcohol use. In addition, the scale has diffi-culty differentiating alcohol abusers from other substance abusers. High scores on the MAC-R scale primarily suggest actual or potential substance abuse but may also suggest extraversion, affiliation, confidence, assertiveness, risk taking, sensation seeking, past school behavior problems, the possibility of having experienced blackouts, and possible difficulties with concentration. Low scores are not only a contraindication of substance abuse but also may suggest introversion, conformity, and low self-confidence. Low scores in a known substance abuser suggest that the abuse is based more on psychological dis-turbance than typical addictive processes. The recommended raw score cutoff to indicate the initial point of drug and/or alcohol problems for males is 26 to 28; for females it is a lower 23 to 25. The MAC-R is not particularly effective with African Americans and other non-Caucasian respondents. High scorers are likely to be extraverted, impulsive risk takers who will benefit from a group-oriented, confrontational treatment approach. Low scorers are more likely to be introverted, withdrawn, depressed risk avoiders who will be more likely to benefit from a supportive and relatively nonconfrontational treatment approach.

AAS/Addiction Acknowledgment Scale. High scores suggest a conscious awareness of and willingness to share information related to drug and/or alcohol-related problems. It is the most sensitive MMPI-2 scale for detecting substance abuse (Rouse, Butcher, & Miller, 1999; L. Stein, Graham, Ben-Porath, & McNulty, 1999). Low scores merely clarify that the person has not acknowledged these problems (although there is still the possibility that the person does have drug and/or alcohol-related difficulties).

APS/Addiction Potential Scale. High scores indicate that the person has a considerable number of lifestyle and personality factors consistent with those who abuse alcohol and/ or drugs. The scale does not necessarily measure the extent of current use but more the potential for developing such problems. This means that if the APS (or MAC-R) is used to identify persons who are actually abusing substances, it is likely to result in a high number of false positives (Rouse et al., 1999). If the person scores in the normal to low range but history reveals a drug and/or alcohol problem, this problem is probably based primarily on psychological maladjustment (drug/alcohol use as self-medication) rather than a typical addictive pattern (harmful habits, peer group issues, physiological impact of the drug). This scale is quite similar to the MAC-R scale, but it uses more of the newer MMPI-2 item pool than the MAC-R. There is some indication that it measures the same factors as the MAC-R and may do so either as effectively (Rouse et al., 1999; L. Stein et al., 1999) or more effectively (Greene, Weed, Butcher, Arredono, & Davis, 1992; Weed, Butcher, Ben-Porath, & McKenny, 1992).

GM/Masculine Gender Role. Persons who score high (both males and females) are likely to be self-confident, deny feeling afraid or worried, and be persistent in pursuing their goals; females scoring high are likely to be honest, unworried, and have a willingness to explore new things; high scores on GM with correspondingly low scores on Gf indicate stereotypic male interests and orientations; high scores on both GM and GF suggest androgyny (the person has both masculine and feminine characteristics); low scores on GM along with high scores on GF suggest stereotypic feminine interests and orientation; low scores on both scales suggest an undifferentiated masculine/feminine orientation. This scale is still experimental and in need of further research.

GF/Feminine Gender Role. High scores suggest the endorsement of stereotypically feminine interests and orientations, and may also suggest religiosity and possibly abuse of alcohol and/or nonprescription drugs; males scoring high may be hypercritical, express religiosity, avoid swearing but act bossy, and have a difficult time controlling their temper. This scale is still experimental and in need of further research.

MMPI-A Supplementary Scales

MAC-R/MacAndrew Alcoholism Scale. High scores suggest that the person is similar to others who have alcohol or drug problems; dominant, assertive, egocentric, self-indulgent, impulsive, unconventional; risk taker and sensation seeker; increased possibility of conduct disorder and legal difficulties. Low scores suggest that the person is dependent, conservative, avoids sensation-seeking activities, is overcontrolled and indecisive.

ACK/Alcohol Drug Acknowledgment Scale. Persons who score high have a conscious awareness of and willingness to admit to alcohol- and/or drug-related problems; includes problem use, reliance on alcohol to cope or as a means of freely expressing feelings, harmful substance abuse habits; friends or acquaintances may tell them that they have alcohol and/or drug problems; they may get into fights while drinking.

PRO/Alcohol Drug Proneness Scale. A high score suggests that the person is prone to developing drug- and/or alcohol-related problems and school and home behavior problems. No obvious items related to drugs and alcohol are included on the scale; therefore, the scale measures personality and lifestyle patterns more consistent with alcohol- and drug-related problems. The scale does not so much measure current alcohol or drug use patterns (although they may still be present; quite similar to the MMPI-2 APS scale).

IMM/Immaturity Scale. High scorers are untrustworthy, undependable, boisterous; quickly become angry, are easily frustrated, may tease or bully others; are resistant, defiant, and likely to have a background of school and interpersonal difficulties.

A/Anxiety. General maladjustment, anxiety, distress, emotionally upset, experiences discomfort.

R/Repression. Submissive, conventional, works hard to avoid unpleasant or disagreeable situations.

MMPI-2-Restructured Form (MMPI-2-RF)

The MMPI-2-Restructured Form (MMPI-2-RF; Ben-Porath & Tellegen, 2008) represents a major revision of the MMPI-2. Indeed, it can be seen as both an alternative to as well as a stand-alone instrument. It is based on a subset of the MMPI-2 pool and utilizes the MMPI-2 normative sample. The validity scales have also been retained. In addition, many of the scales represent a refinement of the standard clinical scales. It has also been reduced in length to 388 items and, as such, represents a good alternative to the MMPI-2 when brevity is critical. At the core of the MMPI-2-RF are the restructured clinical scales and the Psychopathology Five (PSY-5) scales.

MMPI-2 Restructured Clinical Scales

As noted previously, the MMPI clinical scale items were selected based on their ability to distinguish clinical groups from normals. They were not designed to differentiate various clinical groups from each other. The result has been that the MMPI/MMPI-2 clinical scales are good at identifying that psychopathology is present but not what the psychopathology is. In order to counter this difficulty, many strategies have been developed to help clinicians make more nuanced distinctions among various scale elevations. These strategies have included the content scales, Harris and Lingoes subscales, supplementary scales, and critical items. In 2003 a set of restructured clinical scales were made available to help isolate the core features of the clinical scales (Tellegen et al., 2003). The first step was to use factor analysis to develop a general demoralization scale (RCd/Demoralization). By extracting all items in the demoralization scale from any of the clinical scales, initial (or "seed") scales were developed that more closely assessed the core features of the clinical scales. These scales were then further refined to develop the final Restructured Clinical scales (see reviews and debate in a special series of the *Journal of Personality Assessment, 87* (2006): 119–222).

At the present time, the Restructured Clinical scales are recommended to refine the meanings of the clinical scales. For example, a client might have elevations on the so-called psychotic or right side of an MMPI-2 clinical scale profile (Scales 6, 8, and 9). These scores may lead a clinician to wonder if the elevations are due primarily to actual psychotic symptoms or if the elevations are merely due to general distress and demoralization. If the corresponding Restructured Clinical scales (see scales RC6, RC8, and RC9 in the next list) were quite low in comparison to the clinical scales (6, 8, and 9), a clinician could reasonably infer that the "psychotic" scales were elevated primarily due to demoralization (rather than the presence of actual psychotic symptoms).

A listing of the Restructured Clinical scales along with interpretations for high-scoring persons follows (derived from Ben-Porath & Tellegen, 2008; Handel & Archer, 2008; Sellbom et al., 2006; and Tellegen et al., 2003):

RCd/Demoralization. Discouraged, pessimistic, poor self-esteem, insecure, sense of failure, emotional discomfort, poor coping ability, helpless, interpersonally sensitive, depressed, anxious, presence of somatic symptoms.

RC1/Somatic Complaints. Presence of significant health difficulties, may have actual physical condition but with higher scores a significant psychological component is likely, somatization of physical complaints, constant worry related to physical complaints, weakness, fatigue, chronic pain, denies psychological explanations.

RC2/Low Positive Emotions. Withdrawn, passive, self-critical, insufficient energy to deal with life challenges, difficult time accomplishing tasks, isolated, bored, little ability to experience pleasure, interpersonal sensitivity, poor expectations of success, depressed, difficulty becoming engaged with people.

RC3/Cynicism (note that RC3 focuses on the narrow component of Scale 3 that refers to naiveté and is given a reverse scoring). High scorers are perceived as uncaring, untrustworthy, and will readily exploit others; in contrast, low scorers are likely to be gullible, naive, and trust others too readily.

RC4/Antisocial Behavior. Angry, argumentative, aggressive, nonconforming, legal difficulties, lying, cheating, stealing, substance abuse, sexual acting out, conflict with family, poor achievement.

RC6/Ideas of Persecution. Feels they are being controlled and victimized by external forces, feels mistreated, has difficulty trusting others, is suspicious.

RC7/Dysfunctional Negative Emotions. Anxious, irritable, general unhappiness and helplessness, interpersonal sensitivity, feels easily criticized, ruminates, is preoccupied, feels excessive guilt, insecurity.

RC8/Aberrant Experiences. Cognitive, motor, perceptual, and sensory disturbances; possible visual, auditory, or olfactory hallucinations; high scores suggest impaired functioning, bizarre sensory/perceptual experiences, possible thought broadcasting, impaired ability to test reality.

RC9/Hypomanic Activation. High energy, elevated mood, minimal need for sleep, high self-regard, grandiosity, sensation seeking, risk taking, irritability, little ability to control impulses, possible aggression. Extremely high scores (>75) suggest a manic episode but moderate scores (60–70) may indicate persons who are well adapted but high energy.

Personality Psychopathology Five (PSY-5) Scales

The Personality Psychopathology Five (PSY-5) scales represent a special cluster of supplementary scales (Harkness et al., 2002). Item selection was preceded by working with a group of laypersons to develop relevant, distinctive, and easily understandable personality constructs. The five emerging constructs were then used to select the extent of existing MMPI-2 items reflected these constructs. The resulting items were refined by professional reviewers and then submitted to formal psychometric analysis. The descriptors summarized next are from the Harkness et al. (2002) monograph and refer to scores greater than $T = 65$:

AGGR Aggressiveness. Enjoys intimidating others, aggression used to accomplish goals, dominant, extroverted, history of being physically abusive, antisocial. High-scoring men are more likely to have a history of domestic violence; high-scoring women are more likely to have been arrested.

PSYC Psychoticism (PSYC). Delusions of reference, disorganized thinking, tangential, bizarre, disoriented, circumstantial; outpatients were described as having low functioning, few or no friends, depressed; men were rated as sad and depressed, women were more likely to be experiencing hallucinations; inpatient populations are more likely to be psychotic and have paranoid suspiciousness, loose associations, flight of ideas, hallucinations, and ideas of reference.

Disconstraint (DISC). Risk taking, nontraditional, impulsive, easily bored, antisocial, aggressive; history of having been arrested; history of having abused alcohol, cocaine, and marijuana; prefer romantic partners who are also disconstrained. Men have more histories of domestic violence, women are somewhat achievement oriented; low scorers ($T = 40$ or less) have greater self-control, reduced impulsivity, adhere closely to rules, can easily tolerate boredom, are constrained, and prefer romantic partners who are also constrained.

Negative Emotionality/Neuroticism (NEGE). Worry, guilty, self-critical, think in terms of worst-case scenario; outpatients likely to be depressed/dysthymic, low functioning, few/no friends, anxious, sad mood, somatic symptoms. High-scoring men are likely to have engaged in domestic violence related to attempts at maintaining a focus on the flaws, and irritations with their spouse and their future. High-scoring women are likely to be pessimistic, have low achievement, and have histories of alcohol abuse.

Introversion/Low Positive Emotionality (INTR). Depressed, sad, low achievement orientation, introverted, anxious, pessimistic, somatic symptoms; women more likely to have taken antidepressants and to report having few/no friends. Low scorers ($T = 40$ or less) have good capacity to experience pleasure and joy, energized, social, unlikely to be depressed/dysthymic; extremely low scores suggest hypomanic features.

Additional MMPI-2-RF Scales

The MMPI-2-RF has also introduced the following additional scales to help clinicians obtain relevant information. Since these scales can still be considered experimental, they are listed without elaboration. In addition, the titles of the scales closely match the variables they are measuring.

Higher-Order Scales. Emotional/Internalizing Dysfunction (EID), Thought Dysfunction (THD), Behavioral/Externalizing Dysfunction (BXD)

Internalizing Scales. Suicidal/Death Ideation (SUI), Helplessness/Hopelessness (HLP), Self-Doubt (SFD), Inefficacy (NFC), Cognitive Complaints (COG), Stress/Worry (STW), Anxiety (AXY), Anger Proneness (ANP), Behavior-Restricting Fears (BRF), Multiple Specific Fears (MSF)

Externalizing Scales. Juvenile Conduct Problems (JCP), Substance Abuse (SUB), Aggression (AGG), Activation (ACT)

Somatic Scales. Malaise (MLS), Head Pain Complaints (HPC), Neurological Complaints (NUC), Gastro-Intestinal Complaints (GIC)

Interpersonal Scales. Family Problems (FML), Interpersonal Passivity (IPP), Social Avoidance (SAV), Shyness (SHY), Disaffiliativeness (DSF)

Interest Scales. Aesthetic-Literary Interests (AES), Mechanical-Physical Interests (MEC)

RECOMMENDED READING

Archer, R. A. (2005). *MMPI-A: Assessing adolescent psychopathology* (3rd ed.). Hillsdale, NJ: Lawrence Erlbaum.

Butcher, J. N. (2006b). *A beginner's guide to the MMPI-2* (2nd ed.). Washington, DC: American Psychological Association.

Butcher, J. N., & Perry, J. (2008). *Psychological assessment in treatment planning: Use of the MMPI-2 and BTPI.* New York: Oxford University Press.

Caldwell, A. (2001). What do the MMPI scales fundamentally measure? Some hypotheses. *Journal of Personality Assessment, 76,* 1–17.

Finn, S. E. (1996). *A manual for using the MMPI-2 as a therapeutic intervention.* Minneapolis, MN: University of Minnesota Press.

Friedman, A., Lewak, R., Nichols, D., & Webb, J. F. (2000). *Psychological assessment with the MMPI-2.* Mahwah, NJ: Lawrence Erlbaum.

Graham, J. R. (2006). *MMPI-2: Assessing personality and psychopathology* (4th ed.). New York: Oxford University Press.

Lewak, R. W., Marks, P. A., & Nelson, G. E. (1990). *Therapist guide to the MMPI and MMPI-2.* Muncie, IN: Accelerated Development.

Chapter 8

MILLON CLINICAL MULTIAXIAL INVENTORY

The Millon Clinical Multiaxial Inventory (MCMI) is a standardized, self-report questionnaire that assesses a wide range of information related to a client's personality, emotional adjustment, and attitude toward taking tests. It has been designed for adults (18 years and older) who have a minimum of an eighth-grade reading level. The MCMI is one of the few self-report tests that focus on personality disorders along with symptoms that are frequently associated with these disorders. Originally developed in 1977 (Millon, 1977), it has since been through two revisions (MCMI-II; Millon, 1987; MCMI-III; Millon, 1994, 1997). Since its original publication, it has stimulated more than 850 published papers on or about it and has become one of the more frequently used tests in clinical practice (Archer et al., 2006; Camara et al., 2000; C. Piotrowski & Zalewski, 1993). Indeed, it is one of the few tests that has "risen through the ranks" of test usage over the past 30 years. Among objective personality tests for clinical trainees to be familiar with, the MCMI was ranked by directors of clinical training programs second only to the MMPI/MMPI-2 in importance (C. Piotrowski & Zalewski, 1993). Its popularity is further supported by its use in several different countries and its translation into a number of different languages.

The current version, the MCMI-III, is composed of 175 items that are scored to produce 28 scales divided into the following categories: Modifying Indices, Clinical Personality Patterns, Severe Personality Pathology, Clinical Syndromes, and Severe Syndromes (see Table 8.1). The scales, along with the items that comprise the scales, are closely aligned to both Millon's theory of personality and the *DSM-IV* (1994). For example, an item endorsing a person's belief in his or her own superiority would be part of the Narcissistic scale, because the content clearly relates to components of Millon's and the *DSM-IV*'s conceptualization of the narcissistic personality. Many of the scales have both theoretical and item overlap—an important fact to keep in mind when conceptualizing the client and interpreting the scales. Thus, an elevation on both the Antisocial and Sadistic scales would reflect a person who has sadistic features along with legal difficulties and impulsiveness, and who is interpersonally exploitive. Similarly, a person scoring high on the Antisocial scale might have a corresponding elevation on the Alcohol Dependence scale. The corresponding elevations on conceptually related scales allow for a more complete understanding of the client.

In some ways, the MCMI is an alternative or even a competitor to the MMPI. Both instruments cover a wide range of adult pathology that assess both long-standing personality patterns as well as clinical symptomatology. In other ways, the MCMI nicely complements the MMPI as the MMPI focuses primarily on Axis I disorders whereas the MCMI was specifically designed to assist in diagnosing Axis II disorders. One important advantage of the MCMI is that it is considerably shorter than the MMPI-2 (175 versus 567 items) and yet provides a wide range of information. The MCMI takes only 20 to 30 minutes to complete; however, the research base, validity studies, and options for interpretations are clearly more extensive for the MMPI than for the MCMI. Neither instrument

Table 8.1   MCMI-III Scale categories, abbreviations, number of items, and reliabilities

Scale Category/Name	Abbreviation	No. of Items	Alpha
Modifying Indices			
Disclosure	X	NA	NA
Desirability	Y	21	.85
Debasement	Z	33	.95
Validity	V	4	NA
Clinical Personality Patterns			
Schizoid	1	16	.81
Avoidant	2A	16	.89
Depressive	2B	15	.89
Dependent	3	16	.85
Histrionic	4	17	.81
Narcissistic	5	24	.67
Antisocial	6A	17	.77
Aggressive (Sadistic)	6B	20	.79
Compulsive	7	17	.66
Passive-Aggressive (Negativistic)	8a	16	.83
Self-Defeating	8B	15	.87
Severe Personality Pathology			
Schizotypal	S	16	.85
Borderline	C	16	.85
Paranoid	P	17	.84
Clinical Syndromes			
Anxiety	A	14	.86
Somatoform	H	12	.86
Bipolar:Manic	N	13	.71
Dysthymia	D	14	.88
Alcohol Dependence	B	15	.82
Drug Dependence	T	14	.83
Posttraumatic Stress Disorder	PT	16	.89
Severe Syndromes			
Thought Disorder	SS	17	.87
Major Depression	CC	17	.90
Delusional Disorder	PP	13	.79

Source: Adapted from *Millon Clinical Multiaxial Inventory-III Manual* 2nd ed., by T. Millon, 1997, Minneapolis, MN: National Computer Systems.

should be considered to provide diagnosis. Instead, both provide considerable information relevant to diagnosis. In this sense, they place the clinician in the right "diagnostic ballpark," but he or she must then integrate this with other information to make the final diagnosis. In other words, tests (or computer reports) do not diagnose (or make decisions); only practitioners can perform this function.

Factors that greatly assist in useful interpretation are familiarity with the theoretical constructs as well as experience with relevant clinical populations. Theoretical knowledge can be greatly assisted through familiarity with Millon and Davis's (1996) *Disorders of Personality* as well as the diagnostic criteria of the *DSM-IV*. This emphasis on clinical populations also focuses on the principle that the MCMI is intended for psychiatric populations and should not be used with normal persons or those who are merely mildly disturbed. Interpretations should be restricted to persons who scored at or above the designated cutoff scores (75 and 85). Practitioners should resist the temptation to attempt interpretations of persons who have mild "elevations" on the scale but who are still clearly below the formal cutoff.

HISTORY AND DEVELOPMENT

Development of the Original MCMI

Shortly after Millon published his 1969 text, *Modern Psychopathology*, fellow profession-als urged him to develop an instrument that would operationalize and measure the dimen-sions of personality as outlined in the book. By 1972, an initial form was developed: the Millon–Illinois Self-Report Inventory (MI-SRI). Over the next five years, the items were further developed, refined, and coordinated with the upcoming personality disor-ders that were later to be incorporated into *DSM-III* (APA, 1980). When the initial refine-ments were completed, the test was published and renamed the Millon Clinical Multiaxial Inventory (MCMI; Millon, 1977).

The formal development of the original MCMI used a combination of rational theory-based as well as empirical procedures. The first step was the development of a large pool of face valid questions—a total of 3,500 items derived from Millon's (1969) theories. These were then rationally grouped into 20 different scales. The number of items was initially reduced by the test developers by rewording those that were poorly worded and removing those that were redundant. Further refinement was done empirically by hav-ing patients rate the clarity and difficulty of the items. A further procedure involved having clinicians regroup the items into scales to evaluate the extent to which these scales related to those originated by the test developers. Based on these procedures, the items were then grouped into two equivalent provisional research forms, with 556 items in each form. The forms were administered to 200 patients, and their responses were evaluated for their endorsement frequency and item-scale intercorrelations. The highest within-scale item intercorrelations were retained, and items that were either very frequently (> 85%) or very rarely (15%) endorsed were eliminated. The research form was thereby reduced to a test composed of 289 items.

The 289-item research form was given to 167 clinicians who blindly rated 682 of their patients on 20 different variables after having given them the form. The amount of endorse-ment frequency and the degree of scale overlap were then used to reduce the items from 289 to 154. Based on this initial validation procedure, three scales were dropped (Sociopathy, Hypochondriasis, and Obsession-Compulsion), and three new scales were developed and added (Drug Abuse, Alcohol, and Hypomania). This brought the total number of surviving items to 175, with 733 different keyings on the 20 different scales.

The scales were initially standardized on 1,591 clinical subjects used in the construc-tion phase of the test. This sample was used to establish the optimal cutoff scores for determining the presence or absence of certain characteristics. A group of 297 nonclini-cal subjects was used to establish the responses of a normal comparison group. In 1981, the MCMI responses of 43,218 patients were reviewed to further refine and recalculate the cutoff scores.

One feature of the MCMI and its revisions is the use of cutoffs related to Base Rate (BR) scores to designate the presence or absence of a particular characteristic. The BR score, like the more familiar T score, is essentially a means of transforming a raw score into a more meaningful score for interpretation. However, BR scores are derived from the percentage of a population that has been deemed to have a certain characteristic or syndrome. For example, 17% of a psychiatric population can be considered to have clear characteristics of a dependent personality whereas only 1% is considered to have clear features of a sadistic personality. This means that decisions regarding client characteristics are made when a client scores in a range that is consistent with either of these two syndromes. However, the relatively more frequent psychiatric disorders with high BRs (i.e., Dependent) require relatively lower cutoff points than those rare disorders with low BRs (i.e., Sadistic). Millon arbitrarily set a BR score of 85 to indicate that the characteristic(s) in question was definitely present. A lower BR score of 75 indicated that some of the features were present. Additional cutoff or anchor points were set at 35 to represent the median score for normal or nonpsychiatric groups, and at 60, the median for psychiatric populations. This BR approach has been theoretically encouraged by a number of authors (Finn, 1982; Widiger & Kelso, 1983) and empirically demonstrated to increase diagnostic accuracy when compared with the more frequently used T score approach (Duthie & Vincent, 1986).

Development of the MCMI-II

The MCMI-II (Millon, 1987) maintained most of the features of the original MCMI. Its development was motivated by a need to incorporate additional research and theory on personality disorders while remaining aligned with the criteria outlined in *DSM-III* and *DSM-III-R* (APA, 1987). In addition, between 40 and 50 of the original MCMI items were found to be expendable. Items were developed for two new scales, in part by dividing the previous Negativistic scale into separate scales for Passive-Aggressive (Negativistic) and Self-Defeating. Similarly, the earlier Antisocial-Aggressive scale was divided into an Antisocial scale and an Aggressive/Sadistic scale. Additional items were generated with procedures similar to those used for the original MCMI. This resulted in an MCMI-II Provisional Form of 368 items, which was given to 184 patients who had been carefully diagnosed using *DSM-III-R* criteria. Items were retained or deleted based on the extent to which they could differentiate relevant diagnostic criterion groups. Like the earlier MCMI, the MCMI-II totaled 175 items, but they were keyed on 22 (as opposed to only 20) different scales. In an attempt to reduce scale intercorrelation, individual items were given weightings of 1, 2, or 3 points, based on their relative importance for the specific scales they were being keyed on. Optimal BR cutoff scores were based on a standardization group of 1,292 patients who had a wide variety of presenting problems.

Development of the MCMI-III

Ongoing research, new conceptual developments, and the publication of the *DSM-IV* (APA, 1994) contributed to the MCMI-II's revision into its latest version, the MCMI-III (Millon, 1994, 1997; Millon, Millon, Davis, & Grossman, 2006). With procedures similar to those used for the MCMI and MCMI-II, a provisional 325-item test was developed; Depressive and PTSD scales were added. The Self-Defeating and Sadistic Personality Disorder scales were maintained, although these diagnoses were eliminated from the *DSM-IV*. The final MCMI-III still totaled 175 items, but 90 of the items from the MCMI-II were "changed" (85 remained the same). Actually, most of the changed items remained essentially the same in their primary content; the alterations related mostly to increasing the severity of the symptoms. This was done to decrease the number of people endorsing particular items, in the hope that the MCMI-III would be more selective in suggesting pathology. In addition, the items per scale were reduced by half and the number of keyings was reduced from 953 on the MCMI-II to only 440 for the MCMI-III. The possible ratings per item were reduced from 1, 2, or 3 to either 1 or 2. The resulting 28 scales are divided into the categories shown in Table 8.1. Optimal BR cutoff scores were derived from a standardization sample of 1,079 clinical patients who had come from a diversity of backgrounds and treatment settings. In addition, facets, or subcomponents, were developed for each of the personality scales to allow for a more nuanced interpretation of scale elevations (Grossman & del Rio, 2005; Millon et al., 2006).

Theoretical Considerations

The development of the three versions of the MCMI has been partially guided by Millon's theories of personality. One of his core principles is the use of the polarities of pleasure-pain, active-passive, and self-other (R. Davis, 1999; Millon & Davis, 1996; Millon et al., 2006; Strack, 1999). These polarities can be related to the fundamental evolutionary tasks of all people in that they must struggle to exist/survive (pleasure-pain), use various efforts to adapt to their environment or adapt their environment to themselves (passive-active), and invest in other people as well as themselves (other-self). Each of these polarities can be used to describe differences in personality organization for normal persons as well as those with personality disorders. For example, normal levels of functioning can occur on the active-passive dimension but, when either an active or a passive style is exaggerated, then the person can become dysfunctional. Thus, schizoid and avoidant personality disorders are extreme in the direction of passivity. In the self-other dimension, dependent and histrionic personalities are highly oriented toward others, whereas the narcissistic personality is extremely self-oriented. Many of the personality styles can be simultaneously portrayed on each of the three polarities. For example, the histrionic style is quite active and is both other-(dependent) and pleasure-oriented. In some cases, the person is ambivalent on one or more of these dimensions, thereby resembling a person with a passive-aggressive style who is overtly passive and compliant but covertly expresses conflict and anger. Considerably more detail on these polarities, along with other aspects of personality disorders, can be found in Millon and Davis's (1996) *Disorders of Personality: DSM-IV and Beyond*.

Another important point relates to both the test's development and its implications for interpretation: The personality styles are not mutually exclusive. For example, a person with an antisocial style might be frequently uncomfortable with underlying anger and antisocial impulses and thus express them in passive-aggressive modes. This overlap also explains why the diagnosis of personality disorders has been plagued with poor interdiagnostician agreement (poor discriminant validity; R. F. Bornstein, 1998). The expected overlap among characteristics is one reason that the test developers were not overly concerned that many of the scales were highly correlated. Also, the overlap that was present seemed to occur in theoretically consistent patterns. From a practical perspective, this means that combinations of scale elevations can be used to give added meaning to each other. For example, a high score on the Antisocial scale, in combination with an elevation on the Sadistic scale, clearly suggests that the person will act out his or her antisocial feelings in a predictable and potentially dangerous manner. This activity would have very clear implications for case management and treatment planning.

Further, scale elevations should always be placed into the context of the person's life. A high score is not diagnostic of a personality disorder in and of itself. If a person can find an appropriate niche where the expression of his or her personality style is not dysfunctional, that person should not be considered "disordered." Thus, the distinction between a personality "style" and an actual personality "disorder" should be stressed. For example, a salesman with a narcissistic antisocial style might be able to optimize these traits in a way that makes him quite occupationally successful. The diagnostic criteria for personality disorders specifically state that there must be an enduring pattern leading to "clinically significant distress or impairment in social, occupational, or other important areas of functioning" (APA, 2000, p. 686). If there is no or little distress or impairment, a personality disorder should not be diagnosed. This point is particularly crucial for the Compulsive (7), Histrionic (4), and Narcissistic (5) scales since these scales are often elevated among persons without significant psychopathology (Craig, 2005). Thus, it is crucial for clinicians to determine whether a given personality style suggested by the MCMI has actually led to distress and/or impairment.

Finally, the different categories of scales (Clinical Personality Patterns, Severe Personality Pathology, Clinical Syndrome, Severe Syndrome) are conceptually and clinically related (see Table 8.1). The first two categories relate to Axis II diagnoses but are separated to designate the greater levels of severity for the schizotypal, borderline, and paranoid conditions. As was previously pointed out, however, any of the personality styles are not disorders unless there is distress and impairment. The second categories are intended to measure the type and level of distress and thus relate more to Axis I levels of diagnoses. They represent the expression of personality styles that are not working well for the person. For example, if the narcissistic antisocial salesman mentioned previously tries to act toward his spouse as he does toward his business contacts, she may file for divorce. His means of coping with this outcome might be abuse of alcohol. In contrast, an individual with a dependent avoidant style who is undergoing a divorce would be likely to respond with a major depression. This difference underlies the essential interrelationship between Axis I and Axis II diagnoses. It also points out that the MCMI can help to establish the presence of an Axis II diagnosis by noting the type and degree of distress and impairment as expressed in elevations on the scales in the Clinical Syndrome and Severe Syndrome categories.

RELIABILITY AND VALIDITY

Reliability and validity studies on the MCMI indicate that it is generally a well-constructed psychometric instrument. Measures of internal consistency have been particularly strong. For the MCMI-III, alpha coefficients exceed .80 for 20 of the 26 scales, with a high of .90 for the Major Depression scale and a low of .66 for Compulsive (Millon et al., 2006). Test-retest reliabilities have been moderate to high. The MCMI-III manual reports that over a 5- to 14-day interval, test-retest reliability had a median of .91 (the high was .96 for Somatoform and the low was .82 for Debasement). Craig (1999) has summarized three data sets on test reliabilities ranging from 5 days to 6 months by stating that the median reliability was .78 for the Personality scales and .80 for the Clinical Syndrome scales. Much longer term test-retest reliabilities spanning 4 years ranged from a high of .73 for Passive-Aggressive to a low for Dependent of .59 (Lenzenweger, 1999). This is roughly equivalent to other stable dimensions of personality.

Because the personality scales theoretically represent enduring, ingrained characteristics, they should have greater stability than the clinical scales, which are based on more changeable symptomatic patterns. In some cases, this has been found to be true; in others, little difference has been found. Studies on the MCMI-I have indicated the theoretically expected higher stability for the personality scales as opposed to the clinical scales (Piersma, 1986). In contrast, the Craig (1999) summary found very little difference between the mean personality and clinical scales, despite an extended retesting interval. Similarly, the MCMI-III manual reported a mean of .89 for the personality scales and a slightly greater mean of .91 for the clinical scales. This finding suggests that the original MCMI may have had the theoretically higher temporal stability for the personality scales than the clinical scales, but later versions have roughly equivalent temporal stabilities between the two categories of scales.

One central issue when evaluating the validity of the MCMI is the extent to which validity studies on previous versions can be generalized to the newer versions. With appropriate caution, some transferability can be justified because the correlations between the MCMI-II and MCMI-III scales are moderately high. Specifically, the correlations range from a high of .94 for Debasement to a low of .59 for Dependent, with 12 of the 25 scale comparisons above .70. Comparisons between the Depressive and Posttraumatic Stress Disorder scales could not be made because they were uniquely developed for the MCMI-III. However, Marlowe, Festinger, and Kirby (1998) found much lower correlations and little comparability for code types. This should be balanced with their conclusion that the MCMI-III did provide comparable clinical information. It should also be noted that they used a relatively small sample of persons who had a quite specific disorder (cocaine dependence). It would thus be important for future studies to determine the extent to which the MCMI-III code types are actually comparable to the MCMI-II.

More than 20 factor-analytic studies have been performed on the various MCMI versions, and these have generally supported the keying of the items (Retzlaff, Lorr, & Hyer, 1989) as well as the clustering of the factors around Millon's conceptualization of psychopathology (Choca, Retzlaff, Strack, Mouton, & Van Denburg for 1996; Choca & Van Denburg, 1997; McCann, 1991). Factor analysis of the MCMI-II has generally supported the organization of the scales. The most extensive published factor analysis involved 769 cases and resulted in an eight-factor solution (Millon, 1987). The largest factor accounted for 31% of the variance, was related to general Maladjustment, and involved depressed affect, impaired interpersonal relationships, low self-esteem, and unusual cognition and self-behavior. The next two largest factors were Acting Out/Self-Indulgent (13% of the variance) and Anxious and Depressed Somatization (8% of the variance). The final factors, listed according to progressively decreasing proportions of the variance, were Compulsively Defended/Delusional Paranoid, Submissive/Aggressive Sadistic, Addictive Disorders, Psychoticism, and Self and Other Conflictual/Erratic Emotionality. Craig and Bivens (1998) performed a factor analysis on the MCMI-III using 444 outpatients and found three factors they labeled General Maladjustment, Paranoid Behavior/ Thinking with Detached Acting Out, and Antisocial Acting Out.

A variety of correlations have been made between the MCMI and various related instruments, including the Beck Depression Inventory, General Behavior Inventory, Michigan Alcoholism Screening Test, State-Trait Anxiety Inventory, Symptom Checklist-90, and MMPI (Millon, 1994, 1997; Millon et al., 2006). These correlations are reported in detail in the MCMI-III manual. Representative findings include expected correlations between the Beck Depression Inventory and the MCMI-III Major Depression (.74) and Dysthymia (.71) scales. Similarly, high correlations were found between the MMPI-2 Depression scale and the MCMI-III Depression (.71) and Dysthymia (.68) scales. As would be expected, negative correlations were found between the Beck Depression Inventory and MCMI-III scales related to denying pathology (Histrionic, –49; Narcissistic, –40; and Compulsive, –30). An additional representative finding was a .55 correlation between the MCMI-III Somatoform scale and the Symptom Checklist-90-Revised scale for Somatization. One puzzling finding was a low correlation of .29 between the MCMI-III Paranoid scale and the MMPI-2 Paranoia scale. Similar surprising results were moderate correlations between the MMPI-2 Psychopathic deviate scale and the MCMI-III scales for Self-Defeating (.45), Schizotypal (.43), and Depressive (.41). For the most part, however, correlations between the MCMI and external criterion instruments have been in the expected direction.

One of the important and relatively unique contributions of the MCMI has been the development and availability of data on its diagnostic efficiency. This is usually calculated by designating BR scale scores of 75 and/or 85 as *test positives* and comparing these with clinician ratings of whether the characteristics predicted by the scale scores actually matched these clinician ratings. In some settings, however, it is important to take into account the frequency by which a disorder occurs in that setting (base rate of the disorder). For a test to be effective, it must diagnose a disorder more accurately than the chance occurrence as determined by the BR. For example, forensic and/or substance abuse treatment facilities usually have high numbers of persons with antisocial personality styles. In these cases, calculation of the *positive predictive power* of the MCMI for the particular setting is recommended. Essentially, positive predictive power is a calculation of the probability that a test score accurately indicates the presence of a characteristic or diagnosis based on some other measure such as clinical ratings. Such a calculation involves a formula (Gibertini, Brandenberg, & Retzlaff, 1986; see Millon, 1994, pp. 41–43) in which prevalence rates must be inserted (derived from knowledge regarding a specific client population) along with sensitivity and specificity data (available in the MCMI-III manual). Such a calculation provides practitioners with an estimate of the extent to which the instrument performs beyond merely base rate levels levels. For example, if the prevalence (or base rate) of antisocial personalities is .25 but the positive predictive power of the MCMI is .76, the difference (.76 – .25) of .51 indicates that the incremental validity of the instrument is .51 above merely base rate or chance predictions. This emphasis on levels of certainty, with its implications for actual clinical decision making, is one of the strong features of the MCMI.

Calculations of the positive predictive power of the MCMI-II indicated good predictive power ranging between .30 and .80 (Millon, 1987). This was supported by R. Rogers et al. (1999), who pooled existing data on the convergent/divergent validity of the MCMI-II scales and found good support for Avoidant (2A), Schizotypal (S), and Borderline (C); and moderate support for Schizoid (1), Dependent (3), Histrionic (5), Antisocial (6A), Aggressive (6B), Negativistic (8A), Self-Defeating (8B), and Paranoid (P). Little support was found for Compulsive (7%). Positive predictive power for the MCMI-III Axis II scales indicated that the highest accuracy was found for the Dependent (81%), Paranoid (79%), and Compulsive (79%) scales (Millon et al., 2006). In contrast, relatively low positive predictive power was found for the Masochistic (30%), Negativistic (39%), and Depressive (49%) scales. A similar study by R. Davis, Wenger, and Guzman (1997) found that the highest positive predictive power was found for Dependent (.81), Paranoid (.78), and Compulsive (.79), whereas the lowest was found for Masochistic (.30), Negativistic (.39), and Depressive (.49). The low predictive power for Masochistic and Negativistic is consistent with the fact that Masochistic/Self-Defeating was entirely deleted from the *DSM-IV* and Negativistic and Depressive were relegated to the appendix. Deleting these two disorders was thought to be necessary since the *DSM-IV* considered them to be poor diagnoses in the first place; and it also meant that, for the masochistic diagnosis, clinicians did not have the assistance of *DSM-IV* guidelines. Both studies concluded that comparisons of the three generations of the MCMI generally indicate progressive increases in its psychometric characteristics in general and, more specifically, in its diagnostic accuracy (Millon et al., 2006).

ASSETS AND LIMITATIONS

The strategy of developing the MCMI has been commendable and innovative. The history and development section outlines how this has involved a combination of theoretical-conceptual, internal-structural, and external criterion procedures. Each of the procedures has progressed in a stepwise manner; only those items that survived the previous steps were retained. The result has been an instrument that adheres closely to theory, demonstrates good reliability, and, given the limitations of many of the constructs it is measuring, has shown excellent internal and external validity. The use of BR scores has been a noteworthy innovation and has probably resulted in increases in diagnostic accuracy. However, difficulties have been noted related to the extensive item overlap and low level of interdiagnostician agreement among clinicians using methods such as structured interviews and the MMPI. The scale abbreviations are also user unfriendly.

As pointed out previously, the MCMI is a relatively time-efficient test that potentially produces a wide range of information. Of central importance, this information focuses not only on clinical symptomatology (Axis I) but also on the more enduring and potentially more problematic personality disorders (Axis II). These personality disorders can frequently be overlooked. Practitioners might overlook them because (a) the client is more likely to express concern over more overt symptoms, and (b) personality styles are often more hidden and must be inferred. Clients themselves may be unaware of personality styles that have become so automatic that it is difficult to recognize them. They can feel the emotional pain of symptoms but are rarely aware of the recurring patterns of behaviors and cognitions that frequently are at the core of the development and maintenance of these symptoms. In addition to knowing the client patterns that lead to symptoms, considerable literature supports the usefulness of knowing a client's status related to personality disorders. For example, a personality disorder diagnosis suggests that the client is at risk for interpersonal difficulties; these difficulties may complicate the therapeutic relationship and alter the course of Axis I disorders (R. F. Bornstein, 1998). Turkat (1990) has estimated that 50% of clients seeking psychotherapy meet the criteria for a personality disorder. Thus, the MCMI inhabits a crucial niche in objective assessment because it has been designed to better understand personality dysfunction.

Despite the assets of the MCMI, there are a number of inherent difficulties in the assessment of personality disorders. One central issue is that there is no benchmark or gold standard with which to compare the MCMI assessments. Individual clinicians relying on interview information generally have low interdiagnostician agreement (median kappa = .25; J. Perry, 1992). This is sufficiently low enough that it would be unacceptable in any other area of psychological research. Similarly, formal instruments such as the MMPI, MCMI, and structured interviews have shown little agreement (H. Miller, Streiner, & Parkinson, 1992; Streiner & Miller, 1990), which makes it difficult to judge the "true" accuracy of MCMI personality disorder assessment. Several attempts to deal with this have been made. R. F. Bornstein (1998) urges diagnosticians simply to accept that "our ability to describe different personality disorders has outstripped our ability to diagnose them accurately in real-world clinical settings" (p. 334). His solution is to decide whether a client has a personality disorder (which does have very good interdiagnostician agreement; Loranger et al., 1995) and then rate the intensity and level of impairment of various personality characteristics. For example, it might be decided that a client has a personality disorder with dependent (moderate intensity, low impairment levels) and histrionic (low intensity, moderate impairment) features. In contrast, Westen and Shedler (1999a, 1999b) have pointed out that the actual arena of diagnosis by clinicians occurs when they infer personality characteristics from client narratives and match the extent to which these inferences match prototypical conceptions of personality disorders. By rank-ordering composite descriptions of prototypical personality disorders, they developed the Shedler-Westen Assessment Procedure-200 (SWAP-200). Clinicians can then rate a particular client and note the extent to which that client meets the ideal descriptions in the SWAP-200. Initial studies have shown the scale has high alpha (above .90 for 14 of 15 diagnoses), good convergent/divergent validity, and supportive factor analysis (Westen & Muderrisoglu, 2006). These alternatives are consistent with a growing consensus that the personality disorders are not present/nonpresent categories but rather occur on a continuum (Widiger & Trull, 2007). Future research might compare these procedures with MCMI-III data and especially determine the extent to which the MCMI-III might demonstrate incremental validity beyond them.

A related issue is that some of the diagnostic criteria incorporated into the MCMI items are closely tied to the *DSM* criteria, whereas others are more closely linked to Millon's theories. In some cases, these criteria are similar; in others, the criteria are different. This inconsistency related to criteria has led to some controversy regarding the relative advantages and disadvantages of having different criteria (P. Flynn, McCann, & Fairbank, 1995). One disadvantage is that, in many cases, the MCMI should not be considered a *DSM* measure even though the titles of the scales may lead practitioners to think that it is (Wetzler & Marlowe, 1992; Widiger, Williams, Spitzer, & Francis, 1985). However, the differences between the *DSM-IV* and the MCMI-III may actually be an advantage for some of the scales/disorders because the *DSM* criteria have been criticized as being both insufficiently related to theory and clearly inadequate in some areas. Because the MCMI has not strictly adhered to the *DSM* criteria, it can work to remedy some of the *DSM*'s perceived inadequacies. For example, the *DSM-III-R/DSM-IV-TR* diagnosis for antisocial personality has attained high interrater reliability but has done so by sticking closely to clear behavioral criteria primarily related to overt acts against society. The more intangible but crucial issue of poor conscience development has not been sufficiently addressed, which has led to accusations that the *DSM* criteria relate more to a "criminal" disorder than to a "personality" disorder. The theory behind the MCMI antisocial personality disorder items stresses both overt behaviors and the relative lack of conscience, and this conceptualization is reflected in the item content.

One further issue relevant to the diagnosis of personality disorders is the difficulty in distinguishing state and trait. Theoretically, Axis I disorders relate primarily to states and Axis II characteristics relate to traits. In reality, they are highly interdependent, and it is often difficult to separate them. State (clinical) MCMI elevations seem to be closely related to scores on trait (personality) scales. For example, J. Reich and Noyes (1987) found a 50% decrease in MCMI personality disorder prevalence estimates when the MCMI was given during the recovery phase as opposed to measures given during the acute phase. Elevations in MCMI-II personality scales have also been demonstrated to increase the more state-related MMPI-2 F (and other validity) scales (Grillo, Brown, Hilsabeck, Price, & Lees-Haley, 1994). Given this state/trait distinction, it would be predicted that the trait/personality scales would be more stable than the clinical/state scales; yet, in many cases, this has not been demonstrated to be so. A number of sources, including the MCMI-III manual (Craig, 1999; Millon, 1994, 1997; Millon et al. 2006), have demonstrated little difference in the test-retest reliabilities between the two categories of scales. Collectively, these observations indicate that state and trait measures are quite interdependent. Due to this finding, the temporal stability of the personality disorders has been questioned (Widiger & Trull, 2007). To account for the variable stability of personality disorders, Millon has developed, for some of the MCMI-II and MCMI-III scales, a number of adjustments that work similarly to the *K* correction on the MMPI. Also, as with the MMPI *K* correction, it is unclear and controversial as to how effectively they achieve their purpose.

Because of the MCMI's reliance on the *DSM*, efforts have been made to incorporate changes that parallel the ongoing developments of the DSM. Adjusting to these changes has the advantage of keeping the MCMI-III current with changing diagnostic criteria, but it has also meant that the MCMI has been revised relatively frequently (Millon, 1977, 1987, 1994). In contrast, the MMPI and CPI have been through far fewer revisions. The relative frequency of changes to the MCMI means that it takes time before sufficient research is available to establish the relation between the new and previous version and the implications this may have for interpretation.

An important consideration is whether the MCMI measures actual personality "disorders" or, rather, personality "style." As indicated previously, the MCMI-III measures of histrionic, compulsive, and, possibly, narcissistic traits do not seem to be measuring actual disorders but more styles (Craig, 1999). Choca and Van Denburg (1997) prefer to think of the various scales as referring to personality "style" because the inference to disorder requires more information than can realistically be found in scale elevations. Persons with certain personality styles may have been able to find an occupational and/or interpersonal niche that allows them to function adequately. For example, a Schizoid or Avoidant personality may work quite well as a night watchperson. Thus, the inference from style to disorder must be made by the individual practitioner and not by the test. Practitioners who look for the test to include actual diagnosis are overextending its use beyond realistic expectations.

A further issue with the MCMI has been extensive item overlap. The original MCMI (MCMI-I) had its 175 items arranged on 733 different keyings, and the MCMI-II had an even greater 953 keyings. Thus, because many of the items were used to score numerous scales, there were frequently high scale correlations. For example, the MCMI-I's Borderline and Dysthymia scales shared 65% of their items and were highly correlated (.95). Given these characteristics, practitioners might be justifiably concerned that some of the scales were measuring constructs that were too similar and therefore redundant. The defense of the high scale intercorrelation has been that many of the constructs are theoretically and clinically similar, and the similarity would, therefore, be psychometrically reflected in many high scale correlations. Practitioners would then need to look at the relationships between the different scale elevations as a means of fine-tuning their interpretations. For example, Avoidant and Schizoid personalities are similar in their passivity and interpersonal distance. Clinical lore suggests that many persons initially believed to be Schizoids appear more similar to Avoidants as more information is obtained from them. Given the theory and intent of the MCMI, the two scales measuring these styles would be expected to have similar items and to be elevated. Notwithstanding this defense, the recently revised MCMI-III has attempted to reduce the item scale overlap (and resulting intercorrelations) by reducing the number of items per scale, providing item weightings depending on their relative importance for a scale, and reducing the number of keyings to 440 (Millon, 1994). This seems to have been successful in that none of the interscale correlations reported in the manual was above .90 and only three were .80 (the rest were lower). This finding suggests that the MCMI-III scales, compared to the previous versions, are measuring somewhat more independent domains.

When interpreting the MCMI, it is sometimes difficult to know where the interpretive information was derived. That information is based on a combination of theory and empirical relationships determined specifically through validity studies of the MCMI itself. Each of these two interpretive sources has developed over a number of years, during which time three versions of the MCMI have appeared. It is often difficult to know whether the interpretations have been empirically based or theory-based and whether they have been derived from validity studies done on previous versions of the MCMI. If done on previous versions, it can be rightfully argued that most of the interpretations can be transferred from these earlier versions because there has been continuity in theory and scale development. This continuity is particularly reflected in the moderate to high correlations between the new and the older scales. However, practitioners must struggle with which of the interpretations have been empirically versus conceptually derived as well as which are obsolete versus still current. This problem is relevant for the MCMI as well as other similar instruments (i.e., MMPI, CPI), and it highlights the importance of clinicians' working with the test results and integrating them with additional sources. According to Millon (1992), the quality of the interpretive information is dependent on "the overall validity of the inventory, the adequacy of the theory that provides the logic underlying the separate scales, the skill of the clinician, and the interpreter's experience with relevant populations" (p. 424).

A criticism related to this issue is that the MCMI overdiagnoses and overpathologizes (P. Flynn et al., 1995). For example, Wetzler (1990) has noted that MCMI-related diagnoses of personality disorder were 60% higher than diagnoses based on structured interviews. One of the reasons for at least the potential for overdiagnosis among practitioners is the possibly misleading names of the personality scales. They create the external appearance of clear *DSM* diagnostic categories when they are probably best conceptualized as styles that may or may not reflect an actual disorder. This does not mean that the MCMI cannot be extremely useful in diagnosing personality disorders; but it should be more accurately perceived as placing the practitioner in the correct domain or coming halfway (or more) toward diagnosis. A further problem is that the MCMI does not perform well on normal or only mildly disturbed populations. Such persons might have moderate elevations that are still below the BR 75 cutoff, but practitioners might be tempted to interpret these "elevations." This confusion is complicated further if correlations derived from the Modifying Indices bump up the personality or clinical scales into the interpretable range. Unfortunately, the MCMI National Computer System computer interpretations tend to both reinforce interpretations of moderate "elevations" and suggest that *DSM* diagnoses can be made based on MCMI scores. Thus, the MCMI should be used only with clinical populations. A related difficulty is that the scales and their related interpretations tend to emphasize a client's deficiencies without balancing these out with the client's strengths. The result is likely to be an overly negative description of a client's functioning. This occurs despite the fact that many aspects of personality styles might be quite adaptive: for example, the easy sociability of the histrionic style or the adaptability and empathy associated with many persons with depressive styles (see R. F. Bornstein, 1998). In addition to overpathologizing, the MCMI-III has also been found to perform poorly when assessing persons with psychotic disorders (Craig, 1999).

USE WITH DIVERSE GROUPS

One consideration in interpreting the MCMI is the possible influence of gender, age, and ethnicity. Gender influences have been minimized by using separate norms for scoring the profiles of males and females. The gender differences that have emerged on the MCMI are also consistent with prevalence rate estimates. For example, the greater rate of antisocial personalities among males is reflected in the BR scores, which take this greater prevalence rate into account.

Some differences between European American and African American psychiatric patients have been found on 9 of the 20 MCMI-II scales. African Americans scored especially higher on Antisocial, Narcissistic, Paranoid, Hypomania, and Drug Abuse scales (Choca, Shanley, Peterson, & Van Denburg, 1990). However, the meaning attributed to these differences is less clear. For example, the greater elevations on these

MCMI-II scales may mean that these scores are accurate representations of the more difficult circumstances many African Americans encounter. Accuracy of MCMI-III elevations is supported in that self-descriptions by African American clients closely correspond to expected elevations on the MCMI-III (Craig & Olson, 2001).

Finally, there do seem to be age-related differences on the MCMI-II: Older persons score higher on Dependent but lower on Compulsive and Borderline (Choca, Van Denburg, Bratu, & Meagher, 1995). Interpretations among older persons should take these age-related variables into account.

INTERPRETATION PROCEDURE

Effective interpretation of the MCMI requires considerable sophistication and knowledge related to psychopathology in general and personality disorders in particular. At a minimum, practitioners should be familiar with issues related to personality disorders, along with the *DSM-IV-TR* criteria. Ideally, practitioners should also have read Millon and Davis's (1996) definitive *Disorders of Personality: DSM-IV and Beyond*, worked with clients with personality disorders, and administered the MCMI to a number of such clients. Clinicians should also be aware of the previously outlined assets and limitations of the MCMI so that they can most appropriately work with the data. In particular, the MCMI does not provide *DSM-IV* diagnosis; it should be used only with clinical populations; it is not particularly helpful in assessing a person's strengths; and there is a possibility that it might overdiagnose personality disorders and be overinterpreted by clinicians.

The set of procedures outlined in this section is recommended for interpreting the MCMI. The discussion of the various scales and codes represents an integration and summary of current research as well as material included in the MCMI-III manual (Millon, 1994) and interpretive guides developed by Choca and Van Denburg (1997), Craig (2001), and Jankowski (2002). The subsections related to treatment planning have summarized material from Dorr (1999); Goncalves, Woodward, and Millon (1994); Millon and Davis (1996); and Retzlaff and Dunn (2003). Each of the 28 MCMI-III scales is discussed in relation to interpretation, possible interaction with other scales, and implications for treatment planning.

The formal elaboration and separate listing of 2- and 3-point code types are not discussed for several reasons. First, research on the MCMI does not have the well-developed code-type validity literature found for the MMPI. Instead, many of the MCMI code-type descriptions are based on a conceptual integration of the implications of clusters of scale elevations. This means that interpreting patterns of scale elevations is a task that individual practitioners can do themselves by rationally considering the meanings of associated scale elevations. For example, an elevation on Antisocial, combined with a corresponding elevation on Aggressive (Sadistic), would clearly indicate the abusive, combative, and impersonal expression of the person's antisocial tendencies. Second, given that there are fully 28 MCMI-III scales, the total number of possible code types is both unwieldy to list and unrealistic to fully research. However, a short subsection ("Frequent Code Types") under most of the scale descriptions does briefly describe the meanings attached to some of the more important associated scale elevations. Readers are encouraged to read these descriptions and to expand on their meanings by reading the longer interpretive descriptions for the entire associated scale.

1. Determine Profile Validity

Before interpreting the personality and clinical scales, practitioners must be assured that the client has not over- or underreported symptoms or responded in a random manner. The profile validity can be assessed by noting the pattern of scores on the Modifying Indices (validity indicators):

> *Random responding* is suggested by scores of one or more on the three items of the MCMI-III Validity scale ("True" on items 65, 110, and 157).
>
> *Underreporting of difficulties* on the MCMI-III is suggested by low scores (raw score less than 34) on Disclosure (X) and Debasement (Z) and a high score (BR over 75) on Desirability (Y; an "arrow" profile on the Modifying Indices). However, it is sometimes difficult to differentiate persons who are faking good (underreporting) from those who actually have the positive qualities of being cooperative, self-confident, and conscientious. The client's history is often the best tool for making this distinction.
>
> *Fake bad* profiles are suggested by a high score (raw score above 178) on Disclosure (X) and a high score (BR above 75) on Debasement (Z; a "valley" profile on the Modifying Indices). With moderate elevations, this might be a "cry for help"; but with progressively higher scores (BR above 85), the likelihood of an invalid profile is increased.

It should be noted that BR adjustments for certain scales have been made in an effort to increase MCMI-III profile validity. The adjustments serve as correction scores in much the same way as the *K* correction serves for the MMPI. These adjustments are part of the standard scoring and involve adjustments for Disclosure (if either high or low), Anxiety/Depression, Inpatient, and Denial/Complaint.

2. Interpret the Personality Disorder Scales

Retzlaff (1995) recommends that, when interpreting the Personality Disorder scales, practitioners should first check to see whether any of the Severe Personality Disorder scales are elevated. If so, this strongly suggests that one or more of the Clinical Personality Pattern scales will also be elevated. However, the high scale(s) on the Severe Personality Disorder section should take precedence over equivalently elevated scales on the Clinical Personality Pattern scales. The Clinical Personality Pattern scales then serve to color or elaborate on the elevation(s) on the Severe Personality Disorder scale(s). The primary focus for diagnosis, then, should be to rely on the Severe Personality Disorder elevation unless elevations on other categories of scales were extremely elevated compared to the Severe Personality Disorder scales. When that occurs, the extremely elevated scales would take on greater interpretive meaning compared to the more moderately elevated Severe Personality Disorder scale(s). (Interpretive descriptions of each of these scales can be found in the next section.) If there are no elevations on the Severe Personality Disorder scales, practitioners should interpret any elevations on the Clinical Personality Pattern scales.

The interpretive sections under the personality disorder scales are divided into general interpretive descriptions, frequent code types, and treatment implications. Often the descriptors are fairly severe and negative. Interpreters need to determine whether these apply to the individual client, based on how high the scale is elevated, implications of associated scale elevations, and additional data available on the client. For example, some of the descriptors might need to be softened if they are in the marginally elevated range (BR 75 to 80). More severe interpretations might be appropriate for extremely elevated scores or if the elevations are from either the Severe Personality Pathology or Severe Syndromes categories. Millon et al. (2006) specify that scores in the 75 to 84 range indicate the syndrome or pattern is present, whereas scores of 85 or above indicate that it is prominent. The general rule, then, is: The higher the elevation, the more likely that the interpretive descriptions are accurate. Another consideration is the height of elevated scales relative to other elevated scales. If they are approximately the same height, they should be given equal interpretive weight. On the other hand, if there are 20 or more BR points between scales, the lower scale's influence is likely to be so subtle that it can be minimized or even ignored.

The general interpretive descriptions for the Clinical Personality Pattern scales (but not the Severe Personality Disorder) also include paragraphs on possible strengths or positive descriptions. These provide a means of partially balancing the primarily negative descriptions associated with scale elevations. The Frequent Code Types subsection gives a brief description of the meanings attached to frequently associated elevations. Any code types that have been described previously refer the reader back to these earlier descriptions.

3. Interpret Clinical Syndrome Scales

Similar to step 2, Retzlaff (1995) recommends that precedence be given to interpreting any elevations on the Severe Clinical Syndrome scales. Sometimes all or most of these scales are elevated, which should not be considered contradictory; rather, these elevations can be used to complement one another. Any elevations on the Severe Clinical Syndrome scales are usually accompanied by complementary elevations on the Basic Clinical Syndrome scales as well as the Personality Disorder scales. For example, an elevation on the Severe Clinical Syndrome scale of Major Depression might also have corresponding elevations on Drug Dependence, Anxiety, and Avoidant. Interpretations would center on depression but would also include fear of interpersonal involvement, anxiety, and the distinct likelihood that the person is using alcohol as a means of coping with these difficulties. Another example might be a person with an elevation on Anxiety but with a corresponding elevation on Avoidant and Dependent, which suggests he or she is experiencing the anxiety because of conflict between wanting to be accepted and cared for by others and being terrified of criticism and humiliation. In contrast, another person with an elevation on Anxiety but with a corresponding elevation on Narcissistic is most likely experiencing anxiety because of significant challenges to his or her self-inflated sense of importance and superiority. This careful interplay between the scales is crucial for accurate and effective profile interpretation.

One of the unique features of the MCMI is that it is an objective test that measures personality styles/patterns relevant to Axis II disorders. The sections describing each of these scales include subsections on frequent code types (including possible relations with Clinical Syndrome scales) and treatment implications. In contrast, the Clinical Syndrome scale descriptions include descriptions only of the scales, without material on frequent code types or treatment implications, partially because relevant relations with the personality scales are mentioned in the previous section. In addition, there is already a well-developed clinical literature (and extensive time is spent in most training programs) on treating these clinical syndromes (anxiety, depression, etc.). Practitioners who wish to develop detailed treatment procedures for difficulties measured by the Clinical Syndrome scales can consult resources such as Barlow's (2001) *Clinical Handbook of Psychological Disorders* or Gabbard's (2007) *Gabbard's Treatments of Psychiatric Disorders*.

4. Review Noteworthy Responses (Critical Items)

The MCMI-III manual (Millon et al., 2006) has listed a series of Noteworthy Responses in Appendix F (pp. 189–190). These are organized around the topics of Health Preoccupation, Interpersonal Alienation, Emotional Dyscontrol, Self-Destructive Potential,

Childhood Abuse, and Eating Disorder(s). Similar to the MMPI critical items, the MCMI's Noteworthy Responses are not so much formal scales as they are rationally categorized items that might be important for a clinician to more fully understand. Accordingly, they can be used to organize a semistructured interview around relevant responses. They can also be selectively inserted into a psychological report to provide a more concrete qualitative portrayal of the client's attitudes, affect, and behavior.

5. Provide Diagnostic Impressions

Given the interpretive descriptions of a client's profile (steps 2, 3, and 4), along with any other relevant information, clinicians can formulate the most appropriate diagnosis.

6. Elaborate on Treatment Implications and Recommendations

The symptoms reported and reflected in elevations on the Clinical Syndrome scales (Anxiety, Depression, Substance Abuse, etc.) are those that are most problematic and thus should be targeted as high priorities. However, these also need to be understood in the context of the client's personality patterns and pathologies. Under each of the Personality Disorder scales, there are sections with relevant suggestions for treatment recommendations. These can be considered, along with other information, to expand on what would be the most appropriate interventions. Additional useful resources in this process are Chapter 14 of this book ("Psychological Assessment and Treatment Planning"), Millon and Davis's (1996) *Disorders of Personality: DSM-IV and Beyond*, Millon's (1999) *Personality Guided Therapy,* and Magnavita's (2005) chapter "Using the MCMI-III for treatment planning."

MODIFYING INDICES (VALIDITY SCALES)

The MCMI Modifying Indices are adequate at detecting random responding, fake bad, and fake good profiles. However, the detection rate appears lower than for the MMPI (Bagby, Gillis, Toner, & Goldberg, 1991), and, as with the MMPI, fake bad profiles are more accurately detected than fake good (defensive) profiles (Fals-Stewart, 1995; Millon, 1987). Using the decision rules for fake bad profiles, the rate of accurate detection runs between 48% and 92% (Bagby, Gillis, Toner, et al., 1991; Retzlaff, Sheehan, & Fiel, 1991; Schoenberg, Dorr, & Morgan, 2003). However, for severely disturbed clients, high scores on fake bad indices may be more indicative of high distress and a cry for help than an invalid profile (Wetzler & Marlowe, 1990). In contrast to the generally good detection rate for fake bad profiles, persons faking good (defensively) are likely to be detected approximately 50% of the time (Retzlaff et al., 1991), and clients underreporting their substance abuse seem particularly good at avoiding detection (Fals-Stewart, 1995). Thus, the MCMI should be used with extreme caution in situations in which individuals might be likely to underreport their psychopathology.

The most useful tool in making these decisions related to validity is a careful consideration of the client's past and current level of functioning. Specifically, a person who may look as though he or she is faking bad, but whose history reveals someone who is dysfunctional, may be merely expressing distress. In contrast, a relatively highly functioning person with the same scores on Modifying Indices is much more likely to be faking bad. Conversely, a person with a potentially fake good profile but who also has a high level of functioning may be merely expressing actual confidence, assertiveness, and high self-esteem. A person with a similar profile but a history of interpersonal, legal, and/or psychiatric history, however, is much more likely to be underreporting psychopathology.

Validity Index (Scale V)

The MCMI-III Validity Index is composed of three items (numbers 65, 110, 157) that, if endorsed as true, indicate absurd responses. As a result, endorsement of these items strongly suggests that a person has responded randomly. The manual states that one true response should be interpreted as indicating a profile of "questionable validity" and two or more endorsements can clearly be interpreted as an invalid profile. Presumably, the "questionable validity" option is given to suggest that the profile *may* still be valid in the event that the client has misread or randomly responded to only a few items (including one of the three on the Validity Index). Misreading only a few of the items allows the possibility that most of the items were still responded to accurately. In contrast, Bagby, Gillis, and Rogers (1991) recommend that even one endorsed item be used to indicate an invalid profile. One caution: If a person did respond randomly, there is still a 50% chance that he or she may have gotten "lucky" and none of the three items was answered in a true direction, in which case detection on the Validity Index would be avoided (Charter & Lopez, 2002). In addition, a person wishing consciously to fake responses would be able to notice the absurdity of answering "true" to any of the Validity Index questions and would answer them in such a way as to not endorse scorable responses on the Validity Index.

Disclosure Index (X)

The Disclosure Index was designed to measure whether a client's responses were open and revealing as opposed to defensive and secretive. If the MCMI-III raw score on the Disclosure Index is below 34, it most likely indicates a defensive underreporting of psychopathology. It may also mean that the person did not read or understand the questions correctly. A further interpretation is that the client is hesitant, reserved, and overconcerned with seeking social approval. However, low Disclosure Index scores on the MCMI-II were not found to be particularly sensitive because subjects requested to "fake good" still produced generally acceptable Disclosure Index scores (Retzlaff et al., 1991). Thus, when clients do fake good extensively enough to produce a clearly low Disclosure Index, the profile can be considered invalid with a fair degree of certainty.

MCMI-III raw scores above 178 indicate that the individual has extensively exaggerated his or her symptoms. The reporting of symptoms would even exceed fairly disturbed psychiatric populations and, therefore, suggests an overreporting (faking bad) of symptoms. Some caution should be taken in that the scale has been found to be fairly tolerant to overreporting (Morgan, Schoenberg, Dorr, & Burke, 2002). Thus, many persons exaggerating symptoms may still score below the raw score cutoff of 178. If they do score above this cutoff, it can be fairly safely inferred that they are indeed overreporting their symptoms. The Disclosure Index is the only scale on the MCMI that is interpreted if either high or low. The other scales on the MCMI should be interpreted only if they are above the BR 75 cutoff.

Desirability Index (Y)

Similar to the Disclosure Index, the Desirability Index is also a measure of defensive responding. Scores above BR 75 indicate the individual has presented in a manner that is unusually moral, interpersonally attractive, extremely emotionally stable, highly gregarious, organized, and with a high respect for the rules of society. Progressively higher scores suggest that the person is concealing crucial details regarding psychological or interpersonal difficulties. However, this scale is not a particularly good one and results should be interpreted with caution.

Debasement Index (Z)

As the title of the scale suggests, the Debasement Index reflects the extent to which a person is describing himself or herself in negative, pathological terms. Elevated scores on the Debasement Index might include feelings of being empty or angry, crying easily, having low self-esteem, possibly being self-destructive, and frequently feeling tense, guilty, and depressed. Thus, the Debasement Index measures characteristics opposite from those on the Desirability Index. They are rarely both elevated, although, on occasion, someone who is unusually self-disclosing may have high scores on both. Scores above BR 85 indicate either a cry for help resulting from acute psychological distress or a fake bad profile. As with Desirability, this scale is not particularly effective and should be interpreted with caution.

CLINICAL PERSONALITY PATTERNS

Schizoid (Scale 1)

The core characteristic of persons with elevations on this scale is little or no interest in other people. They spend their lives as loners. They are detached, impersonal, withdrawn, unsociable, seclusive, passive, distant, and have few, if any, friends. They rarely initiate conversation, are indifferent to other people, and rarely seek involvement with others. In family, work, or social situations, they prefer to have a peripheral role. As a result, they frequently function on the margins of society. They have little drive to have their needs met, experience few erotic attachments, express little warmth, and are often asexual. Rarely do they experience very much depth of feeling (pleasure, sadness, anger). They are largely indifferent to praise or criticism from others. Their interpersonal distance is not based on a defense stemming from fear of rejection but is, rather, their natural and most comfortable way of functioning. They also lack vitality and are unanimated and almost robotlike in their movements. When they do communicate with others, it is in a vague, distant, unfocused manner. Often the direction of their conversation loses its focus, and whatever information is conveyed is delivered in a circuitous manner. As a result, others are likely to see them as strange or "spacey." They have little self-awareness or insight into the implications of interpersonal relationships. If they are involved in a committed or intimate relationship, a frequent spousal complaint is that there is insufficient closeness, sharing, and understanding.

An asset of this personality style is that these persons typically do not become particularly disturbed by anything. Although they are not particularly involved with or interested in others, when they do interact, they are typically quite comfortable. Decision making is often easier for them because it is not complicated by emotional or interpersonal intricacies. They are also quite self-sufficient—they are comfortable with spending extensive periods of time alone and may have a rich fantasy life. Their hobbies typically involve activities that require only minimal contact with other people.

Frequent Code Types

Clinical scales that are likely to be elevated along with Schizoid are Anxiety and Thought Disorder. This pattern of elevation reflects the sometimes obsessive thinking of the schizoid, along with the possibility that brief psychotic states might occur. Personality scales that are often elevated along with Schizoid are Avoidant, Passive-Aggressive (Negativistic), Dependent, and Compulsive. Each of these adds new variations onto the previous description. A corresponding elevation on Avoidant suggests that these persons are not only uninterested in and unskilled at interpersonal relationships but also uncomfortable around others and fear rejection. However, behind their detachment may be a real desire to become involved. If Schizoid and Avoidant are both elevated, the possibility of problem use of alcohol should be investigated (check Alcohol and Drug Dependence). Elevations on the Passive-Aggressive (Negativistic) scale (along with Avoidant) underscore conflictual feelings and possible resentment toward the few interpersonal relationships they have. This resentment centers on a wish that someone would nurture and guide them (especially if Dependent is also elevated) along with fear that they might be rejected. This conflict results in their frequently being moody and nervous. An elevation on Dependent (along with Avoidant) indicates that they feel less important and capable than others. As a result, they are submissive, humble, and congenial as a means of seeking acceptance and being cared for. When Compulsive is elevated, these persons are disciplined, well organized, emotionally controlled, meticulous, dependable, and persistent. These characteristics are present in part because these persons feel that emotions are threatening and confusing, and their strategy of working with this is to remain disciplined, self-restrained, and proper. They are typically overly polite and even ingratiating toward authority figures but, in contrast, may be somewhat disdainful toward subordinates.

Treatment Implications

The two major goals when working with persons with Schizoid elevations are to (a) encourage at least some increase in social interaction and (b) help them to enhance their ability to experience pleasure. However, these goals are difficult to achieve in a client who is neither likely to become particularly involved in the therapeutic relationship nor ready to place much value in exploration and insight. As a result, the prognosis is poor. In addition, many therapists are likely to feel that schizoids are not particularly rewarding to work with. Therapists must be prepared for long silences and a distant relationship. Yet any relationship that does develop can be extremely important for clients. Problem solving should be directed at concrete, practical matters. Useful techniques might be audiotape or videotape feedback of their behavior and cognitive monitoring and reorientation of their internal processes. Operant conditioning, however, might prove difficult because they have little capacity for external rewards. Similarly, insight might be unproductive because they are not particularly psychologically minded.

Avoidant (Scale 2A)

Both schizoids and avoidants live solitary, often isolated lives. However, schizoids are indifferent to relationships whereas avoidants desperately want to become accepted and involved with other people—a desire that is blocked by an intense fear of being rejected and humiliated. They warily scan their environment for threats and continually try to present themselves in as favorable a manner as possible. This is rarely successful; they feel a continual sense of unease, disquiet, anxiety, and overreaction to minor events. Thus, they are frequently preoccupied with intrusive, fearful, and disruptive thoughts. They perceive themselves as socially inept, inferior, and inadequate, and they continually undervalue their achievements. In addition to fear and self-criticism, they frequently feel alone, empty, and isolated. To protect themselves from these fears, they restrict their social environments, constantly maintaining their distance and privacy. This is unfortunate because it undercuts future opportunities for enhancing relationships and places them in a solitary world where they are more likely to reactivate memories of past social rejections. In addition, they rely extensively on fantasy gratification of their needs for affection and anger. Given these dynamics, they are quite likely to fulfill the formal criteria for a social phobia and are frequently depressed. They are frequently described as withdrawn, insecure, edgy, fretful, insecure, isolated, and rejected.

The positive side of avoidants is that they can be extremely sensitive to the needs and perspectives of others. They can potentially show considerable compassion and understanding, and can be emotionally responsive.

Frequent Code Types

Avoidants, along with borderlines, are likely to experience a wide variety of Axis I-related disorders. As a result, it is quite common to see elevations in several of the clinical syndrome scales. Among the most frequent associated disorders are generalized anxiety, phobias, and social phobias (check Anxiety). Depression (check Dysthymia and Major Depression), hypochondriacal syndromes, and conversion disorders can also occur (check Somatoform). Personality Pattern scales that can be elevated are Dependent, Schizoid, Passive-Aggressive (Negativistic), Narcissistic, and Antisocial. A corresponding elevation on Dependent augments the core dynamics of the avoidant in that the person has even stronger needs not only to become involved with others but also to be supported by and given guidance by them. Avoidant in combination with Schizoid adds the dimension of having a lack of awareness or even of interest in personal feelings. These persons are also likely to be detached, aloof, and apathetic, and they rarely develop strong emotional ties with others. They might have some acquaintances, but they are not likely to have any intimate friendships. Elevations on Passive-Aggressive (Negativistic) suggest moodiness and resentment combined with significant difficulty in trusting others. They might vacillate between being friendly and cooperative and then being hostile, which might be followed by apologies. Because they would feel uncomfortable with their anger, they might resort to covert expressions of hostility, such as passive obstructionism. Whereas many persons with avoidant characteristics have low self-esteem, avoidants with elevations on Narcissistic have an inflated sense of importance, overestimating their own value. They are unappreciative of others and justify this attitude by perceiving themselves as special. Situations are framed in such a way as to enhance their own self-worth, and they describe themselves as intelligent, sophisticated, outgoing, and charming. However, their underlying style is avoidant, so their sense of self-importance is extremely flimsy and easily deflated. Elevations on Antisocial introduce to the avoidants' personality a competitive edge that might be expressed in hostile and exploitive behaviors. They would justify this by fears that others are trying to take advantage of them. They usually describe themselves as self-reliant, strong, realistic, and assertive, and they exhibit a contemptuous attitude toward persons who do not have these qualities. In addition, they are likely to be impulsive, argumentative, guarded, reserved, intimidating, cold, and insensitive to the feelings of others.

Treatment Implications

Avoidants are among the most frequent clients in therapy. A potentially difficult issue is that they reveal only the information they believe will not lead to rejection by the therapist. The central treatment task is to change these clients' self-image, but doing so involves working with interpersonal behavior and helping regulate their mood. Particularly useful techniques would be in vivo exposure based on a graded hierarchy, anxiety management training, cognitive reorientation to challenge thinking errors, assertiveness training, and, possibly, psychopharmacological interventions to deal with anxiety states and possible panic attacks. However, the most difficult challenge is to keep them in therapy long enough to achieve therapeutic gain. Motivating them to remain in therapy would require carefully balancing support, empathy, and trust building while still encouraging them to experience situations that challenge them to work on new behaviors and perceptions. Because their high level of arousal would be the primary reason for their terminating prematurely, techniques of arousal reduction—emotional support, reassurance, relaxation, hypnosis, thought stopping, and supportive interpretation—would be particularly important to use. Typically, these clients make significant therapeutic gains. One area to investigate is the possibility that they are using alcohol to medicate their anxiety. However, referral to Alcoholics Anonymous might be difficult, given their avoidant style; therefore, other forms of intervention should be considered.

Depressive (Scale 2B)

The depressive personality style involves not merely recurrent symptoms of depression but an enduring pattern of thoughts, attitudes, behaviors, and self-concepts related to depression. These clients perceive themselves as worthless, vulnerable, inadequate, unsuccessful, and guilty, and they frequently engage in self-criticism. When possible, they frame events in a defeatist, fatalistic manner. They have learned to expect ridicule and derision. Even extremely slight signs of indifference might be interpreted as contempt and condemnation. Others perceive them as forlorn, somber, discouraged, and hopeless. They similarly describe themselves as discouraged, quiet, drained of energy, and despairing. Initially, their depressive behavior might elicit support and empathy from well-intentioned others. Eventually, however, they end up feeling deserted and abandoned because their interpersonal behavior is likely to either distance others or attract persons who will use their passivity and depression to exploit or otherwise control them. They rarely engage in active, assertive behavior to obtain reinforcement from others. They feel powerless and at the control of forces beyond their control. Although they crave love and support, they fail to act in ways that others find attractive and gratifying. Sometimes their self-criticism is a tactic to diffuse the potential criticism of others and simultaneously solicit support and sympathy. As a result, their interpersonal style serves to further reinforce their depression, and they frequently end up feeling angry, resentful, and pessimistic. Depressive personality disorder can be distinguished from major affective disorder and dysthymia in that, with a depressive personality, there will be an early, extended onset (versus more rapid and intense), along with multiple personality traits consistent with depression.

Because depressives are quite introspective, they have the potential for and the orientation toward developing depth of insight. In addition, they are emotionally responsive and often have depth of feeling. Their level of distress may also be used as an aid in motivating them to change. High-functioning depressives may be able to have genuine close, caring relationships with others and may be articulate, conscientious, responsible, and insightful. They might potentially respond well to humor, elicit liking in others, and be able to effectively take into account alternative points of view.

Frequent Code Types

The most likely elevations on the clinical scales would be on Dysthymia, Major Depression, and, possibly, Bipolar:Manic. Elevations on these scales would be natural extensions of the individual's overall depressive style. Considerable conceptual and clinical overlap with other personality scales is likely, resulting in frequent associated elevations on Schizoid, Avoidant, Passive-Aggressive (Negativistic), Self-Defeating (Masochistic), and

Borderline. An associated elevation on Schizoid would introduce an apathetic, indifferent, self-sufficient element to the depressive style. Because these clients are more likely to be interested in inanimate objects than interpersonal relationships, developing an effective therapeutic working relationship would be difficult. Organizing and logically communicating thoughts is often extremely difficult. If Depressive and Avoidant are both elevated, the depressive style is characterized by anxiety and fear of interpersonal humiliation, which leads to isolation as they attempt to protect themselves. They engage in extreme introspection and have a sense of alienation from themselves. They are inhibited, have few social skills, feel easily embarrassed, and have few close friendships. They are also likely to have difficulty experiencing pleasure and feel inhibited about pursuing goals. An elevation on Passive-Aggressive (Negativistic) flavors the depression with anger, irritability, and sour grumbling. They vacillate between being bitter and resentful toward others and being intropunitive and self-deprecatory. Because they are uncomfortable with their anger and resentment, these feelings are typically expressed in indirect ways, such as through obstinacy, procrastination, and inefficiency. There are clear similarities between Depressive and Self-Defeating (Masochistic). Both of these scales emphasize behaviors that result in the person's not obtaining what he or she wants from life. However, elevation in both of these scales highlights active maneuvers that result in possibly undeserved blame and unjust criticism. These persons present themselves as self-effacing, self-sacrificing, obsequious, and deserving of painful consequences. They are likely to get drawn into relationships that are physically or emotionally abusive, but they respond by being ingratiating and submissive. A Borderline and Depressive configuration emphasizes a serious difficulty with controlling affect and behavior. Cyclical variations of emotional constraint and criticism are followed by impulsive outbursts, sometimes of a self-destructive nature. Suicide potential needs to be carefully monitored. They are likely to have difficulty comforting themselves when distressed and feel that life is meaningless. Problems are typically expanded out of proportion (catastrophized). Accusations may be made that others have mistreated them. Their level of self-identity is extremely weak, and sometimes they have difficulty logically organizing their thoughts and emotions.

Treatment Implications

The major focus of intervention should be to work with their sense of helpless immobility and their belief that emotional pain is an inevitable life condition. Interventions related to interpersonal behavior, cognitive schemas, self-concept, and expectations are often essential. Specific techniques might include social skills and assertiveness training, cognitive interventions that challenge underlying assumptions, behavioral programs that enhance pleasure-related activities, and group involvement that combines support and encouragement for change. Initial contact should be characterized by support that seeks to satisfy some of the client's dependency needs without fostering further helplessness. Psychopharmacology might be considered but should not be an end in itself. Long-standing cognitions, modes of interacting with others, and self-concept persist even after medication might have removed some of the more symptomatic features of the disorder. Therapeutic challenges involve preventing self-harm, preventing the client from proceeding too fast and possibly encountering failure and disillusionment, and preventing relapse. Relapse prevention can be enhanced by realistically advising that some recurrent difficulties are inevitable.

Dependent (Scale 3)

The core characteristic for persons with elevations on this profile is their feeling incapable and incompetent of functioning independently and, therefore, unable to create strong bonds with people whom they perceive as being able to lead and care for them. They quickly create alliances and give up responsibility for decisions. Thus, they feel inadequate and insecure, and they have low self-esteem. They usually describe themselves as placating, insecure, passive, immature, and deserted. A primary way in which they deal with these feelings is to identify with stronger people and define themselves in terms of these people. They are continually concerned with the possibility of losing friends. To maintain friendships, they are extremely submissive and cooperative, and cover up any unpleasant emotions out of fear that the emotions might alienate others. They, therefore, minimize objective problems, rarely disagree with others, and never take a strong position on an issue. Others, therefore, perceive them as gullible, wishy-washy, humble, timid, docile, and passive. Internally, they have a limited range of competencies in reducing tension and stressors. Elevations on this scale are consistent with bulimia (check Noteworthy responses related to eating disorders: items 121, 143, 155, 163).

Often, dependent personalities are well liked because they are cooperative, compliant, and humble, and they value the opinions of others. They are also likely to be loyal, warm, tender, and noncompetitive. They attempt to develop and maintain lasting friendships and do so, in part, by defusing unnecessary conflict.

Frequent Code Types

The most frequent Axis I–related difficulty is likely to be an anxiety disorder (check Anxiety), which might include panic attacks, social phobias, and agoraphobic attacks often related to or triggered by fears of separation. Mood disorders are represented by associated elevations on Dysthymia as well as Bipolar:Manic and Major Depression might also be common. Frequent associated scale elevations on the personality scales include Avoidant, Schizoid (see section on Schizoid), Compulsive, Passive-Aggressive (Negativistic), Histrionic, and Self-Defeating. An associated elevation on Compulsive indicates that dependent characteristics are combined with seeking approval and nurturance from others by acting perfectionistic, disciplined, orderly, industrious, and persistent. They are highly respectful and even ingratiating toward persons in positions of authority. Careful preparation will be made for future events. As a result of their dependency and focus on details, they likely have difficulty making decisions. Elevations on Passive-Aggressive (Negativistic) along with Dependent indicate that although these persons seek the guidance and leadership of others, they are also quite conflicted about these relationships. They may vacillate between appearing to cooperate and then feeling resentful and angry, which leads to resistance toward others in power. Guilt follows, but then the cycle is likely to repeat itself. High scores on Histrionic indicate that these clients are active and outgoing in attempting to get others to notice and take care of them. To this end, they might appear charming, dramatic, seductive, and extroverted. They are often quite sensitive to the moods of others but may have noteworthy difficulty and a feeling of emptiness when they have to act independently. Finally, when Self-Defeating is elevated with Dependent, it highlights these clients' poor self-esteem, based in part on having been in a series of relationships that have been painful. Although they desperately want others to care for them, they present themselves in a negative and pessimistic manner. Eventually, they undermine and sabotage the relationships that, on another level, they seek to create.

Treatment Implications

Dependents frequently seek treatment. Typically, rapport is quite easily established, especially if the therapist responds in an authoritative, comforting, and assertive manner. However, the greatest danger (or challenge) is that a relationship may be created in which the therapist becomes a rescuer, thereby reinforcing the dependent pattern. These clients may prefer the therapist to be directive, but a nondirective, Socratic method is more likely to encourage assertion and independence. An important goal is to reduce their clinging patterns and, instead, encourage their interacting in a more direct, assertive manner. Specific techniques might include assertiveness training, anxiety reduction skills (deep breathing, muscle relaxation, meditation), role playing, group therapy (to explore their impact on others), and psychoanalytic techniques that can probe the origins of their dependent patterns.

Histrionic (Scale 4)

Histrionic persons are dramatic, colorful, and emotional. Their tolerance for boredom is extremely low, and they are constantly seeking new situations. By focusing on the external world, they do not fully digest and integrate their experiences with their inner world. Because experiences are not integrated, they do not grow and learn from them. As a result, their level of maturation does not progress. They typically become highly invested in situations or with friends, but, when the excitement ends, they reinvest their energy and interest elsewhere. They typically describe themselves as active, egocentric, exhibitionistic, flighty, extroverted, and flirtatious. They also see themselves as charming, outgoing, and able to acquire the attention of other people. As a result, they make very good impressions in party-type situations, although sometimes they might be perceived as too loud, demanding, and uncontrollable. In addition, they might be exhibitionistic and seductive, placing excessive reliance on physical appearance. Because they react easily and spontaneously to new situations, it is easy for them to mingle with people and quickly establish friendships. However, behind these seemingly assertive and independent behaviors are strong needs for dependency. Whereas dependents seek the protection and guidance of others, histrionics also need the attention and support of others but seek it in an extroverted, overt manner rather than using more submissive methods. Behind histrionics' dramatics and high level of activity are often conflicted, painful feelings that they avoid focusing on. Thus, their activity allows them to skim the surface of these feelings. Dissociative techniques, including the development of conversion reactions, may even be used. Typically, they communicate in a global, general manner in which they make arbitrary judgments with little focus on the specifics of an event or concept.

Histrionics can be warm, colorful, interesting, engaging, and emotionally responsive; typically, they have a good sense of humor. They easily adapt to new situations and, at least superficially, appear to have little difficulty interacting with and becoming close with others. Elevations on Histrionic are associated with an above-average number of positive life events, low levels of distress, and good social adjustment. As a result, if Histrionic is the only elevated scale, it should not be used to suggest a personality disorder but more a style of adapting.

Frequent Code Types

Because of their underlying feelings of dependency, histrionics are likely to experience separation anxieties or, as an expression of their fears of emptiness, agoraphobia (check Anxiety). Conversion symptoms or hypochondriasis might also be a means of dramatically expressing their needs (check Somatoform), and their need for stimulus seeking may result in substance abuse (check Alcohol Dependence and Drug Dependence). Possible associated elevations on personality scales include Dependent (see section on Dependent), Narcissistic, Passive-Aggressive (Negativistic), Antisocial, and Compulsive. Elevations on Somatoform might indicate conversions. An associated Narcissistic elevation, along with Histrionic, frequently occurs with and is quite consistent with Histrionic in that it exaggerates many of the self-centered qualities of the histrionics. They are also likely to emphasize how charming and capable they are and to belittle those who do not partake in reinforcing their own sense of self-importance. Their descriptions of their competence and exploits are often exaggerated. They continually indicate how they are special and worthy of more attention and praise than others. An associated elevation on Passive-Aggressive (Negativistic) is problematic in that the histrionics do not like to accept their own negative emotions, such as anger and resentment. As a result of this conflict, they are moody, unpredictable, and emotionally reactive. They might overtly criticize or show disdain for others or, in contrast, express these feelings in a more indirect way, such as through obstructionism. Their attempts to repress and overcontrol their anger and resentment may sometimes culminate in explosive outbursts, followed by guilt and apologies. Similarly, an elevation on Antisocial creates conflict for these persons. They are highly dependent on others, but they also realize that their anger, disaffiliation, and resentment are likely to distance the very people whom they so much need. They might begin a relationship by being charming, friendly, and engaging, but eventually their antisocial feelings become expressed in resentment, mistrust, and even anger. In extreme cases, they might fluctuate between overcontrol and occasional extreme emotional or even physical outbursts. They may also seek to cope with this conflict through passive-aggressive strategies. Their world is perceived as a competitive, potentially dangerous place, and, given these perceptions, they have similarly become competitive, tough realists who believe that this is the only means of coping. Elevations on Compulsive along with Histrionic also present a conflicted relationship because part of the person wants to be unrestrained and emotional whereas another part believes in the importance of emotional overcontrol. These clients are likely to seek approval through being orderly, efficient, dependable, and by dressing correctly. Often they have difficulty integrating these two modes of adapting and may become tense and moody.

Treatment Implications

Histrionics are typically motivated to come to therapy because they have been through a time when they have been criticized and feel socially deprived. They describe feeling empty, bored, lonely, and discontented. Because they are emotional, responsive, friendly, and seek the support and approval of others, they are likely to become easily engaged in therapy. These qualities usually lead to an initial high level of motivation and a good prognosis. They are unlikely to develop severe or chronic forms of psychopathology. However, they usually stay in therapy only long enough to become stabilized and rarely engage in deeper levels of self-exploration. One of the primary goals is to reduce their overdramatization. A calm, objective, cognitive approach is often useful in achieving this goal. In addition, group or family interventions can be useful in enhancing and practicing improved interpersonal skills. Given their externalizing coping style, a behavioral approach, combined with the development of specific skills, is likely to be more effective than one attempting to develop extensive insight.

Narcissistic (Scale 5)

The central characteristic of individuals with elevations on this scale is their exaggerated sense of self-importance and competence. Because they perceive themselves as special, they are likely to assume that many of the conventional rules of living with people do not apply to themselves. In addition, they may feel that they deserve special favors without having to reciprocate the time and resources that are given to them. As a result, they are likely to be overrepresented among persons seeking workers' and other forms of legal compensation. Internally, they might be quite creative in developing plausible reasons for their self-centeredness, but, to others, these reasons might seem flimsy and transparent. Their fantasies typically involve immature, self-glorifying situations in which they are the center of attention because they are beloved, admired, successful, and physically attractive. In real life, failures are quickly rationalized and conflicts are minimized, and they are adept at enhancing their sense of pride. In building their image, they might depreciate the value of others to make themselves look superior by comparison. They might, therefore, appear arrogant, haughty, snobbish, pretentious, and conceited. They present themselves as intelligent, sophisticated, outgoing, and charming, with an air of cool optimism and feigned tranquility. Rarely do they express any self-doubt. Interpersonally, they are likely to be exploitive, autocratic, and insensitive to the needs and feelings of others. Thus, they are generally lacking in empathy. They constantly attempt to obtain admiration from others. If they are in situations in which they are criticized, they might become quite competitive and aggressive toward those who criticize them, or they may react with contempt or indifference. Thus, they have a primarily externalizing coping style. If their narcissistic bubble is burst, they are at risk for becoming depressed and potentially involved in substance abuse. A subgroup of high scorers is well adjusted and does not experience much emotional distress (see the following positive descriptions). As such, high scores should be interpreted as merely a style of adapting rather than a possible disorder. In contrast, others are pathologically narcissistic. Thus, a diagnostic challenge is determining in which of the two groups the client best fits. If Narcissistic is only mildly elevated and the only elevation, it strongly suggests that these persons are likely to be in the well-adjusted group.

They frequently make excellent first impressions and might even receive respect and affection from others. Typically, they are articulate, carry themselves with dignity, and have a good sense of humor. Others often perceive them as being proud, independent, confident, and optimistic.

Frequent Code Types

Because narcissistic persons are prone to affective disorders and substance abuse, check relevant clinical scales (Bipolar:Manic, Dysthymia, Alcohol Dependence, Drug Dependence, Major Depression). Personality scales that are likely to be elevated include Avoidant (see section on Avoidant), Histrionic (see section on Histrionic), Antisocial, and Passive-Aggressive (Negativistic). Elevations on Narcissistic and Antisocial emphasize the self-centered, competitive, and possibly aggressive and intimidating character of these persons. They are likely to be hostile and exploitive and justify this conduct by pointing out the competitive and exploitive nature of other people. At times, they might become malicious, cruel, and abusive; at others times, they may be cheerful, gracious, and friendly. Because they fear the criticism and possible exploitiveness of others, they might frequently be guarded, resentful, and reserved. The combination of Passive-Aggressive (Negativistic) and Narcissistic places these persons in a difficult, conflicted position. They seek to perceive themselves as superior and special in relation to others, but they are also acutely aware of their limitations. Thus, they are likely to be apologetic, submissive, compliant, and cooperative on one hand but also hypersensitive, moody, resentful, and angry on the other. They have marked difficulty in accepting criticism, combined with frequent mood changes.

Treatment Implications

Because attending therapy is an implicit admission of imperfections, it is unusual for narcissistic persons to initiate therapy themselves. When they do, it is usually because their narcissistic sense of superiority has been compromised through events such as divorce or loss of employment. Interpersonally, they are likely to remain aloof and often be competitive with the therapist. They might question how someone who is less talented than they are could possibly be of assistance. Alternatively, they might elevate and inflate the status of the therapist because their association with someone who is so accomplished can be used to bolster their own sense of self-esteem. The easiest tactic for returning them to their previous level of functioning is to encourage and support them in recounting their previous successes and achievements. However, this may do them a disservice in the end because they will not learn new strategies of coping and relating. A particularly useful technique might be cognitive reorientation, in which they are helped to challenge the need to be perfect and desensitized to criticism. Group and family therapy might support them in achieving more realistic and adaptive interpersonal skills. Given that they are likely to deny imperfections and resist change, either paradoxical interventions or approaches that use nondirective or self-directed techniques are likely to produce the best outcomes.

Antisocial (Scale 6A)

The central theme for persons with elevations on this scale is competitiveness along with impulsive acting out of antisocial feelings. They are often described as provocative, violent, vicious, self-centered, dominant, dishonest, brutal, and devious. Their actions are often hasty, shortsighted, and imprudent, and they generally ignore the consequences of their actions even to the extent of disregarding the safety of themselves and others. They can be interpersonally irresponsible—they will violate the personal rights of others in occupational, marital, parental, or financial contexts. They can be expected to have legal difficulties because many persons with elevations on Antisocial engage in criminal activities. For others in this category, legal problems are often absent because they confine their acting out to legal domains such as alcohol abuse, interpersonal insensitivity, unreliable work practices, and irresponsible sexual behavior. However, they do not conform to social norms and may even feel and express contempt toward these norms. They enjoy the feeling of not being confined by standard modes of conduct and project the image of being free, flexible, unencumbered, and having little obligation to schedules, commitments, or persons. Unfortunately, this image is usually associated with a lack of compassion, empathy, remorse, and charitableness. They justify frequent expressions of callous competitiveness by pointing out the exploitiveness of others or otherwise conceptualizing the world as functioning according to the law of the jungle. Because of these attitudes, they are mistrustful, suspicious, guarded, and reserved. They might also be aggressive, intimidating, cold, insensitive, or even cruel and malicious, thereby provoking fear. They may treat with contempt those who are considered "weak," or they might ascribe their own malicious tendencies to others. When challenged, they are likely to become impulsively angry or resentful, vindictive, and vengeful.

At their best, antisocials can be gracious, charming, friendly, and cheerful. Some people might perceive them as interesting and exciting, at least in part, because they are not confined by the same rules of conduct and restraints as other people.

Frequent Code Types

Check to see whether the clinical scales of Alcohol Dependence and Drug Dependence are elevated; given the impulsiveness and hedonism of antisocials, they are prone to substance abuse. Although generally free from anxiety, they can develop affective disorders, especially when being held accountable for antisocial acting out (check Bipolar:Manic, Dysthymia, Major Depression). Associated personality scales that are frequently elevated include

Avoidant (see section on Avoidant), Dependent, Narcissistic (see section on Narcissistic), Histrionic (see section on Histrionic), Compulsive, Passive-Aggressive (Negativistic), and Aggressive (Sadistic). High points on Antisocial and Dependent indicate that these persons are extremely conflicted because they perceive the world as a difficult, competitive place; yet at the same time, they feel that they need to rely on others for protection and guidance. They are mistrustful, guarded, and reserved, and, although they know that to function they need to be tough, they do not feel themselves capable of this stance. The combination of Antisocial and Compulsive is also a conflicted combination. These persons feel internally impulsive, but they believe in discipline, control, persistence, and dependability. Their typical strategy is to become emotionally overcontrolled, careful, and deliberate. Perceiving the world as competitive and potentially exploitive, they protect themselves with a strategy of hard work, self-restraint, thorough preparation, and being guarded and mistrustful. Others are likely to perceive them as emotionally distant, tough-minded, formal, perfectionistic, inflexible, and possibly indecisive. When Passive-Aggressive (Negativistic) is high along with Antisocial, the angry, resentful characteristics of the antisocial are brought out; yet the same individuals may desire the closeness and warmth that could be available in relationships. However, they perceive the world as a struggle in which most situations are framed in "win-lose" terms. Thus, they frequently override their need for affection by becoming tough-minded, competitive, and interpersonally superficial. They might excel in individualistic activities—some competitive sports or sales positions, for example—but they would have difficulty working in situations that require loyalty and team coordination. The unusual combination of Antisocial and Aggressive (Sadistic) is noteworthy as it indicates that any acting out will be cruel, malicious, and callous. The elevation on Aggressive (Sadistic) indicates that the expression of antisocial feelings is direct, overt, and abusive. Such persons should be treated with considerable caution.

Treatment Considerations

Antisocials typically do not recognize the need for treatment and are most frequently referred either by the courts or because of threats from spouses that they will leave them. Once in therapy, they are likely to either openly defy therapist interventions or develop a facade of cooperation in the hope that they might be able to somehow exploit the situation. Therapists need to be cautious; they can potentially be conned by these clients, who would then perceive them as weak and not worthy of respect. The therapists may then run the risk of becoming angry, cynical, and punitive—and ineffective. Given that the antisocial's style is one of externally acting out, the most appropriate interventions are ones that are directed toward changing specific forms of behavior with clear limits: behavior modification, behavioral contracting, and external monitoring of behavior. Antisocials are unlikely to be responsive to internalizing, insight-oriented interventions. In addition, because their arousal level is typically low, techniques that increase arousal, distress, or even anxiety serve to increase their level of motivation. A group context might work particularly well, because antisocials are more responsive to peer influence than to authority-directed influence. However, most interventions have not been demonstrated to be effective in changing their underlying personality structure. A more realistic goal is the reduction of specific targeted symptoms or behaviors, particularly their aggression, destruction, impulsiveness, and poor affect. Target behaviors might be framed in the context that change is in the client's self-interest.

Aggressive (Sadistic; Scale 6B)

Individuals scoring high on Aggressive are typically competitive, energetic, hard-headed, authoritarian, and socially intolerant. They are predisposed toward aggressive outbursts, which might be expressed in a callous manner with little awareness of the impact of their verbally or physically aggressive actions. In many ways, their callousness can be seen as a further pathological variation of the antisocial personality. Being in control and exerting power perhaps to the point of intimidating others is a central means they use to achieve their goals. Humiliating their victims also serves to release their own psychological pain. Sometimes they enter socially approved enforcing roles in which their expression of aggression is disguised behind socially sanctioned rules (the strict disciplinarian school principal or overzealous police officer). They are relatively unaffected by pain and punishment and may act in a manner that is both reckless and daring. They have a tough-minded orientation, which might be expressed in a caustic and contemptuous attitude toward social events and is consistent with their prejudice, intolerance, and authoritarianism. At their worst, they might express vicious, explosive, violent, and even brutal behavior. Noticeably absent is a sense of shame, guilt, sentimentality, or internal conflicts. Other persons are perceived as objects to manipulate and control. This attitude might be enhanced and justified if the victims can be considered members of disempowered, marginalized groups.

A positive aspect of persons with this profile is that they can cope effectively with challenges. They can be unflinching and daring, which, if expressed in the right context, can be considered courageous. In reaching a goal, they are relatively unencumbered by subtle ambiguities that might make it difficult for other people to take action.

Frequent Code Types

Fortunately, elevations on Aggressive (Sadistic) are infrequent. When they do occur, noteworthy elevations on other scales include Antisocial (see section on Antisocial), Narcissistic, Compulsive, and Paranoid. When Aggressive (Sadistic) is added to Narcissistic, these individuals do not only have an inflated, unrealistic sense of themselves but also they are likely to be openly hostile and destructive, which is not the case when Narcissistic is elevated by itself. Elevations on the Compulsive scale highlight a methodical and disciplined expression of aggression. A corresponding elevation on Paranoid indicates that these persons' cruelty might be self-justified by suspicions that others would like to exploit or even brutalize them.

Treatment Implications

This difficult-to-treat group almost never reports to therapy on their own initiative. Once in therapy, they are likely to belittle the therapist and may even be overtly hostile. A therapist who responds negatively is likely to be perceived as weak, and clients use this perception to discount therapist interventions. In addition, they typically lack insight into their behavior and can even be indifferent to the damage they inflict. Cognitive interventions are unlikely to be successful because their thought patterns are quite rigid. Potentially useful approaches might be anger and impulse management programs, developing assertive as opposed to hostile communications, and persuading them to see that changing some of their more problematic behavior is actually in their own self-interest.

Compulsive (Scale 7)

The core characteristics for persons with this elevation are conformity, discipline, self-restraint, and formality. They strictly adhere to social norms and may even be upset by novel ideas, especially if they challenge established norms of conduct. They are conscientious, well prepared, righteous, and meticulous; and they perform well when required to work on a schedule. They typically work hard, sometimes to the exclusion of leisure activities. Their emotions and behavior are tightly controlled. Interpersonally, they are formal, moral, perfectionistic, and rigid. They are overrespectful and even ingratiating toward persons in authority. In contrast, they are likely to be demanding, perfectionistic, and even contemptuous of subordinates, insisting that they act in strict adherence to correct and preestablished rules and methods. Self-descriptions include responsible, dependable, orderly, punctual, reliable, and stubborn. Internally, they are rigidly controlled and do not allow themselves to experience any forbidden thoughts or impulses. Their world is constructed in terms of schedules, deadlines, rules, ethics, and prescribed forms of behavior. Although they perform well in structured, concrete working environments, they have difficulty adjusting to changing work situations that require creative, spontaneous responses. These strategies provide them with a high degree of control over their world and their inner impulses, but the price they pay is a grim, tense, joyless life in which warm feelings and spontaneity are kept under tight control.

Positive qualities include loyalty, prudence, consistency, predictability, and a strong sense of duty. Often they are able to approach a difficult situation with maturity and competence. In a work context, they are punctual, thorough, diligent, honest, and rarely make mistakes. Often persons with elevations on Compulsive are high achievers and rarely report psychiatric distress. The evidence is very strong that this scale does not measure aspects of disorder but rather reflects a person's adaptive style. For example, it has been found that persons who have been formally diagnosed with an obsessive-compulsive disorder rarely had significant elevations on the Compulsive scale.

A defensive, fake good profile can produce an elevation on Compulsive. In these cases, the previous scale interpretation should not focus on discipline and restraint but rather on the client's defensiveness.

Frequent Code Types

Typically, elevations on Compulsive are not accompanied by elevations on other scales. However, when comorbid conditions do occur, the most frequent Axis I problems are generalized anxiety disorders (check Anxiety scale) and depression, particularly of an agitated nature (check Dysthymia and, possibly, Major Depression scales). Compared to other personality disorders, compulsives tend to be a better-defined population as there is less overlap with other personality disorders. Nonetheless, associated elevations can occur with Schizoid (see section on Schizoid), Dependent (see section on Dependent), Histrionic (see section on Histrionic), Antisocial (see section on Antisocial), Avoidant, and Narcissistic. Concurrent elevations on Avoidant indicate that these individuals would like to obtain the warmth and affection of others. However, they are extremely hesitant to do so because people are perceived as unpredictable and emotional. Both these aspects of relationships are experienced as risky and are likely to arouse significant anxiety. Compulsives have learned to minimize risk by becoming perfectionistic and relating in a distant, aloof manner. Elevations with Compulsive and Narcissistic suggest individuals who are confident, defensive, and unlikely to concede that they have made a mistake. They rely strongly on their own ideas and are likely to have difficulty accepting the advice, suggestions, and especially the orders of others. Individuals perceive them as inflexible, formal, proper, and distant. As a result, they have difficulty working in supportive team environments where mutual respect and consensus building are crucial factors.

Treatment Implications

Usually compulsives lead controlled, predictable, and generally functional lives. However, when confronted with excessive change or important decisions, they may present to therapy with anxiety-related problems. In particular, these problems might be expressed in somatic complaints because compulsives have a difficult time releasing internal tension. They often view their world in a rigid, inflexible manner. As a result, self-exploration is difficult because it is experienced as a violation of their "character armor" and their personal sense of privacy and conformity. In addition, self-exploration runs the risk of playing into their obsessiveness, so that change never actually occurs. One technique of breaking up their obsessive patterns is to help them access and experience their affect. Other strategies are to work with them to realize the irrationality of their patterns or to use paradoxical interventions (i.e., reframing perfection as actually allowing themselves to make mistakes). Usually the first line of intervention is support, combined with techniques of anxiety reduction: systematic desensitization, relaxation, emotional support, biofeedback, and, possibly, psychopharmacological agents. Any insight-related work should proceed cautiously and with considerable reassurance, so that their defenses are not challenged too quickly. Potentially problematic client-therapist transactions might be therapist boredom, power struggles, or therapist collusion with the client's compulsions in the form of endless but unproductive insights. Despite these potential difficulties, compulsives' prognosis for treatment is quite good.

Passive-Aggressive (Negativistic; Scale 8A)

The core characteristic for clients with elevations in this scale is a mix of passive compliance combined with resentment and opposition. These clients usually act on these resentments in impulsive and erratic ways. Feeding their resentment is a sense that they have somehow gotten a raw deal in life and will inevitably be disappointed in relationships. However, they also feel that their resentment and anger are not acceptable emotions for them to have. As a result, guilt and conflict pervade their lives. This internal conflictual style also becomes externalized and creates problems in interpersonal relationships. They are moody, complaining, and intermittently hostile. One moment they might be angry and stubborn, but the next moment they feel guilty and apologetic. They are likely to express their negativism in indirect ways—procrastination, inefficiency, and contrary behavior that has the effect of undermining the happiness of others. They may also act on their resentment with caustic comments, complaints, and expressions of contempt toward others. One means of coping with these feelings is to deny them and, instead, attribute them to others. Another way is to conceptualize that the resentment and anger are justified because of the numerous reasons to be envious toward others, who are constantly seen as having things so much better. Their resulting chronic unhappiness is expressed through pessimism, disillusionment, and cynicism. Because they blame other people for their misfortunes, they have little insight into how their own behavior and attitudes cause others to reject them. However, when their attitudes and behaviors eventually lead to rejection by others, these clients feel demeaned, abandoned, unappreciated, and disillusioned. Thus, their difficulties are self-fulfilling and self-maintaining. They typically describe themselves as moody, testy, resentful, oppositional, and discontented.

A further core conflict is a feeling that they would like to depend on others, but this dependence is neither socially acceptable nor safe because others inevitably exploit and disappoint them. Thus, they seem moody and unpredictable as they ruminate over these contradictory feelings. They often perceive relationships as a threat to their safety. To protect themselves, they become superficially quite self-sufficient and independent.

At their best, persons with this elevation can be agreeable and friendly. They can also be flexible, changeable, emotionally responsive, and sensitive.

Frequent Code Types

Persons with this code type experience frequent rejection and are likely to experience depression (check Dysthymia and Major Affective Disorder). Their feeling that interpersonal situations are potentially dangerous is capable of producing chronic anxiety (check Anxiety), which might be expressed in indirect ways through psychophysiological disorders or conversions (check Somatoform). Concurrent elevations on personality scales include Schizoid, Avoidant, Dependent, Histrionic, Antisocial, Narcissistic, and Aggressive (Sadistic; check frequent code-type descriptions for each one of these scales in previous sections).

Treatment Implications

The two major areas of intervention involve enabling Passive-Aggressives to be more consistent in their approach to life and to develop insight into the nature of their ambivalent style of responding. However, the therapeutic relationship itself is likely to be complicated by clients' ambivalence. Specifically, they desire caring and support by others but perceive the development of such a relationship as a threat to their independence and fear that it will end up with rejection and disappointment. As a result, they may erratically criticize their therapist or engage in passive resistance. Dealing with this potential difficulty through early behavioral contracting might be particularly useful in keeping these clients engaged in the therapy process. One concern related to clinical management is that their impulsiveness might involve suicide risk. This fact is especially problematic if they decompensate into an anxiety or depressive disorder. Family and marital interventions are likely to be extremely beneficial because passive-aggressive (negativistic) patterns are both initiated by and maintained in these systems. Formal programs of anger management and assertiveness training might also be quite helpful in developing greater control over impulses and learning more effective styles of communication. Their belief in future disappointments, along with their dysfunctional thoughts of having been cheated by life, can be worked on through cognitive interventions that challenge these assumptions. Because they are likely to be resistant, controlling clients, the use of either paradoxical directives or a combination of nondirective and client-directed techniques is likely to optimize outcome.

Self-Defeating (Scale 8B)

High elevations on Self-Defeating indicate aggrieved persons who continually place themselves in situations in which they will be the victims. They present themselves as inferior, nonindulgent, self-effacing, insecure, or otherwise reluctant to accept pleasure and happiness. Somehow, pleasure is seen as something they do not deserve, and they feel that if they allow themselves to experience pleasure, further difficulties or other unpleasant consequences will follow. Anything positive is expressed with very little enthusiasm. Interpersonal relationships are characterized by these clients as servile, self-effacing, self-sacrificing, or otherwise allowing or even encouraging others to exploit or mistreat them. This active involvement in creating situations in which they will be exploited differentiates these types of persons from other depressed clients. Close relationships are usually associated with disappointments and frustrations. Those who do try to support and help them are likely to be ignored or otherwise rendered ineffectual. One purpose of this response is for the client to make him- or herself appear weak and harmless in an effort to discourage possible criticism and aggression from others and evoke guilt instead. In addition, their public displays of dejection initially produce both sympathy and a tacit permission to avoid unpleasant responsibilities. A further purpose is to keep their self-identity organized around being shamed, humbled, and debased. They may be so absorbed in their own suffering and misery that they have few resources for appreciating the dilemmas others might be in. Although superficially, they might be sympathetic to others, underneath they are unempathic and distrustful. They focus and ruminate on past failed relationships and disparage any personal achievements. This results in their being anxious, apprehensive, mournful, anguished, and tormented.

Positive qualities are that, in comparison to disorders such as schizoid, they are involved with and connected to people. Often they can develop a good level of insight into their difficulties. In addition, their level of distress is likely to be sufficiently high that they can and do become engaged in therapy.

Frequent Code Types

The greatest risk for self-defeating persons is the development of depression (check Dysthymia and Major Affective Disorder). If anxiety is present, it is usually diffuse and associated with fears of loss and abandonment. Hypochondriacal strategies might be grafted on to their aggrieved style as a means of channeling anxiety and obtaining support (check Somatoform). The most frequent associated elevations are with Dependent (see section on Dependent), Borderline (see section on Borderline), Depressive (see section on Depressive), and Avoidant. When Self-Defeating and Avoidant are both elevated, it suggests that these persons have found relationships sufficiently painful that they have withdrawn to the extent of rarely interacting and becoming relatively isolated. They would like to be involved with others, but that experience has simply proven to be too painful in the past.

Treatment Implications

The paradox of working with self-defeating persons is that the context of therapy is to make them happier; yet, on one level, they do not want to be happier. These clients might even try to provoke or at least frame situations in such a way that they feel rejected or humiliated by the therapist. To counter this tactic, a sufficient amount of support, understanding, and rapport must be established to work with these clients and make them understand that they do not necessarily have to suffer. Specific self-defeating behaviors need to be identified along with the circumstances that elicit them. Assertiveness training, to help clarify their rights and develop skills to stop exploitation, might be particularly helpful. These skills, and others, might be practiced in the context of role plays and/or couples therapy. Further examination of relationships and the part they play in them can occur both in individual therapy and through supportive group interaction.

SEVERE PERSONALITY PATHOLOGY

Schizotypal (Scale S)

The major characteristics of persons with elevations on Schizotypal are eccentricity, disorganization, and social isolation. These difficulties are usually of a long-term nature. Their eccentricities relate to peculiar mannerisms, strange clothes, and bizarre expressions. They typically look drab, lifeless, apathetic, and joyless. Self-descriptions include alienated, isolated, fragmented, and detached. They may engage in magical behavior and rituals in an attempt to neutralize "evil" thoughts, deeds, or omens. Often there is little distinction between fantasy and reality. Their communication style is characterized by tangential comments, personal irrelevancies, and magical associations.

As a result, they lead empty and meaningless lives in which they drift to and from various locations and sources of employment. Thus, they exist on the fringe of society. Some are detached and emotionally bland; others are more suspicious, anxious, and apprehensive. Because they are mistrustful and communicate poorly, their relationships usually make them quite uncomfortable. As a result, they develop few, if any, close friendships and prefer privacy and isolation. Usually they lack the interest and energy to initiate social interaction. Internally, they have a deep sense of emptiness and meaninglessness, which sometimes is sufficiently severe to prompt a full schizophrenic episode. Their thought processes are scattered, autistic, and disorganized. They are likely to have experiences of depersonalization and dissociation. In summary, schizotypals are cognitively impaired in their ability to comprehend interpersonal motivations and communications.

Frequent Code Types

Diagnostically, schizotypals exist somewhere between the less severe schizoid disorder and the more severe schizophrenic disorders. However, there is conceptual and clinical overlap with both these disorders; therefore, elevations on scales that measure these dimensions should be noted (check Schizoid, Thought Disorder, and Delusional Disorder). Accordingly, schizoid and schizophrenic disorders might coexist with schizotypal. The most likely associated elevations on personality scales are Schizoid, Avoidant, and Paranoid. The Schizoid and Avoidant elevations are important in distinguishing two subtypes of schizotypals. An elevation on Schizotypal in combination with Schizoid indicates a more passive, apathetic, detached expression of schizotypal characteristics. These persons are deficient in their capacity to experience emotions and extremely detached and indifferent toward others. In contrast, an associated elevation on Avoidant indicates a desire for personal contact, but these individuals are more anxious and apprehensive, and actively protect themselves by disengaging from others. If Paranoid is elevated along with Schizotypal, it highlights these clients' suspiciousness along with corresponding ideas of reference. Although their thoughts might be more organized because of the coherence provided by the paranoid content, they still have the tangential thinking and eccentric behavior that are characteristic of persons with elevations on Schizotypal.

Treatment Implications

The prognosis for schizotypal is not good because of the ingrained, long-standing nature of their patterns and the difficulty of engaging them in the therapeutic process. Treatment goals should be tempered accordingly, with a focus on preventing further social isolation and deterioration. Changing these individuals' environment to encourage an increase in supportive interpersonal interaction might be particularly helpful. A further intervention might be to help them express and clarify their thoughts while simultaneously providing emotional support. Psychopharmacological agents might be useful both in helping to organize their thoughts and in reducing the likelihood of their acting on irrational impulses.

Borderline (Scale C)

The core features of individuals with elevations on this scale are instability and unpredictability of mood and behavior. One moment they might feel dejected and disillusioned; sometime later, feelings of euphoria are followed by a phase of intense anger, irritability, and self-destructiveness—possibly even involving self-mutilation. Their self-destructiveness reflects a severely punishing conscience. In addition, much of their unstable behavior seems to be directed by internal factors rather than a reaction to environmental events. They have marked mood swings, intermittent periods of depression, generalized anxiety, and intense emotional attacks on others, followed by apathy and dejection. Although these behaviors often create significant interpersonal difficulties, these clients are also extremely concerned with maintaining the care and emotional support of others. They often elicit rejection, but they react strongly to fears of abandonment. They might intermittently idealize people, but their ambivalence eventually gives way to devaluing and criticizing the same people they have previously idealized. Thus, their relationships are characterized by ambivalence, instability, and intensity. Underlying many of these behaviors is an extremely poorly developed sense of identity, which is at the core of their dissolution of controls. Their poorly defined sense of self might eventually give way to feelings of emptiness and to disorganized thoughts. Under stress, they might have transient psychotic episodes. However, these episodes are rarely sufficient to be considered a formal thought disorder, and these clients usually return fairly quickly to their previous levels of functioning. They typically describe themselves as depressed, impatient, tense, irritable, disturbed, and anxious.

Frequent Code Types

The symptomatology of borderlines can be extremely diverse; elevations may appear on any of the clinical scales. However, mood disorders (check Bipolar:Manic, Dysthymia, Major Depression) and substance abuse (check Alcohol Dependence and Drug Dependence) are among the most common complications. In many ways, borderlines can be conceptualized as exaggerations or extensions of the less dysfunctional personality disorders of self-defeating (masochistic), passive-aggressive (negativistic), dependent, histrionic, and/or narcissistic. As a result, elevations on one or more of the scales representing these constructs would be expected and would provide further information on these individuals' underlying dynamics and particular mode of expression. Because such a broad spectrum of behaviors is encompassed by the borderlines, integrating the meaning of other scale elevations can be crucial information to attend to. One of the most frequent associated scale elevations is when Borderline is combined with Passive-Aggressive (Negativistic), which emphasizes the conflicted aspect of the borderlines. These clients feel intense dependency yet are anxious and extremely ambivalent about it. They also feel intense resentment and anger but simultaneously believe that such feelings are unacceptable. These intense polarities might naturally give way to both a disintegration of the sense of self and clearly unstable, unpredictable behavior. Another important combination is Borderline and Self-Defeating, which would highlight these clients' impulsive and self-destructive characteristics. Behind their unstable emotions and behavior would lie a strong underlying sense that they were not worthy of happiness but, instead, should be exploited and humiliated. Thus, dealing with the client's depression and suicide would be an essential aspect of case management. Elevations on Dependent and Borderline emphasize these clients' low self-esteem, passivity, and apathy, combined with their need for someone else who will care for them and make decisions for them. A corresponding elevation on Histrionic would underscore these persons' dependency but, instead of being apathetic and passive, they would be outgoing, friendly, manipulative, and emotional. When their defenses are challenged, they might increase their activity and attention seeking to intense levels; if this strategy does not work, they may deteriorate into futility and self-destructiveness. When Narcissistic is elevated along with Borderline, it suggests that these individuals' self-inflated sense of importance has collapsed into feelings of shame, insecurity, emptiness, and self-condemnation.

Treatment Implications

Although borderlines are notoriously difficult to work with, they are also more amenable to change than many other personality-disordered individuals. The central, initial goal is to build sufficient rapport so that work can begin on stabilizing their erratic behavior and affect. This might involve a reality-oriented approach emphasizing aspects such as limit setting, sympathy, reassurance, advice, and insight regarding internal processes. Borderlines are capable of a wide range of dysfunctional behaviors, but the highest priority should be given to working with suicidal and self-injurious behavior. In addition, they are an unusually heterogeneous group. For example, depression, anxiety, depersonalization, disorganized thoughts, fears of abandonment, self-destructiveness, and/or ambivalence may all become areas requiring attention. More than for most other client groups, building a strong therapeutic alliance is crucial in helping borderlines to adjust and cope with their many conflicted forms of acting and feeling. Effective treatment has often been achieved using a combination of mindfulness skills, techniques to assist with regulating emotions, strategies to assist with interpersonal effectiveness, and building tolerance to distress. Because many borderlines resist authority-directed interventions, group therapy might be indicated because they are more likely to be responsive to peer influence.

Paranoid (Scale P)

The central issue for persons with elevations on Paranoid is suspiciousness and defensiveness, combined with a feeling of superiority. They are constantly vigilant because they feel others will criticize or deceive them. Innocuous events are perceived as insults or as the workings of a world in which others are trying to control or harm them. They distort their world by interpreting events to fit their idiosyncratic views. Because they feel in frequent danger, they are abrasive, touchy, hostile, and irritable. They are likely to feel bitter toward people who have been successful and to believe that their success has been achieved through dishonesty and possibly illegal activities. This process involves denying their own shortcomings and attributing them to others. Although quick to notice and expand on minor faults in others, they are ignorant of these same faults in themselves. These dynamics are used as a means of establishing their own superiority in relation to others. They often describe themselves as misunderstood, righteous, suspicious, mistreated, and defensive.

If high scorers on Paranoid perceive that anyone is trying to control or influence them, they consider this a personal encroachment on their independence and will attack and humiliate the encroacher. As a result, they frequently induce fear and exasperation in others. Unfortunately, their system of making sense of the world is self-fulfilling. People react negatively to their being mistrustful and even hostile, which provides evidence that indeed the world is a dangerous, insecure place. When other people act in negative ways toward them, this pushes them progressively into a more insular world in which their thinking becomes extremely rigid. The rigidity and insularity are maintained because they depend on their own internal processes for both stimulation and reinforcement. They are terrified of being dominated and consider any sign of dependence an indication of weakness and inferiority. They insist on being the designers of their own fate and, to do so, need to be free from entanglements and obligations. Behind this separateness is a fear of losing their personal control and sense of autonomy. Thus, their extremely tightly organized and coherent personality and cognitive structure makes them feel emotionally and physically disconnected from others. In more extreme cases, these persons may have delusions of grandeur, ideas of reference, and intense fears of persecutory plots.

Frequent Code Types

Given the mistrust and fear expressed by many paranoids, anxiety is probably the most frequent Axis I complication (check Anxiety). Additional difficulties are likely to be obsessive-compulsive syndromes in which they engage in compulsive activities in an attempt to make their world "safe." In severe paranoid states, psychotic symptoms, expressed through delusions and hallucinations, may be present (check Delusional Disorder and Thought Disorder). Related elevations on personality scales include Narcissistic, Passive-Aggressive (Negativistic), Sadistic, and Avoidant. If Narcissistic is elevated, it suggests that, at some earlier stage, these clients' self-inflated sense of importance and superiority has been severely challenged. Paranoid processes become a means to resurrect these beliefs in a way that is further separated from reality and, therefore, requires more drastic measures. The result might be extravagant plans to defend the world from evil, create new societies, or solve insurmountable scientific problems. When an elevation in Passive-Aggressive (Negativistic) is associated with Paranoid, it represents an exaggeration of these persons' fault finding, resentful, and discontented characteristics. These might be expressed as intense feelings of jealously or as claims that they are being cheated and misunderstood. Because their underlying negativism is unacceptable to themselves, they attribute it to the external world, thereby-self-creating the world they are so afraid of. An elevation on both Paranoid and Sadistic suggests that these individuals' paranoia will be expressed in an authoritarian, controlling, intimidating, and belligerent manner. They are likely to ruminate over perceived past wrongs and develop callous plots of revenge. Elevations on Avoidant and Paranoid indicate that these clients are handling their fears and suspicions by becoming progressively more insular, reclusive, and isolated. Insularity helps to protect them from fears that others will be able to influence their thought processes. However, they also feel extremely vulnerable and have serious questions related to their self-esteem.

Treatment Implications

Although paranoid personalities have an intact, organized means of processing their world, they develop and maintain this perspective by insulating themselves from the influence of others and developing extremely rigid cognitive structures. Because therapy tries both to influence clients and to loosen habitual ways of perceiving the world, these people are difficult to work with. As a result, their prognosis is poor. Furthermore, submitting to therapy is an admission of weakness and of giving up self-sufficiency, and both situations are abhorrent to them. A therapist who is too friendly and empathic is likely to be perceived as being deceitful. High empathy by the therapist has even been found to be counterproductive. In contrast, a therapist who is too distant or who challenges these clients' delusions will seem rejecting. Either approach may, therefore, invoke the clients' suspicions. The relationship requires a delicate balance. Trust needs to be slowly built up with gradual but careful encouragement to perceive events from several different perspectives.

CLINICAL SYNDROMES

Anxiety (Scale A)

High scores indicate clients are complaining of tension, difficulty relaxing, indecisiveness, and apprehension. Additional complaints include a highly sensitive startle response, hyperalertness, and fears related to the onset of poorly defined difficulties. Physiological complaints related to overarousal are also common. These might include insomnia, headaches, nausea, cold sweats, upset stomach, palpitations, excessive perspiration, and muscular aches. Anxiety may be either generalized or more focused, as in social situations or specific phobias. Inspection of responses to individual scale items can help to assess the degree of specificity of the anxiety.

Somatoform (Scale H)

Elevations reflect somatic complaints expressed in areas such as generalized pain, fatigue, multiple vague complaints, and/or preoccupation with health-related difficulties. However, these typically represent psychological conflicts that are being expressed through physical means. If clients have legitimate physical illnesses, they are likely to be unduly preoccupied and possibly exaggerating their difficulties. In other words, their difficulties are overinterpreted to signify a major illness when the illness is actually relatively minor. Often the complaints are expressed in a dramatic and/or vague manner. An important function of these complaints is to gain sympathy, attention, or medical reassurance. A careful medical history typically reveals a hypochondriacal pattern in which they are overusers of the health care system.

Bipolar: Manic (Scale N)

High scorers are likely to have mood swings that range from elation to depression. When elated, they are restless and distractible, have an exaggerated sense of self-esteem, and are overly optimistic and impulsive. They have a heightened and general sense of enthusiasm along with unrealistic goals. Interpersonal relationships have a demanding, intrusive, and pressured quality. There is a reduced need for sleep, erratic mood shifts, and flighty ideas. Extreme elevations indicate a psychotic process characterized by delusions and possibly hallucinations.

Dysthymia (Scale D)

Elevations on Dysthymia reflect sadness, pessimism, hopelessness, apathy, low self-esteem, and guilt. These persons continuously feel socially awkward, introverted, sad, useless, and filled with self-doubt. Discouragement and a preoccupation with their own inadequacy are also present. They have a sense of futility and may easily break into tears. Somatic complications might include insomnia, a poor appetite or habitual overeating, poor concentration, a continuous sense of feeling tired, and a marked loss of interest in pleasurable activities. Although they may have reduced effectiveness in competently undertaking daily activities, they still remain involved in everyday life. Suicidal ideation might be present and should be investigated further. This, and other details related to the nature of the depression, can be further understood by noting the responses to particular items. Unless the Major Depression scale is markedly elevated, it is unlikely that the depression will be sufficiently severe to be considered psychotic.

Alcohol Dependence (Scale B)

Individuals scoring high on Alcohol Dependence are likely to have had a history of problem drinking. They may have tried unsuccessfully to curb or discontinue their drinking. High scorers are also likely to be having social, family, and/or occupational distress. However, the degree to which their drinking is problematic needs to be assessed in relation to other information on their level of functioning.

Drug Dependence (Scale T)

High scorers will have had a recurring history of difficulties with drug abuse. Also present are a number of traits associated with drug-related difficulties: hedonism, impulsiveness, difficulty conforming to mainstream standards of behavior, self-indulgence, exploitive-ness, and narcissistic personality characteristics. High scorers are likely to have difficulty organizing daily life activities and experience social, family, legal, and/or occupational distress.

Posttraumatic Stress Disorder (Scale R)

Elevations on this scale suggest that these individuals have experienced an intense life-threatening event that has resulted in extreme fear, helplessness, and arousal. They have reacted by having uncontrolled, intrusive, and recurrent images or emotions related to the event(s): flashbacks, nightmares, or dissociative feelings that reactivate the event(s). Anxiety-related symptoms might include hypervigilance, hyperalertness, overreactive startle reactions, and a compulsive avoidance of circumstances that might be related to the trauma.

SEVERE SYNDROMES

Thought Disorder (Scale SS)

High scores on Thought Disorder suggest these persons have thoughts that are inconsistent, bizarre, fragmented, and disorganized. In addition, their behavior might be regressed, secretive, and incongruous; and they might be confused, withdrawn, and disoriented. Their affect is likely to be blunted, and they may report hallucinations. Possible diagnoses include schizophrenic, schizophreniform, and brief reactive psychosis.

Major Depression (CC)

High scores suggest severe depression, to the extent that these individuals have difficulty with effective daily living. Psychological difficulties include a sense of hopelessness, suicidal ideation, pessimism, ruminating, and fear of the future. Somatic symptoms might include insomnia, poor concentration, psychomotor slowing or agitation, loss of appetite, weight loss, chronic fatigue, early-morning awakening, and loss of sexual desire. They are also likely to feel worthless and to experience guilt. Some high scorers might express their symptoms in an irritable, whining manner, whereas others might be shy, passive, seclusive, and introverted.

Delusional Disorder (PP)

Elevations on this scale indicate acutely paranoid states. These individuals are characterized by irrational but interconnected delusions, persecutory thoughts, and grandiosity. They are hyperalert to possible threats. The most frequent mood is hostile suspiciousness, perhaps to the point of belligerence. They feel mistreated, jealous, and betrayed.

RECOMMENDED READING

Choca, J. P., & Van Denburg, E. (2004). *Interpretive guide to the Millon Clinical Multiaxial Inventory*, 3rd ed. Washington, DC: American Psychological Association.

Jankowski, D. (2002). *A beginner's guide to the MCMI-III*. Washington, DC: American Psychological Association.

Millon, T., & Davis, R. D. (1996). *Disorders of personality: DSM-IV and beyond*. New York: John Wiley & Sons.

Millon, T., & Grossman, S., Millon, C., Meagher, S., & Ramnath, R. (2004). *Personality disorders in modern life* (2nd ed.). Hoboken, NJ: John Wiley & Sons.

Millon, T. (2008). *The Millon inventories: A practitioner's guide to personalized clinical assessment* (2nd ed.). New York: Guilford Press.

Strack, S. (2008). Essentials of Million inventories assessment. (3rd ed.). Hoboken, NJ: Wiley.

Chapter 9

CALIFORNIA PSYCHOLOGICAL INVENTORY

The California Psychological Inventory (CPI) is a self-administered, paper-and-pencil test composed of 434 true-false statements. The test can be administered either to individuals or groups. Although the test has been used to evaluate individuals between the ages of 12 and 70, it was mainly constructed for use with young adults having a minimum of a fourth-grade reading ability. The CPI items request information concerning an individual's typical behavior patterns, usual feelings and opinions, and attitudes relating to social, ethical, and family matters. The results are plotted on 20 scales and 3 vectors (factors) focusing on aspects of interpersonal relationships that are presented in everyday, commonsense descriptions.

The philosophical orientation of the CPI is based on an appreciation of enduring, commonly discussed personality variables that are relevant throughout different cultures. Thus, it uses familiar commonsense terms such as *dominance, tolerance,* and *self-control,* which Gough has referred to as "folk concepts" (Gough, 2000). Accordingly, it has been translated into more than 40 languages. The value of using such common, easy-to-understand constructs is that they already have "functional validity." In other words, they have immediate cross-cultural relevance, are readily understood by a wide range of people, and have a high degree of power in predicting behavior. This is not to imply that untrained persons can competently interpret the CPI, but rather that the test's roots and original constructs are based on conceptions of human behavior held by most people in most cultures. It is up to the skilled clinician to go beyond these common constructs and into a more subtle, broad, and integrated description of the person. Thus, the test does not have as its primary goal psychometric elegance, nor is it derived from any specific personality theory. The focus and concern of the CPI involve practical usefulness and the development of descriptions that strive to be relevant, understandable, and accurate in terms of behavioral predictions. Because of these assets, it has become one of the more frequently used tests by professional psychologists (Camara et al., 2000; C. Piotrowski & Zalewski, 1993; Watkins et al., 1995); more than 2,000 research studies either have been performed on the CPI or have used it.

The CPI was originally developed by Harrison Gough and published in its original form in 1957. Although reviews of the test have been mixed, most reviewers describe it in favorable terms. For example, Bolton (1992) concludes his review in the eleventh *Mental Measurements Yearbook* by stating that the "CPI is an excellent normal personality assessment device, more reliable than the manual advertises, with good normative data and outstanding interpretive information" (p. 139). It has been subjected to more than 50 years of research and continuous improvement. The criticisms that have been directed at the CPI have stimulated extensive efforts toward refinement and improvement, including numerous studies on predictive validity, the development of alternate scales, and expanded normative data. Many of these improvements were incorporated into the 1987 (CPI 462), 1996/2002 (CPI 434), and 2002 (CPI 260) revisions. For these reasons, the CPI has become a respected and frequently used device in personality assessment, particularly in the areas of career development, personnel selection, interpersonal maladjustment, and predicting antisocial behavior (Devine, 2005; Gough, 2000; McAllister, 1996).

HISTORY AND DEVELOPMENT

The CPI was developed as an inventory to assess enduring interpersonal and personality characteristics in a normal population. Gough published his original scales in 1948, but the first copyrighted edition of the initial 15 scales appeared in 1951. However, it was not until 1957 (the "CPI 480") that a completed set of 18 scales was published by Consulting Psychologists Press. It was further revised in 1987 and two new scales (Empathy and Independence) were included, bringing the total number of scales to 20. These 20 scales measure areas such as social ascendancy, social image, intellectual stance, and conceptual interests. Three of these are validity scales, which assess test-taking attitudes including "fake bad" (*Wb*), "fake good" (*Gi*), and the extent to which highly popular responses are given (*Cm*). Because of a combination of continuing research and a wish to conform to the 1990 Americans with Disabilities Act, the CPI was again revised in 1996. Although 28 items were deleted (bringing the total to 434), the 20 scales and 3 vectors from the 1987 version were retained (Gough, 1996/2002). A short form, the CPI 260, was published in 2002 (Gough & Bradley, 2005).

The 1957 version of the CPI was derived from an original item pool of 3,500 questions. Of the 468 items that were eventually selected, 178 were identical to MMPI items, 35 were very similar, and the remaining 255 were developed specifically for the CPI. The items were selected on the basis of both empirical criterion keying and a rational approach in which questions were generated that, from a conceptual point of view, seemed to assess the characteristics the scales were trying to measure. These questions were then given to a sample group and accepted or rejected based on the extent of inter-item correlation. However, the majority of the scales were not developed through the rational approach but rather through empirical criterion keying. Thus, series of questions, which had initially been developed rationally, were administered to different groups having specific, previously assessed characteristics that the scales were eventually intended to measure independently of these groups. Each group was selected using a number of different criteria. For example, ratings by friends and family of an individual's degree of responsibility were used to select a person for inclusion in the sample group for the development of the scale on responsibility. The Achievement via Independence scale was based on college students' grade point averages; the Socialization scale used delinquents and nondelinquents; and Sociability involved the number of extracurricular activities that a student participated in. Items that were found to discriminate between the criterion group (responsibility, sociability, etc.) and a "normal" population were selected for initial inclusion in the scale.

It is important to emphasize that, similar to the MMPI items, the empirical relationships are more important than the "truth" of the content. For example, if a person in the group rated for responsibility answers "true" to the statement "I have never done anything hazardous just for the thrill of it," it does not matter whether he or she has actually performed hazardous behaviors for the thrill of it. The main consideration from a psychometric point of view is that he or she answers "true" to that question, which then indicates the item can be used to help differentiate responsible from nonresponsible persons.

The final step was to cross-validate the items with other populations to determine the extent to which the variable the scale was attempting to measure could be accurately assessed. Of the 18 original scales, 13 used empirical criterion keying, 4 used the rational approach, and the final one (Communality) cannot be easily categorized, although it primarily used a combination of the two techniques. The two new scales in the 1987 (CPI 462) and 1996/2002 (CPI 434) revisions (Empathy and Independence) used a criterion-keying approach to elicit and score items that already existed in the CPI.

Like the MMPI, the CPI scores are given a standard score (T score) with a mean of 50 and a standard deviation of 10. The 1957 scales were standardized on an original normative sample of 6,000 males and 7,000 females having a fairly wide range in age, socioeconomic status, and geographic area. The standardization for the 1996 revision was based on 3,000 participants of each sex selected from the CPI archives to be representative of the U.S. population in age, education, status, and other relevant variables. The 20 scales are arranged so that they relate to the following general domains (Gough, 2000):

- Observable, interpersonal style and orientation (i.e., Sociability, Social Presence).
- Internal normative orientation and values (i.e., Responsibility, Self-Control).
- Aspects of cognitive and intellectual functioning (i.e., Intellectual Efficiency, Achievement via Conformance).
- Measures of role and personal style (i.e., Psychological-Mindedness, Flexibility).

These domains assist interpretation as they help to organize practitioners to provide specific information around these more general domains as well as integrate data with other assessment information. For example, Wechsler IQ scores can be further amplified by noting whether the examinee prefers to work in groups with clear guidelines (conformity) versus more independently. Interpretation is further simplified in that higher scale values are associated with traditionally more favorable qualities and lower scores with more unfavorable qualities (Wallbrown & Jones, 1992). The exception to this is the final scale, F/M, which measures traditionally feminine and masculine characteristics. Gough added three vectors or structural scales to the 1987 version. Rather than organizing these three scales conceptually, he developed them based on factor analysis to measure extraversion-introversion (externality-internality), norm-favoring versus norm-questioning, and degree of self-realization.

The most recent development of the CPI is a short form consisting of 260 items (Gough & Bradley, 2005). The individual scales were developed by selecting the best items that correlated the highest with the longer scales combined with the highest correlations for relevant external test behavior. In addition, all items were assessed for contemporary wording, cross cultural relevance, disability-related content, and tone. The outcome was that all 20 of the CPI 434 scales were retained along with the 3 structural (or vector) scales. Most of the "special purpose" scales (i.e. Managerial Potential, Creative Temperament) were retained. Four of the scales were renamed for ease of understanding and to more accurately describe what the scales measure (Socialization renamed to "Social Conformity," Intellectual Efficiency to "Conceptual Fluency," Psychological Mindedness to "Insightfulness," and Femininity/Masculinity to "Sensitivity"). The revised scales were found to have high correlations with the original CPI 434 scales. The advantage of the CPI 260 is that it takes only 25 to 35 minutes to complete (versus the 45 to 75 minutes for completing the CPI 434; Gough & Bradley, 2005).

The CPI has been put to numerous uses since its initial development in 1957. Megargee (1972) reported that, when the test was first printed, researchers and practitioners used it for many of the more obvious purposes of a psychological test, such as the prediction of scholastic achievement, graduation from high school or college, and performance in specific areas, such as math and English. Later, its uses became much more diversified to the extent that work has now been done on managerial effectiveness, air traffic controllers, stock market speculators, the degree of creativity in fields such as architecture and mathematics, contraceptive practices, and performance in psychiatric residency programs. In the field of counseling, it has been used to predict response to therapy, to aid in the selection of a college major, predict college grade point average (GPA), and to predict the degree of success in graduate education programs such as medicine, dentistry, nursing, and education (see Devine, 2005; Gough, 2000; McAllister, 1996; Megargee, 2002; P. Meyer & S. Davis, 1992; Van Hutton, 1990). Whereas the CPI 434 tends to be somewhat more useful for counseling and clinical psychologists, the CPI 260 has been packaged more for business consultants and human resource professionals (Gough & Bradley, 2005). Surveys indicate that the CPI is one of the more frequently used self-report personality tests (Camara et al., 2000).

Earlier versions of the CPI provided the options of hand as well as computer scoring; the CPI 434 and CPI 260, however, can be scored only using computerized facilities (see Consulting Psychologists Press). A variety of interpretive programs are available as well as additional alternate scales. Should practitioners wish to work with the CPI, they can have protocols scored by Consulting Psychologists Press and interpret the resulting profile themselves, or they can have the results both scored and interpreted by Consulting Psychologists Press (or other providers).

COMPARISON WITH THE MMPI

Because of the similarity in both format and item content, comparisons between the CPI and MMPI are inevitable. Thorndike (1959) has referred to the CPI as "the sane man's MMPI," and there are a number of clear similarities. The 1996 version of the CPI is comprised of more than one-third of the MMPI's questions (171 out of 434); a conversion is made from raw to standard scale scores with a mean of 50 and standard deviation of 10; and the final values are charted on a graph with peaks and valleys.

Despite these similarities, it is essential for any clinician using the CPI to also appreciate the significant conceptual and psychometric differences between the two tests. The general intent of the MMPI is to assess a person's intrapsychic processes and emotional distress as these relate to specific psychodiagnostic categories. Each of these categories has a group of internal dynamics surrounding it, such as depression, which also includes apathy, lowered capacity for pleasure, and feelings of hopelessness and helplessness. The primary task of the MMPI is to identify either the presence or absence of these internal dynamics and to place the examinee in either a normal or one or more psychopathological categories. In contrast, the CPI focuses more on a normal population and is highly interpersonal in nature. In fact, there is a marked absence of symptom-oriented questions. Thus, the CPI is concerned with the presence or absence of specific interpersonal skills. In addition, the CPI avoids complex diagnostic nomenclature and emphasizes practical descriptions that are commonly used in most cultures.

From a psychometric perspective, the MMPI was originally developed from a bimodal distribution in which the main focus of the test was to classify a specific client in either a pathological group or a normal one. The contrast groups were not high or low on a specific trait but, rather, were high in pathology when compared with normals. For example, a group that was high in hysterical traits was contrasted not with a group of persons having superior health but with individuals having only an average number of hysterical traits. In clinical assessment, members of the pathological group are considered to be persons scoring greater than 1.5 standard deviations above the norm ($T = 65$). As a result of this emphasis on differentiating pathological groups from average or normal groups, the interpretation of profiles within "normal" ranges (i.e., $T = 35$ to 60) is uncertain and should be approached with extreme caution. In contrast, the CPI uses a normal distribution within a standardized population. Furthermore, Gough used groups whose behavior was extreme on both high and low dimensions of the characteristic being measured. Thus, normal range scores of less than 1.5 standard deviations from the mean can be interpreted with a fairly high level of confidence. For example, a CPI score on Ac (Achievement via Conformance) of $T = 60$ indicates a fairly high level of this particular attribute and a $T = 40$ score indicates a fairly low level. However, an MMPI T score of 60 on Scale 8 (Schizophrenia) does not indicate a relatively high degree of schizophrenia, nor does a T score of 40 indicate a low level. Thus, relatively normal profiles on the CPI are not only to be expected but also can be interpreted successfully.

RELIABILITY AND VALIDITY

In general, the reliability and validity studies on the CPI compare favorably with those done on other personality inventories. Test-retest reliabilities for individual scales on the CPI 434 have ranged between a low of .51 for Flexibility to a high of .84 for Femininity/ Masculinity. The overall median reliability was reported to be .68 (Gough, 1996) for the CPI 434 and .66 for the CPI 260 (Gough & Bradley, 2005). However, the retest interval was a long one year. Measures of internal consistency indicate considerable variability among the test items, but, overall, the scale constructions are adequate. Internal consistency ranged from a low of .43 for Masculinity/Femininity to a high of .85 for Well Being (median internal consistency was .76; Gough, 1996). Internal consistency for the CPI 260 ranged from a low of .39 for Communality to a high of .87 for Dominance (Gough & Bradley, 2005).

The correlations between the CPI 434 and the much briefer CPI 260 were found to be quite high (ranging between .81 to .97; Gough & Bradley, 2005). As a result, much of the validity that has been derived from the longer CPI 434 can be transferred to the CPI 260. Gough and Bradley (2005) state that "experience with the CPI 260 scales so far suggest[s] that the differences are occasional and relatively minor" (p. 10).

Factor analytic studies have been reported for both a two-factor and four-factor solution. In a general way, the factor structure suggests that elevations on CPI scales suggest personal adjustment whereas low scores indicate psychopathology (Higgins-Lee, 1990; Wallbrown & Jones, 1992). Megargee (1972) reported that the two factors of Internal Controls and Interpersonal Effectiveness accounted for a major portion of the variance on the original 1957 scales. Gough (1996/2002) suggested five factors for the 1996 revision: Ascendance (dominance, empathy), Dependability (self-control, good impression), Conventionality (sociability, communality), Originality (flexibility), and Femininity/Masculinity. Factors I (Ascendance) and III (Dependability) roughly corresponded with the first two vectors or factor scorings that have been included in the 1987 and 1996 revisions. Vector 1 is a measure of introversion-extraversion, and Vector 2 measures the extent to which a person is norm favoring versus norm doubting. An additional factor, Vector 3, provides an index of a person's psychological integration and self-realization. A similar factor structure for the CPI 260 was found but consisted of these four factors: Interpersonal Effectiveness, Dependability, Originality, and Interpersonal Sensitivity (Gough & Bradley, 2005).

The CPI has also been found to relate to most of the core five factors of personality: Neuroticism, Extraversion, Openness to Experience, Agreeableness, and Conscientiousness. Both a conceptual and empirical analysis found that four of these five factors correlated highly with different clusters of CPI scales (Deniston & Ramanaiah, 1993; J. A. Johnson, 2000; McCrae, Costa, & Piedmont, 1993). For example, Openness to Experience was found to correlate most strongly with Achievement via Independence (.41) and Flexibility (.42) but also with Capacity for Status (.38) and Social Presence (.42; McCrae et al., 1993). However, the Agreeableness factor was only minimally represented on the CPI (Deniston & Ramanaiah, 1993; McCrae et al., 1993). This is despite a rational analysis of the CPI scales, which would suggest that Agreeableness would be related to scales such as Socialization, Responsibility, Self-Control, and Good Impression. Despite this, the five-factor model was generally well represented on the CPI. This finding provides support that the CPI is measuring central aspects of personality and suggests the possibility that future CPI scoring might include an option for scoring these factors (Bolton, 1992).

In line with Gough's practical orientation, the main work on validation has been predictive (see Gough, 2000). Thus, the CPI has been less concerned with areas of psychometric elegance, such as whether the scales avoid overlap or measure psychometrically sound traits, than with the practical usefulness of the scales in providing accurate predictions. Specifically, persons scoring high on certain scales are more likely to be described in certain characteristic ways by those who know them. The CPI also focuses on predicting the types of things people do or say when placed in defined situations (i.e., leadership role). The scales themselves or the equations developed from various combinations of scales are able to predict a wide variety of different aspects of behavior. Thus the CPI is not a measure of "traits" but rather an instrument to measure the likelihood that someone would describe the test taker in a certain way. Many of the studies that have found useful levels of predictive validity are summarized later in this chapter in the Configural Interpretation section.

ASSETS AND LIMITATIONS

The CPI focuses on diagnosing and understanding interpersonal behavior in normal populations. Instead of focusing on pathology, it assesses areas such as self-control, dominance, and achievement. However, even though its emphasis is on assessing normal variations, extreme scores can also provide important information about the specifics of a person's expression of maladjustment, particularly with regard to interpersonal relationships (Cook, Young, Taylor, & Bedford, 1996; McAllister, 1996; Sarchione, Cuttler, Muchinsky, & Nelson-Gray, 1998). Whereas the MMPI is limited to use with primarily pathologically oriented populations, the CPI is appropriate for normal persons. Thus, it addresses issues that interest a great many people.

The main thrust of the research and construction of the CPI has been toward developing accurate, long- and short-term behavioral predictions. The focus is not so much on evaluating and predicting a specific, internal, unidimensional trait but more on interpersonal behaviors and orientations. Gough (1968, p. 56) clarifies this by stressing that "a high score on a scale for social status does not mean that the individual has a 'trait' of high status; presumably, therefore, he may be already of high status, or possessed of those talents and dispositions that will lead him toward such attainment." Gough also stresses that certain interpersonal behaviors occur in specific contexts. For example, a person who scores high on dominance would be expected to assume control of a group requiring leadership. Thus, the longitudinal studies on the inventory have developed predictive strategies relating to areas such as change in personality over the life span (Jones, Livson, & Peskin, 2003), police performance (Sarchione et al., 1998), graduation from high school (Gough, 1966), grades in college (Gough & Lanning, 1986), choice of major field in college (Goldschmid, 1967), prediction of delinquent and criminal behavior (DeFrancesco & Taylor, 1993; Gough & Bradley, 1992), persistence among hospice volunteers (Lafer, 1989), and creative potential (Gough, 1992). A number of special scales have been developed for assessing specific areas. These are available through the CPI computer-scored report and include Managerial Potential, Work Orientation, Leadership, Social Maturity Index, Law Enforcement Orientation, and Creative Temperament (see Gough, 2000; McAllister, 1996; P. Meyer & S. Davis, 1992). The test has generally proven to be a useful tool in the area of prediction and, as a result, has been particularly helpful in counseling high school and college students as well as in personnel selection (Devine, 2005; Gough, 2000; P. Meyer & S. Davis, 1992).

Because the CPI's basic concepts were derived from day-to-day social interaction, the test is relatively easily understood by a wide range of persons. Descriptions such as *dominant, achievement oriented*, and *self-controlled* are generally straightforward and are, therefore, not easily misinterpreted by untrained professionals. In contrast, providing feedback to clients who have taken the MMPI requires the clinician to rephrase psychiatric terminology into more approachable, easily understood terminology. Because the CPI relates to ongoing aspects of behavior, CPI interpretations are also likely to have more immediacy, relevancy, and impact on persons receiving feedback from their test results. These "folk concepts" also are generally found in all cultures and societies. Thus, Gough hoped that the inventory would have cross-cultural relevance and validity. Initial research does indicate that the CPI can be adapted to various cultures and that the concepts contained in the inventory do have cross-cultural relevance (Paunonen & Ashton, 1998).

A number of predictive studies have been conducted from a research perspective, and several useful regression equations have been developed as aids in predicting behavior. However, extremely few studies have been performed to test the validity of predictions made by clinicians in actual practice (Gynther, 1978). It may be that clinical judgments based on the CPI are generally accurate, but, at this point, further empirical studies are needed for verification. It is something of a contradiction that a test with an emphasis on practical usefulness has not been sufficiently evaluated in the clinical context. Most predictive studies have attempted to estimate areas such as work outcomes, future college attendance, or GPA in graduate programs. However, college attendance and GPA average do not necessarily correlate with later successful occupational performance. For example, high medical school grades have not been found to correlate with later success as a physician (Loughmiller et al., 1970). This problem is certainly not unique to the CPI but is a general issue with many similar tests and relates to a difficulty in adequately establishing appropriate criterion measures. These issues suggest that test users should develop predictions based on test scores within limited and well-researched contexts. For example, if the CPI is being used to evaluate prospective medical students, it should be made clear that predictions are useful only with regard to the students' academic performance and not to their overall clinical skills or later success as physicians.

A past criticism directed toward the CPI is the lack of factor analysis in the development of the different scales (Eysenck, 1985). Factor-analytic studies suggest that most of the variance can be accounted for by only two factors: interpersonal effectiveness and internal controls (Megargee, 1972). This conclusion is further supported in that many of the scales are highly correlated, are conceptually similar, and have extensive item overlap. Gough (1996/2002, 2000) has responded by pointing out that the scales were designed to assess constructs that are in most people's minds on a daily basis. Any scale overlap, then, might accurately reflect the conceptual overlap in common folk concepts used on a daily basis, such as the self-control and high degree of socialization involved in responsible behavior. Even if many of the scales are quite similar, there is accumulating evidence that the scales measure what they were designed to measure. The lack of factor analysis is further corrected by inclusion in the 1987 and 1996 versions of three different factor-analytically derived scales that measure extraversion-introversion (externality-internality), norm-favoring versus norm-questioning, and degree of self-realization (Gough, 1996). In addition, more recent factor-analytic studies indicate that four of the five core factors of personality are strongly represented in the CPI items and scales (McCrae et al., 1993; Walbrown & Jones, 1992).

A further limitation of the CPI is the insufficient number of studies undertaken on the meaning of pairs or triads of scales (Baucom, 1985). This may result partly from the formidable number of possible CPI code types (compared with the MMPI's more manageable 45 possible combinations). In addition, many persons score within a relatively narrow range, which makes configural interpretation more difficult because there are less likely to be clearly defined clusters of high and low scales (Shaw & Gynther, 1986). In contrast, extensive fruitful research has been conducted on 2- and 3-point codes for the MMPI. Some of the work conducted on CPI code types is summarized later in the Configural Interpretation section. Gough's more recent work on the three vectors (externality-internality, norm-favoring/norm questioning, and realization) has also provided information regarding composite subscale or factor scores (see Vector Scale Interpretation section). In addition, McAllister (1996) has listed 152 different combinations of scale scores based on a combination of empirical research, rational considerations, and clinical experience. However, more research needs to be done on the many possible 2- and 3-point codes that could potentially be derived from the CPI.

In developing accurate clinical interpretations from the CPI, it is essential to consider the implications of factors such as the overall life situation of the examinee. For example, the profile of a 15-year-old on the CPI scale for Psychological-Mindedness (Py) has a meaning different from that of a profile of a person of 55. Another important consideration is the purpose for which the person believes he or she is being examined. A person who is taking the test in a conscious effort to receive a discharge from the military will likely bias his or her responses in a direction different from a person seeking employment. It is also essential to look at overall patterns of scores rather than "single-sign" indicators because corresponding elevations on other scales can elaborate or modify the meaning they have for one another. Thus, clinicians should always keep in mind the implications of an examinee's overall life situation, age, education, perceived reason for assessment, and pattern of scores.

A further issue relates to the degree of comparability between the 1996 revision and previous versions. In the 1996 revision, the total number of items was reduced (from 462 to 434). However, high correlations ranging between .96 and 1.00 indicated sufficient comparability between the scales that previous research and interpretations based on earlier versions can be transferred to the 1996 (Form 434) version. Many of the prediction equations have been (and are being) updated. However, the new scales may be different in some yet-to-be defined ways. Similarly, the high correlations between the CPI 434 and CPI 260 suggest a fairly high level of transferability between the two versions (Gough & Bradley, 2005).

The CPI, then, is an extremely useful test in the assessment of the interpersonal characteristics of relatively normal persons. It measures variables that interest a great number of people, providing helpful behavioral predictions, and uses routine, day-to-day interactional concepts. For these reasons, the CPI is extensively used in personnel selection and vocational guidance (Bolton, 1992; Devine, 2005; Gough, 2000; Gough & Bradley, 2005; McAllister, 1996; Megargee, 2002; P. Meyer & S. Davis, 1992). Significant limitations and cautions relate to limited validity studies in clinical settings, few empirical studies on the meaning of 2- and/or 3-point elevations, and the unknown (but continually emerging) comparability between the 1996 revision and the previous versions.

USE WITH DIVERSE GROUPS

As noted, the CPI was developed using "folk concepts" that appeared to have cross-cultural relevance. From a face validity perspective, it would seem that the CPI is transportable across various cultures. This is one of the reasons it has been used in different cross-national settings and translated into 40 languages. Research in a wide variety of countries has supported its validity, even in countries that are culturally quite different from the United States (i.e., Japan, Taiwan, Egypt; Paunonen & Ashton, 1998). For example, the CPI has been able to make accurate predictions of academic achievement in Greece (Repapi, Gough, Lanning, & Stefanis, 1983), detect faking good among Norwegians (Sandal & Endresen, 2002), and distinguish delinquents from nondelinquents in Sweden (Rosen & Schalling, 1974). The factor structure has also been found to be quite similar between the United States and Japan (Nishiyama, 1973). The cross-cultural use of the CPI has been enhanced by the inclusion of American, British, French, and Italian norms in the *CPI 260 Manual* (Gough & Bradley, 2005).

Research on the CPI within ethnic groups in the United States has noted that some scales are more influenced by ethnicity than others. When compared to European American males, African American males reported being less extraverted, less socially anxious, and more cynical (Cross & Burger, 1982). However, overall scale elevations for African American females were similar to European American females. This is despite the finding that African Americans endorsed different sets of items in order to obtain similar elevations. Research with Native Americans has also found ethnic differences to be gender related. CPI scores for Native American men suggested that, when compared with European American men, they were less conventional and less sensitive to violations of norms (G. L. Davis, Hoffman, & Nelson, 1990). In contrast, Native American females had scores suggesting they were more passive, more likely to seek input in decision making, and less verbally controlling when compared with European American women. Thus, these ethnic differences should be taken into account when making employment and other types of decisions.

The sample of research just discussed provides good support for using the CPI in cross-cultural contexts. However, additional research still needs to be conducted on the relationship between CPI scores and race, socioeconomic status, and other demographic variables. In particular, further research needs to be conducted on the ability of the CPI to predict relevant behaviors in a specific cultural context. Often, knowing that there are differences in various scale scores is not sufficient. We also need to know the meanings of these differences for understanding and predicting relevant external behaviors and internal experiences.

INTERPRETATION PROCEDURES

The examiner should note the length of time it takes a person to complete the test. A person with an IQ within the normal range would be expected to complete the test in 45 to 75 minutes (25–35 minutes for the CPI 260). A computerized administration of CPI 434 items can reduce the time from 25 to 45 minutes. If a person takes 60 to 90 minutes or more to complete the test, one of the following problems is suggested:

1. A major psychological disturbance, such as severe depression or functional psychosis.
2. Obsessive concern with detail and/or indecisiveness.
3. A low IQ combined with poor reading ability.
4. Cerebral impairment.

Tests that are completed in 20 minutes or less suggest:

1. An invalid profile.
2. An impulsive personality.
3. Both 1 and 2.

An alternative form of administration is an oral or tape-recorded format, which would be particularly relevant for persons with unusually low reading skills. If time efficiency is an important consideration, the CPI 260 can be administered.

Scoring for the CPI 434 and CPI 260 must be done by computer through Consulting Psychologists Press or through on-site scanning. Scoring is also performed for additional special-purpose scales (i.e., Managerial Potential, Work Orientation). Examiners may wish to extend the traditional scale information by using regression equations for areas such as high school achievement, parole success, or medical school performance (see Table 9.2).

The steps for interpreting the CPI are described in the next sections.

1. Determine Profile Validity

The CPI, similar to the MMPI, has built-in scales and relevant regression equations to detect invalid profiles. This is important because Gough and Bradley (2005) have estimated that, in large-scale industrial/organizational testing situations, approximately 5% of all profiles are invalid. These include 1% that can be considered fake bad or randomly responded protocols and 4% that were fake good (4.4% for males and 3.8% for females; Gough & Bradley, 2005). As would be expected, invalid profiles may occur more frequently in certain contexts, such as the quite high 7.5% fake good rate noted among males applying to become police officers (Gough, 1996).

An initial consideration in evaluating the profile validity is to note the number of items that have been left blank (available on the computer-generated profile). If 25 or more items on the CPI 434 or 18 or more items on the CPI 260 are blank, the test results may not be valid. The examiner should also make sure the subject has not marked a large number of questions (25/18 or more) with both "true" and "false" on the same item. Yet another area that should be checked is the possibility of random answering. The subject may appear to have answered randomly simply because he or she was out of step between the number's questions in the answer sheet and test booklet, or may answer randomly in an attempt to hide his or her poor reading ability. A good indicator for the possibility of random answering is a low score ($T = 30$ or less) on Cm.

"Faking bad" can usually be detected based on the presence of extremely low scores on Well Being (Wb; $T = 30$ or less) and Communality (Cm; $T = 30$ or less). A low score ($T = 40$ or less) on Good Impression (Gi) is also frequently associated with faking bad. It should be stressed that a subject who fakes bad is not necessarily maladjusted. Rather, it indicates that the specifics of his or her disorder cannot be evaluated because of the distorting effects of the person's need to create an impression of the seriousness of his or her problem. Thus, it is important to assess why the person is faking bad. It might, for example, represent a cry for help in which suicide is a serious possibility, or the person might be malingering because of numerous secondary gains.

To determine whether a subject is "faking good," the most important scale to evaluate is Good Impression (Gi). Fake good profiles usually have high scores ($T = 70$ or higher) on this scale. Usually, when a person is asked to fake good, all the scales with positive social connotations are elevated but Gi is still relatively higher than the others. Sometimes it may be difficult to differentiate between someone who has a superior level of adjustment and a person who is faking good. The most significant consideration in making this distinction is the person's history. An individual with a history of poor adjustment, combined with an unusually high *Gi*, is probably faking good, whereas a person with a history of good adjustment and a moderately high *Gi* is probably expressing his or her superior level of adjustment.

These critical-scale values for the three validity scales can generally serve as clinical tools to detect invalid profiles. However, Gough (1996/2002) notes that a significant number of errors are still likely to occur. In order to increase accuracy, he recommends the following equations (note: *Raw scores must be used in all equations*):

Fake good = 41.225 + .273 *Do* + .198 *Em* + .538 *Gi* − .255 *Wb* − .168 *Fx*
Fake bad = 86.613 − 1.000 *Cm* − .191 *Wb* + .203 *Ac* − .110 *Fx*
Random = 34 .096 + .279 *Gi* + .201 *Wb* + .225 *Py* + .157 *Fx*

The following optimal cutoff scores for these equations should be used:

Fake good = 60.60 or greater
Fake bad = 59.50 or greater (and if the score on random is less than or equal to 48.01)
Random = 48.01 or less (and the score on fake bad is equal to or less than 59.50)

Research using simulators suggests that these equations detect fake bad protocols 84% of the time, fake good protocols 61% of the time, and random protocols about 63% of the time (Gough & Bradley, 2005). It is hoped that clinicians would be able to increase these detection rates by considering the person's overall context—especially his or her reasons for taking the test and past history.

2. Note Vector Scale Patterns

A basic underlying description of core aspects of the person's functioning can be determined by interpreting the three vector scores of internality/externality, norm favoring/norm doubting, and level of realization. These provide a context for understanding other more specific aspects of personality (see Vector Scale Interpretation section).

3. Note General Level of Elevations/Lowerings

Scores of $T = 50$ or more usually suggest a positive area of adjustment. Scales that are well below $T = 50$ indicate specific problem areas. However, the clinician must also interpret these scores in the overall context of assessment, taking into account variables such as the person's age, occupational level, cultural background, and educational level. For example, a high school student with an Intellectual Efficiency (*Ie*) scale score of 60 represents a fairly high level of this characteristic, whereas the same score for a medical student represents a relatively low level when compared with his or her fellow students.

4. Note Patterns of Elevations/Lowerings on Different Clusters and Classes

After looking at possible areas of adjustment and maladjustment, the clinician can then further evaluate the profile by examining the average elevations on the different clusters or classes (Table 9.1) as organized by Gough (1996/2002, 2000) and Gough and Bradley

(2005). For convenience, the clusters are separated on the CPI 434 profile sheets by black, vertical lines. If most or all of the scales in a particular cluster are clearly above $T = 50$, the qualities represented by the cluster are areas of strength. In contrast, scores well below $T = 50$ represent areas of difficulty. Note that the CPI 260 uses somewhat different titles for the clusters that are indicated in parentheses on Table 9.1.

The clusters listed in Table 9.1 are organized according to conceptual similarity rather than statistically derived categories. In contrast, Gough (1987, 1996/2002) also recommends examining the scales based on five factors that have been statistically derived from more empirical relations. Factor 1 (*Do, Cs, Sy, Sp, Sa, In, Em*) indicates a person's level of social poise and interpersonal effectiveness. Factor 2 (*Wb, Re, So, Sc, To, Gi, Ac*) provides a general index of mental health, adjustment, and social conformity. The third factor (*Ai, Fx, To, Ie, Py*) includes scales that are characterized by assessing the extent to which a person can think and behave independently. The fourth factor is composed of scales *Cm, Re, So*, and *Wb* and measures the extent a person adheres to social norms and expectations. High scorers (all above $T = 50$) are likely to be conventional and place a high emphasis on doing and perceiving things correctly, whereas low scorers (all below $T = 50$) are more unconventional, individualistic, and likely to perceive the world in more unusual ways. The final, fifth factor is composed of Femininity/Masculinity and assesses a person's degree of aesthetic interests, dependency, and sensitivity. Clinicians can gain useful information by using either Gough's clusters (classes) or the more empirically derived five factors.

5. Evaluate the Meaning of the Scores on Each Individual Scale

Whereas the different clusters, factors, or vectors provide general impressions for certain areas of functioning, the clinician can obtain more specific information by evaluating each scale individually. Doing this involves looking at the relatively highest and lowest scales and developing a description of the dynamics involved with these scales. The meanings associated with specific high or low scores can be determined by considering the relevant scale descriptions in the Individual Scales section. The general personality descriptions and discussions of the scales have been adapted and modified from the publications of Gough

Table 9.1   Cluster analysis

Cluster	Meaning	Scales
1	Interpersonal style and orientation (Dealing with others)*	Dominance (*Do*), Capacity for Status (*Cs*), Sociability (*Sy*), Social Presence (*SP*), Self-Acceptance (*Sa*), Independence (*In*), Empathy (*Em*)
2	Normative orientation and values (Self-management)	Responsibility (*Re*), Socialization (*So*), Self-Control (*Sc*), Good Impression (*Gi*), Communality (*Cm*), Well Being (*Wb*), Tolerance (*To*)
3	Cognitive and intellectual function (Motivations and thinking style)	Achievement via Conformance (*Ac*), Achievement via Independence (*Ai*), Intellectual Efficiency (*Ie*)
4	Role and personal style (Personal characteristics)	Psychological-Mindedness (*Py*), Flexibility (*Fx*), Femininity/Masculinity (*F/M*)

*The titles in parentheses are used by the CPI 260.

(1975, 1996/2002, 2000), Gough and Bradley (2005), McAllister (1996), and Megargee (2002). Additional relevant material has also been included and is cited accordingly. The short list of most frequently used adjectives (provided at the end of the sections on high and low scores) is based on ratings reported by Gough (1987, 1996/2002). The adjectives were included based on their occurrence in two or more instances from within the different lists of ratings on the Adjective Check List made by peers, spouses, or CPI assessment staff.

6. Note Scale Configurations and Calculate Regression Equations

Initial hypotheses can be evaluated further by consulting the section in this chapter dealing with typical scale configurations for different areas, including intellectual level, achievement, leadership, adjustment, and specific syndromes. This evaluation may also involve calculating and interpreting the regression equations, which are included in the section on configural interpretations and summarized in Table 9.2. One value in using these types of equations is that they typically have been found to make more accurate predictions than relying on clinical judgment (Aegisdottir et al., 2006; Grove, Zald, Lebow, Snitz, & Nelson, 2000). However, some caution should be used because they were derived from previous versions of the CPI and updated versions have not yet been reported. Particular caution should be used with the CPI 260.

7. Integrate Data into a Profile Description

The final step in interpretation is to integrate all the data into a profile description. The clinician's ability to assess the interactions between two or more scales is essential. This suggests that, after a specific trend has been established, the clinician should elaborate on it by evaluating how the other scales change their meaning for the individual (cf. McAllister,

Table 9.2 Summary of CPI equations used for making predictions

1. Achievement (High School) = 20.116 + .317 Re + 192 So − .309 Gi + .227 Ac + .280 Ai + .244 Ie

2. Achievement (High School − Using IQ) = .786 + .195 Re + .244 So − .130 Gi + .19 Ac + .179 Ai + .279 IQ

3. College Attendance = 17.822 + .333 Do + .539 Cs − .189 Gi + .740 Ac

4. Achievement (Introduction to Psychology) = 35.958 − .294 Sy − .180 Sp + .185 Re − .189 Sc − .152 Gi − .210 Cm + .275 Ac + .523 Ai + .241 Ie + .657 Py

5. Male GPA = .16 SAT (Math) + .11 So − .19 Sp + .17 Fe

6. Female GPA = .25 SAT (Verbal) − .14 Sp + .06 Re + .20 Ac + .08 Fe

7. GPA = 30.60 − .26 Wb + .35 Re − .19 Gi + .39 Ai + .22 Ie + .36 Py

8. Teaching Effectiveness = 14.743 + .334 So − .670 Gi + .997 Ac + .909 Py − .446 Fx

9. Medical Promise = .794 Sy + .602 To + 1.114 Cm − .696 Cs

10. Dental Performance = 29.938 − .110 Sp + .148 Re − .262 Gi + .727 Ac + .230 Py

11. Leadership (Social) = 14.130 + .372 Do + .696 Sa + .345 Wb − .133 Gi + .274 Ai

12. Parole Success = 45.078 − .353 Sp − .182 Sa + .532 So + .224 Sc

13. Social Maturity = 25.701 + .408 Re + .478 So − .296 Gi

1996; Meyer & S. Davis, 1992). For example, dominance may be expressed in numerous ways, including rebellion, high achievement, leadership, or delinquency. When these elaborations have been made in the test data, the clinician can then seek outside confirmation through personal history, behavioral observations, and additional test data.

VECTOR SCALE INTERPRETATION

The major addition to the 1987 revision was the development and inclusion of three structural scales. Each of the dimensions was based on a factor analysis of the different items on the CPI. The first theme or factor that seemed to emerge referred to elements of extraversion, self-confidence, assertive self-assurance, and social poise. Items measuring these dimensions were formerly used to develop a scoring for the first vector (or structural scale), which Gough (1987, 1996) referred to as externality-internality. The second factor was related more to the degree to which a person accepted societal norms and included areas such as social conformity, personal integrity, self-control, and disciplined effectiveness. Scoring for these qualities was formally developed into a second vector, which Gough (1987, 1996) referred to as norm-favoring versus norm-questioning. The final, third vector was labeled realization and assesses the degree to which a respondent has developed a sense of self-realization and psychological integration. The CPI 260 has renamed this the Level of Satisfaction scale both to make it more user friendly and to reflect a somewhat different meaning from "self-realization."

On the CPI profile sheet, the first two vectors (externality-internality and norm-favoring versus norm-questioning) are combined to place a person into one of four specific types (Alpha, Beta, Gamma, Delta) based on the interaction between Vectors 1 and 2. The CPI 260 has renamed these types as Implementer, Supporter, Innovator, and Visualizer. The primary emphasis on structural scale interpretation is to understand the meaning associated with these four types. The third vector is used to provide additional meaning to these four types by considering the degree to which the person has managed to integrate them into a fully developed (self-realized) or at least satisfied person. Vector 3 is rated on a scale between 1 and 7, where 1 represents no or little integration (or realization/satisfaction) and 7 represents an unusually high level. Gough (1987, 1996) describes these more specifically as 1 = poor, 2 = distinctly below average, 3 = below average, 4 = average, 5 = above average, 6 = distinctly above average, and 7 = superior.

Any interpretation of type should take into account both the extent to which the person has realized or is satisfied with his or her type (Vector 3) as well as the relative strength with which he or she represents the type. For example, an Alpha (Implementer) combines qualities of extraversion and norm-favoring. These qualities would be far stronger if they scored quite high on both extraversion and norm-favoring (Vectors 1 and 2) than if they scored merely in the borderline areas. Specific interpretations and the implications of their degree of realization are described in the following section and were derived from descriptions provided by Devine (2005), Gough (1996/2002, 2000), Gough and Bradley (2005), and McAllister (1996).

Alphas (Implementers)

Persons scoring in this quadrant tend to be highly extraverted and to adhere to societal norms. They will be good leaders because they are task-focused and productive but also interested in associating with others. Their social style may be somewhat managerial. Externally, they may be assertive, talkative, industrious, ambitious, organized, have high levels of achievement, and social presence. If highly realized (note Vector 3),

Alphas/Implementers may be charismatic leaders and help to create social change. If undeveloped, they might become manipulative, self-centered, and concerned only with achieving their own ends regardless of consequences to others.

Betas (Supporters)

Betas/Supporters combine qualities of both introversion and norm-favoring. Thus, they prefer external structure and are generally most comfortable in the role of a follower. They have a high degree of self-control, are cautious, reserved, conscientious, highly dependable, conservative, value traditions, and may place the needs of others before their own. If highly realized, they can be nurturant, represent ideal models of goodness, and convey conventional sources of wisdom. Poorly developed Betas/Supporters might be nonresponsive, overly conformist, inflexible, constricted, and rigid.

Gammas (Innovators)

Gammas/Innovators are extraverted and, at the same time, question traditional beliefs and values. Thus, they make their questions, beliefs, and challenges quite apparent. These are the skeptics, doubters, and persons who might try to change society. They perceive the world in highly individualistic ways but are still actively involved with others. Often they might try to test limitations imposed on them and do so in a rebellious, self-dramatizing manner. At their best, Gammas/Innovators are visionary, perceptive, and imaginative. They are likely to be inventors, create new ideas, and push their field to new limits. If inadequately developed, they are intolerant, belligerent, self-indulgent, rebellious, and disruptive.

Deltas (Visualizers)

Persons scoring in this quadrant have qualities of introversion and also question traditional values and beliefs. As a result, Deltas/Visualizers are highly reflective, somewhat detached, preoccupied, and possibly overly absorbed in their own fantasies and daydreams. They might prefer that others make decisions for them and, if extreme, may live primarily in their own private world. If fully developed, they might be highly imaginative, artistic, visionary, and innovative. However, they run the risk that their innovations may go unnoticed because they rarely make a production of their activities. If poorly developed, Deltas/Visualizers may be poorly organized, withdrawn, aloof, self-defeating, and at risk of decompensating.

INDIVIDUAL SCALES

1. Dominance (*Do*)

The *Do* scale measures areas of leadership ability and has become one of the most validated scales on the CPI. It includes verbal fluency, persuasiveness, and the extent to which a person is likely to take charge of a situation. Thus, high scorers are persistent in approaching a task and usually take the initiative in interpersonal relationships. However, this description is more characteristic of the style in which high-scoring males express their dominance. High-scoring females express their dominance either by initiating attempts to choose a leader or by being somewhat coercive, aggressive, or impatient. The contents of the items deal with social poise, confidence, verbal fluency, persuasiveness, and a sense of duty.

It should be stressed that the conditions in which leadership occurs are at least as important as the actual trait. This finding means that, when a situation arises requiring leadership, high scorers usually become leaders rather than followers. More specifically, they are more likely to be the ones to set limits, and become more assertive, goal oriented, and clear and direct regarding their requests. They adopt this role relatively comfortably and naturally. In contrast, low scorers experience discomfort when requested to take charge. They may be either more submissive, in which case they prefer others to control and direct them, or merely socially isolated and introverted, in which case they do not want to control others but also do not want others to control them. They may even actively resist efforts that are made to control them.

High *Do* (*T* = 65 or More)

- Strong in expressing opinions and reaching goals.
- Highly assertive; clear and direct in expressing their needs.
- Possibly aggressive and forceful.
- Would rather take charge of a situation and can effectively do so.
- Self-confident when directing others.
- Excellent abilities to plan.
- Can use and develop the resources available to them.
- Often express a sense of optimism.
- Able to define their goals and work persistently to attain them.
- Would not be particularly compromising.
- Would not be the type of person to whom others would feel comfortable admitting their weaknesses.
- Most frequently used adjectives: assertive, confident, dominant, task oriented.

Moderate *Do* (*T* = 50 to 65)

- Have the capacity for leadership but do not, under ordinary circumstances, seek opportunities to use this ability.

Moderately Low *Do* (*T* = 40 to 50)

- Usually feel uncomfortable when leadership is required.
- Prefer being in the follower role.
- Participants rather than organizers.
- Although some persons who are low in dominance are effective in relatively high leadership positions, they are uncomfortable with this aspect of their job and usually have a democratic and participative style of decision making.
- Most persons scoring low have a difficult time planning; may sometimes appear reckless and impulsive.
- Likely to believe and adhere to the beliefs of others; can be easily influenced.
- Have a difficult time making direct requests, nonassertive.
- Described as submissive, shy, timid, inhibited.

Low *Do* (*T* = 40 or Less)

- General pattern of maladjustment.
- Socially withdrawn, insecure, shy.

- Little or no leadership ability.
- Dislike being directly responsible for either their own actions or the actions of others.
- May be passive, require prodding.
- Strongly avoid situations that are likely to produce tension and pressure.
- Most frequently used adjectives: shy, timid, submissive, withdrawn, quiet, retiring, unassuming, silent, and inhibited.

2. Capacity for Status (*Cs*)

An individual's capacity for status has been defined by Gough (1968, p. 61) as equal to the "relative level of income, education, prestige, and power attained in [his or her] social-cultural milieu." This definition focuses on status as it has been achieved, but the *Cs* scale looks at status more as a trait associated with features such as ambition and self-assurance. The specific trait of capacity for status suggests that, eventually, a person will achieve and maintain a position of status. Thus, in creating the scale, Gough looked at the specific trait variables that would eventually lead to a higher status position. These traits include perseverance, self-direction, ambition, and self-confidence. Persons seeking status are usually willing to go through a fairly high degree of discomfort and personal change to achieve their goals. In the scale construction, there is some overlap of test items with Social Presence (*Sp*), Intellectual Efficiency (*Ie*), and Self-Acceptance (*Sa*), indicating that capacity for status also includes dimensions of social poise, efficiency, and self-confidence. The item content also reflects an absence of fears or anxieties, a high degree of social conscience, an interest in belonging to various groups, and an interest in literary and aesthetic activities.

High *Cs* (*T* = 60 or More)
- Independent, imaginative, will take advantage of opportunities.
- Highly self-directed, achievement-oriented.
- Able to respond to their environment in a manner designed to further their own goals.
- High aspirations.
- Excellent verbal fluency.
- Extremely high scores: overbearing, arrogant, aristocratic, feel superior.
- Most frequently used adjectives: ambitious, confident, intelligent, versatile, enterprising, interests wide, assertive, having initiative.

Moderate *Cs* (*T* = 45 to 60)
- Somewhat goal oriented.
- Relatively highly motivated to achieve.
- Willing to change and adapt their lives in order to achieve status.
- Moderately ambitious and self-assured.

Moderately Low *Cs* (*T* = 35 to 45)
- Minimally goal oriented.
- Lack of self-direction is not sufficiently low to impair their level of functioning.
- Unwilling to make many personal sacrifices to achieve power, prestige, or a higher income.
- Indecisive regarding their careers.

Low *Cs* (*T* = 35 or Less)

- Low level of energy.
- Relatively rigid and inflexible.
- Narrow interests, little curiosity about their environment.
- Usually resentful of their current position, which results in tension, restlessness, and depression.
- Faced with difficulties, they usually give up easily and withdraw.
- Their thinking is commonplace, unimaginative, literal, slow.
- Most frequently used adjectives: shy, timid, silent, interests narrow, quiet, simple.

3. Sociability (*Sy*)

The Sociability scale was originally designed to measure the extent to which a person participates in social activities. It was later generalized to differentiate between a person who is outgoing, extraverted, and sociable versus one who is more introverted, withdrawn, and prone to avoid social visibility. There is a great deal of item overlap with Intellectual Efficiency (*Ie*), Social Presence (*Sp*), and Self-Acceptance (*Sa*). The questions deal with enjoyment of social interactions, a sense of poise, self-assurance in dealing with others, and interest in cultural and intellectual activities.

High *Sy* (*T* = 60 or More)

- Many of the same traits as persons scoring high on Capacity for Status (*Cs*); maturity, wide range of interests.
- Outgoing, sociable, confident.
- Feel comfortable in social settings, can easily mix with others.
- Dislike working alone
- Well-developed social skills, generally make a good impression.
- Most frequently used adjectives: outgoing, sociable, confident, ambitious, aggressive, energetic, talkative, assertive, enterprising.

Moderate *Sy* (*T* = 50 to 60)

- Average level of extraversion, are relatively comfortable in most social situations.
- Prefer to be around others but do not exclusively orient their lives in this direction.

Moderately Low *Sy* (*T* = 35 to 50)

- Prefer to be alone but are still relatively comfortable with people.
- Feel somewhat anxious around strangers, strongly prefer to be with persons with whom they are already acquainted.
- Dislike being the center of attention.

Low *Sy* (*T* = 35 or Less)

- Definite awkwardness in social situations, socially anxious.
- Have bitter complaints about their lives.
- Marked lack of confidence in their social skills, avoid most social encounters, especially in unfamiliar settings or with those they do not know.
- Act in self-defeating ways.
- Frequently perceive themselves as underachievers.

- Most frequently used adjectives: withdrawn, shy, retiring, quiet, timid, meek, quitting, reserved, awkward.

4. Social Presence (*Sp*)

The Social Presence scale was intended to serve as a measure of a person's degree of poise, self-confidence, verve, and spontaneity in social interactions. It especially assesses the extent to which the person is self-assured and assertive. *Sp* is very similar to sociability in that an individual scoring high on *Sp* is outgoing, extraverted, and enjoys being around other people. However, a person who is sociable does not necessarily also have social presence, even though this is often the case. Social presence implies not only that the person is sociable but also that he or she has more of a need to have impact on others and is thus likely to be more verbally aggressive, irritable, and sarcastic. A person exerting social presence might manipulate and control others, especially by working on someone else's defenses and self-deceptions. There is some overlap of items with Sociability (*Sy*), Self-Acceptance (*Sa*), and, to a lesser extent, Capacity for Status (*Cs*) and Intellectual Efficiency (*Ie*). The primary content of the questions relates to a person's poise and the degree to which he or she enjoys social interactions.

High *Sp* (*T* = 65 or More)
- Unconventional, spontaneous, witty, perceptive.
- Concerned with their own pleasure in interpersonal relationships.
- Often manipulate interactions to feel a sense of personal power; they not only like to be with other people but also want to be in control.
- Expression of ideas and vocabulary is excellent; socially skilled.
- Imaginative, socially relaxed, generally make a good impression.
- Extremely high scorers: manipulative, highly energetic, feel offended if people do not pay attention to them.
- Most frequently used adjectives: outgoing, confident, versatile, talkative, adventurous.

Low *Sp* (*T* = 40 or Less)
- Extremely cautious and concerned with proper etiquette.
- Others should conform to clear predefined standards.
- Disapproving of nonconforming behavior; their view of what is correct and incorrect falls within relatively narrow limits.
- Emphasize cooperation rather than manipulation.
- Likely to be kind, appreciative, patient, serious; but kindness and appreciation are expressed only when the behavior of others falls within their definition of *conventional.*
- Feel anxious when expected to alter their routine.
- Moralistic regarding the behavior of others; can be made to feel guilty regarding their own behavior.
- Extremely low scores: lack energy, avoid being the center of attention, feel uncomfortable when required to use their influence on others.
- Most frequently used adjectives: shy, withdrawn, retiring, silent, quiet, timid, inhibited.

5. Self-Acceptance (*Sa*)

The Self-Acceptance scale was intended to assess factors such as personal worth, self-acceptance, and capacity for independent thinking and action. Furthermore, it was hoped that *Sa* could "identify individuals who would manifest a comfortable and imperturbable sense of personal worth, and who would be seen as secure and sure of themselves whether active or inactive in social behavior" (Gough, 1987, p. 10). Although persons scoring high on *Sa* would be less likely to become upset, the *Sa* scale should not be used as an index of adjustment and is not related to the absence or presence of pathology. For example, a person might be high in self-acceptance yet still be rebellious, impulsive, and generally indulge in antisocial behavior. In fact, persons scoring extremely high on *Sa* are quite likely to be egocentric and indifferent, sometimes even to the point of narcissism. The scale questions have some overlap with Sociability (*Sy*), Social Presence (*Sp*), and, to a lesser extent, Capacity for Status (*Cs*). There is some negative overlap in which answers are scored in the opposite direction from Capacity for Status (*Cs*). Thus, a number of statements deal with social poise and self-confidence. Additional areas of item content relate to an accepting attitude toward social prohibitions, attention to duty, consideration of others, and an acceptance of human frailties.

High *Sa* (T = 65 or More)

- Comfortable with themselves.
- Self-reliant, independent, polished, sophisticated, enterprising, self-seeking in social relations, adventurous.
- Clear sense of self-definition, self-confident, outgoing (but not necessarily the same as sociability because self-acceptance can be high regardless of the quantity of interaction with others).
- Slight correlation with hypomania, which often has been formulated as a defense against depression. Extremely high scores may suggest an inflated sense of self-acceptance with underlying but unacknowledged feelings of self-criticism, pessimism, and hopelessness.
- Most frequently used adjectives: outgoing, self-confident, talkative, ambitious, and assertive.

Moderate *Sa* (*T* = 50 to 65)

- Average or somewhat above-average level of confidence.
- Generally good sense of harmony and internal balance.
- Somewhat adventurous and outgoing.

Moderately Low *Sa* (*T* = 35 to 50)

- Low in self-confidence, significant doubts about themselves.
- Can usually adequately cope with their lives, but prone to periods of insecurity and depression.
- Often adapt through conformity and conventionality; this usually has the desired effect of making their world safer and more predictable.

Low *Sa* (*T* = 35 or Less)

- Pronounced lack of self-confidence.
- Described as ordinary, have "flat" or unidimensional personalities.

- Achieve a moderate degree of safety in their world by withdrawing, quitting, and maintaining a relatively narrow range of interests.
- Will feel a strong sense of insecurity; afraid to take risks, low levels of self-confidence.
- Usually submissive and conventional but may at times impulsively act out in a reckless manner, almost as a form of rebellion against their largely self-imposed conventionality.
- Most frequently used adjectives: shy, withdrawn, retiring, silent, quiet, timid, and inhibited.

6. Independence (*In*)

The Independence scale measures the extent to which a person strives toward vocational and interpersonal autonomy. Conceptually, it overlaps with *Ai* in that they both assess the value a person places on working away from the restrictions, expectations, and influence of others. It also has similarities with *Sa* because persons high in both *In* and *Sa* are likely to be self-assured and self-reliant. Similarities can also be found with *Sp* (both witty, animated) and *Do* (both like to be in control).

High *In* (*T* = 65 or More)
- Self-assured, confident, possess social presence.
- Vocabulary is likely to be wide.
- Perceived as intelligent, self-reliant, witty, animated; as a result, they are likely to make a good impression.
- Not necessarily affiliative and friendly.
- Perceived as resourceful, confident, self-sufficient, capable.
- Will defend a belief without bending to external pressure.
- Dominant.
- Willing to work to achieve higher status.
- Morally responsible, high levels of self-control.
- Most frequent adjectives: confident, independent, aggressive, (having) initiative, assertive.

Moderately High *In* (*T* = 55 to 65)
- Similar to high scorers: confident, goal-oriented, able to rely on their own evaluations and directions.
- Assertive, can usually can deal effectively with others.

Low *In* (*T* = 30 to 45)
- Rely on others for decisions and directions.
- Likely to avoid conflict, competition; experience discomfort when having to assert themselves.
- Assets: excellent ability to cooperate and blend with the requirements and needs of others.

Extremely Low *In* (*T* = 30 or Less)
- Dependent, lack self-confidence.
- Will accept domination from others, partially because they feel uncomfortable having to face uncertainty.
- Experience worry and anxiety.

- Reluctant to express their own ideas.
- Tolerance, adaptability, generosity, helpfulness.
- Most frequently used adjectives: timid, shy, cautious, meek, submissive, unassuming, nervous.

7. Empathy (*Em*)

The Empathy scale attempts to measure the degree to which a person perceives and can feel the inner experience of others. It also measures related abilities, including social skills, confidence, social presence, leadership, and extraversion. The major underlying themes to the scale are that "empathic persons are characterized by a patient and forbearing nature, by affiliative but socially ascendant tendencies, and by liberal and humanistic political and religious attitudes" (Greif & Hogan, 1973, p. 284).

High *Em* (*T* = 65 or Above)
- Intuitive, perceptive, verbally fluent.
- Have a wide range of interests; usually perceived by others as interesting.
- Highly creative, spontaneous, able to use their imagination.
- Social presence: are animated, witty, and make a good impression.
- Interpersonally effective, independent, flexible.
- Most frequently used adjectives: sociable, outgoing, versatile, spontaneous, interests wide, confident, humorous.

Moderately High *Em* (*T* = 55 to 65)
- Good insight into the feelings and motives of others.
- Friendly, adaptable, comfortable to be around.

Moderately Low *Em* (*T* = 30 to 45)
- Slow to understand the feelings and motives of others.
- Perceived as having narrow interests.
- Shy, withdrawn, narrow-minded, conventional.

Very Low *Em* (*T* = 30 or Lower)
- Often feel bewilderment regarding the reasons others behave as they do.
- Insensitive, inconsiderate.
- Shy, rigid, unfriendly; others find it difficult to please them.
- Uncomfortable with uncertainty.
- Might cling to a rigid set of morals and narrow range of behaviors, often becoming authoritarian and ethnocentric.
- Their fathers were probably distant, cold, taciturn.
- Most frequently used adjectives: shy, silent, interests narrow, and conservative.

8. Responsibility (*Re*)

The intent of the *Re* scale is to assess the degree to which persons are "conscientious, responsible, dependable, [and] articulate regarding rules and order, and who believe life should be governed by reason" (Gough, 1968, p. 65). Although responsibility is somewhat related to sociability and self-control, it also stresses that values and controls are well-defined and significant factors in a person's life. The person who is highly responsible will sacrifice his or her own needs for the benefit of the group. Such people accept the consequences of their behavior, are dependable and trustworthy, and have a sense of obligation to the larger social structure. They are not necessarily leaders, but they do have a high sense of integrity and are committed to follow through on agreements they have made with others. In general, persons who express antisocial behavior score low on *Re*, whereas average or above-average scores are obtained by occupational groups in which responsible behavior and "attention to duty" are required. The *Re* scale is scored positively for items that reflect a high degree of commitment to social, civic, or moral values.

High *Re* (*T* = 60 or More)
- Respond well to tasks in which they are required to be conscientious, dependable, and reasonable.
- Will give up their own personal satisfactions for the sake of the group.
- Will honor any commitments they have made.
- Problem-solving approach is extremely rational and clear.
- Usually have strong religious beliefs, clear sense of ethics, concerned with philosophical issues.
- Work is productive because aspiration levels are high; work style is dependable and responsible.
- Behavior is courteous, polite, alert, energetic, honest, direct.
- Will seek additional information to reduce risk, generally prefer to avoid risky behaviors themselves.
- Most frequently used adjectives: conscientious, responsible, dependable, thorough, industrious, efficient.

Moderate *Re* (*T* = 40 to 60)
- Respond well to tasks in which they are required to be conscientious, dependable, and reasonable.
- Not comfortable taking responsibility for the behavior of others.
- Are seen by others as reasonably conscientious and straightforward.

Low *Re* (*T* = 40 or Less)
- Lack of discipline, usually rebellious, impulsive, seen by others as restless and careless.
- Difficulty budgeting their finances.
- Perceptions are tied to their own personal biases.
- Mainly concerned with their own needs.
- Often behave in exploitive and immature ways.
- First sexual encounters were usually at an early age.
- Underachievers in high school.
- Had considerable disagreements with their parents, fathers were alcoholics.
- Engaged in borderline delinquent behavior.
- Externally: behavior typically crude, unpredictable, rebellious, nonconforming, self-indulgent.
- Internally: feel dissatisfied, moody, cynical, distrustful.
- Most frequently used adjectives: rebellious, reckless, pleasure seeking.

9. Socialization (*So*; CPI 260 renamed Social Conformity/*Sc*)

The Socialization scale was originally called the "Delinquency scale." As the name suggests, its intent was to assess the likelihood of antisocial behavior. The scoring was later reversed, its name changed, and it gradually became a measure of an individual's social maturity, integrity, and rectitude. It is probably Gough's favorite scale and is based on his theory that antisocial behavior is the result of a role that certain individuals assume. There has been an extensive accumulation of literature on this scale, due at least in part to Gough's personal interest in it. The research indicates that the *So* scale has excellent concurrent, predictive, and cross-cultural validity, and is probably the most validated and most powerful scale on the CPI (J. Collins & Griffin, 1998).

The Socialization scale was designed to measure the degree to which social norms are accepted and adhered to. An individual, then, can score on a continuum from extremely well socialized to highly antisocial. The scale also estimates the probability that a person will engage in behavior considered incorrect in his or her culture (J. Collins & Bagozzi, 1999). For example, the *So* scale has been able with relative accuracy to differentiate cheaters from noncheaters in a college population (Kipnis, 1968), and low *So* scores were related to a diagnosis of personality disorder (Kadden, Litt, Donovan, & Cooney, 1996; Standage, 1986, 1990). In addition, low scores were able to predict criminals who would reoffend (DeFrancesco & Taylor, 1993) and differentiate between delinquents and nondelinquents (Gough & Bradley, 1992). Schizophrenics making violent suicide attempts were found to have particularly low scores on *So* (Seeman, Yesavage, & Widrow, 1985). The *So* scale has also differentiated high school dropouts from graduates (Gough, 1966; Hase & Goldberg, 1967). In a further study, Wernick (1955) demonstrated that 50% of the low scorers who were hired as temporary Christmas help stole from the store and none proved to be a satisfactory worker. Several researchers have found a negative correlation between *So* scores and a past lack of family cohesiveness, poor quality of parental care (Kadden et al., 1996; Standage, 1986, 1990), and physical abuse (Barnett & Hamberger, 1992). In addition, low scorers reported having a dysphoric mood (Kadden et al., 1996; Standage, 1990) and are more likely to experience career indecision (F. L. Newman, Ciarlo, & Carpenter, 1999). Thus, many items included in the scale are designed to determine whether the examinees experienced warmth and satisfaction in their family relationships. Some of the items also reflect the presence or absence of pessimism regarding a person's life and environment. The content of several other questions centers on whether examinees can properly evaluate the effects of their behavior as well as the extent to which they can be empathetic and sensitive to the feelings of others.

High *So* (*T* = 65 or More)

- Organized, adaptable, efficient.
- Highly dependable but maintain this level of dependability by being cautious, self-controlled, and inhibited.
- Values are conservative; they behave in an ethically consistent manner.
- Willing to trust others and express a fairly high level of optimism.
- Often described as kind, honest, and practical.
- Typically come from a stable, cohesive family environment where warmth and concern were freely expressed.
- Often were overprotected.
- Behavior is usually relatively conventional.
- External behavior: gentle, considerate, honest, tactful, well organized, capable, and productive.

- Internal experience: feel optimistic, stable, well controlled.
- Most frequently used adjectives: reliable, organized, dependable, stable, cooperative.

Moderate *So* (*T* = 50 to 65)

- Able to trust others.
- Generally accepting of the mores and rules.
- Tend to be inhibited and conventional, sometimes to the point of being overadapted.

Moderately Low *So* (*T* = 30 to 45)

- Impulsive, unreliable, often have a difficult time trusting others.
- Not usually followers; frequently question the rules given to them.
- Generally do not have a high degree of respect for society's prescribed forms of behavior.
- Moderate level of rebelliousness.

Low *So* (*T* = 30 or Less)

- High likelihood of antisocial behavior.
- Usually unreliable, unconventional, rude, defensive, impulsive.
- Reject past family ties, primarily because their past family lives were filled with chaos and were unsatisfying.
- Were unhappy at home; experienced considerable friction with their parents; were underachievers, sexually precocious.
- Experience a deep sense of alienation, have an extremely difficult time trusting people.
- Likely to report dysphoric mood.
- Scores below 25: personality disorder, especially borderlines and antisocial personality
- Others see them as headstrong, unpredictable, deceitful, rebellious, pleasure seeking.
- Internal experience: cynical, moody, often feel that their lives are meaningless.
- Most frequently used adjectives: reckless, impulsive, rebellious, unconventional, bitter, restless, suspicious.

10. Self-Control (*Sc*)

The original intent of the *Sc* scale was to measure the degree to which a person can self-direct his or her own behavior. More specifically, high scores suggest that a person can delay his or her behavior and redirect it in a clear, goal-oriented manner. Thus, a certain degree of similarity exists between self-control and both responsibility and socialization. Gough (in Megargee, 1972) clarifies these concepts by stating that responsibility reflects the "degree to which controls are understood," socialization measures the "extent to which they influence a person's behavior," and self-control assesses the "degree to which the individual approves of and espouses such regulatory dispositions" (pp. 65–66). Persons scoring high on *Sc* are self-directed, inhibited, and withhold their expressions of emotions and behavior. Some types of persons who score extremely high on *Sc* are often overcontrolled to the extent that, for short periods of time, they lose control and become explosive (Megargee, 1966; Megargee, Cook, & Mendelsohn, 1967). Individuals with low scores are impulsive and pleasure seeking, have difficulty delaying their impulses, and are not good at evaluating the consequences of their behavior. Thus, both extremely high and extremely low scorers are similar in that they have significant issues dealing with the management of impulses; however, they use opposite strategies to cope with these impulses.

The primary overlap of items for *Sc* is with *Gi*, and several items are also scored in a direction opposite from *Sp* and *Sa*. Some of the most important items emphasize that thought and rationality are the primary determinants of behavior. Furthermore, high scorers usually endorse items that indicate they take precautions to avoid irrational behavior and are generally socially inhibited.

High *Sc* (*T* = 60 or More)
- Considerate, self-denying, dependable.
- High need for precision, make every attempt to be reasonable.
- Other people perceive them as considerate, wholesome, dependable, but also as stubborn, rigid, overconforming.
- Avoid situations in which they might be tempted to act impulsively.
- Are generally inhibited, lacking in spontaneity, and move slowly.
- External behavior: organized, patient, capable, fastidious
- Conservative, moralistic, behave in an ethical, conscientious, and consistent manner.
- Internal experience: optimistic but serious.
- Most frequently used adjectives: moderate, calm, quiet, conservative, conventional, conscientious.

Moderate *Sc* (*T* = 45 to 60)
- Conventional and somewhat inhibited.
- Carefully consider the consequences of behavior before acting.
- Reasonable and dependable but somewhat lacking in spontaneity.

Moderately Low *Sc* (*T* = 30 to 45)
- Spontaneous, impulsive but can usually delay behavior.
- Impulsiveness is insufficient to impair interpersonal and work relationships.

Low *Sc* (*T* = 30 or Less)
- Marked difficulty delaying behavior, hasty in making decisions.
- Individualistic, self-seeking.
- Impulsiveness may sometimes cause tension in group activities.
- Often regret having acted in inappropriate ways.
- Unrealistic and headstrong.
- Quickly develop relationships that often become chaotic and confused.
- Background reveals that they were sexually precocious, experienced considerable conflicts with parents; academically were both underachievers and unhappy.
- Frequently perceive situations in sexual terms.
- External behavior: restless, excited, outgoing, rebellious, unpredictable.
- Most frequently used adjectives: impulsive, mischievous, restless, humorous, pleasure seeking, adventurous.

11. Good Impression (*Gi*)

Although *Gi* is mainly a validity scale designed to detect persons who are "faking good," it also reflects the degree to which a person with a valid profile is concerned with creating a favorable impression on others. There is a fairly high degree of item overlap with Self-Control (*Sc*), which suggests that an important component of creating a favorable impression is a good ability to delay impulses. Also, a number of items make fairly obvious statements concerning the person's level of functioning, amount of antisocial behavior, the extent to which he or she is goal oriented, and whether he or she has complaints regarding personal failings. High scorers are prone to exaggerate their positive points and minimize their negative qualities. Furthermore, they state that they have a high level of confidence and self-assurance, and minimize anxieties or insecurities. They emphasize that they can adapt well to stress and that they have a stable personality. Finally, there are several items related to the extent to which individuals behave in a socially approved manner and experience harmonious relationships with others.

The *Gi* scale has generally been successful in detecting invalid profiles. For example, Dicken (1960), by using a cutoff score of $T = 60$, was able to detect in 79% of the cases the profiles of persons attempting to make a favorable impression. With somewhat different criteria, only 3% of a total sample of profiles of mixed "normal" and "fake good" were incorrectly classified. In the same study, Dicken also demonstrated that even though persons were, in some of the cases, attempting to fake good on other scales, *Gi* still showed the greatest increase. The practical importance is that *Gi* would still be expected to increase, even though a person might be attempting, for example, to exaggerate his or her level of responsibility. Thus, the use of *Gi* as a validity scale is not restricted to persons attempting to create a favorable impression in a global manner; it can be used to detect persons attempting to fake good along other specific dimensions as well. More precise and accurate classifications can be derived by using the equations summarized in Gough (1996/2002) and included in the previous Determine Profile Validity section.

High Gi (T = 60 or More)

Personal history provides the best guide for determining whether a score in this range reflects a fake good profile or is more likely to indicate a person with an excellent level of adjustment (i.e., alcoholic with a high *Gi* is probably either consciously attempting to create a favorable impression or demonstrating the use of denial, which is often associated with that disorder).

- Ideal cutoff score for detecting a fake good profile: $T = 69$ for males, $T = 71$ for females.
- Person may be unaware of the impression he or she creates on others.
- Has an inflated self-image based on rigidly selective perceptions.
- Self-image would be likely to be maintained by ignoring the feedback received from others and manipulating others to agree with the perceptions they have of themselves.
- May be people pleasers who will do anything to fit in; as a result they are probably liked but not respected by others.
- If profile is only moderately high and valid: person is likely to be conventional, adaptable, self-denying, capable of a high degree of empathy.
- Oversensitive to the criticisms of others, usually respond by attempting to change and adapt to gain approval.
- It is important to please others and to be seen in a favorable light.
- Others see them as kind, warm, considerate, and patient.
- Will probably overcontrol their needs and be moralistic.

- Will try to adapt by becoming considerate and tactful.
- Most frequently used adjectives: calm, conventional, conservative, moderate.

Moderate *Gi* (*T* = 45 to 60)
- Unselfish, concerned with making a favorable impression.
- Able to take feedback from others and use it in a constructive way.
- Peaceable, trusting, understanding, highly concerned with living up to their social responsibilities.

Moderately Low *Gi* (*T* = 30 to 45)
- Minimally concerned with the impression they have on others.
- Sometimes seen as insensitive.
- They alone are the judges of their behavior; rarely listen to others' evaluations.
- Often described as independent, witty, and, occasionally, temperamental, sarcastic.

Low *Gi* (*T* = 30 or Less)
- Arrogant, actively reject the judgments of others.
- Prone to exaggerate their negative behavior in a rebellious way.
- Expect their behavior to be tolerated and even accepted.
- Temperamental, cynical, sarcastic, overly frank to the point of being disagreeable, interpersonal relationships are disrupted.
- Behavior is typically rebellious, undiplomatic, critical, nonconforming, unpredictable, self-indulgent.
- Often come from conflict-ridden families, mothers were nervous and dissatisfied.
- Insensitive, lack qualities of nurturance.
- Internal experience: feel cynical, distrustful, dissatisfied.
- Most frequently used adjectives: temperamental, restless, rebellious.
- Fake bad profile: *T* = 35 or less.

12. Communality (*Cm*)

The *Cm* scale is a validity scale originally designed to detect random answering. The questions are keyed in such a way that normal populations answer 95% of the questions in the keyed direction. Although the scale was not designed to measure personality variables, some personality indicators can tentatively be derived from this scale. Determining personality variables is based mainly on the observation that the content of the items reflects the following areas: good socialization, conformity, optimism, denial of neurotic characteristics, and conventionality of behavior and attitudes. Gough (1996/2002) points out that this is comparable to the "popular" response on the Rorschach in that it reflects the degree to which examinees see their surroundings in ways that are similar to others.

High *Cm* (*T* = 60 or More)
- Adhere to highly conventional attitudes.
- Overly socialized, tending to see world in a stereotyped manner.
- Do not see themselves as particularly unique or special, are conscientious and serious.
- Clear thinking, planful, practical, tactful.

Low *Cm* (*T* = 30 or Less)

- Have chaotic, conflict-ridden family backgrounds.
- Attitudes toward the world typically unusual and idiosyncratic.
- Generally upset, poorly motivated, self-defeating, frail, lack a sense of meaning in life.
- Most frequently used adjectives: reckless, distractible, unconventional, moody, confused.
- Fake bad profile: *T* = 29 for males, *T* = 24 for females; scores below 20 almost always confirm that the profile is invalid (see Determine Profile Validity section)

13. Sense of Well Being (*Wb*)

The Well Being scale was originally developed to help recognize profiles in which the person was "faking bad." Thus, it was initially referred to as the Dissimulation (*Ds*) scale, and fake bad profiles can usually be detected because they are significantly lower than even valid profiles for psychiatric patients. In contrast, persons who score high do not have a need to emphasize psychological or physical complaints. In fact, high scorers play down their worries and, rather, emphasize that they are enterprising, energetic, and experience a sense of security. They are also likely to have effective interpersonal relations, a high level of mental health, and a sense of psychological and physical well-being. Low scorers usually have diminished health and experience difficulty meeting the daily demands of their environment. In general, the *Wb* scale has come to represent a rough estimate of a person's level of adjustment and degree of psychological distress. However, it is more of a "state" scale than the others and is, therefore, somewhat changeable, depending on an individual's mood fluctuations.

The *Wb* scale has a low degree of item overlap with other scales because most of the questions were designed for exclusive use with this scale. The item content usually reflects a denial of various physical and psychological complaints. The second major content area reflects the extent to which a person is self-sufficient and independent.

High *Wb* (*T* = 55 or More)

- Have relaxed and satisfying interpersonal relationships.
- Able to trust others.
- Family backgrounds were stable and supportive.
- Dependable, responsible, value intellectual interests.
- Happily married stable, optimistic, self-confident.
- Most frequently used adjectives: clear thinking, capable.

Moderately Low *Wb* (*T* = 35 to 50)

- Generally feel that life is not going well.
- Meet perceived adversity with apathy and listlessness.
- Passive, awkward, defensive.

Low *Wb* (*T* = 35 or Less)

- Highly alienated, dissatisfied, experience a significant level of maladjustment.
- Extremely distrustful in interpersonal relationships.
- Dwell on real or imagined wrongs.
- Pessimistic, tense, restless, moody, life lacks a sense of meaning.
- Might cope by becoming absorbed in fantasy and daydreams.

- Use test situation as a forum for complaining, examinees who attempt to exaggerate their difficulties often score in this range.
- Most frequently used adjectives: confused, bitter, nagging.
- Temporary mood shift (but person is usually only somewhat maladjusted or even normal).
- Extremely low *Wb* scores: faking bad (see Determine Profile Validity section).

14. Tolerance (*To*)

The Tolerance scale was designed to measure the degree to which persons are socially intolerant versus the extent to which they are accepting, permissive, and nonjudgmental in their social beliefs and attitudes. The content of most of the items focuses on openness and flexibility versus rigidity and dogmatism. Other content areas relate to an interest in intellectual and aesthetic activities, level of trust, and a lack of hostility or resentment toward others. A person scoring high on Tolerance is also indicating that he or she is not alienated, does not feel isolated, rarely feels anxious, and is relatively poised and self-assured. There is a large variety of questions on this scale, but there is also a general lack of adequate validity studies. In fact, Tolerance is one of the poorer scales on the CPI, and its validity has even been questioned. Thus, interpretations based on this scale should be made cautiously and tentatively.

High *To* (*T* = 60 or More)
- Likely to be intelligent, wide range of interests, wide vocabulary, socially tolerant.
- Able to trust others.
- Confident, social poise.
- Nonjudgmental, can easily accept divergent beliefs and values, forgiving, generous, pleasant.
- Interested in philosophical issues.
- Can effectively understand and explain the core of many problems.
- Likable, make a good impression because they are tolerant, permissive, benevolent.
- Extremely high scorers: overly trusting, naive, underestimate potential difficulties.
- Worried about potential confrontations so they become overly adaptable.
- Will fill any role to keep a situation peaceful.
- Most frequently used adjectives: fair-minded, insightful, clear thinking.

Moderate *To* (*T* = 45 to 60)
- Somewhat nonjudgmental and open to the beliefs of others.
- Wide range of interests, informal, independent.

Low *To* (*T* = 40 or Less)
- Judgmental, nonaccepting of the beliefs and values of others.
- Judgmental attitude tends to generalize into other areas of their lives so that, overall, they seem cold, smug, and stern.
- Authoritarian, center their lives on a fixed and dogmatic set of beliefs.
- Mannerly, fearful, arrogant, sarcastic.
- If criticized, they usually become extremely defensive, bitter, and rejecting.
- More likely to judge than to understand others.

- Exert power in relationships by becoming critical, outspoken, and holding unrealistic expectations.
- Internal experience: moody, distrustful, cynical, dissatisfied.
- Most frequently used adjectives: prejudiced, interests narrow, suspicious.

15. Achievement via Conformance (*Ac*)

The *Ac* scale involves not only an orientation toward achievement, but also a need for structure and organization as a means of channeling that achievement. This scale specifically relates to settings in which conformity is an asset and reflects the degree to which persons prefer to have their criteria of performance clearly specified by some outside source. The content of the items relates to how effectively they can perform in an academic setting and how high their relative levels of energy and efficiency are. High scorers also see themselves as being productive workers. Additional content areas relate to the extent to which the examinee is even-tempered, accepts the rules of socially-approved standards of behavior, and dislikes frivolous, unconventional behavior. Persons scoring low dislike externally imposed guidelines, are rebellious and disorganized (Gough, 1996), and are likely to experience career indecision (F. L. Newman et al., 1999).

The *Ac* scale has been one of the more thoroughly researched scales on the CPI, primarily because of its practical relevance for academic personnel. In a review of the literature, Megargee (1972) reported that it has good criterion validity and has been found to correlate significantly (.36 to .44) with GPA and general achievement in high school settings. The correlations are highest for high school performance and somewhat lower for college settings.

High *Ac* (*T* = 60 or More)
- Persistent and industrious, especially when conforming to some external standard.
- Strongly prefer specificity and structure; may have a difficult time when structure is lacking (especially if a high *Ac* is accompanied by a low *Ai*).
- Most comfortable when working in highly organized settings.
- Excel when given specific, well-defined criteria for performance.
- Responsible, capable, ambitious; express these behaviors in a conservative, reserved, and obliging manner.
- Highly value intellectual effort.
- Most frequently used adjectives: responsible, organized, ambitious, persevering, efficient, conscientious.

Moderately High *Ac* (*T* = 50 to 60)
- May question need for structure and organization.
- Prefer not to have structure but can function adequately in a structured situation when required to do so.
- Stable, optimistic, dependable, responsible.

Low *Ac* (*T* = 35 or Less)
- Rejecting of authority and regulations.
- Rebellion may result in achievements far below potential; energy is directed more toward rejecting external organization and rules rather than working within the limits imposed on them.
- Intellectual rebels (especially if Achievement via Independence is relatively high).

- Become disorganized and nonproductive when external demands are placed on them.
- Difficulty committing themselves to organizations or people.
- Experience considerable caregiver indecision.
- Most frequent used adjectives: lazy, impulsive, reckless, rebellious, distractible, mischievous.

16. Achievement via Independence (*Ai*)

Whereas *Ac* can be used to predict achievement in high school, *Ai* was designed to predict achievement in a college environment, where independent initiative is more crucial. Persons who are high in *Ai* succeed in settings that require creativity, self-actualization, and independence of thought. Gough (1968) has clarified this distinction by describing Achievement via Conformance (*Ac*) as "form enhancing" whereas *Ai* is "form creating." *Ai* correlates significantly with college students' GPA (Gough & Lanning, 1986), yet there is only a low correlation with intelligence. Thus, students who have elevated *Ai* scales and who also achieve a high GPA do so mainly on the basis of a high need for achievement and only secondarily on the basis of intelligence. They are able to tolerate a high level of ambiguity and usually reject authoritarian or overly stringent regulations. In some cases, high *Ai* scores can predict achievement in situations in which originality and independence are rewarded. Persons with high scores are unwilling to accept conventional advice unquestioningly but rather prefer to think for themselves. Also, some questions relate to the degree to which individuals appreciate activities involving the intellect. Other content areas attempt to assess their degree of adjustment and the extent to which they are concerned with the deeper aspects of interpersonal relationships.

High *Ai* (*T* = 60 or More)
- Prefer to work without rules and structures.
- Feel restricted in a highly organized environment.
- Value creativity and originality.
- Wide range of interests, high aspirations, concerned with philosophical interests.
- Self-motivated, rejecting of conventional standards of productivity.
- Ability to produce and function is significantly impaired if a great deal of structure is required.
- Produce best when left to regulate their own behavior.
- External behavior: verbally fluent, self-reliant, make a good impression.
- Most frequently used adjectives: intelligent, clear-thinking, logical, foresighted, insightful, interests wide.

Moderate *Ai* (*T* = 40 to 50)
- Able to achieve based on their own self-direction; feel somewhat insecure when doing things completely on their own.
- Can work either with or without structure; prefer a moderate degree of external organization.
- Sometimes can be creative but still need external verification to feel comfortable.

Low *Ai* (*T* = 35 or Less)
- Difficulty trusting their own abilities. This characteristic becomes more exaggerated as the scale score becomes lower.

- Require external definition to establish their self-concept.
- Need others to specify their proper course of action.
- Moderately anxious, depressed, self-doubting.
- Not intellectually inclined, feel out of place in the world of abstract thinking.
- Most frequently used adjectives: confused, interests narrow.

17. Intellectual Efficiency (*Ie*; CPI 260 renamed Conceptual Fluency/*Cf*)

The *Ie* scale was originally called a "nonintellectual intelligence test" and was designed to measure personality traits that coincided with a high level of intellectual ability. High scorers on *Ie* tend to be competent and clear thinking, and to make efficient use of the potential they possess. Thus, it is less an intelligence test than it is a measure of the degree to which persons make efficient use of the intelligence they do possess. There is a moderate amount of item overlap with Sociability (*Sy*), Achievement via Independence (*Ai*), and Social Presence (*Sp*). One important content area of the items relates to the degree to which a person enjoys and is interested in wide-ranging intellectual activities. Also, a number of questions relate to self-confidence and assurance. Other questions relate to good physiological functioning, positive relationships with others, and an absence of irritability and suspiciousness.

A number of representative and noteworthy validity studies have been performed on *Ie*. It is positively correlated with measures of intelligence (Megaree, 1972), and members of MENSA scored significantly higher on *Ie* than the national norms (Southern & Plant, 1968). The scale has also been able to successfully discriminate high school dropouts from students who later graduated (Gough, 1966). The autobiographies of high scorers reveal that they see themselves as well organized, efficient, and committed to pursuing intellectual and cultural activities (A. Hill, 1967).

High *Ie* (*T* = 60 or More)
- Wide range of interests.
- Excellent ability to use their resources.
- Capable, confident, good planning abilities.
- Independent, informal, clear thinking.
- Wide vocabulary, verbally fluent, perceptive, effectively understand subtle nuances of behavior.
- Value intellectual activities, have high levels of aspiration.
- Most frequent used adjectives: intelligent, clear thinking, alert, interests wide (having) initiative.

Moderate *Ie* (*T* = 40 to 60)
- May still be highly competent.
- Likely to have some self-doubts regarding their intellectual capabilities.

Low *Ie* (*T* = 40 or Less)
- Insecure about their intellectual abilities.
- Self-doubt usually sufficient to create a mild degree of depression and anxiety.
- Awkward, shallow, suggestible.
- Might give up easily and feel uncomfortable with uncertainties.

- Alternative interpretation: May merely be uninterested in intellectual activities, which is also likely to be reflected in their choice of occupation; thus would not experience self-doubt and insecurity but merely a lack of interest.
- Most frequently used adjectives: confused, nervous, interests narrow.

18. Psychological-Mindedness (*Py*; CPI 260 renamed Insightfulness/*Is*)

The original intent of the *Py* scale was to identify persons who possess insight into the behavior of others in that they can accurately perceive others' inner needs and motivations. This scale focuses on the ability to figure other people out and does not necessarily indicate people who are empathic and nurturing. To assess the degree of empathy of individuals, it was necessary to consult additional scales, such as Empathy (*Em*), Sociability (*Sy*), and Well Being (*Wb*). However, as further research was done on *Py*, it became clear that it was more an indicator of persons interested in pursuing psychology from an academic perspective. In fact, Megargee (1972) concluded his literature review by stating that the *Py* scale has limited usefulness as an indicator of a person's ability to accurately perceive the inner needs and motivations of others. The content of the items relates to a person's ability to concentrate, his or her effectiveness in dealing with ambiguity, and his or her degree of enjoyment in his or her occupation. Other content areas deal with an ability to stick with long-term goals and an acceptance of unconventional opinions.

High *Py* (*T* = 65 or More)
- Interested in academic pursuits, especially research.
- Can be highly original and creative in their approaches to abstract problems.
- High importance on obtaining recognition for their efforts.
- Perseverance, ability to concentrate for long periods of time, high satisfaction from chosen profession.
- Independent, individualistic, preoccupied, reserved.
- Excellent dealing with abstract situations but generally avoid concrete problem-solving situations.
- Extremely high scorers: distant, aloof, detached.
- Most frequently used adjectives: logical, thorough, clear thinking, foresighted, interests wide (having) initiative.

Low *Py* (*T* = 35 or Less)
- Not inclined toward research or scholarly activities.
- Sociable, talkative, unassuming, conventional.
- Usually accept the behavior and motivation of others at face value.
- More comfortable with concrete situations.
- Most frequently used adjectives: simple, interests narrow.

19. Flexibility (*Fx*)

The *Fx* scale was designed to assess the degree to which an individual is flexible, adaptable, and changeable in his or her thinking, behavior, and temperament. It was originally based on questions relating to rigidity; but as the scale construction evolved, the scoring was reversed and the name changed from the Rigidity scale to the Flexibility scale. Other content areas relate to an ability to tolerate ambiguity, uncertainty, and impulsiveness and to a nonjudgmental, tolerant attitude toward moral and ethical considerations of right and wrong.

The validity studies in part agree with the intent of the scale, as they do support the hypothesis that low-scoring individuals are somewhat rigid. However, there is little evidence to indicate that extremely high scores reflect a high degree of flexibility (Megargee, 1972). Gough (1975) suggests that scores in the higher ranges are curvilinear: A moderately high score suggests that the person is relatively flexible, but with increasing elevation, a person becomes progressively more unstable and unpredictable. Megargee states that, given the weak evidence for the validity of this scale, especially for high Fx, it is one of the least valid scales on the CPI. Thus, any interpretations derived from it should be made with caution.

High Fx ($T = 65$ or More)

- May feel rootless, often emotionally unstable.
- Everything in their lives is open to question, including their sense of values and moral beliefs.
- Difficulty internalizing clear-cut standards.
- Can easily approach situations from a number of varying perspectives.
- Can consider many alternatives but may also have difficulty developing a clearly defined direction.
- Extremely high scorers: volatile, distractible, restless, poorly organized.
- Most frequently used adjectives: logical, thorough, clear thinking, foresighted, wide interests.

Moderate Fx ($T = 50$ to 65)

- Open to considering and experiencing alternative perspectives.
- Nonjudgmental, intellectually flexible, original, able to develop innovative ideas.
- Independent, self-confident, optimistic, value intellectual activities.

Moderately Low Fx ($T = 35$ to 50)

- Prefer structure, like to have things clearly defined and specified.
- Can handle a certain degree of uncertainty, but it usually creates discomfort.
- Cautious, practical, relatively rigid.

Low Fx ($T = 35$ or Less)

- Dislike new ideas and experiences, continually seeking security.
- Strong needs to control their thoughts; rigid, stubborn, defensive.
- Difficulty changing their decisions.
- Often have strong religious beliefs, moralistic, conservative.
- Conscientious, serious, literal-minded, overcontrolled.
- Most frequently used adjectives: organized, efficient, rigid, conservative, interests narrow, conventional, prejudiced.

20. Femininity/Masculinity (F/M; CPI 260 renamed Sensitivity/Sn)

The F/M scale was developed to assess the degree to which examinees were psychologically feminine or masculine, regardless of their actual sex. Its original intent was to detect significant conflicts over sexual identity, but this aspect of the scale has become progressively less emphasized. The scale is currently used to assess the extent to which individuals endorse beliefs, values, and occupations that are traditionally held either by males or by females. The intent of some items is fairly obvious whereas the intent of other items is more subtle. Many items relate to traditional masculine or feminine roles. Additional content areas refer to a person's degree of restraint and impulsiveness as well as the extent to which he or she is emotional during interpersonal relationships. McCrae et al. (1993) found that this was the only scale to correlate strongly (.45) with the core personality factor of Agreeableness. The items also reflect the degree to which a person is interested in politics, current affairs, and achievement. This scale has been well researched, and studies indicate it has a fairly high level of validity.

High *F/M* (*T* = 70 or More)
- Possible difficulties related to sexual identity.
- Males: Highly introspective, philosophical and aesthetic interests, wide-ranging interests, unconventional thought patterns. Most frequent adjectives used to describe them: nervous, worrying, weak, self-pitying, reflective, sensitive.
- Females: Tolerant, permissive, giving, oversensitive. Extremely high scores might be highly affiliative, dependent, submissive, require continual reassurance.
- Both male and females: Might use bodily symptoms to express anxiety and tension.
- Most frequently used adjectives: females—warm, sympathetic, sentimental, and dependent.

Moderately High *F/M* (*T* = 60 to 70 or More)
- Both males and females have significant needs for affiliation and dependency.
- Difficulty dealing with a high degree of autonomy, feel uncomfortable when independent action is required.
- Highly sensitive, quite concerned with not hurting others.

Moderate *F/M* (*T* = 40 to 50)
- Can deal effectively with autonomy; have an average need for dependency and affiliation.
- Practical and self-sufficient but not to an exaggerated extent.

Moderately Low *F/M* (*T* = 40 or Less)
- Task oriented, practical, emotionally self-sufficient, few dependency needs.
- Masculine, robust, tough (even coarse).
- Males: fit the masculine stereotype; are described as masculine, emotionally independent, tough minded, self-sufficient, self-centered; have a clear, stable, internally consistent personality, adhere to conservative values.
- Most frequently used adjectives (males): confident, independent, aggressive, ambitious.
- Females: self-reliant, confident, independent, deliberate, critical, distrustful, cynical, outspoken, motivated by power, have high aspirations.
- Most frequently used adjectives (females): strong, tough, independent.

Low *F/M* (*T* = 30 or Less)
- Exaggeration of above trends (see "moderately low" section).
- Females: likely difficulties related to sexual identity.

SPECIAL PURPOSE SCALES

Several special purpose scales have been included in the Consulting Psychologists Press computer scoring and interpretive report and are summarized next.

Managerial Potential (*Mp*)

This scale identifies people who both seek and have talents in supervising and monitoring others' behavior. Such persons can think clearly, have effective interpersonal behavior, are confident, and are good at setting and following through with goals. At the same time, they do not exploit others and are not self-centered. High scorers ($T = 60$ or more) are trustworthy, efficient, productive, extroverted, well organized, mature, realistic, offer advice, value intellectual activities, make long-term plans, and have high aspirations. In contrast, persons with low scores ($T = 40$ or less) avoid making decisions, give up easily, are easily offended, apathetic, lack confidence, rebellious, dissatisfied, defensive, immature, and become anxious with change.

Work Orientation (*Wo*)

Wo was designed to identify people who have a strong work ethic. Even in routine types of work, they are still likely to put forth their best efforts. Persons with high scores ($T = 60$ or more) are typically described as responsible, dependable, hardworking, self-disciplined, moderate, reasonable, and require little praise or commendation as their attitude toward work is based more on internal values than external reinforcement. Low scorers ($T = 40$ or less) are likely to be distrustful, careless, self-centered, restless, and temperamental.

Creative Temperament (*CT*)

This scale identifies unconventional, artistic people who are likely to perceive the world in unusual, creative ways. High scorers ($T = 60$ or more) are usually described as imaginative, having a wide range of interests, like variety, react strongly to aesthetic material, have progressive social attitudes, and tend to be somewhat rebellious. Persons with low scores ($T = 40$ or less) are typically conventional, overcontrolled, reserved, rigid, have narrow interests, and prefer the status quo.

Leadership Potential (*Lp*)

This scale was designed to identify persons who are effective at and feel comfortable in leadership positions. If persons score high ($T = 60$ or more), they are likely to be enterprising, confident, energetic, alert, ambitious, optimistic, resilient, resourceful, and can elicit cooperation from others. They have good initiative and are unlikely to be affected by criticism and pressure from others. In contrast, low scorers ($T = 40$ or less) can be described as temperamental, pessimistic, ill at ease, have feelings of inadequacy, worry excessively, have low self-confidence, and give up easily.

Amicability (*Ami*)

Ami identifies people who are friendly and considerate of others. Persons who score high ($T = 60$ or more) are ethical, consistent, cooperative, dependable, responsible, optimistic, warm, compassionate, and can easily establish close relationships with others. Some people might perceive them as submissive in that they are mild-mannered, self-controlled, and patient. Low scorers ($T = 40$ or less) are likely to be nonconforming, headstrong, self-centered, dramatizing, opportunistic, uncooperative, self-indulgent, and impatient. They can often be bitter, complaining, argumentative, manipulative, and irritable, particularly if demands are made on them.

Law Enforcement Orientation (*Leo*)

The intention and design of this scale was to identify people who both view societal rules and law enforcement favorably and would also function well working in the law enforcement area. High scores ($T = 60$ or above) indicate someone who is optimistic, stable, ambitious, conscientious, and has leadership abilities. High scorers are also likely to be direct, honest, create a good impression, and have good interpersonal skills. They are also conservative, conventional, moralistic, and hardworking. Persons with low scores ($T = 40$ or less) are described as nonconforming, cynical, distrustful, introspective, changeable, anxious, complicated, irritable, and may be self-defeating.

Tough-Mindedness (*Tm*)

The *Tm* scale measures where a person is on the continuum between tough-mindedness (frank, hard-hearted, unemotional) and tender-mindedness (trusting, reflective, soft-hearted). Persons scoring high ($T = 60$ or above) are likely to be independent, realistic, pragmatic, capable, determined, thorough, and confident. They are also hardworking, organized, have good leadership abilities, and can mobilize their resources quickly and effectively. They take pride in being objective, rational, and unemotional. When making decisions, they rely on facts rather than emotions. In contrast, persons with low scores ($T = 40$ or less) are likely to be sensitive, submissive, anxious, and easily feel inferior and embarrassed. Their motivation may be low, and they are likely to be undependable and have a difficult time dealing with stress.

CONFIGURAL INTERPRETATION

The following material on configural interpretation summarizes most of the empirical research on different code types. Regression equations have been included and are summarized in Table 9.2. The material is organized according to different topics (leadership, achievement, etc.). In contrast, McAllister (1996) has provided a listing of 152 code types arranged according to different patterns of low and high scale scores. Readers wanting to interpret scale scores can refer to McAllister or, alternatively, use the topic listings that follow. They might also wish to make rational interpretations of patterns of scale scores by using this sequence:

1. Note the high (generally above 60) and low (generally below 40) scale scores and read the individual descriptions that correspond with these scores.
2. Write down the key phrases that correspond with these single scales and strengthen, weaken, or alter the descriptions according to their relative elevations or lowerings and their relationships with other scales.
3. Then combine the descriptions to create a more integrated description of the person.

Intellectual Level

Megargee (1972) has reported that *To, Ac, Ai, Ie* (*Cf*), *Py* (*Is*), and *Fx* are all related to an individual's intellectual level. Elevations (*T* = 55 or more) on all or most of these scales strongly indicate that the person has a high interest in intellectual activities and good overall intelligence. Consistently low scores on all or most of these scales reflect limited intellectual ability and are a strong indication that the person has a narrow range of interests. This narrowing of interests may be, in part, a response to an emotionally upsetting event either in the recent past or at a significant time during the person's earlier development.

The particular patterns of high and low scales can provide information on the specific expression of intelligence. For example, it might be noted whether individuals would be more likely to excel in structured (high *Ac*) or nonstructured (high *Ai*) environments (see next subsection on achievement). Similarly, an interpreter can note how tolerant, flexible, or efficient individuals might be.

Achievement

Predicting and Assessing High School Achievement

The CPI is generally effective at detecting bright high school achievers. These students typically have elevated scores on *Ie* (*Cf*) and *Ai*, whereas underachievers are generally low on these scales. Bright achievers also have relatively high scores on *Re, So, To, Ac*, and *Py* (*Is*). Persons who are high achievers but have average IQs have relatively high scores (*T* = 55 or more) on *Re* and *So* and, to a lesser extent, on *Wb, Ac*, and *Ie* (*Cf*).

A number of equations have been developed for use in predicting achievement of high school students (see Megargee, 1972). These equations are composed of weighted combinations of scales and, when computed, provide the best possible prediction of specific abilities. For predicting the achievement of both males and females with combined low, medium, and high IQs, the following equation is recommended:

1. Achievement = 20.116 + .317 *Re* + .192 *So* − .309 *Gi* + .227 *Ac* + .280 *Ai* + .244 *Ie*

This equation correlates from .53 to .56 with overall high school GPA (Gough, 1964). If a student's IQ scores are available, the following equation is recommended:

2. Achievement = .786 + .195 *Re* + .244 *So* − .130 *Gi* + .19 *Ac* + .179 *Ai* + .279 *IQ*

Because *Ie* (*Cf*) is a relatively inefficient measure of IQ, it has been excluded from this equation, and, instead, the exact IQ is from intelligence testing. This equation raises the correlation with overall GPA to .68, which is significantly better than the typical .60 (or lower) correlation found when using only IQ scores.

To evaluate whether students will drop out of high school or graduate and continue to college, social factors as measured by the CPI are at least as important as a student's intellectual ability. The primary scales used to predict high school graduation are *Re, Ac*, and, to a lesser extent, *Wb, To*, and *Ie*, all of which are usually significantly higher for students who graduate from high school than for students who are high school dropouts (Gough, 1964). High school students who later go to college score significantly higher on *Re, Ac*, and *Ie* (Gough, 1968). The following formula correlates at a level of .52 with later college attendance for high school students (Gough, 1968):

3. College Attendance = 17.822 + .333 *Do* +.539 *Cs* − .189 *Gi* + .740 *Ac*

Predicting and Assessing College Achievement

Several studies have been conducted on the relative importance of single-scale and combinations of scale scores in assessing college achievement. Significant correlations have been found among *Re, So, Ai,* and overall GPA (Hase & Goldberg, 1967). Further studies (Flaherty & Reutzel, 1965; Griffin & Flaherty, 1964) likewise stress the importance of *Re, So,* and *Ai* but also include *Ie* (*Cf*) and *Cs*. In female samples, *Do* was significantly correlated with GPA as well (Flaherty & Reutzel, 1965). These scales are somewhat similar to those used to predict achievement in high school students, except that *Ai* becomes more significant for college populations and *Ac* decreases in relative importance. In addition, the likelihood of later upward social mobility is correlated with *Cs* and college GPA.

Although positive correlations were found among these single scales, the magnitude of these correlations was not extremely high, with the highest correlation reaching only .36 for males on *Ai*. Most other significant correlations ranged between .20 and .26. However, weighted combinations of scores produced higher correlations ranging from .35 to .54, depending on the type of population being assessed. Gough (1964) has found a .41 correlation between the following formula and grades for both males and females in introductory psychology classes:

4. Achievement (Introduction to Psychology) = 35.958 − .294 *Sy* − .180 *Sp* + .185 *Re* − .189 *Sc* − .152 *Gi* − .210 *Cm* + .275 *Ac* + .523 *Ai* + .241 *Ie* + .657 *Py*

Weighted combinations of scales in combination with SAT scores for males and females who were National Merit scholars were found to have a .32 and .23 correlation with college GPA, respectively:

5. Male GPA = .16 SAT (Math) + .11 *So* − .19 *Sp* + .17 *Fe*
6. Female GPA = .25 SAT (Verbal) − .14 *Sp* + .06 *Re* + .20 *Ac* + .08 *Fe*

Although the correlations derived from these formulas are somewhat low, they are an improvement on the use of SAT scores alone for this group.

Using a more general sample of college students' CPI scores to predict academic performance, Gough and Lanning (1986) found that *Ai, Ie* (*Cf*), and *Py* (*Is*) correlated at the levels of .28, .25, and .23, respectively. Multiple regression analysis produced the following equation, which had a correlation with later course grades of .38 for males and .36 for females:

7. GPA = 30.60 − .26 *Wb* + .35 *Re* − .19 *Gi* + .39 *Ai* + .22 *Ie* + .36 *Py*

Although the correlation was modest, it predicted academic performance somewhat better than using SAT-V (.31 for males, .38 for females) and SAT-M (.30 for males, .24 for females).

These rather modest correlations indicate that it is more difficult to predict performance for college students than for those attending high school. This fact can be traced to the far greater number and complexity of variables involved in a college setting. Both the selection of curricula and the student's motivation for attending college can result from a variety of situations. Furthermore, significant changes have been made in the curricula and admissions policies of colleges since the early equations (4, 5, and 6) were developed. Finally, a student's lifestyle can be extremely varied. For example, some students may be attempting to struggle through college with a part- or even full-time job, whereas others may be taking relatively few classes and be supported exclusively by their parents. All of these variables are beyond the scope of what can be measured by a test such as the CPI. The practical implication for clinicians predicting college GPA is to consider not only test scores but also as many of the other variables as possible.

Achievement in Vocational Training Programs

Student Teaching

Several studies have been performed to assess the effectiveness of teachers in student-teaching programs. Veldman and Kelly (1965) found that student teachers who were rated highly by their supervisors scored significantly higher on *Ac, Cs, Do, Gi*, and *Py* (*Is*) than those who were rated as less effective. R. Hill (1960) also emphasized the importance of *Ac* but did not find *Do* and *Py* (*Is*) to be important. A further study with a female population again stressed the importance of *Ac* but also included *Re* and *Ie* (*Cf*) as significant factors (Gough, Durflinger, & Hill, 1968). Although these studies consistently emphasized the importance of *Ac*, none of the other individual scales was found to have either consistent or large correlations with teaching effectiveness. However, Gough et al. (1968) found a moderate correlation of .44 between CPI scores and teacher effectiveness by using the following equation based on weighted scales:

8. Teaching Effectiveness $= 14.743 + .334\,So - .670\,Gi + .997\,Ac + .909\,Py - .446\,Fx$

Using this equation, they were able to predict with 65% accuracy the performance of student teachers.

Medical School

Several scales have been found to correlate positively with overall medical school GPA, including *Sy* (.35), *To* (.34), and *Ie* (.40; Gough & Hall, 1964). An equation based on weighted combinations of scores was found to correlate at a magnitude of .43 with both faculty ratings of students and GPA (Gough & Hall, 1964):

9. Medical Promise $= .794\,Sy + .602\,To + 1.114\,Cm - .696\,Cs$

Dental School

Most studies using single-scale correlations with achievement in dental school have not produced significant correlations, although Kirk, Cumming, and Hackett (1963) did report a correlation of .28 between *Ac* and dental school GPA. However, Gough and Kirk (1970) found a .38 correlation with GPA by using the following equation based on weighted combinations of scales:

10. Dental Performance $= 29.938 - .110\,Sp + .148\,Re - .262\,Gi + .727\,Ac + .230\,Py$

Although this correlation is somewhat modest, it is higher than the Dental Aptitude Test's correlation of .29.

Seminary

Query (1966) performed a study on seminary students who were advised to discontinue and those who successfully completed the program. Although he did not develop any equations based on weighted scores, he did find that those who were unsuccessful tended to score higher on *Sy* and *Sa*.

Police and Military Training

Both *Ie* (Hogan, 1973) and *Do* (Hargrave, Hiatt, & Gaffney, 1986) have been found to be related to police effectiveness. Hogan found that *Ie* correlated .40 with ratings of effectiveness made by instructors during training, and it correlated .43 after one year in training when ratings were made by field commanders (Mills & Bohannon, 1980). Other noteworthy correlations with other scales were for *Ac* (.31), *Ai* (.33), and *Sy* (.45; Hogan, 1971). Hargrave et al. (1986) described the most effective deputies as sociable, outgoing, and gregarious, whereas effective traffic controllers were characterized by a high capacity for rewarding social interactions. The most effective persons in both these groups (deputies and traffic controllers) were relatively dominant (high *Do*), energetic (high *Ie*), competitive (high *Ac*), independent (high *Ai*), flexible (high *Fx*), and socially ascendant (high Class 1 scales; Hargrave et al., 1986). Mills and Bohannon (1980) somewhat similarly described effective officers who had been in the field a year or more as independent (high *Ai*), energetic (high *Ie*), and flexible (high *Fx*). Police officers who later developed disciplinary problems were found to have lower scores on *Re, Sc*, and *So* than those who did not (Sarchione et al., 1998).

Pugh (1985) has pointed out that what determines successful police performance changes over time. During their training and first year of employment, the most effective officers were found to be those who were most able to obtain the trust of their coworkers and become an accepted member of their department. After two years, their ability to strive for improvement (high *Cs*) became the best predictor. In contrast, the best predictors after 4.5 years of employment were qualities that indicated a person was stable, socially skilled, and responsible (high *Wb, Re, So*).

A study by D. Collins (1967) rated drill sergeants in a training program on the following four criteria of success: academic grades, an assessment of leadership ability, final class standing, and a field test of combat skills. The only scale to correlate significantly was *Ie*. It is interesting to note that the scales stressing conformity (*Ac*) and dominance (*Do*) had no correlation. This finding is in contrast to the frequent stereotype of drill sergeants as authoritarian, rigid, conformist, and autocratic. It has also been found that women who were successful in Air Force basic training scored higher on all scales except *Sc, Cm, Py* (*Is*), and *Fe* than those who were unsuccessful (Elliot, 1960). A different study found that successful students graduating from an Army language training program scored significantly higher on *Ai* and *Ie* (*Cf*), but not *Ac*, than those who were unsuccessful (Datel, Hall, & Rufe, 1965).

Achievement through Conformance versus Independence

A comparison between *Ac* and *Ai* can provide useful information regarding an individual's typical style or preference toward working. The relation between *Ac* and *Ai* can have important implications for helping a person make a career choice or understanding existing job difficulties. If *Ai* is high (*T* = 55 or more) and significantly higher than *Ac* (10 or more), such persons usually place a high level of trust in their own judgments and conclusions and are likely to reject conventional formulas. Their acceptance of decisions or ideas depends more on inward verification rather than a respect for, or adherence to, external standards. When left on their own, they are highly motivated to achieve, but they may feel restricted if placed in a structured environment. If *Ai* is exceptionally high (*T* = 65 or more), they may spend much of their time rejecting authority. This trend would be further exaggerated with high scores on *Do* and low scores on *Sy*. The result might be an almost obsessional quality in their thinking, characterized by strong themes of rebelliousness. In general, a significantly higher *Ai* than *Ac* is an excellent profile for authors, researchers, and persons in positions of independent leadership.

If *Ac* is high ($T = 55$ or more) and is significantly greater than *Ai* (10 or more), the opposite trend would be apparent. These persons would strongly prefer specificity and external structure. They would be more effective and feel more comfortable when second in command, such as in a middle-management business position. An overall and generally effective combination occurs with high but evenly balanced scores on *Ai* and *Ac*. This finding suggests these individuals have the necessary flexibility both to work in a structured environment and to do effective work independently. The following is a listing of the descriptions given to persons scoring with different high and low combinations of *Ac* and *Ai* (Gough, 1968):

	Ac High		
idealistic	mannerly	intelligent	logical
cautious	shy	rational	interests are wide
praising	conscientious	realistic	inventive
nervous	inhibited	independent	active
helpful	dull	reasonable	stable

Ai Low ———————————————————————————— Ai High

irresponsible	show-off	spunky	tolerant
careless	touchy	reckless	reliable
distrustful	undependable	unexcitable	courageous
disorderly	unstable	foresighted	distractible
indifferent	restless	frank	pleasure-seeking

Ac Low

Leadership and Managerial Style

The CPI has been extensively used with organizations to understand leadership and managerial style. Additional uses have been in team building, consulting with executives, personnel selection, individual development, and filling recently vacated positions with persons within the organization (succession planning). Excellent, practical, case-focused guides toward using the CPI in these areas have been developed by Devine (2005) and P. Meyer and S. Davis (1992). They emphasize that one of the crucial issues to understand is that a person's optimal performance in an organization depends not only on personality but also the degree to which an individual's personality fits into the direction the organization is headed as well as the organizational climate and culture. Thus, any interpretation of the CPI needs to take these factors into consideration. For example, an organization that is quickly undergoing extensive change will benefit from persons who are flexible and adaptable as might be reflected in high scores on the Flexibility scale. In some organizations, a consensus-building style is most appropriate; this might be suggested by high scores on dominance, tolerance, empathy, and *F/M* but with a lower score on Social Presence. In a fast-paced, high-risk organization, this same style might be quite dysfunctional. Thus, any interpretation of CPI profiles needs to integrate test results with the specifics of the organization.

Relevant information on leadership and managerial style often can be found by carefully considering the CPI profile. One way of guiding the questions that can be asked regarding leadership is to consider the following managerial competencies outlined by P. Meyer and S. Davis (1992):

Leadership orientation. Drive for influence, method of working with others to achieve goals, negotiation skills, willingness to take charge, forceful versus low-key style, authoritative versus consensus-building style.

Problem solving. Level of decisiveness, method of analyzing problems, extent to which they use others' input, cautiousness versus impulsivity, likelihood of considering a wide number of alternatives or holding to one or two options and arguing for them, creativity, and independence.

Achievement motivation. The extent or drive to achieve as well as the manner in which the person is likely to achieve, need for approval, need for recognition, achievement through independent efforts (form creating) versus working with and under the direction of others (form enhancing).

Interpersonal skills. Social comfort, extent to which they like to interact, awareness of interpersonal dynamics, concern and support for others, willingness to help and support others, tact, diplomacy, lack of abrasiveness, political astuteness.

Administrative skills. A person's orientation toward planning; need for structure, organization, and planning; attention to details; monitoring and controlling own behavior; focus on short-term as well as long-term planning; degree to which person approaches work in a systematic manner.

Adaptability. Ability to cope with stress, self-reliance, ability to work in a wide number of contexts, tolerance of ambiguity, personal mastery, optimism, ability to be self-directed, possession of a wide number of adaptive behaviors.

Thus, managers might vary on the extent to which they need to take control, carefully consider all options in solving a problem, achieve individually or through conforming to some outside structure, are comfortable with their coworkers, awareness of details, and flexibility. The different high and low points on their CPI results can help to understand and elaborate on these differences in managerial style.

A general overview of a person's managerial and leadership potential can be noted by interpreting the Leadership and Managerial Potential special scales. Interpretations based on these two scales can be further refined by understanding that a person's comfort and wish to lead is largely related to his or her level of dominance. Accordingly, the *Do* scale has consistently proven to be accurate in differentiating leaders from nonleaders. In discussing leadership, it is helpful to describe the difference between an executive leader who has been appointed and a social leader who has been elected. For both types of leaders, the *Do* scale is high. However, for the executive leader, there is considerably more variability among the other scales; the style of expressing leadership is more dependent on the conditions the person is in, and the achievement scales are relatively more important than the other measurements (summarized in Megargee, 1972). This seems reasonable because the success of an executive leader is based more on his or her administrative and supervisory abilities than on his or her popularity. Social leadership is more likely to have a general elevation in Factor 2 scales as well as an elevated *Do.*

For example, if *Do, Cs,* and *Sp* are the high points, the leader is likely to be socially charismatic, persuasive, at the center of attention, and energetic (Heilbrun, Daniel, Goodstein, Stephenson, & Crites, 1962). If *Do* is high along with *Sa* and *Ac*, the person will have a high need for control, fear rejection, demand attention, dislike surprises, and emphasize clear structure (McAllister, 1996). If *Do* and *Ai* are the high points, these individuals are independent achievers who may also be highly creative self-initiators (McAllister, 1996). Further interactions with *Do* can likewise be developed by taking into consideration the specific meanings of additional corresponding high and low scale scores.

Using a combination of weighted scales derived from social leaders in a high school environment, Gough (1969) was able to obtain a modest correlation of .34 between social leadership and weighted CPI scales.

11. Leadership (Social) = 14.130 + .372 *Do* + .696 *Sa* + .345 *Wb* − .133*Gi* + .274 *Ai*

Gough (1968) studied the relationship between *Do* and *Re* and found that the meaning of *Do* is altered by the relative elevation of *Re*. If *Do* and *Re* are both high, a leader is generally progressive, conscientious, and ambitious. In contrast, adjectives describing high-*Do* persons with low *Re* indicate that they are dominant in a more aggressive, rigid, and destructive way. The following is a list of adjectives used to describe various combinations of *Do* and *Re*:

	Do High			
	touchy	dominant	dominant	ambitious
	robust	strong	responsible	foresighted
	cynical	tough	progressive	conscientious
	hardheaded	aggressive	wise	formal
	temperamental	opinionated	stern	alert
Re Low				Re High
	irresponsible	suggestible	quiet	calm
	careless	foolish	peaceable	mild
	unstable	pleasure-seeking	modest	gentle
	apathetic	changeable	reserved	thoughtful
	confused	lazy	cooperative	honest
	Do Low			

Executive Success

Success and effectiveness as an executive are frequently found in a profile in which $T = 60$ on *Do, Cs,* and *Sp*; $T = 40$ to 50 on *Sa, Re, So, Sc*; $T = 55$ or more on *Sy*; $T = 40$ or more on *Wb*; and $T = 50$ or less on *Gi* (in Webb, McNamara, & Rodgers, 1981). The most important variables are the indicated T scores on *Do, Cs, Sp, Sa, Re, So,* and *Sc*. This profile is common among business executives and managers. They are usually able to have others adapt to their plans yet, at the same time, are flexible enough to adapt to the demands that are placed on them. Although they are generally excellent leaders, they may create a certain degree of family discord by attempting to be too demanding and autocratic in the home. If this combination of scores is present for a person under 25 years of age, it can suggest a naive sense of overconfidence in which the person cannot effectively assess his or her personal limitations. However, this profile is generally a good predictor of later success in leadership positions.

Leadership and Empathy

If an individual has elevations on both *Do* ($T = 65$ or more) and *Gi* ($T = 60$ or more), he or she is likely to not only possess excellent leadership abilities but also can demonstrate a concern with, and empathy for, others (Heilbrun et al., 1962). If *Gi* is low in relation to *Do*, the leadership style is usually more critical, domineering, egotistical, and auto-cratic, with a decreased concern for creating and maintaining harmonious interpersonal relationships in the group. A low score on both *Gi* and *Do* reflects a somewhat passive and withdrawn person who is socially inept and resentful, and whose passivity may be expressed in a shy seeking of approval from others.

Decision Making

The interaction between *Sa* and *Wb* reflects the degree to which the examinee turns to himself or herself for decision making or depends on others. If *Wb* is low and *Sa* is mod-erate to high, these persons usually rely on their own self-evaluations and feel that others are inferior and cannot be trusted. This belief may result from their self-assurance and independence as reflected by a *Wb* that is only moderate to slightly low, or they may listen only to their own judgments because of a deep sense of alienation and distrust of others, as reflected in a markedly low *Wb* and high *Sa*.

If *Wb* is moderate to high and *Sa* is low, such individuals tend to believe that the judgment of others is superior to their own judgment, perhaps because they are still fairly accepting of themselves (only slightly low *Sa*) but think even more highly of others. Thus, they may have a high level of loyalty to people who are in superior posi-tions, such as an employer or parent. Such persons may also have a poorly developed abil-ity to accurately perceive the faults and limitations of others and may have developed this loyalty in response to overprotective parents. A further possibility could be that they do not respect their own judgments and perceptions because they are lacking in their own resources.

With both *Sa* and *Wb* low, people are likely to have significant doubts regarding them-selves. There may be an excessive level of dependency, fearfulness regarding their own competence, and a corresponding resentment of continual dependency on others.

Clinical Assessment

The CPI has generally not proven to be as effective in the assessment of psychopathology as it has in the educational and vocational areas. This finding can be traced to several rea-sons, but, primarily, the CPI was not designed for clinical assessment, and thus relatively little research has been conducted in this area. The organization and nature of the scales were not designed to differentiate among the various syndromes of pathology, nor do they provide information relating to a person's intrapsychic areas of functioning. Furthermore, devices such as the MMPI-2 and MCMI-III are clearly superior for the evaluation of pathology.

Despite these limitations, the CPI can make some general, as well as specific, contri-butions. Even though it does not distinguish between the different patterns of pathology, general maladjustment is usually indicated by lowered profiles (Higgins-Lee, 1990). The CPI has also been used effectively to detect and assess criminal and delinquent individu-als, which involves a more interpersonal or, more accurately, an individual versus societal type of conflict. Furthermore, the CPI is a good adjunct to more clinically oriented tests, because it can assess the relative strengths in an otherwise pathological individual and answer questions relating to the type of educational and vocational programs this person might benefit from.

General Maladjustment

An individual's level of maladjustment is indicated by generally lowered profiles (Higgins-Lee, 1990), which are often accompanied by an elevation on *Fe*. The scales found to best predict personal distress were low scores on *Ie*, *Mp*, *So*, and *Py* (Cook et al., 1996). A lowering of Factor 1 scales (especially *Do*, *Re*, *So*, and *Sc*) is often a good indicator of poor adjustment, and men with low *Ac* and *Ie* are especially likely to be maladjusted (Stewart, 1962).

Personality Disorder

Persons with scores below 25 on the *So* scale are likely to have diagnoses of personality disorders, particularly those that are related to dramatic, emotional, or erratic behaviors (borderline, antisocial, histrionic, narcissistic; Kadden et al., 1996; Standage, 1990; Standage, Smith, & Norman, 1988). However, if they score high on items related to "problem behaviors" (indicating denial of these problem behaviors) but low on items reflecting dysphoria and having had an unhappy childhood (thereby agreeing to these difficulties), they would be unlikely to have alcohol or drug problems but may have difficulties with depression. The likelihood that they would have personality disorders would then be intermediate (Standage et al., 1988).

Vulnerability to Stress

Persons with a "V" formation in which *So* is low (*T* = 35 or less), with *Re* and *Sc* significantly higher (*T* = 40 or more), are likely to be defensive and susceptible to the effects of situational stress (in Webb et al., 1981). They usually come from chaotic, stress-filled families in which were episodes of irrational parental abuse. Thus, they have learned that the world is a dangerous place and have developed a precarious balance in which they feel constantly on guard. They keep their emotions carefully controlled, continually attempt to avoid conflict, and feel they need to be constantly prepared to diffuse potentially stress-filled interactions. Their conformity to their environment is based not on an expectation of achieving positive rewards but more on fear and an avoidance of negative consequences. These people may have occasional explosive outbursts in which they have an almost dissociative loss of control. This explosiveness is especially likely if their spouses are manipulative, insensitive, and exploitive. As the discrepancy between *So* and *Sc* increases, these dynamics become more pronounced.

Depression

The Social Ascendency (Class 1) scales are generally lowered by depression, and a *T* score of 40 or less on *Sy, So, Wb*, and *Ie* (*Cf*) is highly typical of depressed populations (Holliman & Montross, 1984). The scales that provided the best indicators of depression in males were *Sy, So*, and *Ie* (*Cf*), whereas for females the best discriminators were *Wb, So,* and *Ie* (*Cf*) (Holliman & Montross, 1984). In most cases, the *Wb* scale is particularly important to notice, because a lowering on scales such as *Do, Cs, Sy, Sp*, and *Sa* might suggest merely a shy, unassertive, socially uninvolved person who is not necessarily depressed (McAllister, 1996). When the depression begins to lift and the person starts to have more optimism and a greater orientation to his or her environment, these scales generally increase. The mental and behavioral apathy often associated with depression can also be reflected by a lowering (*T* = 40 or less) in *Ac, Ai*, and *Ie* (*Cf*).

Psychosomatic Disorders

Although the CPI was not designed to diagnose psychosomatic disorders, it can assess certain personality characteristics that are consistent with individuals who are susceptible to this type of disturbance. Both male and female psychosomatics usually have lowered scores ($T = 40$ or less) on *Wb* and *Sc* and an elevation on *Cm* (Stewart, 1962). In addition, males often have a lowering on *Ie* (*Cf*). When the scores from male and female psychosomatics are compared with persons having behavior disorders, psychosomatics have a relatively higher *So* and *Cm*, with females also having a higher *Re* (Stewart, 1962). All of these scores suggest that psychosomatic patients have a significantly higher level of superego control and socialization. This finding agrees with most formulations of psychosomatic disorders that emphasize the suppression and repression of hostility and antisocial behavior as important predisposing factors. A pattern of psychosomatic disorders is especially likely if *Wb* has a *T* score of 35 or less, accompanied by an *Fe* of 60 or more. This pattern is associated with headaches, gastrointestinal upsets, or functional skin conditions. Such persons are likely to have moderately high needs for dependency, which are not being fulfilled, but they also tend to feel distrustful and alienated in their relationships with others.

Defense Mechanisms

The two basic approaches to defense are either through repression or through sensitization. Whereas repressors attempt to avoid anxiety-arousing stimuli, sensitizers approach and attempt to control situations. Byrne, Golightly, and Sheffield (1965) found that high scorers on *Sy*, *Wb*, *Sc*, *To*, *Gi*, *Ac*, and *Ie* (*Cf*) were more likely to use repression.

Certain types of assaultive offenders usually can be characterized as overcontrolled, but occasionally they drop all inhibitions and impulsively strike out (Megargee, 1964, 1965, 1966). These persons score high on the Overcontrolled Hostility scale (OH) of the MMPI and also have higher scores on *Sc* and *Gi* with a lowering on *Sa* (Megargee et al., 1967). This finding gives further support to the view that *Sc* and *Gi* are associated with the use of repressive defenses.

Juvenile Delinquency and Criminal Behavior

The assessment of antisocial behavior with the CPI has been well researched with generally useful findings. Both delinquents and criminals tend to have lower overall subscale scores, particularly on *Re* and *So* (J. Collins & Bagozzi, 1999; Gough & Bradley, 1992; Laufer, Skoog, & Day, 1982). In addition, persons who scored in either the Gamma or Delta lifestyle categories (questioning of normative beliefs) were more likely to be delinquents than those in the Alpha or Beta categories (Gough & Bradley, 1992). However, level of self-realization or integration (score on Vector 3) is important to consider in that delinquents and criminals had low levels of self-realization. In contrast, persons with high levels of self-realization were found to have a low level of criminal or delinquent behavior regardless of which of the four lifestyles they were in (Gough & Bradley, 1992).

Scores on *Wb*, *To*, and *Ac* are also likely to be somewhat lower (Gough & Bradley, 1992). This pattern suggests that the social poise of delinquents is usually about the same as that of other persons their age; but, in most other respects, their behavior is definitely unconventional, and they usually do not channel these differences into creative or intellectual areas. Mizushima and DeVos (1967) have found significant differences on the CPI between solitary delinquents who have lower scores on *Ie* (*Cf*) and *Fe* (*Sn*) and more socially-oriented delinquents who have significantly higher scores on *Sy*, *Sp*, and *Sa*. They also found violent offenders to be higher on *Sp* and *Sa* but low on *Fe* (*Sn*). However, delinquents who committed extremely violent offenses were especially high on *Sc*, which supports Gough's theory that excessive overcontrol in certain individuals periodically breaks down, leading to assaultive behavior (Megargee, 1966). In summarizing these data on delinquency, it is most important to consider lowerings in *Re* and *So*.

Further information regarding the style of delinquency can be derived by the lowered *Ie* (*Cf*) and *Fe* (*Sn*) for solitary delinquents; higher *Sy*, *Sp*, and *Sa* for social delinquents; higher *Sp*, *Sa*, and low *Fe* (*Sn*) for violent social delinquents; and outstandingly high *Sc* for extremely violent offenders who have periodic excessive losses of control.

The likelihood of successful parole for delinquents can, in part, be predicted in that more successful parolees have higher scores on *Sp* and *Sa*; and less successful parolees have lower scores on *So* and *Sc* (Gough, Wenk, & Rozynko, 1965). Gough and his colleagues have developed the following regression equation to differentiate successful from unsuccessful parolees:

12. Parole Success = $45.078 - .353 \, Sp - .182 \, Sa + .532 \, So + .224 \, Sc$

Using this equation, Gough et al. (1965) were able to predict with 60% accuracy which of a population of California Youth Authority parolees would be successful and which parolees would later become recidivists.

Marital Violence among Males

Males who were found to be physically violent in their marriages generally had lower scores in 10 of the CPI scales including *Re*, *So*, *Sc*, *To*, *Ac*, *Ai*, *Gi*, *Ie*, and *Py* (*Is*) (Barnett & Hamberger, 1992). Low scores on *Re*, *So*, and *Gi* were particularly good predictors and suggested that persons with these scales as their lowest scores had difficulties with impulsivity, problem solving, and intimacy.

Chemical Dependency

Kurtines, Hogan, and Weiss (1975) found that the possibility of potential or actual substance abuse, perhaps to the extent of actual addiction, is suggested by high *Sp* and *Sa* accompanied by low scores on *Re*, *So*, *Sc*, and *Wb*. In a college population, J. Goldstein (1974) somewhat similarly found that students who used drugs were more likely than nonusers to have elevations on Capacity for Status, Social Presence, Self-Acceptance, Psychological-Mindedness (Conceptual Fluency), and Flexibility. In contrast, nonusers scored higher on Well Being, Responsibility, Socialization (Social Conformity), Self-Control, Tolerance, Communality, Achievement via Conformance, and Intellectual Efficiency. The scale with the greatest ability to differentiate the two groups was Socialization, with users having a mean of 41.2 and nonusers having a mean of 52.1.

Social Maturity

The concept of social maturity includes *So* but is more extensive and also includes areas other than that assessed by the *So* scale alone. Specifically, the person who is considered to be socially mature is not merely directed by blind conformance but also has a high level of ethical standards that can even vary from the values held by the majority of people. He or she may, at times, feel a need to resist social pressure. In addition, this person can accurately perceive the faults in a social system and attempt to deal with them in a mature way. Thus, the socially mature person is clearly different from someone who is merely oversocialized or hypernormal. Gough (1966) developed the following multiple regression equation to assess social maturity using combined weighted scores:

13. Social Maturity = $25.701 + .408 \, Re + .478 \, So - .296 \, Gi$

A special Social Maturity scale has also been developed and is available as a portion of the CPI computer report (see Gough, 1996; McAllister, 1996).

RECOMMENDED READING

Devine, R. J. (2005). *CPI 260 Client feedback report guide for interpretation: Strategies for use in business and organizations.* Mountain View, CA: Consulting Psychologists Press.

Gough, H. (1996). *California Psychological Inventory manual.* Mountain View, CA: Consulting Psychologists Press.

Gough, H., & Bradley, P. (2005). *CPI 260 manual.* Mountain View, CA: Consulting Psychologists Press.

McAllister, L. (1996). *A practical guide to CPI interpretation* (3rd ed.). Palo Alto, CA: Consulting Psychologists Press.

Megargee, E. I. (2002). *The California Psychological Inventory handbook* (2nd ed.). San Francisco: Jossey-Bass.

Chapter 10

THE RORSCHACH

The Rorschach is a performance-based test of personality functioning based on interpreting a person's responses to 10 bilaterally symmetrical inkblots. The overall goal of the technique is to assess the structure of personality, with particular emphasis on how individuals construct their experience and the meanings assigned to their perceptual experiences (thematic imagery; Weiner, 2004). The interpretations on Rorschach data can provide information on variables such as motivations, response tendencies, cognitive operations, affectivity, and personal and interpersonal perceptions. Despite attacks from both in and outside the field of psychology, the Rorschach remains one of the most extensively used and thoroughly researched techniques (Archer & Newsom, 2000; Camara et al., 2000; Watkins et al., 1995). This is reflected in the fact that more than 200 books and 10,000 articles have been written about or using the Rorschach (Exner, 2003).

The central assumption of the Rorschach is that stimuli from the environment are organized by a person's specific needs, motives, and conflicts and by certain perceptual "sets." This need for organization becomes more exaggerated, extensive, and conspicuous when subjects are confronted with ambiguous stimuli, such as inkblots. Thus, they must draw on their personal internal images, ideas, and relationships to create a response. This process requires that persons organize these perceptions as well as associate them with experiences and impressions. The central thesis on which Rorschach interpretation is based is this: The process by which persons organize their responses to the Rorschach is representative of how they confront other ambiguous situations requiring organization and judgment. Once the responses have been made and recorded, they are scored according to three general categories: (a) the *location*, or the area of the inkblot on which they focused; (b) *determinants*, or specific properties of the blot they used in making their responses (color, shape, and so on); and (c) the *content*, or general class of objects to which the response belongs (human, architecture, anatomy, etc.). The interpretation of the overall protocol is based on the relative number of responses that fall into each of these categories. Some systems also score for the extent to which subjects organize their responses (organizational activity), the types of verbalizations, and the meaningful associations related to the inkblots.

Although these scoring categories may appear straightforward, the specifics of scoring and interpreting the Rorschach are extremely complex. Furthermore, attempts to develop a precise, universally accepted coding system have not been entirely successful, which creates some confusion and ambiguity in approaching the Rorschach technique itself. Although the primary scoring systems have some agreed-on similarities, there are also significant differences in the elements of these systems. These differences, in turn, reflect the complexity and ambiguity in the nature of the responses made to the cards. Thus, effective use of the Rorschach depends on a thorough knowledge of a scoring system, clinical experience, and adequate knowledge of personality and psychopathology.

The general purpose of this chapter is to provide an overview of administration, scoring, and interpretation using Exner's Comprehensive System. Exner's system was selected because it is the most ambitious and psychometrically sound Rorschach system to date. Furthermore, the most frequently used scorings and interpretations from other systems have been included and integrated into Exner's approach.

Scoring for the Comprehensive System is quite complex, and only a brief overview can be covered in this chapter. Clinicians who wish to use precise scoring tables and criteria, as well as more extensive elaborations on interpretation, are encouraged to consult Exner and his colleagues' original works (Exner, 2000, 2001, 2003; Exner & Weiner, 1995). This chapter cannot stand as a substitute for Exner's work. Its major intent is to familiarize persons with the Rorschach in general and, more specifically, with Exner's approach to interpretation. In addition to students who are learning the system, persons who are already familiar with Exner's system might wish to consult sections of this chapter to obtain summaries of different scoring categories and interpretive hypotheses. This might be most appropriate for practitioners who use the Rorschach only occasionally. Finally, persons who use other scoring systems may wish to consult the different interpretive hypotheses as an aid to interpretation. This is theoretically possible because Exner incorporated the major approaches from other systems into his Comprehensive System. However, variations are likely to occur between the Comprehensive System and other systems; therefore, interpretations should be made with caution.

HISTORY AND DEVELOPMENT

Many inkblot-type tests and games had existed long before Rorschach published his original 10 cards in 1921. For example, da Vinci and Botticelli were interested in determining how a person's interpretations of ambiguous designs reflected his or her personality. This theme was later considered by Binet and Henri in 1895, and by Whipple in 1910. A popular parlor game named Blotto that developed in the late 1800s required players to make creative responses to inkblots. However, Rorschach developed the first extensive, empirically based system to score and interpret responses to a standardized set of cards. Unfortunately, Rorschach died at age 37, shortly after the publication of his major work, *Psychodiagnostik* (1921/1941). His work was continued to a limited extent by three of his colleagues—Emil Oberholzer, George Roeurer, and Walter Morgenthaler.

The main approach used by Rorschach and other early developers of inkblot techniques was to note the characteristic responses of different types of populations. Thus, the initial norms were developed to help differentiate among various clinical and normal populations: schizophrenics, persons with intellectual disabilities (mentally retarded), normals, artists, scholars, and other subgroups with known characteristics. Rorschach primarily wanted to establish empirically based discriminations among different groups and was only minimally concerned with the symbolical interpretation of contents. Many of his original concepts and scoring categories have been continued within current systems of analysis. For example, he noted that depressed, sullen patients seemed to give the fewest responses. Persons giving a large number of very quick responses were likely to be similarly "scattered" in their perception and ideation to nontest situations. He also considered the importance of long latencies (so-called shock responses), and hypothesized that they were related to a sense of helplessness and emotional repression.

Had Rorschach lived longer, the history and development of his test might have been quite different. Without the continued guidance and research from the "founding father," the strands of the Rorschach technique were taken up by persons who had quite different backgrounds from Rorschach and from one another. By 1957, five Rorschach systems were in wide use, the most popular being those developed by Beck and Klopfer.

These two approaches came to represent polarized schools of thought and were often in conflict.

S. J. Beck (1937) adhered closely to Rorschach's format for coding and scoring. He continually stressed the importance of establishing strong empirical relationships between Rorschach codes and outside criterion measures. Beck emphasized that the response to the Rorschach involved primarily a perceptual-cognitive process in which the respondents structure and organize their perceptions into meaningful responses. This perceptual-cognitive process was likely to reflect their responses to their world in general. For example, persons who broke down their perceptions of an inkblot into small details were likely to behave similarly for perceptions outside the testing situation.

In contrast, B. Klopfer (1937) was closely aligned to phenomenology and the theories of personality developed by Freud and Jung. As a result, he emphasized the symbolical and experiential nature of a respondent's Rorschach contents. Thus, Klopfer believed that Rorschach responses were fantasy products triggered by the stimulus of the inkblots. For example, persons who perceived threatening objects on the inkblots would reflect persons who perceive aspects of their world as similarly threatening. Although not as popular, additional systems developed by Piotrowski, Hertz, and Rapaport represented a middle ground between the two extremes taken by Beck and Klopfer.

With five distinct systems available, the Rorschach became not a unitary test but five different tests. Exner (1969) provided a comparative analysis of these different systems and later concluded that "the notion of *the* Rorschach was more myth than reality" (Exner, 1986, p. 19). He pointed out that none of the five systems used the same verbal instructions and only two of the systems required identical seating arrangements. More important, each systematizer developed his or her own format for scoring, which resulted in many differences regarding interpretation, the components required to calculate quantitative formulas, the meanings associated with many of the variables, and the interpretive postulates.

The wide range of often competing approaches resulted in numerous detrimental practices. A survey of practitioners by Exner and Exner (1972) indicated that 22% of all respondents had abandoned scoring altogether and, instead, based their interpretations on a subjective analysis of contents. Of those who did score, 75% used their own personalized integration of scores from a variety of systems. In addition, the vast majority did not follow any prescribed set of instructions for administration. With researchers using a variety of approaches, comparison of the results of different studies was difficult. Researchers in the early 1970s further reported difficulties in recruiting subjects, problems with experimenter bias that needed to be corrected by using multiple examiners, statistical complexities of data analysis, inadequate control groups, and insufficient normative data (Exner, 1993, 2003). Some of the elements had no empirical basis. The general conclusion, based on these findings, was that the research on and the clinical use of the Rorschach were seriously flawed. Despite this, all five systems included some empirically sturdy elements.

To correct the difficulties with both the research and clinical use of the Rorschach, Exner and his colleagues began the collection of a broad normative database and the development of an integrated system of scoring and interpretation. Their initial step was to establish clear guidelines for seating, verbal instructions, recording, and inquiry by the examiner regarding the examinee's responses. The best features for scoring and interpretation, based on both empirical validation and commonality across systems, were adapted from each of the five different systems. A scoring category was included in the new system only after it had achieved a minimum .85 level for interscorer reliability. The final product was first published in 1974 as *The Rorschach: A Comprehensive System* and has since been released in second (1986), third (1993), and fourth (2003) editions. A second volume relating to current research and interpretation has been released in two editions (Exner,

1978, 1991), and two editions of a volume on the assessment of children and adolescents have also been published (Exner & Weiner, 1982, 1995).

Normative data for the Comprehensive System has undergone continual revision. A major reason for these revisions has been to refine stratification. A further impetus was that in 1990 the Comprehensive System eliminated all protocols with fewer than 14 responses because these were likely to have resulted in invalid protocols. The normative base reported in Exner's 1993 (3rd) edition of the Comprehensive System was composed of 700 adult nonpatients and 1,390 nonpatient children and adolescents between the ages of 5 and 16. However, it was discovered in 1999 that more than 200 duplicate adult protocols had inadvertently been included. As a result, a new normative sample was begun. The most recent publication has included 450 contemporary protocols from persons aged 18 to 65+, evenly divided between males and females, with a wide range of education and a variety of ethnic groups (see Appendixes E and F; Exner & Erdberg, 2005). Future publications will include a progressively larger number of participants. In addition, an international normative reference group has been collected by Meyer, Erdberg, and Shaffer (2007). The child and adolescent sample reported in Exner (2003) is the same as that included in 1993 (includes 1,390 nonpatients between the ages of 5 and 16).

Exner's integration of the different Rorschach approaches into his Comprehensive System has been successful in that most research studies over the past 20 years have used his system, and it has become by far the most frequently taught system in graduate training. His attention to empirical validation, combined with a large normative database, has served to increase its acceptance and status. Access to training and interpretive aids has been facilitated through numerous workshops, a scoring workbook (Exner, 2001), ongoing research publications, new editions of earlier volumes, and computer-assisted scoring and interpretation (Exner, 1984, 1986, 1993, 2003).

Debates regarding the psychometric adequacy of the Rorschach have created one of the greatest controversies in the history of psychology. From the beginning, the Rorschach was met with skepticism in the United States; yet it developed a strong following. At one point, the Rorschach was the second most frequently used test, and, in the 1940s and 1950s, the name *Rorschach* was almost synonymous with clinical psychology. Despite this initial (and continuing) popularity, reviews have generally been quite critical. As early as 1954, Shaffer declared that the Rorschach could no longer be considered a promising instrument. Eleven years later, Dana (1965) somewhat prematurely concluded: "Indeed, we have come to the end of an era, preoccupation with the Rorschach as a test" (p. 495). A. R. Jensen (1965) was even more critical when he recommended that "the Rorschach be altogether abandoned in clinical practice, and that students in clinical psychology not be required to waste their time learning the technique" (p. 509). Most recently, Garb (1999) has called for a "moratorium" on its use until research has clarified which scoring categories are valid.

It should be noted that one of the early difficulties in establishing the psychometric properties of the Rorschach was in making meaningful comparisons across various studies. As Exner (1969, 1974, 1986, 1993, 2003) has repeatedly pointed out, there is not *a* Rorschach; rather, at least five different Rorschachs have been created around the five major systems. Reliability and validity studies performed on one system did not necessarily mean that the findings from these studies could be generalized to any of the other systems. However, reviewers often acted as if there were only one Rorschach. Furthermore, many studies were poorly conducted. They were characterized by inadequate controls for age, sex, race, IQ, and socioeconomic status. In addition, many studies had extremely wide variations in the training required for scorers, insufficient protection from experimenter bias, poor validation criteria, and inadequate statistical models. These difficulties were amply demonstrated when Exner (1986) and his associates found it necessary to discard 1,400 research studies of a total of 2,100 studies published before 1970.

More recently, the depth and sophistication of the criticisms have increased. This has resulted in extensive arguments and counterarguments, with each side citing numerous studies in favor of their positions. Between 1998 and 2003, most major assessment journals published special series debating the relative merits of the Rorschach. Challenges were directed at nearly all aspects of the test, including the adequacy of its norms, interscorer reliability, temporal stability, the accuracy of meta-analysis that had found support for the Rorschach, and its level of incremental validity. The central elements of these debates are integrated into the sections on reliability and validity and assets and limitations.

Over the past four decades, Exner has been responsible for much of the leadership and many of the advances regarding the Rorschach. Exner's death in 2006 opened up the possibility of significant changes in his system. Over the next few years, researchers and clinicians will be debating the utility and specifics of these changes.

RELIABILITY AND VALIDITY

As noted previously, Exner originally included only scoring categories that had interscorer reliabilities of .85 or higher. Some controversy has resulted concerning these values in that other researchers have reported greater variability. Parker (1983) analyzed 39 papers using 530 different statistical procedures published in the *Journal of Personality Assessment* between 1971 and 1980. He concluded that, overall, the Rorschach can be expected to have reliabilities in the low to middle .80s. However, only two of his studies used the Comprehensive System. Acklin, McDowell, Verschell, and Chan (2000) found that nearly half of the categories for the Comprehensive System showed excellent reliabilities (>.81) with substantial reliability (.61 to .80) for a third of the categories. They concluded that a majority of the categories had excellent interscorer reliability, but a subset of about a quarter of the variables demonstrated less than adequate (<.61) reliability. The problem with the Acklin et al. data, however, was that the sample sizes were small, with the result that greater variability would be expected.

In the most ambitious, rigorous, and large-scale study to date, G. Meyer et al. (2002) used eight different data sets and employed several different strategies to determine the reliability of the categories for the Comprehensive System. They concluded that it had overall excellent interscorer reliabilities with median correlations ranging from .82 to .97, depending on the data set used. Exner (2003) has recently reported new interscorer reliabilities with agreement ranging from a high of 99% for Texture and Vista responses to a low of 88% for passive movement. These correlations support the claims of Exner and of Gronnerod (2006) that, if scorers are appropriately trained, the system has excellent interscorer reliabilities.

An additional crucial area for reliability is the extent to which clinicians agree on interpretations related to test data. If one clinician made interpretations that were at variance with other clinicians, it would not only indicate low inter-interpreter reliability, but some of the interpretations would necessarily be inaccurate. However, G. Meyer, Mihura, and Smith (2005) found that interpretive agreement among experienced clinicians ranged between .76 and .89.

Test-retest reliabilities for the Comprehensive System have been somewhat variable. Retesting of 41 variables over a one-year interval for a nonpatient group produced reliabilities ranging between .26 and .92 (see Exner, 2003, Table 11.3). Four of the correlations were above .90, 25 were between .81 and .89, and 10 were below .75. Exner has clarified that the 10 variables below .75 would all be expected to have had relatively low reliabilities because they related to changeable state (rather than trait) characteristics of the person. He also pointed out that the most important elements in interpretation are the ratios and percentages, all of which were among the higher reliabilities. Retesting for the same group over a 3-year interval produced a similar but slightly lower pattern of reliability. In contrast, another group of nonpatient adults, retested over a much shorter (3-week) interval, had somewhat higher overall reliabilities than for either the 1-year or 3-year retestings (Exner, 1986). A more extensive summary of test-retest reliability by G. Meyer and Archer (2001) found that the mean reliability was .66 (range from .46 to .84, *Mdn* = .69). This is similar to the .66 to .82 mean reliabilities summarized by Viglione and Hilsenroth (2001) and the .67 for a quite long retesting of 5 years by Gronnerod (2006). Gronnerod (2004) also found that many of the elements of the Rorschach were valid indicators of change following psychotherapy. One issue, however, is that the Rorschach has approximately 125 variables, and some of these do not have known test-retest reliability on them. The number of these untested reliabilities varies across researchers, with Wood and Lilienfeld (1999) stating that 85 variables have missing reliabilities and Viglione and Hilsenroth stating that only 12 variables have unknown test-retest reliabilities.

Long-term retesting for children has not come close to the same degree of stability as for adults (Exner, 2003; Exner & Weiner, 1995). Exner (1986) clarifies that this low stability for test results is to be expected, given that children undergo considerable developmental changes. However, short-term retesting over 7-day (for 8-year-olds) and 3-week (for 9-year-olds) intervals did indicate acceptable levels of stability (Exner, 2003). Only 2 of 25 variables were below .70, with at least 7 above .90 and the remainder from .70 to .90. As with adults, the ratios and percentages demonstrated relatively high stabilities. Although acceptable short-term stability for young children's Rorschach variables was demonstrated, long-term stability was not found to occur until children reached the age of 14 years or older (Exner, 2003; Exner, Thomas, & Mason, 1985).

The primary focus of early validity studies was to discriminate empirically among different populations. These empirically-based discriminations were originally based on past observations of a particular group's responses to the Rorschach, the development of norms based on these responses, and comparisons of an individual's Rorschach responses with these norms. For example, a person with schizophrenia might have a relatively high number of poor-quality responses, or a depressed person might have very few human movement responses. In addition to these empirical discriminations, efforts have been made to develop a conceptual basis for specific responses or response patterns. Thus, it has been conceptualized that people with schizophrenia have poor-quality responses because they do not perceive the world the way most people do; their perceptions are distorted and inaccurate, and their reality-testing is poor. A further approach, which was not extensively developed in the Comprehensive System (nor by Rorschach himself), was the validation of the latent meaning of symbolical content.

These very general approaches have given rise to a surprisingly large number of specific scorings and interpretations, all of which have had various degrees of support. Many of the early validity studies are difficult to evaluate because of the varying scoring systems and poor methodologies. In addition, most early studies depended on inadequate norms (especially for studies conducted on children, adolescents, cross-cultural groups, and persons over 70). Test results might also have been significantly influenced by situational and interpersonal variables, such as seating, instructions, rapport, gender, and personality of the examiner (see review by Masling, 1992). It should then come as no surprise that, for every study supporting an interpretive hypothesis, there would often be another refuting the same hypothesis.

Establishing the validity of the Rorschach as a whole has been further complicated by the many scoring categories and quantitative formulas, each of which has varying levels of validity. Some interpretations have greater validity than others even in a specific category. For example, the number of human movement responses (M) has been used as an index of both creativity and fantasy. A review of the research by Exner (1993) indicates that M relates fairly clearly to fantasy in that it has been correlated with daydreaming, sleep/dream deprivation, dream recall, and total time spent dreaming, whereas associations between M and creativity have been weaker and more controversial. Validity might also depend on the context and population for which the test is used. For example, a depression index (DEPI) based on seven Rorschach combinations of scores has been found to provide low or no associations with the presence of depression among adults (Jorgenson, Anderson, & Dam, 2000; G. Meyer, 2000; Mihura, 2008). Among adolescent populations, the depression index was not successful in distinguishing depressives from schizophrenics (Archer & Krishnamurthy, 1997a; Ball, Archer, Gordon, & French, 1991; Stredny & Ball, 2005). In contrast to DEPI, an index designed to detect thought disorders (Perceptual Thinking Index [PTI]) has been quite successful (Dao & Prevatt, 2006; Mihura, 2008). Additional validity data on specific scoring categories and formulas are included in the Interpretation section of this chapter. These data should be carefully read to more fully understand Rorschach validity.

Probably the best way to provide a global index of validity is to combine the results from a large number of studies. Early meta-analyses indicated that validity ranged from .40 to .50 (L. Atkinson, Quarington, Alp, & Cyr, 1986; Parker, 1983; Parker, Hanson, & Hunsley, 1988; Weiner, 1996). However, these results have been challenged by Garb, Florio, and Grove (1998; Garb, Wood, Nezworski, Grove, & Stejskal, 2001; Hunsley & Bailey, 2001), who reanalyzed the data from Parker et al. and concluded that the overall validity coefficients for the Rorschach were only .29 (in contrast to the significantly higher validity of .48 for the MMPI). This finding produced lively debates in the literature regarding the most appropriate methods of analysis. The majority of recent meta-analyses have continued to support the validity of the Rorschach (R. F. Bornstein, 1999; G. Meyer, 2004; G. Meyer & Archer, 2001; G. Meyer & Handler, 1997; G. Meyer et al., 2005). However, interactions with type of scoring system, experience of the scorer, and type of population used were likely to have complicated the picture.

One of the main efforts on establishing Rorschach validity has been directed toward determining its ability to discriminate among different types of populations. The success of these differentiations has been somewhat equivocal (see Vincent & Harman, 1991; Wood et al., 2000). For example, Wood et al. have indicated that, with the exception of a few disorders (schizophrenia, borderline personality, bipolar disorder), the Rorschach has not been very effective at assisting with making formal psychiatric diagnosis. A defense is that, in contrast to structured interviews or tests such as the MCMI-III, the Rorschach was not designed to accomplish this goal. Since the Rorschach was not designed to provide diagnoses, it means that diagnostic accuracy is conditional in that it is accurate for some diagnoses but not for others. Although the Rorschach is not the optimal instrument for most forms of diagnosis, it has been found to effectively predict variables such as outcome from psychotherapy (using the Prognostic Rating Scale; $r = .45$), detection of psychosis (using the Schizophrenia Index; $r = .44$), and dependent behavior (using the Oral Dependency Scale; $r = .37$; G. Meyer & Archer, 2001).

One major factor that may serve to lower Rorschach validity is the meaning associated with, and the effects of, response productivity. Various interpretations have been associated with extremes of productivity, with low productivity suggesting defensiveness, depression, and malingering, and extremely high productivity suggesting high achievement or an obsessive-compulsive personality. However, response productivity has also been found to be closely tied to age, intellectual level, verbal aptitude, and amount of education. Norms have been provided for different ages (Exner, 1993; Exner & Weiner, 1995), which can be helpful in correcting for the effects of age. However, intellectual level, verbal aptitude, and amount of education can potentially confound the meanings associated with response productivity. A high number of responses does not necessarily represent traditional personality interpretations (obsessiveness, creativity, good impulse control) but might merely indicate a high level of verbal aptitude.

Most early validity studies rarely considered the preceding factors. More important, the number of responses not only affects interpretations related specifically to response productivity, but also productivity affects many other areas of interpretation. For example, a low number of responses is likely to increase the relative number of responses based on the whole inkblot (W). In contrast, a high number of responses would be likely to increase the relative number of small detail (Dd) responses. Because interpretations are frequently based on the relative proportions of different scoring categories (calculated in quantitative formulas), the overall number of responses is likely to influence and possibly compromise the validity of the formulas. However, Exner (1993) has found that lengthy records generally did not result in different interpretations when compared with records from the same persons with average numbers of responses. For practical reasons, he has recommended that the number of responses be limited if the person gives six or more responses to the first card or five or more responses to the second card (see the Administration section). In contrast to lengthy protocols are ones with extremely low numbers of responses. Exner (2003) recommends that brief protocols (fewer than 14) be discarded and the test be readministered. This problem with the meaning of various numbers of responses largely led Holtzman to develop his alternate test (Holtzman Inkblot Test), in which subjects provide only one response for each inkblot in his series (Holtzman, 1988).

A significant and relatively recent concern with the Rorschach is that scores on the test indicate more pathology when compared with indicators from other sources (Hamel, Shaffer, & Erdberg, 2000; Shaffer, Erdberg, & Harioan, 1999). If true, this finding would indicate significant concern related to child custody and other forensic and clinical decisions that might be based on Rorschach data. Advocates of the Rorschach have replied that overpathologizing may appear to be present in part because the Rorschach norms were based on persons who were not merely nonpatients but were rated as being healthy and well functioning (G. Meyer, 2001). The basis for these norms would make it fairly easy for many people to appear relatively pathological compared to them. G. Meyer (in press) also indicated that Rorschach norms, research, and decision rules are being continually revised and improved. One implication of this controversy is that Rorschach scores (and inferences based on them) should be checked against other sources of information. If this information does not support the Rorschach, then the Rorschach inferences should be treated with considerable skepticism. Future research, especially using revised norms based on a sample of the general population, should help inform this crucial issue. The most recent norms have been included in Appendixes E and F, which should be referred to. Any cross-cultural use of the Rorschach should use the international normative reference group published by G. Meyer, Erdberg, & Shaffer (2007).

A further area of difficulty in establishing validity is that Exner cites extensive validity studies throughout his three volumes, but many of these studies were not done using his Comprehensive System. Comparability between the different studies and systems is frequently assumed or at least implied. However, often these studies were performed at a time when norms were inadequate, interscorer reliability was questionable, and little concern was given to the possible confounding effects of age, intellectual level, education, and verbal aptitude. The development of the Comprehensive System itself was largely motivated by the deficiencies (and strengths) inherent in each of the earlier systems. More recently, a greater proportion of studies have used the Comprehensive System, which has helped to reduce the comparability problem. Eventually, these newer studies based on the Comprehensive System will help clarify Rorschach validity without the possible contaminating effects of previous work that used other systems.

The previous overview of Rorschach reliability and validity suggests a number of conclusions. Interscorer and test-retest reliabilities for the Comprehensive System have generally been supported, although there are a number of variables with unknown test-retest reliability. The overall validity of the Rorschach has been found to be moderate (.30–.50). Current reviews are beginning to clarify which of the many variables are the most, versus the least, valid (Mihura, 2008). For example, the Perceptual Thinking Index and Prognostic Rating Scale have been found to predict relevant external behaviors. In contrast, the Depression Index has clearly not been found to be effective with adolescents and children and is only minimally effective with adults. Those variables that have not been found to be valid should be deleted from the Comprehensive System.

ASSETS AND LIMITATIONS

As mentioned, the Rorschach has been surrounded by controversy. Often, battle lines have been polarized into either "clinical loyalists" or "academic iconoclasts" (Parker, 1983). Despite thousands of research studies, these positions have changed only minimally over the past 60 years. Masling (2006) has suggested that the controversial status of the Rorschach may be largely the result of researcher bias in selectively processing the voluminous research. It is hoped that the Comprehensive System, along with reviews such as G. Meyer and Archer (2001) and Mihura (2008), will eventually represent a middle ground that will satisfy hard-nosed empiricists and address areas relevant to clinicians.

Part of the reason the Rorschach has continued to have such high popularity is the number of attractive features associated with it. Perhaps part of its allure is the mystery it frequently invokes. How could something as seemingly simple as 10 inkblots reveal inner aspects of a person's personality? Metaphors such as "X rays of the mind" have certainly served to enhance its mystery and power. Often a Rorschach protocol is perceived as something like a deep well into which a skilled clinician can dip repeatedly, continually coming up with rich and valuable information. The practitioner is framed as a seer and an artist rather than a technician. Indeed, there are many anecdotes in which highly trained Rorschach experts have provided in-depth, nuanced descriptions of a wide range of client characteristics.

One frequently noted asset is that the Rorschach is considered to be excellent at bypassing a person's conscious resistance; instead, it assesses a person's underlying, unconscious structure of personality. This asset might be particularly important if a person appears to have an adequate surface level of adjustment yet the clinician suspects there may be some underlying pathology. In contrast, a structured test, such as the MMPI, may have difficulty assessing these more hidden levels of pathology. It is precisely the difficulty in organizing the ambiguous Rorschach stimuli that is likely to bring out these latent levels of pathology. There is some support for this view in that persons with borderline psychopathology have relatively normal performance on structured tests. In contrast, they tend to show clear indications of thought disorder on the far less structured Rorschach (Edell, 1987). Similarly, a relatively hidden trait such as alexithymia has been found in psychosomatic patients based on their Rorschach responses (Acklin & Bernat, 1987). G. Frank (1990) reviewed the existing literature and found that the Rorschach was sensitive to underlying schizophrenic processes even before their clinical expression.

A related asset is the Rorschach's purported high resistance to faking. It is argued that, because the true meanings of the Rorschach responses are unknown, the subject cannot easily invent faked responses. Some proponents have even stated that it is virtually impossible to fake a Rorschach. Like many other statements about the Rorschach, this one has become quite controversial. Exner (1993, 2003) has presented material, from a theoretical and empirical perspective, suggesting that persons developing a Rorschach response go through a series of six stages, one of which is censorship. Subjects seem to come up with far more responses than they present to the examiner, and they select the ones they feel are most appropriate to reveal. Subjects who feel emotionally close to the examiner tend to provide more responses and conceal less (Leura & Exner, 1978). This finding raises the possibility that they might also have enough control over their responses to effectively fake a protocol. Thus, responses might depend to a certain extent on social desirability, perceptual accuracy, the context of the assessment, and personal needs.

Despite the possibility of censorship, which might potentially lead to undetected faking, Exner and Wylie (1975) have reported that only 1 student in 12 could simulate a schizophrenic profile, even though the students were familiar with protocols from actual schizophrenics. Specifically, malingerers were likely to have longer free associations (presumably because they were censoring and elaborating on their responses), relatively accurate perceptions, and highly dramatic and idiosyncratic responses (i.e., "That's too awful to look at"). Similarly, Frueh and Kinder (1994) found that persons who were malingering with posttraumatic stress disorder provided responses that were overly dramatic, relatively unrestrained, and indicative of an exaggerated sense of impaired reality testing. Finally, Grossman, Wasyliw, Benn, and Gyoerkoe (2001) noted that sex offenders who minimized psychopathology on the MMPI-2 still had Rorschach protocols that indicated psychopathology.

In contrast to this research, Albert, Fox, and Kahn (1980) found that Rorschach experts did poorly when requested to blindly classify protocols from normals who were requested to fake paranoid schizophrenia, normals taking a standard administration, and diagnosed paranoid schizophrenics. Computer analyses of the same protocols were likewise unsuccessful in effectively detecting faking (M. W. Kahn, Fox, & Rhode, 1988). Although this finding clearly challenges the unfakability of the Rorschach, the Albert et al. and Kahn et al. studies did not simulate the manner in which the Rorschach is likely to be used in clinical practice. Typically, practitioners have knowledge regarding the history of the person, context of the assessment, and behavioral observations, all of which potentially sensitize them to the possibility that a protocol might be faked. Consistent with this was the Frueh and Kinder study, which found that relevant behavioral observations were at least as important in detecting malingering as the actual scored protocols.

One clear asset of the Rorschach is its ease of administration. The cards can be easily handled, and the total administration time (including inquiry) is typically 50 minutes (Ball, Archer, & Imhof, 1994). In contrast to the relative ease of administration, scoring and interpretation are often quite complicated and time-consuming. Clinicians report that scoring usually takes 45 minutes and interpretation requires 50 minutes more (Ball et al., 1994). This means that, collectively, the entire procedure takes nearly 2.5 hours. However, computer-assisted scoring and interpretation would be expected to reduce significantly the time for both scoring and interpretation.

Besides the advantages associated with the Rorschach, it has a number of limitations. Although both reliability and validity have generally reached adequate levels, validity is often quite variable across different scoring categories and formulas; some have quite good validity whereas others are moderate, controversial, or even nonexistent (see Mihura, 2008). It is usually difficult for the average user to appreciate and take into account the disparate levels of validity when actually making his or her interpretations.

Because the Rorschach is one of the most complex psychological tests in current use, error can potentially be introduced from many different directions, including censorship by the subject, scoring errors (particularly for infrequently used scorings), poor handling of the subtleties of interpretation, incorrect incorporation of the implications of age or education, or possible examiner bias (illusory correlation, primacy effects, etc.). One temptation is to reduce the complexity of the data by using a single-sign approach rather than viewing each sign in the context of the overall configuration. Rorschach "elevations" are often subject to a number of possible interpretive hypotheses, so a single-sign approach is particularly open to error. Thus, interpretations must be continually checked and rechecked against the overall Rorschach configuration, additional test data, and the patient's history.

The complexity of the Rorschach also requires that potential users undergo extensive training. Each new scoring category and index that is introduced may add to this problem. In the past, graduate schools would sometimes provide a full-semester course on the Rorschach. Some authors, feeling that this is insufficient, have stated that the optimum amount of time is two full-semester courses devoted exclusively to the Rorschach (Hilsenroth & Handler, 1995), a curriculum that is currently difficult for many programs to justify for two reasons. First, many other tests are both more time efficient and are believed to have superior psychometric properties. Second, the past 25 years have brought a significant increase in the roles and skills required of graduate students, including skills in the area of assessment (neuropsychology, behavioral assessment) as well as in other areas of clinical practice (family therapy, rehabilitation, new modes of intervention, treatment of chronic pain, etc.).

The Rorschach has often been considered to have limited use with children, particularly those under the age of 14 years (Klein, 1986). Reliabilities have been found to be adequate for short-term assessments but clearly inadequate over a long-term basis. Thus, for purposes such as child custody decisions, where longer-term predictions are required, the Rorschach would be quite limited. Any use of the Rorschach for children should make clear that descriptions are only for the short term.

A final consideration, which has implications for both research and practice, is that the large number of variables is likely to produce spurious random significance (Karson, 2005). Wechsler subtest interpretation has attempted to correct for this possibility by carefully calculating the significance of subtest differences, including correction factors for the number and reliabilities of variables considered (see Chapter 5). In contrast, it is difficult to know when the numerous variables considered in the Rorschach might indicate "significance" simply because of random fluctuations of scores (i.e., a .05 level of significance would mean that "significance" would happen by chance in 1 of 20 variables considered). Rorschach interpreters must, therefore, take extra caution with their interpretations.

In summary, the Rorschach is difficult to evaluate because of its complexity, its frequent controversy, and considerable variability related to the validity of its variables. The voluminous research associated with the Rorschach is often both an asset and a limitation. Sorting through the maze of sometimes contradictory findings is difficult. Directing this wealth of research toward a clear understanding of the interpretive meanings associated with certain patterns of scores is especially difficult. The specific assets of the Rorschach are potential wealth of information, simplicity of handling, ability to bypass conscious resistance, and possible resistance to faking. Significant weaknesses are moderate and sometimes quite variable reliabilities and validities, time required for scoring and interpretation, limited use with children, extensive time required for training, and possible introduction of error, especially spurious random significance as a result of the large number of areas considered.

USE WITH DIVERSE GROUPS

It has been argued that since the Rorschach is a nonverbal, performance-based measure, it is relatively culture free and therefore ideally suited to assessing ethnic and cross-national populations (Allen & Dana, 2004; Dana 2005). There is some support for this argument. Specifically, G. Meyer (2001) and Meyer, Erdberg, and Shaffer (2007) found that there was no evidence for the differential validity of the Rorschach among various ethnic groups. Similarly, Presley, Smith, Hilsenroth, and Exner (2001) compared 23 core scores for African Americans with a matched group of European Americans and found that only 1 score was significantly different. Finally, G. Meyer et al. (2007) found that there were few major differences among an international set of norms on adults derived from 17 different countries. In contrast, he noted that there was far more variability among children's and adolescent's scores. As a result, he discouraged clinicians from making interpretations of child and adolescent psychopathology.

These findings indicate that clinicians working in cross-national settings should use the international norms published by G. Meyer et al. (2007). In addition, any interpretations should also take into account the cultural context. For example, cultures give different value to introversion versus extroversion. Thus, interpretations should take this into account. In addition, the symbolical value related to qualitative interpretations should be particularly sensitive to various cultural meanings. The client's relative degree of acculturation should also be considered. Finally, it is probably premature to use the Rorschach with cross-national child and adolescent populations until the reasons for the wide differences in scores are better understood.

FUTURE DIRECTIONS

The Rorschach is poised at a potentially important turning point. First, both sides of the most recent intensification of the controversy have had more than a decade to adapt to and investigate various challenges. Second, Exner's death has opened up the possibility of making significant changes. As a result, these areas for change have been considered (Groth-Marnat, 2008):

- Deleting/amalgamating scoring categories based on relative validity, interrater agreement, and clinical utility
- Developing an abbreviated version
- Computerized administration and scoring
- Using international norms (G. Meyer et al., 2007)
- Renaming categories
- Providing more control over number of responses (16–24 responses; G. Meyer, 2007)
- Including a band of error (like Wechsler intelligence scales; G. Meyer, 2007)
- Developing a user-friendly (graphical) profile (Groth-Marnat, in press; G. Meyer, 2007)

One of the most crucial steps would be to develop consensus on those categories that are best validated compared to those that are questionable. To this end, Mihura (2008) reviewed 171 articles that had a total of 2,159 findings investigating the construct validity of the Comprehensive System. The various categories were rated as having "good support," "some support," or "limited, mixed, or absence of evidence." These ratings are included in the relevant categories throughout this chapter. It is quite possible that in the next edition of this book, the categories with minimal support, and possibly even some of those with moderate support, will have been deleted from the Comprehensive System.

Most of the scoring categories have good to excellent interrater agreement. Those with moderate to low interrater reliability include Texture Form (.54), Color' Form (.62), Form Quality+ (.66), Color' (.71), Fictional Animal detail (.72), and Incongruous Combination (.74; G. Meyer et al., 2002). Variables with low (under .70) test-retest reliability (1-year duration) include Inanimate Movement (.26), Diffuse Shading (.31), Pure Color (.56), Color Form (.58), Blends (.62), and Experienced Stimulation (.64; Exner, 2003). It is, however, arguable that some of these categories (i.e., inanimate movement, experienced stimulation) would, as Exner has pointed out, be expected to have low test-retest reliability because they are changeable characteristics of the person.

Research may result in reducing the quite large number of categories. Only those categories that are based on strong evidence, are essential for interpretation, have good clinical utility, have good reliability, and are easy to score might be retained. This eventual "leaner, meaner" version would be quite likely to be highly valid, easier to learn, and far more user-friendly than the current version.

ADMINISTRATION

Examiners should standardize their administration procedures as much as possible. This is particularly important because research has consistently indicated that it is relatively easy to influence a subject's responses. For example, saying the word *good* after each response can increase the overall number of responses on the Rorschach by as much as 50% (Hersen & Greaves, 1971). Similarly, examiners who were told that more experienced examiners elicited a greater proportion of human than animal responses actually produced this pattern from examinees, even though the examiners believed they were providing a standard administration (Exner, Leura, & George, 1976). These findings are consistent with the view that subjects are particularly responsive to subtle influences when attempting to create clarity in an ambiguous situation such as projective testing. However, if the fluctuations in administration style are minor, they are unlikely to significantly influence a subject's responses. In general, examiners should minimize the variations in their administration procedures as much as possible. The following sequence of steps is derived from Exner (2003).

Step 1: Introducing the Respondent to the Technique

One of the most important goals an examiner must initially achieve is to allow the examinee to feel relatively comfortable with the testing procedure. Achieving this goal is complicated by the fact that tests in most cultures are associated with anxiety. Although in some cases, an increase in anxiety may provide some information that cannot be obtained when the subject is relaxed, anxiety is usually regarded as a hindrance. Typically, anxiety interferes with a person's perceptions and with the free flow of fantasy, both of which are essential for adequate Rorschach responses. Thus, subjects should be as relaxed as possible. Their relaxation can be enhanced by giving a clear introduction to the testing procedure, obtaining personal history, answering questions, and generally avoiding any behavior that might increase the subjects' anxiety. In describing the test, examiners should emphasize relatively neutral words such as *inkblot*, *interests*, or *imagination* rather than potentially anxiety-provoking words such as intelligence or *ambiguous*.

For the most part, any specific information regarding what subjects should do or say is to be avoided. The test situation is designed to be ambiguous, and examiners should avoid any statements that might influence the responses. If subjects push for more detailed information about what they should do or what their responses may mean, they should be told that additional questions can be answered after the test is completed.

Step 2: Giving the Testing Instructions

Although some Rorschach systematizers recommend that the subject tell the examiner "everything you see" (S. J. Beck, 1961), the Comprehensive System attempts to keep the task as ambiguous as possible. Thus, Exner (2003) recommends that the examiner hand the subject the first card and ask, "What might this be?"

Commentary on or discussion of the cards by the examiner should be avoided as much as possible. At times, it might be acceptable to briefly describe how the designs were made, or, if questioned regarding what one is supposed to see, the examiner might state, "People see all sorts of things in the blots." Comments from the examiner that indicate the quantity or type of response, or whether the subject can turn the cards, should be strictly avoided. If the subject asks specific questions, such as the type of responses he or she is supposed to give or whether he or she can turn the cards, the examiner might reply that it is up to him or her to decide.

The main objective is to give the subject maximum freedom to respond to the stimuli in his or her own manner. To enhance this, Exner (2003) strongly recommends that the subject and the examiner not be seated face to face but rather side by side, to decrease the possible influence of the examiner's nonverbal behavior. The overall instructions and testing situation should be designed both to keep the task as ambiguous as possible and to keep examiner influence to a minimum. Note that the examinee should be encouraged actually to hold the cards.

Step 3: The Response (Association) Phase

Throughout the testing procedure, the basic conditions of step 2 should be adhered to as closely as possible. However, specific situations often arise as subjects are free-associating to the Rorschach designs. If a subject requests specifics on how to respond or asks the examiner for encouragement or approval, examiners should consistently reply that the subject can respond however he or she likes. The idea that there are no right or wrong answers might sometimes be mentioned.

The examiner should time the interval that begins when subjects first see the card and ends when they make their initial response, as well as the total time they spend with each card. These measurements can be helpful in revealing the general approach to the card and the possible difficulties in coming up with responses. Cards II, III, and V are generally considered relatively easy to respond to and, as a result usually have shorter reaction times. In contrast, Cards VI, IX, and X typically produce the longest reaction times. Because overt timing of subjects' responses is likely to produce anxiety, any recording should be done as inconspicuously as possible. It is recommended that, rather than using a stopwatch, the examiner glance at a watch or clock and record the minute and second positions for the initial presentation, the first response, and the point at which the subject hands the card back to the examiner.

The average number of responses is 22.32 (average range = 17 to 27). Validity can be compromised with a low number of responses (under 14) and may be questionable with a high number of responses (more than 42). Exner (2003) has built in some safeguards to protect against unusually short or extremely long protocols. A client who produces an extremely brief protocol (fewer than 14 responses) should be immediately retested and provided with a clearer request to provide more responses (Exner, 2003). If a client provides more than 5 responses to the first inkblot, the examiner should remove the inkblot. On all subsequent inkblots, the same procedure should be used whenever the client provides 5 or more responses. However, if fewer than 5 responses to the first inkblot are given, no other limits on either the first inkblot or any later inkblots should be provided.

Exner (2003) stresses that all responses must be recorded verbatim. To simplify this process, most clinicians develop a series of abbreviations. A set of abbreviations used throughout all the Rorschach systems consists of the symbols ($\vee$, $<$, $\wedge$, $>$) in which the peak indicates the angle of the card. It is also important to note any odd or unusual responses to the cards, such as an apparent increase in anxiety, wandering of attention, or acting-out on any of the percepts.

Step 4: Inquiry

The inquiry should begin after all 10 cards have been administered. Its purpose is to collect the additional information required for an accurate scoring of the responses. It is intended to clarify the responses that have already been given, not to obtain new responses. The inquiry should not end until this goal has been accomplished. Exner (2003) recommends that the instructions for the inquiry closely approximate these ones:

> Now we are going to go back through the cards again. It won't take very long. I want to see the thing that you said you saw and make sure that I see them like you do. We'll do them one at a time. I'll read what you said and then I want you to show me where it is in the blot and then tell me what there is there that makes it look like that to you, so that I can see it too, just like you did. Is that clear?

Following closely the general theme of the overall administration, the inquiry should not influence the subject's responses. Thus, any questions should be as nondirective as possible. The examiner should begin by merely repeating what the subject has said and then waiting. Usually the subject begins to clarify his or her response. If this information is insufficient to clarify how to score the response, the examiner might become slightly more directive by asking "What about it made it look like a [percept]?" The examiner should *not* ask "Is it mainly the shape?" or "How important was the color?" These questions are far too directive and are worded in a way that can exert influence on the subject's descriptions of his or her responses. The examiner should consistently avoid leading the subject or indicating how he or she should respond. Particular skill is required when clarifying a determinant that has been unclearly articulated but merely implied.

The outcome of a well-conducted inquiry is the collection of information sufficient to decide on scoring for location and determinants. If, on the location, information based on the subject's verbal response is insufficient, the examiner should have the subject point to the percept. An additional feature of the inquiry is to test the subject's awareness of his or her responses. For example, does a strange percept represent coherent creativity, or does it reflect a lack of contact with the environment, with the subject perhaps having no awareness of the strangeness of his or her responses? The overall approach of the inquiry is to word questions in such a way as to be flexible without being too directive.

SCORING

The next step following administration is to code the different categories and calculate the different quantitative formulas in the structural summary. There is general agreement throughout the different Rorschach systems that these categories include location, determinants, content, and popularity. The Comprehensive System also includes 15 special scores for responses such as unusual verbalizations and aggressive movement. After these have been coded and tallied, a series of quantitative summaries, including 6 Special Indices, are created based on reorganizations of, and comparisons among, the scores on the different categories.

The subsections that follow merely list, outline, and define the scoring categories and quantitative summaries. To achieve accurate scoring, it would be necessary to consult Exner's scoring criteria (2003) or to use his workbook (Exner, 2001, *A Rorschach Workbook for the Comprehensive System*, 5th ed.), which includes specific scoring criteria, tables, charts, and diagrams. The inclusion of specific scoring criteria is beyond the scope of this chapter. The focus here is on providing a key to interpretation that is concise, accountable, and clearly organized. The definitions and the accompanying tables serve to outline and briefly define the primary Rorschach factors.

Location

The *location* of the responses refers to the area of the inkblot that is used (Table 10.1). This can vary from the use of the entire blot (whole response) to the use of an unusual detail (Dd). Unusual details are defined as location responses made by less than 5% of subjects. Exner also specifies coding for Developmental Quality, which is determined by evaluating each location score in relation to its degree of integration. Table 10.2 presents the criteria used for scoring the respective Developmental Quality codes. Thus, each location response is given both a designation for the specific area of the blot and a symbol to indicate the quality of that response.

Determinants

Determinants refer to the style or characteristic of the blot to which the examinee responds, such as its shape, color, or texture (Table 10.3). The determinants also receive a scoring for their level of form quality (Table 10.4). The form quality scoring refers to how

Table 10.1   Symbols used for coding the location of Rorschach responses

Symbol	Definition	Criterion
W	Whole response	Where the entire blot is used in the response. All portions must be used.
D	Common detail response	A frequently identified area of the blot.
Dd	Unusual detail response	An infrequently identified area of the blot.
S	Space response	A white-space area is used in the response (scored only with another location symbol, as in WS, DS, DdS).

Source: From *The Rorschach: A Comprehensive System, Volume I: Basic Foundations* (4th ed.), by J. E. Exner Jr., 2003, Hoboken, NJ: John Wiley & Sons. Copyright © 2003 by John Exner Jr. Reprinted with permission.

Table 10.2 Symbols and criteria used for developmental quality

Symbol	Definition	Criterion
+	Synthesized response	Two or more objects are described as separate but related. *At least one* of the objects involved must have a specific form demand, or be described in a manner that creates a specific form demand (e.g., a dog walking among some bushes, a man with a funny hat on, an airplane flying through some clouds, the head of a little girl, she has a hair ribbon).
o	Ordinary response	An area of the blot is identified as a single object that has features that create a natural form demand or the *description of the object is such as to create* a specific form demand (e.g., a fir tree, a cat, a totem pole, a maple leaf, a bat, a flag, a man's head).
v/+	Synthesized response	Two or more objects are described as separate but related. *None of the objects* involved have a specific form demand and the articulation does not introduce a form demand for any of the objects (e.g., clouds coming together, some sort of bay with the vegetation around the shore, a rock and some dirt around it).
v	Vague response	An object is reported that has no specific form demand, *and the articulation does not introduce* a specific form demand for the object (e.g., a cloud, the sky, the colors of sunset, some ice).

Source: From *The Rorschach: A Comprehensive System, Volume I: Basic Foundations* (4th ed.), by J. E. Exner Jr., 2003, Hoboken, NJ: John Wiley & Sons. Copyright © 2003 by John Exner Jr. Reprinted with permission.

Table 10.3 Symbols and criteria for determinant coding

Category	Symbol	Criterion
Form	F	*Form answers.* Used for responses based exclusively on the form features of the blot.
Movement	M	*Human movement response.* Used for responses involving the kinesthetic activity of a human or an animal or fictional character in human-like activity.
	FM	*Animal movement response.* Used for responses involving a kinesthetic activity of an animal. The movement perceived must be congruent to the species identified in the content. Animals reported in movement not common to their species should be coded as M.
	m	*Inanimate movement response.* Used for responses involving the movement of inanimate, inorganic, or insensate objects.
Chromatic color	C	*Pure color response.* Used for answers based exclusively on the chromatic color features of the blot. No form is involved.
	CF	*Color-form response.* Used for answers that are formulated primarily because of the chromatic color features of the blot. Form features are used but are of secondary importance.

Continued

Table 10.3   Continued

Category	Symbol	Criterion
	FC	Form-color response. Used for answers that are created mainly because of form features. Chromatic color is used but is of secondary importance.
	Cn	Color naming response. Used when the colors of the blot are identified by name and with the intention of giving a response.
Achromatic color	C	Pure achromatic color response. Used when the response is based exclusively on the grey, black, or white features of the blot, when they are clearly used as color. No form is involved.
	C'F	Achromatic color-form response. Used for responses that are created mainly because of the black, white, or grey features, clearly used as color. Form features are used but are of secondary importance.
	FC'	Form-achromatic color response. Used for answers that are based mainly on the form features. The achromatic features, clearly used as color, are also included but are of secondary importance.
Shading-texture	T	Pure texture response. Used for answers in which the shading components of the blot are translated to represent a tactual phenomenon, with no consideration to the form features.
	TF	Texture-form response. Used for responses in which the shading features of the blot are interpreted as tactual, and form is used secondarily, for purposes of elaboration and/or clarification.
	FT	Form-texture response. Used for responses that are based mainly on the form features. Shading features of the blot are translated as tactual but are of secondary importance.
Shading-dimension	V	Pure vista response. Used for answers in which the shading features are interpreted as depth or dimensionality. No form is involved.
	VF	Vista-form response. Used for responses in which the shading features are interpreted as depth or dimensionality. Form features are included but are of secondary importance.
	FV	Form-vista response. Used for answers that are based mainly on the form features of the blot. Shading features are also interpreted to note depth and/or dimensionality but are of secondary importance to the formulation of the answer.
Shading-diffuse	Y	Pure shading response. Used for responses that are based exclusively on the light-dark features of the blot that are completely formless and do not involve reference to either texture or dimension.
	YF	Shading form response. Used for responses based primarily on the light-dark features of the blot, not involving texture or dimension. Form features are included but are of secondary importance.
	FY	Form-shading response. Used for responses that are based mainly on the form features of the blot. The light-dark features of the figure, not used to articulate texture or dimension, are included as elaboration and/or clarification and are secondary to the use of form.

Table 10.3 Continued

Category	Symbol	Criterion
Form dimension	FD	*Form-based dimensional response.* Used for answers in which the impression of depth, distance, or dimensionality is created by using the elements of size and/or shape of contours. No use of shading is involved in creating this impression.
Pairs and reflections	(2)	*The pair response.* Used for answers in which two identical objects are reported, based on the symmetry of the blot. The objects must be equivalent in all respects, but must not be identified as being reflected or as mirror images.
	rF	*Reflection-form response.* Used for answers in which the blot or blot area is reported as a reflection or mirror image because of the symmetry of the blot. The object or content reported has no specific form requirement, as in clouds, landscape, shadows, and so on.
	Fr	*Form-reflection response.* Used for answers in which the blot or blot area is identified as reflected or a mirror image, based on the symmetry of the blot. The substance of the response is based on form features, and the object reported as a specific form demand.

Source: From *The Rorschach: A Comprehensive System, Volume I: Basic Foundations* (4th ed.), by J. E. Exner Jr., 2003, Hoboken, NJ: John Wiley & Sons. Copyright © 2003 by John Exner Jr. Reprinted with permission.

Table 10.4 Symbols and criteria for coding form quality

Symbol	Definition	Criterion
+	Ordinary-elaborated	The unusually detailed articulation of *form* in responses that otherwise would be scored ordinary. It is done in a manner that tends to enrich the quality of the response without sacrificing the appropriateness of the form use. The answer is not necessarily original or creative; but, rather, it stands out by the manner in which form details are used and specified.
o	Ordinary	The common response in which general form features are easily articulated to identify an object. These are easy-to-see answers that have been reported by at least 2% of persons in the Form Quality data pool for *W and D* areas, or by at least 50 persons in the pool who responded to *Dd* areas. There is no unusual enrichment of the answer by elaboration of the form features.
u	Unusual	A low-frequency response in which the basic contours involved are appropriate for the response. These are uncommon answers that are seen quickly and easily by the observer.
−	Minus	The distorted, arbitrary, unrealistic use of form in creating a response. The answer is imposed on the blot structure with total, or near total disregard for the contours of the area used. Often, substantial arbitrary lines or contours will be created where none exist.

Source: From *The Rorschach: A Comprehensive System, Volume I: Basic Foundations* (4th ed.), by J. E. Exner Jr., 2003, Hoboken, NJ: John Wiley & Sons. Copyright © 2003 by John Exner Jr. Reprinted with permission.

accurately the percept relates to the form of the inkblot. For example, an angel on Card I is considered to be an "ordinary" form quality response, which is empirically reflected in the fact that nonpsychiatric populations perceive it far more frequently than psychiatric patients. Initially, examiners should give a percept its appropriate classification regarding its determinants. This should then be followed by scoring the determinant for its relative form quality. Descriptions of the different form qualities are included in Table 10.4; however, for specific empirically derived form quality codings, examiners need to consult Exner's (2003) tables.

One relevant coding that should be added to all movement responses is the extent to which the movement is active versus passive. Active movement would include movements such as "fleeing" or "lifting," whereas more passive movements might include "meditating" or "anchored." Whether a movement is active or passive is designated with either an a (for active) or a p (for passive) superscript. The a and p designations are later scored and used for interpretation in the quantitative summaries (see the Ideation Section topic in the Structural Summary section).

In approximately 20% of all responses, more than one determinant is used to make a single response. These are referred to as *blends* and are designated by indicating the two (or more) determinants and placing a full stop (.) between them. The most important determinant is placed in front of the other determinant(s) and is considered the primary determinant. Less important determinants are placed after the primary one and are referred to as secondary or tertiary (if a third one is present).

A further score related exclusively to form determinants is the degree of Organizational Activity (Z) involved in creating the response. However, Organizational Activity is given only if at least one of these four criteria is present:

1. A W response with DQ codings of +, o, v/+ (Wv responses are not scored for Organizational Activity).
2. The response gives some sort of meaningful integration to two or more areas (either adjacent or nonadjacent).
3. Two or more separate objects are identified in distant (nonadjacent) detail areas, and these objects are described in some meaningful relationship.
4. The white space is given some sort of meaningful integration with other areas of the blot.

Specific converted weightings (ranging between 1 and 6) are given to integrative efforts for different types of responses and are provided in Exner (2003; see Table 8.4). For example, the degree of organization required to integrate a whole response to Card I is considered to be much less (Z would equal only 1.0) than that required to integrate the much more fragmented details of Card X (Z would equal a much greater 6.5).

Content

The scoring of content is based on the type and quantity of specific subjects that examinees perceive in their responses. Each Rorschach system uses different lists of content categories, although they all agree on basic contents such as human, human detail, and animal. Table 10.5 provides a listing of Exner's content categories, with the symbol and criterion for each category.

When two or more content categories occur in the same response, they should both be coded and a comma should be placed between the two (or more) codings. If contents

Table 10.5   Symbols and criteria used for coding content

Category	Symbol	Criterion
Whole human	*H*	For responses involving a whole human form. If the response involves a *real* historical figure, such as Napoleon, Joan of Arc, and so on, the content code *AY* should be added as a secondary code.
Whole human, fictional or mythological	*(H)*	For responses involving a whole human form that is fictional or mythological, such as clowns, fairies, giants, witches, fairy-tale characters, angels, dwarfs, devils, ghosts, science-fiction creatures that are humanoid, human-like monsters, silhouettes of human figures.
Human detail	*Hd*	For responses involving an incomplete human form, such as an arm, head, leg, fingers, feet, the lower part of a person, a person without a head.
Human detail, fictional or mythological	*(Hd)*	For responses involving an incomplete human form that is fictional or mythological, such as the head of the devil, the arm of a witch, the eyes of an angel, parts of humanoid science-fiction creatures, jack-o-lantern, and masks *except* animal masks.
Human experience	*Hx*	Usually coded as a secondary content for answers that clearly involve the attribution of a human emotion or sensory experience to the object(s) in the response, such as *two people who are in love looking at each other, a cat that is very sad, people who are angry at each other, a woman smelling something nasty, a very happy person, a man who is very excited, a person in great pain.* The attribution of the motion or sensory experience must be clear and unequivocal. Answers such as *people at a party, an angry-looking face, a mean-looking person, two people who look tired* are not coded *Hx* as the attribution is equivocal. *Hx* is scored as a primary content for formless *M* responses that involve the emotion or sensory experience such as love, hate, depression, happiness, sound, smell, fear, and so on. These answers will also include the use of AB as a special score.
Whole animal	*A*	For responses involving a whole animal form.
Whole animal, fictional or mythological	*(A)*	For responses involving a whole animal that is fictional or mythological, such as a unicorn, dragon, magic frog, flying horse, Black Beauty, Jonathan Livingston Seagull.
Animal detail	*Ad*	For responses involving an incomplete animal form, such as the hoof of a horse, claw of a lobster, head of a dog, animal skin.
Animal detail, fictional or mythological	*(Ad)*	For responses involving an incomplete animal form that is fictional or mythological, such as the wing of Pegasus, the head of Peter Rabbit, the legs of Pooh Bear, and all animal masks.
Anatomy	*An*	For responses in which the content is skeletal, muscular, or of internal anatomy such as bone structure, skull, rib cage, heart, lungs, stomach, liver, muscle fiber, vertebrae, brain. If the response involves a tissue slide, the content *Art* should be added as secondary.

Continued

Table 10.5   Continued

Category	Symbol	Criterion
Art	*Art*	For responses of paintings, drawings, or illustrations, either abstract or definite, art objects such as statues, jewelry, chandelier, candelabra, crests, badges, seals, and decorations. A feather seen worn as a decoration, often seen on Card VII, also should be coded as Art. In many responses coded for Art a second content will also be coded, such as a painting of two dogs would be *Art, A,* a sculpture of two witches would be *Art, (H),* a caricature of two people bending over would be *Art, H.*
Anthropology	*(Ay)*	For responses that have a specific cultural or historical connotation such as totem, roman helmet, Magna Carta, Santa Maria, Napoleon's hat, Cleopatra's crown, arrowhead, prehistoric axe, an Indian war bonnet.
Blood	*Bl*	For responses of blood, either human or animal.
Botany	*Bt*	For responses involving any plant life such as bushes, flowers, seaweed, trees or parts of plant life, such as leaves, petals, tree trunk, root, bird's nest.
Clothing	*Cg*	For responses involving any article of clothing such as hat, boots, belt, dress, necktie, jacket, trousers, scarf.
Clouds	*Cl*	For responses used specifically for the content cloud. Variations of this category, such as fog or mist, are coded *Na.*
Explosion	*Ex*	For responses involving a blast or explosion, including fireworks.
Fire	*Fi*	For responses of fire or smoke.
Food	*Fd*	For responses used for any edible common for humans, such as fried chicken, ice cream, fried shrimp, vegetables, cotton candy, chewing gum, steak, a filet of fish, or for animals eating a food that is natural for their species, such as a bird eating a worm or insect.
Geography	*Ge*	For responses used for the response of a map, specified or unspecified.
Household	*Hh*	For responses used that include household items, such as bed, carving knife, chair, cooking utensils, cup, garden hose, glass, lamp, lawn chair, plate, rug *(animal skin rug should be coded Ad and Hh entered as a secondary content),* silverware. Some items coded *Hh* will also be coded as *Art,* such as candelabra, chandelier, or artistic pieces such as a centerpiece bowl.
Landscape	*Ls*	For responses that involve landscape, such as mountain, mountain range, hill, island, cave, rocks, desert, swamp, or seascapes, such as coral reef or underwater scene.
Nature	*Na*	For responses used for a broad variety of contents from the natural environment that are not coded as *Bt* or *Ls,* such as sun, moon, planet, sky, water, ocean, lake, river, ice, snow, rain, fog, mist, rainbow, storm, tornado, night, raindrop.
Science	*Sc*	For responses that are associated with, or are the direct or indirect products of science or science fiction, such as airplanes, buildings, bridges, cars, light bulb, microphone, motorcycles, motors, musical instrument, radar station, road, rocket ships, ships, space ships, trains, telescope, TV aerial, weapons, and so on.

Table 10.5   Continued

Category	Symbol	Criterion
Sex	*Sx*	For responses involving sex organs or activity of a sexual nature, such as penis, vagina, buttocks, breasts (except when used to identify the sex of a human figure), testes, menstruation, abortion, intercourse. *Sx* is usually scored as a secondary content. Primary contents are typically *H, Hd*, or *An*.
X-ray	*Xy*	For responses used specifically for the content of x-ray and may include either skeleton or organs. When *Xy* is coded, *An* is *not* included as a secondary code.

Source: From *The Rorschach: A Comprehensive System, Volume I: Basic Foundations* (4th ed.), by J. E. Exner Jr., 2003, Hoboken, NJ: John Wiley & Sons. Copyright © 2003 by John Exner Jr. Reprinted with permission.

occur that are not on the list, they should be designated as idiographic (Id) and the unique name of the content should be written out.

Popular Responses

Rorschach Popular (P) scoring refers to the presence of frequently perceived responses. Although different systems have somewhat varying lists of Populars, Exner (2003) has used, as the cutoff for inclusion as a Popular, an occurrence of at least once in every three protocols from nonpsychiatric populations. Exner's list of Popular responses is detailed in Table 10.6.

Special Scores

The Comprehensive System also includes 15 Special Scoring categories that were developed to take into account unusual characteristics of the response, such as unusual verbalizations or inappropriate logic. These, along with their definitions, are listed in Table 10.7. A weighted sum of the first six categories (WSum6) is also required. The weightings are as follows: Deviant Verbalization (DV) = 1, Deviant Response (DR) = 3, Incongruous Combination (INCOM) = 2, Fabulized Combination (FABCOM) = 4, Inappropriate Logic (ALOG) = 5, and Contamination (CONTAM) = 7. A weighted score is given each time the scoring is given. For example, three occurrences of Deviant Response (DR) would equal a sum weighted score of 9.

In addition to the weighting, scoring according to levels are given for the severity of the first six Special Scores. A Level 1 score is considered to be fairly normal, but a Level 2 score is considered to be a more pathological example of the response.

STRUCTURAL SUMMARY

After the examinee's responses have been coded according to locations, determinants, contents, Populars, and special scorings, they are listed and rearranged into frequency summaries and quantitative formulas. The quantitative formulas comprise various ratios, percentages, and derivations. These formulas reflect the proportions of, and comparisons among, various Rorschach factors. After the quantitative formulas have been calculated,

Table 10.6   Popular responses used in the comprehensive system plus the proportions of each appearing in samples of nonpatient and patient protocols

Card	Location	Criterion	Nonpatient %	Patients %
I	*W*	Bat, with the true apex of the blot being identified as the top portion of the bat, and always involving the whole blot.	48	38
I	*W*	Butterfly, with the true apex of the blot being identified as the top portion of the butterfly, and always involving the whole blot.	40	36
II	*D1*	Animal, specifically identified as bear, dog, elephant, or Iamb. The response is usually the head or upper body, but responses involving the whole animal are also coded *P*.	34	35
III	*D9*	Human figures or representations thereof such as dolls, caricatures, and so on. If *D1* is used as two human figures, *D7* or *Dd31* should not be reported as part of the human figure.	89	70
IV	*W* or *D7*	Human or human-like figure such as giant, monster, science-fiction creature, and so on. Animal figures are not coded as *P*.	53	41
V	*W*	Butterfly, with the true apex of the blot being identified as the top portion of the butterfly, and always involving the whole blot. The whole blot *must* be used.	46	43
V	*W*	Bat, with the true apex of the blot being identified as the top portion of the bat, and always involving the whole blot.	36	38
VI	*W* or *D1*	Animal skin, hide, rug, or pelt. Often, the skin, hide, or pelt will be included in the description of a whole animal, such as a cat or fox, in natural or unnatural form. The decision about whether to code *P* in these responses is based on whether the skin or hide is actually mentioned or clearly implied.	87	35
VII	*D1* or *D9*	Human head or face, specifically identified as female, child, Indian, or with gender not identified. This Popular is usually embedded in answers given to the larger areas, *D1*, *D2*, or *Dd23*. If *D1* is used, the upper segment (*D5*) is typically identified as hair or a feather. If the response includes the entire *D2* or *Dd23* areas, *P* is coded only if the head or face is restricted to the *D9* area.	59	47
VIII	*D1*	Whole animal figure, usually of the canine, feline, or rodent varieties, with the head of the animal adjacent to the *D4* area.	94	91

Table 10.6   Continued

Card	Location	Criterion	Nonpatient %	Patients %
IX	*D3*	Human or human-like figures such as witches, giants, science-fiction creatures, monsters, and so on.	54	24
X	*D1*	Spider with all appendages restricted to the *D1* area.	42	34
X	*D1*	Crab with all appendages restricted to the *D1* area. Other variations of multilegged animals are not *P*.	37	38

Source: From *The Rorschach: A Comprehensive System, Volume I: Basic Foundations* (4th ed.), by J. E. Exner Jr., 2003, Hoboken, NJ: John Wiley & Sons. Copyright © 2003 by John Exner Jr. Reprinted with permission.

Table 10.7   Symbols and descriptions for special scores

Special Score (Symbol)	Description
Deviant Verbalization (DV)*	Verbalizations associated with a response, which are odd and suggest some form of cognitive slippage has occurred, such as through neologisms or redundancies (i.e., "pair of two").
Deviant Response (DR)*	Responses that involve a longer segment of the response than verbalizations, such as through inappropriate phrases or circumstantial responses that are long, rambling, and unrelated to the inkblot.
Incongruous Combination (INCOM)*	Images that have been inappropriately merged into a single object.
Fabulized Combination (FABCOM)*	Implausible relationships between two or more portions of the inkblot.
Contamination (CONTAM)*	Two or more impressions that have been inappropriately fused together.
Inappropriate Logic (ALOG)*	Spontaneously offered justification of the response using strained logic.
Perseveration (PSV)	Providing either an identical or almost identical response two or more times in a row, or seeing the same object repeatedly ("There's that man again").
Abstract Content (AB)	Symbolic representation is given to the content.
Aggressive Movement (AG)	Any movement response that is clearly aggressive.
Cooperative Movement (COP)	Any movement response that is clearly cooperative.
Morbid Content (MOR)	Content is characterized by death or damage, or is designated as being dysphoric.
Good Human Representation (GHR)	Positive representation of humans (i.e., Pure Human coding with +, o, or u Form Quality; see Exner, 2003, Table 9.1).

Continued

Table 10.7   Continued

Special Score (Symbol)	Description
Poor Human Representation	Poor representations of humans (i.e., human responses that are Form Quality; see Exner, 2003, Table 9.1).
Personal (PER)	Reference to personal knowledge or experience is used to justify or clarify a response.
Color Projection (CP)	Identification of an achromatic portion of an inkblot as being colored.

* These Special Scores are rated as either Level 1, indicating a mild to modest level of cognitive slippage, or Level 2, indicating that level of cognitive slippage is moderate to severe.
Source: From *The Rorschach: A Comprehensive System, Volume I: Basic Foundations* (4th ed.), by J. E. Exner Jr., 2003, Hoboken, NJ: John Wiley & Sons. Copyright © 2003 by John Exner Jr. Reprinted with permission.

they become the primary focus on which Rorschach interpretations are made. Exner (2003) has categorized the formulas into a Core section followed by sections for Ideation, Affect, Mediation, Processing, Interpersonal, Self-Perception, and Special Indices (Depression Index, Obsessive Style Index, etc.). These sections provide a convenient way to thematically organize the different interpretations. The descriptions and their sequence closely follow those outlined by Exner (2003). The various scorings, frequencies, and formulas can be conveniently summarized on a commercially available record form that includes a *Structural Summary Blank* as well as a *Constellation Worksheet* for calculating the Special Indices.

Core Section

The Core section includes the frequencies for the total number of responses (R), the total number for each of the determinants, and nine quantitative formulas:

1. **Lambda (L):**

$$\frac{\text{F (number of responses having only Pure F determinants)}}{\text{R} - \text{F (total R minus Pure Form answers)}}$$

   In calculating Lambda, only responses involving form are used (F, M, CF, etc.) and not determinants without form (C, C′, T, etc.).

2. **Experience Balance or Erlebnistypus (EB):** EB is the relationship between human movement responses and the weighted sum of the chromatic color responses. The ratio is expressed as Sum M: the Weighted Sum Color (WSumC). The Weighted Sum Color side of the ratio is calculated according to this formula:

$$\text{WsumC} = (0.5) \times \text{FC} = (1.0) \times \text{CF} = (1.5) \times \text{C}$$

   All human movement responses are included in the formula, regardless of whether they are the major determinant of the response. Color naming responses are not included.

3. **Experience Actual (EA):**

$$\text{Sum of Human Movement} + \text{Weighted Sum Color}$$

4. **Experience Pervasive (EBPer):** Experience Pervasive is calculated by dividing the larger number in the EB ratio by the smaller one. This is done only when a marked difference (style) is evident in the EB ratio. This difference occurs when one of these three criteria are met: (a) the value for EA is 4.0 or greater, (b) the value for Lambda is less than 1.0, and (c) "the value of EA falls between 4.0 and 10.0, one side if the EB must be at least two points greater than the other side. If the value of EA is more than 10.0, one side of the EB must be at least 2.5 points greater than the other" (Exner, 2003, p. 237).

5. **Experience Base (eb):** The Experience Base ratio compares all nonhuman movement determinants (FM + m) with the sum of all the shading and achromatic color determinants. It is summarized by this ratio:

$$\text{Sum FM} + m : \text{Sum } C' + \text{Sum } T + \text{Sum } Y + \text{Sum } V$$

6. **Experienced Stimulation (es):** This calculation merely requires adding together the two sides of the Experience Base ratio:

Sum of All Nonhuman Movement + Sum of All Shading or Achromatic Features

or

$$\text{Sum FM} + m + \text{Sum } C' + \text{Sum } T + \text{Sum } Y + \text{Sum } V$$

7. **The D score (D):** This is determined by first subtracting es from EA (EA + es) and designating whether the resulting number is a plus or minus number. The resulting raw score can then be converted into a standard score by consulting a conversion table provided in Exner (2003; Table 10.4, p. 403)

8. **Adjusted es (Adj es):** All but 1m and 1Y (this also includes FY and YF) are subtracted from es.

9. **Adjusted D score (Adj/D):** This is simply calculated by subtracting Adj es from EA (EA − Adj es). This produces a raw score that is converted to a standard score by using the same conversion table used in calculating the standard score for D score (see Exner, 2003; Table 10.4, p. 403).

Ideation Section

This section consists of frequency data for M−, M, number of Level 2 responses, WSum6, and M with no FQ. In addition, there are three formulas:

1. **Active:Passive Ratio (a:p):** This is calculated by adding the total number of active movement responses and comparing it with the total number of passive movement responses:

$$M^a + FM^a + m^a : M^p . FM^p + m^p$$

2. **M Active:Passive Ratio ($M^a:M^p$):** In contrast to the previous active:passive ratio, this ratio refers only to active or passive responses relating to human movement and is calculated by simply inserting the total number of active human movements on the left side of the ratio and the total number of passive human movements on the right side.

3. **The Intellectualization Index:** This is calculated by multiplying the total number of Abstract (AB) responses by 2, and adding the sum of Art and Ay responses according to this formula:

$$2AB + (Art + Ay)$$

Affect Section

Rorschach indicators of affect include frequency of Pure C, S, and CP as well as three quantitative formulas:

1. **Form-Color Ratio [FC:(CF + C)]:** This ratio indicates the total number of form-dominated chromatic color responses, as compared with the absolute number of color-dominant chromatic responses. To calculate this formula, each of the chromatic color determinants is weighted equally as 1. Cn determinants are also included on the left side of the ratio because they are considered color-dominant responses.
2. **Constriction Ratio (Sum C':WSumC):** This is comprised of the total number of C' determinants (Sum C') on the left side of the ration contrasted with the sum of chromatic color (WSumC) on the right side.
3. **Affective Ratio (Afr):** The Affective ratio is composed of the total number of responses to the last three cards, compared with those given to the first seven cards, or:

$$\frac{\text{Number of responses to Cards VIII + IX + X}}{\text{Number of responses to Cards I + II + III + IV + V + VI + VII}}$$

4. **Complexity Ratio (Blends:R):** This compares the total number of blend responses (entered on the left side of the ratio) with the total number of responses (R).

Mediation Section

The Mediation section includes the total number of Popular responses and the total number of S– responses along with these five percentages:

1. **Form Appropriate Extended (XA + %):**

$$\frac{\text{Sum of responses that have an FQ coding of +, o, or u}}{R}$$

2. **Form Appropriate—Common Areas (WDA%):**

$$\frac{\text{Sum of W + D responses with an FQ coding of +, o, or u}}{\text{Sum of W + D}}$$

3. **Distorted Form Quality (X – %):**

$$\frac{\text{Sum FQ–}}{R}$$

4. **Conventional Form (F + %):**

$$\frac{\text{Sum FQx + and O}}{R}$$

5. **Unusual Form (Xu%):** Unusual Form is a measure of the extent to which the contours of the inkblots have been used appropriately but unconventionally.

Processing Section

This section includes three simple sets of frequency data—for Zf (total number of times an Organizational Activity response has occurred), PSV (Perseverations), DQ+ (Developmental Quality+), and DQv (Developmental Quality)—along with the following three ratios:

1. **Economy Index (W:D:Dd):** This index is developed by simply listing the total number of whole (W) responses on the left, the total number of D responses in the middle, and the total number of Dd responses on the right.
2. **Aspirational Ratio (W:M):** The ratio of W to M represents a comparison between the total number of whole responses (placed on the left side of the ratio) and the total number of human movement responses (placed on the right side).
3. **Processing Efficiency (Zd):** Processing Efficiency is a difference score. It is necessary to estimate what the Organizational Activity scores should be (Zest) by first summing the total number of times an Organizational Activity response occurred in a protocol (without taking into account the weightings). Next, the sum of all the weighted scores for Organizational Activity (ZSum) is calculated. Finally, Zest is subtracted from ZSum:

$$\text{Zsum} - \text{Zest}$$

This allows an estimate of how much more Organizational Activity was actually used compared to how much would have been expected to be used, based simply on the total number of Organizational Activity occurrences (without their weightings).

Interpersonal Section

This section is composed of these sets of frequency calculations: sum of Cooperative Movements (COP), Aggressive Movements (AG), primary and secondary Food contents (Fd), sum of Pure H answers, number of PER Special Scores, ratio of GHR:PHR Special Scores, Sum T (transcribed from the Core section), and a:p (transcribed from the Ideation section). The interpersonal section also uses these two formulas:

1. **Interpersonal Interest (Human Content) H:** The sum of responses that are Pure H is entered on the left side, and the sum of human interest contents—Hd and (Hd)—is entered on the right side.

$$H + (H) + Hd + (Hd)$$

2. **Isolation Index (Isolate/R):** Calculation of this index requires noting the total number of content responses for Botany (Bt), Clouds (Cl), Geography (Ge), Landscape (Ls),

and Nature (Na). Contents for Clouds (Cl) and Nature (Na) are then multiplied by 2 and added to the number of responses for the rest of the contents. This sum is then divided by the total number of responses:

$$\frac{Bt + 2Cl + Ge + Ls + 2NA}{R}$$

Self-Perception Section

This section includes five frequency tallies for:

1. Sum of Form-reflection and reflection-Form responses (Fr + rF).
2. Total number of Form Dimension (FD) responses.
3. Total number of responses that have morbid content (MOR).
4. Sum of all responses that have content related to Anatomy (An) or X ray (Xy; primary or secondary).
5. Sum of V (transcribed from Core section).
6. A sixth entry comprises the ratio composed of the number of Pure H contents and the sum of (H) + Hd + (Hd) on the right:

$$H: (H) + Hd + (Hd)$$

The final component of this subsection is a ratio related to the number of pair responses: Egocentricity Index [3r + (2)/R]: This index gives three times the weighting to reflection responses (r) compared to pair responses (2) and compares these to the total number of responses (R):

$$\frac{3 \times (Fr + rF) + Sum(2)}{R}$$

Special Indices

Exner (1993) has developed six Special Indices:

1. Perceptual Thinking Index (PTI).
2. Depression Index (DEPI).
3. Coping Deficit Index (CDI).
4. Suicide Constellation (S-CON).
5. Hypervigilance Index (HVI).
6. Obsessive Style Index (OBS).

The procedure for calculating these indices is more complex than for the other formulas and is not covered in this section. However, scoring criteria and cutoff scores can be found in Exner (2003) and on the commercially available record form under a section designated as the *Constellations Worksheet*. Summaries of interpretive hypotheses for these indices are included in the next section of this chapter.

INTERPRETATION

The following description of interpretive information is meant to serve as a reference guide to alert Rorschach interpreters to a potentially wide range of possible interpretive hypotheses. Although the format is as concise as possible, interpreters should be aware of the tremendous variety inherent in most Rorschach data. Effective interpreters should also have this variety reflected in the wide number of possible interpretive hypotheses they generate. A mere labeling or simplistic "sign" approach should be avoided. Rather, clinicians must begin and end by continually being aware of the total overall configuration of the data. For example, the same number of C responses in two protocols can easily have quite different meanings, depending on the implications from, and interactions with, other aspects of the Rorschach data.

The typical sequence for Rorschach interpretation should follow the general conceptual model for testing developed by Maloney and Ward (1976) and discussed in Chapter 1 (see Figure 1.1). The model requires that clinicians initially take a propositional stance toward the protocol (phase 2). The purpose of this stage is to develop as many tentative hypotheses as possible, based on the quantitative data, verbalizations, and client history. The number and accuracy of these hypotheses depend on the individual richness of the data as well as on the individual skill and creativity of the clinician. The final stage is the integration of the hypotheses into a meaningful and accurate description of the person (phase 4). This involves rejecting, modifying, or confirming previously developed hypotheses (phase 3). When this has been accomplished, clinicians can integrate the Rorschach interpretations into the overall report itself (phases 5, 6, and 7).

In the description of different interpretive hypotheses, continual reference is made to "high" and "low" scores. These relative weightings are based on extensive adult normative data that have been accumulated on the Rorschach. For comparisons of scores on individual protocols with normative ratings, clinicians can refer to Appendixes E and F on pages 623–628, which provides means, standard deviations, and other relevant descriptive statistics for the different Rorschach factors and quantitative formulas (derived from Exner & Erdberg, 2005). Note that normative scores (means and standard deviations), derived from Exner and Erdberg (2005), have been included in each of the interpretive sections for quick reference. The relative validity of various categories is indicated and is based on Mihura (2008). It should be noted that the validity ratings were not done for the individual scores but were provided exclusively for the ratios, percentages, and derivations.

Clinicians interested in child and adolescent assessment (ages 6 to 16 years) can consult the much more extensive age-based norms for children found in Exner (2003) and Exner and Weiner (1995). Cross-national interpretations should refer to the international normative reference group published by G. Meyer et al. (2007).

The sequence of presenting interpretive information is first organized around specific scoring categories (Location, Determinants, Contents, Special Scorings). These are followed by scorings according to the sections in the Structural summary. The scorings for the Structural Summary begin with the Core section and then proceed to the sections for Ideation, Affect, Mediation, Processing, Interpersonal, Self-Perception, and Special Indices. These later groupings should provide a conceptually consistent means of organizing relevant interpretive material around functional domains, thereby enabling the different interpretations to be more easily integrated into the psychological report. For example, if a practitioner is interested in understanding issues related to interpersonal relationships, he or she can note the Rorschach data relevant to this area of functioning. Similarly, information related to dealing with affect can be noted in the section on affect. These interpretations can then be compared, contrasted, and modified with other assessment material on these dimensions. Table 10.8 outlines the different interpretive categories in the sequence in which they are presented for interpretation.

It should be noted that the Comprehensive System initially organizes data according to the sequence provided above (and below in the Interpretation section). However, once this

Table 10.8   Scoring and interpretative domains for the Comprehensive System

Location
  Whole Response (W)
  Common Detail (D)
  Unusual Detail (Dd)
  Space (S)
  Developmental Quality (DQ)

Determinants
  Form (F)
  Human Movement (M)
  Animal Movement (FM)
  Inanimate Movement (m)
  Color Chromatic (C)
  Color Achromatic (C')
  Shading—Texture (T)
  Shading—Dimension (V)
  Form Dimension (FD)
  Pairs (2) and Reflections (Fr)
  Organizational Activity (Z)

Content
  Human and Human Detail (H, Hd)
  Animal and Animal Detail (A, Ad)
  Anatomy and X Ray (An, Xy)
  Food (Fd)

Popular Responses

Special Scores
  Deviant Verbalizations (DV)
  Deviant Responses (DR)
  Incongruous Combinations (INCOM)
  Fabulized Combination (FABCOM)
  Contamination (CONTAM)
  Inappropriate Logic (ALOG)
  Perseveration (PSV)
  Abstract Content (AB)
  Aggressive Movement (AG)
  Cooperative Movement (COP)
  Morbid (MOR)
  Good Human Representation (GHR)
  Poor Human Representation (PHR)
  Personal (PER)
  Color Projection (CP)

Ratios, Percentages, Derivations

Core Section—frequency data (taken from previous sections includes total number of responses plus each of the frequencies of the determinants) and the following nine formulas:

1. Lambda (L)
2. Experience Balance or Erlebnistypus (EB)
3. Experience Actual (EA)
4. Experience Pervasive (EBPer)
5. Experience Base (eb)
6. Experience Stimulation (ES)
7. D Score (D)
8. Adjusted es (Adj es)
9. Adjusted D score (Adj/D)

Ideation Section—frequency data for M-, M, number of Level 2 responses, WSum6, and M with no FQ. In addition:

1. Active; Passive Ratio (a; p)
2. M Active; Passive Ratio (Ma; Mp)
3. The Intellectualization Index [2AB + (Art + Ay)]

Affect Section—frequency of Pure C, S, and CP and the following three formulas:

1. Form-Color Ratio [(FC; CF +C)]
2. Affective Ratio (Afr)
3. Complexity Index (Blend; R)

Mediation Section—number of Popular responses, the total number of S- responses, and the following percentages:

1. Form Appropriate Extended (XA+%)
2. Form Appropriate-Common Areas (WDA%)
3. Distorted Form (X−%)
4. Conventional Form
5. Unusual Form (Xu%)

Processing Section—frequency data for Organization Activity (Zf), Perseverations (PSV), Developmental Quality+ (DQ+), Developmental Quality-v (DQv), and three ratios:

1. Economy Index (W; D; Dd)
2. Aspirational Ratio (W; M)
3. Processing Efficiency (Zd)

Table 10.8   Continued

Interpersonal Section—frequencies of Cooperative Movements (COP), Aggressive Movements (AG), Food Contents, sum of Pure H, number of Perseverations (PER), ratio of Good Human to Poor Human Representation (GHR:PHR), Sum T, and active:passive (a:p), and the following two formulas:

1. Interpersonal Interest (H) + (H) + Hd + (Hd)
2. Isolation Index Bt + 2Cl + Ge + Ge + Ls + 2NA/R

Self-Perception Section—Sum Form-reflection and reflection-Form response, sum Form Dimension responses, sum morbid content, sum Anatomy, sum X ray, sum V, ratio of Pure H; (H) + Hd + (Hd), and the:

1. Egocentricity Index [3r + (2)/R]s

Special Indices
 Perceptual Thinking Index (PTI)
 Depression Index (DEPI)
 Coping Deficit Index (CDI)
 Suicide Constellation Index (S-CON)
 Hypervigilence Index (HVI)
 Obsessive Style Index (OBS)

data is organized, it is then further organized into these eight clusters (see Exner, 2003; Table 13.2, p. 225):

1. Controls and Stress Tolerance
2. Situation
3. Affective Features
4. Self-Perception
5. Information Processing
6. Mediation
7. Ideation
8. Interpersonal Perception

It is believed that the structure provided in the Interpretation section would be relatively easy to follow and understand since it is organized according to the scoring sequence. The organization based on the scoring sequence should provide clinicians with a means of developing some working knowledge of the Rorschach. Once this information is learned, it should then be an easy next step to organize the data according to the eight clusters just listed for the Comprehensive System. The listing of the various clusters of the Rorschach serves as a de facto Rorschach-based theory of personality in that clinicians can conceptualize cases based on these essential aspects of functioning.

The process of reading through the many interpretations in the remainder of the chapter can potentially be tedious because of the sheer quantity. To deal with the quantity of interpretations, it is recommended that the practitioner initially skim over the different sections and interpretations. Next, he or she might obtain a Rorschach protocol through actually administering and scoring a Rorschach, requesting one from a colleague, or using one from one of Exner's books. The practitioner can then go through each of the different categories and generate hypotheses based on the client's results. The hypotheses can be integrated into a description of the person, based on domains measured by the Rorschach variables. This sequence would optimally make the information relevant and engaging as well as enhance the development of actual clinical skills.

Location

In general, the area of the inkblot to which examinees choose to respond is a reflection of the overall style in which they approach their world. This is especially true for the manner in which they confront uncertainties and ambiguities in their lives. For example, one person might perceive only the most obvious and concrete aspects of a situation, whereas another might avoid important aspects of a stimulus by focusing on small details and neglecting potentially more significant issues. An analysis of Rorschach locations does not provide information regarding why people approach their world in a certain manner; rather, it is limited to a description of their particular style.

Rorschach locations can be divided into usual and unusual features, depending on the area of the inkblot that is used. Frequently used locations, if they are within the normal number and of good quality, usually reflect good ties with reality, intelligence, ambition, good reasoning, and an ability to generalize. Unusual locations involving rarely used areas of the blot are associated with neurotic symptomatology, such as fears, anxiety, and obsessive or compulsive tendencies. An extreme use of unusual features may reflect more serious psychopathology (Exner, 2003).

Whole Response (W)

The whole response is related to the degree to which a person can interact in an efficient and active manner with his or her environment. This is particularly true if the quality and organization of the responses are good. Whereas whole responses occur with the greatest frequency in children from 3 to 4 years of age (Exner & Weiner, 1995), there is a gradual decline in later childhood and adolescence until 30% to 40% of normal adult responses are wholes. The average adult ratio of whole:detail is approximately 1:2 (refer also to interpretation of W:M and W:D:Dd formulas).

High W (M = 9.10, SD = 3.70)

- High intellectual activity, good synthesizing ability, good abstract reasoning.
- Good ties with reality.
- Good problem solving abilities.
- The first two interpretations are dependent on the W responses using a high level of organizing activity (check proportion of W+ responses); the more the person can organize the response, the stronger the above interpretations.
- W occurs with greatest frequency for Cards V, I, IV, and VI, and with lowest frequency for Cards X, IX, III, and VIII; W responses for the latter cards require significantly greater organizational activity.

Low W

- Possible depression or anxiety.
- If the frequency, quality, and complexity are low, more serious levels of maladjustment are indicated, such as intellectual deterioration possibly related to brain damage or mental retardation.

Common Detail (D)

Rorschach (1921/1941) originally conceptualized the D response as reflecting the degree to which a person perceives and reacts to the obvious aspects of a situation. This conceptualization is supported by more recent normative data in which adult nonpsychiatric groups and outpatients gave 62% and 67% of their responses, respectively, as D, whereas inpatient nonschizophrenics and inpatient schizophrenics gave 46% and 47% of their responses, respectively, as D (Exner, 1974). D tends to be most frequent for Card X (Exner, 1993). The proportion of D is lowest in young children and gradually increases with age (Ames,

Metraux, Rodell, & Walker, 1974). Any interpretations relating to D should take into account the fact that a greater number of R is likely to increase the relative proportion of D when compared with other locations (also refer to the W:D:Dd ratio).

High D (M = 12.66, SD = 4.75)

- Overemphasis on concrete, obvious aspects of situations, sacrifices full use of intellectual potential by merely focusing on the safe and obvious rather than probing into the more novel and unusual.
- If D+ is high, an excellent level of functioning and a concern with precision are likely.
- If D is high but the quality of responses is low, a severe level of maladjustment is indicated.

Low D

- High experience of stress (if D is low along with a high Dd).
- Poor perceptual abilities possibly consistent with cerebral impairment.

Unusual Detail (Dd)

The Dd response is considered to represent a retreat from a person's environment by focusing on details rather than either perceiving the whole situation or noticing the more obvious elements of the environment. A clinician would expect the number of Dd responses to comprise approximately 6% of the total R for a normal adult. However, Dd is frequently higher in the protocols of normal children and adolescents. For schizophrenics or severely impaired compulsives, the proportion of Dd can increase to 25% or more (Exner, 1974). When Dd is in good proportion to W and D, a healthy adjustment, in which a person combines initiative with an appropriate ability to withdraw, is reflected.

High Dd (M = 1.60, SD = 2.06)

- Need to pull back from the ambiguities that may be contained in a whole response.
- Represents a person's attempt to narrow perceptions of the environment.
- Focus on the details of a situation in an attempt to reduce anxiety and exert more control over perceptions; consistent with a compulsive style.
- Rigid thought processes since the thought processes may not be flexible enough to take into account the ambiguities and complexities of whole responses.

Space (S)

A high number of S responses (three or more) is associated with negativism, difficulty in handling anger, and oppositional tendencies (Exner, 1993, 2003). If S responses are high (three or more) and occur with poor form quality and/or poor primitive movements, a clinician should consider the presence of anger, hostility, and potential acting out (Exner, 1993). There is good support for interpretations based on this variable but only when the space is a "Primary" space (not connected with other aspects of the blot; Mihura, 2008) (M = 2.37, SD = 1.97).

DQ+ and DQv

Developmental quality scores relate to a person's relative ability to analyze and synthesize information. A high DQ+ (above 9 or 10) is consistent with more intelligent, complex, and sophisticated persons. However, this greater complexity does not necessarily mean that the person is well adjusted or even that his or her cognitions are accurate (see Zd for an index of both efficiency and accuracy). A number of disorders are characterized by quite complex cognitive operations, yet they are not well adjusted. In contrast to DQ+, a higher proportion (three or more) of low Developmental Quality (DQv) responses indicates persons who are immature and less sophisticated (children, neuropsychologically impaired, intellectually disabled; Exner, 1993, 2003) (M = 8.43, SD = 3.07, and M = 0.37, SD = 0.72).

Determinants

Because the majority of research has been done on the determinants, they are frequently seen as the core of the Rorschach data. An analysis of a person's determinant score shows the psychological activity that he or she engaged in while the response was being created. It examines his or her unique styles of perception and thinking, and how these interact with one another. In general, research has isolated specific details of the determinants that could possibly lure the clinician into a rigid and potentially inaccurate "single sign" approach. Again, a Rorschach interpreter should focus on the interaction among a large number of variables to modify, confirm, or reject tentative hypotheses derived from any single determinant score.

Form (F)

The amount of pure F in a protocol has generally been used to indicate the extent to which the person can remove affect from a situation. The presence of form in a response represents a certain degree of respect for the standards of the environment and reflects intact reasoning abilities. It is seen both as related to attention and concentration and as an index of affective control or delay (Exner, 1993, 2003). This is reflected in the fact that inpatients with schizophrenia have a relatively higher percentage of Fu and F− responses than other groups. However, pure F is higher among paranoid schizophrenics than among other types of schizophrenics (Rapaport et al., 1968), reflecting their greater degree of organization and caution. In addition, schizophrenics have increases in pure F following treatment (Exner, 1993), and a higher level of pure F for schizophrenics is associated with a better prognosis (Exner & Murillo, 1977). The presence of a pure F response does not necessarily mean that no conflict is present but rather that the person is able to suspend temporarily the affect associated with a conflict. Conversely, people in emotional turmoil are likely to produce a significantly lower number of pure form responses, reflecting their inability to remove their affect from their experience. (See also interpretations for Lambda and the percentages in the Mediation section: X + %, F + %, X − %, S − %, Xu%.)

High Pure F (M = 7.91, SD = 3.70)

- Defensive, constricted.
- Good ability to deliberately suspend or control affect.
- Pure F increases for persons who have been given some prior knowledge of the purpose of the test or who are requested to respond as quickly as possible.

Low Pure F

- Level of turmoil is likely to be sufficiently high to prevent screening out affective response to a situation.
- Acute schizophrenics have difficulty reducing their level of affect and have a low number of pure F responses (Exner & Murillo, 1973). Also organic disorders, in which there is difficulty controlling impulses, have a low number of pure F responses (Exner, 1974).

Human Movement (M)

Probably more research has been done on the M response than on any other Rorschach variable. Most of this research is consistent in viewing M as reflecting inner fantasies connected to the outside world. More specifically, M represents the bridging of inner resources with reality, or what might be described as "internalization of action" (Exner, 1993, 2003). M is also an inhibitor of outward behavior, even though that inhibition may be only temporary. A high proportion of M responses has been associated with creativity (Dudek, 1968) and introverted thinking (Kunce & Tamkin, 1981), and there is a close relationship between M and daydreaming (Dana, 1968; Page, 1957). Schulman (1953) has shown M's relation to abstract thinking in that a high number of M responses reflects both an active inner process and a delay in expressing behavior. Thus, M can be generally understood as involving deliberate inner experience. In its positive sense, M can indicate good ego functioning, ability to plan, impulse control, and ability to withstand frustration. In a more negative vein, it can suggest an over-developed fantasy life.

While interpreting M, it is important to look carefully at the different components of the response. For example, does the movement involve conflict or cooperation? A high number of aggressive movements has been shown to reflect a person who is generally more aggressive and who typically perceives relationships as characterized by aggressiveness (Exner, 1983). The degree of passivity in the movement is also likely to suggest that the person has more dependent and passive behaviors external to the test situation (Exner & Kazaoka, 1978). Specific interests might be projected into the movement responses, such as the increased number of dance movements perceived in the protocols of physical education and dance students (Kincel & Murray, 1984). The clinician should also consider other data both from within the test and external to it. Further elaboration regarding M, especially as it relates to the person's degree of control of impulses, can be derived by referring to the EB and EA ratios.

High M (M = 4.83, SD = 2.18)

- High intelligence (especially if a high number of M are present).
- High creativity.
- Good abstract reasoning.
- Introverted thinking means of processing information.
- Capacity to delay impulses.
- High investment in fantasy life.
- With a high number M+ responses, good prognosis for psychotherapy.
- With high number of M– responses, poorly developed interpersonal relationships (i.e., high M responses have been found among manic patients).

Low M

- Possible depression, consistent with their having a difficult time using inner resources.
- High impulsivity.
- Dementia.
- Rigidity, difficulty accepting and adjusting to change.
- Low empathy, lack of imagination.
- Poor prognosis for psychotherapy due to rigidity, low empathy, and poorly developed inner life.

Animal Movement (FM)

Whereas human movement responses serve to mediate between the inner and outer environment, animal movement has been considered to reflect more unrestrained emotional impulses in which there is less ego control. The impulses are more urgent, more conscious, and provoked by situations beyond the person's control. These observations are reflected in the higher number of FMs in children (Ames et al., 1971) and the aged (B. Klopfer et al., 1956). The number of FM responses for children (ages 8 to 16) is from 3.0 to 3.5, whereas adults have an average of 4.0 (Exner & Erdberg, 2005). However, minimal evidence has been found to support this category (Mihura, 2008).

High FM (M = 4.04, SD = 1.90)

- Thoughts and feelings are beyond the person's control.
- Unrestrained impulses, difficulty delaying gratification, rarely plan toward long-term goals.
- If high number of aggressive FM responses, possibly assaultive.
- Highly defensive with use of intellectualization, rationalization, regression, and substitution as primary means of reducing anxiety.

Low FM

- Overly inhibited in expressing emotions.
- May deny basic needs (i.e., associated with decreased energy level among children).

Inanimate Movement (m)

Similar to FM, the number of inanimate movement responses also provides an index of the extent to which persons are experiencing drives or life events that are beyond their ability to control. The drives reflected by m threaten people's adjustment in that they are helpless to effectively deal with them (B. Klopfer et al., 1956). This helplessness is usually related to interpersonal activities (Hertz, 1976; B. Klopfer et al., 1956; Z. Piotrowski, 1957, 1960). The average number of m responses for adult nonpatients was 1.6 (SD = 1.34; Exner & Erdberg, 2005). The view that m represents threat from the external world is supported by the observation that sailors at sea produced significantly more m during a severe storm (Shalit, 1965). This is also consistent with the finding that normal subjects exposed to uncontrollable laboratory-induced stress (McCown, Fink, Galina, & Johnson, 1992) and those given amphetamines (W. Perry et al., 1995) had temporary increases in m. Similarly, paratroop trainees had an increase in m just before their first jump (Armbuster, Miller, & Exner, 1974), as did elective-surgery patients just before surgery (Exner, 1993; see also the interpretation of experience base [eb]). In contrast, Piotrowski and Schreiber (1952) found no m scores in the records of successfully treated patients. Thus, a number of studies support the interpretations for this scoring category (Hiller et al., 1999; Mihura, 2008). To gain a more complete understanding of the individual meaning of m, clinicians should investigate the possible resources and the characteristic means of resolving conflict by looking at M, sum C, frequency of D and S, and the accuracy of their perceptions as reflected in F + % and X + %.

High m (M = 1.57, SD = 1.34)

- Marked presence of conflict and tension.
- Perception that they are surrounded by threatening persons or events, feel unable to reconcile themselves with their environment.

Color Chromatic (C, CF, FC, Cn)

The manner in which color is handled reflects the style in which a subject deals with his or her emotions. If color dominates (C, CF, Cn), affect is likely to be poorly controlled and disorganized. In such cases, affect is disruptive and the person could be expected to be emotional, labile, and overreactive. If the responses are more dominated by form (FC), affect will be more delayed, controlled, and organized. For example, it has been demonstrated that subjects who could effectively delay their responses in a problem-solving task had a higher number of FC responses in their protocols, whereas those who had difficulty delaying their responses had more CF and C responses (H. Gill, 1966; Pantle, Ebner, & Hynan, 1994). These researchers also found that a positive correlation exists between individuals having color-dominated responses and measurements of impulsiveness. However, if the number of color-dominated responses is used to determine impulsiveness, the implications of D scores, form quality, number of Y responses, and relative number of color-dominated responses (FC:CF + C) should also be taken into account. Furthermore, the chromatic cards produce a greater frequency of aggressive, passive, and undesirable contents than do the achromatic cards (Crumpton, 1956).

Adult nonpatients have between 1.5 to 2.5 times more form-dominated color than color-dominated responses [FC/(CF + C)]. This finding contrasts with the average patient group, which generally has an equal number of FC to CF + C responses (Exner, 1993). Pure C responses are also predominant in the protocols of very young children, as is color naming (Cn; Ames et al., 1974; Exner, 1986). (See also interpretation of the FC: CF + C formula.)

High C and Cn (M = 0.17, SD = 0.45; high C > 1 and M = 0.00, SD = 0.07)

- Little regard for the adaptiveness of expressions, discharge emotions in an impulsive manner.
- Cognitive abilities have been suspended or possibly overwhelmed by affective impulses (possible aggressiveness and assaultive tendencies especially if combined with an absence of human movement).
- Possibly labile, suggestible, sensitive, and irritable.
- Difficulty delaying responses during problem-solving tasks.
- Color naming: indicates concrete, primitive, poorly conceptualized response to the stimuli ("stimulus bound"); this can reflect severe disorders for adults, such as organic impairment. (Note: Cn is not unusual in the protocols of young children, particularly if intellectually disabled.)
- Low C and CF.
- Low spontaneity, overcontrolled emotions (i.e., depression, psychosomatic patients).
- Possible suicidal tendencies if other indicators are present.

High FC (M = 2.97, SD = 1.78)

- Good integration between controlling emotions and appropriately expressing them (moderate FC).
- Good rapport with others (moderate FC).
- Low level of anxiety, capacity to learn under stress, good prognosis for therapy (can conceptualize emotions and give form to their expression; moderate FC).
- May reflect overcompliance and a dependent personality (extremely high FC).
- Among children, may reflect the effects of overtraining with a corresponding decrease in natural spontaneity.

Low FC

- Poor emotional control, difficulties with interpersonal relationships due to the poor control.
- Possible anxiety states.
- Supports hypothesis of schizophrenia if other indicators of schizophrenia are present (i.e., high F– responses).

Color Achromatic (C', C'F, FC')

Achromatic color responses constitute one of the least researched areas of the Rorschach. However, it has been suggested that C' responses reflect constrained, internal, and painful affects. In other words, there is a dampened emotional expressiveness in which the person is cautious and defensive. Exner (1993) has referred to C' as the psychological equivalent of "biting one's tongue, whereby emotion is internalized and consequently creates some irritation" (p. 386). Thus, it relates not only to painful emotions but also to affective constraint and defensiveness. Most Rorschach systematizers have consistently used C' as an index of depression. In considering the meaning of achromatic color responses, a clinician should look at the relative influence of form. If form is dominant (FC'), there is likely to be definition and organization to the affect, with a stronger ability to delay the behavior. Dominant C' responses suggest the immediate presence of painful emotions. The average number of achromatic color responses for nonpatients is 1.49 (Exner, 2003). In contrast, depressives have an average of 2.16 and .83 for character disorders (Exner, 1993). Despite these findings, minimal research has been found to support interpretations of C' (Mihura, 2008).

High C' (M = 1.60, SD = 1.33)

- Highly constrained and painful emotions (i.e., psychosomatics, obsessive-compulsives, depressives).
- Poor overall adjustment.
- Possible suicidality (with absence of shading responses combined with a large proportion of C' responses).

Shading—Texture (T, TF, FT)

Texture responses represent painful emotional experiences combined with needs for supportive interpersonal relationships (S. J. Beck, 1945, 1968; B. Klopfer et al., 1956). For example, recently divorced or separated subjects averaged 3.57 texture responses per protocol (SD = 1.21) as compared with 1.31 for matched controls (SD = 0.96; Exner & Bryant, 1974). Persons with a high number of texture responses reach out, although they do so in a guarded and cautious manner (Hertz, 1976). If form plays a relatively insignificant role and texture is predominant, subjects tend to feel overwhelmed by painful experiences, which would probably be sufficiently intense to disrupt their ability to adapt. Conversely, if form dominates (FT), not only is the pain likely to be more controlled, but also the need for supportive contact from others would be of primary concern (S. J. Beck, 1968; B. Klopfer et al., 1956). Coan (1956) has suggested that a combination of movement and texture responses relates to inner sensitivity and empathy. If chromatic color and texture occur together, the subjects' behaviors would not only be less mature in seeking affection but also more direct and unconstrained (Exner, 1974). Moderate support has been found for this variable (Mihura, 2008).

Responses in which texture dominates show an increase through childhood, reach a maximum by 15 years of age and gradually subside over the next few years until a form-dominated texture response is most characteristic in late adolescence and adulthood (Ames et al., 1971). Nonpatient populations average 1 texture response per record, whereas psychiatric populations average 2 or more per record (Exner, 2003; Exner & Erdberg, 2005). They usually appear 10 times more frequently on Cards IV and VI than on the other cards (Exner, 1993).

High T or TF (for T only M = 1.01, SD = 0.69)

- Intense needs for affection and dependency
- Oversensitivity in personal relationships, difficulty reconciling the intensity of needs for support with what they can realistically expect.
- Open to environment but approach it with a cautious sensitivity.

Low (absent) T

- Emotional "impoverishment," person has ceased to look for meaningful emotional relationships (i.e., inpatient depressives, psychosomatic patients).
- Constrained expression of affect.

Shading—Dimension (Vista; V, VF, FV)

Rorschach systematizers have generally considered Vista responses, especially pure V, to represent a painful process of self-examination in which the person creates a sense of distance from self to introspect (Exner, 1993). This introspection usually involves depression and a sense of inferiority. However, if the V responses are dominated by form, introspection is still suggested, but the process is unlikely to be emotionally painful. This is in contrast to the negative type of self-examination associated with pure V. Even a single pure V response in a Rorschach protocol can be an important indicator. However, minimal research supports this variable (Mihura, 2008).

In normal populations, V responses occur, on average, 0.35 per record (Exner & Erdberg, 2005). Depressed inpatients average 1.09, and schizophrenics and character-disordered persons average 0.60 and 0.24, respectively (Exner, 1993, 2003). It is extremely rare for V to appear in the protocols of children, but it occurs at about the same rate among adolescents as it does for adults (Exner, 1993; Exner & Weiner, 1995).

High V (M = 0.35, SD = 0.77)

- Deep self-critical introspection.
- Possible suicidal risk (see Exner's Suicidal Constellation composed of 12 possible signs including high V, high number of morbid responses, es greater than EA, etc.; cutoff of 8 or more to identify high suicidal risk).

Low V

- Absence of V is a positive sign.
- Presence of a single form-dominated V represents the ability to introspect, suggests the resulting information can be integrated and eventually used productively.

Shading—Diffuse (Y, YF, FY)

B. Klopfer et al. (1956) and S. J. Beck (1945) have described Y as representing a sense of helplessness and withdrawal, which is frequently accompanied by anxiety and is often a response to ambiguity. Beck further elaborated that subjects with a high number of Y responses are experiencing psychological pain and have resigned themselves to their situation. Y increases during stress, such as before examinations (Ridgeway & Exner, 1980), surgery (Exner, Thomas, Cohen, Ridgeway, & Cooper, 1981), uncontrollable laboratory-induced stress (McCown et al., 1992), and situational crises (Exner, 1993, 2003). Good support has been found for this variable (Mihura, 2008).

The same general rule for looking at the influences of form (F) in relation to Vista (V), texture (T), and color (C, C′) also applies for shading-diffuse. When F is dominant, subjects are more able to delay their behavior, and their experience is more controlled, organized, and integrated. This ability to delay behavior also gives them time to mobilize their resources. When Y is dominant, there is a much greater sense of being overwhelmed. Although these individuals are characteristically withdrawn, any expression of pain and helplessness is direct. Because there is little ability to delay their impulses, they do not have enough time to mobilize their resources.

In the general population, 86% of people give at least one Y (Y, YF, or FY) response. Exner's (1993, 2003) normative groups of adult nonpatients had an average of 0.97 Y responses (SD = 1.20; Exner & Erdberg, 2005), compared with 2.12 for schizophrenics (S = 52.62), and 1.81 for depressives (SD = 1.40). The total absence of Y suggests an extremely indifferent attitude toward ambiguity (Exner, 1993). To accurately understand the meaning of Y responses, the clinician should look for other indicators of coping. In particular, these might include the number and manner in which pure form is used, the quality of organization, and the number of human movement responses. If there is a high number of Y and these "coping indicators" are absent, the person is likely to be overwhelmed and probably unable to adapt or respond effectively (Exner, 1993).

High Y (M = 0.97, SD = 1.20)

- Anxiety, constrained expression of emotions.
- Resignation to life events, attempt to create distance between oneself and the environment.

Form Dimension

Form Dimension (FD) is unique to the Comprehensive System and was included because it seemed to be both an empirically distinct category and a source of some interpretive significance. Some research that exists suggests that a high number of FD responses are related to introspection and self-awareness. For example, a relatively high number of FD responses have been found among persons who are introverted and are involved in the later phases of insight-oriented therapy and among patients who have completed a wide number of other forms of therapy (Exner, 1993). FD responses occur more frequently among nonpatients (M = 1.43; Exner & Erdberg, 2005) than among other patient groups—including schizophrenics (M = 0.60) and depressives (M = 0.82), and is particularly low among character disorders (M = 0.33; Exner, 1993, 2003). Most research, however, does not support this variable (Mihura, 2008).

High FD (M = 1.43, SD = 1.15)

- Introspection.
- Self-aware, able to delay and internalize behaviors.

Pairs (2) and Reflections (rF and Fr)

Research on pairs and reflections has been linked both conceptually and empirically to self-absorption (Exner, 1991, 1993, 2003). However, this does not necessarily mean that the individual is pathological. For example, a high number of reflections were found among nonpatients in occupations that encourage a high level of self-worth, such as performing artists and surgeons (Exner, 1993). Whereas reflections occurred in only 7% of adult outpatients, they occurred in a full 20% of the protocols of character disorders and 75% of the records of antisocial groups (Exner, 1993). It is fairly common for children between the ages of 5 and 10 to have a high number of reflection (and pair) responses, but they usually decrease by adolescence, when individuals move to a less egocentric style of functioning (Exner, 1993; Exner & Weiner, 1995). There is moderate support for this variable (Mihura, 2008).

High Pairs (2) and Reflections (rF and Fr) (Fr + rF, M = 0.20, S = 0.67)

- Possible self-absorption.
- Inflated sense of self-worth, exaggerated sense of self-pride, with strong strivings toward status.
- Need for self-affirmation may cause affective or interpersonal difficulties if they do not receive external validation.

Organizational Activity (Z)

The relative extent to which a person efficiently and effectively organizes the disparate aspects of the inkblots will be reflected in the scoring for Organizational Activity. The possibility that Organizational Activity is conceptually related to intelligence is given some empirical support in that moderate correlations (.54) have been found with the Wechsler-Bellevue Full Scale IQ and an even higher correlation of .61 exists with the Wechsler Vocabulary subtest (see Exner, 1993). Adults and younger nonpatients will have frequencies of Organizational Activity (Zf) averaging 13.5 and ranging between 9 and 17.5 (Exner & Erdberg, 2005). Among psychiatric patients, lower organizational activity has been noted among depressed patients (Hertz, 1948). In contrast, quite high levels of organizational activity have been found among patients who projected organized delusions (S. J. Beck, 1945; see also the interpretation for Processing Efficiency in the Processing Section topic later in the chapter). Moderate support has been found for this variable (Mihura, 2008).

High Zf (<13) (M = 13.45, SD = 4.22)

- High intellectual striving.
- Careful, precise work with perceptions.

Low Zf (<9)

- Person expends less effort than needed or required to adequately process information.

Content

The different content categories are generally considered to contain information relating to a person's needs, interests, preoccupations, and social interactions. Positive correlations have been found between a large variety of contents and intelligence (Exner, 1986). Research has also shown that whereas a high variety of contents is associated with intellectual flexibility, a low variety suggests intellectual constriction and rigidity. People's occupational interests are often represented in a higher number of contents relating to their specific career choices. For example, biologists and medical personnel usually give a higher number of anatomy responses than the general population (Exner, 1974). This finding may indicate that these persons merely have an interest in their career, but it could suggest they are overconcerned with their career to the extent that they neglect other areas of their lives, perhaps even impairing their overall level of adjustment. For example, biologists who see only nature contents may be using a preoccupation with their careers to withdraw from interpersonal relationships (Exner, 1974).

When interpreting Rorschach content, it is important to look at the variety of contents, the number of each content, and their overall configuration as well as the implications other Rorschach factors may have for the meaning of the content scorings. It is usually essential to consider the age of the subject and to use age-appropriate norms. For example, children usually have significantly fewer human and human detail responses than adults, and the variety of their contents is also lower (Ames et al., 1974; Exner & Weiner, 1995). Another important step is to study contents relating to aggressiveness (fire, explosions, etc.), facial features, and orality. Although the focus of the Comprehensive System is on a quantitative approach to the Rorschach, symbolical considerations can also be extremely important in conducting a more qualitative analysis. The next section provides general information on the meaning associated with human and animal contents. Further interpretive material can be found in the interpretation of quantitative formulas relating to contents. See Intellectualization Index, Isolation Index, Interpersonal Index, (H) + (Hd):(A) + (Ad), and H + A:Hd + Ad.

Human and Human Detail [H, Hd, (H), (Hd)]

Human responses constitute one of the most thoroughly researched contents. S. J. Beck (1961), in general agreement with other researchers, has found that H and Hd gradually increase with age until the median for 10-year-old children is from 16% to 18%. This remains unchanged through adolescence, and the overall adult proportion of 17% is eventually reached. Exner (1974) found that, whereas adult nonpatient H + Hd responses were 19% of the total adult outpatients' responses, schizophrenics had a lower total of 13%. He also demonstrated that the ratio of human to human detail (H:Hd) for nonpatients was 3:1. In contrast, schizophrenics' average ratio was approximately 1:1 and outpatients' ratio was 2:1. Molish (1967) suggests that when there is an increase in Hd compared with H, the subject is prone to use constricted defenses. Others have theorized that the increase suggests intellectualization, compulsiveness, and a preoccupation with the self that restricts the degree of contact with others (B. Klopfer & Davidson, 1962). S. J. Beck (1945) associated high Hd with anxiety, depression, and a low intellectual level (see also the quantitative formula for Interpersonal Index).

High H (M = 3.18, SD = 1.70)

- Wide-ranging interest in people.
- Possibly good self-esteem and high intelligence.
- Greater likelihood of successful psychotherapeutic treatment.

Low H

- Low level of empathy.
- Withdrawal from interpersonal relationships (i.e., low among schizophrenics).
- Poor prognosis for psychotherapy (with abrupt termination if M responses are low).

Animal and Animal Detail (A and Ad)

Most of the literature indicates that animal content is associated with the obvious aspects of adaptiveness and the most concrete features of reality testing (Draguns, Haley, & Phillips, 1967). Because animal contents are the easiest to perceive, their presence suggests that examinees are using routine and predictable ways of responding. Conversely, a low number of animal responses suggests highly individualistic persons who see their world in their own personal and unique ways.

Animal responses occur more frequently than any other content category with an average of 8.2 (SD = 2.56) for nonpatient adults (Exner & Erdberg, 2005) and a slightly higher amount for children (S. J. Beck, 1961). Schizophrenics and outpatients average 31% and 41%, respectively, whereas depressives score much higher, averaging 41% per protocol (Exner, 1974). Other studies have found that the percentage of A responses is low for manics (Kühn, 1963; H. Schmidt & Fonda, 1954) and high for alcoholics (Buhler & LeFever, 1947).

High A (M = 8.18, SD = 2.56)

- Predictable, stereotyped manner of approaching the world.
- Often associated with depression and the use of constrictive and conforming defenses.

Low A

- Persons who are spontaneous, nonconforming, unpredictable, and of higher intelligence often have a low number of A responses.

Anatomy (An) and X Ray (Xy)— Body Concern

Because An and Xy both measure concern with the body, they are considered together. Anatomy (An) responses have been well researched, and, along with human and animal contents, anatomy is one of the most frequently occurring responses (average of 0.6 for nonpatient adults). Anatomy content has an obvious connection with concern for the body, and the literature supports this connection in that it occurs more frequently for persons preparing to undergo elective surgery (Exner, Armbuster, Walker, & Cooper, 1975) and among psychosomatic patients (Shatin, 1952). Anatomy responses also occur with greater frequency with the onset of psychological difficulties related to pregnancy (Zolliker, 1943). A review of the literature by Draguns et al. (1967) concluded that anatomy content can serve as an index of the degree of involvement persons have in their inner fantasy life or may reflect physical changes such as illness, puberty, or pregnancy. Exner (1993) has also suggested that anatomy content is associated with withdrawal from the environment and obsessive defenses.

The relative proportion of anatomy to Xy responses is an important consideration. Although anatomy responses are generally low for both psychiatric and nonpsychiatric groups, a combined anatomy and Xy score allows for a clearer differentiation between the two groups. Whereas the combined An and Xy responses for a nonpatient group give a combined average of only 0.96 responses (0.88 and .08 respectively; Exner & Erdberg, 2005), outpatients give 1.5, schizophrenics give 1.4, and nonschizophrenic patients give 1.8 (which accounts for 9% of this last group's total number of responses; Exner, 1974, 2003). Xy responses have been found to be particularly high for schizophrenics with bodily delusions (average of 2.2) and depressed patients with concerns related to bodily functioning (1.7; Exner, Murillo, & Sternklar, 1979). Anatomy responses occur most frequently for Cards VIII and IX, and Xy responses are most frequent for Card I. Despite these findings, the overall research for An and Xy has provided minimal support (Mihura, 2008) (Anatomy M = 0.88, SD = 1.05; X Ray M = 0.08, SD = 0.28).

Food (Fd)

A high number (2 or more) of food contents (primary or secondary) suggests dependency. High scorers would be expected to request extensive help and guidance from others, have difficulty making independent decisions, and be naive in their expectations of others (Exner, 1993) (M = 0.26, SD = 0.55).

Popular Responses

The number of Popular responses reflects the subjects' degree of similarity to most people, the extent to which they conform to social standards, and the relative ease with which they can be influenced in interpersonal relationships. Persons who reject conventional modes of thinking give a significantly lower number of Populars than those who are conforming and relatively conventional. Good support has been found for these interpretations (Hiller et al., 1999). With Exner's (2003) scoring system (see Table 10.6), the average number of P responses for nonpatients is 6.28 (SD = 1.53; Exner & Erdberg, 2005). Outpatients and nonschizophrenic patients, likewise, give approximately 7 per record, whereas inpatient schizophrenics give 4 or less, characterologically disordered persons give approximately 5, and depressives have slightly more than 5 (Exner, 1993).

Because Populars are extremely common for Cards I, III, V, and VIII, an absence of them from these cards is significant in that it more strongly suggests the trends just discussed. However, the assumption that low P responses alone confirm maladjustment should be approached with caution. Low P subjects who have good form quality (F + % and X + %) and whose organizational activity is also good are likely to be creative individuals who are avoiding common or ordinary perceptions and want to extend their imagination. If organization and form quality are poor, there is a high likelihood that the psychopathological dimensions are more predominant.

High P (M = 6.28, SD = 1.53; high considered > 7, low considered < 4)

- Conventional, overconforming, guarded, and frequently depressed.
- Anxiety related to a fear of making mistakes and, therefore, clings to common perceptions as a way to achieve approval.

Low P

- Poorly adjusted, detached, aloof from their environment, and unable to see the world as others see it.
- Possible character disorder reflecting their rejection of conventionality and their lack of conformity.
- Highly creative (if F+%, X+%, and organizational activity are high).

Special Scores

Deviant Verbalization (DV), Deviant Responses (DR), Incongruous Combination (INCOM), Fabulized Combination (FABCOM), Contamination (CONTAM), Inappropriate Logic (ALOG)

The first six of the Special Scores were included in the Comprehensive System to detect the presence of cognitive slippage. Illogical, dissociated, fluid, or circumstantial thinking is particularly likely if there are any Level 2 scorings for the first four scores (Exner, 1991). This is consistent with the finding that virtually no Level 2 DV or DR responses occurred among nonpatients but fully 1.90 Level 2 DRs have been noted among schizophrenics (Exner, 1993). However, there is no specific interpretation for each of the six categories. Instead, they are used collectively to detect the presence and seriousness of cognitive distortions. The relative seriousness is indicated in part by the type of Special Score.

Mild distortions are suggested by the presence of scores for DV (Level 1), INCOM (Level 1), or DR (Level 2), and moderate distortions are suggested by the presence of DV (Level 2), FABCOM (Level 1), INCOM (Level 2), and ALOG. The most serious degree of cognitive distortion is suggested if patients have Special Scores for DR (Level 2), FABCOM (Level 2), and CONTAM (Deviant Verbalization M = 0.34, SD = 0.67; Deviant Response M= 0.85, SD = 1.01; Incongruous Combination M = 0.71, SD = 0.93; Fabulized Combination M = 0.45, SD = 0.77; Contamination M = 0.00, SD = 0.00; Inappropriate Logic M = 0.04, SD = 0.21).

A further means of analyzing the first six Special Scores is by noting the relative elevation of WSUM6, which is simply a sum of the different weightings given to the Special Scores (see the Scoring section). The WSum6 for nonpatients is 7.2 (Exner & Erdberg, 2005), indicating that normals do include at least some of the Special Score responses. In striking contrast are schizophrenics, who have a WSum6 of nearly 45 (Exner, 1993). However, the presence of Special Scores does occur among children under 10 but gradually decreases during adolescence (Exner & Weiner, 1995). The general interpretation for the first six high Special Scores is that there is cognitive distortion. The interpretive hypothesis, especially with a high WSum6, is that there is a serious disregard for reality, strained reasoning, faulty cause-and-effect relationships, loose associations, disorganized thinking, and poor ability to focus on tasks (Exner, 1991, 1993). This ability of the Rorschach to detect the bizarre and illogical processes of schizophrenia is probably one of its best-validated features (Hiller, Rosenthal, Bornstein, Berry, & Brunnell-Neuleib, 1999; Mihura, 2008; Vincent & Harman, 1991), and there is some evidence that it is sensitive to these changes in thought processes even before their clinical manifestation (G. Frank, 1990) (WSum6 M = 7.12, SD = 5.74).

Perseveration (PSV)

The presence of perseveration has been considered to represent some difficulty in cognitive shifting. Thus, the individual may have either a permanent or a temporary difficulty with rigidity or inflexibility in information processing or decision making (Exner, 1993). However, minimal support has been found for this variable (Mihura, 2008) (M = 0.99, 1.10).

Abstract Content (AB)

The presence of one or more abstractions suggests intellectualizing defenses (see Intellectualization Index) (M = 0.21, SD = 0.56).

Aggressive (AG) and Cooperative Movement (COP)

It is useful to consider AG and COP together. If there is an absence of scores on either category, it suggests that the individual is aloof, somewhat uncomfortable in social situations, and on the periphery of group situations. In contrast, if COP is high (2 or more) and AG is low (0 or 1), the person is likely to be perceived by others as trustworthy, cooperative, and easy to be around (Exner, 1993). It is also a favorable prognosis for psychotherapy. If COP is low (less than 3 or especially 0) and AG is high (greater than 2), the person's interactions are likely to be forceful or even aggressive and hostile (Exner, 1993). Given these interpretations, it might be speculated that high scores on both COP and AG would suggest some conflict regarding the appropriate and preferred mode of responding and would result in inconsistent interpersonal behaviors (i.e., passive aggressive interactions). Moderate support has been found for these variables (Mihura, 2008) (Aggressive M = 0.89, SD = 1.02 and Cooperative Movement M = 2.07, 1.30).

Morbid Content (MOR)

Although the presence of one MOR is not unusual in the records of nonpatients, two or more suggest pessimism, a negative self-image, and possible depression and is consistent with a diagnosis of PTSD (Weiner, 1996). If three or more MOR responses are present, it is both a strong indicator of depression and one of several indicators for suicide risk (see the Suicide Constellation; Exner, 1991, 1993). Moderate support has been found for this category (Mihura, 2008). MOR content is likely to have unique meaning for the person and can often be interpreted symbolically and qualitatively (M = 0.93, SD = 1.01).

Good Human Representation (GHR) and Poor Human Representation (PHR)

GHR and PHR are considered dichotomous categories. Persons with a high number of GHRs are usually highly regarded by others, well adapted, competent, and are reasonably free from chaos (Exner, 2003). In contrast, persons with psychiatric histories typically give a low number of GHRs. If they also give a high number of PHRs, they are also likely to report histories of interpersonal difficulties, are socially inept, and are interpersonally ineffective (Exner, 2003). Research has provided moderate support for this category (Mihura, 2008) (Good Human Representation M = 5.06, SD = 2.09 and Poor Human Representation M = 2.12, SD = 1.81).

Personal (PER)

Scores of 3 or more suggest a defensive authoritarian stance in which the individual is insecure regarding challenges to his or her sense of self. Interpersonal difficulties may be experienced during attempts to get others to submit to his or her opinions (Exner, 2003) (M = 0.99, SD = 1.10).

Color Projection (CP)

This unusual response indicates persons who deny unpleasant emotions by creating false or substitute emotions instead. Thus, they have difficulty dealing with negative feelings and modulating their emotions, and they bend or even distort reality as a means of adapting (Exner, 1993, 2003). This scoring category should be interpreted only in the context of other indicators for processing and expressing affect (see the Affect Section) (M = 0.01, SD = 0.11).

Ratios, Percentages, Derivations

The quantitative formulas used to develop the different ratios, percentages, and derivations provide a more in-depth and complicated portrayal of the relationships among the locations, determinants, contents, Populars, and special scores. These formulas provide some of the most important, reliable, and valid elements of interpretation. Their numbering and organization correspond with the numbers given to them in the previous listing of the quantitative formulas (see the Structural Summary section).

Core Section

The Core section provides information on the person's dominant personality style, particularly focusing on the level of stress the person is experiencing and how effectively they can tolerate the stress. Seven of the entries for the core section are frequency data providing summaries for total number of responses (R), animal movement (FM), inanimate movement (m), Achromatic color (C'), Shading—Texture (T), Shading—Dimension (V), and Shading—Diffuse (Y). Interpretive material for each of the last six categories can be found in previous sections; the first category, number of responses (R), is detailed in the subsection that follows. The nine quantitative formulas follow the interpretive material on number of responses.

Number of Responses Number of responses is not a quantitative formula (and is, therefore, not numbered). Rather, it is a simple sum of the total number of responses. In using Exner's set of instructions, the mean for the total number of responses for nonpatient adults is 23.36 (SD = 5.68; Exner & Erdberg, 2005). However, different methods of administration can influence this number to a certain extent. For example, Ames et al. (1973) report an overall adult average of 26; S. J. Beck (1961) gives 32 for his adult mean; and both use instructions somewhat different from Exner's. Deviations from the normal range present the following possible interpretive hypotheses. There is good support for interpretations based on R (Mihura et al., 2008).

Low R (Adults, less than 17; Children, less than 15) (M = 23.36, SD = 5.68)

- Defensiveness (possibly consistent with malingering).
- Constriction, depression.
- Invalid profile (is less than 14; see administration instructions).

High R (greater than 27)

- Introversion.
- Above-average intelligence with a relatively high level of academic achievement, high degree of creativity.
- Good ego functioning, including the ability to plan ahead, adequate impulse control, and the ability to tolerate stress.
- Among patient populations: mania obsessive-compulsive disorder.
- Invalidates formulas (higher proportion of D and Dd, more pure F, more Populars, elevated Affective ratio due to greater number of responses to cards VIII and X).

1. Lambda [L; (Pure F:Non-Pure F)]. The Lambda index was developed by S. Beck (1961) as an improvement on the F% that had been used by other Rorschach systematizers. The earlier F% used the total number of R as the denominator, whereas the Lambda uses the total number of non-pure F. The Lambda ratio is used as an overall index of the degree of responsiveness versus lack of responsiveness to stimuli (Exner, 2003). Thus, persons can range from highly constricted and withdrawn to completely emotionally flooded by their responses to stimuli. The Lambda for nonpatients is between 0.11 and 2.33, with a mean of .58. In contrast to this is the much higher range among schizophrenics (.05–29.00), depressives (.08–15.00), and character-disordered persons (0.015–16.00; Exner, 1993, 2003). This greater range among patients reflects their greater tendencies either to overreact to stimuli or, in contrast, to underreact by becoming highly constricted and withdrawn. Thus, a maladjusted person may have a Lambda either greater than 0.99 or less than 0.32. The significance lies in Lambda's ability to provide specifics regarding the form this maladjustment takes. It is also important to look at other information within the test, such as form quality and Experience Balance, to obtain a more complete conceptualization of the meaning of L. However, with adolescents, an interpretation that focuses on maladjustment should be made with caution because adolescents usually have a higher proportion of pure F responses (Ames et al., 1971; Exner, 1995). Despite this research, the preponderance of studies do not provide much support for high (>.86) Lambda (Mihura, 2008). As a result, interpretations should be made with caution.

High L (M = 0.58, SD = 0.37; high L > .99)

- Withdrawal from experiencing a situation fully, avoidance of perceiving all the possibilities that may be present ("tunnel vision").
- Likely to be conservative, insecure, detached, and fearful of involvement.
- Defensive, constricted, unimaginative, anxious.
- Possible depression, guilt, increased potential for suicide.

Low L (low L < 32)

- Overinvolvement with stimuli to the extent that affect disrupts cognitive functioning.
- Inadequate control over emotions; frequent, impulsive acting-out results in difficulty maintaining satisfactory interpersonal relationships.
- Impaired ability to attend to their environment, victims of their needs and conflicts.
- Achievement-oriented persons who deal effectively with their environment (if these indicators in their protocols reflecting control and flexibility are present: average X + %, average number of Populars, good Organizational Activity, above-average W).

2. Experience Balance or Erlebnistypus [EB; (M:C)]. The Experience Balance formula, or Erlebnistypus, was originally devised by Rorschach and is the ratio between the sum of all M responses compared with the sum of all weighted color responses. Rorschach systematizers and researchers have come to view the Experience Balance ratio as the extent to which a person is internally oriented as opposed to being more externally directed and behaviorally responsive to outside stimuli. Although the EB ratio is usually relatively stable (Exner, Armbuster, & Viglione, 1978), it can temporarily change during times of stress or become more permanently altered during the course of successful psychotherapy (Exner, 1974; Exner & Sanglade, 1992). Although the EB ratio is usually stable for adults, there is considerable variability in children until midadolescence (Exner et al., 1985; Exner & Weiner, 1995). In an extensive literature review, J. Singer (1960) described the two sides of the ratio as representing dimensions of "constitutional temperament." These dimensions are introversives (higher M scores), who have a preference for internal experience, as opposed to extratensives (higher weighted C scores), who are more prone to activity and external expression. An introversive can more effectively delay his or her behavior, whereas the extratensive is more emotional and is likely to discharge his or her affect into some form of external behavior. Both types respond differently to stress and to problem-solving tasks (Exner, 1978). It should be emphasized that, in their moderate forms, neither is any more or any less effective than the other, nor is either more prone to psychopathology (Molish, 1967; see also the interpretive meanings associated with M and C and the quantitative formulas dealing with either of these factors [EA, EBPer, D score, Adjusted D score, and W:M]). Despite this research, the preponderance of studies have not provided extensive support for this index (Mihura, 2008), so interpretations should be made with caution.

Higher M (Introversives)

- Oriented toward using their inner fantasy life, directed inward, and use their inner experience to satisfy most of their basic needs (even though externally they may have learned to appear to be extraverted),
- Cautious, deliberate, submissive,
- Less physically active than persons scoring relatively higher on the C side of the ratio,
- Approach problem-solving tasks by internalizing the situation and mentally reviewing possible alternatives,

Higher C (Extratensives)

- Use external interactions as the most important means of satisfying their needs.
- Difficulty delaying their responses.
- Direct their energy toward the outside world.
- Spontaneous and assertive.
- Approach problem-solving situations by experimenting with different behaviors (external trial and error) before achieving solutions.
- Among children, may represent a lack of self-assurance.

M and C Equal (Ambitents)

- Flexible during interpersonal relationships.
- Less sure of themselves during problem solving and tend to vacillate, usually need to verify every sequence in the solution of a problem at hand, do not profit as much from mistakes as either introversives or extratensives.
- Among patient populations, unusually high scores on both M and C suggest a manic condition.

3. Experience Actual [EA; (M + C)]. Whereas the Experience Balance ratio emphasizes the assessment of a person's type, the Experience Actual indicates the "volume of organized activity" (S. J. Beck, 1960). The M side of the formula shows the extent to which persons are able to organize their inner lives, and the C side indicates the extent to which emotions are available. The emphasis here is that both the M and the C represent deliberate, organized activity, which is contrasted with the disorganization associated with nonhuman movement (FM, m) and the responses related to the gray-black features of the blot (T, V, Y).

> For the most part, the adult ratio between M and C is remarkably stable (Exner, 1993), yet the sum of M and C can sometimes fluctuate on a daily basis, which theoretically parallels the effects of changes in mood (Erginel, 1972). After successful psychotherapy, particularly if long term, M and C typically both increase (Exner & Sanglade, 1992; Weiner & Exner, 1991), indicating a greater increase in the degree of organization of the person's inner life and an availability of more emotions. In fact, Exner (1974) found that EA increases significantly more for patients who improved in therapy than for those who showed little or no improvement. Furthermore, persons who underwent long-term insight-oriented treatment showed much more of an increase in EA than those in a treatment that emphasized a combination of support and environmental manipulation (Exner, 1974). This is consistent with the goal of insight therapy, which focuses on helping patients to understand and organize their internal resources. The mean changes for children show a gradual increase (rarely more than 0.5) with each year from the ages of 5 to 13 (Exner, 1993). Although brief retesting for children has shown good stability, long-term retesting (9 months or more) has resulted in wide fluctuations (Exner et al., 1985; Exner & Weiner, 1995). Good support has been found for interpretations based on this index (Mihura, 2008) (M = 9.37, SD = 3.00).

4. Experience Pervasive (EBPer). Because Experience Balance (M:WSumC) is a somewhat crude indicator of how pervasive or dominant the introversive or extratensive style is, Experience Pervasive was designed as a more refined means of indicating how dominant one of the two styles is. Thus, it is an extension of the interpretations described in Experience Balance. It is calculated only when a clear style is indicated, and it takes on interpretive significance only when the value of one style over the other is 2.5 or greater. When this occurs, it clearly indicates that one of the styles is quite pervasive, perhaps to the point of suggesting rigidity in problem-solving style (Exner, 1993). However, there is minimal support for interpretations based on this index (Mihura et al., 2008).

5. Experience Base [eb; (FM + m)/(Y + T + V + C′)]. The Experience Base ratio was originally suggested by B. Klopfer, Ainsworth, Klopfer, and Holt (1956) and later developed in its present form by Exner (1974, 1986). The nonhuman movement side of the ratio reflects tendencies to respond in ways that are not completely acceptable to the ego. These tendencies appear out of control, impinge on the individual, and are disorganized (B. Klopfer & Davidson, 1962). Although the tendencies and feelings may have originally been produced by outside sources, the resulting internal activity is not in the person's control. The opposite side of the ratio, which is a sum of the responses relating to the gray-black features of the blot, is a reflection of the pain and disharmony the person is feeling as a result of unresolved stress. The eb ratio indicates which of these two areas of functioning is more predominant. If the eb is small on both sides, it suggests that the person is not experiencing very much pain and that his or her needs are well organized. Usually the values on either side of the ratio range between 1 and 3 for nonpatients. If either side becomes greater than 5, its interpretive meaning becomes more clear. Despite the conceptual and research findings, only minimal to moderate support has been found for eb (Mihura et al., 2008). (See also the additional interpretive meanings associated with material from the left side of the ratio [FM and m] and the right side [Y, T, V, and C].)

6. Experienced Stimulation [es; (FM + m) + (C′ + T + Y + V)]. Experienced Stimulation is the sum of the nonhuman movement responses and all responses relating to the gray-black features of the inkblot. These are all responses reflecting that the person's functioning is disorganized and that forces are acting on the person and he or she feels they are beyond control. Thus, the es sum is an index of a person's degree of disorganization and helplessness. Persons scoring high on es have a low frustration tolerance, and it is difficult for them to be persistent, even in meaningful tasks (Exner, 1978). This index has received moderate support in the research literature (Mihura et al., 2008).

Important information can be obtained by comparing the amount of organization the person has (as represented by EA) with how much chaos and helplessness he or she experiences (as represented by es). Normal populations usually have a higher EA than es, whereas psychiatric populations have a higher es than EA (Exner, 1974). Exner (1978) has suggested that the ratio between EA and es can provide an index of the degree to which a person can tolerate frustration. Difficulty in dealing with frustration would primarily result from high-scoring es persons' having a limited ability to process and mediate cognitive information (Wiener-Levy & Exner, 1981). As would be expected, a correlate of successful psychotherapy is that there is a decrease in es and a corresponding increase in EA, which suggests that at least some of the patient's activity has become more organized (Exner & Sanglade, 1992; Gerstle, Geary, Himelstein, & Reller-Geary, 1988; Weiner & Exner, 1991). This finding was supported by Exner (1974), who found that subjects rated as unimproved after therapy also showed little change in that their es still remained high in relationship to EA. In another study, Exner (1974) demonstrated that most persons in successful insight therapy had an increase in EA compared with es. This finding suggests that patients in successful insight therapy were able to either neutralize or reorganize the forces that were "acting on" them. In contrast, therapy emphasizing support or environmental manipulation produced no or little change in the es:EA ratio.

High es (M = 9.55, SD = 4.01; high = 13)
- Low frustration tolerance.
- Difficulty following through on tasks.
- Disorganization, distractibility, and a sense of helplessness.

7. D Score (D; EA − es). The D score is a further measure of the client's ability to tolerate stress. It is essentially a means of evaluating the degree of available resources the person has (EA) versus the amount of disorganized events that are occurring beyond the person's control (es). For example, veterans diagnosed with posttraumatic stress disorder have been found to have low D scores (Weiner, 1996). Good support has been found for this scoring category (Mihura, 2008).

Low D Score (M = −0.12, SD = 0.99; Low = −1)

- Person is likely to feel overwhelmed, overloaded, easily distracted, limited psychological resources to deal with stress.
- Unable to deal with complex or ambiguous situations.
- Thoughts, affects, and behaviors might be impulsive and poorly focused; as the D score becomes progressively lower, this trend is likely to become increasingly stronger.

High D Score (high = +0)

- Client can adequately deal with the current level of stress.

8. Adjusted es (Adj es). Because es includes measures of current stimuli impinging on the person (m and Y), a different, adjusted es that excluded m and Y was developed. It is believed that adjusted es represents the more chronic (rather than fluctuating) condition of the person (Exner, 1993). Thus, persons scoring high are likely to feel chronically overstimulated (i.e., racing thoughts, insomnia) and have difficulties organizing their thoughts. However, the main purpose of calculating Adjusted es is to enable the calculation of the Adjusted D score. Even though good support has been reported for D, little research supports interpretations for Adj es (Mihura et al., 2008).

9. Adjusted D score (Adj D). Because the D score includes measures of the current capacity to deal with stress, it may not provide a measure of the person's usual ability to modulate and control his or her behavior. This issue is particularly likely to be present for clients referred for evaluation, because the events surrounding a referral usually involve psychosocial difficulties. These situational uncontrollable stressful events are expressed on the Rorschach (and in the D score) by the presence of m and Y responses (McCown et al., 1992). Adj es has had m and Y subtracted from it, so it theoretically removes the influence of current environmental stressors. What remains in the Adjusted D score is a measure of the person's typical or usual capacity to tolerate stress and to control behaviors (Exner, 1993, 1995). The preponderance of research does not support interpretations based on this variable (Mihura, 2008).

Low Adj D (M = 0.19, SD = 0.83; low = −1)

- Fewer than average resources to adequately cope with stressful situations.
- Function best in routine and predictable situations, adapting to new situations presents difficulties in that they are prone to become distracted, disorganized, and impulsive. (These trends are strengthened with progressively decreasing scores on Adj D.)

High Adj D (high = +1)

- Good ability to deal with stressful situations. (This does not *necessarily* mean that they are also well adjusted; antisocial and paranoid personalities have intricate systems of dealing with stress that are quite effective but they are not well adjusted).

- May use their somewhat limited resources to distance themselves from the types of experiences that might result in increased growth and awareness, low motivational distress.

Ideation Section

The Ideation section focuses on information related to how the client imposes meaningful organization onto his or her perceptions. It includes three quantitative formulas (two ratios and an index) and frequency data for M–, M, number of Level 2 responses, WSum6, and M with no FQ (see the interpretation for each of these frequencies under the listings for human movement and Special Scores).

1. Active:Passive Ratio (a:p). Individuals who have a distinctly higher number of passive responses are likely to be correspondingly more passive in other situations. In contrast, a clearly higher number of active responses indicates a person who is more active in terms of thoughts and behaviors (see also the interpretation for M^a; M^p). However, the contrast or magnitude of differences must be quite clear, as indicated by one of the following conditions: (a) "sum of the values in the ratio is four and one value is zero"; (b) "values in the ratio exceed four, and the value on one side of the ratio is no more than twice that of the other"; or (c) "ratio exceeds four, and the value on one side is two to three times greater than the value on the other side" (Exner, 1993, p. 475).

2. M Active:Passive Ratio (M^a:M^p). A further refinement of the a:p is to consider only the proportion of active and passive responses for human movement scorings. If the summed value of passive Ms (M^p) is greater than active Ms (M^a), it suggests a generally more passive orientation. For example, therapists' ratings of clients with a greater number of passive Ms indicated that they made more requests for directions, seemed more helpless, and exhibited a relatively high number of silences (Exner, 1978). In addition, their daydreams had more passive themes (Exner, 1974) as did their TAT story endings (Exner, 1993). Despite this research and intuitive appeal, most research has not supported interpretations based on active/passive (Mihura, 2008).

3. Intellectualization Index [2Ab + (Art + Ay)]. Earlier research indicated that the presence of three or more summed scores for Abstraction (Ab) and Art (Art) suggests an excessive use of intellectualization (Exner, 2003). Both obsessives and paranoid schizophrenics were often found to have more than three combined Ab and Art frequencies in their protocols (Exner, 1986; Exner & Hillman, 1984), and both these groups are likely to use an intellectual approach to distance themselves from their emotions. This is in contrast to nonpatients who typically reported an average of approximately 2 per protocol (Exner & Erdberg, 2005). Despite this research, much of the research on the intellectualization index has not supported interpretations based on it (Mihura, 2008) (M = 2.17, SD = 2.15).

High Intellectualization Index (5 or More)
- Neutralize emotions through analyzing things from an intellectual perspective, deny or conceal the impact of affect.
- Dealing with emotions is typically circumspect and possibly unrealistic.
- Intellectualization might provide them with a certain degree of control for moderate levels of affect, but much higher levels are likely to overwhelm them, quite possibly resulting in disorganization.

Affect Section

The Affect section provides information on how the person modulates and expresses affect. Because affect is most directly expressed on the Rorschach through color, the different frequencies and formulas are concerned with the various combinations of color with other types of Rorschach responses. Specifically, this section includes frequencies for Pure C, white spaces (S), color projection (CP), and three quantitative formulas.

The sum of C and Cn responses provides an index of the degree to which a person is likely to be overwhelmed by affective impulses. Among nonpatient adults, it is rare to have any C or Cn responses occurring in a protocol (M = 0.12, SD = 0.43), but this increases slightly for patient groups (see discussion in the section on interpretation of color). The degree to which a person uses white spaces (S) has been associated with the person's negativism, means of handling anger, and amount of oppositional tendencies (see Interpretation section on white spaces). Color projection (CP), a rare response included as a Special Score, relates to a tendency for the individual to substitute alternative emotions in place of unacceptable unpleasant ones (in the Interpretation section, see the discussion of color projection [CP]).

1. Form-Color Ratio [FC/(CF + C)]. The ratio of form-dominated color responses to color-dominant responses provides a measure of the degree of control a person has over his or her impulses (also check D score for a tendency to become overwhelmed by stress). If form is predominant (1.5 to 2.5 times greater), it suggests the person has good control over his or her impulses and experiences satisfying interpersonal relationships (Exner, 1969, 1974; B. Klopfer & Davidson, 1962). Exner (1978), for example, has found that schizophrenics who have FC responses greater than CF + C have a better response to psychotherapy and less likelihood of relapse. The high form suggests they can integrate an accurate, reality-oriented interpretation into their perceptions. However, if no or very few color-dominant responses (no CF + C) are present, the person will be overly constricted and have little contact with his or her emotions (Exner, 1978, 1993). This is consistent with the finding that most psychosomatic patients, who are typically constricted, had ratios of 4:1 or greater (Exner, 1993). If the CF + C side of the ratio is relatively high (1:1), it suggests a weak control over a person's impulses, which may be accompanied by impulsiveness (Pantle et al., 1994) or aggressive acting out, perhaps consistent with a narcissistic personality (Exner, 1969; B. Klopfer & Davidson, 1962). The perception of both internal and external events is typically distorted and inaccurate, as are the responses to these events (Exner, 1974). The number of pure C responses increases with pathological groups, as indicated by only 7% of nonpatients giving pure C responses in contrast to 45% of depressives, 32% of schizophrenics, and 27% of character-disordered patients (Exner, 1993). Research has provided moderate support for this index (Mihura, 2008).

2. Affective Ratio [Afr; (R for Cards VIII, IX, X)/(R for Cards I−VII)]. Because the last three cards are chromatic and the first seven are primarily achromatic, the Affective Ratio indicates the extent to which affect (color) makes an impact on the person. Nonpatient adults usually show a mean Afr of .67 (SD = 0.16). However, it is relevant to consider Afr in the context of EB. Introversives (higher M side of EB), who primarily direct their experience inward, have Afr ranges between .50 and .80. In contrast, Extratensives (higher C side of EB) have Afr ranging between .60 and .95 (Exner, 1993, 2003). This means that it is useful to take EB scores into account when judging whether an Afr is high or low. Although the mean Afr for patient groups was not very different from that for nonpatients, the range was much higher for patients and the distribution was bimodal. This higher range among patient groups is consistent with the view that they are more likely to have difficulties with either undercontrolling or overcontrolling affect (Exner, 1993, 2003). However, research has provided little suppor for this category (Mihura, 2008).

High Afr (M = 0.61, SD = 0.17; high > .85)

- Overresponsiveness to affect, person is more receptive to emotional inputs and more likely to respond immediately rather than delay behavior (check FC/(CF + C).

Low Afr (low < .53)

- Tend to withdraw from emotions; if extremely low, persons may attempt to exert an extreme amount of control over their affective responses (note the Intellectualization Index).

3. Complexity Index (Blends:R). Approximately 20% of all Rorschach responses involve blends. To create a blend response, the person must appreciate the complexity of the ink-blot, which requires both analysis and synthesis. Exner (2003) has pointed out that the pure F response is the exact opposite of a blended response in that pure F requires attention to only the most simple, straightforward aspect of the stimulus. Usually there are 1 or more blends in a person's protocol. A complete absence of blends suggests narrowness and con-striction. This is consistent with the finding that blends are less frequent in the protocols of depressives and persons with below-average intelligence (Exner, 1993, 2003). In contrast, an extremely high number of blends (8 or more) suggests an unusual amount of complexity, to the extent that the person may be overly burdened (Exner, 1993, 2003).

A thorough interpretation of blends also requires an understanding of their qualitative aspects. For example, a blend that includes color-dominated determinants implies that the person might be easily overwhelmed by affect, whereas the opposite would be true if the blend were form-dominated. The color-shading blend (combining color with C', Y, T, F, V) implies concern with painful, irritating, confusing emotional experiences, and it is associated with the protocols of depressives. Exner and Wylie (1977) found a moderate correlation with attempted suicide. Accordingly, this blend was included as one of several variables in Exner's (1993) Suicide Constellation. However, the presence of color-shad-ing blends does not seem to be a sufficiently accurate predictor of suicide when used as a single sign (Hansell et al., 1988). Good support has been found for interpretations based on blends (Mihura, 2008) (Blends M = 5.56, SD = 2.55; Blends/R M = 0.24, SD = 0.10).

Mediation Section

The Mediation section uses a series of indicators to measure the extent to which the client is oriented toward making conventional, acceptable responses versus more unique ones. If either one of these directions is extreme and rigid, it suggests difficulties in adapting. This section includes simple frequencies for the total number of Populars and negative white space responses (S–; see previous interpretation for Populars and white space responses) along with the five percentages described next.

1. Conventional Form (X + %). X + % includes the form quality of all the responses in a protocol and, as such, tends to be less subject to distortions than F + % (see next item). The X + % is essentially an indicator of the degree to which a person perceives things in a conventional, realistic manner. Most normal adults have an X + % of 68% (SD + 11%; Exner & Erdberg, 2005). Normal children have a slightly lower mean, ranging between .67 and .78 (Exner & Weiner, 1995). An extremely high percentage (greater than 90%) means that persons perceive their world in an overly conventional manner, to the extent that they might sacrifice their individuality. They are likely to be hypernormal, inflexible, rigid, and overly conventional (Exner, 1993, 2003). This is further supported by, and is consistent with, an elevated number of Populars. In contrast, lowerings in X + % (less than 70%) suggest persons who perceive their world in an unusual manner. This might be simply because they are highly committed to their individuality or, particularly if X + % is unusually low, it might suggest serious psychopathology. For example, schizophrenics have a mean X + % of only 40% (Exner, 1993). There is good support for interpretations based on X = % (Hiller et al., 1999; Mihura, 2008) (M = 0.68, SD = 0.11; low < .55).

2. Conventional Pure Form (F + %). F + % assesses the same dimension as X + % but is limited to a narrower number of responses because it involves only pure F responses rather than other scoring categories (C′, Y, T, and V) that might have been combined with F. Thus, interpretation is similar to the interpretation of X + % but should be done more cautiously. It reflects a person's respect for the conventional aspects of reality and perceptual clarity. The Exner (1993) norms indicate schizophrenics have an F + % of only 42%, in contrast to the average of 71% among normals. In general, a low F + % might suggest limited intellectual endowment (S. J. Beck, 1961), organic impairment (Reitan, 1955b), or schizophrenia (S. J. Beck, 1968; T. Kahn & Giffen, 1960).

3. Distorted Form (X − %). In contrast to X + % (and F + %), X − % is a direct index of the degree to which a person has distorted perceptions of reality. The higher the X − %, the more likely that the person has a significant level of impairment (Mihura, 2008). For example, moderately high percentages (X − % = 20%) are found for depressives, and percentages of 37% are characteristic of schizophrenics (Exner, 1993). Any percentage above 20% suggests that the person will have difficulty, because he or she has poor ties with reality and difficulty developing accurate abstractions (M = 0.11, SD = 0.07; high > .20, very high > .30).

4. White Space Distortion (S − %). Sometimes X + % and F + % can be low; it might then be assumed that this score is a result of a high number of form minus responses. This assumption might then result in incorrect interpretations. One way of checking for this difficulty is to note the percentage of minus responses for the white space (S−). Instead of suggesting the sort of distortions suggestive of schizophrenia (see interpretations for F + % and X + %), a low S − % might be caused by strong negativism or anger (Exner, 1993, 2003), but research supporting this is minimal (Mihura, 2008).

5. Unusual Form (Xu%). Xu% also provides a check for potentially incorrect interpretations derived from low X + % or F + % scores. There might be cases in which X + % and F + % are low primarily as a result of a large proportion of unusual form (Fu) responses. Fu responses are unusual, but they still do not violate reality in the way that minus responses do, and thus they do not reflect severe pathology. In fact, a few Fu responses in a protocol can be a healthy sign that the person is capable of seeing his or her world in a novel manner. However, an overabundance of Fu responses suggests the person is highly committed to an unconventional orientation (Exner, 1993, 2003). Unless the environment is highly tolerant of such an orientation, he or she is likely to have numerous conflicts and confrontations. There is moderate research supporting this variable (Mihura, 2008) (M = 0.20, SD = 0.09; high > .20).

Processing Section

In addition to understanding clients' ideation and mediation, it is also important to assess the quality and efficiency by which they process information. Relevant frequency data are the overall amount of Organizational Activity (Zf; see interpretation under Organization Activity), Perseveration (PER), Developmental Quality+ (DQ+), Developmental Quality v (DQv), and the next three ratios.

1. Economy Index (W:D:Dd). The W:D:Dd ratio compares the degree to which an individual attempts to create a more challenging response that requires a high degree of organization and motivation (W), rather than choosing a less demanding and easily perceived area (D or Dd). Normals and outpatients usually have a W:D ratio of 1:1.2 or even 1:1.8 (Exner, 1993). If a person includes a relatively large number of D responses, it suggests that he or she takes the least challenging and possibly least productive way out of a conflict situation. It could be assumed that his or her characteristic way of dealing with ambiguity is to withdraw from it and focus on the obvious. If W is predominant, the person is perhaps overdriven in his or her attempts to organize perceptions. If, with a high W, both the W and the D responses are of poor quality, it suggests that a person is withdrawn and unrealistically striving for perfection (Exner, 1974). However, when W and D responses are both of good quality, they more likely represent the successful intellectual efforts of a creative person (Exner, 1974). Although this is an intuitively appealing set of interpretations, there is only minimal research supporting the Economy Index (Mihura, 2008).

2. Aspirational Ratio (W:M). The W:M ratio is a rough formula that, at the present time, is somewhat lacking in research (Mihura et al., 2008). As a result, interpretations should be treated with skepticism. It can be generally understood by reconsidering that the W response is an indicator of the degree to which subjects aspire to effectively organize and conceptualize their environments. It is an effort to encompass and include a number of different details in one coherent response. However, determining whether subjects have the resources to actually accomplish an effective organization depends also on M. Although M represents the degree of investment subjects have in their fantasy lives, it also suggests how effectively they can bridge their inner resources with external reality and perform abstract thinking. Thus, the W:M ratio provides a rough comparison between a person's aspiration level, as represented by W, and his or her actual capability, as represented by M (Exner, 1993, 2003). Because introversives have higher M values than extratensives and ambitents, the relative value of EB needs to be taken into account in designating high or low W:M ratios. A high aspirational level is indicated if the W side of the ratio is greater than these values: introversives, 1.5:1; ambitents, 2.2:1; extratensives, 3:1 (Exner, 1993). However, scores with extremely high W components are common in children, which is consistent with the observation that children often underestimate the actual effort required to accomplish a goal (Exner, 1993, 1995). Ratios where the right side (M) is clearly lower than the left (0.5:1 for introversives and 1:1 for extratensives and ambitents) suggest that these persons are extremely cautious and conservative in defining achievable goals (Exner, 1993, 2003). Their motivation to achieve might be low, which would involve their being cautious (not wishing to fail), conservative in defining their objectives, and economical in their expenditure of energy.

3. Processing Efficiency (Zd). Although the frequency of Organizational Activity (Zf) along with the Economy Index (W:D:Dd) and the Aspirational Ratio (W:M) provide information on the motivation and effort that persons place into their perceptions, these indicators do not provide information related to quality or accuracy. In contrast, the Processing Efficiency (Zd) score provides an index not only of effort but also of ease and accuracy of processing. Individuals scoring high on Zd are considered to have an overincorporative style; they invest more effort and are more accurate in their perceptions and conclusions. This seems to be an enduring traitlike feature. In contrast, low scorers have an underincorporative style, which means that they process information in a more haphazard style, often neglecting relevant bits of information. This characteristic seems more amenable to change, as indicated by moves to a more overincorporative style following psychotherapy (Exner, 1978). A review of research on Zd (Exner, 1993) indicates that, consistent with theory, overincorporators (high Zd) have more extensive eye-scanning, make fewer errors on games, and are less likely to make guesses related to requests for factual information. In contrast, underincorporators (low Zd) make fewer eye movements while scanning, are more likely to make errors on games, and are more likely to make guesses related to factual information. Among children, low Zd scores occur among those diagnosed as hyperactive. However, the preponderance of research has not supported the use of Zd (Mihura, 2008).

High Zd (> +3)

- Possibly obsessive or perfectionistic; can also efficiently and accurately process information.

- Exert more effort in information processing.
- Will take care with their perceptions and continually check for accuracy.
- Confident in their abilities.

Low Zd (< −3)

- Likely to be haphazard, might make impulsive decisions without fully taking into account all relevant aspects of a situation.
- Will invest minimal effort into actively working with their perceptions.
- Are typically uneasy with their information-processing ability, may question their efficiency at perceiving, integrating, and responding to information.

Interpersonal Section

Although the Rorschach does not obtain information regarding a person's actual environment or the other persons in that environment, it does provide information related to needs, attitudes, behavioral response sets, and coping styles, all of which are relevant to interpersonal relationships. The Interpersonal section lists several measures relevant to these domains. The person's degree of cooperation with others can be noted through their number of Cooperative Movements (COP). Similarly, Aggressive Movements (AG) provides an index of interpersonal aggression, and a high amount of Food Contents suggests dependency. Additional useful indicators of interpersonal relations include sum of pure H, number of Perseverations (PER), ratio of Good to Poor Human Representations (GHR: PHR), sum T, and active:passive responses (see interpretations under each one of these categories). The next two formulas can also be useful in assessing the extent to which a person is interested in people as opposed to being isolated.

1. Interpersonal Interest [H + (Hd) + Hd + (Hd)]. The Interpersonal Interest ratio index merely adds up the total amount of human content. As such, it represents the degree to which a person is interested in people but there is little research supporting this variable (Mihura, 2008) (M = 6.29, SD = 2.66).
2. Isolation Index (Isolate:R). Exner (1986) points out that the five contents (Botany, Clouds, Geography, Landscape, and Nature) used to develop the Isolation Index are all "nonhuman, nonsocial, inanimate, and usually static objects" (p. 406). If a high proportion of these contents (index score of .25 or greater) occurs in a person's protocol, it suggests the person may be withdrawn or alienated, or may at least have some difficulties related to social isolation (Exner, 1993). This seems to be true for children, adolescents, and adults (Exner, 1986, 1995). However, these interpretations should not necessarily take on a pathological bias. A high score might merely represent less interest in people rather than a negative rejection and alienation from them. There is minial support for this variable (Mihura, 2008) (M = 0.19, SD = 0.09).

Self-Perception Section

The Self-Perception section includes information relevant to the relative assets and limitations of the clients as seen by the clients themselves. These entries are simply frequency tallies: Fr + rF, Form Dimension, sum of Morbid content, and Anatomy/X ray responses, and sum V (see interpretations under relevant sections). The ratio of Pure H:(H) + Hd + (Hd) compares the amount of Pure Human responses with mythical/fictional and part human responses. Two of the human categories on the right side of the ratio relate to fictional/mythical descriptions. As such, they can be considered to represent the extent to which the individual bases his or her perceptions on real versus imaginary aspects of people. Adult and adolescent nonpatients usually give more Pure Human responses than (H) + Hd + (Hd) at a rate of approximately 3:2 (Exner, 1993, 1995, 2003). However, the means for the ratio are different for introversives (3:1) than for either extratensives or ambitents (1.3:1). In contrast, schizophrenics see a much higher proportion of fictional/ mythical and part human responses (1.5:2; Exner, 1993). This low a level of Pure Human responses suggests that they are working from an unrealistic perception of themselves and others. The Self-Perception section also includes one quantitative formula:

1. Egocentricity Index [3r + (2)/R]. The Egocentricity Index (EI) provides information related to whether the client has a sense of self-worth and further relates this to the extent that he or she is absorbed with self. However, there is little support for this variable (Mihura et al., 2003).

High EI (> .44)

- Overinflated sense of self-worth, which reflects underlying dissatisfaction.
- Moderate elevations (index level of .40 to .45) indicate self-focusing and self-concern associated with positive self-esteem.

Low EI (< .33)

- Negative sense of self-worth, conflicted self-image, possible mood fluctuations and dysfunctional behaviors.

Special Indices

In an attempt to increase the robustness and validity of various combinations of Rorschach measures, six Special Indices have been developed based on a composite of scores. For example, a number of different indicators of schizophrenia are found throughout the Rorschach. These include a high number of X – % or M – %, the presence of one or more Level 2 Fabulized Combinations (FAB2), and a high WSum6. These, along with several other indicators, were combined to form the Perceptual-Thinking Index (PTI). Some research has found that this index can discriminate schizophrenia better than any of the single scores (see Exner, 1991, 1993, 2003). A similar strategy was used for the other Special Indices. Collectively, they help to form a nucleus of indices to help with more specific types of diagnostic conditions. Exner (1993, 2003) and the commercially available scoring forms have included Constellation Worksheets for calculating whether the Special Indices are positive (also see Exner, 2003; Table 10.5, p. 405). Caution should be used in interpreting these indices because most have either equivocal or minimal research to support them (see Archer & Krishnamurthy, 2003).

1. Perceptual Thinking Index (PTI). The PTI is a revision of the earlier Schizophrenia Index (SCZI). PTI has the advantage of more accurately identifying persons with thought disorders (Exner, 2003; Dao & Prevatt, 2006; S. Smith et al., 2002). As the name suggests, it is not designed to diagnose schizophrenia but more to assess the array of disorganized or unusual thought processes that may occur with schizophrenia or other forms of thought disorders. It should also be considered as rating a person on a continuum of thought disturbances rather than being designed to place a person in a certain category (diagnosis). This is a well-supported variable (Mihura, 2008). The recommended cutoff score is = 3 (Dao & Prevatt, 2006).

2. Depression Index (DEPI). A DEPI value of 4 raises the possibility that the client is experiencing some depressive symptoms—fluctuations in moods, a sense of dissatisfaction, pessimism, and some mild vegetative symptoms (fatigue, insomnia, slowed thinking, anhedonia). Scores of 5, 6, or especially 7 are far more definitive and strengthen the likelihood of an affective disorder as reflected by an intensification of these symptoms (Exner, 1991, 1993; Exner & Erdberg, 2005). However, the diagnosis of a specifically depressive disorder may not be warranted because depression is generic to a wide variety of disorders, particularly many of the personality disorders and schizophrenia. In addition, the term *depression* might be used to describe people who are emotionally distraught or are pessimistic, self-defeating, and lethargic, as well as those who feel a sense of futility when attempting to function competently in a complex society (Exner, 1993). Depressive symptoms as measured by DEPI may, therefore, relate to both a wide number of types of people and a wide range of possible diagnoses. This index should be used with considerable caution because it has been identified by a number of authors as having questionable validity, especially with children and adolescents (Ball et al., 1991; Jorgenson et al., 2000; G. Meyer & Archer, 2001; Mihura, 2008; Stredny & Ball, 2005).

3. Coping Deficit Index (CDI). It has been conceptualized that clients with scores above 4 or 5 on the CDI are likely to have unsatisfying and somewhat meaningless interpersonal relationships, largely because they find it difficult to effectively deal with everyday requirements (Exner, 1993). Their histories typically include social ineptness, poor success in interpersonal relationships, and times when they have felt overwhelmed by interpersonal demands. Effective moderate- to long-term psychotherapy was found to result in decreases in CDI (Exner & Sanglade, 1992; Weiner & Exner, 1991). However, there is little support for this variable; interpretations should be made with caution (Mihura, 2008).

4. Suicide Constellation (S-CON). The Suicide Constellation comprises 11 variables that collectively are intended to detect persons at risk of attempting suicide. Retrodictive studies indicate that, using a cutoff score of 8, 80% of suicide attempters were accurately identified (Exner, 1986, 1993). However, caution should be exercised in making final decisions. Some clients were incorrectly identified as not being suicidal and yet they later made attempts (false negative rate = 15%). Among depressed populations, a number of clients were incorrectly identified as being at risk of suicide when there was actually no or little risk (false positive rate among depressives = 10%; Exner, 1993). Despite this, there is generally good support for this variable (Mihura, 2008).

5. Hypervigilance Index (HVI). Originally, a series of indicators was isolated from patient protocols that seemed to differentiate paranoid-type patients (paranoid schizophrenics) from other patient groups. This was partially successful in that paranoid schizophrenics and paranoid personalities were correctly identified (88% and 90%, respectively; Exner, 1993). On further investigation, it was found that HVI related more to the hypervigilant aspect of the paranoid style rather than paranoia itself. Thus, persons with positive indicators on HVI are likely to place a large amount of effort into maintaining a high state of preparedness. Motivating this is a sense that they mistrust their environment and experience a chronic sense of vulnerability (Exner, 1993). Before initiating behaviors, they carefully think through why and how they should express them. They are likely to be quite guarded regarding closeness in relationships and initially respond to efforts at closeness with apprehension. As a result, they allow themselves to be close with others only if they feel in control. They are generally quite concerned with issues not only of emotional closeness, but also of personal space in general (Exner, 1993). Moderate support has been found for this variable (Mihura, 2008).

6. Obsessive Style Index (OBS). The Obsessive Style Index was developed by examining the records of clients who had been formally diagnosed as obsessive-compulsive to determine which Rorschach characteristics could distinguish them from other groups. Five characteristics were isolated and, using the designated criteria, they correctly identified 69% of obsessive-compulsives (Exner, 1993). If the OBS is positive (score of

3 or more), it suggests persons who are perfectionistic, indecisive, and preoccupied with details, and who experience difficulty expressing emotion. They are likely to be cautious, conservative, conforming, and conventional (check for high Populars). They process information extremely methodically and, when using the Zd Index definition, are likely to be overincorporators (see interpretation for Zd). However, a positive index does not necessarily indicate psychopathology; rather, it shows a style of approaching the world and processing information. If this style is overly rigid, it can become dysfunctional, particularly when the person is under pressure or is required to achieve goals within a limited time (Exner, 1993). Despite these results, the preponderance of research does not support OBS (Mihura, 2008).

RECOMMENDED READING

Exner, J. E. (2000). *A primer for Rorschach interpretation*. Asheville, NC: Rorschach Workshops.

Exner, J. E. (2001). *A Rorschach workbook for the comprehensive system* (5th ed.). Asheville, NC: Rorschach Workshops.

Exner, J. E. (2003). *The Rorschach: A comprehensive system. Volume 1: Basic foundations* (4th ed.). Hoboken, NJ: John Wiley & Sons.

Exner, J. E., & Weiner, I. (1995). *The Rorschach: A comprehensive system. Volume 3: Assessment of children and adolescents* (2nd ed.). New York: John Wiley & Sons.

Masling, M. (2006). When Homer nods: An examination of some of the systematic errors in Rorschach scholarship. *Journal of Personality Assessment, 87*, 62–73.

Meyer, G. J., & Archer, R. P. (2001). The hard science of Rorschach research: What do we know and where do we go? *Psychological Assessment, 13*, 486–502.

Chapter 11

THEMATIC APPERCEPTION TEST

The Thematic Apperception Test (TAT) is a projective technique consisting of a series of pictures. The examinee is requested to create a story about what he or she believes is occurring in the situations or events depicted by the pictures. Murray (1943) describes the TAT as a "method of revealing to the trained interpreter some of the dominant drives, emotions, sentiments, complexes, and conflicts of personality. Special value resides in its power to expose underlying inhibited tendencies which the subject is not willing to admit, or cannot admit because he is unconscious of them" (p. 1). It differs from projective drawings or inkblot-type tests such as the Rorschach or Holtzman in that the TAT cards present more structured stimuli and require more organized and complex verbal responses. In addition, the TAT typically relies on more qualitative methods of interpretation and assesses the "here and now" features of an individual's life situation rather than the basic underlying structure of personality.

The TAT materials consist of 20 cards with ambiguous pictures on them. The examinee is instructed to make up a story that includes what is occurring in the picture: the thoughts and feelings of the characters, the events that led up to the situation, and the outcome of the story. The examiner can interpret the responses either quantitatively (using rating scales to measure features such as object relations or various needs) or qualitatively (evaluating the story themes using clinical judgment). The results are typically used to supplement other psychological tests because the TAT produces not only highly rich, varied, and complex types of information, but also personal data that theoretically bypass a subject's conscious resistances.

HISTORY AND DEVELOPMENT

The TAT was first conceptualized in a 1935 article by Christina Morgan and Henry Murray but was more fully elaborated in 1938 and 1943 (Gieser & Stein, 1999). Administrators were instructed to give all 20 cards in a given sequence in two separate sessions, which, in total, could last up to two hours. The basic assumption was that unconscious fantasies could be revealed by interpreting the stories subjects told regarding ambiguous pictures. Examiners potentially gained access to things that a client was either unwilling to tell or are unconscious of. Initially, it was believed that the material derived from the test could serve as an "X ray" of personality and would reveal basic themes that might otherwise take months of psychoanalysis to understand. The test immediately had an enthusiastic reception and quickly became used as both a clinical instrument and a research tool. By 1950, several books and more than 100 articles were published either about or using the TAT. The early research studies using the TAT investigated areas such as social attitudes, delinquency, abnormal personality, and variations in the use of language. By the late 1940s, many clinicians were using a limited number of cards and abbreviated scoring systems to reduce the time for administration and scoring. These different TAT systems were elaborated in Shneidman's (1951) *Thematic Test Analysis*. By 1971, more than 1,800 articles had been written based on the TAT.

Despite continuing extensive research, the test is still not considered to have achieved a degree of standardization comparable to the MMPI/MMPI-2 or WAIS-III. There is no clear, agreed-on scoring and interpretive system, and controversy regarding the adequacy of its reliability and validity is ongoing (Hunsley, Lee, & Wood, 2003). Most clinicians vary the methods of administration, especially regarding the number, sequence, and types of cards that are given (Gieser & Stein, 1999). As a result, the TAT is considered a highly impressionistic tool, with interpretation frequently coming from a combination of intuition and clinical experience. Yet, the TAT continues to be extremely popular and currently ranks as the sixth most frequently used test by clinical psychologists (Camara et al., 2000). Fully 63% of psychologists reported using it with adolescent clients (Archer et al., 1991). Clinical psychologists have made it the second most frequently recommended projective test for clinical psychology trainees' competence (Watkins et al., 1995). Furthermore, it has been used in all the European countries, India, South Africa, China, South America, Asia, and the Soviet Union (see Bellak & Abrams, 1997). The TAT (or TAT-type tests) has also been found to be the most frequently used assessment device for cross-cultural research (Dana, 1999, 2005; Retief, 1987).

A number of researchers were dissatisfied with the TAT because they wanted to study different populations (children, the elderly, minorities) and specific problem areas (frustration, stress, social judgment), or because they felt that the TAT produced negative, low-energy stories. These concerns stimulated numerous variations. The most common is the Children's Apperception Test (CAT; Bellak, 1954, 1986, 1993; Bellak & Abrams, 1997) designed for children between the ages of 3 and 10. Only 10 cards are given, and animals are depicted instead of humans. The rationale was that because children have shorter attention spans, they need fewer cards. It was also believed that they could more easily identify with pictures of animals than with pictures of humans. However, Teglasi (2001) determined that stories by children when responding to pictures of animals or humans are equally as meaningful. Subsequently, another version of the CAT was developed depicting humans instead of animals (CAT-Human or CAT-H). The Gerontological Apperception Test (Wolk & Wolk, 1971) and the more frequently used Senior Apperception Test (SAT; Bellak, 1975, 1986, 1993; Bellak & Abrams; 1997, Bellak & Bellak, 1973) are designed for elderly populations and show pictures of elderly people involved in scenes more likely to concern them, such as depictions of loneliness and family conflicts.

One of the most recent additions to child TAT-type assessment is the Roberts Apperception Test for Children (RATC; McArthur & Roberts, 1990) designed to be used for clients between the ages of 5 and 16. There are a total of 27 cards of which 11 are alternate versions for males and females. The cards are organized so that each person is administered a total of 16 cards in a set sequence. It was recently revised and renamed the Roberts-2 (Roberts, 2006). The main new features are an increase in the maximum age to 18 and parallel sets of cards for white, Hispanic, and African American examinees.

The Tell Me A Story Test (TEMAS; Costantino & Malgady, 1999; Costantino, Malgady, & Rogler, 1988), designed for use with child and adolescent minorities, includes 23 cards depicting Hispanic, African American, and Asian American characters in situations of interpersonal conflict (Costantino, Dana, & Malgady, 2007; Costantino & Malgady, 1999). There is also a parallel version for nonminorities. Scoring is made for nine different personality functions (aggression, anxiety, etc.), and the scores have been found to effectively discriminate between minority outpatients and minority normal school children (Costantino, Malgady, Casullo, & Castillo, 1991; Costantino, Malgady,

Rogler, & Tsui, 1988; R. Flanagan & Guiseppe, 1999) as well as nonminority normals and clinical groups (Costantino, Malgady, Colon-Malgady, & Bailey, 1992). The TEMAS is probably the best constructed and most psychometrically sound TAT variation to date (see R. Flanagan & Giuseppe, 1999).

Several TAT-type tests have been designed to study specific problem areas. The Rosenzweig Picture Frustration Study (Rosenzweig, 1976, 1977, 1978) was designed to more fully understand how persons perceive and deal with frustration. The Stress Tolerance Test is an older test that may begin to be used more frequently again in understanding how a subject responds to stressful scenes of combat (Harrower, 1986). More recently, K. Caruso (1988) developed a series of TAT-type cards to study the presence of and dynamics involved in child abuse. Three sets of cards are available: (a) the basic set of 25 cards depicting scenes pulling for possible child abuse; (b) a 10-card set for neglect; and (c) 5 cards to assess attitudes toward different courtroom themes. The Family Apperception Test, composed of 21 pictures of family interactions, is designed to assess family dynamics (Julian, Sotile, Henry, & Sotile, 1991). The Blacky Pictures Test (G. Blum, 1950, 1962, 1968) is another thematic-type test that is closely aligned to psychoanalytic theory. It presents children with pictures of a dog, Blacky, that is involved in situations consistent with psychoanalytic theory, such as themes surrounding oral, anal, and phallic stages of development.

Ritzler, Sharkey, and Chudy (1980) have criticized the TAT for producing negative, low-energy stories and for containing outdated pictures that are difficult for persons to identify with. To counter this, they developed the Southern Mississippi TAT (SM-TAT) using pictures derived from the *Family of Man* (Steichen, 1955) photo collection. They report that using the SM-TAT pictures produces stories with more activity, greater emotional tone, and relatively few variations in thematic content (Sharkey & Ritzler, 1985). More important, the results derived from the SM-TAT were more effective in discriminating different pathological groups than the TAT. Depressives produced gloomy stories, and psychotics demonstrated more perceptual distortions when compared with normals. A more recent but similar attempt is the 8-card Apperceptive Personality Test (APT), which has the advantages of an objective scoring system, a set sequence of card presentations, multiethnic pictures, and initial positive validity outcomes (Holmstrom, Karp, & Silber, 1994; Karp, Holmstrom, & Silber, 1989; Karp, Silber, Holmstrom, Banks, & Karp, 1992). Although the SM-TAT and APT are more modern, are based on a more rigorous methodology, and demonstrate greater diagnostic validity, the long tradition and extensive research associated with the TAT may make it difficult to supplant, even with potentially better instruments.

In addition to the TAT's derivatives, a number of different approaches to scoring and interpreting the TAT itself have been developed. The original approach by Murray involved assessing which character in the story is the "hero" or focal figure, and then quantifying the relative intensity of each expressed need on a 5-point scale. Murray also included measuring the forces of the hero/heroine's environment (press), types of outcomes, basic themes (themas), and interests and sentiments of the hero/heroine. However, Murray's system has not been popular since it is quite cumbersome and time consuming. In addition to Murray's system, many variations have been developed by authors such as Arnold (1962), Bellak (1975, 1986, 1993; Bellak & Abrams, 1997), Chusmir (1985), Cramer (2006), Dana (1955), Eron (1950), McClelland (1971), Sokolowski, Schmalt, Langens, and Puca (2000), A. Thomas and Dudek (1985), Weston (1995), and Wyatt (1947). Most of these have been summarized and evaluated in Jenkins's (2008) *Handbook of Clinical Scoring Systems for Thematic Apperception Techniques.* The extensive diversity of different systems led Murstein, in his 1963 review of the TAT, to remark: "There would seem to be as many thematic scoring systems as there were hairs in the beard of Rasputin" (p. 23).

The most frequently used and updated system has been Bellak's (1975, 1986, 1993; Bellak & Abrams, 1997). His book on the TAT (*The TAT, CAT, and SAT in Clinical Use*) has undergone six editions and is perhaps the simplest and most frequently used of the available systems (Rossini & Moretti, 1997). As a result, his scoring method and interpretive approach have been included in this chapter.

Although the TAT is still relatively popular, there are signs that its use is decreasing for a variety of reasons (C. Piotrowski, 1999). Managed care organizations are increasingly requiring clinicians to use brief, focused, time-efficient, and cost-effective instruments (see Chapter 13; Groth-Marnat, 1999, 2000b). In contrast, the TAT takes considerable time to administer, score, and interpret. Instruments that are far more focused on, and more empirically connected to, treatment planning have also been developed (see Chapter 14). In addition, professional psychologists are being expected to be proficient in an increasingly wider variety of instruments (i.e., neuropsychological assessment, behavioral assessment), leaving less time for the time-consuming training required for projectives. Alternative instruments, such as the rapid proliferation of rating scales during the last half of the 1990s, have helped to supplant the TAT/CAT's use with children and adolescents (Kamphaus et al., 2000). Finally, controversy regarding the psychometric properties of projectives has increased over the past few years (Garb, 1998b, 1999; Garb, 2005a).

Despite these trends, there are a number of noteworthy developments relevant to the TAT and its future. A number of more recent scoring systems that have made useful and valid predictions have been thoroughly researched (see Jenkins, 2008). For example, Weston et al.'s (1995) Social Cognition and Object Relations Scale has predicted relevant dimensions of personality disorders (S. Ackerman, Clemence, Weatherill, & Hilsenroth, 1999), the impact of sexual abuse on clients (Kernhof, Kaufhold, & Grabhorn, 2008), and children's internal representations of their relationships (Niec & Russ, 2002). In general, the object relations school has placed considerable interest in extending the knowledge and usefulness of the TAT. In addition, Cramer's (2006) assessment of defensive styles (denial, projection, identification) using her *Defense Mechanism Manual* has been found to have both good interscorer reliability (.80) and validity (see Meyer, 2004). Finally, the earlier "big three" assessment of motives (achievement, affiliation, power) by McClelland (1971) has been shown to have good interscorer reliability (.85+), relate to a wide number of external measures, and be useful in cross cultural research (Langan-Fox & Grant, 2006; Meyer, 2004).

Finally, there has also been considerable interest in better understanding client narratives as they relate to therapeutic techniques, health outcomes, and the structure of personality (see Special Series in the *Journal of Clinical Psychology*, 1999, 55:1175–1270). This interest has also helped to extend and better understand the meanings of TAT narratives (i.e., Cramer, 1996, 2006; Pennebaker & King, 1999). One possible future for the TAT (and its derivatives) might be that a combination of voice recognition technology and rapid computer analysis and interpretation of word clusters and sequences may make it a more practical, time-efficient technique as well as allow the most validated interpretations to be selected and used (see Fertuck, Bucci, Blatt, & Ford, 2004).

THEORETICAL PERSPECTIVES

The TAT was originally developed based on Murray's concepts of personality. At the core of his concepts was a focus on how individuals interact with their environments—how people are affected by external forces and how their unique sets of needs, attitudes, and values influence their reaction to the world around them. Perhaps more than any other theorist, he has analyzed and clarified the concept of *needs*. The TAT itself was originally conceptualized as a means of measuring the strengths of various needs as expressed by the designated hero in the story. A need can be either provoked by internal processes or, more frequently, the result of specific environmental forces. Murray developed a list of 28 needs that helped to specify the total possible needs that might be expressed in an individual's life (or reflected in TAT stories). To balance and complement the presence of needs, Murray also developed a list of possible forces in a person's environment, which he termed *press*. A total of 24 press were identified, and the relative strength of these press could also be scored on the TAT. As a result, Murray's theory is oftentimes referred to as *needs-press theory*.

To conceptualize units of behavior that result from the interaction between needs and press, Murray developed the term *thema*. A thema is a small unit of behavior that can combine with other thema to form *serial thema*. An individual's *unity thema* is the pattern of related needs and press that gives meaning to the largest portion of his or her behavior. For example, a core and overriding feature of an individual might be rebelliousness or martyrdom. This may be sufficiently well organized and powerful to override even primary (biological) needs, as amply demonstrated in the case of a martyr who is willing to die for his or her beliefs. A unity thema is derived from early infantile experiences and, once developed, repeats itself in many forms during an individual's later life. It operates largely as an unconscious force, and Murray (1938) described it as "a compound of interrelated-collaborating or conflicting-dominant needs that are linked to press to which the individual was exposed on one or more particular occasions, gratifying or traumatic, in early childhood" (pp. 604–605). The TAT was designed to assess both small units of thema and the larger, core aspects of an individual's unity themas.

Murray's theories of personality were obviously the main influence on the early development and use of the TAT. However, psychoanalytic, object relations, and theories of understanding narratives have also had a significant influence on conceptualizing, scoring, and interpreting the TAT. Psychoanalytic conceptualizations easily lend themselves to the interpretation of TAT stories. The cards themselves depict many images that are highly relevant to a psychodynamic perspective, such as possible superego conflicts in Card 1 (boy sitting at a table with a violin in front of him) or castration anxiety related to Card 8BM (a boy in the foreground staring into space with two men in the background performing surgery on a patient lying down). Stories often relate to internal conflict and how the person deals with this conflict. The Bellak scoring system (Bellak & Abrams, 1997) is organized around classic psychodynamic domains, such as the client's conceptualization of parental figures, main defenses against conflicts and fears, adequacy of the superego, and the main drives of the hero. Cramer's (1996) scoring system specifically includes scoring for the defense mechanisms of denial, projection, and identification.

TAT stories can also be understood as depicting the quality of a client's object relations. This is reflected in Weston's coding system (Social Cognition and Object Relations Scale; Weston, 1995), which focuses on understanding these crucial areas of psychological functioning: (a) the client's internal representation of significant others, (b) quality of affect in relationships, (c) capacity for emotional investments and moral integrity, and (d) understanding the extent to which a person can understand interpersonal motivation. The themes surrounding TAT stories can be seen as ideal sources of data to extract and elaborate on these areas of client functioning. As would be expected, researchers have used the TAT to better understand those disorders that lend themselves to poor object relations, such as narcissistic, borderline, and antisocial personalities (Ackerman et al., 1999; Cramer, 1999).

One of the core activities of being human seems to be the importance of constructing a coherent story. Much of therapy can be considered an interaction that helps the client to re-create the story of his or her life in a way that the client can more easily live with. Thus, narrative can both reflect a person's current condition and be used as a means of creating change (Burns, 2001; Groth-Marnat, 1992). Certain patterns of narrative (reflecting on self versus describing external experiences) have been associated with better therapeutic outcomes (Angus, Levitt, & Hardtke, 1999). Research has also found that the word patterns that people use over time are quite reliable and reflect not only how people cognitively organize their world but also relevant dimensions of personality (Pennebaker & King, 1999). Having people write emotionally laden stories for as little as 15 minutes a day for 4 consecutive days has been found to result in less illness, positive increases in markers of immune system, higher grades, and lower reported pain levels (Pennebaker & King, 1999). It also seems that after people have been able to adequately understand how and why an event occurred, they are more able to deal with it the next time it occurs and can also move beyond it. This area of research has had a direct impact on the TAT in the form of new coding systems, greater understanding to how everyday narrative relates to TAT stories, and the factor structure of word patterns on the TAT (Pennebaker & King, 1999).

RELIABILITY AND VALIDITY

A subject's responses to the TAT involve complex, meaningful verbal material. As a result, there are many of possible ways of assessing the meanings of the data. On one hand is a clinical, intuitive approach in which determining reliability and validity is quite problematic. In contrast are the many formal coding systems that have been developed. Many of these systems have been able to establish good reliability and validity. However, reliability (and validity) for one system may not mean that adequate reliability will be present for another system. Some success in achieving adequate interscorer reliability has resulted from the development of the various quantitative scoring strategies and rating scales. This is especially true for the work of McClelland (1961) and Atkinson and Feather (1966), who developed complex scoring schemes for achievement, affiliation, and power. Interscorer reliability across different scoring systems has generally been found to be good, ranging between .37 and .90, with most reports .85 or higher (Meyer, 2004; Pennebaker & King, 1999; Winter, 1999). Although scorers can agree on the quantitative values assigned to different variables, however, these values still constitute raw data and not conclusions. In other words, it remains questionable whether clinicians make the same inferences regarding personality based on the quantitative scores. Briefly, good interscorer reliability relating to areas such as the weighting of different needs has been achieved, but agreement between the conclusions based on these scores typically has not been adequately demonstrated. A further complication is the fact that, in actual practice, clinicians rely primarily on intuitive clinical judgment, use different sets of instructions, and vary the number, type, and sequence of cards from one client to the next (Gieser & Stein, 1999; Karon, 2000). Thus, reliability in clinical contexts is likely to be considerably lower than under experimental conditions.

Another difficulty in determining reliability lies in the wide variability among different stories. If test evaluators wish to determine the internal consistency of the TAT, they are confronted with the fact that the various cards are not comparable (Cramer, 1999; Entwisle, 1972). They were designed to measure separate areas of a person's functioning. Thus, a strategy such as split-half reliability is inappropriate. Not only are different stories in the same administration likely to be different, but so are the stories between two different administrations. Thus, measures of internal consistency have been (and would be expected to be) low (Entwisle, 1972). Likewise, when subjects were asked to tell different stories on different administrations, the test-retest reliabilities derived from quantitative scorings of various needs were low (Lindzey & Herman, 1955). In contrast, Lundy (1985) found that when subjects were requested to tell a similar story between one administration and the next, test-retest reliabilities achieved a respectable .56 (need for affiliation) and .48 (need for achievement). This finding suggests that the test-retest reliability of the TAT might be underestimated. However, the higher reliabilities found by Lundy might reflect merely the quality of memory rather than the stability of personality indices on the TAT.

Reviews of the TAT's validity have shown wide variability. Proponents of the test describe "impressive" and "strong" relationships, whereas critics have said that validity is "almost nonexistent." This disparity can be partially accounted for by differing interpretations of the data. One reviewer might be impressed by a correlation of .25 while another sees it as highly deficient. It would seem that not only is the TAT a projective test itself, but the research done on it likewise allows readers to project their biases, needs, and expectations onto the TAT. One factor that might help to explain the differences in results between studies is that the TAT has been found to be quite sensitive to the effects of instructions. Lundy (1988), for example, found that under conditions that were non-threatening, neutral, and unstructured, there were moderate correlations between outside criterion measures and needs for achievement, affiliation, and power. When instructions were used that presented the TAT as a structured formal test or, especially, when any words were used that might have been interpreted as threatening (will "reveal imperfections" or "minor defects"), the correlations were nonsignificant. This result suggests the interesting possibility that the wide variation in the findings of different studies may have been partially influenced by slight variations in instructions.

Studies attempting to determine criterion validity have shown a balance between positive and negative findings. One major problem lies in establishing agreed-on external criteria. If short-term overt behavior is used as the criterion, there is often little correspondence to test scores. For example, high aggression on TAT scores usually does not reflect the degree to which a person actually expresses aggressive behavior. However, it may still be valuable to understand a person's internal processes even though these are not outwardly expressed. When measures of needs on the TAT were compared with needs measured on tests such as the Personal Research Form, Edwards Personal Preference Schedule, Adjective Check List, and other forms of self-rated questionnaires, there was little correspondence (Megargee & Parker, 1968; Schultheiss & Brunstein, 2001; Spangler, 1992). These findings would seem to call into question the usefulness of TAT protocols. However, a number of positive findings between the TAT and outside criteria have also been reported. An early and frequently cited study by Harrison (1940) found that diagnosis by a trained clinician using the TAT was accurate 75% of the time when assessing broad diagnostic categories. Similarly, a correlation of .78 was found when comparing TAT inferences with data from hospital records. The most extensively studied constructs have been achievement, affiliation, and power (Lundy, 1988; Spangler, 1992; Winter, 1999), and these, too, have had varying degrees of success when they were compared with outside criteria. Examples of positive results include a high need for achievement being associated with greater social attractiveness (Teevan, Diffenderfer, & Greenfield, 1986), need for affiliation being positively correlated with a preference for an internally directed orientation to tasks (Schroth, 1987), and need for achievement being positively related to grade point average (although this might have been confounded by verbal fluency; Lindgren, Moritsch, Thurlin, & Mich, 1986). In addition, Coche and Sillitti (1983) reported that the presence of depressive themes on the TAT was correlated with measures of depression on the MMPI and Beck Depression Inventory. Maitra (1983) found that the fantasies of highly effective executives differed significantly from those of relatively ineffective executives in that the more effective executives had more original themes, expressed a broader range of interests, were more intellectual, and could see beyond the individual details of their work.

In a meta-analysis of 105 studies, Spangler (1992) concluded that, on average, TAT correlations of behavior (.19 to .22) were slightly larger than correlations based on questionnaires (.13 to .15). This is consistent with Meyer's (2004) review, which found a .22 correlation with TAT achievement scores and external spontaneous achievement behavior. Although these correlations were low to moderate, the TAT results were relatively more effective in different situations. The TAT produced quite high correlations (.66) when subjects were required to spontaneously initiate (*internally*) their own behavior to achieve some activity (moderate task risk, task completion, response to time pressure). In contrast, self-report questionnaires were low in making these predictions but relatively effective (.35) in predicting situations involving real-world behavior where social reinforcement (external) was present (Spangler, 1992).

Like the studies on criterion validity, the work on construct validity has shown varying results. A representative confirmatory study provided support for the hypothesis that subjects who were experimentally frustrated produced subsequent stories in which the focal characters in the stories expressed increased aggression (Lindzey & Kalnins, 1958). Somewhat similarly, increased levels of stress have been associated with higher defense-related scores on the TAT (Cramer, 1998). In general, the scoring systems for both the *Defense Mechanism Manual* (Cramer, 2006) and the Social Cognition and Object Relations Scale (Westen, 1995) have shown good validity (see Jenkins, 2008).

An important issue in the interpretation of criterion validity studies on the TAT and other projective devices is understanding the implications of different levels of interpretation. W. Klopfer (1983) summarized the earlier work of Leary (1957) by indicating that behavior can be based on outside observations (direct behavioral data, public communication), self-descriptions, or private symbolization. These three levels are often quite different from one another. For example, the observations by others are frequently quite discrepant from how a particular person perceives himself or herself. Likewise, a person's inner fantasy life (private symbolization) is often quite different from his or her public behavior. Projective tests such as the TAT primarily assess a person's inner life of private symbolization. McClelland, Koestner, and Weinberger (1989) have described the characteristics that the TAT measures as being *implicit* motives as opposed to more conscious self-attributions. Thus, the TAT measured motives and underlying themes that are physiologically and nonconsciously connected to the person, and they influence long-term rather than short-term behaviors. This finding is supported in that TAT results do accurately predict long-term outcomes such as overall success in a person's career (Spangler, 1992). McClelland et al. (1989) even emphasize that it would be unreasonable for the TAT to correlate highly with immediate, conscious, short-term behavior because this is not what the TAT was designed to measure. Furthermore, it may not even be desirable for TAT data to relate to immediate external behavior because it is precisely this ability to access a person's inner life that makes the TAT both unique and valuable. From a practical perspective, each clinician needs to evaluate these issues and establish the importance each places on having access to a person's inner world of private symbolization.

One argument against subjecting the TAT to strict psychometric scrutiny is that rigid objective studies do not represent the way in which the TAT is actually used in clinical practice (Karon, 2000). When experienced clinicians were requested to provide individual descriptions of persons based on TAT stories, the descriptions did tend to match independent descriptions based on case histories (Arnold, 1949; Harrison, 1940; Karon, 2000). However, although the descriptions by individual clinicians were fairly accurate, there was usually little agreement among different clinicians evaluating the same person. It might be argued that, because of the complexity and richness of the material, each clinician was tapping into different (but still potentially valid) aspects of the same person. The poor interrater reliability might then be interpreted not as representing inaccuracy but rather different approaches to the material, with each of these approaches having potentially relevant meanings for the client being evaluated.

ASSETS AND LIMITATIONS

Despite questions related to the TAT's reliability and validity, its frequency of use over the past 40 years has remained essentially unchanged (Archer et al., 1991; Camara et al., 2000; Lubin et al., 1985). It is still rated in the top 10 most frequently used instruments, and it has produced the fourth largest number of research studies (behind the MMPI, Wechsler intelligence scales, and Rorschach). One reviewer has summarized the incongruity between its popularity and its questionable validity by stating "there are still enthusiastic clinicians and doubting statisticians" (Adcock, 1965). In light of this controversy, it is especially important that clinicians fully understand the general assets and limitations involved with the TAT.

Like most projective techniques, it theoretically offers access to the covert and deeper structures of an individual's personality. There also may be less susceptibility to faking because the purpose of projective techniques is usually disguised, and the subject often slackens his or her conscious defenses while releasing unconscious material. However, because the TAT deals with verbally familiar material, there is a somewhat greater potential for the subject to bias and distort his or her responses when compared to the less familiar stimuli of the Rorschach. A further asset is the focus on the global nature of personality rather than on the objective measurement of specific traits or attitudes. These global features include not only emotional, motivational, interpersonal, and defensive characteristics but also general intellectual level, verbal fluency, originality, and style of solving problems. Finally, there is ease of rapport. The TAT is generally regarded as intrinsically interesting and nonthreatening because there are no "wrong" answers and there are no direct questions related to personal and potentially sensitive information. However, certain types of individuals might still feel quite anxious and insecure with the TAT's relative lack of structure.

In contrast to these assets, these general criticisms have been leveled at the TAT (and projective techniques in general). There has typically been difficulty establishing adequate internal consistency and test-retest reliability. Because adequate normative data are generally lacking, clinicians often rely on clinical experience when they interpret the responses. The standardization in respect to administration and scoring is generally lacking. Most clinicians vary the number and types of cards presented and utilize an impressionistic means of interpreting the data. Formal scoring methods are rarely used in clinical practice despite their demonstrated psychometric properties (see Jenkins, 2008). It might be argued that the TAT should not really be considered a "test" unless these formal scoring methods are used. Since these formal scoring methods are used so rarely, the effectiveness of the technique is often more dependent on the clinician's individual skill than on the quality of the test itself. Clinicians relying primarily on their individual skill has resulted in part from an inadequate development of norms and from the fact that the norms that have been created are only a rough approximation of common story themes or the "pull" of each of the cards (see Typical Themes Elicited section). Frequently, in clinical practice, each practitioner develops his or her own individual intuitive norms, based on experience. Thus, the clinician may have a general intuitive conception of what constitutes a "schizophrenic" or "narcissistic" story and will use this subjective schema during diagnostic or interpretive procedures. Reliance on clinical experience becomes indirectly encouraged both by the lack of precise normative data and, more important, by the belief that norms tend to decrease the richness and comprehensiveness of the material being studied.

Most studies on the TAT, as well as the results coming from individual assessments, are confounded by verbal abilities, age, sex, intelligence, and reading ability (Klein, 1986). The TAT has also been shown to be quite sensitive to situational variables such as mood (McFarland, 1984), stress, sleep deprivation, and differences in instruction (Lundy, 1988). These variables can significantly alter test performance, thereby reducing the likelihood that stable aspects of personality are being measured. Finally, many of the validity studies on the TAT have been equivocal. In particular, several researchers have noted that there has been no increase in incremental validity when the TAT and most other projectives are used in a battery of tests (see Garb, 1984, 1998b; Garb, Lilienfeld, & Wood, 2004; Hunsley et al., 2003; Klein, 1986; Lanyon & Goodstein, 1982).

In contrast to these limitations, one important asset is that the responses the TAT produces from clients (verbal stories) are familiar rather than hidden and mysterious. Even a relatively untrained person can appreciate the differing themes, moods, and perspectives portrayed in the stories. The experienced clinician also profits from this inherent familiarity or approachability of the test data.

A further asset of the TAT is its origin within an academic-humanistic environment. It is not closely aligned with any particular school of thought and, therefore, can be approached from, and interpreted by, a number of different theoretical orientations. Furthermore, the TAT was developed from the study of normal individuals rather than by case studies or normative comparisons with disordered populations. This orientation has evolved directly out of Murray's belief that the proper beginning point for understanding personality is the intensive and detailed study of normal persons.

The TAT potentially provides a comprehensive evaluation of personality, which has sometimes been referred to as a *wide-band* approach. For example, among the comprehensive dimensions that the TAT can assess are these: a person's cognitive style, imaginative processes, family dynamics, inner adjustment, emotional reactivity, defensive structure, internal representation of significant people, general intelligence, and sexual adjustment (Bellak & Abrams; 1997; Gieser & Stein, 1999; W. Henry, 1956; Moretti & Rossini, 2004). The TAT also has some potential to evaluate areas such as creativity, level of affect, problem-solving skill, and verbal fluency. Thus, although the TAT is primarily concerned with providing insight into a person's fundamental needs and patterns of interaction, it can potentially give important information about a far wider range of areas. In particular, the TAT may bypass conscious resistance to provide themes that the person may not reveal upon direct questioning. For example, alcoholics who reported high levels of internal locus of control on direct self-report questionnaires typically became highly externally oriented when locus of control was measured using a TAT-type instrument (R. Costello & Wicott, 1984). This finding might be interpreted as the TAT-type test bypassing their conscious denial and assessing a possibly more accurate, or at least different, level of private symbolization.

Although the TAT is potentially quite versatile, it is not self-sufficient. A number of authors have emphasized that the TAT yields optimal results only when included in a battery of tests (Anastasi & Urbina, 1997) and/or as a type of structured clinical interview

(Obrzut & Cummings, 1983). The TAT typically has been found to be a rich source of developing a wide variety of hypotheses. In contrast, it requires other sources of assessment to actually test whether these hypotheses are accurate.

One unresolved dispute surrounding the TAT is the relationship between inner fantasies and overt behavior. It has been assumed by most projective test originators, including Murray, that fantasy productions can be used to predict covert motivational dispositions. However, it is questionable whether high fantasy productions in a certain area actually parallel overt behavior (Klinger, 1966; McClelland, 1966; Skolnick, 1966). In fact, fantasies may even serve to compensate for a lack of certain behaviors. It might be quite consistent for a highly repressed, overcontrolled person to have a high number of inner aggressive fantasies. In a 20-year longitudinal study of adolescents who obtained high TAT scores on need for achievement, the subjects were often *not* among those who subsequently showed upward social mobility. However, individuals who had shown upward social mobility typically obtained higher TAT need-for-achievement scores as adults. The interpretive significance here is that it might be better to see fantasy productions as samples of thoughts that may or may not accurately reflect overt behavior.

Practical difficulties associated with the TAT include the extensive amount of training required to properly learn the technique and its poor cost-effectiveness in terms of the time required for administration and scoring (Groth-Marnat, 1999; Haynes & Peltier, 1985). Simply obtaining biographical information, asking direct questions during an interview, or using rating forms or questionnaires might give similar information in a simpler and quicker manner. It is likely that any major developments in the TAT will occur through the use of computerized content analysis of natural language (Fertuck et al., 2004; Gottschalk, 2000). This may make using it time efficient, provide more versatility in scoring, and possibly help develop stronger psychometric properties.

USE WITH DIVERSE GROUPS

The TAT has been used extensively in clinical and research purposes in various cross-national contexts in South America, Asia, and Europe. However, the original TAT was developed within a European American context. In order to counter this, numerous versions of the TAT have been developed (see History and Development section), including versions for such groups as Chinese, African Americans, and Hispanics. Typically these versions have merely used different cards. For the most part, different norms and scoring categories have not been developed.

Since verbal narratives are likely to be quite influenced by culture, clinicians need to be quite careful in interpreting TAT data for persons from diverse cultural backgrounds. Stories are likely to be influenced by such factors as norms related to denial versus the expression of distress, the influence of religion in stories, beliefs about health/illness, individualism/collectivism, and the extent to which the person relies on internal as opposed to external sources of knowledge (Dana, 2005). For example, Hofer and Chasiotis (2004) compared Zambian and German stories and concluded that the images had different "pull" for these two groups. In order to better situate the TAT narratives, Dana (2005) recommends that the clinician first clarifies the client's understanding of the reason for the assessment. This will lead to clarifying possible conceptions of mental health in general and assessment in particular. Then the clinician should ask questions related to the degree to which the client is acculturated. The less the person is acculturated, the more the clinician needs to be cautious and also to increase his or her understanding of the culture the client is from. In particular, clinicians need to consider whether the TAT narratives represent merely general cultural beliefs or whether they represent personality features that are unique to the person.

In order to optimize the TAT for various groups, relevant stimuli should be used, if available. For example, Chinese images should be used with Chinese clients and Hispanic images for those from Hispanic backgrounds. In addition, scoring variables should be normed in the culture the person is from. Unfortunately, culture specific norms and images are rarely available. Exceptions are TAT versions such as the TEMAS (see Costantino et al., 2007) and the Roberts-2 (Roberts, 2006). Ideally the norms should consider educational level and acculturation, and be developed with the participation of local people. Interpretations should take into account aspects of the culture. For example, clients from a culture that is generally hesitant to reveal personal information should not then be judged as being "defensive" or "restrained" when they might merely be expressing a cultural norm of being slow to disclose information. Clinicians might also wish to collaborate more with their clients to form consensus on the meanings of stories.

ADMINISTRATION

General Considerations

The TAT was intended to be administered in an interpersonal setting in which subjects verbally respond to pictures presented to them. However, when the examiner is absent, responses may be taped or written by the subject. The disadvantage of these latter procedures is that the subject's responses are often more contrived and clichéd, because more time is available to censor fantasy material.

The TAT materials consist of 20 cards on which ambiguous pictures are printed. The cards are numbered so that 20 cards can be presented to four different groups: adult males, adult females, boys, and girls. The back of each card is coded with a number and/or letters to designate which sex and/or age group the card is intended for. A number without a letter indicates the card is to be administered to all subjects regardless of age or sex. A number with "M" or "F" designates that the card is intended for males or females, and "B" or "G" designates boys or girls, respectively. There may also be a number and either BM or GF, indicating the card is to be given to boys/males or girls/females.

Although Murray originally recommended that all 20 cards be given, in actual practice shorter versions typically consisting of 8 to 12 selected cards are used (Bellak & Abrams, 1997; Haynes & Peltier, 1985; Karon, 2000). The selection of cards may be idiosyncratic to the patient's presenting problem or based on previous information derived from relevant history or other test data. For example, if depression and suicide are significant issues for the client, the examiner might administer cards 3BM, 13B, and 14 in an attempt to gather specific information regarding the dynamics of the client's condition. Specific cards may also be selected because they typically produce rich responses. Bellak and Abrams (1997) recommend that the following standard sequence of 10 cards be administered to both females and males in this exact order: 1, 2, 3BM, 4, 6BM, 7GF, 8BM, 9GF, 10, and 13MF. They further recommend that an essential sequence of cards to be administered to all males consist of: 1, 2, 3BM, 4, 6BM, 7BM, 11, 12M, and 13MF. The essential cards for all females are: 1, 2, 3, 3BM, 4, 6GF, 7GF, 9GF, 11, and 13MF. If a reduced number of cards is used, it may be preferable to give the cards in the sequence numbered on the back.

For research purposes, a slightly different listing of card frequencies has been found by Keiser and Prather (1990), who reviewed 26 studies that specified which of Murray's cards were used. The 10 most frequent cards were 1, 2, 3BM, 3GF, 4, 5, 6BM, 6GF, 8BM, and 8GF.

During administration, the subject should be seated beside the examiner, with his or her chair turned away so that he or she cannot see the expressions on the examiner's face. Ideally, this creates a situation in which the subject is comfortable and relaxed, so that his or her imagination can freely respond to the cards. However, if some individuals do not feel comfortable when turned away from the examiner, they should be allowed to sit in a position that is more relaxing for them. Of primary importance are establishing adequate rapport and keeping the subject comfortable and relaxed.

Instructions

Murray's original instructions from the *Thematic Apperception Test Manual* (1943) are as follows:

> This is a test of imagination, one form of intelligence. I am going to show you some pictures, one at a time; and your task will be to make up as dramatic a story as you can for each. Tell what has led up to the event shown in the picture, describe what is happening at the moment, what the characters are feeling and thinking; and then give the outcome. Speak your thoughts as they come to your mind. Do you understand? Since you have fifty minutes for ten pictures, you can devote about five minutes to each story. Here is the first picture. (p. 3)

This set of instructions is suitable for adolescents and adults of average intelligence and sophistication. However, the instructions should be modified for children, adults with minimal education or intelligence, and psychotics. For these types of individuals, Murray (1943) suggests that the examiner state:

> This is a story-telling test. I have some pictures here that I am going to show you, and for each picture I want you to make up a story. Tell what is happening before and what is happening now. Say what the people are feeling and thinking and how it will come out. You can make up any story you please. Do you understand? Well, then, here is the first picture. You have five minutes to make up a story. See how well you can do. (pp. 3–4)

Such instructions may, of course, be modified, elaborated, or repeated to meet the individual needs of each subject. Lundy (1988) recommends that the instructions be given in as neutral and nonthreatening a manner as possible, so that the person does not become defensive. Defensiveness is likely to compromise the quality and accuracy of information. Any references to the TAT as a "test" should be avoided. However, the instructions should clearly indicate that the client is to use some imagination and not merely provide a description of the pictures. Variations on the instructions should also emphasize the four requirements of the story structure:

1. Current situation.
2. Thoughts and feelings of the characters.
3. Preceding events.
4. Outcome.

The instructions, either in whole or in part, may be repeated at any time, particularly if the subject has given a story that is too short or too long, or if he or she has left out one or more of the four requirements. The TAT can potentially be useful for evaluating mentally retarded persons, but particular care needs to be taken to ensure that the instructions are concrete and explicit. The examiner may also want to check whether the instructions have been clearly understood. He or she may need to encourage the person at various times during the storytelling.

Procedure

Time

The time measured should begin when the picture is first presented and end when the subject begins his or her story. It is particularly important to notice any long pauses or hesitations. They may reflect a struggle with conflictual or anxiety-laden material.

Recording

A subject's complete responses should be recorded, along with any noteworthy behavioral observations: exclamations, stuttering, pauses, blushing, degree of involvement, and changes in voice inflection. Thus, the general purpose of recording is not only to develop a reproduction of the verbatim story content but to assess how the person interacts with the picture. As mentioned previously, ongoing verbal involvement with the cards is the preferable form of administration. Having subjects write out their own stories allows time for critically evaluating and censoring their responses. There is no objection to the use of a tape recorder, although, under such conditions, it is helpful to have the examiner record noteworthy behavioral observations and obtain the clients' written consent.

Questioning and Inquiry

If a subject omits certain aspects of the story, such as the outcome or preceding events, the examiner should ask for additional information. This may take the form of questions, such as "What led up to it?" or "How does it end?" However, these requests for clarification or amplification should not be stated in such a way as to bias the stories or reveal the examiner's personal reaction. An optional, more detailed inquiry may be undertaken either after the entire administration of the cards or directly after each story. Murray recommends that the inquiry occur only after the administration of all the cards. Sample inquiry questions may include: "What made you think of this story?" or "Do people you have mentioned in the story remind you of friends or acquaintances?" As with questioning, the inquiry should not be too forceful or it may produce defensiveness and withdrawal. The overall purpose of both the questioning and the inquiry is to produce an unhampered and free flow of the subject's fantasy material.

Order of Presentation

Usually, the cards should be administered according to their sequential numbering system. However, at times, the examiner may be interested in a specific problem and alter the sequence to more effectively obtain information concerning that problem area. For example, if the clinician is particularly interested in problems relating to family constellation in a male subject, the examiner might include some of the female series involving sisters, girlfriends, or wives.

Use of the TAT (or CAT) with Children

Instructions for children should, of course, be modified in accordance with their age and vocabulary. It is usually helpful to describe the test as an opportunity to tell stories or as an interesting game. In general, cards from the TAT should be based on the likelihood that children may easily identify with the characters. For use with children, the TAT cards that have the highest number of interpretable responses and the lowest number of refusals are, in order of usefulness: 7GF, 18GF, 3GF, and 8GF. In contrast, the least helpful cards are 19, 18BM, 11, and 12BG (Bellak & Abrams, 1997).

The stories of children seem to be relatively easily influenced by recent events experienced via television, movies, and computer games. Children also tend to project their problems and conflicts into a story in a more direct and straightforward manner than adults. Often there is little hidden meaning or masking of the relationships involved.

TYPICAL THEMES ELICITED

At the present time, no formal normative standards have been developed for the TAT. The "norms" that are available are descriptions of the typical themes that occur for the different cards combined with clinical experience with these themes. This knowledge should be accompanied by an awareness of possible significant variations from the more Frequent Plots

These can serve to alert the examiner to unique, and, therefore, more easily interpretable, types of stories. Deviations from clichéd or stereotyped responses can be significant in that they may represent important areas of conflict, creative thinking, or important features of the subject's overall personality. If the clinician is equipped with expectations regarding typical versus unusual responses, it will enable him or her to (a) observe more easily specific attitudes toward the central problem; (b) notice gaps where the inquiry can begin; (c) assess which type of information the subject resists, as indicated by the use of noncommittal clichés; and (d) notice any deviation from the expected information that may contain significant and interpretable responses.

Murray's TAT cards and Bellak's original version of the CAT are described and discussed next. The descriptions of each TAT card that follow are divided into three sections:

1. Brief description of card.
2. Plots frequently encountered.
3. A general discussion of the significance and overall usefulness of the card.

The descriptions of each TAT card are this author's characterization of the scene's content; the CAT descriptions are from Bellak and Abrams (1997, pp. 286–289). The discussion of each picture summarizes the work of Bellak and Abrams (1997), Murray (1943), and M. Stein (1981).

Thematic Apperception Test (TAT)

Picture 1

Description of Card   A boy is sitting at a table looking at a violin placed on the table in front of him.

Frequent Plots   Typical stories emerging from this card revolve around either a self-motivated boy who is daydreaming about becoming an outstanding violinist, or a rebellious boy being forced by his parents, or some other significant authority figure, to play the violin.

General Discussion   This is often considered to be the most useful picture in the entire TAT (Bellak & Abrams, 1997). It usually elicits stories describing how the subject deals with the general issue of impulse versus control, or, in a wider sense, the conflict between personal demands and external controlling agents. It also aids in providing information about the client's relationship with his or her parents, by making it relatively easy to see whether the parents are viewed as domineering, controlling, indifferent, helpful, understanding, or protecting (Bellak & Abrams, 1997). This card frequently gives specific information regarding the need for achievement, and it is important to consider how any expressed achievement is accomplished.

Any variations from the frequent plots described should be taken into consideration. They are likely to provide important reflections of the subject's characteristic modes of functioning. For example, the attitude toward, and relationship with, any introduced figures, or their identification as parents or peers, should be given special attention. Also of importance are the way in which the issue of impulse versus control is handled, any themes of aggression that might emerge, and, particularly, the specific outcome of the story.

Picture 2

Description of Card   Country scene with a woman holding a book in the foreground. In the background, a man is working a field while a woman watches.

Frequent Plots   Stories for this card often involve a young girl who is leaving the farm to increase her education or to seek opportunities that her present home environment cannot provide. Usually the family is seen as working hard to gain a living from the soil. The family values often center on maintaining the status quo.

General Discussion   This picture usually provides an excellent description of family relations. As with Picture 1, various themes relate to autonomy from the family versus compliance with the status quo. This is one of the only cards in the series that presents the subject with a group scene and thus gives information relating to how the individual deals with the challenge of people living together. The card itself deals with a younger woman and an older male and female. Thus, it elicits stories dealing with parent-child and heterosexual relationships. There is usually the added dimension of contrasting the new and the old, and demonstrating attitudes toward personal mobility and ambition. This card may elicit stories relating to competition by the younger daughter for the attention of both or one of the parents. In these stories, her rival is either a sibling, particularly an older female, or the other parent. The extent to which separations or alliances occur among the three figures represented can also be quite revealing. For example, the two women may be united against the male who is "merely a hired hand," or the older male and female may be united against the younger female. Within either of these possible formations, it is important to note the attributes of each person and the patterns and styles of interaction. Because this card is relatively complex and has a large number of details, compulsive patients often spend an inordinate amount of time commenting and elaborating on the many small details.

Picture 3BM

Description of Card   A boy is huddled next to a couch. On the floor next to him is an ambiguous object that could be a set of keys or a revolver.

Frequent Plots   The stories usually center on an individual who has been emotionally involved with another person or who is feeling guilty over some past behavior he has committed. Drug abusers often perceive the person in the picture as an addict and interpret the "revolver" as a hypodermic needle.

General Discussion   This has been identified as one of the most useful pictures (Bellak & Abrams, 1997; Keiser & Prather, 1990) because it concerns themes of guilt, depression, aggression, and impulse control. The manner in which the object on the left is seen and described often gives good information regarding problems concerning aggression. For example, if the object is described as a gun, is it used or intended to be used for intra-aggression (the subject is going to use it to do damage to self) or for extra-aggression (the subject has used it, or is going to use it, to harm another person)? If it is used for externally directed aggression, what are the consequences, if any, for the focal figure as portrayed in the outcome? This picture is particularly important for depressed patients, whether male or female, because it can reveal important dynamics regarding the manner in which the depression developed and how it is currently being maintained. For example, denial of aggressive conflict may be represented by completely overlooking the gun or rendering it harmless by depicting it as a toy pistol or a set of keys. Excessive hesitation and detailed consideration of what the object could represent however, a compulsive defense surrounding conflictual aggressive feelings. Because this picture contains a lone figure, attitudes toward the isolated self are often aroused. The picture might be particularly useful for drug abusers because it frequently brings out themes and attitudes toward overdosing, drug use, mechanisms for coping, self-destructive tendencies, and extent of social supports.

Picture 3GF

Description of Card   A woman is standing next to an open door with one hand grabbing the side of the door and the other holding her downcast face.

Frequent Plots   As with Picture 3BM, the stories usually revolve around themes of interpersonal loss and contemplated harm directed internally because of guilt over past behavior.

General Discussion   The same general trends that hold for Picture 3BM are also true here, in that both pictures tend to bring out depressive feelings. Frequently, however, Picture 3BM brings out somewhat richer stories and allows both males and females to identify easily with the central figure.

Picture 4

Description of Card   A woman is grabbing the shoulders of a man who is turning away from her.

Frequent Plots   The primary task is to form some conceptualization as to why the woman is restraining the man. Often the woman is seen as an advice-giving moral agent who is struggling with the more impulsive and irrational man. In approximately half the stories, the vague image of a woman in the background is brought into the story plot.

General Discussion   This picture typically elicits a good deal of information relating to the feelings and attitudes surrounding male-female relationships. Frequently, themes of infidelity and betrayal emerge, and details regarding the male attitude toward the role of women may be discussed. For example, the woman may be seen as a protector who attempts to prevent the man from becoming involved in self-destructive behavior or as a siren who tries to detain and control him for evil purposes. Likewise, a woman's attitude toward past male aggressiveness and impulsiveness may be revealed.

A further area of interest is the vague image of a seminude woman in the background. This often provokes themes of triangular jealousy in which one or more characters have been betrayed. When this picture is described, it is important to note whether the woman is depicted as a sexually threatening person or is seen as more benign.

Picture 5

Description of Card   A woman is looking into a room from the threshold of a door.

Frequent Plots   In the most frequent plot, a mother has either caught her child misbehaving or is surprised by an intruder entering her house.

General Discussion   This picture often reveals information surrounding attitudes about the subject's mother in her role of observing and possibly judging behavior. It is important to note how the woman is perceived and how the situation is resolved. Is she understanding and sympathetic? Does she attempt to invoke guilt? Or is she seen as severely restricting the child's autonomy? Sometimes voyeuristic themes are discussed, including feelings related to the act of observing others' misbehavior. The examiner should note whether these feelings include guilt, anger, indifference, or fear, and the manner in which these feelings are resolved. Often this card elicits paranoid fears of attack or intrusion by an outsider, represented by stories in which the woman is surprised by a burglar.

Picture 6BM

Description of Card   An elderly woman is standing parallel to a window. Behind her is a younger man with his face down. He is holding onto his hat.

Frequent Plots   This picture typically elicits stories of a son who is either presenting sad news to his mother or attempting to prepare her for his departure to some distant location.

General Discussion   This picture can be important to include when testing males. It usually proves to be a rich source of information regarding attitudes and feelings toward their mothers or maternal figures in general. Because the stories usually revolve around a young man striving for independence, the specific manner in which the subject depicts this struggle is important. Does the struggle include an exaggerated amount of guilt? Is there unexpressed or even overt anger toward the older woman? Or does the young man succumb to the woman's wishes? Of equal importance is the mother's reaction to her son's behavior. To what extent does she control him, and how? It is also of interest to note whether the subject accepts the traditional mother-son version, or whether he or she chooses to avoid discussing this relationship directly. If such an avoidance is evident, how are mother-son themes depicted in other cards that may have elicited discussions of this area (i.e., picture 1 or 5)?

Picture 6GF

Description of Card   A young woman sitting on the edge of a sofa looks back over her shoulder at an older man with a pipe in his mouth who seems to be addressing her.

Frequent Plots   The man is usually seen as proposing some sort of an activity to the woman, and the plot often includes her reaction to this suggestion.

General Discussion   This card was originally intended to be the female counterpart to Picture 6BM, and it was hoped that it, too, would elicit attitudes and feelings toward paternal figures. However, because the two figures are often seen as being about equal in age, the card frequently does not accomplish its intended purpose. When clear father-daughter plots are not discussed, the picture reflects the subject's style and approach to unstructured heterosexual relationships. For example, the subject may describe the woman as being startled or embarrassed or, on the other hand, may have her respond in a spontaneous and comfortable manner. It is important to note the manner in which the man is perceived by the woman. Is he seen as a seducer? Does he offer her helpful advice? Is he intrusive? Or is he perceived as a welcome addition? A person who mistrusts interpersonal relationships typically creates a story in which the man is intrusive and the woman's reaction is one of defensiveness and surprise. Subjects who are more trusting and comfortable usually develop themes in which the woman responds in a more accepting and flexible manner.

Picture 7BM

Description of Card   An older man is looking at a younger man, who appears to be peering into space.

Frequent Plots   Stories usually describe either a father-son relationship or a boss-employee situation. Regardless of which of these variations is chosen, the older man is most frequently in the position of advising or instructing the younger one.

General Discussion   This card is extremely useful in obtaining information about authority figures and, more specifically, the subject's own father. The picture deals with hierarchical personal relationships and usually takes the form of an older, more experienced man interacting with a younger, less experienced one. Thus, the card can clearly show how the subject deals with external demands and attitudes toward authority.

Picture 7GF

Description of Card   A young girl is seated on a couch and is holding a doll in her hands. Behind her is an older woman who appears to be reading to her out of a book.

Frequent Plots   This picture is usually perceived as a mother and her daughter, with the mother advising, consoling, scolding, or instructing the child. Less frequently, there are themes in which the mother is reading to the child for pleasure or entertainment.

General Discussion   The intention here is to bring out the style and manner of mother-child interaction. When older women are the subjects, the picture often elicits feelings and attitudes toward children. Because both figures are looking away, either figure is sometimes perceived as rejecting the other. Thus, the card often elicits negative feelings and interactions, and it is important to note how these feelings are resolved, expressed, or avoided. Sometimes the older woman is described as reading a fairy story to the younger girl. Often the most instructive data then comes from the fairy story itself.

Picture 8BM

Description of Card   A young boy in the foreground is staring directly out of the picture. In the background is a hazy image of two men performing surgery on a patient who is lying down.

Frequent Plots   Stories revolve around either ambition (the young man may have aspirations toward becoming a doctor) or aggression. Frequently the aggressive stories relate to fears of becoming harmed or mutilated while in a passive state. Another somewhat less frequent theme describes a scene in which someone was shot and is now being operated on.

General Discussion   The picture can be seen as a thinly veiled depiction of a young man's oedipal conflicts, with concomitant feelings of castration anxiety and hostility. Thus, it is important to note what feelings the boy or other characters in the story have toward the older man performing the surgery. If the story depicts a need for achievement expressed by the younger man, it is also likely that he will identify with the older one and perhaps use him as an example. If this is the case, the details of how the identification takes place and specific feelings regarding the identification may be helpful.

Picture 8GF
Description of Card   A woman is sitting on a chair staring into space with her chin resting in her hand.

Frequent Plots   Because this picture is vague and nonspecific, extremely diverse plots are developed and there are no frequently encountered themes.

General Discussion   This picture is difficult to generalize about. Typically, it produces somewhat shallow stories of a contemplative nature.

Picture 9BM
Description of Card   Four men in a field are lying against one another.

Frequent Plots   Stories typically provide some explanation of why the men are there and frequently describe them either as homeless wanderers or as working men who are taking a much-needed rest.

General Discussion   This picture is particularly helpful in providing information about relations with members of the same sex. Are the men comfortable with one another? Is there any competitiveness? Is the central person in the story merely observing the four men, or is he one of the four men in the picture? Sometimes homosexual tendencies or fears regarding such tendencies become evident in the story plot. Social prejudice surrounding attitudes toward "lazy," lower class, or unemployed persons often becomes apparent, particularly when the men in the picture are seen as homeless.

Picture 9GF
Description of Card   A woman in the foreground is standing behind a tree, observing another woman who is running along a beach below.

Frequent Plots   Usually the two women are seen as being in some sort of conflict, often over a man. Frequently, either in addition to this theme or in a separate story, the woman "hiding behind" the tree has done something wrong. It is very unusual to have a story in which cooperation between the women is the central plot.

General Discussion   This card basically deals with female peer relations and is important in elaborating on issues such as conflict resolution, jealousy, sibling rivalry, and competitiveness. Because the figure standing behind the tree is carefully observing the woman on the beach, stories may provide details surrounding paranoid ideation. At the very least, the dynamics of suspiciousness and distrust are usually discussed. Frequently a man is introduced into the story, often in the role of a long-lost lover whom one or both of the women are running to meet, or a sexual attacker, from whom the woman on the beach is attempting to escape.

Picture 10

Description of Card   One person is holding his or her head against another person's shoulder. The gender of the two persons is not defined.

Frequent Plots   Stories usually center around some interaction between a male and a female, and may involve either a greeting between the two or a departure.

General Discussion   This card often gives useful information regarding how the subject perceives male-female relationships, particularly those involving some degree of closeness and intimacy. It might be helpful to notice the relative degree of comfort or discomfort evoked by emotional closeness. A story of departure or of termination of the relationship may be reflective of either overt or denied hostility on the part of the subject. Sometimes males interpret the embrace as involving two males, which may suggest the possibility of a repressed or overt homosexual orientation.

Picture 11

Description of Card   On a road in a chasm, several figures are proceeding along a path toward a bridge. Above them and against the side of a cliff appears to be a dragon.

Frequent Plot   Typically, stories of attack and escape are elicited in which the subject takes into account the dragon, the path, and the obscure figures in the distance.

General Discussion   Because the form of this picture is quite vague and ambiguous, it is a good test of the subjects' imaginative abilities and their skills in integrating irregular and poorly defined stimuli. The picture also represents unknown and threatening forces, and reflects the manner in which the subjects deal with fear of attack. Thus, the examiner should take note of whether the characters in the story escape or instead become victims of their attackers. If they escape, how effective and coherent was the plan they devised to avoid danger? Were they instead saved by chance or "the forces of fate"? Subjects' stories can often suggest the degree to which they experience a sense of control over their environment and the course of their lives.

The dragon may be seen as coming out of the cliff and attacking people (representing aggressive forces in the environment) or as a protecting creature whom the characters are using for refuge and safety (a need for protection). Such themes can suggest aspects of the subjects' internal framework and mood. For example, stories of "everything being dead" suggest a depressive, impoverished inner state for subjects.

Picture 12M

Description of Card   A man with his hand raised is standing above a boy who is lying on a bed with his eyes closed.

Frequent Plots   Stories center on illness and/or the older man's use of hypnosis or some form of religious rite on the younger, reclining figure.

General Discussion   The picture often elicits themes regarding the relationship between an older (usually more authoritative) man and a younger one. This can be significant in predicting or assessing the current or future relationship between the therapist and the client. The manner in which the older man is perceived is particularly important. Is he sympathetic and giving aid, or is he described in more sinister terms? Thus, the picture can represent specifics of the transference relationship and, as such, can be an aid in interpreting and providing feedback to the client regarding this relationship. It can also be used to predict a client's attitude toward, and response to, hypnotic procedures. Stories related to this picture may also represent whether passivity is compatible with a subject's personality or is regarded with discomfort. In particular, subjects frequently reveal attitudes toward some external controlling force.

Picture 12F
Description of Card   A portrait of a woman is in the foreground; an older woman holding her chin is in the background.

Frequent Plots   Stories center on the relationship or specific communications between the two figures.

General Discussion   This picture elicits descriptions and conceptions of mother figures. The background figure is frequently seen as a mother-in-law who has a variety of evil qualities. Often these negative qualities are feelings that the subject has toward her own mother but can indirectly and, therefore, more safely project onto the figure of a mother-in-law.

Picture 12BG

Description of Card   A country setting depicts a tree, with a rowboat pulled up next to it. No human figures are present.

Frequent Plots   Stories frequently center on themes of loneliness, peace, or enjoyment of nature.

General Discussion   With suicidal or depressed subjects, there may be an elaboration of feelings of abandonment and isolation—for example, someone has been lost or has fallen from the boat. More stable, adjusted subjects are likely to discuss the peace of being alone in the woods and perhaps of fishing or having gone fishing farther down the stream.

Picture 13MF
Description of Card   A young man is standing in the foreground with his head in his arms. In the background is a woman lying in a bed.

Frequent Plots   The most frequent plot centers on guilt induced by illicit sexual activity. Themes involving the death of the woman on the bed and the resulting grief of the man, who is often depicted as her husband, are somewhat less frequent.

General Discussion   This picture is often considered to be helpful in revealing sexual conflicts. In a general way, it provides information on a subject's attitudes and feelings toward his or her partner, particularly attitudes just before and immediately following sexual intercourse. Stories in which there are overt expressions of aggression or revulsion are significant variations and should be noted as relatively unusual. In particular, the relation between a subject's aggressive and sexual feelings is frequently portrayed.

Because this picture has a relatively large number of details, obsessive-compulsive personalities frequently spend an excessive amount of time describing and explaining these details. This approach may be particularly evident when the picture has a shock effect and may, therefore, create anxiety. The obsessive-compulsive's style of handling anxiety by externally focusing on detail is then brought out.

Picture 13B

Description of Card   A boy is sitting in the doorway of a log cabin.

Frequent Plots   Themes of loneliness and stories of childhood are often elicited. However, because the stimulus is somewhat vague, the content and the nature of these stories tend to be extremely varied.

General Discussion   This picture may help both adults and children to reveal attitudes toward introspection or loneliness. In adults, it frequently elicits reveries involving childhood memories.

Picture 13G

Description of Card   A girl is climbing a flight of stairs.

Frequent Plots   The plots are similar to Picture 13B, usually involving themes of loneliness and/or distant childhood memories.

General Discussion   This picture lacks the specificity and impact found in other TAT cards. It usually produces stories that are highly varied but lacking in richness and detail. Like Picture 13B, it can sometimes be useful in depicting a subject's attitude toward loneliness and introspection.

Picture 14

Description of Card   A person is silhouetted against a window.

Frequent Plots   This card produces themes of contemplation, wish fulfillment, or depression, or feelings related to burglary.

General Discussion   If a subject's presenting problem is depression, especially if there is evidence of suicidal ideation, this card, along with Picture 3BM, is essential. This type of subject often describes the figure in the picture and, more important, discusses the events, feelings, and attitudes that led up to the current self-destructive behavior. It becomes important to investigate, during the inquiry phase of examination, the particular methods and styles of problem solving that the story character has attempted or is attempting. Also significant are the character's internal dialogues and personal reactions as he or she relates to different life stresses.

This picture may also reveal the subject's aesthetic interests and personal philosophical beliefs or wish fulfillments. If a story involving burglary is depicted, it can be useful to consider the character's level of impulse control and guilt or the consequences of his or her behavior. For example, is the character apprehended and punished for his or her behavior, or is he or she allowed to go free and enjoy the profits of his or her misdeeds?

Picture 15

Description of Card   A man is standing among tombstones with his hands clasped together.

Frequent Plots   Themes usually revolve around beliefs or events surrounding death and a hereafter.

General Discussion   Stories from Picture 15 reflect the subject's particular beliefs about, and attitudes toward, death and the dying process. For example, death may be viewed as a passive, quiet process, or, in contrast, it can be experienced as a violent, aggressive situation. If the subject is having an extremely difficult time coping with the death of a friend or relative, the themes on Picture 15 can provide useful information as to why this difficulty is being experienced. For example, the story may reveal a method of adjustment based on excessive denial and a seeming inability to engage in grieving, from which a lack of resolution results. The story might also indicate unexpressed and problematic anger directed toward the dead person, because of a sense of abandonment.

Picture 16
Description of Card   Blank card.

Frequent Plots   Stories from this card are highly varied. It frequently elicits narratives related to a person's life (current marital, family, and personal situation) and, to a lesser extent, idyllic, defensive, catastrophic, and achievement-oriented concerns.

General Discussion   Instructions for this card are: "Imagine a picture and then tell a story about it." From subjects with vivid and active imaginations, this card often elicits extremely rich, useful stories; and the amount of detail and complexity in a person's stories have been found to correlate with different measures of creativity (Wakefield, 1986). The card does little to shape or influence the subject's fantasy material and can thus be seen as a relatively pure product of his or her unconscious. However, for anxious, resistant, or noncreative subjects, this card is often of little or no value because the stories are usually brief and lack depth or richness. In considering the story, it is helpful to note whether the depiction involves a scene that is vital and optimistic or one that is desolate and flat. This card's value can be increased by repeating the instructions, which stress that the person must provide a complete story (preceding events, current situation, and outcome), and giving the card as the last one in a series. Its value derives from both its total lack of structure and usefulness across different ages, ethnic backgrounds, and assessment goals.

Picture 17BM
Description of Card   A naked man is climbing up (or down) a rope.

Frequent Plots   Stories usually involve someone escaping from a dangerous situation or an athletic event of a competitive nature.

General Discussion   Because the card depicts a naked man, attitudes regarding the subject's personal body images are often revealed. They in turn may bring out themes of achievement, physical prowess, adulation, and narcissism. Possible homosexual feelings or anxiety related to homosexuality also becomes evident in the stories of some subjects.

Picture 17GF

Description of Card   A female is standing on a bridge over water. Above the bridge is a tall building, and behind the building the sun is shining from behind clouds.

Frequent Plots   A great variety of stories are elicited, although themes surrounding departure and social or emotional distance do occur with some frequency.

General Discussion   Attitudes toward a recent separation or the impending arrival of a loved one are sometimes described. This card can be particularly useful in cases of suicidal depression, where the figure on the bridge is perceived as contemplating jumping off, as a last attempt to resolve her difficulties. As with Pictures 3BM and 14, an inquiry into the specific difficulties the story character has encountered and the manner in which she has attempted to resolve these difficulties can often reflect the subject's manner and style of coping with his or her own difficulties. Personal reactions to, and internal dialogue involving, life stresses can also be extremely informative. However, some of this material is available only through a more detailed inquiry, after the initial story has been given.

Picture 18BM

Description of Card   A man dressed in a long coat is being grabbed from behind. Three hands are visible.

Frequent Plots   Typical themes involve either drunkenness on the part of the figure who is being supported by the three hands or stories in which he is being attacked from behind.

General Discussion   This picture, more than any of the others, is likely to produce anxiety because of the suggestive depiction of invisible forces attacking the figure. Thus, it is important to note how the subject handles his or her own anxiety as well as how the story character deals with his situation. Does the latter see himself as the victim of circumstance in which he is completely helpless? If so, how does he eventually resolve his feelings of helplessness? Is the helplessness a momentary phenomenon, or is it an ongoing personality trait? If the character is seen as the recipient of bad luck, then specifically what situation does the subject perceive as comprising bad luck? Exaggerated aggressiveness or attitudes toward addiction are also sometimes identified with this picture.

Picture 18GF

Description of Card   A woman has her hands around the throat of another woman. In the background is a flight of stairs.

Frequent Plots   Aggressive mother-daughter interactions or sibling relationships are often disclosed in response to this picture.

General Discussion   The manner in which the subject handles aggressive, hostile relationships with other women is the primary type of information this picture elicits. Particular note should be made of what types of events trigger this aggressiveness and of the manner in which the conflict is or is not resolved. Does the character submit passively, withdraw from the relationship, plot revenge, or negotiate change? Feelings of inferiority, jealousy, and response to being dominated are also often described. Although the representation of aggressiveness in the picture is quite explicit, subjects occasionally attempt to deny or avoid this aggressiveness by creating a story in which one figure is attempting to help the other one up the stairs. This may point to general denial and repression of hostility on the part of the subject.

Picture 19

Description of Card   A surreal depiction of clouds and a home covered with snow.

Frequent Plots   Stories are highly varied because of the unstructured and ambiguous nature of the stimuli.

General Discussion   Because this is one of the more unstructured cards, the subject's ability to integrate disparate visual stimuli is tested. For certain subjects, the ambiguous nature of this picture can create anxiety and insecurity. The examiner can then observe how the subject handles his or her anxiety in the context of the story. Often the stories produced deal with impersonal aggression from forces such as nature or the supernatural.

Picture 20

Description of Card   A hazy, nighttime picture of a man leaning against a lamppost.

Frequent Plots   Stories range from the benign theme of a late-evening date to more sinister circumstances, perhaps involving a gangster who is in imminent danger.

General Discussion   The picture often elicits information regarding a subject's attitude toward loneliness, darkness, and uncertainty. Fears may be stated explicitly through gangster stories. As with Picture 18BM, the method of handling these fears and the examinee's response to physical danger should be noted.

Children's Apperception Test (CAT)

The following descriptions of, and typical responses to, pictures on the CAT are adapted from Bellak and Abrams (1997, pp. 286–289).

Picture 1

Bellak's Description   Chicks seated around a table on which is a large bowl of food. Off to one side is a large chicken, dimly outlined.

Discussion   Stories typically revolve around concerns relating to eating or sibling rivalry. The sibling rivalry may center on who is the best behaved, what the consequences of this behavior are, and which one gets more to eat. To obtain useful information on this card, it is particularly important to decide which character the subject identifies with. Food may be seen as reward for "good" behavior or, conversely, when withheld, as punishment for "bad" behavior.

Picture 2

Bellak's Description   One bear is pulling a rope on one side, while another bear and a baby bear pull on the other side.

Discussion   Of particular importance in interpreting this picture is whether the bear who is helping the baby bear is seen as a male (father figure) or a female (mother figure). The struggle depicted can be seen either as a playful game of tug-of-war, or as a struggle involving a high degree of seriousness and aggression. For example, the loser(s) may end up falling off the edge of the rock and into a pool of dangerous animals. In the most recent revision of the CAT, the large bears were made equal in size, to avoid having the largest bear (previously depicted on the right) identified as the father.

Picture 3

Bellak's Description   A lion, with pipe and cane, sits in a chair; in the lower right corner, a little mouse appears in a hole.

Discussion   Because the lion is pictured with the characteristic symbols of authority (pipe and cane), this picture elicits attitudes and feelings toward father figures. It is important to note whether this figure is seen as benevolent and protecting or as dangerous and threatening. Sometimes the subject defensively attempts to minimize the threat of the lion by reducing him to a helpless cripple who needs a cane just to move around.

Most children notice the mouse in the hole and blend it into their stories. Because the mouse and the lion are frequently seen in adversary roles, it is important to note how the threatening presence of the lion is handled. Is the mouse completely under the control of the lion, and does it adapt by being submissive and placating? On the other hand, the mouse may be described as clever and manipulating, to trick and outsmart the lion. When subjects switch their identification back and forth between the lion and the mouse, some role confusion is suggested. This may be particularly true of enmeshed families or families in which the father is unable to set limits effectively.

Picture 4

Bellak's Description   A kangaroo who has a bonnet on her head is carrying a basket with a milk bottle. In her pouch is a baby kangaroo with a balloon; on a bicycle, there is a larger kangaroo child.

Discussion   As in Picture 1, this card elicits themes of sibling rivalry and, occasionally, themes revolving around a wish for regression, as demonstrated when the subject identifies with the baby kangaroo in the pouch. A regressive theme is particularly strong when a subject, who is in reality the oldest or middle child, identifies with the kangaroo in the pouch. A child who is actually the youngest, however, may identify with the oldest kangaroo, thereby suggesting a strong need for autonomy and independence. On occasion, a theme of flight from danger may be introduced.

Picture 5

Bellak's Description   A darkened room contains a large bed in the background and a crib in the foreground in which there are two baby bears.

Discussion   Stories relating to attitudes and feelings about what occurs when parents are in bed are frequent responses to this card. They may involve aspects such as curiosity, conjecture, confusion, rejection, anger, and envy on the part of the children. Descriptions of the two bears in the foreground may also center on themes of sexual manipulation and mutual exploration.

Picture 6

Bellak's Description   A darkened cave shows two dimly outlined bear figures in the background and a baby bear lying in the foreground.

Discussion   This picture and Picture 5 elicit stories of parental bedtime activity. However, this picture tends to enlarge on and extend themes that have only begun to develop in Picture 5. Stories may also revolve around jealousy of the perceived intimacy between parents, or they may reflect possible feelings about masturbation on the part of the baby bear in the foreground.

Picture 7

Bellak's Description   A tiger with bared fangs and claws leaps at a monkey that is also leaping through the air.

Discussion   The subject often discusses his or her fears of aggression and characteristic manner of dealing with it. At times, the anxiety produced by this picture may result in an unwillingness to respond to it at all. On the other hand, the subject's defenses may be either effective enough, or perhaps unrealistic enough, for him or her to transform the picture into a harmless story.

Picture 8

Bellak's Description   Two adult monkeys are sitting on a sofa drinking from teacups. One adult monkey in the foreground is sitting on a hassock talking to a baby monkey.

Discussion   The subject often discusses his or her relative position and characteristic roles in the family. The description of the dominant monkey in the foreground as either a mother or a father figure should be noted as a possible indication of who has more control in the family. It is also significant to note how the dominant monkey is described. Is he or she threatening and controlling or helpful and supportive?

Picture 9

Bellak's Description   A darkened room is seen through an open door from a lighted room. In the darkened one, there is a child's bed in which a rabbit sits up looking through the door.

Discussion   Typically, responses revolve around a subject's fears of darkness, possible desertion by parents, and curiosity as to what is occurring in the next room.

Picture 10

Bellak's Description   A baby dog is lying across the knees of an adult dog; both figures have a minimum of expressive features. The figures are set in the foreground of a bathroom.

Discussion   A child's attitudes and feelings about misbehavior and its resulting punishments are usually discussed in response to this card. In particular, his or her conceptions of right and wrong are often revealed. This picture is a good indicator of the child's degree of impulse control and his or her attitude toward authority figures when their role involves setting limits.

SCORING PROCEDURES

Since the publication of the original *Thematic Apperception Manual* in 1943, there have been numerous methods of scoring and interpretation. The major reason there are so many different systems is due to the type of information that is under investigation. Fantasy productions involve extremely rich and diverse information, which is difficult to place into exact and specific categories. Even the selection of which categories to use is open to question. For example, Murray prefers a listing and weighting of the primary needs and press expressed in the stories, whereas Arnold (1962) emphasizes a restatement of the essential theme of the story on an interpretive level so as to highlight the basic meaning or moral. Cramer (2006) focuses on defense mechanisms, and Westen (1995) has developed a system for scoring object relations. After deciding which method to use and evaluating the stories according to this method, the examiner is able to infer qualities of the subject's personality according to the categorization that is based on the specific method selected. Whether this final inference is valid and accurate is open to question and depends on a number of variables, including the skill and experience of the examiner, comparison with themes derived from other test data, and whether the state of the subject at the time of examination is representative of his or her usual orientation to the world.

For the purposes of this chapter, Bellak's (1954, 1993), and Bellak and Abram's (1997) method of interpretation is described. It is fairly comprehensive, is easy to score, is relatively concise, has been frequently updated, and is the most frequently used of the various systems (Rossini & Moretti, 1997). Bellak's approach involves a certain degree of quantification in that interpreters are requested to rate the stories along several areas, according to the different story styles and contents. The goal is not so much to achieve a diagnosis of the subject as to obtain a description of how the subject confronts and deals with basic universal life situations. Each of the stories can be conceptualized as a series of common social situations depicting interpersonal relations. The manner in which the person constructs what he or she believes is occurring in these situations reveals a dominant pattern of social behavior as well as internal needs, attitudes, and values (Bellak & Abrams, 1997).

The specific scoring of the TAT and CAT cards can be organized on the Bellak TAT and CAT Analysis Sheet (see Figure 11.1). The sheet provides a guide and frame of reference for TAT analysis that can be used later to organize and generate hypotheses about the person. It is intended to be used with a typical administration of 10 cards.

Using the long form of the scoring system, each one of the cards/stories is scored on a single Analysis Sheet. The overall story themes and contents can then be analyzed by noting the common themes and unique features throughout the different sheets. A shorter form is also available, consisting of using the Analysis Sheet as shown in Figure 11.1, but simply having more rows to the right of the 10 scoring categories to indicate the scoring for each card/story (refer to Figure 11.1). Thus, 10 cards/stories might be scored in 10 consecutive rows to indicate Story No. 1, Story No. 2, and so on. At the end of this sequence is a Summary section, which the practitioner can use to organize conclusions. The summary categories are designated as follows:

1–3. Unconscious structure and drives of the subject (derived from scoring categories 1–3: Main Themes, Main Hero, and Main Needs and Drives of Hero).

4. Conception of world.

5. Relationship to others.

6. Significant conflicts.

7. Nature of anxieties.

8. Main defenses used.

9. Superego structure.

10. Integration and strength of ego.

A chart is also included (see Figure 11.2) to provide a format for rating the person's ego functions. The combination of the summaries and ratings of ego functions serves as the actual interpretation of the TAT protocol. A short form is available from C.P.S., Inc.

Figure 11.1   Bellak TAT and CAT analysis sheet

1. **Main theme:** (<u>diagnostic level</u>: if descriptive and interpretive levels are desired, use a scratch sheet or page 5)
2. **Main hero:** age _____ sex _____ vocation _____ abilities _____
   interests _____ traits _____ body image _____
   adequacy (✓,✓,✓✓✓) and/or self-image _____
3. **Main needs and drives of hero:**
   a) behavioral needs of hero (as in story): _____
      implying: _____
   b) figures, objects, or circumstances *introduced:* _____
      implyng need for or to: _____
   c) figures, objects, or circumstanced *omitted:* _____
      implyng need for or to: _____
4. **Conception of environment (world) as:** _____
5. a) Parental figures   (m _____   f _____) are seen as _____
        and subject's reaction to a is _____
   b) Contemp figures   (m _____   f _____) are seen as _____
        and subject's reaction to b is _____
   c) Sibling figures   (m _____   f _____) are seen as _____
        and subject's reaction to c is _____
6. **Significant conflicts:** _____
   _____
7. **Nature of anxieties: (✓)**
   of physical harm and/or punishment _____
   of disapproval _____
   of lack or loss of love _____ of illness or injury _____
   of being deserted _____ of deprivation _____
   of being overpowered and helpless _____ lonely _____
   of being devoured _____ other _____
8. **Main defenses against conflicts and fears: (✓)**
   repression _____ reaction-formation _____ splitting _____
   regression _____ denial _____ introjection _____
   isolation _____ undoing _____
   rationalization _____ other _____
9. **Adequacy of superego as manifested by "punishment" for "crime" being (   )**
   appropriate _____ inappropriate _____
   too severe (also indicated by immediacy of punishment) _____
   inconsistent _____ too lenient _____
   also: _____
   delayed initial response of pauses _____
   stammer _____ other manifestations of superego interference_____
10. **Integration of the ego, manifesting itself in (✓,✓✓,✓✓✓)**
    Hero: adequate _____ inadequate _____
    outcome: happy _____ unhappy _____
            realistic _____ unrealistic _____
    drive control _____
    thought processes as revealed by plot being : (✓,✓✓,✓✓✓)
    stereotyped _____ original _____ appropriate _____
    complete _____ incomplete _____ inappropriate _____
    syncretic _____ concrete _____ contaiminated _____
Intelligence _____
Maturation level _____
Organic signs _____

Note: Reprinted with minor modification by permission of C.P.S. Publications Inc., P.O. Box 345, Englewood, NJ 07631. Courtesy of www.CPSPublishingInc.com.

(see Figure 11.2), and variations on the short form and long forms are available from Harcourt Assessment.

For each of the scoring categories, practitioners should abbreviate their observations about the person. In some sections, practitioners are asked to indicate the levels of importance or strength for the person by putting one check (✓—mere presence of characteristic), two checks (✓✓—moderate), or three checks (✓✓✓—strong). The entire scoring and interpretation procedure typically takes a half-hour. The 10 scoring categories are described in the following sections. An attempt has been made to summarize and clarify as much as possible the descriptions provided by Bellak and Abrams (1997).

1. Main Theme

This section requires the practitioner to restate the essential elements of the story. Each story may have one or more themes that need to be restated. The description of the main theme can vary in terms of its level of inference. On one hand, it might be based on an observation and restatement of the client's story, staying as close as possible to the

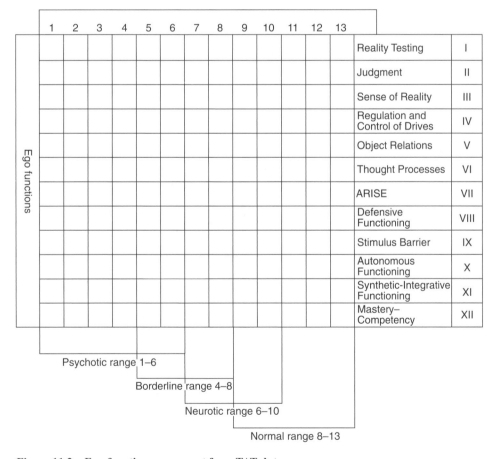

Figure 11.2   Ego function assessment from TAT data

Source: From *Ego Functions in Schizophrenics, Neurotics, and Normals* by L. Bellak, M. Murvich, and H. Gediman. 1973, New York: John Wiley & Sons, Inc. Copyright 1973 by C.P.S. Publications, Inc. Courtesy of www.CPSPublishingInc.com.

client's own words and experience of the story. On the other hand, practitioners may wish to move somewhat further away from the person's description of the story into a more *interpretive* or even *diagnostic* level. Elaboration on the story might even be developed by having the person free-associate to elements in the story. However, for persons who are learning the TAT or who use it infrequently, it is recommended that practitioners stay close to the client's own description. It should be as brief as possible and should aim to extract the essence of what has been described.

2. Main Hero/Heroine

The hero/heroine is usually the person who is most frequently referred to in the story. More information is given on his or her feelings, beliefs, and behaviors than on those of any of the other characters. As a result, the client is assumed to be identifying with this person. In some stories, there might be a degree of uncertainty as to exactly who is the hero/heroine. The practitioner should infer that the story character who is most similar to the client in terms of age, sex, and other characteristics is the hero/heroine. In certain rare cases, there may be one or more heroes/heroines. The Analysis Sheet further requests that the clinician rate the hero in terms of interests, traits, abilities, adequacy, and body image. The adequacy of the hero/heroine refers to an ability to complete tasks in a socially, emotionally, morally, and/or intellectually acceptable manner. This level of adequacy would be directly related to the ego strength of the hero/heroine—or, more inferentially, of the client. The body image refers to the style and qualities with which the body or body representation is depicted. Direct descriptions of the body are usually easy to interpret but a more indirect representation, such as certain symbolical features of the violin in TAT Picture 1, might also be included.

3. Main Needs and Drives of the Hero/Heroine

The *behavioral needs* to be rated in the story refer to the most basic needs expressed in the client's story productions (i.e., affection, aggression, achievement). The descriptions of these needs are fantasy productions by the client and might reflect actual conscious needs as well as more disguised latent needs. The clinician might wish to simply state what the clearest and strongest of these needs are, or make inferences about the actual meaning of these needs for the client. For example, extreme nurturance expressed in the stories might indicate that the client demands nurturance from others or, conversely, that this is a frequent need that he or she expresses. Another example might be extreme avoidance of aggression, which could suggest that the client has a high level of underlying aggression that is being denied.

Clinicians should also note any *figures*, *objects*, or *circumstances* that are *introduced* as well as any that have been *omitted* but perhaps should have been included. Particularly noteworthy omissions include these: no mention of the rifle in Picture 8BM, the gun/keys in Picture 3BM, or the seminude in the background of Picture 4, or no sexual references to Picture 13MF. The implications of these inclusions/omissions should also be noted. For example, the inclusion of a relatively large number of weapons, food, and money might suggest high needs for aggression, nurturance, or financial success. The omission of important objects in the story productions might suggest some areas of repression, denial, or anxiety associated with the omitted objects.

4. Conception of the Environment (World)

Clinicians should summarize the most important and strongest conceptions of the person's environment. They might be alerted to this distinction by noting the number and strength of descriptive words such as hostile, dangerous, or nurturing. The summaries of conceptions of the world might include the overall meaning for the hero/heroine—for example, the environment is overly demanding, a wealth of opportunities, or something to be exploited and used.

5. Figures Seen as. . .

One of the main characteristics of the TAT stories is that they can be seen as "apperceptive distortions of the social relationships and the dynamic factors basic to them" (Bellak, 1993, p. 92). Thus, one of the cornerstones of TAT interpretation is understanding how the client views other persons, as represented in the story productions. This category attempts to elaborate on this by rating the hero/heroine's attitudes and behaviors toward *parental*, *contemporary* (age-related peers), and *junior figures*. For example, the level of aggressiveness of persons of the same gender might be noted, along with the response(s) of the hero/heroine (assertive, placating, hostile, withdrawing).

6. Significant Conflicts

The major conflicts within the hero/heroine should be noted by reviewing the client's current feelings and behaviors and assessing how congruent these are. In particular, clinicians should note any contrast between the *actual* feelings/behaviors and how the client *should* feel. For example, he or she might be trying to accomplish two incongruous goals, such as need for achievement versus need for pleasure or need for hostility versus need for affiliation. Other important conflicts might be between reality and fantasy or between aggression and compliance.

7. Nature of Anxieties

In addition to significant conflicts, clinicians should rate the nature and strength ($\checkmark$, $\checkmark\checkmark$, $\checkmark\checkmark\checkmark$) of the hero/heroine's anxieties in terms of fear of *physical harm* and/or *punishment*, *disapproval, lack or loss of love, illness or injury, being deserted, deprived, overpowered and helpless, devoured*, or *other*.

8. Main Defenses against Conflicts and Fears

The clinician is asked to rate the presence and strength of defenses against anxieties and conflicts. This helps to provide a description of the person's character structure. The strength of the defenses can be assessed by noting their frequency both within each story and among the different stories. For example, intellectualization occurring in six of the stories suggests a rigid and excessive defensive style. In contrast, the use of several different types of defenses suggests that the client has a much greater degree of variety and flexibility. One option might be to formally score for denial, projection, and identification using Cramer's (1996) *Defense Mechanisms Manual*.

9. Adequacy of Superego as Manifested by "Punishment" for "Crime"

Clinicians are requested to rate the relative degree of appropriateness, severity, consistency, and extent of delay of any consequences for potentially punishable behavior. Particular note should be made of the relative strength and type of punishment compared to the seriousness of the "crime." For example, a harsh superego would be suggested when minor infractions by story characters result in imprisonment or even death.

In contrast, a poorly developed superego would be suggested if few or no consequences occurred for a moderate or severe infraction. A section is also included for noting any relevant behavioral observations of the client, such as stammering or blushing, which could suggest an overly harsh superego.

10. Integration of the Ego

In general, the degree of ego integration is indicated by the quality with which the hero/ heroine mediates between different conflicts. This is typically reflected in the effectiveness with which the main character can use interpersonal skills. Specific observations can be made regarding the adequacy, quality, effectiveness, flexibility, and style of problem solving. The overall quality (bizarre, complete, original, etc.) of the thought processes involved should also be rated.

Bellak provides a further unnumbered category for rating the client's intelligence. The traditional classifications of very superior, superior, high average, and so on are used. An additional section allows an overall rating of the client's level of maturity.

In addition to the more traditional TAT areas described, Bellak and Abrams (1997) have provided scales for rating a client's 12 ego functions (I–XII in Figure 11.2). These are based on both the total TAT stories the client has provided and on any relevant behavioral observations. A graph can be created by connecting the ratings summarized on Figure 11.2. The 12 functions are briefly defined as follows.

I. Reality Testing

This variable rates the extent to which the client accurately perceives and relates to his or her external environment. It requires an accurate appraisal of both the physical environment and the social norms and expectations as well as an accurate perception of inner reality testing and level of psychological sophistication. The client's level of reality testing can be partially assessed by noting the extent to which the client can articulate needs, feelings, values, and beliefs. Also included would be accuracy in perceiving time and place.

II. Judgment

What is the client's capacity for understanding a situation, particularly where interpersonal relationships are involved, and translating this understanding into an effective, coherent response? An appraisal of social and physical consequences as well as competent forward planning is involved.

III. Sense of Reality of the World and of the Self

Here the clinician rates disturbances in the client's sense of self, such as dissociative experiences, depersonalization, and deja vu. These also relate to feelings of reality or unreality in the client's perceptions of the environment. In particular, how does this sense of reality/unreality relate to the degree to which the client feels that his or her body parts are well coordinated? Other aspects involved in the rating might be the degree of individuation versus differentiation, the sense of self-esteem, and the extent to which the self is experienced as distinct from others and the external world.

IV. Regulation and Control of Drives, Affects, and Impulses

How direct or indirect is the client's expression of impulses? Can they be appropriately and effectively controlled and delayed? How high a tolerance is there for frustration? Is the client undercontrolled or overcontrolled? Can he or she monitor drives and express them in a modified and adaptive manner? Each of these areas should be considered to make a final rating for this category.

V. Object Relations

To what extent are the client's relationships optimal in that they are appropriately relating to, committed to, and invested in others? What is the typical length of the relationships? What is their overall quality? Any distortions, and the degree to which the client gets his or her needs met, should be noted. How mature is the client and how free from maladaptive interpersonal patterns? To what extent is he or she overinfluenced or underinfluenced by others? This area might be formally evaluated through Westen's (1995) Social Cognition and Object Relations Scale (SCORS) by ratings of these eight dimensions: (1) complexity of representation of people; (2) affective quality of relationships; (3) emotional investment in relationships; (4) emotional investment in values and moral standards; (5) understanding of social causality; (6) experience and management of aggressive impulses; (7) self-esteem; and (8) identity and coherence of self.

VI. Thought Processes

This category requires a rating of the general adequacy and coherence of the client's thought processes. Thus, careful attention should be given to the level of attention, concentration, memory, verbal ability, and abstract reasoning. Are there any distortions, delusions, or unusual associations? Are there clarity and integration in the thought processes? Is the thinking unrealistic, illogical, and characterized by the intrusion of primary process thinking? For example, obsessive-compulsives might be expected to describe minute details of the cards. In contrast, persons with Alzheimer's disease have been found to use fewer words. They typically describe the pictures rather than tell a story about them, and they frequently lose track of the instructions.

VII. ARISE (Adaptive Regression in the Service of the Ego)

Can the client temporarily lower his or her defenses to increase awareness and help with problem solving? Doing this would allow for a relatively free expression of primary process thinking in which the client can approach self and others from different perspectives. Another concern is how adequately he or she can later reintegrate and reorganize the insights and new perspectives resulting from the lowered defenses. The task of responding to the TAT can be seen as an opportunity to allow for this temporary regression into fantasy activity, with the goal of helping to reveal, problem-solve, and understand aspects of self. Relevant questions might involve whether the client approaches the task easily or defensively. Are the story productions rich and creative, or constricted and defended? When they do enter into the fantasies, do they become lost and incoherent or are they able to organize the contents effectively?

VIII. Defensive Functioning

This category requires the clinician to rate the extent to which clients' defenses protect them from internal anxiety-provoking impulses and conflicts. Are they excessive, defective, adaptive/maladaptive? Overall, how successful are they? How much anxiety or depression does the person experience? The specific types and strengths of defenses have been summarized in Category 8 of the Analysis Sheet so that clinicians can refer to these previous summaries to obtain useful detail. However, this Category VIII differs in that it is more a global rating of defensive effectiveness, using all sources of information available to the clinician.

IX. Stimulus Barrier

The client's stimulus barrier refers to how reactive a person is to various events (high/low threshold). Is the person hypersensitive to minor criticisms or low levels of stress? Does he or she react to unpleasant situations with responses such as anger, aggression, assertiveness, withdrawal, disorganization, and/or victimization?

X. Autonomous Functioning

To what extent is the client disrupted by certain ideas, feelings, conflicts, or impulses? If the client feels disrupted, how much does this compromise his or her ability to work and socialize independently? Instead of functioning independently, does the client become highly dependent on others to cope, decide, and initiate what to do? In contrast, has he or she been able to develop autonomous behaviors, such as adaptive habits, time management skills, or hobbies, that help toward functioning relatively independently?

XI. Synthetic-Integrative Functioning

Clinicians must rate the client's ability to actively reconcile difficult needs and conflicts. Are important generalizations and similarities among different ideas, events, and persons perceived? Is there an ability to make necessary compromises between disparate areas of personality and/or interpersonal relationships? How adequately can these integrative abilities be used to work with contradictory behaviors, attitudes, values, and emotions?

XII. Mastery-Competency

This final category requires a rating of the client's overall sense of competency, especially as it relates to the outcome of different story themes. Information useful for this rating might come from a variety of different areas: ability to resolve conflict, quality of ego defenses, ego integrity, creative problem solving, relative degree of rigidity of defenses, self-efficacy, and degree to which the person has an internal versus external locus of control. One important consideration is whether the client's sense of competency is realistic, given his or her actual abilities and achievements. Some clients might either under- or overestimate their level of competency.

INTERPRETATION

When the scoring has been completed, it should be relatively easy to convert this information into a coherent description of the person. The scoring and interpretation can even be considered the same task. In other words, the practitioner can extend on and elaborate on the scoring to make inferences about the client based on the themes occurring in the narratives. Bellak and Abrams (1997) suggest that the three major levels of interpretation are (1) the descriptive, (2) the interpretive, and (3) the diagnostic. The descriptive level is merely a short repeat of the story, as has been outlined in scoring Category 1 of the Analysis Sheet. The interpretive level extends the descriptive level somewhat by an alteration of the descriptive level beginning with "If one...does X, then the outcome will be Y." For example, a descriptive "interpretation" to Card 1 might be: "Boy is practicing to increase his competence." The interpretive level would be "[If one] practices, then he or she will improve." The diagnostic level is a further extension in that an inference is made about the client. Thus, one might infer that, in the story for Card 1, "The client has a high need for achievement with a high level of self-efficacy."

The core features of the client can be organized in the summary section, which has been previously outlined and is included as part of Bellak's Short Form for scoring and interpretation. It is even possible for a report to be organized around the information noted on the 10 different scoring categories. These might be further integrated into these three areas:

1. **Unconscious structure and needs:** Derived from Categories 1 through 3.
2. **Conception of the world and perceptions of significant persons:** Derived from Categories 4 and 5.
3. **Relevant dimensions of personality:** Derived from Categories 6 through 10.

Further ratings can be noted for levels of intelligence and maturational level.

These areas of description tend to be fairly abstract and inferential. One technique for balancing these abstract descriptions is to "anchor" them with actual story segments to illustrate the points or principles that are being described. This should effectively provide a more qualitative, concrete, and impactful description of the client

One useful interpretive consideration regarding the TAT stories is that approximately one-third of the stories are likely to be impersonal renditions or clichés of previously heard information. In the protocols of highly constricted, defensive clients, this proportion is likely to be even higher. Because of the impersonal nature of these stories, it is usually difficult to infer the underlying determinants of personality. In contrast, some stories are extremely rich in that they reveal important core aspects of the client.

Yet another consideration is that, even though, for the most part, high, moderate, or low scores on the stories correspond to high, moderate, and low characteristics within the subject, this is not always the case. For example, Murray found that there was a negative correlation (−.33 to −.74) between n Sex on the TAT and n Sex expressed in overt behavior. Of final and particular note are the subject's current life situation and emotional state at the time of examination. One of the more important variables that can affect the emotional state of the subject, and, therefore, the test results, is the particular interaction between the subject and the examiner. A sensitive and accurate interpretation can be obtained only if the examiner takes into account the existence and possible influence of all these variables.

RECOMMENDED READING

Bellak, L., & Abrams, D. M. (1997). *The TAT, CAT, and SAT in clinical use* (6th ed.). New York: Grune & Stratton.

Costantino, G., Dana, R. H., & Malgady, R. G. (2007). *TEMAS (Tell-Me-A-Story) Assessment in multicultural societies*. Mahwah, NJ: Lawrence Erlbaum.

Jenkins, S. R. (2008). *Handbook of clinical scoring systems for Thematic Apperception techniques*. Mahwah, NJ: Erlbaum.

Meyer, G. J. (2004). The reliability of the Rorschach and Thematic Apperception Test (TAT) compared to other psychological and medical procedures: An analysis of systematically gathered evidence. In M. J. Hilsenroth & D. Segal (Eds.), *Comprehensive handbook of psychological assessment* (Vol. 2) (pp. 315–342). Hoboken, NJ: John Wiley & Sons.

Roberts, G. E. (2006). *Roberts-2 manual*. Los Angeles, CA: Western Psychological Services.

Chapter 12

SCREENING FOR NEUROPSYCHOLOGICAL IMPAIRMENT

An important role in clinical practice is screening and assessing for the presence of possible neuropsychological impairment. The importance of this function is highlighted by data indicating that 20% to 30% of assessment referrals to professional psychologists relate to information regarding central nervous system (CNS) involvement (Camara et al., 2000). This proportion is likely to be even higher for referrals from psychiatric and neurological settings. Information derived from these sorts of assessments might serve as an early warning sign that, if positive, would then result in a more in-depth medical or neuropsychological assessment and/or further monitoring of the patient. Examples of the types of situations where screening might be important would be among substance-abusing populations, persons exposed to neurotoxic substances, or elderly populations where the distinction between depression and organically based dementia might be crucial. Additional situations might occur with a school psychologist who is trying to understand why a student is performing poorly, workers' compensation cases in which brain damage might be suspected, or screening for brain damage among psychiatric populations. Each of these situations would require that the assessing clinician be sensitive to the expression of brain impairment, methods of assessing for it, and the patterns of behavioral and test results that would suggest the presence of such impairment.

This chapter provides introductory knowledge and strategies for screening for CNS involvement. To that end, the chapter provides introductory knowledge into the area combined with a working knowledge of two major screening instruments, the Bender Visual Motor Gestalt Test II (Bender) and the Repeatable Battery for the Assessment of Neuropsychological Status (RBANS). Inclusion of this information is based on the premise that a core competency of professional psychologists is that they should have, at a minimum, knowledge on how to screen for CNS complications. If a more in-depth coverage is required, readers are referred to Groth-Marnat's (2000a) *Neuropsychological Assessment in Clinical Practice: A Guide to Test Interpretation and Integration*.

When appraising clients with suspected CNS involvement, it is important to appreciate that the behavioral manifestation of such involvement is extremely heterogeneous. Some brain-damaged persons might have specific signs, such as aphasia, neglect of a portion of their visual field, or word-finding difficulties. In contrast, others might have widespread impairments, such as a general lowering of cognitive abilities or difficulty regulating their behavior. Deficits might also range in their expression between being extremely subtle to being quite severe. The practical implication is that many screening tests for neuropsychological impairment are likely to assess for a narrow range of abilities. If a client has deficits outside this range, the test is not sensitive to that particular area of difficulties. The result is a high number of false negatives. Indeed, this problem has plagued most screening devices. For example, a test such as the Bender is primarily a test of visuoconstructive abilities. Clients with a wide range of other difficulties are likely to perform quite well on the Bender with the resulting danger that the clinician might erroneously conclude they were not organically impaired. The RBANS covers a much wider range of abilities and, as such, is more likely to be sensitive to a wider range of CNS complications.

The presence of false negatives (or false positives) depends in part on the "narrowness" versus the "width" of the test. For example, a test that measures a specific function, such as ability to name objects, is quite narrow in its focus. Clients who do poorly on such a test would most likely be experiencing neuropsychological impairment (true positives). However, there are also many persons who, despite being neuropsychologically impaired, do quite well on such a test and may be misclassified as normal (false negatives), because most neuropsychologically impaired persons do not experience object-naming difficulties. The sign of object naming, thus, is too specific. If another test is used that casts a wider net by using more general indicators (i.e., concrete thinking, impaired immediate memory, distractibility), not as many persons with neuropsychological impairment will be missed (few false negatives). However, many people will be labeled brain damaged who are not (many false positives). This is likely to be particularly true for severe psychiatric patients. Indeed, neuropsychological tests have had a notoriously difficult time distinguishing psychotics, especially chronic schizophrenics, from brain-damaged persons because they often appear quite similar on test performance (Mittenberg et al., 1989).

The two general strategies in neuropsychological assessment are a qualitative or pathognomonic sign approach and the use of quantitative cutoff scores. The pathognomonic sign approach assumes the existence of distinctive behaviors indicative of brain damage. Distortions in reproducing designs or reproducing the same design repeatedly (so-called perseverations) are examples of such signs. Additional ones might be aphasias, line tremor, rotating a design, difficulty with serial subtraction, clang responses (i.e., ponder meaning "to pound"), neglecting a portion of a visual field (visual neglect), or difficulty distinguishing whether a stimulus is either on the right or left when they are stimulated at the same time (suppressions on bilateral, simultaneous stimulation). In contrast to the sign approach is the use of cutoff scores, which optimally separates a person's performance into either a brain-damaged or normal range. The use of cutoff scores is a major feature of the Halstead-Reitan Neuropsychological Test Battery (HRNTB; Broshek & Barth, 2000; Reitan & Wolfson, 1993) and the Neuropsychological Assessment Battery (Stern & White, 2003).

Similar to other psychological tests, moderator variables, such as age, education, and premorbid intelligence are related to neuropsychological test performance. It has thus been recommended that cutoff scores for determining impairment should use norms corrected for age, education, and sometimes gender. These norms are available in a variety of sources, including the *Handbook of Normative Data for Neuropsychological Assessment* (2nd ed.; Mitrushina, Boone, Razani, & D'Elia's, 2005), *Revised Comprehensive Norms for an Expanded Halstead-Reitan Battery* (Heaton, Miller, Taylor, & Grant, 2004) and *Compendium of Neuropsychological Tests* (3rd ed.; Strauss et al., 2006).

HISTORY AND DEVELOPMENT

Neuropsychological assessment as a well-defined discipline began in the 1950s with the work of Halstead, Reitan, and Goldstein in the United States; Rey in France; and Luria in the Soviet Union. In the United States, the experimental and statistical orientation of American psychology was reflected in test design and use. Norms were refined and used for comparison with an individual patient's performance. Optimal cutoff scores were developed to distinguish impaired from normal performances. In particular, the Halstead-Reitan Neuropsychological Test Battery grew out of an original 27 tests that Ward

Halstead selected in the belief that they measured cerebral functioning based on "biological intelligence." He reduced these to 10 tests, and Reitan (1955a) later reduced these to 7. Cutoff scores were developed on these tests; and, based on the proportion of tests in the impaired range, an Impairment Index could be calculated.

Early success was achieved with the HRNTB in distinguishing not only the presence of brain damage but also the location and nature of lesions (Reitan, 1955a). During the days before sophisticated neuroradiological techniques, this information was extremely useful. These efforts emerged into an emphasis on what has sometimes been referred to as the three Ls of neuropsychology: lesion detection, localization, and lateralization. In contrast, there was a relative neglect in the study of diffuse impairment in favor of the stronger emphasis on focal involvement.

Concomitant with the developments in the United States was the work of Alexander Luria in the Soviet Union and A. Rey in France. They relied extensively on close patient observation and in-depth case histories. They were not so much interested in what score a person might have obtained but rather why the individual performed in a certain manner. Their work has epitomized the flexible pathognomonic sign or qualitative approach. Rather than developing a series of quantitatively oriented tests with optimal cutoff scores, Luria emphasized a series of "procedures" that he believed would help the client to express relevant behavioral domains. His approach relied far more heavily on clinician expertise and observation than formal psychometric data. Although somewhat controversial (see K. Adams, 1980), these procedures were formalized and standardized into the Luria-Nebraska Neuropsychological Battery (Golden et al., 1985).

From these early beginnings, two distinct strategies of approaching neuropsychological assessment emerged. One was the comprehensive battery approach epitomized by Halstead and Reitan and formalized into the Halstead-Reitan Neuropsychological Test Battery; the other was a more flexible, qualitative, hypothesis-testing strategy as represented by Goldstein and Luria. Each of these approaches has different strengths and weaknesses (see Bauer, 2000; Jarvis & Barth, 1994; Russell, 2000). The battery approach has the advantages of assessing both strengths and weaknesses for a broad spectrum of behaviors, is easier to use for research, is more extensively normed and researched, can be administered by trained technicians, and is easier for students to learn. Its disadvantages are that it is typically quite time consuming, may overlook the underlying reasons for a client's specific test score, and is more difficult to tailor toward the unique aspects of the client and referral question. The contrasting qualitative hypothesis-testing approach has the advantages that it can be tailored to the specifics of the client and referral question, emphasizes the processes underlying a client's performance rather than a final score, and is quite time efficient. Measurements of a client's strengths, weaknesses, or certain reasons for ambiguous responses can be pursued in more depth according to decisions made by the examiner. Weaknesses frequently attributed to this approach are that, in practice, it focuses on a client's weaknesses, relies too extensively on clinician expertise, is more difficult to research, is not as extensively researched, and provides a narrower slice of a client's domains of functioning.

Despite the preceding somewhat polarized description, two trends indicate an integration of the quantitative psychometric and the qualitative hypothesis-testing strategies. First, in practice, most neuropsychologists use a combination of the strategies. Surveys of practice indicate that the vast majority of clinical neuropsychological assessments use a "flexible-fixed" battery comprising a relatively short "fixed" or core battery combined with additional flexible tests that can be selected based on the uniqueness of the client and specifics of the referral question (Sweet, Moberg, & Suchy, 2000). The second trend is the development of objective, in-depth, computerized scoring systems that can help clinicians understand the underlying qualitative processes a client makes in responding to test items (i.e., scoring for the California Verbal Learning Test; Delis, Kramer, Kaplan, & Ober, 2000).

Concurrent with the development of the early testing procedures and batteries, there was also an emphasis on brief screening instruments. The Bender Visual Motor Gestalt was one of the earliest of these. It was first developed by Lauretta Bender in 1938 and comprised nine designs that a client was requested to reproduce. A similar but more complex visuoconstructive test was originally devised by Rey in 1941 and expanded by Osterrith in 1944. It has since become refined and referred to as the Rey-Osterrith Complex Figure Test (Meyers & Meyers, 1996; Visser, 1992). Subjects are first asked to complete the drawing while it is directly in front of them and then requested to make a second reproduction of the drawing from memory. Rey also developed the Rey Auditory-Verbal Learning Test (Rey, 1964), which primarily screens for difficulties with short-term auditory memory. Clients are instructed to recall a series of words that are read to them and then repeat back as many of the words as possible. A final example of an early screening test for attentional difficulties is the Stroop procedure (A. R. Jensen & Rohwer, 1966; Stroop, 1935). This test presents clients with a series of names of colors but written in different color ink from the written name of the color given (see Ponsford, 2000). For example, the name *green* might be written in red ink. The client is then asked to read the list and give the name of the color of the ink (i.e., red) rather than merely reading the word (i.e., green).

A frequent goal of many of the early screening tests was to differentiate between organic and functional difficulties. Thus, a referral question was sometimes expressed in terms of "ruling out organicity" or to "differentiate between organic versus functional causes." More recently, the appropriateness of this goal and the assumptions behind it have been questioned. In particular, there has been a gradual disintegration of the distinction between many functional and organic disorders. For example, early conceptualizations of schizophrenia considered it functional. In contrast, current research supports strong genetic, biochemical, and structural correlates in a substantial proportion of schizophrenics (Saran, Phansalkar, & Kablinger, 2007). A second factor is that advances in neuroradiological and other neurologically oriented techniques have greatly refined the diagnosis of brain damage. As a result, the use of neuropsychological techniques in diagnosis has become deemphasized. In contrast, referrals from neurologists and psychiatrists are more likely to request information regarding the nature of already identified lesions.

A further change over time has been that, rather than focusing on measurement, there has been greater emphasis on application (Ponsford, 1988; Stringer & Nadolne, 2000). Thus, it is no longer sufficient merely to state that a client is experiencing cognitive deficits in certain areas. Instead, answers to more functionally relevant questions are being required such as the client's employability, responsiveness to rehabilitation, and the need for certain environmental supports (Sbordone & Long, 1996). Each of these questions can be clarified by considering the differences between impairment and disability. *Impairment* typically reflects normative comparisons and test data. In contrast, the functionally relevant term *disability* more closely takes into account the context of the client, including his or her circumstances, environment, and interests. For example, a client might be statistically in the impaired range on tests requiring sequencing, but if his or her occupation required primarily visuospatial skills, he or she might be able to continue functioning effectively. In contrast, a computer programmer who developed an equal level of sequencing difficulties would be likely to become quite disabled by this problem. Clinicians are increasingly expected to work with both the test data and the specifics of the client to translate the impact of any test-related impairment into a better understanding of the meaning it might have for the client in his or her everyday life. Understanding the meaning of test performance for everyday functioning may also require using methods of analysis other than psychological tests, such as the ratings of relatives, ward observation charts, and simulations (Knight & Godfrey, 1996; Sbordone & Guilmette, 1999).

Consistent with these points is that more recent emphasis has been not so much on measuring "organicity" or "brain damage" but rather on assessing different functions or domains. Possible domains might include attention, short-term memory, or visuoconstructive abilities. Thus, "brain-sensitive" screening tests should not be considered to be tests of brain damage but rather tests of certain functions that *may* be consistent with CNS involvement. A number of these instruments have been developed. One representative screening test is a seven-test battery composed of Trail Making, finger-tapping speed, drawing a Greek cross, the Pathognomonic Scale of the Luria-Nebraska Neuropsychological Battery, the Stroop, and the Logical Memory and Visual Reproduction subtests of the Wechsler Memory Scale (Wysocki & Sweet, 1985). Total administration time is approximately 60 minutes. Another representative screening system is the BNI Screen for Higher Cerebral Functions (Prigatano, Amin, & Rosenstein, 1992a, 1992b). Its purpose is to determine whether patients are capable of taking other neuropsychological tests; it evaluates their level of self-awareness, provides qualitative information regarding cognitive functioning, and assesses a wide range of cerebral functions. The entire procedure typically takes 10 to 15 minutes to complete. There have also been two abbreviated versions of the Halstead-Reitan Battery by Golden (1976) and by Erickson, Caslyn, and Scheupbach (1978).

In addition to these procedures, several short batteries have been developed for reviewing possible neuropsychological impairment with specific types of disorders. Batteries for the evaluation of neurotoxicity are the California Neuropsychological Screening Battery (Bowler, Thakler, & Becker, 1986), Pittsburgh Occupational Exposure Test (C. Ryan, Morrow, Parklinson, & Branet, 1987), and Individual Neuropsychological Testing for Neurotoxicity Battery (R. Singer, 1990). Similar to the previous screening batteries, each of these uses a combination of previously developed tests, such as Trail Making and portions of the Wechsler intelligence scales. Assessment and monitoring of some of the more important domains of dementia might be achieved with the CERAD Battery (Morris et al., 1989) or the Dementia Assessment Battery (Corkin et al., 1986). A similar specialized battery for detecting the early signs of AIDS-related dementia is the NIMH Core Neuropsychological Battery (Butters et al., 1990).

INTERVIEWING FOR BRAIN IMPAIRMENT

Although tests can be quite useful, the strongest tool for a clinician can often be a clear, thorough, and well-informed history. One of the major factors guiding such a history is understanding the types of behavior that are likely to reflect neuropsychological impairment (see Sbordone, 2000a). Table 12.1 provides a summary of possible behavior changes indicative of impaired brain processes. The presence of one of these is not sufficient in and of itself to diagnose pathology, but the presence of several would suggest such a process. An additional tool in extracting the range of possible symptoms is a checklist of potential areas of difficulties that the client can easily complete. Such a checklist might be informally developed by a clinician through simply listing all potentially problematic behaviors, such as difficulties with memory, finding the right word, difficulty organizing thoughts, or confusion. Alternatively, a checklist is commercially available that allows clients to detail the full range of their symptoms (Neuropsychological Symptom Checklist; Schinka, 1983).

Table 12.1.   Examples of behavioral and emotional changes that may indicate pathological processes in the brain

Domain	Behaviors/emotions
Attention	Short term memory complaints Problems staying focused Difficulty shifting attention Repetitive behaviors (perseveration)
Language	Difficulties with reading, writing, or arithmetic Reversals of numbers or letters Problems understanding spoken or written information Word finding difficulties Difficulty pronouncing words
Memory[1]	Short or long term memory problems Memory acquisition, consolidation, retrieval Memory problems can be auditory/verbal or visual/spatial
Spatial	Poor spatial judgment Poor orientation related to spatial material Difficulty with manual skills (i.e. repairs) Problems distinguishing right from left Not attending to left or right visual field
Executive[2]	Difficulty planning Apathy Poor awareness of social impact Difficulty multi-tasking
Perseverations Motor	Poor fine motor coordination Tremors Clumsiness Weakness on right or left side of body
Emotional[3]	Change in grooming (sloppy, not bathing, overly fastidious) Inappropriate social behavior Change in activity level Change in eating, sex, drinking

[1] Note that it is typically difficult to distinguish between memory problems due to neuropathology of the brain and emotional distress caused by environmental factors.

[2] Poor executive functioning can also reflect the apathy and hopelessness consistent with depression.

[3] Change in emotional functioning is often difficult to differentiate between neuropathology and external events.

Any items a client endorses can be further explored in the interview to determine the nature of the symptoms as well as their onset, frequency, intensity, and duration.

A family history should focus on some of the general areas outlined in Chapter 3. The family history for neurological and/or psychiatric complaints should receive particular attention. A family history that includes conditions with a known or suspected genetic component such as schizophrenia, early onset Alzheimer's disease, Huntington's chorea, or hypertension should alert the clinician that similar processes may be occurring with the client. The presence of any early deaths in the family, learning disabilities, or mental retardation would also be important to consider. Because some types of clients have difficulty recalling detailed information, relevant family members might be contacted to help obtain, elaborate, or verify information.

Prenatal and early personal history are also important areas for consideration. The client's prenatal environment might have involved relevant events, such as his or her mother's exposure to alcohol, drugs, pesticides, solvents, or dyes. Complications during pregnancy and birth, such as low birthweight, forceps birth, premature birth, or difficulties related to any anesthetics used, should also be considered. Early developmental milestones, including the age at which the client sat upright, walked, and talked, should be noted and verified with an outside source. Academic history is particularly helpful in determining the person's premorbid level of functioning. Favorite and worst subjects, grades obtained, and highest level of education are all significant. Assessing for possible attentional or learning difficulties is also essential. School records often provide useful information, especially when objective, and outside support is required to verify a client's claims related to his or her premorbid level of functioning.

A client's occupational history also helps establish his or her premorbid level of cognitive and social functioning. Each occupation requires certain skills that might have implications in interpreting test results. For example, test scores indicating average verbal skills would mean something quite different for an unskilled laborer than for a successful attorney. Average scores might be consistent with the former but could very well reflect impairment for the latter. It also might be relevant to note whether the person's occupation has resulted in exposure to potentially neurotoxic substances, such as organic solvents, insecticides, lead, or mercury. If so, the occupational precautions used and occurrence of all incidents would need to be determined. Knowing current and past interests and hobbies can develop a more complete portrayal of the person.

The client's medical history and any available medical records should be obtained from the client as well as from relevant persons close to him or her. The central focus of such a review is to attempt to determine whether the current symptoms can be accounted for based on this history. A person might have had a recent head injury, but inferring that his or her symptoms are partially or wholly the result of this injury might be more difficult. The history might include previous head injuries, high fevers, learning disabilities, or exposure to neurotoxic substances. Any history of a head injury should include details as to the last memory he or she had before the injury, recall of the injury itself, the length of time the person was unconscious, and the first memory following the injury. Any behavioral changes (irritability, poor memory, confusion) should be carefully documented. Further relevant medical complications might include history of high fevers ($103°+F/40°+C$) or significant infectious diseases (meningitis, encephalitis, HIV/AIDS), thyroid dysfunction, diabetes, epilepsy, hypoxia, suicide attempts, hypertension, or neurosurgery for complications such as tumors or aneurysms. If he or she has undergone any surgery, details should be obtained related to anesthetic use, complications, possible loss of consciousness, psychosocial changes following the surgery, and the nature and duration of these changes. Headaches, especially if accompanied by neuropsychological complaints, might suggest a tumor or a vascular disorder. Drug and alcohol use also needs to be carefully documented along with possible changes in prescription or nonprescription medication. Any current or past psychiatric difficulties might also complicate a client's presentation of neuropsychological symptoms.

Any neuropsychological history should provide a careful documentation of current complaints and current overall life situation. Each symptom should be described along with its onset, frequency, duration, intensity, and any changes over time. Asking the client when the symptom first appeared and how it has changed over time often can access much of this information. For example, the abrupt onset of neuropsychological complaints with no clear-cut trauma suggests a cerebral vascular accident. In contrast, gradual change might suggest a dementing condition or a slow-growing tumor. Discrete, temporary symptoms suggest transient ischemic attacks. A complicating factor is that clients vary in relation to their awareness of symptoms. Some might be preoccupied with symptoms, others might be indifferent, while still others might be aware of some difficulties but relatively unaware of others. This varying extent of awareness would then require that the interviewer refer to medical records and relevant persons in the client's life. Doing so would be especially important in conditions such as dementia or frontal lobe impairment in which clients might be both unaware of their deficits and inaccurate regarding details of their personal history (desRosiers, 1992; Gilley et al., 1995). A client's sexual functioning can often reveal relevant information related to neuropsychological status. Changes in sexual desire might be related to certain medications, growth of tumors in strategic areas, affective disorders, infectious diseases, exposure to neurotoxins, or head injuries (especially with frontal lobe involvement). It is also wise for clinicians to investigate the psychosocial factors that might be related to symptoms. Stress, depression, and family turmoil might either cause or serve to exacerbate "neuropsychological" symptoms such as concentration, memory, confusion, and irritability (Burt, Zembar, & Niederehe, 1995; Gorwood, Corruble, Falissard, & Goodwin, 2008; Sherman et al., 2000). Finally, legal complications might be intricately entangled with symptoms. This is especially true for cases involving litigation or workers' compensation.

Whereas the preceding suggestions represent a variety of areas that can be explored flexibly, several structured interviews and questionnaire formats are currently available. The Neuropsychological History Questionnaire (Wolfson, 1985) is an easily completed, 37-page, comprehensive series of questions to be answered by the client. It includes topics such as referral information, academic history, medical and general history, and present status compared with preinjury/preillness status. The Neuropsychological Status Examination (Schinka, 1983) includes a similar organization of topics but is a semistructured interview in which most of the questions are asked by the interviewer. The Neuropsychological Status Examination also includes the previously mentioned Neuropsychological Symptom Checklist, which provides a brief self-report of symptoms that can be used to assist the interview. An extremely detailed and long (3 to 5 hours) structured questionnaire is the Neurobehavioral Assessment Format (A. Siegel, Schechter, & Diamond, 1996). Additional useful tools might be brief, simple rating forms such as the Mini-Mental State (Folstein et al., 1975), Neurobehavioral Rating Scale (H. Levin et al., 1987), or Patient Competency Rating (Prigatano, 1986). Any of these structured formats requires an examiner to integrate the information into the unique characteristics of the client and relevant test data.

DOMAINS OF NEUROPSYCHOLOGICAL FUNCTIONING

Neuropsychological tests have traditionally been organized according to five domains: attention, language, memory, spatial, and executive. Sometimes a measure of achievement is also used and included as part of language functions. These domains cover the primary aspects of a person's cognitive functioning. Table 12.2 lists these domains along with measures that are frequently used to assess them. As can be seen, many of the subtests of the Wechsler intelligence scales are quite useful in providing information for these domains. Often professional psychologists will first administer the Wechsler intelligence scales and then amplify these with more specific cognitive tests. For example, the Wechsler Memory Scale-IV might be used to obtain more in-depth information related to memory functions. Similarly, the Bender-Gestalt II might be administered to better understand a client's spatial abilities. Relevant background information for conducting neuropsychological screening involves a brief understanding of these domains.

Table 12.2.   Domains of cognitive functioning and frequently used tests to measure them

Domain	Tests
Attention	Arithmetic, Digit Span, Letter-Number Sequencing, Trail Making, Stroop Color Word Test
Language	Comprehension, Information, Aphasia Screening Test, Boston Naming, Controlled Oral Word Association Test
Memory	Digit Symbol/Coding, Wechsler Memory Scale, Rey Auditory Verbal Learning Test, Bender Gestalt (recall), Rey-Osterrieth (recall)
Spatial	Block Design, Picture Concepts, Matrix Reasoning, Picture Completion, Bender Gestalt, Rey-Osterrieth Complex Figure Test, Judgment of Line Orientation
Executive	Interview/history, Delis-Kaplan Executive Function System, Category Test, Wisconson Card Sorting Test, Behavioral Assessment of the Dysexecutive Syndrome

Attention

The maintenance of an optimum amount of mental activity involves a complex variety of functions related to filtering, selecting, focusing, shifting, and tracking (see Baddley, 2003; Ponsford, 2000). Because there is typically a large amount of available information to attend to, a person must be able to filter this potential information and attend to only the most relevant sources. Any irrelevant information must be ignored. This filtering, selecting, and focusing process is still not sufficient in and of itself. Unless a person can shift attention, he or she will have difficulty functioning. Attention must strike a balance and be neither overly focused nor too ready to shift. An individual who becomes too focused expresses this symptomatically in perseverations. Such persons then experience difficulty shifting their attention to a new task and are therefore likely to continue with a behavior beyond the point at which it is adaptable. Conversely, people who shift their focus too readily express this symptomatically in distractibility.

Because of the complexity and interrelationship with other tasks, attention is quite sensitive to the effects of CNS complications. It is thus one of the most frequently reported disturbances associated with cerebral impairment (Lezak, 1989b). The most basic form of assessment for attentional deficits is through simple reaction time tasks. For example, reaction time has been found to be sensitive to the effects of head trauma (Van Zomeren & Brouwer, 1990), solvent exposure (Groth-Marnat, 1993), and the early impact of dementia (Teng, Chui, & Saperia, 1990). As attentional tasks become more complex, they become progressively more sensitive to the impact of neuropsychological dysfunction.

A good starting place to understand a client's attentional abilities is to look at the WAIS-IV/WISC-IV Working Memory Indexes and the subtests comprising these indexes (Arithmetic, Digit Span, Letter-Number Sequencing). The Trail Making Test (Army Individual Test, 1944; Reitan & Wolfson, 1993) is a further frequently used measure of attention. It is an easily administered, widely used test that requires clients to draw lines connecting consecutively numbered circles followed by a similar task in which they draw lines connecting alternating numbered and lettered circles (Part B; see Figures 12.1 and 12.2). Scores are based on the total time it takes to complete Part A and the total time it takes to complete Part B. The Stroop is also a frequently used measure of attention (Jensen & Rohwer, 1966; Stroop, 1935). Clients are presented with a series of names

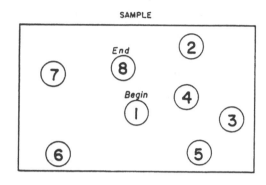

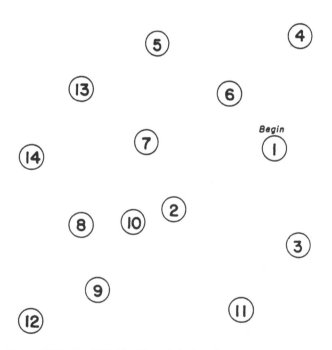

Figure 12.1 Trail Making Part A (abbreviated/child version)

of colors but written in different color ink from the written name of the color given (see Ponsford, 2000). Clients then are asked to read the list and give the name of the color of the ink (i.e., red) rather than merely reading the word (i.e., green). In order to do well, they must be able to disengage their attention from the "pull" of the word in order to name the color of the ink.

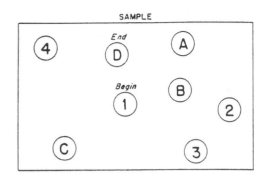

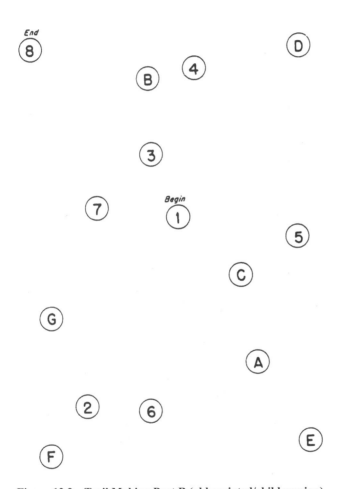

Figure 12.2   Trail Making Part B (abbreviated/child version)

Language

Disturbances of verbal functions are frequently associated with brain damage, particularly when the damage is to the left hemisphere. As a result, any review of neuropsychological functions needs to assess verbal abilities. Often this involves assessing the academic skills that are frequently associated with verbal abilities. The most common disturbances are the aphasias (impaired speech, writing, or understanding spoken or written language) and problems with speech production. These disorders can involve extremely diverse difficulties, including poor articulation, loss of verbal fluency, word-finding difficulty, poor repetition of words or sentences, loss of grammar and syntax, misspoken words (paraphasias), poor auditory comprehension, reading difficulties, and impaired writing (Goodglass & Kaplan, 1983).

Due to the variety of these disorders, neuropsychological screening can assess only a relatively small number of them. For a full assessment of aphasic and related disorders, several comprehensive batteries are available, including the Boston Diagnostic Aphasia Examination (Goodglass & Kaplan, 1983), Communicative Abilities in Daily Living (Holland, 1980), and Multilingual Aphasia Examination (Benton & Hamsher, 1989). In contrast to these formal, comprehensive batteries, Lezak et al. (2004, p. 501) recommends an informal and general clinical review of six major functions:

1. **Spontaneous Speech.** Observe how clients initiate, articulate, and organize their speech.

2. **Speech Repetition.** Ask clients to repeat words, phrases, and sentences. In particular, this might include repeating difficult words, such as *Massachusetts* or *Methodist Episcopal* (see Reitan & Wolfson's, 1993, Aphasia Screening Test), to assess for disorders of articulation.

3. **Speech Comprehension.** Request that they answer simple questions (e.g., Is a ball square?) or obey simple commands (e.g., point to specific objects, put their hands on their chins).

4. **Naming.** Ask clients to name common objects, colors, letters, and actions.

5. **Reading.** Have clients read aloud; for comprehension, have them explain what they have read.

6. **Writing.** Request that the subject copy, write to dictation, and compose a sentence.

The relative difficulty of the verbal tasks should be tailored to additional information regarding client symptoms and behaviors. For example, it would be neither necessary nor appropriate to request that a client with merely mild deficits obey quite simple commands or name common objects. Useful information regarding verbal abilities can often be derived from relevant Wechsler intelligence subtests (Information, Comprehension, Similarities, Vocabulary, Arithmetic).

The most frequently used educational achievement battery in clinical neuropsychology (Camara et al., 2000) is the Wide Range Achievement Test, which is now available in its fourth edition (WRAT-4; Wilkinson & Robertsonh, 2007). The battery is easy to administer, covers a wide range of ages (12 to 75 years), and provides scores for spelling, reading, and arithmetic. These scores can each be conveniently portrayed as school grade equivalents, standard scores, or percentiles. However, it assesses a somewhat narrow range of abilities in these domains and thus should be used only as a crude screening instrument. An increasingly popular, more in-depth assessment of achievement can be obtained from the Wechsler Individual Achievement Test-II (WIAT-II; Psychological Corporation, 2001).

Memory

The types and procedures of memory and learning are complex (see Baddeley, 2002, 2003; see Baddeley, Kopelman, & Wilson, 2002; Helmes, 2000). Aspects of these processes might include sensory memory, short-term memory, rehearsal, long-term memory, consolidation, recall, recognition, and forgetting. In addition, memory and learning can be divided into two major subsystems: declarative memory, which refers to learning about information, objects, and events; and procedural or implicit memory, which refers to automatic, habitual responses. Each of these subdivisions has somewhat different anatomical structures. Additional useful subdivisions of memory are verbal versus spatial, automatic versus effortful, and semantic versus episodic. Studies of brain-lesioned patients indicate that memory can be further divided into extremely specific subareas based on functions such as sensory modality (verbal, tactile, auditory, etc.), type of material (verbal, motor skill, etc.), and content of information (numbers, letters, pictures, names, faces, etc.; see Baddeley et al., 2002; Baddeley et al., 2003). For the practitioner, providing a truly comprehensive evaluation of memory functions is a daunting task.

Fortunately, usually a more limited number of memory domains can provide practitioners with an overview of the general intactness of memory. These include (1) the extent to which the subject can acquire and retain new material, (2) how quickly material is forgotten, (3) the extent to which competing information interferes with learning, (4) the degree of specificity or generality of the deficit, and (5) the stability or fluctuation of the deficits over time (Walsh, 1994). Ideally, these domains should include measurements of both visual and verbal material.

One important distinction is between attention versus memory and learning. In some ways, this distinction is inappropriate because attention is a prerequisite for learning to occur. A person who is easily distracted does not effectively learn and remember relevant information or events. Attention is, therefore, closely linked to learning. However, in other ways attention and learning do represent distinct functions. In particular, it is important to distinguish whether a person is capable of learning but is easily distracted, or whether, even under circumstances in which the person fully attends to a task, he or she still cannot learn very efficiently. Sometimes clients state that they have a memory problem, but, despite their symptom description, they perform learning and memory tasks quite well under the ideal circumstances that often characterize assessment procedures. In contrast, real-world situations frequently mean that they need to exclude a number of distractions and carry on two or more activities simultaneously. Under these conditions, they might have distinct difficulties dividing their attention and, therefore, might not be able to learn and remember particularly effectively. Interviewing them regarding situations in which they do versus do not remember effectively might help the practitioner to understand this issue better. In addition, their test performances would be expected to be lower on tasks that load more heavily on attention (Arithmetic, Digit Span, serial sevens or serial threes) than those that are more pure tests of learning (Wechsler Memory Scales-IV, repeating paragraphs/stories, Bender-Gestalt II recall administration).

A good beginning place to assess memory is in the interview. Details regarding basic information, such as personal, family, educational, and employment history, can be pursued. Interviewers might request dates when the client began or finished employment or education, parents' or children's birthdays, or details related to medical history. Some of this information might be compared with more objective sources to determine its accuracy. In addition, behavioral observations, such as pauses, expressions of uncertainty, or confusion, might suggest difficulties with retrieval.

Current research consistently indicates that there is a mild to moderate relationship between memory impairment and depression. An extensive meta-analysis by Burt et al. (1995) found that memory impairment was most clearly associated with inpatients (versus outpatients) and mixed bipolar and unipolar patients (versus purely unipolar). Similarly, Gorwood et al. (2008) found that frequent, long, and chronic states of depression clearly impaired brain functioning in those areas responsible for memory. In addition, negative affective information was more likely to be remembered accurately than material with a positive or neutral emotional tone (Burt et al., 1995). However, memory impairments were also present among populations of schizophrenics and mixed groups of psychiatric patients but not among patients diagnosed with either anxiety disorders or substance abuse. Interestingly, the association between memory and depression was stronger among younger than older persons (Burt et al., 1995; Gorwood et al., 2008). This is probably because early-onset depression is likely to be more severe and younger persons have a greater amount of memory to lose (greater "ceiling" and "floor") than older persons (narrower range between ceiling and floor). Despite these findings, it should also be stressed that the link between memory impairment (and other forms of neuropsychological functioning) and depression is typically of quite a small magnitude (Burt et al., 1995; Sherman et al., 2000). For example, dementia typically accounts for a far larger proportion of the variance in neuropsychological functioning than depression.

To more fully assess the complex and multifactorial structure of learning and memory, a number of relatively comprehensive memory batteries have been developed. Among the oldest, and certainly the most frequently used (Camara et al., 2000; Robin, et al., 2005), is the Wechsler Memory Scale (WMS; Wechsler, 1945, 1974; see Chapter 6). Its most recent revision is the Wechsler Memory Scale-IV (WMS-IV; Wechsler, 2008), which has five primary indexes, (but only four indexes for the Adult Battery), and assesses both verbal and visual-spatial functions, includes a delayed recall component (see Chapter 6). Additional relatively comprehensive batteries include the Rivermead Behavioral Memory Test (B. Wilson, Cockburn, & Baddeley, 2003), Memory Assessment Scales (J. M. Williams, 1991), and Wide Range Assessment of Memory and Learning-II (Sheslow, & Adams, 2003).

In addition to these comprehensive batteries are a number of brief, narrow, specific tests that measure memory. The Rey Auditory Verbal Learning Test is a relatively short, well-researched, frequently used, individually administered test that presents clients with a series of word lists. Their performance is used to assess short-term verbal memory, their ability to learn new material, the extent to which interference disrupts learning, and their ability to recognize information that might have been previously learned. As the name suggests, however, it is verbally oriented. To include at least some visual-spatial memory assessment, the recall administration of the Bender-Gestalt II can be used. Clinicians might also consider the Benton Visual Motor Retention Test (Benton, 1974) or the Rey-Osterrieth Complex Figure Test (Meyers & Meyers, 1996; Osterrieth, 1944; Rey, 1941; Strauss et al., 2006). In addition, the WAIS-IV/WISC-IV subtests of Digit Symbol-Coding (incidental learning), Information, Digit Span, and Letter-Number Sequencing include potentially valuable information related to learning and memory. However, it should be stressed that Digit Span and Letter-Number Sequencing are primarily attentional tasks rather than pure learning tests.

Spatial Functions

The accurate construction of objects involves intact visual perception along with effective visuospatial and visuomotor abilities. Each one of these three areas (perceptual, spatial, motor) might have disturbances that could make visual construction more difficult. Benton (1979) has listed these as:

1. Visuoperceptual disturbances. Impaired discrimination of complex stimuli, visual recognition, color recognition, figure-ground differentiation, visual integration.

2. Visuospatial disturbances. Impaired localization of points in space, topographic orientation, neglect of part of a person's visual field, difficulties with direction and distance.

3. Visuomotor disturbances. Defective eye movement, assembling, graphomotor performance.

For some patients, these disturbances might occur together, whereas with others, they might occur separately. A patient might have excellent visuoperceptual abilities but still have significant problems making accurate constructions. At other times, poor perception would lead to or occur in combination with poor constructional abilities. In addition, the ability to draw and assemble objects can be quite variable for a particular patient whose ability to assemble objects might be intact (as in Block Design) but whose drawings of human figures or simpler designs might be quite poor.

Each one of the three disturbances is also likely to have somewhat different neuroanatomical pathways. The practical implication is that the clinician should not make any inferences regarding localization of lesion merely by considering a person's overall score on a particular visuoconstructive test. Although overall scores are of limited use, important information and the implications for localization can be derived more appropriately from a careful observation of how the client approaches the task and the types of errors the person makes. In general, patients with lesions in their right hemispheres tend to approach visuoconstructive tasks in a fragmented, piecemeal fashion in which they often lose the overall gestalt of the design. In contrast, patients with left-hemisphere lesions are likely to duplicate the overall gestalt of the design correctly but often omit important details of the drawing.

A number of assessments or visuoconstructive abilities are available. The Bender-Gestalt II is a simple, straightforward task. Its predecessor, the Bender Visual Motor Gestalt test, was extensively researched and frequently used in clinical practice (Brannigan & Decker, 2003; Camara et al., 2000; Lacks, 1999, 2000). The Bender-Gestalt II might be further supplemented with a free drawing task, such as a Human Figure Drawing or House-Tree-Person. Other somewhat simpler drawing tasks, such as drawing a clock, bicycle, or Greek cross, have also been used frequently. Whereas these tasks involve drawing, the Block Design task requires assembling (rather than drawing) designs with the added factor of a time limit.

Executive Functions

Executive functions involve a person's ability to effectively regulate and direct self-behavior. These functions can be subdivided into volition, planning, purposive action, and effective performance (Lezak et al., 2004; Sbordone, 2000b). For example, patients experiencing significant executive impairments might exist in a semivegetative state in which they rarely initiate much activity although other cognitive abilities might be quite intact. Other patients with executive difficulty may have little awareness of their impact on others and thus are unable to effectively direct or regulate their social behavior. Although frontal lobe damage is most typically implicated with executive deficits, damage to subcortical, especially thalamic, regions or the more diffuse damage caused by anoxia or organic solvents can also produce executive impairment (see Sbordone, 2000b).

Despite the importance of executive abilities, they can be overlooked during formal psychological assessment, partially because executive functions can be impaired even though other cognitive functions appear quite intact. As a result, a clinician might look at cognitive test scores such as a composite IQ and erroneously conclude that a patient has made a good or even full recovery. There are even anecdotal reports of patients' IQs actually increasing after frontal lobe damage although they became quite disabled because of a loss of executive abilities.

Another reason executive functioning might be overlooked is that most formal assessment is a structured situation in which the examiner directs the patient to do certain activities. As a result, the patient's ability to self-initiate might be overlooked. This may not occur because examiners must "structure" an unstructured situation in which patients can demonstrate the extent, style, and manner in which they would initiate, develop, plan, and monitor their own behavior. A final assessment issue is that, frequently, depression can produce some of the same behaviors (i.e., apathy, flat affect, lack of direction) that occur with executive loss stemming from brain damage. A clinician might, therefore, erroneously conclude that the executive dysfunctions were the result of depression rather than brain damage (or vice versa).

Interview assessment of executive function might focus on a patient's articulation of future goals along with descriptions of recreational activities. Typically, patients with executive difficulties provide little detail about these areas. If they do provide detail, it may be primarily based on reciting their goals and activities before the injury. For this reason, interviewers need to establish what patients' current activities and goals are and, in particular, what they have done recently to pursue these goals. Interviewers might also establish the extent to which patients can realistically pursue these goals, anticipate and plan relevant activities, develop alternative plans, and give direction to actually putting these plans into action. Because poor executive functions are frequently accompanied by lack of awareness, it might be essential to interview family members who have had a chance to observe the patient on a daily basis. Thus, the client's descriptions can be compared with more objective external descriptions.

In the actual examination itself, various types of behavior can provide information. Does the patient initiate and direct any activity, or does he or she tend to be relatively passive? Are there unusual social behaviors (e.g., poor grooming, discussion of irrelevant tangents, inappropriate jokes) that suggest poor awareness of his or her social impact? The examiner must determine whether such behaviors developed postinjury or were premorbid characteristics. Planning abilities might be estimated based on how well such patients organize their human figure drawings, blocks on Block Design, Bender-Gestalt II drawings, or stories on the TAT. Perseverations suggest poor mental flexibility and difficulty monitoring their behavior; the patient may make too many dots on the Bender-Gestalt II or find it difficult to understand changes in test stimuli (e.g., slow to understand the requirements of WAIS-IV/WISC-IV subtests). Because poor executive functions also include difficulty attending to stimuli while simultaneously performing other tasks, low scores on the Wechsler Working Memory Index or Bannatyne's Sequencing might also reflect poor executive abilities.

A number of informal clinical tests might also help to determine possible executive impairments. For example, the patient might be asked to continue the pattern of a drawing that has various repetitive but alternating small shapes (three circles, two squares, one triangle) and then to repeat this sequence several times (see Goldberg & Bilder, 1987). A similar chain-of-command–type test is having the patient tap the desk with his or her fist, then tap it with the palm, then repeat this pattern several times. A slightly more complicated task might be as follows: The examiner taps his or her foot once, then the patient taps a foot twice. Alternatively, the examiner may tap a foot twice, while then the patient is instructed to tap once (see Lezak et al., 2004). None of these procedures has formal scoring; instead, the examiner must determine, based on observation, whether the patient had relative difficulty with all or any of the activities. Although no single strategy in this section is sufficient to identify executive impairments, collectively, the strategies will help to ensure that this critical domain of functioning is included in a client's assessment.

There are also a number of formal comprehensive batteries to assess for executive function. These include the Behavioral Assessment of the Dysecutive Syndrome (B. Wilson, Alderman, Burgess, Emslie, & Evans, 1999), Frontal Lobe Personality Scale (Grace, Stout, & Malloy, 1999), and Delis-Kaplan Executive Function System (Delis, Kaplan, & Kramer, 1999).

BENDER VISUAL MOTOR GESTALT TEST

History and Development

The Bender Visual Motor Gestalt Test (Bender, 1938), usually referred to as the *Bender-Gestalt* or simply the *Bender*, has been extensively used as a screening device for neuropsychological impairment by assessing a client's visuoconstructive abilities. The original version consisted of nine designs that were sequentially presented to subjects with the request that they reproduce them on a blank, 8.5-by-11-inch sheet of paper. The subject's designs were then rated on their relative degree of accuracy and overall integration. The test's popularity can be partially accounted for in that it is brief, economical, flexible, nonthreatening, nonverbal, and extensively researched.

Despite sometimes-equivocal reviews and ambiguous research findings, the Bender-Gestalt has consistently been one of the five or six most frequently used tests (Camara et al., 2000; Kamphaus et al., 2000). This is consistent with other studies on test usage dating back to 1969. In contrast, Camara et al. found that it was ranked as the 25th most frequently used test by specialty neuropsychologists. This finding likely results from the greater number of options among specialty neuropsychological tests, in addition to the fact that it is not highly regarded among this subgroup.

A wide number of scoring systems for adults and children have been developed for the Bender, each having various advantages and disadvantages. One of the earliest and most widely accepted scoring systems for adults was developed by Pascal and Suttell (1951). Although this system is widely cited in research studies, it has not gained wide acceptance in clinical settings, primarily because of its complexity and time inefficiency. Another early adult system was developed by Hutt in the 1940s and later formally published in 1960 (Hutt & Briskin, 1960). Although his interest in the Bender-Gestalt was primarily for projective personality assessment, he also listed "12 essential discriminators of intracranial damage" (Fragmentation, Closure Difficulty, etc.). Lacks (1984, 2000) adapted this system and provided a detailed scoring manual along with substantial empirical support. In contrast to the Pascal and Suttell (1951) system, it is straightforward and time efficient, typically taking 3 minutes or less to score. Studies using her system have reported good discrimination between brain-damaged and non–brain-damaged populations (Lacks, 1984, 1999, 2000; Lacks & Newport, 1980). The system is limited to persons 12 years of age or older.

A system for children was developed by Koppitz (1963, 1975) and more recently as the Koppitz-2 (Reynolds, 2007). She carried out an extensive standardization of 1,104 children from kindergarten through fourth grade. Her system provided measures of both developmental maturation and neuropsychological impairment. She cautions that, for a diagnosis of brain damage, the examiner needs not only to consider the child's scores but also to observe the time required to complete the test, the amount of space used, and the child's behavior and relative degree of awareness about his or her errors. The original Koppitz system was developed for relatively young children because the scores of children over the age of 10 no longer correlate with either intelligence test results or age. In addition, after the age of 10, most individuals obtain nearly perfect scores. However, more recent research has indicated that the Koppitz system can be used for adolescents between the ages of 12 and 18, although the relation with age is not nearly as strong as with younger children (McIntosh, Belter, Saylor, Finch, & Edwards, 1988; S. Ivnik & Simpson, 1995).

Whereas the use of the Bender-Gestalt in screening for brain dysfunction has been generally accepted, its use in personality assessment has been questionable. Single-sign indicators have rarely been found to be valid. For example, "edging" (consistently drawing the designs along the edge of the paper) has not generally been found to indicate personality variables (Holmes, Dungan, & Medlin, 1984; Holmes & Stephens, 1984). Likewise, projective interpretations that rely heavily on psychoanalytic theory and clinical lore have neither been generally accepted nor sufficiently validated (Sattler, 1985, 1992). However, global ratings that typically sum a series of indicators (size increases, collisions, scribbling, etc.) have had greater validity. For example, accurate discriminations have been made for impulsivity by comparing total scores for impulsive versus nonimpulsive indicators (Oas, 1984). Likewise, Koppitz (1975) has listed emotional indicators that have been found to be good predictors of the general presence of psychopathology when three or more are present (Koppitz, 1975; Rossini & Kaspar, 1987). Thus, the Bender-Gestalt has generally been found to be valid in predicting the absence or presence of psychopathology based on clusters of indicators rather than on single signs. With the possible exception of impulsivity and anxiety, the Bender-Gestalt is probably ineffective in identifying specific personality characteristics or specific psychiatric diagnoses.

A comprehensive revision of the Bender-Gestalt was published in 2003 (Bender-Gestalt II; Brannigan & Decker, 2003, 2006). This revision was partially based on the earlier work of Brannigan and Brunner (1989), who used a scoring system that rated the quality of each of the reproductions of the designs. The ratings were then totaled to form an overall or global rating of all of the designs. Their global rating system is in contrast to other systems (Hutt, Lacks, Koppittz) that focused on types and numbers of specific errors (i.e., perseverations, distortions, rotations). The 2003 revision retained all of the original designs. However, four easier items were added to create a lower "floor" and three more difficult items were added to create a higher "ceiling." These additions enabled the test to be normed on and used with young children down to the age of 4 and adults up to the age of 85+. Children below the age of 8 are given the four easy designs plus the original nine designs (items 1–13). Children above the age of 8, along with adolescents and adults, are given the nine original designs plus the three more difficult ones (items 5–16). The Bender-Gestalt II begins with a copy phase in which the client is shown the designs and requested to copy them. A recall phase follows, in which the client is required to draw as many of the designs as possible from memory.

Norms for the Bender-Gestalt II were based on a large, nationally representative sample that closely paralleled the 2000 U.S. census (based on age, sex, race/ethnicity/ geographic region, and socioeconomic level). These included a total of 4,000 participants between the ages of 4 and 85+. In addition, data was gathered from a sample of persons with mental retardation, learning disabilities, attention deficit hyperactivity disorder (ADHD), serious emotional disturbance, autism, Alzheimer's disease, and giftedness. Scores are compared with age related peers and transformed to standard scores with a mean of 100 and a standard deviation of 15.

Reliability and Validity

Reliabilities for the Bender-Gestalt II indicate it provides stable, consistent measures (Brannigan & Decker, 2003). Test-retest reliability over a 2- to 3-week interval was .85

(range = .80–.88) for the copy phase and .83 (range = .80–.86) for the recall phase. Split-half procedures indicated the overall validity was .91 and the Standard Error of Measurement was 4.55. The developers also provide evidence that there is moderate to high interrater consistency for trained scorers. Rater agreement for the copy phase was .90 (range = .83–.94) and .96 (range = .94–.97) for the recall phase. Even inexperienced scorers had quite high agreement (Copy phase = .85, Recall phase = .92).

Many studies on the previous version of the Bender indicated it has been able to discriminate brain-damaged from non-brain-damaged populations (Hain, 1964; Lacks, 1984, 1999, 2000; Marley, 1982). Studies using the Lacks adaptation have reported diagnostic accuracies of from 64% to 84% with a mean of 80% (Lacks, 1999, 2000; Lacks & Newport, 1980). Its diagnostic accuracy has been questioned, however, when used to assess subtle neuropsychological deficits, such as among many epileptics, or when a differentiation is attempted between functional psychotic patients and brain-damaged patients (Hellkamp & Hogan, 1985). However, this distinction may be inappropriate, because schizophrenia is being progressively conceptualized as an organically based disorder. Further studies have found that Bender-Gestalt performance has been able to differentiate Alzheimer's patients from controls as well as reflect the progression of the disease (Storandt, Botwinick, & Danzinger, 1986). Similarly, Bender-Gestalt scores were able to predict the extent to which head trauma patients could function independently (Acker & Davis, 1989).

Research on the Bender-Gestalt II indicated moderate correlations with similar measures, thereby supporting its construct validity. For example, the Bender-Gestalt II had a moderate correlation ($r = .65$) with the Beery-Buktenica Developmental Test of Visual Organization-IV (Brannigan & Decker, 2003) and a similarly moderate to high correlation (.75) with the WISC-III Perceptual Organization factor (Decker, Allen, & Choca, 2006). Brannigan and Decker (2003) also reported a .80 correlation with the Koppitz Developmental Scoring System. Moderate correlations have also been found with measures of academic skills including the Woodcock Johnson reading cluster (.53) and the Wechsler Individual Achievement Test-II (.41; Brannigan & Decker, 2003). Correlations with the WAIS-III Performance IQ was .52 and Verbal IQ was .47 (Brannigan & Decker, 2003). As expected, correlations were higher for nonverbal abilities than for more verbally oriented skills.

Scores on the Bender-Gestalt II rapidly increase with age, especially between the ages of 5 and 10 (Brannigan & Decker, 2003; Decker, 2007). They increase more gradually between ages 10 and 15 and then remain fairly stable throughout most of adult life. They gradually decrease between ages 40 and 69 and drop off rapidly from 70 to 80+. This finding suggests performance on the Bender-Gestalt II can be used to track developmental changes in visual-motor processes in the 4- to 15-year-old range and again after age 70.

Various groups have scores on the Bender-Gestalt II that roughly correspond to the severity and nature of their cognitive difficulties (see Brannigan & Decker, 2003). A review of Table 12.3 indicates that intellectually gifted persons have the highest scores and mentally retarded persons the lowest. Note that the scores for Alzheimer's patients have copy scores in the average range, indicating that visuoconstructive abilities are relatively spared in the early to middle phases of the disease. As expected given the memory impairment among Alzheimer's patients, the recall phase was found to be quite low. Research indicates that the Bender-Gestalt II has moderate to strong validity.

Assets and Limitations

The Bender-Gestalt II is a brief, user-friendly screening instrument that is easily administered and measures visuoconstructive abilities. The original Bender-Gestalt has a long

Table 12.3. Bender-Gestalt II performance among selected clinical populations

Patient type	B-G II M (SD)	Matched sample M (SD)
Intellectually gifted	copy 110.62 (11.35)	102.83 (11.38)
	recall 114.94 (17.10)	102.77 (12.70)
Reading disabilities	copy 92.33 (11.04)	103.51 (11.22)
	recall 92.96 (10.93)	103.57 (12.79)
Alzheimer's	copy 100.53 (9.59)	100.95 (7.86)
	recall 81.10 (7.10)	100.21 (7.36)
ADHD	copy 91.15 (13.34)	104.65 (9.30)
	recall 93.39 (13.66)	103.89 (12.89)
Mental retardation	copy 75.77 (14.14)	103.01 (11.31)
	recall 83.92 (10.04)	101.97 (11.89)

Data derived from Brannigan and Decker (2003).
Scores are transformed to a standard score ($M = 100$, $SD = 15$).
All score differences with the matched sample were significant (>.001).

history of clinical use and research support. Given that the nine original designs were retained for the Bender-Gestalt II, it is likely that much of the early research on the original test can be cautiously transferred to the newer version. The recent research on the Bender-Gestalt II does provide good support for its validity. Data presented in the manual indicates that it can be reliably scored by both experienced and inexperienced examiners. In addition, it has good internal consistency and test-retest reliability.

The Bender-Gestalt II has a number of new features that suggest it will be an improvement on the earlier version. The norms cover a wide range of ages and are representative of the 2000 U.S. census. Since they include both children and adults, practitioners do not have to use separate scoring systems for children and adults, as was the case with the original Bender-Gestalt. It is also likely that the lower floor/ceiling created by including additional easy/difficult items will increase its sensitivity to both developmental delays as well as acquired cognitive impairment. However, this remains to be determined by future research. A final asset of the Bender-Gestalt II is the inclusion of norms and formal administration and scoring procedures for the recall phase.

Although the Bender-Gestalt has a good track record of achievements, a number of cautions and limitations surround its use. The test has often been described as "assessing" brain damage, yet it is perhaps more accurate to say that it is a "screening" device for brain damage. It does not provide in-depth information about the specific details and varieties of such damage. In fact, the Bender-Gestalt is limited to relatively severe forms of brain damage, especially in the right parietal region of the right hemisphere (Black & Bernard, 1984). Thus, a patient may have significant lesions or subtle deficits that could easily go undetected if the Bender-Gestalt were the sole method used to assess the presence of cerebral impairment. It is more correct to say, then, that the Bender-Gestalt is a screening device for generalized impairment and/or right parietal involvement.

Research on the original version of the Bender-Gestalt found a certain degree of overlap between emotional and organic indicators. For example, one of the better indicators for organic impairment is the presence of difficulties with overlapping, which has been found in the Bender-Gestalt records of 45% of patients with organic impairment. However, Lacks (1984, 1999) also found that overlapping difficulties occurred in the records of 26% of persons with personality disorders and 26% of those with psychosis. The degree of overlap occurring in the scores of different populations has led some reviewers (Dana, Field, & Bolton, 1983; Sattler, 1985) to seriously question the clinical usefulness of the Bender-Gestalt. The Bender-Gestalt II is likely to partially avoid this issue since it uses a global scoring system based on ratings of the overall quality of each of the designs rather than noting various types of errors. However, these qualitative ratings are also based on various errors that might be present in the designs. For example, a rater who notices rotations or difficulty making dots will rate the quality of the design lower. It would thus be likely that emotional difficulties would still have some overlap with the scoring system for the Bender-Gestalt II. Future research will no doubt explore this issue in further detail.

A further difficulty with the original Bender-Gestalt was the absence of a commonly accepted and verified scoring and interpretation system. The result was that different research studies often used different systems, which made it somewhat difficult to compare their conclusions. Clinicians generally begin by learning a system of scoring and interpretation, but end up with their own unique, subjective approach based on clinical impressions. Although this may be a highly workable, flexible approach, disagreements between "experts" can occur because of their differences in approaching the designs. Another difficulty in depending on clinical impressions is continued, unwarranted reliance on unsubstantiated and possibly incorrect clinical "lore." Lacks (1984, 1999) presented evidence that clinicians could increase their diagnostic accuracy for organic impairment on the average of 10% to 15% by using a brief, easily learned, objective scoring system. It is likely that future research on the formal scoring system for the Bender-Gestalt II will also be more accurate when compared with clinical impressions.

A final weakness of the Bender-Gestalt II is the lack of current research. The extensive norms, extended floor/ceiling, good reliability, and inclusion of formal recall phase procedures all seem like improvements. The manual and recent research have certainly supported its validity. However, future research still needs to determine whether it has greater validity than the previous version.

Administration

Administration of the Bender-Gestalt II occurs in two phases. Clients are first requested to draw the designs presented to them one at a time (the "copy" phase). The next, or "recall," phase begins when the examiner removes the designs and the paper with the reproductions on them, gives clients a new blank sheet of paper, and asks them to copy as many of the designs as they can from memory. During the copy phase, the examiner presents the cards directly in front of the client one at a time. The series of cards presented should be appropriate for the client's age (cards 1 to 13 for children 4 to 7 and cards 5 to 16 for persons 8 and older). Clients are asked to copy each design with a number 2 pencil on a single, blank, 8.5-by-11-inch sheet of white paper that has been presented to them in a vertical position. A sharpened backup pencil should be available in case a client breaks the graphite on the pencil. Pencils should include erasers. These verbal directions are taken from Brannigan and Decker (2003) and are recommended as a standard procedure:

> I have a number of cards here. Each card has a different drawing on it. I will show you the cards one at a time. Use this pencil (give pencil to examinee) to copy the drawing from each card onto this sheet of paper (point to drawing paper). Try to make your drawings look just like the drawings on these cards. There are no time limits, so take as much time as you need. Do you have any questions? Here is the first card. (p. 17)

After the person has completed the first design, the next one should be presented until the entire set of designs has been reproduced. Timing should begin immediately following the presentation of the first design. This sequence should be continued and the total time noted after the last drawing has been completed. No comments or additional instructions are to be given while clients are completing the drawings. If clients ask specific questions, they should be given a noncommittal answer, such as "Do the best you can" or "Begin wherever you like."

If clients begin to count the dots on Design 6, the examiner may say, "You don't have to count the dots, just make it look like the picture." If they persist, this may show perfectionistic or compulsive tendencies, and the behavioral observation should be considered when evaluating the test results and formulating diagnostic impressions. Although examinees are allowed to pick up the cards, they are not allowed to turn them unless they are in the process of completing their drawing. If it looks as if they have turned the design and are beginning to copy it in the new position, the examiner should straighten the card and state that it should be copied from this angle. As many sheets of paper may be used as desired, although clients are presented with only one sheet initially. There is no time limit, but it is important to note the length of time required to complete the test, as this information may be diagnostically significant. An observation form is included that enables examiners to note physical and test-taking observations for each of the designs as well as record the scores.

In addition to the copy phase, a memory or "recall" phase is presented. Immediately after having copied the final designs, clients are given a new sheet of paper and given the following instructions (from Brannigan & Decker, 2003):

> Now I want you to draw as many of the designs that I just showed you as you can remember. Draw them on this new sheet of paper. Try to make your drawings just like the ones on the cards that you saw earlier. There are no limits, so take as much time as you need. Do you have any questions? Begin. (p. 18)

Begin timing as soon as clients begin their first drawing and stop when they have indicated that they cannot recall any more of the designs (after approximately 2 minutes). Be sure to label the sheet as "Recall Sheet" and indicate where the top of the page is with an arrow. The recall phase provides an assessment of their level of short-term, visuomotor recall. Typically, adult brain-injured subjects are not able to recall the designs as well as persons who are not brain-injured (Lyle & Gottesman, 1976).

Motor and Perception Procedures (optional/supplemental)

Sometimes it is useful to try to differentiate whether there are motor and/or perceptual difficulties that are interfering with an examinee's performance on the Bender-Gestalt II. One option is to administer the Motor Test, which consists of a sheet of paper with a sample item and four test items. Examinees are first shown the sample item depicting a rectangle with two medium-size dots on either end. A series of smaller dots connect the two medium-size dots. Examinees are given these instructions, which are read from the top of the page of designs:

> For each item, start with the largest figure. For each figure, draw a line connecting the dots without touching the borders. Do not lift the pencil, erase, or tilt the paper while drawing.

Sometimes it might be necessary to demonstrate the procedure by drawing a line between the two medium-size dots in the sample. Begin timing when the examinee begins the first design. Discontinue the procedure and note the time after the examinee either finishes the procedure or after a maximum of 4 minutes has elapsed.

This Motor Test will help detect the presence of motor problems. Another possibility is the presence of perceptual problems. Often these can be detected with the Perception Test, which depicts 10 designs, each of which is followed by 4 designs. One of these 4 is identical to the original design; the others are merely similar. According to the Bender-Gestalt II manual (Brannigan & Decker, 2003), the examiner is to say:

> Look at this picture (point to the design in the first box). There is another picture that looks just like it in this row (run your finger across the first row). Circle or point to the picture that looks just like this one (point again to the designs in the box).

If needed, provide assistance for the first item. Point to each item in the row and say:

> Which one of these pictures looks like this one? (point again to the design in the box). (p. 19)

This procedure should be timed but should be discontinued if it takes more than 4 minutes. If an examinee takes more than 30 seconds to give a response to any of the items, the item should be discontinued and the examinee should be instructed to go to the next item.

Scoring

Scoring for both the copy and recall phases requires examiners to rate each of the designs drawn on a scale between 0 and 4 where:

0 = No resemblance, random drawing, scribbling, lack of design
1 = Slight-vague resemblance
2 = Some-moderate resemblance
3 = Strong-close resemblance, accurate reproduction
4 = nearly perfect (Brannigan & Decker, 2003, p. 20)

Examples are provided in the manual to assist with scoring. The scores are totaled with higher scores indicating better performance. Scores for examinees below age 8 can range between 0 to a maximum of 52. In contrast, scores for examinees above the age of 8 can range from 0 to a maximum of 48. The raw scores are then converted to standard scores (M = 100, SD = 15) using age-referenced tables in the back of the manual.

The Motor Test is scored a 1 if the line touches both of the medium sized dots at either end of the design. The line can touch the border of the design but cannot go over it. In contrast, a 0 is scored if the line extends outside the box or if it does not touch both of the medium-size dots (which represent the end points).

The Perception Test is scored a 1 for a correct response and a 0 for an incorrect response. Thus a total of 10 points is possible. A table at the back of the Observation Form converts both the Motor Test and Perception Test to percentile rankings.

Interpretation Guidelines

In order to perform well on the Bender, clients must have adequate fine motor coordination and the ability to make accurate perceptual discriminations. They must then integrate this into the actual reproduction of the design. In contrast, errors may reflect poor fine motor coordination, difficulties actually perceiving the design, problems executing the drawing itself, or difficulties integrating the perception and motor requirements

(Sattler & Hoge, 2006). Difficulties with poor performance may be the result of delays in visuomotor abilities, brain dysfunction, emotional disturbance, or a combination of all of these factors. Bender performance seems to be only minimally influenced by cultural factors or processing speed (Decker et al., 2006).

The Global Scoring on the Bender-Gestalt II allows for raw scores to be converted into standard scores ranging between 40 and 160. Similar to the Wechsler intelligence, there is a mean of 100 and a standard deviation of 15. Thus a score of 85 on the Bender-Gestalt means the client scored 1 standard deviation below the norm or at the 16th percentile when compared with his or her age-related peers. Brannigan and Decker (2003) state that scores in the lower 25th percentile should signal the need for further evaluation. Often a score in the bottom 2% of the population (2nd percentile, standard score of 70) is considered to be in the "impaired" range. However, these considerations depend largely on the person's history, demographics, and level of functioning. For example, a student who has been functioning near the top of the class but who then begins to have academic difficulties and has Bender-Gestalt II scores at the 20th percentile may indeed suggest a deteriorating condition. In contrast, another student with a marginal academic record, low-average intelligence but who similarly has a Bender-Gestalt II score in the 20th percentile may be merely reflecting overall low-average abilities. Brannigan and Decker (2003) provide these classifications for Bender-Gestalt II standard scores:

Extremely high or extremely advanced	145–160
Very high or advanced	130–144
High or advanced	120–129
High average	110–119
Average	90–109
Low average	80–89
Low or borderline delayed	70–79
Very low or mildly delayed	55–69
Extremely low or moderately delayed	40–54

In a general way, low scores on the Bender-Gestalt II typically represent the person's visuomotor abilities. The listed normative and extra test comparisons represent the most obvious and clear way of making very general sense of the person's scores. Beyond this, three major areas need to be considered in expanding on the meaning of the person's score: (1) distinguishing between perceptual versus motor difficulties, (2) considering the meaning of design construction versus visual memory, and (3) differentiating among developmental delays, brain dysfunction, or emotional disturbance.

Perceptual versus Motor Difficulties

A useful informal guide in distinguishing between whether poor Bender-Gestalt performance is due to perceptual versus motor difficulties is to carefully consider relevant behavioral observations along with qualitative features of the drawings. These observations might include areas such as the client's level of confidence, awareness of errors, completion time, and any comments that are made. The clinician might then look at specific features of the drawings, including figure size, placement, line quality, order of the designs, location of the designs, distortions, erasures, reworking, omissions, and any other unusual treatment. A number of these types of observation can be made on the Bender-Gestalt II protocol in the regions for "Physical Observations" and "Test-taking Observations."

These observations can be useful in determining whether a client's poor Bender-Gestalt II reproductions are the result of inadequate perception (difficulty in receiving visual informal) or inadequate motor abilities (difficulty in reproducing that which might have been accurately perceived). This distinction can sometimes be determined by asking the person to evaluate the accuracy of the drawing he or she has made. If clients feel that poorly reproduced drawings are accurate, then they most likely have receptive difficulties and possibly difficulties with expression. If they recognize that their drawings were done poorly, this suggests their problem might be primarily motor/expressive. Although they might be aware of the inaccuracy of their drawings, they would be expected to have extreme difficulty in correcting the inaccuracies.

The Bender-Gestalt II has formalized this differentiation through the use of the optional Motor and Perception tests. If clients have a poor score on the Bender-Gestalt II but the Motor Test was average or high, it suggests that their perceptual abilities were the major problem. This finding would then be confirmed by whether they had a low score on the Perception Test. Conversely, a poor performance on the Motor Test but an intact performance on the Perception Test would suggest that the problem was due to motor abilities.

Considering Copy versus Recall Performance

A further refinement is to note the relative scores on the Bender-Gestalt copy versus the recall phases. The previous nine design Bender-Gestalt used general or "clinical" norms to indicate low, average, or high performance. Specifically, it was expected that a healthy person of average intelligence would accurately recall and construct four to five designs. An advantage of the Bender-Gestalt II is that the more global scoring allows for a much more precise calculation in which a raw score can be converted to a standard, age-related score. Additional information and validation can be obtained by asking clients for examples in their lives that reflect any difficulties (or strengths) with visual memory. This may include their ability to recall who was at meetings, where they had left things in their homes, or being able to find somewhere that they had been before. If the Wechsler Memory Scale-IV was given, the clinician might make sure the Bender recall score is consistent with Wechsler measures of visual memory.

A normal copy phase with a contrasting poor recall performance indicates good constructional abilities but possible problems with visual memory. This finding may be consistent with a condition such as Alzheimer's disease or the difficulties with memory consolidation that typically follow traumatic brain injury (Brannigan & Decker, 2003).

Possible Causal Patterns

A third and final aspect of Bender-Gestalt II interpretation is inferring causal patterns related to developmental delays, brain dysfunction, or emotional disturbance. Sometimes a combination of all of these problems results in low Bender performance. An important issue is that different clients might have the same score but for different reasons. For example, a poorly drawn design may result from a neurologically based processing deficit in one person; for another it may result from an emotionally based sense of disorientation. Another example may occur when a person with a hesitant, obsessive style but with no indication of brain damage takes considerable time to complete the drawings. Another person with documented brain damage who also takes longer than average but insists on counting each dot may be attempting to compensate for his or her impairment by developing obsessive behaviors. Other factors that might influence Bender-Gestalt II performance are situations that might encourage faking, chronic schizophrenia, older age, or a history of substance abuse. Sattler and Hoge (2006, pp. 218–219) have listed the possible reasons for poor Bender performance as including:

- Visual problems
- Physiological limitations associated with illness, injury, fatigue, or muscular weakness
- Physically disabling conditions, such as low birthweight, cerebral palsy, or sickle cell anemia
- Environmental stresses
- Impulsiveness
- Inadequate motivation
- Emotional problems
- Mental retardation
- Social or cultural deprivation
- Limited experience

Sometimes the presence and severity of different types of errors, along with relevant behavioral observations, can be used to form tentative hypotheses concerning client functioning. In particular, there are often qualitative differences in the performance of persons with lesions in different areas of the brain. Whereas right-hemisphere patients are more likely to make errors related to visuospatial abilities (e.g., rotations, asymmetry, fragmentation, unrecognizable drawings, unjoined lines), persons with left-hemisphere lesions often make drawings that are shaky (line tremors) and smaller in size, with rounded corners and missing parts (oversimplification; Filskov, 1978). However, the Bender-Gestalt II is still more sensitive to being lowered due to right-hemisphere difficulties. In contrast, it is likely to miss patients who have left-hemisphere lesions.

Another pattern may be with clients who might have primary difficulties with incorrectly rotating their reproductions of the designs. This might reflect mirror reversals involved with other tasks, such as reading. In contrast, other clients might have difficulties in sequencing, which could be suggested by a poorly confused sequence in the reproduction of their Bender-Gestalt II designs.

A useful interpretative strategy is to note scores on other relevant tests. If people do poorly on the Bender, it would also be expected that they would do similarly poorly on the WAIS-IV Block Design and Object Assembly subtests. An advantage of both subtests is that careful behavioral observation can help the practitioner more fully understand clients' deficits. Clients with perceptual difficulties do poorly, primarily because they distort and misperceive the design. These difficulties are more consistent with right parietal lesions. In contrast, patients with left parietal lesions are able to correctly perceive the overall gestalt of the design, but their problem-solving style may be confused and simplified. Other clients might be able to understand the task and perceive it correctly but still experience difficulty in actually completing the task. This dissociation between intent and actually being able to make the blocks do what they want is formally referred to as *constructional dyspraxia*. Sometimes clients with a concrete orientation to problem solving do quite poorly on Block Design, because it requires a certain degree of abstraction. Because Object Assembly deals with more concrete objects, these same persons might perform relatively better on it.

In addition, it would also be expected that clients who performed poorly on the Bender also would do poorly on other drawing tests, such as drawings of a clock, human figure, or bicycle. A test like the Bender is quite structured (as would be asking clients to draw a picture of a clock). In contrast, having them perform a free drawing test, such as drawing a picture of a person, is far less structured. Clients must initiate, organize, and monitor their activity to a greater extent. As such, free drawing procedures add a new dimension to the more structured Bender-Gestalt and Wechsler subtest tasks. Formal scoring criteria and norms can be found for clock, bicycle, and house drawings in Lezak et al. (2004, pp. 549–556) and, for clock drawings, in Strauss et al. (2006, pp. 972–983).

Sometimes clients have learned to compensate for visuomotor difficulties caused by CNS complications. As a result, their Bender-Gestalt reproductions might be relatively accurate. This compensation is particularly likely if an injury is not too extensive, there was above-average premorbid intelligence, the location of the lesion is not too critical, and the injury has not been recently acquired. Clinicians sometimes can detect the possible presence of brain damage by becoming sensitized to a wide range of possible compensatory mechanisms. Koppitz (1975) has listed some of these:

- Excessive length of time for completion.
- "Anchoring" designs by placing a finger on them as they attempt to reproduce them.
- Reproducing a design from memory after first glancing at it.
- Checking and rechecking the number of dots, yet still being uncertain regarding the correct number that should be included.
- Rotating either the sheet of paper or the Bender-Gestalt card itself as an aid in reproducing the design.
- Designs that are quickly and impulsively drawn and then corrected with extreme difficulty.
- Expressions of dissatisfaction with the poorly reproduced designs followed by repeated efforts to correct them.

When screening for neuropsychological impairment using the Bender-Gestalt, it is important to be aware that many of the indicators for CNS involvement are also indicators for emotional disturbance. This raises the serious possibility of misclassification. Thus, the results of the Bender-Gestalt alone are rarely sufficient to make a differential diagnosis between neuropsychological impairment and emotional disturbance; additional information is needed to determine both the nature and cause of the individual's problems.

REPEATABLE BATTERY FOR THE ASSESSMENT OF NEUROPSYCHOLOGICAL STATUS

History and Development

The Repeatable Battery for the Assessment of Neuropsychological Status (RBANS; Randolph, 1998) is a relatively brief series of 12 subtests that provide a wide selection of tasks that have been found to be sensitive to neuropsychological impairment. The 12 subtests are organized into five indexes, each of which provides its own score along with a Total Score (see Table 12.4). The test takes 20 to 30 minutes to administer and can be used on persons between the ages of 20 and 89. The author explains that the RBANS was developed to serve as a stand-alone battery for identifying and describing dementia among elderly patients. However, research has found it can be used effectively with a much wider range of patients. The RBANS was also developed to serve as a screening

Table 12.4.   Description of the Repeatable Battery for the Assessment of Neuropsychological Status

Index	Subtest	Description
Immediate Memory	List Learning	List of 10 words read orally; client is requested to learn the words over four trials
	Story Memory	Short story is read orally, client is requested to recall details over two trails
Visuospatial/ Constructional	Figure Copy	Complex picture is presented and client is requested to reproduce it
	Line Orientation	Client is shown one diagram with equal lines radiating from it and must then match it with other diagrams with different patterns of radiating lines
Language	Picture Naming	Client is requested to name pictures of various objects
	Semantic Fluency	Client is requested to name as many words as possible within various categories (i.e. fruits, animals) in one minute
Attention	Digit Span	Lists of numbers are read to the client who is requested to recall as many of the numbers as possible
	Coding	Client is shown rows of boxes and must fill in boxes below these numbers with various matching geometric designs
Delayed Memory	List recall	Client is requested to recall as many of the words from List Learning as possible 20 minutes after having been administered List Learning
	List recognition	Twenty words are read, 10 were on the word list from List Learning and 10 were not; Client is requested to distinguishing between these two categories of words
	Story Memory	Client is requested to recall details from Story Memory following a 20 minute delay
	Figure Recall	Client is requested to draw the design from memory from Figure Copy following a 20 minute delay

Source: Adapted from Randolph, C. (1998) and Struss, Sherman, and Spreen (2006).

battery when longer, more detailed tests are neither practical nor available. As the name suggests, it can also be used to provide repeat evaluations. To reduce the impact of practice effects, it has a parallel form that can administered.

Whereas the Bender focuses on visuomotor abilities, the subtests of the RBANS use a wide range of procedures related to such areas as verbal skills, attention, visual memory, and visuoconstruction. General information on these types of domains can be learned by reading the previous sections on the neuropsychological domains of attention, language, memory, and spatial. The RBANS subtests themselves are variations of commonly used procedures in neuropsychology. For example, learning a list of words, repeating details from a paragraph, and reproducing complex designs are tried and tested procedures. The use of variations from familiar tests should make it easy for practicing professional psychologists to adapt to and interpret many of the RBANS subtests. The procedures are also sufficiently easy for psychologists in training to learn and use. The procedures for the RBANS were, in part, selected to be sensitive to a wide range of conditions. Since the RBANS assesses different domains, it was also hoped that it would be effective at noting different patterns of impairment. For example, one set of patients might present with mainly memory problems whereas another group might primarily have difficulties with attention and verbal fluency. It was hoped that the index score patterns could be used to distinguish among various groups of patients.

In addition to assessing a wide number of discrete domains, the RBANS was also designed to be brief (under 30 minutes), portable, have alternate forms, and have moderate difficulty. The moderate difficulty means that it would be sensitive to early, subtle symptoms of conditions such as dementia. A number of other procedures, such as the Mini Mental Status Examination or the Dementia Rating Scale, have not been found to be particularly sensitive to the early phases of or mild presentation of cognitive difficulties. Many of the other longer, more complex neuropsychological tests are sensitive to subtle cognitive difficulties but are overly challenging for many neuropsychological patients.

The RBANS is an ideal screening procedure. Many acute care settings have patients who present with altered cognitive status and need a fairly brief assessment of their functioning (i.e., anoxia, traumatic brain injury, stroke). The patients' level of cognitive impairment needs to be evaluated quickly so that decisions for level of care or referral to other health professionals can be made. The 20- to 30-minute RBANS measures a wide range of functions and is easy to learn and thus represents an excellent option. In addition, patients often need to have their recovery tracked during rehabilitation. Patients with progressive diseases also need to be monitored to assist with ongoing treatment and decision making. The RBANS is also an ideal instrument for nonneuropsychologists since it is easy to learn, administer, and interpret. A Spanish-language version is available, although no normative data has been collected. Informal versions have been developed for Japan, Hungry, France, Italy, Norway, and Russia.

Norms reported in the RBANS manual were comprised of 540 persons between the ages of 20 and 89 who were representative of the U.S. population based on the 1995 census data. These norms are generally used when calculating the subtest and index scores. However, education can affect cognitive performance on a wide variety of tests. As a result, Duff, Patton, Schoenberg, Mold, Scott, & Adams (2003) developed a larger normative sample of 718 community-dwelling older adults for the RBANS. Tables are provided that allow for conversions of subtest, index, and total scores that include both age and education (also reproduced in Strauss et al., 2006, pp. 240–245). Additional norms are also available for 631 elderly persons (278 men and 353 females) that allow for corrections based on sex and education (Beatty, Mold, & Gontovsky, 2003). Finally, norms for older community-dwelling African Americans are also available (Patton, et al., 2003).

One disadvantage of the norms as they are presented in the RBANS manual is that only index and total scores can be calculated. Unfortunately, if one of the subtests cannot be administered or has been spoiled, neither the index score for that domain nor the total score can be calculated. In order to partially compensate for this, Randolph has made means and standard deviation available for each of the individual subtests (available as a RBANS supplement on the Harcourt Assessment Web site and listed in Lezak et al., 2004,

p. 696). In addition, Patton et al. (2003; also reproduced in Strauss et al., 2006, pp. 241–248) has developed conversions of raw subtest scores into standard scores. These conversions allow for more detailed understanding of the various subtest scores, but they should be made with caution, given the problems associated with interpreting individual subtests for the Wechsler intelligence scales (see discussion of subtest interpretation).

Reliability and Validity

Split-half reliability for the Total Score was an excellent .94 and the individual index scores ranged between .82 for the Language Index to .88 for the Immediate Memory Index (Randolph, 1998). The standard error of measurement (SEM) for the Total Score was a fairly narrow 3.84 with the bands of error for the indexes ranging between 5.31 for the Immediate Memory Index and 6.65 for the Visuospatial/Constructional Index. Specific SEMs for various age ranges in relation to the Total and Index scores are provided in the record forms and manual (Randolph, 1998). Test-retest reliability (mean interval = 38.7 weeks, SD = 2.8) was an average of .88 for the Total Score and ranged between an average of .80 for the Attention Index and .46 for the Language Index. Duff et al. (2005) similarly found test-retest reliabilities for a longer one year duration ranging between .51 and .83. Practice effects were noted to have been absent.

As mentioned, the content of the RBANS subtests is quite similar to other frequently used tests in clinical neuropsychology. In other words, the types of procedures selected have proven their validity within other forms and contexts. Correlations with external measures demonstrate good to excellent convergent and divergent validity. For example, the correlation between the WAIS-R Full Scale IQ and the RBANS Total Score was a quite high .78 (Randolph, 1998). As expected, a quite high correlation was found between the RBANS List Learning subtest and list learning on the California Verbal Leaning Test-II (.70) and the RBANS Coding subtest and Coding on the WAIS-III (.83; McKay, Casey, Wertheimer, & Fichtenberg, 2007). A final example is that the RBANS Visuospatial/Constructional Index had a quite high correlation with the Rey-Osterrieth Complex Figure Test (.79; Randolph, 1998). This is not surprising since most of these RBANS indexes have subtests that are derivatives from earlier "classic" tests in neuropsychology. This similarity of test format combined with the moderate to high correlation with external measures provides good empirical support that the RBANS indexes/subtests rely on and correlate with other well-validated procedures.

A crucial area of validity is the extent the indexes actually measure discrete functions. To a certain extent, this has been supported. For example, high correlations have been found between the similar Immediate Memory Index and the Delayed Memory Index (.63), both of which are measures of memory. In contrast, expected low correlations were found between the other, and more dissimilar, index scores ($r = .21–.82$; Randolph, 1998). There is also evidence that some categories of patients perform in a predicted pattern, given what is known about the disorder. Thus, Alzheimer's disease patients who are known to have particular difficulties with delayed memory scored much lower on the Delayed Memory Index than patients with vascular dementia (Randolph, 1998). A further example is that left-hemisphere stroke patients scored particularly low on the RBANS Language Index and relatively better on the Visuospatial/Constructional Index (Wilde, 2006). The opposite was true for right-hemisphere stroke patients. However, factor analytic studies have supported a two-factor structure for the RBANS rather than the five factors indicated by the index categories (Duff et al., 2006; Wilde, 2006).

Whereas the RBANS was originally intended to be sensitive to early and middle stages of dementia, it has also been found to be sensitive to a wide range of other conditions.

Specifically, the RBANS has been found to be a reliable and valid measure for patients with traumatic brain injury (McKay et al., 2007; Pachet, 2007), stroke (Larson, Kirschner, Bode, Heineman, & Goodman, 2005), schizophrenia (Laurent et al., 2007; Randolph, 1998; Wilk et al., 2004), Huntington's disease, Parkinson's disease, and HIV dementia (Randolph, 1998). RBANS assessment has also been found to predict everyday functioning among patients with dementia (Freilich & Hyer, 2007), stroke (Larson et al., 2005), concussion (Moser & Schatz, 2002; Moser, Schatz, & Jordan, 2005), Parkinson's disease (Beatty, Ryder, Gontkovsky, Scott, & McSwan, 2003), schizophrenia (Gold et al., 2001), and traumatic brain injury (McKay et al., 2007).

Assets and Limitations

The RBANS successfully fills the niche of being a broad band, brief, moderately difficult test that is easy to administer, score, and interpret. It has good reliability and good correlations with relevant outside measures and is effective at differentiating a variety of clinical populations, including patients with cortical and subcortical dementia as well as right- and left-hemisphere stroke. In addition, it can accurately predict relevant aspects of real-world behavior. The subtests themselves are familiar to practitioners in the field, and the tasks seem highly sensitive to cognitive impairment. It is thus an ideal screening instrument that can be used to track a client's improvement as well as deterioration. As a result of these assets, the RBANS has rapidly gained acceptance in clinical and research contexts.

Despite these assets, there are also a number of problems related to its use. The five index scores provide the appearance that a full-range neuropsychological assessment might have been accomplished. Although there is some support that the indexes do indeed measure discrete functions, this has not been supported by factor analysis. In addition, a "pattern analysis" based on the index scores needs to occur only when the differences between the index scores are quite large (typically 10–20 points). Thus minor variations should not be interpreted. Tables provided in the manual allow clinicians to calculate both the statistical significance of differences (Table A.1, pp. 78–79) and the frequency that the differences occur (Table A.2, pp. 80–81). For example, it might seem that a difference of 20 points between the Visuospatial/Constructional Index and the Language Index is quite large. However, this occurs in a full 27% of the standardization sample. Similarly, scores indicating actual change in a client's level of functioning require quite large changes in retest performance (generally at least 15 points in either direction; see Duff et al., 2005; Wilk et al., 2002). In many instances, then, an increase or decrease in scores on retesting merely represents error in measurement rather than actual client change. Strauss et al. (2006) recommend that the relatively stable Total Score and possibly Attention Index should be the preferred measures for tracking client change.

A further area of caution is to take into account factors, particularly educational, that moderate the meaning of scores. The RBANS manual does provide some rough corrections for education (Tables 5.2–5.5), but more precise norms have been provided by Duff et al., 2003). For example, persons with a high school education between the ages of 20 and 49 have been found to have a mean RBANS Total Score of 87.5. Thus, scores from persons with lower education should not be incorrectly inferred to indicate impairment unless the clinician has first taken the effect of education into account. Score reductions for African Americans have also been noted (Patton et al., 2003). Accordingly, clinicians should take this into account when inferring such things as cognitive impairment.

Administration

Administration instructions are clearly indicated on the Record Form and in the RBANS manual. The stimulus material is similarly clear and easy to use. Scoring criteria are straightforward and allow examiners to summarize the results on a graph and table that lists the Total Score, index scores, confidence intervals, and percentiles. However, if a subtest is spoiled or cannot be given due to a disability (aphasia, motor impairment), the value of the test is limited since the related index score and Total Score cannot be calculate. In addition, modifications to accommodate a patient's disabilities or language modifications will not result in a standard administration. Accordingly, the data may not represent accurate information.

Interpretation Guidelines

Similar to the Wechsler intelligence scale and Bender-Gestalt II, the RBANS translates raw scores into standard scores with a mean of 100 and a standard deviation of 15. The Record Form, in combination with the manual, allows these to be described as percentiles and descriptive classifications. Thus a standard Total Score or index score of 70 means that the examinee would have scored in the borderline range or second percentile when compared with their age-related peers. The meaning of a score in the borderline range may need to be modified given the client's educational level and, if sufficient information is present, ethnic identification.

A useful strategy is to begin with the most general level of analysis and then proceed to more specific, qualitative information. A three-step interpretive process is recommended.

Level 1: Total Score

The Total Score is the most stable, well-validated, and general measure on the RBANS. An important consideration is the degree that it agrees with other information about the patient. Thus, a high-functioning professional who scores in the average or low-average range suggests there might have been some sort of acquired difficulty. The clinician would then need to consider if there was something in the person's history that could help to explain this score (set of presenting symptoms, head injury, anoxia, stroke). It should be noted that, since the RBANS is comprised of fluid measures that are highly sensitive to cognitive impairment, RBANS total scores may be significantly lower than something like the Wechsler intelligence scale Full Scale IQ. The Total Score can be used to monitor deterioration or improvement in a client's functioning, assuming the retesting indicates a significantly large difference (generally 15 points or more).

Level 2: Analysis of Index Scores

The five index scores represent five commonly assessed domains of neuropsychological functioning. By comparing and contrasting these domains, a patient's relative strengths and weaknesses can be evaluated. For example, one patient may have poor memory (low scores on the Immediate Memory and Delayed Memory indexes) and have quite good nonverbal abilities (high/intact scores on Visuospatial/Constructional Index). For another patient this may be reversed. These patterns may help to diagnosis different conditions. In addition, inferences can be made related to the patient's everyday functioning.

Randolph (1998) provides examples and evidence that Alzheimer's diseases patients, even in the early stages, are likely to have their lowest scores in Delayed Memory (poor ability to store new information), Immediate Memory (difficulty learning new material), and Language (poor verbal fluency, difficulty with word finding). He thus concludes that the RBANS is not only sensitive to Alzheimer's disease, but its cognitive "signature" can be detected by analyzing the index scores.

Alzheimer's disease typically affects the cortical regions and, as such, is referred to as a "cortical" dementia. Another group of dementias affects primarily the subcortical regions (Parkinson's disease, Huntington's disease, ischemic vascular disease) and is thus referred to as "subcortical" dementias. These dementias are characterized primarily by impairments of attention and visuoconstruction. This is reflected in their RBANS performance in that the Attention and Visuospatial/Construction indexes are lowest. A formal "Cortical-Subcortical deviation score" can be calculated by subtracting the mean for Delayed Memory and Language indexes from the mean of the Attention and Visuospatial/Construction indexes. Patients with scores above 0 can be classified as "cortical"; those with scores below 0 can be considered "subcortical." This classification system was found to correctly classify 37 out of 40 patients correctly (Randolph, 1998). Fink, McCrea, and Randolph (1998) was similarly able to correctly classify 93% of Alzheimer's disease patients and 75% of those with vascular dementia. These differences are likely to be prevalent in the early to moderate stages of the diseases. As the disorder progresses, the high and low scores would be likely to flatten out.

Another pattern of index scores may reflect either left-hemisphere (verbal abilities) or right-hemisphere (nonverbal abilities) involvement. Which hemisphere is affected might be determined by noting whether the RBANS verbal (Language) or nonverbal (Visuospatial/Constructional) indexes were relatively higher.

In interpreting these patterns, clinicians should be guided by and balance between two major principles. The first is psychometric. Difference scores are most likely to be meaningful when the discrepancies have been found to be both significantly different (see Table A.1 in the RBANS manual) and are fairly unusual occurrences (see Table A.2 in the RBANS manual). The second consideration is more clinical and qualitative. Specifically, the pattern of scores needs to be informed by other information about the client, including such areas as medical/psychiatric history, family patterns of illness, other tests scores, presenting problem, and behavioral observations (see Level 3 section).

Level 3: Qualitative Information

The 12 individual subtests comprising the RBANS have mean scores of 10 with standard deviations of 3 (see RBANS supplement on the Harcourt Assessment Web site; conversions in Patton et al., 2003, also reproduced in Strauss et al., 2006, pp. 241–248). Since these subtests are relatively short, they would not be expected to be sufficiently reliable for individual interpretation. However, they do provide what could be considered to be qualitative information when combined with relevant history and behavioral observations. For example, a patient who seems to struggle with finding the correct word and also has low scores on the language subtests (comprising the Language Index) can reasonably be said to have "low verbal fluency" and "problems with word finding." Accordingly, this information can be included with interpretations of the patient's performance. If these difficulties can be supported by sources in the person's life (spouse, children, etc.), these interpretations are further strengthened.

RECOMMENDED READING

Groth-Marnat, G. (Ed.). (2000). *Neuropsychological assessment in clinical practice: A guide to test interpretation and integration*. Hoboken, NJ: John Wiley & Sons.

Lacks, P. (1999). *Bender-Gestalt screening for brain dysfunction* (2nd ed.). New York: John Wiley & Sons.

Lezak, M. D. (2004). *Neuropsychological assessment* (3rd ed.). New York: Oxford University Press.

Snyder, P. J., Nussbaum, P. D., & Robins, D. L. (2006). *Clinical neuropsychology: A pocket handbook for assessment* (2nd ed.). Washington, DC: American Psychological Association.

Strauss, E., Sherman, E. M. S., & Spreen, O. (2006). *A compendium of neuropsychological tests: Administration, norms, and commentary* (3rd ed.). New York: Oxford University Press.

Vanderploeg, R. D. (Ed.). (2001). *Clinicians' guide to neuropsychological assessment* (2nd ed.). Mahwah, NJ: Lawrence Erlbaum.

Chapter 13

BRIEF INSTRUMENTS FOR TREATMENT PLANNING, MONITORING, AND OUTCOME ASSESSMENT

Since the early 1990s, there has been an increasing demand for brief, symptom-focused instruments to assist in the delivery of mental health services. One of the major reasons for this is managed care's emphasis on cost containment and documenting treatment efficacy. Most managed care organizations also have a rather narrow symptom-oriented focus on treatment that is quite consistent with the content of many brief clinical instruments. These instruments can be used to plan, monitor, and evaluate the impact of interventions. Importantly, the use of outcome measures has been found to enhance treatment success by identifying clients who are at risk of not responding to treatment (Lambert & Hawkins, 2004).

Another factor emphasizing the importance of brief, focused tests has been the extensive and continually expanding research on the outcomes of mental health interventions. Pretest and posttest measures have proliferated to the extent that there are now a multitude of options to choose from (see Antony & Barlow, 2002; Maruish, 2004). It is almost a given that training and research clinics monitor their work through tests that typically take less than 10 or 15 minutes to complete. Given the models and procedures present in the research arena, managed care organizations are also expecting clinicians to demonstrate that, indeed, the interventions they are implementing are effective (Callaghan, 2001). As a result, 37% of professional psychologists reported using some form of outcome measure (Hatfield & Ogles, 2004).

The role of brief instruments has expanded in parallel with the dramatic increase in the areas psychologists have become involved in (Maruish, 2004; Stout & Cook, 1999). This has included diverse roles such as prevention; treatment planning; clinical outcomes management; risk management; evaluation of psychoactive medication; uncovering malingering, and detecting undiagnosed psychopathology; assessment of chronic pain; geriatric assessment; and behavioral dentistry. Although the likelihood of using a full battery has decreased, these additional areas that are quite likely to use brief instruments have certainly increased.

One of the major challenges confronting psychologists is demonstrating the financial efficacy of their services. There is considerable evidence that psychosocial interventions are cost-effective in psychotherapy as well as general health care (Groth-Marnat & Edkins, 1996). For example, it has long been known that somatizing patients are high overusers of the medical-surgical system. Significant cost savings can be realized by extracting them from the costly (and relatively ineffective) medical-surgical area and into the mental health area, where they can receive brief, targeted psychotherapy (Cummings, 1991). Unfortunately, there has been little research into the potential cost savings for assessment services. Rational guidelines suggest that assessment is most likely to demonstrate financial efficacy in the areas of risk management, linking assessment and treatment, using computer-assisted assessment, targeting problems most likely to result in cost savings, use of time-efficient instruments, and focusing on domains of greatest relevance to treatment planning and outcome assessment (Groth-Marnat, 1999). Yates and Taub (2003) propose a model of how this can be accomplished by combining measures of cost, procedures, and processes and comparing these with an analysis of outcomes.

SELECTING BRIEF INSTRUMENTS

Before selecting a brief screening instrument, there should be some consideration given to who will administer and interpret it. The majority of instruments (and those included in this chapter) are self-report measures. Such measures have the advantages of reducing clinician time and obtaining clients' own perception of their difficulties. However, they also have the potential for bias by the client's perceptions and are potentially subject to under- or overreporting. Other instruments are administered by professional psychologists or allied health professionals such as primary care physicians, nurses, or clinical social workers (Bufka et al., 2002; Maruish, 2004). On other occasions, a significant other person in the patient's life, such as a parent or spouse, completes the instrument.

The ability of an instrument to assist in planning and outcome assessment is particularly relevant for selecting brief instruments. First, they should not take longer than 15 minutes to complete (and preferably less time). In addition, typically they should be directly relevant to treatment planning and outcome assessment. In contrast, a full-battery approach before psychotherapy often provides a large amount of descriptive information, but most of this information is not directly applicable to treatment planning. A further frequent essential quality is that the instruments be useful for screening purposes. For example, the Beck Depression Inventory (BDI-II) can be used for each of the preceding purposes. A physician might use it to detect the possible presence of depression, a psychologist might administer it to determine the baseline level of severity for a client, and this baseline could then be used to determine the effectiveness of interventions targeted to treat the depression. A managed care company would be particularly interested in this process to monitor quality control over the treatments it reimburses.

In addition to time efficiency and relevance to treatment planning and outcome evaluation, brief instruments should also be relevant to various target groups (F. Newman et al., 1999). For example, specialized variations on the BDI have been developed for children and geriatric populations. The BDI-II has also been found to be valid in the assessment of African Americans (Grothe, Dutton, Jones, Bodenlos, Ancona, & Brantley, 2005) and Hispanic populations (Wiebe & Penley, 2005). Brief instruments should ideally be usable and understandable not only by the therapist but also the client, significant others in the client's life, insurance companies, and researchers. Thus, they should be clear and direct enough such that they can be understood by both a professional and a nonprofessional audience. Because such instruments often are given over several different administrations, they should be sensitive to clinically important levels of change. As with any psychological test used by clinicians, they should also have excellent psychometric properties. Finally, interpreting the results should be uncomplicated and the construct should be clear enough to enable feedback to the client or other relevant persons.

In addition to the many time-honored instruments such as the BDI, instruments have been designed specifically for treatment planning and patient tracking. For example, the Outcome Questionnaire (OQ-45; Lambert et al., 1996) is a 45-item, self-report instrument that requests clients to rate various areas on a 5-point Likert scale. It can be used as an overall measure of client functioning, to establish a baseline, to assist with treatment decisions, and to assess common symptoms (stress, DSM-IV-TR V codes). The results are organized around level and type of symptom distress, interpersonal relations, and relative satisfaction with social role. The Butcher Treatment Planning Inventory (Butcher, 1998) is a 210-item-self-report inventory that assesses issues and challenges that might be particularly relevant to treatment. The scales are organized around validity, treatment issues, and current symptoms. For example, the validity scales measure the extent to which the client has an overly virtuous presentation of self or tends to be close-minded related to his or her difficulties. Treatment issues include areas such as somatization of difficulties, low expectations regarding treatment, and narcissism. A final example, which is discussed in more detail in Chapter 14, is the Systematic Treatment Selection model (Beutler, Clarkin, & Bongar, 2000; Groth-Marnat, Gottheil, Liu, Clinton, & Beutler, 2008), which includes a software package (Beutler & Williams, 1999) and a clinician rating form (STS Clinician Rating Form; D. Fisher, Beutler, & Williams, 1999). Although the preceding instruments show considerable promise, they have not been used or tested as widely as many of the other instruments.

The three instruments selected for this chapter each fulfill the criteria required for treatment planning, monitoring, and outcome assessment. They are time-efficient and directly relevant to treatment planning, can be used to evaluate outcome, are effective as screening instruments, are relevant for a wide range of target groups, are sensitive to change, and the constructs and information they provide are sufficiently clear so that feedback is easy to give. Each also has demonstrated its effectiveness in accurately assessing various ethnic and cross-national groups. As a result of these qualities, they have become the most extensively used brief instruments in both clinical practice and research.

SYMPTOM CHECKLIST-90-R (SCL-90-R) AND BRIEF SYMPTOM INVENTORY (BSI)

The Symptom Checklist 90-R (SCL-90-R; Derogatis, 1994) and its shortened version, the Brief Symptom Inventory (BSI; Derogatis, 1993), are ideally suited to quickly assess a client's type and severity of self-reported symptoms. It should not be regarded as a personality measurement but is more an assessment of the current level of a variety of symptoms as experienced over a 1-week interval. The SCL-90-R was derived from the earlier Hopkins Symptom Checklist (Derogatis, Lipman, Rickels, Uhlenhuth, & Covi, 1974), which in turn had its origins in the much earlier Woodworth Personal Data Sheet (Woodworth, 1918). As the name suggests, the SCL-90-R consists of a series of 90 descriptions of symptoms that a client rates in terms of their severity (ranging from 0 = Not at all to 4 = Extremely). A sixth-grade reading level is required, and it usually takes between 12 and 15 minutes to complete. The symptoms are scored around nine different dimensions (i.e., Somatization, Obsessive-Compulsive) as well as three global indexes (i.e., Global Severity Index). The BSI is a short form of the SCL-90-R composed of 53 of the SCL-90-R items, and it provides scores on the same symptom dimensions and global indexes.

Scores on the SCL-90-R are transferred onto a profile sheet displaying the nine symptom dimensions and three global indexes. Similar to the MMPI-2, each score has a mean of 50 and a standard deviation of 10. One of the unique features of the SCL-90-R is that these scores can be compared with and plotted based on these four normative groups:

1. Norm A: *Psychiatric outpatients* ($N = 1,002$; 425 male, 577 females) approximately two-thirds of whom were White, and the entire sample was slightly skewed toward the lower end of the socioeconomic scale.

2. Norm B: *Nonpatients* ($N = 1,000$; 494 males, 480 female) representing a stratified random sample from a large U.S. eastern state.

3. Norm C: *Psychiatric inpatients* ($N = 313$; two-thirds female) of whom 55.7% were White, 43.6% Black, with a mean age of 33.1.

4. Norm E: *Nonpatient adolescents* ($N = 806$; 60% females, 40% males) ages between 13 and 18 ($M = 15.6$) from two schools and composed primarily of middle-class Whites.

If clinicians wish to make comparisons with a nonpatient group, they can use Norm B. In other situations, it might be advantageous to compare a person with either an outpatient or an inpatient reference group. These norms, combined with the wide diversity of validity studies, suggest that the SCL-90-R can be used with a wide variety of respondents, including medical patients, adolescents, community nonpatients, cross-cultural/national groups as well as inpatients and outpatients. It is also available in more than 26 languages, and computer scoring, administration, and interpretation programs are available.

Scoring and normative comparisons for the BSI follow similar procedures as for the SCL-90-R. The norms used on both scales are the same for psychiatric outpatients, psychiatric inpatients, and nonpatients. The BSI, however, has a larger adolescent normative base composed of 2,408 middle-class students (58% Whites, 30% Blacks, 12% other) between the ages of 13 and 19 ($M = 15.8$) from six different schools. There have also been additional norms developed and published separately for the elderly (Hale, Cochran, & Hedgepeth, 1984) and adolescent students (Canetti, Shalev, & Denour, 1994).

Reliability and Validity

The reliability of the SCL-90-R has consistently been good. The manual reports that internal consistency for the nine symptom dimensions based on psychiatric outpatients ranged from a low of .79 for Paranoid Ideation to a high of .90 for Depression. Internal consistency for "symptomatic volunteers" was slightly lower and ranged from a low of .77 for Psychoticism to .90 for Depression (in Derogatis & Savitz, 1999). Test-retest reliability over a 1-week interval ranged from a low of .78 for hostility to a high of .90 for Phobic Anxiety. Most coefficients were in the mid-80s. As expected, test reliability was slightly lower over a 10-week interval and ranged between .68 for Somatization to .83 for Paranoid Ideation (in Derogatis, 1994; Derogatis & Savitz, 1999).

Reliability for the BSI is similar although slightly lower than the SCL-90-R. Internal consistency ranged between .71 for Psychoticism and .85 for Depression (Derogatis, 1993). Similarly, internal consistency for bereaved parents ranged between .74 for Psychoticism to a quite high .97 on the Global Severity Index (L. C. Johnson, Murphy, & Dimond, 1996). Test-retest reliability over a 2-week interval was a low of .68 for Somatization to .91 for Phobic Anxiety (Derogatis, 1993). One noteworthy feature was that the test-retest reliability was a quite high .91 for the Global Severity Index, indicating that it is a stable measure over time. This is particularly important given that the BSI (and SCL-90-R) Global Severity Indexes are frequently used over repeated administrations to monitor treatment and evaluate its outcome. Stability over a 3-year interval (measures made every 6 months) among a group of schizophrenics was also found to be quite high (Long, Harring, Brekke, Test, & Greenberg, 2007).

Well over 1,000 studies have been done investigating the validity of the SCL-90-R. For example, both MMPI and General Health Questionnaire (GHQ) measures were found to converge with expected dimensions on the SCL-90-R and diverge with other expected measures (see Derogatis, 1994; Schmitz, Kruse, Heckrath, Alberti, & Tress, 1999). The

SCL-90-R Depression dimension has been found to have a high correlation (.80) with the Beck Depression Inventory (Peveler & Fairburn, 1990) and to detect depression equally as effectively (Choquette, 1990).

Expected SCL-90-R profiles have been found for a variety of diagnostic groups, including depression, anxiety, panic, sexual dysfunction, and substance abuse (see Derogatis, 1994; Derogatis & Savitz, 1999). However, other studies have questioned the divergent validity of the SCL-90-R dimensions, and authors have suggested that it be used as a general indicator of distress (Cyr, McKenna-Foley, & Peacock, 1985; Elliot, Fox, Svetlana, Stone, Gunderson, & Zhang, 2006; Vassend & Skrondal, 1999). This controversy is strongly apparent in the findings related to factor structure. On one hand, Derogatis (1994) has reported that factor-analytic research has, with the exception of the Psychoticism dimension, matched the various dimensions of the SCL-90-R (Derogatis, 1994). In contrast, other research has reported anywhere from one to six factors depending on the type of population that has been studied (Cyr et al., 1985; Hayes, 1997; Piersma, Boes, & Reaume, 1994; Vassend & Skrondal, 1999). For example, Vassend and Skrondal generally found a four-factor solution, but this varied depending on the gender and level of negative affect of the sample. They concluded that there was a "profound structural indeterminancy problem" (p. 685). Cyr et al. add that the factor structure becomes particularly uncertain when evaluated beyond the boundaries of neurotic outpatients. In contrast, Hayes found support for a six-factor solution with college students (but not for the nine dimensions listed on the SCL-90-R). The equivocal research on the factor structure of the SCL-90-R suggests that the nine dimensions be interpreted tentatively because most research has not supported their independence.

Although the factor structure of the SCL-90-R has been equivocal, research assessing the sensitivity and specificity for various disorders has been generally supportive. For example, the SCL-90-R detected relevant symptoms among bulimics with a sensitivity of 77% and specificity of 91% (Peveler & Fairburn, 1990). Similar levels of sensitivity (72%) and specificity (87%) for detecting psychological difficulties related to diabetes were also noted. High scores on the Hostility, Paranoid Ideation, Somatization, and Obsessive-Compulsive dimensions were able to detect the presence of Cluster A (paranoid, schizoid, schizotypal) and Cluster B (antisocial, borderline, histrionic, narcissistic) with a quite high sensitivity of 89% and even higher specificity of 97% (Starcevic, Bogojevic, & Marinkovic, 2000). As would be expected given research on a one-factor solution, the SCL-90-R has been found to effectively detect the general level of distress a person is experiencing (Derogatis, 1993, 1994). The SCL-90-R has also been found to be responsive to clinically significant change (Elliot et al., 2006; Schmitz & Hartkamp, 2000) as well as levels of distress for persons with brain injury (Hoofien, Barak, Vakil, & Gilboa, 2005; Westcott & Alfano, 2005) and screening for possible comorbidity among alcohol abusing populations (Benjamin, Mossman, Graves, & Sanders, 2006). In contrast to this favorable research on the diagnostic utility of the SCL-90-R, the Psychoticism dimension was not able to discriminate between psychotic and nonpsychotic patients (Stukenberg, Dura, & Kiecolt-Glaser, 1990). This, in combination with low internal consistency, indicates that the Psychoticism dimension seems to have the weakest psychometric properties of all the SCL-90-R scales.

Validity for the BSI is in part supported by the high correlations between the SCL-90-R and BSI dimensions, which range from a low of .92 for Psychoticism to a high of .98 for Paranoid Ideation (Derogatis & Savitz, 1999). This is sufficiently high so that research on the SCL-90-R not only supports the BSI, but the two tests can be used as alternate forms for each other. Additional studies support the sensitivity of the BSI to distress and suggest that it can be used to track the outcomes of various interventions (Derogatis, 1993; Derogatis & Savitz, 1999). For example, screening of recently diagnosed cancer patients indicates that the BSI was sensitive to varying levels of distress based on ratings using outside criterion measures (Zabora, Smith-Wilson, Fetting, & Enterline, 1990). Similarly, elevated scores on the BSI have been found for bereaved parents (L. C. Johnson et al., 1996). Ratings by experienced clinicians of the level of distress experienced by clients have also been found to have moderate correlations with the expected dimensions on the BSI (Morlan & Tan, 1998). However, correlations between the BSI and client self-ratings of level of satisfaction with psychotherapy were not correlated (Pekarik & Wolff, 1996).

Use with Special Populations

The SCL-90-R has consistently been found to be a reliable and valid instrument in a wide number of cross-cultural contexts. For example, Martinez, Stillerman, and Waldo (2005) concluded that the SCL-90-R measures symptom-related change in a similar way for both Anglo and Hispanic populations. It has also been used to assess level of trauma-related psychopathology in Chinese (Wang, Gao, Shinfuku, Zhang, Zhao, & Shen, 2000) and Vietnamese populations (Hauff & Vaglum, 1994). The normative groups provided in the manual include a reasonable proportion of African Americans, especially for the psychiatric inpatient (43.6%) and community nonpatient (11.6%) populations. As noted, there are also adolescent norms, and the SCL-90-R has been used to document the extent and longitudinal stability of symptoms among elderly populations (Levenson, 1988).

Interpretation

In many ways, "interpretating" the SCL-90-R and BSI is straightforward because the data is descriptive rather than interpretive. In other words, overall severity of a client's symptoms can be assessed through the degree of elevation on the Global Severity Index. Similarly, the severity by which a client is sensitive to the criticisms of others can be gauged based on the relative elevation of the Interpersonal Sensitivity dimension. However, clinicians may also wish to extend beyond these straightforward descriptions based on their clinical knowledge. For example, a person scoring high on Interpersonal Sensitivity is likely to exaggerate criticisms, ruminate over these criticisms, experience irrational thoughts, have low self-esteem, and be low in assertiveness. The severity of a client's condition can be further investigated by taking into account additional data. There may also be patterns of elevations that are consistent with various personality disorders. Avoidant personalities, for example, would be expected to have high scores on Interpersonal Sensitivity, Anxiety, and possibly Phobic Anxiety. In contrast, histrionic personalities would be likely to have elevations on Somatization. These conceptual links can be used as beginning points for further investigation to see if the person does or does not have the suggested personality styles. However, these "interpretations" should be considered more as hypotheses given the questionable independence of the nine SCL-90-R/BSI dimensions.

Interpretation can begin with the global indexes and then proceed to the dimensional and symptom/item level. Accordingly, the following information is a listing and elaboration on the meanings of the elevations in categories under these three general groupings (adapted from Derogatis & Savitz, 1999).

Global Indexes

Global Severity Index (GSI)   This index is a combined rating that takes into account the intensity of experienced stress along with the number of reported symptoms. As such, it is the best single indicator of distress and should be used when a single measure is appropriate. A general rule of thumb is that a T-score above 63 suggests the presence of a clinically significant level of psychological difficulties.

Positive Symptom Distress Index (PSDI)   The PSDI is an average rating for all symptoms that have been endorsed. Thus, it is a measure of symptom intensity (rather than merely the number of symptoms endorsed).

Positive Symptom Total (PST)   Whereas the PSDI is a measure of symptom severity, PST represents the number (or breadth) of symptoms. Thus, a client could theoretically have a low PSDI, indicating that the symptoms they had were not particularly troubling, but might have a high PST, indicating that he or she had a wide, potentially complex array of symptoms.

Symptom Dimensions

Somatization (SOM)   An elevation on SOM indicates that distress is experienced primarily through concerns related to actual, amplified, or imagined physical dysfunction. Complaints might be focused on cardiovascular, gastrointestinal, respiratory, gross musculature, or other bodily areas (note responses to actual items). Pain and anxiety are both likely to be present as well, thereby amplifying any physiologically based disorders. Interventions might involve increasing a client's awareness of how he or she uses somatization as a coping mechanism combined with alternative methods of coping, such as stress management, social skills training, hypnosis, or biofeedback.

Obsessive-Compulsive (O-C)   This dimension focuses on impulses, thoughts, and actions that are irresistible, repetitive, unwanted, and experienced as beyond the person's control. Some of the items also refer to more general cognitive performance deficits (i.e., the person's mind is going blank or he or she has trouble concentrating).

Interpersonal Sensitivity (I-S)   High scores on I-S indicate the respondents have considerable discomfort in interpersonal situations. They have negative expectations regarding relationships and are self-conscious. When they compare themselves with others, they typically feel inferior and thus experience self-doubt and inadequacy. Crucial to any intervention is a supportive therapeutic relationship combined with cognitive restructuring and assertiveness training.

Depression (DEP)   Elevations on DEP indicate the person is experiencing a range of depressive symptoms. These might include loss of pleasure, dysphoria, loneliness, crying, withdrawal, pessimism, sleep disturbance, alterations in appetite, poor motivation, and low energy (check individual items). There may also be the presence of suicidal ideation and other cognitions consistent with depression.

Anxiety (ANX)   This dimension focuses on the presence of apprehension, nervousness, trembling, and dread. High levels of anxiety may or may not be consistent with panic attacks. Physiological components of anxiety, including rapid heart rate, tension, and restlessness, are also likely to be present. Possible interventions include relaxation training, meditation, stress management, assertiveness training (and other forms of skills training), and exercise.

Hostility (HOS)   Persons scoring high on HOS experience resentment, irritability, aggression, and, possibly, rage. Accordingly, anger management might be an appropriate recommendation.

Phobic Anxiety (PHOB)   This dimension focuses on the presence of excessive and irrational fear related to a person, place, object, or situation. He or she might report a fear of open places, anxiety when traveling away from familiar areas, and fear of developing a panic attack. Although the title of the dimension appears to be related to phobias, most of the actual items reflect the more pathological aspect of phobias to the extent that high scores may reflect agoraphobia or panic attacks rather than merely phobias. Interventions can be focused on the areas of greatest anxiety and might include graded exposure, relaxation training, hypnosis, and cognitive restructuring.

Paranoid Ideation (PAR)   Items in this dimension tap into the key dimensions of paranoid thought, including hostility, projection, grandiosity, suspiciousness, and a need for control based on a fear of losing independence. Delusions may also be present and are reflected in items related to fears of being watched, talked about, or not being given credit for achievements.

Psychoticism (PSY)   High scores reflect a person who is extremely withdrawn and isolated and may be experiencing core symptoms of schizophrenia, including hallucinations (hearing voices, thought broadcasting) and thought control. Scores can be seen as being on a psychoticism continuum ranging from minor levels of interpersonal alienation to a full display of severe psychotic symptoms.

   T scores above 63 on two or more of the preceding dimensions suggest that the person has clinically significant levels of psychological distress. Additional potentially important symptom-related items not scored on these dimensions include those related to poor appetite, sleep disturbance, fear of dying, overeating, early-morning awakening, difficulties with sleep maintenance, and guilt. These can be noted to obtain additional information. Researchers have also developed additional scales that may be used some time in the future to extend interpretation (see the SCL-90-R Mania Scale; E. Hunter et al., 2000 and factor-based scales for college students; Hayes, 1997).

Symptom Level/Item

Additional information can be obtained by noting the content of the individual items the client has endorsed. For example, items on the Depression dimension can provide specific information related to the person's depression. Importantly, the presence of Suicidal Ideation (i.e., item related to ending the person's own life) can be noted and should then be followed up by more in-depth assessment for risk of self-harm. The presence and extent of possible vegetative symptoms (low energy, sleep problems, loss of sexual energy) can also be noted; this may have implications for various treatment recommendations. Items that the client has answered either "quite a bit" or "extremely" can be considered critical. These should be given particular attention for assessment, treatment planning, and establishing a relevant baseline and outcome to treatment.

BECK DEPRESSION INVENTORY

The Beck Depression Inventory (BDI) was introduced in 1961 by A. T. Beck, Ward, Mendelson, Mock, and Erbaugh, was revised in 1971, and was copyrighted in 1978 (A. T. Beck, Rush, Shaw, & Emery, 1979). Although the later version, referred to as the BDI-IA, involved a clarification and modification of the items, the two versions were found to be highly correlated (.94; Lightfoot & Oliver, 1985). The BDI underwent a further and major revision in 1996 (BDI-II) to include a wider range of symptoms (A. T. Beck et al., 1996). By so doing, it became more congruent with *DSM-IV* diagnostic criteria for depressive disorders. Four of the items were replaced to reflect symptoms consistent with more severe depression (Agitation, Worthlessness, Concentration Difficulty, and Loss of Energy). A further two items were revised to better reflect decreases in appetite and sleep. In addition, many of the other items were reworded.

Comparisons between the BDI/BDI-IA and the BDI-II indicate that clients are likely to endorse one to two more items/symptoms on the BDI-II when compared with the earlier BDI and BDI-IA (A. T. Beck et al., 1996; Dozois, Dobson, & Ahnberg, 1998; Steer, Rissmiller, & Beck, 2000). More symptoms are likely to be endorsed toward the higher ranges of depression (three or more items/symptoms) than the lower ranges. Using an outpatient sample, BDI-IA/BDI-II correlations were .84, and the mean total scores were slightly higher for the BDI-II than the BDI-IA (21.63 versus 18.15; A. T. Beck et al., 1996). Correlations between the BDI and BDI-II for a university population indicated a slightly higher correlation of .92 (Dozois et al., 1998). Despite the slightly higher scores on the BDI-II, this information indicates that the BDI-II is sufficiently comparable to its predecessors such that, with appropriate caution, much of the research on the BDI/BDI-IA can be generalized to the more recent BDI-II.

The BDI-II and its predecessors have been widely used for the assessment of depression among psychiatric patients (Camara et al., 2000; C. Piotrowski, 1996; Steer, Ball, Ranieri, & Beck, 1999; Steer et al., 2000) as well as depression in normals (A. T. Beck et al., 1996; Steer, Beck, & Garrison, 1986). It has been found to detect depression as effectively as longer and more costly structured interviews (Stukenberg, Dura, & Kiecolt-Glaser, 1990). The popularity of this instrument is amply demonstrated in that, in the nearly 50 years since its introduction, well over 1,000 research studies have been performed either on or using it.

The items in the BDI were originally derived from observing and summarizing the typical attitudes and symptoms presented by depressed psychiatric patients (A. T. Beck et al., 1961). A total of 21 items related to various symptoms were included, and, when completing the inventory, respondents are requested to rate the intensity of these symptoms on a scale from 0 to 3. Typical questions relate to areas such as sense of failure, guilt feelings, irritability, sleep disturbance, and loss of appetite. The inventory is self-administered and takes from 5 to 10 minutes to complete. A fifth- to sixth-grade reading level is required to adequately comprehend the items. The total possible range of scores extends from a low of 0 to a theoretical high of 63. However, only the most severe levels of depression are reflected by scores of 40 or 50. More typically, clinically depressed or maladaptively nonclinical populations score in the 14 to 28 range (A. T. Beck et al., 1996).

Reliability and Validity

Since its initial development in 1961, the BDI has been subjected to extensive psychometric evaluation. A meta-analysis of the original BDI/BDI-IA indicated that internal consistency ranged from .73 to .92 with a mean of .86 (A. T. Beck, Steer, & Garbin, 1988). Test-retest reliabilities have ranged from .48 to .86, depending on the interval between retesting and type of population (Beck et al., 1988). However, repeat administrations over 7 weeks at one administration per week using university students indicated a 40% decline in scores (Ahave, Iannone, Grebstein, & Schirling, 1998). This finding suggests that some of the reduction in scores for clinical populations following interventions may be partially accounted for (approximately 10% of the variance) by a natural reduction rather than the intervention itself. Research with the BDI-II has consistently found a high internal consistency ranging from .89 to .94 even when using a variety of populations

(Arnau, Meagher, Norris, & Bramson, 2001; A. T. Beck et al., 1996; Dozois et al., 1998; Steer et al., 1999, 2000). Test-retest reliability over a 1-week interval was .93 (Beck et al., 1996).

Evaluation of content, concurrent, and discriminant validity as well as factor analysis has generally been favorable. The content of the BDI items was derived by consensus from clinicians regarding symptoms of depressed patients combined with considerations related to the various DSM-IV categories for the diagnosis of depression. Concurrent validity is suggested by high to moderate correlations with clinical ratings for psychiatric patients (A. T. Beck et al., 1996). In addition, moderate correlations have been found with similar scales that also rate depression, such as the Hamilton Psychiatric Rating Scale for Depression (.71), Beck Hopelessness Scale (.68; Beck et al., 1996), and the Depression Anxiety Stress Scale (.88; Osman et al., 1997). The BDI has been able to discriminate psychiatric from nonpsychiatric populations (Beck et al., 1996) as well as discriminate the level of adjustment in psychiatric populations (Arnau et al., 2001; Beck et al., 1996). The BDI-II's ability to discriminate between primarily anxiety as opposed to primarily depressive disorders is supported in that BDI-II scores were more highly correlated with the Hamilton Psychiatric Rating Scale for Depression (.71) compared with the Hamilton Rating Scale for Anxiety (.47). Similarly, Steer et al. (2000) found slightly higher correlations between the BDI-II and the SCL-90-R Depression dimension (.89) than the SCL-90-R Anxiety dimension (.71).

A number of factor-analytic studies indicate that the BDI is composed of a Noncognitive (or Somatic Affective) factor comprising contents related to somatic aspects of depression (loss of energy, changes in sleep patterns, crying) and a Cognitive factor related to self-reported thoughts clients use to describe their attitudes toward themselves and their depression (self-dislike, suicidal thoughts, thoughts of worthlessness; A. T. Beck et al., 1996). These factors have been found to be consistent among various samples including college students (Beck et al., 1996), adolescents (Steer, Kumar, Ranieri, & Beck, 1998), geriatrics (Steer et al., 2000), primary care medical patients (Arnau et al., 2001), geriatric inpatients (Steer et al., 2000), and clinically depressed outpatients (Steer et al., 1999). Most comparisons between the BDI and BDI-II indicate that the factor structure on the BDI-II is more clearly defined, suggesting it is a slightly superior instrument (Dozois et al., 1998).

Despite the frequent finding of two factors on the BDI-II, other research has favored a three-factor solutions (Vanheule, Desmet, Groenvynck, Rosseel, and Fontaine, 2008). For example, Osman et al. (1997) found a factor structure composed of Negative Attitude, Performance Difficulty, and Somatic Elements using a sample of undergraduates. A further three-factor structure comprised of affective, cognitive, and somatic components was found by Vanheule et al. (2008). Ward (2006) analyzed six data sets from previous studies. They found a three-factor solution comprised of a General factor combined with Cognitive and Somatic factors. Vanheule noted that that, across different samples, the Cognitive and Somatic factors were unstable. In other words, the items that loaded on these two factors varied according to different samples that were used. The advantage of the General factor is that it provided most of the "binding" between both factors (internal consistency) and was consistent across the various samples.

Use with Diverse Groups

The BDI-II appears to be an appropriate measure for various ethnic and cross-cultural groups, including African Americans and Hispanics. Specifially, scores do not seem to be different among ethnic groups (Beck et al., 1996), and the factor structure has been found to be quite similar (Grothe et al., 2005; Penley, Wiebe, & Nwosu, 2003). In addition, Spanish translations have been found to maintain assessment utility (Penley et al., 2003; Wiebe & Penley, 2005). The BDI-II has also been found to be effective in assessing the presence and extent of depression in adolescents, although a cutoff of 21 or higher has been recommended (Kumar et al., 2002; Osman, Kopper, Barrios, Gutierrez, & Bagge, 2004). At the other extreme, the BDI-II can be used effectively to assess the level and extent of depression among geriatrics (Steer, Rissmiller, & Beck, 2000).

Interpretation

The following scores can be used to indicate the general level of depression:

0 to 13	No or minimal depression
14 to 19	Mild
20 to 28	Moderate
29 to 63	Severe
Below 4	Possible denial of depression, faking good; lower than usual scores even for normals

Scores significantly above even those of severely depressed persons suggest possible exaggeration of depression, a possible characteristic of histrionic or borderline personality disorders. Significant levels of depression are still possible. Arnau et al. (2001) found that a cutoff score of 18 correctly classified 92% of patients with major depressive disorder.

An ipsative interpretation of BDI responses can be used to specify irrational beliefs and relevant symptoms that are likely to be related to a person's depression. Identification of these beliefs and symptoms can be useful in specifying areas that need to be worked on in therapy. Any of the following (A. T. Beck et al., 1996, p. 5) can be assumed an area of difficulty if a score of 3 is indicated on the numbered item:

1. Sadness.
2. Pessimism.
3. Past failure.
4. Loss of pleasure.
5. Guilty feelings.
6. Punishment feelings.
7. Self-dislike.
8. Self-criticalness.
9. Suicidal thoughts or wishes.
10. Crying.
11. Agitation.
12. Loss of interest.
13. Indecisiveness.
14. Worthlessness.
15. Loss of energy.
16. Changes in sleeping pattern.

17. Irritability.
18. Changes in appetite.
19. Concentration difficulty.
20. Tiredness or fatigue.
21. Loss of interest in sex.

One specific area to be alerted to is the potential for suicide, which can be indicated by strong endorsements (2 or 3) on items 9 (suicidal thoughts or wishes) and 2 (pessimism). Whereas the level of depression (based on total score) and presence of specific item endorsement can assist in suggesting the presence of a formal *DSM-IV* disorder, a definitive diagnosis would still need to be made based on a more thorough review by a clinician.

STATE TRAIT ANXIETY INVENTORY (STAI)

A client's level of anxiety is one of the most crucial dimensions to assess, both for treatment planning as well as to establish the impact of interventions. The State-Trait Anxiety Inventory (STAI; Spielberger, Gorsuch, Lushene, Vagg, & Jacobs, 1983) is ideally suited for this purpose because it is a brief (20-item), self-report inventory that is easy to understand and is sensitive to transitory episodes of anxiety (states) as well as more stable personality features that predispose a client to experiencing more chronic levels of anxiety (traits). It is currently the most frequently used measure of anxiety with over 8,000 studies available in the literature. Research has evaluated its use in the treatment of phobias, test anxiety, panic, generalized anxiety, and the impact of specific types of treatment, such as cognitive behavior therapy, systematic desensitization, relaxation, and rational emotive therapy (Spielberger, Sydeman, Owen, & Marsh, 1999). It has also been used extensively in cross-cultural research and has been translated into more than 60 languages and dialects.

Construction of the STAI began in 1964 with a single set of items that could be used to assess either state or trait anxiety based on rewording the instructions (Form A). The state instructions requested the client to complete items for how they felt "right now, at the moment" whereas the trait descriptions asked them to indicate how they generally feel. The items were originally derived and adapted from existing anxiety inventories, including the Affect Adjective Checklist (see Spielberger & Reheiser, 2004). Items were reduced and the scale refined based on the degree to which individual items correlated with the Manifest Anxiety Scale, Anxiety Scale Questionnaire, and Welsh Anxiety Scale of the MMPI (see Spielberger et al., 1999). Further evaluation with Form A indicated that merely rewording the instructions was not sufficient to eliminate the clear trait connotations of some of the items. For example, the item "I worry too much" was a good measure of trait anxiety, but merely rewording the instructions indicated that it was not a good measure of state anxiety. As a result, a second form (Form X; see Spielberger & Reheiser, 2004) was developed based on the trait and state dimensions having their own individual items. Trait items were selected based on their having the highest correlations with the Manifest Anxiety Scale, Anxiety Scale Questionnaire, and Welsh Anxiety Scale as well as being the most stable over time. The state items were selected based on their being most sensitive to high- versus low-stress conditions (high construct validity) and having the highest internal consistency.

A decade after the publication of Form X, the STAI underwent a further major revision based on factor analysis, a clearer understanding of the concept of anxiety, and an attempt to eliminate item overlap with depression. This resulted in the current (Form Y) version having 10 items for trait and 10 for state anxiety (Spielberger et al., 1983). Form Y was normed on 1,838 employees of the Federal Aviation Administration, 855 university students, 424 high school students, 1,701 Air Force recruits, and 263 naval recruits. Older persons and those with more education scored somewhat lower than those who were either younger or less educated, which suggests it might be important to use age and education-related norms. Additional norms are available for a neuropsychiatric population, general medical/surgical patients, and young prison inmates. A children's form, the State-Trait Anxiety Inventory for Children (STAIC; Spielberger, 1973), is also available.

Reliability and Validity

Test-retest reliability for college students over 30- and 60-day intervals indicated reasonably good coefficients ranging between .73 and .86 for trait anxiety. In contrast, state anxiety test-retest reliabilities were relatively lower, ranging from .51 for males to .36 for females (Spielberger et al., 1983). The lower range for state anxiety is expected given that state anxiety is considered a more changeable construct. Given the expected fluctuations for state anxiety, measures of internal consistency would be more appropriate and important to consider. These have resulted in quite high state anxiety median coefficients ranging between .88 and .93 with a similarly high median trait anxiety coefficient ranging from .92 to .94 (Kabacoff, Segal, Hersen, & Van Hasselt, 1997; Spielberger et al., 1983).

The content validity of the STAI-Trait scale is supported in that five out of a possible eight domains for a *DSM-IV*–based diagnosis of a generalized anxiety disorder were reflected in the items (Okun, Stein, Bauman, & Silver, 1996). Concurrent validity is supported in that correlations with the Manifest Anxiety Scale and the Anxiety Scale Questionnaire have ranged from .73 to .75 (Spielberger & Reheiser, 2004). These correlations are sufficiently high that the STAI can be considered alternative measures of trait anxiety. However, the STAI has the advantage of being shorter and less contaminated by measures of depression. Lower and moderate, but still significant, correlations were found between the STAI-Trait and the Worry Scale (.57) and Padua Inventory (.57; Stanley, Beck, & Zebb, 1996).

The construct validity of the STAI is suggested in that psychiatric patients generally have higher scores on trait anxiety than nonpatient groups (Spielberger et al., 1983; Stanley et al., 1996). One exception is that, as expected, patients with character disorders tended to have lower scores (Spielberger et al., 1983). Kabacoff et al. (1997) also found that patients with anxiety disorders had slightly higher STAI-Trait scores than patients without anxiety disorders. Despite this support for the convergent and divergent validity of the STAI, Kabacoff et al. were not successful in developing adequate cutoff scores for identifying the presence of an anxiety disorder. This was primarily because of difficulty finding a score that produced both good sensitivity (high identification of true positives) as well as good specificity (high identification of true negatives). Construct validity for the validity of STAI-State anxiety is supported in that students during in-class exams and military recruits undergoing stressful training procedures had higher scores when compared to scores taken after relaxation procedures or with age-matched controls (Spielberger et al., 1983). Numerous studies have demonstrated that the STAI is sensitive to the impact of a wide variety of interventions (Spielberger et al., 1983; Speilberger & Reheiser, 2004).

Factor analysis of the STAI has been mixed. According to the STAI scale development, there should ideally be one factor that loads on trait anxiety and another one on state anxiety Spielberger et al., 1983). In contrast, Bieling, Antony, and Swinson (1998) found a higher-order factor derived from the trait anxiety items they referred to as *negative affect* and two lower-order factors that they concluded were organized around *depression* and anxiety. Thus, the trait items seemed not to be pure measures of anxiety but included measures of negative affect and depression as well as anxiety. Whereas Spielberger et al. (1983) did attempt to make Form Y more of a pure measure of anxiety than Form X, this seems to have been only partially successful. The difficulty in developing a pure measure of anxiety underlies the issue, frequently found in other measures of anxiety and depression, that anxiety and depression have overlapping features with correlations typically ranging between .45 and .75 (Lovibund & Lovibund, 1995). The factor structure of the STAI is further complicated in that Kabacoff et al. (1997) found two factors related to whether the items were worded in a positive or negative direction. They concluded that these items were "method factors" unrelated to the constructs of anxiety. An alternative model by Vigneau and Cormier (2008) found a four-factor model based on a combination of state and trait as well as whether the items were worded as these variables being present or absent (State Anxiety positive items, State anxiety negative items, Trait Anxiety negative items, Trait Anxiety positives items). In other words, the bipolar aspects (wording of the items) of trait/state anxiety emerged as independent factors.

Use with Diverse Groups

The utility of the STAI has been demonstrated in a number of cross-cultural contexts. For example, Hishinuma et al. (2000) evaluated the STAI with an Asia Pacific adolescent population and found good internal consistency and a factor structure that was similar to the normative group. A Spanish translation of the STAI has similarly been found to have good internal consistency and a comparable factor structure, suggesting it can be used with Spanish-speaking populations (Novy, Smith, Rogers, & Rowzee, 1995). Overall, the STAI has excellent adaptability across a wide variety of ethnic and cross-cultural groups (Spielberger, Moscoso, & Brunner, 2004; Vigneau & Cormier, 2008).

The STAI has also been found to have good psychometric properties with elderly populations (Kvaal, Ulstein, Nordhus, & Engedal, 2005) and has been both normed for adolescents and been found to have good psychometric properties with this population (Spielberger, 1983). Since both adolescent and elderly populations have been found to be somewhat less anxious than adults, separate norms should be used. As noted previously, a version for children between the ages of 9 and 12 is available (State Trait Anxiety Inventory for Children).

Interpretation

Because the STAI comprises two unidimensional subscales, interpretation is mainly composed of descriptions for the variables being measured. This can be done by considering both the variable itself and the relative magnitude of the person's score.

High T-Anxiety   The person is likely to perceive a wide number of situations as threatening or dangerous; the person is especially likely to be concerned with being evaluated by other people with corresponding threats to self-esteem.

High S-Anxiety   The person has feelings of apprehension, worry, nervousness; unpleasant, consciously perceived feelings of tension; the person is also likely to report corresponding activation of the autonomic nervous system.

High S-Anxiety/Low T-Anxiety   The anxiety the person is reporting is likely to be caused by some external threat or a current situational stressor. As a result, it is likely to resolve itself. If intervention is warranted, it should ideally be directed toward strategies that provide a reduction in arousal, such as increasing the person's social supports, systematic desensitization, providing reassurance, hypnosis, exercise, meditation, or progressive muscle relaxation. There might also be an emphasis on what the current anxiety has taught the person about him- or herself and how this might be used to reduce the likelihood of reducing anxiety in the future.

High T-Anxiety/Low S-Anxiety   Although the person is not currently reporting anxiety, he or she is prone to reacting to situations in such a way as to easily become anxious. He or she is likely to be extremely concerned with threats to self-esteem and, as a result, might be apprehensive in any interpersonal situation in which he or she might be judged.

RECOMMENDED READING

Antony, M. M., & Barlow, D. (Eds.). (2002). *Handbook of assessment, treatment planning, and outcome evaluation: Empirically supported strategies for psychological disorders*. New York: Guilford Press.

Groth-Marnat, G. (1999). Financial efficacy of clinical assessment: Rational guidelines and issues for future research. *Journal of Clinical Psychology, 55*, 813–824.

Maruish, M. (2004). *The use of psychological testing for treatment planning and outcomes assessment* (3rd ed.). Mahwah, NJ: Lawrence Erlbaum.

Chapter 14 ─────────────────────────────────

PSYCHOLOGICAL ASSESSMENT AND TREATMENT PLANNING

The ultimate goal of psychological assessment is to help solve problems by providing information and recommendations relevant to making the optimum decisions related to the client. Doing this involves integrating a wide variety of information including specifics of the problem, client resources, a client's personal characteristics, and environmental circumstances. Practitioners must then work with this information to make recommendations related to treatment setting (inpatient/outpatient), intensity (frequency and duration), goals, mode (individual, group, family), and specific strategies and techniques. The sheer number of these variables can make assessment a daunting task. Thus, the focus of this chapter is to provide a manageable framework for systematically organizing assessment results for planning treatment. Research has shown that following this framework optimizes the outcome of interventions.

The following format for organizing results and developing treatment plans has been guided by several principles and values. When possible, evidence-based information has been provided. This is possible using the knowledge derived from the rather extensive body of research currently available. In fact, treatment that ignores the procedures indicated by current research runs the risk of not offering clients the most effective treatments available. At the same time, it is acknowledged that clinical experience and judgment inevitably needs to interact with the research, assessment results, and the uniqueness of the client to generate the best treatment plan. A further guiding principle underlying this chapter is that the format is both sequential and systematic. It is sequential in that, typically, a series of decisions confronts clinicians, beginning with areas such as how restrictive interventions should be and ending with issues such as specific techniques of therapy and methods of relapse prevention. Finally, the number of variables considered has been reduced to those that seem most relevant, easily manageable, and best supported by research.

Developing effective recommendations requires a number of knowledge and skill areas beyond merely test interpretation. One of the more important areas relates to general case management. Effective case management requires practitioners to survey the general case issues, focus on the most salient features, and make recommendations accordingly. Recommendations should include noting how restrictive treatment should be, which is directly related to the severity of the problem and whether the patient is likely to present a danger to self or others. After reviewing these considerations, practitioners need to be aware of the resources available in the community and make recommendations to the most appropriate one(s), such as a specific inpatient setting or referral to an outpatient clinic, medical facility, suicide prevention center, Alcoholics Anonymous, or a behavioral medicine unit. A variety of self-help resources may also help to enhance treatment. Decisions need to relate to the frequency and duration of treatment. Practitioners should also be able to assess and provide recommendations on how to optimize a client's environment. For example, assessing the client's level of social support might help either in encouraging the person to use available supports or in enhancing only partially adequate supports. Environments might also be changed to increase social interaction or decrease the likelihood of relapse.

Practitioners can and should be able to deliberately tailor their responses toward specific characteristics and circumstances of the client. While this might seem self-evident, many therapists typically provide the same or at least similar interventions for all their clients. Frequently, these interventions are based on the specific school of therapy the therapist is most familiar with (e.g., cognitive therapy for every client who comes in for treatment). Research has demonstrated, however, that whereas cognitive behavior therapy can be effective for patients with externalizing coping styles, a supportive, self-directive method is more effective for patients with internalizing styles of coping (Beutler et al., 2000). A further assumption frequently found in clinical lore is that empathy is an essential ingredient of all effective therapy. Despite this assumption, controlled studies indicate suspicious clients with low motivation do poorly when psychotherapists are empathic, involved, and accepting (Beutler, Crago, & Arizmendi, 1986; Beutler, Harwood, Alimohamed, & Malik, 2002). These examples, and many others, indicate that therapists need to have relational flexibility and a broad range of skills. In contrast, providing clients with a narrow range of possible interventions not only may reduce treatment effectiveness but also raise a question of ethics because the best interventions are not being provided. Recommendations and interventions should, as much as possible, be guided by research as clinical lore can sometimes be misleading.

This brief introduction to treatment planning is not intended to minimize either the tremendous impact that the quality of the treatment relationship has on outcome or of the importance of clinical experience. The overall quality of the therapeutic relationship accounts for at least as much of the outcome variance as specific techniques (Lambert, 2005; Wampold, 2000). Well-defined techniques, however, are often easier to specify and control than the more general quality of the relationship. In addition, techniques that match a client's needs and expectations are likely to enhance the quality of the working relationship. Thus, it is difficult, if not impossible, to separate technique and relationship. For example, relationship quality is likely to deteriorate if a therapist tries highly directive techniques with quite defensive clients (Beutler, Moleiro, & Talebi, 2002; Beutler, Sandowicz, Fisher, & Albanese, 1996). In addition, clinical experience will always be crucial in integrating a diverse range of client information into an optimum set of recommendations. While this process should be generally guided by available research, the specifics of a particular case might be sufficient to alter or even negate the generalities suggested by research data alone. Thus, research findings and clinical information should ideally be in an active interplay such that they optimize each other's strengths and minimize their respective weaknesses.

DEVELOPMENT AND APPROACHES TO TREATMENT PLANNING

One of the central concerns for researchers and clinicians refining treatment planning has been efforts to understand how and why therapeutic interventions do or do not work. Similar to the debates on intelligence, researchers and clinicians can be divided into "splitters," who have focused on the impacts of specific techniques, and "lumpers," who have been more concerned with the common, nonspecific ingredients that facilitate change. A further related theme is the identification of relevant client domains or behaviors needing change and matching these with appropriate interventions. The general purpose of assessment in this process is to identify the most relevant client characteristics or symptom behaviors and match these with optimal interventions. Gordon Paul (1967) ambitiously stated this agenda with a question: "*What* treatment, by *whom*, is most effective for *this* individual with *that* specific problem, and under *which* set of circumstances?" (p. 44).

Ancient traditions of mental health were fully aware of the importance of tailoring interventions toward the specifics of the client. For example, the Vedas discuss the differential effects of telling appropriate metaphors to clients according to their needs. Similarly, Sufism has had a well-developed tradition of storytelling designed to create specific impacts on the participants (Groth-Marnat, 1992). As early as 1919, Freud was concerned with matching patients to different types of psychotherapy. Classical psychoanalysis was recommended for patients who were quite psychologically minded. In contrast, clients who were considered "unanalyzable" because of a lack of psychological sophistication were referred for psychoanalytic psychotherapy that focused on direct suggestion rather than extensive insight and in-depth self-exploration.

Throughout the 1950s and 1960s, an extremely diverse number of therapies were developed. Each one provided a different theoretical model for causation and a wide variety of techniques. Part of what stimulated these developments was the hope that a series of techniques would prove successful in treating certain types of problems. Examples of such techniques included systematic desensitization for phobias or interpreting the transference as a tool in resolving past interpersonal conflicts. In the psychosomatic literature, it was believed that certain disorders (e.g., asthma) were the result of specific types of conflicts (e.g., suppressed dependency needs). Resolving these specific conflicts, it was hoped, would similarly remove the relevant symptoms. This extensive variety and specificity has led to the development of more than 400 different types of psychotherapies, only a few of which have been subjected to any degree of empirical investigation.

Psychological assessment during the 1950s and 1960s closely paralleled the particular school of therapy it was aligned with. Because many assessment procedures were both used in a medical context and relied on projective techniques, they, accordingly, reflected a psychoanalytic perspective. The goal, then, was to list a patient's symptoms along with a dynamic interpretation of the conflicts believed to be causing these symptoms. The specificity of treatment planning was deemphasized in favor of detailed descriptions of inner dynamics. It was assumed that, by describing these conflicts, the therapist would then know better how to proceed. During the 1960s and 1970s, the competing schools of behaviorism and humanism developed their own modes of assessment based on either specifying target behaviors and the antecedent events leading to these behaviors or attending to the ongoing experience of the client. In either case, the value of traditional psychometric procedures was not only deemphasized but even criticized and abandoned.

Understandably, there was considerable competition between the different therapies as to which one was most effective. In 1952, Eysenck stimulated considerable controversy with his verdict that psychotherapy (particularly psychoanalysis) was no more effective than placebo. In contrast, he concluded that behavior therapy has demonstrated positive outcomes beyond merely placebo effects (Eysenck, 1994). Much of the ensuing research became a horse race in which proponents of particular schools wanted to demonstrate the superiority of the chosen therapeutic mode that they had received training in for so many years. The classic and much-cited summary study of therapeutic outcome was M. L. Smith, Glass, and Miller's (1980) meta-analysis, which concluded that all of the evaluated therapies were effective. They also found greater effect sizes for those therapies with a narrow focus than for those with a wider focus. For example, techniques such as systematic desensitization and hypnosis, which typically target a narrow band of behavior (elimination of a phobia, habit modification), were found to have greater impact than client-centered therapy, with its more general goal of personal growth. However, the differences between the various therapies were not extensive, which led many reviewers of the field to agree with Luborsky, Singer, and Luborsky's (1975) earlier verdict that "Everybody has won and all must have prizes" (often referred to as the "dodo bird" verdict). The "dodo bird" verdict is supported by more recent, methodically well-designed studies that have demonstrated little or no differential outcomes between different therapies when targeted at the same problems (Ahn & Wampold, 2001; E. Anderson & Lambert, 1995; Patterson, 1989; Seligman, 1995; Wampold, 2000). For example, current high-quality research (including a meta-analysis) has found that randomly assigned manualized cognitive-behavioral versus psychodynamic-interpersonal interventions for depression had similar effectiveness on therapeutic outcome (Gallagher-Thompson & Steffen, 1994; Leichsenring, 2001; D. A. Shapiro et al., 1994).

The preceding studies, along with responses to these findings, have significant implications for treatment planning. One category of response is an investigation of the *nonspecific features of therapy* common to all systems (see Ahn & Wampold, 2001; Andrews, 2001; Lambert, 2005). Underlying this response is the hope that these nonspecific factors would explain the general equivalence of outcomes across therapies. The earliest formal conceptualization was a 1957 description of "necessary and sufficient conditions of therapeutic change" by C. Rogers (1957/1992). These conditions included genuineness, unconditional positive regard, and accurate empathy. A somewhat similar nonspecific formulation was also proposed by J. Frank (1973), who emphasized that successful therapy involved providing the client with hope, overcoming demoralization, and creating a corrective emotional experience involving benevolent persuasion. This nonspecific focus provides a contrast to the more directive, technique-oriented approaches. In particular, the nonspecific explanations place considerable emphasis on the quality of the therapeutic relationship beyond mere technique (see Norcross, 2002). The implications for assessment and treatment planning are that the technical aspect of assessment (formal tests) recedes in importance compared with the quality of the relationship (Andrews, 2001; Luborsky, 1994). Formal testing may even be perceived as interfering with the development of a positive therapeutic relationship. In addition, the specificity of treatment recommendations is also deemphasized. What still remains, however, are basic case management issues (restrictiveness, format, and intensity of treatment) and enhancing aspects of the relationship that are likely to maximize outcome (i.e., matching client expectations, being perceived as trustworthy and credible).

A second general strategy has collectively been referred to as *differential therapeutics*. This approach focuses on refining intervention techniques based on specific diagnoses combined with additional information related to aspects of the problem (see Antony & Barlow, 2002; Nathan & Gorman, 1998; Sammons & Schmidt, 2001). The general function of assessment in differential therapeutics is to diagnose and evaluate the specifics of a disorder as carefully as possible. Techniques believed to be most effective in optimizing outcome are tailored and directed toward a symptom or symptom cluster. This model closely parallels and draws on procedures used in medicine, which similarly rely on accurate diagnosis before applying the optimal treatment.

The preceding approach has had varying degrees of success. Probably the most noteworthy of these successes has been the development of specific targeted interventions for clusters of anxiety-related symptoms (Barlow, 1988; J. G. Beck & Zebb, 1994; Steketee, 1994). In particular, Barlow, Craske, Cerny, and Klosko (1989) have developed a specific targeted treatment for panic disorder that has been found to be effective for 80% to 100% of those who completed the program. In addition, it has been found to provide outcomes clearly superior to pharmacotherapy (Gould, Otto, & Pollack, 1995).

The treatment involves a combination of muscle relaxation, cognitive restructuring, and exposure to internal sensations linked to training in breathing. Interventions for social phobia and social anxiety have also shown differential effectiveness over other forms of treatment. Such programs involve restructuring cognitions, simulations of feared situations, and homework assignments in which clients gradually expose themselves to actual anxiety-related situations (Hope & Heimberg, 1993). Finally, differentially effective interventions for obsessive-compulsive disorder have primarily centered on gradual exposure to the anxiety-related situations, along with strategies to prevent the occurrence of the compulsive behaviors (Riggs & Foa, 1993).

While most of the anxiety disorders have indicated the advantage of using interventions targeted directly at the subtype of disorder (diagnosis), less success has been achieved for specific interventions in the treatment of depression. The extent of vegetative symptoms, presence of manic episodes (bipolar), and presence of suicidal risk have implications for type of medication and restrictiveness of treatment. Although research has so far not been able to clearly identify the best psychosocial intervention for depression (Gallagher-Thompson & Steffen, 1994; Leichsenring, 2001; Rude, 1986; D. A. Shapiro et al., 1994), some have argued for the differential effectiveness of cognitive-behavioral approaches (see Antonuccio, Danton, & DeNelsky, 1995). Researchers have also had difficulty demonstrating differential effectiveness for specific psychosocial interventions for schizophrenia, sleep disorders, sexual disturbances, generalized anxiety disorder, and personality disorders (Beutler & Crago, 1986; T. Brown, O'Leary, & Barlow, 1993).

A third general response has been to consider the nonequivalence of therapeutic outcomes to be the result of insufficiently explored *client characteristics* (see Beutler et al., 2000; Beutler & Harwood, 2000; Groth-Marnat et al., 2008). Evaluating the relative contribution of client characteristics is based on the finding that some types of clients do quite well when provided with a certain type of therapy and others, given the same therapy, do quite poorly. If those clients who did poorly could have been identified and provided with different strategies, they might have made significant therapeutic gains using an alternate approach. However, the averaged scores on outcome studies using heterogeneous populations have obscured these potentially relevant client differences.

The strategy, then, has been to thoroughly research a wide variety of client characteristics to determine which ones can be used to predict differential response to therapy. Over 200 of these characteristics have been suggested, of which 100 have been subjected to empirical investigation (Beutler et al., 2000; Garfield, 1994; Norcross, 1997). The result has been that, over the past 20 years, there has been increasing delineation and use of the most empirically validated characteristics for systematic treatment planning (Beutler, Harwood, Bertoni, & Thoman, 2006). Reviews of this strategy have indicated that, under optimal matching conditions, up to 64% of the outcome variance can be accounted for (Beutler, 1983, 1989; Berzins, 1977). When client characteristics and treatment matching are combined with the quality of the therapeutic alliance, prediction of outcome increases to 90% (Beutler et al., 1999; Beutler, Moleiro, Malik, & Harwood, 2003). In contrast, providing therapeutic techniques without considering predisposing client characteristics has been found to account for only 10% of the outcome variance (Beutler, 1989; Wampold, 2000).

The implication for assessment is that predisposing client characteristics can and should be used to identify relevant dimensions. Furthermore, these dimensions should then be used to develop optimum treatment plans. This finding emphasizes both the technical and clinical aspects of assessment as well as the specificity of treatment recommendations. It does not negate the importance of common factors (caring, empathy, respect, etc.), but systematic treatment selection can potentially add to the effects of these common factors. It can also improve outcomes beyond merely assigning patients to models of therapy (i.e. cognitive therapy; Beutler et al., 2003).

In addition to the preceding three general strategies, a variety of specific attempts has emerged to provide guidelines for prescriptive matching of client characteristics with therapeutic interventions. Ideally, the *DSM* should be useful in developing treatment plans in a similar manner as occurs for specific disease entities in general medicine. Generally, however, this has not been the case. Although some of the diagnostic categories have implications for different forms of somatic interventions (i.e., antidepressants for depressive disorders), they generally are not particularly helpful for designing psychosocial interventions (Beutler, 1989; Houts, 2002). In an effort to more clearly identify the full array of relevant domains for intervention, Lazarus (1973, 2006) suggested that clinicians analyze a patient's *b*ehaviors, *a*ffects, *s*ensory experiences, *i*magery, *c*ognitions, *i*nterpersonal relationships, and need for *d*rugs (BASIC-ID; see Chapter 4). A somewhat different perspective has been taken by authors who believe that the various stages of therapy or change are crucial to consider in tailoring interventions. Prochaska and DiClemente (1984, 1992) encouraged practitioners to tailor their interventions around the stages of precontemplation, contemplation, preparation, action, and maintenance.

In a behavioral medicine context, Wickramasekera (1995a, 1995b) has developed a high-risk model for identifying and assessing clients likely to have somatizing complaints. The high-risk model makes predictions based on accounting for predisposing factors consisting of either very high or very low hypnotizability, neuroticism (level of sympathetic reactivity), and catastrophizing cognitions. Precipitating factors relate to major life changes or minor hassles, and client factors that are likely to serve as buffers include level of social support and coping ability. Treatment can then be tailored toward the patterns of scores on these client dimensions.

A further strategy has been to determine the factors involved in creating optimal matches between therapist and client. In some ways, similarity between client and therapist has been found to be advantageous, particularly for dimensions such as age, gender, and ethnicity (Beutler & Clarkin, 1990). Similarity is also likely to enhance the value placed on interpersonal treatment goals, friendship, and social recognition (Arizmendi, Beutler, Shanfield, Crago, & Hagaman, 1985; P. Talley, Strupp, & Morey, 1990). In contrast, dissimilarity between patient and client predicted better outcomes when therapists who valued a high level of autonomy worked with clients who had a high need for attachment and dependence. Conversely, therapists who were highly oriented toward attachment and dependency did better with clients who were highly self-sufficient and autonomous (N. Jacobson, Follette, & Pagel, 1986).

Beutler and his colleagues (Beutler & Clarkin, 1990; Beutler et al., 2000; Beutler et al., 2006; Harwood & Williams, 2003) have developed a model of treatment selection based primarily on the identification of relevant client characteristics. This approach relies on systematically identifying these characteristics and making recommendations based on empirically and clinically established relationships with treatment outcomes. These characteristics include degree of functional impairment, social support, level of problem complexity/chronicity, coping style, resistance, and subjective distress. This model, along with stages of change, is emphasized in the remainder of this chapter. The rationale for using this model is that it closely adheres to evidence-based research, uses many of the assessment techniques discussed in previous chapters, follows a clear sequence of decision making, and is comprehensive while detailing a manageable number of variables.

The relevance and urgency of working with evidence-based methods of treatment planning are likely to increase significantly in the future. A powerful factor fueling this urgency is the current managed care movement, which will increasingly demand that both assessment procedures and interventions demonstrate their cost-effectiveness (Groth-Marnat, 1999; Groth-Marnat & Edkins, 1996; Groth-Marnat et al., 1995; Maruish, 2002; Yates & Taub, 2003). As a result, there is increasing pressure to demonstrate that assessment can quickly identify client problems, facilitate optimal treatment recommendations, and show the effectiveness of actual interventions. These "tools of the trade" must be able to provide these services in a way that has been demonstrated to be cost-effective. At the present time, data on the cost-effectiveness of assessment is not yet available, but most likely it will be forthcoming in the near future (Groth-Marnat, 1999, 2000b; Yates & Taub, 2003). Future research should clarify when assessment is and is not cost-effective and, in particular, demonstrate that assessment results can be used to save money by quickly and effectively developing a treatment plan, thereby avoiding misplaced and, possibly, ineffective or unnecessarily long treatment.

A SYSTEMATIC APPROACH TO TREATMENT SELECTION

When a practitioner is confronted with a client, relevant information needs to be acquired; and based on this information, a series of decisions and recommendations should be developed. Beutler and his colleagues (Beutler et al., 2000b; Beutler & Harwood, 2000; Beutler et al., 2006; Harwood & Williams, 2003) have identified six patient dimensions and related these to different types of decisions (see Table 14.1). The first of these relates to *functional impairment* and has clear implications for general case management.

Table 14.1. Systematic steps in treatment planning

Variable	Treatment Considerations
1. Functional impairment	Restrictiveness (inpatient/outpatient)
	Intensity (duration and frequency)
	Medical vs. psychosocial interventions
	Prognosis
	Urgency of achieving goals
2. Social support	Cognitive behavioral vs. relationship enhancement
	Duration of treatment
	Psychosocial interventions vs. medication
	Possible group interventions
3. Problem complexity/chronicity	Narrow symptom focus vs. resolution of thematic unresolved conflicts
4. Coping style	Behavioral symptom-oriented vs. internal insight-oriented interventions
5. Resistance	Supportive, nondirective, or paradoxical vs. structured, directive interventions
6. Subjective distress	Increase/decrease arousal
7. Problem-solving phase	Understanding, exploration, and awareness vs. overt behavioral or interpersonal change

Issues include the relative restrictiveness of therapy (inpatient/outpatient), whether medication should be considered, the intensity of treatment (duration and frequency), and what should be the immediate goals. The other five dimensions relate more to specific techniques of intervention than to general case management. Level of *social support* can be used to determine whether a client's social network can be relied on or whether it needs to be increased. The relative *complexity* (and *chronicity*) of a client's problem is important in considering whether the focus of treatment should be on specific, discrete, environmentally related symptoms, or more internal, chronic areas of conflict. In addition, *coping style* can help guide whether interventions should be on changing external behavior or directed at more internal insight-oriented levels of change, and level of *resistance* (reactance) has implications for how directive interventions should be. *Subjective distress* can be used to guide clinicians in determining whether the client's level of arousal should be increased or decreased. A final, seventh domain developed by Prochaska and DiClemente (1984, 1992) relates to tailoring interventions based on the *problem-solving phase* (stage of change) the client is in.

Each of these dimensions can potentially be assessed with a combination of formal tests, interview data, behavioral observations, and relevant history. Assessing for relevant client characteristics can range from a relatively short interview that focuses on each of the relevant domains, to an extensive battery consisting of a number of formal psychological tests. A rating scale (the *STS Clinician's Rating Form*; D. Fisher, Beutler, & Williams, 1999) has also been developed to assist in summarizing the various ratings. In addition, a software program is available to provide narrative reports, project the course of treatment, graph a patient's relative standing on each of the assessed variables, assess various risks for the client, list most pressing problems, provide a series of brief minimanuals for each problem area, and evaluate outcome (*Systematic Treatment Selection: A Software Package for Treatment Planning*; Beutler & Williams, 1999). Completing the program takes between 20 and 40 minutes. Finally, clients (and clinicians) can enter data through a phone-in service so that the STS dimensions can be rated based on client responses and a treatment plan developed (see additional information at www.systematic-treatmentselection.com or info@cbhti.com; Harwood & Williams, 2003). The following descriptions of these dimensions include a section on describing the construct followed by methods of assessment and different treatment implications based on the information derived from assessment. Although relevant research to support important themes is cited, given the often-immense volume of possible literature, it is not possible to provide an exhaustive listing of citations. Practitioners can use the dimensions that follow to organize their assessment procedures as well as to guide treatment interventions.

FUNCTIONAL IMPAIRMENT

A pressing problem related to any assessment is an evaluation of the severity of the problem. The core issue is to assess the extent to which the patient's problem interferes with his or her ability to deal effectively with everyday social, occupational, and intrapersonal requirements. The degree of functional impairment will have a direct relationship to the client's ability to cope, ego strength, level of insight, and chronicity of symptoms. In most cases, functional impairment relates to the extent to which the client is subjectively distressed. In many instances, however, subjective distress does not relate to the presence of severe problems. Examples include antisocial personalities who create suffering for others but do not feel particularly distressed themselves and schizoid personalities who are functioning on the fringes of society but do not feel particularly worried about their marginal status and level of dysfunction. The major distinction is that functional impairment is reflected in objective indicators of impairment. In contrast, subjective distress does not necessarily mean that the person is also impaired based on objective indicators.

There are numerous formal and informal assessment procedures for assessing functional impairment. Beutler and his colleagues (Beutler & Harwood, 2000; Beutler & Groth-Marnat, 2003; Groth-Marnat et al., in press) have summarized the relevant assessment dimensions to include:

- A problem that interferes with the client's ability to function during the interview.
- Poor concentration during assessment tasks.
- Distraction by minor events.
- General incapacity to function.
- Difficulty interacting with the clinician.
- Multiple impaired areas of performance in the client's daily life.

A Mental Status Examination is a structured means of obtaining useful information related to functional impairment.

One of the more useful psychometric indications of functional impairment is the presence of generally elevated scales on the MMPI-2/MMPI-A. Functional impairment is especially likely if elevations are found on scales on the right side of the profile (Paranoia, Schizophrenia, Hypomania). High Beck Depression Inventory-II (BDI-II) scores (30 or above) also suggest a high level of incapacity. Suicide level should always be assessed if the patient is depressed. Specific signs to alert the clinician to suicide risk are relevant critical items on the MMPI-2/MMPI-A (check critical items listed under Depressed Suicidal Ideation in Appendix H) or items 2 and 9 on the BDI-II. General elevations on the MCMI-III scales also suggest a high level of functional impairment, particularly if elevations occur on the Severe Personality Pathology or Severe Syndrome scales. The multiaxial *DSM-IV-TR* (2000) system also provides methods for summarizing information relevant to estimating functional impairment. Impairment can be generally assessed by the specific type of diagnoses. Impairment is likely to be more severe if there are diagnoses on both Axis I and II and if there is the presence of severe disorders in the psychotic domain (schizophrenia, bipolar). In addition, the *DSM-IV* Global Assessment of Functioning rating specifically requests clinicians to provide an assessment of the level of functioning over the past year on a scale between 1 and 100.

Several noteworthy instruments covered in previous chapters (see Chapters 1 and 13) can also provide useful indicators of functional impairment. A high number of reported problems (*T* above 63) on the Brief Symptom Inventory (BSI; Derogatis, 1992) suggest high functional impairment as do high scores (*T* above 55) on the Trait Anxiety scale of the State-Trait Anxiety Inventory (STAI; Spielberger et al., 1983).

High Level of Functional Impairment

High levels of functional impairment have implications for these five areas: restrictiveness of treatment, intensity of interventions (duration and frequency), use of medical/somatic versus psychosocial interventions, prognosis, and the urgency of achieving initial goals (see Beutler, Harwood, et al., 2003). Severe problems, particularly if the client is suicidal or cannot function in daily activities, may require immediate inpatient care. Examples of diagnoses that may require inpatient care include bipolar mood disorders, psychotic conditions, major depression with suicidal intentions, acute substance abuse requiring detoxification, and some organic conditions that have resulted in significant decompensation. Initial treatment on an inpatient basis might later be reduced to partial hospitalization when the condition has become stabilized. Initial treatment for inpatients might need to be intensive. Outpatient interventions would be appropriate for the vast majority of clients whose problems are of mild to moderate severity (e.g., adjustment reactions, mild to moderate depression) and have greater resources.

The intensity of treatment (duration and frequency) varies from client to client based primarily on functional impairment. Greater duration of treatment is generally suggested for these types of patients:

- Those with more serious diagnoses (e.g., borderline personality).
- Poor premorbid functioning.
- External stress seemingly of minor importance in the development and maintenance of the disorder.
- Age between 25 and 50 years.
- Client expectation that change takes time, and the technique used will be exploratory and insight oriented.
- Low level of social support.

In contrast, these indicators suggest short duration of interventions:

- An acute disorder (e.g., adjustment disorder, acute reactive psychosis).
- External stress that seems to be of primary causal significance.
- Good premorbid level of functioning.
- Clients who expect change to occur quickly.
- Symptom-oriented focus of treatment, or crisis intervention.
- Structured, directive, and active interventions.
- Person who is either child/adolescent or elderly.
- High level of social support.

For some conditions, intermittent brief therapy throughout the life span at critical junctures might be an appropriate recommendation. At times, it might be appropriate to recommend no treatment, particularly if the person might have a negative response (e.g., some borderlines), no response (e.g., some antisocial personalities), spontaneous improvement (e.g., normal grief), or strongly respond to suggestions that he or she will improve rapidly with no treatment. Additional characteristics contraindicating psychotherapy might be a client's associating emotional pain with the change process, suspiciousness toward the therapist, and the client's need for control (Mohr, 1995).

Conditions such as schizophrenia, bipolar disorder, or severe anxiety states might require medical intervention (pharmacotherapy, electroconvulsive therapy) to enable clients to function well enough to become engaged in psychosocial or environmental interventions (see Sammons & Schmidt, 2001). Markers for such interventions might include poor orientation to time and place, poor short-term memory, marked confusion, clearly inappropriate mood, or low level of intelligence. Past clinical and research evidence has suggested severe and/or endogenous depression responds better to pharmacotherapy whereas situationally caused mild and moderate depression responds better to psychosocial interventions. In contrast, the preponderance of current evidence indicates that both severe and endogenous depressions, as well as mild to moderate depression, can be treated at least as effectively with psychotherapy but without the potential for problematic side effects (Antonuccio et al., 1995; Free & Oei, 1989; Garvey, Hollon, & DeRubeis, 1994; McLean & Taylor, 1992; Simons & Thase, 1992). A clearer indication for antidepressant medication is a high number of vegetative symptoms (e.g., fatigue, insomnia, loss of appetite; Preston, O'Neal, & Talaga, 2005). Similar decision processes can be made for anxiety, psychotic, and bipolar disorders (see Preston et al., 2005).

To make prognostic judgments requires considering and integrating a diverse amount of information with particular reference to diagnosis, chronicity, subjective distress, and client resources (employment, abilities, social support). Research on prognosis is somewhat contradictory. On one hand, it might be argued that a person with a severe problem will have difficulty overcoming it because it has progressed to such an extensive level. On the other hand, functional impairment may represent an extreme level in a fluctuating condition so that the person is likely to return spontaneously to an improved level of functioning. In addition, the potential magnitude of change is likely to be greater because the person has so much room for potential improvement. One guideline is that a high degree of psychiatric symptoms associated with the presence of somatic complaints (headaches, irritable bowel syndrome) is likely to suggest a poor prognosis (Blanchard, Schwarz, Neff, & Gerardi, 1988; Jacob, Turner, Szekely, & Eidelman, 1983). In contrast, patients presenting with severe levels of general anxiety and ambulatory depression typically do quite well with either psychosocial or pharmacological interventions (Elkin et al., 1989). Specific diagnosis can also be an important consideration because some diagnoses are likely to have poorer prognoses than others. For example, schizoid and antisocial personalities have difficulty engaging in productive therapy, although certain Axis I conditions related to these personality types often can be targeted and treated effectively. It is a rule of thumb that the greater the chronicity of the disorder, the more difficult it is to treat. A final principle in prognosis is that clients with low levels of social support are not as likely to improve as those with high support (Moos, 1990; Panzaralla, Alloy, & Whitehouse, 2006).

Finally, severe problems suggest that the urgency of treatment is greater and should be focused around working with the symptomatic areas causing the client the greatest distress. Less severe problems mean that the urgency of change is less, and the goals can change and be negotiated over time.

Low Level of Functional Impairment

In contrast to the previously described treatment considerations, low functional impairment suggests that treatment can be in an unrestricted setting (outpatient) and of relatively low frequency and duration. Psychosocial interventions will more likely be the predominant form of intervention, and there will be less urgency to rapidly define and achieve specific, symptom-oriented goals.

SOCIAL SUPPORT

Level of environmental support refers to the presence of a strong cohesive family and a secure form of employment. These external means of support often can modify the impact of other forms of stressors. High social support has also been associated with a favorable response to treatment (Mallinckrodt, 1996; Warren, Stein, & Grella, 2007) as well as the ability to maintain the gains made through treatment (Zlotnick, Shea, Pilkonis, Elkin, & Ryan, 1996). Not only are the treatment gains higher for persons with high social support; they also achieved these gains in a shorter period (Moos, 1990). In contrast, clients with low social support required more time to benefit from therapy.

Informal assessment of social support can be achieved by noting these characteristics:

- The extent to which the client feels trusted and respected by the people in his or her life.
- The extent and quality of people he or she can confide in.
- Level of experienced loneliness.
- The extent he or she feels abandoned by family or friends.
- The extent to which the client feels a part of his or her family network.
- The number of friends the client has common interests with.

It should be stressed that assessing social support should not consider merely the number of people available for the person but the quality the client feels regarding this support. It is one thing to be living with a large number of people and quite another to actually feel that it is possible to confide in those people.

There are also a number of more formal strategies for assessing social support. Probably the most frequently used scale is the Social Support Questionnaire (Sarason, Levine, Basham, & Sarason, 1983). Additional information related to social support might be the relative elevation of MMPI-2 scale 0 (Social Introversion). High scores suggest an inhibited, shy person who may find it difficult to have a large network of friends. In addition, elevations on 6 (Paranoia) and 8 (Schizophrenia) suggest that both the number as well as the quality of social support may be low. High scores on 1 (Hypochondriasis) and 3 (Hysteria) may indicate that, although the number of supports may be high, the quality of these supports may be poor. MCMI-III elevations may also provide useful information related to social support. High scores on Schizoid, Avoidant, Schizotypal, Paranoid, and Thought Disorder each might indicate both a low number and a low quality of social support. Other scale elevations, including Dependent, Histrionic, Narcissistic, Passive-Aggressive (Negativistic), Self-Defeating, and Borderline, may have moderate to high social supports but these supports are also likely to be quite conflicted. For example, Dependents may have social supports but have achieved these supports through sacrificing their autonomy and sense of personal competence. They are also likely to experience some anxiety related to fears that this social support may not be permanent. However, cultural factors, such as whether the person comes from a highly collectivist culture, may need to be taken into account. The Narcissistic may similarly need extensive social supports but needs to manipulate others to maintain these supports, and there may be extensive hostility if there are any threats to the admiration he or she expects from others.

High Social Support

High social support suggests a shorter duration of therapy. Long-term intervention may even be contraindicated. Therapeutic gains are likely to occur relatively rapidly and be maintained. Therapies that enhance the quality of relationships are likely to be particularly effective, presumably because they are enhancing skills the person already has. In contrast, cognitive and behavioral therapies are likely to be less effective (Beutler et al., 2000).

Low Social Support

Low support suggests that cognitive-behavioral therapy is more effective than therapies designed to enhance relationships (Beutler et al., 2000). Both longer duration of therapy and the possibility of medication are indicated. A supportive group intervention might be useful in providing sufficient support to activate additional more relationship/interpersonal types of therapies.

PROBLEM COMPLEXITY/CHRONICITY

Some clients present with problems, such as simple phobias, that are narrow, focused, and either reinforced by or elicited by the environment. In contrast, other clients present problems of a diverse, complex nature. These problems are likely to be pervasive, enduring, and occur in many contexts. Instead of focusing on one or two specific behaviors, they involve diverse themes. A review of past relationships typically reveals that these themes have been enacted with persons in intimate relationships or who were in positions of authority. Examples might include passive-aggressive interactions with authority figures, conflicts between dependency and independence in intimate relationships, or consistently creating problematic relationships by choosing incompatible partners (e.g., alcoholics) despite the availability of more appropriate persons. These themes can be considered reenactments of internal, unresolved conflicts. While the overt goal of becoming involved with such relationships is to somehow resolve the conflicts and achieve a certain level of gratification, the result usually is further suffering. For these sorts of problems, the level of intervention needs to be quite different from problems that are narrow and symptomatic.

Problem complexity can be differentiated from functional impairment in several ways. Whereas *functional impairment* refers to level of dysfunction, *problem complexity* refers to underlying thematic patterns in the person's life that may or may not result in a high level of impairment. For example, a client may be functioning at a rather high level (low functional impairment) but still be quite troubled by chronic dissatisfactions in his or her relationships. These dissatisfactions may be the result of complex themes related to difficulties dealing with anger or issues related to dependency. Such themes may pervade not only one or two primary relationships but most of the people the person comes into contact with. Whereas severe problems might be quite directly caused and reinforced by the environment (e.g., habits, reactions to stress), a complex problem is likely to be strongly related to internal unseen events. Furthermore, complex problems are likely to involve personality patterns that are spread across a wide variety of domains.

Problem complexity is more difficult to measure than most of the other factors relevant for treatment planning, in part because it is more theoretically bound. Clinicians from psychodynamic perspectives are far more likely to frame client difficulties as centering around symbolic, underlying, complex themes, whereas behaviorally oriented practitioners describe problems in narrower, concrete, environmentally oriented language (Witteman & Koele, 1999). Although there is no clear resolution to this dilemma, three main features can be used to indicate problem complexity. The first is the presence of several problem domains or diagnoses (comorbidity), and the second is the presence of pervasive or recurrent patterns and themes of problem behaviors. A third feature suggesting a complex problem is the presence of a personality disorder or, at least, a personality style suggestive of a personality disorder. Beutler and his colleagues (Beutler & Harwood, 2000; Gaw & Beutler, 1995) have summarized indicators of problem complexity based on these background information and behavioral observations:

- Behaviors are repeated as themes across unrelated situations.
- Behaviors are ritualized efforts to resolve underlying interpersonal or dynamic conflicts.

- Interactions seem primarily related to past rather than present relationships.
- Suffering rather than gratification is the result of the repetitive behavior.
- Problems are symbolic expressions of underlying unresolved conflicts.

In contrast, noncomplex problems are more often characterized as being:

- Situation-specific.
- Transient.
- Based on inadequate knowledge or skills.
- Having a direct relationship to initiating events.
- Stemming from chronic habits.

Another reason problem complexity is more difficult to assess is that there are no clear, well-defined instruments. However, some inferences can be made from existing tests. In particular, elevations on the Millon inventories, especially the MCMI-III, are likely not only to suggest the presence of a complex problem but also to provide information related to personality themes (Choca & VanDenberg, 2004; Millon & Bloom, 2008). The presence of a personality disorder as defined by *DSM-IV* (1994) criteria further suggests a complex problem. Additional information can be derived from themes noted in Thematic Apperception Test (TAT) story content or from the client's organization of his or her responses to the Rorschach. Both of these instruments can be quite useful in articulating how a client copes with his or her emotions, responds to stress, resolves conflicts, relates interpersonally, and defends against anxiety. Finally, the MMPI-2/MMPI-A can help clarify not only a client's symptom pattern but also the dynamic interplay among the symptoms, coping strategies, likely patterns in interpersonal relationships, and overall personality structure. A chronic problem is indicated if Scales 1 (Hypochondriasis) and 2 (Depression) are both above 65 but Scale 1 is clearly higher (5 to 10 points or more) than 2. Problem chronicity is also suggested if both Scales 7 (Psychasthenia) and 8 (Schizophrenia) are above 65 but Scale 8 is clearly higher (5 to 10 points or more) than 7 (see Chapter 7).

High Problem Complexity

Complex problems are likely to respond best to broad treatments that are directed toward resolving long-standing underlying conflicts and changing patterns of interpersonal relationships. Depending on the problem, specific techniques might include:

- Two-chair work.
- Group or family therapy exploring patterns of responses.
- Dream work.
- Cathartic discharge.
- Enacting opposite patterns of how the client typically behaves.
- Exploring thematic patterns in behavior and relationships.
- Interpreting the transference.
- Interpreting resistance.
- Free association.

Low Problem Complexity

Noncomplex problems can be treated effectively by targeting specific symptoms, antecedents that elicit these symptoms, and consequences that maintain them. Depending on the problem, specific techniques might include:

- Behavioral contracting.
- Social skills training.
- Graded exposure.
- Reinforcement of target behaviors.
- Contingency management.
- Challenging dysfunctional cognitions.
- Practicing alternative cognitions.
- Practicing new self-statements.
- Self-monitoring.
- Paradoxical strategies.
- Counterconditioning.
- Relaxation.
- Deep muscle relaxation.
- Biofeedback.

COPING STYLE

Theory, research, and clinical observations indicate that client coping style varies on a continuum between externalization to internalization. Externalizers cope with their problems by impulsively acting out, externalizing blame, attributing the cause of their difficulties to bad luck or fate, and actively attempting to avoid their problems. They are not psychologically minded and, as a result, do not respond well to insight. In contrast, internalizers are more prone to blame themselves based in part on the perception that they do not have the sufficient skills or abilities to overcome their difficulties. Accordingly, they tend to experience more subjective distress than externalizers. To cope with this distress, they are likely to attempt to understand their difficulties in more depth.

Clinical indicators for externalization based on history and behavioral observations include (Gaw & Beutler, 1995):

- Projection.
- Blaming others for their problems.
- Paranoia.
- Low frustration tolerance.
- Extroversion.
- Unsocialized aggression.
- Manipulation of others.
- Distraction through seeking stimulation.
- Somatization with a focus on seeking secondary gains.

In contrast, internalizers are more likely to have these characteristics:

- Introversion.
- Intellectualization.
- Constricted or overcontrolled emotions.
- Denial.
- Repression.
- Reaction formation.
- Minimizing difficulties.
- Social withdrawal.
- Somatization with symptoms related to the autonomic nervous system.

MMPI-2/MMPI-A assessment of externalization for clinical populations can be made by finding the sum of T scores on 4 (Psychopathic Deviance), 6 (Paranoia), and 9 (Mania) and then comparing this with the sum of T scores on the internalization measures of 2 (Depression), 7 (Psychasthenia), and 0 (Social Introversion). If the sum of externalization (4 + 6 + 9) is greater than internalization (2 + 7 + 0), the client can be considered an externalizer. Conversely, if the internalizing sum (2 + 7 + 0) is greater than the sum for externalization (4 + 6 + 9), the client is likely to internalize conflicts and stress (Beutler et al., 1991). Note that the preceding ratio has been designed for use with clinical populations who have at least some elevations on the MMPI-2/MMPI-A scales. For depressed patients, greater sensitivity can be achieved by calculating the sum of T scores for Scales 4 (Psychopathic Deviance) and 6 (Paranoia), which should be above 125 to fulfill the criteria for having an externalizing coping style.

Several additional measures might also provide useful information related to coping style. Low scores on the CPI socialization scale suggest an externalizing coping style, whereas high scores suggest a person who is more responsive and compliant (internal). The MCMI scales of Histrionic, Antisocial, Aggressive/Sadistic, and Paranoid conceptually suggest externalizing styles. In contrast, Avoidant, Depressive, Dependent, and Compulsive seem consistent with more internalizing styles of coping.

High Externalizers

Clients using externalizing coping strategies have better treatment outcomes when behavioral, symptom-oriented interventions or specific techniques for building skills are used. In contrast, they do relatively poorly with techniques that attempt to enhance awareness and create insight (Beutler et al., 1991; Beutler & Clarkin, 1990; Beutler, Harwood, et al., 2003; Castonguay & Beutler, 2006; Kadden, Cooney, Getter, & Litt, 1990). Techniques that are likely to be effective with externalizers include:

- Social skills enhancement.
- Assertiveness training.
- Group interventions.
- Anger management.
- Graded exposure.
- Reinforcement.
- Contingency contracting.
- Behavioral contracting.

- Questioning dysfunctional beliefs.
- Practicing alternate thinking.
- Stimulus control.
- Thought stopping.
- Counterconditioning.
- Relaxation.

High Internalizers

High internalizers benefit the most from techniques that emphasize the development of insight and the development of emotional awareness (Beutler et al., 1991; Beutler & Clarkin, 1990; Beutler, Harwood, et al., 2003; Castonguay & Beutler, 2006; Kadden et al., 1990). Specific techniques might include:

- Cathartic discharge.
- Therapist-directed imagery.
- Dream interpretation.
- Direct instruction.
- Outside reading (bibliotherapy).
- Interpreting transference reactions.
- Interpreting resistance.
- Meditation.
- Two-chair work.

RESISTANCE

Clients vary on the extent to which they are accepting and responsive to treatment versus being resistant and oppositional. This resistance is frequently a defense against what they perceive as others attempting to exert or intrude on their sense of control. Those who are most resistant are likely to have a constellation of traits including need for control, hostility, impulsivity, and direct avoidance (Dowd & Wallbrown, 1993; Shen & Dillard, 2007). They may also have difficulty taking feedback and lack empathy. In addition to the preceding trait perspective, resistance can also be a state. The defensive or reactant state usually occurs when the client feels as if his or her freedom is somehow being threatened. Persons who are prone to be resistant are more likely to feel that they have a continual lack of personal control. As a result, they may compensate for this and establish a sense of control by acting in ways that oppose what is being requested or demanded of them. This is most likely to occur when the threatened area of freedom is important to the person and the individual making the request is doing so in an authoritative fashion such as through instruction, confrontation, directives, or structured techniques. Such a structured, directive approach potentially can result in actual increases in client dysfunction. Understandably, highly reactant clients are likely to have a poorer prognosis than those who are more responsive and receptive.

Clinical indicators that may suggest high resistance include (Gaw & Beutler, 1995):

- Extreme need to maintain autonomy.
- Opposition to external influences.

- Dominance.
- Anxious oppositional style.
- History of interpersonal conflict.
- Poor response to previous treatment.
- Refusal to accept therapist interpretations.
- Failure to complete homework assignments.

In contrast, a low level of resistance is suggested by these indicators:

- Seeks direction.
- Submissive to authority.
- Open to experience.
- Accepts therapist interpretations.
- Agrees to and follows through with homework assignments.
- Indicates a tolerance to events beyond his or her control.

Although the MMPI-2/MMPI-A and MCMI-III do not have pure measures of resistance, elevations on some of the scales might be consistent with high resistance. Specifically, high scores on L and K are likely to have oppositional styles as would elevations on 6 (Paranoia) and possibly 1 (Hypochondriasis). Beutler et al. (1991) have used a combination of the MMPI research scales for anxiety (Taylor Manifest Anxiety Scale) and social desirability (Edwards Social Desirability Scale) as a measure of resistance. MCMI-III elevations on scales for Narcissistic, Negativistic (Passive/Aggressive), Paranoid, Aggressive/Sadistic, and Compulsive also suggest a defensive, oppositional person. In contrast, elevations on Dependent and Histrionic suggest a more responsive, compliant style. The most frequently used pure measure of resistance (reactance) is Dowd, Milne, and Wise's (1991) Therapeutic Reactance Scale; scores above 68 indicate sufficient resistance/reactance to have implications for treatment planning.

High Resistance

Strong empirical relationships have been found between positive treatment outcome and the use of nondirective, supportive, self-directed interventions for resistant clients (Beutler & Clarkin, 1990; Beutler, Moleiro, & Talebi, 2002; Beutler et al., 1991, 1996; Castonguay & Beutler, 2006). Specific techniques might include:

- Self-monitoring.
- Therapist reflection.
- Support and reassurance.
- Supportive interpretation of transference.

In addition, paradoxical techniques (double binds) have been found particularly effective with reactant clients and might include:

- Encouraging relapse.
- Prescribing that no change occur.
- Exaggeration of the symptom.

Paradoxical techniques will be more likely to be effective if resistance levels are quite high, as might be reflected in scores above 84 (top 25%) on the Therapeutic Reactance Scale (Beutler et al., 1996; Debord, 1989; Dowd & Wallbrown, 1993; Horvath & Goheen, 1990).

Low Resistance

Clients who are responsive and compliant are likely to achieve the most gains when therapists use a more directive, structured approach (Beutler, Moleiro, & Talebi, 2002; Beutler et al., 1991, 1996; Castonguay & Beutler, 2006; Gaw & Beutler, 1995; Horvath & Goheen, 1990). Specific techniques might include:

- Behavior contracting.
- Contingency management.
- Graded exposure.
- Direct hypnotic suggestion.
- Stimulus control.
- Cognitive restructuring.
- Developing alternative client self-statements.
- Directed imagery.
- Advice.
- Thought stopping.
- Therapist interpretation.

SUBJECTIVE DISTRESS

Subjective distress relates to the degree to which the person subjectively experiences his or her problem and is manifested primarily in heightened anxiety, confusion, or depression. A moderate level of subjective distress is useful because it motivates a client to become involved with change. It can lead to cognitive improvements, including enhanced memory, faster performance, and higher intellectual efficiency. If a client's distress becomes too high, however, it will be disruptive and result in deteriorated ability to function. The person then has difficulty appropriately processing information and concentrating, which interferes with the problem solving and behavioral experimentation required in therapy. A client whose level of subjective distress is too low will have difficulty becoming engaged in actively working to change behavior. Thus, there is an optimum window of distress that clinicians should try to achieve (Beutler & Harwood, 2000; Gaw & Beutler, 1995).

Although there is some overlap with functional impairment and subjective distress, there are also a number of differences. As discussed previously, degree of functional impairment relates to objective indicators of poor functioning, whereas subjective distress is more an internal, subjective phenomenon. In addition, subjective distress can be quite changeable and may be controlled by environmental events. A client's level of subjective distress needs to be monitored from session to session or even within each session. A further contrast exists in the range and types of decisions relevant to either functional impairment or subjective distress. Issues relevant to functional impairment require wide-ranging decisions related to treatment setting (inpatient/outpatient), prognosis, treatment intensity (duration and frequency), and the general goals of intervention. The treatment implications of subjective distress are much narrower in that they provide guidance on whether arousal should be increased or decreased.

Frequent review of interview data, including behavioral observations and relevant history, is one of the best methods of monitoring a client's distress levels. Specific indicators of high distress include (Beutler & Harwood, 2000; Gaw & Beutler, 1995):

- Motor agitation.
- High emotional arousal.
- Poor concentration.
- Unsteady voice.
- Autonomic symptoms.
- Hyperventilation.
- Hypervigilance.
- Excited affect.
- Intense feelings.

In contrast, low levels of distress are indicated by:

- Reduced motor activity.
- Poor emotional investment in treatment.
- Low energy level.
- Blunted or constricted affect.
- Slow speech.
- Unmodulated verbalizations.
- Absence of symptoms.

MMPI-2/MMPI-A scales that are especially sensitive to subjective distress are F, 2 (Depression), and 7 (Psychasthenia). Collectively, these are frequently referred to as the distress scales (see descriptions under *F* scale, Scales 2 and 7, and the 27/72 code type in Chapter 7). However, motivation to change might be undermined if scales related to denial, resistance, and defensiveness are elevated (*L* and *K* as well as 3/Hysteria). A poor prognostic sign is a low 7 (Psychasthenia) with elevations on other scales suggesting psychopathology. This finding suggests that the client might be unrealistically relaxed regarding his or her difficulties or has given in to the inevitability of the problems. Additional measures of subjective distress are the Symptom Checklist 90-R, Brief Symptom Inventory (BSI), and the State-Trait Anxiety Inventory (STAI; see Chapter 13). A high level of distress is suggested if the Global Severity Index on the BSI is above 63 or the State Anxiety Score is in the top quartile.

High Subjective Distress

If subjective distress is quite high, an immediate goal is to reduce the anxiety level. Doing so would be particularly urgent if the distress is sufficiently high to result in a significant disruption in the ability to cope. A wide variety of psychosocial techniques are available but are characterized by being supportive, structured, and designed to enhance relaxation.

If a client's arousal is expressed primarily through physiological signs, techniques targeted at this level are warranted and might include:

- Progressive muscle relaxation.
- Hypnotically assisted physiological relaxation.
- Guided imagery.
- Biofeedback.
- Aerobic exercise.
- Graded exposure.

Arousal that is more socially or cognitively related might be reduced most effectively through these techniques:

- Meditation.
- Reassurance.
- Emotional support.
- Cathartic discharge.
- Supportive challenging of dysfunctional cognitions.
- Time management.
- Thought stopping.

Pharmacotherapy might be useful but should be accompanied by learning new coping skills so that medication can be discontinued as soon as possible. The newly acquired coping skills then decrease the likelihood of relapse after the medication has been discontinued.

Low Subjective Distress

Clients with low subjective distress are likely to be associated with involuntary referrals. Experiential strategies can confront clients with the impact and consequences of their difficulties and are likely to increase distress to a level that makes them more open to changing their behavior. Possible techniques are:

- Two-chair work.
- Symptom exaggeration.
- Experiential role plays.
- Confrontation.
- Family therapy initially focusing on the impact of client behavior on family members.
- Overt practice.
- Predicting the recurrence of symptoms.
- Discussing painful memories.
- Accessing affective responses.
- Directed imagery.
- Interpretation of the transference.
- Interpretation of resistance.

PROBLEM-SOLVING PHASE

Clients undergo a series of steps during the process of change. Accordingly, any client referred for evaluation may be at a different stage in the change process. Some individuals might be simply considering the possibility of change but have not yet struggled with the specifics of how to accomplish it. This might be particularly true for involuntary referrals who are resistant and experiencing a low level of subjective distress. On the other extreme might be a client who has already taken a number of clear steps for change but is seeking help to prevent relapse. According to the stage of change, a client might require somewhat different approaches. However, considering stage of change may not be relevant for disability, medical, or many court assessments (e.g., personal injury) because facilitating change may not be part of the referral question. In these cases, assessment of the current level of functioning or differential diagnosis becomes the focus of the report.

The stages of change are likely to be quite variable. One person might pass through the different stages quite rapidly, and another who is perhaps more ambivalent or less directed might have been considering the possibility of change for years. During the process of successful therapy, it would be expected that the client would have undergone all the different stages at some point. As a result, practitioners need to be continually aware of possible alterations in the stage of change and adapt their interventions accordingly. In addition, a client might have several problem areas, especially if the problem is complex, and each area might be at a different stage in the change process. This variability requires a flexible approach depending on which area is being addressed.

Prochaska and DiClemente (1984, 2005) have described five stages in the change process: precontemplation, contemplation, preparation, action, and maintenance. Each stage has a different set of tasks that must be accomplished before proceeding to the next stage. The first three stages are processes that occur before any actual change or actual attempts at concrete change. In the *precontemplation* stage, people have little intention of changing behavior or attitudes. They might be vaguely aware that change needs to occur, but, for the most part, they are unaware of the possible importance of change. In contrast, other people they relate with can clearly see the need for change. As a result, these clients are likely to be referred or seek treatment when the legal-justice system threatens to punish them, a spouse threatens to leave them, parents threaten to disown them, or an employer threatens to dismiss them. Under these conditions, change is likely to proceed only if there is either continual outside pressure or the client internalizes the need for change. When individuals begin to consider change more seriously, they can be considered to be in the *contemplation* stage. At this point, they are aware that they have a problem and are concerned with how coping with the problem might best be accomplished. However, they have not yet committed themselves to the process. In the *preparation* stage, they have become more committed to change, which is represented by their intent to take action in the near future. This intent may also be accompanied by the possible presence of minor experiments with new behaviors. Because they are not yet clear on how best to accomplish their intended change, they may need help considering all relevant options and choosing the optimal strategy for implementing the change.

The final two steps in the change process focus on actually implementing the change and ensuring that it is maintained. *Action* is the point at which clients actually change their environment, attitudes, or behavior. Often doing this requires a considerable amount of time and energy, and, as a result, individuals must be highly committed. Changes at this point are most clearly visible to others. The preceding preparatory and contemplative processes should not be underestimated, however, because they are crucial in determining the relative success of any change. During the *maintenance* stage, individuals work to consolidate change and prevent relapse.

The following interview questions can help determine the stage of change: Do you intend to change in the near future? Are there current changes you are going through? Have you made changes? Are you currently working to prevent relapse? These questions might also be incorporated into an intake form (Prochaska, Norcross, & DiClemente, 1994). It may be necessary to probe or otherwise obtain clarification to clearly determine the stages of change. Formal assessment of the stages of change can also be made on the 32-item Stages of Change Scale (McConnaughy, Prochaska, & Velicer, 1983).

Research has generally supported the clinical utility and predictive validity of tailoring interventions according to the different stages of change. This research has focused primarily on problems such as addictive behaviors, weight control, eating disorders, sunscreen use, and initiating an exercise program (Geller, Cockell, & Drab, 2001; Prochaska, 2000; Prochaska, DiClemente, & Norcross, 1992; Prochaska, Rossi, & Wilcox, 1991). Further research needs to be conducted to determine its applicability for a wider range of problem areas (Whitelaw, Baldwin, Bunton, & Flynn, 2000). In the areas researched, there is generally evidence that tailoring interventions toward the stage of change can optimize treatment outcome (Petrocelli, 2002; Prochaska, 2000; Prochaska & DiClemente, 2005; Prochaska et al., 1992).

- *Precontemplation Stage.* This stage is often, although not necessarily, consistent with involuntary referrals. As a result, resistance level may be high and subjective distress low, such that interventions would need to be made accordingly (e.g., increase arousal; use nondirective, supportive techniques and paradoxical interventions). Because these clients might feel ambivalent about treatment, it is crucial to spend time building rapport and discussing areas that work or don't work in their lives.

- *Contemplation and Preparation Stages.* As in the previous stage, enhancing the relationship is particularly important. Providing understanding and awareness is also crucial. This should include exploring the client's interpersonal or behavioral patterns, reasons for and against changing, and the different strategies for creating change. An inventory of client strengths or resources and weaknesses might also be useful. The first three stages might be most consistent with humanistic or psychodynamic approaches that stress insight, exploration, value clarification, novel experiences, and clarification of personal goals.

- *Action Stage.* A wide variety of specific, concrete techniques might be used. The selection of these techniques depends in part on areas such as functional impairment, problem complexity, subjective distress, and resistance. Specific strategies can be implemented that might involve changes in concrete behavior, patterns of interpersonal relationships, self-statements, or ways of experiencing the world. Cognitive or behavioral techniques might be most effective at this point, particularly stimulus control, graded exposure, cognitive restructuring, role plays, social skills training, or counterconditioning.

- *Maintenance Stage.* At this point, the therapist can become like a coach or a consultant who advises and encourages the client. A crucial consideration is how relapse is most likely to occur and to develop countermeasures to prevent these situations from occurring or at least to minimize their impact over a longer period. Specific techniques might include stimulus control, social contracting, enhancing social support, anger management, or a behavioral contract requiring the person to take preventive measures if relapse seems likely.

The preceding seven dimensions are intended to be logically consistent as well as manageable. The use of the model might be particularly crucial during training for new clinicians or skill enhancement of more experienced ones. With practice, it is likely that many of the features will become progressively more internalized, perhaps requiring less formal assessment. A briefer, more clinical assessment of the dimensions may also be required when short-term interventions (e.g., crisis intervention) are the only options available.

As further research provides more precise definitions of empirical relationships, additional dimensions will likely be included. There may also be further integration with both differential therapeutics and therapist-client matching. Each of these developments will bring clinicians closer to Paul's (1967) previously stated ultimate goal of combining the best treatment with the optimal mix of therapist, client, problem, and context.

RECOMMENDED READING

Beutler, L. E., & Groth-Marnat, G. (2003). *Integrative assessment of adult personality* (2nd ed.). New York: Guilford Press.

Beutler, L. E., & Harwood, T. M. (2000). *Prescriptive psychotherapy: A practical guide to systematic treatment selection*. New York: Oxford University Press.

Butcher, J. N., & Perry, J. N. (2008). *Personality assessment in treatment planning*. New York: Oxford University Press.

Groth-Marnat, G., Roberts, R., & Beutler, L. E. (2001). Client characteristics and psychotherapy: Perspectives, support, interactions, and implications. *Australian Psychologist, 36*, 115–121.

Jongsma, A. E., & Peterson, L. M. (2006). *The complete adult psychotherapy treatment planner* (4th ed.). Hoboken, NJ: John Wiley & Sons.

Norcross, J. (Ed.). (2002). *Psychotherapy relationships that work: Therapist contributions and responsiveness to patient's needs*. New York: Oxford University Press.

Prochaska, J. O., & DiClemente, C. C. (2005). *The transtheoretical approach*. In J. C. Norcross & M. R. Goldfried (Eds.), *Handbook of psychotherapy integration* (pp. 147–171). (2nd ed.) (pp. 300–334). New York: Oxford University Press.

Chapter 15 ———————————————

PSYCHOLOGICAL REPORT

The psychological report is the end product of assessment. It represents the clinician's efforts to integrate the assessment data into a functional whole so that the information can help the client solve problems and make decisions. Even the best tests are useless unless the data from them is explained in a manner that is relevant and clear, and meets the needs of the client and referral source. Doing this requires clinicians to give not merely test results but also to interact with their data in a way that makes their conclusions useful in answering the referral question, making decisions, and helping to solve problems.

An evaluation can be written in several possible ways. The manner of presentation used depends on the purpose for which the report is intended as well as on the individual style and orientation of the practitioner. The format provided in this chapter is merely a suggested outline that follows common and traditional guidelines. It includes methods for elaborating on essential areas such as the referral question, behavioral observations, relevant history, impressions (interpretations), and recommendations. This format is especially appropriate for evaluations that are problem oriented and that offer specific prescriptions for change. Additional alternatives for organizing the report are to use a letter format, give only the summary and recommendations, focus on a specific problem, summarize the results test by test, write directly to the client, or provide client descriptions around a particular theory of personality. The sample evaluations vary somewhat from the suggested format, although they usually still include the essential categories of information that are discussed in this chapter.

One general style to avoid is sometimes referred to as a shotgun report (Tallent, 1992, 1993). A "shotgun" report provides a wide variety of often-fragmented descriptions in the hope that some useful information can be found within. The shotgun approach is usually vague, stereotyped, and overinclusive. The recommendations for treatment are often neither specific nor practical. The most frequent reason for a shotgun report is a referral question that is too general, vague, and, therefore, poorly understood. In contrast, the "case-focused" report centers on the specific problems outlined by the referring person. It reveals unique aspects of the client and provides specific accurate descriptions rather than portraying stereotypes that may also be overly "theory linked" or "test linked." Furthermore, the recommendations for treatment are both specific and practical. The general approach of the case-focused report is not so much *what* is to be known but rather *why* different types of information are important for the purposes of the report.

The creation of a case-focused report involves understanding and applying several basic principles. First, the report should be integrated rather than organized around disparate portions of test data. In other words, the clinician should describe a person rather than merely reporting test data. Guidelines on how this can be best accomplished will be provided throughout the chapter. Second, the recommendations in a case-focused report need to directly relate to what specifically can be done for this client in his or her particular environment. They may apply to areas such as occupational choice, psychotherapy, institutional programs, or additional evaluation. In certain types of referrals, however, especially clients self-referred for psychotherapy, an important goal may be to help them increase their level of personal insight. In these cases, a wider description of the client that includes a number of different topics might be more appropriate than the narrower, problem-solving approach. In addition, there should be a focus on that which differentiates one person from another. Making these differentiations means avoiding discussions of what is average about the client and emphasizing instead what stands out and is unique to this individual. Case-focused reports also frequently deemphasize diagnosis and etiology. There is, rather, a focus on current descriptions of the person that are tied to specific behaviors. In certain cases, especially in a medical setting, the clinician may still need to provide diagnoses in addition to behaviorally oriented descriptions. Another consideration is that a case-focused report should be written with an awareness of the point of view of the intended readers. Appreciating the readers' perspective includes taking into consideration their level of expertise, their theoretical or professional orientation, the decisions they are facing, and the possible interpretations they are likely to make of the information.

[handwritten margin note: this implies multiple possible interpretations]

A final point is that the quality and usefulness of a report is typically enhanced if the practitioner is knowledgeable about the area or type of issue the client is experiencing. Such knowledge helps to increase the depth of the interpretations and provides relevant information or a general map of the problem area that can be used to help ensure that all relevant aspects have been covered. Importantly, background knowledge on the problem area provides relevant information on a range of interventions as well as the effectiveness of these interventions. For example, knowledge regarding depression means that the practitioner is aware of its causes, variety of ways in which it is expressed, options for interventions, and when further assessment is indicated (for suicide potential). Often consulting a well-written, up-to-date chapter will provide sufficient information. In the general clinical area, useful resources are the *Clinical Handbook of Psychological Disorders* (Barlow, 2001), *Clinician's Handbook of Evidence-Based Practice Guidelines* (Fisher & O'Donahue, 2006), or *Pocket Handbook to Clinical Psychiatry* (Kaplan & Saddock, 2005). Persons doing cognitive evaluations might consult *Neuropsychological Assessment in Clinical Practice: A Guide to Test Interpretation and Integration* (Groth-Marnat, 2000a), *Neuropsychological Assessment* (Lezak, 2004), or *Clinical Neuropsychology: A Pocket Handbook for Assessment* (Snyder & Nussbaum, 2005). Educational report writers might benefit from reading relevant sections in *Assessment of Children* (Sattler & Hoge, 2006; Sattler, 2008) or *Handbook of Clinical Child Psychology* (Walker & Roberts, 2001). A useful resource when doing vocational assessments is *The Essentials of Career Assesssment* (Prince & Heiser, 2000).

GENERAL GUIDELINES

Length

The typical psychological report is between 5 and 7 single-spaced pages (Groth-Marnat & Horvath, 2006). However, the length can vary substantially based on the purpose of the report, context, and expectations of the referral source. In medical contexts, a 2-page report is not uncommon. This parallels the format of many physician reports that are a similar length. In contrast, legal contexts often require reports that are from 7 to 10 pages because of the greater need for documentation combined with more extensive referral questions. It is not unusual for a psychologist serving as an expert witness to not only evaluate a client, but also anticipate and defend him- or herself against rebuttals as well as comment on reports made by other mental health professionals. The more moderate (and frequent) 5- to 7-page report is particularly prevalent in psychological, educational, and vocational contexts. Although this length is fairly typical in clinical practice, one of the most frequent complaints related to psychological reports is that they are too long (Brenner, 2003).

Style

The style or "flavor" of a report is influenced primarily by the training and orientation of the examiner. The clinician can choose from four general report-writing approaches: literary, clinical, scientific, and professional (Ownby, 1997; Tallent, 1992, 1993). Each style has unique strengths, and all have a number of liabilities. The literary approach uses everyday language and is creative and often dramatic. Although it can effectively capture a reader's attention and provide colorful descriptions, it is often imprecise and prone to exaggeration.

The clinical approach focuses on the pathological dimensions of a person. It describes the client's abnormal features, defenses, dynamics involved in maladjustment, and typical reactions to stress. The strength of the clinical approach is that it provides information about areas in need of change and alerts a potential practitioner to likely difficulties during the course of treatment. However, such a report tends to be one-sided in that it may omit important strengths of the person. The result is likely to be more a description of a "patient" than a person. Such a maladjustment bias is a frequent difficulty in clinical psychology and results in a distorted, unrealistic view of the client. Although most clinical reports should describe a person's problem areas, these problem areas should be given appropriate emphasis in the context of the client's relevant strengths and resources.

The scientific approach to report writing emphasizes normative comparisons, tends to be more academic, and, to a lesser extent, relates to the nature of a client's pathology. The scientific style differs from the other two approaches discussed chiefly in its reference to concepts, theories, and data. It looks at and describes test findings in an objective, factual manner. Thus, there might be frequent references to test data, normative comparisons, probability statements, and cutoff scores to be used for decision making. A scientific approach is likely to discuss the person by addressing different, often isolated, segments of personality. Thus, areas such as a client's cognitive, perceptual, and motivational abilities may be described as discrete and often unrelated functions. Although the scientific approach is objective and factual, it has been criticized for violating the unity of personality. Many readers, particularly those from other disciplines, do not respect or empathize with scientific evaluations and perceive them as cold, distant, and overly objective. Purely data-oriented evaluations can potentially do the profession a disservice by reinforcing the view that an assessment is like a laboratory test rather than a professional consultation with a clinician. Furthermore, a focus on factual data may not address the practical decisions the client and referral source are facing.

In actual practice, it is unusual to find a pure example of a literary, clinical, or scientific report. Clinicians generally draw from all three approaches but typically emphasize one. An important part of effective report writing is the ability to evaluate the assets and limitations of each style and to maintain a flexible orientation toward appropriately combining them. In any one report, there may be a need to use creative literary descriptions, elaborate on different pathological dimensions, or provide necessary scientific information. Again, the key is to avoid the pitfalls associated with specializing in any one of these styles and to emphasize instead their relative strengths.

Ownby (1997) stresses that the most important style to use in report writing is what he refers to as a *professional style*. This style is characterized by short words that are in common usage and that have precise meanings. Grammatically, writers should use a variety of sentence constructions and lengths to maintain the reader's interest. The paragraphs should be short and should focus on a single concept. Similar concepts should be located close to one another in the report. Whereas Hollis and Donna (1979) urge writers to use short words, short sentences, and short paragraphs, the *Publication Manual of the American Psychological Association* (5th ed., 2001) recommends varying the lengths of sentences and paragraphs. The result should be a report that combines accuracy, clarity, integration, and readability.

Presenting Test Interpretations

Reports should organize the information around specific referral questions. The result will be a report that is highly focused, well integrated, and avoids any extraneous material. For example, if a referral source asks whether person X is brain-damaged, the interpretations based on the test data are directed toward answering whether this hypothesis is supported.

The interpretations should be organized around specific domains, such as coping style, memory, personality, or interpersonal relations. This approach is comprehensive, indicates the client's strengths and weaknesses, and typically gives the reader a good feel for the person as a whole. The referral question is still answered but is addressed by responding to specific domains relating to the referral question. Readers tend to prefer and better comprehend integrated reports written by addressing functional domains rather than test scores. The weakness of domain-oriented reports lies in the potential to provide too much information, thus overloading the reader.

Some reports present the results test by test, one at a time (WAIS-IV, Bender, MMPI-2, etc.). This approach clarifies the source of the data and enables the reader to understand more clearly how the clinician made his or her inferences. It is also relatively easy for the examiner to organize the results. These advantages are offset by significant disadvantages. The emphasis on tests can distract the reader and tends to reduce the client from a person to a series of test numbers. Readers of reports, regardless of their theoretical or disciplinary background, do not respond well to this style of report writing (Mendoza, 2001; Tallent 1992, 1993). A test-by-test presentation also reflects a failure to integrate the data. A test-by-test format may be a particular issue because it is not uncommon for inconsistencies to occur among different test scores. Often only half of all possible interpretations listed in an interpretive manual or computer narrative are actually true for a particular client. It is up to the clinician to determine which of these do or do not apply for the person. Sometimes a report writer using a test-by-test approach hedges his or her "interpretations" by using a phrase such as "Other persons with similar test profiles have the following qualities." The referral source, however, does not want to know about *other* people but is concerned with *this* client, at this time, living in a certain context. A test-by-test interpretation, then, suggests that the practitioner has neither adequately conceptualized relevant dynamics nor fully understood the area under investigation (Mendoza, 2001; Wolber & Carne, 1993). It also encourages the belief that an examiner is a technician who merely administers tests rather than a clinician who uses multiple sources of information to answer referral questions and help people solve problems they are facing. The existing literature is unanimous in discouraging a test-by-test style and, instead, strongly recommends an integrated, case-focused, problem-solving style (Beutler & Groth-Marnat, 2003; Groth-Marnat, 2003; Groth-Marnat & Horvath, 2006; Kvaal, Choca, & Groth-Marnat, 2003; Mendoza, 2001; Michaels, 2007; Sattler & Hoge, 2006; Sattler, 2008; Tallent, 1992, 1993; Wolber & Carne, 1993; Zuckerman, 2005).

Topics

There is an extremely wide range of topics or domains that clinicians may decide to discuss in their reports. These topics serve as conceptual tools that enable report writers to give form and direction to the information they are trying to communicate. The three most common topics are likely to be related to cognitive functioning, emotional functioning (affect/mood), and interpersonal relations. Many reports can be adequately organized around these three domains. Additional topics include personal strengths, vocational aptitudes, suicidal potential, defenses, areas of conflict, behavior under stress, impulsiveness, or sexuality. Often an adequate case-focused report can be developed by describing just a few of these topics. For example, a highly focused report may elaborate on one or two significant areas of functioning, whereas a more general evaluation may discuss seven or eight relevant topics. Table 15.1 is a representative list of topics that may be considered

Table 15.1. Examples of general topics around which a case presentation may be conceptualized

Achievement	Drives, dynamics	Personal consequences of
Affect	Emotional controls	behavior
Aggressiveness	Emotional functioning	Placement prospects
Antisocial tendencies	Fixations	Problem complexity
Anxieties	Flexibility	Psychopathology
Aptitudes	Frustrations	Rehabilitation needs
Attitudes	Functional impairment	Rehabilitation prospects
Aversions	Goals	Resistance
Awareness	Hostility	Sentiments
Behavioral problems	Identity	Sex
Biological risk factors	Intellectual controls	Sex identity
Cognitive functioning	Intellectual levels	Sex role
Cognitive skills	Interests	Significant others
Cognitive style	Interpersonal relations	Situational factors
Competency	Interpersonal skills	Social consequences of
Conflicts	Irrational cognitions	behavior
Content of consciousness	Lifestyle	Social role
Coping style	Mood	Social structure
Defenses	Needs	Social support
Deficits	Outlook	Special assets
Developmental factors	Perception of environment	Strengths
Diagnostic considerations	Perception of self	Subjective feeling states

Source: Adapted from *Psychological Report Writing* (3rd ed., p.120) by N. Tallent, 1988, Englewood Cliffs, NJ: Prentice Hall.

for inclusion in an evaluation. This list is by no means complete but can provide a general guide for the wide range of possible topics from which a report writer can choose.

Deciding What to Include

The general purpose of a psychological evaluation is to provide information that will be most helpful in responding to the referral question and meeting the needs of the client. In this context, the clinician must strike a balance between providing too much information and providing too little, and between being too cold and being too dramatic. As a rule, information should be included only if it serves to address the referral question and increase understanding of the client. For example, descriptions of a client's appearance should be oriented toward areas such as his or her level of anxiety or resistance. A client might be described as hesitant in his or her approach to tasks and as saying something like "Why do I have to take all these tests anyway?" If the person was dressed in bizarre clothes and his or her hair was unkempt or dyed purple, this information might also be quite important to include. Generally, however, information regarding the types of clothing the person is wearing or color of his or her eyes or hair is not relevant.

The basic guidelines for deciding what to include in a report relate to the needs of the referral setting, background of the readers, purpose of testing, relative usefulness of the information, and whether the information describes unique characteristics of the person. After these general guidelines have been considered, the next step is to focus on and organize the information derived from the tests. For example, if a general review of aspects of personality is the purpose of the report, a clinician can look at each test to determine what information it can provide.

A further general rule is that information should focus on the client's unique method of psychological functioning. A reader is concerned not so much with how the client is similar to the average person as in what ways he or she is different. A common error in psychological reports is the inclusion of generalized statements that are so vague, they could apply to the majority of the population. These vague, generalized statements are likely to be unconditionally accepted as applying to a person even though they are randomly selected. For example, Sundberg (1955) administered a "personality" test to a group of students and gave them all identical "interpretations" based on universal or stereotyped personality descriptions composed of 13 statements, such as:

- You have a great need for other people to like and admire you.
- You have a tendency to be critical of yourself.
- You have a great deal of unused capacity you have not turned to your advantage.
- While you have some personality weaknesses, you are generally able to compensate for them.
- At times, you have serious doubts as to whether you have made the right decision or done the right thing.

Virtually all students used in the study reported that the evaluation statements were accurate descriptions of themselves. Other studies suggest that not only were students unable to discriminate between fictitious and genuine feedback, but they may even have preferred generalized fictitious results, particularly if they were framed within a positive context (Dies, 1972). This uncritical acceptance of test interpretations might be even further encouraged when objective-appearing, computer-generated interpretations are used (Groth-Marnat & Schumaker, 1989). W. Klopfer (1960) has referred to this uncritical acceptance of universally valid statements as the "Barnum effect," in reference to Phineas T. Barnum's saying, "There is a fool born every minute." Although "universal statements" may add to the "subjective" validity of the report when read by the client, such statements should be avoided in favor of stressing the person's essential uniqueness.

After the data, conclusions, and recommendations have been outlined, the next step is to decide on the manner in which to present them. Doing this involves clear communication about the relative degree of emphasis of the results, type of report, proper use of terminology, and the extent to which the raw data will be discussed.

Emphasis

Careful consideration should be given to the appropriate emphasis of conclusions, particularly when indicating the relative intensity of a client's behavior. General summaries may be given, such as "this client's level of depression is characteristic of inpatient populations," or the relative intensity of certain aspects of a client's disorder may be more specifically discussed. To continue with the example of depression, a clinician may discuss the client's cognitive self-criticisms, degree of slowed behavior, extent of social support, level of social skills, or suicidal potential. In addition to discussing and giving the appropriate degree of emphasis to a client's pathology, his or her psychological strengths need to be compared with his or her relative weaknesses. Furthermore, the report should not discuss areas of minor relevance unless they somehow relate to the purpose of the evaluation. To achieve proper emphasis, the examiner and the referral source must clarify and agree on the purpose of the evaluation. Only after this has been accomplished can the examiner decide whether certain information should be elaborated in depth, briefly mentioned, or deleted.

When clinicians present their conclusions, they should indicate their relative degree of certainty. Is a specific conclusion based on an objective fact, or is the clinician merely presenting a speculation? For example, the statement "John scored in the low average range of intelligence" is an objective fact. However, even in this case, examiners may want to give the standard error of measurement to provide an estimate of the probable range of scores. If only mild supporting data is available or if clinicians are presenting a speculation, phrases such as "it appears . . . ," "tends to . . . ," or "probably . . ." should be used. Doing this is especially important when clinicians are attempting to predict a person's behavior, because the predicted behavior has not yet been observed. It may be useful for clinicians to indicate that their predictions cannot be found directly in the tests themselves but rather represent inferences that have been made based on the test data. There should be a clear distinction between what the client did and what he or she anticipates doing. If a statement made in a report is a speculation, it should be clearly indicated that the statement has only a moderate or small degree of certainty. Whenever a speculation is included, it should be relevant to the referral question.

Improper emphasis can reflect an incorrect interpretation by the examiner, and this misinterpretation is then passed down to the reader. Clinicians sometimes arrive at incorrect conclusions because their personal bias results in selective perception of the data. Thus, clinicians can develop an overly narrow focus with which they overlook potentially relevant data. Personal bias may result from factors such as a restrictive theoretical orientation, incorrect subjective feelings regarding the client, or an overemphasis on pathology. Inaccurate conclusions can also result from attempts to please the referral source or from interpretations based on insufficient data. The reader may also be likely to misinterpret the conclusions if the report is generally overspeculative or if speculations are not specified as such but, rather, are disguised as assertions. Overly assertive speculations may not only lead the reader to develop incorrect conclusions; the report may become overly authoritative and dogmatic, perhaps leading readers to become irritated and skeptical.

Misinterpretations can also result from vague and ambiguously worded sentences that place incorrect or misleading emphasis on a client's behavior. A statement such as "the client lacks social skills" is technically incorrect because the client must have some social skills, although these skills may be inadequate. A more correct description would be to state that the client's social skills are "poorly developed" or "below average." Likewise, a statement such as "the client uses socially inappropriate behavior" is subject to myriad interpretations. It could be rephrased to include more behaviorally oriented descriptions, such as "frequently interrupts" or "would often pursue irrelevant tangents."

One technique of emphasizing results is to place the most relevant sections in boldface or italics. For example, the major identified symptoms, most important findings, and the major recommendations could all be placed in boldface. Doing this enables persons reading the report to more easily absorb the most salient features. In addition, they can easily relocate major points that have been made. However, this technique should be used sparingly because readers can become easily saturated with too much boldface print. Instead of placing entire paragraphs or sentences in boldface, only key phrases should be emphasized by this method.

The areas, extent, and method of emphasis significantly contribute to the conclusions of a report. However, responsibility for a report's conclusions rests on the clinician. This responsibility should not and cannot be transferred to the tests themselves. To take this a step further, decisions made about a person should never be in the hands of tests, which may even have questionable validity in certain contexts. Rather, conclusions and decisions regarding people should always be in the hands of responsible persons. Thus, the style of emphasizing results should reflect this. Phrases such as "test results indicate . . ." may give the impression that the examiner is trying to hide behind and transfer responsibility for his or her statements onto the tests. Not only is this not where the responsibility should be, but the reader may develop a lack of confidence in the clinician. If clinicians feel uncertain about a particular area, they should either be clear about this uncertainty or, if they cannot personally stand by the results, exclude the results from the report.

Use of Raw Data

When writing the impressions and interpretation section, a report writer should generally avoid adhering too closely to the raw data. For certain purposes, however, it may be useful to include raw data or even to describe the tests themselves. Test descriptions allow untrained persons to know specific behaviors the client engaged in rather than merely the final inferences. As a result, consumers of reports rate the inclusion of behavioral referents quite favorably (Finn et al., 2001). For example, a report may include a description such as "Mr. A had an average level of recall for short-term visual information, as indicated by his being able to accurately recall and reproduce five out of a possible nine geometric designs that he had previously worked with for five minutes." This sentence provides a more behaviorally referenced description than one like "Mr. A had an average level of recall as measured on the Bender memory." Yet another example might be to include a portion of a Thematic Apperception Test story (i.e., ". . . so he took the violin and, without even thinking about it, threw it into the fire and ran"). These and similar strategies are likely to give the reader a more in-depth, precise, and familiar reference regarding the subject's abilities and personality. However, actual test items should not be included due to copyright and test security restrictions.

It is crucial to stress that the purpose of providing raw data and behavioral descriptions is to enrich and illustrate the topic and not to enable the reader to follow the clinician's line of reasoning or document the inferences that have been made. In developing inferences, clinicians must draw on a wide variety of data. They cannot possibly discuss all the patterns, configurations, and relationships they used to come to their conclusions. Any attempt to do so would necessarily be overly detailed, cumbersome, and incomplete. Statements such as "In considering the pattern of elevated Scales 4 and 9 on the MMPI, it is safe to conclude…" are unnecessary and rarely contribute to a report's overall usefulness. In certain types of reports, such as those for legal purposes, it might be helpful to include some raw data, not so much to repeat the thinking process of the clinician but more to substantiate that the inferences are data based, to provide a point of reference for discussing the results, and to indicate what assessment procedures were used.

Terminology

Several arguments have been made in determining whether to use technical or nontechnical language in psychological reports. It might be argued that technical terminology is precise and economical, increases the credibility of the writer, and can communicate concepts that are impossible to convey through nontechnical language. However, a number of potential difficulties are often encountered with the use of technical language. One of the more frequent problems involves the varying backgrounds and levels of sophistication of the persons reading the report. The most frequent readers of reports include teachers, administrators, judges, attorneys, psychiatrists, nonpsychiatric physicians, and social workers. Increasingly, the clients themselves have access to and read the reports (Harvey, 1997, 2006). Thus, many, if not most, consumers of reports do not have the necessary background to interpret technical terminology accurately. Even psychologists with different theoretical persuasions may be apt to misinterpret some of the terms. Take, for example, the differing uses of *ego* by Freud, Jung, and Erikson. Also, the term *anxiety* might have several different categories of use. Although technical words can undoubtedly be precise, their precision is helpful only in a particular context and with a reader who has the proper background. Generally, reports are rated as more effective when the material is described in clear, basic language (Brenner, 2003; Finn et al., 2001; Harvey, 1997, 2006; Ownby, 1990, 1997; Sandy, 1986; Tallent, 1993). Even among readers who have the proper background to understand technical terms, many prefer a more straightforward presentation (Ownby, 1990, 1997; Tallent, 1992, 1993). Technical terms also run the danger of becoming nominalisms in which, by merely naming the phenomenon, persons develop an illusory sense of understanding more than is actually the case. Terms such as *immature* or *sadistic* cover a great deal of information because they are so general, but they say nothing about what the person is like when he or she is behaving in these maladaptive ways. They also do not adequately differentiate one person from the next and are frequently ambiguous. Furthermore, technical terms are often used inappropriately (e.g., a person who is sensitive and cautious in interpersonal relationships is labeled *paranoid*, or *compulsive* is used to describe someone who is merely careful, conscientious, and effective in dealing with details).

W. Klopfer (1960) provides an excellent and still-relevant rationale for using basic English rather than technical terminology. First, and perhaps most important, the use of basic English allows the examiner, through his or her report, to communicate with and affect a wide audience. This ability is particularly important because the number and variety of persons who read reports is much greater now than 20 or 30 years ago. Furthermore, basic English is more specific and descriptive of an individual's uniqueness, whereas technical terms tend to deal with generalities. Terms such as *sadomasochistic* and *hostile* do not provide essential information about whether the person is assaultive or suicidal. Finally, the use of basic English generally indicates that the examiner has more in-depth comprehension of the information he or she is dealing with and can communicate this comprehension in a precise, concrete manner. Klopfer stresses that any description found in a psychological report should be comprehensible to any literate person of at least average intelligence. In contrast, psychologists have been found to write in a more technical and complex level when compared with the average client (Harvey, 1997, 2006). The first four of the next examples show how to translate technical concepts into basic English (Klopfer, 1960):

> "Hostility toward the father figure" becomes "the patient is so fearful and suspicious of people in positions of authority that he automatically assumes an aggressive attitude toward them, being sure that swift retaliations will follow. He doesn't give such people an opportunity to demonstrate their real characteristics since he assumes they are all alike."
>
> "The patient projects extensively" becomes "the patient has a tendency to attribute to other people feelings and ideas originating within himself regardless of how these other people might feel."
>
> "The defenses the patient uses are. . ." becomes "the methods characteristically employed by the patient for reducing anxiety are. . ."
>
> "Empathy" becomes "the patient can understand and sympathize with the feelings of others, since she finds it relatively easy to put herself in their place." (pp. 58–60)
>
> "The client is hostile and resistant" may be changed to include a behavioral description; "when the client entered the room she stated, 'My dad said I had to come and that's the only reason I'm here'" or "later on in the testing she made several comments such as 'This is a stupid question.'"

The general principle involved in the preceding examples is to translate high-level abstract terms into basic English that provides useful, concrete behavioral descriptions.

Ownby (1990, 1997) recommends combining any conclusion or generalization with specific behaviors or test observations. Recommendations should also be directly linked with the relevant behaviors/generalizations, either in the same place or in the recommendations section. For example, instead of saying a client is "depressed," a writer might state, "The client's behavior, which included self-criticism and occasional crying, suggested he was depressed." Linking generalizations with clear concrete descriptions tends to create reports that are perceived to be relatively credible and persuasive (Ownby, 1990, 1997). If this process is followed, descriptions will be less subject to misinterpretation, less ambiguous, and more likely to convey the unique characteristics of the client. Although abstract technical terms can at times be important components of a psychological report, they should be used sparingly and only when clearly appropriate. An essential aspect of whether or not to include technical information means carefully considering the background of the persons who will read the report. Some authors even recommend collaborating with the relevant recipients of the report, including the client, so that the final report is descriptive rather than interpretive and the readers are not passive recipients of the "higher" wisdom of the psychologist (Fisher, 1985; Sandy, 1986).

Content Overload

There are no specific rules to follow in determining how much information to include in a report. A general guideline is to estimate how much information a reader can realistically be expected to assimilate. If too many details are given, the information may begin to become poorly defined and vague and, therefore, lack impact or usefulness. When clinicians are confronted with a great variety of data from which to choose, they should not attempt to include it all. A statement such as "The client's relative strengths are in abstract reasoning, general fund of knowledge, short-term memory, attention span, and mathematical computation" is likely to overload the reader with too many details. The clinician should instead adequately develop each of the various points and focus on the areas that are most relevant to the purpose of the report.

Feedback

During the earlier days of psychological assessment, examiners often kept the results of psychological assessments carefully concealed from the client. There was often an underlying belief that the results were too complex and mysterious for the client to understand adequately. In contrast, current practices are to provide the client with clear, direct, and accurate feedback regarding the results of an evaluation (S. Ackerman, Hilsenroth, Baity, & Blagys, 2000; Finn, 2007; Finn & Tonsager, 1997; Lewak & Hogan, 2003; K. Pope, 1992).

The change toward providing feedback to clients has been motivated by several factors. First, regulations have supported a growing list of consumer rights, including the right to various types of information. Second, it might be perceived as a violation if the client did not receive feedback regarding the results of testing after he or she had been subjected to several hours of assessment. Even the most secure of clients might easily feel uncomfortable knowing a report with highly personal information might be circulated and used by persons in power to make decisions about his or her future. Such practices could understandably result in suspicion and irritation on the part of the public. Third, examiners cannot safely assume that the original referral source will provide feedback to the client. Even if the referral source does provide feedback, there is no guarantee that the information will be provided in an appropriate manner. Thus, the responsibility for providing feedback is ultimately on the clinician. Finally, there is increasing evidence that providing clients with test feedback can result in significant therapeutic benefits (S. Ackerman et al., 2000; Finn, 2007; Finn & Tonsager, 1992; Gass & Brown, 1992).

The extent to which a clinician providing feedback will allow the client to actually read all or portions of the report varies. The rationale for allowing the client actually to read the report is that doing so enables the client to experience the product of assessment in a direct manner. It also enables a practitioner to explain any areas that are unclear. A significant difficulty is that the client might misinterpret various portions of the report, especially IQ scores and diagnosis. For this reason, most clinicians paraphrase and elaborate on selected portions of the report. This method increases the likelihood that clients will readily understand the most important material and will not be overloaded with too much content.

The likelihood of providing effective feedback can be enhanced by following several guidelines. Initially, the rationale for assessments should be explained and any misconceptions should be corrected. One particularly important misconception is that sometimes clients mistakenly fear that the purpose of assessment is to evaluate their sanity. Practitioners must also select the most essential information to be conveyed to the client. To a large extent, doing this involves clinical judgment. Important considerations include the client's ego strength, life situation, stability, and receptiveness to different types of material. Typically, three to four general and well-developed areas represent an optimum amount of information. The information that is provided should be carefully integrated into the overall context of the person's life. This integration might be enhanced by providing concrete behavioral examples, reflecting on aspects of the client's behavior, referring to relevant aspects of the client's history, or paraphrasing and expanding on a client's self-descriptions. A useful technique is to have the client evaluate the relevance and accuracy of the information. The client might also be asked to give his or her own examples of the trait or pattern of behavior described in the report. Such collaboration with the client helps the clinician to determine how well the client has understood the feedback. Underlying any feedback should be an attempt to provide the information in a clear, intelligible manner. Commonplace language should be used instead of psychological jargon. It is also important to take into account the client's level of intelligence, education, vocabulary, and level of psychological sophistication. Feedback should be not only a neutral conveyance of data but also a clinical intervention. The information should provide the client with new perspectives and options and should aid in the client's own problem solving.

One possibility is to prepare a personalized report designed specifically for the client. Doing this forces the practitioner to write in a clear, straightforward style. Such reports are more likely to emphasize adaptation rather than pathology. In addition, clear recommendations tend to be emphasized. The optimal communication style is an informal letter written to and for the client ("I am writing to communicate the findings of our psychological assessment."). There are currently available a number of computerized reports directed toward providing the client with feedback. There also seems to be a trend for additional resources to include interpretations directed toward the client, such as Lewak, Marks, and Nelson's (1990) *Therapist Guide to the MMPI & MMPI-2: Providing Feedback and Treatments,* and Finn's (2007) *In Our Client's Shoes: Theory and Techniques of Therapeutic Assessment.* These sources should not be seen as substitutes for a dynamic interaction with a client but as adjuncts for enhancing this process.

FORMAT FOR A PSYCHOLOGICAL REPORT

Although no single, agreed-on format exists, every report should integrate old information as well as provide a new and unique perspective on the person. Old information should include identifying information (name, birth date, etc.), reason for referral, and relevant history. New information should include assessment results, impressions, summary/conclusions, and recommendations. At the top of the report, practitioners should indicate its confidential nature by writing "Confidential Psychological Evaluation." A suggested outline follows.

Name:

Age (date of birth):

Sex:

Ethnicity:

Date of Report:

Name of Examiner:

Referred by:

    I.   Referral Question

   II.   Evaluation Procedures

  III.   Behavioral Observations

  IV.   Background Information (relevant history)

   V.   Test Results

  VI.   Impressions and Interpretations

 VII.   Summary and Recommendations

Although this outline represents a frequently encountered format, there are many variations. Some practitioners prefer to include the client's marital status, occupational status, and handedness (for neuropsychological reports) at the top of the report along with the other demographic information. Other practitioners prefer to exclude the test results section or include additional sections on diagnosis, case formulation, or summary. Sometimes it might be more appropriate to write the report directly to the referral source in a letter format ("Dear Dr. Jones:"). The sample reports included later in this chapter have been chosen to demonstrate a variety of different formats in diverse styles and contexts. Each practitioner needs to develop both the format and style that most effectively meet his or her client's and referral source's needs. In addition, different assessment contexts require different styles and areas of focus.

Referral Question

The Referral Question section provides a brief description of the client and a statement of the general reason for conducting the evaluation. In particular, this section should include a brief description of the nature of the problem. If this section is adequately completed, it should give an initial focus to the report by orienting the reader to what follows and to the types of issues that are addressed. This section should begin with a brief, orienting sentence that includes essential information about the client ("Mr. Smith is a 35-year-old, European American, married male with a high school education who presents with complaints of depression and anxiety"). Such a sentence clearly and succinctly introduces the client. A prerequisite for this section is that the clinician has developed an adequate clarification of the referral question. The purpose of testing should be stated in a precise and problem-oriented manner. Thus, phrases such as "the client was referred for a psychological evaluation" or "as a requirement for a class project" are inadequate because they lack focus and precision. It is helpful to include both the specific purpose of the evaluation and the decisions facing the referral source.

Examples of possible reasons for referral include:

- Intellectual evaluation: routine, intellectually disabled (retarded), gifted.
- Differential diagnosis, such as the relative presence of psychological difficulties (i.e., memory problems caused by depression) versus organic impairment (i.e., memory problems because of the early stages of Alzheimer's disease).
- Assessment of the nature and extent of brain damage.
- Evaluation as a component of, and to provide recommendations for, vocational counseling.
- Evaluation of appropriateness for, possible difficulties encountered in, and optimal approach to, psychotherapy.
- Personal insight regarding difficulties with interpersonal relationships.
- Evaluation as an aid in client placement.

These reasons represent general referral questions that, in actual situations, would require further clarification, especially regarding the decisions facing the referral source (see Armengol, 2001). The key should be to find out what the referring person really wants from the report. Doing this may require reading beneath the surface of the referral question(s) and articulating possible hidden agendas and placing the referral question into a wider context than the presenting problem. In some cases, it may be necessary to educate the referral source regarding the strengths as well as the limitations of psychological testing, which may even lead to recommending that the person not be tested. An effective referral question should accurately describe the client's and the referral source's current problems.

After the referral questions have been clarified and outlined, they can be addressed throughout the rest of the report. It is usually helpful to succinctly reiterate and summarize the answers to the referral questions toward the end of the report. A useful strategy is to number each of the referral questions listed in the Referral Question section and then follow this up with succinct answers to each of these questions in the Summary and Recommendations section. The numbers of the questions and corresponding answers to the questions should ideally correspond with each other. Such a procedure is user friendly, provides clear answers to the questions, and allows for symmetry and closure to the report.

Evaluation Procedures

The report section that deals with evaluation procedures simply lists the tests and other evaluation procedures used but does not include the actual test results. Usually full test names are included along with their abbreviations. Later in the report, the abbreviations can be used, but the initial inclusion of the entire name provides a reference for readers who may not be familiar with test abbreviations. For legal evaluations or other occasions in which precise details of administration are essential, it is important to include the date on which different tests were administered and the length of time required to complete each one. For most routine evaluations, however, this degree of detail is not recommended. It may also be important to include whether a clinical interview or mental status examination was given and, if so, the degree of interview structure and the amount of time required for the interview or examination. Evaluation procedures may not necessarily be restricted to testing and interviews with the client. Often evaluation includes a review of relevant records, such as medical reports, nursing notes, military records, police records, previous psychological or psychiatric reports, or educational records. Additional material might come from interviews with individuals such as spouses, children, parents, friends, employers, physicians, lawyers, social workers, or teachers. If any of these sources are used, their dates and, if relevant, who wrote them should be included. This section might end with a statement summarizing the total time required for the evaluation.

Behavioral Observations

A description of the client's behaviors can provide insight into his or her problem and may be a significant source of data to confirm, modify, or question the test-related interpretations. These observations can be related to a client's appearance, general behavioral observations, or examiner-client interaction. Descriptions should generally be tied to specific behaviors and should not represent a clinician's inferences. For example, instead of making the inference that the client was "depressed," it is preferable to state that "her speech was slow and she frequently made self-critical statements such as 'I'm not smart enough to get that one right.'"

Relevant behavioral observations made during the interview include physical appearance, behavior toward the task and examiner, and degree of cooperativeness. A description of the client's physical appearance should focus on any unusual features relating to facial expressions, clothes, body type, mannerisms, and movements. It is especially important to note any contradictions, such as a 14-year-old boy who acts more like an 18-year-old or a person who appears dirty and disheveled but has an excellent vocabulary and high level of verbal fluency. The behaviors the client expresses toward the test material and the examiner often provide a significant source of information. These may include behaviors that reflect the person's level of affect, manifest anxiety, presence of depression, or degree of hostility. The client's role may be as an active participant or generally passive and submissive; he or she may be very much concerned with his or her performance or relatively indifferent. The client's method of problem solving is often a crucial area to note, and it may range from careful and methodical to impulsive and disorganized. It is also important to pay attention to any unusual verbalizations that the client makes about the test material. The level of cooperation expressed by the client should be a factor in assessing the validity of the test results. Level of cooperation is especially important for intelligence and ability tests, because a prerequisite is that the client be alert and attentive, and put forth his or her best effort. It may also be important to note events before testing, such as situational crises, previous night's sleep, or use of medication. If there are situational factors that may modify or bring into question the test's validity, they should be noted with statements such as "The test results should be viewed with caution because. . ." or "The degree of maladjustment indicated on the test scores may represent an exaggeration of the client's usual level of functioning due to conditions surrounding the test administration." Often the most important way to determine test validity in relationship to the client is through a careful look at the client's behaviors relating to the tests and his or her life situation before testing.

Behavioral observations usually should be kept concise, specific, and relevant. If a description does not allow for some insight about the person or demonstrate his or her uniqueness, it should not be included. Thus, if a behavior is normal or average, it is usually not important to discuss other than to briefly mention that the person had, for example, an average level of cooperation, alertness, or anxiety. The focus, then, should be on those client behaviors that create a unique impression. This section usually should not exceed one paragraph. However, in some instances, there may be considerable relevant information that would require two or three paragraphs. The relative importance of this section in relation to the overall report can be quite varied. Sometimes behavioral observations can be almost as important as the test results; at other times, the description might consist of a few minor observations.

Clinicians who prefer behavioral assessment procedures might wish to emphasize the Behavioral Observation section by providing more in-depth descriptions of relevant antecedents. In addition, consequent events surrounding the problem behavior itself might be evaluated in relationship to their onset, duration, frequency, and intensity. Specific strategies of behavioral assessment include narrative descriptions, interval recording, event recording, ratings recordings, and self-report inventories (see Chapter 4).

Some examiners may wish to summarize information from a Mental Status Examination in the Behavioral Observations section. In these cases, there is necessarily a movement away from concrete descriptions of behaviors to inferences about these behaviors. For example, a clinician may infer, based on behavioral observations, that the client was oriented to time and place. Additional categories might include verbalizations, psychomotor activity, affect, thought processes/contents, and insight/judgment (see section on the Mental Status Examination in Chapter 3).

Another exception to adhering closely to concrete behavioral descriptions is that, at the end of the Behavioral Observations section, it is customary and appropriate to include a statement indicating the validity of the assessment procedures. For example, it might state something like: "Given the consistency and detail of the client's responses, the client's high level of motivation, and validity indicators on the MMPI-2, the assessment appears to be an accurate assessment of this person's current level of functioning."

Background Information (also Referred to as Relevant History)

The write-up of a client's background information should include aspects of the person's history that are relevant to the problem the person is confronting and to the interpretation of the test results. The history, along with the referral question, should also place the problem and the test results into the proper context. In accomplishing these goals, the clinician does not need to include a long, involved chronology with a large number of details but rather should be as succinct as possible. Some practitioners even urge that the background information section be kept to one concise paragraph, particularly in medical settings, where there is considerable emphasis on conciseness. In selecting which areas to include and which to exclude, a clinician must continually evaluate these areas in relationship to the overall purpose of the report. It is difficult to specify precise rules because each individual is different. Furthermore, each clinician's own personal and theoretical orientation alters the types of information he or she feels are significant. Whereas one clinician may primarily describe interpersonal relationships, another may focus on intrapsychic variables, birth order, early childhood events, or details about the client's current situation and environment. The key is to maintain a flexible orientation so that the interviewer is aware of the most significant elements in the client's life. In general, the end product should include a good history of the problem along with areas such as important life events, family dynamics, work history, personal interests, daily activities, and past and present interpersonal relationships (see Table 3.1 in Chapter 3).

When describing a client's background, it is important to specify where the information came from ("The client reported that. . ."). This is particularly essential when there may be some question regarding the truth of the client's self-reports or when the history has been obtained from multiple sources.

Usually a history begins with a brief summary of the client's general background. This can be followed by sections describing family background, personal history, medical history, history of the problem, and current life situation.

The extent to which a clinician decides to pursue and discuss a client's family background is subject to a great degree of variability. The primary purpose of such information is to help determine causal factors, what variables might help maintain relevant behaviors, and the extent to which the family should be used as either a focus of systemic intervention or as social support. At a minimum, a brief description of the client's parents is warranted; this description may include whether they are separated/divorced and alive/deceased, and their socioeconomic level, occupation, cultural background, and health status. Sometimes it is important to include information about the emotional and medical backgrounds of parents and close relatives, because certain disorders occur with greater frequency in some families than in the overall population. A description of the general atmosphere of the family is often helpful, including the client's characteristic feelings toward family members and perceptions of their relationships with each other. Descriptions of common family activities and whether the family lived in an urban or a rural environment might also be included. If one or both parents died while the client was young, the clinician can still discuss the speculations the client has about his or her parent(s) and can describe the significant persons for the client as he or she was growing up.

The client's personal history can include information from infancy, early childhood, adolescence, and adulthood. Each stage has typical areas to investigate and problems to be aware of. The information from infancy usually either represents vague recollections or is secondhand information derived from parents or relatives. Thus, it may be subject to a great deal of exaggeration and fabrication. If possible, it may be helpful to have details verified by additional sources, such as through direct questioning of parents or examination of medical records. The degree of contact with parents, family atmosphere, and developmental milestones may all be important areas to discuss. Often it is important to include a client's early medical history since physical and psychological difficulties can be closely linked. The most significant tasks during childhood are the development of peer relationships and adjustment to school. What was the quality of the client's early friendships? How much time did the client spend with others? Were there any fights or rebellious acting out? Was the client basically a loner, or did he or she have a large number of friends? Did the person join clubs and have group activities, hobbies, or extracurricular interests? In the academic area, it may be of interest to note the usual grades, best or worst subjects, and whether the client skipped or repeated grades. Furthermore, what was his or her relationship with parents, and did the parents restrict activities or allow relative freedom? During adolescent years, clients typically face further academic, psychological, and social adjustments to high school. Of particular importance are their reactions to puberty and early heterosexual relationships. Did they have difficulties with sex role identity, abuse drugs or alcohol, or rebel against authority figures? The adult years center around occupational adjustment and establishing marital and family relationships. During early adulthood, what were clients' feelings and aspirations regarding marriage? What were their career goals? Did they effectively establish independence from parents? As adulthood progressed, were there any significant changes in the quality of their close relationships, employment, or expression of sexuality? What activities did they engage in during their leisure time? As clients age, they face challenges in adapting to their declining abilities and limitations, and developing a meaningful view of their lives.

Although the personal history can help place the problem in its proper context and explain certain causative factors, it is usually essential to spend some time focusing directly on the problem itself. Of particular importance are the initial onset and the nature of the symptoms. From the time the client first noticed these symptoms, have there been any changes in frequency, intensity, or expression? If a formal diagnosis will be made, it is particularly important to have a clear description of symptom patterns to substantiate such a diagnosis. It might also be important to determine whether there were any previous attempts at treatment, and, if so, the outcome. In some reports, the history of the problem is the longest and most important part of the history section.

The family and personal histories usually reveal information relating to the predisposing cause of a client's difficulties, whereas the history of the problem often provides an elaboration of the precipitating and reinforcing causes. To complete this picture, the clinician also has to develop a sense of the factors currently reinforcing the problem. Doing this requires information relating to the client's life situation. Significant areas may be the client's life stresses, including changes that he or she is confronting. In addition, what are the nature of and resources provided by his or her family and work relationships? Finally, it is important to understand the alternatives and decisions that the client is facing.

Sometimes an evaluation needs to assess the possible presence and nature of organic impairment. In many cases, the history is of even greater significance than test results; and, often, the most valuable information a psychologist can provide to a referring medical practitioner is a thorough history. Thus, the history needs to be complete and must address a number of areas that are not ordinarily covered in personality evaluations. Several interview aids have been commercially developed to help ensure that most relevant areas are covered (see Chapter 12). If the person reports having had a head injury, it is important to note the length of time the client was unconscious (if at all), whether he or she actually remembers getting hit, the last memory before the injury, and the first thing he or she clearly remembers following the injury. In all neuropsychological assessments, a crucial area is to establish the person's premorbid level of functioning. To do so, the clinician may have to obtain information on his or her grade point average in high school or college, send for any relevant records (e.g., previous IQ results), and determine previous highest level of employment and personal interests or hobbies. Often it may be necessary to verify the client's previous level of functioning with outside sources, such as parents or employers. In determining the probable cause of brain impairment, it may be difficult to rule out other possibilities, such as exposure to toxic substances, strokes, high fevers, or other episodes of head trauma. Areas of current functioning that need to be addressed might include memory problems, word-finding difficulties, weakness on one side of the body, alterations in gait, loss of consciousness, and unusual sensations. Previous assessments with computed tomography/magnetic resonance imaging (CT/MRI) scans, electroencephalograms (EEGs), or neurological physical exams would also be important to obtain. Even though these medical records might be able to identify the site and size of a lesion, it is still the work of the psychologist to describe how the person is functioning as a result of these lesions. It might also be important to obtain current or past information regarding drug intake, especially recent alterations in prescriptions, because these might affect psychological functioning. The interview data and neuropsychological test results from a psychologist should ideally be combined with and complement medical records, such as CT scans and neurological exams. Although the preceding topics are by no means exhaustive, they represent some of the more important areas to consider when taking a history related to possible neuropsychological deficit.

Although the quantity of such information may seem immense, the history format described here is only a general guideline. At times, it may be appropriate to ignore many of the areas mentioned earlier and focus on others. In condensing the client's history into the report, it is important to avoid superfluous material and continually question whether the information obtained is relevant to the general purpose of the report. Thus, the History section should include all relevant information but should not be overly inclusive.

Test Results

For many reports, it may not be necessary to list test scores. Some practitioners do not actually give test scores because they might be misinterpreted and give the impression that the report is too data/test oriented. However, it is often recommended that, at some point, test scores be included, especially in legal reports or when professionals who are knowledgeable about testing will read the report. One option is to include test scores in an appendix. This method has the advantage of removing potentially distracting technical detail from the narrative portion of the report.

If actual test scores are included, standard (rather than raw) scores should be the mode of presentation. Referral sources have consistently indicated that percentiles are preferred over other types of standard scores (Finn et al., 2001). Because various tests use somewhat different types of standard scores, it is recommended that each set of test scores include both the standard score and percentiles. Clinicians may also wish to indicate the relative magnitude of the relevant scores ("Very high," "High," etc.) or whether the scores exceed some clinically meaningful cutoff.

Intelligence test scores are traditionally listed first and, for the Wechsler scales, should include IQ scores (Verbal, Performance, Full Scale IQ), index scores, and subtest scaled scores. Subtests that have been found to be significant strengths should be indicated with an "S" next to the subtest score and significant weaknesses should be indicated with a "W." This listing is often followed by other cognitive test results, such as the Bender or Wechsler Memory Scale-III. Bender results can simply be summarized by a statement such as: "Empirically not in the organic range, although there were difficulties organizing the designs and frequent erasures." MMPI-2/MMPI-A results are often listed in the order in which they appear on the profile sheet. Objective personality tests (MMPI-2, MMPI-A, CPI) should always be referred to by their standardized (usually *T*) scores and not their raw scores. Whereas it is fairly straightforward to list the objective and intelligence test scores, it is considerably more difficult to adequately describe the scores on projective tests. The Rorschach summary sheet can be included, but the results from projective drawings and the Thematic Apperception Test (TAT) are usually omitted. Should a clinician wish to summarize projective drawings, a brief statement is usually sufficient, such as "Human figure drawings were miniaturized and immature, with the inclusion of two transparencies." Likewise, TAT "scores" can be summarized by a brief statement of the most common themes encountered in the stories.

Impressions and Interpretations (also Referred to as Discussion)

This section can be considered the main body of the report. It requires that the main findings of the evaluation be presented in the form of integrated hypotheses. The areas discussed and the style of presentation vary according to the personal orientation of the clinician, the purpose of testing, the individual being tested, and the types of tests administered. As emphasized previously, assessment data should be organized according to different integrated topics. In contrast, a test-by-test presentation is strongly discouraged. To organize the information from an assessment, W. Klopfer (1960) recommends using a grid with the topics for consideration in the left column with the assessment results in the top row. This format enables the practitioner to extract essential findings from the data and list them in the appropriate box where the topic and the method of assessment intersect. When actually writing the Impressions and Interpretations section of the report, the clinician can then review all findings in a particular topic and summarize them on the report. An example of such a grid is given in Table 15.2. The list of assessment methods is dependent on which tests the examiner administered, but the topics can be chosen and arranged according to areas the clinician would like to focus on.

All inferences made in the Impressions and Interpretations section should be based on an integration of the test data, behavioral observations, relevant history, and additional available data. The conclusions and discussion may relate to areas such as the client's cognitive strengths and weaknesses, emotional difficulties, coping style, self-concept,

Table 15.2. Sample grid of assessment domains by tests administered

Topics	Evaluation Procedures				
	Interview	WAIS-IV	MMPI-2	BDI-II	MCMI-III
Cognitive functioning					
Personality					
Interpersonal relations					
Coping style					
Client strengths					
Diagnostic impressions					

Source: Adapted from *The Psychological Report* by W. G. Klopfer, 1960, New York: Grune & Stratton.

dynamics behind the presenting problem, interpersonal relationships, or client strengths. A client's intellectual abilities often provide a general frame of reference for a variety of personality variables. For this reason, a discussion of the client's intellectual abilities usually occurs first. Although this should include a general estimate of the person's intelligence as indicated by IQ scores, it is also important to provide a discussion of more specific abilities. This discussion may include an analysis of areas such as memory, problem solving, abstract reasoning, concentration, and fund of information. If the report will be read by persons who are familiar with test theory, it may be sufficient to include IQ scores without an explanation of their normative significance. In most reports, it is helpful to include the IQ scores as well as the percentile ranking and general intellectual classification (high average, superior, etc.; see Table 5.5). Some examiners may even prefer to omit the actual IQ scores in favor of including only percentile rank and general classification. This method can be useful in cases in which persons reading the report might be likely to misunderstand or misinterpret unexplained IQ scores. After a general estimate of intelligence has been made, it should, whenever possible, be followed by a discussion of the client's intellectual strengths and weaknesses. This discussion may involve elaborating on the meaning of the difference between Verbal IQ and Performance IQ or describing subtest scatter. In addition, it can be useful to compare the client's potential level of functioning with his or her actual performance. If there is a wide discrepancy between these two, reasons for this discrepancy should be offered. For example, the client may be underachieving because of anxiety, low motivation, emotional interference, or perceptual processing difficulties. Practitioners may also wish to discuss additional noncognitive areas of intellectual assessment, which might include the extent to which the person prefers to achieve through independent activities versus a structured environment, the level of motivation, or, the relative intellectual efficiency or hardiness. Cognitive assessments in psychiatric contexts might include any bizarre associations, degree to which the person's thinking is organized, or how concrete or abstract his or her thought processes are.

Whereas a discussion of intellectual abilities is relatively clear and straightforward, the next sections are frequently more difficult to select. There are an extremely wide number of possibilities to choose from, many of which are listed in Table 15.1. Some practitioners recommend including set topics, which typically include the client's level of cognitive functioning, emotional functioning (affect and mood), and interpersonal relationships. A neuropsychological evaluation might divide the impression and interpretation into areas such as memory, language functions, executive abilities, awareness of deficits, sensory/perceptual functions, and personality (Groth-Marnat, 2000a; Hebben & Milberg, 2002). One rationale for not having a preset list of topics to discuss is that the topics should be based primarily on the referral question. This method allows the practitioner to flexibly organize the topics based on the context of the report and the needs of the referral source and client. If the referral question is clearly focused on a specific problem, it may be necessary to elaborate on only two or three topics. A referral question that is more general may require a wider approach in which six or more areas are discussed.

Some additional common and important topics are the client's level of psychopathology, dependency, hostility, sexuality, interpersonal relationships, diagnosis, and behavioral predictions. A client's level of psychopathology refers to the relative severity of the disturbances he or she is experiencing. It is important to distinguish whether the results are characteristic of normals, outpatients, or inpatients, and whether the difficulties are long term or a reaction to current life stresses. Does the client use behaviors that are adaptive or those that are maladaptive and self-defeating? Within the area of ideation, are there persistent thoughts, delusions, hallucinations, loose associations, blocking of ideas, perseveration, or illogical thoughts? It may also be important to assess the adequacy of the client's judgments and relative degree of insight. Can the person effectively make plans, understand the impact he or she has on others, and judge the appropriateness of his or her behavior? To assess the likelihood of successful therapy, it is especially important to assess the client's level of insight. Doing this includes assessing the person's ability to think psychologically, awareness of his or her own changing feelings, understanding of the behaviors of others, and ability to conceptualize and discuss relevant insights.

Usually a client's greatest conflicts center on difficulties with dependency, hostility, and sexuality. In discussing a client's dependency, it is important to discuss the strength of these needs, the typical roles played with others, and current or past significant relationships. In what ways does the client defend him- or herself against, or cope with, feelings of dependency? This evaluation may include a discussion of defense mechanisms, thoughts, behaviors, feelings, or somatic responses as they relate to dependency. The relative intensity of a client's hostility is also important. Is the expression of hostility indirect, or is it direct in the form of either verbal criticisms or actual assaultive behavior? If the expression of hostility is covert, it may be the result of factors such as fear of loss of love, retaliation, or guilt. When the client does feel anger, what are his or her characteristic defenses against these feelings? For example, some clients might express opposite behaviors, with overly exaggerated concern for others, or they might direct their anger inward by developing physical aches and pains that serve as self-punishment for having aggressive impulses. They may also adapt through means such as extreme suspiciousness of others, which has been created by denying their hostility and attributing it to others. A discussion of a client's sexuality usually involves noting the relative intensity of his or her urges and the degree of anxiety associated with the expression of those urges. Does the client inhibit his or her sexuality because of a belief that it is dirty, experience anxiety over possible consequences, or associate it with aggressiveness? Defenses against sexual urges may be handled in ways similar to hostility, such as by performing the opposite behavior through extreme religiosity or celibacy or by denying the feelings and attributing them instead to others. Or clients may impulsively act out their sexual urges, at least in part, out of a need to obtain self-affirmation through sexual contact. Clinicians may want to discuss the dynamics involved in any unusual sexual practices.

Discussing clients' characteristic patterns and roles in interpersonal relationships can also be extremely useful. Often these can be discussed in relation to the dimensions of submissiveness/dominance and love/hate, or the extent to which they orient themselves around the need to be included, control others, or seek affection. Is their style of communicating typically guarded, or is it open and self-disclosing to the extent that they can discuss areas such as painful feelings and fears? Can they deal with the specifics of a situation, or are they usually vague and general? Do they usually appear assertive and direct, or passive and indirect? Finally, it is often important to determine the extent to which they are perceptive about interpersonal relationships and their typical approaches toward resolving conflict.

It may also be appropriate to include descriptions of vocational goals and aptitudes. This information often is quite important in educational reports, especially for students with special educational needs, such as those with disabilities. Many of the tests covered in this text can help in assessing a person's strengths and weaknesses, but practitioners may also need to include further assessment devices, such as the Self-Directed Search, the Strong Interest Inventory, or the Kuder Occupational Interest Survey (see Prince & Heisser, 2000).

A frequent consideration is whether the client's difficulties will continue or, if currently absent, recur. If the client's future prospects are poor, a statement of the rationale for this conclusion should be given. For example, if a clinician predicts that the response to treatment will be poor, he or she should explain that the reason for this conclusion is that the client has a strong need to appear hypernormal, with poor insight, and a high level of defensiveness. Likewise, favorable predictions should include a summary of the client's assets and resources, such as psychological-mindedness, motivation to change, and social supports. If difficulties are likely to be encountered during the course of treatment, the nature and intensity of these difficulties should be discussed. The prediction of suicidal potential, assaultive behavior, child abuse, or criminal behavior is essential in certain types of reports. Often the tests themselves are not useful in predicting these behaviors. For example, one of the best ways of predicting suicidal potential is to evaluate the client's history, current environment, personal resources, and degree of suicide intent (Klespies & Dettmer, 2000; Stelmachers, 1995). However, research indicates that many predictions of behavior, such as dangerousness, are subject to error (Binder, 1999; Freedman, 2001; Megargee, 1995). Making long-term predictions is especially likely to produce a high rate of error. Clinicians thus should exercise appropriate caution in making predictions and not exceed the bounds of reasonable certainty.

Sometimes clinicians may wish to include a separate section on diagnosis. However, whether to include a *DSM-IV* (1994; or *ICD-10*; World Health Organization, 1990) diagnosis has been an area of some controversy. Some clinicians feel that labels should be avoided because they may result in self-fulfilling prophecies, be overly reductionistic, and allow clients to avoid responsibility for their own behavior. Other objections to diagnosis stem from researchers who feel that many of the terms are not scientifically valid (Beutler & Malik, 2002; Rosenhan, 1973) and are not particularly useful in planning interventions (Beutler & Malik, 2002; Groth-Marnat, Roberts, & Beutler, 2001; Houts, 2002). If a clinician does decide to give a diagnosis, he or she must first have a clear operational knowledge of the diagnostic terms. He or she should also include the client's premorbid level of adjustment and the severity and frequency of the disturbance. Instruments such as the Structured Clinical Interview for the *DSM-IV-TR* (SCID; First, Spitzer, et al., 1996; First et al., 1997), Structured Interview for *DSM-IV-TR* Personality (SIDP), or Anxiety Disorders Interview Schedule (T. Brown et al., 1994) might help to increase the reliability of diagnosis. It is also important to include the possible causes of the disorder. A discussion of causes should not be simplistic and one-dimensional but rather should appreciate the complexity of causative factors. Thus, causes may be described from the perspective of primary, predisposing, precipitating, and reinforcing factors. Clinicians may also discuss the relative significance of biological, psychological, and sociocultural variables.

Inclusion of client strengths is becoming increasingly prevalent and relevant. Describing a series of client strengths helps to balance out the typically negative features that occur in many if not most psychological reports (Snyder, Ritschel, Rand, & Berg, 2006). Not only can the inclusion of strengths provide more balance, but when reports are read by clients, it can enhance rapport between the examinee and the mental health profession in general. There is also increasing research evidence that tailoring interventions toward a person's unique pattern of strengths can help improve outcome (Seligman, Steen, Park, & Peterson, 2005).

Summary and Recommendations

The purpose of the Summary subsection is to restate succinctly the primary findings and conclusions of the report. To do so, the practitioner must select only the most important issues and be careful not to overwhelm the reader with needless details. As emphasized previously (see Referral Question section), a useful strategy in the Summary section is to provide brief bulleted/numbered answers to each of the referral questions.

The ultimate practical purpose of the report is contained in the recommendations because they suggest what steps can be taken to solve problems. Such recommendations should be clear, practical, and obtainable, and should relate directly to the purpose of the report. The best reports are those that help the referral sources and/or the clients solve the problems they are facing (Armengol, Moes, et al., 2001; Brenner, 2003; Finn et al., 2001; Ownby, 1997; Tallent, 1993). To achieve this report-writing goal, the clinician must clearly understand the problem, the best alternatives for remediation, and the resources available in the community. One practical implication is that writers can improve their reports by becoming as familiar as possible with the uses to which their reports will be applied. An effective report must answer the referral question and have decisional value. After these factors have been carefully considered, recommendations can be developed.

Chapter 14 elaborated on guidelines for psychotherapy with a focus on selecting the optimum intervention procedures along with considerations for enhancing the therapeutic relationship and decisions related to case management. Often cases will require a wider variety of recommendations than this, especially in forensic, medical, academic, or rehabilitation settings. These recommendations may include treatment options, placement decisions, further evaluation, altering the client's environment, use of self-help resources, and miscellaneous considerations. Clinicians can consult Table 15.3 to see if there might be additional recommendations they would like to include in their report.

Self-help resources have become a particularly well-developed, useful, cost-effective option. Depending on the type of problem and characteristics of the person, research supports that many self-help programs are nearly as effective formal mental health treatment (Norcross, 2006). Norcross et al.'s (2003) *Authoritative Guide to Self-Help Resources in Mental Health* lists a wide variety of resources, rates their quality, and organizes them according to books, autobiographies, films, Internet/online resources, and national support groups (see also Norcross, 2006). There are also a wide variety of computer-assisted psychotherapy programs (Marks, Cavanagh, & Gega, 2007). Self-help resources can be used either in conjunction with formal mental health treatment or as stand-alone interventions.

One clear finding is that reports typically are rated most useful when their recommendations are highly specific rather than general (Armengol, 2001; Finn et al., 2001; Ownby, 1990, 1997; G. White, Nielsen, & Prus, 1984). Thus, a recommendation that states "The client should begin psychotherapy" is not as useful as a statement of the need for

Table 15.3.   Types of treatment recommendations

Recommendation type	Examples
Treatment	Psychotherapy, speech therapy, occupational therapy, medication, meditation, mediation
Placement	Special education, nursing home, 24/7 observation, joint custody, inpatient care
Further evaluation	Re-evaluation with selected portions of current tests, physical exam, CT/MRI
Alteration in environment	Medication alarm, internal/external reminders
Self-help	Self-help books, films, websites, support groups; computer-aided interventions
Miscellaneous	Revoke drivers license, wear Medialert bracelet, probation, homework (gratitude letter, practice self-statements)

"individual therapy focusing on the following areas: increased assertiveness, relaxation techniques for reducing anxiety, and increased awareness of the self-defeating patterns he creates in relationships." Likewise, a recommendation for "special education" can be improved by expanding it to "special education two hours a day, emphasizing exercises in auditory sequencing and increasing immediate recall for verbally relevant information." However, caution should be exercised when providing specific recommendations in some contexts because some health professionals may feel that developing treatment recommendations is primarily their responsibility or perhaps should be made by the overall treatment team. After the report has been submitted, continued contact should be made with the readers(s) to make sure the report has not been filed and forgotten. Even the best report is not useful unless the recommendations are practical, obtainable, and actually put into action (Geffken, Keeley, Kellison, Storch, & Rodrigue, 2006).

SAMPLE REPORTS

The sample reports in this section are from the more common settings in which clinicians work and consult. The dimensions in which the reports vary are:

- Format.
- Referral question.
- Extent to which history rather than test data is emphasized.
- Types of tests used.
- Degree to which they include a variety of descriptions rather than being case-focused with a relatively limited range of topics.

In each setting, specific questions have been presented, along with decisions that must be made related to the client. The different reports illustrate how the clinician has integrated the test data, client's history, and behavioral observations to handle these questions. The reports were selected to illustrate a wide diversity in format, length, type of setting, referral question, and type of tests used.

The first report was written in a psychiatric setting and was intended for use by mental health professionals. As a result, some technical language is used, primarily in the form of a formal *DSM-IV* diagnosis. A further aspect to note is that the evaluation of the patient's cognitive functioning was not based on formal testing but rather on behavioral observations and mental status. The major feature of the report is the extensive development of a detailed treatment plan for psychotherapeutic intervention. This plan was developed based on the Systematic Selection Model detailed in Chapter 14. The recommendations are eclectic in orientation and assume that the treating practitioner can effectively use a number of techniques from a variety of theoretical orientations. Another feature of the report is the absence of psychological test data. Specifically, there is no Test Results section because some, if not many, practitioners believe that the inclusion of detailed test results is both unnecessary and results in cluttering up the report with distracting detail. It is rather assumed that the referral source is most interested in the integration of the overall assessment along with the relevant recommendations.

The second report, written in a legal context, focuses on addressing issues related to comprehension of Miranda warnings, ability to partake in police interrogation, and the possibility of a false confession. As a result, there is a reliance on measures of cognitive abilities and level of achievement. The referral questions are clear and focused. They are numbered in the Referral Question section and then, using the corresponding numbers, are answered in the Summary section. In most reports, it is neither recommended nor necessary to include citations/references. However, they have been included in this report to support the credibility of the assertions. The argument was that, given available research, the client had an optimal set of characteristics for him to have been unable both to comprehend his Miranda rights and to knowingly and intelligently participate in his police interrogation.

The third sample is from an educational context; the client (a 12-year-old Hispanic female) was experiencing emotional and behavioral problems that were impacting her academic performance and peer relations. This report is an important addition not only because it includes a child but also because it demonstrates how the examiner handled ethnic diversity. There is also information on how the combination of emotional difficulties and being bilingual was likely to have lowered her optimal level of cognitive performance. Two noteworthy strengths of the report were the extent to which a wide variety of sources of information were used (previous records, interviews with several different persons, a number of formal tests) and the clear description of the client's assets. The formal tests were targeted toward specific areas (intelligence, achievement, trauma, self-perception) and used a combination of objective and projective/qualitative information.

The final report is in the form of a letter written directly to the client. The language is user-friendly, empathic, and sometimes uses the client's own phrases. It is also clearly organized answering the referral questions. Such a report represents a growing trend toward integrating assessment with therapy. It also reflects a highly collaborative and egalitarian approach to the assessment process.

Psychiatric Setting

NAME: A. G.
DATE OF BIRTH: 5/30/1935
DATE OF EXAMINATION: 12/12/2005
SEX: Female
ETHNICITY: European American
REFERRED BY: Dr. M.

Referral Question

A. G. is a 70-year-old, divorced female with 13 years of education who reported anxiety and episodes of dissociation. The patient reported that she has experienced agoraphobia in the past but now clarifies that her problem is one of motivation rather than panic. She asserted that she is currently not immobilized nor is she extremely anxious when she travels. She acknowledged an "underlying apprehension" that arises when she is scheduled to leave home, however, resulting in her putting off her departure as long as possible. A. G. was referred by her psychiatrist, Dr. M., who has requested an evaluation to clarify the nature of the problem and to develop an optimal treatment plan.

Evaluation Procedures

Life History Questionnaire (12/12/2005).
Clinical Interview (12/12/2005).

Structured Clinical Interview for DSM-IV (SCID; 12/22/2005).
State-Trait Anxiety Inventory (STAI; 12/13/2005).
Millon Clinical Multiaxial Inventory-III (MCMI-III; 12/13/2005).
Personal Attitude Inventory (Dowd Therapeutic Reactance Scale; 12/13/2005).
Beck Depression Inventory (BDI; 12/13/2005).
Beck Hopelessness Scale (BHS; 12/13/2005).
Minnesota Multiphasic Personality Inventory-2 (MMPI-2; 12/21/2005).
Sarason Social Support Questionnaire (SSQ; 1/2/2005).

Behavioral Observations

Throughout the evaluation, A. G. was articulate, introspective, and cooperative. While acknowledging discomfort in talking about her sexual orientation and religious feelings, she was quite forthcoming when questioned directly. A valid MMPI-2 profile, along with her willingness to cooperate and introspect, suggests that the current evaluation presents a valid picture of her current level of functioning.

Relevant History

Personal/Social. A. G. was raised in a middle-class, Jewish family. She was the older of two children, having a brother who is one and a half years her junior. The family always maintained at least a superficial religious identity and a facade of happiness. However, she reported that, behind this facade, there were significant underlying family conflicts. Religion has always been a source of conflict for her as has been her sexual orientation. Moreover, she reported a long family history of mental illness and interpersonal conflict. While she described her parents as emotionally stable, both her parents' families have histories of psychiatric disorders. Her mother was the oldest of nine children; an uncle died in a halfway house with a diagnosis of schizophrenia, another was diagnosed as having bipolar disorder, and still another was diagnosed as having depression. On her father's side, at least one uncle is reported to have had a major depression that was treated with antidepressants.

In her own personal history, A. G. reported that she always felt confused about her sexual orientation. At age 17, she received a proposal of marriage. She declined but he persisted, and she went to live with an uncle to escape his advances. He pursued her and finally, against her "better judgment," he talked her into marriage. The newlyweds moved to Metroville to be with her family, but problems persisted and they separated after about a year. By that time, she had given birth to a daughter. She moved in with her parents, but long-standing conflicts with her mother became more frequent. When her husband contested and prevented the culmination of the divorce, A. G. moved out of the family home and went to work, leaving her daughter with her mother. A. G. blamed her parents for her failed marriage and refused further contact. She did not see or speak with her daughter for two years.

After a period of estrangement from parents and daughter, the patient was contacted by her attorney, who informed her that A. G.'s mother could no longer raise the baby. Her husband was also informed, and he demanded that A. G. reconcile with him to raise the child. A. G. agreed to do so if they would move to Betterville to make a fresh start. Shortly after moving, A. G.'s husband became disillusioned and returned to Metroville, leaving her to raise the child. It was very shortly thereafter that she acknowledged to herself that she was a lesbian. She subsequently engaged in a series of brief lesbian affairs and adopted a "secret life" in which she prevented her parents and husband from an awareness of this emerging sexual orientation.

Still being unable to raise her daughter and work, the client gave up the child to a foster family for temporary care. After a few years, she initiated an effort to again assume care of the child. Concerned about raising the child in a lesbian relationship, she accepted the proposal of marriage from a man who knew about her lesbian lifestyle. He nonetheless agreed to adopt the child and allowed her to continue her lesbian affairs. Their marriage lasted 23 years and produced two sons. Although unsatisfied with her dual life, she waited until her younger son graduated from high school before she left the marriage and began to pursue lesbian relationships exclusively and openly. She met her current lover in 1996. This relationship continues to be close although they ceased sexual contact approximately six years ago.

History of Presenting Problem

A. G. reported symptoms related to agoraphobia, panic attacks, and dissociation. She has a long history of panic attacks without agoraphobia, dating to age 12. The first panic episode occurred when she was babysitting for a family friend. She suddenly hyperventilated, began experiencing heart palpitations, and became afraid that she was going to die. She ran into the street yelling for help, but no one heard her or tried to assist her. The situation was resolved by exerting "self-control."

After her initial panic attacks began, they gradually increased to a frequency of about once per week throughout her teenage years. To protect herself from feared panic and what she perceived as possible death, she frequently slept with her parents and confined herself to known places and locations. At their worst, her panic attacks involved physical symptoms such as nausea, shortness of breath (hyperventilation), and dizziness as well as cognitive symptoms such as fears of losing her mind, dying, of being overwhelmed, and unspecified danger. However, she learned to control these symptoms over time by avoiding such activities as going out, driving, and socializing with groups. These efforts have been successful in that A. G. reported that she had been asymptomatic for agoraphobia and panic for 31 years.

She currently reports that she has become apprehensive about travel and social activity, but the symptoms are confined to initial anticipatory anxiety, gastrointestinal distress, and headaches but with no heart palpitations, shortness of breath, or fainting. She prevents more extensive symptoms by avoiding travel and through a variety of distraction procedures. When she begins to experience the onset of panic, she calls someone or begins to read an interesting book. Her contacts with other people at these times do not include a disclosure of or discussions about the panic but are reported to be simply methods to involve herself with others and to take her mind off her feelings.

She reported that the current symptoms are mild in intensity and include a general discomfort with traveling, difficulty feeling comfortable when alone, and a general heightened sense of vulnerability and apprehension until she is able to return home. She continues to avoid night travel and avoids being alone, if possible, to prevent the associated anxiety.

Since 1996, several dissociative episodes have occurred, which she believes were precipitated by her decision to openly acknowledge her homosexual orientation. The first instance followed a sexual encounter with her current partner during a vacation. After the sexual act, the client experienced an apparent fugue state. She became disoriented, was unable to recall personal information such as that her parents were deceased, and engaged in distraught communication with her lover about "Why am I here." The episodes have subsequently recurred several times: They come on suddenly and without warning and she subsequently has no memory for the events. They uniformly follow a lesbian sexual encounter, and if her partner remains with her during this period (sometimes up to several hours), the fears gradually subside. However, after these dissociative states, she reported having a sense of helplessness, hopelessness, confusion, headaches, and nausea that sometimes lasted for several days. She has been able to successfully avoid these episodes by not engaging in sexual activities for nearly six years.

History of Treatment: A. G. was first treated and hospitalized in 1975 because of agoraphobia. There have been no subsequent hospitalizations. However, she has entered into two treatment relationships in the years since. Her current medication is managed by a psychiatrist, who is treating her with Xanex, Tagamet, and Paxil. She reported that since being on the medication, she has been excessively sleepy and has a difficult time staying awake during the day. She also has experienced an increase in stomach difficulties and diarrhea. She was also treated for a short time in 1995 by an internist and psychiatrist. At that time, she was given tricyclic antidepressants. These drugs produced hallucinations and were discontinued shortly after initiation.

A review of this woman's symptom history also reveals that she has had substantial periods of time in which she has been asymptomatic for fugue states, panic attacks, and agoraphobia. She reported that between August 2003 and June 2004, she was the "best ever." She was able to travel alone, found life enjoyable, and experienced no episodes of discomfort or fear. More recently, she has gradually become more depressed and dysphoric as well as fearful, although there was no obvious precipitator for these feelings.

Medical History. A. G.'s medical history is unremarkable. She currently takes Tagamet for stomach distress and Xanex for anxiety. Aside from some loss of hearing and psychophysiological symptoms, she acknowledges no significant medical problems.

Interpretations and Impressions

Intellectual Ability: While a formal assessment of intellectual level was not undertaken, both A. G.'s verbal conceptual skills and oral presentation suggest at least average and probably bright-normal intellectual performance. Her ideation is dominated by preoccupation with ways to avoid uncomfortable feelings along with concerns with physical symptoms. Collectively, this results in mild impairment to her cognitive efficiency. Her verbal processes are organized, circumstantial, and occasionally dominated by topics about which she has pressing concerns; but they reflect no disorganization, no memory impairment, and moderately well-developed associative and abstract reasoning processes. While she is oriented in all three spheres and manifests no significant mental impairment, she notes having always been concerned with the potential loss of mental functions.

Personality and Symptom Patterns. A. G. experiences ambivalent personality organization, with moderate disturbances to her functional adaptation. Her dominant conflicts involve strong needs for dependency counterbalanced by equally strong strivings for self-definition. A. G. denies dysphoria, depression, and anxiety. She complains of poor sleep, loss of energy, and lack of motivation. Formal assessment confirms the presence of vegetative signs (increased appetite, variable sleep, social withdrawal, loss of interest, reduced libido), consistent with the presence of mild to moderate depression without subjective dysphoria. Trait anxiety levels are within the normal range for her age, and subjective depression is only mild, with the dominant symptoms being psychophysiological. Her affect is appropriate though somewhat variable. Affective responsivity is both dysthymic and blunted.

Coping Style. A. G.'s mood disturbance reflects a chronic condition, against which she has constructed a variety of rigid and brittle defenses. She is excessively sensitive to environmental signals of threat and, at the least suggestion of emotional arousal, engages in both direct and cognitive avoidance patterns. The result is that she prevents the intensification or even emergence of feelings that might overwhelm her. While protecting her somewhat from subjective sensations of anxiety and dysphoria, A. G.'s defenses are not sufficiently strong to prevent the emergence of a variety of secondary symptoms. Denial, phobic avoidance in the face of anticipatory cues, self-criticism, compartmentalization, and somatization are among her most frequently used defenses. As threat intensifies, her fragile denial deteriorates, and both somatization and direct avoidance predominate. Thus, acute stress evokes a variety of stress-related somatic symptoms and phobic behaviors that provide expression for her denial of anxiety and depression.

Her coping style involves both passive and active efforts to reconcile these strong drives. Thus, while she seeks approval and confirmation from others, even to the point of excessive subservience in which she gives up personal strivings, this is frequently a futile effort to ensure the presence of other people in her life. Indeed, these efforts are usually designed to compensate for a host of covert rebellious and angry impulses and by overt efforts to be autonomous and self-guided. Thus, efforts to achieve self-fulfillment and autonomy are followed by guilt, self-doubt, and shame in which fear and withdrawal dominate. These latter symptoms, however, may be so demanding of attention that they are the functional equivalent of interpersonal anger, hurt, and resentment. Thus, her pattern of phobic anxiety and dissociation has led to sexual withdrawal and physical dependency. Her withdrawal may represent an indirect expression of anger yet also be a compromise between asocial impulses and needs for approval. Unfortunately, this compromise also includes low self-regard and restricted mobility. Another consequence of this pattern is the current low level of available others to provide support. In spite of this, A. G.'s satisfaction with the level of interpersonal support available from her significant other is good and suggests the availability of this individual as a support in any treatment program.

Client Strengths. A. G. has good awareness of many of the dynamics underlying her condition combined with a moderate amount of ego strengths. Her cognitive abilities are estimated to be in the average to high-average range and her thought processes are focused and intact. Despite being quite avoidant, her level of distress is at an optimal level to assure her motivation to become engaged in therapy. Her relationship with her partner is both long term and quite supportive.

Diagnostic Impression

AXIS I	(300.22)	Agoraphobia without recent panic disorder (by history)
	(296.3)	Rule out Major Depressive Disorder, recurrent

The diagnosis of Anxiety Disorder is based on history rather than current symptomatology. A major differential question has to do with the relevant salience of Major Depression versus Anxiety Disorder

AXIS II   None
AXIS III   Rule out gastrointestinal disorder
AXIS IV   Problems related to social environment-social isolation, restriction of
               friendships, lifecycle transitions
AXIS V   Current GAF: 62
               Highest GAF past year: 80

Summary and Recommendations

A. G. is a 70-year-old, divorced female with 13 years of education with symptoms related to agoraphobia, panic attacks, and dissociation. These symptoms are of a complex and long-standing nature founded more in dynamic and early developing interpersonal expectations and conflicts than in symptom-contingent events. These core conflicts seem to be largely founded in postpubescent strivings to resolve needs for autonomy and dependency. A. G.'s level of functional impairment is moderate. Numerous areas of functioning are affected, and this, coupled with the chronicity of the condition, suggests the need for long-term treatment. A. G.'s level of distress is well contained since it falls in the average or even below-average range compared with other patients who seek treatment. While her distress increases significantly when exposed to immediate threat, she quickly compensates and so is well versed at avoidance. Client strengths are that she has good awareness, intelllectual level that is both intact and in the average to high-average range, experiences an optimal level of motivational distress, and is in a quite supportive long-term relationship.

An optimal treatment plan would involve the following features:

The dynamic nature of the associated conflicts, and their role in maintaining systemic dysfunction in her relationships with significant others, suggests the need to combine a symptom-focused treatment with efforts to resolve fundamental conflicts. The initial focus of treatment should be on reducing territorial apprehension, with a concomitant increase in social involvement and independent functioning. After initial symptomatic improvement, further interventions should focus on A. G.'s pattern of rebelliousness, which seems to be intertwined with self-incrimination, guilt, and withdrawal. In particular, these interventions might emphasize confirming needs for both autonomy and acceptance, along with greater insight into this pattern.

The patient's level of defense and personal control is sufficient, and the level of subjective despair and hopelessness is within a range that suggests that outpatient care is appropriate. There is no evidence of direct risk to self or others. Anxiolytic or antidepressant medications are contraindicated because of her relative degree of control over her symptoms, combined with the high potential for somatic side effects. Individual treatment may allow a more selective and intensive focus on problematic behaviors. Individual therapy would also be likely to prevent the operation of direct avoidance of discomfort when compared with group treatment.

Despite an optimal level of motivation distress, she may experience difficulty sustaining sufficient motivation for therapy due to her strong avoidant patterns.

Thus, interventions that confront or expose her to feared and avoided circumstances may be helpful to desensitize her to anxiety as well as to maintain her level of motivation to continue treatment.

A. G.'s coping style vacillates between being primarily impulsive and externalizing, to being self-critical and internalizing. This pattern of cyclic coping suggests the need to address her problems at both a behavioral and an insight level. When her impulses and direct avoidance dominate, behavioral strategies should be emphasized. During phases in which she is more introspective and self-blaming, insight-oriented interventions are likely to be more effective. Given the unsustaining nature of her subjective distress, abreactive and sensate-focused, cathartic interventions may prove to be especially helpful during these more introspective phases.

A. G. manifests a pattern of superficial compliance and more covert resistance to the directives of help givers. Thus, special attention should be given to developing a trusting relationship. Even if this is achieved, however, she would still be expected to undermine direct suggestions and specific assignments. The most effective approaches, then, would be collaborative interventions emphasizing clear behavioral change, contingency contracting, or paradoxical interventions such as symptom prescription and "no-change" directives. Particular attention may be given to predicting the exacerbation of physical and phobic symptoms following intense sessions because these sessions may mobilize her resistant impulses in an asymptomatic direction.

Collectively, the symptomatic aspects of the patient's fears and phobias may be susceptible to a combination of structured exposure procedures, cognitive restructuring, and interoceptive awareness (Craske & Barlow, 1993). These procedures circumvent patient resistance by virtue of their reliance on self-monitoring as well as being both symptom and behaviorally focused. The more thematic and dynamic aspects of A. G.'s problem may be addressed by initiating work that specifically mobilizes her anxiety in motivational directions. Confrontation with feared material, along with the use of procedures such as two-chair work and imaginal reliving of unsettling relationships, may be helpful. Imaginal confrontation might be initiated with images and memories of disapproving parents, children, and other significant others, the goals of which may be to help her tolerate discomfort and disapproval. The procedures outlined by Daldrup, Beutler, Engle, and Greenberg (1988, *Focused Expressive Psychotherapy*) for working with the overcontrolled patient may also be particularly helpful.

Sourcenote: Report written and submitted by Larry Beutler, Ph.D., ABPP, Pacific Graduate School of Psychology, Palo Alto, CA.

Legal Context

NAME: Joe Competent
AGE (date of birth): 49 (1/10/58)
SEX: M
ETHNICITY: Hispanic
DATE OF REPORT: 6/25/2007
NAME OF EXAMINER: Frank Clinician, Ph.D., ABPP
REFERRED BY: Harry Hamlin

Referral Question

Mr. Competent is a 49-year-old, right-handed, divorced, Hispanic male who has been previously diagnosed with paranoid schizophrenia and "learning disabilities." I understand that, following apprehension for a suspected burglary, he waived his Miranda rights, was interrogated by the police, and confessed to having broken into a house. I understand that you would like me to determine his cognitive capacity and address the following questions:

1. What is the extent he could comprehend the Miranda rights that were read to him?
2. How competently would he have knowingly and intelligently participated in his interrogation?

Evaluation Procedures

Clinical interview, Neuropsychological Symptom Checklist, Wechsler Adult Intelligence Scale-III, Wechsler Memory Scale-III, Wide Range Achievement Test-III (WRAT-III), Controlled Oral Word Association Test, Bender, Bender Memory, Minnesota Multiphasic Personality Inventory-2 (MMPI-2; questions were read to him), Rey 15 Item, Test of Memory Malingering (TOMM), transcripts of police interrogation, competency evaluation by Jonathan Smith, M.D. (7/22/2005), competency evaluation by Patricia Jones, M.D. (6/15/2005). Total face-to-face evaluation time 5 hours, 40 minutes.

Behavioral Observations

Mr. Competent was seen in the Metrotown County Jail. He was dressed in prison uniform but without restraints. He was missing most of his teeth and the left side of his mouth was slightly lower than the right side. His ability to pronounce words was somewhat poor due to what he described as a "hairlip." His affect was somewhat flat but was otherwise normal. His thoughts were sometimes disorganized and his responses were fairly tangential. However, there did not seem to be any obvious signs of delusions and he denied having any hallucinations. Despite this, he did appear somewhat suspicious and on two occasions asked who would be reading the report I was going to prepare about him. He seemed to have fairly poor insight into his psychiatric difficulties and felt that his suspiciousness toward others was simply due to his having been assaulted when he was in his 20s. When asked why he was taking medication and the impact it had on him, he stated that it made him tired but gave no indication it had any other impact on his emotional or cognitive functioning. The responses he provided on his personal background were quite vague, and on several occasions he altered some of the details. For example, when asked if he was married, he at first said no and then said he had been married but it was in jail. He then said he had gotten divorced but soon afterward said "no, I never did get divorced." Due to these discrepancies, I think he was a fairly poor historian. He did seem to understand the questions I asked him and was usually able to follow instructions. However, on many occasions he needed to have the instructions repeated. On one occasion he appeared to not comprehend the instructions to a task despite repeated attempts at clarification. He did seem to give his best efforts toward the tasks presented to him.

Given the above behavioral observations, I believe some of the history he provided may have been somewhat inaccurate due to his disorganized and tangential thoughts. As a result, I relied on a review of records to develop a complete history. He scored low on measures evaluating the validity of his responses to cognitive testing (so-called fake bad tests). For many clients this might indicate an exaggeration of deficits. However, in Mr. Competent's case, these low scores were consistent with his history, previous evaluations, and quite low performance on other cognitive tests. As a result, I feel the results of testing were generally an accurate assessment of his current level of functioning. However, given his ethnic background, some of the results may be a slight underestimate of his potential. As a result, this has been taken into account during the interpretation of test scores.

Background

(*Note: Background history has been significantly abbreviated and altered to insure anonymity.*)

PERSONAL/SOCIAL: Mr. Competent stated that he was born and grew up in Anytown. He stated that he had two brothers and six sisters but he was unclear as to whether these were biological or foster siblings. English was the main language spoken in the home. Medical records did not refer to him having lived with a foster family. They also indicate he was born in Anytown but about the age of 9 he and his family moved to Metrotown. Mr. Competent reported that his "foster mother" died at age 79 and he doesn't know if his "foster father" is still alive since he said he last saw him in 1986. It is quite possible that when he refers to his "foster" parents, he is actually referring to his biological parents. Mr. Competent said that his father worked on a ranch and his mother cleaned houses.

During high school Mr. Competent stated that he "got along with people" and had many friends. He further stated he liked PE classes and going to parties. Forensic and psychiatric records indicated he had a number of difficulties with the law and spent several years in a Forensic Youth Authority facility beginning in 1976. Medical records indicated he had been married in 1980, but he stated that he did not have any children. In contrast to this, his medical records indicate that he did have three children. Medical records also indicate he has no contacts with either his wife/children or with his family of origin.

ACADEMIC/VOCATIONAL: Mr. Competent stated that during high school he went to "special classes" since he had a difficult time with reading. He said that his most difficult subjects were English, History, and Math. He stated that his grades were a combination of As, Bs, and Cs. He described himself as a "slow learner" and mentioned that he had a "learning disability." Some records indicated he went to Metrotown High School whereas other records indicated he attended Northbridge Special Education School. It should be noted that for at least part of this time he would have attended school at a Forensic Youth Authority facility. No educational records, including formal psychological assessments, were available for review. Employment has been intermittent rarely lasting for more than a few weeks. He clarified he "didn't quit, I just didn't go back to work."

MEDICAL: He denied ever having had a tumor, stroke, unusually high fevers, exposure to neurotoxic substances, and described his use of drugs or alcohol as being moderate (with no use of "hard core" drugs). He has evidently smoked one pack of cigarettes a day for much of his life.

PSYCHIATRIC/LEGAL: Early psychiatric history prior to 1986 was unavailable. It is thus not clear how his first symptoms began and how they were expressed. Review of forensic and psychiatric records indicated he has usually carried a diagnosis of paranoid schizophrenia. Additional diagnoses have included schizoaffective and bipolar disorders. Medication has included Haldol, Zyprexa, Prolixin, Depakote, Risperdal, Cogentin, and Paxil. Complications with his treatment have been poor awareness that he has a mental illness, poor comprehension of his commitment and discharge criteria, difficulty taking care of his health needs, poor medication compliance, social isolation, and suspiciousness. At times he has been able to state that he has a mental illness and that his medication helps him. Most of the time he has expressed that he does not feel he has a mental illness. Substance abuse has been identified as a difficulty, but there was unclear documentation that this had actually been a problem for him. During my interview with him, he minimized any substance abuse, but it is unclear whether this was due to poor insight or whether he simply has not had a substance abuse problem. Treatment has been partially but intermittently successful. One area of success has been that he only rarely seems to experience full-blown psychiatric symptoms such as delusions and hallucinations. Mr. Competent stated that current medication includes Risperdal (4 mg/1Xday) and Cogentin (2 mg/1Xday). Past mental health records are all consistent with him having quite low verbal comprehension, poor insight, low academic achievement, and generally low intellectual abilities. However, these were based on an impressionistic analysis rather than on more formal, precise, psychological measures.

Summary of Alleged Offense

On the evening of 5/25/07, Mr. Competent was apprehended for "prowling." He waived his Miranda rights and, upon questioning, confessed he had been in a house that had been broken into. He was then transferred to Metrotown County Jail, where he is currently incarcerated. He now feels he was manipulated by the police into confessing that he had made an attempted burglary.

Interpretation and Impressions

General Level of Intellectual Function. Overall level of functioning was in the extremely low range or the lower 1% of the population when compared with his age-related peers (Full Scale IQ = 62). This is in the mildly mentally retarded range. Both his verbal knowledge/reasoning abilities as well as his ability to process visual spatial information were equally low. Given his history and previous evaluations, his low intellectual level is likely to be of a long duration.

Attention and Concentration. A noteworthy difficulty was that he has an extremely difficult time paying attention. This means that he is likely to not focus on conversations and have extreme difficulty trying to learn new material. His formal score in this area was in the 0.1 percentile, which means that only one person in 1,000 would perform in this low a range.

Memory. Overall memory was in the extremely low range or the lower 0.1 percent of the population (Immediate Memory Index = 55). This means that he would have a quite difficult time remembering things that people have told him or events that had occurred. For example, he was only able to repeat a maximum of three numbers that had been read to him. His ability to recall a short paragraph that was read to him was extremely limited.

Verbal Skills. Verbal abilities were in the lower 2% of the population (Verbal Comprehension Index = 68). His word knowledge was quite limited as was his fund of information. For example, he defined "tomorrow" as simply "the present" and thought there were "53" weeks in a year. His ability to use everyday reasoning to understand common situations was also quite low. Even though he could name common objects, such as a cross and a square, he could not spell them.

Achievement Level. Formal assessment of his reading indicated he could read up to the fourth-grade level. His spelling was at the first-grade level. Although he was able to spell "cat" and "hut," he was unable to spell "leg" and "shirt." Arithmetic was at the third-grade equivalent. For example, he was able to add and subtract numbers but was unable to do simple division (he thought 20 divided by 4 equaled 30). These scores suggest that he is functionally illiterate in that he would be unable to read newspapers, magazines, books, legal documents, or financial information.

Nonverbal Skills. Mr. Competent's nonverbal abilities were relatively better than his memory and attention. This means that a relative strength is his ability to understand and problem solve information he sees. However, his nonverbal abilities were still in the lower 2% of the population (Perceptual Organization Index = 72). In addition, his ability to reproduce a series of simple designs was clearly in the impaired range.

Speed of Information Processing. The speed by which Mr. Competent processes information is in the lower 1% of the population. This means that explanations and questions would need to be given with extreme care. In order for him to comprehend and solve problems, he would also need to be given extra time. It should be noted, however, that some of his psychiatric medication is sedating so this may have exaggerated Mr. Competent's low processing speed. To compensate for this, I tried to give him tasks requiring speed, concentration, and memory during times in which the impact of his medication would be minimal.

Psychiatric. Review of personality and symptoms indicated an unusual pattern of scores on the MMPI-2. He appeared to exaggerate his symptom complaints. At the same time he minimized them by emphasizing his positive qualities in an unrealistic manner (i.e., he denied ever getting angry and stated that he never felt like swearing). I think this may be due to not adequately understanding the questions since they are at a fifth-grade reading level. At the same time, previous evaluations seem to indicate a style in which he both minimizes his symptoms and yet he still expresses fairly severe psychiatric illness. Despite this, his overall profile was still consistent with his history. There were moderate elevations indicating disorganized thinking, unusual thought processes, tangential thinking, periods of high energy and euphoria, and he is also oversensitive, mistrustful, and suspicious. However, at the time of assessment he was cooperative and did not seem to have any overt delusions or hallucinations.

Summary and Opinion Regarding Questioning

Mr. Competent is a 49-year-old, right-handed, married male with a history of psychiatric illness and legal difficulties. Past treatment has been complicated by low insight, low intellectual level, social isolation, intermittent assaults, suspiciousness, difficulty caring for his medical conditions, and poor compliance. My evaluation found him to be functioning in the mildly mentally retarded range (overall IQ = 62, or the lower 1% of the population) with specific difficulties in verbal comprehension, verbal reasoning, impaired attention, poor memory, low speed of processing information, and impaired ability to construct designs. Academic achievement ranged from a first-grade equivalent in spelling to a fourth-grade equivalent in reading. This is sufficiently low for him to be functionally illiterate. He would also have a difficult time understanding concepts that had even a mild level of complexity. This means that he would need to have information presented in an extremely simple form with clear explanations of the implications of his responses. Due to his poor attention and slow speed of processing information, considerable extra time would be needed for him to comprehend and respond to information. However, he is able to understand things generally when information is explained in simple, uncomplicated terms. Psychiatric symptoms suggest disorganized thinking, unusual thought processes, tangential thinking, oversensitivity, suspiciousness, and periods in which he experiences high energy and euphoria.

1. Concerning waiver of Miranda warnings and competency of waiver:
   Examination of Mr. Competent's reading and language skills in comparison to the comprehension and reading levels required to fully understand the Miranda warnings indicate a significant discrepancy. His verbal abilities and overall mental abilities are in the mild mentally retarded range (lower 1% of the population) and range between the first- and fourth-grade levels. In contrast, grade level for the Miranda warnings typically fall between the sixth- and eighth-grade level (see research review by Helms, 2003). Based on these considerations, it is my opinion, expressed within a reasonable degree of psychological certainty, that Mr. Competent's waiver of his Miranda rights to the Metrotown police was unlikely to be "knowing and intelligent." I believe it was unlikely that he was able to waive these rights with a full awareness of the rights being waived and the consequences of the decision to wave them.

2. Concerning his ability to have knowingly and intelligently been able to respond to interrogation:
   Mr. Competent's low intellectual level along with his chronic mental illness would also have made it difficult for him to knowingly, intelligently, and voluntarily participated in his interrogation. He would have been unlikely to have withstood the stress of interrogation and also to understand the meaning and implications of seemingly "friendly" police. In other words, he would have a difficult time distinguishing between the fact and the appearance of friendliness. Research indicates that a high proportion of persons who are mentally retarded respond with "yes" answers regardless of the content of the questions (see Sigelman et al., 1981; "When in Doubt Say Yes: Acquiescence in Interviews with Mentally Retarded Persons"). Research also indicates that both mentally ill and mentally deficient persons are those who are most likely to provide what are often referred to as false confessions (Clare & Gudjonsson, 1993). They are much more susceptible to leading questions, confabulate more, and are more acquiescent to interrogators (Clare & Gudjonsson, 1993). They are also more likely to believe that falsely confessing will have little or no consequences. Thus Mr. Competent has an ideal set of characteristics that would make him at high risk of providing such "false confession."

Note that the opinions and conclusions herein are clinical in nature, and they do not represent legal conclusions. Ultimate legal questions are solely for the court to decide. I appreciate the opportunity to have been of service. Should you have any questions about the above client, please do not hesitate to contact me at your convenience.

Gary Groth-Marnat, Ph.D., ABPP, ABAP
California State License (PC XXXX)

References

Clare, I.C.H., & Gudjonsson, G.H. (1995). The vulnerability of suspects with intellectual disabilities during police interviews: A review and experimental study of decision-making. *Mental Handicap Research, 8*, 110–128.

Helms, J. L. (2003). Analysis of *Miranda* reading levels across jurisdictions: Implications for evaluating waiver competency. *Journal of Forensic Psychology Practice, 3*, 25–37.

Sigelman, B. E., Spanhel, C., & Schoenrock, C. (1981).When in doubt say yes: Acquiescence in interviews with mentally retarded persons. *Mental Retardation, April, 53–58.*

The Educational Setting*

NAME: Anna S.
DOB: XX/XX/XX
GENDER: Female
DATES OF ASSESSMENT: July 17, 21, 22, 24, 2001
DATE OF REPORT: August 4, 2007
EXAMINER: Annie Chung, Ph.D.

Referral Question

Anna is a 12-year, 1-month-old bilingual, Hispanic female who is currently residing in a foster home due to parental abuse, neglect, and abandonment. Anna presents with irritability, anxiety, and poor peer relations. Additionally, Anna's foster parents indicate that Anna is having problems in school because of interpersonal difficulties with her classmates and problems adjusting to their home (e.g., seeks constant attention, argues with foster siblings). Anna's therapist, Mary Smith, LCSW, requested this psychological evaluation to assist in assessing her current level of cognitive and emotional functioning, clarify her diagnosis, identify her strengths, and provide suggestions that may be useful in helping her to adjust to school.

Evaluation Procedures/Sources of Information

Clinical interview with Anna.
Consultation with Anna's social worker, therapist, teacher, and foster parents.
Wechsler Intelligence Scale for Children-IV (WISC-IV).
Wechsler Individual Achievement Test—Screener (WIAT).
Trauma Symptom Checklist for Children (TSCC).
Personality Inventory for Youth (PIY).
Children's Apperceptive Test.
Draw-A-Person/House-Tree-Person.
Review of social service/family court documents.
Review of current case file.
Child Self-Report and Projective Inventory (Color How You Feel, Critical Items, Color How Others Make You Feel, Perceived Competence, Draw a Child in the Rain, Sentence Completion, Kinetic Family Drawing).

---

* Report written and submitted by Annie Chung, PhD.

Behavioral Observations/Mental Health Status

During the initial testing session, Anna presented as a pleasant and engaging youth who was casually dressed and appropriately groomed. She appeared to be of average size and weight for her gender and chronological age. She willingly accompanied this examiner and appeared eager for individualized attention. Anna remained cooperative, maintained good eye contact, and readily responded to questions with descriptive details. She was clearly oriented to person, place, time, and situation. Her mood was somewhat depressed and her affect was generally constricted. She indicated that the reason for this evaluation "is to see how I'm doing." Anna demonstrated fair insight regarding her current situation, identifying her mother's abandonment of her as the reason for her current foster care placement and her associated feelings of distress. Her responses to hypothetical situations requiring decision-making skills suggest somewhat compromised judgment. Thought content was appropriate to the situation and thought processes were lucid, concrete, and coherent. There was no evidence of perceptual disturbances, flight of ideas, circumstantiality, or loose associations. Cognitive abilities appeared to be within the average range. Although not formally assessed, her conversational English skills were apparently proficient. When responding to direct questions, Anna typically responded in grammatically correct English. At times, she responded in Spanish but quickly restated her response in English, switching between both languages with apparent ease. During subsequent testing sessions, Anna's test-taking behaviors continued to be cooperative. Her approach to each task was marked by diligence, good effort, eagerness to please the examiner, and heightened performance anxiety (e.g., "Am I doing a good job?"). Although Anna exhibited good attention and concentration with the majority of testing activities, she also worked rapidly when given written tasks. Anna reported that she is "good at writing fast" and stated that she wanted this examiner to see how quickly she can work.

Even though Anna appeared to give her best efforts to the tasks presented to her, she is a bilingual youth whose first language is Spanish. Given that the tests administered were not specifically normed on this population, the assessment results should be treated with caution. In addition, she may have somewhat overreported her current level of emotional difficulties.

Background Information

Information obtained from family court documents, consultation with Anna's therapist, her social worker, her current foster parents, and interview with Anna indicates that she has experienced multiple disruptions in her home life events throughout her childhood. These events include physical/emotional abuse, neglect, and abandonment. Anna lived with her biological mother, Lupe S., until she was approximately 6 years old. At that time, Anna and Ms. S. moved in with Juan F., whom Anna refers to as her stepfather. Anna continued to reside primarily with her mother, stepfather, and their two children, Roberto and Juanita, until March 2007.

After moving in with her stepfather, Anna reported that her mother repeatedly stated, "I wish you [Anna] were never born," and that her parents frequently yelled at her, hit her, and did not provide adequate clothing. Furthermore, Anna reported that she and her mother frequently left her stepfather's home to live with other relatives or in homeless shelters because of her stepfather's "mean" behaviors but that her mother always returned to him. Family court documents indicate that there were five substantiated reports of physical/emotional abuse and neglect of Anna and/or her siblings by both her mother and stepfather. Anna's parents reportedly did not comply with family supervision plans as mandated by Child Protective Services. Additionally, Anna explained that over the past several years her mother exhibited "weird" behaviors such as rummaging through garbage cans, forgetting to wash clothes, and most pertinent to the child, witnessing her mother's attempt to choke herself. Anna also reported that her mother has been hospitalized at least four to five times for attempting to kill herself. In the past year, Anna was temporarily placed at the local children's shelter after running away from her home and when her stepfather attempted to abandon her at this facility. Subsequently, Anna resided with a maternal aunt for an undetermined amount of time before returning to her mother's care in the spring of this year.

During the spring of 2007, Anna and Ms. S. resided intermittently with relatives, Ms. S.'s employer, and then in a homeless shelter. Ms. S. then requested that acquaintances from church care for Anna. The acquaintances agreed to this on a temporary basis. However, they reported that Anna began having significant problems at school (e.g., suspended for fighting). Furthermore, these caretakers stated that Anna appeared to have significant "emotional problems" and were, therefore, unwilling to care for her any longer. They contacted Social Services and explained Anna's situation, clarifying that her mother was not available to care for her. As a result, Anna has been a ward of the state since May 2007 and has been placed in the foster home of Mr. and Mrs. G.

Anna's social worker referred Anna for mental health services given her history of neglect and abuse, physical aggression in school, and excessive irritability. On placement in her current foster home, Anna initially appeared very sad and had difficulties interacting with her foster siblings. Anna's foster parents indicated that Anna has not exhibited overt behavioral problems but does appear to be immature (e.g., excessive teasing, difficulty sharing), needs a considerable amount of individual attention, and displays excessive moodiness.

Interpretations and Impressions

Cognitive Functioning. Anna's overall ability was in the low-average range or the 16th percentile (WISC-IV Full Scale IQ = 85) compared with people her own age. A close examination of Anna's relative strengths indicates relatively intact visual-spatial/mechanical skills (Perceptual Reasoning Index = 91) as well as good verbal expression/conceptualization skills associated with school-related learning (Verbal Comprehension Index = 89). She is likely to do particularly well in tasks requiring her to understand social norms and follow the meaning of nonverbal social situations. This was consistent with this examiner's observations of Anna during the interview in which she responded appropriately and answered all questions clearly.

In contrast to these strengths, Anna's responses to tasks that required her to respond quickly and accurately to nonverbal information were quite low (Processing Speed = 67). This finding suggests that even though she can understand what might be expected of her in school, she will do poorly when she is required to perform under time constraints. In these conditions, she would be likely to sacrifice speed for accuracy. In addition, she may have a difficult time concentrating, especially when dealing with numerical information presented to her verbally (e.g., recalling phone numbers, making arithmetical calculations).

Achievement. In comparison to her low-average global cognitive potential (WISC-IV FSIQ = 85), Anna's composite academic achievement skills (WIAT Screener; Total SS = 93) is within the average range. Anna's scores on the Spelling (SS = 102) and Basic Reading (SS = 98) subtests suggest that these are relative strengths while her Mathematical Reasoning (SS = 81) skills are considerably weaker. However, Anna's solid average performance in Spelling and Basic Reading, which actually exceed her global cognitive potential, suggests that Anna's scores on the WISC-IV may be an underestimate of her true cognitive potential. This is likely because of her bilingualism and the absence of normative data pertaining to this specific population's performance on standardized intellectual assessment measures. Her lower scores on the IQ tests are also likely to result from her difficulties working under time constraints.

Emotional Functioning. Anna's reports of multiple and atypically severe intrapersonal discomfort is associated with her traumatic and disruptive childhood experiences. She is experiencing heightened levels of internal anxiety, depression, and uncertainty as well as low self-esteem. For example, she frequently provided self-deprecating remarks about her drawings (e.g., "it's ugly"), and the colors she used to represent her feelings depicted her emotional states as overwhelmingly sad and worried. She seems to harbor feelings of anger but has difficulty expressing these appropriately and, thus, may have a propensity to act out. However, it also appears that she attempts to mask her internal distress by presenting herself as outwardly happy and content. Furthermore, Anna depicts her life experiences as extremely stressful and has significant difficulty coping with such experiences. Her perceptions of her family and others indicate significant ambivalence, isolation, and alienation. For example, when prompted to draw a picture of her family, Anna did not include herself and depicted all family members enjoying activities independent of each other. However, she also incorporated symbols of warmth and closeness in her house drawings. Thus, Anna appears to hold conflictual feelings about her family while she also hopes for safety and support.

In response to questions eliciting Anna's experience of critical life events, she identified three specific traumatic experiences that appear to be associated with her current worries, fears, nightmares, and sadness. Anna reported that when she was about 8 years old, a homeless man attempted to take her while she was walking by herself in the evening but that she never shared this experience with her parents because she felt that it would not be important to them. Additionally, Anna explained that when she was about 10 years old, she witnessed her mother attempting to choke herself and subsequently worries that her mother will kill herself. Most recently, Anna reported that her mother left her with people that she did not know and has been feeling very sad and worried since that time. Anna indicated that she has difficulty staying asleep throughout the night as she has bad dreams about these "scary" events. She also admitted to having considerable difficulty concentrating at school because of intrusive thoughts about her past experiences and worries about her future.

Anna's interpretation of story cards was representative of overwhelmingly negative outcomes for the child figure. Themes included betrayal by mother, excessive worries and fears, abandonment and rejection by others, lack of caring and attention from mother, foreshortened future, harm inflicted by others, and inability to obtain wishes and desires such as reunification with family. Thus, it appears that Anna experiences her world as generally unsafe, unpredictable, and lacking emotional warmth. However, in one story, Anna projected a positive resolution for the child, in which the parents comforted and cared for the child "when she needed them." This suggests that Anna has a strong desire to be nurtured and accepted by caregivers.

Personal Strengths. In spite of Anna's traumatic and stressful life experiences, she is able to identify positive self-attributes related to her academic skills (e.g., spelling, handwriting), personal appearance, and athleticism. It appears that these strengths and perceived competencies bolster Anna's self-esteem and promote her ability to function on a day-to-day basis and hope for positive changes in her life.

Interpersonal Functioning. Anna typically responds to people with the hopes of obtaining attention and acceptance. This has been evident in her interactions with adults, which have been characterized by a strong eagerness to please, requests for individual attention, and gift-giving. However, Anna's negative experiences with her parents have likely bolstered her defenses against continued rejection. Therefore, Anna may respond by rejecting others first. This has been exemplified in her history of aggressive peer interactions, which have led to persistent teasing and fighting at school as well as her own reports of not having any "true" friends. While such behaviors have not been problematic at her current placement, Anna's foster parents have reported that her social interactions with peers have been immature (e.g., whining, teasing, difficulty sharing). Yet when provided with support and nurturing, Anna has become increasingly able to verbalize her difficulties and share painful experiences with adults (e.g., therapist, foster mother).

Behavioral Functioning. Assessment of Anna's overt behavior did not reveal high levels of acting out (e.g., aggression, delinquency). In contrast, she is likely to internalize her distress by becoming anxious and depressed. Anna's foster mother, Mrs. G., described Anna as initially very argumentative and oppositional but said that these behaviors subsided within the first several weeks in the new home. Overall, Mrs. G.'s ratings of Anna's current functioning suggest that Anna is not displaying significant behavioral concerns but that she does demonstrate symptoms of emotional distress at this time. It appears that Anna is responding positively to the structure, consistency, and nurturing provided by her foster parents although concerns associated with Anna's internal turmoil are evident.

Diagnostic Impressions

AXIS I	309.81	Posttraumatic Stress Disorder
	995.5	Neglect/Physical Abuse of Child
AXIS II	v71.09	No Diagnosis on AXIS II
AXIS III		None known/reported
AXIS IV		Abandonment by mother
AXIS V		Current GAF: 60
		Highest GAF past year: 50

Summary and Recommendations

Findings from this psychological evaluation indicate that: (a) Anna's academic skills in reading and spelling exceed her measured cognitive abilities, (b) she does not currently exhibit overt behavioral difficulties although peer/adult interactions have been strained, and (c) she is demonstrating and experiencing significant signs of emotional distress. While Anna's global cognitive ability score is within the low-average range, it is likely an underestimate of her true ability level given her higher-than-expected scores on spelling and reading skills. This finding suggests that Anna's bilingualism and slowed performance may have inhibited her ability to demonstrate her optimal cognitive ability on the WISC-III. It is also quite possible that Anna's exposure to early and persistent abuse/neglect may have impeded the development of her optimal cognitive functioning, which is likely to be in the average range. Anna's experience of multiple traumatic events, including the threat of an abduction by a stranger, witnessing her mother's suicide attempts, and abandonment, have further exacerbated her feelings of fear/uncertainty associated with persistent maltreatment by her parents. It is evident that Anna's worries, sadness, difficulty concentrating, and recurring nightmares are associated with these traumatic experiences. Subsequently, Anna's internal turmoil has been increasingly evident in her interpersonal relationships. With adults, Anna exhibits a strong desire to please and seeks constant individual attention. With peers, her attempts to be recognized have included a large repertoire of negative attention-seeking behaviors. Although obstructive, these patterns of relating to others appear to represent Anna's attempts to obtain any type of personal acknowledgment, albeit negative, in a world that she perceives as largely unsafe and threatening.

However, it is also important to highlight Anna's resiliency in the face of immense risk factors in her young life. Anna's ability to acquire new knowledge (e.g., proficiency in English) and her attempts to initiate relationships with others suggest that she possesses the capability to succeed in academic settings and is receptive to building social support networks outside of her family of origin. In spite of her current and expected difficulties associated with trauma, Anna presents as a likable youth who desires acceptance from others. Ensuring placement in a loving, consistent, and structured home environment that provides unconditional acceptance is absolutely crucial in supporting Anna's cognitive and socioemotional development and long-term stability. This is also likely to improve her cognitive level of functioning and enhance her academic performance.

Given the previous findings, the following recommendations seem appropriate:

1. Ensure regular attendance at school to bolster Anna's academic skills. Providing extra assistance/tutoring for mathematics and strategies on how best to work with timed tasks would be particularly helpful.
2. Provide Anna with opportunities to participate in structured community activities of interest to her (e.g., sports team) to promote her sense of self-efficacy and enable her to develop positive peer relationships in natural settings.
3. Provide Anna's foster parents with ongoing parenting education and parenting skills training to promote their understanding of Anna's needs (e.g., supportive structure, limit setting, explanations, consistency, acceptance) and use of specific strategies to promote Anna's positive adjustment to her new placement, as well as school.

4. Reevaluate Anna's cognitive and academic functioning, including language proficiency in English and Spanish, after stable home and academic placements are secured, to determine if a need for additional educational interventions are warranted.

5. Provide Anna with individual therapy that uses supportive as well as cognitive-behavioral strategies to enhance her ability to further process her thoughts/feelings about her situation, promote her self-esteem, facilitate her use of positive coping strategies when distressed, and alleviate her trauma-related symptoms. As therapy progresses, it would be important to help Anna understand and process her experience of her family, her abandonment, and abuse. Integrating and resolving these issues will be essential in assisting her to become a well-adapted adolescent and young adult.

Sourcenote: Report written and submitted by Annie Chung.

Psychology Clinic*

Mr. S.
100 Main Street
Smalltown, TX 7XXXX

Dear Mr. S.

This is the letter I promised you summarizing the results of the psychological assessment we did together this past month. As I did in our last session, I'll structure the letter by addressing each of your questions for the assessment:

Why can't I cry?

Mr. S., as you may remember, we worked mainly with two major personality tests, the Minnesota Multiphasic Personality Inventory-2 (MMPI-2)— the long true-false test you took—and the Rorschach inkblots. The combination of your scores on these two tests helped me understand why you can't cry at those times you wish you could.

The MMPI-2 excels at measuring people's outside "persona"—the way they present themselves to the world and generally think about themselves. Your results showed that you have *very* strong psychological coping mechanisms and that these help you keep difficult feelings "under wraps" and out of awareness. I believe these skills led to your reporting much less depression, anger, and anxiety than do most people who fill out the MMPI-2. This "picture" of you from the MMPI-2 is likely very similar to how you and others usually think of you—as a sturdy, non-reactive guy who is slow to anger, resilient, and not easily upset. This view of you captures important truths about who you are.

In contrast, the Rorschach excels at revealing "underlying" feelings—those that are affecting us at some level but of which we may be unaware. On this test you scored very much like people who are dealing with severely painful feelings, including sadness, anxiety, anger, remorse, alienation, and self doubt. I suspect these feelings also capture an important reality about you—that is, that you carry a lot of pain inside that is left over from difficult events earlier in your life. By

*Report contributed by Stephen Finn, Ph.D., Center for Therapeutic Assessment.

necessity, you found a way to put this pain aside when it first arose. Now it feels threatening to get too in touch with any feelings related to these "stored" emotions, so they're in "deep storage" and you're unable to cry even when you feel upset.

The Rorschach also suggests another another factor in your not crying: your emotional "controls" appear to be less developed than would be optimal for your age. As you so aptly said, at this point you have more of an "on-off" switch for emotions rather than a "rheostat." This situation is common when one has had to shut off and avoid feelings early in life in order to be safe. While this coping strategy served you well, your emotional management skills didn't get to grow up as fast as the rest of you. Now, if you open up inside to strong emotions, they are likely to flood you, overwhelm you, disrupt your ability to think clearly, and leave you feeling confused and out of control. Thus, you generally keep the switch turned "off."

So, in short, until you've had a chance to develop better emotional controls and to find support from someone who is knowledgeable about emotional blockages, it may be too scary to cry. In the meantime, it does seem that you are developing more access to your feelings and finding that this helps you rather than hurts you (e.g., in intimate relationships).

Why do I remember so little of my childhood?

Mr. S., as you know, for your assessment I talked with Dr. Smith (your therapist from ages 7–14) and he told me his impressions of your childhood. I also know some things about your family situation from talking to your parents when I assessed them and your sister. Last, you did write about some early events on the Early Memory Procedure. (I'm returning the original booklet to you with this letter.)

From all accounts, when you were little, you experienced some traumatic abandonments and violent family scenes that would have been quite emotionally overwhelming for any small child. On top of this, you didn't have adequate emotional support at that time from those around you so you could process these experiences and the feelings they must have generated. So at least some of the time, you reportedly "tuned out" or "dissociated" as a coping mechanism. This is very much like an emotional "fuse" blowing to shut down certain parts of the brain when it is flooded and overwhelmed. Typically this is a last-ditch survival mechanism when one is unable to physically flee or fight in a terrifying situation.

What all this means is that some of your childhood memories were probably not even "encoded" at the time, because you were so overwhelmed and in a state of emotional shock. (Shock is an altered state where our senses screen out incoming data to keep us from getting more overwhelmed.) In addition, it's likely that some memories are still there, but they are currently being kept out of awareness because you aren't yet ready to face the feelings that would result if you had those memories back. Such feelings could overwhelm you even now until you develop better emotional controls. Plus, as you yourself said, you're not ready to deal with the effects on your relationship with your parents of knowing all that went on when you were a child. Thus, you have been intuitively taking care of yourself by not remembering much from your childhood.

Why did I repeatedly put myself in the role of a caregiver with girlfriends and women friends?

Let me remind you of some things you already know: You and your father have been caregivers in the past of your mother, so this role was familiar to you and modeled to you as the way to be with women. Also, the caregiver role has been a way to feel good about yourself; there is a part of you that genuinely wants to help people and feels good when you can, and such behavior has been rewarded in the past. Third, from watching your mother, you decided you never wanted to lean too much on others; this pushed you to "overcorrect"—that is, to deny your own needs to be cared for and to focus mainly on caring for others.

The testing adds the following pieces to the puzzle: Because your feelings were shut down to protect you, you weren't very in touch with your anger and thus couldn't realize that at times you felt taken advantage of by women who were leaning on you heavily. Also, for many of us, when we are focused outside ourselves on helping other people with their emotional pain, it helps keep our own pain at bay. Last, I believe all this is a way we go about healing also. We project our own sad and hurt feelings out on others (or find people who seem to embody these feelings) and then we try to "fix" the problem outside ourselves. Eventually, if all goes well, we eventually are forced into a major confrontation with ourselves—that we too have needs for support and caring—and that we can't address those needs by simply caring for others. You seem to have been having such a realization lately.

It's so great to see the progress you've made in this area, Mr. S. The testing says you are still at risk to fall into caregiver roles, so you'll want to keep an eye out for this and pay attention to any anger you feel about supporting others. Such anger could be a sign that you are doing too much.

Why do I often not know how I am feeling?

Mr. S., you described a shift around ninth grade when you started to feel more in control and more sure of yourself. I wonder if this is the time when you finally achieved some success in shutting down your own feelings so you would not feel anxious, stirred up, and overwhelmed all the time. However, you were probably already using pieces of this coping mechanism much earlier. Again, I believe such a strategy would have helped you not "rock the boat" at home—which would have helped keep your mom stable and your parents from fighting. Your coping style was modeled after someone you admired and were close to—your dad. And as we talked about, as a child you also got rewards from other people when you didn't show normal feelings of anger, impatience, or irritation—for being so "adult," "precocious," and "well mannered."

Last, what I understand from the testing is this: After a while, the feelings you had put aside were so huge and painful that you would need help accessing them and managing them. Plus, experience had taught you that the people you loved most—your parents—were not really able to help you process painful emotions. This left you with few choices. Since you, like the rest of us, don't like feeling out of control of your emotions, you did what made sense: kept your feelings out of awareness. As we discussed, I believe that when you are ready, it will be very helpful to "open up" some of these feelings—with the support of a therapist—and that doing so will help you succeed in your intimate relationships.

Mr S., I very much enjoyed working with you and I hope the assessment and this letter are helpful. Please don't hesitate to call, visit, or e-mail me if you have any questions about the results of your assessment.

> Last, I have a request for you. Would you be willing to fill out the enclosed forms giving me feedback about the assessment and mail them back to me? Your honest comments would help me serve other people in the future.
>
> With my very best wishes for your future,
> Stephen E. Finn, Ph.D.
> Licensed Psychologist
>
> _____
>
> Sourcenote: Report written and submitted by Stephen E. Finn, PH.D. Center for Therapeutic Assessment.

RECOMMENDED READING

Finn, S. E. (2007). *In our client's shoes: Theory and techniques of therapeutic assessment*. Mahwah, NJ: Lawrence Erlbaum.

Groth-Marnat, G. (2006). The psychological report: A review of current controversies. *Journal of Clinical Psychology, 62*, 73–81.

Harvey, V. S. (2006). Variables affecting the clarity of reports. *Journal of Clinical Psychology, 62*, 5–18.

Norcross, J. C. (2006). Integrating self-help into psychotherapy: 16 practical suggestions. *Professional Psychology: Research & Practice, 37*, 683–693.

Norcross, J., Santrock, J. W., Campbell, L. F., Smith, T. P., Sommer, R., & Zuckerman, E. L. (2003). *Authoritative guide to self-help resources in mental health*. New York: Guilford Press.

Zuckerman, E. L. (2005). *The clinician's thesaurus: A guidebook for wording psychological reports* (6th ed.). Pittsburgh, PA: Three Wishes Press.

TEST PUBLISHERS/DISTRIBUTORS

American Guidance Service, Inc.

Publisher's Building

Circle Pines, MN 55014-1796

1-800-328-2560

List includes: Kaufman Assessment Battery for Children-II, Kaufman Adolescent and Adult Intelligence Test, Kaufman Brief Intelligence Test

Center for Behavioral Health Care Technologies, Inc.

3600 S. Harbor Boulevard, #86

Oxnard, CA 93035

1-805-677-4501

e-mail: info@cbhti.com

www.systematictreatmentselection.com

List includes: Systematic Treatment Selection software

Consulting Psychologists Press

1055 Joaquin Road, 2nd Floor

Mountain View, CA 94043

1-650-969-8901

1-800- 624-1765

Fax: 1-650-969-8608

www.cpp.com

List includes: California Psychological Inventory, Fundamental Interpersonal Relations Orientation-B, Myers Briggs Type Indicator, Strong Interest Inventory

Harcourt Assessment (see Pearson Assessment)
Jastak Associates, Inc.

1526 Gilpin Avenue

Wilmington, DE 19806

1-800-221-WRAT

List includes: Wide Range Achievement Test

Lafayette Instrument Company
P.O. Box 5729
Lafayette, IN 47903
1-800-428-7545
List includes: Hand dynamometer (grip strength)

NFER-Nelson Publishing Co.
Darville House
2 Oxford Road
East Windsor
Berkshire 21A IDF, UK
List includes: National Adult Reading Test

National Computer Systems, Inc. (NCS; see **Pearson Assessment**)
Neuropsychology Laboratory
University of Victoria
P.O. Box 1700
Victoria, BC CANADA
List includes: Paced Auditory Serial Addition Test, Stroop Color-Word Test (Victoria version)

Pearson Assessment (previously Harcourt Assessment, Psycholgical Corporation, and National Computer Systems)
P.O. Box 599700
   San Antonio, TX 78259
1-800-211-8378
Fax: 1-800-232-1223

List includes: Beck Depression Inventory-II, Bender Visual Motor Gestalt-II, Brief Symptom Inventory, California Verbal Learning Test, Career Assessment Inventory, Children's Depression Inventory, Children's Category Test, Children's Memory Scale, Kaufman Assessment Battery for Children-II, Kaufman Adolescent and Adult Intelligence Test, Kaufman Test of Educational Achievement, Millon Behavioral Heatlh Inventory, Millon Clinical Multiaxial Inventory-III, Minnesota Multiphasic Personality Inventory-2, Minnesota Multiphasic Personality Inventory-2-RC Paced Auditory Serial Addition Test, Repeatable Battery for the Assessment of Neuropsychological Status, Rorschach, Sixteen Personality Factors (16 PF), Symptom Checklist 90-R, Wechsler Adult Intelligence Scale-IV, Taylor Johnson Temperament Analysis, Thematic Apperception Test, Test of Memory Malingering, Wechsler Individual Achievement Test-II, Wechsler Intelligence Scale for Children-IV, Wechsler Preschool and Primary Scale for Children-III, Wechsler Memory Scale-IV, Wechsler Test of Adult Reading, Wide Range Test of Memory and Learning

Psychological Assessment Resources

16204 N. Florida Avenue

Lutz, FL 33549

1-800-331-8378

Fax: 1-800-727-9329

Tech Support: 1-800-899-8378

www.parinc.com

List includes: BarOn Emotional Quotient Inventory, Behavioral Assessment of the Dysecutive Syndrome, Bender Visual Motor Gestalt Test, Benton Visual Retention Test, Boston Diagnostic Aphasia Examination, Boston Naming Test, Category Test (computer version), Children's Apperception Test, Children's Auditory Verbal Learning Test, Children's Category Test, Cognitive Assessment System, Color Trails Test, Connor's Rating Scales, Finger Tapping, Hand Dynamometer, Hare Psychopathy Checklist-Revised, House Tree Person, Kaufman Adolescent and Adult Intelligence Test, Kaufman Assessment Battery for Children-II, KOPPITZ-2 (Koppitz Developmental Scoring System fo the Bender, NEO-PI-R, Personality Assessment Inventory, Personality Disorder Interview-IV, Repeatable Battery for the Assessment of Neuropsychological Status, Rey Auditory Verbal Learning Test, Rey Complex Figure and Recognition Trial, Rivermead Behavioural Memory Test, Rorschach Self Directed Search, Sentence Completion Series, State Trait Anger Expression Inventory, State Trait Anxiety Inventory, State Trait Anxiety Inventory for Children, Stroop Neuropsychological Screening Test, Stroop Color and Word Test, Tactual Performance Test, Taylor Johnson Temperament Analysis, Test of Everyday Attention, Test of Nonverbal Intelligence, Thematic Apperception Test, Wide Range Achievement Test, Wide Range Assessment of Memory and Learning, Wisconson Card Sorting Test

Psychological Corporation (see Pearson Assessment)

Reitan Neuropsychology Laboratory

2920 South 4th Avenue

Tucson, AZ 85713-4819

List includes: Halstead Reitan Neuropsychological Test Battery, Neuropsychological History Questionnaire

Riverside Publishing Co.

8420 Bryn Mawr Avenue

Chicago, IL 60631

1-201-729-6031

List includes: Bender Visual Motor Gestalt Test-II, Das Naglieri Cognitive Assessment System, Stanford-Binet, Woodcock Johnson-III

Western Psychological Services

12031 Wilshire Boulevard

Los Angeles, CA 90025-1251

1-800-222-2670

www.wpspublish.com

List includes: AAMR Adaptive Behavior Scales, Adolescent Apperception Test, Behavior Rating Inventory of Executive Functions, Bender Visual Motor Gestalt Test, Children's Category Test, Children's Depression Inventory, Comprehensive Test of Nonverbal Intelligence, Connor's Rating Scales, Draw-a-Person, Eating Disorders Inventory, House-Tree-Person, Human Figure Drawing Test, Family Apperception Test, Kaufman Adolescent and Adult Intelligence Test, Kaufman Assessment Battery for Children, Luria Nebraska Neuropsychological Battery, Millon Index of Personality Styles, Personality Assessment Inventory, Personality Inventory for Children, Psychopathy Checklist, Rey Auditory and Verbal Learning Test, Rivermead Behavioral Memory Test, Rey Auditory Verbal Learning Test, Roberts Apperception Test, Rorschach, Sixteen PF (16 PF), Self-Directed Search, State Trait Anger Expression Inventory, Symbol Digit Modalities Test, Thematic Apperception Test, Taylor Johnson Temperament Analysis, Test of Everyday Attention, Tell Me A Story, Wide Range Achievement Test, Wisconsin Card Sorting

TESTING ORGANIZATIONS

American Psychological Association
750 First Street, NE
Washington, DC 20002-4242
1-800-374-2721
1-202-336-5500
www.apa.org

Board on Testing and Assessment
The National Academies
500 Fifth Street, NW, 11th Floor
Washington, DC 20001
1-202-334-3462
Fax: 1-202-344-1294
www7.nationalacademies.org/bota/

Buros Institute of Mental Measurements
University of Nebraska, Lincoln
21 Teachers College Hall
Lincoln, NE 68588-0348
1-402-472-6203
www.unl.edu/buros/bimm

Institute for Personality and Ability Testing
1801 Woodfield Drive
Savoy, IL 61874
1-800-225-4728
1-217-352-4739
Fax: 1-217-352-9674
www.ipat.com/

International Neuropsychological Society
700 Ackerman Road, Suite 625
Columbus, Ohio 43202

1-614-263-4200
Fax: 1-614- 263-4366
www.the-ins.org/contact/

National Academy of Neuropsychology
2121 South Oneida Street, Suite 550
Denver, CO 80224-2594
1-303-691-3694
Fax: 1-303-691-5983
www.nanonline.org

National Council on Measurement in Education (NCME)
Central Office
2810 Crossroads Drive, Suite 3800
Madison, WI 53718
1-608-443-2487
Fax: 1-608-443-2474
www.ncme.org/contact.cfm

Society for Industrial and Organizational Psychology
P.O. Box 87
520 Ordway Avenue
Bowling Green, OH 43402-0087
1-419-353-0032
Fax: 1-419-352-2645
www.siop.org/contact.aspx

Society for Personality Assessment
6109H Arlington Boulevard
Falls Church, Virginia 22044
1-703-534-4SPA (1-703-534-4772)
Fax: 1-703-534-6905
www.personality.org

Appendix C

WISC-IV NORMS TABLES FOR CLINICAL CLUSTERS

Table C.1.   Fluid reasoning (*Gf*) cluster equivalent of sums of scaled scores for matrix reasoning, picture concepts, and arithmetic

Sum of scaled scores	*Gf* cluster	95% Confidence interval	Percentile rank
3	50	42–58	.05
4	52	44–60	.07
5	54	46–62	.11
6	55	47–63	.16
7	57	49–65	.20
8	59	51–67	.30
9	61	53–69	.49
10	62	54–70	1
11	64	56–72	1
12	66	58–74	1
13	67	59–75	1
14	69	61–77	2
15	71	63–79	3
16	73	65–81	3
17	75	67–83	5
18	77	69–85	6
19	78	70–86	7
20	80	72–88	9
21	82	74–90	12
22	84	76–92	14
23	86	78–94	17
24	88	80–96	21
25	90	82–98	25
26	92	84–100	29
27	94	86–102	35

Tables in Appendix C reprinted with permission from: D.P. Flanagan & A.S. Kaufman (2004). Essentials of WISC-IV Assessment (pp. 336-357). John Wiley & Sons, Inc., Hoboken:NY.

Continued

Table C.1.   Continued

Sum of scaled scores	Gf cluster	95% Confidence interval	Percentile rank
28	96	88–104	40
29	98	90–106	45
30	100	92–108	50
31	102	94–110	55
32	104	96–112	62
33	106	98–114	65
34	109	101–117	73
35	111	103–119	77
36	113	105–121	81
37	115	107–123	84
38	117	109–125	87
39	119	111–127	89
40	121	113–129	92
41	123	115–131	93
42	125	117–133	95
43	127	119–135	97
44	129	121–137	97
45	131	123–139	98
46	132	124–140	98
47	134	126–142	99
48	136	128–144	99
49	137	129–145	99
50	139	131–147	99.57
51	141	133–149	99.70
52	142	134–150	99.75
53	144	136–152	99.84
54	146	138–154	99.89
55	147	139–155	99.93
56	149	141–157	99.94
57	150	142–158	99.95

Table C.2. **Visual processing (*Gv*) cluster equivalent of sums of scaled scores for block design and picture completion**

Sum of scaled scores	*Gv* cluster	95% Confidence interval	Percentile rank
2	50	41–59	.05
3	53	44–62	.09
4	56	47–65	.16
5	59	50–68	.30
6	62	53–71	1
7	65	56–74	1
8	67	58–76	1
9	70	61–79	2
10	72	63–81	3
11	75	66–84	5
12	78	69–87	7
13	80	71–89	9
14	83	74–92	13
15	86	77–95	17
16	88	79–97	21
17	91	82–100	27
18	94	85–103	35
19	97	88–106	43
20	100	91–109	50
21	103	94–112	57
22	106	97–115	65
23	108	99–117	71
24	111	102–120	77
25	114	105–123	83
26	117	108–126	87
27	120	111–129	91
28	123	114–132	93
29	126	117–135	96
30	130	121–139	98
31	133	124–142	99
32	135	126–144	99
33	138	129–147	99
34	140	131–149	99.64
35	143	134–152	99.80
36	145	136–154	99.87
37	148	139–157	99.93
38	150	141–159	99.95

Table C.3.   Nonverbal fluid reasoning (*Gf*-nonverbal) cluster equivalent of sums of scaled scores for matrix reasoning and picture concepts

Sum of scaled scores	*Gf*-nonverbal cluster	95% Confidence interval	Percentile rank
2	50	41–59	.05
3	53	44–62	.09
4	55	46–64	.16
5	58	49–67	.25
6	61	52–70	.49
7	64	55–73	1
8	67	58–76	1
9	69	60–78	2
10	71	62–80	3
11	74	65–83	4
12	77	68–86	6
13	79	70–88	8
14	82	73–91	12
15	85	76–94	16
16	88	79–97	21
17	91	82–100	27
18	94	85–103	35
19	97	88–106	43
20	100	91–109	50
21	103	94–112	57
22	106	97–115	65
23	109	100–118	73
24	112	103–121	79
25	115	106–124	84
26	118	109–127	88
27	121	112–130	92
28	124	115–133	95
29	127	118–136	97
30	130	121–139	98
31	133	124–142	99
32	135	126–144	99
33	138	129–147	99
34	140	131–149	99.64
35	143	134–152	99.80
36	145	136–154	99.87
37	148	139–157	99.93
38	150	141–159	99.95

Table C.4.   Verbal fluid reasoning (*Gf*-verbal) cluster equivalent of sums of scaled scores for similarities and word reasoning

Sum of scaled scores	*Gf*-verbal cluster	95% Confidence interval	Percentile rank
2	50	40–60	.05
3	52	42–62	.07
4	55	45–65	.16
5	58	48–68	.25
6	61	51–71	.49
7	63	53–73	1
8	66	56–76	1
9	69	59–79	2
10	72	62–82	3
11	75	65–85	5
12	78	68–88	7
13	81	71–91	11
14	84	74–94	14
15	86	76–96	17
16	89	79–99	21
17	92	82–102	29
18	94	84–104	35
19	97	87–107	43
20	100	90–110	50
21	102	92–112	55
22	105	95–115	65
23	108	98–118	71
24	111	101–121	77
25	113	103–123	81
26	116	106–126	86
27	120	110–130	91
28	123	112–133	93
29	126	116–136	96
30	129	119–139	97
31	132	122–142	98
32	135	125–145	99
33	137	127–147	99
34	140	130–150	99.64
35	142	132–152	99.75
36	145	135–155	99.87
37	147	137–157	99.93
38	150	140–160	99.95

Table C.5.   Lexical knowledge (*Gc*-VL) cluster equivalent of sums of scaled scores for word reasoning and Vocabulary

Sum of scaled scores	*Gc* -VL cluster	95% Confidence interval	Percentile rank
2	50	41–59	.05
3	53	44–62	.09
4	56	47–65	.16
5	59	50–68	.30
6	62	53–71	1
7	65	56–74	1
8	68	59–77	2
9	71	62–80	3
10	74	65–83	4
11	76	67–85	5
12	79	70–88	8
13	81	72–90	11
14	84	75–93	14
15	86	77–95	17
16	89	80–98	21
17	91	82–100	27
18	94	85–103	35
19	96	87–105	40
20	99	90–108	48
21	102	93–111	55
22	105	96–114	65
23	108	99–117	71
24	110	101–119	75
25	113	104–122	81
26	116	107–125	86
27	120	111–129	91
28	123	114–132	93
29	126	117–135	96
30	129	120–138	97
31	132	123–141	98
32	135	126–144	99
33	137	128–146	99
34	140	131–149	99.64
35	142	133–151	99.75
36	145	136–154	99.87
37	147	138–156	99.93
38	150	141–159	99.95

Table C.6.   General information (*Gc*-K0) cluster equivalent of sums of scaled scores for comprehension and information

Sum of scaled scores	*Gc* -K0 cluster	95% Confidence interval	Percentile rank
2	50	40–60	.05
3	53	43–63	.09
4	56	46–66	.16
5	59	49–69	.30
6	62	52–72	1
7	65	55–75	1
8	68	58–78	2
9	71	61–81	3
10	73	63–83	3
11	76	66–86	5
12	78	68–88	7
13	81	71–91	11
14	83	73–93	13
15	85	75–95	16
16	88	78–98	21
17	91	81–101	27
18	94	84–104	35
19	97	87–107	43
20	99	89–109	48
21	102	92–112	55
22	105	95–115	65
23	108	98–118	71
24	111	101–121	77
25	114	104–124	83
26	117	107–127	87
27	120	110–130	91
28	123	113–133	93
29	126	116–136	96
30	129	119–139	97
31	131	121–141	98
32	133	123–143	99
33	136	126–146	99
34	139	129–149	99.57
35	142	132–152	99.75
36	145	135–155	99.87
37	148	138–158	99.93
38	150	140–160	99.95

Table C.7.   Long-term memory (*Gc*-LTM) cluster equivalent of sums of scaled scores for vocabulary and information

Sum of scaled scores	*Gc*-LTM cluster	95% Confidence interval	Percentile rank
2	50	42–58	.04
3	54	46–62	.11
4	57	49–65	.20
5	60	52–68	.36
6	63	55–71	1
7	66	58–74	1
8	69	61–77	2
9	72	64–80	3
10	74	66–82	3
11	77	69–85	6
12	79	71–87	8
13	81	73–89	11
14	84	76–92	14
15	87	79–95	19
16	89	81–97	21
17	91	83–99	27
18	94	86–102	35
19	97	89–105	43
20	99	91–107	48
21	102	94–110	55
22	105	97–113	65
23	108	100–116	71
24	111	103–119	77
25	113	105–121	81
26	116	108–124	86
27	119	111–127	89
28	122	114–130	92
29	125	117–133	95
30	127	119–135	97
31	130	122–138	98
32	133	125–141	99
33	136	128–144	99
34	138	130–146	99
35	141	133–149	99.70
36	144	136–152	99.84
37	147	139–155	99.93
38	150	142–158	99.95

Table C.8.   Short-term memory (*Gsm*-WM) cluster equivalent of sums of scaled scores for letter-number sequencing and digit span

Sum of scaled scores	*Gsm*-WM cluster	95% Confidence interval	Percentile rank
2	50	42–58	.05
3	52	44–60	.07
4	54	46–62	.11
5	56	48–64	.16
6	59	51–67	.30
7	62	54–70	1
8	65	57–73	1
9	68	60–76	2
10	71	63–79	3
11	74	66–82	4
12	77	69–85	6
13	80	72–88	9
14	83	75–91	13
15	86	78–94	17
16	88	80–96	21
17	91	83–99	27
18	94	86–102	35
19	97	89–105	43
20	99	91–107	48
21	102	94–110	55
22	104	96–112	62
23	107	99–115	67
24	110	102–118	75
25	113	105–121	81
26	116	108–124	86
27	120	112–128	91
28	123	115–131	94
29	126	118–134	96
30	129	121–137	97
31	132	124–140	98
32	135	127–143	99
33	138	130–146	99
34	141	133–149	99.70
35	144	136–152	99.84
36	146	138–154	99.89
37	148	140–156	99.93
38	150	142–158	99.95

Note: The *Gsm*-WM Cluster is identical to the WISC-IV Working Memory Index (WMI).

Appendix D

DIRECTIONS FOR HAND SCORING THE MINNESOTA MULTIPHASIC PERSONALITY INVENTORY (MMPI-2) VALIDITY AND CLINICAL SCALES

1. Separate the Scale 5 (Mf) scoring keys by sex to correspond with the sex of the person who has taken the test.

2. With a colored pen, cross out items that have been either omitted or double marked. Count them as cannot say (?) responses, and enter the raw score (total number) on the profile sheet indicated to the right of "? Raw Score."

3. Then place scoring keys for the validity and clinical scales over the "softcover answer sheet." Be sure to match the horizantal black rectangles on the top and bottom right side of the templates with the horizantal black rectangles on the top and bottom right side of the "softcover answer sheet." Count the total number of marked items to determine the raw scores for each of the scales. Ignore items marked with a colored pen to designate they are cannot say (?) responses. Enter the raw scores for each of the scales in the designated sections on the profile sheet. Examiners should make sure that the gender indicated on the profile sheet matches the gender of the examinee.

4. Before plotting the profile, add K corrections to the raw scores for Hs, Pd, Pt, Sc, and Ma. First calculate the appropriate fractions of K (.5K to Hs; .4K to Pd; 1K to Pt; 1K to Sc; and .2K to Ma) using the box to the far left of the profile sheet designated as "Fractions of K." The raw score of K that was derived from scoring K can be located in the far left column of the "Fractions of K" box. The three numbers to the right of the raw score of K are the correct fractions of K. For example, if a raw score for K was 15, then .5K, .4K, and .2K would be 8, 6, and 3, respectively. Then add the correct fractions of K to the raw scores for Hs, Pd, and Ma. Pt and Sc both have a full K correction added to them.

5. When K corrections have been added to Hs, Pd, Pt, Sc, and Ma, the raw scores for the clinical scales can be plotted on the profile sheet. Note the lower-scale labels (Hs1.5K, etc.) and find the correct raw score on the profile sheet directly above them. Then mark these raw scores with a dot, circle, or cross. When they have all been marked, draw a line connecting the 10 clinical scales. The T scores can be found by lining up the raw scores with the correct T scores on either the far right or the far left of the profile sheet (designated as "T or Tc"). For example, a raw score of 25 on Scale 1 (Hs) converts to a T score of 80.

6. The final step is calculating the scores for VRIN and TRIN. A separate answer (or "Recording Grid") sheet is required. First, transfer all items for the VRIN scale from the main answer sheet to the VRIN answer sheet/recording grid. (See the number of items listed on the right side of the answer sheet/recording grid to identify which

of the items need to be transferred.) For example, if the response for item 3 was "True," then mark the "True" circle on the VRIN answer sheet/recording grid.

7. Next, place the VRIN-1 scoring template over the grid. Be sure to match up the two vertical black rectangles on the template with the two vertical black rectangles on the answer sheet/recording grid.

8. If both pairs of boxes on the grid have a blackened response, record a "+" sign on the far right side of the answer sheet/recording grid. Do the same for the template indicated as VRIN-2, then total the +s and record the total score.

9. The TRIN answer sheet/recording grid is on the opposite side of the answer sheet/recording grid as that for VRIN. In order to score for TRIN, first transfer the item pairs from the main answer sheet to the TRIN answer sheet/recording grid (as was done for VRIN).

10. Then place the TRIN-1 scoring template over the answer sheet/recording grid (as was done for VRIN). If both item pairs have blackened responses, enter a "+" sign on the line to the far right of the answer sheet/recording grid. Count the total number of +s and write this down on the line just to the right of "TRIN-1."

11. Next place the TRIN-2 scoring template over the answer sheet/scoring grid. Whenever both item pairs have blackened responses, write down a "–" sign on the far right line of the answer sheet/recording grid. Count the total number of –s and write this down on the line just to the right of "TRIN-2."

12. Subtract the total TRIN-2 score from the total TRIN-1 score and enter the result to the right of where it says =. Add 9 points to calculate the TRIN Total.

13. Enter the VRIN and TRIN Totals on the validity/clinical scale profile sheet. Like the other scales, the VRIN and TRIN scores can be plotted with a dot, circle, or cross. When all the validity scales (including VRIN and TRIN) have been recorded and plotted, a line can be drawn connecting each of the validity scales (as was done for the 10 clinical scales). The T scores can be found by lining up the raw scores with the correct T scores on either the far right or the far left of the profile sheet.

Appendix E

RORSCHACH NORMS FOR SCORING CATEGORIES

Table E.1.   Descriptive statistics for 450 nonpatient adults

Variable	Mean	SD	Min	Max	Freq	Median	Mode	SK	KU
AGE	34.90	13.42	19.00	86.00	450	31.00	27.00	1.20	1.24
Years Education	14.00	1.99	8.00	21.00	450	14.00	12.00	0.91	0.89
R	23.36	5.68	14.00	59.00	450	23.00	22.00	1.89	6.75
W	9.10	3.70	2.00	37.00	450	8.00	8.00	2.12	9.48
D	12.66	4.75	0.00	36.00	448	13.00	14.00	0.29	1.92
Dd	1.60	[2.06]	0.00	21.00	317	1.00	1.00	3.77	24.48
S	2.37	[1.97]	0.00	17.00	407	2.00	1.00	2.27	9.69
DQ+	8.43	3.07	1.00	21.00	450	8.00	9.00	0.64	1.47
DQo	14.29	4.66	4.00	40.00	450	14.00	14.00	1.30	4.26
DQv	0.37	[0.72]	0.00	4.00	119	0.00	0.00	2.34	6.36
DQv/+	0.27	[0.61]	0.00	6.00	97	0.00	0.00	3.46	19.76
FQx+	0.54	[0.93]	0.00	7.00	153	0.00	0.00	2.32	7.87
FQxo	15.09	3.22	6.00	29.00	450	15.00	16.00	0.02	0.87
FQxu	4.85	2.93	0.00	24.00	448	4.00	4.00	1.99	7.10
FQx−	2.73	2.01	0.00	18.00	425	2.00	2.00	2.21	9.86
FQxNone	0.15	[0.41]	0.00	3.00	57	0.00	0.00	3.09	10.65
MQ+	0.42	[0.72]	0.00	4.00	136	0.00	0.00	1.71	2.54
MQo	3.74	1.79	0.00	9.00	443	4.00	3.00	0.29	−0.35
MQu	0.44	0.81	0.00	5.00	139	0.00	0.00	2.65	9.45
MQ−	0.23	[0.57]	0.00	5.00	81	0.00	0.00	3.48	17.58
MQNone	0.01	[0.08]	0.00	1.00	3	0.00	0.00	12.16	146.64
SQual−	0.58	[0.89]	0.00	6.00	182	0.00	0.00	2.13	6.33
M	4.83	2.18	0.00	12.00	449	5.00	4.00	0.44	0.18
FM	4.04	1.90	0.00	10.00	441	4.00	4.00	0.33	0.36
m	1.57	1.34	0.00	10.00	361	1.00	1.00	1.57	5.33
FC	2.97	1.78	0.00	11.00	416	3.00	2.00	0.59	0.71
CF	2.80	1.64	0.00	12.00	426	3.00	2.00	0.99	3.42
C	0.17	[0.45]	0.00	3.00	64	0.00	0.00	3.02	10.37
Cn	0.00	[0.07]	0.00	1.00	2	0.00	0.00	14.95	222.48
Sum Color	5.95	2.47	0.00	14.00	448	6.00	5.00	0.38	0.16
WSumC	4.54	1.98	0.00	15.00	448	4.50	4.00	0.74	2.06
Sum C'	1.60	[1.33]	0.00	9.00	371	1.00	1.00	1.58	4.62
Sum T	1.01	[0.69]	0.00	4.00	364	1.00	1.00	0.76	1.86
Sum V	0.35	[0.77]	0.00	5.00	106	0.00	0.00	2.88	9.92
Sum Y	0.97	[1.20]	0.00	9.00	261	1.00	0.00	2.27	8.62
Sum Shading	3.94	2.45	0.00	21.00	445	3.00	3.00	2.24	8.97
Fr+rF	0.20	[0.67]	0.00	7.00	54	0.00	0.00	5.08	34.50

Source for table in this Appendix: From *The Rorschach: A Comprehensive System, Volume 2. Advanced Interpretation* (3rd ed.) by J.E. Exner, Jr. & Philip Erdberg. Hoboken, NJ: John Wiley & Sons. Copyright © 2005 by John Exner, Jr. and Philip Erdberg with permission.

Continued

Table E.1   Continued

Variable	Mean	SD	Min	Max	Freq	Median	Mode	SK	KU
FD	1.43	[1.15]	0.00	8.00	360	1.00	1.00	1.21	3.10
F	7.91	3.70	0.00	32.00	449	7.00	7.00	1.56	6.00
(2)	8.82	3.08	2.00	30.00	450	9.00	8.00	1.54	7.18
3r+(2)/R	0.40	0.10	0.12	0.87	450	0.39	0.38	0.77	2.23
Lambda	0.58	0.37	0.00	2.33	449	0.47	0.50	1.56	2.82
FM+m	5.61	2.51	0.00	20.00	449	5.00	5.00	1.06	4.02
EA	9.37	3.00	2.00	24.00	450	9.50	8.00	0.51	1.64
es	9.55	4.01	2.00	34.00	450	9.00	8.00	1.91	8.12
D Score	−0.12	0.99	−7.00	3.00	142	0.00	0.00	−1.84	9.39
AdjD	0.19	0.83	−3.00	3.00	167	0.00	0.00	−0.19	3.07
a (active)	6.76	2.87	0.00	19.00	447	7.00	7.00	0.29	0.84
p (passive)	3.73	2.34	0.00	17.00	430	3.00	3.00	1.41	4.48
Ma	2.93	1.67	0.00	10.00	423	3.00	3.00	0.59	0.84
Mp	1.93	1.37	0.00	10.00	395	2.00	1.00	1.17	3.43
Intellect	2.17	2.15	0.00	15.00	360	2.00	1.00	1.78	4.82
Zf	13.45	4.22	2.00	41.00	450	13.00	14.00	1.81	6.72
Zd	0.25	3.71	−13.50	12.00	420	0.00	−2.00	0.06	0.79
Blends	5.56	2.55	0.00	20.00	446	5.00	5.00	0.77	2.88
Blends/R	0.24	0.10	0.00	0.71	446	0.24	0.17	0.43	1.03
Col-Shd Blends	0.67	[0.93]	0.00	6.00	207	0.00	0.00	2.02	6.35
Afr	0.61	0.17	0.18	1.42	450	0.60	0.50	0.45	1.22
Populars	6.28	1.53	1.00	12.00	450	6.00	7.00	0.02	0.69
XA%	0.88	0.07	0.57	1.00	450	0.89	0.88	−0.71	0.77
WDA%	0.91	0.06	0.69	1.00	450	0.91	0.95	−0.66	0.47
X+%	0.68	0.11	0.33	0.95	450	0.70	0.67	−0.58	0.20
X−%	0.11	0.07	0.00	0.38	425	0.11	0.10	0.72	0.73
Xu%	0.20	0.09	0.00	0.49	448	0.19	0.17	0.42	−0.01
Isolate/R	0.19	0.09	0.00	0.60	440	0.18	0.14	0.55	0.92
H	3.18	1.70	0.00	10.00	432	3.00	3.00	0.43	0.30
(H)	1.35	1.12	0.00	8.00	348	1.00	1.00	1.19	3.11
Hd	1.14	[1.26]	0.00	11.00	293	1.00	1.00	2.16	9.83
(Hd)	0.62	0.87	0.00	5.00	191	0.00	0.00	1.64	3.11
Hx	0.15	[0.50]	0.00	4.00	47	0.00	0.00	4.45	23.71
H+(H)+Hd+(Hd)	6.29	2.66	0.00	20.00	449	6.00	5.00	0.93	2.32
A	8.18	2.56	2.00	25.00	450	8.00	7.00	1.08	3.79
(A)	0.42	[0.69]	0.00	5.00	151	0.00	0.00	2.02	5.81
Ad	2.90	[1.65]	0.00	15.00	438	3.00	2.00	1.60	7.20
(Ad)	0.13	[0.38]	0.00	2.00	53	0.00	0.00	2.92	8.36
An	0.88	[1.05]	0.00	7.00	258	1.00	0.00	1.87	5.53
Art	1.19	1.42	0.00	14.00	282	1.00	0.00	2.60	15.24
Ay	0.56	[0.69]	0.00	4.00	211	0.00	0.00	1.23	1.98
Bl	0.24	[0.51]	0.00	3.00	93	0.00	0.00	2.25	5.40
Bt	2.22	1.52	0.00	7.00	388	2.00	2.00	0.47	−0.18
Cg	2.16	1.57	0.00	9.00	391	2.00	2.00	0.98	1.64
Cl	0.16	[0.41]	0.00	2.00	61	0.00	0.00	2.71	6.99
Ex	0.21	[0.47]	0.00	4.00	87	0.00	0.00	2.65	10.68
Fi	0.81	[0.84]	0.00	4.00	264	1.00	0.00	1.01	1.08
Food	0.26	[0.55]	0.00	3.00	99	0.00	0.00	2.21	5.16
Ge	0.14	[0.45]	0.00	3.00	45	0.00	0.00	3.81	15.82
Hh	1.24	1.06	0.00	5.00	327	1.00	1.00	0.69	0.10
Ls	0.93	1.04	0.00	9.00	275	1.00	1.00	2.11	9.71
Na	0.45	[0.81]	0.00	6.00	144	0.00	0.00	2.74	11.51

Table E.1 Continued

Variable	Mean	SD	Min	Max	Freq	Median	Mode	SK	KU
Sc	1.64	[1.41]	0.00	13.00	360	1.00	1.00	1.87	9.44
Sx	0.19	[0.53]	0.00	4.00	67	0.00	0.00	3.62	16.81
Xy	0.08	[0.28]	0.00	2.00	32	0.00	0.00	3.81	14.87
Idiographic	0.34	[0.65]	0.00	6.00	121	0.00	0.00	2.87	14.37
DV	0.34	[0.67]	0.00	5.00	117	0.00	0.00	2.84	12.10
INCOM	0.71	[0.93]	0.00	5.00	212	0.00	0.00	1.47	2.30
DR	0.85	[1.01]	0.00	7.00	251	1.00	0.00	1.89	6.82
FABCOM	0.45	[0.77]	0.00	6.00	147	0.00	0.00	2.39	9.13
DV2	0.00	[0.07]	0.00	1.00	2	0.00	0.00	14.95	222.48
INC2	0.06	[0.25]	0.00	2.00	23	0.00	0.00	4.74	24.02
DR2	0.03	[0.18]	0.00	1.00	15	0.00	0.00	5.21	25.33
FAB2	0.05	[0.24]	0.00	2.00	23	0.00	0.00	4.49	20.83
ALOG	0.04	[0.21]	0.00	1.00	20	0.00	0.00	4.43	17.76
CONTAM	0.00	[0.00]	0.00	0.00	0	—.—	0.00	—.—	—.—
Sum 6 Sp Sc	2.54	1.90	0.00	14.00	394	2.00	2.00	1.25	3.67
Lvl 2 Sp Sc	0.15	[0.39]	0.00	2.00	60	0.00	0.00	2.65	6.69
WSum6	7.12	5.74	0.00	38.00	394	6.00	0.00	1.49	3.99
AB	0.21	[0.56]	0.00	4.00	69	0.00	0.00	3.25	12.09
AG	0.89	1.02	0.00	7.00	254	1.00	0.00	1.46	3.34
COP	2.07	1.30	0.00	6.00	401	2.00	2.00	0.36	−0.24
CP	0.01	[0.11]	0.00	1.00	5	0.00	0.00	9.35	85.98
GOODHR	5.06	2.09	0.00	13.00	444	5.00	5.00	0.21	0.29
POORHR	2.12	1.81	0.00	15.00	380	2.00	1.00	1.71	6.43
MOR	0.93	[1.01]	0.00	6.00	267	1.00	0.00	1.35	2.85
PER	0.99	[1.10]	0.00	8.00	274	1.00	0.00	1.76	6.04
PSV	0.12	[0.38]	0.00	2.00	43	0.00	0.00	3.45	11.91

RORSCHACH NORMS FOR RATIOS, PERCENTAGES, AND SPECIAL INDICES

Table F.1. Demography data and frequencies for 36 variables for 450 nonpatient adults

DEMOGRAPHY VARIABLES

MARITAL STATUS		AGE		RACE	
Single 145	32%	18−25. . 119	26%	White. . . .374	83%
Lives w/S.O. 20	4%	26−35. . 158	35%	Black. 39	9%
Married 210	47%	36−45. . . 85	19%	Hispanic. 30	7%
Separated. 13	3%	46−55. . . 45	10%	Asian. 7	2%
Divorced 53	12%	56−65. . . 26	6%	Other. 0	0%
Widowed 9	2%	OVER 65. . . 17	4%		

SEX				EDUCATION	
				UNDER 12. 8	2%
Male 220	49%			12 Years. . . .117	26%
Female. 230	51%			13−15 Yrs. . . .216	48%
				16+ Yrs. . . .109	24%

RATIOS, PERCENTAGES AND SPECIAL INDICES

STYLES		FORM QUALITY DEVIATIONS	
Introversive 173	38%	XA% > .89. . . .203	45%**L**
Pervasive introversive 27	6%	XA% < .70. 4	1%
Ambitent 80	18%	WDA% < .85. . . .72	16%**H**
Extratensive. 138	31%	WDA% < .75. 7	2%
Pervasive extratensive. 20	4%	X+% < .55. 55	12%**H**
Avoidant 59	13%	Xu% > .20. . . .202	45%**H**
		X−% > .20. . . .46	10%
D-SCORES		X−% > .30. 4	1%
D Score > 0 64	14%		
D Score = 0 308	68%	**FC:CF+C RATIO**	
D Score < 0 78	17%	FC > (CF+C) + 2. 68	15%**L**
D Score < −1 28	6%	FC > (CF+C) + 1. . . .118	26%**L**
		(CF+C) > FC+1. . . .117	26%**H**
Adj D Score > 0 122	27%	(CF+C) > FC+2. 62	14%**H**
Adj D Score = 0 283	63%		
Adj D Score < 0 45	10%		
Adj D Score < −1. 14	3%		
		S-Constellation Positive. 11	2%
		HVI Positive. 20	4%
Zd > +3.0 (Overincorp). 89	20%	OBS Positive. 3	1%
Zd < −3.0 (Underincorp) . . .64	14%		

PTI = 5 0	0%	DEPI = 7. . . . 2	0%	CDI = 5. 9	2%
PTI = 4 1	0%	DEPI = 6. . . 16	4%	CDI = 4. 30	7%
PTI = 3 1	0%	DEPI = 5. . . 44	10%		

Source for table in this Appendix: From *The Rorschach: A Comprehensive System, Volume 2. Advanced Interpretation* (3rd ed.) by J.E. Exner, Jr. & Philip Erdberg. Hoboken, NJ: John Wiley & Sons. Copyright © 2005 by John Exner, Jr. and Philip Erdberg with permission.

Continued

Table F.1.   Continued

MISCELLANEOUS VARIABLES

MARITAL STATUS			AGE	RACE		
R < 17	26	6%		(2AB+Art+Ay) > 5	35	8%
R > 27	65	14%		Populars < 4	16	4%
DQv > 2	8	2%L		Populars > 7	81	18%L
S > 2	169	38%H		COP = 0	49	11%L
Sum T = 0	86	19%		COP > 2	164	36%
Sum T > 1	77	17%		AG = 0	196	44%
3r+(2)/R < .33	89	20%		AG > 2	32	7%
3r+(2)/R > .44	134	30%		MOR > 2	30	7%
Fr + rF > 0	54	12%		Level 2 Sp.Sc. > 0	60	13%
PureC > 0	64	14%		GHR > PHR	384	85%
PureC > 1	10	2%		Pure H < 2	76	17%
Afr < .40	41	9%		Pure H = 0	18	4%
Afr < .50	107	24%H		p > a+1	44	10%
(FM+m) < Sum shading	81	18%		Mp > Ma	103	23%H

H or L = Differs by more than 7% from sample of 600: (H = higher; L = lower)

Progress in Building a New Nonpatient Sample #

References

Achenbach, T. M., & Rescorla, L. A. (2001). *Manual for ASEBA School-Age Forms & Profiles.* Burlington, VT: University of Vermont, Research Center for Children, Youth, & Families.

Acker, M. B. (1990). A review of the ecological validity of neuropsychological tests. In D. E. Tupper & K. D. Cicerone (Eds.), *The neuropsychology of everyday life: Assessment and basic competencies* (pp. 19–55). Boston: Kluwer Academic.

Acker, M. B., & Davis, J. R. (1989). Psychology test scores associated with late outcome head injury. *Neuropsychology, 3,* 1–10.

Ackerman, M. J. (2006a). *Clinician's guide to child custody evaluations* (3rd ed.). Hoboken, NJ: John Wiley & Sons.

Ackerman, M. J. (2006b). Forensic report writing. *Journal of Clinical Psychology, 62,* 59–72.

Ackerman, P. T., Peters, J. R., & Dykman, R. A. (1971). Children with specific learning disabilities: Bender Gestalt Test findings and other signs. *Journal of Learning Disabilities, 4,* 437–446.

Ackerman, S. J., Clemence, A. J., Weatherill, R., & Hilsenroth, M. J. (1999). Use of the TAT in the assessment of DSM-IV personality disorders. *Journal of Personality Assessment, 73,* 422–448.

Ackerman, S. J., Hilsenroth, M. J., Baity, M. R., & Blagys, M. D. (2000). Interaction of therapeutic process and alliance during psychological assessment. *Journal of Personality Assessment, 75,* 82–109.

Acklin, M. W., & Bernat, E. (1987). Depression, alexithymia, and pain prone disorder: A Rorschach study. *Journal of Personality Assessment, 51,* 462–479.

Acklin, M. W., McDowell, C. J., Verschell, M. S., & Chan, D. (2000). Interobserver agreement, intraobserver reliability, and the Rorschach Comprehensive System. *Journal of Personality Assessment, 74,* 15–47.

Adams, K. M. (1980). In search of Luria's battery: A false start. *Journal of Consulting and Clinical Psychology, 48,* 511–516.

Adcock, C. J. (1965). Thematic Apperception Test: A review. In O. K. Buros (Ed.), *The sixth mental measurements yearbook* (Vol. 1, pp. 533–535). Highland Park, NJ: Gryphon Press.

Aegisdottir, S. et al. (2006). The meta-analysis of clinical judgment project: Fifty-six years of accumulated research on clinical versus statistical prediction. *Counseling Psychologist, 34,* 341–382.

Ahava, G. W., Iannone, C., Grebstein, L., & Schirling, J. (1998). Is the Beck Depression Inventory reliable over time? An evaluation of multiple test-retest reliability in a nonclinical college student sample. *Journal of Personality Assessment, 70,* 222–231.

Ahn, H., & Wampold, B. E. (2001). Where oh where are the specific ingredients? A meta-analysis of component studies in counseling and psychotherapy. *Journal of Counseling Psychology, 48,* 251–257.

Aiken, L. R., & Groth-Marnat, G. (2006). *Psychological testing and assessment* (12th ed.). Boston, MA: Pearson Education.

Albert, S., Fox, H. M., & Kahn, M. W. (1980). Faking psychosis on the Rorschach: Can expert judges detect malingering? *Journal of Personality Assessment, 44,* 115–119.

Alessi, G. J. (1980). Behavioral observation for the school psychologist: Responsive-discrepancy model. *School Psychology Review, 9,* 31–45.

Alfonso, V. C., Johnson, A., Patinella, L., & Radar, D. E. (1998). Common WISC-III examiner errors: Evidence from graduate students in training. *Psychology in the Schools, 35*, 119–125.

Allen, J. J. (1998). Personality assessment with American Indians and Alaska Natives: Instrument considerations and service delivery style. *Journal of Personality Assessment, 70*, 17–42.

Allen, J. J. (2004). Methodological issues in cross-cultural and multicultural Rorschach research. *Journal of Personality Assessment, 82*, 189–206.

Allen, J. J., Iacono, W. G., & Danielson, K. (1992). The identification of concealed memories using the event-related potential and implicit behavioral measures: A methodology for prediction in the face of individual differences. *Psychophysiology, 29*, 504–522.

Allison, J., Blatt, S. J., & Zimet, C. N. (1968). *The interpretation of psychological tests.* New York: Harper & Row.

Alloy, L. B., Abramson, W. G., Whitehouse, W. G., Hogan, M. E., Tashman, N. A., Steinberg, D. L., et al. (1999). Depressogenic cognitive styles: Predictive validity, information processing, and personality characteristics, and developmental origins. *Behavior Research and Therapy, 37*, 503–531.

Alnacs, R., & Torgerson, S. (1989). Clinical differentiation between major depression only, major depression with panic disorder, and panic disorder: Childhood personality, and personality disorder. *Acta Psychiatrica Scandinavica, 79*, 370–377.

Amabile, T. M. (1983). *The social psychology of creativity.* New York: Springer-Verlag.

Ambrosini, P. J. (2000). Historical development and present status of the Schedule for Affective Disorders and Schizophrenia for School-Age Children (K-SADS). *Journal of the American Academy of Child and Adolescent Psychiatry, 39*, 49–58.

Ambrosini, P. J., Metz, C., Prabucki, K., & Lee, J. (1989). Videotape reliability of the third revised edition of K-SADS. *Journal of the American Academy of Child and Adolescent Psychology, 28*, 723–728.

American Educational Research Association. (1999). *Standards for educational and psychological testing.* Washington, DC: Author.

American Journal of Managed Care. (1999). Introduction. *American Journal of Managed Care, 5*, S764–S766.

American Psychiatric Association. (1968). *Diagnostic and statistical manual of mental disorders* (2nd ed.). Washington, DC: Author.

American Psychiatric Association. (1980). *Diagnostic and statistical manual of mental disorders* (3rd ed.). Washington, DC: Author.

American Psychiatric Association. (1987). *Diagnostic and statistical manual of mental disorders* (3rd ed., rev.). Washington, DC: Author.

American Psychiatric Association. (1994). *Diagnostic and statistical manual of mental disorders* (4th ed.). Washington, DC: Author.

American Psychiatric Association. (2000). *Diagnostic and statistical manual of mental disorders* (4th ed., text rev.). Washington, DC: Author.

American Psychological Association. (1987). General guidelines for providers of psychological services. *American Psychologist, 42*, 7.

American Psychological Association. (1988). *Computer use in psychology.* Washington, DC: Author.

American Psychological Association. (1992). Ethical principles of psychologists and code of conduct. *American Psychologist, 47*, 1597–1611.

American Psychological Association. (1994). Guidelines for child custody evaluations in divorce proceedings. *American Psychologist, 49*, 677–680.

American Psychological Association. (2001). *Publication manual of the American Psychological Association* (5th ed.). Washington, DC: Author.

American Psychological Association. (2002). Ethical principles of psychologists and code of conduct. *American Psychologist, 57*, 1060–1075.

American Psychological Association Committee on Professional Practice and Standards. (1998). *Guidelines for psycholotgical evaluations in child protection matters.* Washington, DC: American Psychological Association.

Ames, L. B., Metraux, R. W., Rodell, J. L., & Walker, R. N. (1973). *Rorschach responses in old age* (rev. ed.). New York: Brunner/Mazel.

Ames, L. B., Metraux, R. W., Rodell, J. L., & Walker, R. N. (1974). *Child Rorschach responses: Developmental trends from two to ten years* (rev. ed.). New York: Brunner/Mazel.

Anastasi, A., & Urbina, S. (1997). *Psychological testing* (7th ed.). Upper Saddle River, NJ: Prentice-Hall.

Anastopoulos, A. D., Spisto, M. A., & Maher, M. C. (1994). The WISC-III Freedom from Distractibility Factor: Its utility in identifying children with Attention Deficit Hyperactive disorder. *Psychological Assessment, 6,* 368–371.

Anderson, E. M., & Lambert, M. J. (1995). Short-term dynamically oriented psychotherapy: A review and meta-analysis. *Clinical Psychology Review, 15,* 503–514.

Anderson, K. E., & Savage, C. R. (2004). Cognitive and neurobiological findings in obsessive-compulsive disorder. *Psychiatric Clinics of North America, 27,* 37–47.

Anderson, T. K., Cancelli, A. A., & Kratochwill, T. R. (1984). Self-reported assessment practices of school psychologists: Implications for training and practice. *Journal of School Psychology, 22,* 17–29.

Andrews, H. B. (2001). Back to basics: Psychotherapy is an interpersonal process. *Australian Psychologist, 36,* 107–114.

Angus, L. E., Levitt, H., & Hardtke, K. (1999). The narrative process coding system: Research applications and implications for psychotherapy. *Journal of Clinical Psychology, 55,* 1255–1270.

Antonuccio, D. O., Danton, W. G., & DeNelsky, G. Y. (1995). Psychotherapy versus medication for depression: Challenging the conventional wisdom with data. *Professional Psychology: Research and Practice, 26,* 574–585.

Antony, M. M., & Barlow, D. (Eds.). (2002). *Handbook of assessment, treatment planning, and outcome evaluation: Empirically supported strategies for psychological disorders.* New York: Guilford Press.

Apter, A., Bleich, A., Plutchik, R., Mendelsohn, S., & Tyrano, S. (1988). Suicidal behavior, depression, and conduct disorder in hospitalized adolescents. *Journal of the American Academy of Child and Adolescent Psychiatry, 27,* 696–699.

Aram, D. M., & Ekelman, B. L. (1986). Cognitive profiles of children with early onset unilateral lesions. *Developmental Neuropsychology, 2,* 155–172.

Arbisi, P. A., & Ben-Porath, Y. S. (1995). An MMPI-2 infrequent response scale for use with psychopathological populations: The Infrequency Psychopathology Scale, F(p). *Psychological Assessment, 7,* 424–431.

Arbisi, P. A., & Ben-Porath, Y. S. (1998). Characteristics of the MMPI-2 F(p) Scale as a function of diagnosis in an inpatient VA sample. *Psychological Assessment, 10,* 221–228.

Archer, R. P. (2005). *MMPI-A: Assessing adolescent psychopathology* (3rd ed.). Hillsdale, NJ: Lawrence Erlbaum.

Archer, R. P. (1984). Use of the MMPI with adolescents: A review of salient issues. *Clinical Psychology Review, 4,* 241–251.

Archer, R. P. (1987). *Using the MMPI with adolescents.* Hillsdale, NJ: Lawrence Erlbaum.

Archer, R. P. (1992a). MMPI-A: Assessing adolescent psychopathology. Hillsdale, NJ: Lawrence Erlbaum.

Archer, R. P. (1992b). *Review of the Minnesota Multiphasic Personality Inventory-2.* In J. J. Kramer & J. C. Conoley (Eds.), *Eleventh mental measurements yearbook* (pp. 558–562). Lincoln, NE: Buros Institute of Mental Measurements.

Archer, R. P. (2006). *Forensic uses of clinical assessment instruments.* Mahwah, NJ: Lawrence Erlbaum, 2006.

Archer, R. P., Buffington-Vollum, Stredny, J. K., & Handel, R. W. (2006). A survey of test use patterns among forensic psychologists. *Journal of Personality Assessment, 87*, 64-94.

Archer, R. P., Griffin, R., & Aiduk, R. (1995). MMPI-2 clinical correlates for ten common codes. *Journal of Personality Assessment, 65*, 391–407.

Archer, R. P., & Jacobson, J. M. (1993). Are critical items "critical" for the MMPI-A? *Journal of Personality Assessment, 61*, 547–556.

Archer, R. P., & Krishnamurthy, R. (1997a). MMPI-A and Rorschach indices related to depression and conduct disorder: An evaluation of the incremental validity hypothesis. *Journal of Personality Assessment, 69*, 517–533.

Archer, R. P., & Krishnamurthy, R. (1997b). MMPI-A scale-level factor structure: Replication in a clinical sample. *Assessment, 4*, 337–349.

Archer, R. P., & Krishnamurthy, R. (2003). The Rorschach. In L. E. Beutler & G. Groth-Marnat (Eds.), *Integrative assessment of adult personality* (2nd ed.). New York: Guilford Press.

Archer, R. P., Maruish, M. E., Imhof, E. A., & Piotrowski, C. (1991). Psychological test usage with adolescent clients: 1990 survey findings. *Professional Psychology: Research and Practice, 22*, 247–252.

Archer, R. P., & Newsom, C. R. (2000). Psychological test usage with adolescent clients: Survey update. *Assessment, 7*, 227–236.

Archer, R. P., Pancoast, D. L., & Klinefelter, D. (1989). A comparison of MMPI code types produced by traditional and recent adolescent norms. *Psychological Assessment, 1*, 23–29.

Arizmendi, T. G., Beutler, L. E., Shanfield, S., Crago, M., & Hagaman, R. (1985). Client-therapist similarity and psychotherapy outcome: A microscopic approach. *Psychotherapy: Theory, Research, and Practice, 22*, 16–21.

Armbuster, G. L., Miller, A. S., & Exner, J. E. (1974). Rorschach responses of parachute trainees at the beginning of training and shortly before their first jump. Rorschach Workshops (Study No. 201, unpublished).

Armengol, C. G. (2001). The referral process. In C. G. Armengol, E. Kaplan, & E. J. Moes (Eds.), *The consumer-oriented neuropsychological report* (pp. 47–60). Lutz, FL: Psychological Assessment Resources.

Armengol, C. G., Moes, E. J., Penney, D. L., & Sapienza, M. M. (2001). Writing client-centered recommendations. In C. G. Armengol, E. Kaplan, & E. J. Moes (Eds.), *The consumer-oriented neuropsychological report* (pp. 141–160). Lutz, FL: Psychological Assessment Resources.

Army Individual Test Battery. (1944). *Manual of directions and scoring.* Washington, DC: War Department, Adjutant General's Office.

Arnau, R. C., Meagher, M. W., Norris, M. P., & Bramson, R. (2001). Psychometric evaluation of the Beck Depression Inventory-II with primary care medical patients. *Health Psychology, 20*, 112–119.

Arnold, M. B. (1949). A demonstration analysis of the TAT in a clinical setting. *Journal of Abnormal and Social Psychology, 44*, 97–111.

Arnold, M. B. (1962). *Story sequence analysis: A new method of measuring and predicting achievement.* New York: Columbia University Press.

Aronow, E., Reznikoff, M., & Moreland, K. L. (1995). The Rorschach: Projective technique or psychometric test? *Journal of Personality Assessment, 64*, 213–228.

Arvey, R. D., & Campion, J. E. (1982). The employment interview: A summary and review of recent research. *Personnel Psychology, 35*, 281–322.

Asaad, G. (2000). Somatization disorder. In M. Hersen & M. Biaggio (Eds.), *Effective brief therapies: A clinicians guide* (pp. 179–190). San Diego, CA: Academic Press.

Association of Test Publishers. (2000). *Guidelines for computer-based testing.* Washington, D.C.: Association of Test Publishers.

Atkinson, J. W., & Feather, N. T. (Eds.). (1966). *A theory of achievement motivation.* New York: John Wiley & Sons.

Atkinson, L., Quarington, B., Alp, I. E., & Cyr, J. J. (1986). Rorschach validity: An empirical approach to the literature. *Journal of Clinical Psychology, 42*, 360–362.

Ax, A. F. (1953). The physiological differentiation between fear and anger in humans. *Psychosomatic Medicine, 15*, 433–442.

Axelrod, B. N. (2001). Administration duration for the Wechsler Adult Intelligence Scale-III and Wechsler Memory Scale-III. *Archives of Clinical Neuropsychology, 16*, 293–301.

Axelrod, B. N., Ryan, J. J., & Ward, L. C. (2001). Evaluation of seven-subtest short forms of the Wechsler Adult Intelligence Scale-III in a referred sample. *Archives of Clinical Neuropsychology, 16*, 1–8.

Axelrod, B. N., Ryan, J. J., & Woodward, J. L. (2001). Cross-validation of prediction equations for Wechsler Memory Scale-III. *Assessment, 8*, 367–372.

Axelrod, B. N., Vanderploeg, R. D., & Schinka, J. A. (1999). Comparing methods for estimating premorbid intellectual functioning. *Archives of Clinical Neuropsychology, 14*, 341–346.

Axelrod, B. N., & Woodward, J. L. (2000). Parsiminous prediction of Wechsler Memory Scale-III memory indices. *Psychological Assessment, 12*, 431–435.

Baade, L. E., & Schoenberg, M. A. (2004). A proposed method to estimate premorbid intelligence utilizing group achievement measures from school records. *Archives of Clinical Neuropsychology, 19*, 227–244.

Baddeley, A. D. (2003). Working memory: Looking back and looking forward. *Nature Reviews Neuroscience, 4*, 829–839.

Baddeley, A. D., Kopelman, M. D., & Wilson, B. A. (Eds.) (2002). *Handbook of memory disorders* (2nd ed.). Hoboken, NJ: John Wiley & Sons.

Baer, J. S., Holt, C. S., & Lichtenstein, E. (1986). Self-efficacy and smoking re-examined: Construct validity and clinical utility. *Journal of Consulting and Clinical Psychology, 54*, 846–852.

Baer, J. S., & Lichtenstein, E. (1988). Classification and prediction of smoking relapse episodes: An exploration of individual differences. *Journal of Consulting and Clinical Psychology, 56*, 104–110.

Baer, R. A., Kroll, L. S., Rinaldo, J., & Ballenger, J. (1999). Detecting and discriminating between random responding and overreporting on the MMPI-A. *Journal of Personality Assessment, 72*, 308–320.

Baer, R. A., Wetter, M. W., & Berry, D. T. (1995). Effects of information about validity scales underreporting symptoms on the MMPI-2: An analogue investigation. *Assessment, 2*, 189–200.

Baer, R. A., Wetter, M. W., Nichols, D. S., Greene, R., & Berry, D. T. (1995). Sensitivity of MMPI-2 validity scales to underreporting of symptoms. *Psychological Assessment, 7*, 419–423.

Bagby, R. M., Buis, T., & Nicholson, R. A. (1995). Relative effectiveness of the standard validity scales in detecting fake-bad and fake-good responding: Replication and extension. *Psychological Assessment, 7*, 84–92.

Bagby, R. M., Gillis, J. R., & Rogers, R. (1991). Effectiveness of the Millon Clinical Multiaxial Inventory Validity Index in the detection of random responding. *Psychological Assessment, 3*, 285–287.

Bagby, R. M., Gillis, J. R., Toner, B. B., & Goldberg, J. (1991). Detecting fake-good and fake-bad responding on the Millon Clinical Multiaxial Inventory-II. *Psychological Assessment, 3*, 496–498.

Bagby, R. M., Marshall, M. B., Basso, M. R., Nicholson, R. A., Bacchiochi, J. & Miller, L. S. (2005). Distinguishing bipolar depression, major depression, and schizophrenia with the MMPI-2 Clinical and Content Scales. *Journal of Personality Assessmen. 84*, 89-95

Bagby, R. M., Rogers, R., Nicholson, R. A., Buis, T., Seeman, M. V., & Rector, N. A. (1997). Effectiveness of the MMPI-2 validity indicators in the detection of defensive responding in clinical and nonclinical samples. *Psychological Assessment, 9*, 406–413.

Bakker, C., Bakker-Rabdau, M., & Breit, S. (1978). The measurement of assertiveness and aggressiveness. *Journal of Personality Assessment, 42*, 277–284.

Ball, J. D., Archer, R. P., Gordon, R. A., & French, J. (1991). Rorschach Depression Indices with children and adolescents: Concurrent validity findings. *Journal of Personality Assessment, 57*, 465–476.

Ball, J. D., Archer, R. P., & Imhof, E. A. (1994). Time requirements of psychological testing: A survey of practitioners. *Journal of Personality Assessment, 63*, 239–249.

Bamgbose, O., Smith, G. T., Jesse, R. C., & Groth-Marnat, G. (1980). A survey of the current and future directions of professional psychology in acute general hospitals. *Clinical Psychologist, 33*, 24–25.

Bandura, A. (1986). *Social foundations of thought and action: A social cognitive theory.* Englewood Cliffs, NJ: Prentice-Hall.

Bandura, A. (1997). *Self-efficacy: The exercise of control.* New York: W.H. Freeman.

Bannatyne, A. (1974). Diagnosis: A note on recategorization of the WISC scaled scores. *Journal of Learning Disabilities, 7*, 272–273.

Barber, T. X., & Silver, M. J. (1968). Fact, fiction and the experimenter bias effect. *Psychological Bulletin Monograph Supplement, 70*, 1–29.

Barlow, D. H. (1988). *Anxiety and its disorders: The nature and treatment of anxiety and panic.* New York: Guilford Press.

Barlow, D. H. (Ed.). (2001). *Clinical handbook of psychological disorders* (3rd ed.). New York: Guilford Press.

Barlow, D. H., Craske, M. G., Cerny, J. A., & Klosko, J. S. (1989). Behavioral treatment of panic disorder. *Behavior Therapy, 20*, 261–282.

Barnett, O. W., & Hamberger, L. K. (1992). The assessment of maritally violent men on the California Psychological Inventory. *Violence and Victims, 7*, 15–28.

Bar-On, R. (1998). *Bar-On Emotional Quotient Inventory (EQ-itm): Technical manual.* Toronto, Canada: Multi Health Systems.

Barona, A., Reynolds, C., & Chastain, R. (1984). A demographically based index of premorbid intelligence for the WAIS-R. *Journal of Consulting and Clinical Psychology, 26*, 74–75.

Barrios, B. A., & Hartman, D. P. (1988). *Fears and anxieties in children.* In E. J. Mash & L. G. Terdel (Eds.), *Behavioral assessment of childhood disorders* (2nd ed., pp. 196–262). New York: Guilford Press.

Barrios, B. A., & O'Dell, S. (1998). *Fears and anxieties.* In E. J. Mash & R. A. Barkley (Eds.), *Treatment of childhood disorders* (2nd ed., pp. 249–337). New York: Guilford Press.

Barthlow, D. L., Graham, J. R., Ben-Porath, Y. S., & McNulty, J. L. (1999). Incremental validity of the MMPI-2 content scales in an outpatient mental health setting. *Psychological Assessment, 11*, 39–47.

Bartholomew, D. J. (2006). *Measuring intelligence: Facts and fallacies.* Cambridege: Cambridge University Press.

Bartlett, J. A., Schleifer, S. J., Johnson, R. L., & Keller, S. E. (1991). Depression in inner city adolescents attending an adolescent medicine clinic. *Journal of Adolescent Health, 12*, 316–318.

Basham, R. B. (1992). Clinical utility of the MMPI research scales in the assessment of adolescent acting out. *Psychological Assessment, 4*, 483–492.

Basso, M. B., Harrington, K., Matson, M., & Lowery, N. (2000). Sex differences on the WMS-III: Findings concerning verbal paired associates and faces. *Clinical Neuropsychologist, 14*, 231–235.

Baucom, D. H. (1985). Review of the California Psychological Inventory. In J. V. Mitchel (Ed.), *The ninth mental measurements yearbook.* Highland Park, NJ: Gryphon Press.

Baucom, D. H., Epstein, N., Rankin, L. A., & Burnett, C. K. (1996). Assessing relationship standards: The Inventory of Specific Relationship Standards. *Journal of Family Psychology, 10*, 72–88.

Baucom, D. H., Sayers, S. L., & Duhe, A. (1989). Marital attributions: Issues concerning attributional pattern and attributional style. *Journal of Personality and Social Psychology, 56*, 596–607.

Bauer, R. M. (2000). The flexible battery approach to neuropsychological assessment. In R. D. Vanderploeg (Ed.), *Clinician's guide to neuropsychological assessment* (2nd ed., pp. 419–448). Hillsdale, NJ: Lawrence Erlbaum.

Beatty, W. W., Mold, J. W., & Gontkovsky, S. T. (2003). RBANS performance: Influence of sex and education. *Journal of Clinical and Experimental Neuropsychology, 25*, 1065–1069.

Beatty, W. W., Ryder, K. A., Gontkovsky, S. T., Scott, J. G., McSwan, K. L., & Bharucha, K. J. (2003). Analyzing the subcortical dementia syndrome of Parkinson's disease using the RBANS. *Archives of Clinical Neuropsychology, 18*, 509–520.

Beck, A. T. (1967). *Depression: Clinical, experimental, and theoretical aspects.* New York: Harper & Row.

Beck, A. T., Rush, A. J., Shaw, B. F., & Emery, G. (1979). *Cognitive therapy of depression.* New York: Guilford Press.

Beck, A. T., Steer, R. A., & Brown, G. K. (1996). *BDI-II manual.* San Antonio, TX: Psychological Corporation.

Beck, A. T., Steer, R. A., & Garbin, M. (1988). Psychometric properties of the Beck Depression Inventory: Twenty-five years of evaluation. *Clinical Psychology Review, 8*, 77–100.

Beck, A. T., Ward, C. H., Mendelson, M., Mock, J., & Erbaugh, J. (1961). An inventory for measuring depression. *Archives of General Psychiatry, 4*, 561–571.

Beck, J. G. (1994). *Cognitive therapy: Basics and beyond.* New York: Guilford Press.

Beck, J. G., & Zebb, B. J. (1994). Behavioral assessment and treatment of panic disorder: Current status, future directions. *Behavior Therapy, 25*, 581–611.

Beck, S. J. (1937). Introduction to the Rorschach method: A manual of personality study. *American Orthopsychiatric Association Monograph, 1.*

Beck, S. J. (1945). *Rorschach's test: A variety of personality pictures* (Vol. *2*). New York: Grune & Stratton.

Beck, S. J. (1951). The Rorschach Test: A multi-dimensional test of personality. In H. H. Anderson & G. Anderson (Eds.), *An introduction to projective techniques.* Englewood Cliffs, NJ: Prentice-Hall.

Beck, S. J. (1960). *The Rorschach experiment.* New York: Grune & Stratton.

Beck, S. J. (1961). *Rorschach's test: Basic processes* (Vol. 1). New York: Grune & Stratton.

Beck, S. J. (1968). Reality, Rorschach and perceptual theory. In A. I. Rabin (Ed.), *Projective techniques in personality assessment.* New York: Springer.

Beebe, D. W., Pfiffner, L. J., & McBurnett, K. (2000). Evaluation of the validity of the Wechsler Intelligence Scale for Children-3rd ed. Comprehension and Picture Arrangement subtests as measures of social intelligence. *Psychological Assessment, 12*, 97–101.

Behnke, S. (2004, November). Ethics rounds: Release of test data and the new ethics code. *Monitor, 35*, 90–91.

Beier, E. G. (1966). *The silent language of psychotherapy.* New York: Aldine.

Bellack, A. S., & Hersen, M. (Eds.). (1988). *Behavioral assessment: A practical handbook* (3rd ed.). New York: Pergamon Press.

Bellack, A. S., & Hersen, M. (Eds.). (1998). *Behavioral assessment: A practical handbook* (4th ed.). New York: Pergamon Press.

Bellack, A. S., Hersen, M., & Turner, S. M. (1979). Relationship of roleplaying and knowledge of appropriate behavior to assertion in the natural environment. *Journal of Consulting and Clinical Psychology, 47*, 670–678.

Bellak, L. (1954). *The Thematic Apperception Test and the Children's Apperception Test in clinical use.* New York: Grune & Stratton.

Bellak, L. (1975). *The TAT, CAT, and SAT in clinical use* (3rd ed.). New York: Grune & Stratton.

Bellak, L. (1986). *The TAT, CAT, and SAT in clinical use* (4th ed.). New York: Grune & Stratton.

Bellak, L. (1993). *The TAT, CAT, and SAT in clinical use* (5th ed.). New York: Grune & Stratton.

Bellak, L., & Abrams, D. M. (1997). *The TAT, CAT, and SAT in clinical use* (6th ed.). Boston: Allyn & Bacon.

Bellak, L., & Bellak, S. S. (1973). *Manual: Senior Apperception Test.* Larchmont, NY: CPS.

Bender, L. (1938). *A visual motor gestalt test and its clinical uses* (Research Monograms No. 3). New York: American Orthopsychiatric Association.

Benjamin, A. B., Mossman, D., Graves, N. S., & Sanders, R. D., (2006). Tests of a symptom checklist to screen for comorbid psychiatric disorders in alcoholism. *Comprehensive Psychiatry, 47,* 227–233

Ben-Porath, Y. S., & Butcher, J. N. (1989). The psychometric stability of rewritten MMPI items. *Journal of Personality Assessment, 53,* 645–653.

Ben-Porath, Y. S., Butcher, J. N., & Graham, J. R. (1991). Contribution of the MMPI-2 content scales to the differential diagnosis of schizophrenia and major depression. *Psychological Assessment, 3,* 634–640.

Ben-Porath, Y. S., Hostetler, K., Butcher, J. N., & Graham, J. R. (1989). New subscales for the MMPI-2 Social Introversion (Si) Scale. *Psychological Assessment, 1,* 169–174.

Ben-Porath, Y. S., McCulley, E., & Almagor, M. (1993). Incremental validity of the MMPI-2 content scales in the assessment of personality and psychopathology by self-report. *Journal of Personality Assessment, 61,* 557–575.

Ben-Porath, Y. S., Shondrick, D. D., & Stafford, K. P. (1995). MMPI-2 and race in a forensic diagnostic sample. *Criminal Justice and Behavior, 22,* 19–32.

Ben-Porath, Y. S., & Tellegen, A. (2008). *Minnesota Multiphasic Personality Inventory-2 Restructured Form manual.* Minneapolis, MN: Pearson Assessments.

Benton, A. L. (1968). Differential behavioral effects in frontal lobe disease. *Neuropsychologia, 6,* 53–60.

Benton, A. L. (1974). *The Revised Visual Retention Test* (4th ed.). New York: Psychological Corporation.

Benton, A. L. (1979). Visuoperceptive, visuospatial, and visuoconstructive disorders. In K. M. Heilman & E. Valenstein (Eds.), *Clinical neuropsychology* (pp. 186–232). New York: Oxford University Press.

Benton, A. L., & Hamsher, K. (1983). *Multilingual Aphasia Examination.* Iowa City, IA: AJA Associates.

Benton, A. L., & Hamsher, K. (1989). *Multilingual Aphasia Examination* (2nd ed.). Iowa City, IA: AJA Associates.

Berg, F. W., Franzen, M. D., & Wedding, D. (1987). *Screening for brain impairment.* New York: Springer.

Bergin, A. E. (1971). The evaluation of therapeutic outcomes. In A. E. Bergin & S. L. Garfield (Eds.), *Handbook of psychotherapy and behavior change* (pp. 217–270). New York: John Wiley & Sons.

Berry, D. T., Baer, R. A., & Harris, M. J. (1991). Detection of malingering on the MMPI: A meta-analysis. *Journal of Personality Assessment, 11,* 585–598.

Beutler, L. E. (1979). Toward specific psychological therapies for specific conditions. *Journal of Consulting and Clinical Psychology, 47,* 882–897.

Beutler, L. E. (1983). *Eclectic psychotherapy: A systematic approach.* New York: Pergamon Press.

Beutler, L. E. (1989). Differential treatment selection: The role of diagnosis in psychotherapy. *Psychotherapy, 26,* 271–281.

Beutler, L. E. (1995). Integrating and communicating findings. In L. E. Beutler & M. R. Berren (Eds.), *Integrative assessment of adult personality* (pp. 25–64). New York: Guilford Press.

Beutler, L. E. (2000). David and Goliath: When empirical and clinical standards of practice meet. *American Psychologist, 55,* 997–1007.

Beutler, L. E., Albanese, A. L., Fisher, D., Karno, M., Sandowicz, M., Williams, O. B., et al. (1999). *Selecting and matching to patient variables.* Paper presented at the annual meeting of the Society for Psychotherapy Research, Braga, Portugal.

Beutler, L. E., & Berren, M. R. (Eds.). (1995). *Integrative assessment of adult personality.* New York: Guilford Press.

Beutler, L. E., & Clarkin, I. F. (1990). *Systematic treatment selection: Toward targeted therapeutic interventions.* New York: Brunner/Mazel.

Beutler, L. E., Clarkin, I. F., & Bongar, B. (2000). *Guidelines for the systematic treatment of the depressed patient.* New York: Oxford University Press.

Beutler, L. E., & Crago, M. (1986). Strategies and techniques of prescriptive psychotherapeutic intervention. In R. E. Hales & A. J. Francis (Eds.), *American Psychiatric Association Annual Review* (Vol. *6*, pp. 378–397). Washington, DC: American Psychiatric Press.

Beutler, L. E., Crago, M., & Arizmendi, T. G. (1986). Therapist variables in psychotherapy process and outcome. In S. L. Garfield & A. E. Bergin (Eds.), *Handbook of psychotherapy and behavioral change* (3rd ed., pp. 257–310). New York: John Wiley & Sons.

Beutler, L. E., Engle, D., Mohr, D., Daldrup, R. J., Bergan, J., Meredith, K., et al. (1991). Predictors of differential response to cognitive, experiential, and self-directed psychotherapeutic procedures. *Journal of Consulting and Clinical Psychology, 59*, 1–8.

Beutler, L. E., & Groth-Marnat, G. (2003). *Integrative assessment of adult personality* (2nd ed.). New York: Guilford Press.

Beutler, L. E., & Harwood, T. M. (2000). *Prescriptive psychotherapy.* New York: Oxford University Press.

Beutler, L. E., Harwood, T. M., Alimohamed, S., & Malik, M. (2002). Functional impairment and coping style. In J. C. Norcross (Ed.), *Psychotherapy relationships that work: Therapist contributions and responsiveness to patient's needs* (pp. 145–170). New York: Oxford University Press.

Beutler, L. E., & Malik, M. (Eds.). (2002). *Rethinking the DSM: A psychological perspective.* Washington, DC: American Psychological Association.

Beutler, L. E., & Moleiro, C. (2001). Clinical versus reliable and significant change. *Clinical Psychology: Science and Practice, 8*, 441–445.

Beutler, L. E., Moleiro, C., Malik, M., & Harwood, T. M. (2003). A new twist on empirically supported treatments. *Internal Journal of Clinical and Health Psychology, 3*, 423–437.

Beutler, L. E., Moleiro, C., & Talebi, H. (2002). Resistance. In J. C. Norcross (Ed.), *Psychotherapy relationships that work: Therapist contributions and responsiveness to patient's needs* (pp. 129–444). New York: Oxford University Press.

Beutler, L. E., Sandowicz, M., Fisher, D., & Albanese, A. L. (1996). Resistance in psychotherapy: What can be concluded from empirical research. In *Session: Psychotherapy in Practice, 2*, 77–86.

Beutler, L. E., & Williams, O. B. (1999). *Systematic treatment selection: A software package for treatment planning.* Ventura, CA: Center for Behavioral Technology.

Beutler, L. E., Williams, R. E., Wakefield, P. J., & Entwistle, S. R. (1995). Bridging scientist and practitioner perspectives in clinical psychology. *American Psychologist, 50*, 984–994.

Bieling, P. J., Antony, M. M., & Swinson, R. P. (1998). The State-Trait Anxiety Inventory, Trait version: Structure and content re-examined. *Behaviour Research and Therapy, 36*, 777–788.

Bienvenu, O. J., Samuels, J. F., Riddle, M. A., Hoehn-Saric, R., Liang, K., Cullen, B. A. M., et al. (2000). The relationship of obsessive-compulsive disorder to possible spectrum disorders: Results from a family study. *Biological Psychiatry, 48*, 287–293.

Bigler, E. D., Rosa, L., Schultz, F., Hall, S., & Harris, J. (1989). Rey Auditory Verbal Learning and Rey-Osterrieth Complex Figure Design Test performance in Alzheimer's diseases and closed head injury. *Journal of Clinical Psychology, 45*, 277–280.

Billings, A. G., & Moos, R. H. (1986). Psychosocial processes of remission in unipolar depression: Comparing depressed patients with matched community controls. *Journal of Consulting and Clinical Psychology, 3*, 314–325.

Binder, R. L. (1999). Are the mentally ill dangerous? *Journal of the American Academy of Psychiatry and the Law, 27*, 189–201.

Birchler, G. R. (1989). Review of behavioral assessment: A practical handbook (3rd ed.). *Behavioral Assessment, 11*, 384–388.

Birchler, G. R., & Fals-Stewart, W. (2006). *Marital dysfunction.* In M. Hersen (Ed.), *Clinician's handbook of adult behavioral assessment* (pp. 297–324). New York: Elsevier.

Black, F. W., & Bernard, B. A. (1984). Constructional apraxia as a function of lesion locus and size in patients with focal brain damage. *Cortex, 20*, 111–120.

Blanchard, E. B., Schwarz, S. P., Neff, D. F., & Gerardi, M. A. (1988). Prediction of outcome from the self-regulatory treatment of irritable bowel syndrome. *Behavior Research and Therapy, 26*, 187–190.

Blatt, S. J., Zuroff, D. C., Quinlan, D. M., & Pilkonis, P. A. (1996). Interpersonal factors in brief treatment of depression: Further analysis of the National Institute of Mental Health Treatment of Depression Collaborative Research Program. *Journal of Consulting and Clinical Psychology, 64*, 162–171.

Blount, A., Schoenbaum, M., Kathol, R., Rollman, B. L., Marshall, T., O'Donohue, W., & Peek, C. J. (2007). The economics of behavioral health services in medical settings: A summary of evidence. *Professional Psychology: Research and Practice, 38*, 290–297.

Blum, G. S. (1950). *The Blacky pictures and manual.* New York: Psychological Corporation.

Blum, G. S. (1962). A guide for research use of the Blacky pictures. *Journal of Projective Techniques, 26*, 3–29.

Blum, G. S. (1968). Assessment of psychodynamic variables by the Blacky pictures. In P. McReynolds (Ed.), *Advances in psychological assessment* (Vol. 1, pp. 150–168). Palo Alto, CA: Science and Behavior Books.

Boccaccini, M. T., & Brodsky, S. L. (1999). Diagnostic test usage by forensic psychologists in emotional injury cases. *Professional Psychology: Research and Practice, 30*, 252–259.

Bockian, N., Meagher, S., & Millon, T. (2000). Assessing personality with the Millon Behavioral Health Inventory, the Millon Behavioral Medicine Diagnostic, and the Millon Clinical Multiaxial Inventory. In R. J. Gatchel & J. N. Weisberg (Eds.), *Personality characteristics of patients with pain* (pp. 61–88). Washington, DC: American Psychological Association.

Boerger, A. R. (1975). *The utility of some alternative approaches to MMPI scale construction.* Unpublished doctoral dissertation, Kent State University, Kent, OH.

Boll, T. J. (1974). Behavioral correlates of cerebral damage in children age 9–14. In R. M. Reitan & L. A. Davison (Eds.), *Clinical neuropsychology: Current status and application.* Washington, DC: V. H. Winston & Sons.

Bolton, B. (1992). Review of the California Psychological Inventory, revised edition. In J. J. Framer & J. C. Conely (Eds.), *Eleventh mental measurements yearbook* (pp. 558–562). Lincoln, NE: Buros Institute of Mental Measurements.

Bonarius, H. (1984). Prediction or anticipation: Some implications of personal construct psychology for professional practice. *Jyvaskyla Studies in Education: Psychology and Social Research, 54*, 190–206.

Boone, K. B. (2007). *Assessment of feigned cognitive impairment: A neuropsychological perspective.* New York: Guilford.

Bornstein, R. A. (1983). Verbal I.Q.-Performance I.Q. discrepancies on the Wechsler Adult Intelligence Scale-Revised in patients with unilateral or bilateral cerebral dysfunction. *Journal of Consulting and Clinical Psychology, 51*, 779–789.

Bornstein, R. A., & Chelune, G. J. (1988). Factor analysis of the Wechsler Memory Scale-Revised. *Clinical Neuropsychologist, 2*, 107–115.

Bornstein, R. A., & Matarazzo, J. D. (1982). Wechsler VIQ versus PIQ differences in cerebral dysfunction: A literature review with emphasis on sex differences. *Journal of Clinical Neuropsychology, 4*, 319–334.

Bornstein, R. A., Suga, L., & Prifitera, A. (1987). Incidence of verbal I.Q.-Performance I.Q. discrepancies at various levels of education. *Journal of Clinical Psychology, 43*, 387–389.

Bornstein, R. F. (1999). Criterion validity of objective and projective dependency tests: A meta-analytic assessment of behavioral prediction. *Psychological Assessment, 11*, 48–57.

Bornstein, R. F. (2007). From surface to depth: Diagnosis and assessment in personaltiy pathology. *Clinical Psychology: Science and Practice, 14*, 99–101.

Borus, J. F., Howes, M. J., Devins, N. P., & Rosenberg, R. (1988). Primary health care providers' recognition and diagnosis of mental disorders in their patients. *General Hospital Psychiatry, 10*, 317–321.

Botwinick, J., Storandt, M., Berg, F. W., & Boland, S. (1988). Senile dementia of the Alzheimer type: Subject attrition and testability in research. *Archives of Neurology, 45*, 493–496.

Bowden, S. C., Dodds, B., Whelan, G., Long, C., Dudgeon, P., Ritter, A., et al. (1997). Confirmatory factor analysis of the Wechsler Memory Scale-Revised in a sample of clients with alcohol dependence. *Journal of Clinical and Experimental Neuropsychology, 19*, 755–762.

Bowden, S. C., & Smith, L. C. (1994). What does the Austin Maze measure? *Australian Psychologist, 29*, 34–37.

Bowler, R. M., Thakler, C. D., & Becker, C. E. (1986). California Neuropsychological Screening Battery (CNC/BI & II). *Journal of Clinical Psychology, 42*, 946–955.

Bowman, M. L. (1996). Ecological validity of neuropsychological and other predictors following head injury. *Clinical Neuropsychologist, 10*, 382–396.

Bracken, B. A., & McCallum, R. S. (1998). *Examiner's manual: Universal Nonverbal Intelligence Test (UNIT).* Itasca, IL: Riverside Publishing.

Brannigan, G., & Decker, S. L. (2003). *Bender Visual-Motor Gestalt Test II examiner's manual.* Itasca, IL: Riverside Publishing.

Brar, H. S. (1970). Rorschach content responses of East Indian psychiatric patients. *Journal of Projective Techniques and Personality Assessment, 34*, 88–94.

Brawman-Mintzer, O., Lydiard, R. B., Emmanuel, N., Payeur, R., Johnson, M., Roberts, J., et al. (1993). Psychiatric comorbidity in patients with generalized anxiety disorder. *American Journal of Psychiatry, 150*, 1216–1218.

Brayfield, A. H. (Ed.). (1965). Testing and public policy. *American Psychologist, 20*, 857–1005.

Breen, M. J. (1982). Comparison of educationally handicapped student's scores on the Revised Developmental Test of Visual-Motor Integration and Bender-Gestalt. *Perceptual and Motor Skills, 54*, 1227–1230.

Breitholtz, E., Johansson, B., & Ost, L.-G. (1999). Cognitions in generalized anxiety disorder and panic disorder patients: A prospective approach. *Behavior Research and Therapy, 37*, 533–544.

Brenner, E. (2003). Consumer-focused psychological assessment. *Professional Psychology: Research and Practice, 34*, 240–247.

Brewin, C. R. (1985). Depression and causal attributions: What is their relation? *Psychological Bulletin, 98*, 297–309.

Brewin, C. R. (1996). Theoretical foundations of cognitive-behavior therapy for anxiety and depression. *Annual Review of Psychology, 47*, 33–57.

Bricklin, H. (1984). *Bricklin Perceptual Scales.* Furlong, PA: Village Publishing.

Brooks, B. L., & Hosie, T. W. (1984). Assumptions and interpretations of the SOMPA in estimating learning potential. *Counselor Education and Supervision, 23*, 290–299.

Brooks, B. L., Iverson, G. L., Holdnack, J. A., & Feldman, H. H. (2008). The potential for misclassification of mild cognitive impairment: A study of memory scores on the Wechsler Memory Scale-III in healthy older adults. *Journal of the International Neuropsychological Society, 14*, 463–478.

Broshek, D. K., & Barth, J. T. (2000). The Halstead-Reitan Neuropsychological Test Battery. In G. Groth-Marnat (Ed.), *Neuropsychological assessment in clinical practice: A guide to test interpretation and integration* (pp. 457–532). New York: John Wiley & Sons.

Broughton, R. (1984). A prototype strategy for construction of personality scales. *Journal of Personality and Social Psychology, 47*, 1334–1346.

Brown, L. (1990). Taking account of gender in the clinical assessment interview. *Professional Psychology, 21*, 12–17.

Brown, T. A., DiNardo, P. A., & Barlow, D. H. (1994). *Anxiety Disorders Interview Schedule for DSM-IV.* Albany, NY: Graywind.

Brown, T. A., O'Leary, T. A., & Barlow, D. H. (1993). Generalized anxiety disorder. In D. H. Barlow (Ed.), *Clinical handbook of psychological disorders* (2nd ed., pp. 127–188). New York: Guilford Press.

Brtek, M. D., & Motowidlo, S. J. (2002). Effects of procedure and outcome accountability on interview validity. *Journal of Applied Psychology, 87*, 185–191.

Bufka, L. F., Crawford, J. I., & Levitt, J. (2002). Brief screening instruments for managed care and primary care. In M. M. Antony & D. Barlow (Eds.), *Handbook of assessment, treatment planning, and outcome evaluation: Empirically supported strategies for psychological disorders* (pp. 49–62). New York: Guilford Press.

Buhler, C., & LeFever, D. (1947). A Rorschach study on the psychological characteristics of alcoholics. *Quarterly Journal of Studies on Alcoholism, 8*, 197–260.

Burns, G. (2001). *101 healing stories*. Hoboken, NJ: John Wiley & Sons.

Burt, D. B., Zembar, M. J., & Niederehe, G. (1995). Depression and memory impairment: A meta-analysis of the association, its pattern, and specificity. *Psychological Bulletin, 117*, 285–305.

Butcher, J. N. (1990). *The MMPI-2 in psychological treatment*. New York: Oxford University Press.

Butcher, J. N. (Ed.). (1996). *International adaptations of the MMPI-2*. Minneapolis: University of Minnesota Press.

Butcher, J. N. (1998). *Butcher Treatment Planning Inventory*. San Antonio, TX: Psychological Corporation.

Butcher, J. N. (2004). Personality assessment without borders: Adaptation of the MMPI-2 across cultures. *Journal of Personality Assessment, 83*, 90–104.

Butcher, J. N. (2006a). *A beginner's guide to the MMPI-2* (2nd ed.). Washington, DC: American Psychological Association.

Butcher, J. N. (2006b). *MMPI-2: A practitioner's guide* (2nd ed.). Washington, DC: American Psychological Association.

Butcher, J. N. (Ed.). (2000). *Basic sources of the MMPI-2*. Minneapolis: University of Minnesota Press.

Butcher, J. N., Dahlstrom, W. G., Graham, J. R., Tellegen, A., & Kaemmer, B. (1989). *Manual for administration and scoring: MMPI-2*. Minneapolis: University of Minnesota Press.

Butcher, J. N., Graham, J. R., Ben-Porath, Y. S., Tellegen, A., Dahlstrom, W. G., & Kaemmer, B. (2001). *Minnesota Multiphasic Personality Inventory-2: Manual for administration and scoring* (2nd ed.). Minneapolis: University of Minnesota Press.

Butcher, J. N., Graham, J. R., Williams, C. L., & Ben-Porath, Y. S. (1990). *Development and use of the MMPI-2 content scales*. Minneapolis: University of Minnesota Press.

Butcher, J. N., & Han, K. (1995). Development of an MMPI-2 scale to assess the presentation of self in a superlative manner: The S scale. In J. N. Butcher & C. D. Spielberger (Eds.), *Advances in personality assessment* (Vol. 10, pp. 25–50). Hillsdale, NJ: Lawrence Erlbaum.

Butcher, J. N., & Hostetler, K. (1990). Abbreviating MMPI item administration: What can be learned from the MMPI for the MMPI-2? *Psychological Assessment, 2*, 12–21.

Butcher, J. N. & Perry, J. (2008). *Psycholgoical assessment in treatment planning: Use of the MMPI-2 and BTPI*. New York: Oxford University Press.

Butcher, J. N., Perry, J. N., & Hahn, J. (2004). Computers in clinical assessment: Historical developments, present status, and future challenges. *Journal of Clinical Psychology, 60*, 331–345.

Butcher, J. N., & Williams, C. L. (2000). *Essentials of MMPI-2 and MMPI-A interpretation* (2nd ed.). Minneapolis: University of Minnesota Press.

Butcher, J. N., Williams, C. L., Graham, J. R., Archer, R. P., Tellegen, A., Ben-Porath, Y. S., et al. (1992). *MMPI-A (Minnesota Multiphasic Personality Inventory-Adolescent): Manual for administration, scoring, and interpretation*. Minneapolis: University of Minnesota Press.

Butler, M., Retzlaff, P., & Vanderploeg, R. (1991). Neuropsychological test usage. *Professional Psychology, 22*, 510–512.

Butters, N., Grant, I., Haxby, J., Judd, L. L., Martin, A., McClelland, J., et al. (1990). Assessment of AIDS-related cognitive changes: Recommendations of the NIMH Workgroup on neuropsychological assessment approaches. *Journal of Clinical and Experimental Neuropsychology, 12*, 963–978.

Byrne, D., Golightly, C., & Sheffield, J. (1965). The Repression-Sensitization Scale as a measure of adjustment: Relationship with the CPI. *Journal of Consulting Psychology, 29*, 585–589.

Cacciola, J. S., Alterman, A. I., Rutherford, M. J., McKay, J. R., & May, D. J. (1999). Comparability of telephone and in-person structured clinical interview for DSM-III-R (SCID) diagnoses. *Assessment, 6*, 235–242.

Cacioppo, J. T., Glass, C. R., & Merluzzi, T. V. (1979). Self-statements and self-evaluations: A cognitive response analysis of heterosocial anxiety. *Cognitive Therapy and Research, 3*, 249–262.

Caldwell, A. B. (1988). *MMPI Supplemental Scale manual.* Los Angeles: Caldwell Report.

Caldwell, A. B. (2001). What do the MMPI scales fundamentally measure? Some hypotheses. *Journal of Personality Assessment, 76*, 1–17.

Callaghan, G. M. (2001). Demonstrating clinical effectiveness for individual practitioners and clinics. *Professional Psychology: Research and Practice, 32*, 289–297.

Calvin, J. (1975). *A replicated study of the concurrent validity of the Harris subscales for the MMPI.* Unpublished doctoral dissertation, Kent State University, Kent, OH.

Camara, W. J., Nathan, J. S., & Puente, A. E. (2000). Psychological test usage: Implications in professional psychology. *Professional Psychology: Research and Practice, 31*, 141–154.

Campbell, J. (1998). Internal and external validity of seven Wechsler Intelligence Scale for Children (3rd ed., short forms in a sample of psychiatric inpatients). *Psychological Assessment, 10*, 431–434.

Campbell, K. A., Rohlunan, D. S., Storybach, D., Binder, L., Anger, W. K., Kovera, C. A., et al. (1999). Test-retest reliability of psychological and neurobehavioral tests set administered by computer. *Assessment, 6*, 21–32.

Canetti, L., Shalev, A. Y., & De-Nour, A. K. (1994). Israeli adolescent norms of the Brief Symptom Inventory (BSI). *Israel Journal of Psychiatry and Related Sciences, 31*, 13–18.

Canter, A. (1983). *The Canter Background Interference Procedure for the Bender Gestalt Test.* Los Angeles: Western Psychological Services.

Carkhuff, R. R. (1969). *Helping and human relations. I: Selection and training. II: Practice and research.* New York: Holt, Rinehart and Winston.

Carlson, J. G. (1982). Some concepts of perceived control and their relationship to bodily self-control. *Journal of Biofeedback and Self-Regulation, 7*, 341–375.

Carnes, G. D., & Bates, R. (1971). Rorschach anatomy response correlates in rehabilitation of failure subjects. *Journal of Personality Assessment, 35*, 527–537.

Cartwright, R. D. (1986). Affect and dream work from an information processing point of view. *Journal of Mind and Behavior, 7*, 411–428.

Caruso, J. C., & Cliff, N. (1999). The properties of equally and differentiated weighted WAIS-III factor scores. *Psychological Assessment, 11*, 198–206.

Caruso, K. R. (1988). *Manual for the Projective Storytelling Cards.* Sarasota, FL: Professional Resource Exchange.

Cashel, M. L. (2002). Child and adolescent psychological assessment: Current clinical practices and the impact of managed care. *Professional Psychology, 33*, 446–453.

Castonguay, L. G., & Beutler, L. E. (2006). Common and unique principles of therapeutic change: What do we know and what do we need to know? In L. G. Castonguay & L. E. Beutler (Eds.), Principles of therapeutic change that work. (pp. 353–370). New York: Oxford University Press.

Cella, D. (1984). The modified WAIS-R: An extension and revision. *Journal of Clinical Psychology, 40*, 801–804.

Chambers, W. J., Puig-Antich, J., Hirsch, M., Paez, P., Ambrosini, P. J., Tabrizi, M. A., et al. (1985). The assessment of affective disorders in children and adolescents by semistructured interview: Test-retest reliability of the Schedule for Affective Disorders and Schizophrenia for School Age Children, Present Episode version. *Archives of General Psychiatry, 42*, 696–702.

Charter, R. A., & Lopez, M. N. (2002). Millon Clinical Multiaxial Inventory (MCMI-III): The inability of the validity conditions to detect random responders. *Journal of Clinical Psychology, 58*, 1615–1617.

Chelune, G. J., & Bornstein, R. A. (1988). WMS-R patterns among patients with unilateral brain lesions [Special issue]. *Clinical Neuropsychologist, 2*, 121–132.

Chiles, J. A., Lambert, M. J., & Hatch, A. L. (1999). The impact of psychological interventions on medical cost offset: A meta-analytic review. *Clinical Psychology: Science and Practice, 6*, 204–220.

Chisholm, S. M., Crowther, J. H., & Ben-Porath, Y. S. (1997). Selected MMPI-2 Scales' ability to predict premature termination and outcome from psychotherapy. *Journal of Personality Assessment, 69*, 127–144.

Choca, J. P., Retzlaff, P., Strack, S., Mouton, A., & Van Denburg, E. (1996). Factorial elements in Millon's personality theory. *Journal of Personality Disorders, 10*, 377–383.

Choca, J. P., Shanley, L. A., Peterson, C. A., & Van Denburg, E. (1990). Racial bias and the MCMI. *Journal of Personality Assessment, 54*, 479–490.

Choca, J. P., & Van Denburg, E. (2004). *Interpretive guide to the Millon Clinical Multiaxial Inventory* (3rd ed.). Washington, DC: American Psychological Association.

Choca, J. P., Denburg, E., Bratu, M. E., & Meagher, S. (1995, March). *Personality changes of psychiatric patients with aging.* Paper presented at the midwinter meeting of the Society for Personality Assessment, Denver, CO.

Chojnacki, J. T., & Walsh, W. B. (1992). The consistency of scores and configural patterns between MMPI and MMPI-2. *Journal of Personality Assessment, 59*, 276–289.

Choquette, K. A. (1990). Assessing depression in alcoholics with the BDI, SCL-90-R, and DIS criteria. *Journal of Substance Abuse, 6*, 295–304.

Chusmir, L. H. (1985). Short-form scoring for McClelland's version of the TAT. *Perceptual and Motor Skills, 61*, 1047–1052.

Ciarrochi, J. V., Chan, A. Y. C., & Caputi, P. (2000). A critical evaluation of the emotional intelligence construct. *Personality and Individual Differences, 28*(3), 539–561.

Cicchetti, D. V. (1994). Guidelines, criteria, and rules of thumb for evaluating normed and standardized assessment instruments in psychology. *Psychological Assessment, 6*, 284–290.

Ciminero, A. R., Calhoun, K. S., & Adams, H. E. (Eds.). (1977). *Handbook of behavioral assessment.* New York: John Wiley & Sons.

Claassen, C. A., & Lovitt, R. (2001). Solving ethical problems in medical setting druing psychological assessment: A decisional model. *Journal of Personality Assessment, 77*, 214–230.

Clark, C. G., & Miller, H. L. (1971). Validation of Gilberstadt and Duker's 8–6 profile type on a black sample. *Psychological Reports, 29*, 259–264.

Clawson, A. (1962). *The Bender Visual Motor Gestalt for children: A manual.* Los Angeles: Western Psychological Services.

Coan, R. (1956). A factor analysis of Rorschach determinants. *Journal of Projective Techniques, 20*, 280–287.

Coche, E., & Sillitti, J. A. (1983). The Thematic Apperception Test as an outcome measure in psychotherapy. *Psychotherapy: Theory, Research, and Practice, 20*, 41–46.

Cojnacki, J. T., & Walsh, W. B. (1992). The consistency of scores and configural patterns between the MMPI and MMPI-2. *Journal of Personality Assessment, 59*, 278–289.

Colby, F. (1989). Usefulness of the K correction in MMPI profiles of patients and non-patients. *Psychological Assessment, 1*, 142–145.

Colligan, R. C., & Offord, K. P. (1989). The aging MMPI: Contemporary norms for contemporary teenagers. *Mayo Clinic Proceedings, 64*, 3–27.

Collins, D. J. (1967). Psychological selection of drill sergeants: An exploratory attempt in a new program. *Military Medicine, 132*, 713–715.

Collins, J. M., & Bagozzi, R. P. (1999). Testing the equivalence of the socialization factor structure for criminals and noncriminals. *Journal of Personality Assessment, 72*, 68–73.

Collins, J. M., & Griffin, R. (1998). The psychology of underlying counterproductive job performance. In R. W. Griffin, A. O'Leary-Kelly, & J. M. Collins (Eds.), *Dysfunctional work behavior in organizations: Monographs in organizational behavior and industrial relations* (Vol. 23, Pt. B). Stamford, CT: JAL.

Cone, J. D. (1977). The relevance of reliability and validity for behavioral assessment. *Behavior Therapy, 8*, 411–426.

Cone, J. D. (1978). The behavioral assessment grid (BAG): A conceptual framework and taxonomy. *Behavior Therapy, 9*, 882–888.

Cone, J. D. (1998). Psychometric considerations: Concepts, contents, and methods. In A. S. Bellack & M. Hersen (Eds.), *Behavioral assessment: A practical handbook* (4th ed., pp. 22–46). Boston: Allyn & Bacon.

Conners, C. K. (1997). *Conners' Parent Rating Scale—Revised.* North Tonawanda, NY: Multi-Health Systems.

Conners, C. K. Sitarenios, G., Parker, J. D., & Epstein, J. N. (1998). Revision and restandardization of the Conners' Teacher Rating Scale (CTRS-R): Factor structure reliability and criterion validity. *Journal of Abnormal Child Psychology, 26*, 279–291.

Cooney, N. L., Kadden, R. M., & Litt, M. D. (1990). A comparison of methods assessing sociopathy in male and female alcoholics. *Journal of Studies on Alcohol, 51*, 42–48.

Cooper, H. M., & Rosenthal, R. (1980). Statistical versus traditional procedures for summarizing research findings. *Psychological Bulletin, 87*, 442–449.

Cooper, W. H. (1981). Ubiquitous halo. *Psychological Bulletin, 90*, 218–244.

Cooper, Z., & Fairburn, C. G. (1987). The eating disorder examination: A semistructured interview for the assessment of the specific psychopathology of eating disorders. *International Journal of Eating Disorders, 6*, 136–141.

Cordoni, B. K., O'Donnell, J. P., Ramaniah, N. V., Kurtz, J., & Rosenshein, K. (1981). Wechsler Adult Intelligence Scale patterns for learning disabled young adults. *Journal of Learning Disabilities, 14*, 404–407.

Corkin, S., Growdon, J. H., Sullivan, E. V., Nissen, M. J., & Huff, F. J. (1986). Assessing treatment effects: A neuropsychological battery. In L. W. Poon (Ed.), *Handbook for clinical memory assessment of older adults* (pp. 156–167). Washington, DC: American Psychological Association.

Cormier, W. H., & Cormier, L. S. (1998). *Interviewing strategies for helpers: Fundamental skills and cognitive behavioral interventions* (4th ed.). Monterey, CA: Brooks/Cole.

Coryell, W. H., Akiskal, H. S., Leon, A. C., Winokur, G., Masur, J. D., Mueller, T. I., et al. (1994). The time course of nonchronic major depressive disorder. *Archives of General Psychiatry, 51*, 405–410.

Costa, P. T., Zonderman, A. B., Williams, R. B., & McRae, R. R. (1985). Content and comprehensiveness of the MMPI: An item factor analysis in a normal adult sample. *Journal of Personality and Social Psychology, 48*, 925–933.

Costantino, G., Dana, R. H., & Malgady, R. G. (2007). *TEMAS (Tell-Me-A-Story) Assessment in multicultural societies.* Mahwah, NJ: Lawrence Erlbaum.

Costantino, G., & Malgady, R. G. (1999). The Tell-Me-A-Story Test: A multicultural offspring of the Thematic Apperception Test. In L. Gieser & M. I. Stein (Eds.), *Evocative images: The Thematic Apperception Test and the art of projection* (pp. 177–190). Washington, DC: American Psychological Association.

Costantino, G., Malgady, R. G., Casullo, M. M., & Castillo, A. (1991). Cross-cultural standardization of the TEMAS in three Hispanic subcultures. *Journal of Behavioral Sciences, 13*, 48–62.

Costantino, G., Malgady, R. G., Colon-Malgady, G., & Bailey, J. (1992). Clinical utility of the TEMAS with nonminority children. *Journal of Personality Assessment, 59*, 433–438.

Costantino, G., Malgady, R. G., & Rogler, L. H. (1988). *Technical manual: TEMAS Thematic Apperception Test.* Los Angeles: Western Psychological Services.

Costantino, G., Malgady, R. G., Rogler, L. H., & Tsui, E. C. (1988). Discriminant analysis of clinical outpatients and public school children by TEMAS: A Thematic Apperception Test for Hispanics and Blacks. *Journal of Personality Assessment, 52,* 670–678.

Costello, E. J., Benjamin, R., Angold, A., & Silver, D. (1991). Mood variability in adolescence: A study of depressed and nondepressed comorbid patients. *Journal of Affective Disorders, 23,* 199–212.

Costello, E. J., Edelbrock, C. S., & Costello, A. J. (1985). Validity of the NIMH Diagnostic Interview Schedule for Children: A comparison between psychiatric and pediatric referrals. *Journal of Abnormal and Child Psychology, 13,* 579–595.

Costello, E. J., Edelbrock, C. S., Duncan, M. K., & Kalas, R. (1984). *Testing of the NIMH Diagnostic Interview Schedule for Children (DISC) in a clinical population.* Final report to the Center for Epidemiological Studies, National Institute for Mental Health. Pittsburgh, PA: University of Pittsburgh.

Costello, R. M., & Wicott, K. A. (1984). Impression management and testing for locus of control in an alcoholic sample. *International Journal of the Addictions, 19,* 45–56.

Craig, R. J. (1995). Clinical diagnoses and MCMI codetypes. *Journal of Clinical Psychology, 51,* 352–360.

Craig, R. J. (1999). Overview and status of the Millon Clinical Multiaxial Inventory. *Journal of Personality Assessment, 72,* 390–406.

Craig, R. J. (2001). Adjectival descriptions of personality disorders: A convergent validity study of the MCMI-III. *Journal of Personality Assessment, 77,* 259–271.

Craig, R. J. (2005). Alternative interpretations for the histrionic, narcissistic, and compulsive personality disorder scales of the MCMI-III. In R. J. Craig (Ed.), *New directions in interpreting the Millon Clinical Multiaxial Inventory-III*(pp. 71–93). Hoboken, NJ: John Wiley & Sons.

Craig, R. J., & Bivens, A. (1998). Factor structure of the MCMI-III. *Journal of Personality Assessment, 70,* 190–196.

Craig, R. J., & Olson, R. E. (2001). Adjectival descriptions of personality disorders: A convergent validity study of the MCMI-III. *Journal of Personality Assessment, 77,* 259–271.

Cramer, P. (1996). *Storytelling, narrative, and the Thematic Apperception Test.* New York: Guilford Press.

Cramer, P. (1998). Threat to gender representation: Identity and identification. *Journal of Personality Assessment, 66,* 335–357.

Cramer, P. (1999). Future directions for the Thematic Apperception Test. *Journal of Personality Assessment, 72,* 74–92.

Cramer, P. (2006). *Protecting the self: Defense mechanisms in action.* New York: Guilford Press.

Crary, W. G., & Johnson, C. W. (1981). Mental status examination. In C. W. Johnson, J. R. Snibbe, & L. A. Evans (Eds.), *Basic psychopathology: A programmed text* (2nd ed., pp. 56–57). Lancaster, PA: MTP Press.

Craske, M. G., & Barlow, D. H. (1993). Panic and agoraphobia. In D. H. Barlow (Ed.), *Clinical handbook of psychological disorders* (pp. 1–47). New York: Guilford Press.

Crawford, J. R., Millar, J., & Milne, A. B. (2001). Estimating premorbid IQ from demographic variables: A comparison of a regression equation vs. clinical judgment. *British Journal of Clinical Psychology, 40,* 97–105.

Cronbach, L. J. (1978). Black Intelligence Test of Cultural Homogeneity: A review. In O. K. Buros (Ed.), *The eighth mental measurements yearbook* (Vol. 1, p. 250). Highland Park, NJ: Gryphon Press.

Cross, D. T., & Burger, G. (1982). Ethnicity as a variable in responses to California Psychological Inventory items. *Journal of Personality Assessment, 46,* 153–158.

Crumpton, E. (1956). The influence of color on the Rorschach Test. *Journal of Projective Techniques, 20,* 150–158.

Cuellar, I., Arnold, B., & Maldonado, R. (1995). Acculturation Rating Scale for Mexican Americans-II: A revision of the original ARSMA scale. *Hispanic Journal of Behavioral Science, 17*, 275–304.

Cummings, N. A. (1991). The somatizing patient. In C. A. Austad & W. A. Berman (Eds.), *Psychotherapy in managed care: The optimal use of time and resources* (pp. 234–237). Washington, DC: American Psychological Association.

Cummings, N. A. (1999). Medical cost offset, meta-analysis, and implications for future research and practice. *Clinical Psychology: Science and Practice, 6*, 221–224.

Cunningham, T. R., & Thorp, R. G. (1981). The influence of settings on accuracy and reliability of behavioral observation. *Behavioral Assessment, 3*, 67–78.

Cyr, J. J., McKenna-Foley, J. M., & Peacock, E. (1985). Factor structure of the SCL-90-R: Is there one? *Journal of Personality Assessment, 49*, 571–578.

Dahlstrom, W. G. (1969). Recurrent issues in the development of the MMPI. In J. N. Butcher (Ed.), *MMPI: Research developments and clinical applications* (pp. 1–40). New York: McGraw-Hill.

Dahlstrom, W. G., & Welsh, G. S. (1960). *An MMPI handbook: A guide to use in clinical practice and research.* Minneapolis: University of Minnesota Press.

Dahlstrom, W. G., Welsh, G. S., & Dahlstrom, L. E. (1972). *An MMPI handbook. Vol. 1: Clinical Interpretation.* Minneapolis: University of Minnesota Press.

Dahlstrom, W. G., Welsh, G. S., & Dahlstrom, L. E. (1975). *An MMPI handbook. Vol. 2: Research developments and applications.* Minneapolis: University of Minnesota Press.

Daldrup, F. J., Beutler, L. E., Engle, D., & Greenberg, L. S. (1988). *Focused expressive psychotherapy: Freeing the overcontrolled patient.* New York: Pergamon Press.

Dao, T. K., & Prevatt, F. (2006). A psychometric evaluation of the Rorschach System's Perceptual Thinking Index. *Journal of Personality Assessment, 86*, 180–189.

Dana, R. H. (1955). Clinical diagnosis and objective TAT scoring. *Journal of Abnormal and Social Psychology, 50*, 19–24.

Dana, R. H. (1965). Review of the Rorschach. In O. K. Buros (Ed.), *Sixth mental measurements yearbook* (pp. 492–495). Highland Park, NJ: Gryphon Press.

Dana, R. H. (1968). Six constructs to define Rorschach M. *Journal of Projective Techniques and Personality Assessment, 32*, 138–145.

Dana, R. H. (1999). Cross-cultural-multimethod use of the Thematic Apperception Test. In L. Gieser & M. I. Stein (Eds.), *Evocative images: The Thematic Apperception Test and the art of projection* (pp. 177–190). Washington, DC: American Psychological Association.

Dana, R. H. (2000). *Handbook of cross-cultural and multi-cultural personality assessment.* Mahwah, NJ: Lawrence Erlbaum.

Dana, R. H. (2005). *Multicultural assessment: Principles, applications, and examples.* Mahwah, NJ: Lawrence Erlbaum.

Dana, R. H., Field, K., & Bolton, B. (1983). Variations of the Bender-Gestalt Test: Implications for training and practice. *Journal of Personality Assessment, 47*, 76–84.

Daniel, M. H. (1997). Intelligence testing: Status and trends. *American Psychologist, 52*, 1038–1045.

Das, J. P., & Naglieri, J. A. (1994). *Das-Naglieri Cognitive Assessment System: Standardization Test Battery.* Chicago: Riverside Press.

Datel, W. E., Hall, F. D., & Rufe, C. P. (1965). Measurement of achievement motivation in army security agency foreign language candidates. *Educational and Psychological Measurement, 25*, 539–545.

Davis, G. L., Hoffman, R. G., & Nelson, K. S. (1990). Differences between Native Americans and Whites on the California Psychological Inventory. *Psychological Assessment, 2*, 238–242.

Davis, R. G. (1999). Millon: Essentials of his science, theory, classification, assessment, and therapy. *Journal of Personality Assessment, 72*, 330–352.

Davis, R. G., Wenger, A., & Guzman, A. (1997). *Validation of the MCMI-III.* In T. Millon (Ed.), *The Millon inventories: Clinical and personality assessment* (pp. 327–362). New York: Guilford Press.

Dawes, R. M., & Corrigan, B. (1974). Linear models in decision making. *Psychological Bulletin, 81*, 95–106.

Dean, R. S. (1982). Neuropsychological assessment. In T. Kratochwill (Ed.), *Advances in school psychology* (Vol. 2). Hillsdale, NJ: Lawrence Erlbaum.

Deardorff, W. W. (2000). The MMPI-2 and chronic pain. In R. J. Gatchel & J. N. Weisberg (Eds.), *Personality characteristics of patients with pain* (pp. 109–125). Washington, DC: American Psychological Association.

Debord, J. B. (1989). Paradoxical interventions: A review of the recent literature. *Journal of Counseling and Development, 67*, 394–398.

Decker, S. L. (2007). Measuirng growth and decline in visual-motor processes with the Bender-Gestalt second edition. *Journal of Psychoeducational Assessment, 10*, 1–13.

Decker, S. L., Allen, R., & Choca, J. P. (2006). Construct validity of the Bender-Gestalt II: Comparison with the Wechlser Intelligence Scale for Children-III. *Perceptual and Motor Skills, 102*, 133–141.

DeFrancesco, J. J., & Taylor, J. (1993). A validation on the revised Socialization Scale of the California Psychological Inventory. *Journal of Psychopathology and Behavioral Assessment, 15*, 53–56.

DeGood, D. E., Crawford, A. L., & Jongsma, A. E. (1999). *The behavioral medicine treatment planner.* New York: John Wiley & Sons.

Del Greco, L., Breitbach, L., & McCarthy, R. H. (1981). The Rathus Assertiveness Schedule modified for early adolescents. *Journal of Behavioral Assessment, 3*, 321–328.

Delis, D. C., Kaplan, E., & Kramer, J. H. (2001). *Delis-Kaplan Executive Function System.* San Antonio, TX: Psychological Corporation.

Delis, D. C., Kramer, J. H., Kaplan, E., & Ober, B. A. (2000). *California Verbal Learning Test-II: Adult version.* San Antonio, TX: Psychological Corporation.

Deniston, W. M., & Ramanaiah, N. V. (1993). California Psychological Inventory and the five-factor model of personality. *Psychological Reports, 73*, 491–496.

Derogatis, L. R. (1992). *BSI: Administration, scoring, and procedures manual-II* (2nd ed.). Baltimore: Clinical Psychometric Research.

Derogatis, L. R. (1993). *Brief Symptom Inventory (BSI) administration, scoring, and procedures manual* (3rd ed.). Minneapolis, MN: National Computer Systems.

Derogatis, L. R. (1994). *SCL-90-R: Administration, scoring, and procedures manual.* Minneapolis, MN: National Computer Systems.

Derogatis, L. R., Lipman, R. S., Rickels, K., Uhlenhuth, E. H., & Covi, L. (1974). The Hopkins Symptom Checklist (HSCL): A self-report symptom inventory. *Behavioral Scientist, 19*, 1–15.

Derogatis, L. R., & Savitz, K. L. (1999). The SCL-90-R, Brief Symptom Inventory, and matching clinical rating scales. In M. E. Maruish (Ed.), *The use of psychological testing for treatment planning and outcomes assessment* (pp. 679–724). Mahwah, NJ: Lawrence Erlbaum.

desRosiers, G. (1992). Primary or depressive dementia: Clinical features. *International Journal of Geriatric Psychiatry, 7*, 629–638.

Devine, R. J. (2005). *CPI 260 Client feedback report guide for interpretation: Strategies for use in business and organizations.* Mountain View, CA: Consulting Psychologists Press.

Dicken, C. F. (1960). Simulated patterns on the California Psychological Inventory. *Journal of Counseling Psychology, 7*, 24–31.

DiClemente, C. (1986). Self-efficacy and the addictive behaviors. *Journal of Social and Clinical Psychology, 4*, 302–315.

Dies, R. R. (1972). Personal gullibility or pseudodiagnosis: A further test of the "fallacy of personal validation." *Journal of Clinical Psychology, 28*, 47–50.

Diller, L., Ben-Yishay, Y., Gertsman, L. J., Goodkin, R., Gordon, W., & Weinberg, J. (1976). *Studies in cognition and rehabilitation in hemiplegia* (Rehabilitation Monograph, No. 50). New York: New York University Medical Center, Institute of Rehabilitation Medicine.

Dixon, W. E., & Anderson, T. (1995). Establishing covariance continuity between the WISC-R and the WISC-III. *Psychological Assessment, 7*, 115–117.

Dobbins, C., & Russell, E. W. (1990). Left temporal lobe brain damage pattern on the Wechsler Adult Intelligence Scale. *Journal of Clinical Psychology, 46*, 863–868.

Dodrill, C. B., & Troupin, A. S. (1975). Effects of repeated administration of a comprehensive neuropsychological battery among chronic epileptics. *Journal of Nervous and Mental Diseases, 161*, 185–190.

Dolman, R., Roy, E. A., Dimeck, P. T., & Hall, C. R. (2000). Age, gesture span, and dissociation among component subsystems of working memory. *Brain, Cognition, and Rehabilitation, 43*, 164–168.

Dorr, D. (1999). Approaching psychotherapy of the personality disorders from the Millon perspective. *Journal of Personality Assessment, 72*, 407–425.

Dougherty, T. W., Ebert, R. J., & Callender, J. C. (1986). Policy capturing in the employment interview. *Journal of Applied Psychology, 71*, 9–15.

Dowd, E. T., Milne, C. R., & Wise, S. L. (1991). The Therapeutic Reactance Scale: A measure of psychological reactance. *Journal of Counseling and Development, 69*, 541–545.

Dowd, E. T., & Wallbrown, F. (1993). Motivational components of client reactance. *Journal of Counseling and Development, 71*, 533–538.

Dozois, D. J., Dobson, K. S., & Ahnberg, J. L. (1998). A psychometric evaluation of the Beck Depression Inventory-II. *Psychological Assessment, 10*, 83–89.

Draguns, J. G., Haley, E. M., & Phillips, L. (1967). Studies of the Rorschach content: A review of the research literature. Part 1: Traditional content categories. *Journal of Projective Techniques and Personality Assessment, 31*, 3–32.

Drake, L. E. (1946). A social I. E. scale for the MMPI. *Journal of Applied Psychology, 30*, 51–54.

Dritschel, B. H., Williams, K., & Cooper, P. J. (1991). Cognitive distortions among women experiencing bulimic episodes. *International Journal of Eating Disorders, 10*, 547–555.

DuAlba, L., & Scott, R. L. (1993). Somatization and malingering for workers' compensation applicants: A cross-cultural MMPI study. *Journal of Clinical Psychology, 49*, 913–917.

Dubois, B., Feldman, H. H., Jacova, C., Dekosky, S. T., Barberger-Gateau, O., et al. (2007). Research criteria for the diagnosis of Alzheimer's Disease: Revising the NINCDS-ADRDA criteria. *Lancet Neurology, 6*, 734–746.

Duff, K., Langbehn, D. R., Schoenberg, M. R., Moser, D. J., Baade, L. E., Mold, J., Scott, J., & Adams, R. L. (2006). Examining the Repeatable Battery for the Assessment of Neuropsychological Status: Factor analytic studies in an elderly sample. *American Journal of Geriatric Psychiatry, 14*, 976–979.

Duff, K., Leigh, J. B., Schoenberg, M. R., Patton, D. E., Mold, J., Scott, J. G., & Adams, R. (2005). Test-retest stability and practic effects of the RBANS in a community dwelling elderly sample. *Journal of Clinical and Experimental Neuropsychology, 27*, 565–575.

Duff, K., Patton, D., Schoenberg, M. R., Mold, J., Scott, J. G., & Adams, R. (2003). Age and education-corrected independent normative data for the RBANS in a community dwelling elderly sample. *Clinical Neuropsychologist, 17*, 351–366.

Durand, V. M., & Crimmins, D. B. (1992). *The Motivation Assessment Scale administrative guide.* Topeka, KS: Monaco & Associates.

Duthie, B., & Vincent, K. R. (1986). Diagnostic hit rates of high point codes for the Diagnostic Inventory of Personality and Symptoms using random assignment, base rates, and probability scales. *Journal of Clinical Psychology, 42*, 612–614.

Dye, O. A. (1979). Effects of practice on Trail Making performance. *Perceptual and Motor Skills, 48*, 296.

Earls, R., Reich, W., Jung, K. G., & Cloninger, C. R. (1988). Psychopathology in children of alcoholic and antisocial parents. *Alcoholism: Clinical and Experimental Research, 12*, 481–487.

Eaton, W. W., Neufeld, K., Chen, L., & Cai, G. (2000). A comparison of self report and clinical diagnostic interviews for depression. *Archives of General Psychiatry, 57*, 217–222.

Edell, W. S. (1987). Role of structure in disordered thinking in borderline and schizophrenic disorders. *Journal of Personality Assessment, 51*, 23–41.

Edwards, A. L. (1957). *The social desirability variables in personality assessment and research.* New York: Dryden Press.

Edwards, A. L. (1964). Social desirability and performance on the MMPI. *Psychometrika, 29*, 295–308.

Edwards, D. W., Morrison, T. L., & Weissman, H. N. (1993). The MMPI and MMPI-2 in an outpatient sample: Comparisons of code types, validity scales, and clinical scales. *Journal of Personality Assessment, 61*, 1–18.

Egeland, B. R. (1969). Examiner expectancy: Effects on the scoring of the WISC. *Psychology in the Schools, 6*, 313–315.

Eichler, R. M. (1951). Experimental stress and alleged Rorschach indices of anxiety. *Journal of Abnormal and Social Psychology, 46*, 169–177.

Eidelson, R. J., & Epstein, N. (1982). Cognitive and relationship adjustment: Development of a measure of dysfunctional relationship beliefs. *Journal of Consulting and Clinical Psychology, 50*, 715–720.

Eisman, E. J., Dies, R. R., Finn, S. E., Eyde, L. D., Kay, G. G., Kubiszyn, T. W., et al. (2000). Problems and limitations in using psychological assessment in the contemporary health care delivery system. *Professional Psychology: Research and Practice, 31*, 131–140.

Elashoff, J., & Snow, R. E. (Eds.). (1971). *Pygmalion revisited.* Worthington, OH: C. A. Jones.

Elion, V. H., & Megargee, E. I. (1975). Validity of the MMPI Pd Scale among black males. *Journal of Consulting and Clinical Psychology, 43*, 166–172.

Elkin, I., Shea, T., Watkins, J. T., Imber, S. D., Sotsky, S. M., Collins, J. F., et al. (1989). National Institute of Mental Health treatment of depression collaborative research program. *Archives of General Psychiatry, 46*, 971–982.

Elliot, A.J., Mittenberger, R.G., Kaster-Bundgaard, J., & Lumley, V. (1996). A national survey of assessment and therapy techniques used by behavior terapists. *Cognitive and Behavioral Practice, 3*, 107–125.

Elliot, L. L. (1960). *WAF performance on the California Psychological Inventory* (Wright Air Development Division Technical Note 60–218). San Antonio, TX: Air Research and Development Command, Lackland AFB.

Elliot, R., Fox, C. M., Svetlana, A., B., Stone, G. E., Gunderson, J., & Zhang, X. (2006). Deconstructing therapy outcome measurement with Rasch analysis of a measure of general clinical distress: The Symptom Checklist-90-Revised. *Psychological Assessment, 18*, 359–372.

Ellis, M. V., Robbins, E. S., Schult, D., Ladny, N., & Baker, J. (1990). Anchoring errors in clinical judgments: Type I error, adjustment or mitigation. *Journal of Counseling Psychology, 37*, 343–351.

Elwood, R. W. (1991). The Wechsler Memory Scale-Revised: Psychometric characteristics and clinical application. *Neuropsychology Review, 2*, 179–201.

Embretson, S., Schneider, L. M., & Roth, D. L. (1986). Multiple processing strategies and the construct validity of verbal resoning tests. *Journal of Educational Measurement, 23*, 13–32.

Endicott, J., & Spitzer, R. L. (1978). A diagnostic interview: The schedule for affective disorders and schizophrenia. *Archives of General Psychiatry, 35*, 837–844.

Entwisle, D. R. (1972). To dispel fantasies about fantasy-based measures of achievement motivation. *Psychological Bulletin, 77*, 377–391.

Eppinger, M. G., Craig, P. L., Adams, R. L., & Parsons, O. A. (1987). The WAIS-R Index for estimating premorbid intelligence: Cross-validation and clinical utility. *Journal of Consulting and Clinical Psychology, 55*, 86–90.

Epstein, J., & Klinkenberg, W. D. (2001). From Eliza to Internet: A brief history of computerized assessment. *Computers in Human Behavior, 17*, 295–314.

Equal Employment Opportunity Commission. (1970). Guidelines on employee selection procedures. *Federal Register, 35*, 12333–12336.

Erginel, A. (1972). On the test-retest reliability of the Rorschach. *Journal of Personality Assessment, 36*, 203–212.

Erickson, R. C., Caslyn, D. A., & Scheupbach, C. S. (1978). Abbreviating the Halstead-Reitan Neuropsychological Test Battery. *Journal of Clinical Psychology, 42*, 946–955.

Eron, L. D. (1950). A normative study of the Thematic Apperception Test. *Psychological Monographs, 64*, 315.

Exner, J. E. (1969). *The Rorschach systems.* New York: Grune & Stratton.

Exner, J. E. (1974). *The Rorschach: A comprehensive system. Volume 1: Basic foundations.* New York: John Wiley & Sons.

Exner, J. E. (1978). *The Rorschach: A comprehensive system. Volume 2: Current research and advanced interpretations.* New York: John Wiley & Sons.

Exner, J. E. (1979). *The effects of voluntary restraint on Rorschach retests.* Rorschach Workshops (Study No. 258, unpublished).

Exner, J. E. (1983). Rorschach assessment. In I. B. Weiner (Ed.), *Clinical methods in clinical psychology* (2nd ed.). New York: John Wiley & Sons.

Exner, J. E. (1984). *A computer program to assist in Rorschach interpretation* (rev. ed.). Bayville, NY: Rorschach Workshops.

Exner, J. E. (1986). *The Rorschach: A comprehensive system. Volume 1: Basic foundations* (2nd ed.). New York: John Wiley & Sons.

Exner, J. E. (1988). Problems with brief Rorschach protocols. *Journal of Personality Assessment, 52*, 640–647.

Exner, J. E. (1991). *The Rorschach: A comprehensive system. Volume 2: Current research and advanced interpretation* (2nd ed.). New York: John Wiley & Sons.

Exner, J. E. (1993). *The Rorschach: A comprehensive system. Volume 1: Basic foundations* (3rd ed.). New York: John Wiley & Sons.

Exner, J. E. (1995). *The Rorschach: A comprehensive system. Volume 3: Assessing children and adolescents.* New York: John Wiley & Sons.

Exner, J. E. (1997). The future of Rorschach in personality assessment. *Journal of Personality Assessment, 68*, 37–46.

Exner, J. E. (2000). *A primer for Rorschach interpretation.* Asheville, NC: Rorschach Workshops.

Exner, J. E. (2001). *A Rorschach workbook for the comprehensive system* (5th ed.). Asheville, NC: Rorschach Workshops.

Exner, J. E. (2003). *The Rorschach: A comprehensive system. Volume 1: Basic foundations* (4th ed.). New York: John Wiley & Sons.

Exner, J. E., Armbuster, G. L., & Viglione, D. (1978). The temporal stability of some Rorschach features. *Journal of Personality Assessment, 42*, 474–482.

Exner, J. E., Armbuster, G. L., Walker, E. J., & Cooper, W. H. (1975). *Anticipation of elective surgery as manifest in Rorschach records.* Rorschach Workshops (Study No. 213, unpublished).

Exner, J. E., & Bryant, E. L. (1974). *Rorschach responses of subjects recently divorced or separated. Rorschach Workshops* (Study No. 206, unpublished).

Exner, J. E., & Erdberg, P. (2005). *The Rorschach: A comprehensive system, Advanced Interpretation,* Vol. 2 (3rd ed.). Hoboken, NJ: John Wiley & Sons.

Exner, J. E., & Exner, D. E. (1972). How clinicians use the Rorschach. *Journal of Personality Assessment, 36*, 403–408.

Exner, J. E., & Hillman, L. (1984). *A comparison of content distributions for the records of 76 paranoid schizophrenics and 76 nonparanoid schizophrenics.* Rorschach Workshops (Study No. 293, unpublished).

Exner, J. E., & Kazaoka, K. (1978). *Dependency gestures of 16 assertiveness trainees as related to Rorschach movement responses.* Rorschach Workshops (Study No. 261, unpublished).

Exner, J. E., Leura, A. V., & George, L. M. (1976). *A replication of the Masling study using four groups of new examiners with two seating arrangements and ride evaluation.* Rorschach Workshops (Study No. 256, unpublished).

Exner, J. E., & Murillo, L. G. (1973). Effectiveness of regressive ECT with process schizophrenics. *Diseases of the Nervous System, 34*, 44–48.

Exner, J. E., & Murillo, L. G. (1977). A long-term follow up of schizophrenics treated with regressive ECT. *Diseases of the Nervous System, 38*, 162–168.

Exner, J. E., Murillo, L. G., & Sternklar, S. (1979). *Anatomy and X-ray responses among patients with body delusions or body problems.* Rorschach Workshops (Study No. 257, unpublished).

Exner, J. E., & Sanglade, A. A. (1992). Rorschach changes following brief and short term therapy. *Journal of Personality Assessment, 59*, 59–71.

Exner, J. E., Thomas, E. A., Cohen, J. B., Ridgeway, E. M., & Cooper, W. H. (1981). *Stress indices in the Rorschachs of patients recovering from myocardial infarctions.* Rorschach Workshops (Study No. 286, unpublished).

Exner, J. E., Thomas, E. A., & Mason, B. (1985). Children's Rorschachs: Descriptions and prediction. *Journal of Personality Assessment, 49*, 13–20.

Exner, J. E., & Weiner, I. B. (1982). *The Rorschach: A comprehensive system. Volume 3: Assessment of children and adolescents.* New York: John Wiley & Sons.

Exner, J. E., & Weiner, I. B. (1995). *The Rorschach: A comprehensive system. Volume 3: Assessment of children and adolescents* (2nd ed.). New York: John Wiley & Sons.

Exner, J. E., & Wylie, J. R. (1975). *Attempts at simulation of schizophrenia-like protocols by psychology graduate students* (Workshops Study No. 211, unpublished). Bayville, NY: Rorschach Workshops.

Exner, J. E., & Wylie, J. R. (1977). Some Rorschach data concerning suicide. *Journal of Personality Assessment, 41*, 339–348.

Exner, J. E., Wylie, J. R., Leura, A. V., & Parrill, T. (1977). Some psychological characteristics of prostitutes. *Journal of Personality Assessment, 41*, 474–485.

Exner, J. E., Zalis, T., & Schumacher, J. (1976). *Rorschach protocols of chronic amphetamine users.* Rorschach Workshops (Study No. 233, unpublished).

Eysenck, H. J. (1985). *Review of the California Psychological Inventory.* In J. V. Mitchell (Ed.), *The ninth mental measurements yearbook* (pp. 252–253). Highland Press, NJ: Gryphon Press.

Eysenck, H. J. (1994). The outcome problem in psychotherapy: What have we learned? *Behavior Research and Therapy, 32*, 477–495.

Fals-Stewart, W. (1995). The effect of defensive responding by substance-abusing patients on the Millon Clinical Multiaxial Inventory. *Journal of Personality Assessment, 64*, 540–541.

Faust, D. (1991). Forensic neuropsychology: The art of practicing a science that does not yet exist. *Neuropsychology Review, 2*, 205–231.

Faust, D., & Ziskin, J. (1989). Computer-assisted psychological evaluation as legal evidence: Someday my prints will come. *Computers in Human Behavior, 5*, 23–36.

Feighner, J. P., Robins, E., Guze, S. B., Woodruff, R. A., Winokur, G., & Munoz, R. (1972). Diagnostic criteria for use in psychiatric research. *Archives of General Psychiatry, 26*, 57–63.

Feingold, A. (1983). The validity of the information and vocabulary subtests of the WAIS for predicting college achievement. *Educational and Psychological Measurement, 43*, 1127–1131.

Feldman, S. E., & Sullivan, D. S. (1971). Factors mediating the efforts of enhanced rapport on children's performance. *Journal of Consulting and Clinical Psychology, 36*, 302.

Fernandez-Ballesteros, R., & Staats, A. W. (1992). Paradigmatic behavioral assessment, treatments, and evaluation: Answering the crisis in behavioral assessment. *Advances in Behavior Research and Therapy, 14*, 1–27.

Fertuck, E. A., Bucci, W., Blatt, S., & Ford, R. Q. (2004). Verbal representation and therapeutic change in anaclitic and introjective inpatients. *Psychotherapy: Theory, Research, Practice, Training, 41*, 13–25.

Filskov, S. B. (1978). *The prediction of impairment from figure copying.* Paper presented at the Southeastern Psychological Association convention, Atlanta, GA.

Fincham, F. D., & Bradbury, T. N. (1992). Assessing attributions in marriage: The Relationship Attribution Measure. *Journal of Personality and Social Psychology, 62*, 457–468.

Finger, M. S., & Ones, D. S. (1999). Psychometric equivalence of the computer and booklet forms of the MMPI: A meta-analysis. *Psychological Assessment, 11*, 58–66.

Fink, J., McCrea, M., & Randolph, C. (1998). Neuropsychological differentiation of vascular dementia and Alzheimer's disease: A neurocognitive profile approach using a short battery. *Journal of the International Neuropsychological Society, 4*, 30.

Finlayson, M. A. J., & Bird, D. R. (1991). Psychopathology and neuropsychological deficit. In H. O. Doerr & A. S. Carlin (Eds.), *Forensic neuropsychology: Legal and scientific basis* (pp. 123–140). New York: Guilford Press.

Finn, S. E. (1982). Base rates, utilities, and the DSM-III: Shortcomings of fixed rule systems of psychodiagnostics. *Journal of Abnormal Psychology, 48*, 294–302.

Finn, S. E. (1996). A manual for using the MMPI-2 as a therapeutic intervention. Minneapolis: University of Minnesota Press.

Finn, S. E. (2007). *In our client's shoes: Theory and techniques of therapeutic assessment.* Mahwah, NJ: Lawrence Erlbaum.

Finn, S. E., Moes, E. J., & Kaplan, E. (2001). The consumer's point of view. In C. G. Armengol, E. Kaplan, & E. J. Moes (Eds.), *The consumer-oriented neuropsychological report* (pp. 13–46). Lutz, FL: Psychological Assessment Resources.

Finn, S. E., & Tonsager, M. E. (1992). Therapeutic effects of providing MMPI-2 test feedback to college students awaiting therapy. *Psychological Assessment, 4*, 278–287.

Finn, S. E., & Tonsager, M. E. (1997). Information gathering and therapeutic models of assessment: Complementary paradigms. *Psychological Assessment, 9*, 374–385.

Fischer, C.T. (1985). *Individualizing psychological assessment.* Monterey, CA: Brooks/Cole.

Fischer, J. & Corcoran, K. (2007). *Measures for clinical practice: A sourcebook.* New York: Free Press.

Fischer, J. E., & O'Donohue, W. T. (2006). *Clinician's handbook of evidence-based practice guidelines.* New York: Springer.

First, M. B., Frances, A., Widiger, T. A., Pincus, H. A., & Davis, W. W. (1992). DSM-IV and behavioral assessment. *Behavioral Assessment, 14*, 297–306.

First, M. B., & Gibbon, M. (2004). The Structured Clinical Interview for DSM-IV Axis I Disorders (SCID-I) and the Structured Clinical Interview for DSM-IV Axis II Disorders (SCID-II). In M. J. Hilsenroth & A. L. Segal (Eds.) *Comprehensive handbook of psychological assessment* (Vol. 2, pp. 134–143. Hoboken, NJ: John Wiley & Sons.

First, M. B., Gibbon, M., Williams, J. B., & Spitzer, R. L. (1996). *Users manual for the Auto SCID-II (for DSM-IV).* North Tonawanda, NY: Multi-Health Systems.

First, M. B., Spitzer, R. L., Gibbon, M., & Williams, J. B. W. (1995). The Structured Clinical Interview for DSM-III-R Personality disorders (SCID-II): Description. *Journal of Personality Disorders, 9*, 83–91.

First, M. B., Spitzer, R. L., Gibbon, M., & Williams, J. B. W. (1996). *Structured Clinical Interview for Axis I DSM-IV: Disorders Research version—Patient edition (SCID-I/P, Version 2.0).* New York: New York State Psychiatric Institute, Biometrics Research Department.

First, M. B., Spitzer, R. L., Gibbon, M., & Williams, J. B. W. (1997). *Structured Clinical Interview for DSM-IV Axis I Disorders (SCID-I)—Clinician version.* Washington, DC: American Psychiatric Press.

Fisher, D. C., Beutler, L. E., & Williams, O. B. (1999). Making assessment relevant to treatment planning: The STS Clinician Rating Form. *Journal of Clinical Psychology, 55*, 825–842.

Fisher, D. C., Ledbetter, M. F., Cohen, N. J., Marmor, D., & Tulsky, D. S. (2000). WAIS-III and WMS-III profiles of mildly to severely brain-injured patients. *Applied Neuropsychology, 7*, 126–132.

Flaherty, M. R., & Reutzel, G. (1965). Personality traits of high and low achievers in college. *Journal of Educational Research, 58*, 409–411.

Flanagan, D. P., & Harrison, P. L. (Eds.). (2005). *Contemporary intellectual assessment* (2nd ed.). New York: Guilford Press.

Flanagan, D. P., & Kaufman, A. S. (2004). *Essentials of WISC-IV assessment.* Hoboken, NJ: John Wiley & Sons.

Flanagan, D. P., & Ortiz, S. O. (2001). *Essentials of cross-battery assessment.* New York: John Wiley & Sons.

Flanagan, R., & Guiseppe, R. D. (1999). Critical review of the TEMAS: A step within the development of thematic apperception instruments. *Psychology in the Schools, 36*, 21–30.

Flaugher, R. L., & Schrader, W. B. (1978). *Eliminating differentially difficult items as an approach to test bias (RB-78-4).* Princeton, NJ: Educational Testing Service.

Flynn, P. M., McCann, J. T., & Fairbank, J. A. (1995). Issues in the assessment of personality disorder and substance abuse using the Millon Clinical Multiaxial Inventory (MCMI-II). *Journal of Clinical Psychology, 51*, 415–421.

Follette, W. C., & Hayes, S. C. (1992). Behavioral assessment in the DSM era. *Behavioral Assessment, 14*, 293–295.

Folstein, M. F., Folstein, S. E., & McHugh, P. R. (1975). Mini-mental state. *Journal of Psychiatric Research, 12*, 189–198.

Folstein, M. F., Romanoski, A. J., Nestadt, G., Chahal, R., Merchant, A., Shapiro, S., et al. (1985). Brief report on the clinical reappraisal of the Diagnostic Interview Schedule carried out at the Johns Hopkins site of the Epidemiological Catchment Area Program of the NIMH. *Psychological Medicine, 15*, 809–814.

Forbey, J. D., & Ben-Porath, Y. S. (2007). Computerized adaptive personality testing: A review and illustration with the MMPI-2 computerized adaptive version. *Psychological Assessment, 19*, 14–24.

Foster, S. L., & Cone, J. D. (1995). Validity issues in clinical assessment. *Psychological Assessment, 7*, 248–260.

Frank, G. (1990). Research on the clinical usefulness of the Rorschach: The diagnosis of schizophrenia. *Perceptual and Motor Skills, 71*, 573–578.

Frank, J. D. (1973). *Persuasion and healing: A comparative study of psychotherapy* (rev. ed.). Baltimore: Johns Hopkins University Press.

Franzen, M. D. (2004). Behavioral neuropsychology. In S. N. Haynes & E. M. Heiby (Eds.) *Comprehensive handbook of psychological assessment. Behavioral assessment* (Vol. 3, pp. 386–401). Hoboken, NJ: John Wiley & Sons.

Franzen, M. D., & Iverson, G. L. (1998). *Detecting negative response bias and diagnosing malingering: The dissimulation exam.* In P. J. Snyder & P. D. Nussbaum (Eds.), *Clinical neuropsychology: A pocket handbook for assessment* (pp. 88–101). Washington, DC: American Psychological Association.

Franzen, M. D., & Iverson, G. L. (2000). The Wechsler Memory Scales. In G. Groth-Marnat (Ed.), *Neuropsychological assessment in clinical practice: A guide to test interpretation and integration* (pp. 195–222). Hoboken, NJ: John Wiley & Sons.

Fray, P. J., Robbins, T. W., & Sahakian, B. J. (1996). Neuropsychological applications of CANTAB. *International Journal of Geriatric Psychiatry, 11*, 329–336.

Free, M. L., & Oei, T. P. S. (1989). Biological and psychological processes in the treatment and maintenance of depression. *Clinical Psychology Review, 9*, 653–688.

Freed, E. X. (1969). Acturial data on Bender Gestalt rotations in a psychiatric hospital. *Journal of Clinical Psychology, 25*, 252–255.

Freedman, D. (2001). False prediction of future dangerousness: Error rates and Psychopathy Checklist-Revised. *Journal of the American Academy of Psychiatry and the Law, 29*, 89–95.

Freilich, B. M., & Hyer, L. A. (2007). Relation of the Repeatable Battery for the Assessment of Neuropsychological Status to measures of daily functioning in dementia. *Psychological Reports, 101*, 119–129.

Friedman, A., Lewak, R., Nichols, D., & Webb, J. F. (2000). *Psychological assessment with the MMPI-2.* Mahwah, NJ: Lawrence Erlbaum.

Friman, P. C., Handwerk, M. L., Smith, G. L., Larzelere, R. E., Lucas, C. P., & Shaffer, D. M. (2000). External validity of conduct and oppositional defiant disorders determined by the NIMH Diagnostic Interview Schedule for Children. *Journal of Abnormal Child Psychology, 28*, 277–286.

Frueh, B. C., & Kinder, B. N. (1994). The susceptibility of the Rorschach Inkblot Test to malingering of combat-related PTSD. *Journal of Personality Assessment, 62*, 280–298.

Fuchs, D., & Fuchs, L. S. (1986). Test procedure bias: A meta-analysis of examiner familiarity effects. *Review of Educational Research, 56*, 243–262.

Fuld, P. A. (1983). Psychometric differentiation of the dementias: An overview. In_B. Reisberg (Ed.), *Alzheimer's disease: The standard reference* (pp. 201–210). New York: Free Press.

Fuld, P. A. (1984). Test profile of cholinergic dysfunction and of Alzheimer's-type dementia. *Journal of Clinical Neuropsychology, 6*, 380–392.

Fyer, A. J., Endicott, J., Manuzza, S., & Klein, D. F. (1985). *Schedule of Affective Disorders and Schizophrenia—Lifetime version (modified for the study of anxiety disorders).* New York: New York State Psychiatric Institute, Anxiety Disorder Clinic.

Fyer, A. J., Endicott, J., Manuzza, S., & Klein, D. F. (1995). *Schedule for Affective Disorders and Schizophrenia—Lifetime version (modified for the study of anxiety disorders, updated for DSM-IV; SADS-IV).* Unpublished measure, New York State Psychiatric Institute, Anxiety Genetics Unit.

Gabbard, G. (2007). *Gabbard's treatments of psychiatric disorders* (4th ed.). Arlington, VA: American Psychiatric Publishing.

Gainotti, G., & Marra, C. (1994). Some aspects of memory disorders clearly distinguish dementia of the Alzheimer's type from depressive pseudo-dementia. *Journal of Clinical and Experimental Neuropsychology, 16*, 65–78.

Gale, S. D., Johnson, S. C., Bigler, E. D., & Blatter, D. D. (1995). Nonspecific white matter degeneration following traumatic brain injury. *Journal of the International Neuropsychological Society, 1*, 17–28.

Gallagher-Thompson, D., & Steffen, A. M. (1994). Comparative effects of cognitive-behavioral and brief psychodynamic psychotherapies for depressed family caregivers. *Journal of Consulting and Clinical Psychology, 62*, 543–549.

Gallucci, N. T. (1994). Criteria associated with clinical scales and Harris-Lingoes subscales of the Minnesota Multiphasic Personality Inventory with adolescent inpatients. *Psychological Assessment, 6*, 179–187.

Gambrill, E. D., & Richey, C. A. (1975). An assertion inventory for use in assessment and research. *Behavior Therapy, 6*, 550–561.

Garb, H. N. (1984). The incremental validity of information used in personality assessment. *Clinical Psychology Review, 4*, 641–655.

Garb, H. N. (1989). Clinical judgment, clinical training, and professional experience. *Psychological Bulletin, 105*, 387–396.

Garb, H. N. (1992). The trained psychologist as expert witness. *Clinical Psychology Review, 12*, 451–467.

Garb, H. N. (1994a). Judgment research: Implications for clinical practice and testimony in court. *Applied and Preventive Psychology, 3*, 173–183.

Garb, H. N. (1994b). Toward a second generation of statistical prediction rules in psychodiagnostics and personality assessment. *Computers in Human Behavior, 10*, 377–394.

Garb, H. N. (1998a). Recommendations for training in the use of the Thematic Apperception Test (TAT). *Professional Psychology: Research and Practice, 29*, 621–622.

Garb, H. N. (1998b). *Studying the clinician.* Washington, DC: American Psychological Association.

Garb, H. N. (1999). Call for a moratorium on the use of the Rorschach Inkblot Test in clinical and forensic settings. *Assessment, 6*, 313–317.

Garb, H. N. (2000). Computers will become increasingly important for psychological assessment: Not that there's anything wrong with that. *Psychological Assessment, 12*, 31–39.

Garb, H. N. (2003). Incremental validity and the assessment of psychopathology in adults: Incremental validity and utility in clinical assessment, *Psychological Assessment, 15*, 508–520.

Garb, H. N. (2005a). Roots of the Rorschach controversy. *Clinical Psychology Review, 25*, 97–118.

Garb, H. N. (2005b). Clinical judgment and decision making. *Annual Review of Psychology, 1*, 67–89.

Garb, H. N. (2007). Computer-administered interviews and rating scales. *Psychological Assessment, 19*, 4–13.

Garb, H. N., Florio, C. M., & Grove, W. M. (1998). The validity of the Rorschach and the Minnesota Multiphasic Personality Inventory: Results from a meta-analysis. *Psychological Science, 9*, 402–404.

Garb, H. N., Lilienfeld, S. O., & Wood, J. M. (2004). Projective techniques and behavioral assessment. In S. N. Haynes, & E. M. Heiby (Eds.). *Comprehensive handbook of psychological assessment, Vol 3: Behavioral assessment* (pp. 453–469). Hoboken, NJ: John Wiley & Sons.

Garb, H. N., Wood, J. M., Lilienfeld, S. O., & Nezworski, M. T. (2002). Effective use of projective techniques in clinical practice: Let the data help with selection and interpretation. *Professional Psychology: Research and Practice, 33*, 454–463.

Garb, H. N., Wood, J. M., Nezworski, M. T., Grove, W. M., & Stejskal, W. J. (2001). Toward a resolution of the Rorschach controversy. *Psychological Assessment, 13*, 433–448.

Gardner, H. (1999). *Intelligence reframed: Multiple intelligences for the 21st century.* New York: Basic Books.

Gardner, H. (2006). *Multiple intelligences: The theory in practice* (2nd ed.) New York: Basic Books.

Garfield, S. L. (1994). Research on client variables in psychotherapy. In A. E. Bergin & S. L. Garfield (Eds.), *Handbook of psychotherapy and behavior change* (4th ed., pp. 190–228). New York: John Wiley & Sons.

Garner, D. M., & Garfinkel, P. E. (1979). The Eating Attitudes Test: An index of the symptoms of anorexia nervosa. *Psychological Medicine, 9*, 273–279.

Garratt, G., Ingram, R., Rand, K. L. & Sawalani, G. (2007). Cognitive processes in cognitive therapy: Evaluation of the mechanisms of change in the treatment of depression. *Clinical Psychology: Science and Practice, 14*, 224–239.

Garvey, M. J., Hollon, S. D., & DeRubeis, R. J. (1994). Do depressed patients with higher pretreatment stress levels respond better to cognitive therapy than imiprimine? *Journal of Affective Disorders, 32*, 45–50.

Gass, C. S. (1991). MMPI-2 interpretation and closed-head injury: A correction factor. *Psychological Assessment, 3*, 27–31.

Gass, C. S. (1992). MMPI-2 interpretation of patients with cerebrovascular disease: A correction factor. *Archives of Clinical Neuropsychology, 7*, 17–27.

Gass, C. S. (2000). Assessment of emotional functioning with the MMPI-2. In G. Groth-Marnat (Ed.), Neuropsychological assessment in clinical practice: A guide to test interpretation and integration (pp. 457–532). Hoboken, NJ: John Wiley & Sons.

Gass, C. S., & Apple, C. (1997). Cognitive complaints in closed-head injury: Relationship to memory test performance and emotional disturbance. *Journal of Clinical and Experimental Neuropsychology, 19*, 290–299.

Gass, C. S., & Brown, M. C. (1992). Neuropsychological test feedback to patients with brain dysfunction. *Psychological Assessment, 4*, 272–277.

Gaudino, E. A., Geisler, M. W., & Squires, N. K. (1995). Construct validity in the Trail Making Test: What makes Part B harder? *Journal of Clinical and Experimental Neuropsychology, 17*, 529–535.

Gaw, K. F., & Beutler, L. E. (1995). *Integrating treatment recommendations*. In L. E. Beutler & M. R. Berren (Eds.), *Integrative assessment of adult personality* (pp. 280–319). New York: Guilford Press.

Geffken, G. R., Keeley, M. L., Kellison, I., Storch, E. A. & Rodrigue, J. R. (2006). Parental adherence to child psychologists' recommendations from psychological testing. *Professional Psychology: Research & Practice, 37*, 499–505.

Geisinger, K. F. (2003). Testing and assessment in cross-cultural psychology. In J. R. Graham & Jack A. Naglieri (Eds.), *Handbook of psychology* (Vol. 10, pp. 95–117). Hoboken, NJ: John Wiley & Sons.

Geisinger, K.F., Spies, R.A., Carlson, J.F., & Plake, B.S., (eds.)(2007). *The Seventeenth Mental Measurements Yearbook*. Lincoln, NE: Buros Institute.

Geller, J., Cockell, S. J., & Drab, D. L. (2001). Assessing readiness for change in the eating disorder: The psychometric properties of the Readiness and Motivation Interview. *Psychological Assessment, 13*, 189–198.

Gerstle, R. M., Geary, D. C., Himelstein, P., & Reller-Geary, L. (1988). Rorschach predictors of therapeutic outcome for inpatient treatment of children: A proactive study. *Journal of Clinical Psychology, 44*, 277–280.

Gibertini, M., Brandenberg, N. A., & Retzlaff, P. D. (1986). The operating characteristics of the Millon Clinical Multiaxial Inventory. *Journal of Personality Assessment, 50*, 554–567.

Gieser, L., & Stein, M. I. (1999). *Evocative images: The Thematic Apperception Test and the art of projection*. Washington, DC: American Psychological Association.

Gilley, D. W., Wilson, R. S., Fleischmann, D. A., Harrison, D. W., Goetz, C. G., & Tanner, C. M. (1995). Impact of Alzheimer's-type dementia and information source on the assessment of depression. *Psychological Assessment, 7*, 42–48.

Gilmore, D. C., Beehr, T. A., & Love, K. G. (1986). Effects of applicant sex, applicant physical attractiveness, and type of job on interview decisions. *Journal of Occupational Psychology, 59*, 103–109.

Glass, C. R., & Merluzzi, T. V. (2000). Cognitive and behavioral assessment. In C. E. Watkins & V. L. Campbell (Eds.), *Testing and assessment in counseling practice* (pp. 175–224). Mahwah, NJ: Lawrence Erlbaum.

Glass, C. R., Merluzzi, T. V., Biever, J. L., & Larsen, K. H. (1982). Cognitive assessment of social anxiety: Development and validation of a self-statement questionnaire. *Cognitive Therapy and Research, 6*, 37–55.

Glutting, J. J., McDermott, P. A., Konold, T. R., Snelbaker, A. J., & Watkins, M. W. (1998). More ups and downs of subtest analysis: Criterion validity of the DAS with an unselected cohort. *School Psychology Review, 27*, 599–612.

Glutting, J. J., Watkins, M. W., Konold, T. R., & McDermott, P. A. (2006). Distinctions without a difference: The utility of observed versus latent factors from the WISC-IV in estimating reading and math achievment. *Journal of special Education, 40*, 103–114.

Gocka, E. (1965). *American Lake norms for 200 MMPI scales*. Unpublished raw data.

Godber, T., Anderson, V., & Bell, R. (2000). The measurement and diagnostic utility of intrasubtest scatter in pediatric neuropsychology. *Journal of Clinical Psychology, 56*, 101–112.

Gold, J. M., Goldberg, R., MnNary, S., Dixon, L., & Lehman, A. (2002). Cognitive correlates of job tenure among patients with severe mental illness. *American Journal of Psychiatry, 159*, 1395–1402.

Goldberg, E., & Bilder, R. M. (1987). The frontal lobes and heirarchical organization of cognitive control. In E. Perecman (Ed.), *The frontal lobes revisited* (pp. 159–187). New York: IRBN Press.

Golden, C. J. (1976). The identification of brain damage by an abbreviated form of the Halstead-Reitan Neuropsychological Battery. *Journal of Clinical Psychology, 32*, 821–826.

Golden, C. J., Purisch, A. D., & Hammeke, T. A. (1985). *Luria-Nebraska Neuropsychological Battery: Forms I and II (Manual).* Los Angeles: Western Psychological Services.

Goldfried, M. R. (1982a). Behavioral assessment: An overview. In A. S. Bellack, M. Hersen, & A. E. Kazdin (Eds.), *International handbook of behavior modification and therapy.* New York: Pergamon Press.

Goldfried, M. R. (1982b). On the history of therapeutic integration. *Behavior Therapy, 13*, 572–593.

Goldfried, M. R. (1983). A behavior therapist looks at reapproachment. *Journal of Humanistic Psychology, 23*, 97–107.

Goldfried, M. R., Stricker, G., & Weiner, I. B. (1971). *Rorschach handbook of clinical and research application.* Englewood Cliffs, NJ: Prentice-Hall.

Goldschmid, M. L. (1967). Prediction of college majors by personality tests. *Journal of Counseling Psychology, 14*, 302–308.

Golstein, A,M. (2007). Forensic psychology: Emerging topics and expanding roles. Hoboken, NJ: John Wiley & Sons, Inc.

Goldstein, J. W. (1974). Motivations for psychoactive drug use among students. In B. Kleinmuntz (Ed.), *Readings in the essentials of abnormal psychology* (pp. 371–375). New York: Harper & Row.

Goncalves, A. A., Woodward, M. J., & Millon, T. (1994). The Millon Clinical Multiaxial Inventory-II. In M. E. Maruish (Ed.), *The use of psychological testing for treatment planning and outcome assessment* (pp. 161–184). Hillsdale, NJ: Lawrence Erlbaum.

Goodglass, H., & Kaplan, E. (1983). *Boston Diagnostic Aphasia Examination (BDAE).* Philadelphia: Lea & Febiger. (Distributed by Psychological Assessment Resources)

Gordon, N. G., & Swart, E. C. (1973). A comparison of the Harris-Lingoes subscales between the original standardization population and an inpatient Veterans Administration hospital population. *Newsletter for Research in Mental Health and Behavioral Sciences, 15*, 28–31.

Gorwood, P., Corruble, E., Falissard, B., & Goodwin, G. M. (2008). Toxic effects of depression on brain function: Impairment of brain recall and the cumulative length of depressive disorder in a sample of depressed outpatients. *American Journal of Psychiatry, 165*, 731–739.

Gottschalk, L. A. (2000). The application of computerized content analysis of natural language in psychotherapy research now and in the future. *American Journal of Psychotherapy, 54*, 305–311.

Gough, H. G. (1948). A new dimension of status. I: Development of a personality scale. *American Sociological Review, 13*, 401–409.

Gough, H. G. (1957). *California Psychological Inventory manual.* Palo Alto, CA: Consulting Psychologists Press.

Gough, H. G. (1964). Academic achievement in high school as predicted from the_California Psychological Inventory. *Journal of Educational Psychology, 65*, 174–180.

Gough, H. G. (1966). Graduation from high school as predicted from the California Psychological Inventory. *Psychology in the Schools, 3*, 208–216.

Gough, H. G. (1968). An interpreter's syllabus for the California Psychological Inventory. In P. McReynolds (Ed.), *Advances in psychological assessment* (Vol. 1, pp. 55–79). Palo Alto, CA: Science and Behavior Books.

Gough, H. G. (1969). A leadership index on the California Psychological Inventory. *Journal of Counseling Psychology, 16*, 285–289.

Gough, H. G. (1975). *Manual for the California Psychological Inventory* (rev. ed.). Palo Alto, CA: Consulting Psychologists Press.

Gough, H. G. (1987). *California Psychological Inventory: Administrator's guide* (2nd ed.). Palo Alto, CA: Consulting Psychologists Press.

Gough, H. G. (1992). Assessment of creative potential in psychology and the development of a creative temperament scale for the CPI. In J. C. Rusen & P. McReynolds (Eds.), *Advances in psychological assessment* (Vol. *8*, pp. 225–257). New York: Plenum Press.

Gough, H. G. (1996/2002). *California Psychological Inventory manual.* (3rd ed.). Palo Alto, CA: Consulting Psychologists Press.

Gough, H. G. (2000). *The California Psychological Inventory.* In C. E. Watkins & V. L. Campbell (Eds.), *Testing and assessment in counseling practice* (2nd ed., pp. 45–71). Mahwah, NJ: Lawrence Erlbaum.

Gough, H. G., & Bradley, P. (1992). Delinquent and criminal behavior as assessed by the revised California psychological Inventory. *Journal of Clinical Psychology, 48*, 298–308.

Gough, H., & Bradley, P. (2005). *CPI 260 manual.* Mountain View, CA: Consulting Psychologists Press.

Gough, H. G., Durflinger, G. W., & Hill, R. E., Jr. (1968). Predicting performance in student teaching from the California Psychological Inventory. *Journal of Educational Psychology, 52*, 119–127.

Gough, H. G., & Hall, W. B. (1964). Prediction of performance in medical school from the California Psychological Inventory. *Journal of Applied Psychology, 48*, 218–226.

Gough, H. G., & Kirk, B. A. (1970). Achievement in dental school as related to personality and aptitude variables. *Measurement and Evaluation in Guidance, 2*, 225–233.

Gough, H. G., & Lanning, K. (1986). Predicting grades in college from the California Psychological Inventory. *Educational and Psychological Measurement, 46*, 205–213.

Gough, H. G., Wenk, E. A., & Rozynko, V. V. (1965). Parole outcome as predicted from the CPI, the MMPI, and a Base Expectancy Table. *Journal of Abnormal Psychology, 70*, 432–441.

Gould, R. A., Otto, M. W., & Pollack, M. H. (1995). A meta-analysis of treatment outcome for panic disorder. *Clinical Psychology Review, 15*, 819–844.

Grace, J., Stout, J., & Malloy, P. F. (1999). Assessing frontal lobe behavioral syndromes with the Frontal Lobe Personality Scale. *Assessment, 6*, 269–284.

Graham, J. R. (2006). *MMPI-2: Assessing personality and psychopathology* (4th ed.). New York: Oxford University Press.

Graham, J. R., Ben-Porath, Y. S., & McNulty, J. L. (1999). *MMPI-2 correlates for outpatient mental health settings.* Minneapolis: University of Minnesota Press.

Graham, J. R., & Lilly, R. S. (1984). *Psychological testing.* Englewood Cliffs, NJ: Prentice-Hall.

Graham, J. R., Smith, R. L., & Schwartz, G. F. (1986). Stability of MMPI configurations for psychiatric inpatients. *Journal of Consulting and Clinical Psychology, 49*, 477–484.

Graham, P., & Rutter, M. (1968). The reliability and validity of the psychiatric assessment of the child. II: Interview with the parent. *British Journal of Psychiatry, 114*, 581–592.

Graves, R. E., Carswell, L. M., & Snow, W. G. (1999). An evaluation of the sensitivity of premorbid IQ estimators for detecting cognitive decline. *Psychological Assessment, 11*, 29–38.

Green, R. E., Melo, B., Christensen, B., Ngo, L. A., Monette, G., & Bradbury, C. (2008). Measuring premorbid IQ in traumatic brain injury: An examination of the validity of the Wechsler Test of Adult Reading. *Journal of Clinical and Experimental Neuropsychology, 30*, 163–172.

Green, S. B., & Kelley, C. K. (1988). Racial bias in prediction with the MMPI for a juvenile delinquent population. *Journal of Personality Assessment, 52*, 263–275.

Greenbaum, P. F., Prange, M. E., Friedman, R. M., & Silver, S. E. (1991). Substance abuse prevalence and comorbidity with other psychiatric disorders among adolescents with severe emotional disorders. *Journal of the Academy of Child and Adolescent Psychology, 30*, 575–583.

Greenberg, L. S. (2007). Emotion coming of age. *Clinical Psychology: Science and Practice, 14*, 414–421.

Greene, R. L. (1987). Ethnicity and MMPI performance: A review. *Journal of Consulting and Clinical Psychology, 55*, 497–512.

Greene, R. L. (1991). *The MMPI-2/MMPI: An interpretive manual.* Boston: Allyn & Bacon.

Greene, R. L. (2000). *The MMPI-2: An interpretive manual* (2nd ed.). Boston: Allyn & Bacon.

Greene, R. L., & Clopton, J. R. (1994). Minnesota Multiphasic Personality Inventory-2. In M. E. Maruish (Ed.), *The use of psychological testing for treatment, planning and outcome assessment* (pp. 137–159). Hillsdale, NJ: Lawrence Erlbaum.

Greene, R. L., & Clopton, J. R. (1999). Minnesota Multiphasic Personality Inventory-2 (MMPI-2). In M. E. Maruish (Ed.), *The use of psychological testing for treatment, planning and outcomes assessment* (2nd ed., pp. 1023–1049). Mahwah, NJ: Lawrence Erlbaum.

Greene, R. L., Weed, N. C., Butcher, J. N., & Arredondo, R. (1992). A cross validation of MMPI-2 substance abuse scales. *Journal of Personality Assessment, 58,* 405–410.

Greenspan, S., & Driscoll, J. (1997). The role of intelligence in a broad model of personal competence. In D. P. Flanagan, J. L. Genshaft, & P. L. Harrison (Eds.), *Contemporary intellectual assessment: Theories, tests, and issues* (pp. 131–150). New York: Guilford Press.

Greenway, P., & Milne, L. (1999). Relationship between psychopathology, learning disabilities, or both and WISC-III subtest scatter in adolescents. *Psychology in the Schools, 36,* 103–108.

Gregory, M. L. (1977). Emotional indicators on the Bender Gestalt and the Devereux Child Rating Scale. *Psychology in the Schools, 14,* 433–437.

Gregory, R. J. (1999). *Foundations of intellectual assessment: The WAIS-III and other tests in clinical practice.* Boston: Allyn & Bacon.

Greif, E. B., & Hogan, R. (1973). The theory and measurement of empathy. Journal of Counseling Psychology, *20,* 280–284.

Greiffenstein, M. F., Fox, D., & Lees-Haley, P. R. (2007). The MMPI-2 Fake Bad Scale in the detection of noncredible brain injury claims. In K. Boone (Ed.), *Assessment of feigned cognitive impairment: A neuropsychological perspective* (pp. 210–235). New York: Guilford Press.

Gresham, F. M. (1984). Behavioral interviews in school psychology: Issues in psychometric adequacy and research. *School Psychology Review, 13,* 17–25.

Grice, J. W., Krohn, E. J., & Logerquist, S. (1999). Cross-validation of the WISC-III factor structure in two samples of children with learning disabilities. *Journal of Psychoeducational Assessment, 17,* 236–248.

Griffin, M. L., & Flaherty, M. R. (1964). Correlation of CPI traits with academic achievement. *Educational and Psychological Measurement, 24,* 369–372.

Grigorenko, E. L., & Sternberg, R. J. (1998). Dynamic testing. *Psychological Bulletin, 124,* 75–111.

Grillo, J., Brown, R. S., Hilsabeck, R., Price, J. R., & Lees-Haley, P. (1994). Raising doubts about claims of malingering: Implications of relationships between MCMI-II and MMPI-2 performances. *Journal of Clinical Psychology, 50,* 651–655.

Gronnerod, C. (2004). Rorschach assessment of changes following psychotherapy: A meta-analytic review. *Journal of Personality Assessment, 83,* 256–276.

Gronnerod, C. (2006). Reanalysis of the Gronnerod (2003) Rorschach temporal stability meta-analysis data set. *Journal of Personality Assessment, 86,* 222–225.

Grossman, L. S. Wasyliw, O. E., Benn, A. F., & Gyoerkoe, K. L. (2002). Can sex offenders who minimize on the MMPI conceal psychopathology on the Rorschach? *Journal of Personality Assessment, 78,* 484–501.

Grossman, S., & del Rio, C. (2005). The MCMI-III facet scales. In Craig, R. J. (Ed.) *New directions in interpreting the Millon Clinical Multiaxial Inventory-III (MCMI-III).* Hoboken, NJ: John Wiley & Sons.

Groth-Marnat, G. (1985). Evaluating and using psychological testing software. *Human Resource Management Australia, 23,* 16–21.

Groth-Marnat, G. (1988). A survey of the current and future direction of professional psychology in acute general hospitals in Australia. *Australian Psychologist, 23,* 39–43.

Groth-Marnat, G. (1991). Hypnotizability, suggestibility, and psychopathology: An overview of research. In J. F. Schumaker (Ed.), *Human suggestibility: Advances in theory, research, and application* (pp. 219–234). New York: Routledge.

Groth-Marnat, G. (1992). Past cultural traditions of therapeutic metaphor. *Psychology: An International Journal of Human Behavior, 29*, 1–8.

Groth-Marnat, G. (1993). Neuropsychological effects of styrene exposure: A review of current literature. *Perceptual and Motor Skills, 77*, 1139–1149.

Groth-Marnat, G. (1995). *The Rey Auditory Verbal Learning Test: A manual for administration, scoring, and interpretation* (Tech. and Res. Rep.). Perth, Australia: Curtin University of Technology, Research Center for Applied Psychology.

Groth-Marnat, G. (1999). Financial efficacy of clinical assessment: Rational guidelines and issues for future research. *Journal of Clinical Psychology, 55*, 813–824.

Groth-Marnat, G. (Ed.). (2000a). *Neuropsychological assessment in clinical practice: A guide to test interpretation and integration.* Hoboken, NJ: John Wiley & Sons.

Groth-Marnat, G. (2000b). Visions of clinical assessment: Then, now, and a brief history of the future. *Journal of Clinical Psychology, 56*, 349–365.

Groth-Marnat, G., (2001). Learning disabilities assessment with the Wechsler intelligence scales (WAIS-III/WISC-III). In A. Kaufman & N. Kaufman (eds.), *Learning disabilities assessment: Psychological assessment and evaluation* (pp. 29–52). Cambridge, UK: Cambridge University Press.

Groth-Marnat, G. (2003). The psychological report. In R. Fernandez-Ballesteros (Ed.), *Encyclopedia of psychological assessment* (pp. 812–817). Thousand Oaks, CA: Sage.

Groth-Marnat, G. (2006). The psychological report: A review of current controversies. *Journal of Clinical Psychology, 62*, 73–81.

Groth-Marnat, G. (2008, March). The five assessment issues you meet when you go to heaven. Paper presented at the Society for Personality Assessment 2008 annual meeting, New Orleans, LA.

Groth-Marnat, G. (in press). *The five assessment issues you meet when you go to heaven. Journal of Personality Assessment.*

Groth-Marnat, G., & Edkins, G. (1996). Professional psychologists in general health care settings: A review of the financial efficacy of direct treatment interventions. *Professional Psychology: Research and Practice, 27*, 161–174.

Groth-Marnat, G., Edkins, G., & Schumaker, J. F. (1995). Psychologists in disease prevention and health promotion: A review of the cost-effectiveness literature. *Psychology, 32*, 127–135.

Groth-Marnat, G., Gallagher, R. E., Hale, J. B., & Kaplan, E. (2000). The Wechsler intelligence scales. In G. Groth-Marnat (Ed.), *Neuropsychological assessment in clinical practice: A practical guide to test interpretation and integration* (pp. 129–194). Hoboken, NJ: John Wiley & Sons.

Groth-Marnat, G., Gottheil, E., Liu, W., Clinton, D., & Beutler, L. E. (2008). Personality and treatment planning for psychotherapy: The Systematic Treatment Selection Model. In G. Boyle, G. Matthews, & D. Saklofske (Eds.) (pp. 620–634). *Handbook of personality and testing.* Thousand Oaks, CA: Sage Publishers.

Groth-Marnat, G., & Roberts, L. (1998). Indicators of psychological health on Human Figure Drawings and the House Tree Person: A search for concurrent validity. *Journal of Clinical Psychology, 46*, 219–222.

Groth-Marnat, G., Roberts, R., & Beutler, L. E. (2001). Client characteristics and psychotherapy: Perspectives, support, interactions, and implications. *Australian Psychologist, 36*, 115–121.

Groth-Marnat, G., & Schumaker, J. (1989). Computer-based psychological testing: Issues and guidelines. *American Journal of Orthopsychiatry, 59*, 257–263.

Groth-Marnat, G., & Teal, M. (2000). Block Design as a measure of everyday spatial ability: A study of ecological validity. *Perceptual and Motor Skills, 90*, 522–526.

Grothe, K. B., Dutton, G. R., Jones, G. N., Bodenlos, J., Ancona, M., & Brantley, P. J. (2005). Validation of the Beck Depression Inventory-II in a low income African American sample of medical outpatients. *Psychological Assessment, 17*, 110–114.

Grove, W. M., Zald, D. H., Lebow, B. S., Snitz, B. E., & Nelson, C. (2000). Clinical versus mechanical prediction: A metanalysis. *Psychological Assessment, 12*, 19–30.

Guevremont, G. C., & Spiegler, M. D. (1990, November). *What do behavior therapists really do? A survey of the clinical practice of AABT members.* Paper presented at the 24th annual convention of the Association for Advancement of Behavior Therapy, San Francisco.

Gutkin, T. B., & Reynolds, C. R. (1981). Factorial similarity of the WISC-R for white and black children from the standardization sample. *Journal of Educational Psychology, 73*, 227–231.

Gynther, M. D. (1978). The California Psychological Inventory: *A review.* In O. K. Buros (Ed.), *The eighth mental measurements yearbook* (Vol. *1*, pp. 733–737). Highland Park, NJ: Gryphon Press.

Gynther, M. D. (1979). Aging and personality. In J. N. Butcher (Ed.), *New developments in the use of the MMPI* (pp. 240–256). Minneapolis: University of Minnesota Press.

Gynther, M. D., & Green, S. B. (1980). Accuracy may make a difference, but does a difference make for accuracy? A response to Pritchard and Rosenblatt. *Journal of Consulting and Clinical Psychology, 48*, 268–272.

Gynther, M. D., & Shimkuras, A. M. (1966). Age and MMPI performance. *Journal of Consulting Psychology, 30*, 118–121.

Haaga, D. A., Dyck, M. J., & Ernst, D. (1991). Empirical status of cognitive theory of depression. *Psychological Bulletin, 110*, 215–236.

Haas, A. P., Hendin, H., & Singer, P. (1987). Psychodynamic and structured interviewing: Issues of validity. *Comprehensive Psychiatry, 28*, 40–53.

Haddad, F. A. (1986). The performance of learning disabled children on the Kaufman Assessment Battery for Children and the Bender-Gestalt Test. *Psychology in the Schools, 23*, 342–345.

Hain, J. D. (1964). The Bender Gestalt Test: A scoring method for identifying brain damage. *Journal of Consulting Psychology, 28*, 34–40.

Hale, W. D., Cochran, C. D., & Hedgepeth, B. E. (1984). Norms for the elderly on the Brief Symptom Inventory. *Journal of Counsulting and Clinical Psychology, 52*, 321–322.

Hall, C. (1983, December 6). Psychiatrist's computer use stirs debate. *The Wall Street Journal, 35*, 39.

Hall, G. C. N., Bansal, A., & Lopez, I. R. (1999). Ethnicity and psychopathology: A meta-analytic review of 31 years of comparative MMPI/MMPI-2 research. *Psychological Assessment, 11*, 186–197.

Hall, H. V., & Sbordone, R. J. (Eds.). (1993). *Disorders of executive function.* Winter Park, FL: PMD Publishers.

Hamel, M., Shaffer, T. W., & Erdberg, P. (2000). A study of nonpatient preadolescent Rorschach protocols. *Journal of Personality Assessment, 75*, 280–294.

Hammen, C. L. (1978). Depression, distortion, and life stress in college students. *Cognitive Therapy and Research, 2*, 189–192.

Hammen, C. L., & Krantz, S. (1976). Effect of success and failure on depressive cognitions. *Journal of Abnormal Psychology, 85*, 577–586.

Hammill, D. D., Pearson, N. A., & Wiederholt, J. L. (1997). *Comprehensive Test of Nonverbal Intelligence.* Austin, TX: Pro-Ed.

Handel, R. W., & Archer, R. P. (2008). An investigation of the psychometric properties of the MMPI-2 Restructured Clinical (RC) scales with mental health patients. *Journal of Personality Assessment, 90*, 239–249.

Handel, R. W., & Ben-Porath, Y. S. (2000). Multicultural assessment with the MMPI-2: Issues for research and practice. In R. H. Dana (Ed.), *Handbook of cross-cultural and multicultural personality assessment* (pp. 229–245). Mahwah, NJ: Lawrence Erlbaum.

Handelsman, M. M., & Galvin, M. D. (1988). Facilitating informed consent for outpatient psychotherapy: A suggested written format. *Professional Psychology: Research and Practice, 19*, 223–225.

Hansell, A. G., Lerner, H. D., Milden, R. S., & Ludolph, P. (1988). Single-sign Rorschach suicide indicators: A validity study using a depressed inpatient population. *Journal of Personality Assessment, 52*, 658–669.

Hanson, R. K., Hunsley, J., & Parker, K. C. H. (1988). The relationship between WAIS subtest reliability, "g" loadings, and meta-analytically derived validity estimates. *Journal of Clinical Psychology, 44*, 557–562.

Hanson, R. K., & Thornton, D. (1999). *Static-99: Improving acturial risk assessment for sex offenders* (User Rep No.1999-02). Ottawa, Ontario: Department of the Solicitor General of Canada.

Hargrave, G. E., Hiatt, D., & Gaffney, T. W. (1986). A comparison of MMPI and CPI test profiles for traffic officers and deputy sheriffs. *Journal of Police Science and Administration, 14*, 250–258.

Hargrave, G. E., Hiatt, D., Ogard, E. M., & Karr, C. (1994). Comparison of the MMPI and MMPI-2 for a sample of peace officers. *Psychological Assessment, 6*, 27–32.

Harkness, A. R., McNulty, J. L., Ben-Porath, Y. S. & Graham, J. R. (2002). *MMPI-2 Personality Psychopathology Five (PSY-5) Scales: Gaining an overview for case conceptualization and treatment planning.* Minneapolis: University of Minnesota Press.

Harrell, T. H., Honaker, L. M., & Parnell, T. (1992). Equivalence of the MMPI-2 with the MMPI in psychiatric patients. *Psychological Assessment, 4*, 460–465.

Harris, R. E., & Lingoes, J. C. (1968). *Subscales for the MMPI: An aid to profile interpretation.* Los Angeles: University of California, Department of Psychiatry. (Original work published 1955.)

Harrison, R. (1940). Studies in the use and validity of the Thematic Apperception Test with mentally disordered patients. II: A quantitative validity study. III: Validation by blind analysis. *Character and Personality, 9*, 122–133, 134–138.

Harrower, M. (1986). The Stress Tolerance Test. *Journal of Personality Assessment, 50*, 417–427.

Hartshorne, H., & May, M. A. (1928). *Studies in deceit.* New York: Macmillan.

Harvey, V. S. (1997). Improving readability of psychological reports. Professional Psychology: *Research and Practice, 28*, 271–274.

Harvey, V. S. (2006). Variables affecting the clarity of reports. *Journal of Clinical Psychology, 62*, 5–18.

Harwood, T. M., & Williams, O. (2003). *Identifying treatment relevant assessment: The STS.* In L. E. Beutler & G. Groth-Marnat (Eds.), *Integrative assessment of adult personality (*pp. 65–81). New York: Guilford Press.

Hase, H. D., & Goldberg, L. R. (1967). Comparative validity of different strategies of constructing personality inventory scales. *Psychological Bulletin, 67*, 231–248.

Hathaway, S. R., & McKinley, J. C. (1940). A Multiphasic Personality Schedule (Minnesota). I: Construction of the schedule. *Journal of Psychology, 10*, 249–254.

Hathaway, S. R., & Monachesi, E. D. (1963). *Adolescent personality and behavior: MMPI patterns of normal, delinquent, dropout, and other outcomes.* Minneapolis: University of Minnesota Press.

Hauff, E., & Vaglum, P. (1994). Chronic posttraumatic stress disorder in Vietnamese refugees. A prospective community study of prevalence, course, psychopathology, and stressors. *Journal of Nervous and Mental Disease, 182*, 85–90.

Haverkamp, B. E. (1993). Confirmatory bias in hypothesis testing for client-identified and counselor self-generated hypotheses. *Journal of Counseling Psychology, 40*, 303–315.

Hawkins, K. A. (1998). Indicators of brain dysfunction derived from graphic representations of the WAIS-III/WMS-III Technical manual clinical sample data: A preliminary approach to clinical utility. *Clinical Neuropsychologist, 12*, 535–551.

Hawkins, K. A., Sullivan, T. E., & Choi, E. J. (1997). Memory defects in schizophrenia: Inadequate assimilation or true amnesia? Findings from the Wechsler Memory Scale-Revised. *Journal of Psychiatry and Neuroscience, 22*, 169–179.

Hawkins, S. A., & Hastie, R. (1990). Hindsight: Biased judgments of past events after the outcomes are known. *Psychological Bulletin, 107*, 311–327.

Hayes, J. A. (1997). What does the Brief Symptom Inventory measure in college and university counseling center clients? *Journal of Counseling Psychology, 44*, 360–367.

Haynes, J. P., & Howard, R. C. (1986). Stability of WISC-R scores in a juvenile forensic sample. *Journal of Clinical Psychology, 42*, 534–537.

Haynes, J. P., & Peltier, J. (1985). Patterns of practice with the TAT in juvenile forensic settings. *Journal of Personality Assessment, 49*, 20–29.

Haynes, S. N. (1991). Clinical applications of psychophysiological assessment: An introduction and overview. *Psychological Assessment, 3*, 307–308.

Haynes, S. N. (1995). Introduction to the special section in chaos theory and psychological assessment. *Psychological Assessment, 7*, 3–4.

Haynes, S. N. (2006). Psychometric considerations. In M. Hersen (Ed.). *Clinician's handbook of adult behavioral assessment* (pp. 17–42). New York: Elsevier.

Haynes, S. N., & Heiby, E. M. (Eds.). (2004). *Comprehensive handbook of psychological assessment. Behavioral assessment* (Vol 3). Hoboken, NJ: John Wiley & Sons.

Haynes, S. N., & O'Brien, W. H. (1988). The Gordian knot of DSM-III-R use: Integrating principles of behavior classification and complex causal models. *Behavioral Assessment, 10*, 95–106.

Haynes, S. N., & O'Brien, W. H. (2000). *Principles and practice of behavioral assessment.* New York: Kluwer Academic.

Haynes, S. N., & Yoshioka, D. T. (2007). Clinical assessment applications of ambulatory sensors. *Psychological Assessment, 19*, 44–57.

Heaton, R. K., Beade, L. E., & Johnson, K. L. (1978). Neuropsychological test results associated with psychiatric disorders in adults. *Psychological Bulletin, 85*, 141–162.

Heaton, R. K., Grant, I., Razani, J., & Mathews, C. G. (2004). *Revised comprehensive norms for an expanded Halstead-Reitan Battery.* Lutz, FL: Psychological Assessment Resources.

Heaton, R. K., Miller, S. W., Taylor, M. J., & Grant, I. (2004). Revised Comprehensive Norms for an Expanded Halstead-Reitan Battery: Demographically adjusted for neuropsychological norms for African American and Caucasian adults. Lutz, FL: Psychological Assessment Resources.

Heaton, R. K., Taylor, M. J., & Manly, J. (2003). Demographic effects and use of demographically corrected norms with the WAIS-III and WMS-III. In D. S. Tulsky, D. H. Saklofske, G. J. Chelune, R. K. Heaton, & R. J. Ivnik, *Clinical interpretation of the WAIS-III and WMS-III. (pp.* 183–204). San Diego, CA: Academic Press.

Hersen, M. (Ed.). (2005). *Clinicians handbook of child behavioral assessment.* New York: Elsevier.

Hersen, M. (Ed.). (2006). *Clinicians handbook of adult behavioral assessment.* New York: Elsevier.

Hersen, M., & Bellack, A. (Eds.). (2002). *Dictionary of behavioral assessment.* New York: Pergamon Press.

Hebb, D. O. (1972). *Textbook of psychology* (3rd ed.). Philadelphia: Saunders.

Hebben, N., & Milberg, W. (2002). *Essentials of neuropsychological assessment.* Hoboken, NJ: John Wiley & Sons.

Hedlund, J. L., Sletten, I. W., Evenson, R. C., Altman, H., & Cho, D. W. (1977). Automated psychiatric information systems: A critical review of Missouri's Standard System of Psychiatry (SSOP). *Journal of Operational Psychiatry, 8*, 5–26.

Heflinger, C. A., Cook, V. J., & Thackrey, M. (1987). Identification of mental retardation by the System of Multicultural Pluralistic Assessment: Nondiscriminatory or nonexistent? *Journal of School Psychology, 25*, 177–183.

Heilbrun, A. B., Daniel, J. L., Goodstein, L. D., Stephenson, R. R., & Crites, J. O. (1962). The validity of two-scale pattern interpretation on the California Psychological Inventory. *Journal of Applied Psychology, 46*, 409–416.

Heilbrun, K., Marczyk, G. G., & Dematteo, D. (2002). *Forensic mental health assessment: A casebook.* New York: Oxford University Press.

Heimberg, R. G. (1994). Cognitive assessment strategies and the measurement of outcome of treatment for social phobia. *Behavior Research and Therapy, 32*, 269–280.

Heimberg, R. G., Harrison, D. F., Goldberg, L. S., Desmarais, S., & Blue, S. (1979). The relationship of self-report and behavioral assertion in an offender population. *Journal of Behavior Therapy and Experimental Psychiatry, 10*, 283–286.

Hellkamp, D. T., & Hogan, M. E. (1985). Differentiation of organics from functional psychiatric patients across various I.Q. ranges using the Bender-Gestalt and Hutt scoring system. *Journal of Clinical Psychology, 41*, 259–264.

Helmes, E. (2000). Learning and memory. In G. Groth-Marnat (Ed.), *Neuropsychological assessment in clinical practice: A guide to test interpretation and inte*gration (pp. 293–334). Hoboken, NJ: John Wiley & Sons.

Helmes, E., & Reddon, J. R. (1993). A perspective on development in assessing psychopathology: A critical review of MMPI and MMPI-2. *Psychological Bulletin, 113*, 453–471.

Helzer, J. E., & Robins, L. N. (1988). The Diagnostic Interview Schedule: Its development, evolution and use. *Social Psychiatry and Psychiatric Epidemiology, 23*, 6–16.

Helzer, J. E., Robins, L. N., Croughan, J. L., & Welner, A. (1981). Renard Diagnostic Interview: Its reliability and procedural validity with physicians and lay interviewers. *Archives of General Psychiatry, 38*, 393–398.

Helzer, J. E., Robins, L. N., McEvoy, L. F., Spitznagel, E. L., Stolzman, R. K., Farmer, A., et al. (1985). A comparison of Clinical and Diagnostic Interview Schedule diagnoses: Physician re-examination of lay-interviewed cases in the general population. *Archives of General Psychiatry, 42*, 657–666.

Helzer, J. E., Spitznagel, E. L., & McEvoy, L. (1987). The predictive validity of lay Diagnostic Interview Schedule diagnoses in the general population: A comparison with physician examiners. *Archives of General Psychiatry, 44*, 1069–1077.

Henry, B., Moffitt, T. E., Caspi, A., Langley, J., & Silva, P. A. (1994). On the "remembrance of things past": A longitudinal evaluation of the retrospective method. *Psychological Assessment, 6*, 92–101.

Henry, W. E. (1956). The analysis of fantasy: The Thematic Apperception Test in the study of personality. New York: John Wiley & Sons.

Herjanic, B., & Campbell, W. (1977). Differentiating psychiatrically disturbed children on the basis of a structured interview. *Journal of Abnormal Child Psychology, 51*, 127–134.

Herjanic, B., & Reich, W. (1982). Development of a structured psychiatric interview for children: Agreement on diagnosis comparing child and patient interviews. *Journal of Abnormal Psychology, 10*, 325–336.

Hersen, M. (1988). Behavioral assessment and psychiatric diagnosis. *Behavioral Assessment, 10*, 107–121.

Hersen, M. (2008). *Handbook of psychological assessment, case conceptualization, and treatment.* Hoboken, NJ: John Wiley & Sons.

Hersen, M., & Bellack, A. S. (1976). *Behavioral assessment: A practical handbook.* New York: Pergamon Press.

Hersen, M., & Bellack, A. S. (1988). DSM-III and behavioral assessment. In A. S. Bellack & M. Hersen (Eds.), *Behavioral assessment: A practical handbook* (3rd ed., pp. 67–84). New York: Pergamon Press.

Hersen, M., & Bellack, A. S. (Eds.). (2002). *Dictionary of behavioral assessment techniques* (2nd ed.). New York: Pergamon Press.

Hersen, M., & Greaves, S. T. (1971). Rorschach productivity as related to verbal performance. *Journal of Personality Assessment, 35*, 436–441.

Hertz, M. R. (1948). Suicidal configurations in Rorschach records. *Rorschach Research Exchange, 12*, 3–58.

Hertz, M. R. (1976). Detection of suicidal risks with the Rorschach. In M. Abt & S. L. Weissman (Eds.), *Acting out: Theoretical and clinical aspects* (2nd ed.). New York: Aronson.

Herzog, D. B., Keller, M. B., Sacks, N. R., Yeh, C. J., & Lavori, P. W. (1992). Psychiatric comorbidity in treatment-seeking anorexics and bulimics. *Journal of the American Academy of Child and Adolescent Psychiatry, 31*, 810–818.

Higgins, R. L., Alonso, R. R., & Pendleton, M. G. (1979). The validity of roleplay assessments of assertiveness. *Behavior Therapy, 10*, 655–662.

Higgins-Lee, C. (1990). Low scores on California Psychological Inventory as predictors of psychopathology in alcoholic patients. *Psychological Reports, 67*, 227–232.

Hill, A. H. (1967). Use of a structured autobiography in the construct validation of personality scales. *Journal of Consulting Psychology, 31*, 551–556.

Hill, R. E., Jr. (1960). Dichotomous prediction of student teaching excellence employing selected CPI scales. *Journal of Educational Research, 53*, 349–351.

Hiller, J. B., Rosenthal, R., Bornstein, R. A. , Berry, D. T. R., & Brunnell-Neuleib, S. (1999). A comparative meta-analysis of Rorschach and MMPI validity. *Psychological Assessment, 11*, 27–66.

Hilsenroth, M. J., & Handler, L. (1995). A survey of graduate students' experiences, interests, and attitudes about learning the Rorschach. *Journal of Personality Assessment, 64*, 243–257.

Hilsenroth, M., & Stricker, G. (2004). A consideration of challenges to psychological assessment instruments used in forensic settings. *Journal of Personality Assessment, 83*, 141–152.

Hishinuma, E. S., & Yamakawa, R. (1993). Constructional and criterion related validity of the WISC-III for exceptional students and those at risk. In B. A. Braken & R. S. McCullum (Eds.), *Wechsler Intelligence Scales for Children* (3rd ed.)(pp. 94–104). Brandon, VT: Clinical Psychology.

Hofer, J., & Athanasios, C. (2004). Methodological considerations of applying TAT-type picture story test in cross-cultural research. *Journal of Cross-Cultural Psychology, 35*, 224–241.

Hoofien, D., Barak, O. Vakil, E, & Gilboa, A. (2005). Symptom Checklist-90 Revised scores in persons with traumatic brain injury: Affective reactions or neurobehavioral outcomes of the injury? *Applied Neuropsychology, 12*, 30–39

Hogan, R. (1971). Personality characteristics of highly rated policemen. *Personnel Psychology, 24*, 679–686.

Hogan, R., Hogan, J., & Roberts, B. W. (1996). Personality measurement and employment decisions: Questions and answers. *American Psychologist, 51*, 469–477.

Hoge, R. D., Andrews, D. A., Robinson, D., & Hollett, J. (1988). The construct validity of interview-based assessments in family counseling. *Journal of Clinical Psychology, 44*, 563–571.

Holland, A. L. (1980). *Communicative abilities in daily living: A test of functional communication for aphasic adults.* Austin, TX: ProEd.

Holliman, N. B., & Montross, J. (1984). The effects of depression upon responses to the California Psychological Inventory. *Journal of Clinical Psychology, 40*, 1373–1378.

Hollis, J. W., & Donna, P. A. (1979). *Psychological report writing: Theory and practice.* Muncie, IN: Accelerated Development.

Hollon, S. D., & Kendall, P. C. (1980). Cognitive self-statements in depression: Development of an automatic thoughts questionnaire. *Cognitive Therapy and Research, 4*, 383–395.

Holmes, C. B., Dungan, D. S., & Medlin, W. J. (1984). Reassessment of inferring personality traits from Bender-Gestalt drawing styles. *Journal of Clinical Psychology, 40*, 1241–1243.

Holmes, C. B., & Stephens, C. L. (1984). Consistency of edging on the Bender-Gestalt, Memory for Designs, and Draw-A-Person Tests. *Journal of Psychology, 117*, 269–271.

Holmstrom, R. W., Karp, S. A., & Silber, D. E. (1994). Prediction of depression with the Apperceptive Personality Test. *Journal of Clinical Psychology, 50*, 234–237.

Holtzman, W. H. (1988). Beyond the Rorschach. *Journal of Personality Assessment, 52*, 578–609.

Hope, D. A., & Heimberg, R. G. (1993). Social phobia and social anxiety. In D. H. Barlow (Ed.), *Clinical handbook of psychological disorders* (pp. 99–136). New York: Guilford Press.

Hopwood, C. J., & Richard, D. C. S. (2005). Graduate student WAIS-III scoring accuracy is a function of full scale IQ and complexity of examiner tasks. *Assessment, 12*(4), 445–454.

Horn, J. L. (1985). Remodeling old models of intelligence. In B. Wolman (Ed.), *Handbook of intelligence* (pp. 267–300). New York: John Wiley & Sons.

Horn, J. L., & Cattell, R. B. (1966). Refinement and test of the theory of fluid and crystalized intelligence. *Journal of Educational Psychology, 57*, 253–270.

Horn, J. L., & Noll, J. (1997). Human cognitive capabilities: Gf-Gc theory. In D. P. Flanagan, J. L. Genshaft, & P. L. Harrison (Eds.), *Contemporary intellectual assessment: Theories, tests, and issues.*(pp. 53–91). New York: Guilford Press.

Horowitz, M. J. (1985). *Report of the program on conscious and unconscious mental processes of the John D. and Catherine T. MacArthur Foundation.* San Francisco: University of California.

Horvath, A. O., & Goheen, M. D. (1990). Factors mediating the success of defiance- and compliance-based interventions. *Journal of Consulting and Clinical Psychology, 37*, 363–371.

Horvath, A. O., & Symonds, B. D. (1991). Relations between working alliance and outcome in psychotherapy: A meta-analysis. *Journal of Counseling Psychology, 38*, 139–149.

Houts, A. C. (2002). Discovery, invention, and the expansion of the modern Diagnostic and Statistical Manuals of Mental Disorders. In L. E. Beutler & M. L. Malik (Eds.), *Rethinking the DSM: A psychological perspective* (pp. 17–69). Washington, DC: American Psychological Association.

Hoyt, M. F. (1994). Single session solutions. In M. Hoyt (Ed.), *Constructive therapies* (pp. 140–159). New York: Guilford Press.

Huffcutt, A. I., & Arthur, W. (1994). Hunter and Hunter. (1984). revisited: Interview validity for entry-level jobs. Journal of Applied Psychology, *79*, 184–194.

Humphrey, D. H., & Dahlstrom, W. G. (1995). The impact of changing from the MMPI to the MMPI-2 on profile configurations. *Journal of Personality Assessment, 64*, 428–439.

Hunkin, N. M., Stone, J. V., Isaac, C., Holdstock, J. S., Butterfield, R., Wallis, L. I., et al. (2000). Factor analysis of three standardized tests of memory in a clinical population. *British Journal of Clinical Psychology, 39*, 169–180.

Hunsley, J., & Bailey, J. M. (2001). Whither the Rorschach? *Psychological Assessment, 13*, 472–485.

Hunsley, J., Hanson, R. K., & Parker, K. C. H. (1988). A summary of the reliability and stability of MMPI scales. *Journal of Clinical Psychology, 44*, 44–46.

Hunsley, J., Lee, C., & Wood, J. M. (2003). Controversial and questionable assessment techniques. In S. O. Lillienfeld, S. J. Lynn, & J. M. Lohr (Eds.), Science and pseudoscience in clinical psychology (pp. 39–76). New York: Guilford Press.

Hunsley, J., & Mash, E. J. (Eds.). (2008). *Assessments that work.* New York: Oxford University Press.

Hunsley, J., & Meyer, G. (2003). The incremental validity of psychological testing and assessment: Conceptual, methodological, and statistical issues. *Psychological Assessment, 15*, 446–455.

Hunter, E. E., Powell, B. J., Penick, E. C., Nickel, E. J., Othmer, E., & DeSouza, C. (2000). Development and validation of a mania scale for the Symptom Checklist-90-R. *Journal of Nervous and Mental Diseases, 188*, 176–179.

Hunter, J. E. (1986). Cognitive ability, cognitive aptitudes, job knowledge, and job performance. *Journal of Vocational Behavior, 29*, 340–362.

Hunter, J. E., & Hunter, R. F. (1984). Validity and utility of alternative predictors of job employment. *Psychological Bulletin, 96*, 72–98.

Hunter, J. E., & Schmidt, F. L. (1996). Intelligence and job performance: Economic and social implications. *Psychology, Public Policy, and Law, 2*, 447–472.

Hunter, J. E., & Schmidt, F. L. (2000). Racial and gender bias in ability and achievement tests. *Psychology, Public Policy, and Law, 6*, 151–158.

Hutt, M. L. (1985). *The Hutt adaptation of the Bender-Gestalt Test* (4th ed.). New York: Grune & Stratton.

Hutt, M. L., & Briskin, G. J. (1960). *The clinical use of the revised Bender-Gestalt Test.* New York: Grune & Stratton.

Iacano, W. G., & Patrick, C. J. (2006). Polygraph ("lie detector") testing: Current status and emerging trends. In I. B. Weiner & A. K. Hess (Eds.), *The handbook of forensic psychology* (3rd ed.)(pp. 552–588). Hoboken, NJ: John Wiley & Sons.

Ingram, R. E., Kendall, P. C., Siegle, G., Guarino, J., & McLaughlin, S. C. (1995). Psychometric properties of the Positive Automatic Thoughts Questionnaire. *Psychological Assessment, 7,* 495–507.

Ireland-Galman, M., Padilla, G., & Michael, W. (1980). The relationship between performance on the mazes subtest of the Wechsler Intelligence Scale for Children-Revised (WISC-R) and speed of solving anagrams with simple and difficult arrangements of letter and order. *Educational and Psychological Measurement, 40,* 513–524.

Iverson, G. L. (1999). In terpreting change on the WAIS-III/WMS-III following traumatic brain injury. *Journal of Cognitive Rehabilitation, 17*:16–20.

Iverson, G. L., Franzen, M. D., & Hammond, J. A. (1995). Examination of inmate's ability to malinger on the MMPI-2. *Psychological Assessment, 7,* 115–117.

Jackson, D. N., Fraboni, M., & Helms, E. (1997). MMPI-2 content scales: How much content do they measure? *Assessment, 4,* 111–117.

Jacob, R. G., Turner, S. M., Szekely, B. C., & Eidelman, B. H. (1983). Predicting outcome of relaxation therapy in headaches: The role of "depression." *Behavior Therapy, 14,* 457–465.

Jacobson, J. W., & Mulick, J. A. (Eds.). (1996). *Manual of diagnosis and professional practice in mental retardation.* Washington, DC: American Psychological Association.

Jacobson, N. S., Follette, W. C., & Pagel, M. (1986). Predicting who will benefit from behavioral marital therapy. *Journal of Consulting and Clinical Psychology, 54,* 518–522.

Jankowski, D. (2002). *A beginner's guide to the MCMI–III.* Washington, DC: American Psychological Association.

Janus, M., Tolbert, H., Calestro, K., & Toepfer, S. (1996). Clinical accuracy ratings of MMPI approaches for adolescents: Adding ten years and the MMPI-A. *Journal of Personality Assessment, 67,* 364–383.

Jarvis, P. E., & Barth, J. (1994). *The Halstead-Reitan Neuropsychological Battery: A guide to interpretation and clinical application.* Odessa, FL: Psychological Assessment Resources.

Jenkins, S. R. (2008). *Handbook of clinical scoring systems for Thematic Apperception techniques.* Mahwah, NJ: Lawrence Erlbaum.

Jensen, A. L., & Weisz, J. R. (2002). Assessing match and mismatch between practitioner-generated and standardized interview-generated diagnosis for clinic-referred children and adolescents. *Journal of Consulting and Clinical Psychology, 70,* 158–168.

Jensen, A. R. (1965). Review of the Rorschach. In O. K. Buros (Ed.), *The sixth mental measurements yearbook* (pp. 501–509). Highland Park, NJ: Gryphon Press.

Jensen, A. R. (1969). How much can we boost I.Q. and scholastic achievement? *Harvard Educational Review, 39,* 1–23.

Jensen, A. R. (1972). *Genetics and education.* New York: Harper & Row.

Jensen, A. R. (1984). The black-white difference on the K-ABC: Implications for future tests. *Journal of Special Education, 18,* 377–408.

Jensen, A. R., & Rohwer, W. D. (1966). The Stroop Color-Word Test: A review. *Acta Psychologica, 25,* 36–93.

Johnson, D. L., & Danley, W. (1981). Validity: Comparison of the WISC-R and SOMPA estimated learning potential scores. *Psychological Reports, 49,* 123–131.

Johnson, J. A. (2000). Predicting observers' ratings of the Big Five from the CPI, HPI, and NEO-PI-R: A comparative validity study. *European Journal of Personality, 14,* 1–19.

Johnson, J. H., Null, C., Butcher, J. M., & Johnson, K. N. (1984). Replicated item level factor analysis of the full MMPI. *Journal of Personality and Social Psychology, 47,* 105–114.

Johnson, J. W., & Williams, T. A. (1977). Using on-line computer technology to improve service response and decision-making effectiveness in a mental health admitting system. In J. B. Sidowski & T. A. Williams (Eds.), *Technology in mental health care delivery systems* (pp. 237–249). Norwood, NJ: Ablex.

Johnson, L. C., Murphy, S. A., Dimond, M. (1996). Reliability, construct validity, and subscale norms of the Brief Symptom Inventory when administered to bereaved parents. *Journal of Nursing Measurement, 4,* 117–127.

Johnson, M. H., Margo, P. A., & Stern, S. L. (1986). Use of the SADS-C as a diagnostic and symptom severity measure. *Journal of Consulting and Clinical Psychology, 54,* 546–551.

Jones, M. C. (1924). The elimination of children's fears. *Journal of Experimental Psychology, 7,* 382–390.

Jones, C. J., Livson, N., & Peskin, H. (2003). Longitudinal hierarhical linear modeling analyses of California Psychological Inventory data from age 33 to 75: An examinatin of stability and change in adult personality. *Journal of Personality Assessment, 80,* 294–308.

Jones, R. G. (1969). A factored measure of Ellis's Irrational Belief System. *Dissertation Abstracts International, 29* (43), 4379B–4380B. (UMI No. 69–64)

Jongsma, A. E., & Peterson, L. M., & Bruce, T. J. (2006). *The complete adult psychotherapy treatment planner* (4th ed.). Hoboken, N.J.: John Wiley & Sons.

Jorgensen, K., Anderson, T. J., & Dam, H. (2000). The diagnostic efficiency of the Rorschach Depression Index and the Schizophrenia Index: A review. *Assessment, 7,* 259–280.

Julian, A., Sotile, W. M., Henry, S. H., & Sotile, M. O. (1991). *Technical manual: The Family Apperception Test.* Beverly Hills, CA: Western Psychological Services.

Kabacoff, R. I., Segal, D. L., Hersen, M., & Van Hasselt, V. B. (1997). Psychometric properties and diagnostic utility of the Beck Anxiety Inventory and the State-Trait Anxiety Inventory with older adult psychiatric outpatients. *Journal of Anxiety Disorders, 11,* 33–47.

Kadden, R. M., Cooney, N. L., Getter, H., & Litt, M. D. (1990). Matching alcoholics to coping skills or interactional therapies: Post-treatment results. *Journal of Consulting and Clinical Psychology, 57,* 698–704.

Kadden, R. M., Litt, M. D., Donovan, D., & Cooney, N. L. (1996). Psychometric properties of the California Psychological Inventory Socialization Scale in treatment-seeking alcoholics. *Psychology of Addictive Behaviors, 10,* 131–146.

Kahn, M. W., Fox, H., & Rhode, R. (1988). Detecting faking on the Rorschach: Computer versus expert clinical judgment. *Journal of Personality Assessment, 52,* 516–523.

Kahn, R. L., & Cannell, C. F. (1961). *The dynamics of interviewing: Theory, technique, and cases.* New York: John Wiley & Sons.

Kahn, T. C., & Giffen, M. B. (1960). Psychological techniques in diagnosis and evaluation. New York: Pergamon Press.

Kamin, L. J. (1974). *The science and politics of I.Q.* Hillsdale, NJ: Lawrence Erlbaum.

Kamphaus, R. W., Petoskey, M. D., & Rowe, E. W. (2000). Current trends in psychological testing of children. *Professional Psychology: Research and Practice, 31,* 155–164.

Kane, R. L. (1991). Standardized and flexible batteries in neuropsychology: An assessment update. *Neuropsychology Review, 2,* 281–337.

Kane, R. L. (2007). Introduction to this supplement (Automated Neuropsychological Assessment Metric). *Archives of Clinical Neuropsychology, 22,* S3–S5.

Kanfer, F. H., & Grimm, L. G. (1977). Behavioral analysis: Selecting target behaviors in the interview. *Behavior Modification, 4,* 419–444.

Kanfer, F. H., & Saslow, G. (1969). Behavioral diagnosis. In C. M. Franks (Ed.), *Behavior therapy: Appraisal and status.*(pp. 417–444). New York: McGraw-Hill.

Kaplan, E., Fein, D., Morris, R., & Delis, D. (1991). *The WAIS-R as a neuropsychological instrument.* San Antonio, TX: Psychological Corporation

Kaplan, E., Fein, D., Morris, R., Kramer, J. H., & Delis, D. C. (1999). *The WISC-III as a process instrument.* San Antonio, TX: Psychological Corporation.

Kaplan, E., Fein, D., Morris, R., Kramer, J. H., Maerlender, A., & Delis, D. C. (2004). *The Wechsler Intelligence Scale for Children—Fourth Edition Integrated.* San Antonio, TX: Psychological Corporation.

Kaplan, R. M., & Saccuzzo, D. P. (1993). *Psychological testing: Principles, applications and issues* (3rd ed.). Belmont, CA: Wadsworth.

Kaplan, R. M., & Saccuzzo, D. P. (2005). *Psychological testing: Principles, applications, and issues* (5th ed.). Pacific Grove, CA: Brooks/Cole.

Kareken, D. A., & Williams, J. M. (1994). Human judgment and estimation of premorbid intellectual function. *Psychological Assessment, 6,* 83–91.

Karon, B. P. (2000). The clinical interpretation of the Thematic Apperception Test, Rorschach, and other clinical data: A reexamination of statistical versus clinical prediction. *Professional Psychology: Research and Practice, 31,* 230–233.

Karp, S. A., Holstrom, R. W., & Silber, D. E. (1989). *Manual for the Apperceptive Personality Test (APT).* Orland Park, IL: International Diagnostic Systems.

Karp, S. A., Silber, D. E., Holstrom, R. W., Banks, V., & Karp, J. (1992). Outcomes of Thematic Apperceptive Test and Apperceptive Personality Test stories. *Perceptual and Motor Skills, 74,* 479–482.

Karson, M. (2005). Overinterpretation of the Rorschach and the MMPI-2 when standard error is ignored. *Scientific Review of Mental Health Practice, 3,* 25–29.

Katon, W. J., & Walker, E. A. (1998). Medically unexplained symptoms in primary care. *Journal of Clinical Psychiatry, 59,* 15–21.

Kaufman, A. S. (1975). Factor analysis of the WISC-R at eleven ages between 6.2 and 16.2 years. *Journal of Consulting and Clinical Psychology, 43,* 135–147.

Kaufman, A. S. (1990). *Assessing adolescent and adult intelligence.* Boston: Allyn & Bacon.

Kaufman, A. S. (1994). *Intelligent testing with the WISC-III.* New York: John Wiley & Sons.

Kaufman, A. S. (2000). Seven questions about the WAIS-III regarding differences in abilities across the 16 to 89 year life span. *School Psychology Quarterly, 15,* 3–29.

Kaufman, A. S. (2001). WAIS-III IQs, Horn's theory, and generational changes from young adulthood to old age. *Intelligence, 29,* 131–167.

Kaufman, A. S., Kaufman, J. C., Balgopal, R., & McLean, J. E. (1996). Comparison of three WISC-III short forms: Weighing psychometric, clinical, and practical factors. *Journal of Clinical Child Psychology, 25,* 97–105.

Kaufman, A. S., & Kaufman, N. L. (1993). *Manual for the Kaufman Adolescent and Adult Intelligence Test (KAIT).* Circle Pines, MN: American Guidance Service.

Kaufman, A. S., & Kaufman, N. L. (Eds.) (2001). *Specific learning disabilities and difficulties in children and adolescents: Psychological assessment and evaluation.* Cambridge, England: Cambridge University Press

Kaufman, A. S., & Kaufman, N. L. (2004). *Kaufman Assessment Battery for Children—second edition.* Minneapolis, MN: Pearson Assessments.

Kaufman, A. S., & Lichtenberger, E. O. (1999). *Essentials of WAIS-III assessment.* New York: John Wiley & Sons.

Kaufman, A. S., & Lichtenberger, E. O. (2000). *Essentials of WISC-III and WPPSI-R assessment.* Hoboken, NJ: John Wiley & Sons.

Kaufman, A. S., & Lichtenberger, E. O. (2002). *Assessing adolescent and adult intelligence* (2nd ed.). Boston: Allyn & Bacon.

Kaufman, A. S., Lichtenberger, E. O., & Fletcher-Janzen, E. (2005). *Essentials of KABC-II assessment.* Hoboken, NJ: John Wiley & Sons.

Kaufman, A. S., & Lichtenberger, E. O. (2006). *Assessing adolescent and adult intelligence* (3rd ed.). Boston: Allyn & Bacon.

Kaufman, A. S., McLean, J. E., & Reynolds, C. R. (1988). Sex, race, residence, region, and education differences on the 11 WAIS-R subtests. *Journal of Clinical Psychology, 44*, 231–248.

Kaufman, J., & Kaufman A. (2001). Time for the changing of the guard: A farewell to short forms of IQ tests. *Journal of Psychoeducational Assessment, 19*, 245–267.

Kaslow, N. J., Bollini, Druss, B., Glueckauf, R. L., Goldfrank, R. R., Kelleher, K. J., et al. (2007). Health care for the whole person: Research update. *Professional Psychology: Research and Practice, 38*, 278–289.

Kazdin, A. E. (1988). The diagnosis of childhood disorders: Assessment issues and strategies. *Behavioral Assessment, 10*, 67–94.

Kearney, C. A., Cook, A. C., Chapman, C., & Bensaheb, A. (2006). Exploratory and factor analysis of the Motivation Assessment Scale and the Resident Choice Assessment Scale. *Journal of Developmental and Physical Disabilities, 18*, 1–11.

Keiller, S., & Graham, J. R. (1993). The meaning of low scores on the MMPI-2 clinical scales of normal subjects. *Journal of Personality Assessment, 61*, 211–223.

Keiser, R. E., & Prather, E. N. (1990). What is the TAT? A review of ten years of research. *Journal of Personality Assessments, 55*, 800–803.

Keith, T. Z., Fine, J. D., Taub, G. E., Reynolds, M. R., & Kranzler, J. H. (2006). Higher order, multisample, confirmatory factor analysis of the Wechsler Intelligence Scale for children—Fourth Edition: What does it measure? *School Psychology Review, 35*, 108–127.

Kelly, E. L., & Fiske, D. W. (1951). *The prediction of performance in clinical psychology.* Ann Arbor: University of Michigan Press.

Kendall, P. C., & Hollon, S. D. (Eds.). (1981). *Assessment strategies for cognitive-behavioral interventions.* New York: Academic Press.

Kendall, P.C. & Treadwell, K. (2007). The role of self-statements as a mediator in treatment for anxiety-disordered youth. *Journal of Consulting and Clinical Psychology, 75*, 380–389.

Kernhof, K., Kaufhold, J., & Grabhorn, R. (2008). Object relations and interpersonal problems in sexually abused female patients: An empirical study with the SCORS and the IIP. *Journal of Personality Assessment, 90*, 44–51.

Kerns, L. L. (1986). Falsifications in the psychiatric history: A differential diagnosis. *Psychiatry, 49*, 13–17.

Killgore, W. D. S., & Dellapietra, L. (2000). Item response biases on the logical memory delayed recognition subtest of the Wechsler Memory Scale-III. *Psychological Reports, 86*, 851–857.

Kim, B. S., Atkinson, D. R., & Yang, P. H. (1999). The Asian Values Scale: Development, factor analysis, validation, and reliability. *Journal of Counseling Psychology, 46*, 342–352.

Kincel, R. L., & Murray, S. C. (1984). Kinesthesias in perception and the experience type: Dance and creative projection. *British Journal of Projective Psychology and Personality Study, 29*, 3–7.

Kinder, B. N. (1994). Where the action is in personality assessment. *Journal of Personality Assessment, 62*, 585–588.

Kipnis, D. (1968). Social immaturity, intellectual ability, and adjustive behavior in college. *Journal of Applied Psychology, 52*, 71–80.

Kirk, B. A., Cumming, R. W., & Hackett, H. H. (1963). Personal and vocational characteristics of dental students. *Personnel and Guidance Journal, 41*, 522–527.

Klassen, R.M. (2004). Optimism and realism: A review of self efficacy from a cross-cultural perspective. *International Journal of Psychology, 39*, 205–230.

Klein, R. G. (1986). Questioning the usefulness of projective psychological tests for children. *Journal of Developmental and Behavioral Pediatrics, 7*, 378–382.

Kleinmuntz, B. (1990). Why we still use our heads instead of formulas: Toward an integrative approach. *Psychological Bulletin, 107*, 296–310.

Klespies, P. M., & Dettmer, E. L. (2000). An evidence-based approach to evaluating and managing suicidal emergencies. *Journal of Clinical Psychology, 56*, 1109–1130.

Klinefelter, D., Pancoast, D. L., Archer, R. P., & Pruitt, D. L. (1990). Recent adolescent MMPI norms: T score elevation comparisons to Marks and Briggs. *Journal of Personality Assessment, 54*, 379–389.

Klinger, E. (1966). Fantasy need achievement as a motivational construct. *Psychological Bulletin, 66*, 291–308.

Klopfer, B. (1937). The present status of the theoretical development of the Rorschach method. *Rorschach Research Exchange, 1*, 142–147.

Klopfer, B., Ainsworth, M. D., Klopfer, W. G., & Holt, R. R. (1956). *Developments in the Rorschach technique* (Vol. 2). Yonkers, NY: World Books.

Klopfer, B., & Davidson, H. (1962). *The Rorschach technique: An introductory manual.* New York: Harcourt, Brace, Jovanovich.

Klopfer, W. G. (1960). *The psychological report.* New York: Grune & Stratton.

Klopfer, W. G. (1983). Writing psychological reports. In A. Walker (Ed.), *The handbook of clinical psychology: Theory, research, and practice.* Homewood, IL: Dow Jones-Irwin.

Knight, R. G., & Godfrey, H. P. D. (1996). Psychosocial aspects of neurological disorders: Implications for research in neuropsychology. *Australian Psychologist, 31*, 48–51.

Konold, T. R., Glutting, J. J., McDermott, P. A., Kush, J. C., & Watkins, M. W. (1999). Structure and diagnostic benefits of a normative taxonomy developed from the WISC-III standardization sample. *Journal of School Psychology, 37*, 29–48.

Koppitz, E. M. (1958). Relationships between the Bender-Gestalt Test and the Wechsler Intelligence Scale for Children. *Journal of Clinical Psychology, 14*, 413–416.

Koppitz, E. M. (1963). *The Bender Gestalt Test for Young Children* (Vol. 1). New York: Grune & Stratton.

Koppitz, E. M. (1975). *The Bender Gestalt Test for Young Children. Vol. 2: Research and Applications 1963–1973.* New York: Grune & Stratton.

Koss, M. P. (1979). MMPI item content: Recurring issues. In J. N. Butcher (Ed.), *New developments in the use of the MMPI* (pp. 3–38). Minneapolis: University of Minnesota Press.

Kostlan, A. (1954). A method for the empirical study of psychodiagnosis. *Journal of Consulting Psychology, 18*, 83–88.

Kramer, J. H. (1993). Interpretation of individual subtest scores on the WISC-III IQ and index scores. *Psychological Assessment, 5*, 193–196.

Kramer, J. H., Kaplan, E., & Huckeba, W. (1999). Configural errors on WISC-III Block Design. *Journal of the International Neuropsychological Society, 5*, 518–524.

Kratochwill, T. R. (1985). Selection of target behaviors in behavioral consultation. *Behavior Assessment, 7*, 49–61.

Kubiszyn, T. W., Meyer, G. J., Finn, S. E., Eyde, L. D., Kay, G. G., Moreland, K. L., et al. (2000). Empirical support for psychological assessment in clinical care settings. *Professional Psychology, 31*, 119–130.

Kühn, R. (1963). Über die kritische Rorschach-Forschung und einige ihrer Ergebnisse. *Rorschachiana, 8*, 105–114.

Kurtines, W., Hogan, R., & Weiss, D. (1975). Personality dynamics of heroin use. *Journal of Abnormal Psychology, 84*, 87–89.

Kvaal, S., Choca, J., & Groth-Marnat, G. (2003). The integrated psychological report. In L. E. Beutler & G. Groth-Marnat (Eds.), *Integrated assessment of adult personality* (2nd ed.)(pp. 398–434). New York: Guilford Press.

Lachar, D., & Gruber, C. P. (2001). *Personality inventory for Children, Second Edition (PIC-2) Standard Form and Behavioral Summary manual.* Los Angeles: Western Psychological Services.

Lacks, P. (1984). Bender-Gestalt screening for brain dysfunction. New York: John Wiley & Sons.

Lacks, P. (1996). *Bender Gestalt screening for brain dysfunction* [Computer software]. Odessa, FL: Psychological Assessment Resources.

Lacks, P. (1999). *Bender-Gestalt screening for brain dysfunction* (2nd ed.). New York: John Wiley & Sons.

Lacks, P. (2000). Visuoconstructive abilities. In G. Groth-Marnat (Ed.), *Neuropsychological assessment in clinical practice: A guide to test interpretation and integration* (pp. 401–436). Hoboken, NJ: John Wiley & Sons.

Lacks, P., & Newport, K. (1980). A comparison of scoring systems and level of scorer experience on the Bender-Gestalt Test. *Journal of Personality Assessment, 44*, 351–357.

Lafer, B. (1989). Predicting performance and persistance in hospice volunteers. *Psychological Reports, 65*, 467–472.

Lamb, D. G., Berry, D. T., Wetter, M. W., & Baer, R. A. (1994). Effects of two types of information on malingering of closed head injury on the MMPI-2: An analog investigation. *Psychological Assessment, 6*, 8–13.

Lambert, M. J., Hansen, N. B., Umphress, V., Lunnen, K., Okiishi, J., Burlingame, G. M., et al. (1996). *Administration and scoring manual for the Outcome Questionnaire (OQ45.2).* Wilmington, DE: American Professional Credentialing Services.

Lambert, M. J., & Hawkins, R. J. (2004). Measuring outcome in professional practice: Considerations in selecting brief outcome measures. *Professional Psychology: Research and Practice, 35*, 492–499.

Landrine, H., & Klonoff, E. A. (1994). The African American Acculturation Scale: Development, reliability, and validity. *Journal of Black Psychology, 20*, 104–127.

Langan-Fox, J., & Grant, S. (2006). The Thematic Apperception Test: Toward a standard measure of the big three motives. *Journal of Personality Assessment, 87*, 277–291.

Lanning, K. (1989). Detection of invalid response patterns on the California Psychological Inventory. Applied Psychological Measurement, *13*, 45–56.

Lanyon, R. I. (1997). Detecting deception: Current models and directions. *Clinical Psychology: Science and Practice, 4*, 377–387.

Lanyon, R. I., & Goodstein, L. D. (1982). *Personality assessment* (2nd ed.). New York: John Wiley & Sons.

Lapouse, R., & Monk, M. A. (1958). An epidemiologic study of behavior characteristics of children. *American Journal of Public Health, 48*, 1134–1144.

Lapouse, R., & Monk, M. A. (1964). Behavior deviations in a representative sample of children: Variations by sex, age, race, social class, and family size. *American Journal of Orthopsychiatry, 34*, 436–446.

Larkin, K. T. (2006). Psychophysiological assessment. In M. ,Hersen (Ed.), *Clinician's handbook of behavioral assessment* (pp. 165–185). New York: Elsevier.

Larrabee, G. J. (2005). Assessment of malingering. In G. J. Larrabee (Ed.), *Forensic neuropsychology: A scientific approach.* (pp. 115–158). New York: Oxford University Press.

Larrabee, G. J. (1986). Another look at VIQ-PIQ scores and unilateral brain damage. *International Journal of Neuroscience, 29*, 141–148.

Larson, E. B., Kirschener, K., Bode, R., Heinemann, A., & Goodman, R. (2005). Construct and predicitve validity of the Repeatable Battery for the Assessment of Neuropsychological Status in the evaluation of stroke patients. *Journal of Clinical and Experimental Neuropsychology, 27*: 16–32).

La Rue, A., & Jarvik, L. R. (1987). Cognitive function and prediction of dementia in old age. *International Journal of Aging and Human Development, 25*, 78–89.

Laufer, W. S., Skoog, D. K., & Day, J. M. (1982). Personality and criminality: A review of the California Psychological Inventory. *Journal of Clinical Psychology, 38*, 562–573.

Laurent, H., Chinot, L., Laure, J., Plancherel, B., Sofia, C., Halfon, O., & Randolph, C. (2007). Detection of cognitive impairment with the Repeatable Battery for the Assessment of Neuropsychological Status (RBANS) in adolescents with psychotic symptomology. *Schizophrenia Research, 95*, 48–53.

Lawrence, S. B. (1984). *Lawrence Psychological-Forensic Examination (Law-PSI)*. San Bernadino, CA: Lawrence Psychological Center.

Lazarus, A. A. (1973). Multimodel behavior therapy: Treating the "BASIC ID." *Journal of Nervous and Mental Diseases, 156*, 404–411.

Lazarus, A. A. (1989). *The practice of multi-modal therapy*. Baltimore, MD: Johns Hopkins University Press.

Lazarus, A. A., (2005). Multimodal therapy. In R.J. Corsini & D. Wedding (eds.) Current psycho-therapies (pp. 737–371). Belmont, CA: Thomson Brooks/Cole.

Leary, T. (1957). *Interpersonal diagnosis of personality*. New York: Ronald Press.

Lees-Haley P. R., English L.T., & Glenn W.J. (1991). A Fake Bad Scale on the MMPI-2 for personal injury claimants. *Psychological Reports, 68*, 203–210.

Lefebvre, M. F. (1981). Cognitive distortions and cognitive errors in depressed and low back pain patients. *Journal of Consulting and Clinical Psychology, 49*, 517–525.

Leffard, S. A., Miller, J. A., Bernstein, J., DeMann, J. J., Mangis, H. A., & McCoy, E. L. B. (2006). Substantive validity of working memory measures in major cognitive functioning test batteries for children. *Applied Neuropsychology, 13*, 230–241.

Lefkowitz, J., & Fraser, A. W. (1980). Assessment of achievement and power motivation of blacks and whites, using a black and white TAT with black and white administrators. *Journal of Applied Psychology, 65*, 685–696.

Leichsenring, F. (2001). Comparative effects of short-term psychodynamic psychotherapy and cognitive-behavioral therapy in depression: A meta-analytic approach. *Clinical Psychology Review, 21*, 401–419.

Leigh, J., & Zaylor, C. (2000). Cyberspace: Creating a therapeutic environment for telehealth applications. *Professional Psychology: Research and Practice, 31*, 478–483.

Lemsky, C. (2000). Neuropsychological assessment and treatment planning. In G. Groth-Marnat (Ed.), Neuropsychological assessment in clinical practice: A guide to test interpretation and integration (pp. 535–576). Hoboken, NJ: John Wiley & Sons.

Lenzenweger, M. F. (1999). Stability and change in personality disorder features: The longitudinal study of personality disorders. *Archives of General Psychiatry, 56*, 1009–1015.

Leon, G. R., Gillum, B., Gillum, R., & Gouze, M. (1979). Personality stability and change over a 30-year period—middle age to old age. *Journal of Consulting and Clinical Psychology, 47*, 517–524.

Lerner, E. A. (1972). *The projective use of the Bender-Gestalt Test*. Springfield, IL: Charles C Thomas.

Lesiak, J. (1984). The Bender Visual Motor Gestalt Test: Implications for the diagnosis and prediction of reading achievement. *Journal of School Psychology, 22*, 391–405.

Leura, A. V., & Exner, J. E. (1978). *Structural differences in the records of adolescents as a function of being tested by one's own teacher* (Workshops Study No. 265, unpublished).

Levenson, M. R. (1988). Emotionality and mental health: Longitudinal findings from the normative aging study. *Journal of Abnormal Psychology, 97*, 94–96.

Levin, H. S., High, W. M., Goethe, K. E., Sisson, R. A., Overall, J. E., Rhoades, H. M., et al. (1987). The Neurobehavioral Rating Scale: Assessment of the behavioral sequalae of head injury by the clinician. *Journal of Neurology, Neurosurgery, and Psychiatry, 50*, 183–193.

Levine, A. (2007). Cultural beliefs keep many Hispanics away from getting mental health care. *Psychiatric News, 42*, 8–9.

Levine, D. (1981). Why and when to test: The social context of psychological testing. In A. I. Rabin (Ed.), Assessment with projective techniques (pp. 553–580). New York: Springer.

Lewak, R., & Hogan, L. (2003). Applying assessment information. In L. E. Beutler & G. Groth-Marnat (Eds.), *Integrative assessment of adult personality* (2nd ed.). New York: Guilford Press.

Lewak, R. W., Marks, P. A., & Nelson, G. E. (1990). *Therapist guide to the MMPI and MMPI-2.* Muncie, IN: Accelerated Development.

Lewinsohn, P. M., Rohde, P., Klein, D. N., & Seeley, J. R. (1999). Natural course of adolescent major depressive disorder. I: Continuity into young adulthood. *Journal of the American Academy of Child Adolescent Psychiatry, 38,* 56–63.

Lezak, M. D. (1982). *The test-retest stability and reliability of some tests commonly used in neuropsychological assessment.* Paper presented at the 5th European conference of the International Neuropsychological Society, Deauville, France.

Lezak, M. D. (1983). *Neuropsychological assessment* (2nd ed.). New York: Oxford University Press.

Lezak, M. D. (1988). IQ: RIP. *Journal of Experimental and Clinical Neuropsychology, 10,* 351–361.

Lezak, M. D. (1989a). *Assessment of the behavioral consequences of brain injury: Frontiers of clinical neuroscience* (Vol. 7). New York: Alan R. Liss.

Lezak, M. D. (1989b). Assessment of psychosocial dysfunctions resulting from head trauma. In M. D. Lezak (Ed.), *Assessment of the behavioral consequences of head trauma: Frontiers of clinical neuroscience* (Vol. 7). New York: Alan R. Liss.

Lezak, M. D., Howieson, D. B., & Loring, D. W. (2004). *Neuropsychological assessment* (4th ed.). New York: Oxford University Press.

Lichtenberger, E. O. (2006). Computer utilization and clinical judgment in psychological assessment reports. *Journal of Clinical Psychology, 62,* 19–32.

Lichtenberger, E. O., Kaufman, A. S., & Lai, Z. C. (2002). *Essentials of WMS-III assessment.* Hoboken, NJ: John Wiley & Sons.

Lichtenstein, S., & Fischoff, B. (1977). Do those who know more also know more about how much they know? *Organizational Behavior and Human Performance, 20,* 159–183.

Lightfoot, S. L., & Oliver, J. M. (1985). The Beck Inventory: Psychometric properties in university students. *Journal of Personality Assessment, 49,* 434–436.

Lindgren, H. C., Moritsch, B., Thurlin, E. K., & Mich, G. (1986). Validity studies of three measures of achievement motivation. *Psychological Reports, 59,* 123–136.

Lindsay, D. S., & Read, J. D. (1995). "Memory work" and recovered memories of childhood sexual abuse: Scientific evidence and public and professional issues. *Psychology, Public Policy, and Law, 1,* 846–908.

Lindzey, G., & Herman, P. S. (1955). Thematic Apperception Test: A note on reliability and situational validity. *Journal of Projective Techniques, 19,* 36–42.

Lindzey, G., & Kalnins, D. (1958). Thematic Apperception Test: Some evidence bearing on the "hero assumption." *Journal of Abnormal and Social Psychology, 57,* 76–83.

Linger, M. L., Ray, G. E., Zachar, P., Underhill, A. T., & LoBello, S. G. (2007). Decreasing scoring errors on Wechsler scale Vocabulary, Comprehension, and Similarities subtests: A preliminary study. *Psychological Reports, 101,* 661–669.

Linscott, J., & DiGiuseppe, R. (1998). Cognitive assessment. In A. S. Bellack & M. Hersen (Eds.), *Behavioral assessment: A practical handbook* (pp. 104–125). Boston: Allyn & Bacon.

Little, K. B., & Shneidman, E. S. (1959). Congruencies among interpretations of psychological test and anamnestic data. *Psychological Monographs, 73* (6, Whole No. 476).

Little, S. G. (1992). The WISC-III: Everything old is new again. *School Psychology Quarterly, 7,* 138–142.

LoBello, S. G., Thompson, A. P., & Venugopala, E. (1998). Supplementary WAIS-III tables for determining subtest strengths and weaknesses. *Journal of Psychoeducational Assessment, 16,* 196–200.

Lodge, J., Tripp, G., & Harte, D. K. (2000). Think aloud, thought listing, and video-mediated recall procedures in the assessment of children's self talk. *Cognitive Therapy and Research, 24,* 399–418.

Loe, S. A., Kadlubek, R. M., & Marks, W. (2007). Administration and scoring errors for the WISC-IV among graduate stuednt examners. *Journal of Psychoeducational Assessment, 25*, 237–247.

Loenberger, L. T. (1989). The question of organicity: Is it still functional? *Professional Psychology: Research and Practice, 20*, 411–414.

Loftus, E. F. (1993). The reality of repressed memories. *American Psychologist, 48*, 518–537.

Long, J. D., Harring, J. R., Brekke, J. S., Test, M. A., & Greenberg, J. (2007). Longitudinal construct validity of Brief Symptom Inventory Subscales in schizophrenia. *Psychological Assessment, 19*, 298–308.

Lopez, E. C. (1997). The cognitive assessment of limited English proficient and bilingual children. In D. P. Flanagan, J. L. Genshaft, & P. L. Harrison (Eds.), *Contemporary intellectual assessment: Theories, tests, and issues* (pp. 503–518). New York: Guilford Press.

Loranger, A. W. (1988). *Personality Disorder Examination (PDE) manual.* Yonkers, NY: DV Communications.

Loranger, A. W., Sartorius, N., Andreoli, A., Berger, P., Buchheim, P., Channabasavanna, S. M., et al. (1995). The International Personality Disorder Examination. *Archives of General Psychiatry, 51*, 215–224.

Lorber, M. F. Psychophysiology of aggression, psychopathy, and conduct problems: A metaanalysis. *Psychological Bulletin, 130*, 531–552.

Loring, D. W., Lee, G. P., Martin, R. C., & Meador, K. J. (1989). Verbal and visual memory index discrepancies from the Wechsler Memory Scale—Revised: Cautions in interpretation. *Psychological Assessment: A Journal of Consulting and Clinical Psychology, 3*, 198–202.

Lovibund, P. F., & Lovibund, S. H. (1995). The structure of negative emotional states: Comparison of the Depression Anxiety Stress Scale (DASS) with the Beck Depression Inventories. *Behaviour Research and Therapy, 33*, 335–342.

Lowman, R. L. (1991). *The clinical practice of career assessment: Interests, abilities and personality.* Washington, DC: American Psychological Association.

Lubin, B., Larsen, R. M., & Matarazzo, J. D. (1984). Patterns of psychological test usage in the United States: 1935–1982. *American Psychologist, 39*, 451–454.

Lubin, B., Larsen, R. M., Matarazzo, J. D., & Seever, M. (1985). Psychological test usage patterns in five professional settings. *American Psychologist, 40*, 857–861.

Lubin, B., Larsen, R. M., Matarazzo, J. D., & Seever, M. (1986). Selected characteristics of psychologists and psychological assessment in five settings: 1959–1988. *Professional Psychology: Research and Practice, 17*, 155–157.

Luborsky, L. (1994). Therapeutic alliances as predictors of psychotherapy outcomes: Factors explaining predictive success. In A. O. Horvath & L. S. Greenberg (Eds.), *The working alliance: Theory, research, and practice* (pp. 38–50). New York: John Wiley & Sons.

Luborsky, L., Singer, B., & Luborsky, L. (1975). Comparative studies of psychotherapies. *Archives of General Psychiatry, 32*, 995–1008.

Lucas, C. P., Zhang, H., Fisher, P. W., Shaffer, D., Regier, D. A., Narow, W. E., et al. (2001). The DISC Predictive Scales (DPS): Efficiently screening for diagnosis. *Journal of the Academy of Child and Adolescent Psychiatry, 40*, 443–449.

Luciano, M. (2003). Practitioner review: Computerized assessment of neuropsychological function in children: Clinical and research applications of the Cambridge Neuropsychological testing Automated Battery (CANTB). *Journal of Child Psychology and Psychiatry, 44*, 649–663.

Luckasson, R., Coulter, D. L., Polloway, E. A., Reiss, S., Schalock, R. L., Snell, M. E., et al. (1992). *Mental retardation: Definition, classification, and systems of support.* Washington, DC: American Association on Mental Retardation.

Lundy, A. (1985). The reliability of the Thematic Apperception Test. *Journal of Personality Assessment, 49*, 141–145.

Lundy, A. (1988). Instructional set and Thematic Apperception Test validity. *Journal of Personality Assessment, 52*, 309–320.

Luria, A. R. (1973). *The working brain.* New York: Basic Books.

Luria, A. R. (1980). *Higher cortical functions in man* (2nd ed.). New York: Basic Books.

Lynn, R. (1977). The intelligence of the Japanese. *Bulletin of the British Psychological Society, 30*, 69–72.

Macmann, G. M., & Barnett, D. W. (1997). Myth of the master detective: Reliability of interpretations for Kaufman's "intelligent testing" approach to the WISC-III. *School Psychology Quarterly, 12*, 197–234.

Maddox, T. (2003). *Tests: A comprehensive reference for assessments in psychology, education, and business* (5th ed.). Austin, TX: ProEd.

Magnavita, J. J. (2005). Using the MCMI-III for treatment planning and to enhance treatment efficacy. In R. J. Craig (Ed.), *New directions in interpreting the Millon Clinical Multiaxial Inventory-III* (pp. 478–494). Hoboken, N.J.: John Wiley & Sons.

Maitra, A. K. (1983). Executive effectiveness: Characteristic thematic phantasy. *Managerial Psychology, 4*, 59–68.

Makatura, T. J., Lam, C. S., Leahy, B. J., Castillo, M. T., & Kalpakjian, C. Z. (1999). Standardized memory tests and the appraisal of everyday memory. *Brain Injury, 13*, 355–367.

Mallinckrodt, B. (1996). Change in working alliance, social support, and psychological symptoms in brief therapy. *Journal of Counseling Psychology, 43*, 448–455.

Maloney, M. P., & Ward, M. P. (1976). *Psychological assessment: A conceptual approach.* New York: Oxford University Press.

Malpass, R. S., & Kravitz, J. (1969). Recognition for faces of own and other race. *Journal of Personality and Social Psychology, 13*, 330–334.

Marchese, M. C., & Muchinsky, P. M. (1993). The validity of the employment interview: A meta-analysis. *International Journal of Selection and Assessment, 1*, 18–26.

Margolin, D. I., Pate, D. S., Friedrich, F. J., & Elia, E. (1990). Dysnomia in dementia and in stroke patients: Different underlying cognitive deficits. *Journal of Clinical and Experimental Neuropsychology, 12*, 597–612.

Margolin, G., Hattem, D., John, R. S., & Yost, K. (1985). Perceptual agreement between spouses and outside observers when coding themselves and a stranger dyad. *Behavioral Assessment, 7*, 235–247.

Marks, I. M., Cavanagh, K., & Gega, L. (2007). *Hands-on help: Computer aided psychotherapy.* London: Taylor & Francis.

Marley, M. L. (1982). *Organic brain pathology and the Bender Gestalt Test: A differential diagnostic scoring system.* New York: Grune & Stratton.

Marlowe, D. B., Festinger, D. S., & Kirby, K. C. (1998). Congruence of the MCMI-II and MCMI-III in cocaine dependence. *Journal of Personality Assessment, 71*, 15–28.

Martin, J. D., Pfaadt, N. K., & MaKinster, J. G. (1983). Relationship of hostility and white space responses on the Rorschach. *Perceptual and Motor Skills, 57*, 739–742.

Martin, P., Churchard, M., Kotcher, S., & Korenblum, M. (1991). Diagnostic utility of the Beck Depression Inventory with adolescent psychiatric outpatients and inpatients. *Canadian Journal of Psychiatry, 36*, 428–431.

Martinez, S., Stillerman, L., & Waldo, M. (2005). Reliability and validity of the SCL-90-R with Hispanic college students. *Hispanic Journal of Behavioral Sciences, 27*, 254–264.

Maruish, M. E. (Ed.). (2000). *Handbook of psychological testing in primary care settings.* Mahwah, NJ: Lawrence Erlbaum.

Maruish, M. E. (2002). *Psychological testing in the age of managed behavioral health care.* Mahwah, NJ: Erlbaum.

Maruish, M. E. (2004). *The use of psychological testing for treatment planning and outcomes assessment* (3rd ed.). Mahwah, NJ: Lawrence Erlbaum.

Masling, J. (1992). The influence of situation and interpersonal variables in projective testing. *Journal of Personality Assessment, 59*, 616–640.

Masling, M. (2006). When Homer nods: An examination of some of the systematic errors in Rorschach scholarship. *Journal of Personality Assessment, 87*, 62–73.

Mason, B., & Exner, J. E. (1984). *Correlations between WAIS subtests and nonpatient adult Rorschach data*. Rorschach Workshops (Study No. 289, unpublished).

Massman, P. J., & Bigler, E. D. (1993). A quantitative review of the diagnostic utility of the WAIS-R Fuld Profile. *Archives of Clinical Neuropsychology, 8*, 417–428.

Matarazzo, J. D. (1965). The interview. In B. B. Wolman (Ed.), *Handbook of clinical psychology* (pp. 403–450). New York: McGraw-Hill.

Matarazzo, J. D. (1972). *Wechsler's measurement and appraisal of adult intelligence* (5th ed.). Baltimore: Williams & Wilkins.

Matarazzo, J. D. (1990). Psychological assessment versus psychological testing: Validation from Binet to the school, clinic, and courtroom. *American Psychologist, 45*, 999–1017.

Matarazzo, J. D., Daniel, M. H., Prifitera, A., & Herman, D. O. (1988). Inter-subtest scatter in the WAIS-R standardization sample. *Journal of Clinical Psychology, 44*, 940–950.

Matarazzo, J. D., & Prifitera, A. (1989). Subtest scatter and premorbid intelligence: Lessons from the WAIS-R standardization sample. *Psychological Assessment, 1*, 186–191.

Mauger, P. A. (1972). The test-retest reliability of persons: An empirical investigation utilizing the MMPI and the personality research form. *Dissertation Abstracts International, 33*, 2816B.

Mayes, S. D., & Calhoun, S. L. (2007). Wechsler Intelligence Scale for Children—Third and—Fourth Edition predictors of academic achievement in children with Attention-Deficit/Hyperactivity Disorder. *School Psychology Quarterly, 22*, 234–249.

Mayes, S. D., Calhoun, S. L., & Crowell, E. W. (1998). WISC-III profiles for children with and without learning disabilities. *Psychology in the Schools, 35*, 309–316.

Maziade, M., Roy, A. A., Fournier, J. P., Cliche, D., Merette, C., Caron, C., et al. (1992). Reliability of best-estimate diagnosis in genetic linkage studies of major psychoses. *American Journal of Psychiatry, 149*, 1674–1686.

McAllister, L. (1996). *A practical guide to CPI interpretation* (3rd ed.). Palo Alto, CA: Consulting Psychologists Press.

McArthur, D. S., & Roberts, G. E. (1990). *The Roberts Apperception Test for Children manual*. Los Angeles, CA: Western Psychological Services.

McCall, R. B., Appelbaum, M. I., & Hogarty, P. S. (1973). Developmental changes in mental performance. *Monographs of the Society for Research in Child Development, 38*(3, Serial No. 150), 1–83.

McCallum, R. S., & Bracken, B. A. (1997). The Universal Nonverbal Intelligence Test. In D. P. Flanagan, J. L. Genshaft, & P. L. Harrison (Eds.), *Contemporary intellectual assessment* (pp. 268–280). New York: Guilford Press.

McCallum, R. S., Bracken, B. A., & Wasserman, J. (2001). *Essentials of nonverbal assessment*. Hoboken, NJ: John Wiley & Sons.

McCann, J. T. (1991). Convergent and discriminant validity of the MCMI-II and MMPI personality disorder scales. *Psychological Assessment, 3*, 9–18.

McClelland, D. C. (1961). *The achieving society*. Princeton, NJ: Van Nostrand.

McClelland, D. C. (1966). Longitudinal trends in the relation of thought to action. *Journal of Consulting Psychology, 30*, 479–483.

McClelland, D. C. (1971). *Assessing human motivation*. New York: General Learning Press.

McClelland, D. C., Koestner, P., & Weinberger, J. (1989). How do self-attributed and implicit motives differ? *Psychological Review, 96*, 690–702.

McCloskey, G., & Maerlander, A. (2005). The WISC-IV integrated. In A. Prifitera, D.H. Saklofske, & L.G. Weiss (Eds.) *WISC-IV clinical use and interpretation: Scientist practitioner perspectives* (pp. 101–149). San Diego, CA: Elsevier.

McConnaughy, E. A., Prochaska, J. O., & Velicer, W. (1983). Stages of change in psychotherapy: Measurement and sample profiles. *Psychotherapy: Theory, Research, and Practice, 20*, 368–375.

McConnell, O. L. (1967). Koppitz's Bender Gestalt in relation to organic and emotional problems in children. *Journal of Clinical Psychology, 23*, 370–374.

McCormick, I. A. (1984). A simple version of the Rathus Assertiveness Schedule. *Behavioral Assessment, 7*, 95–99.

McCown, W., Fink, A. D., Galina, H., & Johnson, J. (1992). Effects of laboratory-induced controllable and uncontrollable stress on Rorschach variables m and Y. *Journal of Personality Assessment, 59*, 564–573.

McCrae, R. R., Costa, P. T., & Piedmont, R. L. (1993). Folk concepts, natural language, and psychological constructs: The California Psychological Inventory and the five-factor model. *Journal of Personality Assessment, 61*, 1–25.

McCurry, S. M., Fitz, A. G., & Terri, L. (1994). Comparison of age-extended norms for the Wechsler Adult Intelligence Scale-Revised in patients with Alzheimer's disease. *Psychological Assessment, 6*, 231–235.

McDaniel, M. A., Whetzel, D. L., Schmidt, F. L., & Maurer, S. D. (1994). The validity of employment interviews: A comprehensive review and meta-analysis. *Journal of Applied Psychology, 79*, 599–616.

McDermott, P. A., Fantuzzo, J. W., Glutting, J. J., Watkins, M. W., & Baggaley, M. (1992). Illusions of meaning in the ipsative assessment of children's abilities. *Journal of Special Education, 25*, 504–526.

McFall, R. M., & Lillesand, D. V. (1971). Behavior rehearsal with modeling and coaching in assertive training. *Journal of Abnormal Psychology, 77*, 313–323.

McFarland, R. A. (1984). Effects of music upon emotional content of TAT stories. *Journal of Psychology, 116*, 227–234.

McFie, J. (1960). Psychological testing in clinical neurology. *Journal of Nervous and Mental Diseases, 131*, 383–393.

McFie, J. (1969). The diagnostic significance of disorders of higher nervous activity syndromes related to frontal, temporal, parietal, and occipital lesions. In P. J. Vinken & G. W. Bruyn (Eds.), *Handbook of clinical neurology* (Vol. 4). New York: American Elsevier.

McGlyn, F. D., & Rose, M. P. (1998). Assessment of anxiety and fear. In A. S. Bellack & M. Hersen (Eds.), *Behavioral assessment: A practical handbook* (pp. 179–209). Boston: Allyn & Bacon.

McGrath, R. E. (2001). Toward more clinically relevant research. *Journal of Personality Assessment, 77*, 307–332.

McGrath, R. E., & Ingersoll, J. (1999a). Writing a good cookbook. I: A review of MMPI high-point code system studies. *Journal of Personality Assessment, 73*, 149–178.

McGrath, R. E., & Ingersoll, J. (1999b). Writing a good cookbook. II: A synthesis of MMPI high-point code system study effect sizes. *Journal of Personality Assessment, 73*, 179–198.

McGrath, R. E., Powis, D., & Pogge, D. L. (1998). Code type-specific tables for interpretation of MMPI-2 Harris and Lingoes Subscales: Consideration of gender and code definition. *Journal of Clinical Psychology, 54*, 655–664.

McIntosh, J. A., Belter, R. W., Saylor, C. F., Finch, A. J., & Edwards, G. L. (1988). The Bender-Gestalt with adolescents: Comparison of two scoring systems. *Journal of Clinical Psychology, 44*, 226–230.

McKay, C., Wertheimer, J. C., Fichtenberg, N. L., & Casey, J. E. (2007). The Repeatable Battery for the Assessement of Neuropsychological Status (RBANS): Clinical utility in a traumatic brain injury sample. *Clinical Neuropsychology, 28*, 1–14.

McLean, P., & Taylor, S. (1992). Severity of unipolar depression and choice of treatment. *Behavior Research and Therapy, 30*, 443–451.

McLeod, C. C., Budd, M. A., & McClelland, D. C. (1997). Treatment of somatization in primary care. *General Hospital Psychiatry, 19*, 251–258.

McMinn, M. R., Buchanan, T., Ellens, B. M., & Ryan, M. K. (1999). Technology, professional practice, and ethics: Survey findings and implications. *Professional Psychology: Research and Practice, 30*, 165–172.

McMinn, M. R., Ellens, B. M., & Soref, E. (1999). Ethical perspectives and practice behaviors involving computer-based test interpretation. *Assessment, 6*, 71–77.

McNulty, J. L., Ben-Porath, Y. S., & Graham, J. R. (1998). An empirical examination of the correlates of well-defined and not-defined MMPI-2 code types. *Journal of Personality Assessment, 71*, 393–410.

McNulty, J. L., Graham, J. R., Ben-Porath, Y. S., & Stein, L. A. R. (1997). Comparative validity of MMPI-2 scores of African American and Caucasian mental health center clients. *Psychological Assessment, 9*, 464–470.

McShane, D. A., & Plas, J. M. (1984). The cognitive functioning of American Indian children: Moving from the WISC to the WISC-R. *School Psychology Review, 13*, 16–73.

Meehl, P. E. (1954). *Clinical versus statistical prediction: A theoretical analysis and a review of the evidence.* Minneapolis: University of Minnesota Press.

Meehl, P. E. (1965). Seer over sign: The first good example. *Journal of Experimental Research in Personality, 1*, 27–32.

Megargee, E. I. (1964). Undercontrol and overcontrol in assaultive and homicidal adolescents (Doctoral dissertation, University of California, Berkley, 1964). *Dissertation Abstracts International* (UMI No. 64–9923).

Megargee, E. I. (1965). Assault with intent to kill. *Trans-Action, 2*, 27–31.

Megargee, E. I. (1966). Undercontrolled and overcontrolled personality types in extreme anti-social aggression. *Psychological Monographs, 80*(611).

Megargee, E. I. (1972). *The California Psychological Inventory handbook.* San Francisco: Jossey-Bass.

Megargee, E. I. (1995). Assessing and understanding aggressive and violent patients. In J. Butcher (Ed.), *Clinical personality assessment: Practical approaches* (pp. 395–409). New York: Oxford University Press.

Megargee, E. I. (2002). *California Psychological Inventory handbook* (2nd ed.). San Francisco: Jossey-Bass.

Megargee, E. I., Cook, P. E., & Mendelsohn, G. A. (1967). Development and evaluation of an MMPI scale of assaultiveness in overcontrolled individuals. *Journal of Abnormal Psychology, 72*, 519–528.

Megargee, E. I., & Mendelsohn, G. A. (1962). A cross-validation of twelve MMPI indices of hostility and control. *Journal of Abnormal Psychology, 65*, 431–438.

Megargee, E. I., & Parker, G. V. (1968). An exploration of the equivalence of Murrayan needs as assessed by the Adjective Check List, the TAT, and the Edwards Personal Preference Schedule. *Journal of Clinical Psychology, 24*, 47–51.

Mehrabian, A. (1972). *Nonverbal communication.* Chicago: Aldine-Atherton.

Melzack, R. (1975). The McGill Pain Questionnaire: Major properties and scoring methods. *Pain, 1*, 277–299.

Mendez, F. (1978). *Adult Neuropsychological Questionnaire.* Odessa, FL: Psychological Assessment Resources.

Mendoza, J. (2001). Reporting the results of the neuropsychological evaluation. In_C. G. Armengol, E. Kaplan, & E. J. Moes (Eds.), *The consumer-oriented neuropsychological report* (pp. 95–122). Lutz, FL: Psychological Assessment Resources.

Mercer, J. R. (1979). In defense of racially and culturally non-discriminatory assessment. *School Psychology Digest, 8*, 89–115.

Mercer, J. R., & Lewis, J. F. (1978). *System of multicultural pluralistic assessment.* San Antonio, TX: Psychological Corporation.

Mermelstein, J. J. (1983). The relationship between rotation on the Bender-Gestalt Test and ratings of patient disorientation. *Journal of Personality Assessment, 47,* 490–491.

Messick, S. (1995). Validity of psychological assessment: Validation of inferences from persons' responses and performances as scientific inquiry into score meaning. *Psychological Assessment, 7,* 741–749.

Meyer, G. J. (1997). On the integration of personality assessment methods: The Rorschach and the MMPI. *Journal of Personality Assessment, 68,* 297–330.

Meyer, G. J. (2000). On the science of Rorschach research. *Journal of Personality Research, 75,* 46–81.

Meyer, G. J. (2001). Evidence to correct misperceptions about Rorschach norms. *Clinical Psychology: Research and Practice, 8,* 389–386.

Meyer, G. J. (2002). Exploring possible ethnic differences and bias in the Rorschach Comprehensive System. *Journal of Personality Assessment, 78,* 104–129.

Meyer, G. J. (2004). The reliability of the Rorschach and Thematic Apperception Test (TAT) compared to other psychological and medical procedures: An analysis of systematically gathered evidence. In M. J. Hilsenroth & D. Segal (Eds.), *Comprehensive handbook of psychological assessment* (Vol. 2, pp. 315–342). Hoboken, NJ: John Wiley & Sons.

Meyer, G. J. (2007, March). *Steps towards a lean, clean, assessment machine.* Paper presented at the annual meeting of the Society of Personality Assessment, Arlington, VA.

Meyer, G. J., & Archer, R. P. (2001). The hard science of Rorschach research: What do we know and where do we go? *Psychological Assessment, 13,* 486–502.

Meyer, G. J., Erdberg, P., & Shaffer, T. W. (2007). Towards international normative reference data for the Comprehensive System [Special issue]. *Journal of Personality Assessment, 89,* S201–S216.

Meyer, G. J., & Handler, L. (1997). The ability of the Rorschach to predict subsequent outcome: A meta-analysis of the Rorschach Prognostic Rating Scale. *Journal of Personality Assessment, 69,* 1–38.

Meyer, G. J., Hilsenroth, M. J., Baxter, D., Exner, J. E., Fowler, J. C., Piers, C. C., et al. (2002). An examination of interrater reliability for scoring the Rorschach Comprehensive System in eight data sets. *Journal of Personality Assessment, 78,* 219–274.

Meyer, G. J., Mihura, J., & Smith, B. (2005). The interclinician reliability of Rorschach interpretation in four data sets. *Journal of Personality Assessment, 84,* 296–314.

Meyer, P., & Davis, S. (1992). *The CPI applications guide: An essential tool for individual, group, and organizational development.* Palo Alto, CA: Consulting Psychologists Press.

Meyer, R. G. (1996). *The clinician's handbook: Integrated diagnostics, assessment and intervention in adult and adolescent psychopathology* (3rd ed.). Needham Heights, MA: Allyn & Bacon.

Meyers, J. E., & Meyers, K. R. (1996). *Rey Complex Figure Test and recognition trial: A professional manual.* Odessa, FL: Psychological Assessment Resources.

Michaels, M. (2007). *Professional guide to psychological report writing.* New York: Oxford University Press.

Mihura, J. (2008, March). *A review of the validity research on the Rorschach Comprehensive System variables.* Workshop presented at the Society for Personality Assessment conference, New Orleans, LA.

Milberg, W. P., Hebben, N., & Kaplan, E. (1996). The Boston Process Approach to neuropsychological assessment. In I. Grant & K. M. Adams (Eds.), *Neuropsychological assessment of neuropsychiatric disorders* (2nd ed., pp. 58–80). New York: Oxford University Press.

Miller, D. N. (2007). Projective techniques and the school-based assessment of childhood internalizing disorders: A critical analysis. *Journal of Projective Psychology and Mental Health, 14,* 48–58.

Miller, H. R., Streiner, D. L., & Parkinson, A. (1992). Maximum likelihood estimates of the ability of the MMPI and the MCMI personality disorder scales and the SIDP to identify personality disorders. *Journal of Personality Assessment, 59*, 1–13.

Miller, L. (1993, January/February). Toxic torts: Clinical neuropsychological and forensic aspects of chemical and electrical injuries. *Journal of Cognitive Rehabilitation, 11*, 6–18.

Millis, S. R., Malina, A. C., Bowers, D. A., & Ricker, J. H. (1999). Confirmatory factor analysis of the Wechsler Memory Scale-III. *Journal of Clinical and Experimental Neuropsychology, 21*, 87–93.

Millon, T. (1969). *Modern psychopathology: A biosocial approach to maladaptive learning and functioning.* Philadelphia: Saunders.

Millon, T. (1977). *Millon Clinical Multiaxial Inventory.* Minneapolis, MN: National Computer Systems.

Millon, T. (1987). *Manual for the MCMI-II* (2nd ed.). Minneapolis, MN: National Computer Systems.

Millon, T. (1992). Millon Clinical Multiaxial Inventory: I & II. *Journal of Counseling and Development, 70*, 422–426.

Millon, T. (1993). *The MACI manual.* Minneapolis, MN: National Computer Systems.

Millon, T. (1994). *Manual for the MCMI-III.* Minneapolis, MN: National Computer Systems.

Millon, T. (1997). *Millon Clinical Multiaxial Inventory-III manual* (2nd ed.). Minneapolis, MN: National Computer Systems.

Millon, T. (1999). *Personality guided therapy.* New York: John Wiley & Sons.

Millon, T., & Bloom, C. (2008). *Millon inventories: Personality guided assessment.* New York: Guilford Press.

Millon, T., & Davis, R. D. (1996). *Disorders of personality: DSM-IV and beyond* (2nd ed.). New York: John Wiley & Sons.

Millon, T., Green, C. J., & Meagher, R. B. (2000). *Manual for the Millon Behavioral Health Inventory.* Minneapolis, MN: National Computer Systems.

Millon, T., Millon, C., Davis, R., & Grossman, S. (2006). *MCMI-III Manual* (3rd ed.). Minneapolis, MN: NCS Pearson.

Mills, C. J., & Bohannon, W. E. (1980). Personality characteristics of effective state police officers. *Journal of Applied Psychology, 65*, 680–684.

Milne, D. (1984). Improving the social validity and implementation of behavior therapy training for psychiatric nurses using a patient-centered learning format. *British Journal of Clinical Psychology, 23*, 313–314.

Mischel, W. (1968). Personality and assessment. New York: John Wiley & Sons.

Mitrushina, M., Boone, K., Razani, J., & D'Elia, L. F. (2005). *Handbook of normative data for neuropsychological assessment* (2nd ed.). New York: Oxford University Press.

Mittenberg, W., Hammeke, T. A., & Rao, S. M. (1989). Intrasubtest scatter on the WAIS-R as a pathognomonic sign of brain injury. *Psychological Assessment, 1*, 273–276.

Mittenberg, W., Patton, C., Canyock, E. M., & Condit, D. C. (2002). Base rates of malingering and symptom exaggeration. *Journal of Clinical and Experimental Neuropsychology, 24*, 1094–1102.

Mizes, J. S., & Christiano, B. A. (1994). Assessment of cognitive variables relevant to cognitive behavioral perspectives on anorexia nervosa and bulimia nervosa. *Behavior Research and Therapy, 33*, 95–105.

Mizushima, K., & DeVos, G. (1967). An application of the California Psychological Inventory in a study of Japanese delinquency. *Journal of Clinical Psychology, 71*, 45–51.

Mohr, D. C. (1995). The role of proscription in psychotherapy. *Psychotherapy, 32*, 187–193.

Molish, H. B. (1967). Critique and problems of the Rorschach: A survey. In S. J. Beck & H. B. Molish (Eds.), *Rorschach's test. Vol. 2: A variety of personality pictures* (2nd ed., pp. 45–48). New York: Grune & Stratton.

Monahan, J., & Steadman, H. J. (2001). Violence risk assessment: A quarter century of research. In L. E. Frost & R. J. Bonnie (Eds.), *The evolution of mental health law* (pp. 195–211). Washington, DC: American Psychological Association.

Monahan, J., Steadman, H. J., Appelbaum, P. S., Robbins, P. C., Mulvey, E. P., Silver, E., et al. (2000). Developing a clinically useful actuarial tool for assessing violence risk. *British Journal of Psychiatry, 176*, 312–319.

Moon, G. W., Blakey, W. A., Gorsuch, R. L., & Fantuzzo, J. W. (1991). Frequent WAIS-R administration errors: An ignored source of inaccurate measurement. *Professional Psychology, 22*, 256–258.

Moon, G. W., Fantuzzo, J. W., & Gorsuch, R. L. (1986). Teaching WAIS-R administration skills: Comparison of the MASTERY model to other existing clinical training modalities. *Professional Psychology, 17*, 31–35.

Moos, R. H. (1990). Depressed patients' life context, amount of treatment, and treatment outcome. *Journal of Nervous and Mental Diseases, 178*, 105–112.

Morena, D. (1981). The healthy drawing. In G. Groth-Marnat & D. Morena (Eds.), *Handbook of psychological assessment* (pp. 80–85). Unpublished manuscript.

Moretti, R. J., & Rossini, E. D. (2004). The Thematic Apperception Test. In M. J. Hilsenroth & D. L. Segal (Eds.) *Comprehensive handbook of psychological assessment, Vol. 2: Personality assessment* (pp. 356–371). Hoboken, NJ: John Wiley & Sons.

Morey, L. C., Blashfield, R. K., Webb, W. W., & Jewell, J. (1988). MMPI scales for DSM-III personality disorders: A preliminary validation study. *Journal of Clinical Psychology, 44*, 47–50.

Morgan, C. D., & Murray, H. A. (1935). A method for investigating fantasies. *AMA Archives of Neurology and Psychiatry, 34*, 389–406.

Morgan, C. D., Schoenberg, M. R., Dorr, D., & Burke, M. J. (2002). Overreport on the MCMI-III: Concurrent validation with the MMPI-2 using a psychiatric inpatient sample. *Journal of Personality Assessment, 78*, 288–300.

Morgan, G., Gliner, J. A., & Harmon, R. J. (2001). Measurement validity. *Journal of the American Academy of Child and Adolescent Psychiatry, 40*, 729–731.

Morlan, K. K., & Tan, S.-Y. (1998). Comparison of the Brief Psychiatric Rating Scale and the Brief Symptom Inventory. *Journal of Clinical Psychology, 54*, 885–894.

Morris, J. C., Heyman, A., Mohs, R. C., Hughes, J. P., van Belle, G., Fillenbaum, G., et al. (1989). The consortium to establish a registry for Alzheimer's disease (CERAD). Part 1: Clinical and neuropsychological assessment of Alzheimer's disease. *Neurology, 39*, 1159–1165.

Morrow, L. A., Furman, J. M. R., Ryan, C. M., & Hodgson, M. J. (1988). Neuropsychological deficits associated with verbatim abnormalities in solvent exposed workers. *Clinical Neuropsychologist, 2*, 272–273.

Moser, R. S., & Schatz, P. (2002). Enduring effects of concussion in youth athletes. *Archives of Clinical Neuropsychology, 17*, 91–100.

Moser, R. S., Schatz, P., & Jordan, B. D. (2005). Prolonged effects of concussion in high school atheletes. *Neurosurgery, 57*, 300–306.

Mostofsky, D., & Barlow, D. H. (2000). *The management of stress and anxiety in medical disorders.* Needham Heights, MA: Allyn & Bacon.

Mueller, H. H., Dash, V. N., Matheson, D. W., & Short, R. H. (1984). WISC-R subtest patterning of below average, average, and above average I.Q. children: A meta-analysis. *Alberta Journal of Educational Research, 30*, 68–85.

Mulvey, E., & Cauffman, E. (2001). The inherent limits of predicting school violence. *American Psychologist, 56*, 797–802.

Munley, P. H. (1991). Confidence intervals for the MMPI-2. *Journal of Personality Assessment, 57*, 52–60.

Murdoch, B. E., Chenery, H. J., Wilks, V., & Boyle, R. S. (1987). Language disorder in dementia of the Alzheimer's type. *Brain and Language, 31*, 122–137.

Murphy, J. M., Monson, R. R., Laird, N. M., Sobol, A. M., & Leighton, A. H. (2000). A comparison of diagnostic interviews for depression in the Stirling County Study: Challenges for psychiatric epidemiology. *Archives of General Psychiatry, 57*, 230–236.

Murphy, L. L., Spies, R. A., & Plake, B. S. (Eds.). (2006). *Tests in print VII.* Lincoln, NE: Buros Institute of Mental Measurements.

Murphy, M.J., Levant, R.G., Hall, J.E., & Glueckauf, R.L. (2007). Distance Education in Professional Training in Psychology. *Professional Psychology: Research and Practice, 38*, 97–103.

Murray, H. A. (1938). *Explorations in personality.* New York: Oxford University Press.

Murray, H. A. (1943). *Thematic Apperception Test manual.* Cambridge, MA: Harvard University Press.

Naglieri, J. A. (1993). Pairwise and ipsative comparisons of WISC-III IQ and index scores. *Psychological Assessment, 5*, 113–116.

Naglieri, J. A. (1999). *Essentials of CAS assessment.* New York: John Wiley & Sons.

Naglieri, J. A., & Das, J. P. (1997). *Cognitive Assessment System Administration and Scoring manual.* Itasca, IL: Riverside.

Nathan, P. E., & Gorman, J. M. (Eds.). (1998). *A guide to treatments that work.* New York: Oxford University Press.

Neale, M. D., & McKay, M. F. (1985). Scoring the Bender-Gestalt Test using the Koppitz Developmental System: Interrater reliability, item difficulty, and scoring implications. *Perceptual and Motor Skills, 60*, 627–636.

Neisser, U., Boodoo, G., Bouchard, T. J., Boykin, A. W., Brody, N., Ceci, S. J., et al. (1996). Intelligence: Knowns and unknowns. *American Psychologist, 51*, 77–101.

Nelson, H. E., & Williams, J. R. (1991). *National Adult Reading Test (NART): Test manual.* Windsor, England: NFER-Nelson.

Nelson, J. R., Roberts, M. L., Rutherford, R. B., Mathur, S. R., & Aaroe, L. A. (1999). A statewide survey of special education administrators and school psychologists regarding functional behavioral assessment. *Education and Treatment of Children, 22*, 267–279.

Nelson, N. W., Sweet, J. J., & Demakis, G. J. (2006). Meta-analysis of the MMPI-2 Fake Bad Scale: Utility in forensic practice. *Clinical Neuropsychologist, 20*, 39–58.

Nelson, R. E., & Maser, J. D. (1988). The DSM-III and depression: Potential contributions of behavioral assessment. *Behavioral Assessment, 10*, 45–66.

Nelson-Gray, R. O., & Farmer, R. F. (1999). Behavioral assessment of personality disorders. *Behavior Research and Therapy, 37*, 347–368.

Nelson-Gray, R. O., & Paulson, J. (2004). Behavioral assessment and the *DSM system.* In S. N. Haynes & E. M. Heiby (Eds.), *Comprehensive handbook of psychological assessment. Behavioral assessment* (Vol. 3, pp. 470–488). Hoboken, NJ: John Wiley & Sons.

Newman, F. L., Ciarlo, J. A., & Carpenter, D. (1999). Guidelines for selecting psychological instruments for treatment planning and outcome assessment. In M. E. Maruish (Ed.), *The use of psychological testing for treatment planning and outcomes assessment* (pp. 153–170). Mahwah, NJ: Lawrence Erlbaum.

Nezu, A. M., Nezu, C. M., Peacock, M. A., & Girdwood, C. P. (2004). Case formulation in cognitive-behavior therapy. In S. N. Haynes & E. M. Heiby (Eds.), *Comprehensive handbook of psychological assessment. Behavioral assessment* (Vol. 3, pp. 402–426). Hoboken, NJ: John Wiley & Sons.

Nguyen, L., Huang, L. N., Arganza, G. F., Liao, Q. (2007). The influence of race and ethnicity on psychiatric diagnoses and clinical characteristics of children and adolescents in children's services. *Cultural Diversity and Ethnic Minority Psychology, 13*, 18–25.

Nicholi, A. M. (1978). History and mental status. In A. M. Nicholi (Ed.), *The Harvard guide to modern psychiatry.* Cambridge, MA: Harvard University Press.

Niec, L. N., & Russ, S. W. (2002). Children's internal representations, empathy, and fantasy play: A validity study of the SCORS-Q. *Psychological Assessment, 14*, 331–338.

Nishiyama, T. (1973). Cross cultural invariance of the California Psychological Inventory, *Psychologia, 16*, 75–84.

Norcross, J. C. (1997). Emerging breakthroughs in psychotherapy integration: Three predictions and one fantasy. *Psychotherapy, 34*, 86–90.

Norcross, J. C. (Ed.). (2002). *Psychotherapy relationships that work: Therapist contributions and responsiveness to patient's needs.* New York: Oxford University Press.

Norcross, J. C. (2006). Integrating self-help into psychotherapy: 16 practical suggestions. *Professional Psychology: Research & Practice, 37*, 683–693.

Norcross, J. C., & Beutler, L. E. (1997). Determining the therapeutic relationship of choice in brief therapy. In J. N. Butcher (Ed.), *Objective psychological assessment in managed health care: A practitioner's guide* (pp. 42–60). New York: Oxford University Press.

Norcross, J. C., Santrock, J. W., Campbell, L. F., Smith, T. P., Sommer, R., & Zuckerman, E. L. (2003). *Authoritative guide to self-help resources in mental health.* New York: Guilford Press.

Oakland, T. D. (1980). An evaluation of the ABIC, pluralistic norms, and estimated learning potential. *Journal of School Psychology, 18*, 3–11.

Oas, P. (1984). Validity of the Draw-A-Person and Bender Gestalt as measures of impulsivity with adolescents. *Journal of Counsulting and Clinical Psychology, 52*, 1011–1019.

Ober, B. A., Koss, E., Friedland, R. P., & Delis, D. C. (1985). Processes of verbal memory failure in Alzheimer-type dementia. *Brain and Cognition, 4*, 90–103.

O'Brien, W. H., Kaplar, M. E., & McGrath, J. J. (2004). Broadly based causal models of behavior disorders. In S. N. Haynes & E. M. Heiby (Eds.), *Comprehensive handbook of psychological assessment. Behavioral assessment* (Vol. 3, pp. 69–93). Hoboken, NJ: John Wiley & Sons.

Obrzut, J. E., & Cummings, J. A. (1983). The projective approach to personality assessment: An analysis of thematic picture techniques. *School Psychology Review, 12*, 414–420.

Office of Science and Technology. (1967). *Privacy and behavioral research.* Washington, DC: U.S. Government Printing Office.

Office of Strategic Services Staff. (1948). *Assessment of men.* New York: Holt, Rinehart and Winston.

Okun, A., Stein, R. K., Bauman, L. J., & Silver, E. J. (1996). Content validity of the Psychiatric Symptom Index, CES Depression Scale, and State-Trait Anxiety Inventory from the perspective of DSM-IV. *Psychological Reports, 79*, 1059–1069.

Ollendick, T. H. (1978). *The Fear Survey Schedule for Children—Revised.* Unpublished manuscript, Indiana State University, Terre Haute.

Ollendick, T. H. (1983). Reliability and validity of the revised Fear Survey Schedule for Children (FSSC-R). *Behavior Research and Therapy, 21*, 685–692.

Ollendick, T., Alvarez, H. K., & Greene, R. W. (2004). Behavioral assessment: History of underlying concepts and methods. In S. N. Haynes & E. M. Heiby (Eds.), *Comprehensive handbook of psychological assessment. Behavioral assessment* (Vol. 3, pp. 19–34). Hoboken, NJ: John Wiley & Sons.

Orne, M. T. (1962). On the social psychology of the psychological experiment: With particular reference to demand characteristics and their implications. *American Psychologist, 17*, 766–783.

Osman, A., Downs, W., Barrios, F. X., Kopper, B. A., Gutierrez, P. M., & Chiros, C. E. (1997). Factor structure and psychometric characteristics of the Beck Depression Inventory-III. Journal of Psychopathology and Behavioral Assessment, *19*, 359–376.

Osman, A., Kopper, B. A., Barrios, F., Gutierrez, P. M., & Bagge, C. L. (2004). Reliability and validity of the Beck Depression Inventory-II with adolescent psychiatric inpatients. *Psychological Assessment, 16*, 120–132.

Osterrith, P. A. (1944). Le test de copie d'une figure complexe. *Archives de Psychologie, 30*, 206–356.

Othmer, E., & Othmer, S. C. (2002). *The clinical interview using DSM-IV. Vol. 1: Fundamentals.* Washington, DC: American Psychiatric Press.

Otto, R. K., & Heilbrun, K. (2002). The practice of forensic psychology: A look toward the future in light of the past. *American Psychologist, 57*, 5–10.

Ownby, R. L. (1990). A study of the expository process model in mental health settings. *Journal of Clinical Psychology, 46*, 366–371.

Ownby, R. L. (1997). *Psychological reports: A guide to report writing in professional psychology* (3rd ed.). Brandon, VT: Clinical Psychology.

Ownby, R. L., & Wallbrown, F. H. (1983). Evaluating school psychological reports. Part I: A procedure for systematic feedback. *Psychology in the Schools, 20*, 41–45.

Pachet, A. (2007). Construct validity of the Repeatable Battery of Neuropsychological Status (RBANS) with acquired brain injury patient. *Clinical Neuropsychologist, 21*, 286–297.

Page, H. A. (1957). Studies in fantasy-daydreaming frequency and Rorschach scoring categories. *Journal of Consulting Psychology, 21*, 111–114.

Palmer, B. W., Boone, K. B., Lesser, I. M., & Wohl, M. A. (1998). Base rates of "impaired" neuropsychological test performance among healthy older adults. *Archives of Clinical Neuropsychology, 13*, 503–511.

Pancoast, D. L., & Archer, R. P. (1988). MMPI adolescent norms: Patterns and trends across four decades. *Journal of Personality Assessment, 52*, 691–706.

Pantle, M. L., Ebner, D. L., & Hynan, L. S. (1994). The Rorschach and the assessment of impulsivity. *Journal of Clinical Psychology, 50*, 633–638.

Panzarella, C., Alloy, L., & Whitehouse, W. G. (2006). Extended hopelessness theory of depression: On the mechanisms by which social support protects against depression. *Cognitive Therapy and Depression, 30*, 307–333.

Parker, K. C. H. (1983). A meta-analysis of the reliability and validity of the Rorschach. *Journal of Personality Assessment, 47*, 227–231.

Parker, K. C. H., Hanson, R. K., & Hunsley, J. (1988). MMPI, Rorschach, and WAIS: A meta-analytic comparison of reliability, stability, and validity. *Psychological Bulletin, 103*, 367–373.

Parks, C. W. (1982). *A multi-dimensional view of the imagery construct: Issues of definition and assessment.* Unpublished manuscript.

Parks, C. W., & Hollon, S. D. (1988). Cognitive assessment. In A. S. Bellack &_M. Hersen (Eds.), *Behavioral assessment: A practical handbook* (3rd ed., pp. 161–212). New York: Pergamon Press.

Parks, R. W., Loewenstein, D. A., Dodrill, K. L., Barker, W. W., Yoshii, F., Chang, J. Y., et al. (1988). Cerebral metabolic effects of a verbal fluency test: A PET scan study. *Journal of Clinical and Experimental Neuropsychology, 10*, 565–575.

Pascal, G. R., & Suttell, B. J. (1951). *The Bender Gestalt Test: Quantification and validity for adults.* New York: Grune & Stratton.

Patterson, C. H. (1989). Foundations for a systematic eclectic psychotherapy. *Psychotherapy, 26*, 427–435.

Patton, D. E., Duff, K., Schoenberg, M. R., Mold, J., Scott, J. G., & Adams, R. (2003). Performance of cognitively normal African Americans on the RBANS in community dwelling older adults. *Clinical Neuropsychologist, 17*, 515–530.

Paul, G. L. (1967). Behavior modification research: Design and tactics. In C. M. Franks (Ed.), *Handbook of psychotherapy integration* (pp. 300–334). New York: Basic Books.

Paunonen, S. V., & Ashton, M. C. (1998). The structured assessment of personality across cultures. *Journal of Cross-Cultural Psychology, 29*, 150–170.

Pearson (2009a). Wechsler Memory Scale—Fourth Edition technical and interpretive manual. San Antonio, TX: Author

Pearson (2009b). Wechsler Memory Scale—Fourth Edition administration and scoring manual. San Antonio, TX: Author.

Pearson (2009c). *WAIS-IV/WMS-IV Advanced clinical solutions.* San Antonio, TX: NCS Pearson, Inc. San Antonio, TX: NCS Pearson, Inc.

Pekarik, G., & Wolff, C. B. (1996). Relationship of satisfaction to symptom change, follow-up adjustment, and clinical significance. *Professional Psychology: Research and Practice, 27*, 202–208.

Penley, J. S., Wiebe, J. S., & Nwosu, A. (2003). Psychometric properties of the Spanish Beck Depression Inventory-II in a medical sample. *Psychological Assessment, 15*, 569–577.

Pennebaker, J. W., & King, L. A. (1999). Linguistic styles: Language use as an individual difference. *Journal of Personality and Social Psychology, 77*, 1296–1312.

Pennebaker, J. W., & Seagal, J. D. (1999). Forming a story: The health benefits of narrative. *Journal of Clinical Psychology, 55*, 1243–1254.

Perez, R. G., Ascaso, E. E., Massons, J. M. D., & Chaparro, N. (1998). Characteristics of the subject and interview influencing the test-retest reliability of the Diagnostic Interview for Children and Adolescents—Revised. *Journal of Child Psychology and Psychiatry, 39*, 963–972.

Perkins, D. N., & Grotzer, T. A. (1997). Teaching intelligence. *American Psychologist, 52*, 1125–1133.

Perry, J. C. (1992). Problems and considerations in the valid assessment of personality disorders. *American Journal of Psychiatry, 149*, 1645–1653.

Perry, W., Sprock, J., Schaible, D., McDougall, A., Minassian, A., Jenkins, M., et al. (1995). Amphetamine use on Rorschach measures in normal subjects. *Journal of Personality Assessment, 64*, 456–465.

Persons, J. B., Mooney, K., & Padesky, C. A. (1995). Interrater reliability of cognitive behavioral case formulations. *Cognitive Therapy and Research, 19*, 21–34.

Petrocelli, J. V. (2002). Processes and stages of change: Counseling with the transtheoretical model of change. *Journal of Counseling and Development, 80*, 22–30.

Peveler, R. C., & Fairburn, C. G. (1990). Measurement of neurotic symptoms by self report questionnaire: Validity of the SCL-90-R. *Psychological Medicine, 20*, 873–879.

Pfeifer, C., & Sedlacek, W. (1971). The validity of academic predictors for black and white students at a predominantly white university. *Journal of Educational Measurement, 8*, 253–261.

Piasecki, T. M., Hufford, M. R., Solhan, M., & Trull, T. J. (2007). Assessing clients in their natural environments with electronic diaries: Rationale, benefits, limitations, and barriers. *Psychological Assessment, 19*, 25–43.

Piedmont, R. L., Sokolov, R. L., & Flemming, M. Z. (1989a). An examination of some diagnostic strategies involving the Wechsler intelligence scales. *Psychological Assessment, 1*, 181–185.

Piedmont, R. L., Sokolov, R. L., & Flemming, M. Z. (1989b). On WAIS-R Difference Scores in a psychiatric population. *Psychological Assessment, 1*, 155–159.

Piersma, H. L. (1986). The stability of the Millon Clinical Multiaxial Inventory for psychiatric patients. *Journal of Personality Assessment, 50*, 193–197.

Piersma, H. L., Boes, J. L., & Reaume, W. M. (1994). Unidimensionality of the Brief Symptom Inventory (BSI) in adult and adolescent inpatients. *Journal of Personality Assessment, 63*, 338–344.

Pilowski, I., Spence, N., Cobb, J., & Katsikitis, M. (1984). The Illness Behavior Questionnaire as an aid in clinical assessment. *General Hospital Psychiatry, 6*, 123–130.

Pincus, H.A., Pechura, C., Keyser, D., Bachman, J., & Houtsinger, J. K. (2006). Depression in primary care: Learning lessons in national quality improvement. *Administration and Policy in Mental Health and Mental Health Services Research, 33*, 2–15.

Piotrowski, C. (1984). The status of projective techniques: Or, "Wishing won't make it go away." *Journal of Clinical Psychology, 40*, 1495–1502.

Piotrowski, C. (1996). Use of the Beck Depression Inventory in clinical practice. *Psychological Reports, 6*, 74–82.

Piotrowski, C. (1999). Assessment practices in the era of managed care: Current status and future directions. *Journal of Clinical Psychology, 55*, 787–796.

Piotrowski, C., & Keller, J. W. (1984). Psychodiagnostic testing in APA-approved clinical psychology programs. *Professional Psychology: Research and Practice, 15*, 450–456.

Piotrowski, C., & Keller, J. W. (1989). Psychological testing in outpatient mental health facilities: A national study. *Professional Psychology: Research and Practice, 20*, 423–425.

Piotrowski, C., & Zalewski, C. (1993). Training in psychodiagnostic testing in APA-approved PsyD and PhD clinical training programs. *Journal of Personality Assessment, 61*, 394–405.

Piotrowski, Z. A. (1937). The Rorschach Ink-Blot Method in organic disturbances of the central nervous system. *Journal of Nervous and Mental Disorders, 86*, 525–537.

Piotrowski, Z. A. (1957). *Perceptanalysis.* New York: Macmillan.

Piotrowski, Z. A. (1960). The movement score. In M. Rickers-Ovsiankina (Ed.), *Rorschach psychology* (pp. 49–58). New York: John Wiley & Sons.

Plake, B. S., Impara, J. C., & Spies, R. A. (2003). Fifteenth Mental Measurements Yearbook. Lincoln, NE: Buros Institute.

Ponsford, J. L. (1988). Neuropsychological assessment: The need for a more pragmatic approach. *Australian Psychologist, 23*, 349–360.

Ponsford, J. L. (2000). Attention. In G. Groth-Marnat (Ed.), *Neuropsychological assessment in clinical practice: A guide to test interpretation and integration* (pp. 355–400). Hoboken, NJ: John Wiley & Sons.

Pope, K. S. (1992). Responsibilities in providing psychological test feedback to clients. *Psychological Assessment, 4*, 268–271.

Pope, K. S. (2007). Informed consent in psychotherapy and counseling: Forms, standards, guidelines, and references. Retrieved November 2, 2007, from http://kspope.com/consent/index.php.

Pope, K. S. (2007). Responsibilities in providing psychological test feedback to clients. Retrieved November 2, 2007, from http://kspope.com/assess/feedabs1.php.

Pope, K. S., Butcher, J. N., & Seelen, J. (2000). *The MMPI, MMPI-2 and MMPI-A in court: A practical guide for expert witnesses and attorneys* (2nd ed.). Washington, DC: American Psychological Association.

Porter, E. H. (1950). *An introduction to therapeutic counseling.* Boston: Houghton-Mifflin.

Poythres, N., Nicholson, R., Otto, R. K., Edens, J. F., Bonnie, R. J., & Monahan, J., et al. (1999). *The MacArthur Competence Assessment Tool-Criminal Adjudication: Professional Manual.* Odessa, FL: Psychological Assessment Resources.

Presley, G., Smith, C., Hilsenroth, M., & Exner, J. (2001). Rorschach validity with African Americans. *Journal of Personality Assessment, 77*, 491–507.

Preston, J., O'Neal, J. H., & Talaga, M. C. (2005). *Handbook of clinical psychopharmacology for therapists* (4th ed.). Oakland, CA: New Harbinger.

Pretzer, J. L., Epstein, N., & Fleming, B. (1992). The Marital Attitude Survey: A measure of dysfunctional attitudes and expectancies. *Journal of Cognitive Psychotherapy, 5*, 131–148.

Price, L., Tulsky, D., Millis, S., & Weiss, L. (2002). Redefining the factor structure of the Wechsler Memory Scale-III: Confirmatory factor analysis with cross validation. *Journal of Clinical and Experimental Neuropsychology, 24*, 574–585.

Prigatano, G. P. (1986). *Neuropsychological rehabilitation after brain injury.* Baltimore, MD: Johns Hopkins University Press.

Prigatano, G. P. (1987). Personality and psychosocial consequences after brain injury. In M. Meir, A. Benton, & L. Diller (Eds.), *Neuropsychological rehabilitation* (pp. 335–378). New York: Plenum Press.

Prigatano, G. P. (1992). Personality disturbance associated with traumatic brain injury. *Journal of Consulting and Clinical Psychology, 60*, 360–368.

Prigatano, G. P. (1999). Impaired awareness, finger tapping, and rehabilitation outcome after brain injury. *Rehabilitation Psychology, 44*, 145–159.

Prigatano, G. P., Amin, K., & Rosenstein, L. D. (1992a). *Manual for the BNI Screen for Higher Cerebral Functions.* Phoenix, AZ: Barrow Neurological Institute.

Prigatano, G. P., Amin, K., & Rosenstein, L. D. (1992b). Validity studies of the BNI Screen for Higher Cerebral Functions. *Barrow Neurological Institute Quarterly, 9*, 2–9.

Prince, J. P., & Heisser, L. J. (2000). *Essentials of career interest assessment.* Hoboken, NJ: John Wiley & Sons.

Prochaska, J. O. (2000). Change at differing stages. In C. R. Snyder & R. E. Ingram (Eds.), Handbook of psychological change: Psychotherapy processes and practices for the 21st century (pp. 109–127). Hoboken, NJ: John Wiley & Sons.

Prochaska, J. O., & DiClemente, C. C. (1984). The transtheoretical approach: Crossing the traditional boundaries of therapy. Homewood, IL: Dow Jones-Irwin.

Prochaska, J. O., & DiClemente, C. C. (2005). The transtheoretical approach. In J. C. Norcross & M. R. Goldfried (Eds.), *Handbook of psychotherapy integration* (pp. 147–171; 2nd ed., pp. 300–334). New York: Oxford University Press.

Prochaska, J. O., DiClemente, C. C., & Norcross, J. C. (1992). In search of how people change: Applications to addictive behaviors. *American Psychologist, 47*, 1102–1114.

Prochaska, J. O., Norcross, J. C., & DiClemente, C. C. (1994). *Changing for good.* New York: Morrow.

Prochaska, J. O., Rossi, J. S., & Wilcox, N. S. (1991). Change processes and psychotherapy outcome in integrative case research. *Journal of Psychotherapy Integration, 1*, 103–120.

Pruitt, J. A., Smith, M. C., Thelen, M. H., & Lubin, B. (1985). Attitudes of academic clinical psychologists toward projective techniques: 1968–1983. *Professional Psychology: Research and Practice, 16*, 781–788.

Psychological Corporation. (1997). *WAIS-III/WMS-III technical manual.* San Antonio, TX: Psychological Corporation.

Psychological Corporation. (1999). *Wechsler Abbreviated Scale of Intelligence.* San Antonio, TX: Author.

Psychological Corporation (2001). Wechsler Individual Achievement Test (2nd ed.). San Antonio, TX: Psychological Corporation.

Psychological Corporation. (2002). *Technical manual for the WPPSI-III.* San Antonio, TX: Psychological Corporation.

Pugh, G. (1985). The California Psychological Inventory and police selection. *Journal of Police Science and Administration, 13*, 172–177.

Puig-Antich, J., & Chambers, W. (1978). *The schedule for affective disorders and schizophrenia for school aged children.* New York: New York State Psychiatric Institute.

Putzke, J. D., Williams, M. A., Daniel, F. J., & Boll, T. (1999). The utility of K-Correction to adjust for defensive response set on the MMPI. *Assessment, 6*, 61–70.

Query, W. T. (1966). CPI factors and success of seminary students. *Psychological Reports, 18*, 665–660.

Quillan, J., Besing, S., & Dinning, D. (1977). Standardization of the Rathus Assertiveness Schedule. *Journal of Clinical Psychology, 33*, 418–422.

Rabin, L. A., Barr, W. B., & Burton, L. A. (2005). Assessment practices of clinical neuropsychologists in the United States and Canada: A survey of INS, NAN, and APA division 40 members. *Archives of Clinical Psychology, 20*, 33–65.

Randolph, C. (1998). *Repeatable Battery for the Assessment of Neuropsychological Status manual.* San Antonio, TX: The Psychological Corporation.

Rao, S. M. (1990). Neuroimaging correlates of cognitive dysfunction. In S. M. Rao (Ed.), *Neurobehavioral aspects of multiple sclerosis* (pp. 118–135). New York: Oxford University Press.

Rapaport, C., Gill, M., & Schafer, J. (1968). *Diagnostic psychological testing* (Vol. 1, rev. ed.). Chicago: Year Book.

Rapport, L. J., Webster, J. S. & Dutra, R. L. (1994). Digit Span performance and unilateral neglect. *Neuropsychologia, 32*, 517–525.

Rathus, S. A. (1972). An experimental investigation of assertive training in a group setting. *Journal of Behavior Therapy and Experimental Psychiatry, 3*, 81–86.

Rathus, S. A. (1973). A 30-item schedule for assessing assertive behavior. *Behavior Therapy, 4*, 398–406.

Rathus, S. A., & Nevid, J. S. (1977). Concurrent validity of the 30-item assertiveness schedule with a psychiatric population. *Behavior Therapy, 8*, 393–397.

Redfering, D. L., & Collings, J. (1982). A comparison of the Koppitz and Hutt techniques of Bender-Gestalt administration correlated with WISC-R performance scores. *Educational and Psychological Measurement, 42*, 41–47.

Rees, L. M., Tombaugh, T. N., Gansler, D. A., & Moczynski, N. P. (1998). Five validation experiments of the Test of Memory Malingering (TOMM). *Psychological Assessment, 10*, 10–20.

Reich, J. H., & Noyes, R. (1987). A comparison of DSM-III personality disorders in acutely ill panic and depressed patients. *Journal of Anxiety Disorders, 1*, 123–131.

Reich, W. (2000). Diagnostic Interview for Children and Adolescents (DICA). *Journal of the Academy of Child and Adolescent Psychiatry, 39*, 59–66.

Reichenberg, N., & Raphael, A. R. (1992). *Advanced psychodiagnostic interpretation of the Bender Gestalt Test.* New York: Praeger.

Reid, D. B., & Kelly, M. P. (1993). Wechsler Memory Scale-Revised in closed head injury. *Journal of Clinical Psychology, 49*, 245–254.

Reinecke, M. A., Beebe, D. W., & Stein, M. A. (1999). The third factor of the WISC-III: Its (probably) not freedom from distractibility. *Journal of the American Academy of Child and Adolescent Psychiatry, 38*, 322–328.

Reitan, R. M. (1955a). Certain differential effects of left and right cerebral lesions in human adults. *Journal of Comparative and Physiological Psychology, 48*, 474–477.

Reitan, R. M. (1955b). Validity of the Rorschach Test as a measure of the psychological effects of brain damage. *Archives of Neurology and Psychiatry, 73*, 445–451.

Reitan, R. M. (1974a). Methodological problems in clinical neuropsychology. In R. M. Reitan & L. A. Davison (Eds.), *Clinical neuropsychology: Current status and applications* (pp.19–46). New York: John Wiley & Sons.

Reitan, R. M. (1974b). Psychological effects of cerebral lesions in children of early school age. In R. M. Reitan & L. A. Davison (Eds.), *Clinical neuropsychology: Current status and applications* (pp. 53–90). Washington, DC: Winston & Sons.

Reitan, R. M., & Wolfson, D. (1985). *The Halsted-Reitan Neuropsychological Test Battery: Theory and clinical interpretation.* Tucson, AZ: Tucson Neuropsychology Press.

Reitan, R. M., & Wolfson, D. (1992). *Neuropsychological education of older children.* Tucson, AZ: Neuropsychology Press.

Reitan, R. M., & Wolfson, D. (1993). *The Halstead-Reitan Neuropsychological Test Battery: Theory and clinical interpretation* (2nd ed.). Tucson, AZ: Neuropsychology Press.

Repapi, M., Gough, H., Lanning, K., & Stefanis, C. (1983). Predicitng academic achievment of Greek secondary school students from family background and California Psychological Inventory scores. *Conemporary Educational Psychology, 8*, 181–188.

Retief, A. (1987). Thematic appercetion testing across cultures: Tests of selection versus tests of inclusion. *South African Journal of Psychology, 17*, 47–55.

Retzlaff, P. D. (1995). *Tactical psychotherapy of the personality disorders: An MCMI-III-based approach.* Boston: Allyn & Bacon.

Retzlaff, P. D., & Dunn, T. (2003). The Millon Clinical Multiaxial Inventory. In L. E. Beutler & G. Groth-Marnat (Eds.), *Integrative assessment of adult personality* (pp. 192–226). New York: Guilford Press.

Retzlaff, P. D., Lorr, M., & Hyer, L. (1989). *An MCMI-II item-level component analysis: Personality and clinical factors.* Unpublished manuscript.

Retzlaff, P. D., Sheehan, E. P., & Fiel, A. (1991). MCMI-II report style and bias: Profile and validity scales analysis. *Journal of Personality Assessment, 56,* 478–486.

Rey, A. (1941). Psychological examination of traumatic encephalopathy. *Archives de Psychologie, 28,* 286–340.

Rey, A. (1964). *The clinical exam in psychology.* Paris: Presses Universitaires de France.

Reynolds, C. R. (1986). Wide Range Achievement Test (WRAT-R), 1984 edition. *Journal of Counseling and Development, 64,* 540–541.

Reynolds, C. R. (2000). Why is psychometric research on bias in mental testing so often ignored? *Psychology, Public Policy, and Law, 6,* 144–150.

Reynolds, C. R. (2007). *The Koppitz Developmental System for the Bender Gestalt Test, (2nd ed.).* Austin, TX: Pro-Ed.

Reynolds, C. R., Chastain, R. L., Kaufman, A. S., & McLean, J. E. (1987). Demographic characteristics and IQ among adults: Analysis of the WAIS-R standardization sample as a function of the stratification variables. *Journal of School Psychology, 25,* 323–324.

Reynolds, C. R., & Hartlage, L. (1979). Comparison of WISC and WISC-R regression lines for academic prediction with black and white referred children. *Journal of Consulting and Clinical Psychology, 47,* 589–591.

Reynolds, C. R., & Kamphaus, R. W. (2004). *Behavior assessment system for children* (2nd ed.). Minneapolis, MN: Pearson Assessments.

Ridgeway, E. M., & Exner, J. E. (1980). *Rorschach correlates of achievement needs in medical students under an arousal state.* Rorschach Workshops (Study No. 274, unpublished).

Riessman, F., & Miller, S. M. (1958). Social class and projective tests. *Journal of Projective Techniques, 22,* 432–439.

Riggs, D. S., & Foa, E. B. (1993). Obsessive compulsive disorder. In D. H. Barlow (Ed.), *Clinical handbook of psychological disorders* (2nd ed., pp. 189–239). New York: Guilford Press.

Riskind, J. H., Beck, A. T., Berchick, R. J., Brown, G., & Steer, R. A. (1987). Reliability of DSM-III diagnoses for major depression and generalized anxiety disorder using the Structured Clinical Interview for DSM-III. *Archives of General Psychiatry, 44,* 817–820.

Ritzler, B. A., Sharkey, K. J., & Chudy, J. F. (1980). A comprehensive projective alternative to the TAT. *Journal of Personality Assessment, 44,* 358–362.

Roberts, G. E. (2006). *Roberts-2 manual.* Los Angeles, CA: Western Psychological Services.

Robin, R. W., Greene, R. L., Albaugh, B., Caldwell, A., & Goldman, D. (2003). Use of the MMPI-2 in American Indians: I Comparability of the MMPI-2 between two tribes and with the MMPI-2 normative group. *Psychological Assessment, 15,* 351–359.

Robins, L. N., Cottler, L. B., Bucholz, K. K., & Compton, W. (1996). *The Diagnostic Interview Schedule (Version IV).* St. Louis, MO: Washington University School of Medical.

Robins, L. N., & Helzer, J. E. (1994). The half life of a structured interview: The NIMH Diagnostic Interview Schedule (DIS). *International Journal of Methods in Psychiatric Research, 4,* 95–102.

Robins, L. N., Helzer, J. E., Cottler, L. B., & Goldring, E. (1989). *NIMH Diagnostic Interview Schedule (Version III-Revised).* St. Louis, MO: Washington University School of Medicine.

Robins, L. N., Helzer, J. E., Croughan, J. L., & Ratcliff, K. S. (1981). National Institute of Mental Health Diagnostic Interview Schedule. *Archives of General Psychiatry, 38,* 381–389.

Robinson, J. (2001). *Brain calipers: Descriptive psychopathology and the mental status examination* (2nd ed.). Port Huron, MI: Rapid Psychler Press.

Robinson, J. D., & Baker, J. (2006). Psychological consultation and services in a general medical hospital. *Professional Psychology: Research and Practice, 37,* 264–267.

Rodenhauser, P., & Fornal, R. E. (1991). How important is the mental status examination? *Psychiatric Hospital, 22*, 256–262.

Rodgers, D. A. (1972). The MMPI: A review. In O. K. Buros (Ed.), *Seventh mental measurements yearbook* (Vol. 1, pp. 243–250). Highland Park, NJ: Gryphon Press.

Roe, A. (1952). Analysis of group Rorschachs of psychologists and anthropologists. *Journal of Projective Techniques, 16*, 212–242.

Rogers, C. R. (1961). *On becoming a person.* Boston: Houghton Mifflin.

Rogers, C. R. (1992). The necessary and sufficient conditions of therapeutic personality change. *Journal of Consulting and Clinical Psychology, 60*, 827–832. (Original work published 1957.)

Rogers, R. (2001). *Handbook of diagnostic and structured interviewing.* New York: Guilford.

Rogers, R. (2008). *Clinical assessment of malingering and deception* (3rd ed.). New York: Guilford Press.

Rogers, R., Bagby, R. M., & Chakraborty, D. (1993). Feigning schizophrenic disorders on the MMPI-2: Detection of coached simulators. *Journal of Personality Assessment, 60*, 215–226.

Rogers, R., Jackson, R. L., & Cashiel, M. (2004). The Schedule for Affective Disorders and Schizophrenia (SADS). In M. Hilsenroth & D. L. Segal (Eds.), *Comprehensive handbook of psychological assessment* (Vol. 2, pp. 144–152). Hoboken, N. J.: John Wiley & Sons.

Rogers, R., Salekin, R. T., & Sewell, K. W. (1999). Validation of the Millon Clinical Multiaxial Inventory for Axis II disorders: Does it meet the Daubert standard? *Law and Human Behavior, 22*, 425–443.

Rogers, R., Sewell, K. W., Martin, M. A., & Vitacco, M. J. (2003). Detection of feigned mental disorders: A meta-analysis of the MMPI-2 and malingering. *Assessment, 10*, 160–177.

Rogers, R., Sewell, K. W., & Ustad, K. L. (1995). Feigning among chronic outpatients on the MMPI-2: A systematic examination of fake-bad indicators. *Assessment, 2*, 81–89.

Rogers, R., Tillbrook, C. E., & Sewell, K. W. (2004). *Evaluation of competence to stand trial—revised: Professional manual.* Odessa, FL: Psychological Assessment Resources.

Roid, G. H., Prifitera, A., & Ledbetter, M. (1988). Confirmatory analysis of the factor of the Wechsler Memory Scale-Revised. *Clinical Neuropsychologist, 2*, 116–120.

Romanczyk, R. G., Kent, R. N., Diament, C., & O'Leary, K. D. (1973). Measuring the reliability of observational data: A reactive process. *Journal of Applied Behavior Analysis, 6*, 175–184.

Rorschach, H. (1941). *Psychodiagnostik* (Hans Huber Verlag, Trans.). Bern, Switzerland: Bircher. (Original work published 1921)

Rosen, A., & Schalling, D. (1974). On the validity of the California Psychological Inventory Socialization scale. *Journal of Consulting and Clinical Psychology, 42*, 765–757.

Rosen, B. M., Bahn, A. K., & Kramer, M. (1964). Demographic and diagnostic characteristics of psychiatric clinic patients in the U.S.A., 1961. *American Journal of Orthopsychiatry, 34*, 455–468.

Rosenhan, D. L. (1973). On being sane in insane places. *Science, 179*, 250–257.

Rosenthal, M. J. (1989). Towards selective and improved performance of the mental status examination. *Acta Psychiatrica Scandinavica, 80*, 207–215.

Rosenthal, R. (1966). *Experimenter effects in behavioral research.* New York: Appleton-Century-Crofts.

Rosenthal, R., & Fode, K. L. (1963). The effects of experimenter bias on the performance of the albino rat. *Behavioral Science, 8*, 183–189.

Rosenthal, R., & Jacobson, L. (1968). *Pygmalion in the classroom.* New York: Holt, Rinehart and Winston.

Rosenzweig, S. (1976). *Manual for the Rosenzweig Picture-Frustration Study, adolescent form.* St. Louis, MO: Author.

Rosenzweig, S. (1977). *Manual for the Children's Form of the Rosenzweig Picture-Frustration (P-F) Study.* St. Louis, MO: Rana House.

Rosenzweig, S. (1978). *Adult form supplement to the Basic Manual of the Rosenzweig Picture Frustration (P-F) Study.* St. Louis, MO: Rana House.

Rosqvist, J., Sundsmo, A., MacLane, C., Cullen, K., Norling, D. C., Davies, M., & Maack, D. (2006). Analogue and virtual reality assessment. In M. Hersen (Ed.), *Clinician's handbook of adult behavioral assessment* (pp. 43–63). New York: Elsevier.

Ross, L. D. (1977). The intuitive psychologist and his shortcomings: Distortions in the attribution process. In L. Berkowitz (Ed.), *Advances in experimental social psychology* (Vol. 10, pp. 173–220). New York: Academic Press.

Rossini, E. D., & Kaspar, J. C. (1987). The validity of the Bender-Gestalt emotional indicators. *Journal of Personality Assessment, 51,* 254–261.

Rossini, E. D., & Moretti, R. J. (1997). Thematic Apperception Test (TAT) interpretation: Practice recommendations from a survey of clinical psychology doctoral programs by the American Psychological Association. *Professional Psychology: Research and Practice, 28,* 393–398.

Roth, D. L., Hughes, C. W., Mankowski, P. G., & Crosson, B. (1984). Investigation of validity of WAIS-R short forms for patients suspected to have brain impairment. *Journal of Consulting and Clinical Psychology, 52,* 722–723.

Rouse, S. V., Butcher, J. N., & Miller, K. B. (1999). Assessment of substance abuse in psychotherapy clients: The effectiveness of the MMPI-2 substance abuse scales. *Psychological Assessment, 11,* 101–107.

Royer, F. L., & Holland, T. R. (1975). Rotations of visual design in psychopathological groups. *Journal of Consulting and Clinical Psychology, 43,* 346–356.

Rude, S. R. (1986). Relative benefits of assertion or cognitive self-control treatment for depression as a function of proficiency in each domain. *Journal of Consulting and Clinical Psychology, 54,* 390–394.

Ruegg, R. G., Ekstrom, D. E., Evans, D. L., & Golden, R. N. (1990). Introduction of a standardized report form improves the quality of mental status examination reports by psychiatric residents. *Academic Psychiatry, 14,* 157–163.

Ruscio, J. (2000). The role of complex thought in clinical prediction: Social accountability and the need for cognition. *Journal of Consulting and Clinical Psychology, 68,* 145–154.

Rushton, J. P. (1994). The equalitarian dogma revisited. *Intelligence, 19,* 263–280.

Russ, S. W. (2001). Tackling ethical dilemmas in personality assessment. *Journal of Personality Assessment, 77,* 255–258.

Russell, E. W. (1975). A multiple scoring method for the assessment of complex memory functions. *Journal of Consulting and Clinical Psychology, 43,* 800–809.

Russell, E. W. (1979). Three patterns of brain damage on the WAIS. *Journal of Clinical Psychology, 35,* 611–620.

Russell, E. W. (1988). Renorming Russell's version of the Wechsler Memory Scale. *Journal of Clinical and Experimental Neuropsychology, 10,* 235–249.

Russell, E. W. (2000). The cognitive-metric, fixed battery approach to neuropsychological assessment. In R. D. Vanderploeg (Ed.), *Clinician's guide to neuropsychological assessment* (2nd ed., pp. 449–483). Hillsdale, NJ: Lawrence Erlbaum.

Ryan, C. M., Morrow, L., Parklinson, D., & Branet, E. (1987). Low level lead exposure and neuropsychological functioning in blue collar males. *International Journal of Neuroscience, 36,* 29–39.

Ryan, J. J. (1999). Two types of tables for use with the seven-subtest short forms of the WAIS-III. *Journal of Psychoeducational Assessment, 17,* 145–151.

Ryan, J. J., Georgemiller, R., & McKinney, B. (1984). Application of the four-subtest WAIS-R short form with an older clinical sample. *Journal of Clinical Psychology, 40,* 1033–1036.

Ryan, J. J., Glass, L. A., Brown, C. N. (2007). Administration time estimates for Wechsler Intelligence Scale for Children-IV subtests, composites, and short forms. *Journal of Clinical Psychology, 63,* 309–318.

Ryan, J. J., Lopez, S. J., & Werth, T. R. (1998). Administration time estimates for WAIS-III sub-tests, scales, and short forms in a clinical sample. *Journal of Psychoeductional Assessment, 16,* 315–323.

Ryan, J. J., Lopez, S. J., & Werth, T. R. (1999). Development and preliminary validation of a Satz-Mogel short form of the WAIS-III in a sample of persons with substance abuse disorders. *International Journal of Neurosciences, 98,* 131–140.

Ryan, J. J., Paolo, A. M., & Brungardt, T. M. (1990). Standardization of the Wechsler Adult Intelligence Scale-Revised for persons 75 years and older. *Psychological Assessment, 2,* 404–411.

Ryan, J. J., & Paul, C. A. (1999). Who is president of the United States? *Perceptual and Motor Skills, 89,* 595–596.

Ryan, J. J., Paul, C. A., & Arb, J. D. (1999). Intrasubtest scatter on the WAIS-III Information subtest and psychometrically defined retrieval deficits. *Perceptual and Motor Skills, 89,* 1052–1058.

Ryan, J. J., Rosenberg, S. J., & Mittenberg, W. (1984). Factor analysis of the Rey Auditory Verbal Learning Test. *International Journal of Clinical and Experimental Neuropsychology, 5,* 249–253.

Ryan, J. J., & Schnakenberg-Ott, S. D. (2003). Scoring reliability on the Wechsler Adult Intelligence Scale-Third Edition (WAIS-III). *Assessment, 10*(2), 151–159.

Ryan, J. J., & Ward, L. C. (1999). Validity, reliability, and standard errors of measurement for two seven subtest short forms of the Wechsler Adult Intelligence Scale-III. *Psychological Assessment, 11,* 207–211.

Sackett, P. R., Borneman, M. J., & Connelly, B. S. (2008). High-stakes testing in higher education and employment: Appraising evidence for validity and fairness. *American Psychologist, 63,* 215–227.

Sadock, B. J., & Sadock, V. A. (2005). *Kaplan & Sadock's pocket handbook of clinical psychiatry* (4th ed.). Philadelphia: Lippincott.

Saklofske, D. H., Hildebrand, D. K., & Gorsuch, R. L. (2000). Replication of the factor structure of the Wechsler Adult Intelligence Scale-Third Edition with a Canadian sample. *Psychological Assessment, 12,* 436–439.

Sales, J., & Miller, P. (1994). *Psychology in litigation and legislation.* Washington, DC: American Psychological Association.

Sameroff, A. J., Seifer, R., Baldwin, A., & Baldwin, C. (1993). Stability of intelligence from pre-school to adolescence: The influence of social and family risk factors. *Child Development, 64,* 80–97.

Sammons, M. T., & Schmidt, N. B. (2001). *Combined treatment for mental disorders: A guide to psychological and pharmacological interventions.* Washington, DC: American Psychological Association.

Sandal, G. M., & Endersen, I. M. (2002). The sensitivity of the CPI Good Impression scale foe detecting "Faking Good" among students and job applicants. *International Journal of Selection and Assessment, 10,* 304–311.

Sandoval, J. (1979). The WISC-R and internal evidence of test bias with minority groups. *Journal of Consulting and Clinical Psychology, 47,* 919–927.

Sandy, L. R. (1986). The descriptive-collaborative approach to psychological report writing. *Psychology in the Schools, 23,* 395–400.

Saran, M., Phansalkar, S., & Kablinger, A. S. (2007). Biological markers and the future of early diagnosis and treatment of schizophrenia. *Psychiatric Times, 24,* 1–3.

Sarason, I. G., Levine, H. M., Basham, R. B., & Sarason, B. R. (1983). Assessing social support: The Social Support Questionnaire. *Journal of Personality and Social Psychology, 44,* 127–139.

Sarchione, C. D., Cuttler, M. J., Muchinsky, P. M., & Nelson-Gray, R. O. (1998). Prediction of dys-functional job behaviors among law enforcement officers. *Journal of Applied Psychology, 83,* 904–912.

Sattler, J. M. (1973a). Examiners scoring style, accuracy, ability, and culturally disadvantaged children. In L. Mann & D. Sabatino (Eds.), *The first review of special education* (Vol. 2). Philadelphia: J. S. E. Press.

Sattler, J. M. (1973b). Racial experimenter effects. In K. S. Miller & R. M. Dreger (Eds.), *Comparative studies of blacks and whites in the United States* (pp. 8–32). New York: Seminar Press.

Sattler, J. M. (1985). Review of the Hutt adaptation of the Bender-Gestalt Test. In J. V. Mitchell (Ed.), *The ninth mental measurements yearbook* (Vol. 1, pp. 184–185). Highland Park, NJ: Gryphon Press.

Sattler, J. M. (1992). *Assessment of children* (3th ed. rev.). San Diego, CA: Author.

Sattler, J. M. (2001). *Assessment of children: Cognitive functions* (4th ed.). San Diego, CA: Author.

Sattler, J. M. (2008). *Assessment of children: Cognitive functions* (5th ed.). San Diego, CA: Author.

Sattler, J. M., & Atkinson, L. (1993). Item equivalence across scales: The WPPSI-R and WISC-III. *Psychological Assessment, 5,* 203–206.

Sattler, J., & Dumont, R. (2004). *Assessment of children: WISC-IV and WPPSI-III supplement.* San Diego: Jerome M. Sattler.

Sattler, J. M., & Gwynne, J. (1982). White examiners generally do not impede the intelligence test performance of black children: To debunk a myth. *Journal of Consulting and Clinical Psychology, 50,* 196–208.

Sattler, J. M., Hillix, W. A., & Neher, L. A. (1970). Halo effect in examiner scoring of intelligence test responses. *Journal of Consulting and Clinical Psychology, 34,* 172–176.

Sattler, J. M. & Hoge, R. D. (2006). *Assessment of children: Behavioral, social and clinical foundations* (5th ed.). San Diego, CA: Jerome M. Sattler.

Sattler, J. M., & Ryan, J. J. (1998). *Assessment of children, revised and updated 3rd ed. WAIS-III supplement.* San Diego, CA: Jerome M. Sattler.

Sattler, J. M., & Winget, B. M. (1970). Intelligence testing procedures as affected by expectancy and I.Q. *Journal of Clinical Psychology, 26,* 446–448.

Satz, P., & Mogel, S. (1962). An abbreviation of the WAIS for clinical use. *Journal of Clinical Psychology, 18,* 77–79.

Sayers, S. L., & Tomcho, T. J. (2006). Behavioral interviewing. In M. Hersen (Ed.). *Clinician's handbook of adult behavioral assessment* (pp. 63–84). New York: Elsevier.

Sbordone, R. J. (2000a). The assessment interview in clinical neuropsychology. In G. Groth-Marnat (Ed.), *Neuropsychological assessment in clinical practice: A guide to test interpretation and integration* (pp. 94–128). Hoboken, NJ: John Wiley & Sons.

Sbordone, R. J. (2000b). The executive functions of the brain. In G. Groth-Marnat (Ed.), *Neuropsychological assessment in clinical practice: A guide to test interpretation and integration* (pp. 437–456). Hoboken, NJ: John Wiley & Sons.

Sbordone, R. J., & Guilmette, T. J. (1999). Ecological validity: Prediction of everyday and vocational functioning from neuropsychological test data. In J. Sweet (Ed.), *Forensic neuropsychology: Fundamentals and practice* (pp. 223–250). New York: Swets.

Sbordone, R. J., & Long, C. J. (Eds.). (1996). *Ecological validity of neuropsychological testing.* Odessa, FL: Psychological Assessment Resources.

Schalock, R. L., Luckasson, R. A., Shogren, K. A., Borthwick-Duffy, S., Bradley, V., et al. (2007). The renaming of mental retardation: Understanding the change to the term intellectual disability. *Intellectual and Developmental Disabilities, 45,* 116–124.

Schinka, J. A. (1983). *Neuropsychological Status Examination.* Odessa, FL: Psychological Assessment Resources.

Schinka, J. A., LaLone, L., & Greene, R. (1998). Effects of psychopathology and demographic characteristics on MMPI-2 scale scores. *Journal of Personality Assessment, 70,* 197–211.

Schmidt, F. L., & Hunter, J. E. (1998). The validity and utility of selection methods in personnel psychology: Practical and theoretical implications of 85 years of research findings. *Psychological Bulletin, 124,* 262–274.

Schmidt, F. L., & Hunter, J. E. (2004). General mental ability in the work place. *Journal of Personality and Social Psychology, 86*, 162–173.

Schmidt, F. L., Ones, D. S., & Hunter, J. E. (1992). Personnel selection. *Annual Review of Psychology, 43*, 627–670.

Schmidt, H. O., & Fonda, C. P. (1954). Rorschach scores in the manic state. *Journal of Psychology, 38*, 427–437.

Schmidt, M., Trueblood, W., Merwin, M., & Durham, R. L. (1994). How much do "attention" tests tell us? *Archives of Clinical Neuropsychology, 9*, 383–394.

Schmitz, N., & Hartkamp, N. (2000). Assessing clinically significant change: Application to the SCL-90-R. *Psychological Reports, 86*, 263–274.

Schmitz, N., Kruse, J., Heckrath, L., Alberti, L., & Tress, W. (1999). Diagnosing mental disorders in primary care: The General Health Questionnaire (GHQ) and the Symptom Check List (SCL-90-R) as screening instruments. *Social Psychiatry and Psychiatric Epidemiology, 34*, 360–366.

Schoenberg, M. R., Dorr, D., & Morgan, C. D. (2003). The ability of the Millon Clinical Multiaxial Inventory-Third Edition to detect malingering. *Psychological Assessment, 15*, 198–204.

Schoenberg, M. R., Duff, K., Scott, J. G., & Adams, R. L. (2003). An evaluation of the clinical utility of the OPIE-3 as an estmate of premorbid WAIS-III FSIQ. *Clinical Neuropsychology, 17*, 308–321.

Schoenberg, M. R., Lange, R. T., Brickell, T. A, & Saklofske, D. H. (2007). Estimating premorbid general cognitive functioning for children and adolescents using the American Wechsler Intelligence Scale for Children—Fourth Edition: Demographics and current performance approaches. *Journal of Child Neurology, 22*, 379–388.

Schraa, J. C., Jones, N. F., & Dirks, J. E. (1983). Bender-Gestalt recall: A review of the normative data and related issues. In J. N. Butcher & C. D. Spielberger (Eds.), *Advances in personality assessment* (Vol. 2, pp. 125–138). Hillsdale, NJ: Lawrence Erlbaum.

Schroth, M. L. (1987). Relationships between achievement-related motives, extrinsic conditions, and task performance. *Journal of Social Psychology, 127*, 39–48.

Schuerger, J. M., & Witt, A. C. (1989). The temporal stability of individually tested intelligence. *Journal of Clinical Psychology, 45*, 294–302.

Schultheiss, O. C., & Brunstein, J. C. (2001). Assessment of implicit motives with a research version of the TAT: Picture profiles, gender differences, and relations to other personality measures. *Journal of Personality Assessment, 77*, 71–86.

Schultz, C. B., & Sherman, R. H. (1976). Social class, development, and differences in reinforcer effectiveness. *Review of Educational Research, 46*, 25–59.

Schwab-Stone, M., Fisher, P., Piacentini, J., Shaffer, D., Davies, M., & Briggs, M. (1993). The Diagnostic Interview Schedule for Children-Revised version (DISC-R). II: Test-retest reliability. *Journal of the American Academy of Child and Adolescent Psychiatry, 32*, 651–657.

Schwartz, G. E. (1982). Testing the biopsychosocial model: The ultimate challenge facing behavioral medicine? *Journal of Consulting and Clinical Psychology, 50*, 1040–1053.

Schwartz, L., & Levitt, E. E. (1960). Short forms of the WISC for children in the educable, non-institutionalized mentally retarded. *Journal of Educational Psychology, 51*, 187–190.

Schwartz, R. M., & Garamoni, G. L. (1989). Cognitive balance and psychopathology: Evaluation of an information processing model of positive and negative states of mind. *Clinical Psychology Review, 9*, 271–294.

Schwartz, S., & Wiedel, T. C. (1981). Incremental validity of the MMPI in neurological decision-making. *Journal of Personality Assessment, 45*, 424–426.

Seeman, K., Yesavage, J., & Widrow, L. (1985). Correlations of self-directed violence in acute schizophrenics with clinical ratings and personality measures. *Journal of Nervous and Mental Diseases, 173*, 298–302.

Seligman, M. E. P. (1995). The effectiveness of psychotherapy: The Consumer Reports study. *American Psychologist, 50*, 965–974.

Seligman, M. E. P., Abramson, L. Y., Semmel, A., & von Baeyer, C. (1979). Depressive attributional style. *Journal of Abnormal Psychology, 88*, 242–247.

Seligman, M. E. P., Steen, T., Park, N., & Peterson, C. (2005). Positive psychology progress: Empirical validation of interventions. *American Psychologist, 60*, 410–421.

Sellbom, M., Ben-Porath, Y., & Graham, J. (2006). Correlates of the MMPI-2 Restructured Clinical (RC) scales in a college counseling setting. *Journal of Personality Assessment, 86*, 89–99.

Sewitch, T., & Kirsch, I. (1984). The cognitive content of anxiety: Naturalistic evidence for the predominance of threat-related thoughts. *Cognitive Therapy and Research, 8*, 49–58.

Shaffer, D., Fisher, P. W., Lucas, C. P., Dulcan, M. K., & Schwab-Stone, M. E. (2000). NIMH Diagnostic Interview Schedule for Children (Version IV; NIMH DISC-IV): Description, differences from previous versions, and reliability of some common diagnosis. *Journal of the American Academy of Child and Adolescent Psychiatry, 39*, 28–38.

Shaffer, D., Schwab-Stone, M., Fisher, P., Cohen, P., Piacentini, J., Davies, M., et al. (1993). The Diagnostic Interview Schedule for Children-Revised version (DISC-R). I: Preparation, field testing, interrater reliability, and acceptability. *Journal of the American Academy of Child and Adolescent Psychiatry, 32*, 643–650.

Shafer, T. W., Erdberg, P., & Haroian, J. (1999). Current nonpatient data for the Rorschach, WAIS-R, and MMPI-2. *Journal of Personality Assessment, 73*, 305–316.

Shalit, B. (1965). Effects of environmental stimulation on the M, FM, and m response to the Rorschach. *Journal of Projective Techniques and Personality Assessment, 29*, 228–231.

Shapiro, D. A., Barkham, M., Rees, A., Hardy, G. E., Reynolds, S., & Startup, M. (1994). Effects of treatment duration and severity of depression on the effectiveness of cognitive-behavioral and psychodynamic-interpersonal psychotherapy. *Journal of Consulting and Clinical Psychology, 62*, 522–534.

Shapiro, P. N., & Penrod, S. (1986). Meta-analysis of facial identification studies. *Psychological Bulletin, 100*, 139–156.

Shapiro, S. K., & Simpson, R. G. (1995). Koppitz scoring system as a measure of Bender-Gestalt performance in behaviorally disturbed adolescents. *Journal of Clinical Psychology, 51*, 108–112.

Sharkey, K. J., & Ritzler, B. A. (1985). Comparing diagnostic validity of the TAT and a new Picture Projective Test. *Journal of Personality Assessment, 49*, 406–412.

Shatin, L. (1952). Psychoneurosis and psychosomatic reactions: A Rorschach contrast. *Journal of Consulting Psychology, 16*, 220–223.

Shaw, D. S., & Gynther, M. D. (1986). An attempt to obtain configural correlates for the California Psychological Inventory. *Psychological Reports, 59*, 675–678.

Shear, M. K., Greeno, C., Kang, J., Ludewig, D., Frank, E., Swartz, H. A., et al. (2000). Diagnosis of nonpsychotic patients in community clinics. *American Journal of Psychiatry, 157*, 581–587.

Sheikh, A. A. (2003). *Healing images: The role of imagination in health.* Amityville, NY: Baywood.

Shen, L., & Dillard, J. P. (2007). Reactance proneness assessment. In R. A. Reynolds, R. Woods, & J. D. Baker (Eds.), *Handbook of research on electronic surveys and measurements* (pp. 323–329). Hershey, PA: Idea Group Reference.

Sherman, E. M. S., Strauss, E., Slick, D. J., & Spellacy, F. (2000). Effect of depression on neuropsychological functioning in head injury: Measurable but minimal. *Brain Injury, 14*, 621–632.

Sheslow, D., & Adams, W. (2003). *WRAML-II manual.* Wilmington, DE: Jastak Associates.

Shneidman, E. S. (Ed.). (1951). *Thematic test analysis.* New York: Grune & Stratton.

Shorkey, C. L., Reyes, E., & Whiteman, V. L. (1977). Development of the rational behavior inventory: Initial validity and reliability. *Educational and Psychological Measurement, 37*, 527–534.

Shrauger, J. S., & Osberg, T. M. (1981). The relative accuracy of self-predictions and judgments of others in psychological assessment. *Psychological Bulletin, 90*, 322–351.

Sieber, K. O., & Meyers, L. S. (1992). Validation of the MMPI-2 social introversion subscales. *Psychological Assessment, 4*, 185–189.

Siegel, A. W., Schechter, M. D., & Diamond, S. P. (1996). Neurobehavioral assessment format. In R. J. Sbordone & C. J. Long (Eds.), *Ecological validity of neuropsychological testing* (pp. 429–504). Delray Beach, FL: St. Lucie Press.

Siegel, L. S. (1999). Issues in the definition and diagnosis of learning disabilities: A perspective on *Guckenberger v. Boston University*. *Journal of Learning Disabilities, 32*, 304–319.

Silverstein, A. B. (1990). Short forms of individual intelligence tests. *Psychological Assessment, 2*, 3–11.

Silverstein, A. B., & Mohan, P. J. (1962). Bender-Gestalt figure rotations in the mentally retarded. *Journal of Consulting Psychology, 26*, 386–388.

Simon, W. E. (1969). Expectancy effects in the scoring of vocabulary items: A study of scorer bias. *Journal of Educational Measurement, 6*, 159–164.

Simons, A. D., & Thase, M. E. (1992). Biological markers, treatment outcome, and 1 year follow-up in endogenous depression: Electroencephalographic sleep studies and response to cognitive therapy. *Journal of Consulting and Clinical Psychology, 60*, 392–401.

Singer, J. L. (1960). The experience type: Some behavioral correlates and theoretical implications. In M. Rickers-Ovsiankina (Ed.), *Rorschach psychology.* Hoboken, NJ: John Wiley & Sons New York: Wiley.

Singer, R. M. (1990). *Neurotoxicity guidebook.* New York: Van Nostrand-Reinhold.

Sipps, G. J., Berry, G. W., & Lynch, E. M. (1987). WAIS-R and social intelligence: A test of established assumptions that uses the CPI. *Journal of Clinical Psychology, 43*, 499–504.

Skolnick, A. (1966). Motivational imagery and behavior over twenty years. *Journal of Consulting Psychology, 30*, 463–478.

Slate, R. J., & Hunnicutt, L. C. (1988). Examiner errors on the Wechsler scales. *Journal of Psychoeducational Assessment, 6*, 280–288.

Slate, R. J., Jones, C. H., & Murray, R. A. (1991). Teaching administration and scoring of the Wechsler Adult Intelligence Scale-Revised: An empirical evaluation of practice administrations. *Professional Psychology, 22*, 375–379.

Smith, C. P., & Graham, J. R. (1981). Behavioral correlates for the MMPI standard F scale and the modified F scale for black and white psychiatric patients. *Journal of Consulting and Clinical Psychology, 49*, 455–459.

Smith, D., & Dumont, F. (1995). A cautionary study: Unwarranted interpretations of the Draw-A-Person Test. *Professional Psychology: Research and Practice, 26*, 298–303.

Smith, G. T. (2005). On construct validity: Issues of method and measurement. *Psychological Assessment, 17*, 396–408.

Smith, G. T., & McCarthy, D. M. (1995). Methodological considerations in the refinement of clinical assessment instruments. *Psychological Assessment, 7*, 300–308.

Smith, M. L., Glass, G. V., & Miller, T. L. (1980). *The benefits of psychotherapy.* Baltimore: Johns Hopkins University Press.

Smith, S. R., Baity, M. R., Knowles, E. S., & Hilsenroth, M. J. (2002). Assessment of disordered thinking in children and adolescents: The Rorschach Perceptual-Thinking Index. *Journal of Personality Assessment, 76*, 333–351.

Smith, S. R., Hilsenroth, M. J., Castlebury, F. D., & Durham, T. W. (1999). The clinical utility of the MMPI-2 Antisocial Practices Content Scale. *Journal of Personality Disorders, 13*, 385–393.

Snyder, P. J., Nussbaum, P. D., & Robins, D. L. (Eds.). (2006). *Clinical neuropsychology: A pocket handbook for assessmen.* (2nd ed.).Washington, DC: American Psychological Association.

Snyder, W. V. (1945). An investigation of the nature of nondirective psychotherapy. *Journal of General Psychology, 33*, 139–223.

Snyderman, M., & Rothman, S. (1987). Survey of expert opinion on intelligence and aptitude testing. *American Psychologist, 42*, 137–144.

Sobel, D. S. (2000). Mind matters, money matters: The cost effectiveness of mind-body medicine. *Journal of the American Medical Association, 284*, 1705.

Sokolowski, K., Schmalt, H.-D., Langens, T., & Puca, R. M. (2000). Assessing achievement, affiliation, and power motives all at once: The Multi-Motive Grid (MMG). *Journal of Personality Assessment, 74*, 126–145.

Sommer, R., & Sommer, D. (1958). Assaultiveness and two types of Rorschach color responses. *Journal of Consulting Psychology, 22*, 57–62.

Sommers-Flanagan, R., & Sommers-Flanagan, J. (2003). *Clinical interviewing* (2nd ed.). Hoboken, NJ: John Wiley & Sons.

Southern, M. L., & Plant, W. T. (1968). Personality characteristics of very bright adults. *Journal of Social Psychology, 75*, 119–126.

Spangler, W. D. (1992). Validity of questionnaire and TAT measures of need for achievement: Two meta-analyses. *Psychological Bulletin, 112*, 140–154.

Sparrow, S. S., Balla, D. A., & Cicchetti, D. V. (1984). *Vineland Adaptive Behavior Scales.* Circle Pines, MN: American Guidance Service.

Spielberger, C. D. (1973). *Manual for the State-Trait Anxiety Inventory for Children.* Palo Alto, CA: Consulting Psychologists Press.

Spielberger, C. D., Gorsuch, R. L., Lushene, R., Vagg, P. R., & Jacobs, G. A. (1983). *Manual for the State-Trait Anxiety Inventory.* Palo Alto, CA: Consulting Psychologists Press.

Spielberger, C. D., Moscoso, M. S., & Brunner, T. M. (2005). Cross-cultural assessment of emotional states and personality traits. In R. K. Hambleton, C. D. Spielberger, & P. F. Merenda (Eds.), *Adapting educational and psychological tests for cross cultural assessment* (pp. 343–368). Mahwah, NJ: Lawrence Erlbaum.

Spielberger, C. D., & Piotrowski, C. (1990). Clinician's attitudes toward computer-based testing. *Clinical Psychologist, 43*, 60–63.

Spielberger, C. D., & Reheiser, E. C. (2004). Measuring anxiety, anger, depression, and curiosity as emotional states and personality traits with the STAI, STAXI, and STPI. In M. J. Hilsenroth & D. L. Segal (Eds.), *Comprehensive handbook of psychological assessment* (Vol. 2, pp. 70–86). Hoboken, NJ: John Wiley & Sons, Inc.

Spiker, D. G., & Ehler, J. G. (1984). Structured psychiatric interviews for adult. In G. Goldstein & M. Hersen (Eds.), *Handbook of psychological assessment* (pp. 291–304). New York: Pergamon Press.

Spitzer, R. L., Endicott, J., & Cohen, J. (1974). Constraints on the validity of computer diagnosis. *Archives of General Psychiatry, 31*, 197–203.

Spitzer, R. L., Endicott, J., & Robins, E. (1978). Research diagnostic criteria: Rationale and reliability. *Archives of General Psychiatry, 35*, 773–782.

Spitzer, R. L., Williams, J. B. W., & Gibbon, M. (1987). *Structured clinical interview for DSM-III-R (SCID).* New York: State Psychiatric Institute.

Spitzer, R. L., Williams, J. B. W., Gibbon, M., & First, M. B. (1990). *Structured clinical interview for DSM-III-R personality disorders (SCID-II).* Washington, DC: American Psychiatric Press.

Springer, S. P., & Deutsch, G. (1998). *Left brain right brain: Perspectives from cognitive neuroscience* (5th ed.). New York: Freeman.

Standage, K. (1986). Socialization scores in psychiatric patients and their implications for the diagnosis of personality disorders. *Canadian Journal of Psychiatry, 31*, 138–141.

Standage, K. (1990). A classification of respondents to the CPI Socialization scale: Associations with diagnosis and other clinical variables. *Personality and Individual Differences, 11*, 335–341.

Standage, K., Smith, D., & Norman, R. (1988). A classification of respondents to the CPI Socialization Scale: Associations with psychiatric diagnosis and implications for research. *Personality and Individual Differences, 9*, 231–236.

Stanley, M. A., Beck, J. G., & Zebb, B. J. (1996). Psychometric properties of four anxiety measures in older adults. *Behaviour Research and Therapy, 34*, 827–838.

Stanton, H. C., & Reynolds, C. R. (1998). *Configural frequency analysis as a method of determining Wechsler profile types.* Paper presented at the annual meeting of the American Psychological Association, San Francisco, CA.

Starcevic, V., Bogojevic, G., & Marinkovic, J. (2000). The SCL-90-R as a screening instrument for severe personality disturbance among outpatients with mood and anxiety disorders. *Journal of Personality Disorders, 14*, 199–207.

Steadman, H. J., Silver, E., Monahan, J., Appelbaum, P. S., Clark, R. P., Mulvey, E. P., et al. (2000). A classification tree approach to the development of actuarial violence risk assessment tools. *Law and Human Behavior, 24*, 83–100.

Steer, R. A., Ball, R., Ranieri, W. F., & Beck, A. T. (1999). Dimensions of the Beck Depression Inventory-II in clinically depressed outpatients. *Journal of Clinical Psychology, 55*, 117–118.

Steer, R. A., Beck, A. T., & Garrison, B. (1986). *Applications of the Beck Depression Inventory.* In N. Sartorius & T. A. Ban (Eds.), *Assessment of depression* (pp. 121–142). Geneva, Switzerland: World Health Organization.

Steer, R. A., Kumar, G., Ranieri, W. F., & Beck, A. T. (1998). Use of the Beck Depression Inventory-II with adolescent depressed outpatients. *Journal of Psychopathology and Behavioral Assessment, 20*, 127–137.

Steer, R. A., Rissmiller, D. J., & Beck, A. T. (2000). Use of the Beck Depression Inventory-II with depressed geriatric inpatients. *Behaviour Research and Therapy, 38*, 311–318.

Steichen, E. (1955). *Family of man.* New York: Simon & Schuster.

Stein, L. A. R., Graham, J. R., Ben-Porath, Y. S., & McNulty, J. L. (1999). Using the MMPI-2 to detect substance abuse in an outpatient mental health setting. *Psychological Assessment, 11*, 94–100.

Stein, L. A. R., Graham, J. R., & Williams, C. L. (1995). Detecting fake-bad MMPI-A profiles. *Journal of Personality Assessment, 65*, 415–427.

Stein, M. (1981). *The Thematic Apperception Test: An introductory manual for its clinical use with adults* (2nd ed.). Springfield, IL: Charles C Thomas.

Steinberg, M. (1993). *Interviewer's guide to the Structured Clinical Interview for DSM-IV Dissociative Disorders (SCID-D).* Washington, DC: American Psychiatric Press.

Steiner, J. L., Tebes, J. K., Sledge, W. H., & Walker, M. L. (1995). A comparison of the structured clinical interview for DSM-III-R and clinical diagnosis. *Journal of Nervous and Mental Diseases, 183*, 365–369.

Steketee, G. (1994). Behavioral assessment and treatment planning with obsessive compulsive disorder: A review emphasizing clinical application. *Behavior Therapy, 25*, 613–633.

Stelmachers, Z. T. (1995). Assessing suicidal clients. In J. N. Butcher (Ed.), *Clinical personality assessment: Practical approaches* (pp. 367–379). New York: Oxford University Press.

Stern, R. A., & White, T. (2003). *Manual for the Neuropsychological Assessment Battery.* Lutz, FL: Psychological Assessment Resources.

Sternberg, R. J. (2003). Wisdom, intelligence, and creativity synthesized. New York: Cambridge University Press.

Sternberg, R. J., & Grigorenko, E., (1997). *Intelligence, heredity, and environment.* New York: Cambridge University Press.

Sternberg, R. J., & Kaufman, J. C. (1998). Innovation and intelligence testing: The curious case of the dog that didn't bark. *European Journal of Psychological Assessment, 12*, 175–182.

Stewart, L. H. (1962). Social and emotional adjustment during adolescence as related to the development of psychosomatic illness in adulthood. *Genetic Psychology Monographs, 65*, 175–215.

Stompe, T., Ortwein-Swoboda, G., Strobl, R., & Freidman, A. (2000). The age of onset of schizophrenia and the theory of anticipation. *Psychiatry Research, 93*, 125–134.

Storandt, M., Botwinick, J., & Danziger, W. L. (1986). Longitudinal changes: Patients with mild SDAT and matched health controls. In L. W. Poon (Ed.), *Handbook for clinical memory assessment of older adults.* Washington, DC: American Psychological Association.

Stout, C. E. (1997). Psychological assessment in managed care. New York: John Wiley & Sons.

Stout, C. E., & Cook, L. P. (1999). New areas for psychological assessment in general health care settings: What to do today to prepare for tomorrow. *Journal of Clinical Psychology, 55,* 797–812.

Strack, S. (1999). Millon's normal personality styles and dimensions. *Journal of Personality Assessment, 72,* 426–436.

Strauss, E., Sherman, E. M. S., & Spreen, O. (2006). *A compendium of neuropsychological tests: Administration, norms, and commentary* (3rd ed.). New York: Oxford University Press.

Stredny, R. V., & Ball, J. D. (2005). The utility of the Rorschach Coping Deficit Index as a measure of depression and social skills deficits in children and adolescents. *Assessment, 12,* 295–302.

Streiner, D. L., & Miller, H. R. (1990). Maximum likelihood estimates of the accuracy of four diagnostic techniques. *Educational and Psychological Measurement, 50,* 653–662.

Stringer, A. Y., & Nadolne, M. J. (2000). Neuropsychological assessment: Contexts for contemporary clinical practice. In G. Groth-Marnat (Ed.), *Neuropsychological assessment in clinical practice: A guide to test interpretation and integration* (pp. 26–47). Hoboken, NJ: John Wiley & Sons.

Stroop, J. R. (1935). Studies of interference in serial verbal reactions. *Journal of Experimental Psychology, 18,* 643–662.

Strupp, H. H. (1958). The psychotherapist's contribution to the treatment process. *Behavioral Science, 3,* 34–67.

Stukenberg, K. W., Brady, C., & Klinetob, N. (2000). Psychiatric inpatients and the MMPI-2: Providing benchmarks. *Journal of Clinical Psychology,* 747–756.

Stukenberg, K. W., Dura, J. R., & Kiecolt-Glaser, J. K. (1990). Depression screening scale validation in an elderly, community-dwelling population. *Psychological Assessment, 2,* 134–138.

Sturgis, E. T., & Gramling, S. E. (1998). Psychophysiological assessment. In A. S. Bellack & M. Hersen (Eds.), *Behavioral assessment: A practical handbook* (pp. 126–178). Boston: Allyn & Bacon.

Suen, H. K., & Rzasa, S. R. (2004). Psychometric foundations of behavioral assessment. In M. Hersen (Ed.), *Comprehensive handbook of psychological assessment (Vol. 3): Behavioral assessment* (pp. 37–56). Hoboken, NJ: John Wiley & Sons.

Sullivan, K. (2000). Examiners errors on the Wechsler Memory Scale-Revised. *Psychological Reports, 87,* 234–240.

Sullivan, K., & Bowden, S. C. (1997). Which tests do neuropsychologists use? *Journal of Clinical Psychology, 53,* 657–661.

Summerfeldt, L. J., & Antony, M. M. (2002). Structured and semistructured diagnostic interviews. In M. M. Antony & D. H. Barlow (Eds.), *Handbook of assessment and treatment planning for psychological disorders* (pp. 3–37). New York: Guilford Press.

Sundberg, N. D. (1955). The acceptability of "fake" versus "bona fide" personality test interpretations. *Journal of Abnormal and Social Psychology, 50,* 145–147.

Suzuki, L. A., Meller, P. J., & Ponterotto, J. G. (Eds.). (1996). *Handbook of multicultural assessment: Clinical, psychological, and educational applications.* Englewood Cliffs, NJ: Prentice-Hall.

Swartz, M. S., Blazer, D. G., George, L. K., Winfield, I., Zakris, J., & Dye, E. (1989). Identification of borderline personality with the NIMH Diagnostic Interview Schedule. *American Journal of Psychiatry, 146,* 200–205.

Sweet, J. J., Moberg, P. J., & Suchy, Y. (2000). Ten-year follow-up survey of clinical neuropsychologists. Part I: Practices and beliefs. *Clinical Neuropsychologist, 14,* 18–37.

Swensen, W. M., Pearson, J. S., & Osborne, D. (1973). *An MMPI source book: Basic item, scale, and pattern data on 50,000 medical patients.* Minneapolis: University of Minnesota Press.

Szasz, T. (1987). Justifying coercion through religion and psychiatry. *Journal of Humanistic Psychology, 27,* 158–174.

Taft, R. (1955). The ability to judge people. *Psychological Bulletin, 52*, 1–23.

Tallent, N. (1992). *The practice of psychological assessment.* Englewood Cliffs, NJ: Prentice-Hall.

Tallent, N. (1993). *Psychological report writing* (4th ed.). Englewood Cliffs, NJ: Prentice-Hall.

Talley, P. F., Strupp, H. S., & Morey, L. C. (1990). Matchmaking in psychotherapy: Patient-therapist dimensions and their impact on outcome. *Journal of Consulting and Clinical Psychology, 58*, 182–188.

Taylor, R. L., Kaufman, D., & Partenio, I. (1984). The Koppitz developmental scoring system for the Bender-Gestalt: Is it developmental? *Psychology in the Schools, 21*, 425–428.

Taylor, R. L., Sternberg, L., & Partenio, I. (1986). Performance of urban and rural children on the SOMPA: Preliminary investigation. *Perceptual and Motor Skills, 63*, 1219–1223.

Teevan, R. C., Diffenderfer, D., & Greenfield, N. (1986). Need for achievement and sociometric status. *Psychological Reports, 58*, 446.

Teglasi, H. (2001). *Essentials of TAT and other storytelling techniques of assessment.* Hoboken, NJ: John Wiley & Sons.

Tellegen, A., & Ben-Porath, Y. S. (1992). The new uniform T scores for the MMPI-2: Rationale, derivation, and appraisal. *Psychological Assessment, 4*, 145–155.

Tellegen, A., & Ben-Porath, Y. S. (1993). Code-type comparability of the MMPI and MMPI-2: Analysis of recent findings and criticisms. *Journal of Personality Assessment, 61*, 489–500.

Tellegen, A., Ben-Porath, Y. S., McNulty, J. L., Arbisi, P. A., Graham, J., & Kaemmer, B. (2003), *The MMPI-2 restructured clinical (RC) scales.* Minneapolis: University of Minnesota Press

Temp, G. (1971). Test bias: Validity of the SAT for blacks and whites in thirteen integrated institutions. *Journal of Educational Measurement, 8*, 245–251.

Teng, E. L., Chui, H. C., & Saperia, D. (1990). Senile dementia: Performance on a neuropsychological test battery. *Recent Advances in Cardiovascular Disease, 11*, 27–34.

Terman, L. M. (1916). *The measurement of intelligence.* Boston: Houghton Mifflin.

Terman, L. M., & Miles, C. C. (1936). *Sex and personality: Studies in masculinity and femininity.* New York: McGraw-Hill.

Terrell, F., Taylor, J., & Terrell, S. L. (1978). Effects of types of social reinforcement on the intelligence test performance of lower-class black children. *Journal of Consulting and Clinical Psychology, 46*, 1538–1539.

Thelen, M. H., Farmer, J., Wonderlich, S., & Smith, M. (1991). A revision of the Bulimia Test: The BULIT-R. *Psychological Assessment, 3*, 119–124.

Thomas, A. D., & Dudek, S. Z. (1985). Interpersonal affect in Thematic Apperception Test responses: A scoring system. *Journal of Personality Assessment, 49*, 30–36.

Thompson, G. M. (1948). MMPI correlates of movement responses on the Rorschach. *American Psychologist, 3*, 348–349.

Thorndike, R. L. (1959). The California Psychological Inventory: A review. In O. K. Buros (Ed.), Fifth mental measurements yearbook (p. 99). Highland Park, NJ: Gryphon Press.

Thurstone, L. L. (1938). *Primary mental abilities.* Chicago, IL: University of Chicago Press.

Timbrook, R. E., & Graham, J. R. (1994). Ethnic differences on the MMPI-2. *Psychological Assessment, 6*, 212–217.

Todd, J., Coolidge, F., & Satz, P. (1977). The Wechsler Adult Intelligence Scale Discrepancy Index: A neuropsychological evaluation. *Journal of Consulting and Clinical Psychology, 45*, 450–454.

Tolor, A. (1956). A comparison of the Bender Gestalt Test and the digit-span test as measures of recall. *Journal of Consulting Psychology, 20*, 305–309.

Tolor, A., & Brannigan, G. C. (1980). *Research and clinical applications of the Bender-Gestalt Test.* Springfield, IL: Charles C Thomas.

Tolman, A. O., & Rotzien, A. L. (2007). Conducting risk evaluations for future violence: Ethical practice is possible. *Professional Psychology: Research and Practice, 38*, 71–79.

Tombaugh, T. N. (1997). The Test of Memory Malingering (TOMM): Normative data from cognitively intact and cognitively impaired individuals. *Psychological Assessment, 9*, 260–268.

Tombaugh, T. N., McDowell, I., Kristjansson, B., & Hubley, A. M. (1996). Mini-mental state examination (MMSE) and the Modified MMSE (3MS): Psychometric comparison and normative data. *Psychological Assessment, 8*, 48–59.

Tranel, D. (1994). The release of psychological data to nonexperts: Ethical and legal considerations. *Professional Psychology: Research and Practice, 25*, 33–38.

Truax, C. B., & Carkhuff, R. R. (1967). *Toward effective counseling and psychotherapy.* New York: Aldine.

Tucker, R. K., Weaver, R. L., Duran, R. L., & Redden, E. M. (1983). Criterion-related validity of three measures of assertiveness. *Psychological Record, 33*, 361–370.

Turk, D., & Salovey, P. (1985). Cognitive structures, cognitive processes, and cognitive behavior modification. *Cognitive Therapy and Research, 9*, 19–33.

Turkat, I. D. (1990). *The personality disorders: A psychological approach to clinical management.* New York: Pergamon Press.

Turner, S. M., DeMers, S. T., Fox, H. R., & Reed, G. M. (2001). APA's guidelines for test user qualifications. *American Psychologist, 56*, 1099–1113.

Twentyman, C. T., & McFall, R. M. (1975). Behavioral training of social skills in shy males. *Journal of Consulting and Clinical Psychology, 53*, 393–401.

Ullman, L. P., & Krasner, L. A. (1965). *Case studies in behavior modification.* New York: Holt, Rinehart and Winston.

Ulrich, L. P., & Trumbo, D. (1965). The selection interview since 1949. *Psychological Bulletin, 63*, 100–116.

United States Census Bureau News. (2007, May 17). *Minority population tops 100 million.* Washington, DC: U.S. Department of Commerce.

Vakil, E., & Blachstein, H. (1993). Rey Auditory Verbal Learning Test: Structure analysis. *Journal of Clinical Psychology, 49*, 883–890.

Vance, B., Fuller, G. B., & Lester, M. L. (1986). A comparison of the Minnesota Perceptual Diagnostic Test Revised and the Bender-Gestalt. *Journal of Learning Disabilities, 19*, 211–214.

Vanderploey, R. D. (Ed.). (2000). Clinicians guide to neuropsychological assessment (2nd ed.). Mahwah, NJ: Lawrence Erlbaum.

Vanderploeg, R. D., Schinka, J. A., & Axelrod, B. N. (1996). Estimation of WAIS-R premorbid intelligence: Current ability and domographic data used in a best-performance fashion. *Psychological Assessment, 8*, 404–411.

Vanderploeg, R. D., Schinka, J. A., Baum, K. M., Tremont, G., & Mittenberg, W. (1998). WISC-III premorbid prediction strategies: Demographic and best performance approaches. *Psychological Assessment, 10*, 277–284.

Vandiver, T., & Sheer, K. J. (1991). Temporal stability of the diagnostic interview schedule. *Psychological Assessment, 3*, 277–281.

Vane, J. R., & Guarnaccia, V. J. (1989). Personality theory and personality assessment measures: How helpful to the clinician? *Journal of Clinical Psychology, 45*, 5–19.

Vanheule, S., Desmet, M., Groenvynck, H., Roseel, Y., & Fontaine, J. (2008). The factor structure of the Beck Depression Inventory-II: An evaluation. *Assessment, 15*, 177–187.

Van Hutton, V. (1990). Test review: The California Psychological Inventory. *Journal of Consulting and Development, 69*, 75–77.

Van Zomeren, A. H., & Brouwer, W. H. (1990). Attentional deficits after closed head injury. In B. G. Deelman, R. J. Saan, & A. H. Van Zomeren (Eds.), *Traumatic brain injury: Clinical, social, and rehabilitation aspects.* Amsterdam: Swets & Zeitlinger.

Vassend, O., & Skrondal, A. (1999). The problem of structural indeterminancy in multidimensional symptom report instruments: The case of the SCL-90-R. *Behaviour Research and Therapy, 37*, 685–701.

Veiel, H. O. F., & Koopman, R. F. (2001). The bias in regression-based indices of premorbid IQ. *Psychological Assessment, 13*, 356–368.

Veldman, D. J., & Kelly, S. J. (1965). Personality correlates of a composite criterion of teaching effectiveness. *Alberta Journal of Educational Research, 11*, 702–707.

Vernon, P. E. (1964). *Personality assessment: A critical survey.* London: Methuen.

Vieta, E., Colum, F., Martinez-Aran, A., Benabarre, A., Reinares, M., & Gasto, C. (2000). Bipolar II disorder and comorbidity. *Comprehensive Psychiatry, 41*, 339–343.

Viglione, D. J., & Hilsenroth, M. J. (2001). The Rorschach: Facts, fictions, and future. *Psychological Assessment, 13*, 452–471.

Vigneau, F., & Cormier, S. (2008). The factor structure of the State-Trait Anxiety Inventory: An alternative view. *Journal of Personality Assessment, 90*, 280–285.

Vilkki, J., Ahola, K., Holst, P., Ohman, J., Servo, A., & Heiskanen, O. (1994). Prediction of psychosocial recovery after head injury with cognitive tests and neurobehavioral ratings. *Journal of Clinical and Experimental Neuropsychology, 16*, 325–338.

Vincent, K. R. (1991). Black/white differences: Does age make the difference? *Journal of Clinical Psychology, 47*, 266–270.

Vincent, K. R., Castillo, I., Hauser, R., Stuart, H. J., Zapata, J. A., Cohn, C. K., et al. (1983). MMPI code types and DSM-III diagnosis. *Journal of Clinical Psychology, 39*, 829–842.

Vincent, K. R., & Harman, M. J. (1991). The Exner Rorschach: An analysis of its clinical validity. *Journal of Clinical Psychology, 47*, 596–599.

Visser, R. S. H. (1992). *Manual for the Complex Figure Test.* Amsterdam: Swets & Zeitlinger.

Vogt, A. T., & Heaton, R. L. (1977). Comparison of WAIS indices of cerebral dysfunction. *Perceptual and Motor Skills, 45*, 607–615.

Wagner, R. K. (1949). The employment interview: A critical review. *Personnel Psychology, 2*, 17–46.

Wagner, R. K. (1997). Intelligence, training, and employment. *American Psychologist, 52*, 1059–1069.

Wakefield, J. F. (1986). Creativity and the TAT blank card. *Journal of Creative Behavior, 7*, 127–133.

Walker, C. E., & Roberts, M. C. (2001). Handbook of clinical child psychology (3rd ed.). Hoboken, NJ: John Wiley & Sons.

Wallbrown, F. H., & Jones, J. A. (1992). Reevaluating the factor structure of the revised California Psychological Inventory. *Educational and Psychological Measurement, 52*, 379–386.

Walsh, K. (1994). Neuropsychological assessment of patients with memory disorders. In S. Toyz, D. Byrne, & A. Gilandas (Eds.), *Neuropsychology in clinical practice* (pp. 107–127). New York: Academic Press.

Wampold, B. E. (2000). *The great psychotherapy debate: Models, methods, and findings.* Hillsdale, NJ: Lawrence Erlbaum.

Wang, X., Gao, L., Shinfuku, N., Zhang, H., Zhao, C., & Shen, Y. (2000). Longitudinal study of earthquake-related PTSD in a randomly selected community sample in north China. *American Journal of Psychiatry, 157*, 1260–1266.

Ward, L. C. (1991). A comparison of the MMPI and the MMPI-2. *Psychological Assessment, 3*, 688–690.

Ward, L. C. (2006). Comparison of factor structure models for the Beck Depression Inventory-II. *Psychological Assessment, 18*, 81–88.

Ward, L. C., Ryan, J. J., & Axelrod, B. N. (2000). Confirmatory factor analysis of the WAIS-III standarization data. *Psychological Assessment, 12*, 341–345.

Ward, S. B., Ward, T. J., Hatt, C. V., Young, D. L., & Mollner, N. R. (1995). The incidence and utility of the ACID, ACIDS, and SCAD profiles in a referred population. *Psychology in the Schools, 32*, 267–276.

Warren, J. I., Stein, J. A., & Grella, C. E. (2007). Role of social support and self-efficacy in treatment outcomes among clients with co-occurring disorders. *Drug and Alcohol Dependence, 89*, 267–274.

Watkins, C. E. (1991). What have surveys taught us about the teaching and practice of psychological assessment. *Journal of Personality Assessment, 56*, 426–437.

Watkins, C. E., Campbell, V. L., & McGregor, P. (1990). What types of psychological tests do behavioral (and other) counseling psychologists use? *Behavior Therapist, 13*, 115–117.

Watkins, C. E., Campbell, V. L., Nieberding, R., & Hallmark, R. (1995). Contemporary practice of psychological assessment by clinical psychologists. *Professional Psychology: Research and Practice, 26*, 54–60.

Watkins, M. W., Glutting, J. J., & Lei, P. (2007). Validity of the Full Scale IQ when there is significant variability among the WISC-III and WISC-IV factor scores. *Applied Neuropsychology, 14*, 13–20.

Watkins, M. W., Wilson, S. M., Kotz, K. M., Carbone, M. C., & Babula, T. (2006). Factor structure of the Wechsler Intelligence Scale for Children-Fourth Edition among referred students. *Educational and Psychological Measurement, 66*, 975–983.

Watson, D., & Friend, R. (1969). Measurement of social-evaluative anxiety. *Journal of Consulting and Clinical Psychology, 33*, 448–457.

Watzlawick, P., Beavin, J. H., & Jackson, D. D. (1966). *Pragmatics of human communication.* New York: Norton.

Waugh, K. W., & Bush, W. J. (1971). *Diagnosing learning disorders.* Columbus, OH: Merrill.

Webb, J. T., McNamara, K. M., & Rodgers, D. A. (1981). *Configural interpretation of the MMPI and CPI.* Columbus: Ohio Psychology Publishing.

Webster, C. D., Douglas, K. S., Eaves, D., & Hart, S. D. (1997). *HCR-20: Assessing risk for violence (Version 2).* Vancouver, British Columbia, Canada: Mental Health, Law, and Policy Institute, Simon Fraser University.

Wechsler, D. (1945). A standardized memory scale for clinical use. *Journal of Psychology, 19*, 87–95.

Wechsler, D. (1949). *Manual for the Wechsler Intelligence Scale for Children.* New York: Psychological Corporation.

Wechsler, D. (1955). *Manual for the Wechsler Adult Intelligence Scale.* New York: Psychological Corporation.

Wechsler, D. (1958). *The measurement and appraisal of adult intelligence* (4th ed.). Baltimore: Williams & Wilkins.

Wechsler, D. (1967). *Manual for the Wechsler Preschool and Primary School of Intelligence.* New York: Psychological Corporation.

Wechsler, D. (1974). *Wechsler Memory Scale manual.* San Antonio, TX: Psychological Corporation.

Wechsler, D. (1981). *Manual for the Wechsler Adult Intelligence Scale-Revised.* New York: Psychological Corporation.

Wechsler, D. (1987). *Wechsler Memory Scale-Revised manual.* San Antonio, TX: Psychological Corporation.

Wechsler, D. (1989). *Manual for the Wechsler Preschool and Primary Sale of Intelligence-Revised (WPPSI-R).* San Antonio, TX: Psychological Corporation.

Wechsler, D. (1991). *Manual for the Wechsler Intelligence Scale for Children* (3rd ed.). New York: Psychological Corporation.

Wechsler, D. (1992). *Wechsler Individual Achievement Test.* San Antonio, TX: Psychological Corporation.

Wechsler, D. (1997a). *WAIS-III Administration and Scoring manual.* San Antonio, TX: Psychological Corporation.

Wechsler, D. (1997b). Wechsler *Memory Scale: Administration and Scoring manual* (3rd ed.). San Antonio, TX: Psychological Corporation.

Wechsler, D. (2001). *Wechsler Test of Adult Reading*. San Antonio, TX: Psychological Corporation.

Wechsler, D. (2002a). *WAIS-III/WMS-III technical manual, updated*. San Antonio, TX: Psychological Corporation.

Wechsler, D. (2002b). *Wechsler memory scale-Third Edition, abbreviated*. San Antonio, TX: Psychological Corporation.

Wechsler, D. (2002c). *Wechsler Preschool and Primary Scale of Intelligence—3rd Ed*. San Antonio, TX: Harcourt Assessment.

Wechsler, D. (2003a). *Wechsler Intelligence Scale for Children—4th ed.: Administration and scoring manual*. San Antonio, TX: Psychological Corporation.

Wechsler, D. (2003b). *Wechsler Intelligence Scale for Children—4th ed.: Technical and interpretive manual*. San Antonio, TX: Psychological Corporation.

Wechsler, D. (2008a). *Wechsler Adult Intelligence Scale—4th ed*. San Antonio, TX: NCS Pearson, Inc.

Wechsler, D. (2008b). *Wechsler Intelligence Scale for Children—4th ed.: Administration and scoring manual*. San Antonio, TX: NCS Pearson, Inc.

Wechsler, D. (in press). *WAIS-IV/WMS-IV Advanced clinical solutions*. San Antonio, TX: NCS Pearson Inc.

Wechsler, D., Kaplan, E., Fein, D., Kramer, J., Morris, R., Delis, D., et al. (2004). *WISC-IV Integrated: Technical and research manual*. San Antonio, TX: Psychological Corporation.

Wechsler, D., & Naglieri, J. A. (2006). *Wechsler Nonverbal Scale of Ability*. San Antonio, TX: Harcourt Assessment.

Wedding, D., & Faust, D. (1989). Clinical judgment and decision making in neuropsychology. *Archives of Clinical Neuropsychology, 4*, 233–265.

Weed, L. L. (1968). Medical records that guide and teach. *New England Journal of Medicine, 278*, 593–600.

Weed, N. C., Butcher, J. N., McKenna, T., & Ben-Porath, Y. S. (1992). New measures for assessing alcohol and drug abuse with the MMPI-2. The APS and AAS. *Journal of Personality Assessment, 58*, 389–404.

Weed, N. C., Butcher, J. N., & Williams, C. L. (1994). Development of MMPI-A Alcohol/Drug problem scales. *Journal of Studies on Alcohol, 55*, 296–302.

Weinberg, R. A. (1989). Intelligence and IQ: Landmark issues and great debates. *American Psychologist, 44*, 98–104.

Weiner, I. B. (1966). *Psychodiagnosis in schizophrenia*. New York: John Wiley & Sons.

Weiner, I. B. (1986). Conceptual and empirical perspectives on the Rorschach assessment of psychopathology. *Journal of Personality Assessment, 50*, 472–479.

Weiner, I. B. (1996). Some observations on the validity of the Rorschach Inkblot Method. *Psychological Assessment, 8*, 206–213.

Weiner, I. B. (1999). Incremental validity of the Rorschach. *Assessment, 6*, 327–338.

Weiner, I. B. (2004). Rorschach assessment: Current status. In M. J. Hilsenroth & D. L. Segal (Eds.), *Comprehensive handbook of psychological assessment* (Vol. 2, pp. 343–355). Hoboken, NJ: John Wiley & Sons.

Weiner, I. B., & Exner, J. E. (1991). Rorschach changes in long-term and short-term psychotherapy. *Journal of Personality Assessment, 56*, 453–465.

Weiss, L., & Price, L. (2002). An update on the factor structure of the WMS-III. www.psychcorp.com/catg/Wms/wmsfactor.html.

Weiss, L. G., Prifitera, A., & Roid, G. H. (1993). The WISC-III and the fairness of predicting achievements across ethnic and gender groups. *Monograph Series of the Journal of Psychoeducational Assessment: Wechsler Intelligence Scale for Children, 3rd ed*. 35–42.

Weissman, A., & Beck, A. T. (1978, November). Development and validation of the Dysfunctional Attitude Scale (DAS). Paper presented at the 12th annual meeting of the Association for the Advancement of Behavior Therapy, Chicago, IL.

Weller, R. A., Penick, E. C., Powell, B. J., Othmer, E., Rice, A. S., & Kent, T. A. (1985). Agreement between two structured psychiatric diagnostic interviews: DIS and the PDI. *Comprehensive Psychiatry, 26*, 157–163.

Wernick, R. (1955, September 12). The modern-style mind reader. *Life,* 95–108.

Westcott, M. C., & Alfano, D. P. (2005). The Symptom Checklist-90-Revised and mild traumatic brain injury. *Brain Injury, 19*, 1261–1267

Weston, D. (1995). *Revision of Social Cognition and Object Relations Scale: Q sort for projective stories (SCORS-Q).* Unpublished manuscript, Cambridge Hospital and Harvard Medical School, Department of Psychiatry, Cambridge, MA.

Westen, D., & Muderrisoglu, S. (2006). Clinical assessment of pathological personality Traits. *American Journal of Psychiatry, 163*, 1285–1287.

Wetter, M. W., Baer, R. A., Berry, D. T., Robinson, L. H., & Sumpter, J. (1993). MMPI-2 profiles of motivated fakers given specific symptom information: A comparison to matched patients. *Psychological Assessment, 5*, 317–323.

Wetter, M. W., & Deitsch, S. E. (1996). Faking specific disorders and temporal response consistency on the MMPI-2. *Psychological Assessment, 8*, 39–47.

Wetzler, S. (1990). The Millon Clinical Multiaxial Inventory (MCMI): A review. *Journal of Personality Assessment, 55*, 445–464.

Wetzler, S., & Marlowe, D. (1990). "Faking bad" on the MMPI, MMPI-2 and Millon-II. *Psychological Reports, 67*, 1117–1118.

Wetzler, S., & Marlowe, D. (1992). What they don't tell you in the test manual: A response to Millon. *Journal of Counseling and Development, 70*, 427–428.

White, G. W., Nielsen, L., & Prus, J. S. (1984). Head start teacher and aide preferences for degree of specificity in written psychological recommendations. *Professional Psychology: Research and Practice, 15*, 785–790.

White, S., & Edelstein, B. (1991). Behavioral assessment and investigatory interviewing. *Behavioral Assessment, 13*, 245–264.

Whitelaw, S., Baldwin, S., Bunton, R., & Flynn, D. (2000). The status of evidence and outcomes in stages of change research. *Health Education Research, 15*, 707–718.

Wickramasekera, I. E. (1995a). A model of people at high risk to develop chronic stress-related somatic symptoms: Some predictions. *Professional Psychology: Research and Practice, 17*, 437–447.

Wickramasekera, I. E. (1995b). Somatization: Concepts, data, and predictions from the high risk model of threat perception. *Journal of Nervous and Mental Diseases, 186*, 15–23.

Widiger, T. A., & Clark, L. A. (2000). Toward DSM-V and the classification of psychopathology. *Psychological Bulletin, 126*, 946–963.

Widiger, T. A., & Kelso, K. (1983). Psychodiagnosis of Axis II. *Clinical Psychology Review, 3*, 491–510.

Widiger, T. A., Williams, J., Spitzer, R., & Francis, A. (1985). The MCMI as a measure of DSM-III. *Journal of Personality Assessment, 49*, 366–378.

Wiebe, J. S., & Penley, J. A. (2005). A psychometric comparison of the Beck Depression Inventory-II in English and Spanish. *Psychological Assessment, 17*, 481–485.

Wielkiewicz, R. M. (1990). Interpreting low scores on the WISC-R Third Factor: It's more than distractibility. *Psychological Assessment, 2*, 91–97.

Wiener-Levy, D., & Exner, J. E. (1981). The Rorschach Comprehensive System: An overview. In P. McReynolds (Ed.), *Advances in psychological assessment* (Vol. 5). San Francisco: Jossey-Bass.

Wiens, A. N. (1976). The assessment interview. In I. B. Weiner (Ed.), *Clinical methods in psychology* (pp. 3–60). New York: John Wiley & Sons.

Wiesner, W., & Cronshaw, S. (1988). A meta-analytic investigation of the impact of interview format and the degree of structure on the validity of the employment interview. *Journal of Occupational Psychology, 67*, 189–205.

Wiggins, J. S. (1966). Substantive dimensions of self-report in the MMPI item pool. *Psychological Monographs, 80*(630).

Wiggins, J. S. (1971). *Content scales: Basic data for scoring and interpretation.* Unpublished raw data.

Wilde, M. C. (2006). The validity of the Repeatable Battery of Neuropsychological Status in acute stroke. *Clinical Neuropsychologist, 20,* 702–715.

Wilde, N. J., Strauss, E., Chelune, G. J., Hermann, B. P., Hunter, M., Loring, D. W. et al. (2003). Confirmatory factor analysis of the WMS-III in patients with temporal lobe epilepsy. *Psychological Assessment, 15,* 56–63.

Wilke, C. M., Gold, J., Bartko, J. J., Dickerson, F., Fenton, W. S., Knable, M. Randolph, C., & Buchanaan, R. W. (2002). Test-retest stability of the Repeatable Battery for the Assessment of Neuropsychological Status in schizophrenia. *American Journal of Psychiatry, 159,* 838–844.

Wilke, C. M., Gold, J., Humber, K., Dickerson, F., Fenton, W. S., & Buchanan, R. W. (2004). Brief cognitive assessment in schizophrenia: Normative data for the Repeatable Battery for the Assessment of Neuropsychological Status. *Schizophrenia Research, 70,* 175–186.

Wilkinson, G. S., & Robertson, G. J. (2007). *Wide Range Achievement Test-IV.* Wilmington, DE: Jastak.

Williams, C. L., & Butcher, J. N. (1989a). An MMPI study of adolescents. I: Empirical validity of the standard scales. *Psychological Assessment, 1,* 251–259.

Williams, C. L., & Butcher, J. N. (1989b). An MMPI study of adolescents. II: Verification and limitations of code type classifications. *Psychological Assessment, 1,* 260–265.

Williams, C. L., Butcher, J. N., Ben-Porath, Y. S., & Graham, J. R. (1992). *MMPI-A content scales: Assessing psychopathology in adolescents.* Minneapolis: University of Minnesota Press.

Williams, J. E., & Weed, N. C. (2004). Review of computer-based test interpretation software for the MMPI-2. *Journal of Personality Assessment, 83,* 78–83.

Williams, J. B. W., Gibbon, M., First, M. B., Spitzer, R. L., Davies, M., Borus, J., et al. (1992). The Structured Clinical Interview for DSM-III-R (SCID). II: Multisite test-retest reliability. *Archives of General Psychiatry, 49,* 630–636.

Williams, J. M. (1991). Memory Assessment Scales. Odessa, FL: Psychological Assessment Resources.

Williams, W. M. (2000). Perspectives on intelligence testing, affirmative action, and educational policy [Special series]. *Psychology, Public Policy, and Law, 6* (1), 5–19.

Williamson, D. A., Veron-Guidry, S., & Kiper, K. (1998). Assessment of health-related disorders. In A. S. Bellack & M. Hersen (Eds.), *Behavioral assessment: A practical handbook* (pp. 256–270). Boston: Allyn & Bacon.

Wilson, B. A., Alderman, N., Burgess, P., Emslie, H., & Evans, J. J. (1999). *Behavioural assessment of the dysexecutive syndrome manual.* Odessa, FL: Psychological Assessment Resources.

Wilson, B. A., Cockburn, J., & Baddeley, A. (2003). *The Rivermead Behavioral Memory Test-II.* Gaylord, MI: National Rehabilitation Services.

Wilson, T. E., & Evans, I. M. (1983). The reliability of target behavior selection in behavioral assessment. *Behavioral Assessment, 5,* 33–54.

Wing, J. K., Cooper, J. E., & Sartorius, N. (1974). *Description and classification of psychiatric symptoms.* Cambridge, England: Cambridge University Press.

Winter, D. G. (1999). Linking personality and "scientific" psychology: The development of empirically derived Thematic Apperception Test measures. In L. Gieser & M. I. Stein (Eds.), *Evocative images: The Thematic Apperception Test and the art of projection* (pp. 177–190). Washington, DC: American Psychological Association.

Witmer, J. M., Bornstein, A. V., & Dunham, R. M. (1971). The effects of verbal approval and disapproval upon the performance of third and fourth grade children of four subtests of the Wechsler Intelligence Scale for Children. *Journal of School Psychology, 9,* 347–356.

Witt, J. C., & Elliott, S. N. (1983). Assessment in behavioral consultation: The initial interview. *School Psychology Review, 12*, 42–49.

Witteman, C. L. M., & Koele, P. (1999). Explaining treatment decisions. *Psychotherapy Research, 9*, 100–114.

Wittman, C. L. M., & van den Bercken, J. H. L. (2007). Intermediate effects in psychodiagnostic classification. *European Journal of Psychological Assessment, 23*, 56–61.

Wolber, G. J., & Carne, W. F. (1993). *Writing psychological reports: A guide for clinicians.* Sarasota, FL: Professional Resource Press.

Wolfson, D. (1985). *Neuropsychological History Questionnaire.* Tucson, AZ: Reitan Neuropsychology Laboratory.

Wolk, R., & Wolk, R. B. (1971). *Manual: Gerontological Apperception Test.* New York: Behavioral Publications.

Wolpe, J., & Lang, P. J. (1964). A fear survey schedule for use in behavior therapy. *Behavior Research and Therapy, 2*, 27–30.

Wolpe, J., & Lang, P. J. (1969). *Fear Survey Schedule.* San Diego, CA: Educational and Industrial Testing Service.

Wolpe, J., & Lang, P. J. (1977). *Manual for the Fear Survey Schedule.* San Diego, CA: EdITS.

Wolpe, J., & Lazarus, A. (1966). *Behavior therapy techniques.* New York: Pergamon Press.

Wood, J. M., & Lilienfeld, S. O. (1999). The Rorschach Inkblot Test: A case of overstatement? *Assessment, 6*, 341–349.

Wood, J. M., Lilienfeld, S. O., Garb, H. N., & Nezworski, M. T. (2000). The Rorschach Test in clinical diagnosis: A critical review, with a backward look at Garfield (1947). *Journal of Clinical Psychology, 56*, 395–430.

Wood, J. M., Nezworski, M. T., & Garb, H. N. (2003). What's right with the Rorschach? *Scientific Review of Mental Health Practice, 2*, 142–146.

Woodcock, R. W. (1990). Theoretical foundations of the WJ-R measures of cognitive ability. *Journal of Psychoeducational Assessment, 8*, 231–258.

Woodcock, R. W., McGrew, K. S., & Mather, N. (2001). *Woodcock-Johnson III.* Itasca, IL: Riverside.

Woodruff, R. A., Goodwin, D. W., & Guze, S. B. (1974). *Psychiatric diagnosis.* New York: Oxford University Press.

Woodworth, R. S. (1918). *Personal data sheet.* Chicago: Stoelting.

Woody, R. W. (Ed.). (1980). *Encyclopedia of clinical assessment* (Vol. 1). San Francisco: Jossey-Bass.

Wooten, A. J. (1983). MMPI profiles among neuropsychology patients. *Journal of Clinical Psychology, 39*, 392–406.

World Health Organization. (1990). *The ICD-10 classification of mental and behavioural disorders: Clinical description and diagnostic guidelines.* Geneva, Switzerland: Author.

Wright, D., & DeMers, S. T. (1982). Comparison of the relationship between two measures of visual-motor coordination and academic achievement. *Psychology in the Schools, 19*, 473–477.

Wurtz, R. G., Sewell, T. E., & Manni, J. L. (1985). The relationship of estimated learning potential to performance on learning task and achievement. *Psychology in the Schools, 22*, 293–302.

Wyatt, F. (1947). The scoring and analysis of the Thematic Apperception Test. *Journal of Psychology, 24*, 319–330.

Wyndowe, J. (1987). The microcomputerized Diagnostic Interview Schedule: Clinical use in an outpatient setting. *Canadian Journal of Psychiatry, 32*, 93–99.

Wysocki, J. J., & Sweet, J. J. (1985). Identification of brain-damaged schizophrenic, and normal medical patients using a brief neuropsychological screening battery. *International Journal of Clinical Neuropsychology, 7*, 40–44.

Yaloff, J., & Brabender, V. (2001). Ethical dilemmas in personality assessment courses: Using the classroom for in vivo training. *Journal of Personality Assessment, 77*, 203–213.

Yates, B., & Taub, J. (2003). Assessing the costs, benefits, cost effectiveness, and cost benefit of psychological assessment: We should, we can, and here's how. *Psychological Assessment, 15*, 478–495.

Yudin, L. W. (1966). An abbreviated form of the WISC for use with emotionally disturbed children. *Journal of Consulting Psychology, 30*, 272–275.

Zabora, J. R., Smith-Wilson, R., Fetting, J. H., & Enterline, J. P. (1990). An efficient method for psychosocial screening of cancer patients. *Psychosomatics, 31*, 192–196.

Zedeck, S., Tziner, A., & Middlestadt, S. E. (1983). Interviewer validity and reliability: An individual analysis approach. *Personnel Psychology, 36*, 355–370.

Zilmer, E. A., Bell, J. D., Fowler, P. C., Newman, A. C., & Stutts, M. L. (1991). Wechsler Verbal-Performance I.Q. discrepancies among psychiatric inpatients: Implications for subtle neuropsychological dysfunctioning. *Archives of Clinical Neuropsychology, 6*, 61–71.

Zilmer, E. A., Waechtler, C., Harris, B., Khan, F., & Fowler, P. C. (1992). The effects of unilateral and multifocal lesions on the WAIS-R: A factor analytic study of stroke patients. *Archives of Clinical Neuropsychology, 7*, 29–40.

Zimbardo, P. G. (1977). *Shyness: What it is and what to do about it.* Reading, MA: Addison-Wesley.

Ziskin, J., & Faust, D. (2008). Coping with psychiatric and psychological testimony (4th ed.). Los Angeles, CA: Law and Psychology Press.

Zlotnick, C., Shea, M. T., Pilkonis, P., Elkin, I., & Ryan, C. (1996). Gender dysfunctional attitudes, social support, life events, and depressive symptoms over naturalistic follow-up. *American Journal of Psychiatry, 153*, 1021–1027.

Zolliker, A. (1943). Schwangerschaftsdepression and Rorschach'scher formdeutversuch. *Schweiz Archeives Neurologie und Psychiatri, 53*, 62–78.

Zotter, D. L., & Crowther, J. H. (1991). The role of cognitions in bulimia nervosa. *Cognitive Therapy and Research, 15*, 413–426.

Zuckerman, E. L. (2003). *The paper office: Forms, guidelines, and resources to make your practice work ethically, legally, and profitably.* New York: Guilford Press.

Zuckerman, E. L. (2005). *The clinician's thesaurus three: A guidebook for wording psychological reports* (6th ed.). New York: Guilford Press.

Author Index

Subject Index